October 7–10, 2012
Cambridge, Ma, USA

Association for Computing Machinery

Advancing Computing as a Science & Profession

UIST'12

Proceedings of the 25th Annual ACM Symposium on User Interface Software and Technology

Sponsored by:

SIGCHI, ACM SIGGRAPH

Supported by:

Autodesk, Synaptics, Perceptive Pixel, NOKIA, Google, Microsoft, GRAND, WACOM, Disney Research, United Technologies Research Center, Adobe, FX PAL, IBM Research, DiamondTouch, University of Rochester

Association for Computing Machinery

Advancing Computing as a Science & Profession

The Association for Computing Machinery
2 Penn Plaza, Suite 701
New York, New York 10121-0701

Notice to Past Authors of ACM-Published Articles
ACM intends to create a complete electronic archive of all articles and/or other material previously published by ACM. If you have written a work that has been previously published by ACM in any journal or conference proceedings prior to 1978, or any SIG Newsletter at any time, and you do NOT want this work to appear in the ACM Digital Library, please inform permissions@acm.org, stating the title of the work, the author(s), and where and when published.

ISBN: 978-1-4503-1582-1 (Digital)

ISBN: 978-1-4503-1581-4 (Print)

Additional copies may be ordered prepaid from:

ACM Order Department
PO Box 30777
New York, NY 10087-0777, USA

Phone: 1-800-342-6626 (USA and Canada)
+1-212-626-0500 (Global)
Fax: +1-212-944-1318
E-mail: acmhelp@acm.org
Hours of Operation: 8:30 am – 4:30 pm ET

Printed in the USA

Foreword

Welcome to UIST 2012, the Twenty-Fifth Annual ACM Symposium on User Interface Software and Technology.

UIST is the premier forum for the presentation of research innovations in the software and technology of human-computer interfaces. Sponsored by ACM's special interest groups on computer-human interaction (SIGCHI) and computer graphics (SIGGRAPH), UIST brings together researchers and practitioners from many areas, including web and graphical interfaces, new input and output devices, information visualization, interactive displays, tangible computing, and computer supported cooperative work. The single-track schedule, intimate size, and location in Cambridge, Massachusetts, a place rich in history of technical innovations, make UIST 2012 an ideal place to exchange results and to forge future collaborations.

We received a record 288 paper submissions from more than 20 countries. After a thorough review process, the program committee accepted 62 papers (21.5%). Each anonymous submission was first reviewed by a primary program committee member and three external reviewers. If any of the four reviewers deemed a submission to pass a rejection threshold we asked the authors to submit a short rebuttal addressing the reviewers' concerns. The secondary committee member then wrote a fifth review of the paper taking into account the authors' rebuttal. The program committee met in person in Redmond, WA, on June 7–8, 2012, to select the papers for the conference. Submissions were finally accepted only after the authors provided a final revision addressing the committee's comments.

In addition to the presentations of accepted papers, this year's program includes a keynote by Margaret Livingstone (Harvard Medical School neuroscientist) on how art affects the brain. Posters, demos, the ninth annual Doctoral Symposium, and the fourth annual Student Innovation Contest (this year focusing on a new touch-sensitive device from Synaptics called Jedeye) complete the program.

UIST is made possible by the efforts of many volunteers. We would like to express our deepest gratitude to the program committee and all external reviewers for their hard work. Also, the organizing committee worked tirelessly to solicit and organize the extensive variety of content presented this year. Finally, we wish to thank our corporate supporters, as well as ACM SIGCHI and SIGGRAPH, for supporting UIST's tradition of research and innovation.

We hope you enjoy the conference!

Rob Miller
UIST'12 General Chair
MIT CSAIL, USA

Hrvoje Benko
UIST'12 Program Co-Chair
Microsoft Research, USA

Celine Latulipe
UIST'12 Program Co-Chair
UNC Charlotte, USA

Table of Contents

Session 3: Hands & Fingers
Session Chair: Chris Harrison *(Carnegie Mellon University)*

Session 4: Toolkits
Session Chair: Krzysztof Gajos *(Harvard University)*

Session 5: Interactions 1
Session Chair: Shahram Izadi *(Microsoft Research)*

Session 6: Pen

Session Chair: Daniel Vogel *(University of Waterloo)*

Session 7: Interactions II

Session Chair: Dan Olsen *(Brigham Young University)*

Session 8: Augmented Reality

Session Chair: Daniel Avrahami *(Intel)*

Session 9: Multi-touch

Session Chair: Patrick Baudisch *(Hasso Plattner Institute, University of Potsdam)*

Session 10: Tactile & Grip

Session Chair: Andy Wilson *(Microsoft Research)*

Session11: Fabrication & Hardware

Session Chair: Xiang Cao *(Microsoft Research Asia)*

UIST 2012 Conference Organization

General Chair: Rob Miller *(MIT CSAIL, USA)*

Program Chairs: Hrvoje Benko *(Microsoft Research, USA)*
Celine Latulipe *(University of North Carolina at Charlotte, USA)*

Treasurer: Maria Rebelo *(MIT CSAIL, USA)*

Sponsorship Chair: Daniel Wigdor *(University of Toronto, Canada)*

Poster Chairs: Mira Dontcheva *(Adobe, USA)*
Amy Karlson *(Microsoft Research, USA)*

Demo Chairs: Christian Holz *(Hasso Plattner Institute, Germany)*
Scott Saponas *(Microsoft Research, USA)*

Doctoral Symposium: Maneesh Agrawala *(University of California Berkeley, USA)*
Steven Feiner (chair) *(Columbia University, USA)*
mc schraefel *(University of Southampton, UK)*
Desney Tan *(Microsoft Research, USA)*

Student Innovation Contest Chairs: Gabriel Reyes *(Georgia Tech, USA)*
Julia Schwarz *(Carnegie Mellon University, USA)*
Kayur Patel *(University of Washington, USA)*

Student Volunteer Chairs: Chinmay Kulkarni *(Stanford University, USA)*
Sean Follmer *(MIT Media Lab, USA)*

Registration Chairs: Merve Keles *(New York University, USA)*
Sean White *(Nokia, USA)*

Proceedings Chairs: Daniel Ashbrook *(Nokia Research, USA)*
Ari Rapkin Blenkhorn *(Orbis Technologies, USA)*
Nirmal Patel *(Georgia Tech, USA)*

Publicity Chairs: Paul André *(Carnegie Mellon University, USA)*
mc schraefel *(University of Southampton, UK)*

Program Committee:

Daniel Avrahami *(Intel, USA)*
Patrick Baudisch *(Hasso Plattner Institute, University of Potsdam, Germany)*
Jeff Bigham *(University of Rochester, USA)*
Joel Brandt *(Adobe Research, USA)*
Xiang Cao *(Microsoft Research Asia, China)*
Géry Casiez *(INRIA Lille, France)*
Mira Dontcheva *(Adobe Research, USA)*
Pierre Dragicevic *(INRIA, France)*
Cliff Forlines *(Draper Labs, USA)*
Krzysztof Gajos *(Harvard University, USA)*
Chris Harrison *(Carnegie Mellon University, USA)*
Bjoern Hartmann *(University of California Berkeley, USA)*
Jeff Heer *(Stanford University, USA)*
Otmar Hilliges *(Microsoft Research, UK)*
Scott Hudson *(Carnegie Mellon University, USA)*
Takeo Igarashi *(University of Tokyo, Japan)*
Shahram Izadi *(Microsoft Research, UK)*
Shaun Kane *(University of Maryland, USA)*
Ed Lank *(University of Waterloo, Canada)*
Tessa Lau *(IBM Research, USA)*
Yang Li *(Google Research, USA)*
Jeff Nichols *(IBM Research, USA)*
Dan Olsen *(Brigham Young University, USA)*
Ivan Poupyrev *(Disney Research, USA)*
Merrie Ringel Morris *(Microsoft Research, USA)*
Scott Saponas *(Microsoft Research, USA)*
m.c. schraefel *(University of Southampton, UK)*
Dan Vogel *(University of Waterloo, Canada)*
Sean White *(Nokia Research, USA)*
Daniel Wigdor *(University of Toronto, Canada)*
Andy Wilson *(Microsoft Research, USA)*
Tom Yeh *(University of Maryland, USA)*

UIST 2012 Sponsors & Supporters

UIST 2012 gratefully acknowledges our sponsoring SIGs and the support of the following corporations:

Sponsors

SIGCHI

ACMSIGGRAPH

Platinum Supporter

Autodesk

Gold Supporters

Synaptics

PERCEPTIVE PIXEL

Silver Supporters

NOKIA

Google

Microsoft

GRAND — Graphisme, animation et nouveaux médias — Graphics, Animation and New Media

wacom

Bronze Supporters

Disney Research

Adobe

IBM Research

DiamondTouch ... by Circle Twelve Inc

United Technologies Research Center

FXPAL Palo Alto Laboratory

University of Rochester

Keynote Talk

What Art Can Tell Us about the Brain

Margaret Livingstone
Harvard University

Abstract:
Artists have been doing experiments on vision longer than neurobiologists. Some major works of art have provided insights as to how we see; some of these insights are so fundamental that they can be understood in terms of the underlying neurobiology. For example, artists have long realized that color and luminance can play independent roles in visual perception. Picasso said, "Colors are only symbols. Reality is to be found in luminance alone." This observation has a parallel in the functional subdivision of our visual systems, where color and luminance are processed by the newer, primate-specific What system, and the older, colorblind, Where (or How) system. Many techniques developed over the centuries by artists can be understood in terms of the parallel organization of our visual systems. I will explore how the segregation of color and luminance processing are the basis for why some Impressionist paintings seem to shimmer, why some op art paintings seem to move, some principles of Matisse's use of color, and how the Impressionists painted "air". Central and peripheral vision are distinct, and I will show how the differences in resolution across our visual field make the Mona Lisa's smile elusive, and produce a dynamic illusion in Pointillist paintings, Chuck Close paintings, and photomosaics. I will explore how artists have intuited important features about how our brains extract relevant information about faces and objects, and I will discuss why learning disabilities may be associated with artistic talent.

ACM Classifiers: H.5.m

Author Keywords: Keynote Talk; Brain; Art

Bio:
Margaret Livingstone is Professor of Neurobiology at Harvard Medical School. She has done research on hormones and behavior, learning, dyslexia, and vision. Livingstone has explored the ways in which vision science can understand and inform the world of visual art. She has written a popular lay book, Vision and Art, which has brought her acclaim in the art world as a scientist who can communicate with artists and art historians, with mutual benefit. She generated some important insights into the field, including a simple explanation for the elusive quality of the Mona Lisa's smile (it is more visible to peripheral vision than to central vision) and the fact that Rembrandt, like a surprisingly large number of famous artists, was likely to have been stereoblind.

UIST'12, October 7–10, 2012, Cambridge, Massachusetts, USA.
ACM 978-1-4503-1580-7/12/10.

RevMiner: An Extractive Interface for Navigating Reviews on a Smartphone

Jeff Huang
University of Washington
uist@jeffhuang.com

Oren Etzioni
University of Washington
etzioni@cs.washington.edu

Luke Zettlemoyer
University of Washington
lsz@cs.washington.edu

Kevin Clark
University of Washington
kevinc22@cs.washington.edu

Christian Lee
University of Washington
clee@cs.washington.edu

ABSTRACT

Smartphones are convenient, but their small screens make searching, clicking, and reading awkward. Thus, perusing product reviews on a smartphone is difficult. In response, we introduce REVMINER—a novel smartphone interface that utilizes Natural Language Processing techniques to analyze and navigate reviews. REVMINER was run over 300K Yelp restaurant reviews extracting attribute-value pairs, where attributes represent restaurant attributes such as *sushi* and *service*, and values represent opinions about the attributes such as *fresh* or *fast*. These pairs were aggregated and used to: 1) answer queries such as "cheap Indian food", 2) concisely present information about each restaurant, and 3) identify similar restaurants. Our user studies demonstrate that on a smartphone, participants preferred REVMINER's interface to tag clouds and color bars, and that they preferred REVMINER's results to Yelp's, particularly for conjunctive queries (*e.g.*, "great food and huge portions"). Demonstrations of REVMINER are available at `revminer.com`.

ACM Classification: H.5.2 [Information interfaces and presentation]: User Interfaces – graphical user interfaces.

Keywords: opinion mining; user reviews; information extraction; information retrieval.

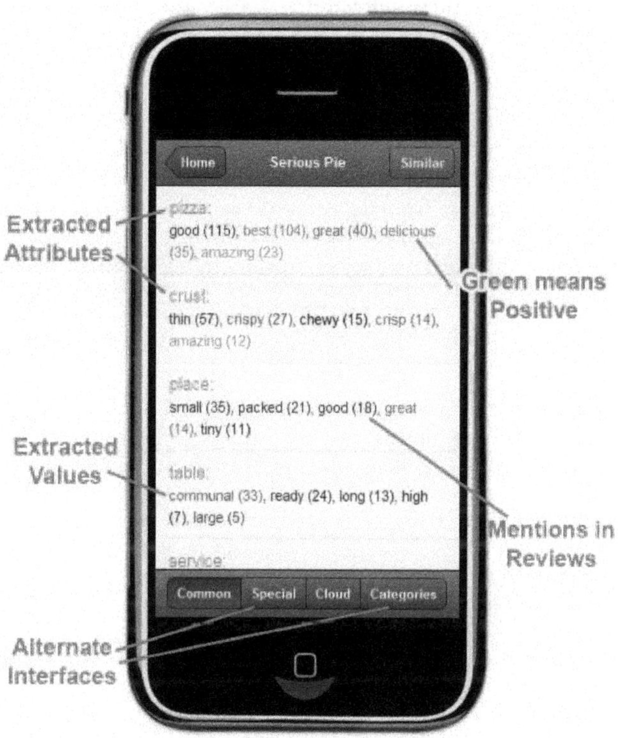

Figure 1: The REVMINER interface listing attributes and associated values extracted from Yelp reviews for the Serious Pie pizza restaurant in Seattle.

INTRODUCTION

People are using smartphones to access a wealth of information on the Web at an unprecedented rate. Yet, the phones' tiny screens make searching for Web pages, and reading them, far less convenient and efficient than on the desktop. To address this challenge, we investigate *extractive interfaces*—user interfaces that utilize attribute-value pairs automatically extracted from unstructured text to summarize the text concisely.

This automatically-extracted summary obviates reading the original text in many cases, and enables new approaches to information navigation and retrieval. Instead of keyword search, which often yields a long list of snippets that are awkward to read on the phone, an extractive interface supports querying by a particular attribute-value pair (*e.g.*, "surprising ending" for movies or "high in vitamin C" in the descriptions of fruit and vegetables). Reviews for businesses and products are particularly helpful on mobile devices when a user is ready to act "then and there". Thus, we investigate extractive smartphone interfaces to reviews.

UIST'12, October 7–10, 2012, Cambridge, Massachusetts, USA.

We focused, in particular, on the familiar task of selecting a restaurant based on user reviews. Reviews for businesses and products are particularly appropriate on mobile devices, which are often used when a user is prepared to shop and eat, then and there. We introduce REVMINER, which summarizes reviewer opinions by extracting the most-mentioned attributes (*e.g.*, dim sum, happy hour, service, *etc.*) and associated values (*e.g.*, fresh, outstanding, slow) utilizing state-of-the art Natural Language Processing (NLP) methods. Like earlier work on review mining [12, 13, 21], REVMINER analyzes each value to determine its polarity and strength (*e.g.*, "exquisite" is stronger than "good"). Next, REVMINER assigns a color in the green-red spectrum based on this analysis. Adjacent to each value, REVMINER records the number of reviews in which this particular attribute-value pair appeared (see Figure 1).

Compared with the standard keyword search interfaces, extractive interfaces, like REVMINER's, offer a more structured way to both query and navigate text. Instead of long lists of snippets, REVMINER returns a short list of attributes and their associated values. If more detail is necessary, the user can "click through" to the original text, establishing the provenance of the extraction. In contrast, with interfaces that highlight *phrases* from the text, the structured attribute-value representation enables querying by conjunctions and disjunctions of attributes, and sorting results by the strength of the values.

In summary, REVMINER's compact extractive interface enables smartphone users to conveniently:

query: for restaurants matching one or more attribute-value pairs (*e.g.*, "good margaritas and large portions"),

rank: obtain a list of restaurants sorted on the strength of values for the queried attribute (*e.g.*, a restaurant with "exquisite margaritas" is ranked above one with "good margaritas"),

summarize: view a concise summary of hundreds of reviews organized by attribute and associated value,

identify: restaurants similar to a particular one based on its attributes and peoples' opinions of the attributes

elaborate: access the source of any particular value in its original sentences, and in the underlying reviews.

Finally, the interface also supports querying by restaurant name which brings up a concise summary of the corresponding reviews, culling and aggregating information from a large number of different documents.

In this paper, we ran REVMINER on a set of 300K Yelp reviews about Seattle restaurants; REVMINER has also been run on user reviews covering hotels, beauty salons, and more, demonstrating its generality. In contrast, most previous work on opinion mining was run at far smaller scales. The massive review corpus enables both higher-accuracy extraction and interface elements that rely on statistics computed over the corpus (see the Extraction and Processing section).

Our main contributions are to:

- Articulate and analyze the extractive interface abstraction for smartphones.
- Design and implement the REVMINER extraction system and associated user interface.
- Assess REVMINER's overall performance in a user study that contrasted its interface with the Yelp Android app and a re-implementation of alternate interfaces (*e.g.*, a tag cloud and color bar).

The web site `http://revminer.com` allows anyone to experiment with a version of the interface for the desktop, for the iPhone, and also to download the Android app used in our experiments.

The remainder of this paper is organized as follows. In the next section, we describe the related work and how REVMINER builds on the latest research in review interfaces and NLP. The Extraction and Processing section presents the review data along with how we processed the extractions. The Mobile App section describes the applications of using the extractions to build a full-featured mobile app that allows users to search and be informed about particular restaurants. Finally, we present a user study of two common restaurant tasks where participants evaluate the app. We wrap up with a discussion about going beyond reviews, and conclude.

RELATED WORK

There has been extensive work on opinion mining [12] and even more on Information Extraction (IE) from the Internet [4]. For instance, the OPINE system introduced an unsupervised method for identifying product features and the associated opinions (including their strength and polarity) [13]. While there are technical differences between REVMINER's extraction methods and previous work, our focus in this paper is on the novel *extractive interface* embodied in REVMINER, not on creating a novel extraction algorithm.

While there is an extensive body of work on opinion mining and IE, there has been little work on extractive user interfaces, and none of that work has investigated opinion mining as a substrate for a smartphone interface. One notable exception is the innovative Review Spotlight system, which introduced a tag cloud interface based on adjective-noun pairs extracted from reviews [21].

REVMINER builds on the ideas described by Yatani *et al.* but there are key differences from Review Spotlight. REVMINER utilizes statistical NLP methods for extracting attribute-value pairs, identifies synonyms, and determines the polarity and strength of opinions. These capabilities are enabled by our 300K review dataset which supports probabilistic learning techniques, whereas Review Spotlight generates a tag cloud directly from each review. REVMINER's attribute-value pairs differ from Review Spotlight's adjective-noun pairs. Attributes relate to restaurants, and the values are opinions of the attributes; for example, "only thing" and "other person" are adjective-nouns from the Review Spotlight paper but not attribute-values in REVMINER. Regarding the interface, REVMINER also produces attribute-value summaries in addition to a tag cloud. While Rivadeneira et al. [16] finds that tag clouds are good at impression formation, other in-

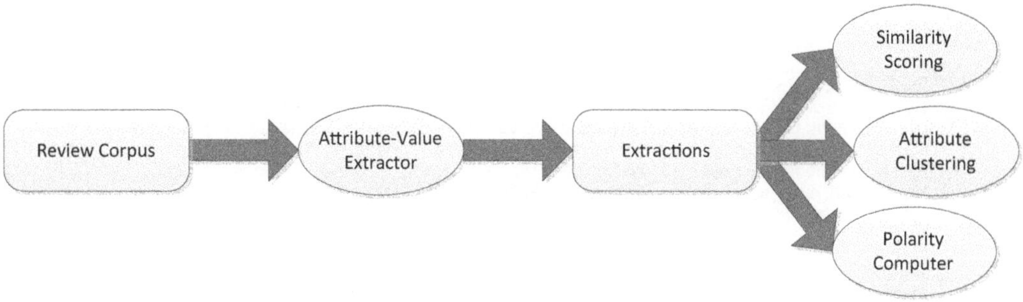

Figure 2: Architecture of the REVMINER offline system. The attributes and values are extracted from the review corpus, which are further processed for other applications. The extraction is performed solely on the review text without any structured data.

terfaces may be better for the browsing and searching tasks that Rivadeneira poses. REVMINER parses search queries to perform a semantic search (*e.g.*, "cheap mexican food free parking" will match places where the *food* is noted to be both *cheap* and *mexican*, at the same time the *parking* is noted to be *free*). Finally, unlike Review Spotlight, our focus is on an extractive interface for a smartphone as evident from our user studies.

Von Reischach et al. evaluate the interaction with product reviews on mobile phones. They remark, "we consider todays product reviews not suitable for mobile phones" [20], referring to review text in their unabbreviated form. Later work by Von Reischach et al. [19] find that text is still rated highest by users for "perceived utility", but star ratings were read more than twice as fast as text. The authors concede, "While almost half the users prefer pure text recommendation or text combined with stars, the consumers who use the ratings have a high preference for text." Thus, there seems to be value in text over a simple rating score, since the text provides more informational depth.

Other research enables similar features to ours but utilizes non-extractive methods. Collaborative filtering, often used in recommender systems, identifies similar objects given one object's user ratings and structured metadata [2, 18]. Document similarity techniques such as the vector space model [17] treat text as a bag-of-words to retrieve similar documents. In contrast, REVMINER uses the extracted attributes and their distributions of values from the unstructured review text to identify similar restaurants. Our work also relates to semantic search [6], where the search system seeks a "shallow" understanding of the meaning in the query and documents, and use this understanding to provide better results. REVMINER also builds on shallow understanding of text in the extraction of attributes and values, and in its parsing of queries into attribute searches.

Faceted search is another method for navigating documents. It entails using metadata (what we extract from unsupervised text and call 'attributes') to browse a collection of documents [7]. Hearst et al. explore faceted search for browsing images, using attributes such as "material", "location", and "view". While we opt for a search interface rather than a browsing interface for the attribute-value extractions, the extraction technology in REVMINER can enable faceted search as well.

Karlson et al. develop a faceted search interface on mobile devices, emphasizing the importance of a compact interface [10]. These techniques can potentially be used to navigate user reviews as well, complementing our work.

Finally, Hoffmann et al. [8] take a similar approach to ours but rather than extracting attributes and values from reviews, they extract programming keywords from source code and documentation. This allows developers to perform programming-related queries over computer programs.

EXTRACTION AND PROCESSING

REVMINER consists of an offline system that extracts information from a corpus of reviews (see Figure 2), and a user interface that enables users to query for restaurants based on the extracted information. The interface is described in the Mobile App section.

The offline system consists of the following key components:

1. **Attribute-Value Extractor:** The main module that generates extractions from a corpus of reviews.
2. **Polarity Computer:** Generates a table from Yelp review scores that associates each value with a score on the positive-negative scale.
3. **Attribute Clustering:** Clustering algorithm that groups together related attributes to form categories used in the Color Bar interface.
4. **Similarity Scoring:** Computes a similarity score between each pair of restaurants.

The offline system in REVMINER automatically learns, given a corpus of reviews, the set of attributes that are discussed (*e.g.*, dim sum, happy hour, service, *etc.*), their associated values (*e.g.*, fresh, outstanding, slow), the polarity of values (*e.g.*, "exquisite" is stronger than "good"), clusters of similar attributes (*e.g.*, food, which would contain pizza, tofu, and seafood), and similarity scores between restaurants. We now describe each of the components from the architecture diagram shown in Figure 2.

Learning to Extract Attributes and Values

Our goal was to design an approach for automatically inducing a set of attribute-value pairs, which we will call extractions, with no pre-existing bias toward the vocabulary that would be used.

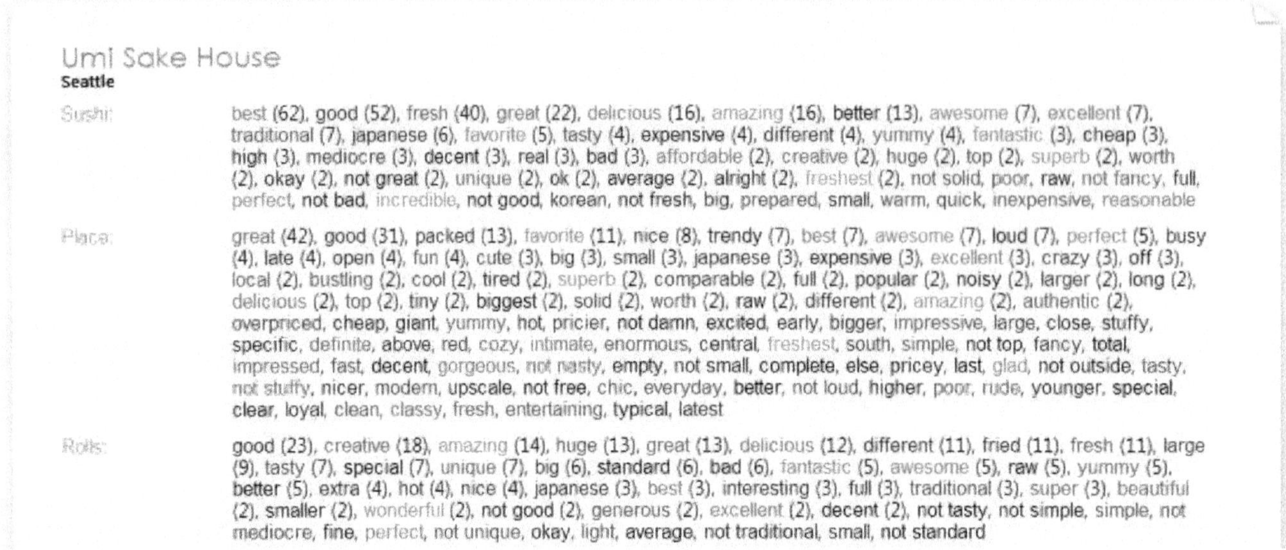

Figure 3: An example of the "raw" extracted values for the three most-frequent attributes for the Umi Sake House restaurant. The number beside the value represents how often that value has been used to describe the attribute in the reviews. A small subset of these values is presented to the user in the REVMINER app.

We developed an automated bootstrapping method, through empirical experimentation on a development corpus. This approach is based on earlier work on bootstrapping patterns for information extraction tasks [1, 3, 14, 15]. As we describe below, the redundancy in reviews provides powerful leverage for utilizing relatively simple extraction templates, and filtering the results to ensure quality.

The bootstrapping method is initialized with a small list of seed extractions that provide the initial cues for learning. These included, *food* as potentially *tasty*, *delicious*, or *disgusting*, and *service* as potentially *fast*, *helpful*, or *polite*. Given a set of extractions, the bootstrapping process repeatedly builds 'phrase templates'[1] that can, with high reliability, be used to expand the set of extractions. These templates include all of the words that occur between an attribute-value pair. For example, the phrase "parking here is terrible" would provide the template "[attribute] here is [value]" for the attribute *parking* with value *terrible*. We extract templates that commonly occur with arguments in our current extraction set and apply them to the complete corpus to grow the extraction set. Figure 4 shows pseudo-code for the full process. At each round, we (1) fix the extractions and update the templates, (2) fix the templates and values to extract new attributes, and (3) fix the templates and attributes to extract new values. This process is performed repeatedly, each time with higher frequency thresholds for whether the new templates or extractions can be included, until the set of extractions converges.

In general, each extraction comprises one word for an attribute with one word for the value. However, we sometimes allow multi-word extractions and multiple extractions per sentence or phrase. Two-word attributes are constructed when two nouns (identified by a part-of-speech tagger) appear together. This allowed REVMINER to include attributes such as *wait staff*, *wine list*, and *pad thai*. We also apply simple rules to identify boolean patterns in sentences. For example, REVMINER understands "and" as an operator over sentences such as "The service we received was both fast and friendly." This allows REVMINER to do multiple extractions, to extract *fast* and *friendly* as values associated with *service*. Finally, we extract multi-word values for negations that appear in templates by prepending the negative word to the extracted value. For example, for the sentence "Fries are not quite crispy" and the template "[attribute] are not quite [value]" we would extract the attribute *fries* with value *not crispy*.

We found during development that this bootstrapping provided many high-quality extractions but also over-generated by producing a much larger number of spurious extractions such as "guys = happy" for the "The guys were happy with the food." or "hand = tiny" for "My hand was tiny compared to the burger." This led us to refine the process with a number of filters. First, we expect extractions, across a large corpus, to appear with and without good patterns. For example, both "parking here is terrible" and "terrible parking" should be seen. If the more compact version is not seen for at least 5% of the extractions for a pattern, we discard the pattern. Additionally, we drop a number of qualifier words from the patterns, for example "lots" or "plenty," to avoid confusions they can cause. Finally, we used a part of speech tagger to ensure that in extractions with no pattern, such as "terrible parking," the first word is an adjective and the second is a noun. Together, these filters reduced the number of undesirable extractions shown in the extractive interface.

In total, 200 unique attributes and 1,536 unique values were extracted from the review data.

[1]These are sometimes called 'lexical patterns' in the literature.

Inputs: A large corpus of reviews R.

Definitions:

- Let E be a set of extractions. Each $e \in E$ is an attribute, value pair, for example $e = (a = \textit{parking}, v = \textit{terrible})$. Define $A(E)$ to be the set of attributes that exist in some pair in E and $V(E)$ to be the set of values in E. Let T be the set of extraction templates. One example $t \in T$ might be "[attribute] here is [value]." Define γ to be a count cutoff threshold.

Initialization:

- Create the empty template set $T = \emptyset$. Set ϵ based on dataset size ($\epsilon = 6$ for Yelp Seattle data). Set the cutoff to $\gamma = \epsilon$. Initialize E with a small set of seed extractions. For example, *food* paired with *tasty*, *delicious*, and *disgusting*.

Algorithm:

Do until the size of E does not grow:

Step 1: (Template Induction)

a. Find the set of templates T' that appear with attribute-value pairs in E somewhere in the corpus R. See text for full details.

b. Filter T' to remove templates that do not match the frequency threshold δ, and also as described in the main text.

c. Set $T = T'$.

Step 2: (Attribute Induction)

a. Let E' be every extraction from the corpus R for a template in T that contains a value in $V(E)$.

b. Filter E' according to the frequency cutoff δ.

c. Set $E = E'$.

Step 3: (Value Induction)

a. Let E' be every extraction from the corpus D for a template in T that contains an attribute in $A(E)$.

b. Filter E' according to the frequency cutoff δ.

c. Set $E = E'$.

Step 4: Update cutoff $\delta = \delta + \epsilon$.

Output: The final extraction set E.

Figure 4: REVMINER's bootstrapping algorithm for extracting attribute-value pairs from a large corpus of reviews.

Polarity

To determine the polarity of a value (*e.g.*, whether *delicious* is a positive or negative value), we use a simple method that works well on a large dataset such as ours. For each value, we compute the average of the Yelp ratings for all reviews it appears in. If this value is above or below empirically set thresholds, we label it as positive or negative. Otherwise, it is neutral. Across the potentially tens of thousands of reviews containing the value, this technique yielded high-quality polarity scores for nearly all values.

To evaluate the polarity generated from extracted values and their corresponding review ratings, we compared REVMINER and SentiWordNet (used in Review Spotlight [21]) to a gold standard of labels. SentiWordNet is a manually constructed resource that assigns positive and negative scores to subjective adjectives [5]. We selected the most appropriate word form from SentiWordNet based on the context and labeled it positive if the positive score was greater than the negative score, and negative if vice versa. This seemed to be a heuristic in which SentiWordNet performed well. Two judges labeled 199 values as either positive, negative, or neutral (with a weighted Kohen's kappa of $\kappa = 0.80$, representing high inter-rater agreement) and resolved differences. We then compared both REVMINER and SentiWordNet's labels with the judges' labels. REVMINER's labels agreed with the gold standard more often than SentiWordNet ($\kappa = 0.52$ for REVMINER, $\kappa = 0.48$ for SentiWordNet), demonstrating the effectiveness of our polarity computing method over this dataset.

Attribute Clustering

The Color Bar interface in Figure 6 displays attributes in five categories (*food*, *service*, *decor*, *overall*, other), each of which is a cluster that averages over a large number of primitive attributes. We manually selected the five clusters and seeded each with a small set of example attributes. For example, *decor* included *atmosphere* and *view*. We also define the distance between two attributes to be the Kullback-Leibler divergence [11] of the normalized count vectors for all values they appear with in the corpus. The clustering algorithm then simply places the remaining attributes in the cluster which has the closest seed attribute, according to this metric. This approach worked well for the small set of clusters we were interested in, outperforming other techniques such as k-means or agglomerative clustering in our development experiments.

Restaurant Similarity

We can use the extractions to compare different restaurants, rather than structured metadata or bag-of-words, as is often used. To determine which restaurants are most similar to a target restaurant, we iterate through each attribute, comparing their distributions of associated values. We experimented with a few metrics and found empirically that macro-averaging per attribute the Kullback-Leibler divergence of values returned the most intuitive results. The Kullback-Leibler divergence [11] (with a smoothing parameter) measures how far apart the restaurants' attributes are from each other. The attributes are weighted by how many values they are associated with, and summed together. The restaurants with the lowest divergence from the target restaurant are deemed the most similar and are presented in the REVMINER mobile app. For example, the two businesses most similar to Agua Verde Cafe (a traditional Mexican restaurant) were Cactus Restaurant and Rositas Mexican Grill.

Similarity based on fine-grained attributes automatically extracted from reviews differs from similarity based on Yelp metadata. Take for example, the restaurant called Paseo in the Fremont neighborhood. Yelp places it in the cuisine categories of Caribbean, Sandwiches, and Cuban. Its price range is $ for "Cheap, Under $10". Very different from Salumi Artisan Cured Meats in Pioneer Square, which Yelp categorized as Italian, Delis, Meat Shops with a $$ price range (*i.e.*, "Moderate, $11-$30"). Yet REVMINER identifies Salumi as its most similar restaurant to Paseo. Can that be right?

Careful inspection of the extracted attributes (Figure 5) in REVMINER for Paseo and Salumi finds the following: 78 mentions of a "long line" at Paseo, 76 mentions of a "long

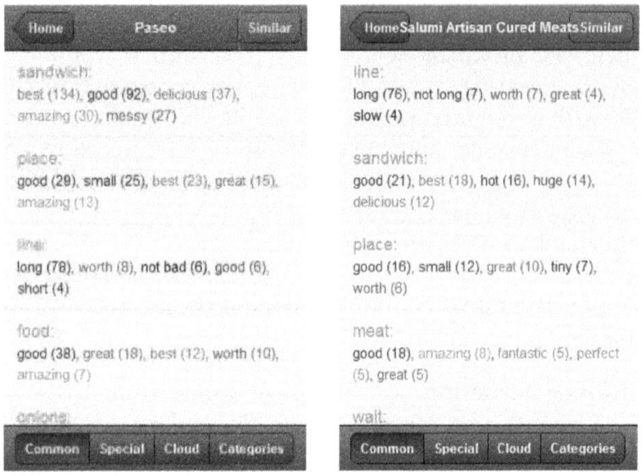

Figure 5: An example where two restaurants *seem* unrelated based on Yelp's cuisine and price meta-data, but are noticeably similar when inspecting the finer-grained attributes extracted from reviews by REVMINER.

line" at Salumi; raving descriptions of the sandwiches and food at both restaurants, many mentions of the place being "small" as well as the seating being "limited" at Paseo and Salumi. From this, we can infer that these both attract lunch crowds where the long lines in front of small store with limited seating are worth the wait for delicious sandwiches. Thus, the metadata presented in the Yelp app's search results page suggests there is little similarity between the two restaurants, but a deeper inspection by the similarity scoring system identifies a surprising similarity based on the extractions. Of course, REVMINER also performs well in common cases of finding similarity by typical attributes relating to cuisine, foods offered, service quality, etc.

MOBILE APP

The REVMINER Android app enables users to search and learn about the restaurants mentioned in our review corpus. The app consists of three capabilities: *search* for restaurants by listing attributes of interest, *view* information about each restaurant via four compact interfaces (Figure 6), and *suggest* similar restaurants. Each capability is described below.

Attribute Search

The REVMINER app enables users to query by attribute, and view restaurant results ranked by the polarity, strength, and frequency of the extracted values for those attributes.

Given a query, REVMINER first identifies which terms are attributes and which terms are values, and then pairs each value with the closest preceding attribute. For example, the query "free parking cheap mexican food" is parsed as the attribute = value assignments: parking = free, food = cheap, and food = mexican. Now, given a set of assignments, restaurants are ranked according how often their review text mentioned that pair by matching the assignments with extractions.

For the above example query on the Yelp Seattle corpus, this approach would return Rancho Bravo, a local taco shop with a parking lot in the back, as the top result. These types of queries are difficult to process in a traditional information retrieval system which cannot identify attributes and values in the query, and relies on seeking the words in the document. Thus, a review noting "free food" would score well in traditional information retrieval systems even though that is not the intent in the query "free parking cheap mexican food".

REVMINER's attribute search also distinguishes between subjective and objective searches. When a user searches for "good service", they do not literally mean "service that people said was good". Instead, they mean "service that people said was good or better". Therefore, we treated some values such as *best, good, great, amazing* as subjective values, which switched the query into finding the restaurant that maximizes the associated attribute (based on the polarities of values for the restaurant's attribute). For example, if the query is "good margaritas", REVMINER will return restaurants where the margaritas are called "exquisite" and "amazing" ahead of ones where the margaritas are merely "good", even though the values are not a literal match to the query. For objective values such as *creamy* or *chinese*, this behavior would not be desirable.

Note that we could easily supplement attribute searches with traditional information retrieval techniques. For example, we could fall back to a bag-of-words technique like the vector space model if our attribute searches return no results. We have not done so to focus on assessing the behavior of a "pure" extractive interface.

Presenting Restaurant Information

Reducing large numbers of reviews into a set of extractions allows REVMINER to summarize a restaurant on a single interactive page. Rather than presenting dozens or hundreds of reviews to the user as on a typical review website, REVMINER lays out the aggregated extractions for a restaurant, allowing the user to see what attributes other users comment most frequently about for a restaurant, what opinions they held about particular attributes for the business, and which were the most common extractions.

For example, Umi Sake House is a sushi bar with over a thousand reviews listed across 40 pages. The extractions for Umi Sake House comprise 101 attributes with an average of 12 distinct values each. Many attribute-value pairs are mentioned numerous times like "best sushi" (62) and "great place" (42). This collapses the information substantially, trading 40 pages of text for a table of extractions. The extractions are then sorted and laid out differently depending on the interface currently chosen. Four distinct interfaces are offered in the REVMINER mobile app.

The default REVMINER interface (the **Common** interface) lists the attributes vertically, with the most frequent values associated with the attribute shown underneath. The attributes themselves are sorted in descending order based on the number of values associated with them. The values are color-coded according to their polarity and strength (the greener the more positive, the redder the more negative). This gives the user a sense of the most common things reviewers say about the restaurant's attributes. Users can scroll down to less frequent attributes using the familiar swipe-to-scroll gesture.

(a) Common (b) Special (c) Tag Cloud (d) Color Bars

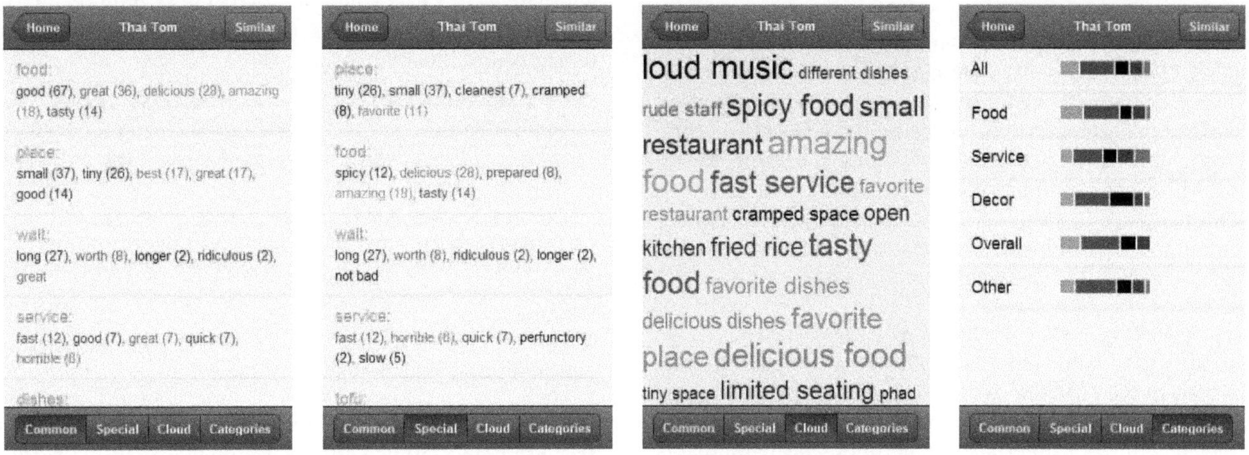

Figure 6: The four interfaces available to view information about Thai Tom in REVMINER. The default Common interface is a list of most-frequent attributes paired with their most-frequently-associated values. Compared to the Common interface, the Special interface selects more unusual values to show, the Tag Cloud interface lays out the attribute-value pairs differently, while the Color Bar interface clusters the attributes into categories and shows the values in a color-coded stacked bar chart.

Tapping on the attribute would show the source sentences containing that attribute, and tapping the sentence would show the entire review containing the sentence. This allowed users to zoom into a particularly interesting attribute.

The **Special** interface presents the attributes in the same manner, but sorts the values based on different criteria. The values are sorted not just by frequency, but also how unusual the value is. This resembles the tf-idf equation used in information retrieval systems [9], where the inverse of the term's frequency is multiplied by its frequency in the document (in our case, the reviews). We hypothesized that this presentation surfaced the more interesting aspects of a restaurant. For example, in Figure 6, key aspects of the restaurant become more prominent: the small tiny place, spicy food, and minority of customers who thought the service was horrible.

We implemented a **Tag Cloud** with some features similar to those from Review Spotlight[2] [21], which differed from a typical tag cloud by treating attribute-value pairs as a single term, placing them adjacent to each other in the cloud. The size of the words represented their frequency in the reviews. For example, "fresh sushi" in large font would indicate that many reviewers noted the sushi was fresh (possibly in multiple different lexical forms). Users could use this to gain an immediate impression of which attribute-value pairs were most pronounced in the reviews.

The final interface was **Color Bars** for attribute clusters, similar to those used in shopping websites like Google Shopping. Like Google Shopping, REVMINER's color-coded stacked bar charts presented the polarities drawn from the values for different attribute clusters (*e.g.*, food, service, decor). The color bars show at a glance the proportion of positive, neutral, and negative values describing each attribute. Clicking on the attribute cluster presented either a list (like the Common interface) or a Tag Cloud interface for that attribute cluster, depending on what was last selected by the user.

Similar Restaurants

Through the similarity scores computed in the offline processing, users had the option to view restaurants similar to the one they were already viewing. The app retrieved the five most similar restaurants and allowed the user to navigate to the information about those retrieved restaurants. From there, REVMINER would again retrieve the five most similar restaurants, thus allowing the user to browse similar restaurants indefinitely.

USER STUDY

We conducted a user study of REVMINER to address two key questions:

1. What is a compelling way to display the attribute-value information extracted by REVMINER on a smartphone?
2. What "natural" queries take advantage of an extractive interface over a search interface in the restaurant domain?

To answer the first question, we compared REVMINER's interface to three alternatives: a Tag Cloud interface which re-implements portions of the Review Spotlight interface, a Color Bar interface based on Google's shopping interface, and a Special interface, which highlights the distinctive values associated with each attribute (instead of the most common ones as in REVMINER's default interface). To answer the second question, we compared REVMINER's interface to Yelp's returned results on a set of attribute queries crawled from Twitter (described in the next subsection).

[2]Review Spotlight's tag cloud presented their pairs differently and included interactive features that REVMINER did not. Notably, the noun and adjective could be different sizes and were laid out more sparsely than a typical tag cloud. The user could also interact with the tag cloud—the source sentences were revealed by clicking the pairs, and adjectives for each noun were combined but were shown when hovering over the pair.

Method

Fourteen participants helped in evaluating REVMINER using two Android smartphones with the REVMINER app preinstalled. The participants were mostly recruited from mailing lists for graduate students; the recruitment email asked for participants who had lived in Seattle for at least two years, and frequently dined out. This allowed us to acquire participants who were familiar with many of the restaurants they would encounter in study. The study lasted approximately 90 minutes per participant, and we compensated them with snacks and a gift card drawing.

For the **interface** task, each participant was asked to list 10 restaurants they were familiar with. They looked up each restaurant in REVMINER and were presented with the four interfaces described earlier. The participant then studied and interacted with each interface; sometimes, the participants would use both phones provided to them for side-by-side comparisons. The participants rated the interfaces based on how well the interface accurately reflected what they knew about the restaurant, and whether it was useful for presenting attributes about the restaurant.

For the **search** task, participants evaluated how well REVMINER compared to Yelp in returning restaurant results related to a search query. REVMINER was loaded on one phone, while the Yelp app was loaded on another phone with geolocation features disabled. Therefore, the geographical scope of REVMINER and Yelp were the same (Seattle area), and the underlying dataset was the same, except Yelp's dataset had an additional 8 months of data accrued after the development of REVMINER.

We collected actual questions people had about restaurants automatically by searching Twitter. First, we copied 48 messages (originally 50, but 2 were discarded as irrelevant to restaurants) that contained "What restaurant has" or some variation of that phrase, from public Twitter messages. These messages typically asked for recommendations of restaurants with particular attributes, specifying an information need. For example, "What restaurant makes the best mexican food in Seattle?" Participants were then asked to formulate queries that could satisfy the information need from a selection of 10 such messages. They entered the query into the search box of REVMINER and Yelp, and rated the quality of the ranked list of results, providing us with a comparison between REVMINER and Yelp.

We examined the results from the search task and noticed that REVMINER performed particularly well for queries that contained more than one attribute. For example, one information need was "Which restaurant has the best wings for best price?" Queries containing multiple attributes took advantage of the attribute association and scoring mechanism used with the REVMINER extractions. However, since these queries only comprised a small portion of the original evaluation, we asked our last four participants to evaluate the efficacy of these 'conjunctive queries'. Four of the 48 Twitter messages were conjunctive information needs, and these last participants formulated and evaluated queries for each of the four conjunctive information needs.

Table 1: REVMINER's default interface compared with three alternatives in a user study. REVMINER's Common interface is preferred over Tag Cloud, Color Bar, and Special by a statistically significant margin.

Comparison	Yes	No	Tie	p-value
Common > Tag Cloud	46%	20%	33%	< 0.05
Common > Color Bar	73%	10%	18%	< 0.05
Common > Special	54%	14%	32%	< 0.05

Results

We present here the quantitative results for the two tasks and our qualitative interpretations of them.

Our first task resulted in 114 **interface** comparisons from the 14 participants (some participants did not perform the full 10 comparisons due to time constraints).

Comparing Common to Special: Both interfaces have the same layout, and thus can show the same amount of information on the screen. The difference is in the values chosen to display—whether REVMINER displayed the most frequent values for each attribute, or gave preference to the unusualness of the values as well. In our study, we found that participants rated Common higher in 54% cases, Special higher in 14% cases, and rated them equally in 32% cases. Thus, while there were several cases where unusual values were useful as they highlighted aspects of the restaurant that deviated from the norm, in most cases, they were outliers and detracted from the understanding of the restaurant.

Comparing Common to Tag Cloud: Both interfaces choose the content to show in order of frequency, but use a different layout. Common presents a list of attributes along with their values, while Tag Cloud is a similar implementation to the tag cloud in Review Spotlight [21]. Participants preferred Common to Tag Cloud in 46% cases, while the inverse was true in 20% cases, and participants rated them equally in 33% cases. One participant reasoned that the Common interface was able to pack more information in the same screen space, while being faster to glance. However, other participants did prefer the Tag Cloud because the most important terms "popped out of the screen" in large font. We found this comparison to be the most polarizing among participants.

Comparing Common to Color Bar. We experimented with adding an additional layer of abstraction above the Common interface. The stacked bar charts for each category, which comprised multiple related attributes, showed the distribution of polarities for the values in that category. Participants preferred Common 73% to 10% of the time, with 18% having same ratings. Participants rating Common higher explained that many restaurants had similar bar charts, and it was difficult to compare between bar charts. They preferred having descriptive values to understand the attributes in a richer way.

We used a two-tailed Sign Test to test for differences in the $N = 114$ interface comparisons. We found the differences between Common and the other three interfaces were statistically significant at the $p < 0.05$ level after applying the Bonferroni correction.

Table 2: REVMINER's restaurant results compared with restaurant results in the Yelp mobile app.

Result	Frequency
REVMINER Favored	45%
Yelp Favored	30%
REVMINER and Yelp Tied	25%

In the **search** comparison between Yelp and REVMINER, participants performed 115 comparisons (not all participants did 10 comparisons due to time constraints). The findings showed that in 9 cases (8% of queries), REVMINER produced no results. This was due to terms in the query not matching any of the attributes of values extracted by REVMINER (*e.g.*, mac n cheese). Yelp's bag-of-words representation enables it to produce some results for these queries. For the rest of the queries, participants preferred REVMINER in 45% cases and preferred Yelp in 30% cases. Yelp and REVMINER scored the same in the remaining cases.

Upon closer inspection of the queries where REVMINER produced substantially better results, we found that conjunctive needs were a particular strong point for REVMINER. We asked our last four participants to select the Twitter questions with conjunctive information needs to focus on evaluating these. For the conjunctive queries, participants preferred REVMINER more than twice as often as Yelp (62% preferring REVMINER, 27% preferring Yelp). This suggests that an extractive approach may perform better than the traditional information retrieval approach that Yelp uses for conjunctive queries. One explanation is that a system understanding how the values are associated with different attributes can identify relevant restaurants better than a bag-of-words approach to query-restaurant matching.

DISCUSSION

Contrasting with Information Retrieval

Extractive interfaces such as REVMINER differ from traditional information in a few ways. First, extractive interfaces can treat words as ordinal values. This means understanding that *great* and *good* are both subjective values, and that *great* is more positive than *good*. Thus, values can be placed on a scale and compared. Second, extracting the attribute-value pairs allow an extractive interface to aggregate attributes and values in many ways. This enables applications such as clustering and similarity which depend on the distributions of aggregated values. Furthermore, documents (restaurants in our case) can then be ranked based on a scoring function using the aggregated query terms. Third, values are associated with attributes when appropriate, and thus the query and document are not treated as a bag of words, as is typical in information retrieval. The query "Free parking amazing desserts" will not match reviews containing mentions of "free desserts" and "amazing parking". Finally, we able to take advantage of boolean-like operators in sentences such as "not" and "and" to generate more extractions.

Meaning in Review Language

During the processing of extracting attributes and values from the reviews, we learned two lessons about meaning inherent in the language used in reviews. First, words can have different meanings when it is written in a review, versus when it is issued in a query. For example, people who mention that the food at a restaurant is *cheap* does not necessarily mean it cost little. What they mean is the food is good value compared to their expectations. Few people will remark that McDonald's was *cheap*, but people will declare *cheap* over a $30 3-course special at an exclusive establishment. But when searching for "cheap restaurant", the same people seek cheap eats in absolute terms, rather than somewhat cheaper than they would typically expect. An edge case such as this can cause problems for both traditional information retrieval and extraction-based search.

The meaning in a query itself can also be ambiguous. Someone looking for "good dim sum" is not looking for dim sum where people have noted is "good". In fact, our polarity calculations show that "good" is barely a positive complement in reviews. Instead, the searcher is looking for "good or better" dim sum, including dim sum that others have described as "great" or "amazing". Not all values are subjective in this way, as others such as "spicy" or "italian" describe a specific quality in the attribute. REVMINER is able to understand this and by identifying subjective values such as *good* in the query, to give the searcher what they really want: dim sum restaurants sorted by quality.

Extending Similarity

Item similarity typically uses a collaborative filtering algorithm such as k-nearest neighbors applied to user browsing data or user ratings. As part of REVMINER, we have developed a good similarity scoring function based solely on user reviews. Thus, as an independent source of data, user reviews can be combined with other user data to develop even more accurate similarity-based applications.

Beyond Restaurant Reviews

There is a growing dataset of reviews on the Web, such as product reviews and movie reviews. While we have used REVMINER on other types of non-restaurant reviews business reviews, non-business reviews may pose other interesting challenges. For example, movie reviews often contain more descriptions of the movie content, but some attribute-value extractions are still quite useful, such as "surprise ending", "predictable plot", "poor acting". Mining the reviews to produce similarity scores may be useful as a supplement to existing methods.

User-Review Behavior

Our research presents a new opportunity for users of review websites. It is currently common to read reviews after finding a particular business or product, rather than using reviews to discover new products. This may be due to the large amount of review text that one has to wade through. An extractive interface may enable a change in this behavior, by presenting aggregate review information as extractions and enabling better searching capabilities in reviews. Perhaps this may change peoples' behavior so that reading reviews might not remain the last action in a shopping process. Instead, people may go to the reviews first to find a particular business or product matching their needs.

Limitations

We acknowledge some limitations to our evaluation of REVMINER. In evaluating the extractive interface, we focused on the choice of which extractions to present and how to present them. We did not compare the interface with the full Yelp mobile app because the Yelp app also displays metadata such as photos, the address, opening hours, etc. which were beyond the scope of this paper. Additionally, we did not perform rigorous counterbalancing of the order we presented the interfaces to the participants. Participants browsed the four extractive interfaces on two phones informally, sometimes side-by-side, sometimes one after another.

CONCLUSION

This paper described a method for extracting attribute-value pairs from a large corpus of user reviews. These extractions provide a structured representation of the opinions people have about restaurants and their attributes. Using the extractions, we developed REVMINER, which enables searching based on attributes, presenting information for restaurants, and identifying similar restaurants. We created an Android app, which offers four compact presentations of the extracted information, and carried out a user study.

Our user study helped to quantify the advantage of the extractive interface over both earlier research and over Yelp's smartphone app. We believe that our experiments, and the REVMINER system demonstrate the potential of extractive interfaces to enable a better experience for shoppers navigating product reviews on smartphones.

ACKNOWLEDGMENTS

This research was supported in part by NSF grant IIS-0803481, ONR grant N00014-08-1-0431, a gift from Google, and carried out at the University of Washington's Turing Center. The authors thank James Fogarty for helpful discussions about study design, and Dan Weld and Raphael Hoffman for reviewing earlier drafts of the paper.

REFERENCES

1. Agichtein, E., and Gravano, L. Snowball: Extracting relations from large plain-text collections. In *Proceedings of DL* (2000), 85–94.

2. Breese, J., Heckerman, D., and Kadie, C. Empirical analysis of predictive algorithms for collaborative filtering. In *Proceedings of UAI* (1998), 43–52.

3. Brin, S. Extracting patterns and relations from the world wide web. *The World Wide Web and Databases* (1999), 172–183.

4. Chang, C.-H., Kayed, M., Girgis, M. R., and Shaalan, K. F. A survey of web information extraction systems. *IEEE Trans. on Knowl. and Data Eng. 18*, 10 (Oct. 2006), 1411–1428.

5. Esuli, A., and Sebastiani, F. Sentiwordnet: A publicly available lexical resource for opinion mining. In *Proceedings of LREC*, vol. 6 (2006), 417–422.

6. Guha, R., McCool, R., and Miller, E. Semantic search. In *Proceedings of WWW* (2003), 700–709.

7. Hearst, M., Elliott, A., English, J., Sinha, R., Swearingen, K., and Yee, K.-P. Finding the flow in web site search. *Commun. ACM 45*, 9 (Sept. 2002), 42–49.

8. Hoffmann, R., Fogarty, J., and Weld, D. S. Assieme: finding and leveraging implicit references in a web search interface for programmers. In *Proceedings of UIST* (2007), 13–22.

9. Jones, K. S. A statistical interpretation of term specificity and its application in retrieval. *Journal of Documentation 28*, 1 (1972), 11–20.

10. Karlson, A. K., Robertson, G. G., Robbins, D. C., Czerwinski, M. P., and Smith, G. R. Fathumb: a facet-based interface for mobile search. In *Proceedings of CHI* (2006), 711–720.

11. Kullback, S., and Leibler, R. A. On information and sufficiency. *Ann. Math. Statist. 22*, 1 (1951), 79–86.

12. Pang, B., and Lee, L. Opinion mining and sentiment analysis. *Found. Trends Inf. Retr. 2*, 1-2 (Jan. 2008), 1–135.

13. Popescu, A.-M., and Etzioni, O. Extracting product features and opinions from reviews. In *Proceedings of HLT* (2005), 339–346.

14. Probst, K., Ghani, R., Krema, M., Fano, A., and Liu, Y. Semi-supervised learning of attribute-value pairs from product descriptions. In *Proceedings of IJCAI* (2007), 2838–2843.

15. Riloff, E., and Jones, R. Learning dictionaries for information extraction by multi-level bootstrapping. In *Proceedings of AAAI* (1999), 474–479.

16. Rivadeneira, A. W., Gruen, D. M., Muller, M. J., and Millen, D. R. Getting our head in the clouds: toward evaluation studies of tagclouds. In *Proceedings of CHI* (2007), 995–998.

17. Salton, G., Wong, A., and Yang, C. S. A vector space model for automatic indexing. *Commun. ACM 18*, 11 (Nov. 1975), 613–620.

18. Su, X., and Khoshgoftaar, T. M. A survey of collaborative filtering techniques. *Adv. in Artif. Intell. 2009* (Jan. 2009), 4:2–4:2.

19. von Reischach, F., Dubach, E., Michahelles, F., and Schmidt, A. An evaluation of product review modalities for mobile phones. In *Proceedings of MobileHCI* (2010), 199–208.

20. von Reischach, F., Guinard, D., Michahelles, F., and Fleisch, E. A mobile product recommendation system interacting with tagged products. In *Proceedings of PerCom* (2009), 1–6.

21. Yatani, K., Novati, M., Trusty, A., and Truong, K. N. Review spotlight: a user interface for summarizing user-generated reviews using adjective-noun word pairs. In *Proceedings of CHI* (2011), 1541–1550.

Cross-Device Interaction via Micro-mobility and F-formations

Nicolai Marquardt[1,2], Ken Hinckley[1], Saul Greenberg[2]

[1]Microsoft Research
One Microsoft Way, Redmond WA 98052
kenh@microsoft.com

[2]University of Calgary, Dept. of
Computer Science, Calgary, AB, Canada
{nicolai.marquardt, saul}@ucalgary.ca

ABSTRACT

GroupTogether is a system that explores cross-device interaction using two sociological constructs. First, *F-formations* concern the distance and relative body orientation among multiple users, which indicate when and how people position themselves as a group. Second, *micro-mobility* describes how people orient and tilt devices towards one another to promote fine-grained sharing during co-present collaboration. We sense these constructs using: (a) a pair of overhead Kinect depth cameras to sense small groups of people, (b) low-power 8GHz band radio modules to establish the identity, presence, and coarse-grained relative locations of devices, and (c) accelerometers to detect tilting of slate devices. The resulting system supports fluid, minimally disruptive techniques for co-located collaboration by leveraging the *proxemics of people* as well as the *proxemics of devices*.

Author Keywords

Proxemics; F-formations; micro-mobility; tablets; sensors

ACM Classification Keywords

H.5.2 [Information Interfaces and Presentation]: Input

INTRODUCTION

Despite the ongoing proliferation of devices and form-factors such as slates and electronic whiteboards, technology often hinders (rather than helps) informal small-group interactions. Whereas natural human conversation is fluid and dynamic, discussions that rely on digital content—slides, documents, clippings—often remain stilted due to the awkwardness of manipulating, sharing, and displaying information on and across multiple devices.

To address these shortcomings, we leverage two sociological constructs that have been observed in human-human social activity: first, the interpersonal (*proxemic*) dynamics of small-group gatherings known as *F-formations*; and second, how people employ *micro-mobility* of physical artifacts to afford nuanced collaboration. Multiple sensing modalities enable us to capture and make use of these constructs in novel multi-device interaction techniques. Paired together, these approaches afford a lightweight federation of multiple devices and displays that leverage proxemic cues derived from: (a) the human-to-human proxemic relationships resulting from the spacing and relative body orientation among people; and (b) the distance and relative orientation between the devices themselves. We believe that recognizing and respecting the *proxemics of devices* as a related yet nonetheless separate construct from the *proxemics of people* is an important conceptual distinction contributed by our work.

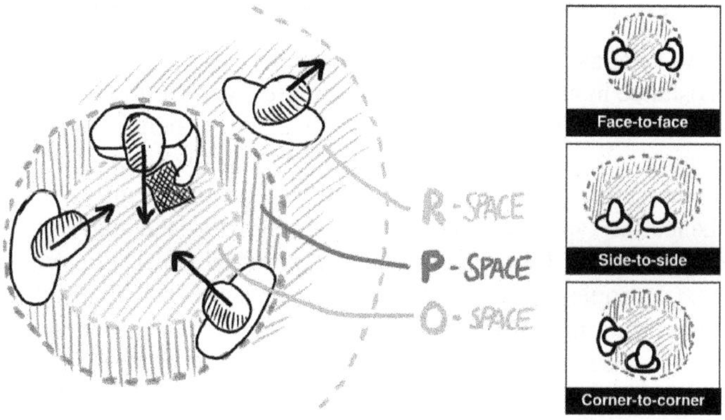

Fig. 1. An F-formation consists of two or more persons engaged in joint activity. Their bodies define three, roughly circular, regions: the inner o-space, the ring of p-space, and the surrounding r-space.

Our paper contributes the following. Using the theoretical lenses of F-formations and micro-mobility (detailed in depth in the following sections), and further informed by an observational study we conducted of people working together with foam-core mock-ups of mobile displays, we designed a number of cross-device interaction techniques that support nuanced gradations of sharing, from the subtle to the overt, with the goal of minimizing the transaction costs—and social disruption—of sharing information across a small-group ecology of digital devices and situated displays. The techniques are unique in that they consider device-to-device relationships as well as the context of the social group to mediate interaction. Our system realizes this through a hybrid of on-device sensors (motion sensors and 8GHz band radios) as well as extrinsic sensors in the environment (depth cameras and fixed-location radios).

The remaining sections of this paper first delve further into the theory of proxemics, F-formations, and micro-mobility that motivate our work, and discuss additional related work. Next, we present an observational study which informs the behaviors that serve as the building blocks of our interaction techniques. We then detail the interaction techniques and sensing system implementation. We close with an informal evaluation of the techniques as well as a discussion of salient issues raised by this research.

UIST '12, October 7–10, 2012, Cambridge, Massachusetts, USA.

BACKGROUND THEORY AND MOTIVATION

Our research leverages insights from three sociological concepts: proxemics, F-formations, and micro-mobility.

Proxemics

The sociological field of proxemics [4,10] studies people's use of personal space to mediate social interactions. While proxemics has many aspects (e.g. nonverbal cues, body orientation, and cultural variation), the defining characteristic is that people equate interpersonal physical distance with social distance. Hall [10], for example, describes social zones based on physical distance between people, ranging from *intimate* (0-50cm), *personal* (1m), *social* (4m), and *public* (>4m) distances. In the context of ubiquitous computing, the implication is that proximity becomes, in part, an estimation of people's desire to communicate with one another via the devices they carry.

The Focused Encounter: F-formations

Distance in and of itself is not a complete description of the social connectedness of co-located persons. Whereas Hall's notion of proxemics primarily concerns the impact of *distance* on the perceptions available to the organism—and hence the types of communications afforded—the study of *F-formations* further considers the *physical arrangements* that people adopt when they engage in focused conversational encounters. Specifically, F-formations [5,17] are a macro-level theoretical lens through which one observes small-group interactions. F-formations consider the spatial relationships that occur as people arrange themselves during face-to-face interaction for optimal task-dependent communication and clarity of perception (Fig. 1). A typical arrangement is a roughly circular cluster that contains 2-5 persons who are actively part of the group. The inner space of that circle (called *o-space*) is reserved for the main activity the group is pursuing. The ring of space occupied by the people (*p-space*) determines group membership. The surrounding region (*r-space*) buffers the group from the outside world. Thus persons who are nearby but not in p-space are excluded from the fine-grained social circle that defines the F-formation. Still, the group monitors r-space to see others who may be trying to join. For example, an approaching person in r-space may be greeted via eye contact, while a person who is facing away, even if close to the group, is not treated as a potential member.

F-formations are nuanced. They need not be circular. Different relative body orientations— face-to-face, side-by-side (as in Fig. 1), or corner-to-corner (L-shaped)— afford different types of collaborative tasks: competitive, collaborative, or communicative, respectively [26]. Group size varies, but tends to be small. Freely forming groupings rarely surpass 5 persons; 95% are 4 persons or less, and more than half are dyadic [7]. Gestures made or objects held within the o-space become the focus of conversation, whereas objects held down (in p-space) or outside the circle (in r-space) are excluded [5]. Fixed or semi-fixed features of a room, such as walls and furniture, can also influence the structure of F-formations [5]. As we will see, these observations—as further reinforced by our own behavioral study—inform the sensing requirements and desired transactional properties of our interaction techniques.

Micro-Mobility

The *micro-mobility* of physical artifacts is the fine-grained orientation and repositioning of objects so that they may be fully viewed, partially viewed, or concealed from other persons. For example, Luff & Heath [20] reported on patient-doctor consultations via paper records and observed how individuals rely on the micro-mobility of these physical artifacts to facilitate communication. The doctor might gesture at a record, orient it such that it invites the patient to view material, or pull it back to give the doctor time to read information. These subtle manipulations of the paper record afford the shifting demands of an activity.

Thus micro-mobility posits that orienting an artifact towards other persons, moving it closer to them, or even subtly tilting it towards or away from that person affords powerful and nuanced ways for individuals to share (or not share) information, as well as to fluidly manage the focus of conversation and make their intentions clear to others.

Using Theory to Motivate Group Interaction Techniques

Our belief is that ubiquitous computing environments can sense social proximity of people in the form of F-formation assemblages as well as the micro-mobility of the physical devices used by the group. In particular, we sense F-formations of both the people and the devices they carry to automatically federate devices and mediate cross-device interaction in a way that corresponds to real-time social groupings. Physically nearby people in the r-space, especially those facing away, are recognized as socially distant from the current assemblage of users and therefore can be excluded from the exchange. If people within the F-formation then orient their devices towards (say) the central o-space (i.e., using micro-mobility), the system can offer lightweight ways to share device contents across the group.

ADDITIONAL RELATED WORK

Previous efforts have explored techniques for mediating cross-device interaction, sometimes informed by proxemics [10] or a more general notion of proximity sensing, but past work rarely applies the multiple lenses of proxemics, F-formations, and micro-mobility in unison.

Sensing Presence, Proximity, and F-Formations

Various early systems sense and take action based on the distance between people and a device. However, what often goes unrecognized is that the fidelity of sensing (*coarse-grained* vs. *fine-grained* detection of physical distance) as well as the sensing approach itself (*intrinsic* sensors on the device or worn by the user, vs. *extrinsic* sensors mounted in the environment) entail many tradeoffs that speak to the nature and type of interactions that can be supported.

For example, sensing mere presence represents one very coarse-grained type of ubicomp proxemics, with correspondingly limited interactive capabilities, such as turning on the lights when a user enters a room [4]. If a rough measure of distance is available, more fine-grained interaction is afforded by sensing proximity in several discrete zones (akin to Hall's proxemic zones [10]). For example, Vogel [28] describes an ambient wall display that exhibits responses ranging from public to semi-private interaction depending on what zone a person is in, a theme further explored by Ju [16]. Systems may also provide proximity-ordered lists of nearby resources [25,30].

Greenberg [9] argues that computing systems—which are carried about as well as embedded in the world around us—could be enhanced by sensing proxemic dimensions such as distance, orientation, movement, identity, and location. Ballendat [1], for example, describes a proxemic media player that responds to movement, proximity, and relative body orientation of multiple persons. Other examples include games, advertising displays, and presentation systems based on nuanced notions of proximity [9,21,29]. Such systems typically leverage environments augmented with sensing technologies [1,3,28,31], though approaches such as orienting proximate mobile devices using their back-facing cameras have also been explored [6].

In computing, F-formations have been used to analyze social interactions in crowded environments [14,22], but they have rarely been applied to interaction technique design. Models have been proposed for federating sets of cooperating devices, such as Rodden's awareness model for groupware applications [24], or the boundary principle [18] articulated by Kindberg & Fox. F-formations offer a lens grounded in sociological theory to enrich these approaches.

Micro-mobility for Tabletops and Other Interactions

Luff and Heath [20] introduced micro-mobility and its implications for the design of groupware systems mostly as a cautionary tale, i.e., that new technologies may disrupt the natural movement of artefacts necessary for effective communication. Micro-mobility has since been applied to other areas, particularly the spacing and orientation [8,19] of digital objects on tabletop systems to denote personal territoriality as well as groupings of objects. Other related techniques include adjusting the posture of dual-screen devices [13], bumping and pouring [12], stitching [23], and "chucking" content from one device to another [11].

Implications

Our work differs from this prior work in several ways. First, we apply the above concepts in unison. By explicitly incorporating sensing mechanisms for both interpersonal proxemics (via F-formations) as well as device-to-device orientation and identification (via micro-mobility), our system embraces these approaches in a hybrid design.

Second, our focus is on cross-device interaction methods, and in particular how to decide when devices should be federated (by sensing F-formations) and how that information should be shared (by sensing micro-mobility).

Third, the sociological study of proxemics and F-formations has primarily considered interpersonal distance. As such, this literature rarely concerns itself with "object territoriality" – for our purposes, that is, the *proxemics of devices* such as slates or mobiles. Our work, including our formative study, seeks to explicitly address this gap.

DESIGN STUDY: PROXEMICS OF PEOPLE & DEVICES

We conducted an exploratory design study to gain insight into: (a) how people vary proxemic variables, such as distance and orientation, while interacting with one another; and (b) the less well-studied proxemic relationships of device to people, and device to device. Our goal was to inform the behaviors we should look for with our sensing system, as well as to provide fodder for naturally occurring gestures and device movements that we might leverage—or need to disregard—for our interaction techniques.

Participants performed joint activities, consisting of both cooperative and competitive tasks, using handheld displays of different sizes (slate, reader, and phone; 30.5 x 21 cm, 15 x 21cm, and 6 x 12cm, respectively). Tasks included *collaborative* (discuss and compare graphics divided across displays), *competitive* (find locations on a map as quickly as possible), and *co-present but individual* work: memorize a list of items, and then enumerate them while the other participant checks the list. We also included scenarios where participants read pre-printed "private" emails.

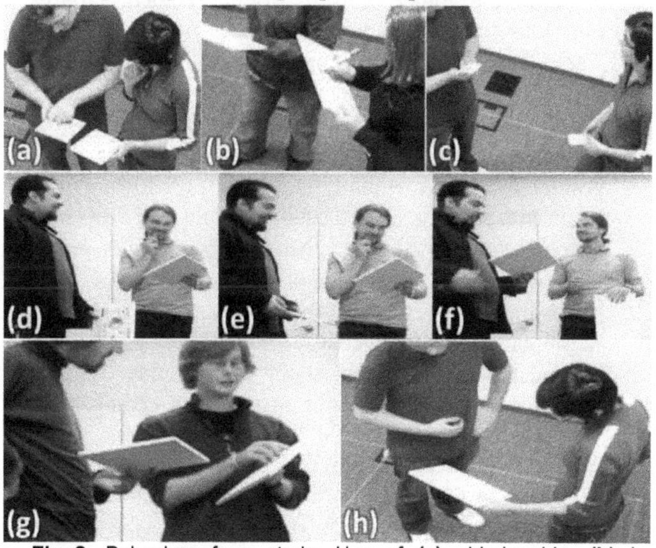

Fig. 2. Behaviors from study. Use of **(a)** side-by-side, **(b)** L-shaped, and **(c)** face-to-face formations depends on task. Devices shift in and out **(d,e,f)** of the shared o-space as users attend to them. Tilting **(g)** while pointing to an item on the display. Moving a display into o-space **(h)** and orienting to a compromise viewpoint.

We videotaped ten paired participants (2 pairs male-female, 3 pairs male-male) as they worked with 1cm thick foam-core mock-ups of slates, readers, and phones fitted with paper "displays." We used foam-core models so that we could focus on the human behaviors of micro-mobility and F-formations, rather than limitations induced by the affordances (weight, screen glare, etc.) of current devices.

From these sessions we observed the following behaviors (B1-B8) that illustrate interpersonal postures, movements, and gestures that people naturally exhibit in such situations:

B1. Device as extension of person. Participants treated the devices as part of their person (Fig. 2a). They were reluctant to bring displays into direct contact or to touch one another's displays (though they sometimes did so, albeit briefly). Users clearly exhibited a notion of "personal space" surrounding their devices, but the socially acceptable *device-space* was compressed as compared to normal interpersonal distances.

B2. Distance and shape of F-formations vary by task. In the presence of hand-held devices, the task influenced the choice of formation, reinforcing related findings from the proxemics literature [26]. For collaborative tasks that required synthesis of information across displays, users moved close together and adopted side-by-side formations (Fig. 2a). For parallel individual work, users moved apart, often in L-shaped formations (Fig. 2b). For competitive or private tasks, users often moved face-to-face (Fig. 2c), as well as further apart.

B3. Movement of devices in and out of focal zone. Users extended displays into the o-space defined by their joint gaze when discussing content. Displays not the topic of communication moved into p-space at the user's side, with the display facing inward (Fig. 2d,e,f).

B4. Incidental tilting. As long as a display was not oriented towards the other person, users seemed largely oblivious to the particular tilt angles of their device. That is, any particular tilt angle is not a definitive cue in and of itself, but rather has to be interpreted in the context of the F-formation (e.g. Fig. 2d, e).

B5. Pointing while tilting within the o-space. People often pointed to an item while tilting the display towards the other person (Fig. 2g). That is, people often discuss *specific pieces of content* rather than the entire display.

B6. Reorientation with gradation in response. As with micro-mobility [20], we observed subtle tilting and reorientation to nonverbally indicate when people wanted to say something about their display. Larger, more overt movement of the display to a compromise viewpoint was a powerful cue to redirect the other person's attention (Fig. 2h). That is, people employed a gradation in response, from the subtle to the overt, to suit the current communicative need.

B7. Avoid persistent spatial invasion. When users gestured at each other's display, such intrusions always remained brief, typically just a second or two. Users often want to indicate referents on the other's display, yet doing so may be uncomfortable; this suggests cross-device interactions should avoid direct interaction with another user's display [23].

B8. Matching pose while side-by-side. When actively working on a joint task, users tended to mirror the tilt angle of one another's slates (e.g. Fig. 2a), suggesting that equal tilt angles offer a context where it might be useful to reduce the barriers to sharing across devices.

Our intent is not to mimic B1-B8 in our design *per se*, but rather to use them as building-blocks, or points of departure. Furthermore, some of the above points—while perhaps obvious in retrospect—did not strike us as important observations until after we had completed our initial implementation and usability study. These we will return to later as we discuss the strengths, weaknesses, and possible extensions to our techniques.

THE GROUPTOGETHER SYSTEM

The GroupTogether system explores these concepts in action. We implemented a prototype "informal information workspace" where users can freely arrange collected content (photos, sketches, clippings, etc.) on an interactive canvas. We implemented the application for both slates and digital whiteboards, and each instance of the application may connect to others nearby, as mediated by our sensing of F-formations and device micro-mobility. We chose this application context because collecting and loosely organizing content is a common need of information workers, such as during active reading (e.g. [13,27]).

In the following sections we describe four main interaction techniques supported by GroupTogether, focusing initially on the micro-mobility aspects. We then describe how we extend these techniques to federated devices held by users in F-formations consisting of two or more persons. We also consider the case where the F-formation encompasses a digital whiteboard. We then describe our implementation.

INTERACTION TECHNIQUES

We developed four interaction techniques facilitating the sharing of digital information between the devices of people standing in an F-formation. These techniques are directly inspired by behaviors B1-B8 noted above, and as we discuss each technique we will refer back to these behaviors to reinforce our rationale, design considerations, and behavioral constraints. Note, however, that B1 and B2 are more meta-observations underlying all our techniques: they validate our preconception that there exists a proxemics of devices (B1), reinforce our design approach (devices must be proximal, but do not have to touch; again B1), and furthermore that a variety of F-formation structures must be properly sensed and supported in a consistent manner by the interaction techniques (B2). Furthermore, while in the following descriptions of specific techniques we primarily focus on micro-mobility gestures, keep in mind that these gestures are only active when the user is currently sensed as standing in an F-formation.

Our interaction techniques facilitate transient sharing, copying, transfer, and reference to digital information across federated devices. These actions suit our application context and allow us to explore various possibilities in order to generate design insights. In particular, the system offers multiple ways to support co-located collaborative activity, ranging from the subtle to the more overt, with various and nuanced semantics of what it means to "share" content. For clarity, in the following we refer to a two-user F-formation involving handheld devices: the user initiating the interaction is the ***sender***; and the other person is the

recipient. We later describe how our techniques work with more than two people, and also with a large display.

Tilt-to-Preview Selected Content

The *Tilt-to-Preview* technique provides an extremely lightweight way to *transiently share* selected digital content across devices. The receiving user can then elect to *grab a copy* of the transiently shared information.

Following the example of behavior B5, *Pointing while tilting within the o-space*, the sender shares a selected piece of content by holding his finger on said content while simultaneously tipping the slate slightly (by a minimum of 10 degrees, Fig. 3). This gesture is only active when the tablet is held up within o-space; when triggered it causes a transient semi-transparent representation of the selected item to appear on the display of all devices in the current F-formation. To make it easy for recipients to identify who is offering an item, an animation slides-in the shared item from the side of the screen where the sender is standing.

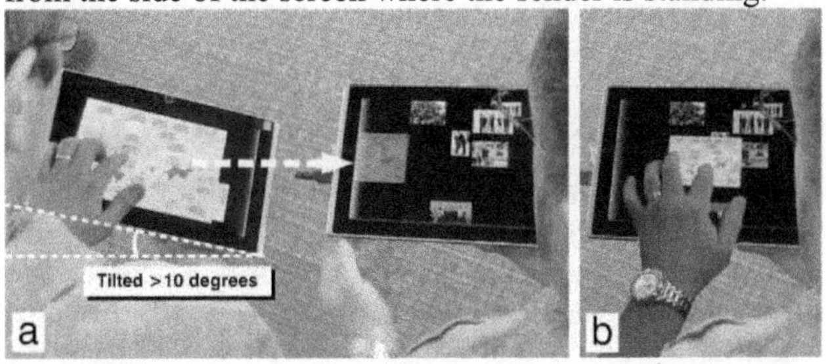

Fig. 3. Tilting tablet and touching content to transfer temporary copy (a), touch copy on second tablet to keep permanent copy (b).

We employ a tilt threshold of 10 degrees: during pilot testing we found this angle well beyond the *incidental tilting* (B4) that users typically exhibit while holding a slate. Tipping a slate beyond this threshold serves both as a gesture to trigger the behavior as well as a social cue observable to the recipient (and any other people nearby) that the sender wishes to share something. The gesture therefore also leverages observation B6, *Reorientation with gradation in response*, with a fairly subtle overture. Note also that the recipient can ignore such an overture merely by leaving his tablet down, in p-space (as in B3, *Movement in/out of focal zone*), or accept it by holding the tablet up.

When the sender lets go of the transiently shared content, it disappears from the recipient's screen. However, the recipient can choose to keep a *copy* of the transiently shared content by touching a finger down and grabbing it while it remains visible. This precludes any need for either user to reach onto the other's display, in accordance with observation B7 (*Avoid persistent spatial invasion*).

In dyadic F-formations the sender just tips the slate towards the other user. Alternatively, or if there are more than two people in the F-formation, the user can also tip the slate towards the o-space (i.e., the center of the formation).

Face-to-Mirror the Full Screen

As noted in B6, *Reorientation with gradation in response*, we observed both subtle and overt tipping gestures in the course of our design study. As we observed there, a user can employ a larger tilt as a more demanding nonverbal request to interrupt the current thread of conversation and introduce something else. We also noticed that users often employed larger tilts to show content to their more distant partner in face-to-face formations (B2, but not pictured).

Face-to-Mirror explores how we might provide digital affordances based on these observed behaviors. Using this technique, a person can share the full screen view of the primary digital content displayed on their screen to the other tablets in the social group of an F-formation.

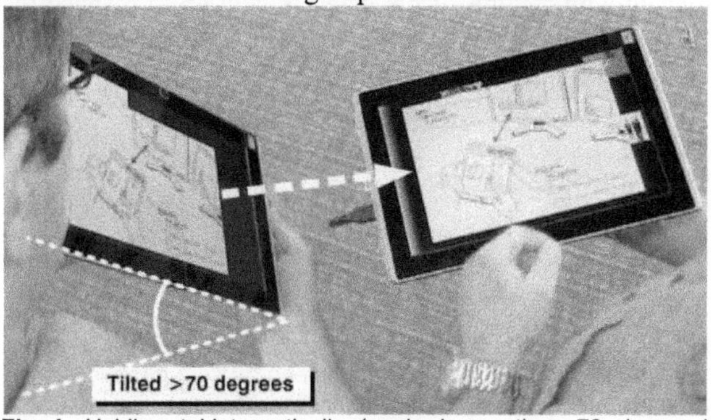

Fig. 4. Holding tablet vertically (angle larger than 70 degrees) shows a full screen copy on the other tablet.

When a person holds their tablet vertically (at an angle larger than 70 degrees), the interactive canvas is mirrored, at full-screen scale, to the display of all other tablets of the group (Fig. 4). Note that unlike Tilt-to-Preview, this is a pure tilting gesture; the user does not have to touch the screen to explicitly select content. Thus, while the tilting motion is larger, the transaction cost of sharing is potentially lower because the required action is simply "show your screen to the others." Again, the tilting motion is large enough that incidental tilting (B4) is not an issue with this technique, and furthermore we only observed the *Tilting while pointing* behavior (B5) in the context of more subtle tilting motions, so requiring pointing during Face-to-Mirror would run counter to our design study observations.

As with Tilt-To-Preview, Face-to-Mirror begins as a transient sharing technique that ends when the sender moves his slate away from the vertical posture, but where recipients can retain a copy by grabbing the mirrored item.

Portals

The above two techniques both share either a transient representation of an item, or a permanent copy if the recipient touches down and grabs it.

To explore an alternative semantic of *transferring* content from one device to another (that is, moving rather than copying content), we implemented the Portals technique, which builds on the notion of dragging items across federated devices (as explored in previous systems such as ARIS [2] and PointRight[15]). The difference here is the sensing approach to federate the devices in the first place, plus tilting as a micro-mobility gesture to establish a Portal.

When tilting a tablet (more than 10 degrees) towards the device of any other group member, a tinted edge appears along the shared screen edge of the two slates (Fig. 5a). By dragging an item through this edge and releasing the touch, the item is (permanently) transferred to the other device (Fig. 5b). A continuous cross-display animation reinforces the metaphor of the gesture: the content slides off the sender's screen, and slides into the recipient's screen. The recipient can then drag, resize, and otherwise manipulate the content that was transferred to their tablet (Fig. 5c). As with Tilt-to-Preview, the recipient will only receive items sent through a Portal if his tablet is held up in o-space (as opposed to moving it down to p-space), as observed in B3.

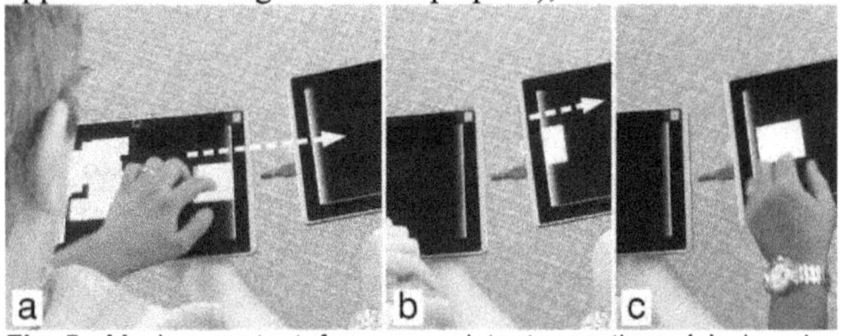

Fig. 5. Moving content from one slate to another: **(a)** dragging content through the tinted edge of screen,**(b)** item moves onto the other slate, and **(c)** the recipient repositions the item.

Note that in one sense the gesture for Portals is a hybrid of Tilt-to-Preview and Face-to-Mirror: the user performs a fairly subtle (>10 degree) tilting motion (like Tilt-to-Preview) to create the portal, but does not have to touch the screen while doing so. On the one hand this means that Portals may be more prone to incidental tilting (B4). On the other hand, the feedback for Portals (a visually unobtrusive tinting along the matching edge of the devices) as well as the semantics of using the Portal (a transfer only occurs if the user explicitly passes an item through the shared edge of the Portal) means that there is very little impact if accidental activation of a Portal does occur.

In our evaluation (see below) users liked the Portals technique but found our distinction between *copy* and *transfer* confusing. We are therefore currently considering alternate mappings that treat all sharing as a copy, and thus free up tilting (any amount) for full-screen sharing.

Cross-Device Pinch-to-Zoom

Cross-Device Pinch-to-Zoom was motivated in part by B8, *Matching pose while side-by-side*. Here, we explore ways that users can explicitly share items when the slates are *not* tilted (e.g. as shown in Fig. 2a), but just held together side-by-side in o-space (B3 and B7) and at the same relatively flat angle (B8).

This technique allows viewing content across multiple tablet devices when using a pinch-to-zoom gesture. As typical of freeform canvas interfaces, a person can use a two finger pinch gesture to enlarge any content on the screen (Fig. 6a). But since our technique leverages the GroupTogether system's knowledge of F-formations and the pose of nearby devices, when the sender enlarges the zoomed content beyond the visible area of the slate's display, the remaining content expands onto the surrounding tablets in o-space (Fig. 6b). That is, while the person zooms in, the content is displayed on the combined screen area of the tablets that form a particular f-formation (i.e., a larger cross-device virtual canvas is created).

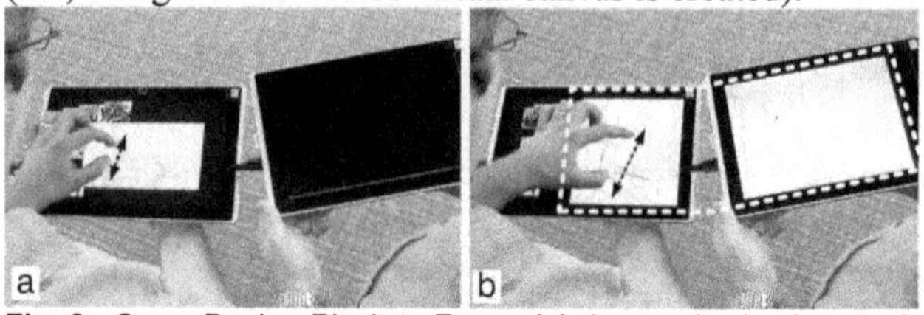

Fig. 6. Cross-Device Pinch-to-Zoom: **(a)** the sender begins pinch-to-zoom on the first slate; **(b)** the zoomed content is displayed on surrounding slates that are part of the F-formation.

Propagation through F-formations

While the above interactions illustrate how our ideas apply to two-person F-formations, the techniques also apply to larger groups (Fig. 7a). For *Tilt-to-Preview* and *Face-to-Mirror*, for example, a person can share content with the entire group by tilting their tablet towards the center of the formation (i.e., towards o-space) rather than just tilting towards a single person.

Furthermore, we implement the techniques described above for all three types of F-formations (side-by-side, face-to-face, and corner-to-corner). While it would be possible to support assemblage-specific gestures, we felt that this might not be intuitive to users. However, we do adapt the feedback on the screen (e.g. placement of the tinting indicating an active Portal) to match the spatial arrangement of users.

Likewise, users who are sensed as external to the F-formation cannot participate in group interactions, unless of course they move to stand within the group. While it might be interesting to explore various techniques for beyond-arms-reach interaction [3]—for example, to allow distant persons to send items to an F-formation, or to the digital whiteboard— by the same token in the context of GroupTogether this would go against the simplicity of the natural human behaviors that we observed in our design study, so we chose not to pursue such mechanisms here.

While we have fully implemented F-formation tracking and propagations, and performed pilot tests with groups of 3-4 persons, we did not include groups of this size in our informal user studies (see below). As such, while we believe propagation micro-mobility gestures through F-formations of more than two persons represents an important concept, as of this writing this aspect of our system has not yet been fully explored and evaluated.

A Digital Whiteboard as Part of an F-formation

Because F-formations can implicitly encompass fixed or semi-fixed features of the environment [5], we included a large screen digital whiteboard in our system as an exemplar. Users within a sensed F-formation can share content with the digital whiteboard in a manner analogous to sharing content to slates held by other participants. For example, consider the *Hold-to-Mirror* technique. A person can hold their tablet vertically towards the large display, and a temporary copy of the tablet's content appears on the large screen (Fig. 7b). Similarly, a person standing next to the whiteboard can use the Portals technique to move content to the large display by dragging content onto the edge of the slate facing towards the whiteboard.

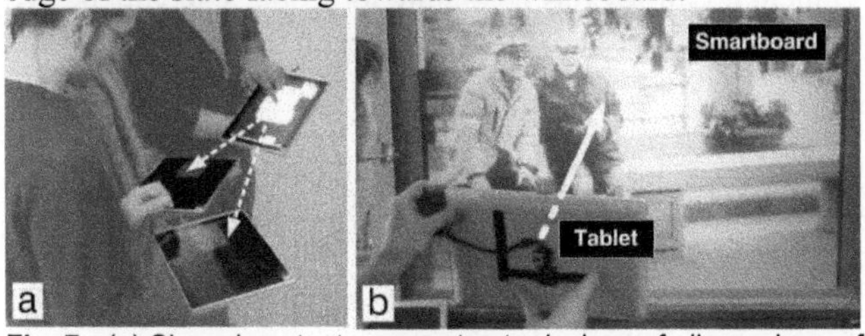

Fig. 7. (a) Shared content propagates to devices of all members of the current F-formation. **(b)** Using the Face-to-Mirror technique with a large digital whiteboard display sensed as part of an F-formation.

Our implementation considers the digital whiteboard in a manner similar to the human participants in an F-formation; that is, it has a particular location and a facing vector. When it falls along the perimeter of p-space it is treated as part of the F-formation, but if it falls outside the huddle, in r-space, it is not. For example, if a circle of users stands in front of the digital whiteboard, with one user's back to the display, and another user performs a Face-to-Mirror gesture, the content will be mirrored to the F-formation but not to the whiteboard. But if the same circle expands to encompass the whiteboard, then the content would be sent to the whiteboard as well.

IMPLEMENTATION

We now describe the major system components of GroupTogether, including the hardware and sensors, how we employ 8GHz band radios to associate devices to people, and how we process the raw Kinect depth data to sense F-formations.

Hardware System Components

We implemented all techniques on Asus EP121 slates (1.16 kg, 312 x 207 x 17 mm), with two-point capacitive multitouch screens running Windows 7. To the back of each slate, we attached a Phidgets Spatial 3/3/3 motion sensor and a Qualcomm Short Range Communication Technology ("QSRCT") 8GHz band radio module.

We mounted a pair of Kinect depth cameras in the ceiling above our prototyping environment. This enabled us to sense users in a roughly L-shaped active area (Fig. 8). The wall display was a fifty inch diagonal SmartBoard with single-point optically-sensed touch. We mounted fixed QSRCT radio modules on either side of the SmartBoard to enable triangulation of the slate-mounted radio modules. This enabled identification of specific devices (by their radio ID) as well as coarser-grained proximity sensing of devices that were nearby, but not held by a user within the viewing area of the Kinect cameras.

System Architecture

All the GroupTogether system components were connected via TCP over wireless Ethernet. We implemented a message protocol using Windows Communication Framework (WCF) to transmit all application and sensor state. A central server maintained a global model of all spatial relationships, and notified clients of state changes.

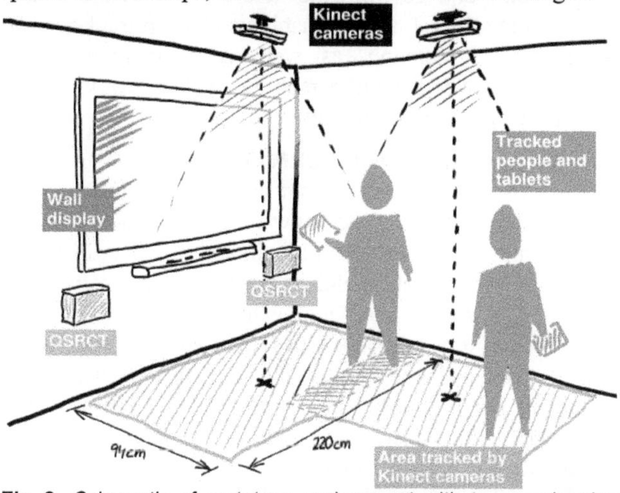

Fig. 8. Schematic of prototype environment with two overlapping Kinect cameras, and wall display with 8GHz band QSRCT radios (a radio was also attached to the back of the tablets, not shown).

Associating Devices to People via 8GHz Band Radios

The overhead Kinect cameras allow us to track moving blobs that we recognize as people, but this tells us nothing about the *devices* that they carry. We employ the QSRCT radios via *wireless radio signal trilateration* to associate devices to sensed persons.

The Qualcomm Short Range Communication Technology (QSRCT) radio modules transmit signals in the 8 GHz band, which avoids interference with the popular 2.4 GHz WLAN band, but also restricts QSRCT to line-of-sight communication. An advantage of this property is that the signals tend to stay within the social boundaries of meeting spaces delineated by walls, partitions, furniture, etc. The QSRCT radios have a maximum range of 15m and also *sense approximate distance* between radio modules (10 cm accuracy at 90% confidence). We employ *three point location trilateration* where we put three QSRCT radio nodes at fixed locations in the space around the edges of the area tracked by the depth cameras. The mobile radio sends range-finding requests to each fixed node and we Kalman-filter the resulting measurements to reduce noise. The device location is then the intersection of the three circles.

The server matches the device to a person by assigning the device to the person who is standing closest (as sensed by the Kinect cameras) to the triangulated location. If the distance between the device and all currently tracked people is above a tolerance threshold (currently 1m), the device remains unassigned. To assign all other devices, the process is repeated with the remaining QSRCT radios attached to the tablets.

Trilateration with the QSRCT radios—and matching these radio ID's to the devices held by people tracked via the Kinect depth cameras—allows us to not only associate each device to a particular person, but also to identify a person based on the device they carry (under the assumption that each person carries their own device). Furthermore, when people come and go from the field-of-view of the Kinect camera, the QSRCT radios enable us to keep track of *who* is entering or leaving, as well as to maintain some awareness of whether the person has walked away, or still remains nearby but out of depth-camera view.

KINECT TRACKING OF F-FORMATIONS

We use overhead Kinect depth cameras, mounted in the ceiling and looking downwards, to track spatial relationships between people, including the distance, viewing direction, and relative body orientation between persons. Our system then aggregates these sensed persons into F-formations and classifies the type of assemblage (that is, face-to-face, side-by-side, corner-to-corner, or as singletons not a member of any formation). We note that our implementation assumes users are *standing*, and does not yet handle seated participants.

The Kinect field-of-view of 58.5 degrees, with the cameras mounted 200cm above the floor, produces a 220x94cm tracking area per camera. We arrange the Kinects in an L-shaped sensing region (Fig. 8) and, with a one-time calibration step, compose the data into a combined depth image. For each depth image we calculate the orthographic projection of the camera view, and then use filters and linear interpolation to remove noise resulting from the partial overlap of the Kinects' structured light patterns.

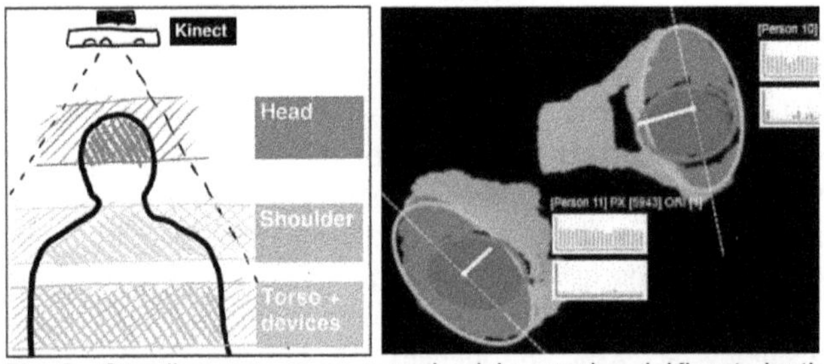

Fig. 9. Standing person as perceived by overhead Kinect depth cameras, with schematic (left) and raw depth image (right) labeled with recognized head, shoulders, and torso/arms. Note the facing vector (white line segments) and principal body axis (dotted lines).

Processing Pipeline for F-Formation Detection

We process the combined depth image in multiple steps to identify the location, orientation, and formations of people.

1. ***Filter.*** We first filter out all connected components too small or too large to be an actual person, leaving just those components most likely to represent a person.

2. ***Normalize height.*** Next, the height of all detected people is normalized to match. The algorithm finds the highest point of all detected people identified in the previous step, and shifts the depth values of all remaining outlines of people by the difference in height.

3. ***Detect heads.*** We assume the topmost depth band represents people's heads (Fig. 9). Our algorithm identifies all connected components in this separated 2D image. The results are ellipsoidal outlines of people's heads. We take the major axis of the ellipse as the orientation of the head.

4. ***Calculate body orientation.*** The second depth band (Fig. 9) includes all regions belonging to people's shoulders. We assign each detected shoulder region to the person it is closest to. We then take the convex hull (since the shoulder is not necessarily a single connected component) to get an ellipsoidal outline of a person's shoulders. The major axis of that ellipse gives us the orientation of the person's body.

5. ***Determine which way people face.*** The orientations calculated in steps 3-4 still have a 180-degree ambiguity. To determine which way the user is facing, we take a third depth band that corresponds to the user's torso, including their arms and hands (Fig. 9). We then identify which side of the major body axis a person's arms and hands appear on, as well as which side the head is shifted towards, and take this as the front. We further apply hysteresis to prevent momentary flips in the facing vector due to noise.

6. ***Detect F-Formations.*** Finally, our algorithm identifies F-formations. Two people can be in an F-formation if: (a) they are not standing behind each other, (b) the angle between their orientation vectors is smaller than 180 degrees (otherwise they would face away from each other), and (c) the distance between individuals is small enough so they can comfortably communicate and their o-spaces (Fig. 1) overlap. Our algorithm iterates over all pairs of people, calculates the distance and angle between them, and assigns an F-formation type (i.e., side-by-side, L-shaped, face-to-face, or none) based on tolerance thresholds. Hysteresis prevents frequent switching of detected formations if measurements lie close to a threshold. We also detect and tag singletons and persons in R-space (outside a formation).

We have not formally evaluated the error rates of our F-formation sensing approach; the current system is intended only as a proof-of-concept to illustrate that small groups can be sensed, as well as to suggest some directions as to how such sensing can be leveraged for small-group interaction. We have pilot tested the sensing with various arrangements of 2-4 person groups, including groups with nearby persons outside the formation (in R-space).

Note that in our system, sensed formations lead only to federated groups where the barriers for sharing are lowered: we do not necessarily assume that people in a group want to share. Indeed, this is precisely why we pursued a hybrid approach (of sensed F-formations + device micro-mobility) to initiate the actual cross-device sharing of content. We believe this approach appropriate for contexts such as small-group meeting spaces, where people have freedom of movement, but it might not be suitable for crowded environments such as a conference hall or subway station.

INFORMAL EVALUATION & REACTIONS FROM USERS

We conducted an informal evaluation to gather feedback of people using our techniques in practice. We recruited 6 participants for our experiments (all male, age 29-50, part of the same organization but not members of our group) paired into groups of two. Each was given a slate running our software. The experimenter explained the four main cross-device interaction techniques. We asked participants to use the technique for basic information-sharing and viewing tasks. They then responded to several 7-point Likert scale questions, discussed what the best and worst thing was about each technique. and ranked them for overall preference.

Results

We observed that participants were quickly able to perform each of the four techniques, and that they generally found them intuitive, quick, and easy to perform. Likert responses confirmed their overall positive feedback regarding ease-of-use, where they particularly liked the notion of lightweight sharing across devices. They ranked *Portals* as their favorite technique (and also gave it the highest average rating on a "comfortable to perform" Likert scale question), followed by *Tilt-to-Preview*, *Cross-Device Pinch-to-Zoom*, and *Face-to-Mirror*. However, a number concerns were raised by our participants or from our own observations, as summarized below.

Physical effort and tilting. Participants felt comfortable performing the smaller tilting gestures, such as that used for *Tilt-to-Preview*. They usually quickly moved the tablet back to the horizontal position after performing one of the sharing interactions. Yet the size, weight, and fragility of the sensor-augmented slates were an issue, as some participants found it difficult to hold the tablet in one hand while touching an item with the other hand. However, this points more to the limitations of these particular tablets and attached sensors than any particular failing of the micro-mobility idea: recall that people had no problem with tis using the lighter foam-core models during the design study.

Participants commented on the "intuitive" use of *Face-to-Mirror*: "this is like... I show it to you" or that there was "even less work to do" than the other techniques (i.e., just hold the slate vertically, with no touch required). Yet participants did raise concerns about the large tilting gesture (>70 degrees) required for *Face-to-Mirror*, particularly for side-by-side interaction. One user stated "you have to tilt too much" and another reported that the technique "required extreme tilt." Observations of people using the technique also revealed difficulties repeatedly holding the slate in the vertical position; users often changed grips to avoid fatigue and maintain a secure grip on the slate with both hands. This issue can be mitigated simply by relaxing the required angle.

Copy vs. move. The semantics of *copy* vs. *transfer* actions adopted by our techniques sometimes caused confusion for participants ("not sure when it copies vs. moves the image"). Our feedback did not make it sufficiently clear which type of "sharing" a particular gesture enabled.

Ownership, control, and handover. For all but the *Cross-Device Pinch-to-Zoom* technique (for the reasons described above), participants felt in control of what content was shared, transferred and kept between devices and the minimal effort required to do so. Participants commented positively: "it felt natural to either 'take it' or 'leave it'," or that the "receiving user decides to keep [it]." However, a few difficulties arose when users attempted to simultaneously share items (such as by dragging through Portals): "when both of us were trying to transfer images at the same time, it became confusing / difficult."

Structure of F-formations. Most participants agreed that the physical distance between themselves and the second person felt appropriate to enable sharing of data. Participants mostly stood in a side-by-side formation during the experiment, usually faced slightly inwards towards the o-space. Users also clearly expected the techniques to extend to more than two users ("Will this work in groups?"). As noted above, groups of more than two people were implemented in our system and tested in pilot sessions, but not were not included in this evaluation. Therefore the suitability of our techniques for larger groups of people remains to be fully demonstrated.

Overall preference. Participants ranked *Portals* as their favorite technique (and also gave it the highest average rating on a "comfortable to perform" Likert scale question), followed by *Tilt-to-Preview*, *Cross-Device Pinch-to-Zoom*, and *Face-to-Mirror*.

In future studies, we would like to evaluate our techniques more systematically for a variety of F-formation types as well as for larger groups of users (3-5 people). It would also be interesting to explore further variations of the techniques, such as *Face-to-Mirror* with a less extreme requirement for the tilt angle.

DISCUSSION

While our system explored a number of novel ideas, it is clear that much more could be done. For example, we explored a pair of techniques—*Tilt-to-Preview* and *Face-to-Mirror*—that looked at two extremes in gradation of response (B6). But from our observational studies, as well as from the commentary of Luff & Heath [20], it is clear that people's use of micro-mobility is more nuanced still. Therefore, it would be interesting to explore similarly nuanced techniques that explore this continuum further. These might include both implicit ways of using device tilt and motion for context sensing, as well as explicit gestures or posturing of devices (as explored in this paper) to support finely delineated notions of sharing content.

The observations in our design study, as well as those resulting from our implementation and informal evaluation, strongly suggest that people treat handheld objects as extensions of their person (B1). Yet by the same token the sociological rules governing "object territoriality" are clearly not the same as those governing our physical bodies. To our knowledge the notion of object territoriality has never been systematically studied, which suggests the need for further experimental and observational studies to better understand behavioral principles that might inform interaction design for micro-mobility and F-formations.

Several sensing platforms currently exist that we could exploit for sensing the presence and location of people and devices (such as high-fidelity Vicon-based tracking [1,28], the proximity toolkit [21], etc.). In the present research, we deliberately wanted to design a practical, low-cost sensing system to illustrate that such systems could realistically be deployed in the near–rather than the far–future. While the implementation we pursued still requires equipment installation within a room, it could be practically and affordably done within (say) a small dedicated meeting room context such as a breakout room.

More generally, further investigation of lower-cost, coarser-grained, or more easily deployable sensing modalities to detect micro-mobility and F-formations remains important. Exploring the tradeoffs inherent in this liminal zone of imperfect sensing—rather than assuming high-fidelity optical sensing of fully tagged persons and devices, for example—is a worthy area of continuing research.

CONCLUSION AND FUTURE WORK

We have described GroupTogether, a sensing system that jointly brings into play the sociological constructs of micro-mobility and F-formations. We contributed a design study that illustrates how the *proxemics of people* as well as the *proxemics of devices* surface during joint activity. We then demonstrated how the attributes sensed by our system leverage these behaviors to enable a number of novel interactions that employ both the micro-mobility of devices and the social structure of F-formations. We described how the system senses these interactions using a combination of motion sensors, radio modules with coarse-grained range finding capability, and overhead Kinect-based depth camera tracking. And finally, we have presented an informal study illustrating user reactions to the techniques.

We believe we have only scratched the surface of a potentially rich space of such techniques. As devices become thinner and lighter, the opportunities for socially-situated interactions continue to expand. Likewise, systems and techniques that leverage ubiquitous proxemics should benefit from ongoing developments in spatially-aware technologies such as the Kinect depth cameras and QSRCT radio modules utilized in this research. These should be welcome developments for the many contexts where users need to share and discuss digital artifacts while remaining fully engaged in the seamless flow of social exchange with friends and colleagues.

REFERENCES

1. Ballendat, T., et al., Proxemic Interaction: Designing for a Proximity and Orientation-Aware Environment. *ITS '10.*
2. Biehl, J.T., Bailey, B.P. ARIS: An Interface for Application Relocation in an Interactive Space. *Proc. Graphics Interface (GI '04).*
3. Bragdon, A., et al., Code Space: Combining Touch, Devices, and Skeletal Tracking to Support Developer Meetings. *ITS '11.*
4. Buxton, W., Living in augmented reality: Ubiquitous Media and Reactive Environments, in *Video Mediated Communication*, ed. by K. Finn, Sellen, A., & Wilber, S. 1997, Erlbaum. p. 363-384.
5. Ciolek, T.M., Kendon, A., Environment and the Spatial Arrangement of Conversational Encounters. Sociological Inquiry 1980. **50**(3-4): p. 237-271.
6. Dearman, D., Guy, R., Truong, K. Determining the Orientation of Proximate Mobile Devices using their Back Facing Camera. *CHI'12.*
7. Dunbar, R., Duncan, N., Nettle, D., Size and Structure of Freely Forming Conversational Groups. Human Nature, 1995. **6**(1): p. 67-78.
8. Everitt, K., Shen, C., Ryall, K., Forlines, C. MultiSpace: Enabling Electronic Document Micro-mobility in Table-Centric, Multi-Device Environments. *Proc. IEEE TABLETOP '06.*
9. Greenberg, S., et al., Proxemic Interactions: The New Ubicomp? Interactions, 2011. **18**(1): p. 42-50.
10. Hall, E.T., *The Hidden Dimension*. 1966, New York: Doubleday.
11. Hassan, N., Rahman, M., Irani, P., Graham, P. Chucking: A One-Handed Document Sharing Technique. *INTERACT'09.*
12. Hinckley, K. Synchronous Gestures for Multiple Users and Computers. *UIST'03.*
13. Hinckley, K., Dixon, M., Sarin, R., Guimbretiere, F., Balakrishnan, R. Codex: A Dual-Screen Tablet Computer. *CHI'09.*
14. Hung, H., Kröse, B.J.A. Detecting F-formations as dominant sets. *Proc ICMI '11 Conf. on Multimodal Interfaces.*
15. Johanson, B., et al., PointRight: experience with flexible input redirection in interactive workspaces. *UIST'02.*
16. Ju, W., Lee, B.A., Klemmer, S.R. Range: Exploring Implicit Interaction through Electronic Whiteboard Design. *CSCW '08.*
17. Kendon, A., Spacing and orientation in co-present interaction, in *COST'09 Proceedings 2nd Int'l Conf on Development of Multimodal Interfaces: Active Listening and Synchrony*, Springer-Verlag Berlin: Heidelberg. p. 1-15.
18. Kindberg, T., Fox, A., System Software for Ubiquitous Computing. IEEE Pervasive Computing, 2002. **1**(1): p. 70-81.
19. Kruger, R., Carpendale, M., Scott, S.D., Greenberg, S. How People Use Orientation on Tables: Comprehension, Coordination and Communication. *Proc. ACM Group 2003 Conference.*
20. Luff, P., Heath, C. Mobility in collaboration. *CSCW '98.*
21. Marquardt, N., Diaz-Marino, R., Boring, S., Greenberg, S. The Proximity Toolkit: Prototyping Proxemic Interactions in Ubiquitous Computing Ecologies. *UIST '11.*
22. Marshall, P., Rogers, Y., Pantidi, N. Using F-formations to analyse spatial patterns of interaction in physical environments. *CSCW '11.*
23. Ramos, G., et al., Synchronous Gestures in Multi-Display Environments. Human-Comp. Interaction, 2009. **24** (1-2): p. 117-169.
24. Rodden, T. Populating the application: a model of awareness for cooperative applications. *CSCW '96.*
25. Schilit, B., Adams, N., Want, R. Context-Aware Computing Applications. *Proc. IEEE Workshop on Mobile Computing Systems and Applications.* 1994.
26. Sommer, R., *Personal space*. 1969: Prentice-Hall.
27. Tashman, C., Edwards, W.K. LiquidText: A Flexible, Multitouch Environment to Support Active Reading. *CHI'11.*
28. Vogel, D., Balakrishnan, R. Interactive public ambient displays: transitioning from implicit to explicit, public to personal, interaction with multiple users. *UIST'04.*
29. Wang, M., Boring, S., Greenberg, S., Proxemic Peddler: A Public Advertising Display that Captures and Preserves the Attention of a Passerby. *ACM 2012 Int'l Symp. on Pervasive Displays.*
30. Want, R., et al, The active bage location system. ACM Trans. Information Systems, 1992. **10**(1): p. 91-102.
31. Wilson, A.D., Benko, H. Combining multiple depth cameras and projectors for interactions on, above and between surfaces. *UIST'10.*

Real-Time Captioning by Groups of Non-Experts

Walter S. Lasecki[1], Christopher D. Miller[1], Adam Sadilek[1], Andrew Abumoussa[1]
Donato Borrello[1], Raja Kushalnagar[2], and Jeffrey P. Bigham[1]

University of Rochester[1]
Computer Science, ROC HCI
Rochester, NY 14623 USA
{wlasecki,sadilek,abumouss,jbigham}@cs.rochester.edu
{c.miller,donato.borrello}@rochester.edu

Rochester Institute of Technology[2]
Computer Science and NTID
Rochester, NY 14623 USA
rskics@rit.edu

ABSTRACT

Real-time captioning provides deaf and hard of hearing people immediate access to spoken language and enables participation in dialogue with others. Low latency is critical because it allows speech to be paired with relevant visual cues. Currently, the only reliable source of real-time captions are expensive stenographers who must be recruited in advance and who are trained to use specialized keyboards. Automatic speech recognition (ASR) is less expensive and available on-demand, but its low accuracy, high noise sensitivity, and need for training beforehand render it unusable in real-world situations. In this paper, we introduce a new approach in which groups of non-expert captionists (people who can hear and type) collectively caption speech in real-time on-demand. We present LEGION:*S*CRIBE, an end-to-end system that allows deaf people to request captions at any time. We introduce an algorithm for merging partial captions into a single output stream in real-time, and a captioning interface designed to encourage coverage of the entire audio stream. Evaluation with 20 local participants and 18 crowd workers shows that non-experts can provide an effective solution for captioning, accurately covering an average of 93.2% of an audio stream with only 10 workers and an average per-word latency of 2.9 seconds. More generally, our model in which multiple workers contribute partial inputs that are automatically merged in real-time may be extended to allow dynamic groups to surpass constituent individuals (even experts) on a variety of human performance tasks.

ACM Classification Keywords

H.5.2 [Information interfaces and presentation]: User Interfaces. - Graphical user interfaces.

General Terms

Design, Human Factors, Experimentation

Author Keywords

real-time; captioning; transcription; deaf; hard of hearing; text alignment; crowdsourcing

UIST'12, October 7–10, 2012, Cambridge, Massachusetts, USA.

INTRODUCTION

Real-time captioning converts aural speech to visual text to provide access to speech content for deaf and hard of hearing (DHH) people in classrooms, meetings, casual conversation, and other live events. Current options are severely limited because they either require highly-skilled professional captionists whose services are expensive and not available on demand, or use automatic speech recognition (ASR) which produces unacceptable error rates in many real-world situations [30]. This paper introduces a new approach of having groups of non-expert captionists (people who can hear and type, but are not trained stenographers) collectively caption speech in real-time, and explores this new approach via LEGION:*S*CRIBE (henceforth *S*CRIBE), our end-to-end system allowing collective instantaneous captioning for live events on-demand. Since each individual is unable to type fast enough to keep up with natural speaking rates, *S*CRIBE automatically combines multiple inputs into a final caption.

While visual access to spoken material can also be achieved through sign language interpreters, many DHH people do not know sign language. This is particularly true of the large (and increasing) number of DHH people who lost their hearing later in life [15]. Captioning may also be preferred by some to sign language interpreting for technical domains because it does not involve translating from the spoken language to the sign language[1], but rather transliterating an aural representation to a written one. Finally, like captionists, sign language interpreters are also expensive and difficult to schedule.

Professional captionists (stenographers) provide the best real-time (within a few seconds) captions. Their accuracy is generally over 95%, but they must be arranged in advance for blocks of at least an hour, and cost between $120 and $200 per hour, depending on skill [30]. As a result, they cannot be used to caption a lecture or other event at the last minute, or provide access to unpredictable and ephemeral learning opportunities, such as conversations with peers after class.

Automatic speech recognition (ASR) is inexpensive and available on-demand, but its low accuracy in many real settings makes it unusable. For example, ASR accuracy drops below 50% when it is not speaker-trained, captioning

[1]Sign languages, such as American Sign Language (ASL) are not simply codes for an aural language, but rather an entirely different languages with their own vocabulary, grammar, and syntax.

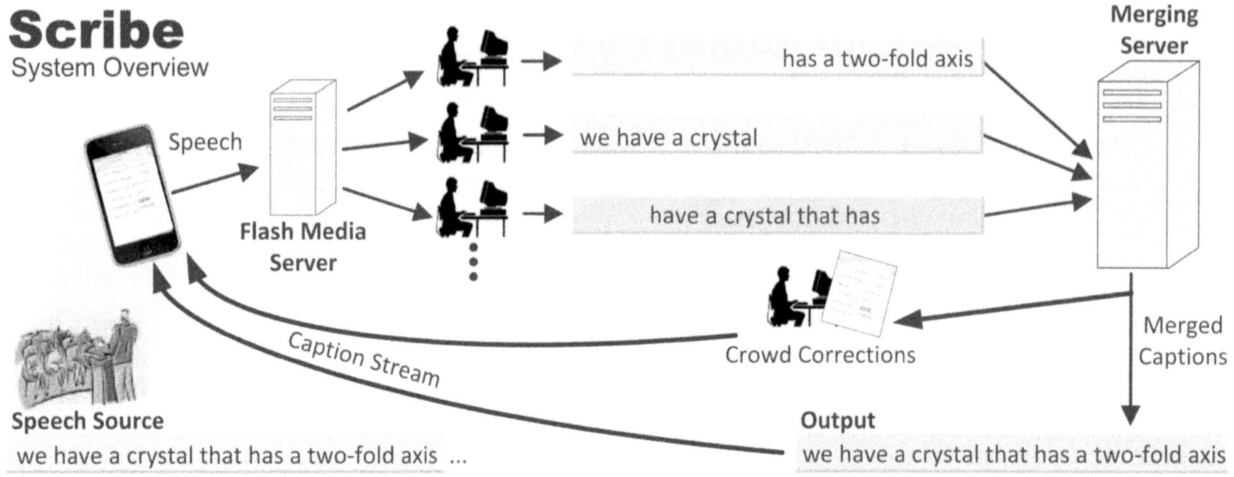

Figure 1. SCRIBE allows users to caption audio on their mobile device. The audio is sent to multiple amateur captionists who use the SCRIBE web-based interface to caption as much of the audio as they can in real-time. These partial captions are sent to our server to be merged into a final output stream, which is then forwarded back to the user's mobile device. Crowd workers are optionally recruited to edit the captions after they have been merged.

multiple speakers, or when not using a high-quality microphone located close to the speaker [12, 7]. Both ASR and the software used to assist real-time captionists often make errors that significantly distort the meaning of the original speech. As DHH people use context to compensate for errors, they often have trouble following the speaker [12].

Non-expert captionists can be drawn from more diverse labor pools than professional captionists, and so we expect captioning by groups of non-experts to be cheaper and more easily available on demand. Recent work has shown, for instance, that workers on Mechanical Turk can be recruited within a few seconds [2, 5]. Recruiting from a broader pool allows workers to be *selectively* chosen for their expertise not in captioning but in the technical areas covered in a lecture. While professional stenographers type faster and more accurately than most crowd workers, they are not necessarily experts in other fields, which often distorts the *meaning* of transcripts of technical talks [30]. SCRIBE will allow student workers to serve as non-expert captionists for $8-12 per hour (a typical work-study pay). Therefore, we could hire several students for less than the cost of one professional captionist.

SCRIBE can benefit people who are not DHH as well. For example, students can easily and affordably obtain searchable text transcripts of a lecture even before the class ends, enabling them to review earlier content they may have missed. Furthermore, we all are subject to a situational disability from time to time [27]. Even a person with excellent hearing can have trouble following a lecture when sitting too far from the speaker, when acoustics are poor, or when it is too noisy.

The key contributions of this paper are as follows:

- We introduce the idea of using non-expects to caption audio in real-time, and present SCRIBE—an end-to-end system that has advantages over current state of the art in terms of availability, cost, and accuracy.
- We show that non-experts can collectively cover speech at rates similar to or above that of a professional (over 93%).
- We demonstrate that SCRIBE can produce transcripts that both cover more of the input signal and are more accurate than either ASR or any single constituent worker.
- More generally, we introduce the idea of automatically merging the real-time inputs of dynamic groups of workers to outperform individuals on human performance tasks.

CURRENT APPROACHES FOR REAL-TIME CAPTIONING

In this section, we first overview current approaches for real-time captioning, introduce our data set, and define evaluation metrics used in this paper. Methods for producing real-time captioning services come in three main varieties: (1) verbatim computer-aided real-time translation, (2) non-verbatim systems, and (3) automatic speech recognition.

Communications Access Real-Time Translation (CART): CART is the most reliable real-time captioning service, but is also the most expensive. Trained stenographers type in shorthand on a "steno" keyboard that maps multiple key presses to phonemes that are expanded to verbatim text. Stenography requires 2-3 years of training to consistently keep up with natural speaking rates that average141 words per minute (WPM) and can reach 231 WPM [17].

Non-Verbatim Systems: In response to the cost of CART, computer-based macro expansion services like C-Print were introduced [30]. C-Print captionists need less training, and generally charge around $60 an hour. However, they normally cannot type as fast as the average speaker's pace, and cannot produce a verbatim transcript. SCRIBE employs captionists with no training and compensates for slower typing speeds and lower accuracy by combining the efforts of multiple parallel captionists.

Automated Speech Recognition: ASR works well in ideal situations with high-quality audio equipment, but degrades quickly in real-world settings. ASR is speaker-dependent, has difficulty recognizing domain-specific jargon, and adapts poorly to changes, such as when the speaker has a cold [12, 9]. ASR systems can require substantial computing power

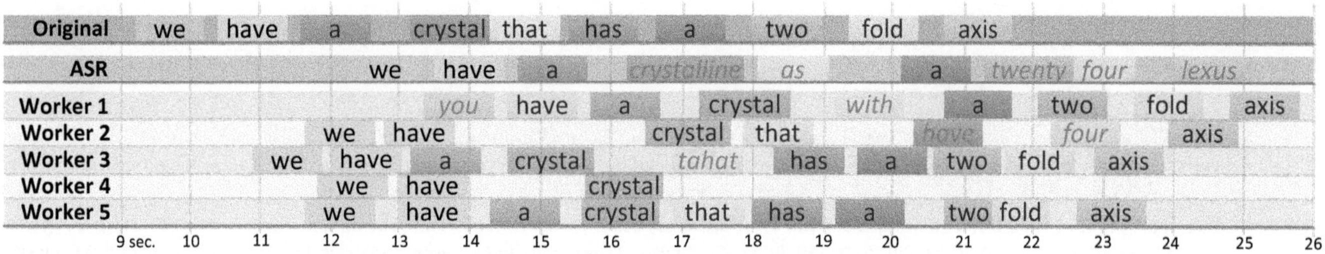

Figure 2. Captions by ASR and five Mechanical Turk workers for a segment of speech. Our results show that merging the input of multiple non-expert workers results in accurate, real-time captions. The left edge of each box represents the time when the typed word was received. Boxes are color-coded to show word position (red denotes incorrect text).

and special audio equipment to work well, which lowers availability. In our experiments, we used Dragon Naturally Speaking 11.5 for Windows.

Another approach is *respeaking*, where a person in a controlled environment is connected to a live audio feed and repeats what they hear to an ASR that is extensively trained for their voice [16]. Respeaking works well for offline transcription, but simultaneous speaking and listening requires professional training. By contrast, SCRIBE enables non-experts to contribute without any special training or skill.

REAL-TIME CAPTIONING WITH NON-EXPERTS

Non-expert captionists can be anyone who can type what they hear. People are able to understand spoken language with ease, but most lack the ability to record it with sufficient speed and accuracy to generate an exact transcript of audio in real-time. As we will see, no single person achieves an acceptable level of coverage when captioning extended audio clips. SCRIBE overcomes this problem by automatically unifying input from multiple workers. Additionally, SCRIBE's user interface encourages different workers to concentrate on different segments of the speech by adjusting audio saliency.

Our approach only requires workers to be able to hear and type. Non-expert captionists can be drawn from the general population, micro-task marketplaces (such as Amazon's Mechanical Turk), groups of volunteers, and students. The pool of workers is dynamic. As a result, no specific worker can be relied upon to be available at a given time or to continue working on a job for any amount of time. Workers cannot be relied upon to provide high-quality work of the type one might expect from a traditional employee. This stems from the lack of direct control, misunderstanding of the task, or delays that are beyond their control, such as network latency. Using multiple workers decreases the likelihood that no worker will be able to provide a correct caption quickly.

Aural speech is often noisy and ambiguous. Speakers may make mistakes, use unfamiliar terms, or have a unique accent. In these cases, people have the advantage of *understanding* the context the word was spoken in, unlike ASR. This makes people less likely to mistake a word for another that does not fit the current context. Furthermore, ASR is unlikely to recognize unusual words or terms the speaker defined during the presentation, whereas human workers may have prior knowledge of the topic, and can learn new terms on-the-fly. In most cases workers are only delayed by their typing rate, not comprehension, allowing faster responses than most ASR, without sacrificing accuracy.

We focus on two types of worker: *local* and *remote*. Local workers are able to hear the audio with no communication delay, and at the original audio quality. These workers may be more familiar with the topic being discussed, and may already be used to the style of the speaker. Remote workers are easier to recruit on-demand, and are generally cheaper. However, remote workers will not be trained on the specific speaker, and may lack the background knowledge of a local worker. These two types of workers can be mixed in order to extract the best properties of each. For instance, using local workers to take advantage of the low latency when possible, while using remote workers to maintain enough captionists to ensure consistent coverage.

In order to successfully generate complete and accurate captions, we need to intelligently merge all of the noisy partial inputs into a single stream. Workers have different typing speeds, captioning styles, and connection latencies, making time alone a poor signal for word ordering. Aligning based on word matching can be more consistent between workers, but spelling mistakes, typographical errors, and confusion on the part of workers make finding a consensus difficult. A robust alignment method must be able to handle these inconsistencies, while not overestimating the similarity of two inputs.

Using worker input exclusively fails to take advantage of existing knowledge of languages and common errors. We use additional information about the most likely intended input from a worker by making use of language and typing models. For the language model, we use bigram and trigram data from Google's publicly available N-gram corpus. This provides prior probabilities on sets of words, which we use to resolve ordering conflicts in workers' input. To determine *equivalent* words, we use the Damerau-Levenshtein distance [10] between the words, weighted using the manhattan distance between the letters on a QWERTY keyboard.

Metrics for Evaluation

Determining the quality of captions is difficult [31]. The most common method is word error rate (WER), which performs a best-fit alignment between the caption and the ground truth. The WER is then calculated as the sum of the substitutions S, the deletions D, and the insertions I needed to make the two transcripts match divided by the total number of words in the ground truth N, or $\frac{S+D+I}{N}$. A key advantage of human captionists over ASR is that humans tend to make more reasonable errors because they are able to infer meaning from context, influencing their prior probability toward words that make sense in context. We anticipate this will make SCRIBE more usable than automated systems even when the results of

```
1:    learn  g is such      a  suitcase word though right  so          has a lot of there     s a lot
2:  o learning is such                                                          there a are a lot
3:    learning ss such      a  suitcase word though           learning has              is a lot
4:    lea ning is su h      a                       right  so learning                     a lot
5: so learning is such      a  suitcase      though           learning has                   lot
6:    learning is such      a  suitcfse word though right                           this    in a lot
F: so learning is such      a  suitcase word though right  so learning has a lot of there   is a lot
```

Figure 3. Example output of our MSA algorithm. Each line is a partial caption input by a worker, and the final merged caption (F). Dashes represent "gaps" inserted to attain an optimal alignment given our language model. While individual workers provide noisy and incomplete data, merging multiple captions significantly improves coverage and precision.

traditional metrics are similar. Figure 2 gives an example of the confusing errors often made by ASR, substituting "twenty four lexus" for "two-fold axis".

We define two other metrics in addition to WER to help characterize the performance of real-time captioning. We believe these metrics are particularly useful in understanding the potential of various approaches. The first is *coverage*, which represents how many of the words in the true speech signal appear in the merged caption. While similar to 'recall' in information retrieval, we choose to use 'coverage' because we augment the definition of recall in calculating coverage by requiring that a word in the caption appear no later than 10 seconds after the word in the ground truth, and not before it, to count. Similarly, *precision* is the fraction of words in the caption that appear in the ground truth within 10 seconds.

Finally, for real-time captioning, latency is also important. Calculating latency is not straightforward because workers' noisy partial captions differ from the ground truth. In this paper, we measure latency by first aligning the test captions to the ground truth using the Needleman-Wunsch sequence alignment algorithm [24], and then averaging the latency of all matched words. In order for DHH individuals to participate in a conversation or in a lecture, captions must be provided quickly (within about 5 seconds) [30].

BACKGROUND

In addition to alternative approaches to real-time captioning, SCRIBE also builds from prior work in (i) real-time human computation and (ii) multiple sequence alignment.

Real-Time Human Computation

Historically, people with disabilities have attempted to solve their accessibility problems with the support of people in their community [4]. Increasing connectivity has made remote services possible that once required human supporters to be co-located. Real-time captioning by non-experts is a type of human computation [28], which has been shown to be useful in many areas, including writing and editing [3], image description and interpretation [5, 29], and protein folding [8]. Existing abstractions obtain quality work by introducing redundancy and layering into tasks so that multiple workers contribute and verify results at each stage [22, 19]. For instance, the ESP Game uses answer agreement [29] and Soylent uses the multiple-step find-fix-verify pattern [3]. SCRIBE presents a model of crowdsourcing that uses workers in parallel, not sequentially, to improve performance on real-time tasks.

Human computation has been applied to offline transcription with great success [1], but has not been previously applied to real-time captioning. Scribe4Me allowed deaf and hard of hearing people to receive a transcript of a short sound sequence in a few minutes, but was not able to produce verbatim captions over long periods [23]. SCRIBE enables real-time transcription from multiple non-experts and uses crowd agreement to ensure quality.

Real-time human computation has only started to be explored. VizWiz [5], was one of the first systems to target nearly real-time response from the crowd. It introduced a queuing model to help ensure that workers were available quickly on-demand. For SCRIBE to be available on-demand multiple users are required to be available at the same time so that multiple workers can collectively contribute. Prior systems have shown that multiple workers can be recruited for collaboration by having workers wait until enough workers have arrived [29, 6]. Adrenaline combines the concepts of queuing and waiting to recruit crowds (groups) in less than 2 seconds from existing sources of crowd workers [2]. SCRIBE also uses the input of multiple workers, but differs because it engages workers for longer continuous tasks.

Legion enables real-time control of an existing user interface by allowing the crowd to collectively act as a single operator [20]. Each crowd worker submits input independently of other workers, then the system uses an *input mediator* to combine the input into a single control stream. Our input combination approach could be viewed as an instance of an input mediator. A primary difference is that while Legion selected from individual user inputs, we use a synthesis of the crowd's input to create the final stream.

Multiple Sequence Alignment (MSA)

Our transcription problem is an instance of the general problem of multiple sequence alignment with an additional merging step. Much work in bioinformatics concentrates on aligning multiple related sequences of nucleotides and other chemical compounds. The main biological motivation for this process is to gain insights into the relationships between organisms based on their respective genomes. While finding the globally optimal alignment is an NP-hard problem [13] (in our case, the runtime is exponential in the number of workers), effective approximate solutions have been developed. One of our input combiners extends the MUSCLE package [11] with a language model for English in order to align partial captions in a meaningful way (Figure 3).

SCRIBE

SCRIBE gives users on-demand access to real-time captioning from groups of non-experts via their laptop or mobile devices (Figure 1). When a user starts SCRIBE, it immediately

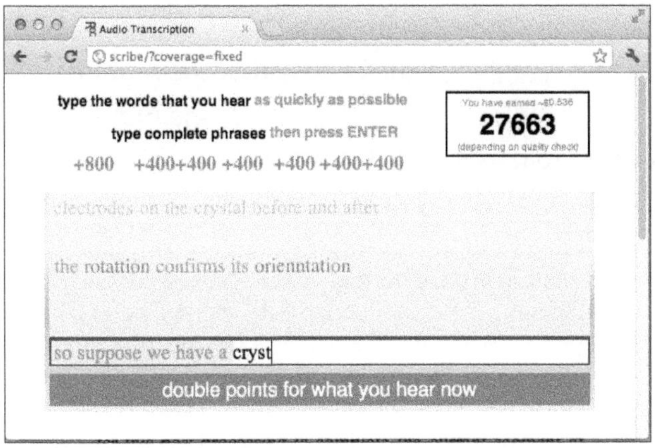

Figure 4. The worker interface encourages captionists to type audio quickly by locking in words soon after they are typed. To encourage coverage of specific segments, visual and audio cues are presented, and the volume is reduced during off periods. Rewards are increased for words typed during these segments.

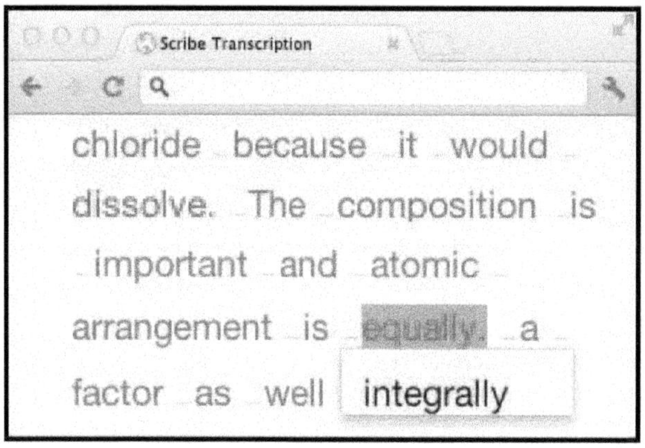

Figure 5. The web-based interface for users to see and correct the live caption stream returned by $\mathcal{S}$**CRIBE.**

begins recruiting workers for the task from Mechanical Turk, or a pool of volunteer workers, using quikTurkit [5]. When users want to begin captioning audio, they press the start button, which forwards audio to Flash Media Server (FMS) and signals the $\mathcal{S}$CRIBE server to begin captioning.

Workers are presented with a text input interface designed to encourage real-time answers and increase global coverage (Figure 4). A display shows workers their rewards for contributing in the form of both money and points. In our experiments, we paid workers $0.005 for every word the system thought was correct. As workers type, their input is forwarded to an *input combiner* on the $\mathcal{S}$CRIBE server. The input combiner is modular to accommodate different implementations without needing to modify $\mathcal{S}$CRIBE. The combiner and interface are discussed in the next section.

The user interface for $\mathcal{S}$CRIBE presents streaming text within a collaborative editing framework (see Figure 5). $\mathcal{S}$CRIBE's interface masks the staggered and delayed format of real-time captions with a more natural flow that mimics writing. In doing this, the interface presents the merged inputs from the crowd workers via a dynamically updating web page, and allows users to focus on reading, instead of tracking changes. $\mathcal{S}$CRIBE also supports real-time editing by users or other crowds. The web interface visually presents relevant information, such as the confidence of each spelling and possible word and arrangement alternatives. These cues both reduce the attention that must be paid to the editing process, and encourage users to focus their efforts on specific problems in the caption. For example, conflicted words or spellings are highlighted and, when selected, alternatives are displayed and can be agreed with or new answers can be added. These updates are then forwarded back to the combiner.

When users are done, pressing the stop button will end the audio stream, but let workers complete their current transcription task. Workers are asked to continue working on other audio for a time to keep them active in order to reduce the response time if users need to resume captioning.

Collaborative Editing

We expect that multiple users will often want to use $\mathcal{S}$CRIBE to generate captions for the same event. $\mathcal{S}$CRIBE's interface supports this by allowing users to share the link to the web interface for a given session to view the generated captions. This allows more captionists from the worker pool to be used for a single task, improving performance. Additionally, the joint session acts as a collaborative editing platform. Each participant in this shared space can submit corrections to the captions, adding their individual knowledge to the system.

Adjustable Quality

$\mathcal{S}$CRIBE allows for placing emphasis on either coverage or precision. However, these two properties are at odds: using more of the worker input will increase coverage, but maintain more of the individual worker error, while requiring more agreement on individual words will increase precision, but reduce the coverage since not all workers will agree on all words. We allow users to either let the system choose a default balance, or select their own balance of precision versus coverage by using a slider bar in the user interface. Workers can select from a continuous range of values between 'Most Accurate' and 'Most Complete' which are mapped to settings within the combiner.

Co-Evolving Systems

Our solution to the transcription problem is two-fold. First, we have designed an interface that facilitates real-time captioning by non-experts and encourages covering the entire audio signal. Second, we have developed an algorithm for merging partial captions to form one final output stream. The interface and algorithm have been developed to address these

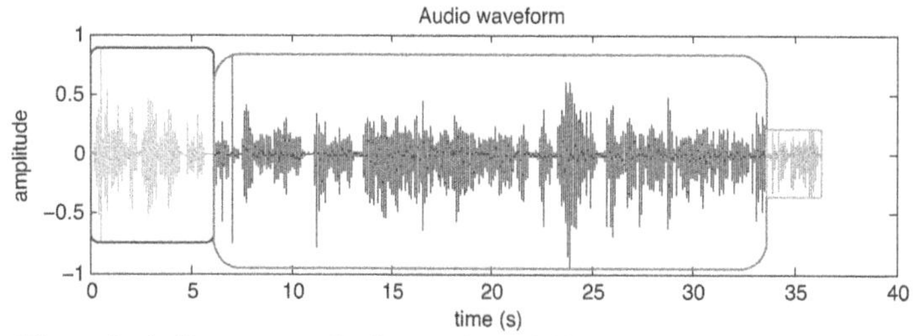

Figure 6. Audio segmented using our kernel SVM method. Each segment contains audio from one speaker, and is sent to different workers.

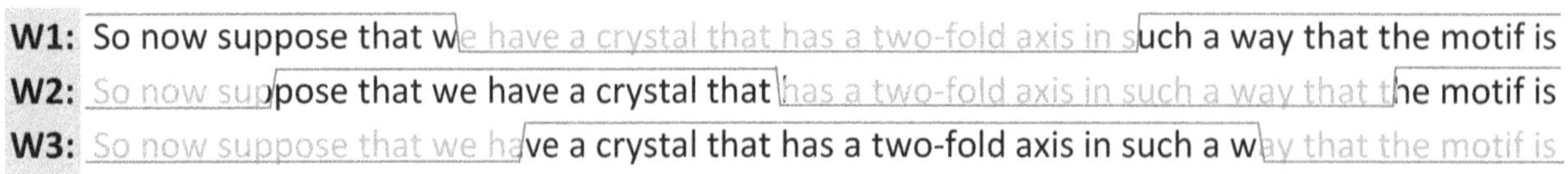

Figure 7. ***S*****CRIBE encourages workers to type different portions of the input speech by raising and lowering the volume of the audio, as depicted visually here. Artificially adjusting saliency while streaming the signal improves overall coverage.**

problems jointly. For instance, determining where each word in a partial caption fits into the final transcript is difficult, so the interface was designed to encourage workers to type continuous segments then signal breaks. We detail the co-evolution of the worker interface and algorithm for merging partial captions in order to form a final transcript. By developing the interface and merging algorithm to best suit each other, we can create a system that efficiently uses the imperfect captioning abilities of workers to create transcripts.

Transcribing a Dialogue

Interleaving different speakers adds an additional layer of complexity to the transcription task. ASR attempts to adapt to a particular speaker's voice; however, if speakers constantly change, this adjustment often reduces the quality of the transcription further [7]. In order to address this problem and enable accurate transcriptions of conversations, even those between individuals with very different speaking styles, systems must be able to either dynamically adjust to the variances, or isolate the separate components of the audio.

Though this paper has focused on transcribing a single person speech so far, *S*CRIBE can handle dialogues using automated speaker segmentation techniques (Figure 6). We combine a standard convolution-based kernel method for identification of distinct segments in a waveform with a one-class support vector machine (SVM) classifier to each segment to assign it a speaker ID [18]. Prior work has shown such segmentation techniques to be accurate even in the presence of severe noise, such as when talking on a cell phone while driving [26, 18]. The segmentation allows us to *decompose* a dialogue in real-time, then caption each part individually.

AN INTERFACE FOR REAL-TIME CAPTIONING

The first component of *S*CRIBE is the interface that non-expert captionists will use to provide their captions (Figure 4). The web-based interface streams audio to the captionists who are instructed to type as much of it as they can. Furthermore, Workers are told to separate contiguous sequences of words by pressing [enter]. Knowing which word sequences are likely to be contiguous can help later when recombining the partial captions from multiple captionists.

To encourage real-time entry of captions, the interface "locks in" words a short time after they are typed (800 milliseconds). New words are identified when the captionist types a space after the word, and are sent to the server. The delay is added to allow workers to correct their input while adding as little additional latency as possible to it. When the captionist presses [enter] (or following a 2 second timeout during which they have not typed anything), the line is confirmed and animates upward. During the 10 second trip to the top of the display, words that *S*CRIBE determines were entered correctly (by either a spelling match or overlap with another worker) are colored green. When the line reaches the top, a point score is calculated for each word based on its length and whether it has been determined to be correct.

To recover the true speech signal, non-expert captions must *cover* all of the words in that signal. A primary reason why the partial transcriptions may not fully cover the true signal relates to *saliency*, which is defined in a linguistic context as "that quality which determines how semantic material is distributed within a sentence or discourse, in terms of the relative emphasis which is placed on its various parts." [14]. Numerous factors influence what is salient, and so it is likely to be difficult to detect automatically. Instead, we inject saliency artificially by systematically varying the volume of the audio signal that captionists hear. The web-based interface that we use is able to vary the volume over a given a period with an assigned offset. It also displays visual reminders of the period to further reinforce this notion. Figure 7 shows how the volume can be systematically varied to maximize coverage over the whole signal.

In preliminary work, we instead divided the audio signal into segments that we gave to individual workers to transcribe. We found a number of problems with this approach. First, workers tended to take longer to provide their transcriptions as it took them a bit to get into the flow of the audio. A continuous stream avoids this problem. Second, the interface seemed to encourage workers to favor quality over speed, whereas a stream that does not stop is a reminder of the real-time nature of the transcription. The continuous interface was designed using an iterative process involving tests with 57 remote and local users with a range of backgrounds and typing abilities. These tests demonstrated that workers generally tended to provide chains of words rather than disjoint words, and that workers needed to be informed of the motivations behind aspects of the interface to use them properly.

A non-obvious question is what the period of the volume changes should be. In our experiments, we chose to play the audio at high volume for four seconds and then at a lower volume for six seconds. This seems to work well in practice, but it is likely that it is not ideal for everyone. Our experience suggested that keeping the on period short is preferable even when a particular worker was able to type more than the period because the latency of a worker's input tended to go up as they typed more consecutive words.

REAL-TIME INPUT COMBINER

The second primary component of *S*CRIBE is the merging server, which uses a selectable algorithm to combine partial

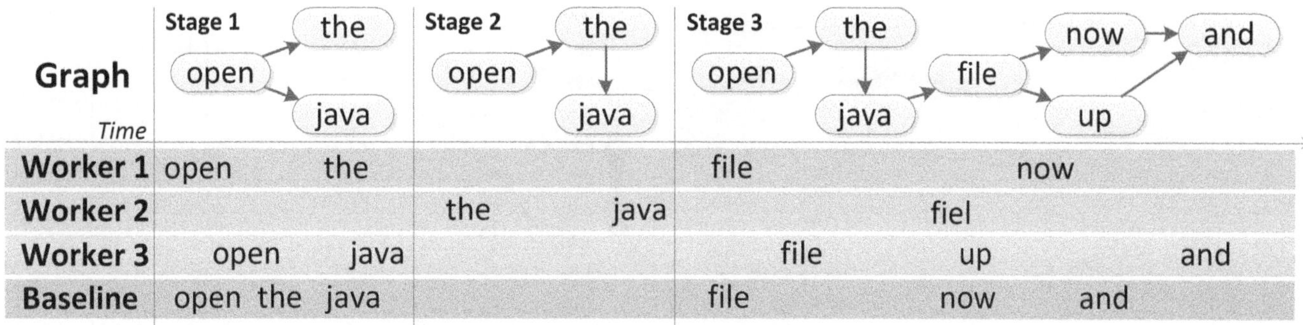

Figure 8. Graph building for three workers captioning the spoken sentence *"Open the Java code up now and ... "*. The top section shows the current state of the graph after each stage. The bottom shows the corresponding input. Note that Worker 2 spelling 'file' incorrectly does not adversely affect the graph since a majority of the workers still spell it correctly.

captions into a single output stream. A naive approach would be to simply arrange all words in the order in which they arrive, but this approach does not handle reordering, omissions, and inaccuracy within the input captions. Instead, our algorithm combines timing information, observed overlap between the partial captions, and models of natural language to inform the construction of the final output. In this section, we first describe our straightforward adaptation of multiple sequence alignment (MSA) to the caption combination problem, and then describe the reformulation of this algorithm that enables $\mathcal{S}$CRIBE to overcome many of the run-time and scalability issues associated with MSA.

Multiple Sequence Alignment

To use MSA, we replaced the mutation model for nucleotides used in the MUSCLE bioinformatics package with a spelling error model based on the physical layout of a keyboard. For example, when a person intends to type [a], he is more likely to mistype [q] than [m]. The model is further augmented with context-based features learned from spelling corrections drawn from the revisions of Wikipedia articles.

Learning a substitution matrix for each pair of characters along with character insertion and deletion penalties allows us to run a robust optimization technique that finds a near-optimal joint alignment [11]. Even though finding the best alignment is computationally expensive, our system operates in real-time by leveraging dynamic programming and approximations. Once the partial captions are aligned, we need to merge them into a single transcript, as shown in Figure 3. We perform a majority vote for each column of aligned characters, then remove the gaps in a post-processing step. The entire computation takes only a few seconds for input several minutes in length. To apply our MSA model to longer audio signals while maintaing the real-time aspect of the system, a sliding window can be used to bound the runtime.

Online Dynamic Sequence Alignment

In order to achieve the response-time and scalability required for real-time captioning of longer sessions, we create a version of MSA that aligns input using a graphical model. Worker captions are modeled as a linked list with nodes containing equivalent words aligned based on sequence order submission time. As words are added, consistent paths arise. We maintain the longest self-consistent path between any two nodes to avoid unnecessary branching. Figure 8 shows an example of the graph building process.

Reconstructing the Stream

Using a greedy search of the graph, in which we always follow the highest weight edge (a measure of the likelihood of two words appearing in a row), we derive a transcript in real-time. The greedy search traverses the graph between inferred instances of words by favoring paths between word instances with the highest levels of confidence derived from worker input and n-gram data. Ideally, we imagine using n-gram corpora tailored to the domain of the audio clips being transcribed, either by generating them in real time along with our graph model, or by pre-processing language from similar contexts. Specific n-gram data should allow more accurate transcriptions of technical language by improving the accuracy of the model used to infer word ordering in ambiguous cases.

The greedy graph traversal favors paths through the graph with high worker confidence, and omits entirely words contained within branches of the graph that contain unique instances of words. A post-processing step augments the initial sequence by adding into it any word instances with high worker confidence that were not already included. Because the rest of the branch is not included, these words can be disconnected from words adjacent in the original audio The positioning of these words are added back into the transcript by considerng the most likely sequence given their timestamps and the bigrams and trigrams that result from their insertion into the transcription. After this post-processing is complete the current transcript is forwarded back to the user.

Run-time

Each time a worker submits new input, a node is added to the worker's input chain. A hash map containing all existing unique words spoken so far in the stream is then used to find a set of equivalent terms. The newest element can always be used since the guarantee of increasing timestamps means the the most recent occurrence will always be the best fit. The match is then checked to see if a connection between the two nodes would form a back-edge. Using this approach allows us to reduce the runtime from worst-case $O(n^k)$ to $O(n)$. We can further reduce the runtime of this algorithm by limiting the amount of data stored in the graph at any one time – since we can safely assume that the latency with which any worker submits a response is limited. In practice, a 10 second time

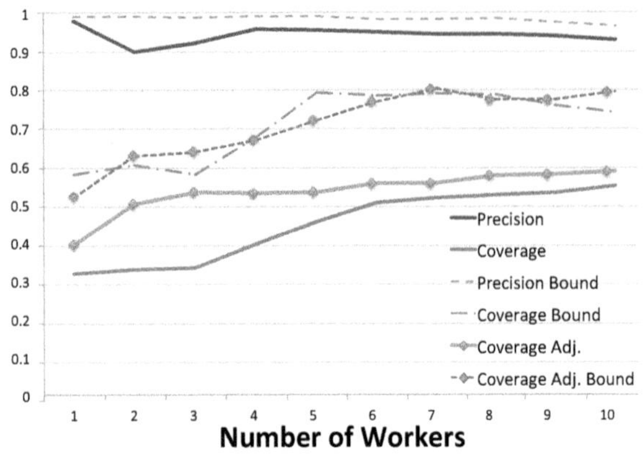

Figure 9. Precision and coverage plots for MSA with artificial saliency adjustments (Adj.) and without, and their theoretical upper bounds. We see that the adjustments significantly improve SCRIBE's coverage.

Figure 10. Optimal coverage reaches nearly 80% when combining the input of four workers, and nearly 95% with all 10 workers. This demonstrates that captioning audio in real-time with non-experts is feasible.

window is effective, though SCRIBE was able to incrementally build the graph and generate output within a few milliseconds for time windows beyond 5 minutes.

Our approach does not have the optimality guarantees of offline MSA; however, we show that this approach is effective in the real-time captioning domain, due to properties such as the relatively low frequency of repeated words. In the future, we will extend this model to handle general online sequence alignment, given statistical information about the domain.

EXPERIMENTS

We ran experiments to test the ability of non-expert captionists drawn from both local and remote crowds to provide captions that cover speech, and then evaluate our approaches for merging the input from these captionists into a final real-time transcription stream. We collected a data set of speech selected from freely available lectures on MIT OpenCourseWare (http://ocw.mit.edu/courses/). These lectures were chosen because one of the main goals of SCRIBE is to provide captions for classroom activities, and because the recording of the lectures roughly matches our target as well – there is a microphone in the room that often captures multiple speakers, *e.g.*, students asking questions. We chose four 5-minute segments that contained speech from courses in electrical engineering and chemistry, and had them professionally transcribed at a cost of $1.75 per minute. Despite the high cost, we found a number of errors and omissions, and corrected these to obtain a completely accurate baseline.

Our study used 20 local participants. Each participant captioned 23 minutes of aural speech over a period of approximately 30 minutes. Participants first took a standard typing test and averaged a typing rate of 77.0 WPM (SD=15.8) with 2.05% average error (SD=2.31%). We then introduced participants to the real-time captioning interface, and had them caption a 3-minute clip using it. Participants were then asked to caption the four 5-minute clips, two of which were selected to contain saliency adjustments.

One key question as to the effectiveness of our approach is whether or not groups of non-experts can effectively *cover* the speech signal. If some part of the speech signal is never typed then it will never appear in the final output, regardless of merging effectiveness. We also measure the precision and WER of the captions, which influence the overall readability.

Multiple Sequence Alignment

Figure 9 shows precision and coverage plots for the MSA algorithm using multiple workers. The metrics are calculated at a character level and averaged over all subsets of workers and over all audio clips. We see that precision is not significantly impacted by the number of workers, whereas coverage significantly improves as we use additional captionists. The theoretical upper bounds in Figure 9 for both precision and coverage shows what can be attained by a fully informed MSA with access to ground truth. This shows that SCRIBE is extracting nearly all of the information it can in terms of precision, but could improvement in terms of coverage. Narrowing this gap is a key direction of our future work.

Note that adjusting the saliency dramatically improves coverage, as compared to no adjustments (Figure 9). For example, only 2 workers are needed to achieve 50% coverage when using adjustments, while 6 workers are required to produce the same level with no adjustments. We discuss this in more in more detail later in this section.

Real-time Combiner

In our tests, an average worker achieved 29.0% coverage, ASR achieved 32.3% coverage, CART achieved 88.5% coverage and SCRIBE reached 74% out of a possible 93.2% coverage using 10 workers (Figure 10). Groups of workers also had an average latency of 2.89 seconds (including network latency), significantly improving on CART's latency of 4.38 seconds. Results show that SCRIBE is easily able to outperform the coverage of both ASR and lone workers. Additionally, the number and types of errors in ASR captions make it far less useful to a user trying to comprehend the content of the audio. Our naive approach (optimal coverage curve), which combines input based only on timestamp, shows that multiple workers have the potential to surpass CART with respect to coverage. Latency is also improved since multiple concurrent workers will naturally interleave answers, so that no one worker falling behind will delay the whole system, unlike a single-captionist approach such as CART.

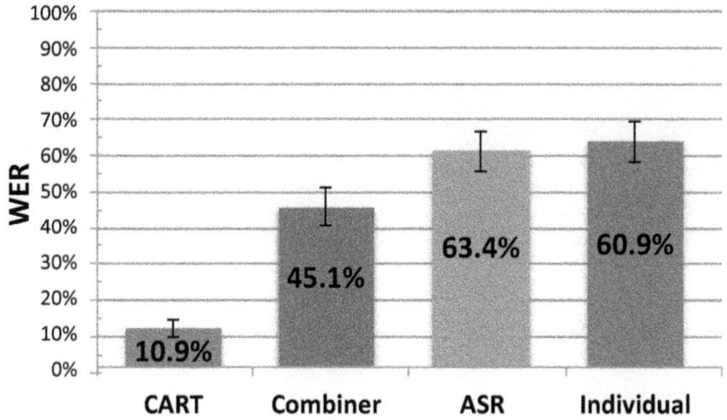

Figure 11. Word error rate (WER) results for the captioning systems. Our combiner outperforms both individual workers and ASR.

Figure 11 shows WER results from the captioning systems. For this example, we tuned our combiner to balance coverage and precision, getting an average of 66% and 80.3% respectively. As expected, CART outperforms the other approaches. However, our combiner presents a clear improvement over both ASR and a single worker. The precision of each system is shown in Figure 12. Because the input of multiple workers is merged, our combiner occasionally includes repeated words, which are marked as incorrect by our metrics. The difference is that SCRIBE can be tuned to reach arbitrarily high accuracies, at the expense of coverage. This tradeoff is discussed in the next section.

Adjusting Tradeoffs

The input combiner is parameterized and allows users to actively adjust the tradeoff between improving coverage and improving precision while they are viewing the captions. To increase coverage, the combiner reduces the number of workers required to agree on a word before including it in the final caption. To increase accuracy, the combiner increases the required agreement. Figure 13 shows tradeoffs users can make by adjusting these settings.

Saliency Adjustment

We also tested the interface changes designed to encourage workers to type different parts of the audio signal. For all participants, the interface indicated that they should be certain to type words appearing during a four second period followed by six seconds in which they could type if they wanted to. The 10 participants who typed using the modified version of the interface for each 5-minute file were assigned offsets ranging from 0 to 9 seconds.

In our experiments, we found that the participants consistently typed a greater fraction of the text that appeared in the periods in which the interface indicated that they should. For the electrical engineering clip, the difference was 54.7% (*SD*=9.4%) for words in the selected periods as compared to only 23.3% (*SD*=6.8%) for word outside of those periods. For the chemistry clips, the difference was 50.4% (*SD*=9.2%) of words appearing inside the highlighted period as compared to 15.4% (*SD*=4.3%) of words outside of the period.

Mechanical Turk

We were curious to see if the interface and captioning task would make sense to workers on Mechanical Turk since we would not be able to provide directions in person. We used quikTurkit to recruit a crowd of workers to caption the four clips (20 minutes of speech). Our HITs (Human Intelligence Tasks) paid $0.05 and workers could make an additional $0.002 bonus per word. We asked workers to first watch a 40-second video in which we describe the task. In total, 18 workers participated, at a cost of $13.84 ($36.10 per hour).

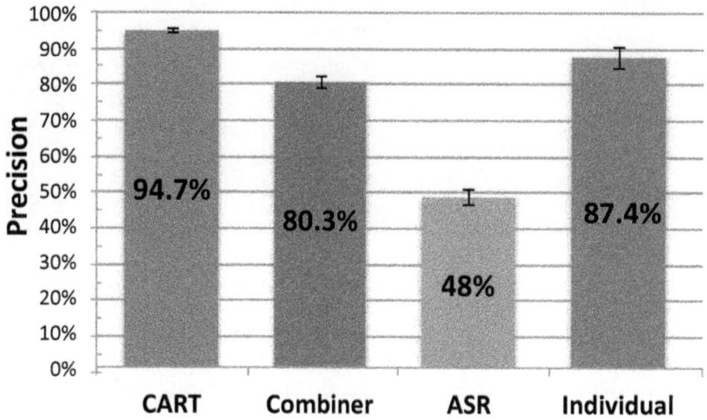

Figure 12. Precision results for the captioning systems.

Workers collectively achieved a 78.0% coverage of the audio signal. The average coverage over just three workers was 59.7% (*SD*=10.9%), suggesting we could be conservative in recruiting workers and cover much of the input signal. Participating workers generally provided high-quality captions, although some had difficulty hearing the audio. Prior work has shown that workers remember the content of prior tasks, meaning that as more tasks are generated, we expect the size of the trained pool of workers available on Mechanical Turk will increase [21]. The high cost of alternatives means that we can pay workers well and still provide a cheaper solution.

DISCUSSION AND FUTURE WORK

Our results show that groups of non-experts have the ability to achieve better coverage and less latency than a professional captionist. Furthermore, we can encourage workers to focus

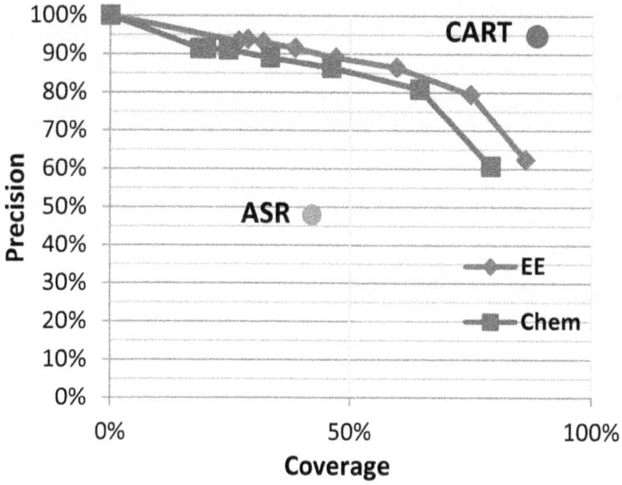

Figure 13. Precision-coverage curves for the electrical engineering (EE) and chemistry (Chem) lectures using different combiner parameters with 10 workers. In general, increasing coverage reduces accuracy.

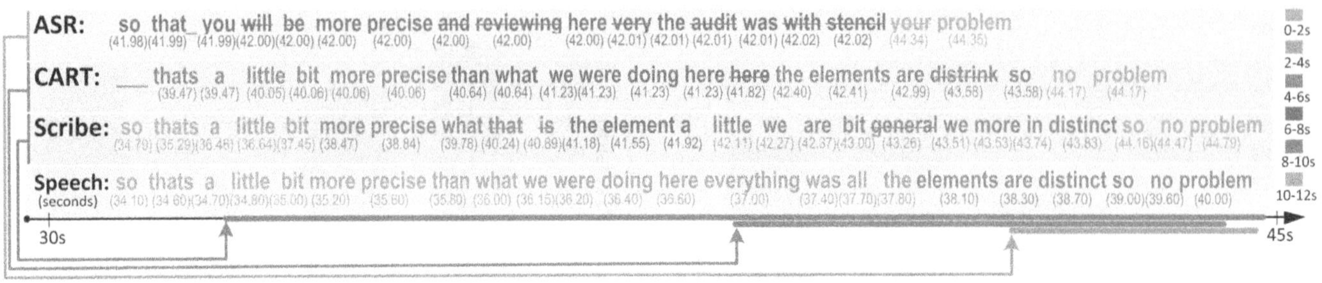

Figure 14. Captions by CART, SCRIBE, and ASR illustrating common errors and tradeoffs. Words are colored based on 2-second time spans. ASR and (to a lesser extent) CART captions arrive in bursts, disrupting the 'flow'. The timeline shows the duration of output from each system. SCRIBE repeats some content, but creates a significantly more accurate and meaningful transcript than ASR.

on specific portions of the speech to improve global coverage, and it is possible to recombine partial captions while effectively balancing coverage and precision. This presents opportunities for future work that aims to improve the quality, availability, and cost of real-time captioning.

Covering the Input Signal

For our approach to work, the captions provided by workers must fully cover the original content. We have shown that a single worker is unable to cover even one third of the speech, but groups can collectively cover over 93%. Many of the remaining gaps measured are due to differences in phrasing (e.g. "anybody" vs. "anyone") that do not affect the usability of the system, meaning our combiner will likely perform better in real settings than the results indicate.

We have also shown that we can effectively encourage workers to cover portions of speech that we want, and future work will seek to further improve the interface and worker feedback to increase coverage even more with fewer workers. In particular, our current approach does not reward workers sufficiently for typing long or complicated words, and so these are often missed. For instance, the word "non-aqueous" was used in a clip about chemistry but no workers typed it.

Our saliency adjustment is currently defined to be the same for all workers.Personalizing the on and off periods for each worker could improve results while requiring fewer workers by letting more experienced and skilled workers be used to their full potential, while not overwhelming newer workers. Several workers (both local and on Mechanical Turk), made a point of mentioning that they enjoyed the captioning task and were interested in continued participation as a SCRIBE captionist. Reporting scores, most common mistakes, and other information back to workers may help them improve their typing ability, resulting in a more skilled set of available worker in future tasks. Adding multiple classes of continuous workers will make some alternate approaches more viable. For example, using a separate group of workers to provide information such as the number of words said reduces the amount of uncertainty that needs to be handled by the model.

We expect that leveraging a more rich probabilistic language model will help improve SCRIBE's performance. Currently, the input combination algorithm is agnostic to part-of-speech tags, sentence structure, and other linguistic features. A unified conditional random field model [25] that finds the most likely sequence of words given partial worker captions *along with* language-based features, semantics, and context, will not only yield better accuracy, but may even produce a transcript that is more comprehensible than verbatim.

Leveraging Hybrid Workforces

ASR is not reliable on its own, but may be useful as a supplement to (or eventually replacement of) the input of human workers by including ASR systems as contributors. This is especially useful with small groups of workers. For example, supplementing the captions of a single worker with ASR brings the optimal coverage up from 28.5% to 55.3%, and for 10 workers, from 93.2% to 95.1%. Additionally, our tests found that the errors made by ASR differ from those made by humans: ASR tends to replace words with others that are phonetically similar, but differ in meaning, while humans tend to replace words with ones that have the same meaning, but may sound different. Thus, we expect that using a hybrid approach will be more effective than either humans or ASR alone by using these difference to increase coverage while maintaining accuracy even with lower agreement. For example, if a human worker and ASR both agree on a word and its position, it is more likely to be correct than if two workers (who make similar mistakes) agree on it. As ASR improves, SCRIBE can reduce its reliance on human contributors, and transition towards a fully automatic system that is more robust and faster than any single ASR.

Real-World User Testing

The utility of captioning in real-world settings is dependent on both the information content retained and the ease by which the captions can be read. Spoken language often flows differently than written text. Speakers pause, change subjects, and repeat phrases – all of which can make exact transcripts difficult to read (Figure 14). A language model may help make SCRIBE captions more readable. Captioning methods such as C-Print paraphrase speech to keep up, often making them easier to read but also leaving out content. ASR often produces nonsensical errors, which is likely to confuse users, even though ASR can appear competitive on automatic metrics. Models could be individually customized to a user's preferred style. We plan to test these tradeoffs in real settings with DHH and hearing students.

Extending to New Problems

SCRIBE uses a new model of human computation to allow groups to collectively out-perform individuals on a difficult human performance task (real-time captioning). The general idea of combining partial inputs automatically may be extended to new domains and new problems thus far limited by individuals' abilities. Groups composed of multiple contributors collectively possess superior motor and cognitive abilities, but how to effectively harness those abilities in general remains an open research question. We believe the model introduced in this paper is a valuable first step.

CONCLUSIONS

In this paper, we have introduced a new model of crowdsourcing in which multiple workers provide simultaneous input that is then combined into a final answer. This approach enables workers to collectively complete tasks that they may otherwise be unable to perform individually. As a specific instance of this framework, we presented LEGION:SCRIBE, an end-to-end system enabling real-time captioning by non-experts. We showed that groups of workers can outperform both individuals and ASR in terms of coverage, precision, and latency, and introduced a new algorithm for aligning and merging partial text captions as they arrive. We have furthermore demonstrated that groups of non-experts can achieve better coverage and latency than a professional captionist, and that we can encourage them to focus on specific portions of the speech to improve global coverage. Finally, we have shown that it is possible to recombine partial captions and effectively tradeoff coverage and precision. Our results demonstrate the feasibility of this approach and open a number of interesting opportunities for future research.

ACKNOWLEDGMENTS

This work was supported by National Science Foundation grants #IIS-1149709 and #IIS-1016486, and by Google.

REFERENCES

1. Y. C. Beatrice Liem, H. Zhang. An iterative dual pathway structure for speech-to-text transcription. In *Proc. of the 3rd Workshop on Human Computation*, HCOMP 2011. 2011.
2. M. S. Bernstein, J. R. Brandt, R. C. Miller, and D. R. Karger. Crowds in two seconds: Enabling realtime crowd-powered interfaces. In *Proc. of the 24th annual ACM Symp. on User Interface Software and Technology*, UIST '11, p33–42. 2011.
3. M. S. Bernstein, G. Little, R. C. Miller, B. Hartmann, M. S. Ackerman, D. R. Karger, D. Crowell, and K. Panovich. Soylent: a word processor with a crowd inside. In *Proc. of the 23rd Annual ACM Symp. on User Interface Software and Technology*, UIST '10, p313–322. 2010.
4. J. P. Bigham, R. E. Ladner, and Y. Borodin. The Design of the Human-Backed Access Technology *Conf. on Computers and Accessibility*, ASSETS 2011, p3–10. 2011.
5. J. P. Bigham, C. Jayant, H. Ji, G. Little, A. Miller, R. C. Miller, R. Miller, A. Tatarowicz, B. White, S. White, and T. Yeh. Vizwiz: nearly real-time answers to visual questions. In *Proc. of the 23rd Annual ACM Symp. on User Interface Software and Technology*, UIST '10, p333–342. 2010.
6. L. Chilton. Seaweed: A web application for designing economic games. Master's thesis, MIT, 2009.
7. M. Cooke, P. Green, L. Josifovski, and A. Vizinho. Robust automatic speech recognition with missing and unreliable acoustic data. *Speech Comm.*, 34(3):267–285, 2001.
8. S. Cooper, F. Khatib, A. Treuille, J. Barbero, J. Lee, M. Beenen, A. Leaver-Fay, D. Baker, Z. Popovic, and F. Players. Predicting protein structures with a multiplayer online game. *Nature*, 466(7307):756–760, 2010.
9. X. Cui, L. Gu, B. Xiang, W. Zhang, and Y. Gao. Developing high performance asr in the IBM multilingual speech-to-speech translation system. In *IEEE Intl. Conf. on Acoustics, Speech and Signal Processing*, ICASSP 2008, p5121–5124. 2008.
10. F. J. Damerau. A technique for computer detection and correction of spelling errors. In *Commun. ACM.*, 7(3):171–176. March 1964.
11. R. Edgar. Muscle: multiple sequence alignment with high accuracy and high throughput. *Nucleic acids research*, 32(5):1792–1797. 2004.
12. L. B. Elliot, M. S. Stinson, D. Easton, and J. Bourgeois. College Students Learning With C-Print's Education Software and Automatic Speech Recognition. In *American Ed. Research Assoc. Annual Meeting*, 2008.
13. J. Felsenstein. Inferring phytogenies. Sinauer Associates, Sunderland, Massachusetts. 2004.
14. J. L. Flowerdew. Salience in the performance of one speech act: the case of definitions. *Discource Processes*, 15(2):165–181. April-June 1992.
15. J. Holt, S. Hotto, and K. Cole. Demographic Aspects of Hearing Impairment: Questions and Answers. 1994. http://research.gallaudet.edu/Demographics/factsheet.php.
16. T. Imai, A. Matsui, S. Homma, T. Kobayakawa, K. Onoe, S. Sato, and A. Ando. Speech recognition with a re-speak method for subtitling live broadcasts. In *Intl. Conf. on Spoken Lang. Processing*, ICSLP-2002, p1757–1760. 2002.
17. C. Jensema, R. McCann, S. Ramsey. Closed-captioned television presentation speed and vocabulary. In *Am Ann Deaf.* 141(4):284–92. October 1996.
18. H. Kadri, M. Davy, A. Rabaoui, Z. Lachiri, N. Ellouze, et al. Robust audio speaker segmentation using one class SVMs. In *Proc of the European Signal Processing Conf.*, EUSIPCO 2008. 2008.
19. A. Kittur, B. Smus, S. Khamkar and R. E. Kraut. Crowdforge: Crowdsourcing complex work. In *Proc. of the 24th Symp. on User Interface Software and Technology*, UIST '11, p43–52. 2011.
20. W. S. Lasecki, K. I. Murray, S. White, R. C. Miller, and J. P. Bigham. Real-time crowd control of existing interfaces. In *Proceedings of the 24th ACM Symp. on User Interface Software and Technology*, UIST '11, p23–32. 2011.
21. W. S. Lasecki, S. White, K. I. Murray, and J. P. Bigham. Crowd memory: Learning in the collective. In *Proc. of Collective Intelligence 2012*, CI 2012. 2012.
22. G. Little, L. B. Chilton, M. Goldman, and R. C. Miller. Turkit: human computation algorithms on mechanical turk. In *Proc. of the 23rd ACM Symp. on User interface software and technology*, UIST '10, p57–66. 2010.
23. T. Matthews, S. Carter, C. Pai, J. Fong, and J. Mankoff. Scribe4me: evaluating a mobile sound transcription tool for the deaf. In *Proc. of the 8th Intl. Conf. on Ubiquitous Computing*, UbiComp '06, p159–176. 2006.
24. S. B. Needleman and C. D. Wunsch. A general method applicable to the search for similarities in the amino acid sequence of two proteins. In *Journal of Molecular Biology*. 48 (3):443-53. 1970.
25. C. Sutton and A. McCallum. *An introduction to conditional random fields for relational learning*. Introduction to statistical relational learning. MIT Press, 2006.
26. A. Tritschler and R. Gopinath. Improved speaker segmentation and segments clustering using the bayesian information criterion. In *Sixth European Conf. on Speech Communication and Technology*, 1999.
27. C. Van Den Brink, M. Tijhuis, G. Van Den Bos, S. Giampaoli, P. Kivinen, A. Nissinen, and D. Kromhout. Effect of widowhood on disability onset in elderly men from three european countries. *Journal of the American Geriatrics Society*, 52(3):353–358. 2004.
28. L. von Ahn. Human Computation. Ph.D. Thesis. 2005.
29. L. von Ahn and L. Dabbish. Labeling images with a computer game. In *Proc. of the Conf. on Human Factors in Computing Systems*, CHI '04, p319–326. 2004.
30. M. Wald. Creating accessible educational multimedia through editing automatic speech recognition captioning in real time. *Interactive Technology and Smart Education*, 3(2):131–141. 2006.
31. A. A. Ye-Yi Wang and C. Chelba. Is word error rate a good indicator for spoken language understanding accuracy. In *IEEE Workshop on Automatic Speech Recognition and Understanding*. 2003.

Carpus: A Non-Intrusive User Identification Technique for Interactive Surfaces

Raf Ramakers **Davy Vanacken** **Kris Luyten** **Karin Coninx** **Johannes Schöning**
Hasselt University - tUL - IBBT
Expertise Centre for Digital Media
Wetenschapspark 2, 3590 Diepenbeek, Belgium
firstname.lastname@uhasselt.be

ABSTRACT
Interactive surfaces have great potential for co-located collaboration because of their ability to track multiple inputs simultaneously. However, the multi-user experience on these devices could be enriched significantly if touch points could be associated with a particular user. Existing approaches to user identification are intrusive, require users to stay in a fixed position, or suffer from poor accuracy. We present a non-intrusive, high-accuracy technique for mapping touches to their corresponding user in a collaborative environment. By mounting a high-resolution camera above the interactive surface, we are able to identify touches reliably without any extra instrumentation, and users are able to move around the surface at will. Our technique, which leverages the back of users' hands as identifiers, supports walk-up-and-use situations in which multiple people interact on a shared surface.

Author Keywords
Interactive tabletops; surface computing; multi-touch interaction; multi-user applications; user identification.

ACM Classification Keywords
H.5.2 [Information interfaces and presentation]: User Interfaces: Input devices and strategies; I.4.9 [Image Processing and Computer Vision]: Applications

General Terms
Design, Experimentation, Human Factors.

INTRODUCTION
Interactive tabletops and surfaces are well suited to co-located collaboration because of their ability to track multiple inputs simultaneously. However, the multi-user experience on these devices can be enriched significantly if touch points can be associated with the user performing an action. New opportunities are, for example, customizing functionalities (e.g. multi-user undo [29]) or personalizing the appearance of the interface, such as providing automatic translations or help cues for novice users [31]. When the user's identity is readily available with every touch, it is also possible for the system to enforce social protocols in multi-user applications [19, 26].

Figure 1. Carpus recognizes users by observing the dorsal region of their hands with a high-resolution camera mounted above an interactive surface.

Although several approaches exist for identifying users of a touch display, each has important limitations. Some techniques require additional instrumentation of the users at the start of each session [15, 16, 28] or the use of a mobile device [32], while others are easy to spoof because they identify the shoe that the user is currently wearing [27]. DiamondTouch [7] and Medusa [2] assign an identity to fixed positions around an interactive table, making them unsuitable for free-flow environments. In contrast to these approaches, Schmidt et al. [30] presented a system that uses a biometric technique. However, very specific hand postures are required each time the user's identity is needed, which impedes the 'naturalness' of the interaction.

In this paper, we present a novel technique to associate touch points with a user with high accuracy. Our system, Carpus, supports walk-up-and-use scenarios in which each touch can be identified transparently once users have been registered. By mounting a high-resolution camera above an interactive surface (Figure 1), we are able to extract identifying information from the back of the human hand (also known as the *dorsal* region) during traditional multi-touch interactions. As a result, our technique is non-intrusive and can be used in combination with a large range of touch technologies, including sensor-based, optical-based and vision-based hardware. Carpus supports user identification for setups intended for ad-hoc or informal collaboration [10], with users collaborating in unplanned fashion.

Among the many possible applications of Carpus, we envision new interactive setups deployed in shops and travel agencies. The system can differentiate between actions of customers searching together for information about new products, a task that frequently involves collaboration [17]. In such a situation, it is possible for the system to interpret two-handed touch gestures unambiguously while multiple users are interacting simultaneously. In addition, a profile can be created for each customer, making it possible for the system to track a user's interests in order to recommend other relevant products. We also expect that Carpus can satisfy the demand for easy to deploy techniques to identify users in groupware studies, such as studies regarding territoriality [33]. With Carpus, analysis of users' behavior will be significantly less time consuming, as each action is automatically associated with a particular user.

Our main contribution is a new technique to *identify touch points non-intrusively by observing the back of the users' hands*. Our approach is robust for hand postures that are common during the practical use of multi-touch systems. For traditional pointing, which is most common in touch interaction [29], Carpus uniquely identifies both hands of a user with more than 97% accuracy, even when 20 users are registered. As a result, it becomes possible to differentiate between actions performed by a user's right and left hand in order to support non-symmetric division of labor [9]. For more complex hand postures, which are less common, the recognition rates drop to 82% in the worst case scenario. A smaller group size is recommended to achieve higher recognition rates in these situations.

RELATED WORK

Identifying users is a challenging and prominent issue in surface computing research. In this section, we will review the previous efforts in more depth. Existing approaches to user identification have at least one of the following limitations: (1) The naturalness of the interaction is impeded due to users being required to wear additional instrumentation or because of limitations on the supported hand postures; (2) Users need to stay at a fixed position around the surface; (3) Associating an identity to a touch point can be difficult, resulting in accuracy problems. A summary of existing approaches can be found in Table 1.

Visual tags [15] can be easily used to identify users. Electronic tags such as the IdWristband [16] or the IR-Ring [28] are also able to identify users reliably, in this case by flashing a unique sequence in the infrared spectrum to the interactive surface. However, these techniques require users to wear equipment. This overhead can be a burden, especially when the system is used for short, spontaneous and unplanned interactions. Schöning et al. [32], on the other hand, require the use of a mobile device to authenticate with the system, while

	Non-intrusive	Position invariant	Unambiguous association
DiamondTouch [7]	√	–	√
Medusa [2]	√	–	–
IdWristbands [16]	–	√	–
IR-Ring [28]	–	√	–
Tagged gloves [15]	–	√	√
HandsDown [30]	–	√	√
Mobile Phone [32]	–	√	–
Bootstrapper [27]	√	√	–
Carpus	√	√	√

Table 1. A summary of the strengths and weaknesses of related user identification techniques for interactive surfaces.

Schmidt et al. [30] extract biometric geometry features from the human hand. In order to measure these metrics reliably, however, a hand needs to be placed flat on the interactive surface. These approaches require either additional equipment or unusual hand postures, interrupting the 'naturalness' of multi-touch interaction.

Other researchers have presented non-intrusive user identification by associating touches to users' positions around an interactive tabletop. DiamondTouch [7] leverages a specialized capacitive surface to transmit an electrical charge through a user's body when touching it. A receiver unit inside each user's chair is used to register all touch events of the user that is currently sitting on that chair. If users swap chairs, their identity will change. Annett et al. [2] instrumented a tabletop with arrays of proximity sensors to relate each touch to a user's position. Although this technique can track users' bodies that are moving near the tabletop, the system cannot preserve identities when users move further away. These identification techniques can be practical in situations where the users' positions around the table are fixed, but they cannot be used in free-flow environments where the interaction is interrupted frequently by other activities and the users' positions around the table are likely to vary.

A few projects have demonstrated the potential of revealing identities by observing shoes or gait. Bootstrapper [27] extracts features from the top of a user's shoes, whereas Multitoe [3] observes shoe sole patterns. Orr et al. [23] took another approach, identifying users by analyzing the forces and timings while walking on custom-built floor plates. However, these extracted features are not unique, as users can wear the same shoes or walk with an abnormal gait. Furthermore, relating touches to these identified regions requires additional tracking, and is therefore challenging and error-prone.

CARPUS

Our approach uses a high-resolution overhead camera (Figure 1) and works as follows: (1) Carpus continuously captures frames from above the interactive surface and extracts the visible dorsal hand regions; (2) Only when a user performs a "touch down" event, unique features are extracted from the hand region visible at the location of the touch in the last captured frame; (3) These unique features are matched against a database of feature-user pairs that was constructed beforehand during a very short training session; (4) The resulting user identity associated with that touch becomes available to

Figure 2. Unique features are extracted from the dorsal hand region. Fingers are excluded from the region.

the application running on the interactive surface. The surface then tracks the touch point to automatically identify subsequent finger movements.

The dorsal hand region (Figure 2) is well suited to user identification in a collaborative environment for several reasons. To begin with, each person's dorsal hand regions have many strongly identifying characteristics, such as lines, grooves, folds and furrows [20]. Furthermore, the dorsal hand region is quite large and is also the part of the hand that is the least flexible [20], making it possible to capture consistent patterns in the skin over many frames. The dorsal hand region is visible to an overhead camera throughout the majority of hand postures encountered during interaction with a tabletop, something that is not true of fingers (e.g. when performing vertical touches [36]).

BENEFITS AND LIMITATIONS

Carpus overcomes some drawbacks of current identification approaches (Table 1). Our technique provides transparent identification of users by extracting unique features directly from the back of the hand. Once registered with the system, Carpus supports real walk-up-and-use scenarios. The camera can be mounted above any type of interactive surface and captures the entire interaction. As a result, each touch point can be unambiguously related to an identified skin region. This enables identification of touches even when arms of multiple users overlap. Furthermore, Carpus is able to differentiate between the two hands of a user, which enables non-symmetric devision of labor [9].

Carpus is, however, subject to a few limitations. First, the dorsal hand region needs to be clearly captured by the camera. When performing very fast movements, it is possible that the camera cannot capture a sharp image of the hand. This can be addressed by using a camera with an appropriate shutter speed. Furthermore, while Carpus can handle most common hand postures encountered during multi-touch interactions, some techniques [18, 11] require the user's hand to be in such a position that the back is not visible to an overhead camera. In order to get a clear image of the dorsal region in those circumstances, we can add multiple cameras to our setup, capturing the hand from different points of view.

Secondly, Carpus has not been designed to offer authentication for privacy or security reasons. The current version of our algorithm can differentiate between users working simultaneously on an interactive surface, but has difficulties eliminating users that are not registered. As a result, the automatic detection of a 'new' unregistered user is unreliable, and thus the users' hands need to be registered beforehand to achieve higher recognition rates. However, registration is only a one-time cost compared to techniques that require configuration at the start of each session [16, 28]. We are exploring several interactive widgets for registration purposes that can be easily integrated in applications. Registration can be as simple as performing a single gesture before first usage (e.g. similar to the interactions required to unlock a smartphone).

Lastly, the reported recognition rates are only representative for groups of people with Caucasian skin. We intentionally recruited people with similar skin color for the evaluation of Carpus, because the similarity makes it harder to find unique features. Further research is needed to investigate the effect of different skin types on the accuracy of Carpus.

SKIN REGION AND IDENTITY EXTRACTION

In order to identify a hand that is visible in a captured frame, Carpus performs the following four steps: (1) extraction of the dorsal hand region; (2) feature extraction; (3) feature matching; (4) relating touches to identified regions.

Step 1: Extraction of the Dorsal Hand Region

First, the dorsal hand region needs to be detected in a captured frame. When a touch event occurs, Carpus does this in three sub-steps: (A) extraction of the skin region; (B) detection of visible fingers; (C) detection of the position of the wrist. Two iterations of this algorithm are executed for each detected skin region. During the second run, a more accurate segmentation is used in order to detect the dorsal region of the hand more precisely in particular situations, as we explain below.

Skin Detection

Skin segmentation [25] involves finding ranges of intensity values for which most skin pixels fall in a given color space. The image is first converted to the YCrCb color space [24] to obtain a decision rule that is robust under varying illumination conditions. To support various types of human skin, all pixels in a relatively large intensity range are classified as skin:

$$Y>20, 85<Cb<135, 135<Cr<180 \qquad (1)$$

Figure 3-A1 shows areas of pixels that were selected using this static segmentation rule. Because of the large intensity range, shadowed regions between fingers are erroneously classified as skin pixels. Therefore, a second, more dynamic skin segmentation rule is used after the position of the wrist and the fingers are detected. This dynamic segmentation rule is based on the average (μ) and standard deviation (σ) of the intensity of the pixels in the detected dorsal region:

$$\begin{gathered} \mu_Y - 2\sigma_Y < Y < \mu_Y + 2\sigma_Y \\ \mu_{Cr} - 2\sigma_{Cr} < Cr < \mu_{Cr} + 2\sigma_{Cr} \\ \mu_{Cb} - 2\sigma_{Cb} < Cb < \mu_{Cb} + 2\sigma_{Cb} \end{gathered} \qquad (2)$$

In Figure 3-A2 the shadowed regions between the fingers are correctly excluded with dynamic segmentation. Parts of an arm or finger are sometimes erroneously classified as non-skin regions because of variations in the observed skin color. However, this does not influence the outcome of our algorithm, since only the back of the hand is used.

Finger Detection

Once the skin regions are extracted from a captured frame, fingers need to be detected in order to exclude these regions from the final contour. We first detect the tips and then the phalanges of the fingers. To detect fingertips, we use a curvature-based approach similar to Malik and Laszlo [14] and Segen and Kumar [34]. The vectors from each contour point k to $k + n$ and $k - n$ are computed (n is a fixed value and depends on the distance between two contour points). If the angle between the two vectors is below some threshold, then the contour point is marked as a fingertip (Figure 3-B). We use a relatively high angular threshold value of 60 degrees to make the fingertip detection algorithm more 'greedy'. Our algorithm even classifies the knuckles of folded fingers as fingertips (Figure 3-B), because we want to exclude all visible finger regions from our contour and are not interested in the exact position of the real fingertips. The misclassification of finger valleys is avoided by taking into account the sign of the angle between two vectors while processing the contour in counterclockwise direction. Finally, non-maximal suppression is used to avoid detecting fingertips too close to each other.

In order to extract entire finger regions, the phalanges of the fingers also need to be detected. Boreki and Zimmer [5] do this by finding the position of finger valleys between two consecutive fingertips. However, we need to support all hand postures, even when only one finger is visible (e.g. pointing). Therefore, we take a different approach. Our algorithm starts roaming the skin contour from each detected fingertip to the left and right. Each contour point is then classified as part of a finger phalange until the length of the finger has reached a maximum value or the angle between two phalanges exceeds an angular threshold value (Figure 3-B). This threshold is inversely proportional to the length of the finger and ranges between 40 and 60 degrees in our algorithm.

Wrist Detection

Before we are able to detect the position of the wrist, we need to determine its orientation. The orientation of the wrist is based on the orientation of the arm, which is given as the principal axis of inertia of the extracted skin region. The orientation of the principal axis (Figure 3-C) can be computed from the image moments up to the second order, as described by Freeman et al. [8]. When the aspect ratio of the skin region along the direction of the principal axis is almost equal to 1:1 (e.g. a user with long sleeves performing a vertical touch), this approach is less reliable. In that case, we use the principal axis of the entire arm region, obtained by doing an additional background subtraction step.

Once the orientation of the wrist is known, the precise position of the wrist can be determined. Kioke et al. [12] assume that this position is always located at a fixed distance from the top of the hand. However, we observed that the distance from

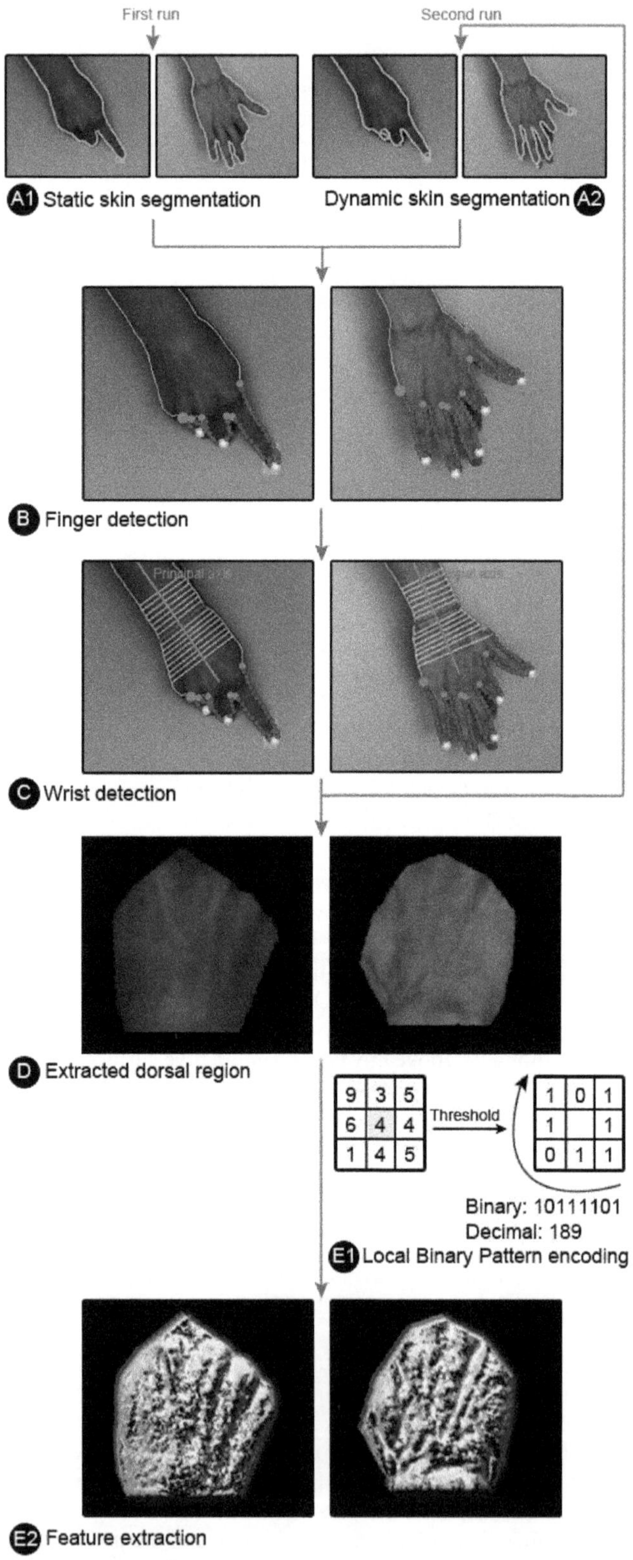

Figure 3. Extracting fine-grained details from the dorsal hand region (step 1 and step 2): (A) The skin region is detected in the image; (B) The fingers are detected; (C) The direction and position of the wrist is detected; (D) The dorsal hand region is extracted; (E) Fine-grained details are encoded using the Local Binary Pattern operator.

the wrist to the top of the hand can vary extensively, even when fingers are detected, because hands are free to move in three dimensions when working on an interactive surface. Therefore, we take an approach similar to Choi et al. [6], and evaluate the width of the contour along the direction of the principal axis from the finger tips to the arm region. The width of the contour has very specific characteristics at the position of the wrist. In the direction of the fingertips, the width will vary significantly, but in the direction of the arm, the width will be fairly constant. We consider the wrist to be located outside the finger regions, at the position where the width ratio reaches its maximum value (Figure 3-C).

Step 2: Feature Extraction

Once the dorsal hand region is detected using the algorithm described in the previous step, unique features need to be extracted from this region (Figure 3-D). There are several interest point detectors, such as SIFT [13] and SURF [4]. However, the skin of the hand is flat and does not contain a lot of these interest points. Therefore, we use the pattern of the entire skin region as a feature. Before we can compare skin patterns in different images (step 3), a texture descriptor is needed to quantize these patterns. Color histograms [35] are the most straightforward image descriptors, but this technique is very sensitive to changes in illumination. During preliminary studies, we noticed that color histograms are not able to capture unique information consistently over time, because the illumination of the hand changes significantly due to shadows cast by the user's body.

Local Binary Patterns (LBP) [21] is a technique to describe very fine-grained details of textures in images. In contrast to color histograms, LBP is invariant to any monotonic change in intensity values. The LBP-operator labels the pixels of an image by thresholding the 3x3-neighborhood of each pixel with the center value. The decimal representation of the number formed by the concatenation of all binary digits in the neighborhood is the intensity value of the central pixel in the local pattern (Figure 3-E1). Carpus uses Circular Local Binary Patterns (CLBP) [22], an extension to the basic LBP. The CLBP-operator samples the neighborhood circularly with a variable radius. If a point on the circle does not correspond to image coordinates, the point gets interpolated. The CLBP-operator is thus able to capture patterns at different scales: a small radius captures local details, whereas a larger radius captures more global information.

In our preliminary exploration, we noticed that the luminance component of the hand's skin texture (i.e. the hairs, lines, grooves, folds and furrows) contains most of the discriminative information. The color information was not very discriminative. Therefore, we only capture information in the luma (Y) component of the extracted skin regions. When capturing details at radii 2, 5 and 10 using the CLBP-operator, we can describe most of the unique features of the dorsal region of the human hand (Figure 3-E2).

Step 3: Feature Matching

To identify users, Carpus matches descriptions of textures captured using the CLBP-operator with a database of previously captured features. Before features of different images can be compared, we need to ensure that these features are captured at the same scale. Therefore, we only process a detected dorsal hand region when a "touch down" event is performed. A naive approach to comparing descriptions of textures would be a simple histogram comparison. When using this approach, however, all spatial information is lost. Through experiments, we discovered that without this spatial information, the extracted features are not very discriminative. Therefore, we use a technique similar to Ahonen et al. [1]. First, the skin region is divided into square patches of equal size (Figure 4). We currently use patches of 20 by 20 pixels. Next, histograms of these local micropatterns are computed. Histograms of the same patch, which contain information of fine-grained details at different scales, are concatenated to form a single description of the patch.

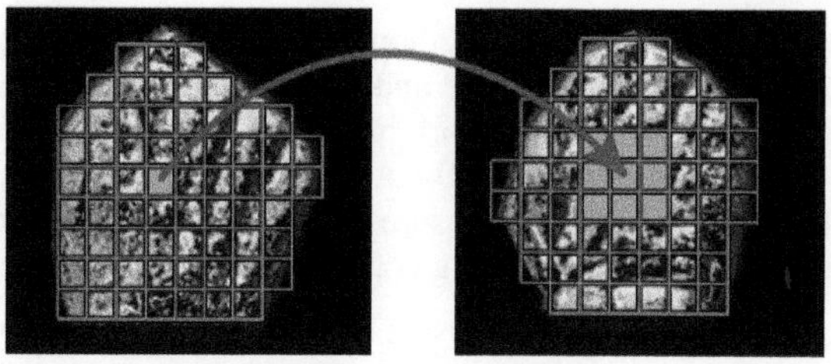

Figure 4. Feature matching (step 3): finding similar patches in a predefined neighborhood.

Opposed to the approach of Ahonen et al. [1], the local histograms of all patches in an image are not concatenated. Concatenation of these local histograms implies the integration of the hand's shape as a feature. Since the shape of the hand can vary significantly under different postures, we take another approach. Carpus compares two images by finding the best match for each patch in a predefined neighborhood around the corresponding position in the other image (Figure 4). We use a neighborhood of two times the patch size.

Experimenting with different histogram comparison metrics, we found that the histogram intersection technique provides the best matching of patches. As a result, the similarity between features extracted from two dorsal hand regions is the sum of the number of similar pixels for each of the patch's best matches. An unknown hand is assigned the identity of the dorsal hand region in the training set with the highest number of similar pixels.

Step 4: Relating Touches to Identified Regions

Once the identities of all extracted dorsal hand regions are known, each touch point needs to be related to an identified skin region. In contrast to other touch identification techniques [27, 16], Carpus is able to relate touch points to identified skin regions unambiguously. Each touch position is directly related to a single dorsal hand region by the contour of the fingers detected in step 1.

SYSTEM SPECIFICATIONS AND PERFORMANCE

For our experiments, we use a Philips BDT4225EM/06 42" multi-touch display, mounted horizontally on a table (Carpus was also informally tested in combination with other technologies, such as an FTIR tabletop). A Point Grey Grasshopper2 camera with a resolution of 1624 by 1224 pixels is mounted above the surface and transmits 22 frames per second at 45 dpi via the network interface of the camera to a PC (2.1 GHz Intel Core 2, 4 GB RAM) running Carpus. Artificial light sources are used to ensure that over different sessions of our experiment, the lighting conditions remain unchanged.

Carpus is able to identify users in real-time and scales well to higher resolutions. However, we did not focus on the performance of our algorithm, so many optimizations are possible. The extraction of the dorsal hand region (step 1) takes 28 ms on our system if only one hand is visible in a single frame with a resolution of 1100 by 790 pixels, 41 ms if two hands are visible and 52 ms if three hands are visible. When using a higher resolution camera, as in our setup, this step can still be performed at the specified lower resolution without reducing the accuracy of our identification technique. After the position of the dorsal hand region is detected, features can be extracted from the original high-resolution image. The feature extraction and matching step is only executed on a hand that is detected at the position of the "touch down" event in the last frame, to ensure that all extracted features have the same scale. This process takes on average 43 ms when the hand is captured at 45 dpi. When 16 samples are used for each registered hand, matching features of a single hand takes on average 68 ms if 4 hands are registered and 155 ms if 8 hands are registered.

UNIQUENESS OF THE DORSAL HAND REGION

In this first experiment, we evaluate the uniqueness of the dorsal hand region over different users, as well as over different hands of the same user. Here, we only consider the hands-down posture [30], because in this posture the overhead camera can capture clear images of the dorsal region. The robustness of Carpus with regard to posture changes will be tested in a second experiment, which we discuss in the next section.

Tasks

We recruited 22 participants (5 female) between 22 and 50 years old. We instructed them to take off all jewelry (jewelry could actually increase the recognition rates, because it often provides very unique features). Each participant sat down at an interactive tabletop and placed her/his left and right hand flat on the surface with fingers spread. They did this at 15 predefined positions that were evenly distributed over the entire surface area. In each position, our camera captured a single image. These images are used to train and test our system.

Procedure

From a set of 660 images, we simulated six scenarios that differed in the number of hands registered with the system (4, 10 and 20 users, each registering one or two hands). For each scenario, we generated 25 sets of randomly drawn groups. For each set, a 10-fold cross-validation with a stratified random selection of training images is performed, resulting in a total of 34000 trials (for each scenario 25 sets x 10 trials x 2 hands x number of users). A hand region is correctly identified if the system can not only match it to the correct user, but also to the correct hand of that user.

Results

Table 2 lists the recognition rates of our technique for the six scenarios. The accuracy is very high in all scenarios, although it slightly decreases when larger groups of users are registered with the system. These results demonstrate that our extracted features are unique, even for fairly large groups of users. In addition, note that if both hands of a user are registered, our system can distinguish between each hand the vast majority of the time. This enables identification of both hands and thus non-symmetric devision of labor [9].

	Group size		
	4	10	20
One hand registered	99.5%	99.4%	99.1%
Two hands registered	99.4%	99.4%	99.0%

Table 2. Recognition rates for the hands-down posture when one or both hands of 4, 10 and 20 users are registered with the system.

ROBUSTNESS AGAINST POSTURE VARIATIONS

In the first study, we showed that the dorsal hand region can be used to reliably map hands to users. The goal of this second study is to show that Carpus is sufficiently robust for postures that are common during the practical use of multi-touch systems. When interacting on a tabletop, the overhead camera often gets a clear view of the dorsal hand region, e.g. when clicking a button (Figure 5-A). When scaling or rotating an object (Figure 5-B-C), however, the captured dorsal hand region can be skewed, potentially influencing the accuracy of the recognition. To evaluate to what extent Carpus can handle posture variations, we ran a second experiment.

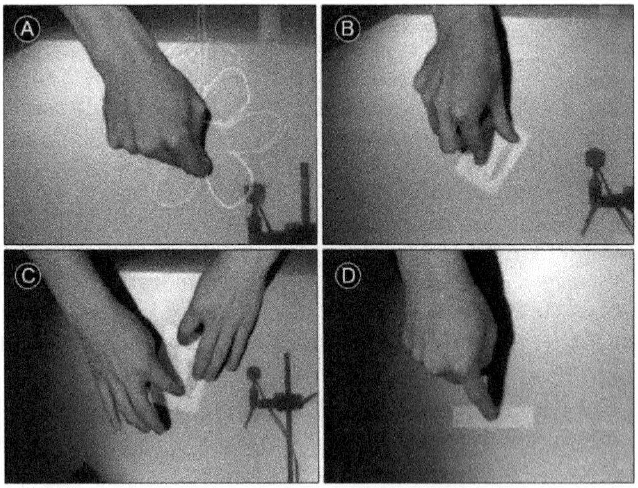

Figure 5. The four tasks in our second experiment: (A) painting a flower; (B) scaling and rotating images using one hand; (C) scaling and rotating images using two hands; (D) pressing buttons.

Tasks

We asked our 22 participants to perform four additional tasks. During these tasks, we did not give any instructions regarding hand postures with the purpose of capturing natural interaction. (1) In the first task, participants were asked to color the contours of a flower in a painting application using only their right hand (Figure 5-A). The application showed a preview of the flower, with the colors we expected the participants to use. (2) In the second task, participants scaled and rotated 10 images (evenly spread out over the surface area) to fit them in a box using traditional free transformation gestures (Figure 5-B). This task was first performed with the right hand and afterwards repeated with the left hand. The center points of the images were fixed, so that there was no need to move them. (3) In the third task, those same images were displayed and participants were asked to scale and rotate them using both their left and right hand together (Figure 5-C). (4) Finally, each participant was asked to click 15 buttons that were spread out over the surface area, first with their right hand and afterwards with their left hand (Figure 5-D).

Data Collection

During this experiment, all interaction was captured by our overhead camera and streamed to a PC, together with all touch events ('down', 'move' and 'up'). Afterwards, all frames were extracted in which one or more 'down' events were registered, and these frames were used in simulations as training and test data. For the first, second and third task, we collected on average 35.5, 82.8 and 39.7 images per participant, respectively. For the last task, 30 images per participant were captured. In total, we collected 5009 images. For the third task, in which two hands are visible at the same time, we provided the position of the left and right hand to the system by processing those images by hand. With this data, the correctness of the result of our hand identification algorithm can be verified.

Procedure

Using our collection of captured frames, we simulated six scenarios that differed in the number of hands registered with the system (4, 10 and 20 users, each registering one or two hands). For each scenario, we generated 25 sets of randomly drawn groups. We trained the system with randomly drawn samples for each hand that needed to be registered. This training set consisted of four samples of hands in the hands-down posture from the previous experiment, and four samples of the pointing task (task 2) and the free transformation task with one (task 3) and both hands (task 4). We determined that this collection of 16 training samples per hand is needed if a large range of postures is to be supported. After this training phase, we tested our system with 10 randomly drawn samples for each hand in each of the four tasks (the randomly drawn samples were always different from the training samples), resulting in a total of 136000 trials (for each scenario 25 groups x 10 trials x 2 hands x 4 tasks x number of users). As in the first experiment, a hand region is correctly identified if the system can relate it to the correct user and the correct hand of that user.

Results

Figure 6 summarizes our findings of the second experiment. These results show that hands in a pointing posture can be identified very accurately, because the overhead camera has a clear view on the dorsal hand region. Carpus had the greatest difficulty identifying a single hand in a free transformation gesture (Figure 5-B). We observed that users often rotated their hand in various directions while performing such a gesture. As a result, the dorsal hand region was highly skewed in many of the captured frames. In that case, matching features is much more difficult. We also noticed that, because of tilting of the hand, the space between two fingers was sometimes almost entirely occluded. That makes it harder for our algorithm to detect all fingers correctly, in order to exclude them. Parts of fingers still present in the feature extraction step will produce unreliable data, which can influence the accuracy of our technique. However, even for these challenging hand postures, the recognition rate for a smaller group of users is still relatively high.

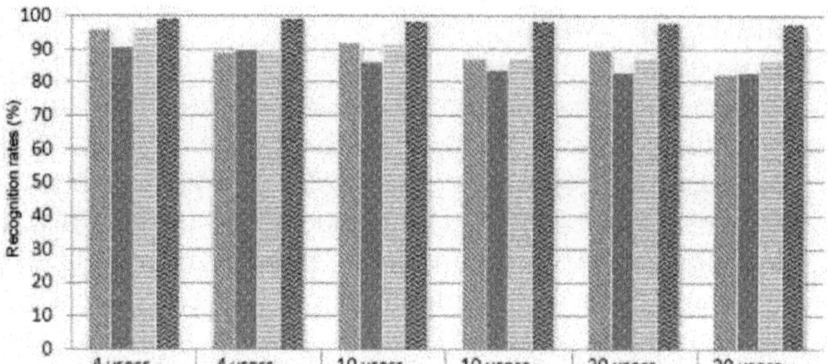

	4 users - 1 hand registered	4 users - 2 hands registered	10 users - 1 hand registered	10 users - 2 hands registered	20 users - 1 hand registered	20 users - 2 hands registered
Painting task	95,7	89	91,8	86,7	89,7	82,2
Free transformation task using 1 hand	90,5	89,6	85,9	83,8	83	83
Free transformation task using 2 hands	96	89,7	91,3	87,4	87,1	86,5
Pointing task	99,1	98,9	98,2	98,3	97,6	97,3

Figure 6. The recognition rates for different group sizes for all four tasks of our second experiment.

The accuracy for the painting task was somewhat surprising, as we anticipated that this recognition rate would be almost identical to the pointing task because of the similarity of the expected hand posture. After analyzing our captured data, we noticed that some users tilted their hand during this task to reduce the occlusion of the active painting area, in order to paint the contour more precisely. This behavior causes the extracted dorsal hand region to be skewed, and makes feature matching more difficult. However, the results of this experiment show that, even when no instructions are given and the user can naturally interact with the surface, Carpus provides an accurate technique for identifying touches of a small group of users.

We reproduced our entire experiment, after adding four randomly drawn images of the painting task to the training set. The recognition rate of the painting task was significantly higher (97%, 96,5%, 97,8%, 96,2%, 96,1% and 95,5% for the six scenarios). The accuracy for the other tasks remained almost unchanged. This suggests that the recognition rate can be improved by training the system with samples of hand postures that are more similar to the hand postures that will occur in the application.

One can imagine many other hand postures that can be used on interactive surfaces. However, our tasks produced a wide range of postures that are very common during the practical use of multi-touch systems.

USAGE SCENARIO

Carpus enables non-intrusive and transparent identification of users on interactive surfaces. This allows an entire range of new applications in which people collaborate on a shared surface, such as buying new products [17]. We developed an interactive application that can be deployed in, for example, a mobile phone retail environment. Families or friends shopping together for a new mobile phone can collaborate on a multi-touch tabletop located inside the store to find more information about products and compare specifications.

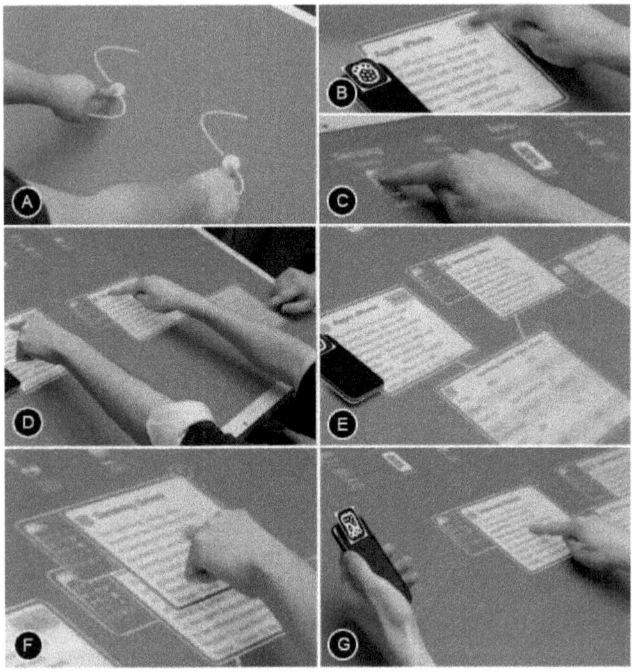

Figure 7. Carpus enables non-intrusive identification of (both hands of) users, for example in a mobile phone retail environment, allowing users to find more information about products and compare specifications.

Figure 7 illustrates a typical usage scenario. John and Jane are looking for a new mobile phone. A nice looking phone catches John's eye and they both walk to the interactive display to get more information about this product. (A) Because it is the first time that they have visited the store, a simple widget allows them to very quickly register both hands with the system. (B) John then puts the phone on the interactive display to get more information (the device is currently recognized by a visual tag). (C) Identity information from Carpus is used to create a temporary profile for each customer. This makes it possible to track the user's interests in order to provide product recommendations. (D) While Jane reads through the specifications of recommended phones, John finds another nice mobile phone and compares two products using a two-handed gesture. (E) Carpus unambiguously recognizes this gesture because the system can distinguish between touch points of both users. (F) Jane notices John's actions and also wants to take a look at the product in which he is interested. John then makes a copy of the information by moving it with his left hand to Jane. (G) John and Jane are now both interested in the phone suggested by the system and go find it in the shop. When returning back to the interactive display, they notice that other customers started a new session. However, when they touch the display, the system uses the identify information to restore their session.

DISCUSSION

Carpus extracts identity features from the back of the human hand. However, as mentioned in the benefits and limitations section, the detection of this region is difficult in two particular situations. The first situation is when identification is needed while performing a very fast gesture, such as a swipe-gesture. It is possible that the camera cannot capture a sharp image of the dorsal region. This problem can be addressed by using a camera with an appropriate shutter speed, or by adding tracking capabilities to the algorithm in order to identify the dorsal region during slow movements, and track the arm during fast movements. Secondly, researchers have investigated new types of interactions in which the dorsal hand region is not always clearly visible to the overhead camera [18, 11]. Using multiple cameras that observe the dorsal hand region from different points of view may alleviate this problem, making it much more likely that the system can capture a clear image of the dorsal hand region. Such a multi-camera setup can also be used to reduce occlusion problems that are inherent to the use of overhead cameras. This is especially the case when vertical displays or tilted tables are used in combination with Carpus.

In our first study, we found that the dorsal hand region is unique over a large group of users. In a second study, we demonstrated the robustness of our technique for a range of hand postures. Carpus has the highest recognition rate (97,3% when 20 users register both hands) when a user clicks buttons, which is a very common action in interfaces. Since we only identify a user when a "touch down" event occurs, a lot of other interactions are actually reduced to clicking (e.g. moving sliders, scrollbars, objects, etc.). The recognition rate was the lowest when identifying scale and rotate actions performed by a single hand (Figure 5-B). This is expected, because users rotate their hands in all directions when performing such gestures. As a result, the camera captures a skewed view of the dorsal region that is more difficult to match with the training set. However, user identification during these actions is only needed in very specific circumstances and the vast majority of applications will only need the user's identity during pointing actions [29].

We also found that the recognition rate is higher when training the system with samples of hand postures that are more similar to the hand postures that occur in the application. This suggest that the accuracy of our technique could be improved for some hand postures by refining the training set over time with samples of hand postures that are performed in the actual application. Future versions of Carpus will implement this by tracking users' hands during interaction with the application. Samples for which no good match is found in the training set can be added to the training data after a reliable sample has been detected during the same hand movement. Tracking was not yet integrated in Carpus because it could bias the results of our studies depending on the type of user interface (e.g. how frequently users' hands leave the surface area).

The recognition rate of Carpus is most likely sufficiently accurate for all postures when a small group of users are registered with the system. However, even in these situations, Carpus is currently not intended for applications that require real security (e.g. accessing emails, online banking). As the dorsal hand region contains no papillary ridges, our extracted features are not as persistent and immutable as fingerprints. It is, for example, possible for the skin to get a tan, and wounds can result in permanent scars. However, more long-term research is needed in this area to investigate the effects of these changes on the recognition rate of Carpus.

As already mentioned in the benefits and limitations section, our technique has some difficulties eliminating users that are not registered. In an additional study, we tested our system with four known and four unknown users, which resulted in an acceptance rate of 87% and a false acceptance rate of 7%. These results indicate that explicit registration is needed when higher reliability is required. However, registering with the system is only a one-time cost compared to systems that require configuration at the start of each session. When a reduced reliability is acceptable, for example in case of very short interactions with non-crucial applications, spontaneous registration is possible. We already demonstrated the potential use of interactive widgets as a means for transparent registration in our usage scenario. However, more experiments are needed to make sure that a sufficient number of different hand postures are captured during the interaction with this widget to get the best possible accuracy rates.

CONCLUSION

In this paper, we presented Carpus, a novel, non-intrusive technique for identifying users of interactive surfaces. Our approach relies on the extraction of unique information from the back of the human hand. This hand region is extracted from high-quality images captured by an overhead camera. Fine-grained features are encoded using a special pattern description technique. For traditional pointing tasks, Carpus can uniquely identify both hands of a user with 97.3% accuracy, even when large groups of users are registered. For more complex gestures that occur less often, smaller group sizes are recommended to achieve a higher recognition rate. Carpus enables touch identification for non-crucial applications in walk-up-and-use scenarios in which users interact frequently and in an unplanned fashion. In addition, our presented technique is able to differentiate between the two hands of a user, opening up even more interaction possibilities. Carpus is also easy to deploy and can be used in combination with all existing touch technologies. This makes our approach suitable in many situations in which touch identification can enrich the multi-user experience.

ACKNOWLEDGMENTS

We would like to thank Brent Hecht for his valuable comments and language editing.

REFERENCES

1. Ahonen, T., Hadid, A., and Pietikäinen, M. Face recognition with local binary patterns. In *Proceedings of the 8th European Conference on Computer Vision (ECCV '04)*, Springer (2004), 469–481.
2. Annett, M., Grossman, T., Wigdor, D., and Fitzmaurice, G. Medusa: a proximity-aware multi-touch tabletop. In *Proceedings of the 24th annual ACM symposium on User interface software and technology (UIST '11)*, ACM (2011), 337–346.
3. Augsten, T., Kaefer, K., Meusel, R., Fetzer, C., Kanitz, D., Stoff, T., Becker, T., Holz, C., and Baudisch, P. Multitoe: high-precision interaction with back-projected floors based on high-resolution multi-touch input. In *Proceedings of the 23rd annual ACM symposium on User interface software and technology (UIST '10)*, ACM (2010), 209–218.
4. Bay, H., Ess, A., Tuytelaars, T., and Van Gool, L. Speeded-up robust features (SURF). *Computer Vision and Image Understanding 110*, 3 (2008), 346–359.
5. Boreki, G., and Zimmer, A. Hand geometry: a new approach for feature extraction. In *Proceedings of the 4th IEEE Workshop on Automatic Identification Advanced Technologies (AUTOID '05)*, IEEE Computer Society (2005), 149–154.
6. Choi, J., Seo, B.-K., and Park, J.-I. Robust hand detection for augmented reality interface. In *Proceedings of the 8th International Conference on Virtual Reality Continuum and its Applications in Industry (VRCAI '09)*, ACM (2009), 319–321.
7. Dietz, P., and Leigh, D. DiamondTouch: a multi-user touch technology. In *Proceedings of the 14th annual ACM symposium on User interface software and technology (UIST '01)*, ACM (2001), 219–226.
8. Freeman, W. T., Anderson, D. B., Beardsley, P. A., Dodge, C. N., Roth, M., Weissman, C. D., Yerazunis, W. S., Kage, H., Kyuma, K., Miyake, Y., and Tanaka, K. Computer vision for interactive computer graphics. *IEEE Computer Graphics and Applications 18*, 3 (1998), 42–53.
9. Guiard, Y. Asymmetric division of labor in human skilled bimanual action: the kinematic chain as a model. *Journal of Motor Behavior 19* (1987), 486–517.
10. Gutwin, C., Greenberg, S., Blum, R., Dyck, J., Tee, K., and McEwan, G. Supporting informal collaboration in shared-workspace groupware. *Journal of Universal Computer Science 14*, 9 (2008), 1411–1434.
11. Harrison, C., Schwarz, J., and Hudson, S. E. TapSense: enhancing finger interaction on touch surfaces. In *Proceedings of the 24th annual ACM symposium on User interface software and technology (UIST '11)*, ACM (2011), 627–636.
12. Koike, H., Sato, Y., and Kobayashi, Y. Integrating paper and digital information on EnhancedDesk: a method for realtime finger tracking on an augmented desk system. *ACM Transactions on Computer-Human Interaction 8*, 4 (2001), 307–322.

13. Lowe, D. G. Object recognition from local scale-invariant features. In *Proceedings of the 1999 International Conference on Computer Vision (ICCV '99)*, IEEE Computer Society (1999), 1150–1157.

14. Malik, S., and Laszlo, J. Visual touchpad: a two-handed gestural input device. In *Proceedings of the 6th international conference on Multimodal interfaces (ICMI '04)*, ACM (2004), 289–296.

15. Marquardt, N., Kiemer, J., Ledo, D., Boring, S., and Greenberg, S. Designing user-, hand-, and handpart-aware tabletop interactions with the TouchID toolkit. In *Proceedings of the 2011 ACM International Conference on Interactive Tabletops and Surfaces (ITS '11)*, ACM (2011), 21–30.

16. Meyer, T., and Schmidt, D. IdWristbands: IR-based user identification on multi-touch surfaces. In *Proceedings of the 2010 ACM International Conference on Interactive Tabletops and Surfaces (ITS '10)*, ACM (2010), 277–278.

17. Morris, M. R. A survey of collaborative web search practices. In *Proceedings of the 26th annual SIGCHI conference on Human factors in computing systems (CHI '08)*, ACM (2008), 1657–1660.

18. Morris, M. R., Huang, A., Paepcke, A., and Winograd, T. Cooperative gestures: multi-user gestural interactions for co-located groupware. In *Proceedings of the 24th annual SIGCHI conference on Human Factors in computing systems (CHI '06)*, ACM (2006), 1201–1210.

19. Morris, M. R., Ryall, K., Shen, C., Forlines, C., and Vernier, F. Beyond "social protocols": multi-user coordination policies for co-located groupware. In *Proceedings of the 2004 ACM conference on Computer supported cooperative work (CSCW '04)*, ACM (2004), 262–265.

20. Napier, J., and Tuttle, R. *Hands*. Princeton Science Library. Princeton University Press, 1993.

21. Ojala, T., Pietikäinen, M., and Harwood, D. A comparative study of texture measures with classification based on featured distributions. *Pattern Recognition 29*, 1 (1996), 51–59.

22. Ojala, T., Pietikäinen, M., and Mäenpää, T. Multiresolution gray-scale and rotation invariant texture classification with local binary patterns. *IEEE Transactions on Pattern Analysis and Machine Intelligence 24*, 7 (2002), 971–987.

23. Orr, R. J., and Abowd, G. D. The smart floor: a mechanism for natural user identification and tracking. In *CHI '00 extended abstracts on Human factors in computing systems*, ACM (2000), 275–276.

24. Phung, S. L., Bouzerdoum, A., and Chai, D. A novel skin color model in YCbCr color space and its application to human face detection. *Proceedings of the 2002 IEEE International Conference on Image Processing (ICIP '02) 1* (2002), 289–292.

25. Phung, S. L., Bouzerdoum, A., and Chai, D. Skin segmentation using color pixel classification: analysis and comparison. *IEEE Transactions on Pattern Analysis and Machine Intelligence 27*, 1 (2005), 148–154.

26. Piper, A. M., O'Brien, E., Morris, M. R., and Winograd, T. SIDES: a cooperative tabletop computer game for social skills development. In *Proceedings of the 2006 ACM conference on Computer supported cooperative work (CSCW '06)*, ACM (2006), 1–10.

27. Richter, S., Holz, C., and Baudisch, P. Bootstrapper: recognizing tabletop users by their shoes. In *Proceedings of the 30th annual conference on Human factors in computing systems (CHI '12)*, ACM (2012), 1249–1252.

28. Roth, V., Schmidt, P., and Güldenring, B. The IR ring: authenticating users' touches on a multi-touch display. In *Proceedings of the 23nd annual ACM symposium on User interface software and technology (UIST '10)*, ACM (2010), 259–262.

29. Ryall, K., Esenther, A., Forlines, C., Shen, C., Shipman, S., Morris, M. R., Everitt, K., and Vernier, F. D. Identity-differentiating widgets for multiuser interactive surfaces. *IEEE Computer Graphics and Applications 26*, 5 (2006), 56–64.

30. Schmidt, D., Chong, M. K., and Gellersen, H. HandsDown: hand-contour-based user identification for interactive surfaces. In *Proceedings of the 6th Nordic Conference on Human-Computer Interaction (NordiCHI '10)*, ACM (2010), 432–441.

31. Schmidt, D., Chong, M. K., and Gellersen, H. IdLenses: dynamic personal areas on shared surfaces. In *Proceedings of the 2010 ACM International Conference on Interactive Tabletops and Surfaces (ITS '10)*, ACM (2010), 131–134.

32. Schöning, J., Rohs, M., and Krüger, A. Using mobile phones to spontaneously authenticate and interact with multi-touch surfaces. *PPD '08 workshop on designing multi-touch interaction techniques for coupled public and private displays* (2008).

33. Scott, S. D., Sheelagh, M., Carpendale, T., and Inkpen, K. M. Territoriality in collaborative tabletop workspaces. In *Proceedings of the 2004 ACM conference on Computer supported cooperative work (CSCW '04)*, ACM (2004), 294–303.

34. Segen, J., and Kumar, S. Gesture VR: vision-based 3D hand interace for spatial interaction. In *Proceedings of the 6th ACM international conference on Multimedia*, ACM (1998), 455–464.

35. Swain, M. J., and Ballard, D. H. Color indexing. *International Journal of Computer Vision 7*, 1 (1991), 11–32.

36. Wang, F., Cao, X., Ren, X., and Irani, P. Detecting and leveraging finger orientation for interaction with direct-touch surfaces. In *Proceedings of the 22nd annual ACM symposium on User interface software and technology (UIST '09)*, ACM (2009), 23–32.

Low-cost Audience Polling Using Computer Vision

Andrew Cross, Edward Cutrell, and William Thies
Microsoft Research India
{t-across, cutrell, thies}@microsoft.com

ABSTRACT

Electronic response systems known as "clickers" have demonstrated educational benefits in well-resourced classrooms, but remain out-of-reach for most schools due to their prohibitive cost. We propose a new, low-cost technique that utilizes computer vision for real-time polling of a classroom. Our approach allows teachers to ask a multiple-choice question. Students respond by holding up a *qCard*: a sheet of paper that contains a printed code, similar to a QR code, encoding their student IDs. Students indicate their answers (A, B, C or D) by holding the card in one of four orientations. Using a laptop and an off-the-shelf webcam, our software automatically recognizes and aggregates the students' responses and displays them to the teacher. We built this system and performed initial trials in secondary schools in Bangalore, India. In a 25-student classroom, our system offers 99.8% recognition accuracy, captures 97% of responses within 10 seconds, and costs 15 times less than existing electronic solutions.

Author Keywords

Education; audience polling; low-cost; electronic response system; clickers; ICT4D

ACM Classification Keywords

H.4.1 [*Information Interfaces and Presentation*]: Group and Organization Interfaces; K.3.1 [*Computers and Education*]: Computer Uses in Education

INTRODUCTION

Contemporary research has shown that there is educational value in promoting interactive and collaborative learning in the classroom [2,8,11]. In addition to keeping students engaged with the material, interactive classroom exercises enable teachers to monitor the interests and understanding of students and to adjust the content and pacing of their lectures accordingly. Collaborative learning between peers can offer additional benefits, as students receive (and give) personalized attention and can discuss pertinent topics using their own language and metaphors.

A common requirement in many interactive and collaborative lessons is the ability to *poll* students regarding their views or comprehension of a subject. While there is no shortage of everyday polling techniques, each has its limitations. A show of hands is subject to peer pressure, where students who are shy or unsure may align themselves with popular opinion. Conversely, asking for feedback from one student at a time – either volunteered, or "cold-called" – does not paint a complete picture of the class. While a written test achieves the goals of accuracy and completeness, it is typically too slow to be administered and checked within the span of an interactive lesson.

UIST '12, October 7–10, 2012, Cambridge, Massachusetts, USA.

Figure 1: Students respond to a multiple-choice question using qCards. Each card has a unique code that encodes the student's ID. The rotation of the card encodes the student's answer. Codes are recognized by a webcam (mounted at front) and aggregated for display on the teacher's computer.

To overcome these challenges, many classrooms have embraced *electronic response systems*, in which networked devices called *clickers* are distributed to students, allowing them to submit answers to multiple-choice questions (or occasionally, to submit richer data). Student responses are automatically aggregated and displayed to the teacher in real-time. Clickers have been commercially successful; the i>clicker company alone claims usage by 2 million students in over 1,000 institutions [17]. In terms of pedagogical benefits, reports are mixed, with reactions ranging from extremely positive to, at worst, distracting. However, in general, teachers trained to respond to their audience and prepared to alter a lesson based on feedback can use clickers to improve teaching where the worst result is no change in learning outcomes [1,4,7,15]. The consensus is that, when paired with appropriate pedagogy, clickers offer strong benefits by increasing interactivity, enjoyment, participation, attentiveness, and learning outcomes [1,4,7].

Despite their benefits, clickers remain out of reach for the vast majority of educational institutions due to their high cost. For example, the i>clicker handsets mentioned previously cost about $30 each, plus $200 for a central receiver. Thus, even if a classroom already has a computer, an additional $950 is needed to equip 25 students with clickers. While systems such as Poll Everywhere aim to reduce device costs by leveraging students' cell phones as handsets, these systems face other challenges in the classroom. Cell phones distract students from the lesson, and are often banned from school for this reason. Also, they would impose usage fees (SMS or data connections) on students, and would disadvantage those who do not own appropriate phones.

In this paper, we propose a new approach to classroom polling that maintains the benefits of clickers while drastically reducing costs. Our system enables teachers to ask a multiple-choice question to students and receive their feedback without individual active components or a costly external receiver. Students respond by holding up a *qCard*: a sheet of normal paper that has a printed code, similar to a QR code. The code indicates the student's ID, while the rotation of the card indicates the student's answer (see Figure 1). Using a computer vision algorithm, an inexpensive, off-the-shelf webcam can automatically recognize and aggregate the students' responses for immediate evaluation by the teacher.

We have built this system and performed initial trials in government schools outside of Bangalore, India. Our results show that our system captures 97% of students' votes within the first 10 seconds of a poll, maintains 99.8% recognition accuracy, and costs at least 15 times less than alternative electronic solutions.

RELATED WORK

High-end electronic clickers have been commercialized by many companies, including i>clicker, Meridia, IML, Fleetwood, Qwizdom, and eInstruction. There is substantial literature that studies the benefits and drawbacks of electronic clickers as educational tools. As we do not aim to advance this discourse within the current paper, we refer readers to other excellent reviews on the subject [1,5,7,9].

Within the HCI community, there are two main thrusts of research surrounding audience polling. The first is in response to the CHI 2004 Student Design Competition, which challenged participants to design an audience voting system for the Olympic Games. Nineteen solutions were published as Extended Abstracts. Of these, the majority propose that each audience member use an active electronic device, not unlike a clicker. However, three submissions propose using computer vision to recognize printed signs, containing numeric scores, in the audience [6,12,16]. The PHOTOVOTE system also proposes to recognize colored signs, as a simple alternative to numbers [16].

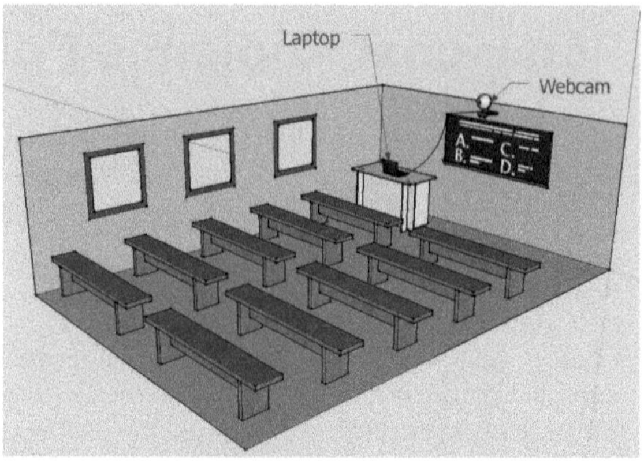

Figure 2: Physical components of our system in a classroom. A webcam is mounted above the chalkboard, tilted downward to see the entire class, and connected to a laptop for processing student responses.

While these solutions have some resemblance to ours, there are three key differences. First, we are unaware of any prior proposal to use a machine encoding (such as QR codes) to represent a user's choice in an audience response system. In addition to encoding more bits than a simple gesture or printed number, a machine encoding preserves the privacy of the respondent relative to peers; his/her choice is undecipherable to everyone except for the computer. Second, prior systems utilizing computer vision encode each respondent's answer, but do not explicitly encode a unique ID number for the respondent. This lack of identity encoding prevents tracking the answers of individuals over time. Finally, we are unaware of any implementation or evaluation of an audience response system based on computer vision in a real-world classroom setting.

The second thread of research is in using computer vision to solicit other kinds of participation and feedback from the audience. Maynes-Aminzade et al. engaged audiences in creative ways, including a pong game controlled by the tilt of audience members' bodies and an audience poll where answers are submitted according to the focus of laser pointers [10]. BallBouncer is another game enabled by computer vision, in which audience members volley a virtual ball from side to side [14]. Cinematrix enables audience polling using two-sided reflective panels [18]. Unlike our system, these polling techniques do not encode the identity of each participant, or preserve participants' anonymity relative to peers.

SYSTEM OVERVIEW

Our system can be instantiated in several different forms. The instantiation used for our experiments is illustrated in Figure 2. The fundamental elements of our design are as follows:

1. **A printed qCard** for each student. The qCard (see Figure 3) encodes the student's ID in a unique bit

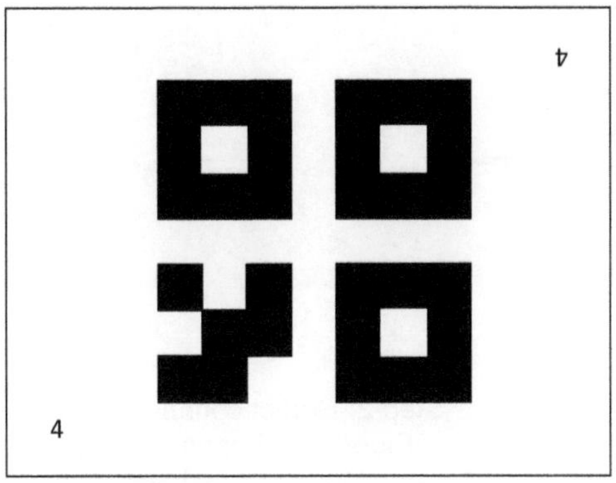

(a) Front view. The three black squares are used to locate the card and determine its orientation. The student ID is encoded in the fourth quadrant. The human-readable labels are useful for classroom management of the cards, but are not recognized by the algorithm.

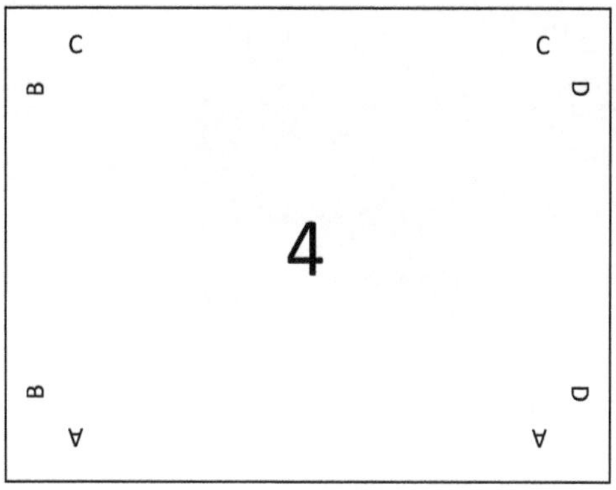

(b) Back view. Students rotate the card so their answer is at the top, cover their answer with their fingers, then raise the card with the front side facing the camera. The assignment of answers (A, B, C, D) to edges is randomized in order to further conceal a student's response from peers.

Figure 3: A sample qCard (for student 4).

pattern. On the back of the card, each orientation is labeled with an answer (A, B, C, or D). Students encode a response by rotating the card such that their intended answer is on top, and then showing the card to the camera. qCards are printed on A4 paper using a normal black-and-white printer.

2. **Camera-enabled computing device.** In our experiments, we utilize a laptop with a USB webcam (Logitech Pro 9000, 2.0 megapixel video). We envision that a mobile phone can substitute for the laptop and webcam in the future. (We have completed initial feasibility tests on phones, but do not report them in this paper.)
3. **(Optional) LCD projector.** If available, an LCD projector can be used to display the results of each poll to the class. We utilized such a projector in our initial prototyping, but not in our final tests, as the school where we ran our experiment did not have a projector in the classroom. For each question asked by the teacher, the options were written on the board prior to initiating a poll.

To utilize these elements, teachers need to follow the following basic procedure:

1. **Mount the camera** in an elevated location that can read all qCards simultaneously, without some students obscuring others. For our classroom experiments, we taped a webcam to the wall above the chalkboard (see Figure 2).
2. **Distribute qCards** to students. If the teacher desires to log each student's responses, then student names need to be mapped to qCard IDs in the computer software.
3. **(Optional) Calibrate the software** to the lighting conditions of the room. The key parameter is the threshold for distinguishing black and white elements of the cards. It may help to adjust any irregular lighting conditions, e.g., to close or open window blinds.
4. **Ask students questions, and see the results.** Each polling period is started and stopped via a keypress on the computer. In order to ensure that students understand the multiple-choice options, we recommend writing each option on the board (or projecting on a slide).

While these steps cover the mechanical operation of the system, additional attention is needed to adjust the pedagogy to benefit from the technology. We briefly discuss such pedagogies near the end of the paper.

DESIGN AND RECOGNITION OF THE QCARDS

The central goal in designing the qCards is to encode information that can be quickly and robustly recognized by a low-end camera. A key parameter of interest is the number of bits encoded per card. As the number of bits increases, it becomes possible to support more students (each with a unique ID). However, the recognition accuracy also decreases, as the cards become more densely coded and thus more difficult to reliably decode. Our initial design encodes 9 bits of information, which would support up to 512 students – far more than we aspire to test in our initial trials. In settings with fewer students, the extra bits can be used for error correction.

Our starting point for the design was a 2-dimensional barcode, such as the QR code. However, traditional 2-dimensional barcode designs are optimized to encode high levels information (at least 231 bits, some used for error correction, in the case of QR codes). The primary use case for industry standard designs assumes the scanner is close to the code in relation to its size, and is targeted at a single

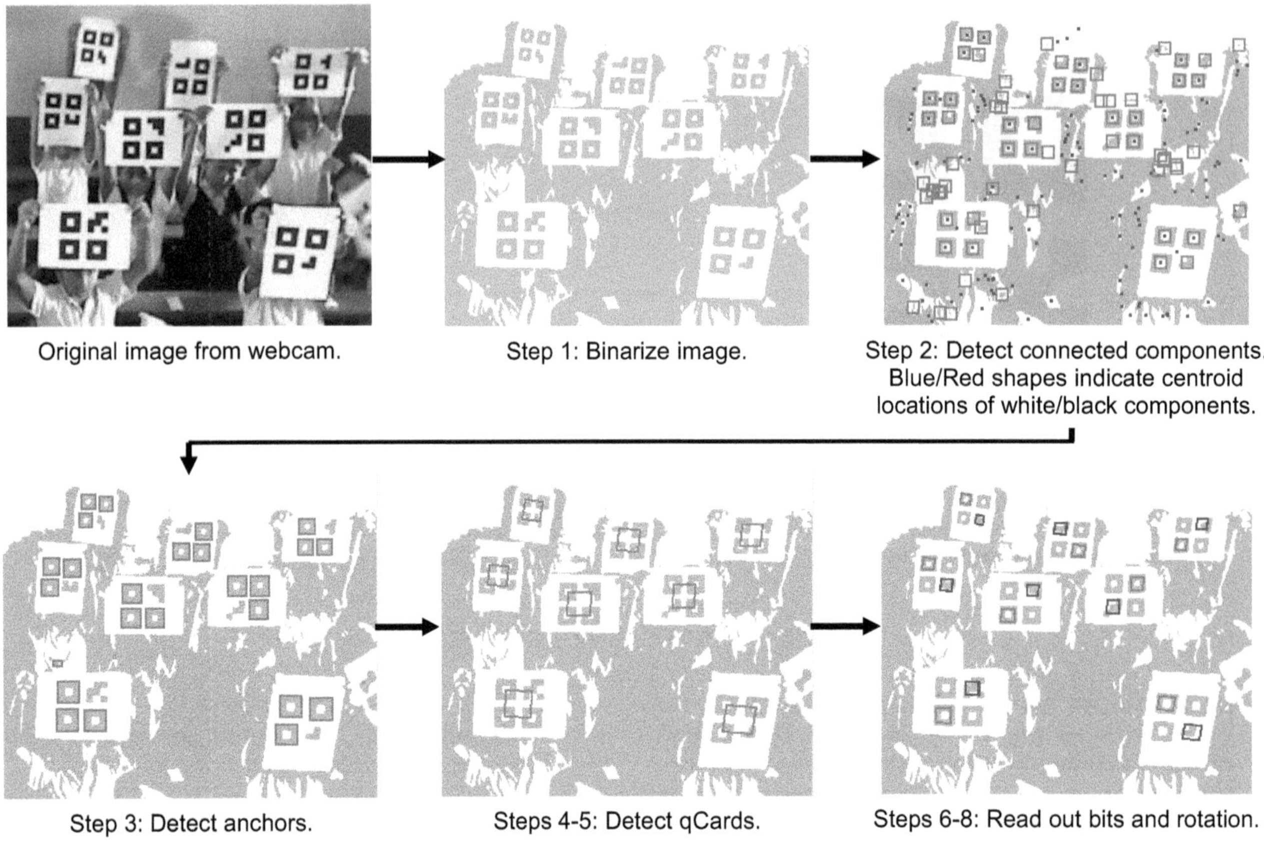

Figure 4: Example execution of qCard recognition algorithm.

code at any given time. Advanced algorithms exist to increase successful reading rates in low-resolution environments, but do not optimize for distance [13].

Thus, we designed a simplified QR code that increases the size of each symbol, thereby facilitating recognition by an ordinary webcam, even at a long distance or under imperfect lighting conditions. To further facilitate recognition accuracy, each code is printed on a full sheet of paper (in our experiments, we used A4 paper size).

Design Specification

The qCard design (see Figure 3) is a 7x7 square with a 1-unit quiet zone around the image. There are four regions of interest. The first three are 3x3 black areas with a 1x1 white center. These three "anchors" are used for locating the code in a frame, and determining orientation and rotation in 3-space. The fourth region consists of the 9-bit code.

Leveraging Video to Improve Accuracy

A distinct difference from other 2-dimensional barcode scanning algorithms is that the algorithm presented below does not require a "perfect" scan on a single photo frame. Instead, the system relies on a majority of reads over the duration of the poll in different frames of a video stream to account for false positives. The algorithm processes each frame individually, and does not require every qCard present to be recognizable in a single frame. It continually scans images from the instantiation of a "poll" until its close, tabulating how many of each code it has read. If it reads more than one response for a given student, the code it read the most times is deemed the final answer.

Recognition Algorithm

Apart from its use of video to improve accuracy, our recognition algorithm follows the general principles of other barcode scanning algorithms in isolating regions of importance based on high-contrast locators in the image.

An example operation of our algorithm is illustrated in Figure 4. Each frame is processed in the following way:

1. Binarize the image according to a predetermined brightness which can be calibrated for the entire class or by region in difficult environments.
2. Scan the binarized image for connected components of black or white pixels. At the same time, compute the centroid of each connected component based on the number of pixels in the object, and their relative positions. This is the most computationally-intensive step of the algorithm; it is critical to use an incremental algorithm (linear in the number of pixels in the image) to compute the connected components and their centroids.
3. Pair black and white components whose centroids are closely aligned, pairing components separated by no

more than a given threshold. This step isolates the anchors – black squares with white centers – which in groups of three define the position and orientation of a card. Each anchor is assigned a "weight" determined by the number of pixels in the connected components of that anchor.

4. Group sets of three anchors based on location and weight to determine where a qCard likely exists. This grouping uses a nearest-neighbors algorithm.
5. Calculate the orientation and rotation in 3-space of the card from the distance and angle between the three anchors. The rotation encodes the student's answer.
6. Calculate the location of the center of the fourth quadrant where the student ID is encoded.
7. Given the angles in 3-space at which the card is being held, calculate the locations of the centers of the 9 bits where the information is encoded.
8. Read the binary bits given the contrast of the region.
9. Combine the encoded bits and the card rotation to register a response for a given student.

IMPLEMENTATION

We implemented our system in C#. It consists of three parts: an image processing library that implements the algorithm detailed above; a GUI wrapper that maps found codes and orientations to students and answer choices, presents calibration options, and visually confirms card reads; and a webcam driver to pull in live images for processing. The image processing library consists of 1500 lines of non-comment, non-blank lines of C# code. The GUI wrapper consists of another 1600 lines of code, and the webcam drivers consist of another 250 lines of code.

The runtime performance of our system depends on the scene, lighting environment, and number of cards present. For the experiment environment, in a sunlit classroom with 25 students, the algorithm processes at about 12fps. For more varied environments, including multiple light sources, shadows, "border" threshold regions with many small connected components, or very large numbers of cards, our implementation can run as slow as 2fps.

The cost of the setup is the price of a laptop/netbook and the Logitech 9000, 2MP camera (available on Amazon.com for $61). By way of comparison, it would cost about $950 to provide i>clicker units for our classroom of 25 students. Thus, assuming that a computer is already available to utilize both systems, our approach represents about a 15-fold cost savings in this case. As the number of students increases, our system becomes even more economical, because our marginal cost is simply the cost of printed cards (rather than a $30 device per student).

Figure 5: A simulated 100-person classroom. Our algorithm recognizes all 100 qCards in under 5 seconds from a webcam video stream, or in 85ms from this high-quality still image.

INITIAL EXPERIMENTS

We conducted three stages of early experiments culminating in a test of our system within a real classroom environment. Our goals were to assess the technical feasibility of accurately recognizing student responses as well as to gauge the usability and overall experience of students.

Stage 1: Laboratory Environment

For this stage of testing, we wanted to test the limits of the system design without the behavioral effects of students holding the cards. We set up 100 chairs in an auditorium (see Figure 5) to simulate a 100-person classroom. On each chair, we taped a qCard in alternating rotations within view of the webcam, mounted at the front of the room and looking down as it would in a classroom setting.

Our system correctly recognized all 100 qCards from the webcam video feed; however, this required processing 30 frames over a period of 4.4 seconds. Though the scene was static, processing multiple frames improved the recognition for two reasons. First, the contrast threshold was manually altered over the polling period to capture cards in different lighting conditions (the auditorium had rows of lights at fixed intervals, providing variable lighting for chairs). Second, due to the limited quality and resolution of the webcam, pixels on the border of a given threshold "flickered" from black to white across frames of the binarized image sequence. For larger cards in the front rows, single pixel changes do not affect the algorithm's pairing of black and white components; however, with smaller cards toward the back, single pixel shifts have a more significant effect. Figure 6 shows the average time to recognize the cards for a given row, where the first four rows average about 250ms (recognized on the first frame) and the last row averages about 1.8 seconds.

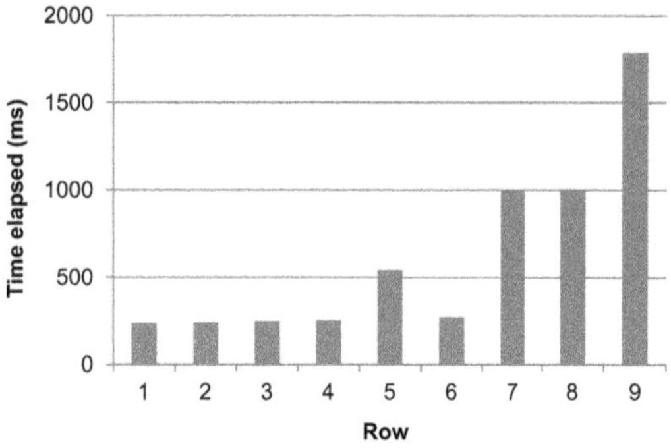

Figure 6: Average time needed to recognize qCards in each row of the simulated 100-student classroom (Figure 5).

The recognition speed can be improved by using a higher-quality camera. To demonstrate this, we took a high-quality still photo using a 14 MP camera (Sony NEX-3). Using this image, the algorithm recognizes all 100 cards in 518ms (a single frame). Recognition is also successful when the high-quality image is resized to 2 megapixels, corresponding to the resolution of the webcam. In this case, recognition requires only 85ms.

Stage 2: After-School Program

Our first field deployment was with a non-profit partner, the Children's Lovecastles Trust (CLT India), which runs a "computer clubhouse" that hosts after-school enrichment activities for low-income children in peri-urban Bangalore. Students between the ages of 9 and 19 voluntarily come to the clubhouse to explore their own ideas (often utilizing computers) with support from peers and adult mentors. For our experiments, we interacted with students from both private and government schools. They were mostly in the 5th and 6th standard. While they were most comfortable speaking the local language (Kannada), they were also able to interact in English.

The goal of our experiments in the after-school program was to perform a simple litmus test: can students understand the concept of using encoded cards to submit an answer, and are they engaged by interactive activities enabled by the technology?

To engage with students, we created a participatory quiz show game that was themed after "Kaun Banega Crorepati" (the Indian equivalent of "Who Wants to Be A Millionaire?") We utilized an LCD projector to show multiple-choice questions to a group (see Figure 7). The projector indicated which students have answered a given question in real-time, enabling them to lower their cards (decreasing congestion) once their answers were recognized. After each question, the system displayed the distribution of student responses, the correct response, as well as a leaderboard that listed the names of students with the highest score so far.

Figure 7: Experiments with a projected quiz show in an after-school program.

We conducted five quiz events over the course of three days. Between 12 and 19 students participated in each quiz (with significant overlap between sessions). While we did not attempt to rigorously evaluate these sessions, the feedback was overwhelmingly positive. Despite the low lighting conditions, qCards were recognized consistently and almost instantaneously. Students found the cards easy to use and were extremely engaged in the game. In fact, our most significant lesson learned was that the camera was almost too sensitive: it frequently read a card that was still in a student's lap, as the student prepared to answer the question. We addressed this in two ways in advance of stage 3. First, we instructed students to shield their card from the camera, except when they intended to answer. Second, we changed the recognition algorithm to a majority vote, so that even if the student revealed an unintended answer, his or her final answer would appear for a longer time and thus would be prioritized by the recognition algorithm.

Stage 3: Government School

Encouraged by our experience in an informal setting, we proceeded to test the system in an actual classroom. With the help of CLT India, we made contact with a Kannada-medium government school and received their permission to use the system to administer and review a test that was pertinent to their curriculum. Our participants were 7th-grade students.

We performed trials on three separate days, in three different classes. Trials lasted for between 45 minutes and

1.5 hours. We limit our presentation to the third trial, as it contained the most refined software and experimental protocol. The first two trials contained similar procedures and results, but evaluated an earlier version of the qCards in which students encoded their answers by choosing one of four different cards, instead of rotating a single card into different orientations.

Study Goals

Our study was designed to answer two distinct questions:

Q1: Technology assessment. Once a student has decided on an answer, how do cards compare with traditional polling methods (clickers and hand-raising) in relaying that answer to the teacher? We are interested in two metrics: accuracy (does the teacher see the answer that the student intends) and speed (how long does it take for students to indicate their answer and have it recognized by the system).

Q2: Behavioral assessment. Does the polling technology affect which answer the student *intends* to submit? For example, with a show of hands, one might expect shy or unsure students to change their answer depending on answers observed from other students. This behavior is inhibited using clickers or cards, since answers are (mostly) private with respect to peers.

For clarity, we also specify a question that the current study does **not** intend to address, and that is whether cards offer pedagogical benefits in an Indian classroom. Though our ultimate goal is to impact educational outcomes, our scope in the current paper is to demonstrate that cards preserve the salient benefits of clickers (which have been demonstrated to impact education) while greatly reducing costs.

Experimental design

To answer the questions posed above, we structured our study as follows. We developed a multiple-choice test (details below), and administered each question as follows:

1. A facilitator wrote the question and multiple-choice answers on the board, and read them aloud.
2. Students indicated their answers using i>clickers.
3. Students indicated their answers again using qCards.
4. Students indicated their answer a third time with a show of hands. That is, the teacher asked students to raise their hand if their answer was A, followed by B, C, and D.

Steps 2 and 3 were interchanged on alternate questions so that clickers and cards were balanced with respect to ordering. Step 4 was always last, because showing hands revealed students' answers and could impact the answers gathered by clickers or cards. At each step, we waited for all students to respond before moving on. Students were told not to submit any answer until the teacher had finished reading the question and all the answer choices. Students were not allowed to talk during the exercise.

This experimental design allowed us to probe Q1 (technology assessment) by comparing the answers reported via the three polling technologies. The accuracy was assessed in two ways. First, we examined the answers to *stock questions*: questions on the exam that simply instructed students to respond with a given answer. These questions enabled us to compare the measured answers with what the student likely intended. Second, we examined the consistency of replies: the answers reported via clickers and cards should be identical for each student. Finally, the speed of the techniques was measured with a simple timer.

To probe Q2 (behavioral assessment), we compared the answers reported with a show of hands to the automated polling techniques. A systematic difference would suggest that students behave differently when everyone reports their answers openly.

Methodology

To obtain a test of appropriate difficulty, we used a test that had been given to a previous class and resulted in an average score of about 60%. It was prepared in English and Kannada, and presented to the class in Kannada. The test contained 5 "real" questions and 16 "stock" questions; the stock questions simply requested students to submit a particular answer, in order to test the voting technologies. The stock questions were inserted between the real questions, each time requesting students to answer A, B, C, and D, in sequence. All (real) questions included four possible answers.

The participants in this experiment were 25 students (13 female), all in the 7th standard. We utilized a medium-sized classroom, typical of government schools in Bangalore and the usual setting for this class. The lighting in the room was 100% natural, with sunlight coming through open windows on both sides. We closed some of the window blinds prior to the experiment to obtain more uniform lighting of the room. The room was organized into two sections, boys on one side and girls on the other side, with an aisle in between.

At the start of the experiment, each student received a clicker and a qCard. The teacher explained how to use the clickers and how to use the cards. Since the clickers supported 5 choices, students were told to ignore the "E" choice since there was no equivalent for the cards.

During the testing phase, responses were collected by a researcher who was monitoring the laptop running the qCard recognition software. Responses for clickers and cards were recorded in real time (and archived for later analysis). The researcher confirmed that all responses were received prior to initiating the next poll with students. In a handful of cases, a response was outstanding for a long period, and the researchers offered assistance to the student in question. Assistance included: replacing the expired battery of four i>clicker units, instructing two students to

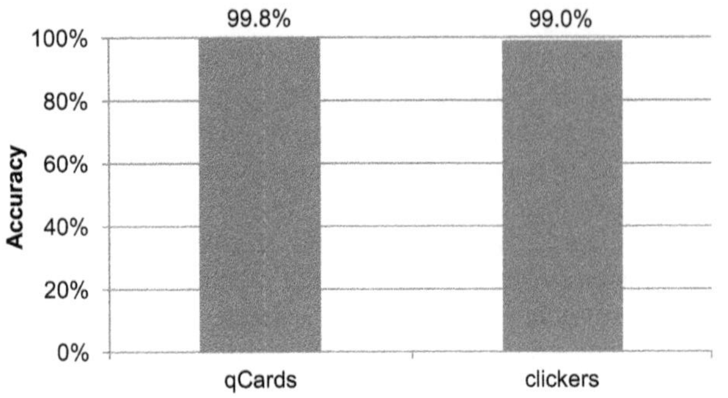

Figure 8: Accuracy of responses read via qCards and clickers for questions with known answers.

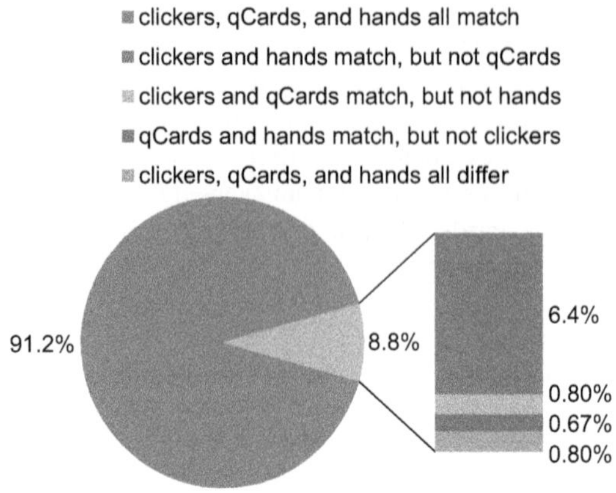

Figure 9: Comparison of responses received by clickers, cards, and a show of hands for 25 students across 5 questions.

raise their qCards higher, and reminding a few students not to obstruct the qCard with their hands. Each poll continued until all students successfully submitted an answer.

Responses to the hand-raising questions were videotaped for later analysis. The responses were not counted in real-time, as we suspected this approach would be too slow to represent a viable model for real-time interaction.

Results: Technology Assessment (Q1)

As outlined previously, we assess the polling techniques according to their accuracy and speed. Accuracy is measured both in terms of correctness relative to known answers and consistency across techniques.

Figure 8 illustrates the absolute accuracy of clickers and cards for questions with "known" answers. For clickers, these correspond to the stock questions only. For cards, the analysis also encompasses the real questions, as we manually decoded students' answers using the video logs. Clickers received 4 incorrect answers out of 400 data points, yielding an accuracy of 99.0%. All four errors came from the same student; we later verified that the clicker was not malfunctioning, so this likely represents an error on the student's part. qCards decoded the correct answer on all of the stock questions, but made one error on a real question, leading to an overall accuracy of 99.8% (one error out of 525 cases). Inspection of video logs reveals that the mistake occurred for a student that changed their answer after raising the card. While such changes are typically detected by our algorithm, in this case the student also changed the card's position such that the new answer was partially obscured by another student's card. Thus, our algorithm recognized the first answer only.

Figure 9 compares the answers received by cards, clickers, and hands, encompassing 375 responses (25 students answering 5 real questions in 3 different ways). In the vast majority of cases (91.2%), all polling techniques report the same answer from a student. In cases where one technique led to a different answer, the most common outlier was cards (6.4%), followed by hands (0.80%) and clickers (0.67%). In only 0.80% of cases did all three techniques give a different answer. We are not sure why answers reported using qCards were a more frequent outlier compared to the other polling techniques, particularly since answers to stock questions were 100% accurate with cards. Inspection of video logs did not reveal any clear explanations for this trend, e.g., due to copying from other students, or confusion/carelessness with the cards. It is possible that using qCards is a bit more cognitively demanding than clickers or hand-raising, thus leading to these differences. We note that one of the outlying points corresponds to the decoding error for qCards; correcting this, the techniques are in agreement 92.0% of the time.

Given the high correspondence between the techniques, it is not surprising that students' overall performance on the test is measured similarly with each method. The class average based on responses received by clickers is 31%; the average based on cards is 31%; and the average based on a show of hands is 33%. These scores are much lower than anticipated, and only marginally better than answering randomly. On further investigation, we believe that for these particular students, the material tested may not have been taught yet during this school year. However, in a trial of students during the preceding school year, the average was over 60%, and the correspondence between polling techniques remained high (ranging from 61% to 66%). This suggests that each method would provide similar guidance to the teacher regarding potential customization of lesson plans.

The speed of responses using clickers and cards is illustrated in Figure 10. Our goal was to measure the time taken for students to use the technology, rather than time spent thinking about the question at hand. Toward that end, we present timings for the stock questions only, and time each response relative to the *first* response received for that question. Results show that both clickers and cards are quite fast; after 10 seconds, 97.0% of qCard results are in, while 98.0% of clicker results are in. After 25 seconds, both techniques have read 99% of replies. Responses requiring longer than this represent exceptional situations, e.g., requiring a battery replacement on a clicker. Even then, no response required longer than one minute to read.

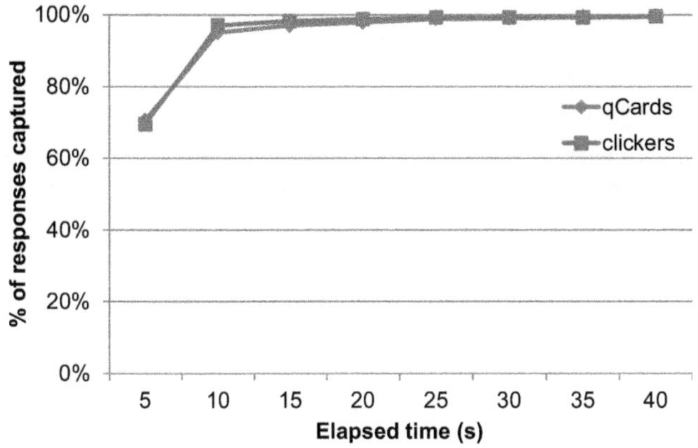

Figure 10: Speed of audience polling technologies: fraction of student responses captured over time.

We also analyzed the speed of hand raising, by analyzing the recoded video feed. We find that an entire hand-raising exercise (spanning all four answers) requires an average of 15 seconds per test question (stdev = 4.6 seconds), though this does not include the time needed to count (or estimate) the number of raised hands for each condition. Thus hand-raising is generally competitive with both clickers and cards as a way to survey the entire class; however, cards and clickers can give a partial estimate in less time.

Results: Behavioral Assessment (Q2)

Our second question of interest is whether students may have *intended* to submit different answers using different polling technologies. Though we conjectured that hand-raising would lead to perturbed results relative to cards and clickers, our data give no evidence for such an effect. The responses from hand-raising agree with responses from clickers 99% of the time, and they agree with qCards 93% of the time. In cases where clickers and cards agreed, the response with hand-raising was different only 1.2% of the time. While these cases could represent a deliberate change in behavior, additional study would be needed to further explicate this effect.

Discussion

We are pleased with the overall performance of qCards. As an initial exploration into this design space, an accuracy of 99.8% (one mis-read in 525 trials) is strong evidence for the feasibility of the system. Whether this accuracy is sufficient depends on the application. If the goal of the system is to give teachers a sense of where their students stand on a question, this accuracy seems well within the bounds of error. However, if the system is used as a graded assessment tool, then additional care may be needed to ensure that every single answer is read as intended.

We note that even the i>clicker system is not perfect; it admitted four errors on stock questions, leading to an accuracy of 99%. This illustrates the limits of accurate classroom polling. Also, i>clickers are subject to battery failure, which could conceivably impact the reports.

Regarding the behavioral assessment, we were surprised with students' consistency (and bravery!) in responding to the show of hands. On several occasions a lone student boldly raised his/her hand and kept it raised, even when it must have become immediately clear that the answer was incorrect. We conjecture that this bold behavior may have been influenced by certain aspects of our study, in particular, by the order of polls conducted. The students were told to vote first by clickers and cards, and then to vote publicly by hands. It is possible the students were more prone to answer honestly feeling the computer had already registered the first responses and that they were locked in. Another possibility is internal to the culture and environment of an Indian primary school classroom. Perhaps students in this environment are less inhibited by fear of standing out than researchers have documented in other primary-school contexts [3,15]. In either case, the influence of peers on student responses merits further research and exploration.

Pedagogies and Usage Scenarios

Due to the high cost of electronic clickers, their use to date has been tightly associated with rich environments. By reducing the cost of electronic response systems, we extend their traditional benefits to low-income environments, and also enable new capabilities that are uniquely tailored to low-income regions.

Traditional benefits of electronic response systems are documented elsewhere [1,4,7]. These include enabling interactive and collaborative pedagogies, as well as enabling teachers to customize lessons to the knowledge and understanding of the class. We believe that techniques to facilitate interactive lessons are especially valuable in developing-country contexts, as current lessons are often delivered by rote with minimal participation of students.

One usage scenario for qCards that may have particular relevance in low-income contexts is that of distance education. Distance-education programs aspire to bring quality teaching from urban centers to rural areas. The physical separation of teachers and students makes it more difficult for remote teachers to assess their students in real-time.

Our project originated with a visit to one such distance-education program, which is run by CLT India. With the help of a large corporation, CLT runs daily distance-education classes, connecting premier teachers in Bangalore with live audiences of students in rural areas. Though there is a high-bandwidth two-way video feed connecting the teacher and the classroom, it remains challenging for the teacher to monitor the progress of each student. The organization perceived that monitoring student progress is even more important in the distance-education scenario, since even the bright and attentive students may fall behind if there is any glitch in the technology (audio, video, volume, etc.) The system proposed in this paper is especially well-suited to this scenario, because there is already a webcam mounted at the front of the class.

There are also several applications for low-cost audience polling outside of a classroom context. Examples include market research, audience choice awards, conference surveys, and anonymous polls for sensitive topics. We envision that the technology developed in this paper would apply equally well in these scenarios.

CONCLUSIONS

Electronic response systems such as clickers have had a demonstrated impact in making classrooms more interactive. However, to date these benefits have been restricted to wealthy environments, due to the prohibitive costs of clickers.

This paper proposes a replacement for clickers that utilizes computer vision to offer the same benefits at drastically lower cost. By replacing electronic handsets with sheets of printed paper, and replacing an expensive receiver with an ordinary webcam, our solution is about 15 times cheaper than clickers. This innovation makes real-time audience polling (and associated pedagogies) accessible to low-resource schools for the first time. While our study was performed in India, we believe the solution would also be valuable for schools in developed countries, where budget constraints often prohibit costly educational technologies.

Our field trials, though exploratory in nature, confirm the technical feasibility of our approach. Our system recognizes answers with almost 100% accuracy. Moreover, students immediately take to the system, and have no trouble interacting with the technology despite their limited exposure to hi-tech artifacts.

In the future, it will be important to undertake long-term trials to assess the learning outcomes that are enabled via usage of our system. We are also working on porting the system to a mobile phone, which could lower the price even further and simplify distribution in emerging markets.

ACKNOWLEDGEMENTS

We would like to thank Bhagya Rangachar and the entire CLT India team for helping us connect with the school for the experiment as well as giving us access to the after-school program for initial prototyping of the design. A special thanks to Jona, Hemalatha, Nireeksha, and Chethan for creating, translating, and administering the tests. Additionally, we would like to thank Manik Varma, P. Anandan, Samar Singh and especially Andy Wilson for helpful conversations about the project.

REFERENCES

1. Caldwell, J.E. Clickers in the large classroom: current research and best-practice tips. *CBE— Life Sciences Education 6*, 1 (2007), 9-20.
2. Cramer, M., Beauregard, R., and Sharma, M. An investigation of purpose built netbooks for primary school education. *8th International Conference on Interaction Design and Children*, 2009.
3. Crozier, W. The influence of shyness on children's test performance. *British Journal of Educational 73*, 3 (2003), 317-328.
4. Fies, C. and Marshall, J. Classroom response systems: A review of the literature. *Journal of Science Education and Technology 15*, 1 (2006), 101–109.
5. De Gagne, J.C. The impact of clickers in nursing education: A review of literature. *Nurse Education Today 31*, 8 (2011), e34 - e40.
6. Hawkey, K., Kellar, M., MacKay, B., Parker, K., and Reilly, D. From cookies to puppies to athletes: designing a visual audience voting system. *CHI*, (2004).
7. Kay, R.H. and LeSage, A. Examining the benefits and challenges of using audience response systems: A review of the literature. *Computers & Education 53*, 3 (2009), 819-827.
8. Looi, C.-K., Chen, W., and Ng, F.-K. Collaborative activities enabled by GroupScribbles (GS): An exploratory study of learning effectiveness. *Computers & Education 54*, 1 (2010), 14-26.
9. MacArthur, J.R. and Jones, L.L. A review of literature reports of clickers applicable to college chemistry classrooms. *Chemistry Education Research and Practice 9*, 3 (2008), 187.
10. Maynes-Aminzade, D., Pausch, R., and Seitz, S. Techniques for interactive audience participation. *4th International Conference on Multimodal Interfaces*, IEEE Comput. Soc (2002), 15-20.
11. Nussbaum, M., Alvarez, C., Mcfarlane, A., Gomez, F., Claro, S., and Radovic, D. Technology as small group face-to-face Collaborative Scaffolding. *Computers & Education 52*, 1 (2009), 147-153.
12. Schalleck, R., Bober, M., and Drewes, H. Design of an audience voting system for the Olympic games. *CHI EA* (2004).
13. Shams, R. Bar code recognition in highly distorted and low resolution images. *Acoustics, Speech and Signal Processing*, (2007).
14. Sieber, J., McCallum, S., and Wyvill, G. BallBouncer: Interactive Games for Theater Audiences. *Crowd Computer Interaction (Workshop at CHI)*, (2009).
15. Stowell, J.R., Oldham, T., and Bennett, D. Using Student Response Systems ("Clickers") to Combat Conformity and Shyness. *Teaching of Psychology 37*, 2 (2010), 135–140.
16. Unger, P., Forsberg, K., and Jacobsen, J.H. PHOTOVOTE: Olympic judging system. *CHI Extended Abstracts* (2004).
17. i-clicker website. 2012. http://www.iclicker.com/Products/iclicker/.
18. Cinematrix website, 2012. http://usa.cinematrix.info/.

CrowdScape: Interactively Visualizing User Behavior and Output

Jeffrey M. Rzeszotarski, Aniket Kittur
Human-Computer Interaction Institute
Carnegie Mellon University
{jeffrz, nkittur}@cs.cmu.edu

ABSTRACT

Crowdsourcing has become a powerful paradigm for accomplishing work quickly and at scale, but involves significant challenges in quality control. Researchers have developed algorithmic quality control approaches based on either worker outputs (such as gold standards or worker agreement) or worker behavior (such as task fingerprinting), but each approach has serious limitations, especially for complex or creative work. Human evaluation addresses these limitations but does not scale well with increasing numbers of workers. We present CrowdScape, a system that supports the human evaluation of complex crowd work through interactive visualization and mixed initiative machine learning. The system combines information about worker behavior with worker outputs, helping users to better understand and harness the crowd. We describe the system and discuss its utility through grounded case studies. We explore other contexts where CrowdScape's visualizations might be useful, such as in user studies.

ACM Classification:

H5.m. Information interfaces and presentations (e.g., HCI).

General terms:

Design, Human Factors, Measurement

Keywords:

Crowdsourcing, Visualization, Interfaces, Event Logging, User Behavior, Quality Control, Performance

INTRODUCTION

Crowdsourcing markets help organizers distribute work in a massively parallel fashion, enabling researchers to generate large datasets of translated text, quickly label geographic data, or even design new products [4,11,20]. However, distributed work comes with significant challenges for quality control. Approaches include algorithmically using tools such as gold standard questions that verify if a worker is accurate on a prescribed baseline, majority voting where more common answers are weighted, or behavioral traces where certain behavioral patterns are linked with outcome measures [4,6,10,16]. Crowd organization algorithms such as *Partition-Map-Reduce, Find-Fix-Verify,* and *Price-Divide-Solve* distribute the burden of breaking up, integrating, and checking work to the crowd [2,14,15].

These algorithmic approaches can be effective in deterministic or constrained tasks such as image transcription or tagging, but they become less effective as tasks are made more complex or creative [7,13,14]. For example, subjective tasks may have no single "right" answer, and in generative tasks such as writing or drawing no two answers may be identical. Conversely, looking at the way workers behave when engaged in a task (e.g., how they scroll, change focus, move their mouse) rather than their output can overcome some of these challenges, but may not be sufficiently accurate on its own to determine which work to accept or reject [16]. Furthermore, two workers may complete in a task in very different ways yet both provide valid output.

We present CrowdScape, a system that supports the evaluation of complex and creative crowdwork by combining information about worker behavior with worker outputs through mixed initiative machine learning (ML), visualization, and interaction. By connecting multiple forms of data, CrowdScape allows users to develop insights about their crowd's performance and identify hard workers or valuable products. The system's machine learning and dynamic querying features support a sensemaking loop wherein the user develops hypotheses about their crowd, tests them, and refines their selections based on ML and visual feedback. CrowdScape's contributions include:

- An interface for interactive exploration of crowdworker results that supports the development of insights on worker performance by combining information on worker behavior and outputs;
- Novel visualizations for crowdworker behavior
- Novel techniques for exploring crowdworker products
- Tools for grouping and classifying workers
- Mixed initiative machine learning that bootstraps user intuitions about a crowd.

In the remainder of this paper we will describe the technical details of the visualization system and illustrate its utility through several grounded case studies.

QUALITY CONTROL IN CROWDSOURCING

Low quality work is common in crowdsourcing markets, comprising up to an estimated one third of all submissions

UIST'12, October 7–10, 2012, Cambridge, Massachusetts, USA.

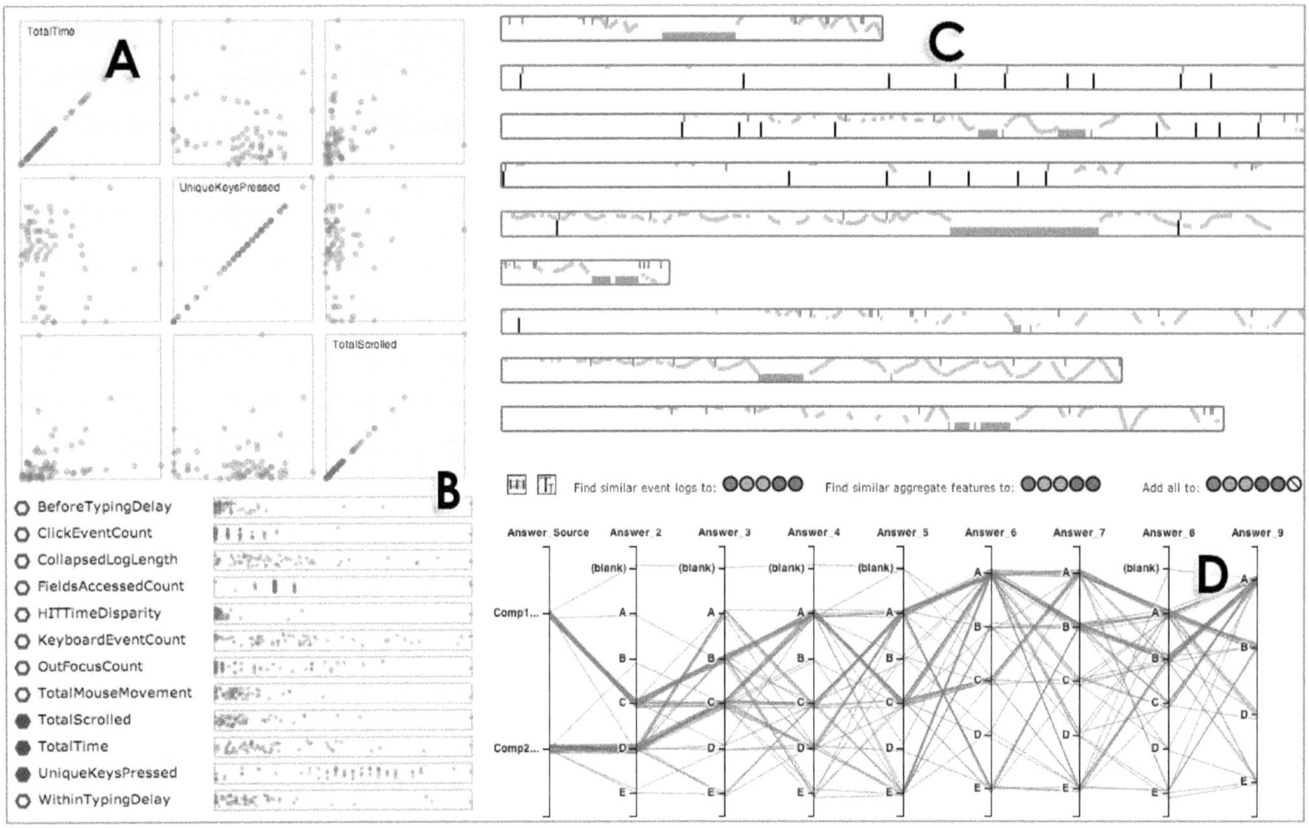

Figure 1: The CrowdScape interface. (A) is a scatter plot of aggregate behavioral features. Brush on the plot to filter behavioral traces. (B) shows the distribution of each aggregate feature. Brush on the distribution to filter traces based a range of values. (C) shows behavioral traces for each worker/output pair. Mouseover to explore a particular worker's products. (D) encodes the range of worker outputs. Brush on each axis to select a subset of entries. Next to (B) is a control panel where users can switch between parallel coordinates and a textual view of worker outputs (left buttons), put workers into groups (colored right buttons), or find points similar to their colored groups (two middle button sets).

[2]. As a result, researchers have investigated several ways of detecting and correcting for low quality work by either studying the post-hoc pool of outputs or the ongoing behavior of a worker.

Post-hoc output evaluations

Validated 'gold standard' questions can be seeded into a task with the presumption that workers who answer the gold standard questions incorrectly can be filtered out or given corrective feedback [4,8]. In the case of well defined tasks such as transcribing a business card, it is easy to insert validated questions. However, in more complex tasks such as writing validation questions often do not apply. Other researchers have suggested using trends or majority voting to identify good answers, or to have workers rate other workers' submissions [2,4,18]. While these techniques can be effective (especially so when the range of outputs is constrained) they also are subject to gaming or majority effects and may completely break down in situations where there are no answers in common such as in creative or generative work.

Another method researchers have employed relies on organizing and visualizing crowd workflows in order to guarantee or work towards better results. Turkomatic and CrowdWeaver use directed graph visualizations to show the organization of crowd tasks, allowing users to better understand their workflow and design for higher quality [13,15]. CrowdForge and Jabberwocky use programmatic paradigms to similarly allow for more optimal task designs [1,14]. These tools can provide powerful ways of organizing and managing complex workflows, but are not suited to all tasks and require iteration to perfect.

Behavioral traces

Another line of research suggests that looking at the manner in which workers complete a task might provide enough information to make inferences about their final products [16,19]. For example, a worker who quickly enters tags one after the other may be doing a poorer job than a worker who enters a tag, pauses to glance back at the image, and then enters another. While harnessing these implicit behavioral features can be effective, it requires that at least some of the feature vectors be labeled by examining and evaluating worker outputs manually. CrowdFlower's analytics tools address this issue, aligning post-hoc outcomes such as gold standard question responses with individual workers in visual form [5]. As a result, this tool can surface general worker patterns, such as failing certain gold questions or spending too little time on a task. However, without access to detailed behavioral trace data, the level of feedback it can provide to task organizers is limited.

Integrated Quality Control

While each of these categories has advantages and disadvantages, in the case of creative or complex work neither are sufficient alone. There may not be enough data to train predictive models for behavioral traces, or it may be difficult to seed gold standard questions. Yet, in concert both post-hoc output analysis and behavioral traces provide valuable complementary insights. For example, imagine the case of image tagging. We may not have enough labeled points to build a predictive model for a worker who enters tags in rapid succession, but we may recognize that this worker submits two short tags. Another worker may also enter the same two tags and share a similar behavioral trace. From this we might posit that those two tags are indicators of workers who behave in a slipshod manner. By combining both behavioral observations and knowledge of worker output, we gain new insight into how the crowd performs.

CROWDSCAPE

CrowdScape, as illustrated in Figure 1, is built on top of Mechanical Turk, a crowdsourcing market, capturing data from both the MTurk API in order to obtain the products of work done on the market and Rzeszotarski and Kittur's Task Fingerprinting system in order to capture worker behavioral traces [16]. CrowdScape uses these two data sources to generate an interactive data visualization which is powered by Javascript, JQuery, and D3.js [3].

Scenario

Imagine a requester has two hundred workers write short synopses of her collection of YouTube physics tutorials so that she can pick the best ones to use as her video descriptions. She turns to CrowdScape to parse through her pool of submissions. Since she added code to log worker behavior and has stored her collection of worker outputs, she inputs them into the interface and begins exploring her data.

She wants to be sure that people actually watched her video before summarizing, so she locates the 'Total Time' aggregate feature (a behavioral trace of actual time spent working). She then brushes the scatter plot, selecting workers who spent a minimum reasonable amount of time on the task. The interface dynamically updates all other views, filtering out several non sequiturs and one-word summaries in the worker output panel.

She now looks through a few worker's logs and end products by hovering over their behavioral trace timelines for more details. She finds several that submitted good descriptions of her videos, so she places them into the same colored group. She uses the mixed-initiative machine learning feature to get suggestions for submissions similar to her labeled group of 'good' submissions. The list reorders, and she quickly adds some similarly good-sounding summaries to her final list. After repeating the process several times, she feels she has a good list of candidates, and exports her submissions so that she can add them to YouTube.

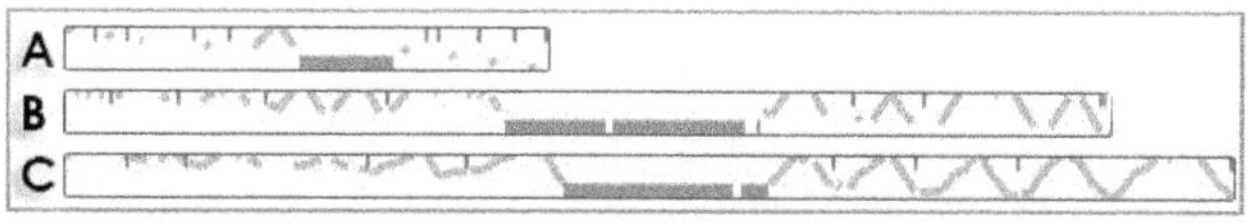

Figure 2: Workers clicking radio buttons while referring to a source passage at the top of their view.

WORKER BEHAVIOR

CrowdScape utilizes two data sources: worker behavior and output. Each has important design considerations for interaction and visualization. In the case of worker behavior, there are two levels of data aggregation: raw event logs and aggregate worker features.

Individual Traces

Raw event logs measure worker behavior on a highly granular, user interface interaction level, providing time-series data for user mouse mouse movements, clicks, scrolls, keypresses, and focus changes. A key challenge in CrowdScape is representing this time series data in a way that is accurate yet easy to interpret and detect differences and patterns in worker behavior.

To address this challenge we developed a method for generating an abstract visual timeline of a trace. Our designs focused on promoting rapid and accurate visual understandings of worker behavior. We represent the time a worker takes to do certain tasks horizontally, and place indicators based on the different activities a worker logs. Through iteration we determined that representing keypresses, visual scrolling, focus shifts, and clicking provided a meaningful level of information. Representing mouse movement greatly increased visual clutter and in practice did not appear to provide useful information for the user. Keypress events are logged as vertical red lines that form blocks during extended typing, and help to differentiate behaviors such as copy-pasting versus typing. Clicks are blue flags that rise above other events so they are easily noticed. Browser focus changes are shown with black bars to suggest the 'break' in user concentration. Scrolling is indicated with orange lines that move up and down to indicate page position and possible shifts in user cognitive focus. To make it easy to compare workers' completion times we used an absolute scale for the length of the timeline; this proved more useful than normalizing all timelines to the same length as it also allowed accurate comparison of intervals within timelines.

The colors and flow of the timelines aim to promote quick, gestalt understandings of a user's behavior. For instance, compare the three timelines in Figure 2. *A* is a *lazy* worker who picks radio buttons in rapid succession. *B* is an *eager* worker who refers to the source text by scrolling up to it in between clicking on radio buttons and typing answers. *B*'s scrolling manifested in the U-shaped orange lines as they jump from the button area to the source text as well their

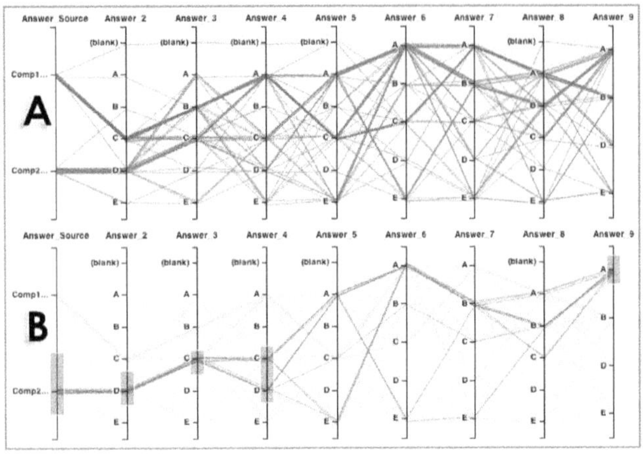

Figure 3: Two views of submission parallel coordinates for a text comprehension quiz. (A) shows all points while (B) uses brushing to show a subset.

keyboard entry. Such patterns manifest in other diligent workers within the same task (such as *C*).

To support larger scale exploration over hundreds or thousands of worker submissions we provide a means to algorithmically cluster traces. The user first provides a cluster of exemplar points such as the group of similarly behaving users in the earlier example (workers *B* and *C*). We compute the average Levenshtein distance from the exemplar cluster to each of the other workers' behavioral traces and order them based on their 'closeness'. This allows users to quickly specify an archetypical behavior or set of behaviors and locate more submissions that exhibit this archetype.

Aggregate Features

We also visualize aggregate features of worker behavioral traces. These have been shown to be effective in classifying the workers into low and high performing groups, or identifying cheaters. Making these numerous multi-dimensional features understandable is a key challenge for CrowdScape. We first reduced the number of dimensions by eliminating redundant or duplicate features in favor of features shown to be effective in classifying workers in previous research [16]. This resulted in twelve distinct aggregate features.

Given our list of twelve features, we use a combination of 1-D and 2-D matrix scatter plots to show the distribution of the features over the group of workers and enable dynamic exploration. For each feature we use a 1-D plot to show its individual characteristics (Figure 1B). Should the user find it compelling, they can add it into a 2-D matrix of plots that cross multiple features in order to expose interaction effects (Figure 1A).

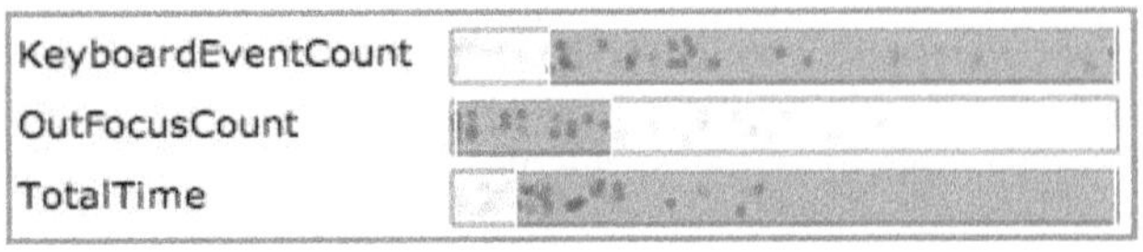

Figure 4: Brushing ranges of aggregate features

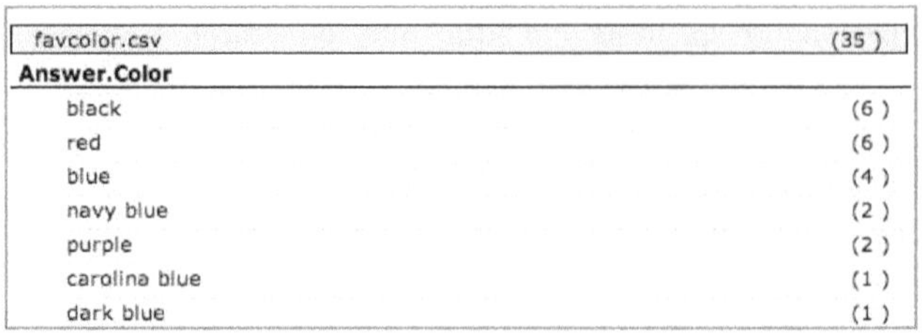

Figure 5: The text view of submissions for a survey. This view is useful if the parallel coordinates (Fig. 3) are saturated with singletons or large text entries.

While these static visuals are effective at showing distributions and correlations, we further use dynamic querying to support interactive data analysis. Users can brush a region in any 1D or 2D scatter plot to select points, display their behavioral traces, and desaturate or filter unselected points in all other interface elements. This interactivity reveals multidimensional relationships between features in the worker pool and allows users to explore their own mental model of the task. For example, in Figure 4 the user has selected workers that spent a fair amount of time on task, haven't changed focus too much, and have typed more than a few characters. This example configuration would be useful for analyzing a task that demands concentration.

Yet, it still may be difficult to spot multi-dimensional trends and explore the features of hundreds or thousands of points. As a result we provide a means to cluster submissions based on aggregate event features. Similar to the ML behavioral trace algorithm, the user provides exemplars, and then similar examples are found based on distance from a centroid computed from the selected examples' aggregate features. The system computes the distance for all non-example points to the centroid and sorts them by this similarity distance. This allows users to find more workers whose behavior fits their model of the task by triangulating on broad trends such as spending time before typing or scrolling.

WORKER OUTPUT

Though visualizing worker behavior is useful, users still require an understanding of the final output a worker produced. One challenge for CrowdScape is representing worker output in a meaningful way. For a scale larger than ten or twenty workers, serially inspecting their contributions can be intractable and inefficient. Instead, we chose to focus on two different characteristics of worker submissions.

The first characteristic is that worker submissions often follow patterns. For example, if a user is extracting text from a document line-by-line, the workers that get everything right will tend to look like each other. In other words, workers that get line 1 correct are more likely to get line 2 correct and so forth. These sorts of aggregate trends over multiple answer fields are well suited for parallel coordinates visualizations [9]. For each answer section, the system finds all possible outcomes and marks them on parallel

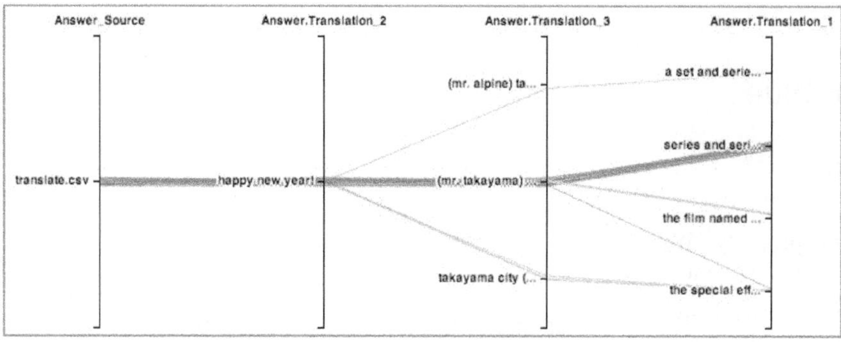

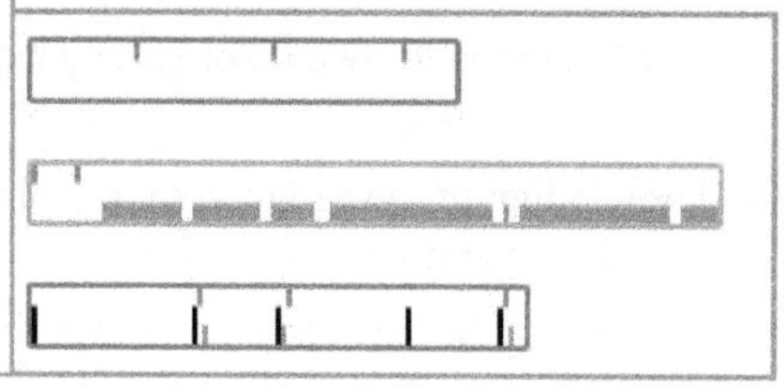

Figures 6 and 7: Figure 6 shows the parallel coordinates for a 21 translations of 3 sentences. Note that only one translator (green) was successful. Red and orange translators copies from machine translation services. Observe the green translator's markedly different behavioral trace.

vertical axes. Each submission then is graphed as a line crossing the axes at its corresponding answers. Figure 6 shows one such trend, highlighting many workers who answer a certain way and only a few workers who deviate. Figure 3 shows a far more complex relationship. To help disambiguate such complex output situations, the system allows for dynamic brushing over each answer axis. This allows a user to sift through submissions, isolating patterns of worker output (Figure 3B).

Not all tasks generate worker output that is easy to aggregate. For writing a review of a movie, few if any workers will write the exact same text (and those that did would likely be suspect). The system provides a means to explore the raw text in a text view pane, which users can view interchangeably with the parallel coordinates pane. The text view pane shows answers sorted by the number of repeat submissions of the same text. For example if one were to ask workers to state their favorite color, one would expect to find lots of responses to standard rainbow colors, and singleton responses to more nuanced colors such as "fuschia" and "navy blue" (Figure 5). The text pane view is also linked with the other views; brushing and adding items to categories is reflected through filtering and color-coded subsets of text outputs, respectively.

INTEGRATING BEHAVIOR AND OUTPUT

While on their own behavioral traces and worker output visualizations can provide useful insights to crowd organizers, together they can provide far more nuanced information. For instance, imagine the case where users are translating a passage sentence-by-sentence. Worker agreement in this case may identify a cluster of identical good translations, but also a cluster of identical poor translations copy-pasted into translation software. Behavioral trace visualization can provide additional insights: the software group may show evidence of taking very little time on the task, or using copy-paste rather than typing. They may change focus in their behavioral traces. The typing group may show large typing blocks in their traces, delays of deliberation, and take longer to complete the task. Thus combining behavioral traces and worker outputs can provide more insight than either alone.

It is through dynamic querying and triangulation that CrowdScape helps users to develop mental models of behavior and output like described above. Dynamic queries update the interface in realtime as filters are applied and data is inspected [17]. Such interaction techniques augment user understanding through instantaneous feedback and enabling experimentation. Thus, by brush-selecting on the aggregate feature of time spent in CrowdScape, the parallel coordinate display of worker output as well as behavioral traces update accordingly. Picking one point highlights it in every axis at once. Even further, the interface supports assigning group identities to points using color. This allows users to color-code groups of points based on their own model of the task and then see how the colors cluster along various features.

This unity between behavior and output fosters insights into the actual process workers use to complete a task. Users develop a mental model of the task itself, understanding how certain worker behaviors correlate with certain end products. In turn, they can use this insight to formulate more effective tasks or deal with their pool of worker submission data.

CASE STUDIES

To illustrate the different use cases of CrowdScape, we posted four varieties of tasks on the Amazon Mechanical Turk crowdsourcing market and solicited submissions. We logged worker behavior (with explicit worker consent), recorded output, generated raw traces and aggregate features, and then imported them into CrowdScape for study.

Translation

CrowdScape reveals patterns in workers that help to unveil important answers that majority-based quality control may miss. We posted a task asking for workers to translate text from Japanese into English, figuring that lazy Turkers would be likely to use machine translation to more quickly complete the task. We chose three phrases: a conventional "Happy New Year" phrase which functioned as a gold standard test to see if people were translating at all, a sentence about Gojira that does not parse well in mechanical translators, and a sentence about a village that requires do-

Figure 8: Traces for two color survey workers

main knowledge of geography to translate properly. We had 21 workers complete this task at a pay rate of 42 cents.

After importing the results of the task into CrowdScape, one feature in the output of the workers is immediately revealed by the parallel coordinates interface of worker products in Figure 6. All workers passed our gold, translating 'Happy New Year" properly. However, 16 out of 21 workers submitted the same three sentences; this pattern is clearly delineated by the dark line of multiple submissions (red in the figure). Examining their submissions shows that they likely used Google Translate, which is able to translate the first two sentences properly, but stumbles on the Gojira film sentence. Another bold line at the bottom shows a grouping of workers who used a different machine translation service (orange).

Eliminating those two groups, two workers are left. The orange line at the top shows one such worker. Note that the grammatical errors in their third submission are rather similar to the red machine translation group, suggesting more machine translation. The alignment of the parallel coordinates helps to expose these patterns. We are left with only one worker who likely translated the task manually, producing a reasonably accurate translation of the final sentence. This is confirmed by their behavioral traces (the green bar in Figure 7), which show evidence of time spent thinking, lack of focus changes (e.g., to copy-paste to and from translation software), and significant time spent typing (as opposed to copy-pasting).

This case study demonstrates the power of CrowdScape in identifying outliers among the crowd. By examining the pattern of worker submissions, one can quickly hone in on unique behaviors or outputs that may be more valuable than common behaviors or submissions made by the crowd.

Picking a Favorite Color

CrowdScape can also support or refute intuitions about worker cognitive processes as they complete tasks. We posted a task asking workers to use an HSV color picker tool to pick their favorite color and then tell us its name. 35 workers completed the job for 3 cents each. With this task in mind, we developed the model that workers who spent a long time picking a color were likely trying to find a more specific shade than 'red' or 'blue' which are easy to obtain using the color picker. In turn, we posited that workers that identified a very specific shade were more likely to choose a descriptive color name since they went to the trouble.

As anticipated, CrowdScape showed that the three most common colors were black, red, and blue (Figure 5). In order to explore our theory about worker cognition, we

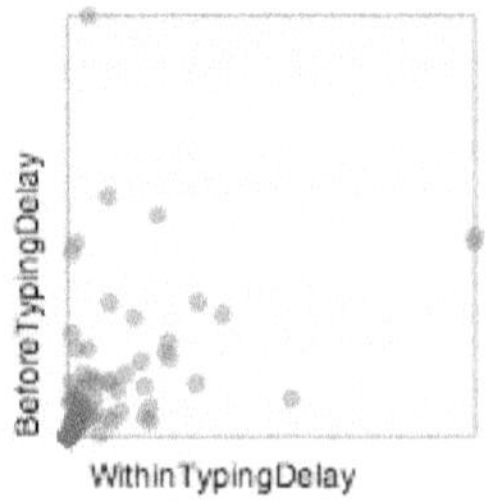

Figure 9: Scatter plot for workers who summarized and tagged (red) and only tagged (blue)

filtered submissions by the amount of time workers waited before typing in their color. This reduced the amount of submissions, revealing workers who wrote colors such as "Carolina blue", "hot pink", or "teal". The difference is evident in the workers' behavioral traces as well (Figure 8).

This case demonstrates that CrowdScape supports the investigation of theories about worker cognitive processes and how they relate to workers' end products. By simply following our intuition that more deliberation may suggest more descriptive colors, we were able to locate an interesting set of minority submissions.

Writing About a Favorite Place

CrowdScape supports feedback loops that are especially helpful when worker output is extremely sparse or variable. We asked 50 workers to describe their favorite place in 3-6 sentences for 14 cents each. No two workers provided the same response, making traditional gold standard and worker majority analysis techniques inapplicable. Instead, we explored the hypothesis that good workers would deliberate about their place and description and then write about it fluidly. This would manifest through a higher time before typing and little time spent between typing characters. After configuring the scatterplot matrix to pair the two aggregate features for typing delays (similar to Figure 9) we selected a region on the graph that described our hypothesis and were left with 10 selected points. By hovering over each one, we quickly scanned their responses, binning good ones into a group. We then used the machine learning similarity feature to find points that had similar aggregate behavioral features. We chose this over finding similar traces because workers in practice did not scroll, click, or change focus much. After we found points with similar features, we repeated the same process, quickly binning good descriptions. After one more repetition, we had a sample of 10 acceptable descriptions.

Our ending response set satisfices our goal of finding a diverse set of well-written favorite places. Descriptions ranged from the beaches of Goa, India, a church in Serbia, a park in New York, and mountains in Switzerland. By progressively winnowing our submissions by building a feedback loop using recommendations and binning, CrowdScape allowed us to quickly develop a successful final output set.

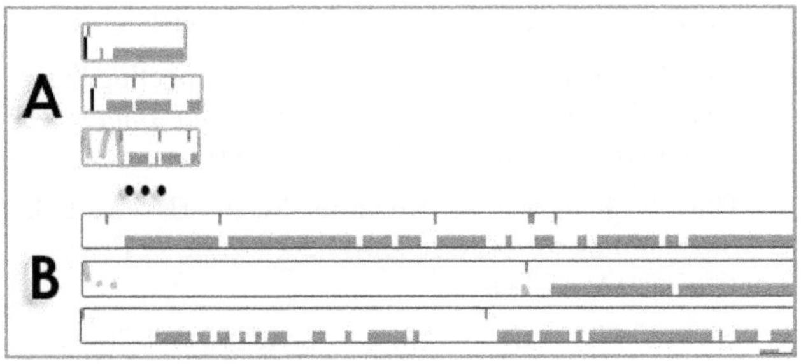

Figure 10: Traces for workers who only tagged videos (A) and for workers who tagged and summarized videos (B)

Tagging a Video

To explore this feedback loop in more detail, we had 96 workers tag science tutorial videos from YouTube for either 25 or 32 cents. Some workers also summarized the video, based on Kittur et al.'s design pattern for having easily monitored tasks that engage workers in task-relevant processing [12]. Binning the workers into two groups immediately shows that workers who only gave tags (in blue) spent less time than summarizers (in red) deliberating before and during their text entry (Figure 9).

The behavioral traces also expose another nuance in the pool of workers: some workers watch the whole video then type, other workers type while watching, and some seemingly don't watch at all. We first scrolled through the entire pool of traces, looking for telltale signs of people who skipped the video such as no focus changes (interactions with the flash video player) and little white space (pauses). After identifying several of these traces, we had the machine learning system generate similarity ratings for the rest of the traces based on the traces of our group of exemplars. This yielded several more similar cases where workers did not watch the video and instead added non-sequitur tags such as "extra", "super" and "awesome". Among these cases were some good submissions, suggesting that our initial insight that shorter traces might correlate to worse tags is incomplete. However, when examining strings highly *dissimilar* to our bad examples, they were almost universally good. This was extreme enough that we felt we could take the bottom half of the list of submissions sorted by similarity to the bad examples and have a sufficient set of good tags. Figure 10 illustrates the contrast between our bad exemplars and the set of good 'dissimilar' points.

This case demonstrates the sorts of detailed insights that CrowdScape promotes by unveiling the intersection between output and behavior. We were able to find evidence supporting our hypothesis that asking workers to summarize produced better tags, while also identifying an usable subset of valid outputs.

DISCUSSION, LIMITATIONS, AND FUTURE WORK

CrowdScape links behavioral information about workers with data about their output through an interactive visualization and mixed-initiative machine learning. While past work in crowdsourcing has focused on worker output or worker behavior alone, combining them has several advantages. In the case of purely generative tasks (such as describing one's favorite place), this combination helps a user quickly explore the space of worker submissions, facilitating their development a mental model of the behavior of workers who have good or bad outputs. This model helps them identify further good workers and output in a sort of positive feedback loop. Visualizing the process workers use to complete a task can contradict or reinforce our conception of the cognitive processes they use to complete a task, which in turn informs our understanding of the task's end products (as in the favorite color case). The video tagging case illustrates the value of mixing the two data sources together, permitting organizers to understand their crowd's collective action in greater detail.

These contributions may have use beyond crowdsourcing, for example in supporting studies of user interface design. By pairing the behavioral traces of users as they interact with an interface with outputs such as whether they completed the task successfully, CrowdScape could quickly unveil elements of tasks or designs that might be improved over iteration. This would enable deeper analysis of user study data, as well as dealing with some of the challenges inherent in remote user studies (in which users are typically unobserved).

There are some limitations to CrowdScape's current approach. In some situations it may not be possible to capture worker behavior easily; currently, CrowdScape is limited to online web pages in which Javascript can be inserted. Thus the approach may not be applicable to non-web interfaces, pages where the requester does not have access to inject Javascript, or when the worker blocks scripting (though the latter can be tested for). In the case of generative tasks like describing favorite places, the parallel coordinates view becomes saturated and the linear list can become quite long. Techniques for filtering the data (e.g., by behavior in the "favorite place" case study) can help alleviate this issue. Furthermore, it is unclear whether the set of aggregate features included will always be useful, and whether similarity based on distance will always provide useful feedback.

There are situations in which learning to use CrowdScape and employing it may not be appropriate. For instance, in cases where there are clear, consensus ground truths such as identifying a spelling error, CrowdScape does not provide a significant advantage compared to preexisting quality control measures. There may also be situations in which the behavioral traces analyzed are not very indicative of the way that work is done. For example, if users complete most of the task in a separate text editor and paste the text in at the end, their behavioral trace will contain very little info (other than focus changes and that someone pasted, which can itself be informative). Taken further, tasks that are completely offline or primarily cognitive (such as considering the next move in a game of chess) may not be amenable to the generalized approach espoused by

CrowdScape. Further work is needed to test the approach on a wider variety of tasks.

One other potential weak point of CrowdScape is in the detail level of the behavioral traces. Currently it relies on mouse movement, scrolling, keypresses, focus events, and clicks. This may not be sufficient for determining, for instance, where the fovea of the user is currently focused. However, we could design tasks to provide more detailed feedback in exchange for increasing obtrusiveness. For instance, we could only play a video if the mouse is hovered over it, allowing us to measure when it is playing. Or, we could require a text area to be clicked and held to show its actual text, allowing us to accurately estimate where and when the user is directing their attention. However, advantages in measuring user behavior more accurately must be balanced against increases in intrusiveness and decreases in efficiency.

CrowdScape aims to unify different quality control approaches, benefiting from their synergy. Gold standard and worker majority can help task organizers immediately evaluate worker output. Aggregate behavioral traces can help isolate target worker clusters. Individual traces can provide insight into actual worker behaviors. By unifying these approaches, CrowdScape allows users to develop and test their mental models of tasks and worker behaviors, and then ground those models in worker outputs and majority or gold standard verifications. Furthermore, CrowdScape's dynamic querying system permits the rapid analysis of large sets of data by providing immediate feedback to users. As crowd work becomes increasingly creative, collaborative, and complex, we hope that integrated systems such as CrowdScape will enable organizers to better understand and harness the nature of their crowd.

ACKNOWLEDGMENTS

We thank Paul André, Rebecca Gulotta, Lisa Yu, and our reviewers among many others for their feedback and support. This research was supported by NSF grants OCI-09-43148, IIS-0968484, IIS-1111124, and a grant from Carnegie Mellon's Center for the Future of Work.

REFERENCES

1. Ahmad, S., Battle, A., Malkani, Z., and Kamvar, S. The Jabberwocky programming environment for structured social computing. *In Proc. UIST '11*, (2011), 53-64.
2. Bernstein, M.S., Little, G., Miller, R.C., et al. Soylent: a word processor with a crowd inside. *In Proc. UIST '10,* ACM (2010), 313–322.
3. M. Bostock, V. Ogievetsky, and J. Heer. D3: Data-driven documents. *IEEE Transactions on Visualization and Computer Graphics 17,12*. (2011), 2301–2309.
4. Callison-Burch, C. Fast, cheap, and creative: evaluating translation quality using Amazon's Mechanical Turk. *In Proc. Empirical Methods in Natural Language Processing*. (2009), 286–295.
5. CrowdFlower. www.crowdflower.com. (2012).
6. Dekel, O. and Shamir, O. Vox populi: collecting high-quality labels from a crowd. *In Proc. 22nd Annual Conference on Learning Theory*, (2009).
7. Dow, S., Kulkarni, A., Klemmer, S., and Hartmann, B. Shepherding the crowd yields better work. *In Proc. CSCW '11*, (2011).
8. Downs, J.S., Holbrook, M.B., Sheng, S., and Cranor, L.F. Are your participants gaming the system?: Screening Mechanical Turk workers. *In Proc. CHI '10*, (2010).
9. Inselberg, A. and Dimsdale, B. Parallel coordinates: a tool for visualizing multi-dimensional geometry. *IEEE Visualization*, (1990), 361-378.
10. Ipeirotis, P.G., Provost, F., and Wang, J. Quality management on Amazon Mechanical Turk. *In Proc. ACM SIGKDD workshop on human computation*, (2010).
11. Ishikawa, S. Clickworkers interactive: towards a robust crowdsourcing tool for collecting scientific data. *Lunar and Planetary Institute*, (2012), 2-3.
12. Kittur, A., Chi, E., and Suh, B. Crowdsourcing user studies with Mechanical Turk. *In Proc. CHI '08*, (2008).
13. Kittur, A., Khamkar, S., André, P., and Kraut, R. CrowdWeaver: Visually managing complex crowd work. *In Proc. CSCW '12*, (2012).
14. Kittur, A., Smus, B., and Khamkar, S. Crowdforge: Crowdsourcing complex work. *In Proc. UIST '11*, (2011).
15. Kulkarni, A., Can, M., and Hartmann, B. Collaboratively crowdsourcing workflows with Turkomatic. *In Proc. CSCW '12*, (2012).
16. Rzeszotarski, J.M. and Kittur, A. Instrumenting the crowd: using implicit behavioral measures to predict task performance. *In Proc. UIST '11*, (2011).
17. Shneiderman, B. Dynamic queries for visual information seeking. *Software, IEEE*, (1994).
18. Snow, R., O'Connor, B., Jurafsky, D., and Ng, A.Y. Cheap and fast—but is it good?: Evaluating non-expert annotations for natural language tasks. *In Proc. Empirical Methods in Natural Language Processing*, (2008), 254–263.
19. Vanderaalst, W., Vandongen, B., Herbst, J., Maruster, L., Schimm, G., and Weijters, a. Workflow mining: a survey of issues and approaches. *Data & Knowledge Engineering 47*, 2 (2003), 237-267.
20. Yu, L. and Nickerson, J. Generating creative ideas through crowds: an experimental study of combination. *In Proc. ICIS*, (2011), 1-16.

Learning Design Patterns with Bayesian Grammar Induction

Jerry O. Talton
Intel Corporation
jerry.o.talton@intel.com

Lingfeng Yang
Stanford University
lfyg@stanford.edu

Ranjitha Kumar
Stanford University
ranju@stanford.edu

Maxine Lim
Stanford University
maxinel@stanford.edu

Noah D. Goodman
Stanford University
ngoodman@stanford.edu

Radomír Měch
Adobe Corporation
rmech@adobe.com

ABSTRACT

Design patterns have proven useful in many creative fields, providing content creators with archetypal, reusable guidelines to leverage in projects. Creating such patterns, however, is a time-consuming, manual process, typically relegated to a few experts in any given domain. In this paper, we describe an algorithmic method for learning design patterns directly from data using techniques from natural language processing and structured concept learning. Given a set of labeled, hierarchical designs as input, we induce a probabilistic formal grammar over these exemplars. Once learned, this grammar encodes a set of generative rules for the class of designs, which can be sampled to synthesize novel artifacts. We demonstrate the method on geometric models and Web pages, and discuss how the learned patterns can drive new interaction mechanisms for content creators.

ACM Classification Keywords

H.1.2. [Models and Principles]: User/Machine Systems – Human factors.

General Terms

Algorithms, Human Factors.

Author Keywords

Design patterns; grammar induction.

INTRODUCTION

As creative fields mature, a set of best practices emerge for design. Often, attempts are made to codify these practices into a set of formal rules for designers which set out principles of composition, describe useful idioms, and summarize common aesthetic sensibilities. Such *design patterns* have proven popular and influential in fields such as architecture [3], software engineering [14], interaction [7], and Web design [13].

Despite their popularity, design patterns are also problematic. For one, they are difficult to operationalize: users bear the burden of locating reputable sources of design knowledge, assimilating that knowledge, and applying it to their own problems. For another, patterns must be painstakingly formulated and compiled by experts, resulting in guidelines that may be less descriptive of actual practice than prescriptive of a particular designer's point of view.

A more attractive proposition is to learn design patterns directly from data, and encapsulate them in a representation that can be accessed algorithmically. In this paper, we address this problem for one common class of designs: those comprising a hierarchy of labeled components. Such hierarchies abound in creative domains as diverse as architecture [39], geometric modeling [35], document layout [21], and Web design [25].

To learn patterns in a principled way, we leverage techniques from natural language processing and structured concept learning. In particular, we cast the problem as *grammar induction*: given a corpus of example designs, we induce a probabilistic formal grammar over the exemplars. Once learned, this grammar gives a design pattern in a human-readable form that can be used to synthesize novel designs and verify extant constructions.

The crux of this induction is learning how to generalize beyond the set of exemplars: we would like to distill general principles from the provided designs without extrapolating patterns that are not supported by the data. To this end, we employ an iterative structure learning technique called Bayesian Model Merging [41], which formulates grammar induction as Bayesian inference. The method employs an inductive bias based on the law of succinctness, also known as Occam's razor, searching for the simplest grammar that best fits the examples. Since compactness and generality are inexorably linked in grammar-based models, the method provides a data-driven way to learn design patterns that are neither too specific nor overly general.

We demonstrate the method on two distinct classes of designs: geometric models (based on scene graphs), and Web pages (based on Document Object Model trees). We report on statistical analyses of the grammars induced by our technique, share the results from a small user study, and discuss how these sorts of probabilistic models could lead to better tools and interaction mechanisms for design.

UIST'12, October 7–10, 2012, Cambridge, Massachusetts, USA.

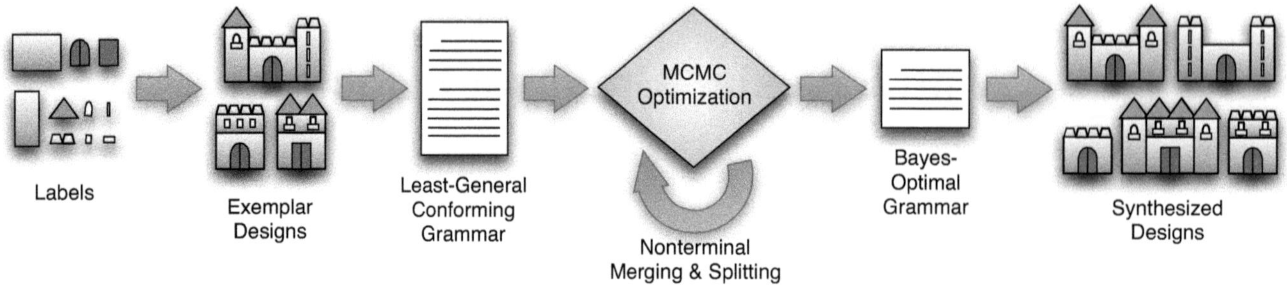

Figure 1. The pipeline for learning design patterns with grammar induction. A set of example designs, each comprising a hierarchy of labeled components, are used to produce an initial, specific grammar. Then, Markov chain Monte Carlo optimization is employed to explore a space of more general grammars, balancing the descriptive power of each one against its representation complexity. At the end of this process, the best scoring grammar is returned, and can be sampled to generate new designs.

BACKGROUND

The use of grammars as generative models has a long history in design. Grammar-based procedural models have seen extensive use in architecture [39, 8, 12], product design [24, 1, 34], document layout [9, 44], and 3D modeling [33, 31, 29]. However, despite the proven utility of grammars as a computational mechanism for design, the overwhelming majority of these models are coded painstakingly by hand. Although a few attempts have been made to learn deterministic rules from patterns [38] and adapt texture synthesis techniques to geometric modeling [28, 6], relatively little work has been done on learning grammars from designs in a principled way.

In formal language theory, the problem of grammar induction was first introduced by Solomonoff [37], who posed the fundamental question of language learning: given a sequence of words from a formal language, is it possible to learn an automaton capable of recognizing that language? The classical result, due to Gold [15], is negative, and states that no superfinite language class is learnable in the limit from positive examples. This means that none of the languages in the Chomsky hierarchy—regular, context-free, context-sensitive, or recursively enumerable—can be learned in this way, regardless of how many samples from the language the induction algorithm is allowed to inspect, or how long it is allowed to process them.

Horning [19] showed that things are not quite so grim for *probabilistic* languages: in fact, stochastic context-free grammars can—in theory—be induced from positive examples. Learning these grammars in practice, however, is a challenging problem: even deciding whether or not there exists an n-state automaton which agrees with some finite set of data is known to be $\mathcal{NP}$-complete [16]. Accordingly, no general algorithm for learning stochastic context-free grammars in the limit has been proposed [10], although several authors have demonstrated natural language induction from large corpora by leveraging domain-specific linguistic features [22, 23].

One popular strategy for making the grammar induction problem tractable is the introduction of an inductive bias. In this paper, we use a technique called Bayesian Model Merging [41] which employs an inductive bias based on the cognitive principle of Occam's razor: specific, complex models are deemed less likely than simple, general ones [26]. In particular, we formulate a posterior probability distribution over the space of possible grammars, and then attempt to maximize this posterior via Markov chain Monte Carlo (MCMC) optimization. This gives a principled, flexible method for inducing design patterns from data.

ALGORITHM OVERVIEW

The method takes as input a set of designs in the form of labeled trees, where each label is drawn from a discrete dictionary $\mathbf{C}$. The algorithm begins by traversing each tree and creating a production rule for every node to generate a *least-general conforming grammar* (LGCG). The grammar is conforming in the sense that every exemplar is a valid derivation from it; it is the least-general such grammar because it derives only the exemplars, with no additional generalization capacity.

Once this grammar is constructed, Markov chain Monte Carlo optimization is used to explore a series of more general conforming grammars by merging and splitting nonterminal symbols. Each merge operation takes two nonterminals, rewrites them to have a common name, and unions their productions; each split operation is the reverse of a merge.

To judge the quality of each candidate grammar, we adopt a Bayesian interpretation that balances the likelihood of the exemplar designs against the description length of the grammar. At each step in the optimization, we randomly select a split or merge move to apply, and evaluate the posterior of the resultant grammar. This search procedure is run until it exhausts a predetermined computational budget and the *maximum a posteriori* estimate is returned. This process is outlined in Figure 1.

GRAMMAR FORMULATION

In order to describe the grammar induction framework, we must first define some basic concepts. A stochastic, context-free grammar (SCFG) is a tuple

$$\mathbf{G} = \langle V, T, \omega, R, \theta \rangle,$$

where V is the set of *nonterminals*, T is the set of *terminals*, $\omega \in (V \cup T)^+$ is the *axiom*, $R \subset V \times (V \cup T)^+$ is a finite set of *production rules*, and $\theta : R \rightarrow (0, 1]$ is a *probability function*. Each production $\rho \in R$ is written as $A \to \chi$, where $A \in V$ is called the *predecessor*, and $\chi \in (V \cup T)^+$ is called the *successor*. For any $A \in V$, the sum of the probabilities for all the rules in R with predecessor A is 1. In the context of structure learning, the set $S_\mathbf{G} = \langle V, T, \omega, R \rangle$ is called the grammar's *structure*, and $\theta_\mathbf{G}$ is said to comprise its *parameters*.

The set $\mathcal{L}(\mathbf{G})$ of all strings which the grammar can generate is called the *language* of $\mathbf{G}$. Given a string $m \in \mathcal{L}(\mathbf{G})$, there is at least one *derivation tree* τ for m. Each such tree is rooted on ω, and every subsequent level in τ consists of a string produced by applying a matching production to each nonterminals in the level above. The last level of the tree contains m.

BAYESIAN INFERENCE FOR GRAMMARS

Given a set of example designs $\mathbf{M}$, we formulate a posterior probability distribution over the space of possible grammars

$$p(\mathbf{G}|\mathbf{M}) \propto P(\mathbf{M}|\mathbf{G})\pi(\mathbf{G}) \qquad (\star)$$

where $P(\mathbf{M}|\mathbf{G})$ is the likelihood of the set of example designs given the grammar and $\pi(\mathbf{G})$ is the grammar prior. Finding the optimal grammar for the exemplars then reduces to maximizing this posterior.

From a strict Bayesian perspective we should formulate this inference as a search for the optimal grammar *structure*, integrating over the associated parameters to compute

$$P(\mathbf{M}|S_\mathbf{G}) = \int_{\theta_\mathbf{G}} P(\theta_\mathbf{G}|S_\mathbf{G}) P(\mathbf{M}|S_\mathbf{G}, \theta_\mathbf{G}) d\theta_\mathbf{G}. \qquad (\diamond)$$

Since this integral has no analytic solution, it would have to be approximated numerically via a costly Monte Carlo simulation for each candidate grammar structure, making inference intractable. Instead, we make a Viterbi assumption that the maximum likelihood parameters for any given structure will dominate in ($\diamond$), which simplifies the inference procedure by identifying a unique set of parameters with each candidate grammar.

Design Likelihoods

With this assumption, given a grammar $\mathbf{G}$ comprising structure $S_\mathbf{G}$ and parameters $\theta_\mathbf{G}$, we can calculate the likelihood of the exemplar set under the grammar

$$P(\mathbf{M}|\mathbf{G}) = \prod_{m \in \mathbf{M}} P_\mathbf{G}(m),$$

where $P_\mathbf{G}(\cdot)$ is the probability of deriving a design. The probability of a model m is the sum over all possible derivation trees yielding m,

$$P_\mathbf{G}(m) = \sum_{\tau \Rightarrow m} P(\tau) = \sum_{\tau \Rightarrow m} \prod_{\rho \in \tau} \theta_\mathbf{G}(\rho),$$

where the probability of a tree is just the product of the probabilities of the rules used in its derivation.

Grammar Priors

To calculate the second term in the posterior ($\star$), the grammar prior, we decompose the grammar into structure and parameters, and apply the chain rule to write

$$\pi(\mathbf{G}) = P_G(\theta_\mathbf{G}|S_\mathbf{G})\pi_G(S_\mathbf{G}),$$

where $P_G(\cdot|\cdot)$ is the probability of the grammar's parameters given its structure, and $\pi_G(\cdot)$ is a structure prior.

To compute the probability of the grammar's parameters, we examine each nonterminal $v \in V_\mathbf{G}$ and observe that the subset of parameters $\theta_v \subseteq \theta_\mathbf{G}$ associated with it form a multinomial. Then, we write the probability as a product of Dirichlet distributions

$$P_G(\theta_\mathbf{G}|S_\mathbf{G}) = \prod_{v \in V_\mathbf{G}} P_G(\theta^v) = \prod_{v \in V_\mathbf{G}} \frac{1}{B(\alpha)} \prod_{\rho \in R|v} \theta^v(\rho)^{\alpha - 1},$$

where $B(\cdot)$ is the multinomial beta function, and α is a concentration parameter. By setting $\alpha = 1$, we obtain a uniform distribution over all possible production probabilities; when $\alpha < 1$ we prefer grammars in which most of the probability mass is concentrated in a few productions; when $\alpha > 1$ we give preference to distributions in which all of the probabilities are equal.

To compute the prior probability of the grammar structure, we take

$$\pi_G(S_\mathbf{G}) = \exp\left[-\ell(S_\mathbf{G})\right]^\lambda,$$

where $\ell(\cdot)$ is an approximation of the description length of the grammar and λ is a weighting term. We encode the grammar as a string of productions separated by a special termination character, starting with the axiom and continuing with the predecessor and successor of the remaining rules. Each symbol in the string then contributes $\log_2(|V| + |T|)$ bits to the length. Since our formulation measures model complexity syntactically and fit to data semantically, we use λ to adjust the balance between these two intrinsically incommensurable quantities.

MODEL MERGING

With this formulation, we use Markov chain Monte Carlo optimization to seek a grammar that maximizes the posterior. The key idea behind this optimization is that we can explore a family of related, conforming grammars by merging and splitting nonterminal symbols. While the original Bayesian Model Merging algorithm used only merge operations in a beam search, we employ both merges and splits in a full MCMC framework to prevent the search procedure from getting "stuck" in local maxima.

Initial Grammar Creation

The algorithm begins by processing the exemplars to create a least-general conforming grammar, which is used to initialize the optimization. To produce this grammar, one nonterminal symbol is created for each instanced label used in $\mathbf{M}$, and a counter i is initialized. Then, each hierarchical design is traversed recursively. As each label g with children $c_1, \ldots, c_k$ is encountered, the traversal generates a new production $A_i \to g A_{i+1} \ldots A_{i+k}$, pushes productions

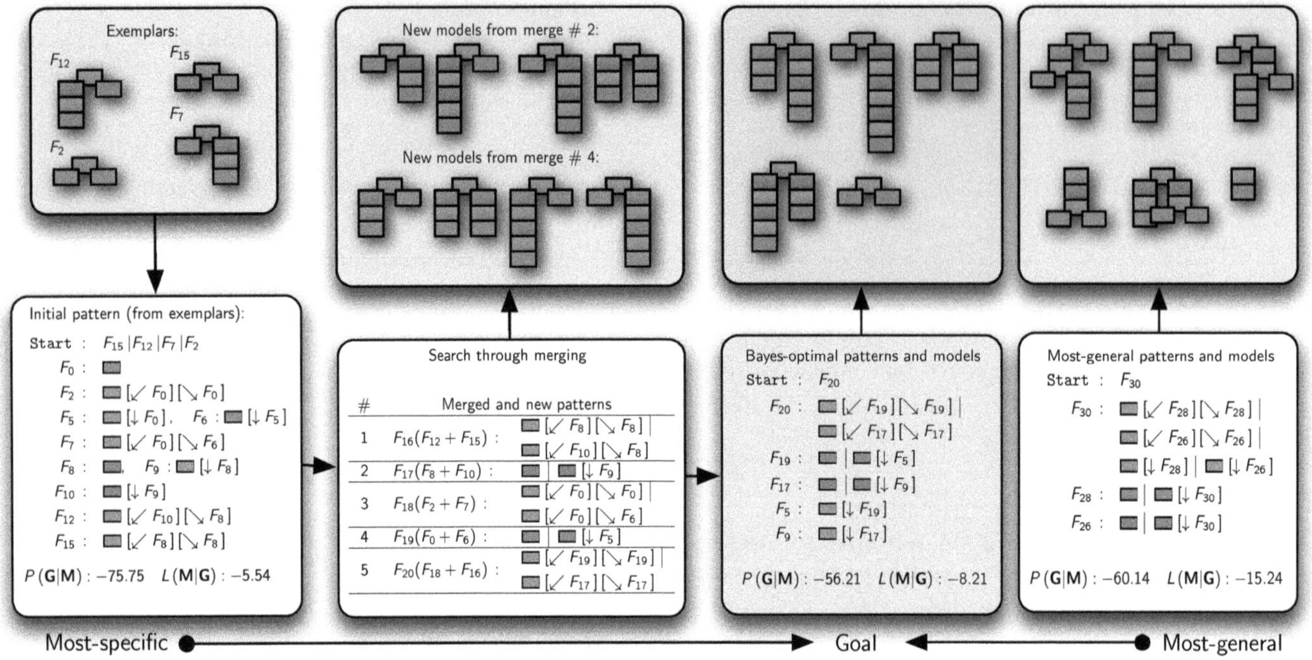

Figure 2. The grammar induction pipeline applied to a simple design space of blocks in a pattern. (left) The initial exemplars and the least-general conforming grammar generated from them. (mid left) The set of merges used to collapse the grammar. (mid right) The optimal grammar, and a set of random samples drawn from it. (right) The most-general conforming grammar, and a set of random samples drawn from it. The design pattern learned with our method generalizes beyond the exemplars in a reasonable way.

$A_{i+1} \rightarrow \ldots$ through $A_{i+k} \rightarrow \ldots$ onto the stack, and increments i by $k+1$. At the end of this process, the starting nonterminals for each of the distinct designs are set as successors of the axiom S. The resultant grammar generates input example m with probability $1/|\mathbf{M}|$.

Merging and Splitting

From the LGCG, the method explores a space of more general grammars by merging and splitting nonterminal symbols. Each merging operation adds to the grammar's generalization capacity and decreases its description length. With successive merges, the cardinality of $\mathcal{L}(\mathbf{G})$ increases: accordingly, each merging operation can only decrease the likelihood of the examples. Occasionally, a merge will create a loop in the grammar structure, making the resultant language superfinite.

Each merge operation takes two nonterminals $A_i, A_j \in V$ and their productions

$$A_i \rightarrow \chi_1 \mid \ldots \mid \chi_k \quad \text{and} \quad A_j \rightarrow \psi_1 \mid \ldots \mid \psi_l,$$

and collapses them to a single, new nonterminal A_{ij} whose successors are the union of the productions of the original symbols

$$A_{ij} \rightarrow \chi_1 \mid \ldots \mid \chi_k \mid \psi_1 \mid \ldots \mid \psi_l.$$

A split operation is the reverse of a merge: it takes a single nonterminal A_i and randomly splits its productions between two new nonterminals A_{i1} and A_{i2}. Then, every instance of A_i in the grammar is replaced by one of these new nonterminals selected at random.

Type Restrictions

In general language learning applications, any two nonterminal symbols can be merged. In particular design domains, however, the semantics of the symbols can be used to restrict the set of potential merge operations and reduce the size of the search space. Since every merge operation represents a determination by the learning algorithm that two symbols can be used interchangeably and identically, we can improve performance by identifying symbols that are fundamentally incomparable *a priori*. In essence, we impose a type system for nonterminals, and only consider merges amongst type-compatible symbols. This type system comprises a discrete set of types $\mathcal{T}$, and an assignment for each variable $\mathbf{t} : V \rightarrow \mathcal{T}$.

Parameter Estimation

While each merge or split operation defines a new grammar structure, to evaluate the posterior we must also have corresponding parameters. In particular, given a grammar structure $S_{\mathbf{G}}$, we wish to find maximum likelihood values for $\theta_{\mathbf{G}}$ such that

$$\theta_{\mathbf{G}} = \underset{\theta}{\operatorname{argmax}}\, P(\mathbf{M}|S_{\mathbf{G}}, \theta).$$

This problem is solved using expectation maximization via the Inside-Outside algorithm [5], a generalization of the classical Baum-Welch algorithm for hidden Markov models. Given a current estimate for the probabilities θ, we update

Domain	|M|	|C|	λ	Least-General		Most-General			Bayes-Optimal		
				DL	L	DL	L	p200	DL	L	p200
Spaceship	5	51	1.15	402	3.2×10^{-4}	369	1.0×10^{-27}	.34	389	1.9×10^{-11}	.85
Castle	6	37	1.05	739	2.1×10^{-5}	662	1.1×10^{-88}	.0045	718	6.9×10^{-18}	.92
Seussean	9	29	1.2	376	2.6×10^{-9}	341	4.2×10^{-32}	.62	346	1.2×10^{-27}	.77
Sakura	8	19	1.2	463	6.0×10^{-8}	406	6.5×10^{-73}	1.3×10^{-7}	433	3.0×10^{-29}	.14
Web page	30	30	1.0	733	4.9×10^{-45}	67	1×10^{-1546}	-	602	8.8×10^{-101}	.37

Table 1. For each of the example domains, the number of exemplars; the number of components; the parameter from the grammar prior; the description length; and the likelihood for the least-general, most-general, and Bayes-optimal grammars. For these latter two grammars, we also report the probability mass occupied by the two-hundred highest-probability designs as a measure of the grammar's generalization capacity.

the probability of a rule $A \to \chi$ by

$$\hat{\theta}(A \to \chi) = \frac{\sum_{m \in \mathbf{M}} c_\theta(A \to \chi; m)}{\sum_{m \in \mathbf{M}} \sum_\gamma c_\theta(A \to \gamma; m)},$$

where $c_\theta(\cdot;\cdot)$ is the expected count of the number of times that a particular rule is used in the derivation of a given model. Since each $c_\theta(\cdot;\cdot)$ depends on the current value of θ, the algorithm is iterative: we initialize the probabilities to be uniform for all rules associated with a given nonterminal, and then update and recompute the counts until θ converges.

Parsing

To compute the expected count of the number of times a particular rule is used, we must find derivation trees for each of the designs in $\mathbf{M}$. In linguistic theory, this process is known as *parsing*. Because the number of possible derivations for any particular design can be exponential in the size of the tree, we cannot enumerate these derivations and count the number of occurrences of each rule. Instead, we employ a bottom-up, chart-based parser similar to the CYK algorithm [2], but adapted for labeled trees instead of strings. Once constructed, the chart can be used to efficiently compute both the the total probability of deriving a model $P_{\mathbf{G}}(\cdot)$ and the expected count of a rule in a derivation $c_\theta(\cdot;\cdot)$ via dynamic programming [27].

Markov chain Monte Carlo

With this machinery in place, the Bayes-optimal grammar can be sought via Markov chain Monte Carlo search using the Metropolis-Hastings algorithm [4]. The state space is a graph where every node is a grammar, and adjacencies between nodes represent merging and splitting operations. The score of each node is the posterior probability ($\star$), and the starting node is the LGCG.

At the ith iteration of the optimization, a split or merge move is chosen at random in the current grammar $\mathbf{G}$, and a new grammar $\mathbf{G}'$ is generated. This new grammar is then accepted as the current search state with probability

$$\alpha(\mathbf{G}'|\mathbf{G}) = \min\left(1, \frac{p^{1/T_i}(\mathbf{G}'|\mathbf{M})q(\mathbf{G}|\mathbf{G}')}{p^{1/T_i}(\mathbf{G}|\mathbf{M})q(\mathbf{G}'|\mathbf{G})}\right),$$

where $q(\cdot|\cdot)$ is the probability of splitting or merging one grammar to generate the other and T_i is a decreasing cooling schedule with $\lim_{i\to\infty} T_i = 0$. After the algorithm has been run for a fixed number of iterations, the grammar with the highest posterior is returned.

To calculate $q(\mathbf{G}'|\mathbf{G})$, consider a split move where nonterminal A_i is broken into two new nonterminals A_j and A_k. First, A_i is selected uniformly from amongst the $|V_{\mathbf{G}}|$ nonterminals. Then, each of the $|R_{A_i}|$ productions that have A_i as their predecessor are assigned randomly to A_j or A_k. Finally, each of the f instances of A_i in the grammar are randomly replaced by one of A_j or A_k. In this case, the reverse distribution $q(\mathbf{G}|\mathbf{G}')$ measures the probability of selecting A_j and A_k from the set of $|V_{\mathbf{G}'}|$ nonterminals to merge. In the absence of type restrictions, this gives

$$q(\mathbf{G}'|\mathbf{G}) = \frac{1}{|V_{\mathbf{G}}| 2^{|R_{A_i}|+f}}, \; q(\mathbf{G}|\mathbf{G}') = \frac{2}{|V_{\mathbf{G}'}|(|V_{\mathbf{G}'}|-1)}.$$

EVALUATION

To test our framework for inducing design patterns, we experimented with two distinct classes of hierarchical, labeled designs: Web pages constructed from Document Object Model (DOM) trees, and geometric models constructed from scene graphs.

Web Pages

We built a corpus of thirty Web pages, harvested from design blogs and popular business sites. We used the Bento page segmentation algorithm [25] to decompose each page into a visual information hierarchy bootstrapped by the DOM. Then, we assigned each element in the hierarchy one of thirty distinct labels describing its semantic properties. These labels were chosen in the spirit of the semantic tags included in HTML 5, comprising concepts like page, text, image, header, navigation, container, subheading, link, hero image, and logo. In the induction, we use the type system to prevent the "page" label from being merged with any other labels.

Geometric Models

We also constructed collections of geometric models for several different classes of objects: alien spaceships, Japanese castles, sakura trees, and Seussian architecture. Each class is built with a collection of modular 3D components, which comprise the labels in our framework [32]. These components are assembled into a scene graph, which imposes a tree topology over them, specifying parent/child relationships and relative transformations between nodes. In these examples, we employ the type system to disallow merges between components with differing labels, which helps preserve geometric semantics.

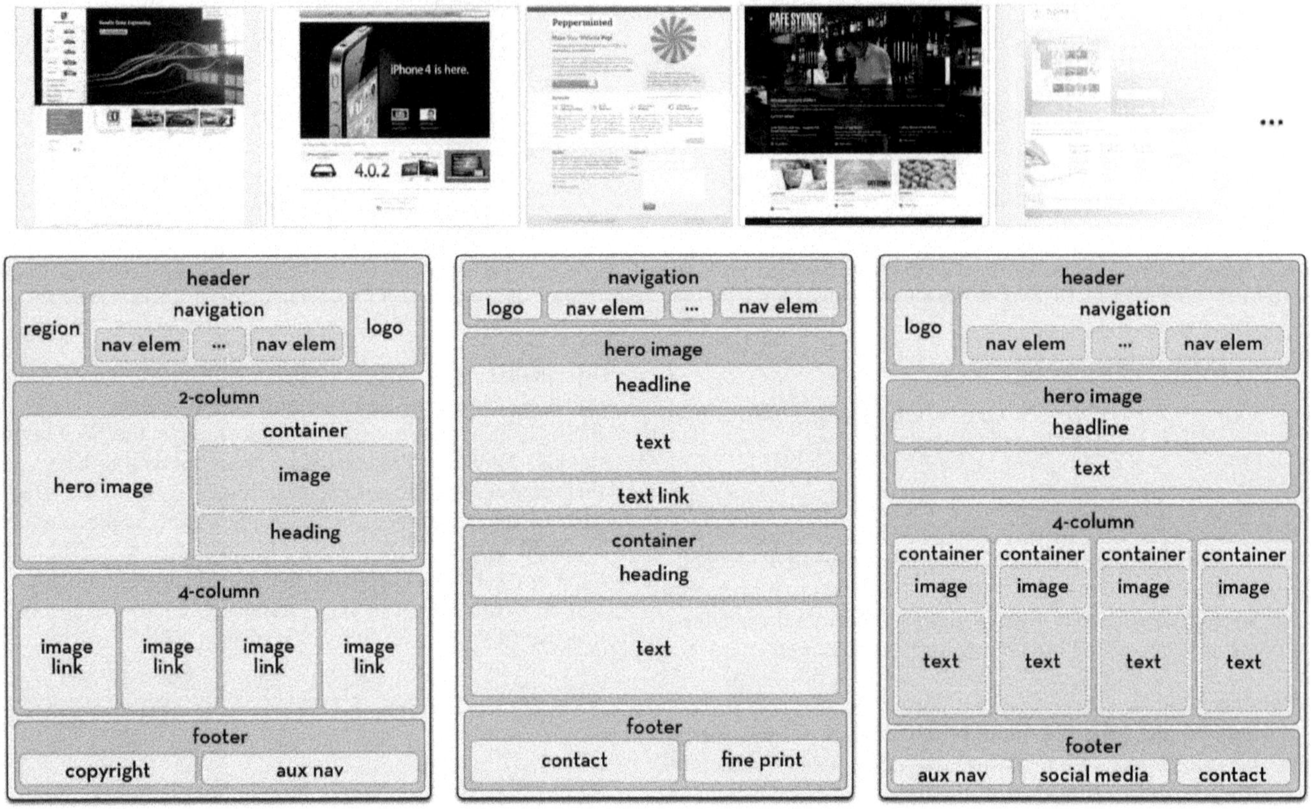

Figure 3. (top) A small sampling of the Web pages in our corpus. (bottom) Three random derivations from the grammar induced over that corpus.

RESULTS

Figure 2 illustrates the algorithm applied to a simple geometric block space, showing the initial examples, least-general conforming grammar, set of merges chosen in the search, the optimal grammar, and some random derivations sampled from the induced design pattern. In this example, the algorithm is able to generalize beyond the initial exemplar set in a sensible way.

The last column in the figure shows the *most-general conforming grammar* (MGCG) over the exemplars. This grammar provides a useful benchmark by which to judge the quality of the induction. The MGCG is obtained in the limit of the merging process, when all type-compatible symbols have been merged. Accordingly, the MGCG's description length is small and its generalization capacity is large, but the likelihood of the exemplar set is low. In essence, the MGCG makes a Markov assumption of stationarity that is not well-founded in design domains. In fact, the MGCG is precisely the grammar that is generated by model synthesis techniques that are popular in visual computing applications today [28, 6].

By varying the parameter λ in the grammar prior, we can smoothly interpolate along the space of grammars between the LGCG and the MGCG. Good design patterns will naturally fall somewhere in the middle of these two extremes. Table 1 gives statistics for the grammars induced in this paper, including the description length, likelihood of the exemplar set under the grammar, and cumulative probability of the two-hundred most likely designs generated by the grammar. This latter quantity is useful as a measure of the capacity of the grammar to generalize beyond the set of exemplars on which it was trained.

Figure 4 shows typical samples from the MGCG and the optimal grammar induced from a set of spaceship models. Models produced from the MGCG resemble the exemplar models only locally; conversely, the models synthesized with our technique exhibit similar global structure. Figure 5 shows fifty distinct random samples from a design pattern induced from six Japanese castle models; Figure 6 shows fifty distinct random samples from a design pattern induced from eight different sakura tree models.

Figure 7 shows modes from the distribution defined by the grammar of Seussian architecture, along with their probabilities. While the majority of the produced designs are plausible, these samples also highlight some of the limitations of our framework (highlighted in red). Because we induce context-free grammars, it is not possible for these design patterns to reliably learn high-level semantic constraints like "every building must have at least one door." Similarly, since our models are specified as hierarchies, relationships between subtrees which are very far apart in the derivation are difficult to capture: thus, some models have stairways that are not connected to the ground.

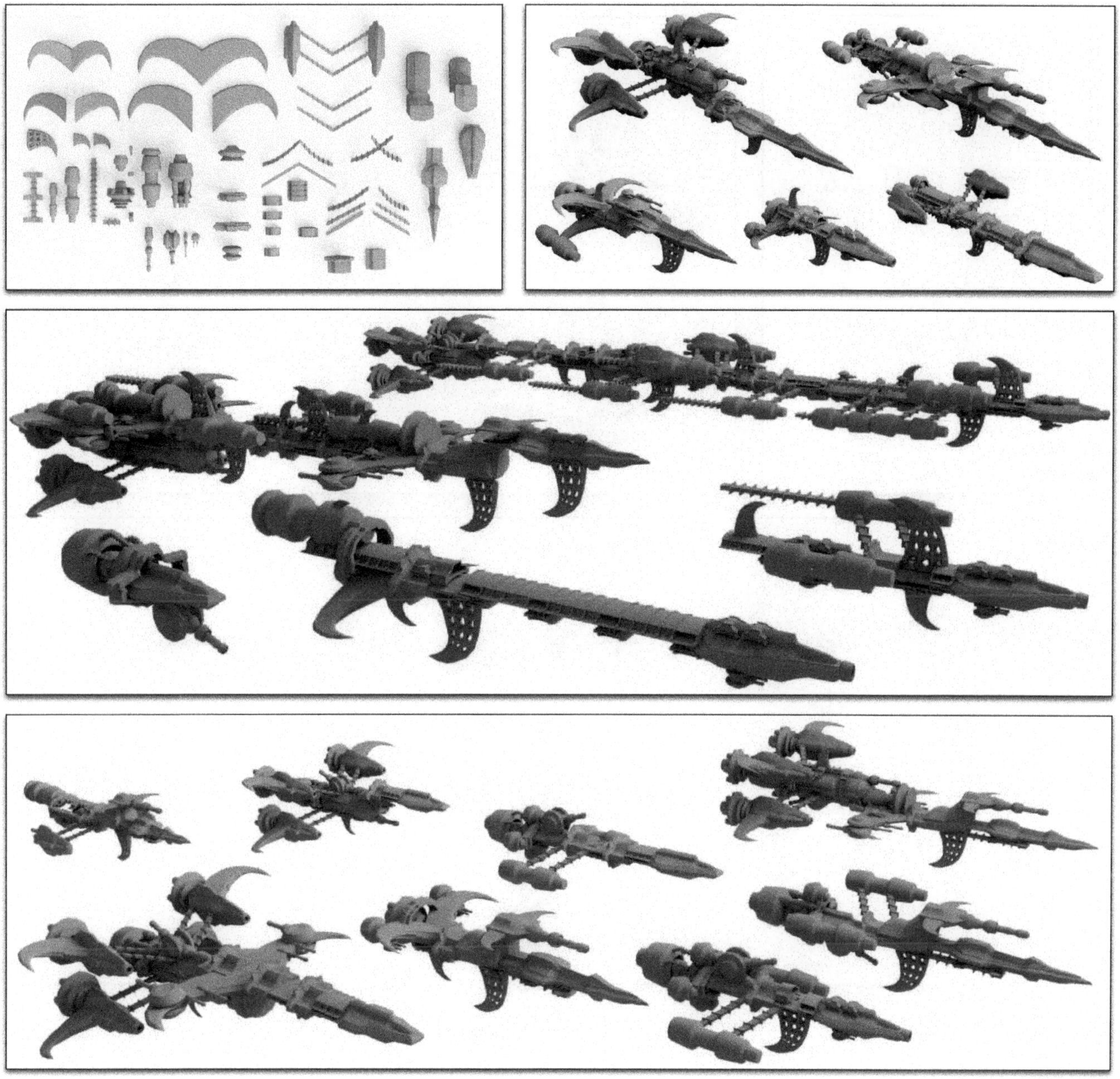

Figure 4. Spaceships. (top left) The set of components. (top right) The exemplars. (mid) Random samples from the MGCG: observe how these designs resemble the exemplars only locally. (bottom) Random samples from the induced design pattern: note the more plausible global structure.

We can also gain insight about the patterns induced by our technique by inspecting the grammar itself. For instance, when we examine the grammar we induce over Web pages, we see one rule that differentiates between two classes of designs. Each consists of a header and a common center structure comprising either two or four columns; one class has a hero image, while the other does not. Figure 3 shows a small portion of our page corpus, as well as a few random derivations from the learned model of page structures.

User Study

To assess how effectively the presented technique is able to generalize beyond the set of exemplars, we conducted a cognitive evaluation on Amazon's Mechanical Turk for three of the geometric domains. In each experiment, we sampled a collection of two-hundred designs from our induced grammars and the MGCGs. One-hundred test subjects were then shown the set of exemplar designs and a single sampled design below, and asked to answer the question "How similar in style is this design to the ones above?" on a four-point Likert scale ranging from "not at all similar" to "very similar." This process was repeated until each participant had rated twenty random designs. Responses were normalized to $[0, 1]$.

Table 2 shows the results from this study. We see higher average ratings for the designs sampled from our learned grammars by proportions of between 7% and 21%, all with $p < 0.001$ two-tailed using a Mann-Whitney-Wilcoxon test.

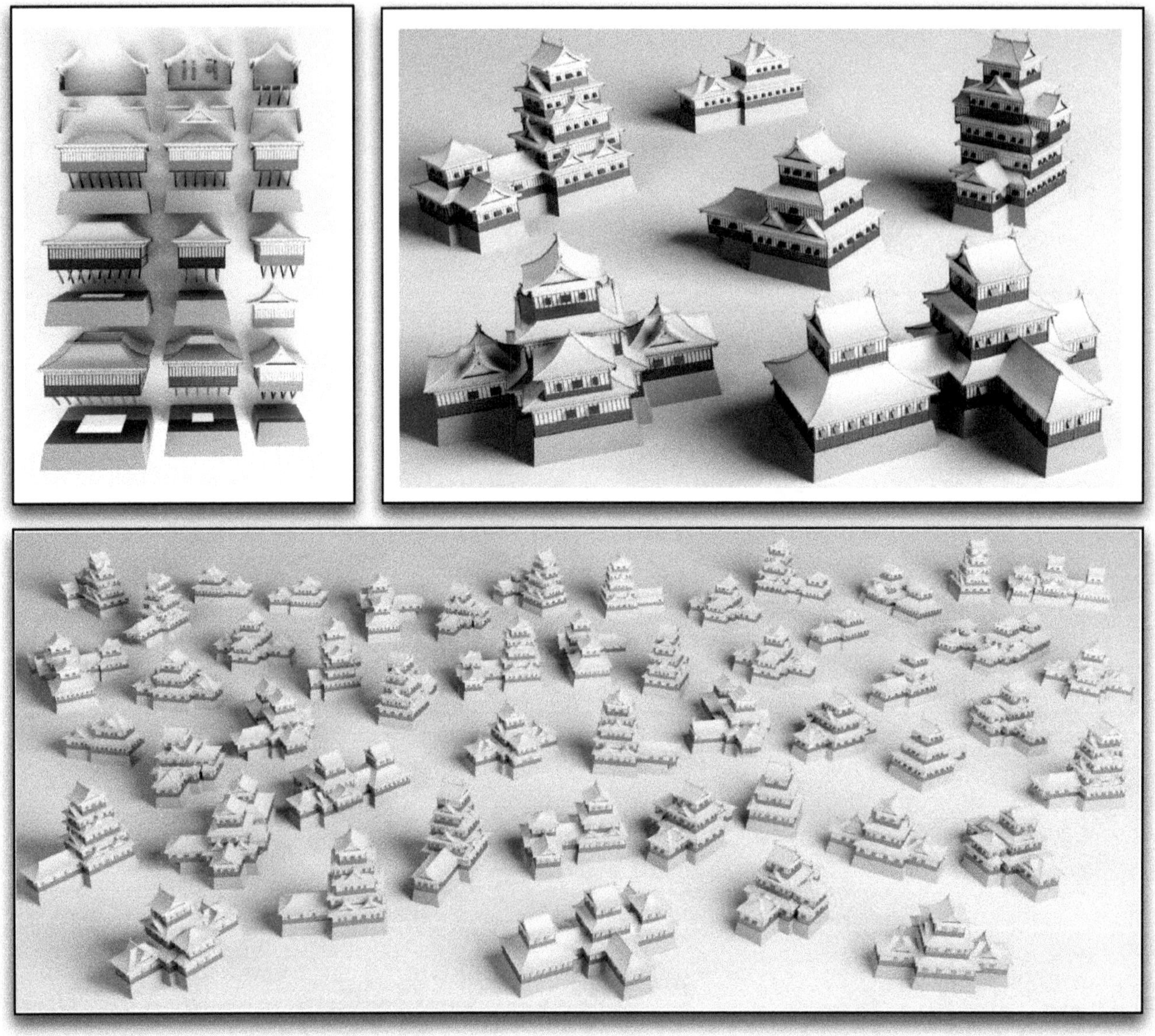

Figure 5. Japanese castles. (top left) The set of components. (top right) The exemplar designs. (bottom) Fifty distinct random derivations from the induced design pattern.

Although this is only a preliminary validation of our approach, this study seems to indicate that the grammars induced by our technique are better predictors of stylistic similarity than existing model synthesis methods.

DISCUSSION AND FUTURE WORK

Although the method we describe in this paper is just a first step towards learning design patterns from data in a principled way, it raises several interesting avenues for future work. Inducing patterns for other design domains is one obvious next step: even for classes of data that lack explicit hierarchical structure, it may be possible to infer hierarchies as part of the learning process [36]. Similarly, extending the induction to scale efficiently to training sets of thousands or millions of examples is another important direction for future research [40]: imagine learning a generative model of page designs that is trained over the entire Web.

	MGCG	Bayes-optimal	U
Seuss	.69	.76	15288
Sakura	.54	.75	8990
Spaceship	.58	.67	14777

Table 2. Average ratings for the three domains in our user study, along with the Mann-Whitney U value.

Data-Driven Design Tools

Another area ripe for further investigation is leveraging the induced patterns to build better tools and interaction mechanisms for content producers and designers. We hope that general, principled techniques for learning design patterns will reinvigorate the study of data-driven design in HCI. A few directions seem particularly promising.

Figure 6. Sakura trees. (top left) The set of components. (top right) The exemplar designs. (bottom) Fifty distinct random derivations from the induced design pattern.

For one, generative models like the ones learned in this paper provide a simple algorithmic mechanism for producing design alternatives. Given a small set of representative examples, techniques like grammar induction can be used to quickly and easily generate a diverse selection of new designs that are stylistically similar—but not identical—to the exemplars. Furthermore, by varying the weighting parameter λ in the induction process, the degree to which the grammar generalizes can be controlled. In this manner, it seems likely that a whole host of tools for automatically populating scenes, galleries, and virtual environments with content could make use of design pattern learning.

In addition, it has been well established that considering alternatives in the design process itself facilitates discussion, improves the rate of convergence, and increases the quality of productions [43, 18, 11]. One can imagine a workflow à la active learning in which patterns are induced in the background during design and sampled to suggest new constructions which are then assimilated by users in turn.

Perhaps most intriguing is the potential for exploiting the rich mathematical structure of generative probabilistic models in tool-building. In particular, it seems likely that many common design tasks can be formulated as probabilistic inference problems over a particular design pattern, and solved with Monte Carlo methods [42, 45]. For instance, we can write down a smooth function that scores page designs based on how closely they conform to a particular specification, and perform MAP estimation via MCMC to find a page from our learned Web grammar that has a four-column layout, a single navigation bar with four navigation elements, a header, and a hero image (see inset).

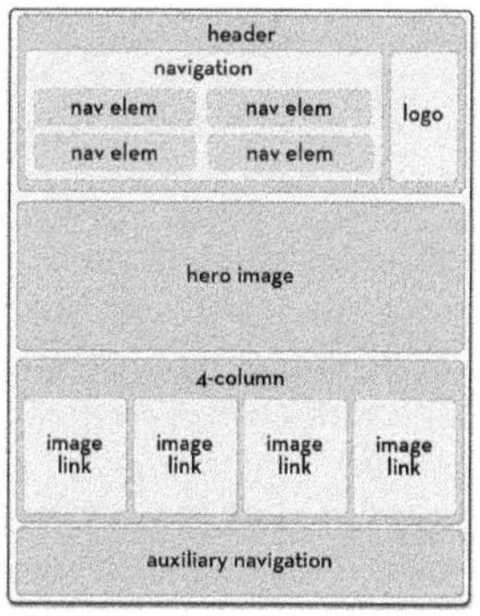

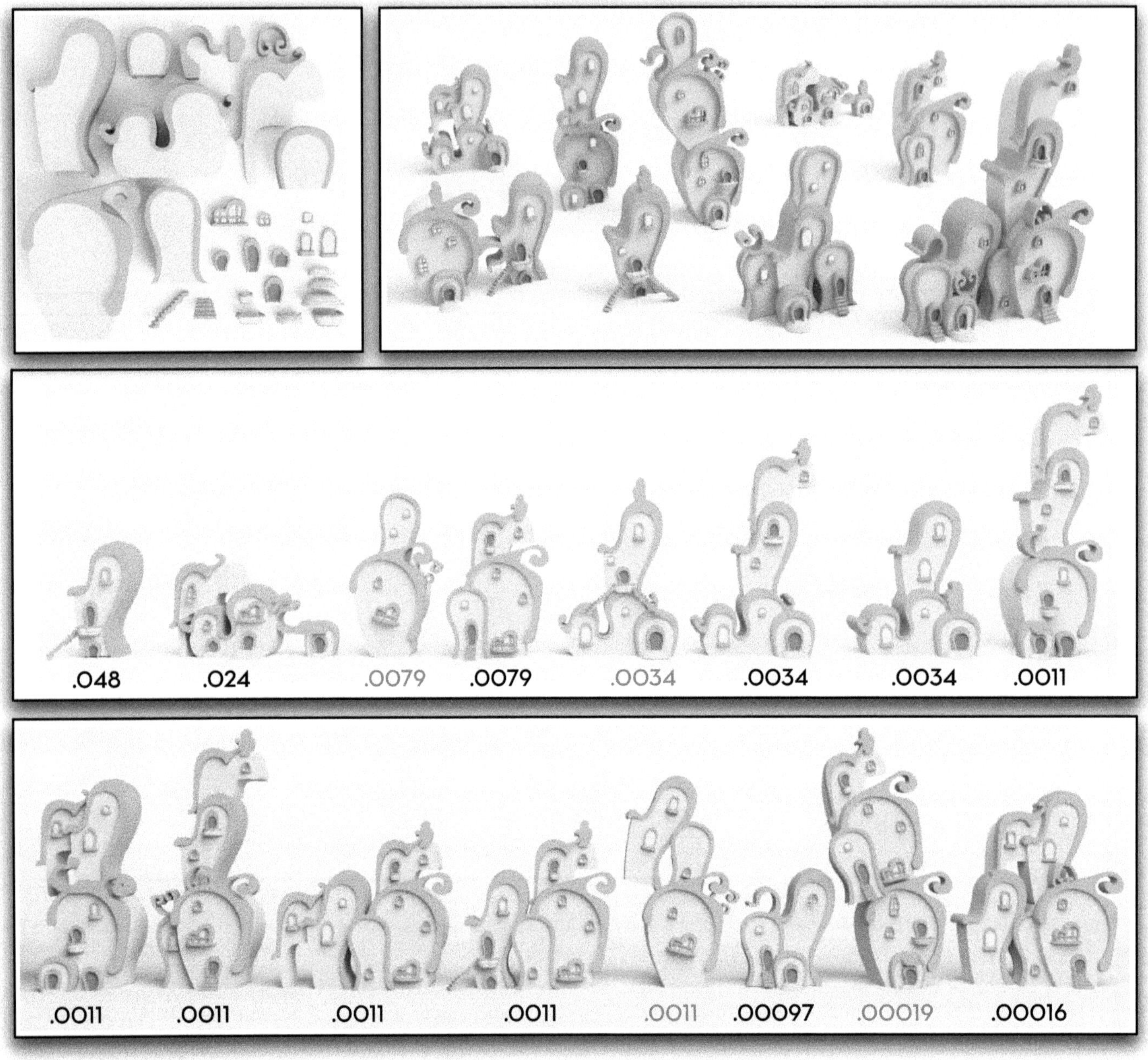

Figure 7. Seussian architecture. (top left) The set of components. (top right) The exemplar designs. (bottom) Modes from the distribution defined by the induced grammar, along with their probabilities. Models with questionable structure are highlighted in red.

New Computational Models

One final direction for investigation is learning more powerful computational models for design. Although stochastic context-free grammars provide a useful and compact generative representation, they are subject to a number of limitations which have led content creators to seek out more powerful graphical models [30]. For one, SCFGs automatically assign higher probabilities to shorter derivations, an assumption well-founded neither in natural language nor design, where model size typically peaks at some intermediate length. For another, the independence assumptions inherent in SCFGs prevent them from accurately representing models which have more general graph (rather than tree) structure, precluding them from capturing symmetries or other distant relationships between disjoint subtrees in a derivation. Similarly, CFGs are fundamentally discrete representations, and cannot easily encode continuous variability.

Recent work in probabilistic program induction suggests ways to overcome some of these limitations [20]: although the induction problem is more difficult with less structure *a priori*, universal probabilistic programming languages like Church [17] are capable of encoding any computable function.

ACKNOWLEDGMENTS

We thank Chris Platz for designing, building, and texturing all the 3D models used in this paper; Yu Lou for his work building an early version of our codebase; Tony Kaap for his invaluable Maya support; Haden Lee for his work on the Web examples; and Scott Klemmer—along with several members of the Stanford Graphics Laboratory—for providing valuable feedback on this research. This material is based upon work supported by the National Science Foundation under Grant No. 0846167, and a Google PhD Fellowship.

REFERENCES

1. Agarwal, M., and Cagan, J. A blend of different tastes: the language of coffee makers. *Environment and Planning B: Planning and Design 25*, 2 (1998), 205–226.
2. Aho, A. V., and Ullman, J. D. *The theory of parsing, translation, and compiling*. Prentice-Hall, 1972.
3. Alexander, C. *The Timeless Way of Building*. Oxford University Press, 1979.
4. Andrieu, C., de Freitas, N., Doucet, A., and Jordan, M. I. An introduction to MCMC for machine learning. *Machine Learning 50*, 1 (2003), 5–43.
5. Baker, J. K. Trainable grammars for speech recognition. In *Speech Communications for the 97th Meeting of the Acoustical Society of America.*, ASA (June 1979), 31–35.
6. Bokeloh, M., Wand, M., and Seidel, H.-P. A connection between partial symmetry and inverse procedural modeling. In *Proc. SIGGRAPH*, ACM (2010).
7. Borchers, J. *A Pattern Approach to Interaction Design*. John Wiley & Sons, 2001.
8. Buelinckx, H. Wren's language of City church designs: a formal generative classification. *Environment and Planning B: Planning and Design 20*, 6 (1993), 645–676.
9. Conway, A. Page grammars and page parsing: a syntactic approach to document layout recognition. In *Proc. ICDAR* (1993).
10. de la Higuera, C. *Grammatical inference: learning automata and grammars*. Cambridge University Press, 2010.
11. Dow, S. P., Glassco, A., Kass, J., Schwarz, M., Schwartz, D. L., and Klemmer, S. R. Parallel prototyping leads to better design results, more divergence, and increased self-efficacy. *ACM Trans. Comput.-Hum. Interact. 17*, 4 (2010), 18:1–18:24.
12. Duarte, J. P., Rocha, J. M., and Soares, G. D. Unveiling the structure of the Marrakech Medina: A shape grammar and an interpreter for generating urban form. *Artificial Intelligence for Engineering Design, Analysis and Manufacturing 21*, 4 (2007), 317–349.
13. Duyne, D. K. V., Landay, J., and Hong, J. I. *The Design of Sites*. Addison-Wesley, 2002.
14. Gamma, E., Helm, R., Johnson, R., and Vlissides, J. *Design Patterns: Elements of Reusable Object-Oriented Software*. Addison-Wesley, 1995.
15. Gold, E. M. Language identification in the limit. *Information and Control 10*, 5 (1967), 447–474.
16. Gold, E. M. Complexity of automaton identification from given data. *Information and Control 37*, 3 (1978), 302 – 320.
17. Goodman, N. D., Mansinghka, V. K., Roy, D. M., Bonawitz, K., and Tenenbaum, J. B. Church: A language for generative models. In *Proc. UAI* (2008), 220–229.
18. Hartmann, B., Yu, L., Allison, A., Yang, Y., and Klemmer, S. R. Design as exploration: creating interface alternatives through parallel authoring and runtime tuning. In *Proc. UIST*, ACM (2008), 91–100.
19. Horning, J. J. *A study of grammatical inference*. PhD thesis, Stanford University, Stanford, CA, USA, 1969.
20. Hwang, I., Stuhlmüller, A., and Goodman, N. D. Inducing probabilistic programs by Bayesian program merging. *CoRR abs/1110.5667* (2011).
21. Jacobs, C., Li, W., and Salesin, D. H. Adaptive document layout via manifold content. In *Workshop on Web Document Analysis* (2003).
22. Klein, D., and Manning, C. D. A generative constituent-context model for improved grammar induction. In *Proc. ACL* (2002), 128–135.
23. Klein, D., and Manning, C. D. Corpus-based induction of syntactic structure: models of dependency and constituency. In *Proc. ACL* (2004), 478–487.
24. Knight, T. W. The generation of Hepplewhite-style chair-back designs. *Environment and Planning B: Planning and Design 7*, 2 (1980), 227–238.
25. Kumar, R., Talton, J. O., Ahmad, S., and Klemmer, S. R. Bricolage: Example-based retargeting for web design. In *Proc. CHI*, ACM (2011).
26. MacKay, D. J. C. *Information Theory, Inference, and Learning Algorithms*. Cambridge University Press, 2003.
27. Manning, C., and Schutze, H. *Foundations of Statistical Natural Language Processing*. MIT Press, 1999.
28. Merrell, P. Example-based model synthesis. In *Proc. I3D*, ACM (2007), 105–112.
29. Müller, P., Wonka, P., Haegler, S., Ulmer, A., and Van Gool, L. Procedural modeling of buildings. In *Proc. SIGGRAPH*, ACM (2006), 614–623.
30. Měch, R., and Prusinkiewicz, P. Visual models of plants interacting with their environment. In *Proc. SIGGRAPH*, ACM (1996), 397–410.
31. Parish, Y. I. H., and Müller, P. Procedural modeling of cities. In *Proc. SIGGRAPH*, ACM (2001), 301–308.
32. Perry, L. Modular level and component design. *Game Developer Magazine* (2002).
33. Prusinkiewicz, P., and Lindenmayer, A. *The algorithmic beauty of plants*. Springer-Verlag New York, Inc., 1990.
34. Pugliese, M. J., and Cagan, J. Capturing a rebel: modeling the Harley-Davidson brand through a motorcycle shape grammar. *Research in Engineering Design 13* (2002), 139–156.
35. Shuey, D., Bailey, D., and Morrissey, T. P. PHIGS: a standard, dynamic, interactive graphics interface. *IEEE Comput. Graph. Appl. 6*, 9 (Aug 1986), 50–57.
36. Socher, R., Manning, C., and Ng, A. Learning continuous phrase representations and syntactic parsing with recursive neural networks. In *NIPS Workshop on Deep Learning and Unsupervised Feature Learning* (2010).
37. Solomonoff, R. J. A formal theory of inductive inference. *Information and Control 7* (1964).
38. Stava, O., Beneš, B., Měch, R., Aliaga, D., and Kristof, P. Inverse procedural modeling by automatic generation of L-systems. *Computer Graphics Forum 29*, 2 (2010).
39. Stiny, G., and Mitchell, W. J. The palladian grammar. *Environment and Planning B: Planning and Design 5*, 1 (1978), 5–18.
40. Stolcke, A. *Bayesian Learning of Probabilistic Language Models*. PhD thesis, University of California at Berkeley, 1994.
41. Stolcke, A., and Omohundro, S. M. Inducing probabilistic grammars by Bayesian model merging. In *Proc. International Colloquium on Grammatical Inference and Applications* (1994), 106–118.
42. Talton, J., Lou, Y., Lesser, S., Duke, J., Měch, R., and Koltun, V. Metropolis procedural modeling. *ACM Trans. Graphics 30*, 2 (2010).
43. Tohidi, M., Buxton, W., Baecker, R., and Sellen, A. Getting the right design and the design right. In *Proc. CHI*, ACM (2006), 1243–1252.
44. Weitzman, L., and Wittenburg, K. Relational grammars for interactive design. In *IEEE Workshop on Visual Languages* (1993), 4–11.
45. Yeh, Y.-T., Yang, L., Watson, M., Goodman, N., and Hanrahan, P. Synthesizing open worlds with constraints using locally annealed reversible jump MCMC. In *Proc. SIGGRAPH* (2012).

Adding Structured Data in Unstructured Web Chat Conversation

Min Wu, Arin Bhowmick, Joseph H. Goldberg
Oracle Corporation
500 Oracle Parkway, Redwood Shores, CA 94065
{min.wu, arin.bhowmick, joe.goldberg}@oracle.com

ABSTRACT
Web chat is becoming the primary customer contact channel in customer relationship management (CRM), and Question/Answer/Lookup (QAL) is the dominant communication pattern in CRM agent-to-customer chat. Text-based web chat for QAL has two main usability problems. Chat transcripts between agents and customers are not tightly integrated into agent-side applications, requiring customer service agents to re-enter customer typed data. Also, sensitive information posted in chat sessions in plain text raises security concerns. The addition of web form widgets to web chat not only solves both of these problems but also adds new usability benefits to QAL. Forms can be defined beforehand or, more flexibly, dynamically composed. Two preliminary user studies were conducted. An agent-side study showed that adding inline forms to web chat decreased overall QAL completion time by 47 percent and increased QAL accuracy by removing all potential human errors. A customer-side study showed that web chat with inline forms is intuitive to customers.

Author Keywords
Web Chat; CRM; Human Performance

ACM Classification Keywords
H.5.2 [Graphical user interfaces (GUI)]: User Interfaces

INTRODUCTION
Web-based live chat, a standard communication channel in social network and collaboration, is becoming the primary customer contact channel for companies, especially in sales and customer service. Fifty-eight percent of US consumers have interacted with an e-retailer using web chat [5]. A well-implemented chat strategy can transform a business's ability to drive sales, increase productivity, achieve operational savings, and deliver an excellent customer experience. Moreover, web chat is a jumping-off point for advanced web collaboration (such as co-browsing and remote control) between agents and customers to further improve the support metrics (such as first-contact resolution, average talk time, and incident handling time).

UIST '12, October 7–10, 2012, Cambridge, Massachusetts, USA.
Copyright 2012 ACM 978-1-4503-1580-7/12/10...$15.00.

Question/Answer/Lookup (QAL) is the dominant communication pattern in the agent-to-customer chat in customer relationship management (CRM). In the question phase, an agent asks a customer a question (for example, "May I have your name and your company's name?"); in the answer phase, the customer replies to the agent (for example, "My name is Leslie Hahn, and my company's name is Kingos."); and in the lookup stage, the agent uses the submitted answer in the chat session to look up information (for example, to find the corresponding customer record) or to perform other actions (for example, to create a new customer record if the customer is not already in the database).

Two main usability problems arise from the QAL pattern in web chat. First, because chat transcripts (the text content in the chat session) are unstructured and not integrated into other system applications, in order to use the data typed by a customer, copy-and-paste functionality or duplicated typing across different user interfaces is required. For example, when identifying a customer, an agent asks for the customer's full name and company name and has to *copy and paste* the customer's response from the chat window to the customer profile management application. Sometimes, the free-form chat response from a customer has to be mentally processed by an agent and then confirmed with the customer. As another example, if a customer types that her company should be available "next Friday" for an onsite visit, in order to follow the grammatical rules specified by the customer service policy, an agent has to figure out the exact date, confirm it with the customer, and enter it into the company's calendar to create an event. Unstructured chat data that requires the data re-entry among different interfaces makes web chat inefficient and error-prone.

The second usability problem pertains to security and privacy concerns because chat transcripts are in plain text. Even though the security of chat sessions is guaranteed by HTTPS, concerns arise when customers have to enter sensitive information such as their PINs or the last four digits of their social security numbers in plain text in order to verify their identities [6, 11].

In order to solve these two usability problems, we propose the addition of web form widgets to web chat conversation, as shown in Figure 1. Instead of asking questions in free-form text, an agent sends a customer a web form as a chat messages. The customer then completes the form in the chat

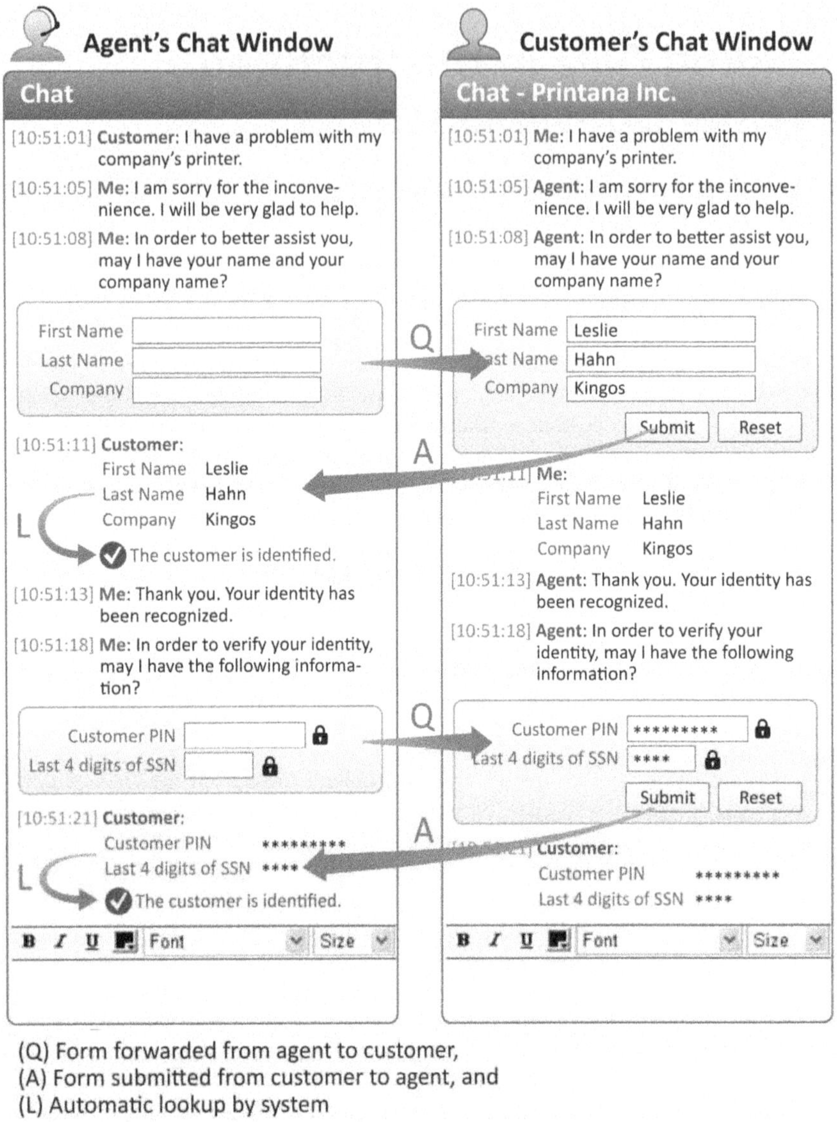

Figure 1: Web chat with inline form for QAL

window. Clicking the Submit button in the form sends the completed data from the customer to the agent as another chat message. Inline forms structure customer input data so that it can be interpreted and used by system applications automatically. In Figure 1, the system automatically identifies and verifies the customer after form submissions. Agents do not need to manually re-enter or copy and paste customer data across different interfaces.

We make two main contributions with this paper. First, we design and develop web chat with inline forms to facilitate the data transfer between two parties during QAL. Form can be inserted either by selecting pre-defined forms or, more flexibly, by dynamically building a form using existing form widgets in other interfaces. Our chat application creates a single complete view of the chat conversation, supports efficient data input and automatic data processing, and can be extended as a collaboration tool that supports fine-grained joint form filling and control sharing.

Second, we conduct two preliminary user studies in the customer service context to show that compared with text-only communication, chat with inline forms improved the QAL efficiency by 47 percent and removed all potential human errors from the agent side. Additionally, we show that customers find chat with inline forms to be an intuitive means of communication when responding to agent questions.

RELATED WORK

Different approaches have been taken in order to address the two usability problems presented in this paper.

Pre-Chat Survey

Pre-chat surveys [1] with sets of questions presented to customers before chats start have been used to collect necessary information to identify customers and their problems. However, pre-chat surveys are known to create a barrier between agents and customers, potentially causing up to 39 percent of customers to abandon the chats at that point [1, 14]. Asking personal information before customers actually use the online service is expected to be the main reason that causes the high abandonment rate [3]. Second, these surveys cannot be used during chat sessions. Third, the questions covered by pre-chat surveys have to be defined beforehand so that when agents want to ask questions that are not covered by the pre-chat survey, they have to use text chat.

Sensitive Information Submission

To address security concerns from customers, some websites advise customers not to enter personal or sensitive information into web chat [13]. Instead, customers are asked to use pre-chat surveys or are redirected to separate SSL-protected web pages. Other websites provide a web chat service only to authenticated customers but not to the general public [10], which limits the usage of web chat.

LivePerson uses pattern matching to mask certain types of sensitive information (for example, US Social Security Numbers and credit card numbers) in chat transcript display and storage [8]. However, masking does not work for sensitive information that lacks a specific pattern, such as account IDs and passwords.

Data Integration from Chat

As a text-based communication channel, chat generally has its content opaque to the underlying computer system. Facilitating machines to understand chat content would help data integration from chat to other applications and thus achieve software or web automation triggered from chat channels.

Natural language processing (NLP) can help systems understand live chat content, but is currently used only for certain data types in certain tasks, such as an NLP tool that can schedule meetings during a chat session by determining meeting participants and available times from unformatted chat content [18]. A more generic approach is needed to communicate structured data among chatters.

The semistructured messages project [9] used different message templates to create collaboration objects such as calendar events and group tasks. It concentrated on the backend automation of structured messages.

Collaborative data objects (CDOs) can be added into chat sessions to enhance collaboration [16]. CDOs are created, viewed, and edited by launching a separate form-based dialog window from the chat window, which, however, fragments the chat conversation and requires users to switch windows during chat. Moreover, the data communication in the separate dialog window is lost from the chat transcript, causing an incomplete chat conversation. Third, the supported types of CDOs have to be defined beforehand, causing the same issue as pre-chat survey.

PlayByPlay (PBP) is a web collaboration tool that provides two mechanisms for data communication through the chat channel: regular text messages and clips of web pages [15]. Its clip feature supports joint form filling by allowing two chat parties to share web forms, although the interactive clips are displayed in a separate browser window rather within the chat transcript. The clip feature is useful in personal collaboration when both parties can see and access the same form, but could be problematic in the CRM context, where the forms in the agent's console should not be shared with customers. While the features of PBP could be used to approximate some of the features of our solution, PBP in general would be overly complex for the QAL communication pattern.

WEB CHAT WITH INLINE FORMS

Web forms can structure the chat data transmitted in the QAL pattern, making it directly available to other applications.

Form as Chat Messages

In the question phase, instead of typing a question in plain text, an agent forwards a form to a customer. The form is posted as a chat message into the chat transcript, ready for the customer to complete. In the answer phase, the customer completes the form that appears in the chat transcript and clicks the Submit button. The submission generates a new chat message with a list of read-only name-value pairs from the customer input data. Because form data is structured, the lookup phase can be automated with the lookup results appended at the end of the form submission message in the agent-side chat transcript.

Treating form forwarding and form submission as separate chat messages guarantees a single complete view of the chat session for both agents and customers. Form interaction is no longer in a separate window and won't get lost from the conversation archive. Moreover, because form submission happens in the chat transcript area instead of the chat input area, customers can send other text messages (such as clarification requests) while they are facing the form to complete.

Usability Enhancement in CRM Chat

In addition to automating the lookup phase without requiring agents to manually "move" data between the chat window and other applications, web forms in chat enhance the user experience of the QAL pattern in CRM chat by exploiting the existing form features.

First, web forms can mask sensitive data submission. Therefore, the same sense of security gained from web form submission can be achieved during a chat session. The backend application that uses customer's sensitive data can be automatically launched without revealing data to the agent, as shown in the verification flow in Figure 1.

Second, existing form widgets, such as a date/time picker, choice list, or input with auto-complete, can be leveraged to improve the input efficiency at the customer side. For example, instead of typing in a long string of the model number of her problematic printer, a customer can choose the model from a choice list populated by the model numbers from all the printers that her company has bought. Moreover, customers need to type in only the required values (for example, "John Smith") without the extra typing to describe what the values are about (for example, "my name is John Smith").

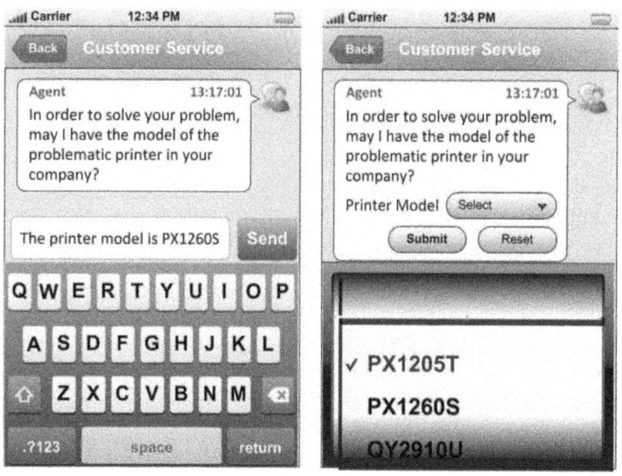

Figure 2: Input efficiency improvement in smartphones

Such input efficiency improvement can be significant to the customers who are using mobile devices to chat because typing in mobile devices is slow and unwieldy. As shown in Figure 2, picking a value from a choice list (right) is much easier and faster than typing in text (left). Auto-complete can be added to further improve the efficiency when the choice list is long. Additionally, by applying new input types from HTML 5 into the form, the soft keyboard in the mobile device can be automatically adjusted based on the focused input field.

Third, data validation supported by forms can automatically detect certain types of input errors from customers and thus prevent invalid data from being submitted, which is impossible with text-based chat. Form-based data validation not only reduces network traffic, but also relieves agents from manually validating customer data.

Form Creation

We propose two mechanisms to create forms and insert them into chat.

Predefined Forms

CRM agents can use predefined forms that are designed beforehand from a list of customer's frequently asked questions. Each form is for a single question. At the front end, appropriate form widgets are chosen for efficient input. Input masking for sensitive data and data validation are added if necessary. At the back end, the system flow is defined to automatically process the customer's form submission.

Those predefined forms can be inserted into the chat input area either by clicking an Insert button or, more efficiently, by typing a special prompt in the chat input area (Figure 3). Moreover, when agents see a predefined form in the agent's console, they can click the associated button to push the form into the chat input area without selecting it from the predefined form list. If agents change their mind, they can close the form to undo the insertion. Eventually, pressing the ENTER key posts the form into the chat transcript.

The list of predefined forms can be dynamic and context sensitive. For example, before a customer is identified, only the forms can be answered anonymously as well as the customer identification form are available, while all the customer-specific forms are hidden until the customer is identified. The predefined form list can thus serve as handy guidance for agents to follow when they are solving customer problems.

Dynamic Form Generation

Inserting predefined forms has its limitation in that all the forms have to be designed beforehand. We propose a more flexible approach to solve this limitation, where agents push input fields from other applications in the agent's console into the chat input area, as shown in Figure 4. Instead of sharing existing forms as PBP does [15], our solution dynamically builds a *new* form using the pushed input fields so that confidential information (for example, the customer value) that is contained in the form in the agent's console won't be exposed to the customer side.

Chat-aware inputs are the input fields from the agent's console that can be pushed into chat, each marked with a special icon. Clicking the icon pushes the input field along with its label into the chat input area. The pushed input field is then highlighted, indicating that the chat is expected to supply its value. In the chat input area, agents can edit the labels of pushed input fields in case the existing labels are not understood by customers. Agents can type help text before or after each pushed input field, and can undo the push by clicking the close icon associated with each field.

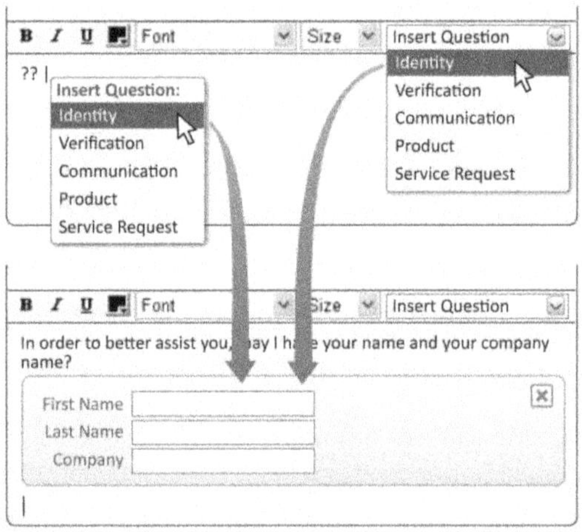

Figure 3: Form creation using predefined forms

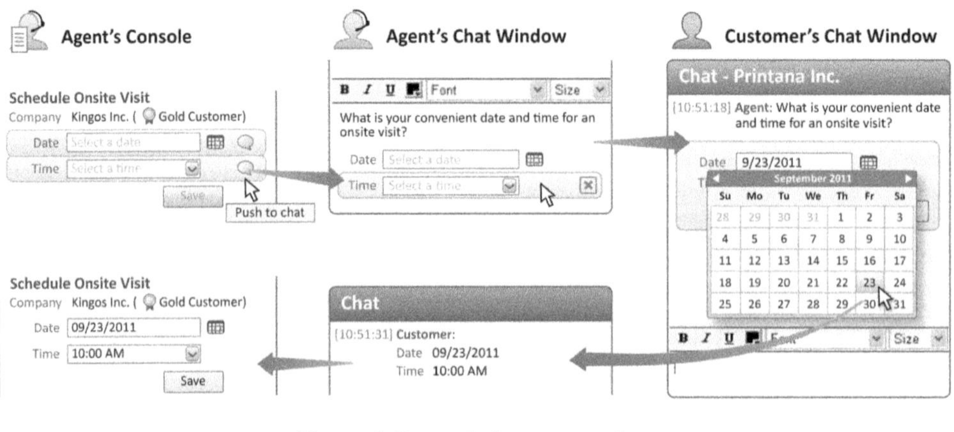

Figure 4: Dynamic form generation

When agents are satisfied with the dynamically composed form in the chat input area, they presses the ENTER key to post the form into the chat transcript. After the customer completes the form and submits the data, the submitted values are automatically populated into the corresponding input fields on the original form in the agent's console. No copy and paste or re-entry is necessary. Agents only need to click the action button on the agent's console to continue.

In the CRM context, dynamic form generation can be combined with predefined forms. Repetitively pushing certain input fields into chat suggests new pre-defined forms.

Web Chat with Inline Forms as Collaboration Tool

Web chat with inline forms can be extended as a collaboration tool for fine-grained joint form filling and control sharing without co-browsing [4], wherein users share their screens with or grant remote access to their computers to other users in real time.

Similar to PBP [15], our chat application can be placed in browser sidebars. With inline form enhancement, any form input field from any website is chat-aware and can be pushed into the chat sidebar so that web forms can be filled collaboratively.

In addition to form's input fields, other control widgets available in web interfaces can also be pushed into chat. Chat therefore becomes a novel lightweight control sharing tool that improves end-user productivity.

Consider the following scenarios. User A wants to open a document in an enterprise document sharing application, but the document is locked by User B. User A could ask User B to stop his current work, open the same application, go to the same section that she is already in, and unlock the specific document that she wants to open. However, with our solution, User A has a more efficient option by pushing the document entry and the Unlock button from the interface into the chat. User B can then click the Unlock button in the chat session to unlock the document. Chat, in this example, provides a shortcut to the exact control point for users to perform certain actions with their appropriate privileges. The fine-grained control sharing is more efficient and less error prone for mobile users because they do not have to navigate through multiple pages in their devices in order to perform certain actions. Instead, they can leverage the shortcuts to those actions in chat.

USER STUDY I: AGENT SIDE

In order to determine the degree to which chat with inline forms can improve the efficiency and accuracy of QAL at the agent side, we ran a controlled experiment.

Methodology

Tested Interfaces

Three chat interfaces were tested. Users either typed text (*Text*) or inserted one of the five predefined questions in the format of either plaintext (*Question*) or inline form (*Form*) into the chat input area. Then they pressed the ENTER key to post the text or the form into the chat transcript. The five predefined questions were specific for the five study tasks.

Tasks

Each 30-minute study session included five typical agent tasks focused on the QAL pattern, in which an agent asked some questions (Q) and used the submitted data to conduct lookup (L) either manually (using Text or Question) or automatically (using Form). The task selection was based on a year-long set of service and support department observational studies at more than 10 companies and a survey of 90 global call center agents. The tasks were:

- *Identification (ID):* An agent asked a customer her name and company name (Q) and then searched for the customer (L).
- *Verification (VE):* After the customer was identified, an agent asked for the customer's account ID and PIN as the security questions (Q), and then matched the answer against the system record (L).
- *Checking a service request status (SR):* An agent asked for the service request numbers and the associated asset numbers (Q), and then searched the service request (L).
- *Finding a solution for a technical problem (SL):* An agent asked for the machine model and the problem details (Q), and then searched for the solution (L).
- *Scheduling an onsite visit (OV):* An agent asked a customer for a convenient date for the onsite visit (Q), and then used the customer's suggested data to schedule the visit in the system calendar (L).

Study Implementation

A web-based chat prototype was built using jQuery, PHP, and MySQL. In order to insert forms in the chat input area, we customized CKEditor[1], a web-based rich text editor. The chat messages with their senders and their post timestamps were stored in a MySQL database on the server. The browser pulled new messages from the server every second and displayed these messages in the chat transcript.

The agent console contained a chat interface and a work area where the agent could search customers, service requests, and solutions, and schedule onsite visits. The customer side had only a chat interface in a browser.

Study Procedure

We hypothesized that the Form user interface (UI) was significantly faster than both the Question UI and the Text UI across all the five QAL tasks, and thus we measured the completion time of each task.

[1] http://ckeditor.com/

Participants were assigned the personas of customer service agents from Printana Inc, a fictitious printer company. They were asked to strictly follow a printed agent manual that described the steps and communication rules for each task. The experimenter acted as the customer, chatting in real time from a separate computer, using a script to insert appropriate messages into the chat with minimal latency. The customer always posted the same chat messages within each task:

- ID: The customer provided the correct identification information (name and company name) on the first time.
- VE/SR/SL: On the first response, the customer provided either an incorrect account ID, service request number, or printer model number, which led to verification failure or no matched result. When asked again, the customer provided the correct information.
- OV: The customer's first suggested date was unavailable. When the agent asked for another date, the alternative date was available. When the customer typed the dates in plaintext, a relative date was used (that is, "Let's say next Friday."). As one of the communication rules, the agent had to translate the relative date to the exact date and confirm it in the month-day-year format (that is, "Do you mean September 23, 2011?").

Task completion time was determined by the difference between the task start time when the experimenter clicked the Start button and the end time when the participant typed or posted an ending message into the chat transcript. Ending messages included "Thank you" after the customers were verified (ID and VE tasks), or the request status, solution, or schedule confirmation (SR, SL, and OV tasks).

Participants
Eighteen professional colleagues (nine males and nine females) with online chat experience participated in the study. Each had previously performed tasks similar to customer service agents in interacting synchronously with customers.

Experimental Design
A within-participant design was used. The three chat interfaces were exposed to participants in one of six possible orders (Text-Question-Form, Text-Form-Question, and so on). The three specific tasks (SR, SL, and OV) were sent to participants in one of three counterbalanced orders (SR-SL-OV, OV-SR-SL, SL-OV-SR). A total of 18 experimental conditions (six chat interface orders × three task orders) were presented across the participants. In each session, both ID and VE were done three time with all three chat interfaces (Text, Question, and Form), but SR, SL, and OV were done once, each with a different chat interface.

Results

Efficiency
Task completion times were analyzed statistically to determine the impact of each chat interface on each task.

A total of 162 observations were made in this study. Fifty-four observations were from ID and VE each because each of the 18 participants did these two tasks with all three chat interfaces. Eighteen observations were from SR, SL, and OV each because each participant did these three tasks only once. Three invalid observations were removed because three validation tasks failed when the participants passed the verification step and continued with the invalid security answers from the customer. As a result, 159 valid observations were available for statistical analysis.

Two-factor ANOVA on completion times considered both chat interface and task type as main effects. Significant differences among factor levels were explored using Tukey's pairwise comparisons (α=.05). The chat interface was quite significant ($F_{2,\ 144} = 43$, $P < 0.001$), with the Form UI resulting in the shortest completion time (mean=57 seconds), which was significantly faster than both the Question UI (88 seconds) and the Text UI (108 seconds). Figure 5 shows the mean and the standard deviation of the completion time of each task by each chat interface. The Form UI reduced the agent QAL time by 47 percent compared with the Text UI, and by 35 percent compared with the Question UI.

Accuracy
Three verification failures and two input errors were made using the Text or Question UI, and date confusion was also observed. However, no errors were made with the Form UI.

Three verification failures were observed when customer answers were incorrect (one with Text UI and two with Question UI) with no confirmation by the participants to make sure that customer security answers matched those in the system. Two data entry errors were made (both Text and Question UIs) by re-entering the customer name with a typo, and copying the wrong service request number from the chat transcript to the search interface. Four of 12 participants using the Text or Question UI confused in scheduling the onsite visit date from a relative date input. They interpreted

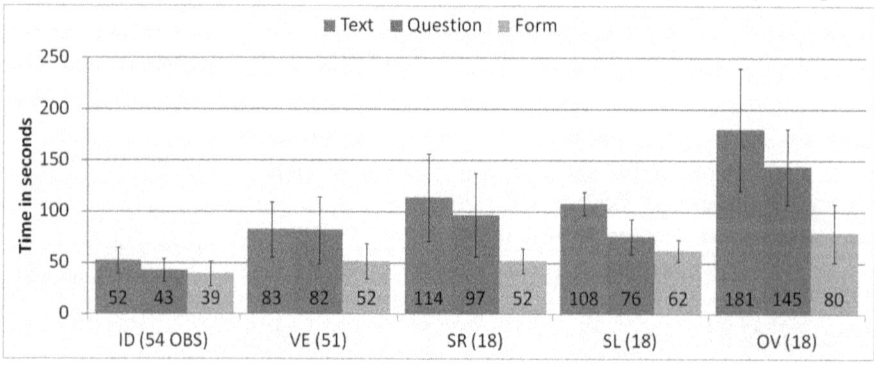

Figure 5: Task completion time with different chat UIs

"next Friday" to mean the Friday in the current week, which resulted in additional required confirmation time with the customer.

Discussion

Efficiency

The Form UI was most efficient across the tasks, because the submitted form data was already structured. The identification and verification processes were automatically loaded with customer data without the agent's involvement (ID and VE), and the agent was automatically notified regarding successful customer identification and verification. Customer data was populated from form to the agent's work area (SR, SL, and OV), and clicking an action button immediately searched for a service request or solution, or scheduled an onsite visit.

Extensive research on improving call center efficiency has been conducted [2, 12, 17]. A one-minute reduction per call is significant for call centers with at least 1 million calls each year [2]. An efficiency gain of 47 percent by chat agents in QAL is thus very significant in CRM.

Accuracy

The Form UI was error-free mainly because the lookup phase was automated. As a result, verification did not require agent involvement, customer's input was either automatically used by the system or directly populated into the agent's search interface, and the date picker used for date entry didn't require any additional date translation.

Customer service chat agents make errors, due to intense workloads, working multiple chat sessions in parallel [7]. This agent-side study showed that chat with inline forms minimizes the chances for potential errors, which should dramatically improve agent performance.

USER STUDY II: CUSTOMER SIDE

Unlike customer service agents who are oriented to maximizing efficiency, customers using web chat to obtain help are more concerned with learnability and satisfaction. A formative customer-side study was conducted to determine whether customers could understand and correctly use an inline form that has been posted within a chat transcript by agents.

Methodology

Two chat interfaces were tested: one where customers could use inline forms in the chat transcript (*Form*), and one without this support (*Text*). Participants, given the persona of an IT support specialist to solve a printer problem, initiated two chat requests to a customer service agent at Printana Inc. One request was to find a solution to a technical problem, and the other was to schedule an onsite visit (as for the SL and OV tasks in Study I). Participants had to first pass identification/verification steps, as well as their account IDs and customer PINs. The experimenter acted as the agent, chatting with the participants from a separate computer in real time.

Eight professional colleagues (five males and three females) with online chat experience participated in the study. The study design included four experimental conditions (two chat interface orders × two chat request orders), and two participants were assigned to each condition in a counterbalanced way. Each session lasted 30 minutes.

Results and Discussion

All participants found the Form UI to be intuitive; requested data was submitted to the agent without difficulty. Five participants preferred the Form UI. Four were more comfortable providing sensitive information because the secure form masked the account ID and the customer PIN, compared with the Text UI that exposed the sensitive information in plain text. Four felt the inline form provided more structured and well-defined guidance; e.g., they did not need to type the label for the provided data (for example, "First name is …"). Two participants felt the date picker was easy to use and that they wanted to have the same auto-suggestion support for all input fields whose values were hard to type. For example, after a customer is identified, the printer model input field should have a drop-down list with all the models that the customer had purchased.

However, two preferred the text chat over the chat with inline forms. They thought that forms in chat were too impersonal and made them think that they were talking to a "chat bot." Conversely, another mentioned that he did not care about impersonal chat as long as his issue was resolved. Sometimes, customers provided required information before the form was forwarded to them, causing agents to re-enter the data from the chat transcript into the search interface.

The inline form should be an add-on feature to the text chat. If an agent notices that certain customers do not like the inline form or is inappropriate, the agent does not have to use it and can stick with text chat. The customer-side user study has shown that chat with inline forms is intuitive to customers and that they can immediately use the forms without any difficulty or training.

CONCLUSION AND FUTURE WORK

We propose to embed inline forms into web chat so that the structured form data can be automatically interpreted and used by the system. Powered by inline forms, web chat is no longer a separate standalone tool, but can be presented as a tightly integrated input channel directly interfacing with the underlying applications. Data in the chat transcript does not have to be re-entered or copy-and-pasted into other interfaces. Moreover, chat with inline forms provides a sense of security for customers who need to share sensitive information. We showed that chat with inline forms can improve the experience of web chat for both agents and customers in CRM. The agent-side study showed that chat with inline forms dramatically improves the agent's efficiency and accuracy, while the customer-side study showed that chat with inline forms is intuitive and can be used without any difficulty or training. The next phase of the agent-side study will include customer service agents performing the tasks in their real work environments and locations.

Chat with inline forms can be extended from the CRM agent-customer environment to other collaboration environments, supporting joint form filling and control sharing. Future work will implement and evaluate a browser-based chat interface as a browser sidebar, as well as assess its security, trust, and cultural implications.

ACKNOWLEDGEMENTS

This research was funded by the Applications User Experience organization at Oracle. The authors would like to thank Sam Ting, Rami Musa, and Allison Farrell for their interaction and visual design contributions. The opinions expressed are solely the authors' and do not necessary reflect those of Oracle.

REFERENCES

1. Bold Software. Live Chat Performance Benchmarks. October 2009. http://www.boldchat.com/live_chat_software/files/Live_Chat_Performance_Benchmarks_Oct_2009_I.pdf.
2. Bond, C. Time Is Money: Impacts of Usability at a Call Center. *Ergonomics in Design: The Quarterly of Human Factors Applications 15*, 4 (2007), 17-22.
3. Chellappa, R and Sin, R. Personalization Versus Privacy: An Empirical Examination of the Online Consumer's Dilemma. *Information Technology and Management 6*, 2-3 (2005), 181-202.
4. eGain. Chat and Cobrowse. eGain Best Practice Series. 2011.
5. Enright, A. Live chat use is on the rise, survey says. May 10, 2011. http://www.internetretailer.com/2011/05/10/live-chat-use-rise-survey-says.
6. Flavián, C. and Guinalíu, M. Consumer trust, perceived security and privacy policy: Three basic elements of loyalty to a web site. *Industrial Management & Data Systems 106*, 5 (2006), 601-620.
7. Gliedman, C. The ROI of Interactive Chat. *Forrester Research* (2008). http://www.moxiesoft.com/uploadedFiles/tal_resources/ForrestWP_ROI_of_chat.pdf.
8. Live Person. Security Model Overview. January 2011. http://www.liveperson.com/sites/default/files/pdfs/LivePerson%20Security%20White%20Paper.pdf.
9. Malone, T., Grant, K., Lai, K.-Y., Rao, R., and Rosenbiltt, D. Semistructured Messages Are Surprisingly Useful for Computer-Supported Coordination. In *Proc. CSCW (1986)*, ACM Press (1986), 102-114.
10. Provide Support LLC. The Benefits of Live Chat for E-Commerce. http://www.providesupport.com/about-us/articles/benefits-live-chat-ecommerce.html.
11. Ray, S., Ow, T., and Kim, S. Security Assurance: How Online Service Providers Can Influence Security Control Perceptions and Gain Trust. *Decision Sciences 42*, 2 (2011), 391-412.
12. Sapounakis, E. Efficiency: The second essential of a customer centric business. *UX Magazine* (2011). http://uxmag.com/articles/efficiency.
13. Security4web. Instant Messaging and Chat Rooms: DO's and Don't's. http://www.security4web.org/page.php?id=25.
14. Tabibian L. Understanding Missed Chat Opportunities and How to Reduce Them. May 24, 2010. http://community.liveperson.com/docs/DOC-1242.
15. Wiltse, H. and Nichols, J. PlayByPlay: Collaborative Web Browsing for Desktop and Mobile Devices. In *Proc. CHI 2009*, ACM Press (2009), 1781-1790.
16. Winkowski, D. and Krutsch, M. Collaborative Data Objects Enhanced Chat in Support of Net-Centric Collaboration - Collaborative Technologies for Network-Centric Operations. In *13th ICCRTS: C2 for Complex Endeavors* (2008).
17. Zapata, C. Evaluating UX by Measuring Task Efficiency. *UX Magazine* (2011). http://uxmag.com/articles/evaluating-ux-by-measuring-task-efficiency.
18. Zurko, M. E. Instance Messaging Auto-Scheduling. U.S. Patent 7,853,471 B2 (2010).

Waken: Reverse Engineering Usage Information and Interface Structure from Software Videos

Nikola Banovic[1,2], Tovi Grossman[1], Justin Matejka[1], and George Fitzmaurice[1]

[1]Autodesk Research
210 King St. E., Toronto, Ontario, Canada
{firstname.lastname@autodesk.com}

[2]Dept. of Computer Science
University of Toronto, Ontario, Canada
nikola@dgp.toronto.edu

ABSTRACT

We present *Waken*, an application-independent system that recognizes UI components and activities from screen captured videos, without any prior knowledge of that application. *Waken* can identify the cursors, icons, menus, and tooltips that an application contains, and when those items are used. *Waken* uses frame differencing to identify occurrences of behaviors that are common across graphical user interfaces. Candidate templates are built, and then other occurrences of those templates are identified using a multiphase algorithm. An evaluation demonstrates that the system can successfully reconstruct many aspects of a UI without any prior application-dependant knowledge. To showcase the design opportunities that are introduced by having this additional meta-data, we present the *Waken Video Player*, which allows users to directly interact with UI components that are displayed in the video.

Author Keywords

Videos; tutorials; pixel-based reverse engineering.

ACM Classification Keywords

H.5.2 [Information Interfaces and Presentation]: User Interfaces - Graphical user interfaces.

INTRODUCTION

In recent years, video tutorials have become a prevalent medium for delivering software learning content [21, 26]. Recent research projects have attempted to pre-capture usage meta-data in order to enhance the video tutorial viewing experience by marking up the video timeline [10, 13, 22]. While such systems show promise, the vast collection of existing online videos will not possess such meta-data.

We build upon recent work in reverse engineering user interfaces [5, 30], and explore the possibilities related to reverse engineering the video tutorials. This is a challenging task, as information from cursor movements, mouse clicks, and accessibility API's is not available to aid recognition. Previous research systems have provided promising results, but have relied on explicit application-dependant rules [21] or templates [26] that may not generalize.

UIST '12, October 7–10, 2012, Cambridge, Massachusetts, USA.

In this paper, we present *Waken*, an application-independent system that recognizes UI components and activities, from an input set of video tutorials. *Waken* does not require any prior knowledge of the appearance of an applications icons or its interface layout. Instead, our system identifies specific motion patterns in the video and extracts the visual appearance of associated widgets in the application UI (Figure 1). Template matching can then be performed on the extracted widgets to locate them in other frames of the video.

Waken is capable of tracking the cursor, identifying application icons, and recognizing when icons are clicked. We also explore the feasibility of associating tooltips to icons, and reconstructing the contents of menus. An initial evaluation of our system on a set of 34 Google SketchUp video tutorials showed that the system was able to successfully identify 14 cursors, 8 icons, and accurately model the hotspot of the system cursor. While the accuracy levels have room for improvement, the trends indicate that with enough samples, all elements could get recognized.

We then present the *Waken Video Player*, to showcase the design opportunities that are introduced by having the meta-data associated with videos. The video player allows users to directly explore and interact with the video itself, almost as if it were a live application. For example, users can click directly on icons in the video, to find related videos in the library that use that particular tool. Users can also hover over icons in the video to display their associated tooltips, or hover over menus to reveal their contents. These techniques are all enabled without any prior knowledge of specific interface layouts or item appearances. We conclude with a discussion of lessons learned and limitations of our work, and outline possible lines of future work.

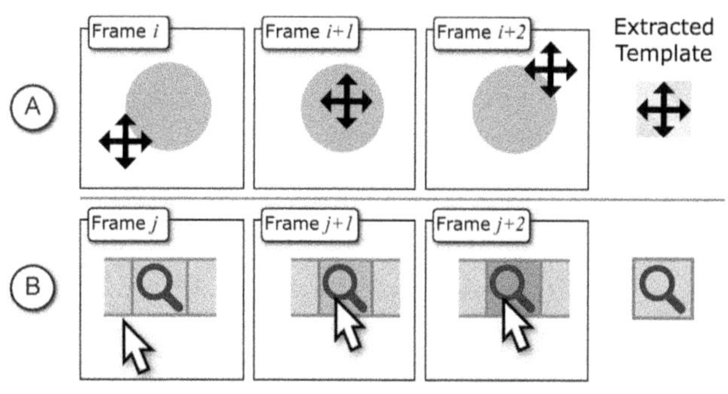

Figure 1. *Waken* uses frame differencing to extract UI elements, such as cursors (a) and icons (b).

RELATED WORK

In this section we discuss previous research on video tutorials, tutorial authoring, and reverse engineering UIs.

Video Tutorials

Video tutorials have become a prevalent instructional aid for learning software [21, 26]. One of the main reasons for the popularity of such tutorials could be due to the benefits of learning software application by directly observing expert use [28]. However, there are also some drawbacks.

One major drawback is navigation issues within longer video tutorials which could lead to misunderstandings of the content [14]. Additionally, users may be unable to keep up with the pace of the instructions, which could lead to reduced knowledge retention [23]. Although Grossman and Fitzmaurice [12] showed benefits of short contextual video clips, longer tutorials could still pose difficulty for the user.

Past research has shown that navigation of recorded software workflows can be aided by visualizing operation history [22]. Chronicle [13] combines operational history visualizations and timeline-based video summarization and browsing, to aid in exploration of high-level workflows in video tutorials. Ambient Help [21] and Pause-and-Play [26] also provide video timelines based on operation histories.

Our enhanced player provides similar operation history and timeline-based browsing interactions. However, we also extend this literature by exploring how direct manipulation of the user interface in the video tutorial itself could enhance the user experience. While direct manipulation of videos has been previously explored [9] we are unaware of any implementations specific to software tutorial videos. Motivation for such interaction is provided by evidence that users sometimes try to interact with the elements within a documentation article directly [20]. Allowing the user to explore the target application interface directly in the video could also reduce switching between the video and target application [26], and support discovery-based learning [8].

Tutorial Authoring and Usage Data Capture

Video tutorials are typically built from screen capture videos demonstrating usage of the target application. Unfortunately, tutorials authored in this way do not contain additional metadata required for reconstructing operation histories and providing interactive timelines. Existing research has explored ways to automatically capture workflow information [1, 10, 11, 13, 17, 22]. However, those approaches often require special recording tools and instrumentation of the target applications. Additionally, there is already a large collection of tutorial videos on the Internet that were not recorded using such tools. It would be useful to be able to extract workflow information from videos themselves.

Some partial solutions to this problem have been explored through computer visions techniques. Matejka *et al.* [21] reconstructed tool usage information by performing explicit text-based template matching on the AutoCAD command line. While effective for AutoCAD, the technique would not work on other software applications. Pongnumkul *et al.* [26] described a technique to infer icon usage data from existing video tutorials. However, their implementation was also application specific, as it performed template matching on the target application's tool palette. While it may be possible to provide such templates for any application of interest, it would be helpful if such application-dependant templates were not required. We explore an approach, which does not require prior training data.

Reverse Engineering User Interfaces

Advances in computer vision have enabled techniques to identify user interface elements from live applications. Sikuli [30] uses computer vision to identify GUI components in screen captures, search for GUI elements in the interface [1], and automate GUI tasks [2]. However, the underlying computer vision algorithms in Sikuli identify GUI elements based on templates from sample image data.

To minimize the time required for collecting training data, past research [3, 5, 18, 21] explored abstracting identification of different GUI elements and decoupling GUI element representation from predefined image templates. Hurst *et al.* [18] combined a number of useful computer vision techniques with mouse and accessibility API information to automatically identify clickable targets in the interface. Chang *et al.* [3] proposed an accessibility and pixel-based framework, which also allowed for detecting text and arbitrary word blobs in user interfaces. However, when working with video tutorials, mouse information and data from the accessibility API is not available.

Prefab [5] identified GUI elements by using GUI specific visual features, which enabled overlaying of advanced interaction techniques on top of existing interfaces [6, 7]. We build on the insight from Prefab [5] that "it is likely not necessary to individually define each widget in every application, but may instead be possible to learn definitions of entire families of widgets." However, instead of using interactive methods to identify visual features of widgets, we propose an automated application-independent method that learns widget representations from the source video itself.

SYSTEM GOALS AND CHALLENGES

Our work is a first step towards an ultimate goal of automatically constructing interface façades [27], from only an input set of videos. Previous work on reverse engineering user interfaces rely mainly on "pixels", but have access to other forms of information, such as the cursor position, click and keystroke events, and accessibility information. In contrast, with a video, the only source of information is the pixels of the video. Our work provides a first effort at addressing unique challenges when working with videos:

Where is the cursor?

The mouse cursor is a core mechanism for interacting with typical graphical user interfaces. As such, to reverse engineer the activities the user caries out, it is important to know where the cursor is [18]. This stream of information is trivial to access on live applications via global hooks. In videos, this information is absent.

When does the mouse button click?

Related to the cursor position, is understanding when the mouse button clicks. This is another stream of information that can be obtained from a live application, but is absent when working with videos.

Cursor Occlusion

In videos, the screen contents behind the cursor are occluded and unknown. In a live application, taking screenshots by default hides the cursor, so no pixels are occluded. This can be problematic, for example, when trying to understand the appearance of an icon that the cursor has just clicked.

Video Artifacts

When analyzing video screen recordings, there may be artifacts in the video due to lossy codecs being used. The resulting artifacts could be problematic for template matching and frame differencing algorithms.

WAKEN SYSTEM OVERVIEW

The core insight we use in the implementation of *Waken* is that GUI elements possess certain behaviours across applications (Figure 3). Our approach is to use the computer vision technique of frame differencing to identify occurrences of such behaviors, or *motions*, and then extract the associated widgets.

Another insight we build from is that there will be access to a potentially large training set of videos. We can thus use conservative rules to identify target motions. As long as such motion occurs somewhere within the videos, a widget can be extracted. These widgets can then be located in other videos and frames through template matching.

A final insight is that video processing does not need to be accomplished in real time. In contrast, techniques like Prefab [5] need to work in real-time to enable interactive techniques [7]. We thus have the advantage of being able to split the processing of tutorial videos into multiple phases.

Video Processing

Waken processes a set of videos over a sequence of four phases (Figure 2). Phase 1 makes a pass to identify possible cursors from the motions in the video. Phase 2 tracks the cursor in individual frames through template matching. Phase 3 combines the cursor position information with frame differencing to identify and extract clickable icons

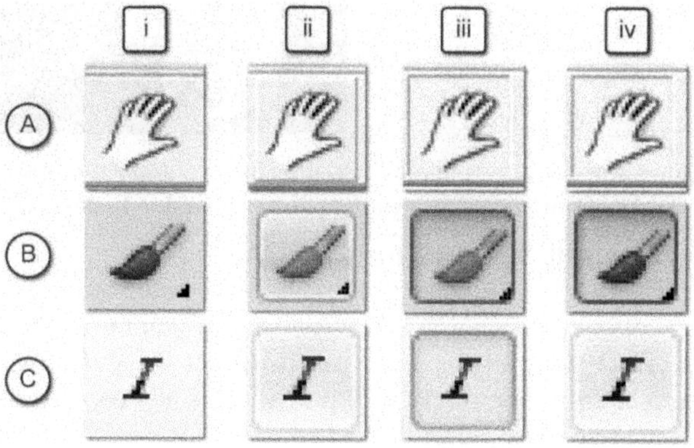

Figure 3. UI Buttons states in a) Google SketchUp, b) Adobe Photoshop, and c) Microsoft Word: i) default, ii) highlighted, iii) clicked, and iv) active.

in the videos. Phase 4 identifies the icons in all other frames and detects when they are clicked. The final phase is also used to identify and associate icons with their tooltips, and menus with their top-level contents.

Source Videos

We make several simplifying assumptions about the source library of videos: 1) we assume that the input videos are from the same version of a software application, 2) that videos are captured at a 1 to 1 scale, and 3) that the video is encoded with a reasonable quality. We discuss the limitations imposed by these assumptions later in this paper.

ELIMINATING CODEC ARTIFACTS

One of the difficulties of reverse engineering videos, in comparison to live applications, is that individual frames may not be pixel perfect representations, due to video compression artifacts. In the presence of a lossy codec, there is a significant amount of noise when comparing consecutive frames (Figure 4), which our algorithms handle.

To compensate for this noise, we filter any small frame-to-frame differences. We first convert the consecutive frames to grayscale and then apply an absolute difference on the two frames. We then apply a threshold function and filter out any difference that is less than 20 on the grayscale (from 0 to 255). This approach preserves the pixels as much as possible, where as a more traditional Gaussian filter would contaminate them.

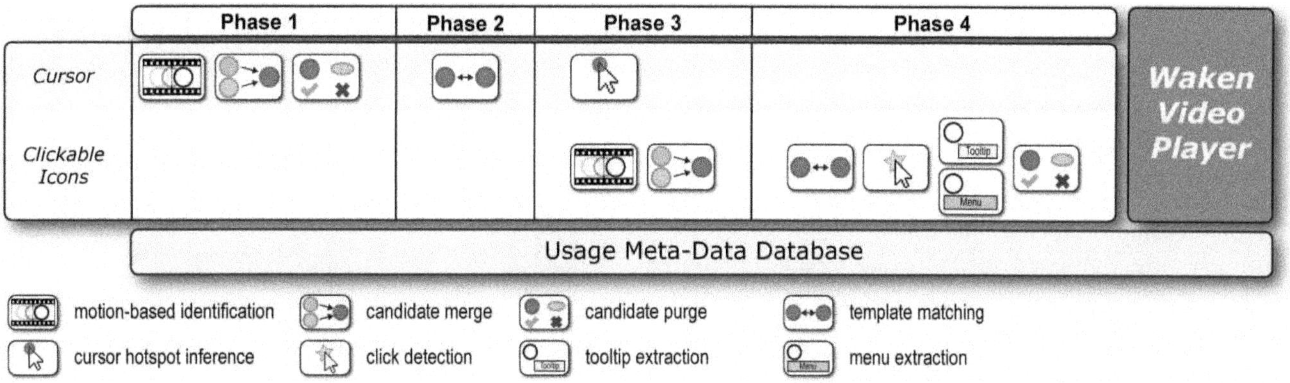

Figure 2. The four main phases of the *Waken* processing system.

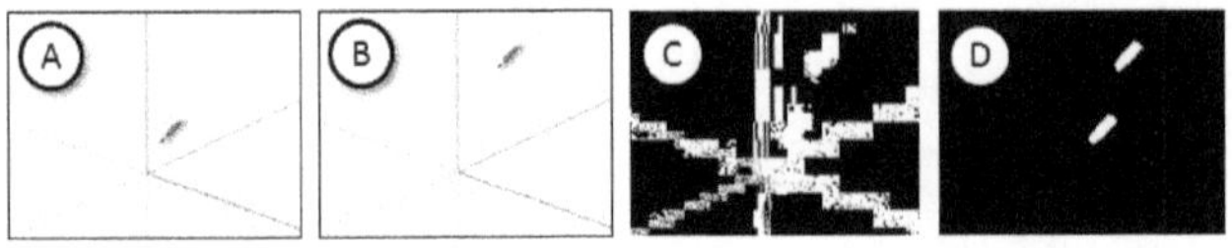

Figure 4. Pixel differences between frames (a) and (b) is show in (c). Applying our filter removes differences due to noise (d).

PHASE 1 AND 2: CURSOR TRACKING

Our first goal is to identify and track the cursor. To remain application independent, we make no assumptions about the cursor appearance, but instead extract the cursor appearance from motion patterns in the video. We do this in a two-phase process described below.

Phase 1: Cursor Identification

In this first phase, we identify the cursor appearance based on specific patterns in frame differences, and then generate a cursor model that can be then used for template matching.

Identifying Cursor Candidates

To identify cursor candidates, we search for frames where only the cursor moves, which creates an easily recognizable pattern (Figure 5). Considering any 3 consecutive frames, if the absolute difference between the first and the second frame, and the absolute difference between the second and the third frame, each contain exactly two blobs, then there is a high likelihood that the blobs identify cursor regions. As an additional confirmation, we compute the contours of the blobs [29] and then match the shapes of the four contours using the OpenCV Hu invariants based [16] shape matching function. If the result of the comparison is greater or equal to 0.95 between all four of the contours then we consider this a candidate cursor match. We store the associated regions from the 3 frames into a new cursor candidate *bucket*. This is repeated for every set of 3 consecutive frames across all videos.

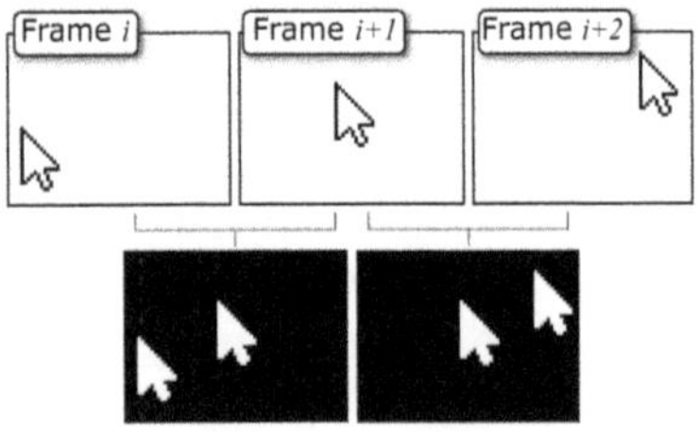

Figure 5. (Top) Consecutive frames and the corresponding blobs in each of the two absolute differences when only the cursor moves (Bottom).

Short Cursor Movements

When the cursor moves by a short distance, the two absolute difference frames might contain only one blob each (Figure 6). In this case, the intersection of the two blobs from the two absolute differences may contain the cursor. We only attempt to identify the cursor in such situations when there are 4 absolute differences between any 5 consecutive frames, each containing a single blob. If this occurs, we calculate the three interactions of the 4 consecutive difference blobs. If the result of comparing the contours of these three intersection blobs is greater than 0.95 we consider this to be three samples of the same cursor in the second, third, and fourth frames and we add the samples to a new *bucket*.

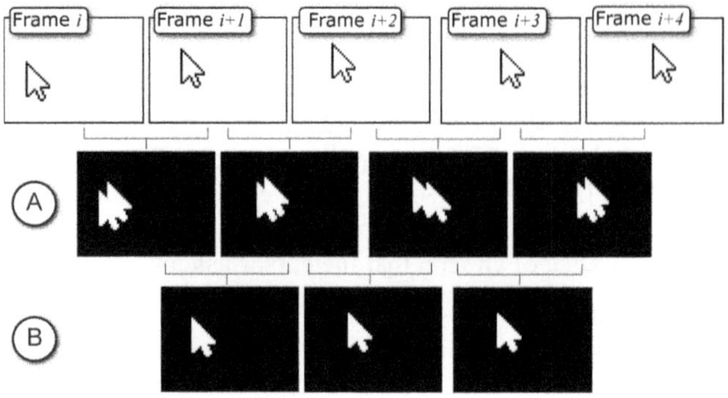

Figure 6. Consecutive frames and a) corresponding single blobs in the absolute difference frames when cursor moves a short distance. b) Cursor shapes in intersection of differences.

Grouping Cursors Together

In most software applications, there are multiple visual representations of the cursor depending on its location and system mode. We group different cursor *buckets* whose average contour match is equal or greater to 0.95. The templates can then be created from these merged buckets.

Generating Cursor Estimate

The individual instances in each bucket will not be identical. Differences can be due to video artifacts, or transparency in the cursor. In particular, a cursor with high transparency would look much different depending on the background color in the frame it was captured from. Thus, using any single instance for template matching may fail. To determine what the cursors actually look like, we look at all of the captured cursor images for each cursor *bucket*. To build a model of the cursor, we first align all images from a *bucket*, by minimizing the distance between pixels, in RGB space. We then calculate the mean values and variances for the RGB channels for each pixel in the cursor area, across all images in the bucket. This probabilistic template model can subsequently be used for template matching.

To visualize the generated templates, we built a cursor viewer. The cursor viewer shows a 2D representation of the mean pixel values, a 2D representation of the variances, and a 3D representation of the mean pixel values, with height mapped to variance (Figure 7). It can be seen that variance levels are higher when there is transparency or drop-shadows in a cursor.

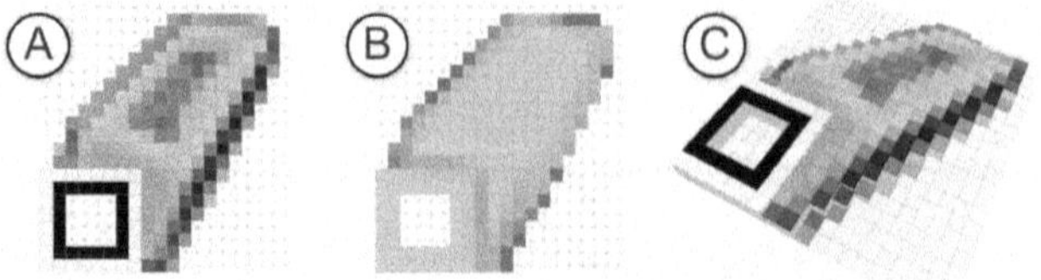

Figure 7. The cursor viewer application visualizes cursor templates we generate. Variance is represented by color in (b) and height in (c).

Phase 2: Cursor Template Matching

In the Phase 2, we iterate through every frame for which a cursor has not already been found, and search for the cursor. We use a probabilistic template matching algorithm against the templates generated in Phase 1. A brute force approach searches for every cursor in every frame.

We consider an individual pixel match when the RGB value of a pixel is within 4 standard deviations of the mean for the corresponding pixel in the cursor model. We consider a template match if 95% of the individual pixels match.

If multiple matches are found, we keep the cursor with the highest template match score. If any cursor achieves a match score of 100%, we keep that cursor and move to the next frame. To improve processing time, we first look for the same cursor as the previous frame, in the proximity of the previous cursor position. If that old cursor is found with a 95% match, we keep that cursor and move to the next frame. If a frame contains no cursor matches, then we assume that the cursor is not present in that frame.

A filtering heuristic is used to account for potential false positives when static icons take on the appearance of a cursor. For each cursor, we generate the distribution of (x, y) coordinates that it was found at. If the number of occurrences at any single (x, y) coordinate is more than 4 times the standard deviation of this distribution, then those matches are discarded, and the template matching is repeated to find a new cursor in the associated frames.

PHASE 3 AND 4: ICON IDENTIFICATION

The technique described above allows us to infer the location of the cursor. In this section, we describe how the cursor information can be leveraged to identify clickable icons in a user interface video.

As with cursor tracking, icon identification is accomplished across two phases, Phase 3 and 4 of our algorithm. We first identify candidate icons based on consecutive frame image differences. We then use this information to locate candidates in other frames of the video.

Phase 3: Icon Identification

As with cursor identification, we identify icons using a conservative set of rules. Imposing such rules reduces the number of icons which are identified in Phase 3. Remaining icons are located in Phase 4 through template matching.

We identify candidate icons from instances when they are clicked in the video. We look for a visual pattern that is common across typical user interfaces, where the cursor: enters the icon region causing the region to highlight, briefly pauses, clicks the icon causing the icon region to switch to a "depressed" state, and exits the icon.

To identify such patterns, we start by searching across all instances where there cursor location changes across 3 consecutive frames, i, $i+1$, and $i+2$. We then look at the differences between frames i and $i+1$. We consider the movement a potential candidate if there is a blob that intersects the cursor position from frame $i+1$, that does not intersect the cursor position from frame i. This indicates that the cursor has potentially moved into an icon, and the icon has highlighted. We then require that blob to *not* be present in the difference of frame $i+1$ and $i+2$, which ensures that the cursor has remained within the icon. This pattern identifies a highlighted icon, and the associated region (Figure 8).

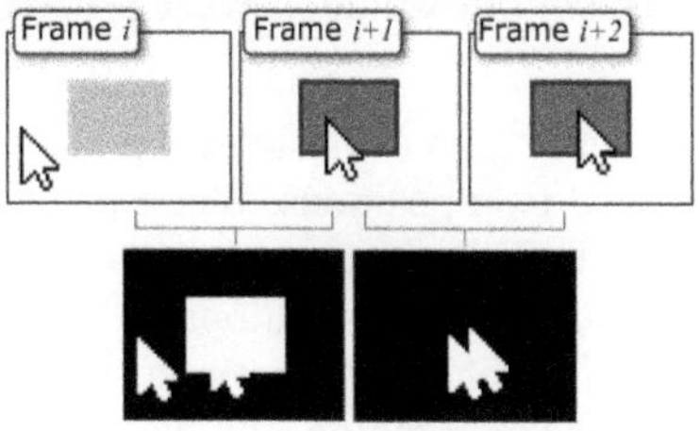

Figure 8. Typical cursor movement when approaching and acquiring an icon and resulting frame differences.

We then test to see if the icon which was highlighted gets clicked. As long as the cursor remains within the highlighted region, we search for 3 consecutive frames, j, $j+1$, and $j+2$. To detect a click, we require the cursor to be stationary, within 2 pixels, between frames j and $j+1$, and fully stationary between frames $j+1$ and $j+2$. In addition, there must be a new difference blob between frames $j+1$ and $j+2$, which intersects the highlight region. This indicates the icon has been clicked (Figure 9). This identification process will identify root level menu clicks as well.

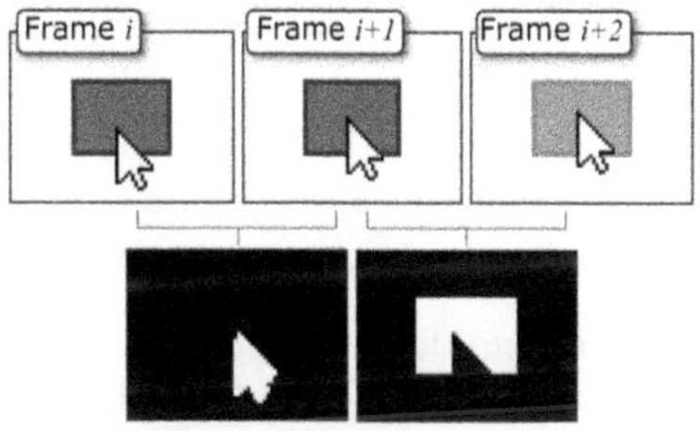

Figure 9. Typical cursor movement when clicking an icon and resulting frame differences.

To extract the appearance of the icon, we store the image of the highlight region from frame i (before it was occluded by the cursor), and from the first frame after the click which the cursor is no longer occluding the region.

Grouping Icons Together

Each time we extract an icon, we check if it matches the appearance of previously detected icons, using OpenCV's standard template matching algorithm, with a 0.95 threshold. If there is no match, the icon is added. If it matches with a previous icon, they are grouped together. The final icon templates are generated by averaging the pixel values of all icons in a group.

Inferring the Cursor Hotspot

In Phase 3, we also infer the cursor hotspot. Each time an icon is highlighted, we detect which cursor pixels intersect the highlighted region. We define the hotspot as the region of pixels which are in the highlight region at least 95% of the time an icon is highlighted. We use this hotspot to test when the cursor enters the area of an icon in Phase 4.

Phase 4: *Detecting Icons, Tooltips, and Menus*

In Phase 4 we use template matching to find instances of the icons extracted from Phase 3. For simplicity, in our implementation, we only search a small area around the initial location where we found the icon. However, this could be extended to the whole frame to account for customized layouts, but this would increase processing time.

Icon Click Detection

We can now identify icon clicks by using knowledge of the cursor hotspot and icon positions. While the cursor hotspot is in an icon, we look for 3 consecutive frames, i, $i+1$, and $i+2$, where the cursor remains stationary. To detect a click, there must be a difference blob between frames i and $i+1$, which intersects the icon region, and that blob cannot be in the difference between frames $i+1$ and $i+2$. When this occurs, we record a click in frame $i+1$. Blob larger than the icon region we classify as a menu.

Purging Icons

We developed two simple mechanisms to reduce occurrences of false positives. First, any icon that has only a solid color is dismissed. Second, we remove icons that were rarely identified via template matching: we discard an icon if it was identified is Phase 3 95% of the time, relative to the total number of times it is identified in Phases 3 and 4.

Tooltip and Menu Identification

In addition to identifying clickable icons, we can begin to reconstruct other UI information associated with the icons. An ultimate goal would be to automatically construct interface façades [27] from the videos. We take an initial step in this direction, and infer the tooltip information associated with icons, and the top-level items associated with menus.

To detect a candidate tooltip, we consider consecutive frames in which the cursor is within an icon and does not move. If the difference between consecutive frames contains a single blob that does not intersect with the highlighted area of the icon, it is considered a tooltip. To capture the tooltip appearance, we take the region of the blob in the last frame that blob is detected. This ensures the tooltip is captured at full opacity, to account for user interfaces where tooltips gradually fade-in. We calculate the mean value of RGB for each pixel in the tooltip from all occurrences for that particular icon. This gives us the final appearance of the tooltip that we use.

We use a similar approach to detect the top-level contents associated with a menu. When we detect the click of an icon that has been classified as a menu, we capture the image of the top-level menu items, defined as the blob area, with the icon area subtracted. As with tooltips, we take the image from the last frame which the blob occurs, and we average the RGB value across all occurrences, to get its final appearance.

One limitation of this approach is that it does not handle menu or tooltip associations changing due to application context. Inferring the correct context is a more challenging task, which requires additional research.

IMPLEMENTATION AND INITIAL RESULTS

We implemented *Waken* using the C++ implementation of OpenCV[1] version 2.3 on Windows 7. The system used a Postgres[2] version 9.1.3 database to store and access processed usage data. The system ran on a 64-bit Windows 7 Enterprise with Intel Xeon 2 quad-core 2.53GHz processors and 12GB or RAM.

We ran *Waken* on a library of 34 Google SketchUp[3] videos downloaded from the Google SketchUp training website[4]. The videos were in the Apple QuickTime format with *H264 – MPG-4 AVC* codec. The resolution of the videos was 640×480, with a 1:1 scale, and frame rates ranged from 8fps to 24fps. The videos lasted from 1-8 minutes, and totaled 2 hours and 22 minutes of playing time.

Total analysis time for all videos was approximately 50 hours. The large majority of time was spent searching for cursor templates in Phase 2. Although processing time is high, the system implementation is highly parallelisable, and the process time could decrease with more processors.

Below we provide some of the results and observations from this test set on the core features of our algorithm: cursor tracking, icon identification, and icon click detections. Refining and evaluating the UI reconstruction techniques (*i.e.* tooltip and menu recognition) is left for future work.

We do not expect to be able to reconstruct all cursors and icon clicks in this test, with this relatively small input set of videos. Our goal in this initial evaluation is to get an indication of how well the system will work, and identify limitations that can guide future work and improvements.

Results

We discuss the results and observations for each of the phases of the *Waken* processing system. In order to obtain the ground truth, one of the authors manually coded all cursor changes and icon click events in the videos. Phase 1 was performed on all 34 videos. However, we removed 18 videos as outliers due to the large number of frames that were not at 1 to 1 scale, due to zooming effects. In Phases 2 to 4, we ran on the remaining 16 videos. We present the results based on the data from these 16 videos.

Phase 1: Cursor Identification and Template Generation

The total number of frames that contributed to motion-based identification of cursors was 1,847 frames out of 96,223 (1.9%). This provides a rough guideline as to how often cursors will exhibit the required behavior to be tracked by our algorithm.

The system was able to successfully recognize 14 different cursors, leaving 5 cursors unrecognized and no false positives. In most cases, the unrecognized cursors were rarely used. However, larger data sets could alleviate this and increase the chances of each cursor being recognized.

[1] http://opencv.willowgarage.com
[2] http://www.postgresql.org/
[3] http://sketchup.google.com/
[4] https://sites.google.com/site/sketchupvideo/

The quality of the template cursors depended on how frequently the cursor was observed. Figure 10 shows mean pixel RGB values and variance for the cursor with the greatest number of templates (N=656). A side by side comparison with the actual cursor icon shows that the templates can be extremely accurate with enough samples to build from. Overall we feel these results are impressive, given that we had *no* a priori knowledge of cursor appearance.

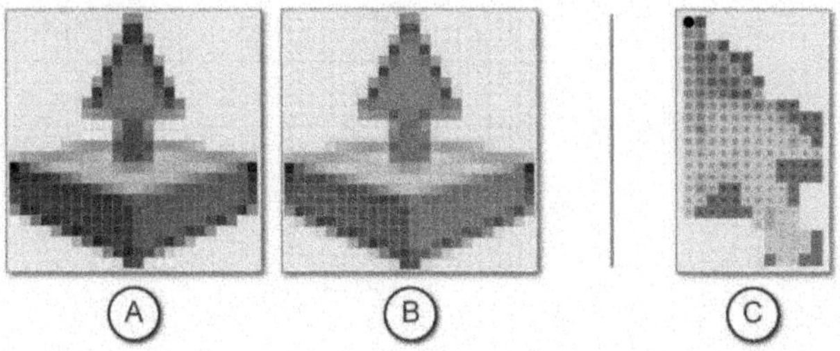

Figure 10. a) Cursor reconstructed using our algorithm on the test data. b) Actual cursor icon. c) System cursor with hotspot estimate (solid black dot indicates 95% confidence).

Phase 2: Cursor Tracking Results

Attempting to track the cursors in every individual frame resulted in an accuracy of 77.28% (SD=13.19) and recall of 72.67% (SD=14.48) (Figure 11). There were no false positives. Individual cursors accuracy varied greatly, depending on the number of samples used to build its template (Figure 12). When removing the 8 cursors whose templates were generated from less than 10 samples, the average accuracy increased to 81.39% (SD=5.98) and the average recall increased to 81.28% (SD=12.78) (Figure 11).

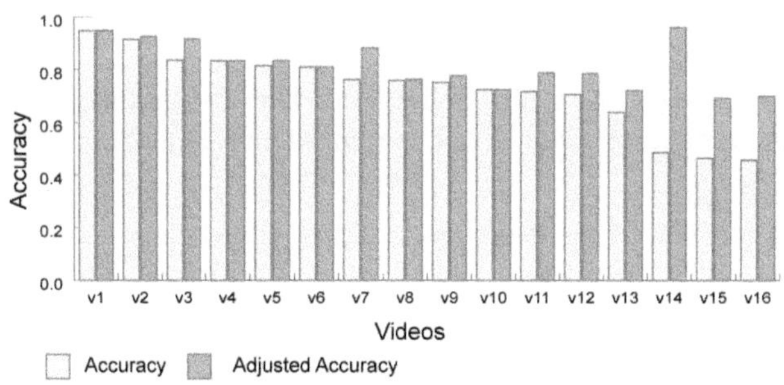

Figure 11. Cursor tracking accuracy by video. Adjusted accuracy shows results when the low-sampled cursors are removed from the data set.

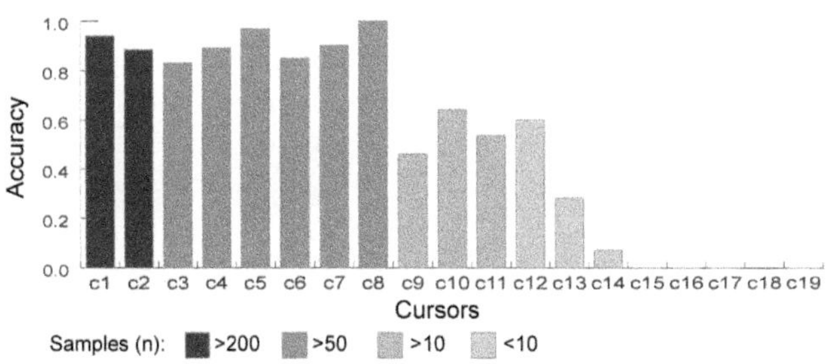

Figure 12. Cursor tracking accuracy by cursor.

Phase 3: Icon Identification Results

Phase 3 was not able to identify any icons in the videos with 8 and 15fps, suggesting that the frame rate could affect the identification accuracy. We therefore continued our phase 3 analysis on the 4 videos that had 24fps frame rate.

In these 4 videos, the system was able to successfully identify 8 icon buttons. Five buttons were not recognized, and there was one false positive. However, any button that was clicked at least four times was accurately recognized. The system successfully identified the cursor that clicked on the icons, and accurately estimated its hotspot (Figure 10.c).

Phase 4: Click Tracking Results

While we didn't manually calculate tracking accuracy of the icons which were identified in Phase 3, our observations indicated that accuracy was above 99%.

The precision and recall of click tracking was 81.79% and 29.48% respectively. However, for videos with 24fps the precision was 87.97% and recall was 66.04%. This suggests that the click usage data can only be usable from videos with larger frame rates, but on the other hand the user interface reconstruction works with videos with very low frame rates.

Lessons Learned

Given this is a first effort in reconstructing UI elements from videos, without any application dependant knowledge, we are encouraged by these results. *Waken* was able to successfully recognize 14 cursors, 8 icons, and accurately model the hotspot of the system cursor. While the accuracy levels have room for improvement, the trends indicate that with enough samples, all elements could get recognized.

More importantly, the analysis has identified a number of challenges leaving room for future improvements.

We found some cursors were not recognized because they were rarely used. However, one of the cursors appeared frequently in the videos, but was rarely recognized in Phase 1. It turned out that this cursor was used in drawing content and almost was always associated with other movements in the working area. It would be helpful to enhance Phase 1 so that it could identify the cursor, even when other content in the frames are changing.

Low frame rate was also problematic preventing icon click identification. The problem is that key frames required for our rules may be skipped when the video has a low frame rate (for example, the cursor remaining stationary for one frame after a click event). To overcome this problem, we could attempt to generate templates for "active" states of the buttons. We could then perform template matching to determine if an icon has taken on its active state, similar to the strategy used in Pause-and-Play [26].

Finally, the lack of false positives in the tests suggests that heuristics we use to identify and track cursors and icon buttons describe the motion well. However, there is a potential to, in the future, relax some of the rules and test how that affects the overall accuracy of the system.

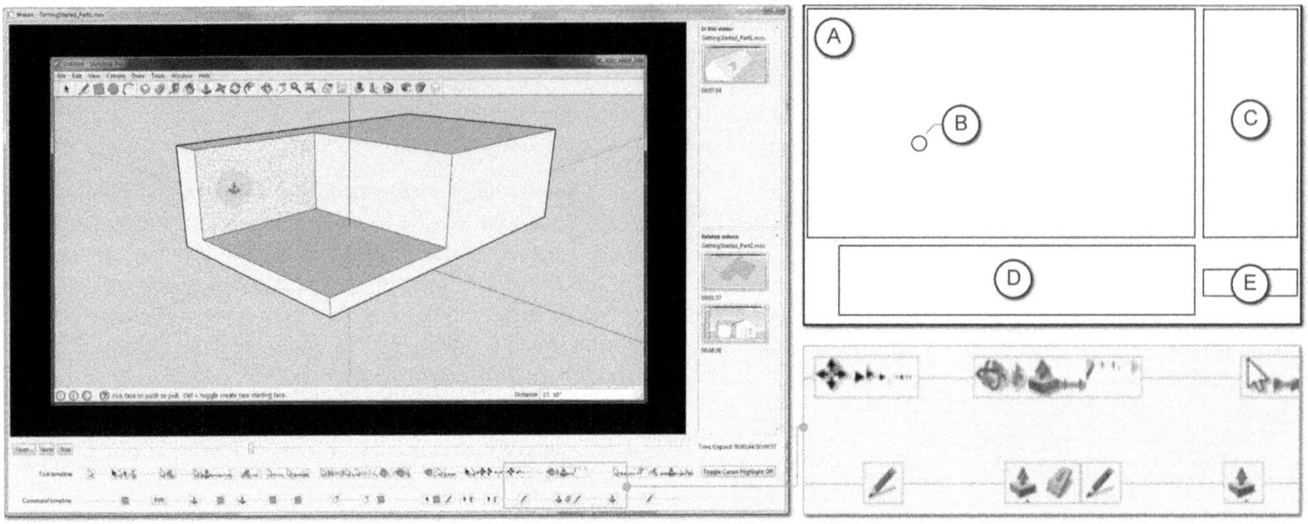

Figure 13. The *Waken Video Player* user interface components. a) The playback area. b) Highlighted cursor. c) Navigation panel. d) Event based timelines. e) Cursor highlight toggle.

WAKEN VIDEO PLAYER

We developed a video player that serves as a demonstration of some of the design opportunities that our video analysis system enables. The *Waken Video Player* brings the videos to life, by allowing users to directly interact with them.

System Implementation

The video player was implemented on the Java 6 SE platform, using Xuggle, a free open source video manipulation library. A Postgres version 9.1.3 database was used to store and access the tutorial video usage meta-data.

Main Player Components

Figure 13 shows the main components of the video player. These components include a playback area (Figure 13a), event-based timelines (Figure 13d), a navigation panel (Figure 13c), and a toggle button for cursor highlighting (Figure 13e). Users can open video files, which automatically loads the associated meta-data from the database.

Cursor Highlighting

The player contains a toggle to highlight the cursor. This is an effect in many screen captured videos, but must be hard-coded into the video. Viewers thus have no capability to enable or disable it. By leveraging the cursor location data generated by *Waken*, we can allow users to dynamically enable or disable cursor highlighting (Figure 13b).

Enhanced Timeline Navigations

Similar to previous systems [13, 21, 26] we mark up the timeline with the icons the tutorial author clicked on. Users can click on the icons to navigate to associated time in the video. While the design is similar to previous systems, the technique to obtain this data, without any prior knowledge of the UI appearance, is novel.

We also visualize the cursor representation in the timeline to show the user when cursor changes occur. This may help users locates areas of the video where a mode changes or a specific type of action occurs that did not result from an icon click.

Direct Video Navigation

Users can interact with the individual icons that are recognized in any frame of the video. When a user pauses the video, bounding box overlays are rendered on top of the video indicating any recognized component. Users can then click directly on an icon to search for other moments in the video when that icon is used. This is similar to previous direct video navigation techniques [9], but is novel for software videos. When the user clicks on an icon, a panel on the right shows thumbnails representing all the times in the video when that icon was used. A second section shows instances of when that icon was used in other videos. Thus, a user can select a tool in the current video and see a list of frames from related videos which also use the tool. Clicking on a related video opens the video and seeks to the frame when that tool is being used. This can be thought of as event-based interactive hyperlinks between videos.

UI Exploration

In our player, we can show tooltips within the video canvas, even if the video itself contains no tooltips. To see a tooltip, the user simply hovers over the corresponding icon of interest while the video is paused. A bounding box is drawn around the tooltip to distinguish it from actual content from the video. Tooltips within the video allow users to get simple information about tools, just like they would in a live user interface (Figure 14a). We also added the ability to expand and collapse top-level menu contents, by hovering over the root menu. This adds further abilities for a user to explore an interface directly from the video itself. As with tooltips, a bounding box distinguishes the menu from an actual menu in the video (Figure 14b).

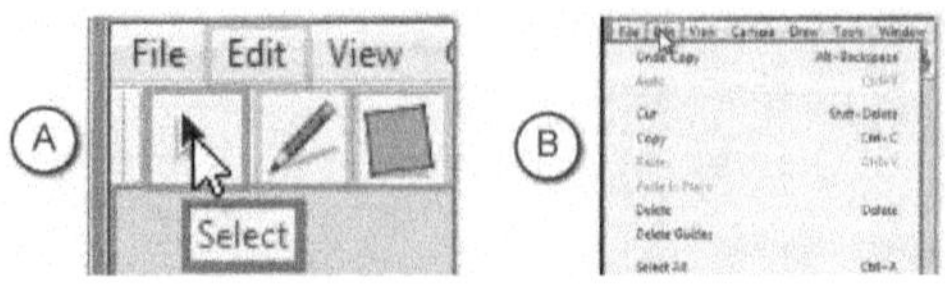

Figure 14. a) A tooltip is rendered over the video b) Menu contents are rendered over the video.

DISCUSSION AND LIMITATIONS

We have demonstrated an application independent system that is able to reconstruct events which occur in video tutorials. We have also shown how this data can allow for a set of novel, direct manipulation interactions, on the videos themselves. Results from an initial test of 16 videos provided some encouraging results, but there are still a number of ways our work can be extended and improved.

Waken has some inherent limitations. For example, we cannot capture interactions resulting from keyboard usage. Furthermore, if, across the entire library of videos, an icon is *never* clicked, or a tooltip is *never* shown, then it will not be recognized. Other limitations are addressable. For example, we did not try to account for repositioning or customization of palettes, but searching the entire frame for template icons would likely address this challenge.

Our study showed that the performance of *Waken* is dependent on the quality of the videos. Today's CPU capabilities and network infrastructure do make it easier to record and share high-quality videos. As such, limitations regarding video quality will not likely be an important issue in the years to come. That being said, it would still be desirable for the system to work well on lower quality videos.

Our initial tests with loseless videos showed very high accuracy rates. Our evaluation was performed on a set of videos that had been compressed with a lossy codec, and accuracy rates were still acceptable. However, as the amount of loss increases, more codec artifacts will begin to impact accuracy. While such artifacts can be overcome by tuning the thresholds we used, at some point, alternative strategies would need to be considered. Similarly, at 8 frames per second, accuracy levels begin to degrade. Refinements to account for low-quality videos should be explored.

Our work was also limited to videos that were recorded at a 1 to 1 scale. The main impact of analyzing downscaled videos would be on the quality of the cursor templates our system generates. Generating templates for multiple resolutions could be a strategy to overcome the scale issue [26]. This type of technique could also be used to account for pan and zoom operations that may occur in the videos.

One of the main advantages of our work is that there is no application-specific information required for the algorithms to work. However, if the end goal is to run our system on a large library of videos, from multiple applications or application versions, there would need to be a way to distinguish what application was in the video. Otherwise, the system would try to match icons from one application to another. In our study, the system was run on a library of videos from a single application. However, future work could look at techniques to automatically distinguish or group applications from the video itself.

Our system depends of finding consecutive frames in a video that have specific patterns in their differences. If a region of the video is changing throughout the entire video, this could prevent any recognition from occurring. For example, if an animation or video is playing within the video itself. One way to address this could be to mask areas of the video that are changing for large periods of time.

A strength of our system is that information from all videos in the library are combined. For example, no cursors may be found in a video from Phase 1, but in Phase 2, the cursor can be tracked through template matching. Similarly, users can view tooltips in videos which they never appeared in.

While our system does not require any application-dependant rules or templates, it does depend on some high-level rules. For example, the recognition of clickable elements requires those elements to become highlighted when the cursor enters, and to provide an additional highlight when the element is clicked. Although this type of behavior is prevalent in most of today's user interfaces, there will be instances of widgets that do not elicit such behaviors.

Finally, while *Waken* was designed to be application-independent, our test was performed only for one application. However, our informal tests on videos for Microsoft Word and Adobe Photoshop found comparable identification and tracking accuracy for cursors and clickable icons to results from our study (Figure 15). Unless the UI mechanics are much different, we expect our system to work for most software applications.

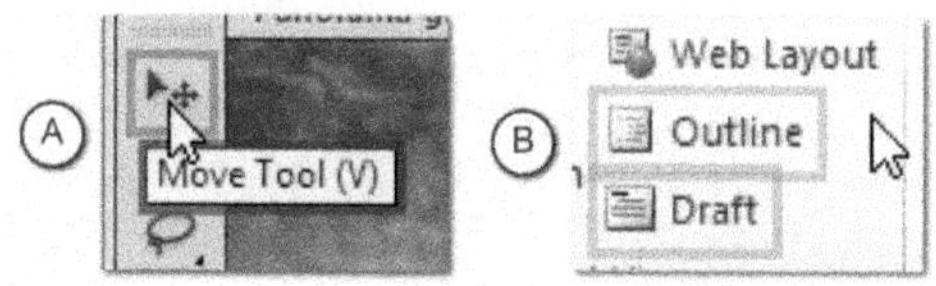

Figure 15. Cursor and clickable icon recognition from Adobe Photoshop (a) and Microsoft Word (b).

FUTURE WORK

Our work opens up a number of interesting opportunities for future research. With respect to the recognition system, new techniques to address the limitations described in the previous section could be developed. In particular the ability to automatically recognize software and versions, or the recording resolution, could help improve the robustness of the system. Also, some motion pattern recognition rules may have been stricter than necessary, although our current implementation was intentionally biased towards avoiding false positives. One of our goals for future work is to explore how to relax some of these rules without sacrificing identification accuracy. Further investigating and addressing the issue of codec artifacts would also increase the scope of videos where our work would be applicable.

Our work was guided by numerous previous systems that have performed recognition of on-screen activities. We used a combination of frame differencing and template matching. However, our algorithms could likely be improved by integrating other concepts that have been seen in prior art, such as interpreting interface hierarchy [6].

We leveraged the information collected by the recognizer to provide an enhanced video player. However, this information opens up alternative design opportunities. For example, it would be interesting to investigate the feasibility of automatically translating a recorded video into a different language, similar to live user interface translations [6].

Finally, the menu reconstruction provides an initial step towards automatically reconstructing an entire user interface façade [27]. It would be interesting to explore how close to a full reconstruction could be obtained by extending our work. This would require modelling a much deeper set of application components, such as application states, hierarchal menus, and floating palates.

CONCLUSION

We have presented *Waken*, a new system that leverages computer vision techniques to extract usage information from tutorial videos, such as the movement of the cursor, the icons which are clicked, and the tooltips associated with interactive elements. A main contribution of this system is that it does not require any application specific rules or templates. We have demonstrated a number of novel interactions that are enabled, such as allowing the user to interact directly with the video itself. Results from our initial test indicate a number of fruitful areas for future work.

REFERENCES

1. Bergman, L., Castelli, V., Lau, T., and Oblinger, D. 2005. DocWizards: a system for authoring follow-me documentation wizards. *ACM UIST*, 191-200.
2. Chang, T., Yeh, T., and Miller, R. C. 2010. GUI testing using computer vision. *ACM CHI*, 1535-1544.
3. Chang, T., Yeh, T., and Miller, R. C. 2011. Associating the visual representation of user interfaces with their internal structures and metadata. *ACM UIST*, 245-256.
4. Cheng, K., Luo, S., and Chen, B. 2009. SmartPlayer: user-centric video fast-forwarding. *ACM CHI*, 789-798.
5. Dixon M. and Fogarty, J. 2010. Prefab: implementing advanced behaviors using pixel-based reverse engineering of interface structure. *ACM CHI*, 1525-1534.
6. Dixon, M., Leventhal, D., and Fogarty, J. 2011. Content and hierarchy in pixel-based methods for reverse engineering interface structure. *ACM CHI*, 969-978.
7. Dixon M., Fogarty, J., and Wobbrock, J. 2012. A general-purpose target-aware pointing enhancement using pixel-level analysis on graphical interfaces. *ACM CHI*, 3167-3176.
8. Dong, T., Dontcheva, M., Joseph, D., Karahalios, K., Newman, M. W., and Ackerman, M. S. 2012. Discovery-based Games for Learning Software. *ACM CHI*, 2083-2086.
9. Dragicevic, P., Ramos, G., Bibliowitcz, J., Nowrouzezahrai, D., Balakrishnan, R., and Singh, K. 2008. Video browsing by direct manipulation. *ACM CHI*, 237-246.
10. Fernquist, J., Grossman, T., and Fitzmaurice, G. 2011. Sketch-sketch revolution: an engaging tutorial system for guided sketching and application learning. *ACM UIST*, 373-382.
11. Grabler, F., Agrawala, M., Li, W., Dontcheva, M., and Igarashi, T. 2009. Generating photo manipulation tutorials by demonstration. *ACM SIGGRAPH*. 66. 9 pages.
12. Grossman, T. and Fitzmaurice, G. 2010. ToolClips: an investigation of contextual video assistance for functionality understanding. *ACM CHI*, 1515-1524.
13. Grossman, T., Matejka, J., and Fitzmaurice, G. 2010. Chronicle: capture, exploration, and playback of document workflow histories. *ACM UIST*, 143-152.
14. Harrison, S. M. 1995. A comparison of still, animated, or nonillustrated on-line help with written or spoken instructions in a graphical user interface. *ACM CHI*, 82-89.
15. Hategekimana, C., Gilbert, S., and Blessing, S. 2008. Effectiveness of using an intelligent tutoring system to train users on off-the-shelf software. *Society for Info. Tech. and Teacher Education Int'l Conf.*, AACE.
16. Hu, M. 1962. Visual pattern recognition by moment invariants. *IRE Trans. Inf. Theory* IT-8, 8, 1409-1420.
17. Huang, J. and Twidale, M. B. 2007. Graphstract: minimal graphical help for computers. *ACM UIST*, 203-212.
18. Hurst, A., Hudson, S. E., and Mankoff, J. 2010. Automatically identifying targets users interact with during real world tasks. *ACM IUI*, 11-20.
19. Kelleher, C. and Pausch, R. 2005. Stencils-based tutorials: design and evaluation. *ACM CHI*, 541-550.
20. Knabe, K. 1995. Apple guide: a case study in user-aided design of online help. *ACM CHI*, 286-287.
21. Matejka, J., Grossman, T., and Fitzmaurice, G. 2011. Ambient help. *ACM CHI*, 2751-2760.
22. Nakamura, T. and Igarashi, T. 2008. An application-independent system for visualizing user operation history. *ACM UIST*, 23-32.
23. Palmiter, S. and Elkerton, J. 1991. An evaluation of animated demonstrations of learning computer-based tasks. *ACM CHI*, 257-263.
24. Petrovic, N., Jojic, N., and Huang, T. S. 2005. Adaptive Video Fast Forward. *Multimed. Tools Appl.* 26, 3.
25. Pongnumkul, S., Wang, J., Ramos, G., and Cohen, M. 2010. Content-aware dynamic timeline for video browsing. *ACM UIST*, 139-142.
26. Pongnumkul, S., Dontcheva, M., Li, W., Wang, J., Bourdev, L., Avidan, S., and Cohen, M. F. 2011. Pause-and-play: automatically linking screencast video tutorials with applications. *ACM UIST*, 135-144.
27. Ramesh, V., Hsu, C., Agrawala, M., and Hartmann, B. 2011. ShowMeHow: translating user interface instructions between applications. *ACM UIST*, 127-134.
28. Shneiderman, B. 1983. Direct Manipulation: A Step Beyond Programming Languages. *Compt.* 16, 8, 57-69.
29. Suzuki, S. and Abe, K. 1985. Topological structural analysis of digitized binary images by border following. *Comput. Vision Graph.*, 30(1), 32-46.
30. Yeh, T., Chang, T., and Miller R. C. 2009. Sikuli: using GUI screenshots for search and automation. *ACM UIST*, 183-192.
31. Yeh, T., Chang, T., Xie, B., Walsh, G., Watkins, I., Wongsuphasawat, K., Huang, M., Davis, L. S., and Bederson, B. B. 2011. Creating contextual help for GUIs using screenshots. *ACM UIST*, 145-154.

MixT: Automatic Generation of Step-by-Step Mixed Media Tutorials

Pei-Yu (Peggy) Chi[1], Sally Ahn[1], Amanda Ren[1], Mira Dontcheva[2], Wilmot Li[2], Björn Hartmann[1]

[1]University of California, Berkeley — Computer Science Division
{peggychi, sallyahn, aren, bjoern}@berkeley.edu

[2]Advanced Technology Labs, Adobe
{mirad, wilmotli}@adobe.com

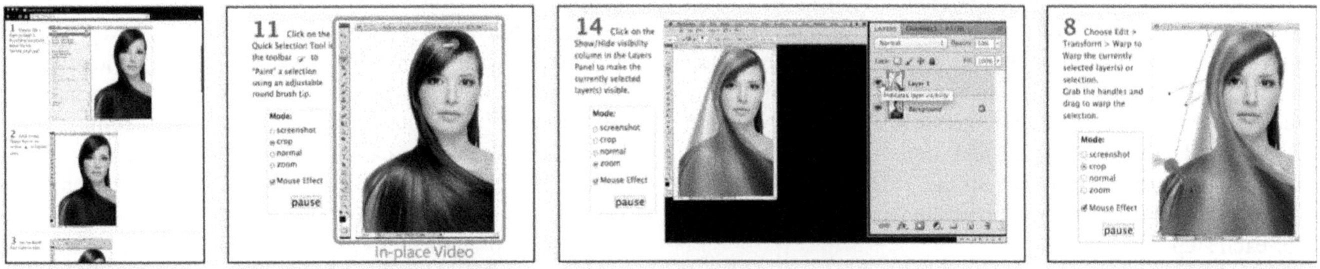

A User browses the static view of a MixT tutorial in a browser.

B Clicking on a step image replaces the image with video in a ***crop view***, showing a panel and a canvas.

C User chooses ***zoom mode*** to see an enlarged UI panel composited onto video of the entire application for additional context.

D MixT mouse trails show continuous manipulations in video clips.

Figure 1: MixT generates tutorials that contain static and video information from task demonstrations. Videos are automatically edited and offer different views to highlight the most relevant screen areas for a step. Visualizing mouse movement helps user understand a complex action.

ABSTRACT

Users of complex software applications often learn concepts and skills through step-by-step tutorials. Today, these tutorials are published in two dominant forms: *static tutorials* composed of images and text that are easy to scan, but cannot effectively describe dynamic interactions; and *video tutorials* that show all manipulations in detail, but are hard to navigate. We hypothesize that a mixed tutorial with static instructions and per-step videos can combine the benefits of both formats. We describe a comparative study of static, video, and mixed image manipulation tutorials with 12 participants and distill design guidelines for mixed tutorials. We present MixT, a system that automatically generates step-by-step mixed media tutorials from user demonstrations. MixT segments screencapture video into steps using logs of application commands and input events, applies video compositing techniques to focus on salient information, and highlights interactions through mouse trails. Informal evaluation suggests that automatically generated mixed media tutorials were as effective in helping users complete tasks as tutorials that were created manually.

ACM Classification: H5.2 [Information interfaces and presentation]: User Interfaces. - Graphical user interfaces.

Author Keywords: Software tutorials; instructions; video

UIST '12, October 7–10, 2012, Cambridge, Massachusetts, USA.

INTRODUCTION

Learning how to use software applications often happens opportunistically as users need to accomplish specific tasks. When it is unclear how to achieve the desired results, many users turn to step-by-step tutorials, which describe the set of operations required to complete a task. Visual editing applications, such as applications for drawing, photo editing, and 3D modelling, require visual tutorials that show not only how to navigate the user interface but also how to manipulate the canvas, image, or 3D model.

There are two main forms of visual step-by-step tutorials. *Static tutorials* use text and images to describe the set of operations required to accomplish a task. *Video tutorials* are screen recordings of the tutorial author performing the the task. Both forms of instructional content have strengths and weaknesses. Static tutorials are easy to scan forward and backward because they show all instructions. Offering both text and images, they are well suited for people who prefer to learn by looking at images and those who prefer to learn by reading text [11]. However, it can be difficult for users to understand continuous, complex manipulations such as painting a region, adjusting control points, or rotating a 3D object in static tutorials. In contrast, videos are effective at showing exactly how an application responds to user interaction, but it is hard to navigate back to previous steps or to look ahead in a video timeline [18].

We hypothesize that a combination of static and video instructions can improve users' success in following tutorials. We focus on image-editing software in particular, because it is widely used and has a large collection of tutorials accessible in bookstores (books and magazines) and on the web (e.g., user forums and video sharing sites), but we suspect that our findings are generally applicable to visual editing software. With mixed static and video tutorials, users may effectively learn complicated actions (e.g., applying brush strokes) from tutorial video clips, and quickly access basic actions (e.g., copying a layer) from static text and images.

To test our hypothesis, we carried out a within-subjects study comparing static, video, and mixed media tutorials. 12 participants completed three workflows, one for each format. We found that videos are especially valuable for actions that involve brushing, control point manipulation, and adjustment of continuous parameters. We also found that the availability of video reduces the number of repeated attempts users make to execute a step. The study results led to four design guidelines for mixed media tutorials: 1) offer a scannable overview of steps; 2) include small but legible videos; 3) add visualizations of canvas interactions such as brushing to the videos, and 4) enable users to choose the most appropriate visual representation for each step.

To enable instructors to create mixed media tutorials, we introduce MixT, a system that takes a user demonstration and automatically generates mixed tutorials that show static step-by-step content and also include in-place video clips for each operation (Figure 1). MixT generates these materials from screencapture video and recorded traces of application commands and input device events. MixT segments video into steps, applies video compositing techniques to focus on salient screen regions, and highlights canvas interactions through mouse trails. The web-based tutorials give users interactive control over when to see images or videos, and how to render videos. A quantitative analysis of nine automatically generated MixT tutorials indicates that our algorithms for segmenting videos into steps and detecting salient regions within frames are effective (<8% error rates). In addition, informal user feedback suggests that MixT tutorials were as effective as manually created tutorials in helping users complete tasks.

In summary, the main contributions of this paper include:

- a categorization of the types of user operations for which video is useful.
- a set of design principles for how to embed video in step-by-step tutorials, derived from a formative study.
- a general approach for automatically generating mixed media tutorials from demonstrations, and algorithms for implementing this approach for Adobe Photoshop.
- an evaluation of automatically generated mixed media tutorials.

RELATED WORK

Previous HCI research on instructional content falls into four main categories: 1) new tutorial formats and interfaces [1,6,9,12,14,15,18]; 2) automated methods for generating tutorials [3,8,10,18]; 3) studies evaluating the effectiveness of different instructional formats [8,9,11,16,17]; and 4) techniques for searching and analyzing collections of tutorials [5,13]. Our work on generating and evaluating mixed-media tutorials addresses the first three of these topics. In this section, we describe related work on new tutorials formats and automatic generation of instructional content. The following section discusses previous studies on tutorial effectiveness in the context of our own formative study.

New forms of instructional content: While static step-by-step and video tutorials are the most prevalent forms of instructional content, researchers have been exploring new formats and interfaces for learning materials. Many efforts propose instructional aids that work in conjunction with the target application, including in-application step-by-step wizards [1,12,6] and Q&A forums [15], video-based tooltips [9], interactive video tutorials [18], command recommenders [14], and interface facades for mapping commands between applications [19]. Some systems also include features that facilitate navigation within tutorials, such as annotated video timelines [10,18] and reactive "current step" indicators [6]. Our work introduces an interactive mixed-media tutorial format that combines aspects of both step-by-step and video-based learning aids.

Automatic generation of learning materials: One of our key contributions is a method for automatically generating mixed-media tutorials from user demonstrations. Most existing tutorial generation approaches analyze traces of user interactions through the application or screencast video of the demonstration. Methods that analyze user action traces [8,3,10] often capture application-level semantics about specific tools and their purpose, while techniques that analyze screen recordings [18,20,4] use computer vision to identify GUI interactions such as clicking on an icon or button. In MixT, we combine and extend these approaches to create step-by-step tutorials that incorporate text, images, and several formats of video.

FORMATIVE USER STUDY

Researchers provide different findings on the effectiveness of media formats of software tutorials. Evaluating the instructional potential of videos began in the 1990s. Palmiter, Elkerton [16,17], and Harrison [11] studied the effect of animated demonstrations on learning and instruction recall. More recently, Grabler *et al.* compared how users followed book tutorials, videos, and automatically generated static tutorials [8]. Their results showed that automatically generated text and image tutorials outperformed video or book instructions on time and errors. Grossman *et al.* studied the effectiveness of embedding short (10-25 second) video clips in applications [9]. They found that participants who had access to video-based tooltips were significantly faster in completing tasks than those who viewed static ones.

While these studies suggest that there is still some debate over the tradeoffs between step-by-step static and video tutorials, they provide strong support for two key claims: step-by-step tutorials help users make fewer errors by allowing them to work at their own pace, while videos can help provide subtle details of complex interactions that are difficult to represent statically. Based on these findings, we

Figure 2: In our formative study, participants completed three tutorials with images similar but not identical to the originals.

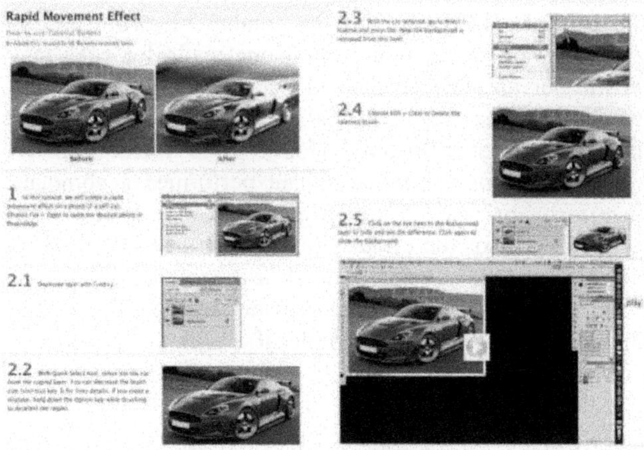

Figure 3: In the mixed condition, participants saw an HTML page with static images and text; they could expand each step to view a video of that step (here: step 2.5).

designed a formative user study that investigates whether video clips can be incorporated into a step-by-step framework to help users follow certain types of image-editing tasks within a tutorial.

Study Design

Hypotheses. Our formative study aims to test the following two hypotheses:

H1 Image manipulation tutorials that mix static images and video clips are more effective than all-static or all-video tutorials.

H2 Users benefit more from seeing video clips instead of static text and images for certain types of commands.

Participants. We recruited 12 participants (5 males and 7 females, aged 20-52), 4 from a campus student design group and 8 from a computer software company, and compensated each with a $15 gift card for participating. Our tutorials focused on achieving specific tasks in Adobe Photoshop. We recruited participants who had prior expertise with Adobe Photoshop, but who were not expert users. To demonstrate expertise, potential participants first completed an online screening test that asked them to follow a short image manipulation tutorial and submit the resulting file. The selected participants had between 1 and 20 years of experience using Photoshop.

Tasks and Material. The study was based on a within-subject design. We looked through Photoshop books and selected 3 different image manipulation tasks with similar levels of difficulty and complexity (see Figure 2). Each tutorial comprised 15-20 steps. We focused on tutorials that included new, less common features such as the *liquify* tool, *gradient warp* tool, and *puppet warp* tool to increase the chance that participants would encounter unfamiliar tools. For each tutorial, we created three types of presentations: 1) *static* (in HTML format displayed on the screen), 2) *video* (on YouTube with audio narration), and 3) *mixed* (web interface shown in Figure 3 without audio). To ensure that different formats presented equivalent information where possible, we first recorded and narrated our video tutorials, then manually generated the static version by writing text instructions based on the narration and annotating and cropping frames of the video. To create mixed tutorials we started with the static tutorials and added the corresponding screencapture video segment for each step. To view the video segment for a step in the mixed tutorial, the user had to click on the image for that step. We scaled these videos to a fixed resolution of 800x500 pixels so that at least 2-3 steps would fit on screen when the videos were expanded. Many online tutorials do not offer full-screen resolution videos; even when high-resolution videos are available, they are hard to use as they force users to continually switch between the video and application windows. We disabled the soundtrack in the mixed tutorial to avoid situations when users only relied on auditory instructions instead of learning from static or video formats.

For each task, participants were given a source image that was distinct, but thematically similar to the image manipulated in the tutorial itself. This study design choice was motivated by the fact that users typically want to transfer the techniques found in tutorials to their own images.

Procedure and Environment. Each session consisted of 1 warm-up task and 3 experimental tasks. The warm-up task was a short 5-step static tutorial. In the 3 experimental tasks the format and task order were randomized. Each 60-minute session was conducted in a lab environment, using computers running Mac OS X, Adobe Photoshop CS5.1 and a web browser (Google Chrome) for viewing tutorials. Each participant was provided with a keyboard and a mouse and was allowed to adjust the equipment setting such as the monitor position and mouse tracking speed during the warm-up task. Photoshop and the web browser were arranged side-by-side on a 30-inch monitor with a resolution of 2048x1280 pixels. During the study, we used screen capture software to record user performance.

Measurement

To evaluate **H1**, we report the number of *errors* and *repeated attempts* that the participants made for each task. While our ultimate goal is skill acquisition and retention, we focus on the pragmatic goal of improving users' success in following tutorials and performing the instructions. We record an *error* if the participant performed a command incorrectly or skipped a step in the tutorial. While errors give a sense for the effectiveness of the tutorials, they do not measure the extraneous work users might have to perform when they have trouble understanding the correct outcome of a step. For example, if a user makes an error and then correctly executes several steps before recognizing the problem, we count this as a single error, even though the user must go back to fix the problem and then redo the subsequent steps. In addition, users may select the right command, but be dissatisfied with the result of their image and try again (e.g., redrawing a gradient). In such cases, we record all executions of the same step following the first attempt as a *repeated attempt.* Note that we do not count adjustments of continuous parameters or refinements of selection regions as repeated attempts because in these cases, the user is focusing on a single action rather than repeating a previously executed step. We do count a repeated attempt if the user entirely undoes a step to then retry it.

To evaluate **H2**, we count the number of different users who click on the video for each step in the mixed tutorials. To determine whether some types of commands benefit from videos more than others, we bin each step into one of the following five command categories based on the types of user interaction and UI elements it involves: brushing/drawing, manipulating control points (e.g., mesh-based warping, spline editing), parameter adjustment (e.g. using a slider to change opacity), UI navigation (e.g., switching tools, finding menu items), and layer operations.

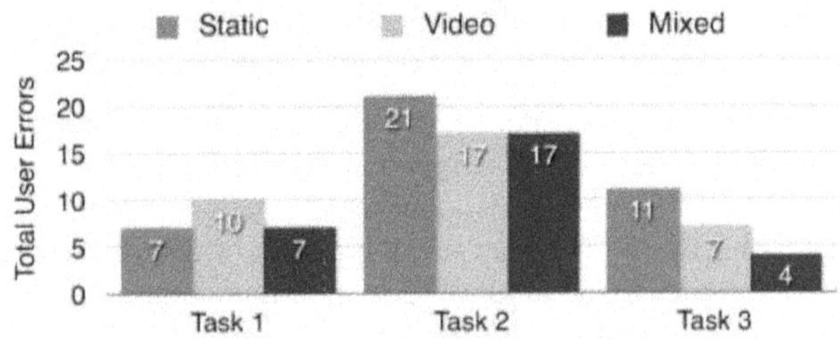

Figure 4: Users tied for fewer errors with mixed tutorials.

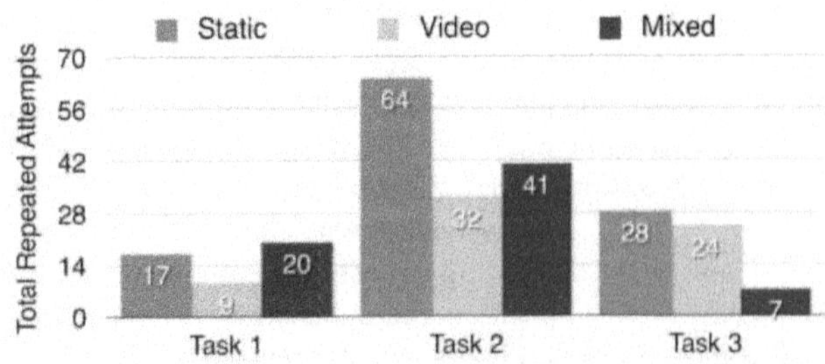

Figure 5: In two of three tasks, participants made more repeated attempts at executing steps with static tutorials than with mixed tutorials. Video tutorials had the fewest attempts.

We also collect qualitative data by observing how users follow the presented information and obtain additional feedback via 5-point Likert-scale questions (e.g., "The <condition> tutorial was easy to follow.") and open-ended questions (e.g., "Compared with static tutorials, what were the pros and cons of the mixed media tutorial?").

RESULTS OF FORMATIVE STUDY

Based on the quantitative data and observations from our study, we gained several insights about how users interact with static and video content.

User Performance on Image Editing Tasks

Our analysis of user performance supports **H1**. As Figure 4 shows, mixed tutorials resulted in the fewest total number of errors (28 for mixed, 34 for video, 39 for static) across all three tasks and produced an equivalent or fewer number of errors compared to static and video for any given task. In terms of extraneous work, the mixed condition resulted in many fewer repeated attempts than static tutorials and slightly more than video tutorials (65 for video, 68 for mixed, 109 for static, see Figure 5). Although the differences in errors and repeated attempts are not statistically significant – likely due to the small study size and differences between the tasks – the overall trends suggest that mixed tutorials help users make fewer errors and do less extraneous work compared to static and video tutorials.

In addition to these quantitative results, we observed a few specific behaviors that had an impact on user performance:

The scannable nature of the static and mixed tutorial formats helped users follow along and avoid missing steps that might result in errors. In the video condition, users were more likely to accidentally skip steps because they were working at a different pace than the video. They also had trouble finding previous steps when trying to identify the source of an error.

In the static condition, users had trouble understanding how to perform steps that involve complex or unfamiliar UI elements and interactions. As we discuss in the following subsection, these were often the same steps where users decided to play the videos in the mixed condition. With only static text and images, users often made errors or had to repeat such steps multiple times.

Participants used the video clips in the mixed condition in a few different ways. Some users played the video *before* attempting the step to familiarize themselves with the relevant UI elements and interactions. In some cases, users also played the video at the same time as they performed the action, which corresponds to what Palmiter and Elkerton described as "mimicking actions" [10]. We suspect both of these behaviors helped reduce errors, especially for complex or unfamiliar steps. In addition, several users also played the video *after* completing a step, as a way to confirm that they had performed the step correctly and "debug" what went wrong if they made an error. This confirmation behavior helped reduce repeated attempts by making it easier to recognize and fix errors sooner.

In some cases, users had trouble seeing all of the relevant details in the mixed videos because the videos were scaled down to 800x500 pixels. For example, when using the *puppet warp* tool, users missed that dragging in the vicinity of a control point (instead of on top of the control point) initiated a control wheel for a rotation rather than a translation maneuver. Although participants neither complained about not being able to resize the video in the MixT condition nor chose full-screen mode in the video condition, they explained that they would hope to clearly see the key part of the video.

Which Commands Led to Video Views?

Our analysis of which mixed steps prompted users to click on the corresponding videos suggests that users did indeed find the video clips more beneficial for some types of steps over others (**H2**). To compute the *likelihood of a video view* (L_V) for the five command categories described earlier, we first determine L_V for each individual step (across all three mixed tutorials) by computing the fraction of users who clicked to view the video for that step, and then we average likelihoods across all the steps in each command category.

As Table 1 shows, L_V is highest for steps that involve brushing/drawing, manipulating control points and parameter adjustments. Based on our observations, videos help users perform the first two types of commands (brushing/drawing and manipulating control points) by explicitly demonstrating the necessary mouse movements rather than requiring the user to infer what to do from text and images alone. In addition, we noticed that some participants used the video clips to determine how precise they needed to be for certain brushing or selection tasks, which is hard to convey with a static representation. Text descriptions such as "rough" and "detailed" are relative and can be interpreted differently by individuals, but seeing how much time the demonstrator devotes to the task provides a much clearer estimate of the required precision for that task. As for parameter adjustments, users may be relying on the videos to provide some context about the range of visual effects the relevant parameters cover in order to determine what parameter values to use for their own image. Unlike static images, which only show the final parameter values and resulting effect, video demonstrations often show how the canvas changes as continuous parameters are updated (often via sliders), which may give users a better sense for the desired outcome of the step.

User Preferences for Tutorial Types

The results of our questionnaire show that while participants had varying opinions on the static and video tutorials, all users strongly agreed that the mixed tutorial was easy to follow. Participants had difficulty finding the tools that the static tutorials referenced and remarked that there were not enough visuals. For full-length videos, participants disliked having to pause the video to complete each step. For the mixed tutorial, half the participants found that video was the most useful among different media components for understanding a step instruction. One participant acknowledged that because the mixed tutorial allowed him to "break down the process into simple steps," he was able to easily find the point where he had made a mistake. Another user explained that videos would be most helpful if the tasks were more advanced and in-depth. On the other hand, users had different preferences within a task. Expertise could be tool-specific: users might find static instructions sufficient for one set of operations (e.g., duplicating layers), and needed to watch videos for another set they were less familiar with (e.g., the *puppet warp* tool). Overall, these responses suggest that users appreciated being able to choose from static and video features in mixed tutorials.

Command Type	L_V: Likelihood of a video view	Steps of this type in corpus
Brushing, Drawing (e.g., Gradient, Brush tool)	35.4%	12
Manipulating Control Points (e.g., Warping)	25.0%	9
Parameter Adjustment (e.g., Levels, Curves)	19.4%	9
UI Navigation (e.g., finding a submenu)	5.4%	37
Layer operations (e.g, Duplicate Layer)	0%	13

Table 1: Participants watched videos most often for brushing, control point manipulation, and parameter adjustments.

DESIGN GUIDELINES

Based on the findings from our formative study, we propose four design guidelines for creating effective mixed media tutorials that combine text, images and videos.

Scannable steps: Scannable steps provide valuable context and facilitate navigation within tutorials. To leverage these benefits, videos in mixed tutorials should be presented in a format that supports scanning.

Small but legible videos: To make mixed media tutorials scannable and enable users to work with the tutorial and their application side-by-side, the videos for individual steps should use the minimum amount of screen real estate while still being legible. Ideally, videos should clearly depict the most important portions of the UI for each step (e.g., dialog boxes, panels, or canvas) while hiding or deemphasizing less relevant regions.

Visualize mouse movement: Our study indicates that videos are most useful for steps that involve brushing, drawing and manipulating control points, but even in videos, it can be difficult to see the exact motion or path of the mouse during such interactions. Visualizing mouse movement and events helps viewers understand the relevant spatio-temporal characteristics of the demonstration.

Give control to the user: Our observations of user behavior suggest that expertise and familiarity with the specific tools or interactions in a tutorial is likely to have an impact on which instructional format (static or video) is best for a given user. Videos help users understand, confirm and debug steps with unfamiliar tools, while static images and text are quicker and easier to skim. Thus, mixed tutorials should let users choose the most appropriate format at the granularity of individual steps.

Figure 6: MixT offers three video playback options: Normal mode (A), zoom mode (B) and crop mode (C).

GENERATING MIXED MEDIA TUTORIALS WITH MIXT

The benefits of mixed media tutorials are unlikely to be realized if creating such materials is too tedious, time-consuming, or if it requires more expertise than creating other tutorial formats. To lower the authoring barrier, we designed MixT, a system that automatically generates mixed media tutorials from user demonstrations. While the MixT architecture can apply to different media creation applications, our current implementation is specific to creating tutorials for Adobe Photoshop.

Tutorial Format

MixT generates HTML tutorials with embedded videos that follow the design guidelines identified in our study. By default, our interface presents a textual description and screenshot for each step, just like a standard static tutorial (see Figure 1A). Clicking on the screenshot replaces the static image with a video player that plays the segment of the original demonstration that corresponds to the written step instructions. For example, a screenshot of a layer panel enhances the instruction "*Select Soft Light from the drop-down menu for Blend Mode*," and the corresponding video clip shows continuous mouse action to the menu, expanding the drop-down menu, moving down to click on the feature, and shows the canvas change. By presenting steps as text and images with video clips that are accessible on demand, MixT tutorials retain the scannability of static tutorials while giving users the option of static- or video-based instruction at each step. To ensure that steps remain scannable and that the tutorial can still be viewed alongside the image editing application (without window switching), we scale each in-place video to at most 700 pixels wide and display text instructions on the left.

Video Playback Options

The MixT video player gives users additional control over the format of playback. Three different modes (normal, zoom, and crop) each emphasize different types of information (Figure 6). In addition, users can display a pointer trace visualization to clarify the path of mouse interactions.

Normal mode shows the entire application window (Figure 6A). This mode preserves all context, but because MixT scales videos down to at most 700x440 pixels positioned next to the text instructions, it may be hard to see precise manipulation or small widgets or handles in the UI.

Zoom mode also shows the entire application window, but performs a non-uniform enlargement of specific UI regions. In particular, the application area being manipulated (e.g., a menu, dialog, or the canvas) is enlarged to fill the full height of the frame and composited on top of the original video in another video layer (Figure 6B). If a dialog also modifies pixels on the canvas, both areas are enlarged and positioned such that they do not overlap. This video composition effectively creates a focus-plus-context view that makes important regions easier to see at a given video resolution [7]. Commercial screencasting software commonly includes a pan-and-zoom technique to make interactions legible in small videos. However, testing early prototypes of MixT suggested that such a technique is not appropriate for brief, single-step videos, as it is hard to establish application context in such short video segments.

Crop mode does not show the entire application — it only shows the currently active area (a tool bar, dialog, main menu, or a panel) and the canvas if being changed (Figure 6C). This offers the unique benefit of showing both a user interface manipulation (e.g., moving a layer opacity slider), and the effect on the image (e.g., parts of the image becoming transparent), while minimizing all other visual distractions. Like the zoom mode, cropped videos are very compact since only the relevant portions of the UI are shown.

Mouse visualization: To help video viewers understand interactions with the canvas, MixT can render a trace visualization of the mouse (Figure 7). These traces show a fading path of the most recent positions of the cursor and encode mouse state using color: *click* events are shown in green (mouse down) and red (mouse up), while mouse *movement* events are shown in purple, and mouse *dragging* events are shown in yellow. Commercial screencasting software also includes mouse visualization techniques. However, they are usually limited to clicking, and the visualizations are typi-

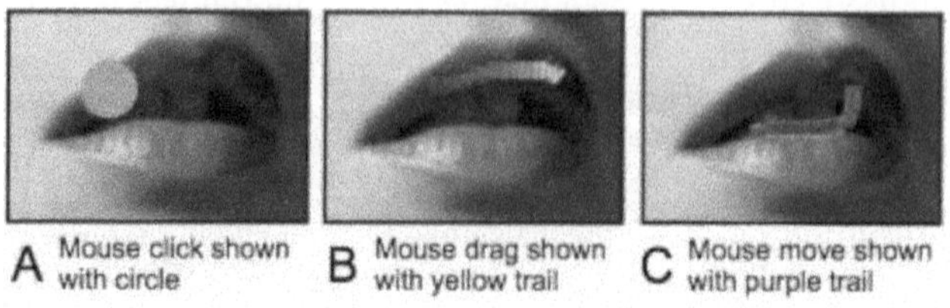

Figure 7: Mouse visualization distinguishes moving and dragging.

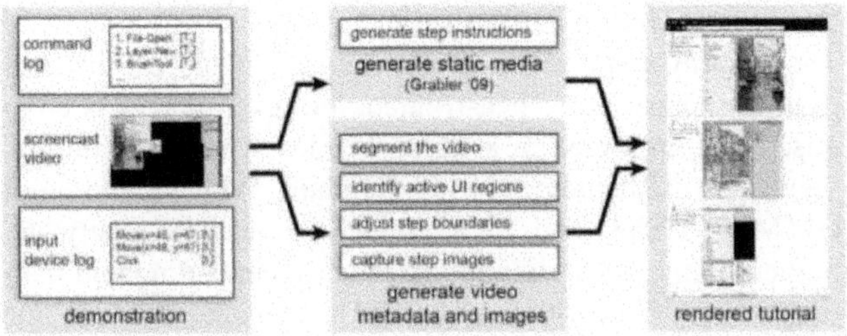

Figure 8: MixT generates tutorials from video and log files.

cally rendered into the final video. In contrast, MixT emphasizes dragging because such interactions are especially relevant for image manipulation. Furthermore, our trace visualizations can be toggled on and off interactively in real-time. By default, the visualizations are enabled for all steps. However, users can change this behavior through an option in the video player.

AUTOMATIC GENERATION PIPELINE

To generate mixed media tutorials, tools can either help authors create new tutorials (e.g., [8]), or they can reformat existing video tutorials into step-by-step videos (e.g., [18]). Our system adopts the former approach and extends Grabler *et al.*'s system for generating static tutorials from demonstration to include videos [8]. Producing mixed media tutorials requires three steps (Figure 8). First, MixT captures an application command log, screencast video and an input device event log and synchronizes them. Second, MixT generates appropriate media files and descriptions: it transforms the log into text instructions, segments the video into steps, and identifies active UI regions, which inform the different video playback modes. Finally, MixT composes the text, images, and video into one document and adds mouse interactions as visualizations on top of the videos. For each step in the tutorial, MixT produces the three video formats and one representative step image.

Recording the Demonstration

MixT records three different time-synchronized data streams during a demonstration: a history of executed application commands; a trace of mouse events; and screencapture video of the entire application interface. To capture application commands, such as opening a file, selecting a region, or hiding a layer, we use Tutorial Builder[1], a freely available Photoshop plug-in that records commands and transforms them into text instructions through text templates. To synchronize Tutorial Builder output with the screencast video and mouse streams, we timestamp the command log during the user demonstration. We obtain mouse event traces on Apple's OS X operating system through the Event Taps[2] API, which observes system-wide input events. We record full-screen video with the commercial Camtasia application[3].

[1] http://labs.adobe.com/technologies/tutorialbuilder/

[2] http://developer.apple.com/library/mac/#documentation/Carbon/Reference/QuartzEventServicesRef/Reference/reference.html

[3] http://www.techsmith.com/camtasia.html

Generating Video Metadata and Step Images

After acquiring the time-synchronized data, there are three technical challenges:

1) Segmenting the video into steps: MixT segments the screencapture video into individual steps based on the timestamps for individual commands in the command log. We map each command Cmd_i with timestamp T_i to a video segment that starts at T_i and ends at T_{i+1}.

2) Identifying active UI regions for zooming and cropping: MixT uses zooming and cropped side-by-side views to preserve legibility for videos at small video frame sizes. To create these specialized views, MixT needs metadata describing the relevant pixel coordinates for each step. Each command in the command log contains information about the logical UI regions that are involved (*e.g.*, the toolbar, a dialog box, or the canvas). However, many commands can be invoked in multiple ways. For example, the *New-Layer* command can be accessed through the application menu, or an icon on the Layer Palette. Therefore, MixT must find and select the correct UI regions from a set of candidates. MixT first uses pixel-based template matching [18] to locate these areas on the screen. MixT then identifies the active UI region by inspecting the mouse event log to see which candidate region received a mouse click at the recorded timestamp T_i of Cmd_i. If there are no mouse clicks detected (e.g., a command invoked via keyboard shortcut), MixT treats the entire frame as the active UI region to ensure the application response is visible in the video.

3) Adjusting segmentation boundaries: While segmenting the video based on the command log timestamps produces a reasonable rough alignment between steps and video segments, there are some cases where a command is recorded after important UI events have taken place. One typical case is menu navigation. For example, to use the *Replace Color* operation, the user moves from the *Image* menu through the *Adjustment* sub menu to the *Replace Color* option. The entire traversal sequence is relevant information as it explains how to reach the menu item. However, the command log only records *Replace Color* when the operation is invoked, which means that a video segment generated based solely on command timestamps would not include the menu traversal.

MixT adjusts step boundaries by leveraging template matching and the mouse event log. To compute the start time of the tutorial step for Cmd_i, our algorithm starts at the command timestamp T_i, looks backward for all mouse clicks that occur within any visible candidate UI region for the command (e.g., menus, panels, toolbar) between T_i and the recorded T_{i-1} of the previous command, and sets the adjusted start time of the step T_i' to the time of the earliest mouse click. Adjusting step boundaries in this manner ensures that the step video clip shows all the relevant actions associated with the command.

4) Capturing screenshots and after images: Finally, in order to generate a representative static image for each step, MixT selects the most informative frame of UI interaction

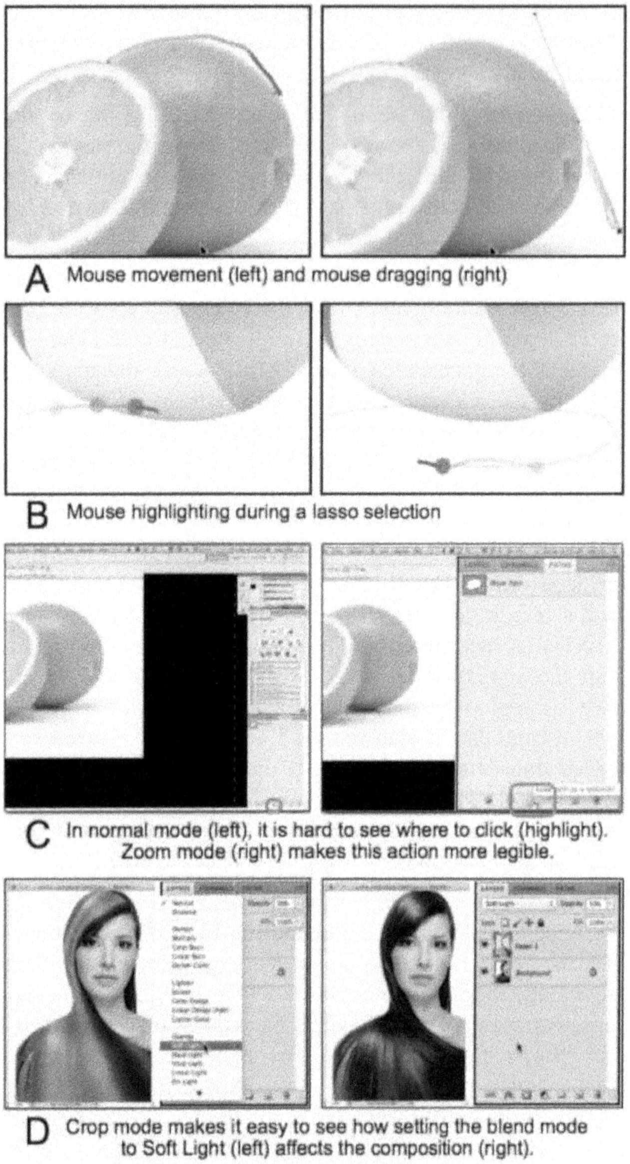

Figure 9: Automatically-generated MixT results.

from the video. For example, if the step changes the layer blend mode, we show an image of the expanded blend mode menu where the appropriate option is highlighted. If the command involves a dialog box, we show the final frame when the dialog is visible. To do so, MixT selects the last frame that includes any candidate UI region within the duration of the step [T_i', T_{i+1}'] and crops the frame to the UI region to produce the representative static image. Furthermore, MixT also captures the state of the canvas from the last frame of the step as an "after" image that helps viewers understand how the canvas was affected.

The MixT video analysis is implemented in MATLAB. In our dataset of nine test tutorials (see Table 2), the average duration of a step video is 12.4 seconds – our analysis takes an average of 6.3 seconds to process each step.

Composing the Mixed Tutorial

The step-by-step mixed-media tutorial with text instructions, structured screencast video, and step images is composed and presented in a web interface. The MixT tutorial viewer is implemented with standard Web technologies (HTML5, CSS3, and JavaScript) so it can be easily deployed online. In particular, all video compositing and matting is done in real-time using HTML5 video. Just-in-time compositing enables users to change viewing options *on the fly* without pre-rendering multiple video presentations. For example, during the video playback users can choose to show the enhanced mouse movement inside its frame for additional detail of a brush stroke, or disable the effect and focus on the incremental change on a canvas in real-time.

RESULTS

We gathered nine different tutorials and recorded working through each tutorial in Photoshop. We then used MixT to automatically generate mixed media tutorials from these demonstrations. This section describes this corpus. The following section then evaluates the generated tutorials quantitatively and qualitatively.

Our tutorials came from both online and book sources: two from "Adobe Photoshop CS5 Classroom in a Book," five from `photoshopstar.com`, one from `makeuseof.com`, and one from `icanbecreative.com`. All are popular resources for Photoshop learners. Two of the tutorials were also used in the formative user study. The selected tutorials had a total of 165 steps and covered all five command types: they contained 15 brushing/drawing operations, 14 control point manipulations, 30 parameter adjustments, 67 UI navigations, and 39 layer operations. The demonstrations were recorded on three different laptops running Photoshop in full screen with native resolutions of 1680x1050, 1440x900, and 1280x800 pixels.

Overall, the MixT tutorials that we generated exhibit the desired characteristics that we identified in our formative study: scannable steps, small but legible videos, visualized mouse operations, and user control over presentation format. We highlight some interesting results generated by MixT and also refer readers to the provided video figure, which has additional examples.

Scannability: The step-by-step layout of our tutorials makes them easy to scan. For example, at a glance, we see that the tutorial "Turning an Image into an Old Photo" involves several adjustment layer operations, while the tutorial "Creating Artistic Effects" involves more parameter adjustments and brushing commands.

Mouse visualization: Our mouse visualizations help clarify several interactions. They clearly communicate the difference between clicking and dragging, a distinction that is fundamental to operations such as path manipulation but hard to glean from screen capture video. For example, Figure 9A shows the difference between moving around the contour of an object without drawing a path (left), and dragging a Bézier handle to adjust a path segment (right).

Mouse trails and click markers were also useful for showing the trajectory of lasso selections (Figure 9B).

Zoom and crop modes: For many steps, the zoom and crop videos offer clear legibility benefits over the normal video mode. In our corpus, zoom mode was especially valuable for highlighting actions on small buttons that occurred near the frame boundaries, e.g., in the layers palette (Figure 9C right). Such operations are easy to miss in a normal, scaled video (Figure 9C left). Crop mode was useful in showing the effect that parameter selection has on the canvas. Figure 9D shows two successive frames that illustrate how changing a layer's blending mode affects the image. Enlarging the canvas in these modes also helps users see the details of effects, such as applying the *eraser* tool on the canvas to enhance the underlying layer (Figure 7).

EVALUATION

To evaluate MixT, we measure the performance of our automatic tutorial generation pipeline and gather user feedback on the effectiveness of the resulting MixT tutorials.

Expert Inspection of Generated Results

We examined the segmented and cropped videos for each step of our nine converted tutorials and recorded the following errors. If a clip does not include all actions of the current step, we record a *segmentation error*. If the screenshots or zoom/crop videos do not show the appropriate application regions, we record a *region finding error*; if the system fails to identify the active region and shows the overall UI instead, we record a *region finding miss*; if they show some relevant regions but omit others, we record an *incomplete region*.

Table 2 shows the results of our inspection. On average, MixT correctly segmented steps around 92% and found relevant regions of complete views 92% of the time. These error rates suggest that our automatic generation pipeline performs reasonably well for a variety of real-world tutorials, but there is room to improve our segmentation and region-finding accuracy.

User Experiences: Working with MixT Tutorials

We conducted a small user evaluation with four participants (2 males and 2 females, aged 25-29, with 5-12 years of Photoshop experience) to gather feedback on the usability of our MixT tutorials. We selected four of our nine evaluation tutorials with features such as the *brush* tool, *pen* tool, *puppet warp* tool, and *gradient warp* tool – commands that led to many video views in our formative study (Table 1). These test tutorials were generated with an earlier version of MixT that did not use the mouse event log to refine the step segmentation and active UI region finding as described earlier. This previous implementation relied solely on the command log and computer vision, which resulted in lower segmentation accuracy (84%) and region-finding accuracy (90%).

Table 2. Error rates for automatically generated tutorials.

Task (time)	Steps	Segmentation Error	Region Error	Region Miss	Incomplete Region
T1 (2'30)	19	15.8%	0.0%	0.0%	10.5%
T2 (3'19)	21	19.0%	0.0%	14.3%	0.0%
T3 (6'02)	30	3.3%	3.3%	0.0%	10.0%
T4 (2'44)	16	12.5%	0.0%	0.0%	0.0%
T5 (4'37)	9	0.0%	0.0%	0.0%	0.0%
T6 (6'10)	21	4.8%	0.0%	0.0%	0.0%
T7 (2'58)	21	4.8%	0.0%	0.0%	4.8%
T8 (3'59)	16	5.6%	11.1%	5.6%	5.6%
T9 (1'41)	12	0.0%	0.0%	0.0%	8.3%
AVG (3'46)	**18**	**7.3%**	**1.6%**	**2.2%**	**4.4%**

Participants were introduced to the MixT system and then asked to work through the set of tutorials, analogously to our formative study. We asked participants to comment on their process using the think-aloud method, and afterwards asked open-ended questions to elicit additional detail.

Successes. The participants found the same benefits in automatically-generated MixT tutorials as earlier participants found in manually-created tutorials. Participants commented that videos helped them understand steps that were complicated or text that was ambiguous or did not contain explanations why certain steps were taken: *"Videos were convenient when trying to get a sense of a complex operation." / "I tended to watch the videos when the text wasn't clear."* Examples included making a selection from a path (1.75 views per user) and the *puppet warp* tool (2.75 views). Note that a clip might be viewed more than once by a single user. Participants also watched videos to confirm their results because *"The photo/screenshot (...) wasn't as actively helpful in guiding what I needed to do or confirming that I was doing the right thing."*

Multiple participants commented positively on the utility of automatically segmented videos that focus on short step clips about the task at hand: *"I didn't have to sit through 5 mins of intro to get a video description of the task I was interested in" / "What I liked the most about the mixed tutorial was the ability to only watch short segments of video that was relevant. Often with video tutorials I find myself sitting and waiting for the content that I need. Because of this, I tend to avoid video tutorials in favor of text. The mixed tutorial was a nice way to achieving the best of both worlds."*

Shortcomings. Our participants identified useful suggestions for improving our tutorial design. Currently, static images do not provide sufficient *information scent* about the contents of the video – it was hard to judge how long each video was and whether there were remaining important actions in a clip. Therefore, participants sometimes skipped important information that resulted in editing errors (e.g., not adjusting the pose after placing pins using the *puppet warp* tool). In addition, the minimal play/pause interface was deemed insufficient: *"Navigating the videos was difficult [...] It was also hard to go back in the video to observe missed steps. Adding standard playback controls might help."* One approach to remedy this would be to analyze the video and provide thumbnail frames of the video clip that highlight the clip's content and length.

As mentioned earlier, our automatic tutorial generation pipeline computes the correct video segments and finds the right spatial regions to highlight for most steps. However, the few segmentation and region finding errors that users encountered sometimes caused important information to be hidden in crop or zoom mode. As a result, participants referred back to the normal video mode more often than we expected, even though the crop and zoom videos were typically more legible. For the 41 video segments that were watched, the average view counts per step were 0.66 for crop mode, 0.24 for zoom mode, and 1.8 for normal mode. Participants commented on the impact of segmentation errors: *"Sometimes the video doesn't line up – and you have to go to the step before to see what's going on."* We consider this as an opportunity to include the tutorial authors in the loop to modify computer-generated tutorials.

LIMITATIONS AND FUTURE WORK

The current MixT implementation has some important limitations that should be addressed in future work. One missing yet interesting component is the audio content, such as a tutorial author's narration in the video demonstrations. Spoken explanations of the demonstrated actions can help viewers understand the rationale behind a sequence of steps. However, narration and interactions may not always occur in synchrony and it is an open problem to segment combined audio and video tracks appropriately into steps. MixT also does not provide opportunities for the tutorial creator to edit a demonstration. To maximize the benefits of mixed media tutorials, we are interested in exploring ways to provide an editing interface for tutorial authors to easily examine and modify automatic results, and to add annotations that can provide rationale in a lightweight way before sharing their demonstrations.

CONCLUSION

This paper introduced MixT, a system that automatically generates step-by-step mixed media tutorials from user demonstrations. We motivated the design of MixT through a formative study that suggested that step videos help users understand complex direct manipulation operations. MixT's architecture uses a command log, an input device log, and screencapture video to generate tutorials. It applies video compositing techniques to focus on salient information, and highlights interactions through mouse trails. Our informal evaluation suggests that automatically generated MixT tutorials were as effective in helping users complete tasks as tutorials that were created manually.

ACKNOWLEDGMENTS

Work at Berkeley was supported by Adobe, Google, a Berkeley Fellowship for Graduate Studies, and a Siebel Foundation Fellowship.

REFERENCES

1. Bergman, L., Castelli, V., Lau, T., and Oblinger, D. DocWizards: a System for Authoring Follow-me Documentation Wizards. In *Proc. UIST '05*, ACM Press (2005).
2. Brunelli, R. Template Matching Techniques in Computer Vision: Theory and Practice. *Wiley* (2009)
3. Denning, J. D., Kerr, W. B., and Pellacini, F. MeshFlow: Interactive Visualization of Mesh Construction Sequences. In *Proc. SIGGRAPH '11*, ACM Press (2011).
4. Dixon, M. and Fogarty, J. Prefab: Implementing Advanced Behaviors Using Pixel-Based Reverse Engineering of Interface Structure. In *Proc. CHI '10*, ACM Press (2010).
5. Ekstrand, M., Li, W., Grossman, T., Matejka, J., and Fitzmaurice, G. Searching for Software Learning Resources using Application Context. In *Proc. UIST '11*, ACM Press (2011).
6. Fernquist, J., Grossman, T., and Fitzmaurice, G. Sketch-Sketch Revolution: An Engaging Tutorial System for Guided Sketching and Application Learning. In *Proc. UIST '11*, ACM Press (2011).
7. Furnas, G. W. Generalized Fisheye Views. In *Proc. CHI '86*, ACM Press (1986).
8. Grabler, F., Agrawala, M., Li, W., Dontcheva, M., and Igarashi, T. Generating Photo Manipulation Tutorials by Demonstration. In *Proc. SIGGRAPH '09*, ACM Press (2009).
9. Grossman, T., and Fitzmaurice, G. ToolClips: an Investigation of Contextual Video Assistance for Functionality Understanding. In *Proc. CHI '10*, ACM Press (2010).
10. Grossman, T., Matejka, J., and Fitzmaurice, G. Chronicle: Capture, Exploration, and Playback of Document Workflow Histories. In *Proc. UIST '10*, ACM Press (2010).
11. Harrison, S. A Comparison of Still, Animated, or Nonillustrated On-line Help with Written or Spoken Instructions in a Graphical User Interface. In *Proc. CHI '95*, ACM Press (1995).
12. Kelleher, C., and Pausch, R. Stencils-based Tutorials. In *Proc. CHI '05*, ACM Press (2005).
13. Kong, N., Grossman, T., Hartmann, B., Fitzmaurice, G. and Agrawala, M. Delta: A Tool for Representing and Comparing Workflows. In *Proc. CHI '12*, ACM Press (2012).
14. Matejka, J., Li, W., Grossman, T., & Fitzmaurice, G. CommunityCommands: Command Recommendations for Software Applications. In *Proc. UIST '09*, ACM Press (2009).
15. Matejka, J., Grossman, T., and Fitzmaurice, G. IP-QAT: In-Product Questions, Answers & Tips. In *Proc. UIST '11*, ACM Press (2011).
16. Palmiter, S. and Elkerton, J. Animated Demonstrations vs Written Instructions for Learning Procedural Tasks: a Preliminary Investigation. In *International Journal of Man-Machine Studies* (1991), 34, pp. 687-701.
17. Palmiter, S. and Elkerton, J. Animated Demonstrations for Learning Procedural Computer-Based Tasks. *Human-Computer Interaction*. 8, 3 (1993), pp. 193–216.
18. Pongnumkul, S., Dontcheva, M., Li, W., Wang, J., Bourdev, L., Avidan, S., and Cohen, M. F. Pause-and-Play: Automatically Linking Screencast Video Tutorials with Applications. In *Proc. UIST '11*, ACM Press (2011).
19. Ramesh, V., Hsu, C., Agrawala, M., and Hartmann, B. ShowMeHow: Translating User Interface Instructions Between Similar Applications. In *Proc. UIST '11*, ACM Press (2011), 1–8.
20. Yeh, T., Chang, T.-H., and Miller, R.C. Sikuli: Using GUI Screenshots for Search and Automation. In *Proc. UIST '09*, ACM Press (2009), 183–192.

GamiCAD: A Gamified Tutorial System For First Time AutoCAD Users

Wei Li, Tovi Grossman, and George Fitzmaurice
Autodesk Research
firstname.lastname@Autodesk.com

ABSTRACT
We present GamiCAD, a *gamified* in-product, interactive tutorial system for first time AutoCAD users. We introduce a *software event driven finite state machine* to model a user's progress through a tutorial, which allows the system to provide real-time feedback and recognize success and failures. GamiCAD provides extensive real-time visual and audio feedback that has not been explored before in the context of software tutorials. We perform an empirical evaluation of GamiCAD, comparing it to an equivalent in-product tutorial system without the gamified components. In an evaluation, users using the gamified system reported higher subjective engagement levels and performed a set of testing tasks faster with a higher completion ratio.

Author Keywords: Game; tutorial; learning; gamification

ACM Classification: H5.2 [Information interfaces and presentation]: User Interfaces. - Graphical user interfaces.

INTRODUCTION
Today's software applications can contain hundreds or thousands of features [27], making the process of learning to use the software difficult for new users [20]. A long line of HCI literature has investigated the problems associated with learning and many types of learning aids have been proposed. Common formats include online help [4, 5, 41], discussion boards [16, 39], and video assistance [19, 33].

For new users, documentation may not be effective. Carroll suggests a user has a *production bias* which "reduces their motivation to spend any time just learning about the system" [4]. A more promising approach may be to provide interactive tutorials, where users get to learn by accomplishing tasks in the application itself [2, 14, 17, 24].

While many types of interactive tutorials exist, they may lack a level of engagement that will provide enough motivation for the user to follow through with required or recommended lessons.

One technique to increase engagement levels, which recently has become commonly used in many domains, is gamification [10]. Gamification is commonly defined as using elements of video games in non-game situations to enhance user experience and engagement levels with a product [38, 36]. Gamification has been rapidly growing in popularity, with workshops [9] and entire conferences[1] now being dedicated to the topic.

Given its current popularity, it is reasonable to consider the appropriateness of gamification for software tutorials. Some previous commercial systems have developed tutorial systems that contain some gamified elements[2 3]. However, little research literature exists on this topic [12]. In particular, it is unclear if there are any empirical advantages of a gamified software tutorial compared to a non-gamified counterpart [25, 31]. Without data to refer to, software designers must make uninformed decisions to develop gamified tutorials, without an awareness of the benefits or tradeoffs.

In this paper, we investigate the use of gamified tutorials to help new users both learn and improve their performance with a software system. Our work is composed of two main contributions:

First, we present GamiCAD, a gamified tutorial system for AutoCAD[4]. GamiCAD builds upon the recent work of Dong et al's Jigsaw system [12], introducing several novel features. In particular, a *software event driven finite state machine* is used to model a user's progress through a tutorial, which allows the system to provide real-time feedback and recognize success and failures. In addition, GamiCAD provides extensive real-time visual and audio feedback that has not been explored before in the context of software tutorials.

Our second core contribution is an empirical evaluation of GamiCAD, comparing it to an equivalent in-product tutorial system without the gamified components. Our evaluation shows that not only does a gamified tutorial increase subjective engagement and enjoyment levels, it can also improve learning. In particular, users completed 10% more testing tasks and were 20%-76% faster after using the tutorial with the gamified components.

UIST '12, October 7–10, 2012, Cambridge, Massachusetts, USA.

[1] The Gamification Summit
http://www.gsummit.com (retrieved April 13, 2012)
[2] http://success.adobe.com/microsites/levelup/ (retrieved April 13, 2012)
[3] http://www.ribbonhero.com/ (retrieved April 13, 2012)
[4] http://usa.autodesk.com/autocad/

RELATED WORK

In this section, we discuss previous research in the areas of software learning, tutorial systems, gamification, and software gamification.

Software Learning

Software learnability [11, 30] is an important research problem that has been prevalent since the beginnings of HCI. Important early work includes Carrol et al.'s investigations of learning within word processing tools [4, 5, 26].

A recent survey of software learnability is provided by Grossman et al [20]. Their taxonomy of learnability distinguished between *initial learnability*, the initial performance with a system and *extended learnability*, the change in performance over time. In targeting new users, GamiCAD focuses mostly on initial learnability.

In the psychology literature, the Dreyfus model proposes that a learner passes through five distinct stages during the skill acquisition (Figure 1) [13]. This indicates that tutorial systems for novice users should provide a high level of guidance and feedback. Using game mechanics may be one way to do so.

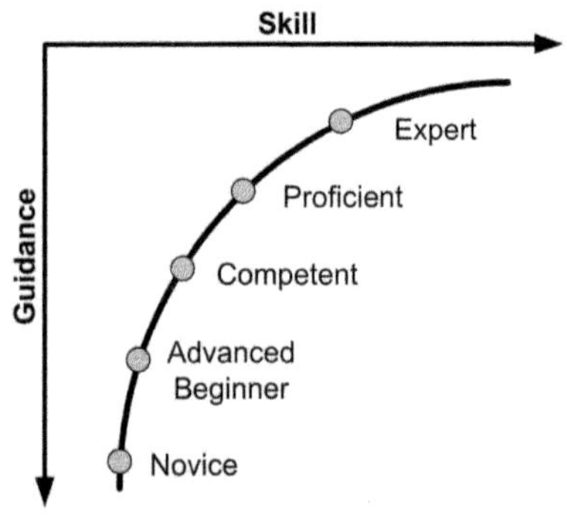

Figure 1. Dreyfus model of skill acquisition.

Tutorial Systems

Delivering effective help material and documentation can be a challenging task, because of the active user's *production bias* [4]. Early efforts to improve software documentation included minimalist and task-centered help [4, 5, 41].

An alternative to static help systems is animated assistance [19, 32, 33]. Such materials typically enforce a passive learning process, or force users to work at the pace of the video [17]. Pause-and-Play is an interesting new system that aims to improve upon this limitation, by automatically pacing the video based on a user progress [33].

Alternatively, tutorial systems can also be integrated within the software application itself, providing a rich interactive learning experience [2, 14, 24, 33, 35]. For example, Stencils-based tutorials [24] guide a user to perform the correct step by overlaying a stencil with a hole to click-through. The level of engagement they provide could potentially be increased even more by integrating gaming components.

In particular, Fernquist et al. suggest that tutorial experiences should be *as compelling as possible*, so that users stay engaged [14]. One guideline for creating such experiences is Csikszentmihalyi's concept of flow [8], which describes a user's state of "optimal experience". Qualifying factors for achieving flow include: perceptions of clear goals, immediate feedback, and matched skills and challenges [6]. GamiCAD is designed with these factors in mind.

Gamification

Gamification is the use of design elements, which are characteristic for games, in non-game contexts [10]. Gamification has been used in numerous domains, such as work environments [15, 36], the design industry [23], marketing [43] and, particularly, educations [18, 34, 37].

One main motivation for gamifying a learning experience is to make the experience more engaging for the user [38]. However, there is "a lack of empirical evidence" that the use of gamification is effective in learning contexts [25]. Previous studies of gamified learning environments [7, 31] have been confounded in that "positive educational outcomes can be attributed to the instructional design of the educational programs and not to games as a medium" [25]. Our work contributes empirical data from a controlled experiment, comparing a gamified and non-gamified learning experience with equivalent instructional design.

Software Gamification

There are several games designed for learning software applications. Commercial examples include Microsoft Ribbon Hero[1], and the now expired Adobe LevelUp[2]. In the research literature Jigsaw [12] is also related to our work.

In these examples, users need to finish small tasks to collect points and badges. Jigsaw promotes discovery-based learning, where users can explore multiple strategies for completing a task. While Dong et al. found that users enjoyed the Jigsaw system [12]; none of these systems have been empirically compared to non-gamified counterparts.

Furthermore, in these examples, the extent of the gamified components is limited. For example, Ribbon Hero provides a game like menu system for choosing levels, but once a task is chosen, the system runs like a typical in-product tutorial. In addition, these previous systems give users exposure to a broad range of tools, but users do not necessarily learn the best way to use them.

GamiCAD builds upon these systems and increases the extent of which gamified mechanics are used during individual levels. Furthermore, GamiCAD exposes users to multiple ways to use individual tools, so users learn how to use tools in both basic and advanced ways.

Summary

A large amount of literature exists on software learning and tutorial systems. Results from this literature indicate promise in providing interactive tutorial systems, and using gamified mechanics to achieve high engagement levels. While

[1]http://www.ribbonhero.com/ (retrieved April 13, 2012)
[2]http://success.adobe.com/microsites/levelup/ (retrieved April 13, 2012)

some gamified software tutorial systems exist, the extent to which they are gamified is limited, and no empirical evaluations have been performed. In general, there is a lack of empirical evidence that the use of gamification is effective in learning contexts.

GAMIFICATION ELEMENTS

In our work we aim to push the envelope in terms of the extent of gamified mechanics which are included in our tutorial system. For a complete discussion of gaming elements, we direct the reader to existing surveys [29, 22, 28, 40]. Here, we specifically discuss the gaming elements most appropriate for use in a software tutorial system. Each of these elements will be integrated into GamiCAD.

Fantasy

According to Maloney [29], "Fantasy is probably the most important feature of computer games that can be usefully included in other user interfaces." Fantasy evokes images of objects or situations that aren't actually present. This can make the experience more emotionally appealing to users.

Clear Goals

An aspect of games that has been strongly correlated with game popularity is the presence of clear goals [29, 40]. Clear goals are important so that players understand the task which they are trying to complete, so that they will stay engaged with the system [8].

Feedback and Guidance

Typical video games provide immediate feedback to users based on their progress and goals. Providing such feedback can also increase users' engagement levels [6, 8, 40]. In addition, if a user makes a mistake, they can become lost and disoriented [12]. As such, the system should lead users to recovering from error states [40].

Progressive Disclosure

A game helps players to continuously increase their skills by progressive disclosure of both knowledge *and* challenge [40]. This will help ensure that the challenges in the game match the player's skill levels [8]. For example, the system could provide more strict guidance to a novice user or more freedom to proficient learners.

Time Pressure

Time pressure is commonly considered an important and effective aspect of games. Adding time pressure is effective as it establishes clear and challenging goals [42, 29, 36].

Rewards

A common approach to directly motivate users is to provide points and rewards [36, 42]. Performance feedback can be provided by assigning scores after the completion of a game level, which can facilitate a user's progress assessment. Another type of reward mechanism is to unlock new levels based on the user's achievements.

Stimuli

To ensure high engagement levels, games should provide stimuli that is worth attending to [1, 40]. High-quality stimuli can be provided in a number of different formats, such as unique animations, sounds, and appearances.

GAMICAD SYSTEM AND IMPLEMENTATION

We now described GamiCAD, a new gamified software tutorial system, designed for new AutoCAD users. GamiCAD consists of several components which interact with one another (**Figure 2**). The Mission Console is used to select levels to complete. The in-product task panel is used to provide instructions and feedback during individual levels. For accurate feedback to be provided, the in-product task panel requires knowledge of the tasks, knowledge of how the tools work, and also needs to be able to monitor events and data from the AutoCAD environment. The system is implemented as an AutoCAD plugin using the AutoCAD ObjectArx SDK.

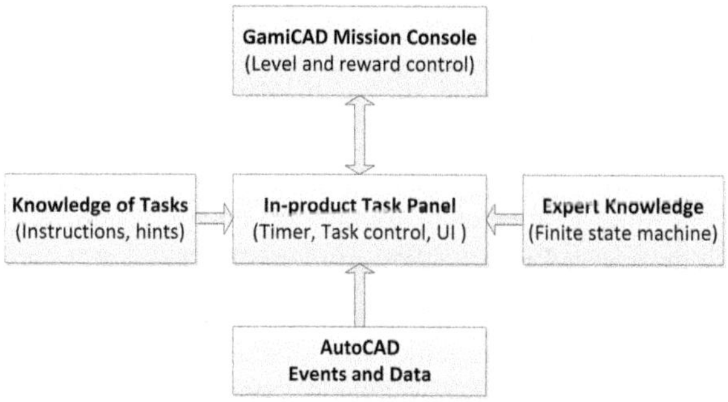

Figure 2. GamiCAD Architecture.

System Goals and Contributions

Our ultimate motivation is to provide an *effective* and *engaging* learning system for new users. In terms of *effectiveness*, we aim to help users learn basic *and* efficient ways to accomplish tasks. In terms of *engagement*, we aim to provide an environment that users will enjoy, and be motivated to repeat tasks to improve their own performance levels.

Compared with previous systems, GamiCAD contributes several novel features: 1) GamiCAD provides learning tasks in two level formats. Highly structured guided tasks are provided for first-time users, but as users progress, they are rewarded with "arcade style" bonus levels. 2) GamiCAD stimulates repetition of tasks through level unlocking mechanics. GamiCAD uses approaches to make repetitive tasks challenging and interesting, so that users can refine and improve their skills before advancing to the next level. 3) GamiCAD provides immediate feedback to help users recover from errors. An event driven finite state machine is used to model possible states of a task. This allows the system to guide users back from incorrect states, preventing user frustration. 4) GamiCAD provides multiple detailed lessons for similar tasks, so that users can be exposed to alternative task flows to accomplish a task. This allows users to learn how to not only use a command, but use it efficiently.

Target Application and Content

We study our gamified learning system in the context of AutoCAD, a software application for both 2D and 3D design. AutoCAD is considered challenging for novices, making it a good candidate for our efforts.

We focus the learning content of GamiCAD on two fundamental CAD commands, LINE and TRIM. Both LINE and TRIM tools have complex subtleties and are difficult for novices to learn, yet fundamental for achieving higher level expertise. The lessons are delivered in a set of comprehensive in-product learning modules covering multiple options and parameters for working with these functions. In addition, the learning modules also provide basic skills of using AutoCAD, including command line input, document navigation skills and object selection.

Command Flow Modeling

Many AutoCAD commands are designed to follow a specific action sequence. For example, with the TRIM command, a set of cutting edges has to be selected before selecting the objects to trim. If the system lacks an awareness of a user's progress through these steps, adequate real-time feedback cannot be provided, which can cause users to become lost and confused [10]. In GamiCAD we use an event driven finite state machine to monitor a user's progress, and help the user actively recover from incorrect states.

Finite state machines (FSMs) have been broadly used in video games. Popular games like Quake II and Warcraft III take advantage of FSM systems to control their levels, environmental conditions and computer-controlled characters.

In our FSM, the transition from one state to another is triggered by software events or messages. Our FSM is also enhanced with parameters, for example, to keep track of the number of points in a line. Most software applications can formally abstract their features or specifications using event driven FSMs [21]. In AutoCAD, the LINE and TRIM command can be represented by the FSMs in Figure 3.

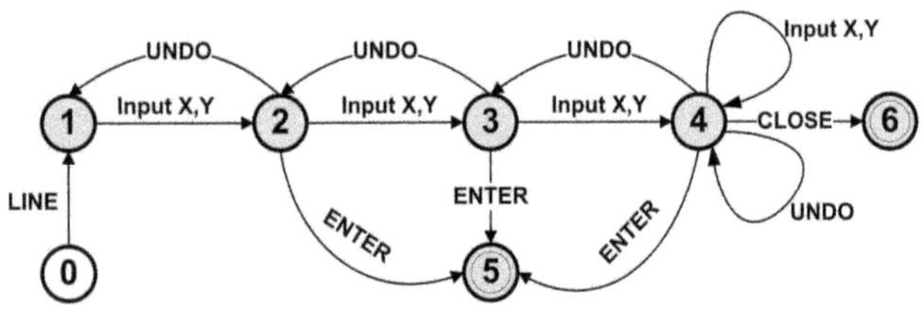

Figure 3. FSMs for LINE command.

We define a *command flow* by a specific path to reach a final state. For example, the *command flow* for drawing a triangle with the LINE command is [LINE]→[Input X,Y] →[Input X,Y]→[Input X,Y]→[CLOSE]. This will trigger the transitions of the FSM from states 0 to 6.

In GamiCAD, once the user begins a task, the finite state machine begins to parse the user's action stream and match it with the associated command flow, so their progress throughout the task can be accurately monitored.

This is particularly helpful for guiding users to recover from error states. When the user makes an error, GamiCAD searches the FSM to find the shortest path to return to the last correct state. We use Figure 4 as an example, where a user's task is to draw a single line segment. If the user instead draws two line segments, using three points, the FSM will incorrectly be in state 4. To guide the user back to the *command flow* path, the system can prompt the user to return to state 3 by typing UNDO.

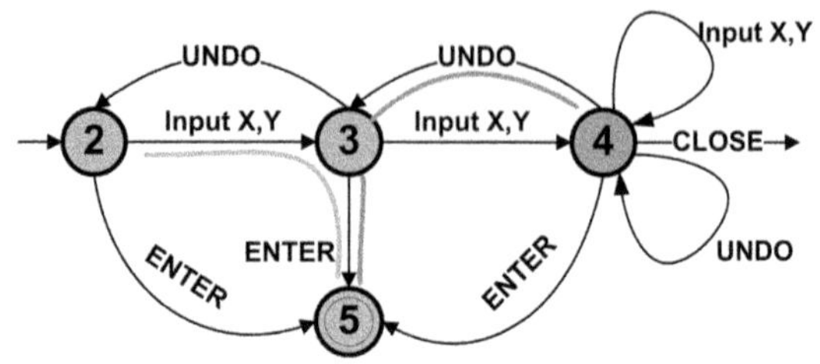

Figure 4. Error recovery. User currently in state 4. Correct flow is green line connecting states 2→3→5. Orange line shows the error recovery path 4→3→5.

GAMICAD DESIGN

We now discuss the design of GamiCAD, highlighting which design choices utilize the previously described Gamification Elements, shown in italicized brackets.

The Mission Console

The *Mission Console* is the top-level interface used to navigate through the game and its levels. The mission console is displayed in an external window.

We choose to use the design intensive Apollo program as the backstory for GamiCAD (*Fantasy)*. Users are introduced to a story in an initial screen when they first launch the game, which explains that the user will be responsible for helping NASA build components of a spacecraft.

In addition to the initial start-up screen, the Mission Console contains four Mission Pages. Users can navigate through the mission console with Forward and Back arrows. Initially the user can only access the first mission, with missions 2-4 being locked.

The four missions are sorted by topic (**Figure 5**). Each mission contains multiple levels. The individual levels take one of three mini-game formats. SkillBuilder provides a guided task level, and QuickClick and TrimMaster provide arcade style bonus levels.

The Bonus Missions are designed to be rewarding experiences (*Rewards*). To unlock the next mission, users must achieve at least 4 stars in each level of the current mission (*Progressive Disclosure*). This can encourage learning through repetition.

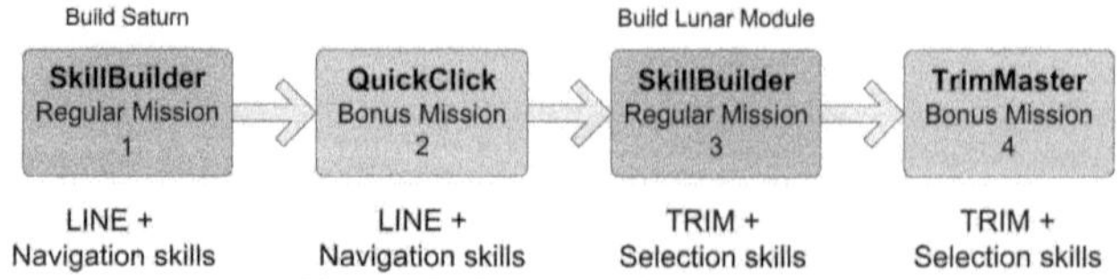

Figure 5. Four mission topics.

Mission Pages

Each Mission has a dedicated mission page in the Mission Console (Figure 6). Each mission page lists the individual levels within that mission. The levels are carefully ordered to first expose users to the basic functionality, and then more advanced options and features. Users must complete the tasks in order (*Progressive Disclosure*). Clicking on a level launches the level inside of AutoCAD.

For each completed level, the user's best score and highest number of stars achieved are displayed (*Feedback and Guidance*). An icon is used to indicate the levels which are still locked.

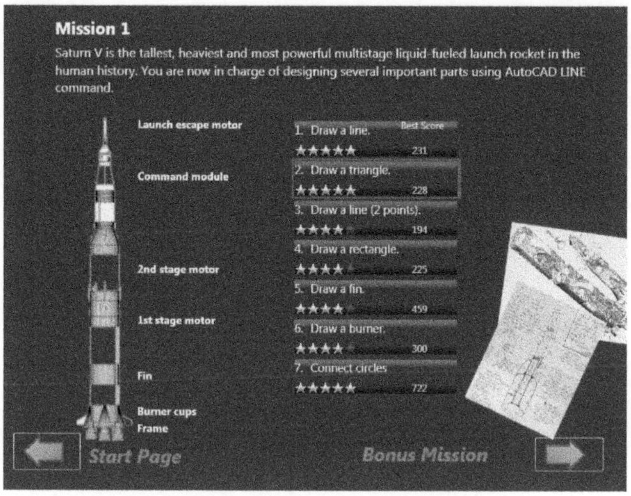

Figure 6. Mission Page with 7 completed levels.

SkillBuilder

SkillBuilder provides a structured task with step-by-step guidance to learn a new skill. A palette in AutoCAD is used to show the instructions and information about the task (Figure 7). An image and instructions describing the goal of the task are displayed at the top of the palette (*Clear Goals*) (Figure 7A). Users click a "Start" button to begin a level.

Step-by-step instructions

Under the task description, an area is reserved to show step-by-step instructions. The step-by-step instructions are hidden by default, so users can try to complete the task without assistance. A "show hints" button can be clicked to reveal the hints. When visible, each step contains a simple and clear instruction (*Clear Goals*) (Figure 7B).

After the completion of a step, the FSM will trigger a step complete message, and a green check mark is displayed next to that step (*Feedback and Guidance*). If the user makes an error, a message is displayed directing the user to the required corrective action (*Feedback and Guidance*). If a user diverges from the required command path by more than two steps, a message informs the user that they must start over. This is equivalent to dying/failing a level in a video game, and prevents users from becoming too lost.

Some steps have a hint button, which provides an animated visual aid to help the user locate an associated component or tool from the AutoCAD UI (*Stimuli*) (Figure 7C).

Speed bonus

At the bottom of the palette, a timing progress bar and Speed Bonus Points are displayed (*Time Pressure*). The Speed Bonus Points start at 150, and begin to continually decrease immediately after the task is activated, decreasing by 1 every 0.2 seconds until it reaches 0. The progress bar also reflects this time pressure by shortening its length and changing its color from green to red (Figure 7D).

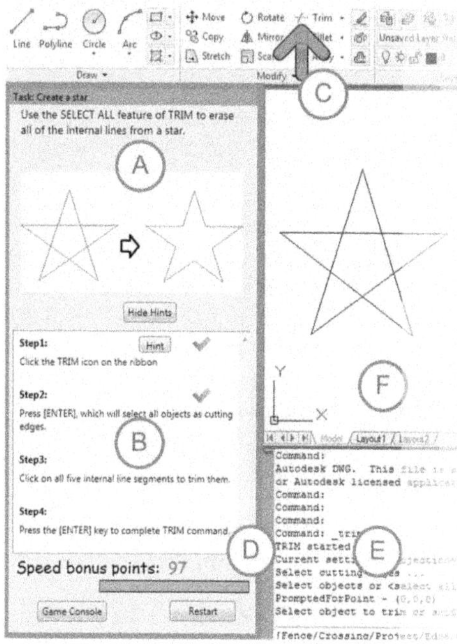

Figure 7. Task panel for SkillBuilder (A) Task description; (B) Step-by-step instructions; (C) UI element visual aid; (D) Speed bonus; (E) AutoCAD command line; (F) Drawing area.

Scoring

When the user completes a level, a display provides feedback on how they performed (*Rewards*). We display a total score, bonus points, and 0 to 5 stars (Figure 8). A customized message is also displayed based on their performance.

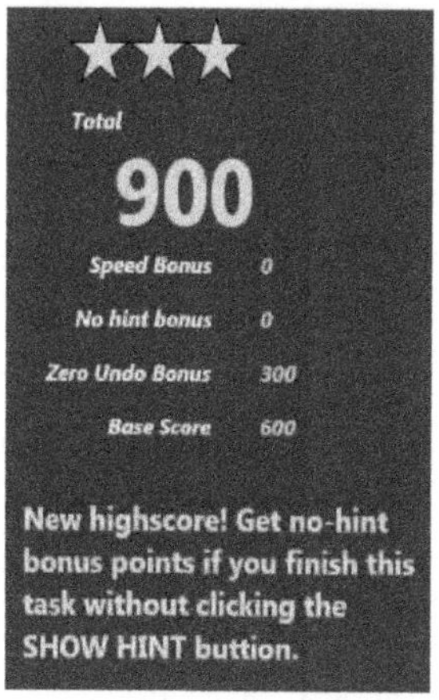

Figure 8. SkillBuilder score board.

The score and stars earned per task are computed based on four factors:

$$total\ score = base\ score + speed\ bonus$$
$$+no\ hint\ bonus + zero\ undo\ bonus$$

The base score is pre-assigned to each task according to its complexity, varying from (50 to 600). The no hint bonus is either 0, if the user viewed the hints, or 50% of the base score, if they did not. Similarly, the zero undo bonus is either 0, if the user used an undo operation, or 50% of the base score if they did not. The number of stars assigned is based on the ratio of the current score over the total score.

Bonus Mission: QuickClick Game

Once all tasks for the LINE tool are completed in Mission 1, users are rewarded with an arcade-style QuickClick bonus Mission, where they can apply their newly obtained skills.

QuickClick is a connect-the-dots tracing game that requires efficient use of the LINE command and navigation tools to complete (Figure 9). The player is required to navigate in the drawing area and connect a series of small circles by using the LINE command. Only one dot is displayed at a time. When the user successfully clicks within the displayed dot, the next dot is revealed.

The dots are extremely small, so the user must zoom in to be able to click within their boundaries. A larger blue circle is displayed around the next goal dot, so that the user knows where the target is. The trick of the game is to quickly locate the next dot, zoom in to it, and then zoom out or pan to the next target location. This is a common and important behavior for efficient use of AutoCAD.

For Mission 2 there are 3 QuickClick levels. In each level, the dots get smaller making the task more difficult, as more zooming is required (*Progressive Disclosure*).

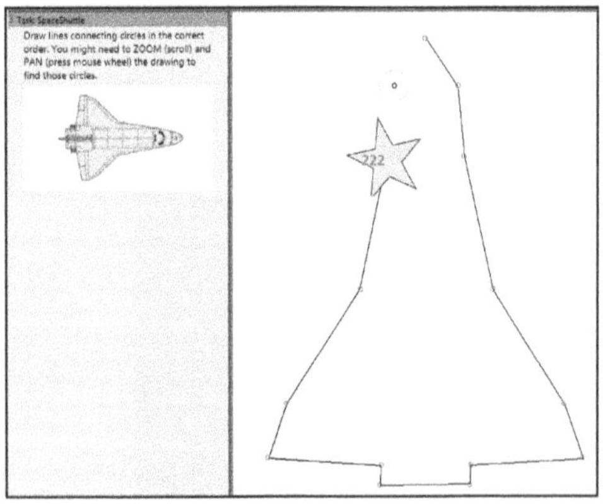

Figure 9. QuickClick bonus game.

Scoring

QuickClick provides feedback every time a user successfully clicks a dot (*Feedback and Guidance*). A step score is calculated based on how fast the user clicked the dot (*Time Pressure*). An overlay displays the step score and a spinning star animation when the user successfully clicks on a dot (*Stimuli*). Higher scores generate bigger stars. The total score of the task is the sum of each step score.

Bonus Mission: TrimMaster Game

TrimMaster is the other bonus game that users can play after completing the TRIM tool levels in Mission 3. In TrimMaster, players are required to remove the internal boundaries among geometries and maximize the internal area of merged geometries (Figure 10). Similar to puzzle-arcade games like Tetris, TrimMaster keeps adding new geometry, so that the level gets more difficult as it continues. Figure 10 shows the progression of levels. Each time the user executes the TRIM command, a new object is added to the scene, until a predetermined number of objects have been added. If the player performs perfectly, the final object will have no internal lines.

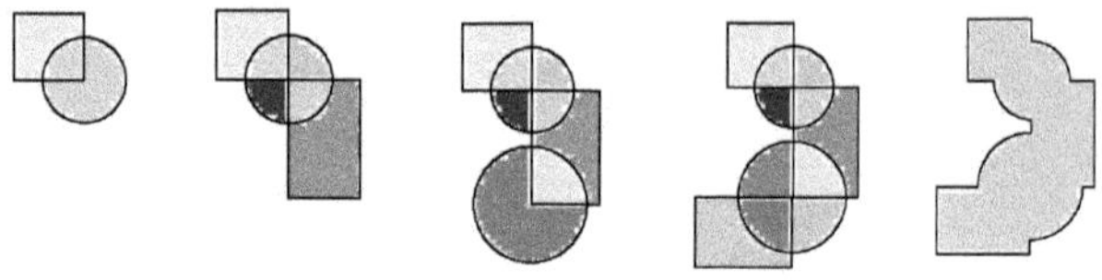

(1) (2) (3) (4) (5)

Figure 10. (1-4) TrimMaster getting harder from round 1 to round 4. (5) The final geometry if the player successfully merged all geometries

Scoring

As in the QuickClick bonus game, no step-by-step instructions are provided, but feedback is provided each time a user executes the TRIM command (*Feedback*). The same animated visual overlay from QuickClick is displayed, each time a TRIM is completed (*Stimuli*). The score is based on the largest internal area in the geometry, and the time taken to complete the step (*Time Pressure*). The higher the score is, the bigger the star will be. The total level score is the sum of these scores.

Music and Sound Effects

To provide a more immersive experience, GamiCAD uses real time sound effects and dynamic background music (*Stimuli*). Sound effects are played throughout the game. For example, a sound effect is played: when a user changes pages in the mission console; when the user completes each step in the bonus mission levels; and when a level is completed and the score is displayed.

In addition, background music is played throughout the entire game, and is updated dynamically based on the user's progress and the game's state. Each mission has its own background music, with the bonus levels having faster paced music. While viewing the Mission console, the background music is more ambient. The Mission console background music updates each time a user completes an entire mission, to strengthen the user's sense of progress. The background music was taken from the award winning Assassin's Creed II video game original sound track[1].

[1] http://www.amazon.com/Assassins-Creed-Original-Game-Soundtrack/dp/B002TURE9E

We direct the reader to our video figure to hear the sound effects and background music.

USER STUDY

While informal subjective evaluations of gamified software tutorials have been previously conducted, there is a lack of empirical evidence studying the differences between gamification and non-gamified counterparts in the learning domain [10, 31]. Our goal of this comparative study is to answer two main questions: 1) Does the inclusion of gamified elements provide a more engaging learning experience? 2) Does a gamified software tutorial have a positive impact on learning? We hypothesize that the gamified components will increase user engagement levels, which will in turn, also positively impact learning.

Conditions

To truly understand the impact of gamification, GamiCAD needs to be compared to a system with equivalent instructional design. As such, we built an in-product tutorial system that contains the exact same tasks and instructions but without the gamified mechanic. By comparing these gamified vs. non-gamified learning systems, we are able to conduct a controlled quantitative and qualitative analysis of the impact of gamifying software tutorials.

As such, there were two conditions in our study, associated with the two tutorial systems. The first tutorial system was *GamiCAD*. The second system, *TutorCAD*, was the equivalent version of the tutorial system, where only the gamified features were removed (Figure 11). The features which were removed were: the mission console (replaced with a tutorial list panel, Figure 11a), scoring system, animated feedback, music, sound effects, timers, and mission/level unlocking mechanism. Users were asked to complete tasks following the same order in the game. *TutorCAD* still provides many of the interactive features possessed by GamiCAD, such as the step-by-step instructions, step completion feedback, error recovery guidance, and UI element visual aids (Figure 11b).

Once a tutorial is selected in TutorCAD, a task panel will be opened in AutoCAD. The task panel looks almost the same as GamiCAD's SkillBuilder task panel, but the speed bonus points, progress bar and the game console buttons have been removed. Bonus levels were included, but presented as regular tasks in the tutorial list panel. The actual tasks were identical, with the exception of the TrimMaster tasks. Instead of presenting geometry one object at a time, the final round is present at the beginning of the task.

Apparatus

Our user study was conducted using a HP workstation with AutoCAD 2012 installed and a 24 inch monitor with a resolution of 1920×1200. A standard mouse, keyboard, and set of speakers were connected to the workstation.

Participants

Fourteen participants (10 female) between the ages of 19 and 62 without any AutoCAD experience were recruited via online postings. Five participants were regular gamers, eight played games occasionally. Only one participant reported not playing any video games at all.

Procedure and Design

A within participant design was used for the study, where task order was fixed but condition order was counterbalanced. All participants completed LINE tasks first and TRIM tasks second. Half the participants used GamiCAD for LINE (first) and the other half used TutorCAD for LINE (first). We fixed the order of the tasks to maintain progressive disclosure of the relevant AutoCAD skills. In the *GamiCAD* condition, users needed to achieve 4 or 5 stars in all regular levels to unlock the bonus levels. In the *TutorCAD* condition, subjects were told that they could repeat tasks, but there was no unlocking mechanism.

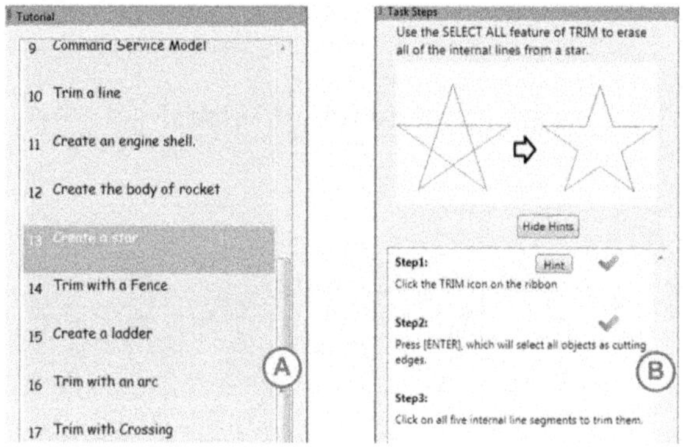

Figure 11. TutorCAD a) Tutorial list. b) Task panel.

After completing each block, a set of testing tasks were administered to evaluate the user's abilities to complete related tasks without system assistance. We designed 6 tasks, two for "LINE and navigations" and four for "TRIM and selections." shows all six test tasks.

ID	Drawing	Task	Knowledge
1	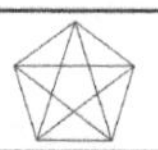	Draw the pentagon and star (coordinates were provided)	Line, coordinates
2	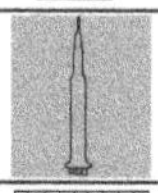	Draw the rocket by connecting circles	Pan, Zoom, Line
3	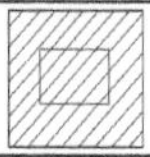	Remove lines inside small rectangle	Trim, crossing
4	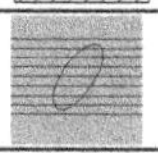	Remove lines inside ellipse	Trim, fence
5	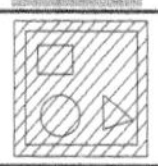	Remove lines between 3 shapes and rectangle	Trim, crossing
6		Remove lines inside star	Trim, fence

Table 1. Test tasks.

A moderator was present during the study to take observations. The moderator provided assistance if the user failed to complete a task after 8 minutes (480 seconds). The moderator recorded anytime assistance was provided. Upon completion of the study, a questionnaire was administered to collect qualitative data and subjective feedback.

Quantitative Results

The main quantitative measures for the study were the completion time and completion rate of the testing tasks that were presented at the end of each block.

Analyzing task completion times can provide an indication of how well users learned the concepts of the tools during the tutorials. In calculating testing task completion times, we assigned the maximum duration (480s) to any task which the user did not complete. The average task completion times were 111s for *GamiCAD* and 261s for *TutorCAD*. Figure 12 shows the testing completion time for each of the six tasks. It can be seen that the times were faster for *GamiCAD* in all of the tasks. A paired sample t-test showed that this difference was significant for testing tasks 1, 3, 4, and 6 ($p<.05$).

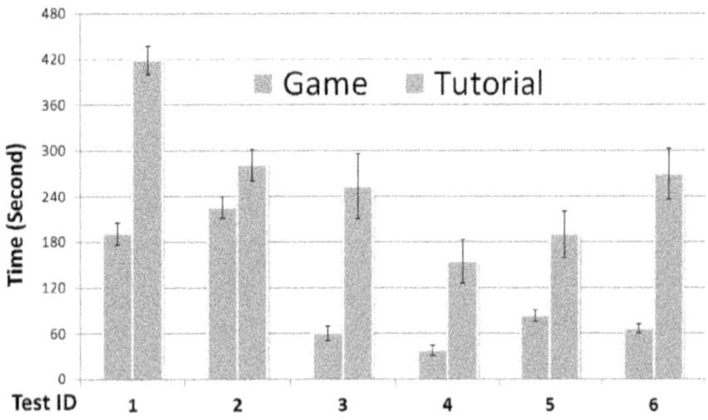

Figure 12. Completion times for 6 testing tasks.

We also performed an analysis of task completion rates. We considered a task to be completed if the user was able to successfully finish the task within the allotted 8 minutes. The testing task completion rate for *GamiCAD* was 100%. For *TutorCAD*, 90.5% of tasks were completed within the allotted time.

These results indicate that users hadn't fully understood the concepts after using the *TutorCAD* system. We believe the performance gains were in large part due to unlocking mechanism present in the *GamiCAD* condition, requiring user's to repeat levels to improve their performance. On average, tasks were repeated 7.8 times for the *GamiCAD* tasks and 1.1 times for the *TutorCAD* tasks.

As such, the above results should be considered with a degree of caution, due to unbalanced learning times. However, the results we find are important: without enforcing a threshold level of performance, users may struggle through a tutorial without adequately learning the core concepts, as evident by the lower completion rates and higher completion time in the *TutorCAD* condition.

Qualitative Results

Figure 13 shows the results of our subjective questionnaire. In general, participants found the game condition more enjoyable, fun, engaging and effective. It is interesting to note that three participants strongly preferred the standard tutorial style condition. Based on their comments, one participant did not like the fast paced music. The other two felt too much time pressure during the game.

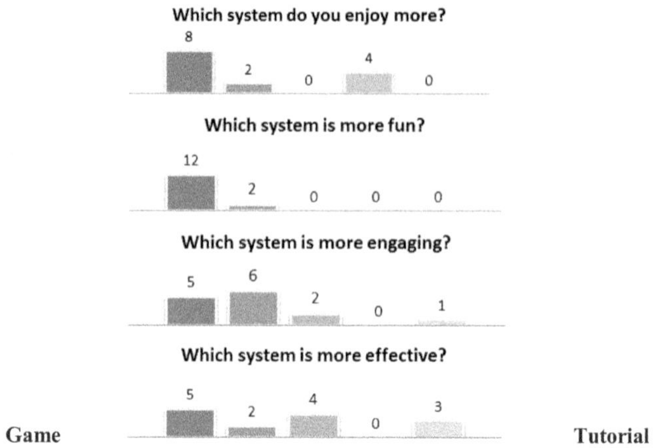

Figure 13. Results from subjective questionnaires comparing the game and the tutorial systems.

In the post-study questionnaire, participants were asked to rate 8 questions on a (strongly disagree) 1 to 5 (strongly agree) Likert scale for each system. We ran Mann-Whitney's U tests to evaluate their difference. The responses to question A, B, D, and H were significantly different ($p<0.05$).

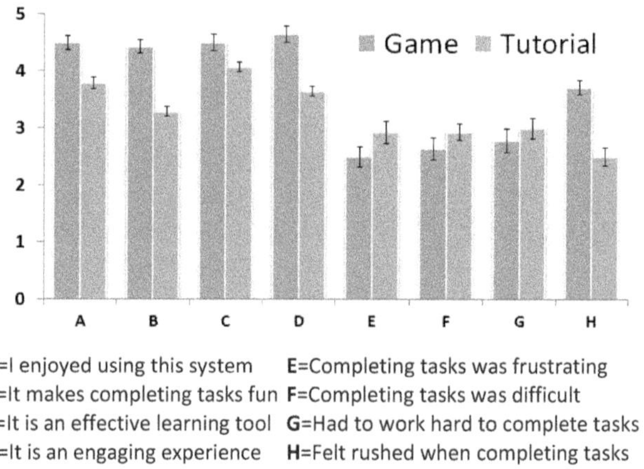

Figure 14. Subjective results comparing the game and the tutorial systems.

Engagement

In general, users commented that the game condition was fun and engaging. P1: "*Game [is] more fun – [it] didn't seem as hard. You tend to forget you're learning*" P2: "*The game was a lot more engaging and it made me excited to learn the task.*" P3: "*The game was definitely more engaging. You had to work hard in order to go to the next level.*" In contrast, the tutorial system received some negative feedback. P11: "*The tutorial was somewhat boring compared to the game.*" P3: "*Not engaging. Feels like it was just testing my skills to follow instructions in order.*" P6: "*Tutorial [feels] dry, hard to do many lessons in one sitting.*"

Challenge

We observed many users wanting to challenge themselves and repeat tasks to achieve higher scores or levels. P1: "*Completing against myself is fun.*" P2: "*I liked that 'mis-*

sion' format of the game and the element of challenge (timer, points, etc)." P10: "*I am very competitive myself. I enjoyed adding the speed component even though it challenged me more.*" P11: "*Good level of stress involved to keep me engaged (i.e. timed exercises).*"

There were participants who disliked the pressure and stress of the game. P5: "*I felt more pressured to do well.*" P6: "*Time pressure could be exhausting after a few sessions* (suggesting a slower tempo)", P13: "*However, the game was fun but stressful with the clock, and the tutorial was a little boring but definitely made this a[n] easy learning experience.*"

Feedback

Almost every participant commented on the gaming feedback. P4: "*[I] like [the] animation and score system.*" P5: "*[I like] the fact it animated a task.*" P12: "*game [is] fun, colorful, engaging, and appealing to the eye.*" We did observe a diversity of preference about the game feedback. For example, P2 commented that the speed bonus was too fast. P1 wrote "*[game] graphics are a little distracting.*" P4, P6 and P11 commented that the "*music was distracting*" or "*too rushing.*"

Some participants did like the simplicity of the tutorial. P13: "*Tutorial: easier to use, clear interface, no rush/clock, simple to follow, quite effective at getting job done.*"

DISCUSSION

In both the GamiCAD and TutorCAD learning conditions, users were able to have a sense of accomplishment in completing tasks and progressing through levels of a structured system. This is often not the case when users try to learn by only reading instructional content or reference material outside of an interactive in-product tutorial system.

Using the within-subject design, participants were able to compare both systems, and required fewer participants [15]. The risk of good-participant effects exists but quantitative results also indicate benefits of the GamiCAD condition. In our study, we also notice some ordering effects in users' AutoCAD familiarity. For example, several participants had trouble using the command line panel in the first system, but none of them had any problem in the second system. However, we believe the counter-balancing mitigated this ordering effect.

Within the consumer game industry, missions and levels are designed by professional level designers who use game level editors to create new environments and scenarios. For a CAD learning system, potentially the best level designers are the actual software users. Thus, GamiCAD is able to load AutoCAD drawing files and then automatically generate new levels for QuickClick and TrimMaster. We used these authoring features to create all of the levels for both games within a couple of hours.

CONCLUSIONS AND FUTURE WORK

GamiCAD provides guided training tasks for first-time users utilizing an "arcade style" gamification of the tasks to facilitate learning. By developing challenging levels, providing motivational feedback and encouraging repetitive task completions through score improvement, we are able to make improvements to the learning process compared to a standard in-product tutorial system.

In addition, the introduction of a finite-state system offers customized feedback and error-recovery messages. We believe this approach could serve to correct mistakes more quickly before the user gets frustrated by a lack of progress in learning. In the future, we would like to explore methods to model a user's task progress given uncertainty and implicit user observations.

Our user study comparing a gamified with a non-gamified in-product interactive tutorial system showed that the gamified system produced significantly faster test task completion times. Users also felt that the game condition was more enjoyable, fun, engaging and effective.

In the future, we wish to continue to study additional aspects of game design to facilitate guided instructions. We are also curious to determine if there is a minimal level of gamification possible that still yields similar performance and learning benefits. For example, in our GamiCAD system, can we remove the gaming music without reducing the performance benefits?

It would be interesting to conduct a longitudinal study on the operating speed of users trained on a gaming system compared to a standard in-product training system. Are game-trained users faster than standard-trained users outside of the learning environment?

Finally, since GamiCAD provides an authoring capability for AutoCAD users, it would be interesting to find out if we can leverage the existing AutoCAD users' community to create new gamified tutorials.

REFERENCES

1. Andersen, E., Liu, Y., Snider, R., Szeto, R., and Popović, Z. (2011). Placing a value on aesthetics in online casual games. *ACM CHI, 1275-1278.*
2. Bergman, L., Castelli, V., Lau, T., and Oblinger, D. (2005). DocWizards: a system for authoring follow-me documentation wizards. *ACM UIST. 191-200.*
3. Card, S. K., Moran, T. P., and Newell, A. (1983). *The Psychology of Human-Computer Interaction*, CRC Press.
4. Carroll, J. M., and Rosson, M. B. (1987). *Paradox of the active user. Interfacing Thought Cognitive Aspects of Human-Computer Interaction.* MIT Press, 80-111.
5. Carroll, J. M. (1990). *The Nurnberg Funnel: Designing Minimalist Instruction for Practical Computer Skill.* MIT Press.
6. Chen, H., Wigand, R.T. and Nilan, M.S. (1999). Optimal experience of web activities. *Computers in human behavior.* 15(5), 585-608.

7. Clark, R.E. (1983) Reconsidering research on learning from media. *Review of Educational Research, 53, 4,* 445-459.
8. Csikszentmihalyi, M. (1988). The flow experience and its significance for human psychology. *Optimal Experience: Psychological Studies of Flow in Consciousness.*15-35.
9. Deterding, S., Sicart, M., Nacke, L., O'Hara, K., and Dixon, D. (2011). *CHI 2011 Workshop Gamification: Using Game Design Elements in Non-Game Contexts.*
10. Deterding, S., and Dixon, D. (2011). From Game Design Elements to Gamefulness : Defining " Gamification. *ACM MindTrek.* 9-15.
11. Dix, A., Finlay, J. E., Abowd, G. D. and Beale, R. (2003). Human Computer Interaction. Prentice-Hall.
12. Dong, T., Dontcheva, M.., Joseph, D., and Karahalios, K., Newman, M. W., Acherman, M. S., (2012). Discovery-based Games for Learning Software, *ACM CHI.* 2083-2086.
13. Dreyfus, S. E., and Dreyfus, H. L. A Five-Stage Model of the Mental Activities Involved In Directed Skill Acquisition. *Technical report*, 1980.
14. Fernquist, J., Grossman, T. and Fitzmaurice, G. (2011) Sketch-sketch revolution: an engaging tutorial system for guided sketching and application learning. *ACM UIST.* 373-382.
15. Flatla, D., Gutwin, C., Nacke, L., Bateman, S. and Re-Mandryk, R. (2011) Calibration games: making calibration tasks enjoyable by adding motivating game elements. *ACM UIST.* 403-412.
16. Fiore, A.T., Tiernan, S.L., Smith, M.A. (2002). Observed behavior and perceived value of authors in usenet newsgroups: bridging the gap. *ACM CHI*, 323-330.
17. Grabler, F., Agrawala, M., Li, W., Dontcheva, M. and Igarashi, T. (2009). Generating photo manipulation tutorials by demonstration. *ACM SIGGRAPH.* 28(3):66.
18. Gee, J.P. (2003) *What Video Games Have to Teach Us About Learning and Literacy*. New York: Palgrave Macmillan.
19. Grossman, T., Fitzmaurice, G. (2010) ToolClips: an investigation of contextual video assistance for functionality understanding. *ACM CHI.* 1515-1524.
20. Grossman, T., Fitzmaurice, G. and Attar, R. (2009) A survey of software learnability: metrics, methodologies and guidelines. *ACM CHI.* 649-658.
21. Harel, D. (1987). A Visual Formalism for Complex Systems. *Science of Computer Programming* , 231–274.
22. Hunicke, R., LeBlanc, M., Zubek, R. (2004) MDA: A Formal Approach to Game Design and Game Research. *Proc.AAAI04 WS on Challenges in Game AI*, 1-5.
23. Inbar, O., Tractinsky, N., Tsimhoni, O. and Seder, T. (2011) Driving the Scoreboard: Motivating Eco-Driving Through In-Car Gaming, *CHI Gamification Workshop.*
24. Kelleher, C. and Pausch, R. (2005). Stencils-based tutorials: design and evaluation. *ACM CHI.* 541-550.
25. Linehan, C., Kirman, B., Lawson, S., and Chan, G. (2011). Practical, appropriate, empirically-validated guidelines for designing educational games. *ACM CHI.* 1979-1988.
26. Mack, R. L., Lewis, C. H., and Carroll, J. M. (1983). Learning to use word processors: problems and prospects. *ACM Trans Inf Syst.* 1, 254-271.
27. McGrenere, J., and Moore, G. (2000). Are We All In the Same "Bloat"? ACM GI, 187-196.
28. Malone, T. (1981) Toward a Theory of Intrinsically Motivating Instruction. *Cognitive Science*, 4, 333-370.
29. Malone, T. W. (1982). Heuristics for designing enjoyable user interfaces: Lessons from computer games. *ACM CHI.* 63-68.
30. Nielsen, J. (1994). *Usability Engineering*. Morgan Kaufmann.
31. O'Neil, H.F., Wainess, R. and Baker, E.L. (2005). Classification of Learning outcomes: evidence from the computer games literature. *The Curriculum Journal,* 16. 455-474.
32. Palmiter, S. and Elkerton, J. (1991). An evaluation of animated demonstrations of learning computer-based tasks. *ACM CHI.* 257-263.
33. Pongnumkul, S., Dontcheva, M., Li, W., Wang, J., Bourdev, L., Avidan, S. and Cohen, M. F. Pause-and-play: automatically linking screencast video tutorials with applications. *ACM UIST.* 135-144.
34. Prensky, M. (2001). *Digital Game-Based Learning.* McGraw-Hill.
35. Ramesh, V., Hsu, C., Agrawala, M. and Hartmann, B. (2011) ShowMeHow: translating user interface instructions between applications. *ACM UIST.* 127-134.
36. Reeves, B. and Read, J.L. (2009). *Total Engagement: Using Games and Virtual Worlds to Change the Way People Work and Businesses Compete.* Harvard Business School Press.
37. Rosas, R., Nussbaum, M., Cumsille, P., Marianov, V. etc. (2003) Beyond Nintendo: design and assessment of educational video games for first and second grade students. *Computers& Education,* 40 71–94.
38. Shneiderman, B. (2004). Designing for fun: how can we design user interfaces to be more fun?.*Interactions* 11, 5, 48-50.
39. Singh V, Twidale MB, and Rathi D. (2006). Open Source Technical Support: A Look at Peer Help-Giving. *IEEE HICSS*, 6, 118c.
40. Sweetser, P., and Wyeth, P. (2005). GameFlow: a model for evaluating player enjoyment in games. Computer Entertainment, 3, 3.
41. Tuck, R. and Olsen, D. R. (1990). Help by Guided Tasks: Utilizing UIMS Knowledge. *ACM CHI.* 71-78.
42. Von Ahn, L. and Dabbish, L. (2008). Designing games with a purpose. *Communications Of ACM* 51, 8, 58-67.
43. Zichermann, G. and Linder, J. (2010). *Game-Based Marketing: Inspire Customer Loyalty Through Rewards, Challenges, and Contests.* Wiley.

Tutorial-based Interfaces for Cloud-enabled Applications

Gierad Laput, Eytan Adar
School of Information
University of Michigan
Ann Arbor, MI 48109
{glaput,eadar}@umich.edu

Mira Dontcheva, Wilmot Li
Advanced Technology Labs
Adobe
San Francisco, CA 94103
{mirad,wilmotli}@adobe.com

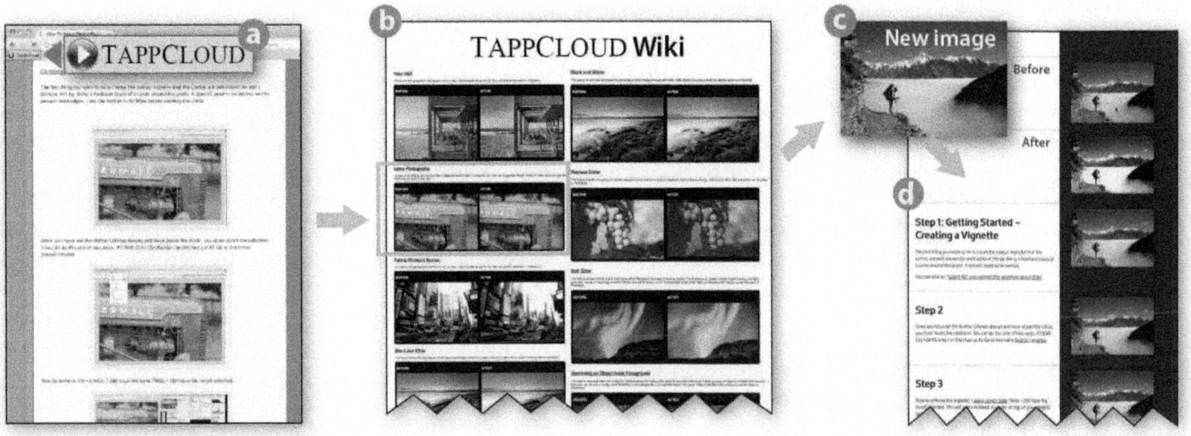

Figure 1: TAPPCLOUD turns static online tutorials into *tutorial-based applications* (tapps). Once a tapp has been created, a TAPPCLOUD bookmarklet appears on the source tutorial page (a). Clicking on the bookmarklet opens the TAPPCLOUD wiki that hosts all created tapps (b). Users can upload their own images (c) to a tapp to apply the target technique (d).

ABSTRACT

Powerful image editing software like Adobe Photoshop and GIMP have complex interfaces that can be hard to master. To help users perform image editing tasks, we introduce *tutorial-based applications* (tapps) that retain the step-by-step structure and descriptive text of tutorials but can also automatically apply tutorial steps to new images. Thus, tapps can be used to batch process many images automatically, similar to traditional macros. Tapps also support interactive exploration of parameters, automatic variations, and direct manipulation (e.g., selection, brushing). Another key feature of tapps is that they execute on remote instances of Photoshop, which allows users to edit their images on any Web-enabled device. We demonstrate a working prototype system called TAPPCLOUD for creating, managing and using tapps. Initial user feedback indicates support for both the interactive features of tapps and their ability to automate image editing. We conclude with a discussion of approaches and challenges of pushing monolithic direct-manipulation GUIs to the cloud.

ACM Classification: H.5.2 [Information interfaces and presentation]: User Interfaces. - Graphical user interfaces.

Keywords: tutorials, macros, cloud computing.

INTRODUCTION

Advances in camera technology have made it easier than ever to capture high quality images. As a result, photo editing, which has traditionally been the domain of experienced photographers and creative professionals, has become a common task for the general population, many of whom want to edit their own digital photos to improve image quality, refine composition, or create specific stylized effects. Tools such as the Instagram and Hipstamatic mobile applications offer simple one-button image manipulation solutions. However these applications are limited to reproducing a single specific effect that may not correspond to what the user wants to do. At the other extreme are full image-editing packages such as Adobe Photoshop and GIMP. While these tools are powerful (with hundreds of different features and parameters), they are also difficult to learn and seem like overkill for many of the relatively simple image-editing tasks that users often want to perform (e.g., red-eye removal, cropping, simple filters).

Tutorials and application-specific macros offer two potential solutions. It is easy to find a wide variety of step-by-step tutorials that explain how to accomplish many different photo editing tasks in Photoshop. Unfortunately, such tutorials can be hard to follow, especially for inexperienced users who may not have the necessary prior knowledge or familiarity with the user interface to understand the steps. Even, if the user succeeds in following the tutorial, he still has to manually apply the technique to every image he wants to edit. On the other hand, macros allow users to automatically apply a technique to their own images without actually performing the steps in the target application. However, a typical macro does not expose any of the underlying details of the image editing technique that it encodes, which makes it difficult for the user to explore the space of possible effects that the technique can generate or adapt the technique to different images. In most cases, the macro simply acts as a black-box that takes an image as input and produces a modified image as output (e.g., transforming a photograph into a watercolor picture). Moreover, using a macro requires the presence of the target application. Applications such as Adobe Photoshop require fairly powerful hardware and high resolution displays to execute effectively, which makes it impossible to run macros on cameras and other mobile devices.

In this work, we introduce *tutorial-based applications* (tapps) that address some of the limitations of tutorials and macros. A tapp is a specialized application that encodes a target technique as an ordered set of commands that are executed on a traditional monolithic GUI application (possibly hosted elsewhere). In the context of Adobe Photoshop, tapps enable users to apply image editing techniques described in online Adobe Photoshop tutorials directly to their own images. Tapps have several important features:

Generated from tutorials. Our system provides semi-automated tools that help users generate tapps from input tutorials by mapping tutorial steps to Photoshop commands. Once a tapp is created, it can be shared with other users.

Step-by-step structure. Instead of applying Photoshop commands as a black box macro, a tapp retains the step-by-step structure and descriptive text of the original tutorial and presents this structure as an interface for applying the target technique. This approach allows users to see and understand the sequence of manipulations that are applied to new input images.

Interactive steps. When executing a tapp, users can customize the technique for different images by interactively modifying the parameters of individual steps. As the user changes a parameter setting, the tapp interface shows real-time updates to the manipulated image. This design allows users to apply tapps in a flexible manner without having to familiarize themselves with the entire application UI.

Automatic variations. To help users explore the design space of the target technique, we support parameter variations in the interface (e.g., the radius on a blur filter). Variations can be pre-calculated and displayed in a "gallery" mode next to the step or explored interactively. These variants are also pushed through what remains of the tutorial to demonstrate the effects of the setting on all later steps. Because TAPPCLOUD can use many instances of Photoshop running in parallel, variants can be calculated as quickly as a single execution of the tutorial.

Separate interface from application. By separating the tapp interface from the original application we are able to push the application itself into the cloud, which allows a user to access many instances of an application from a single interface. The difficultly we begin to address in this paper is how to take a monolithic, direct-manipulation GUI and make it function effectively as a cloud-based application. We start by eliminating as much direct-manipulation interactions as possible but add new techniques to support direct-manipulation of parallel versions of the same application. The advantage of this architecture is that it allows users to run tapps on any device that is connected to the Internet, even if it does not have Photoshop installed. Furthermore, connecting to multiple Photoshop instances enables tapps to work with multiple images or generate many variations in a responsive manner.

We demonstrate these features in our TAPPCLOUD system, which consists of the TAPPCLOUD server and a collection of application servers (see Figure 2). The TAPPCLOUD server includes three modules: the *tutorial parser* helps users convert existing tutorials to tapps by automatically extracting application commands and parameter values from tutorial text; for commands that cannot be extracted automatically, the *programming-by-demonstration (PBD) mapper* allows users to interactively associate tutorial steps with commands and expose adjustable parameters by demonstrating them in the application; finally, the TAPPCLOUD *wiki* hosts the converted tapps. The application servers, which are hosted in the cloud, run instances of the target application that execute commands when a user runs a tapp.

Our work makes several contributions:

- We present an approach for transforming tutorials into applications that leverages both automated analysis and demonstration interfaces. We demonstrate a few forms of these applications including a wiki-style interface and file browser extensions.
- We propose interaction techniques for making tutorials act as applications (parameter setting, mixed access when direct manipulation is necessary).
- Finally, we introduce a framework for pushing desktop-based applications to the cloud, including strategies for keeping the application servers synchronized and interaction techniques for working with multiple application instances.

RELATED WORK

Our system design is inspired by work in three main areas: instructional content analysis, authoring instructional content with demonstrations, and virtual computing.

Instructional content analysis

Interest in improving Web search and use of online help resources has spurred a number of research efforts in analyzing webpages to extract deeper structure, including application commands. One class of approaches uses a list of all possible application commands [6, 8, 24] to search learning documents for exact or approximate string matches. Unfortunately, many application commands use words that are common in the English language, such as "image," "select," or "copy," which leads to errors. Lau et. al. [18] take a more principled approach and compare three approaches for extracting commands from written instructions for Web-based tasks, such as creating an email account or buying a product. They compare a keyword-based interpreter, a grammar-based interpreter, and a machine learning-based interpreter and find that the machine learning approach is best in recognizing

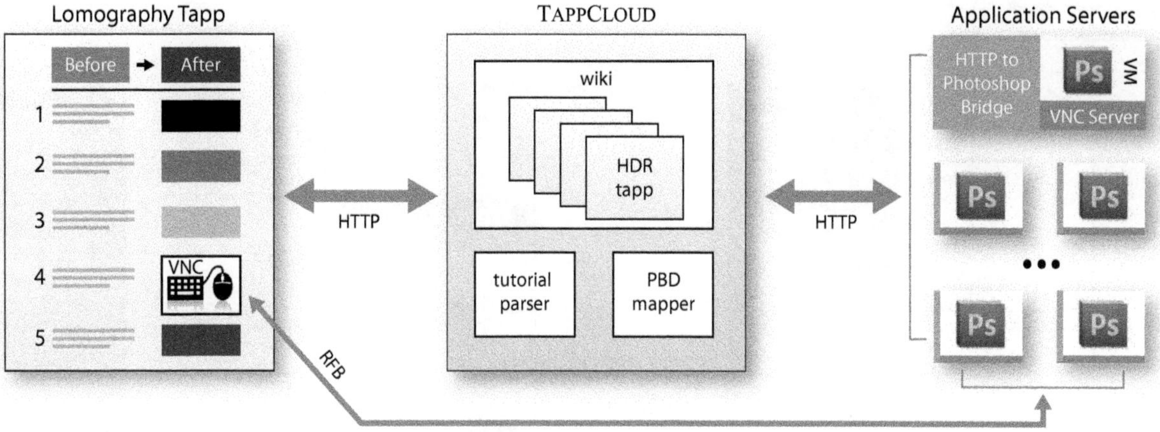

Figure 2: The TAPPCLOUD architecture. The main server (center) serves individual tapps to the user. Here it is serving a tapp that generates Lomo-style images (left). The server also acts to manage the creation and modification of tapps. The application servers (right) run in the cloud and interact with the server or with the user through our parallel-VNC system.

commands in written instruction (82% accuracy) and the keyword-based interpreter is best at interpreting an instruction (59% accuracy). Interpreting an instruction is inherently more difficult because it requires putting together multiple pieces of information. For example, in the instruction "Create a gaussian blur with $Filter > Blur > Gaussian\ Blur$ and change the radius to 10 pixels," it is easier to identify the gaussian blur command as a valid command than it is to interpret that the radius is a parameter of the command and that it should be set to 10. In recent work Fourney et al. [7] show that it is possible to recognize commands from step-by-step desktop application tutorials with up to 95% accuracy. We build on these approaches and use a Conditional Random Field (CRF) extractor augmented with heuristics. Our text-analysis approach performs on par with previous approaches though we identify a larger number of entity classes (menu commands, tools, parameters, etc.).

Tutorials and macros from demonstrations

Even in the limited domain of instructional content, natural language understanding is a challenging problem. Thus, some researchers have developed systems for producing instructional content from example demonstrations [3, 19, 9]. Tutorials that are produced by demonstration are generally easier to author but also have the added benefit of being highly structured. Thus, they can easily be embedded in applications and offer step-by-step instruction as the user needs it. TAPPCLOUD makes use of demonstrations to enhance tutorial analysis. When our tutorial parser fails to interpret a command, we let users give TAPPCLOUD a demonstration of how to accomplish the task. We present both automatically extracted and demonstrated commands as text using text templates. This approach was inspired by Grabler et al.'s system for authoring tutorials for image-editing applications from demonstrations [9].

In many ways TAPPCLOUD tutorials are closer in spirit to application macros than to traditional tutorials, as they are not explicitly trying to teach users how to use an application. They are simply enabling users to accomplish a particular task while leveraging the familiar paradigm of tutorials. Creating generalizable macros in the context of visual editing was first introduced by the Chimera system [13], which used heuristics to generalize macros for manipulating 2D graphics. More recently Berthouzoz et al. [4] presents a framework and interface for content-adaptive macros for image editing. Their macros automatically adapt parameter settings, selections, and brush strokes based on the user's image. TAPPCLOUD does not currently adapt tutorial settings automatically, but such functionality would be a nice addition to the existing system. As TAPPCLOUD tutorials interact with multiple application instances, users can explore the parameter design space for one or more images in parallel. Interacting with variations has been explored in the context of specific interface elements [28]. TAPPCLOUD builds on this work and allows users to explore variations across an entire workflow.

Virtual computing

There are several commercial Virtual Network Computing (VNC) systems that offer the ability to access remote desktop applications. Commercial vendors have also begun to port their desktop applications to the Web (e.g., Photoshop Express [25]) though these interfaces are generally much more limited than their desktop counterparts. Additionally, these systems are intended to support one-to-one (one user to one application) or collaborative (multiple users to one application) interactions. In contrast, TAPPCLOUD is designed to allow single users to interact with multiple application instances simultaneously. Sophisticated systems such as Façade [26], Prefab [5], Sikuli [32], and WinCuts [27] allow users to crop and manipulate GUIs both in local and remote settings but are similarly intended for single-user or single-application domains.

Another line of research focuses on enabling what is normally possible in a desktop browser on a mobile phone (e.g., Highlight [20]). These systems allow users to run macros authored by demonstration remotely on a server that is running a full browser. While we build on the ideas introduced by these systems, the direct-manipulation aspect of our image editing cloud-enabled applications requires the development of new interaction techniques.

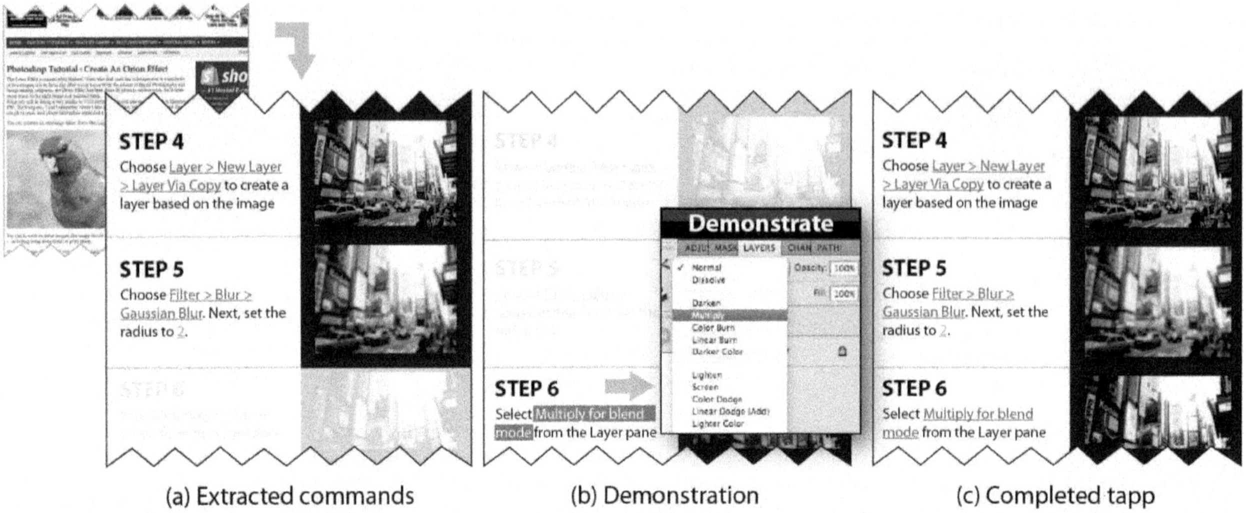

Figure 3: Authoring a tapp. To convert an existing online tutorial (top left), the user first applies our tutorial parser to automatically link commands to tutorial text (a). Next, he manually links unparsed steps and selects adjustable parameters to expose using our PBD mapper (b). The final tapp is saved to the TAPPCLOUD wiki (c).

TAPP WORKFLOW

We begin by describing how users author tapps and apply them to their own images with TAPPCLOUD. The next section provides details on the system implementation.

Tapp Authoring Scenario

Let's follow Mario as he uses TAPPCLOUD to create a new tapp from an online "Orton effect" tutorial. Mario opens the tutorial page and clicks the "Convert to Tapp" bookmarklet. TAPPCLOUD generates a new tapp wiki page. All of the steps where the system is able to extract the corresponding application command are highlighted (Steps 4 and 5 in Figure 3a). For all other steps, Mario manually specifies the appropriate command by demonstration. Here, he selects the relevant command text in Step 6 ("Multiply for blend mode") and performs the action in Photoshop, as shown in Figure 3b. Based on this demonstration, the TAPPCLOUD Programming-by-Demonstration (PBD) mapper automatically links the command with the step. Once a step is associated with an executable command, Mario can expose adjustable parameters by selecting the relevant text and indicating that it represents a parameter value. For example, if the tutorial parser failed to identify the parameter in Step 5, Mario can select the "2" (the blur radius), and TAPPCLOUD binds this text to the corresponding command parameter. If the command has more than one adjustable parameter, TAPPCLOUD lets the user select the appropriate one from a list. Once Mario is done linking steps to commands and exposing adjustable parameters, he saves the tapp to the wiki (Figure 3c).

Tapp Use Scenario

Let's follow Julie as she uses TAPPCLOUD to edit some of her photos. Julie finds a tutorial describing a "Lomo effect" and wants to apply it to one of her images. She clicks the "TAPPCLOUD" bookmarklet (Figure 1a), which takes her to the TAPPCLOUD wiki where she sees the "Lomo" tapp that corresponds to that webpage (Figure 1b). Julie clicks on the "Upload your own image" button and selects her image. Julie sees the steps of the tutorial applied to her own photo (Figure 1d) with intermediate images visualizing the effect of each step. Julie changes the opacity parameter for the black fill layer to create more contrast (Figure 4a). She clicks on "View as Gallery," which shows her the effect of the layer opacity at a glance (Figure 4b). She then clicks "Apply to the rest of the steps" and sees a grid of images that describe the effect of the layer opacity on the intermediate and final images. Julie likes the way the middle column looks, so she double clicks the middle image to choose this setting. The TAPPCLOUD wiki saves all of Julie's selected settings so that she can access them at any time.

Some tapps include steps that require direct interaction with the canvas. For example, when Julie wants to remove a stranger from a vacation photo, she opens the "Remove object" tapp, which asks her to select the region of the image to remove. She clicks on "Demonstrate" to open a live view editing window and selects the relevant image region (Figure 5). When she is done, the rest of the steps are applied to her selection. To explore the parameter space of a direct manipulation step, Julie can use a parallel live view mode that allows her to perform a single interaction with several different parameter settings. For example, Julie can specify different brush parameters for a step that involves painting on the canvas. When she paints, our system dispatches the mouse actions to multiple Photoshop instances, each of which uses a different brush setting. Julie can switch between the live view windows to see how the parameters affect the results.

Finally, Julie can apply tapps that do not require canvas interactions to multiple images in a batch processing mode. For instance, Julie can upload several images via the TAPPCLOUD wiki. Similarly, she can apply a tapp to local images on her computer through a custom context menu item. Julie can click on a folder with the right mouse button to open the context menu and select the menu item that invokes the tapp. The images in the folder are pushed to the TAPPCLOUD server, and when the processing is complete the results are saved in Julie's original folder.

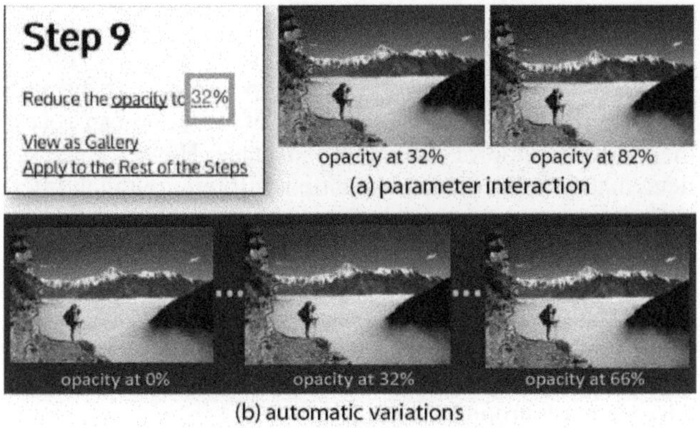

Figure 4: Interacting with parameters. Within a tapp, users can directly modify parameter settings and see the results of the change (a) or view galleries of images that show a range of results across a variety of parameter values (b).

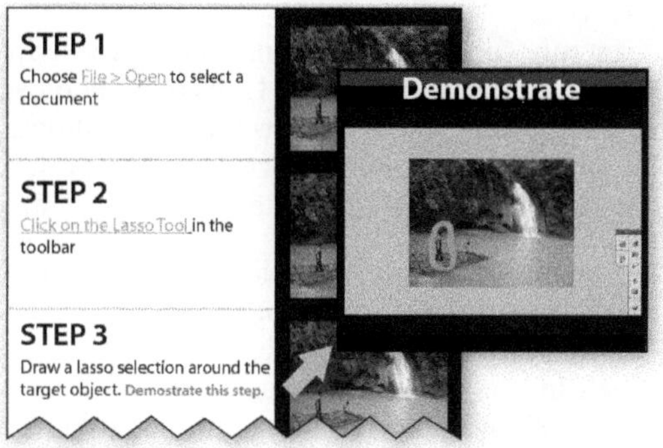

Figure 5: Live editing. TAPPCLOUD provides a live editing interface that allows users to perform steps interactively. Here, the user selects a specific region of the image to remove.

THE TAPPCLOUD SYSTEM

We now describe the TAPPCLOUD system in more detail.

Tutorial Parser

Ideally, tutorial text would function as a form of literate programming [11]. However, because of the extensive direct manipulation directives issued by the authors of the tutorials (e.g., "paint a few more smoke lines using the brush tool") and the highly informal writing (e.g., "Anyway, on top of the other layers just add the Invert adjustment") it is extremely difficult to transform an arbitrary tutorial into a program that can be directly executed. Nonetheless, there are many steps that can be extracted automatically by our parser. The parser generates a "skeleton" program for a tapp that can then be augmented, modified, or extended through the tapp construction interface.

In order to automatically detect instructions and parameters in tutorial text found on the Web, we implemented a Conditional Random Field (CRF) extractor augmented with some heuristics. The complete set of features for this extractor are described in Appendix 1.

Our working dataset included 630 tutorials pulled from two websites: psd.tutsplus.com (549 tutorials) and psdbox.com (81 tutorials). Because of the regular structure of tutorials on these sites, each tutorial was automatically deconstructed into individual steps (14,345 in total). A training set was constructed using 400 tutorials (748,780 labeled tokens including 1,762 MENU entities, 3,018 TOOL entities, and 12,189 PARAMETERS). The remaining 230 tutorials were used as a test collection (722 MENUS, 1,221 TOOLS, and 4,677 PARAMETERS). The CRF extractor attained a precision/recall/F1 of .95/.99/.97 for menus, .97/.98/.98 for tools, and .67/.25/.36 for parameters.

In order to associate parameter values with the parameter names, a simple heuristic creates an association between the nearest numerical value found in the text to the parameter name (without passing over "boundary" signals such as semicolons, commas, the token 'and,' or periods). Once identified, commands and parameters are associated to the tutorial step where they are located, and a programmatic "stub" in ExtendScript (a JavaScript variant that is understood by Adobe applications) is generated. In a test set of 4,482 steps, we were able to extract entities (tools, menus, etc.) in 2,072 of them (46%). While we believe this number may be somewhat improved, a completely unsupervised system would be difficult to achieve. Because of this, we extend our system with support for programming by demonstration and direct modification to these skeleton scripts.

Programming-by-Demonstration (PBD) Mapper

For commands that are not detected by the tutorial parser, we provide a demonstration interface for associating commands with tutorial text. The tapp author selects the relevant text, opens Photoshop, and then performs the appropriate action. The PBD Mapper automatically captures the relevant ExtendScript code for the demonstrated command (using Photoshop's built-in ScriptListener plugin) and associates it with the selected text.

While a tapp author may demonstrate a specific step to be included in the program, we also allow the user to demonstrate all of the steps in the tutorial at one time. We convert the trace created by the demonstration into a step-by-step tutorial using the technique described in [9] and [14] and map it to the pre-processed tapp skeleton. To map the executable commands output from the demonstration to the partial extractions obtained by the CRF or other annotation process, we compare each step in the user's trace to the existing tapp stubs. Commands in the trace for which there is a match can be automatically copied into the tapp. For those commands that cannot be matched, we rely on the fact that both traces and tutorials are roughly linear. An unmatched trace command(s) is frequently book-ended by commands that do match. This allows for an approximate association between the commands and tapp steps.

Running tutorials as applications

When users want to use a tapp on their own images, they can access TAPPCLOUD through a webpage from the TAPPCLOUD wiki (see Figure 2) or directly from their file system through a JSON API [10]. The TAPPCLOUD server selects an available application server and sends each user's image along with the list of programmatic stubs that correspond to the tapp steps. Because of our focus on Photoshop, TAPPCLOUD uses ExtendScript. We note that currently TAP-

TAPPCLOUD can only support applications that have a scripting interface. Many complex, monolithic GUIs (e.g., Photoshop, Illustrator, Word, Excel, etc.) offer scripting capabilities. Alternatively, automation systems external to the application may also be used (e.g., AutoIt [2], Sikuli [32], or Prefab [5]).

TAPPCLOUD talks to multiple application servers to distribute calculations required to execute the tapp. For a tapp handling batch image requests, for example, TAPPCLOUD can map each image to a different application server. Our TAPPCLOUD implementation provides a simple FIFO queue when the number of requests exceed the number of available servers. Clearly, other complicated schemes are possible and we briefly suggest an example in the Discussion Section.

Although the wiki provides a convenient front-end for users, because we use a JSON API, there are many other possibilities for interaction. For example, we have implemented a custom menu item for the desktop. We created a Python shell extension [23] which calls the TAPPCLOUD server using a remote URL request. We scan for images within the folder and use them as inputs for the tapp request. Once processed, the results are saved back to the original folder.

Tapp interaction

Real-time parameter modification For commands that are bound to specific parameters, TAPPCLOUD provides a level of interaction which allows a user to see the immediate effect of a given value. We use the Tangle library [30] for binding tutorial text to corresponding controls for parameter adjustment (e.g., sliders and text input). Users can adjust parameter-bound elements by clicking on the parameter and dragging the mouse to the left or right to increase or decrease the parameter value. The effect of this change is displayed automatically within the current and subsequent steps.

Exploring parameter ranges TAPPCLOUD also provides a gallery mode to support the exploration of parameter values. The gallery mode provides a side-by-side comparison of the effect of a parameter value. When enabled, a row of images along with the parameter value used in the step are displayed (see Figure 4). We further support exploration by allowing the user to see the effects of parameter values as they propagate throughout the rest of the steps via an image gallery "grid." Users can explore the gallery and immediately see how a given value can affect the overall result. By clicking on a particular image in the gallery, the tapp is set to those parameter values and saved for subsequent steps.

Rich interactions through VNC When direct manipulation of graphical content is necessary, TAPPCLOUD provides a limited "window" to the remote application by means of a Virtual Network Computing (VNC) client. VNC uses the Remote Framebuffer (RFB) protocol to send bitmap images of the remote server to a local client and to convey interactions (mouse movements, key presses, etc.) from the client to the server. Because of the relative simplicity of the protocol, many clients have been built including ones that run natively in the browser (using the HTML5 canvas), as applets, or as independent applications. For our purposes, we utilize a modified version of TightVNC [29] that we execute as an applet.

When a direct-manipulation interaction or demonstration is necessary, an embedded applet window allows the user to directly control the remote Photoshop instance. If the user needs to demonstrate a complex set of steps, he can access the entire desktop of the remote instance. However, we believe that a more common situation will require quick interactions with the drawing surface alone. Because of this, we have written a small program to calculate the coordinates of the Photoshop window and modified the VNC client to crop to that region. By programmatically pre-selecting the appropriate tool for the user, they can control the drawing surface to accomplish a task before moving on to the next step (e.g., "draw a mask around the hair.").

A more critical limitation of VNC is that it is intended to pair one client to one server. Instead of requiring users to perform their actions on each instance serially–as the VNC architecture would require–we modified TightVNC to support simultaneous connections to multiple VNC servers. The user has access to any of the drawing surfaces of the servers they are connected to. However, any user interaction is dispatched to all servers by "broadcasting" the RFB protocol packet. Users may "disentangle" some portion of the servers (manipulate one set one way, and another set another) or choose to interact with only one at a time. We have also implemented a feature to support divergent editing of any text dialog (e.g., specifying the feathering on a selection tool or color on a paintbrush). A user currently does this by opening a dialog in our VNC client and entering a comma-delimited list of values. Each of these values is sent to a different server (e.g., a GUI version of a "Map" step in a Map/Reduce operation). The user may now continue to perform parallel manipulation, but potentially may be drawing with a differently configured tool–allowing them to quickly test different ideas in parallel (e.g., recoloring the sky in different shades, smudging at different levels, or sampling differently in a clone stamp).

Experimental Platform

To test TAPPCLOUD in a realistic environment we deployed our system on Amazon's EC2 cloud running 8 machines (4 small and 4 medium instances running Windows). Small instances are configured with 1 core, 1.7GB RAM, and 160 GB storage whereas a medium instance is 2 cores, 3.75GB RAM, and 410 GB in storage. All instances are running Microsoft Windows Server 2008 with both Photoshop CS5 and a beta version of Photoshop CS6 installed. The cost to operate an instance is $.115 and $.230 per hour for the small and medium instances respectively (at a cost of roughly $1000 per year per machine if running continuously). To construct our instances, one initial machine was configured and then cloned to ensure identical set up.

In addition to Photoshop, each machine also runs a VNC server and a small Java-based Web service that converts HTTP requests to the Photoshop remote connection protocol. This architecture allows TAPPCLOUD to pass ExtendScript commands over the Web and collect thumbnail snapshots of the current image. The main TAPPCLOUD server (Figure 2) is built in Ruby on Rails. We note that our implementation works as effectively on the local desktop with direct-manipulation steps performed by simply switching to

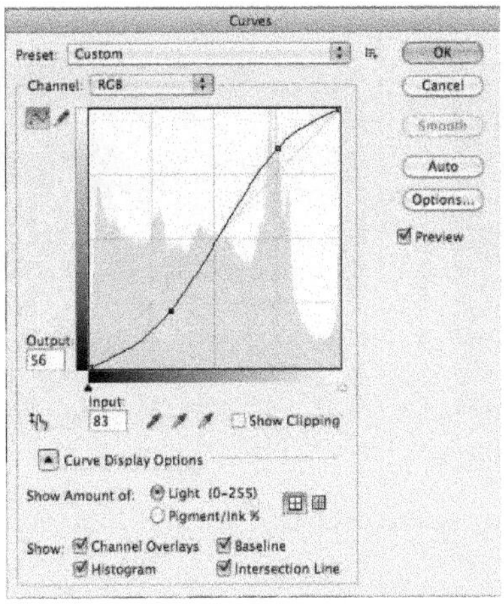

Figure 6: The curves image adjustment allows users to manipulate contrast with a tone curve. TAPPCLOUD doesn't currently support interaction with this type of interface element. To edit an image with this command, the user has to go into "live view" mode and directly interact with Photoshop.

the locally-running Photoshop (though at a loss of features such as cropping to the drawing area). Much of our early testing was done in this configuration.

DISCUSSION

As we developed TAPPCLOUD, and on receiving informal feedback, we were able to identify potential issues in cloud-enabling applications. A number of these issues were fixed through various design features (described throughout this paper). However, we have also identified other areas for future development.

Awareness

Designers of direct-manipulation systems build features into their systems to provide feedback even when the system is busy. At the simplest, progress bars or busy icons indicate that the system is "thinking." More complex solutions, such as displaying partial results, also indicate to the user what is happening (or more critically, that something is happening). Within the context of TAPPCLOUD, this is a much more difficult proposition. A tapp may include multiple automated steps when only limited feedback is provided. During this time, the system may be queuing a job, processing–multiple, computationally intensive steps–at the instance nodes, or transferring data. Awareness of what is going on, how much work is left to do, if the system has crashed, and so on, is crucial and more work is necessary to decide how best to convey this.

A second form of "awareness" in the context of parallel instances is how a user tracks divergent workflows and maintains an understanding of how the work is split up and which instance is running which image with which parameters. Others have worked on graphical representations to show high-level system state (i.e., trees or directed acyclic graphs) or interaction techniques such as Side Views [28]. Currently, we provide this information through the gallery view, which is a basic grid representation. This is appealing as it is easy to understand, but does not capture all possible workflow paths.

User Interface

We feel that we have only begun to explore how to enable users to explore the design space of an image editing technique. Our current interface allows users to manipulate parameters one step at a time. But parameters and steps can interact and to truly understand their interaction, the user must be able explore parameter variations in parallel. Of course even a small number of parameters can quickly lead to combinatorial explosion of possible paths, so we have to carefully consider how to enable such an interface. Berthouzoz et al. [4] present a framework for creating content-adaptive macros from multiple examples. Automatically adapting parameter settings based on the user's image will be very useful for those who want a one button solution, but modeling the relationship between images and user operations could also be useful in building an exploratory interface.

Another future direction is improving the step-by-step tutorial presentation. By experimenting with different tutorials, we found that tutorials often include steps that don't affect the canvas. Some tutorial steps, such as manipulating layers, describe how to manipulate the user interface, not how to edit the image. In future work we plan to group steps that do not have a visible effect. Automatically collapsing the text for such steps may be hard to do fully automatically. Our wiki approach enables users to modify the text and remove unnecessary text or add rationale for a specific step. Our current system doesn't support tying multiple application commands to one step, but extending the system with this support is straightforward. What is less clear is how to provide a rich text editor for the tapp, while still maintaining a mapping between the text and application commands.

Unfortunately, tutorials don't offer a natural interface for all image editing commands. For example, to adjust contrast in an image, photographers often use the *Curves Adjustment* (see Figure 6). In handwritten tutorials, authors often include screenshots showing how to adjust the curves, but applying the curves adjustment often requires image-specific changes. Furthermore, it is unclear how to parameterize this type of control to allow users to easily explore variations. The space of all curves is equivalent to the space of all images.

Live Demonstration

Our implementation uses a web-based VNC client to perform commands on the remote application server. An alternative to the VNC strategy–which we do not implement in this version of the system–is to create a thin "client" that uses a locally-managed drawing surface (e.g., the canvas or an application such as Deviant Art's Muro [1]) that acts as a proxy to the remote instance. This may work in situations where a selection can be encoded and transmitted programmatically (e.g., specifying a path, converting that to the appropriate ExtendScript command, and pushing the program to the remote instance). This has a number of benefits in situations when security needs to be maintained or a network connection is slow. Conversely, the solution adds to implementation complexity that can grow with the expanding features of the underlying GUI.

Synchronization

An issue unaddressed in our current system is synchronization between multiple application instances. The virtual ma-

Orton Effect Fake HDR Remove an Object Watercolor

Figure 7: Before-After results of example tapps ranging from Macro-like (Orton and Fake HDR) to those that require direct manipulation (Object removal) and a multi-image processing (Watercolor).

chines running each instance may become out of sync for a number of reasons ranging from low-level issues (different machine specifications, different latencies to the machines, reboots, etc.) to application issues (divergent parameters on an operation taking a different amount of time, the GUIs placed in incompatible states, errors on a machine, etc.). There are two fundamental issues that need to be resolved: detection of unintentional divergence of state, and reconciling unsynchronized VMs. Both problems are well beyond the scope of this paper, though notably there are a number of new VM technologies that support synchronization–generally by logging VM behavior, checkpointing, and transferring over the deltas [16]. Such systems can also support bringing up a new VM set to the state of a currently executing one (live replication) which would allow for dynamic, demand-based VM creation (presently we pre-instantiate a cluster). A similar, high-level, solution would be to checkpoint at the application level to support "resetting" to a known state.

A second synchronization issue is how to reconcile instances that have been made explicitly divergent in response to parameter variants introduced by the user. In this case, a user creates divergent instances (e.g., trying color or font variants) and then wants to pick a dominant one to continue from. In part, this is an awareness problem (how has a tapp diverged and converged), but technically might be addressed through similar techniques to those described above: checkpointing, synchronization, and live-replication.

Lastly, our TAPPCLOUD implementation uses a FIFO queue when the number of processing requests exceed the total number of application servers. Clearly, more sophisticated schemes are possible. For example, when parameter variation occurs in only one step of the entire tapp, overall throughput may be optimized by using a single application server that reverts the step with the variation and re-executes it with a new parameter value rather than sending the complete tapp to multiple application servers to execute the entire tapp.

Security

In addition to the replication issue, there are a number of security concerns that will need to be addressed if TAPPCLOUD or other "cloudified" GUIs are deployed. Some security complications may be mitigated by creating instances that can only be accessed by a single user at any one time (rather than a shared instance) and encrypting communication. The addition of this security will by necessity create additional overhead, but would be necessary for a live deployment.

USER FEEDBACK

To solicit user feedback, we carried out two sets of evaluations with Photoshop users (n=13, 5 female/8 male, 25-45 years old). Our goals were 1) to gauge users' response to using tutorial-based applications, and 2) to understand whether users would be interested in exploring the design space of a technique by scrubbing parameter values and using galleries. In our initial evaluation, we demonstrated several tapps to eight users and had an informal discussion about the concept. In our second evaluation, we gathered feedback by asking five users to interact with the TAPPCLOUD wiki, upload photos and edit them with various tapps.

We found consistent positive feedback about the idea of tutorial-based applications. All of the participants expressed that tapps provide an efficient way to get results quickly. The majority of the interviewees agreed that tapps let them skip the workflow details and focus on the result. One user said, "it's really great to just load an image and see it executed in action." One user was particularly positive about the idea of the TAPPCLOUD wiki, and exclaimed that, "the draw of contributing to the wiki and gaining benefits from other tapps is particularly strong." All users said that they would see themselves using tapps in a variety of ways. One particular user said "I want it for mobile!"

Most users agreed that text descriptions were necessary to understand certain steps, especially those that require them to complete direct manipulation steps (e.g., selecting a specific object). Not surprisingly, some users interested in learning were concerned that tapps might conflict with the learning benefits associated with manually going through a tutorial. In fact, some users felt the text was not necessary or too verbose for some steps. Tutorial-based applications are not meant to replace tutorials and could be used in parallel. For example, tapps might offer a debugging interface for someone who gets stuck going through the steps of tutorials. In addition, tutorial text is still useful for automated command extraction and to indicate what commands the user must perform using the demonstration interface.

With regards to the exploration interfaces, users were generally receptive about the instant feedback when changing specific parameters. One particular user said that being able to easily explore the design space was beneficial, as long as enough context about the parameter was available to make better sense of the effect. Another user felt overwhelmed by the gallery mode. He said, "I usually have a narrow browser window, so this might be too much." More research is needed to establish the best interfaces for exploring the design space of a workflow.

Overall, all interviewed users expressed positive views about the core idea of tutorial-based applications, and they consistently stated that TAPPCLOUD provides a convenient image editing interface.

CONCLUSIONS

We present an approach and a working implementation for tutorial-based applications that provide web interfaces to traditional desktop applications running in the cloud. We demonstrate the feasibility of this approach with a complex image-editing application, Adobe Photoshop. Early user feedback confirms that enabling users to embed their images in tutorials has benefits and argues for further research in interfaces for exploring the design space of editing workflows.

We have yet to explore the social aspect of tutorial-based applications. The TAPPCLOUD wiki faces some of the same challenges as the AdaptableGIMP [15] and CoScripter [19], including how to fail gracefully, how to manage customizations, and how to surface relevant content. Kong et al. [12] present possible interfaces for our wiki, while Lau et al. [17] suggest reusing repositories of macros to enable speech interfaces. In the future, we hope to identify other mechanisms for invoking and interacting with tapps on different devices and through different modalities (e.g., mobile) that can benefit from the availability of cloud-hosted interfaces.

ACKNOWLEDGEMENTS

We would like to thank our study participants and the reviewers for their time and feedback. We thank Jason Linder for his help with the figures and Ryan Oswald for early work on the CRF system.

REFERENCES

1. Deviant Art. Muro. http://muro.deviantart.com/. Online; accessed April 10, 2012.
2. AutoIt. AutoIt/autoItScript home. http://www.autoitscript.com. Online; accessed April 10, 2012.
3. Lawrence Bergman, Vittorio Castelli, Tessa Lau, and Daniel Oblinger. Docwizards: a system for authoring follow-me documentation wizards. In *Proceedings of UIST*, pages 191–200. ACM, 2005.
4. Floraine Berthouzoz, Wilmot Li, Mira Dontcheva, and Maneesh Agrawala. A framework for content-adaptive photo manipulation macros: Application to face, landscape, and global manipulations. *ACM Trans. Graph.*, 30(5):120:1–120:14, October 2011.
5. Morgan Dixon and James Fogarty. Prefab: implementing advanced behaviors using pixel-based reverse engineering of interface structure. In *Proceedings of SIGCHI*, pages 1525–1534. ACM, 2010.
6. Michael Ekstrand, Wei Li, Tovi Grossman, Justin Matejka, and George Fitzmaurice. Searching for software learning resources using application context. In *Proceedings of UIST*, pages 195–204. ACM, 2011.
7. Adam Fourney, Ben Lafreniere, Richard Mann, and Michael Terry. "then click ok!" extracting references to interface elements in online documentation. In *Proceedings of the SIGCHI*. ACM, 2012.
8. Adam Fourney, Richard Mann, and Michael Terry. Query-feature graphs: bridging user vocabulary and system functionality. In *Proceedings of UIST*, pages 207–216. ACM, 2011.
9. Floraine Grabler, Maneesh Agrawala, Wilmot Li, Mira Dontcheva, and Takeo Igarashi. Generating photo manipulation tutorials by demonstration. *ACM Trans. Graph.*, 28(3):66:1–66:9, July 2009.
10. JSON. JavaScript Object Notation. http://www.json.org. Online; accessed April 10, 2012.
11. D.E. Knuth and Stanford University. Computer Science Dept. *Literate programming*. Center for the Study of Language and Information, 1992.
12. Nicholas Kong, Tovi Grossman, Björn Hartmann, George Fitzmaurice, and Maneesh Agrawala. Delta: A tool for representing and comparing workflows. In *Proceedings of the SIGCHI*. ACM, 2012.
13. David Kurlander and Steven Feiner. A history-based macro by example system. In *Proceedings of UIST*, pages 99–106. ACM, 1992.
14. Adobe Labs. Tutorial builder. http://labs.adobe.com/technologies/tutorialbuilder/. Online; accessed June 25, 2012.
15. Benjamin Lafreniere, Andrea Bunt, Matthew Lount, Filip Krynicki, and Michael A. Terry. AdaptableGIMP: designing a socially-adaptable interface. In *Adjunct proceedings of UIST*, pages 89–90. ACM, 2011.
16. H.A. Lagar-Cavilla, J.A. Whitney, A.M. Scannell, P. Patchin, S.M. Rumble, E. De Lara, M. Brudno, and M. Satyanarayanan. Snowflock: rapid virtual machine cloning for cloud computing. In *Proceedings of the 4th ACM European conference on Computer systems*, pages 1–12. ACM, 2009.
17. Tessa Lau, Julian Cerruti, Guillermo Manzato, Mateo Bengualid, Jeffrey P. Bigham, and Jeffrey Nichols. A conversational interface to web automation. In *Proceedings of UIST*, pages 229–238. ACM, 2010.
18. Tessa Lau, Clemens Drews, and Jeffrey Nichols. Interpreting written how-to instructions. In *Proceedings of IJCAI*, pages 1433–1438. Morgan Kaufmann Publishers Inc., 2009.

19. Gilly Leshed, Eben M. Haber, Tara Matthews, and Tessa Lau. Coscripter: automating & sharing how-to knowledge in the enterprise. In *Proceedings of SIGCHI*, pages 1719–1728. ACM, 2008.

20. Jeffrey Nichols, Zhigang Hua, and John Barton. Highlight: a system for creating and deploying mobile web applications. In *Proceedings of UIST*, pages 249–258. ACM, 2008.

21. Naoaki Okazaki. CRFsuite: a fast implementation of conditional random fields (CRFs), 2007.

22. Hoifung Poon and Pedro Domingos. Joint inference in information extraction. In *Proceedings of AAAI*, pages 913–918. AAAI Press, 2007.

23. Mark Hammond. Pywin32 - Python for Windows Extensions `http://starship.python.net/crew/mhammond/win32/`. Online; accessed July 3, 2012.

24. Vidya Ramesh, Charlie Hsu, Maneesh Agrawala, and Björn Hartmann. Showmehow: translating user interface instructions between applications. In *Proceedings of UIST*, pages 127–134. ACM, 2011.

25. Adobe Software. Photoshop Express. `http://www.photoshop.com/tools/expresseditor`. Online; accessed April 10, 2012.

26. Wolfgang Stuerzlinger, Olivier Chapuis, Dusty Phillips, and Nicolas Roussel. User interface façades: towards fully adaptable user interfaces. In *Proceedings of UIST*, pages 309–318. ACM, 2006.

27. Desney S. Tan, Brian Meyers, and Mary Czerwinski. Wincuts: manipulating arbitrary window regions for more effective use of screen space. In *CHI '04 extended abstracts on Human factors in computing systems*, pages 1525–1528. ACM, 2004.

28. Michael Terry and Elizabeth D. Mynatt. Side views: Persistent, on-demand previews for open-ended tasks. In *Proceedings of UIST*, pages 71–80. ACM Press, 2002.

29. TightVNC. TightVNC: Remote control / remote desktop software. `http://www.tightvnc.com`. Online; accessed April 10, 2012.

30. Bret Victor. tangle: explorable explanations made easy. `http://worrydream.com/#!/Tangle`. Online; accessed April 10, 2012.

31. Wavii. Pretty Fast Parser (pfp). `https://github.com/wavii/pfp`. Online; accessed June 25, 2012.

32. Tom Yeh, Tsung-Hsiang Chang, and Robert C. Miller. Sikuli: using gui screenshots for search and automation. In *Proceedings of UIST*, pages 183–192. ACM, 2009.

Feature Description	*Example*
First token in sentence	*Hello* world
Last token in sentence	Hello *world*
numeric	99 ; 93.5
greater-than symbol	>
single character	j ; I ; z
capitalized	Gradient
punctuation	. ; ?
unit	px ; pixels ; inches
percent	%
command key	cmd ; ctrl ; alt
token itself	Holding
normalized token	hold
Part of Speech (POS) of token [31]	VB ; IN ; DT
previous/next tokens (window size 1 to 3)	
normalized previous/next tokens	
POS of previous/next tokens	

Table 1: CRF Features

APPENDIX 1: CRF Extractor

To preform command extraction from unstructured text we make use of the CRFsuite package [21]. We utilize the features described in Table 1.

To create a training set, we utilized a self-supervised training technique that automatically identified high-quality matches for menus, parameters, and tools in the text. This was done by forcing a direct text match to menu commands that was generated semi-automatically (a total of 1,168 menus, panel names, tool names, etc. for Photoshop). For example, the command list might include the menu command "*Filter > Blur > Lens Blur*" which brings up a dialog with the parameters *noise*, *radius*, etc. To generate a training set, all menu and tool commands found in our data collection were marked as matches (e.g., every instance of "*Filter > Blur > Lens Blur*" was marked as a match to the MENU class and all matches to the *Recompose Tool* was marked as a TOOL). If a menu or tool match was identified, a second pass through the text marked all parameters related to those items as PARAMETER matches (in those tutorial steps were the original match was found). This two-step process ensured that common words were not likely to be marked as parameters when in the wrong context. For example, *shape* is a common word that appears throughout tutorials but is often a parameter in the context of the *Lens Blur* command.

Though we leave this to future work, we note that there is an opportunity to improve the extraction through joint-inference [22] (e.g., the strings *10px*, *radius*, and "*Filter > Blur > Box Blur*" appearing near each other can be mutually reinforcing).

Facet: A Multi-Segment Wrist Worn System

Kent Lyons, David H. Nguyen, Daniel Ashbrook, Sean White
Nokia Research Center
200 S. Mathilda Ave. Sunnyvale, CA 94086 USA
{kent.lyons, david.h.nguyen, daniel.ashbrook, sean.white}@nokia.com

ABSTRACT
We present Facet, a multi-display wrist worn system consisting of multiple independent touch-sensitive segments joined into a bracelet. Facet automatically determines the pose of the system as a whole and of each segment individually. It further supports multi-segment touch, yielding a rich set of touch input techniques. Our work builds on these two primitives to allow the user to control how applications use segments alone and in coordination. Applications can expand to use more segments, collapses to encompass fewer, and be swapped with other segments. We also explore how Facet concepts could apply to other devices in this design space.

ACM Classification Keywords
H.5.2 [Information interfaces and presentation]: User Interfaces. - Graphical user interfaces.

Author Keywords
wearable; multi-display; multi-segment touch; watch; bracelet

INTRODUCTION
Multi-screen displays are becoming increasingly common: from multi-screen desktop PCs or laptops with external displays to walls with dozens of screens. At the same time, the lowering costs of display technology is enabling an explosion of multi-display devices. Large screens are not the only ones increasing in number; small screens are multiplying as well. For example, Siftables [20] consist of multiple 1.5" display devices. When considering very small displays, one of the smallest practical screen sizes is the watch. Researchers have explored interaction with watches [2, 3, 4, 6, 16, 22, 24] and the challenges of input with other small screens [1, 25, 27]. While both watch interactions and numerous small devices have been investigated independently, multi-display watch-sized wearable systems have yet to be considered. In this paper, we introduce Facet, a segmented multi-display bracelet system for input and output.

Facet is segmented, comprised of multiple small I/O elements, and worn about the wrist (Figures 1 and 3). Facet's segmented nature enables affordances that would not be possible with a unified display. Users can create a one-to-one mapping of applications, activities, or people to specific segments; for example, one segment could be allocated to messaging and another to social network streams. This design creates an opportunity to make information that is important to the user quickly accessible. Much like the functional benefit for wearing a wrist watch to get time at a glance, Facet allows the user to glance at different segments that have information important to the user. Although segmented watches exist (*e.g.*, the Diesel DZ9024 has several watch faces), Facet is more analogous to an interactive charm bracelet where each segment is a physical artifact and has meaning for the wearer. Users can interact with and customize the system in a direct, tangible manner: gaps between segments allow quick display location by sight or touch, while applications can be easily swapped by replacing one segment with another. Finally, users can expand applications to encompass more segments when needed, and Facet's circular nature allows the user to view more content than there is physical space.

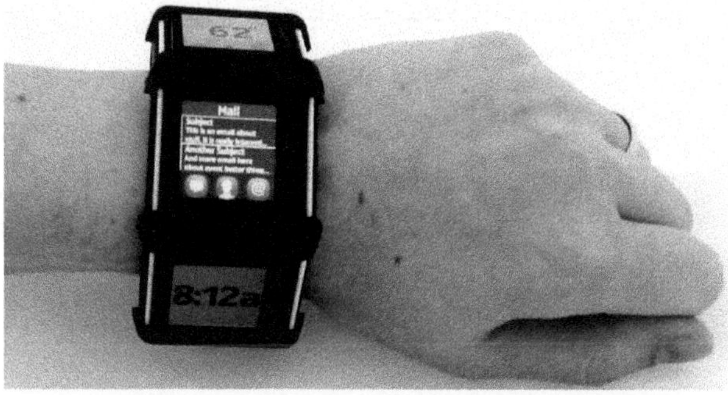

Figure 1: The Facet prototype, consisting of six WIMM One devices mounted in a bracelet such that they are removable.

Scenario
The following scenario illustrates the use of Facet. Karen uses Facet in both her work and personal life. Every morning, she slips on Facet and adds her work email and calendar segments (Figure 2a). Walking to work, she feels a buzz, and a glance shows an important email. Unable to see the entire message, Karen performs a open-pinch gesture to expand the email to the next segment (2b), where she sees she is needed in an afternoon meeting. Her calendar segment only shows the morning; expanding it to show the afternoon (2c), she finds she can attend. She pinches to collapse her email (2d), rotates Facet to find Messaging and sends a confirmation.

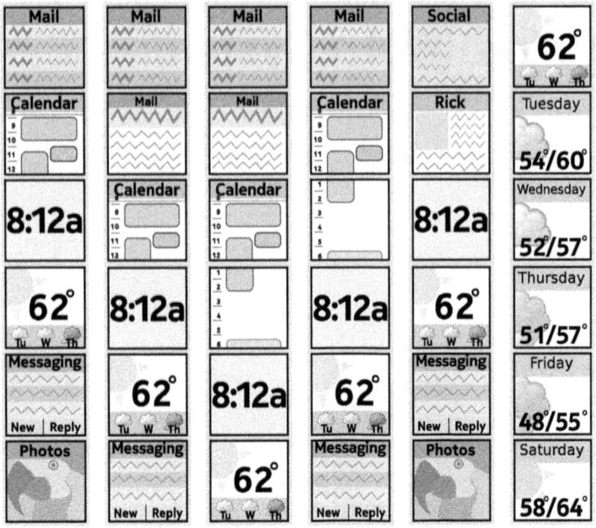

(a) (b) (c) (d) (e) (f)

Figure 2: Illustration of our scenario. Each vertical strip indicates the state of Facet at a given point.

That evening, getting ready for dinner with her fiancé, Rick, Karen swaps her work email and calendar segments for a social networking segment and a *Rick* segment, which shows private information such as his location (Figure 2e). Walking to meet Rick, she thinks ahead to their weekend plans and checks the weather. Facet is only showing the next few days; tapping the weather and two other segments expands the application to the entire bracelet (2f). As she turns Facet, she sees the ten days forecast, with Facet cleverly allowing more days than segments. Satisfied, a quick shake of the wrist resets Facet to its default state and she continues to dinner.

Contributions

Facet makes a number of contributions to the field. Although multi-display systems are not new, there have been few investigations into multiple wearable displays. We introduce multi-segment touch, illustrate how the device can use each segment's pose to configure the system, and present a variety of interaction techniques. We discuss the design and implementation of the window manager-like Facet Manager (which allows the user to manipulate applications) and discuss how Facet's core principles could be extended to other systems.

RELATED WORK

Facet has commonalities with other wrist-based computing platforms. There have been numerous research projects investigating smart watches: researchers from IBM created a Linux-based watch [22]; Hutterer *et al.* created the infrastructure for a thin client watch [15]; and Martin examined the history of the watch including the transition from pocket to wrist-watches [19]. Smart watches have been commercially available for years (Hutterer *et al.* give an overview in [15]), and currently a new generation is entering the market such as WIMM Labs' "WIMM One" developer platform[1].

[1] http://www.wimm.com

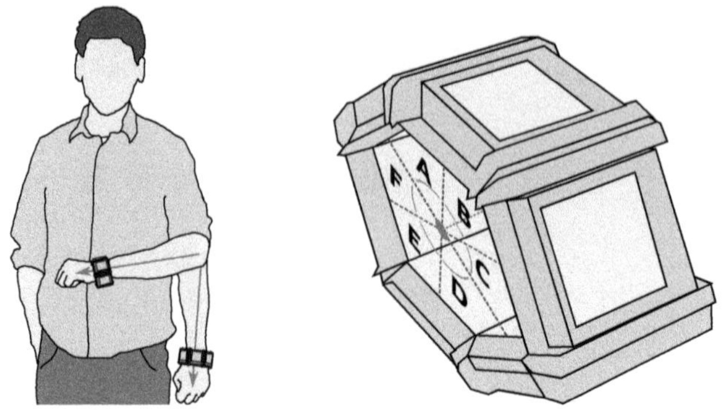

(a) (b)

Figure 3: Image (a) shows the common axis shared by the segments as a green arrow, at two different arm angles. Image (b) shows how the relative order of the segments is determined. Each angle A–F (red solid curved lines) is 60° different from the preceding angle.

One piece of previous research that has explored multiple watch-sized displays is Merrill *et al.*'s Siftables [20]. Individual Siftable elements have a form factor similar to Facet's segments; however, these were not intended to be worn or attached and used together. Furthermore the hardware itself and the interaction space are quite different. Siftables lack a touchscreen, and interactions between multiple elements are enabled through motion gestures (such as tilting or shaking) and IrDA-based neighbor sensing.

Other work has begun to explore multifaceted systems. Tuister has six displays arranged in a similar configuration as Facet [5]. Instead of being worn on the wrist, the Tuister displays encircle a handle. With Facet we explore touch screen interactions on small high resolution displays whereas Tuister explores a complementary interaction space using rotation. Poupyrev *et al.* also explore multifaceted interactions with their 20 sided D20 and consider how several faces can be seen and used simultaneously [21]. Their prototype utilized a physical 3D model that was tracked and 3D computer graphics simulated the display of D20.

Work on multi-screen systems is also relevant to Facet. There are different systems that allow users to bring together mobile devices such as phones [17] or tablets [11, 18]. Hinckley *et al.*'s Codex [12] uses two small tablets that work together while attached with a flexible interconnect, but also supports a configuration where each device can be removed. Some previous work has investigated multiple display elements on the wrist by using LEDs. Hansson and Ljungstrand's Reminder Bracelet used three LEDs for subtle notifications [8], while Williams *et al.* explored a six-LED bracelet where each of five of the lights represented the status of a different individual [26]. Similarly, Facet can dedicate a single segment to one type of content such as an individual's status.

Other systems have used inertial sensing for input, both deliberate and contextual: the work by Harrison *et al.* [9] is one of the earliest examples of intentionally moving a device for input. Rekimoto [23] utilized tilt for input for small screen devices and Harrison and Hudson [10] explored input using magnetic fields for wrist worn I/O . Hinckley *et al.* demonstrated early contextual response to sensor input such as switching between portrait and landscape modes [13]. Facet continues these traditions by enabling pose-dependent meaning for explicit input, as well as implicit automatic self-configuration with orientation.

Facet is made of components that are physically similar to watches and Siftables, and shares some of the multi-screen aspects of Codex and the segmented nature of Tuister. Facet explores the intersection of this prior work through multiple small interconnected wearable screens, leading to unique affordances different than a single smart watch, larger multi-screen systems, or the multi-device and multi-display non-wearable nature of Siftables and Tuister respectively.

FACET PLATFORM

Facet consists of an application stack with several components (Figure 4) and a hardware platform consisting of multiple WIMM One (hereafter simply "WIMM") devices. Each WIMM is a 667 MHz Android OS-based computer with a 1 x 1" (25.4 x 25.4 mm) 160 x 160 pixel capacitive touch bi-modal color display, an accelerometer and magenetometer, and WiFi and Bluetooth wireless communication. Each WIMM measures roughly 1.3 x 1.4 x .5" (32 x 36 x 13 mm) and weighs .78 oz (22g). The WIMMs form individual segments of Facet, which are joined together to form a bracelet (Figure 1). This design allows for quick removal, insertion, and placement of the bracelet segments. Our prototype allows up to six segments to be snapped in, but can easily adapted for wrist size or preference with more or fewer segments.

Coordination of multiple segments is handled by a distributed architecture. The segments use a custom inter-device communication framework that can use either WiFi or Bluetooth radios. This framework is built on top of the Open Sound Control protocol and provides a mechanism to pass human readable messages amongst our segments and a computer. Each segment provides input and output resources that are exposed remotely via a simple API. Currently each segment supports streaming sensor data (accelerometer, magnetometer, and touch). The software supports a very simple drawing interface where images can be shown, moved, removed, and animated. The software is implemented in Java as an Android application and the same software runs on all of the WIMMs.

We use a laptop running a custom Python program attached to the communication framework. This software provides a centralized point for processing sensor data and touch events. Currently, it also simulates application logic. Applications are implemented using sets of static images and by issuing the correct set of drawing commands via the framework to segments. This choice of implementation was to simplify development and this functionality could be distributed across the segments or placed into a master segment in the future.

INTERACTION COMPONENTS

Facet's construction enables two unique affordances that can be used as building blocks for interaction: pose detection and multi-segment touch.

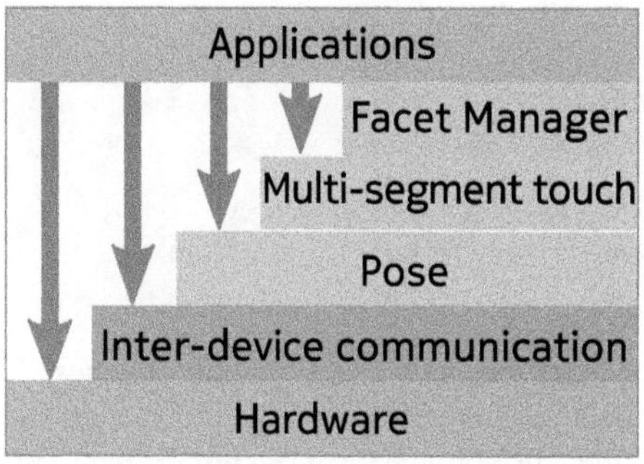

Figure 4: Facet system stack. Each layer takes advantage of the lower layers. Applications can use each layer directly. In this paper, we focus on the interaction components (pose and multi-segment touch) and the Facet Manager.

Pose

Using each segment's accelerometer and magenetometer, we extract orientation (pitch, roll and yaw) for each device with respect to a common coordinate system. This data allows us to dynamically calculate the relative ordering of segments in the bracelet, the angle of the user's forearm, and which segments are part of the bracelet.

Because the bracelet form factor imposes a circular arrangement, the segments all share a common axis running roughly along the user's forearm (Figure 3a). This property allows Facet to deduce the ordering of the segments by sorting each device's angle relative to their common axis. In our current six-segment prototype, each segment is rotated on this axis approximately 60° relative to the previous one (Figure 3b). The same data also provides information about the rotation of the bracelet around the wrist: by comparing the segments' common axis to the gravity vector extracted from the accelerometers, facet can calculate the orientation of the user's forearm. For example, when this common axis is approximately 90° from the gravity vector, the forearm is horizontal.

The pose data also provides an indication of membership—that is, whether an individual segment is physically attached to the bracelet. We compare each segment's orientation relative to the median orientation for all segments; segments within 1.2 medians are considered to be part of the bracelet. This technique can lead to false positives if disconnected segments are by chance oriented similar to the bracelet. Additional methods for finding connected devices could be applied, such as detecting common accelerations [14].

The order, arm angle, and membership data can be used in isolation by other parts of the system. They can also be used to form higher-level interaction primitives—for example, a quick rotation of the wrist back and forth is easy to detect as an oscillation in orientation about the forearm axis.

Multi-Segment Touch

Due to the limitations of the WIMMs, Facet segments do not individually support multi-touch. However, having several touch screens in direct proximity enables multi-segment touch, where each finger touches a different segment. Like traditional multi-touch we sense the number of touches and

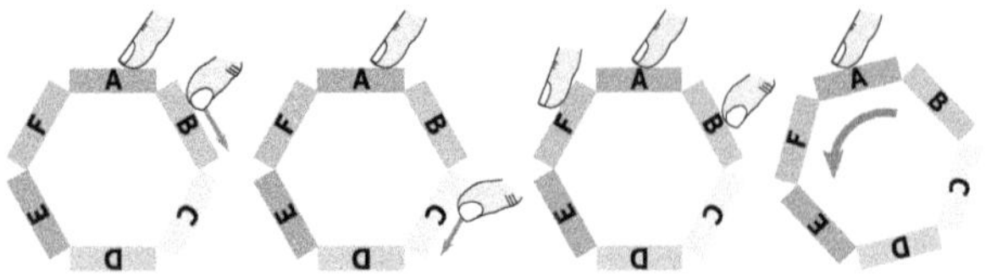

(a) (b) (c) (d)

Figure 5: Side views of Facet showing touches: (a) is a two-finger pinch on adjacent segments; (b) is a two-finger pinch on non-adjacent segments; (c) is a three-finger chord; and (d) illustrates rotating Facet while touching a segment.

the position of the touch within each screen. However, the information generated by the Pose component provides additional information. First, because we know the relative ordering of the segments, we know relative touch position; for example, two adjacent segments, or two segments separated by one or two other segments. We can further augment the touch data with information about the pose of the entire bracelet. When Facet is being held in front of the user, the segments take on meaningful positions such as top, bottom and inside, and thus absolute segment positions can become meaningful. Using this information, a multi-segment touch on the top and bottom segments is distinct from the (relatively speaking) same touch on inside and outside segments (Figure 5a and b).

Multiple touches without movement form a chord; when moved, they become gestures. With three fingers (likely the maximum practical) the possibilities increase (Figure 5c). The user can also tap on one or more segments in different sequences. Touch can be used in conjunction with pose. For instance, spinning Facet around the wrist with a segment touched could result in a different action from spinning with nothing pressed (Figure 5d).

FACET MANAGER

Pose and multi-segment touch provide basic interaction components for Facet; however, we also provide a higher-level system that manages the mapping between applications and individual segments with the Facet Manager. An affordance of Facet's individual segments is enabling a one-to-one mapping between segment and content as illustrated in our scenario above. However, we want to allow the user to temporarily break this mapping to overcome the limited interaction space of individual segments. For example, when reading email the user might want to temporarily expand the application to an adjacent segment to have more space to read a message. Akin to a desktop operating system's window manager, the Facet Manager provides generalized capabilities for moving and resizing applications running on different segments.

At the core of the Facet Manager is a mechanism for mapping applications to individual segments and specifying how the segments work together. It provides a way for applications—at the user's request—to grow to encompass more segments, and to revert back to a single segment. The Facet Manager allows users to reorder applications on the bracelet without physically moving the segments. It also enables virtual segments—segments that are logically part of the circular configuration of Facet yet do not have associated physical segments. Although there are many possibilities for touch interaction (both on-screen and movement-based) to control the Facet Manager, we decided to use just three: a two-segment pinch, a two-segment "rotate", and a three-segment chord. This allows any touch events occurring on a single segment, and any other multi-segment touches, to be passed through to applications. Furthermore, there are potentially many different interactions that could be used to perform these operations; although we believe our selection make sense, there is room to investigate more optimal configurations.

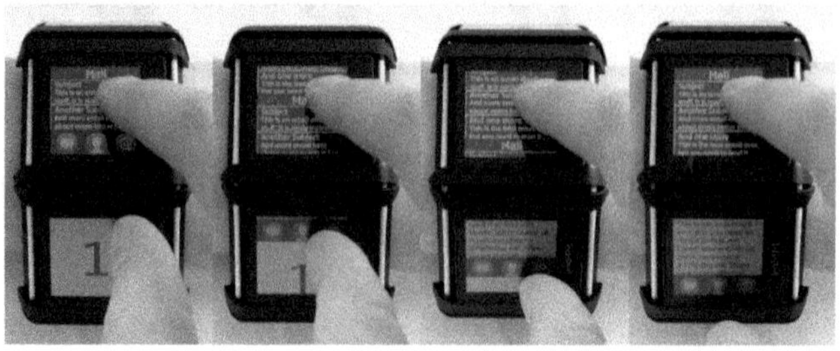

Figure 6: The *expand* operation. The user touches first on the top to indicate which segment to expand, then drags in the segment to which the application should expand. In this case, the application uses the extra segment to show more text. (View right-to-left for the *collapse* operation).

In addition to providing the above capabilities for Facet, the Facet Manager serves as a way to validate the overall system and interaction components. In particular, we use several of the interaction components in the context of a system with key functional capabilities.

Expand

Facet Manager allows the user to annex additional segments for an application. This *expand* operation is performed with a multi-segment touch reverse pinch (Figure 6). The segment of the first touch specifies which application to expand, while the second touch indicates which segment to expand onto. As the user expands the pinch, the new content from the application slides onto the second segment. Once the user slides the second finger past a threshold (currently 2/3 of the screen), the fingers can be lifted and the expansion completes. Lifting before the threshold is reached cancels the operation, reverting the system to its previous state. Expansion need not be just to adjacent segments; the user can skip intervening segments depending on their needs and the application's capabilities (Figure 5b).

Content shown on the new segment is application-dependent. One application might show more content, while another might show a keyboard or a menu. Additionally, the application can respond differently based on the initial touch points: when an expand is initiated, the Facet Manager provides the starting point to the application, which can perform a *contextual expand* based on the content touched (Figure 7).

When expanding, the new content displaces content on the affected segments. The visual effect of this operation is to

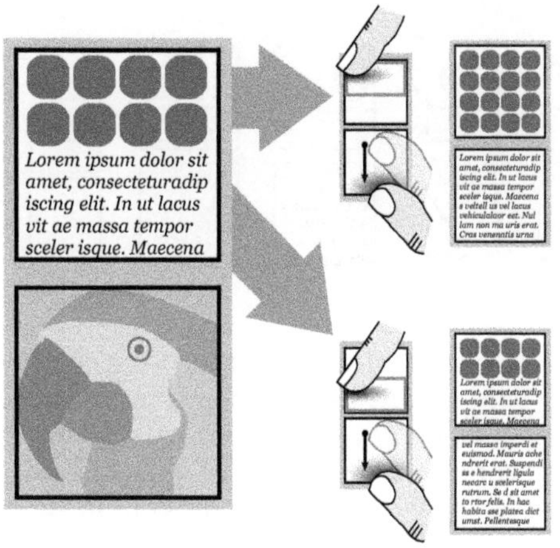

Figure 7: Two options for context-based expansion with the initial state (left), the orange rectangles showing where the user starts a touch (middle), and the results (right).

push all of the content around the bracelet by one segment. With the addition of the new application screen, the system now has more logical segments than physical devices it can show creating *virtual segments*. For a short interaction with a piece of expanded content, this mismatch is not likely to be an issue; however, in some cases the user may wish to see the hidden information. We include one mechanism (discussed below) for easily accessing the virtual segments.

Collapse
The logical inverse of *expand* is *collapse*, allowing the user to shrink an application taking up multiple segments. The collapse interaction is the opposite of expand (Figure 6, viewed right-to-left). As with expand, applications can respond to collapse differently based on context: if an application is using three segments, collapsing the first and second might have a different effect than collapsing the second and third.

Swap
The contents of two segments can be exchanged with the *swap* operation, which uses a touch interaction similar to the "rotate" gesture on larger multi-touch systems (Figure 8). With Facet, the two fingers used for the touch specify which segments to swap.

Expand All
While the expand operation can be used repeatedly to grow an application to multiple segments, there may be times when the user wishes to expand an application to all of the segments, allowing for interaction with a single application for a period of time. The *expand all* operation uses a three-finger chord (Figure 5c), with the first finger to touch indicating which segment to expand. The other two fingers are placed on the directly adjoining segments; when any finger is lifted, the application receives the expand all event and gains access to all of the segments. In some cases, an application may have fewer or more screens to show than there are segments. If fewer, the application expands to its maximum state, and the remaining segments show their original content. If an

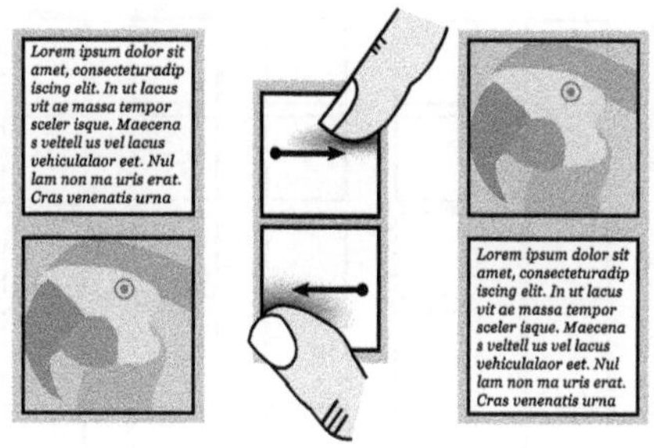

Figure 8: *Swap* exchanges the contents of two segments.

application has more content than available segments, it creates *virtual segments*, which can be accessed with the rotation mechanism described below.

Collapse All
To reverse the expand all, or collapse one or more segments that have been expanded, the user can employ the *collapse all* operation, which is simply a rapid back and forth wrist rotation, reminiscent of re-seating a traditional watch on one's wrist. This operation uses wrist angle data provided by the pose subsystem, looking for a rapid sequence of positive and negative changes in angle. To minimize false positives, the collapse all operation is only triggered when Facet is likely in use with the arm approximately horizontal ($\pm 30°$, as detected by the pose subsystem).

Virtual Segments
The Facet Manager support operations such as expand and expand all that may cause applications to occupy more segments than are physically available, resulting in hidden, or *virtual* segments. In order to view the virtual segments, the user can rotate the bracelet about the wrist. As it rotates, Facet shows all of the application screens in order. With this capability the user could, for example, rotate through nine virtual screens on six physical segments, with all of the content appearing in order (Figure 9).

To accomplish this effect, we create a discontinuity between segments that are difficult to see when in normal use. We use the pose subsystem to find the bottom segment, and the adjacent segment facing away from the user (segments D and E in Figure 5). Between these two segments is the discontinuity which is updated as Facet is rotated, so the user always sees the correct set of continuous segments. To see all of the segments, the user must rotate Facet more than 360°; for example, with nine segments, the user would rotate Facet 540°. Although not implemented currently, we have considered an "infinite" mode that would continually update as the user rotates; such a mode might be useful for long textual content or other widgets utilizing the continuous nature of the system.

DISCUSSION
The design and implementation of Facet allowed us to explore a number of issues and opportunities raised by its unique form factor. Facet's automatic pose calculation capability, coupled with multi-segment touch enabled us to build the Facet Manager, which in turn provides a platform for managing applications. We have shown how Facet allows applications to use

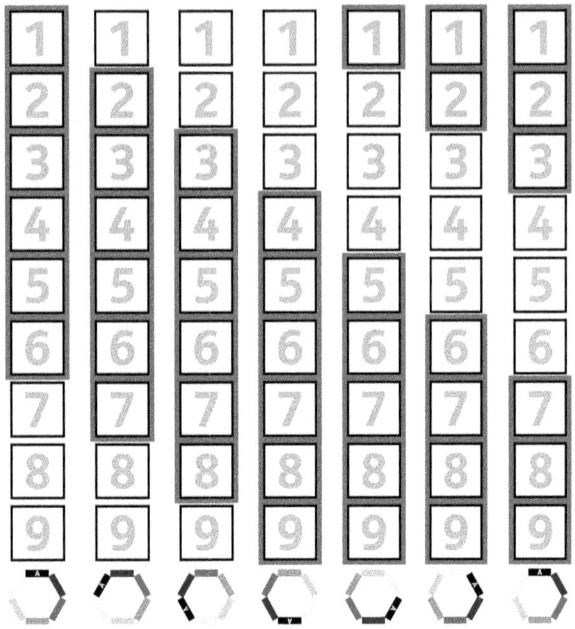

Figure 9: Progression of virtual segments. The dark green box indicates which virtual segments are visible, while the side view of Facet at the bottom shows its pose.

additional space, move between segments, and show more content than fits on the available segments. Facet in its current form is very much a prototype, but many of the lessons we have learned in its creation can be generalized.

From the beginning, we conceptualized Facet as a collection of identical segments that can be attached and removed by the user. If a device similar to Facet *was* to be constructed without removable segments some aforances would be lost, but much of the redundancy in hardware could be eliminated. It would require multiple touch screens to retain the segmented nature of the device, but the processing, storage, radios, and sensors could be consolidated. Most of the Facet Manager's interaction language could be retained: expansion, contraction, swapping and virtual segments would all still work. Taking the integration a step farther, one could imagine using a single curved touch screen wrapped around the user's wrist. In this configuration, the user would further lose the landmarks provided by segment boundaries which could result in different usage patterns as found in the use of multiple larger displays [7]. Explicitly comparing the relative affordances of these hardware configurations would be a useful area for future research.

Another design possibility would be to use heterogenously-sized hardware: it might be useful to have one segment larger than the others—analogous to a traditional watch face—with the others comprising a "band". Segments of differing aspect ratios—short and wide versus narrow and tall—could lend themselves to different application uses and touch affordances. A different point in a heterogeneous design space could be offering segments that are touch-only with no display, display-only with no touch, or segments with different sensing capabilities. The segment on the bottom of the wrist

(a) (b)

Figure 10: Proposed extensions to Facet. Image (a) shows menuing where a slight slide upwards from the bottom "pulls up" a menu; then a downward slide "pushes" the menu to the next segment. For notifications (b), a bar appears on the side of all segments. The user slides a finger from the side, and the notification appears on the segment where the touch occurred.

might be touch-only and offer indirect input as suggested by Baudisch and Chu's nanoTouch [1]. Depending on configuration, devices would lose some of Facet's application management and ability to interchange segments on an as needed basis but might gain in simplicity of use or cost.

A unique aspect of Facet is multi-segment touch. Superficially, this is similar to multi-touch on other devices. However, Facet's touch functionality has unique properties. Due to its segmented nature, the user can distinguish between segments by touch alone, similar to a touch-typist's ability to feel the keys on a keyboard. In addition to the physical affordance of the touch-sensitive segments, Facet offers parameterization for input: the *pose* of the segment being touched can be significant even if the touches are otherwise the same.

FUTURE WORK

Our Facet prototype provides an excellent jumping-off point for future work. As a platform with unique affordances, there is an opportunity to develop additional interaction techniques. For example, a "slide up then down" gesture could summon a menu that is hidden at the bottom of a segment, using similar semantics to the *expand* operation (Figure 10a). Facet could receive and show notifications, but what if the relevant application segment is not visible to the user? One solution is to show the notification on *all* segments (Figure 10b); the user could then choose which segment to view the notification on.

Facet could be combined with other devices in a complementary way. For example, a phone's orientation sensor could be compared with each segment of Facet and detect which segment the phone has been tapped against. This would then pair that segment with the phone, providing an expanded application view, system configuration, or a larger input surface.

When wearing Facet on the wrist, visibility varies from segment to segment: those towards to the top and inward side (A–C in Figure 5) are more private; segments on the outside (E and F) are more visible to others; and the bottom segment (D) is difficult for anyone to see. Applications might leverage these varying levels of privacy: a social application might just show photos when publicly-visible, but display updates in the "private" position. Applications might also support collaboration by mirroring content among segments.

Facet could be used in other ways besides on the wrist: it can be held in the hand and rotated, collapsed flat to a double-sided three-segment-long display, or unbuckled and laid out flat in a row. These modes of operation could yield other interesting affordances to explore.

CONCLUSION

In this paper we presented Facet, a wearable segmented multi-display system. We described the technical platform as well as unique interaction components afforded by the platform and interaction techniques supported by the Facet Manager.

Facet simultaneously provides the capabilities of individual independent segments and of a cohesive collection. By taking advantage of the physicality of individual components, segments can be customized—manipulated as individual devices to run different applications in a wearable form factor with unique affordances.

Furthermore, Facet facilitates bringing those individual components together as a cohesive whole. The bracelet form factor enables a user to put several segments together and physically manipulate them as one device through pose detection and multi-segment touch, unique affordances that could be applied elsewhere. The pose detection further enables cohesion by managing the relationship between segments.

Finally, the Facet Manager allows the user to manage both the individual and collective nature of the system. The user can expand, move, collapse, and swap applications as needed. Virtual segments provide a mechanism for moving beyond the fixed set of segments by leveraging the continuous circular nature of Facet. Based on this work, we believe Facet points to a novel class of wearable device.

REFERENCES

1. Baudisch, P., and Chu, G. Back-of-device interaction allows creating very small touch devices. In *Proc. of the 27th international conference on Human factors in computing systems*, CHI '09 (2009), 1923–1932.
2. Blasko, G., and Feiner, S. An interaction system for watch computers using tactile guidance and bidirectional segmented strokes. In *Proceedings of the Eighth International Symposium on Wearable Computers*, ISWC '04 (2004), 120–123.
3. Blasko, G., and Feiner, S. Evaluation of an eyes-free cursorless numeric entry system for wearable computers. In *Proc. of the 10th International Symposium on Wearable Computers*, ISWC '06 (2006), 21–28.
4. Blasko, G., Narayanaswami, C., and Feiner, S. Prototyping retractable string-based interaction techniques for dual-display mobile devices. In *Proceedings of the SIGCHI conference on Human Factors in computing systems*, CHI '06 (2006), 369–372.
5. Butz, A., Groß, M., and Krüger, A. Tuister: a tangible ui for hierarchical structures. In *Proceedings of the 9th international conference on Intelligent user interfaces*, IUI '04, ACM (New York, NY, USA, 2004), 223–225.
6. Crossan, A., Williamson, J., Brewster, S., and Murray-Smith, R. Wrist rotation for interaction in mobile contexts. In *Proceedings of the 10th international conference on Human computer interaction with mobile devices and services*, MobileHCI '08 (2008), 435–438.
7. Grudin, J. Partitioning digital worlds: focal and peripheral awareness in multiple monitor use. In *Proceedings of the SIGCHI conference on Human factors in computing systems*, CHI '01 (2001), 458–465.
8. Hansson, R., and Ljungstrand, P. The reminder bracelet: subtle notification cues for mobile devices. In *CHI '00 extended abstracts on Human factors in computing systems*, CHI EA '00 (2000), 323–324.
9. Harrison, B. L., Fishkin, K. P., Gujar, A., Mochon, C., and Want, R. Squeeze me, hold me, tilt me! an exploration of manipulative user interfaces. In *Proceedings of the SIGCHI conference on Human factors in computing systems*, CHI '98 (1998), 17–24.
10. Harrison, C., and Hudson, S. E. Abracadabra: wireless, high-precision, and unpowered finger input for very small mobile devices. In *Proceedings of the 22nd annual ACM symposium on User interface software and technology*, UIST '09 (2009), 121–124.
11. Hinckley, K. Synchronous gestures for multiple persons and computers. In *Proceedings of the 16th annual ACM symposium on User interface software and technology*, UIST '03 (2003), 149–158.
12. Hinckley, K., Dixon, M., Sarin, R., Guimbretiere, F., and Balakrishnan, R. Codex: a dual screen tablet computer. In *Proc. of the 27th international conference on Human factors in computing systems*, CHI '09 (2009), 1933–1942.
13. Hinckley, K., Pierce, J., Sinclair, M., and Horvitz, E. Sensing techniques for mobile interaction. In *Proc. of the 13th annual ACM symposium on User interface software and technology*, UIST '00 (2000), 91–100.
14. Holmquist, L. E., Mattern, F., Schiele, B., Alahuhta, P., Beigl, M., and Gellersen, H.-W. Smart-its friends: A technique for users to easily establish connections between smart artefacts. In *Proceedings of the 3rd international conference on Ubiquitous Computing* (2001), 116–122.
15. Hutterer, P., Smith, M. T., Thomas, B. H., Piekarski, W., and Ankcorn, J. Lightweight user interfaces for watch based displays. In *Proceedings of the Sixth Australasian conference on User interface - Volume 40*, AUIC '05 (2005), 89–98.
16. Kim, J., He, J., Lyons, K., and Starner, T. The gesture watch: A wireless contact-free gesture based wrist interface. In *Proceedings of the 2007 11th IEEE International Symposium on Wearable Computers*, ISWC '07 (2007), 1–8.
17. Lucero, A., Keränen, J., and Korhonen, H. Collaborative use of mobile phones for brainstorming. In *Proceedings of the 12th international conference on Human computer interaction with mobile devices and services*, MobileHCI '10 (2010), 337–340.
18. Lyons, K., Pering, T., Rosario, B., Sud, S., and Want, R. Multi-display composition: Supporting display sharing for collocated mobile devices. In *Proceedings of the 12th IFIP TC 13 International Conference on Human-Computer Interaction*, INTERACT '09 (2009), 758–771.
19. Martin, T. Time and time again: Parallels in the development of the watch and the wearable computer. In *Proc. of the 6th IEEE International Symp. on Wearable Computers*, ISWC '02 (2002), 5–11.
20. Merrill, D., Kalanithi, J., and Maes, P. Siftables: towards sensor network user interfaces. In *Proc. of the 1st international conference on Tangible and embedded interaction*, TEI '07 (2007), 75–78.
21. Poupyrev, I., Newton-Dunn, H., and Bau, O. D20: interaction with multifaceted display devices. In *CHI '06 extended abstracts on Human factors in computing systems*, CHI EA '06, ACM (New York, NY, USA, 2006), 1241–1246.
22. Raghunath, M. T., and Narayanaswami, C. User interfaces for applications on a wrist watch. *Personal Ubiquitous Computing 6* (January 2002), 17–30.
23. Rekimoto, J. Tilting operations for small screen interfaces. In *Proceedings of the 9th annual ACM symposium on User interface software and technology*, UIST '96 (1996), 167–168.
24. Rekimoto, J. Gesturewrist and gesturepad: Unobtrusive wearable interaction devices. In *Proceedings of ISWC '01* (2001), 21–27.
25. Vogel, D., and Baudisch, P. Shift: a technique for operating pen-based interfaces using touch. In *Proceedings of the SIGCHI conference on Human factors in computing systems*, CHI '07 (2007), 657–666.
26. Williams, A., Farnham, S., and Counts, S. Exploring wearable ambient displays for social awareness. In *CHI '06 extended abstracts on Human factors in computing systems*, CHI EA '06 (2006), 1529–1534.
27. Yatani, K., Partridge, K., Bern, M., and Newman, M. W. Escape: a target selection technique using visually-cued gestures. In *Proceedings of the twenty-sixth annual SIGCHI conference on Human factors in computing systems*, CHI '08 (2008), 285–294.

iRing: Intelligent Ring Using Infrared Reflection

Masa Ogata[1], Yuta Sugiura[2], Hirotaka Osawa[1], Michita Imai[1]

[1] Graduate School of Science and Technology,
Keio University,
3-14-1 Hiyoshi, Kohoku,
Yokohama 223-8522, Japan
{ogata, osawa, michita}@ayu.ics.keio.ac.jp

[2] Graduate School of Media Design,
Keio University,
4-1-1 Hiyoshi, Kohoku,
Yokohama 223-8526, Japan
y-sugiura@kmd.keio.ac.jp

ABSTRACT
We present the iRing, an intelligent input ring device developed for measuring finger gestures and external input. iRing recognizes rotation, finger bending, and external force via an infrared (IR) reflection sensor that leverages skin characteristics such as reflectance and softness. Furthermore, iRing allows using a push and stroke input method, which is popular in touch displays. The ring design has potential to be used as a wearable controller because its accessory shape is socially acceptable, easy to install, and safe, and iRing does not require extra devices. We present examples of iRing applications and discuss its validity as an inexpensive wearable interface and as a human sensing device.

Author Keywords
Multiple sensors; wearable computing; finger gesture; skin sensing; photo reflectivity;

ACM Classification Keywords
H5.2 [Information interfaces and presentation]: User Interfaces. - Input devices and strategies.

INTRODUCTION
Along with advancing mobile computing, research on human sensing is being applied to understand human behavior and input control. However, finger input is still a primary method of user manipulation in the field of Human–Computer Interaction (HCI). Information on finger gesture and interaction with the hand provides special meaning and very specific information because the hand has high flexibility resulting from its several joints and agility, which helps reflect human intention [1]. Thus, there are many sensory techniques addressing finger and hand gestures using wearable devices or tracking systems. As an example wearable device, a data glove is an accurate method for sensing finger bending and distance between fingers. However, several expensive sensors are required and users are deprived of tactile sensitivity on the fingers.

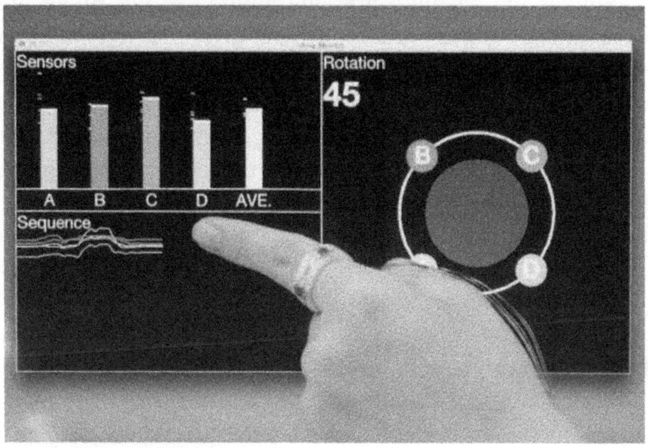

Figure 1: iRing senses finger gestures. Bending, pressure, and rotation are shown on the visualizer.

iRing is an intelligent input device that recognizes finger gestures and external force. The sensing information only consists of skin infrared (IR) reflectance under an IR reflection sensor installed inside of iRing. Different reflectance for each gesture and situation is observed depending on the distance between the skin and the sensor, and skin protuberance. Using a reflection sensor guarantees safety and robustness against rough use in daily life. Four sensors are used to detect the finger, recognize the angles of iRing when worn, and identify the type of pressure applied internally or externally. After calibration, iRing recognizes the finger state, namely, straight, bent, bent backward, and clenched. If the finger bends, reflectance of all sensors increases, but if the finger bends backward, reflectance of the sensor on the palm of the hand decreases. Rotation is also recognized by calculating differences between values of the four sensors because finger skin has different reflectance on each side where the ring is located.

iRing is standalone, an accessory shape device, and the user does not have to wear extra devices. Further, it is suitable as a wearable interface and controller device. Being ring-shaped, iRing can be used by one hand for a few controls, but by using both hands more controls can be integrated when one of the hands touches the ring on the other hand. In this paper, we describe the principles and characteristics of finger skin that we leveraged in developing iRing, the calculation algorithm for recognizing finger gesture and external input, sensor reflectance for each situation, limitation of this work, and application in using input, controlling, and human sensing including rehabilitation.

RELATED WORK

To recognize hand gestures, Rekimoto et al. developed GestureWrist, a wrist device equipped with electrodes to measure conductivity [2]. Fukui et al. proposed a method of wearing a sensor device around the wrist to recognize hand gestures by using an array of infrared distance sensors [3]. Concerning gesture recognition, the purpose is similar to that of these developed devices, but our device iRing recognizes the absolute pressure applied to the finger and the extent of finger bending.Research on devices that can be worn only on the finger has revealed reduced difficulty in using these devices. Several ring-shaped devices are available, but not all can sense finger joint movements, and some require the user to wear them over the entire finger in order to be able to measure the finger's extent of bending; further, some other devices are expensive for consumer use and require extra pieces of equipment. Ubi-Finger is a gesture input device that uses a bending sensor over the entire finger [4]. Ring controllers are another invention in this field. For example, Ashbrook's Nenya is a small ring controller equipped with only a magnet [5]. The extra sensor on the wrist measures the strength of the magnetic field emitted from the ring's magnet. A jog dial and button input interface are obtained by rotating and shifting the ring. Although the ring contains an extra magnet sensor, iRing can support these interfaces using only the ring device. Finally, we mention other studies involving the use of IR sensors. Rhee et al. developed a medical ring device to sense a patient's pulse rate by measuring rays reflected from the inner skin [6]. Our method, however, measures reflectance at the skin surface to determine the distance between the device and the skin. Sugiura et al. proposed a method to measure cotton density [7]. By using an IR sensor, this method sensed the reflection of IR rays from cotton; in contrast, iRing senses the reflection from the skin. Mascaro et al. developed photoplethysmograph fingernail sensors to sense pressure when the finger touches an object [8]. Our method is obviously different from other such methods in this field because it is based on the principle of sensing finger bending movements and pressure accurately and externally by using an IR distance sensor.

PRINCIPLE

iRing leverages three characteristics of the skin. First, the finger has softness owing to its skin, muscle, and tendon, a factor that can be used to adjust IR reflectance. Second, skin absorption of IR light can be changed depending on situations such as stretching or pressing of skin. Last, the finger skin where the ring is located has different reflectances. We tested these characteristics from two dimensions listed below that are described in the experiment section.

Measurement of Distance and Softness

We found that the pressure on the finger device can be measured by a photoreflector that measures distance by detecting the emitted IR ray. In other words, skin reflectance can be used to measure the distance between the skin and the ring device. The pressure applied on iRing approximates the finger movement and the interaction with fingers. Hence, this method is suitable because of its high responsiveness, low power, and noninvasive nature.

Non-uniform Reflectance on Textures of Skin Surface

Human skin has an uneven surface texture, which is called the epidermis. IR radiation causes light to spread through reflection from the epidermis. Most of the incident light received by the phototransistor is reflected from the surface, and the surface texture determines the sensor reflectance. The finger has a different texture on the palm, back, and side, as described in Figure 2. The order of reflectance on the finger is as follows: top, side, and bottom. iRing exploits this property by capturing the absolute number of ring rotations.

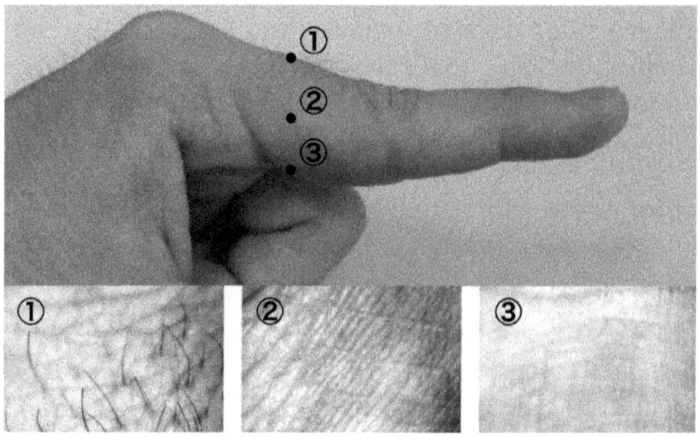

Figure 2. Surface texture has different reflectances.

CHARACTERISTIC EXPERIMENT

Experiment #1 (Reflectance with Pressure)

We inspected the relationship between pressure and reflectance acquired by the sensor that is shown in figure 3, using implemented iRing prototype. The maximum force is 920 g. The graph is approximately linear until about 7 N, but for higher values seems to curve along the upper line.

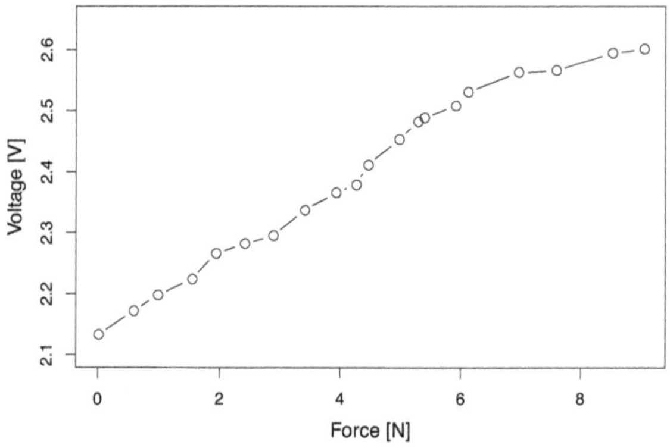

Figure 3. Voltage and applied force in Newtons.

Experiment #2 (Reflectance of Skin Surface)

We used one of the sensors installed in iRing to measure accurate reflectance when a user wears iRing. The subject is the first author of this paper who is originally Japanese; the sensing location is the root side of the left index finger. The interval was set to 10° and the start point is the palm side, going toward the thumb. Figure 4 illustrates the finger cross section and shows a photo that describes the measuring direction with a real finger.

In figure 5, there is a gap at around 150° that seems to be caused by a part that has different reflectance. However, this graph was estimated as a normal distribution by a one-sample Kolmogorov-Smirnov test ($p = 0.1929$).

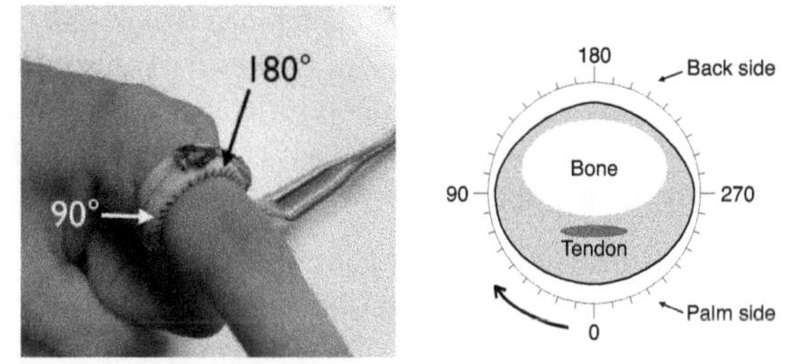

Figure 4. Measuring reflectance using iRing marked with a blue line that expresses angles by 10°.

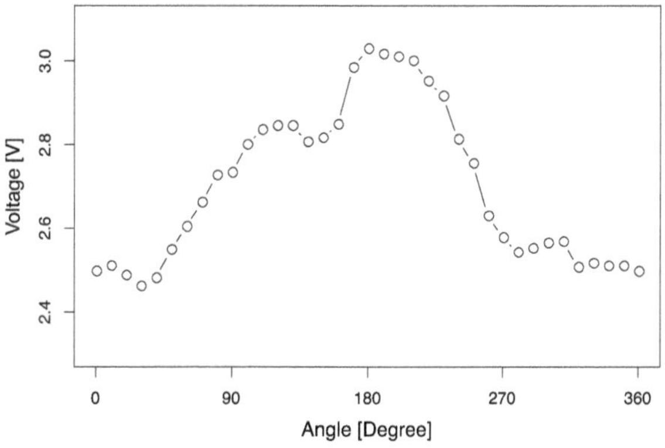

Figure 5. Reflectance of the first author's finger skin at 10° intervals expressed by voltage.

Experiment #3 (Reflectance of many people)

To gather more reliable data from a large group of people, we acquired finger skin reflectance of 22 subjects when using the ring-shaped rigid device. Subjects are Japanese undergraduate and graduate students including one Nordic and one black. Subjects were tested using two types of ring. One is the same device described in the implementation section and the other one is a device that was made for people with slim fingers. Data in figure 6 show the sensed values at 8 points. As the top and bottom reflectance in each point is different for each person because of the finger size, color of skin, and level of wrinkles, all data are normalized in figure 7. Although 20 out of 22 are Asian subjects, we also included non-Asian people who work at the laboratory. Data of the black and Nordic subjects are 1.47 and 0.36 times against the average of the 22 subjects, respectively. Though these data show that a multiethnic group has uneven skin reflectance that seems to be caused by melanin, the distribution is along the average data.

As compared to the result in experiment #2, the value at 180° is lower than the nearby value, because the back of the finger is not round but almost flat. However, the standard deviation in figure 7 shows that the reflectance of each point can be distinguished even if we consider the deviation that is expressed as a line that does not cover to the other point on the y axis. This graph is also estimated as follow-ing a normal distribution ($p = 0.8748$).

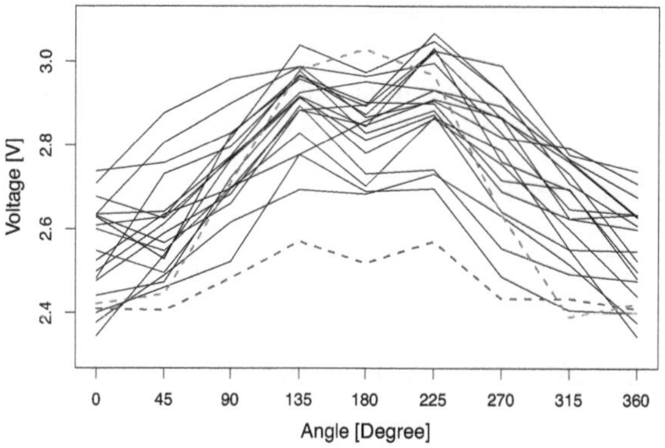

Figure 6. Raw data from A/D converter of 22 skin reflectances from 22 subjects, with 8 points by 45°. The value at 360° is the same as that at 0°. The red line denotes the data for black people while the blue line denotes Nordic ethnicity.

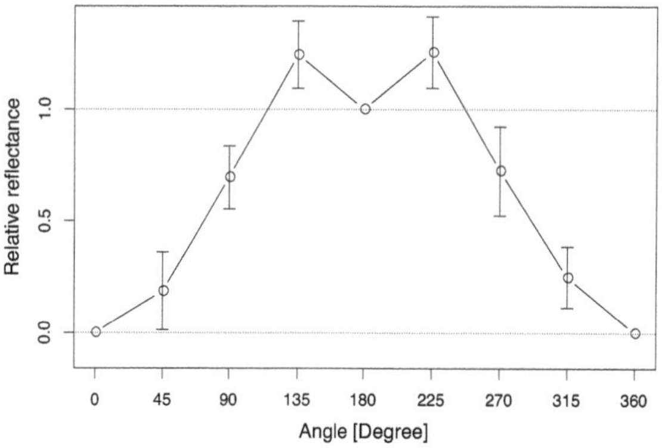

Figure 7. Average and standard deviation of figure 6. As the baseline of raw data is scattered, data are normalized with values of zero° and 180° corresponding to 0.0 and 1.0 on the y axis, respectively. Hence, there is no standard deviation at 0°, 180°, and 360°.

RING DESIGN

Similar to an accessory, iRing consists of a rigid body made from polycarbonate that works with four sensors to guarantee valid sensing when pressure is applied. The relation between the finger skin and the ring can be classified into two states. First, distance exists between iRing and the finger skin that can be detected by the IR reflection sensor when inner or external pressure is weak. Second, there is no distance between the ring and the finger skin, but the sensor cannot measure how strong the applied pressure is. Considering the sensor characteristics, the ring size should fit the finger to measure accurate reflectance. If the ring is tight, reflectance becomes higher than in the normal state and is near to the pressured state. After soldering, iRing is coated by acrylic resin (Figure 8).

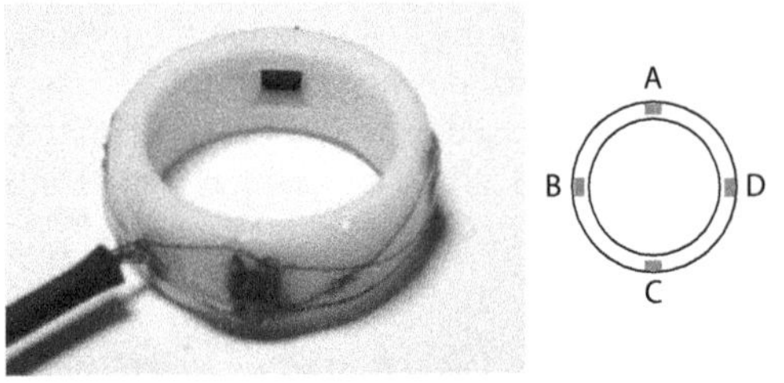

Figure 8. Rigid body of iRing and photoreflector. The four sensors are named A, B, C, and D.

Hole inside the iRing

If pressure is applied, a small part of the finger skin goes into the hole because skin is soft and wrinkled, as described in Figure 9. Even in the straight finger state, the distance between the skin and the sensor will be zero if the sensor touches the skin when the user wears the device. Making a hole on the inner ring allows measuring strong pressure even when the distance between the skin and the ring is zero. The hole height is 1.0 mm, an optimized distance between the skin and the photoreflector. This design allows sensing the protuberance of finger skin when the user bends the finger and also when he/she clenches his/her fist, because this movement generates inner pressure on the finger. Furthermore, when the fist is clenched, the device can sense the power level, which cannot otherwise be measured by a bend sensor.

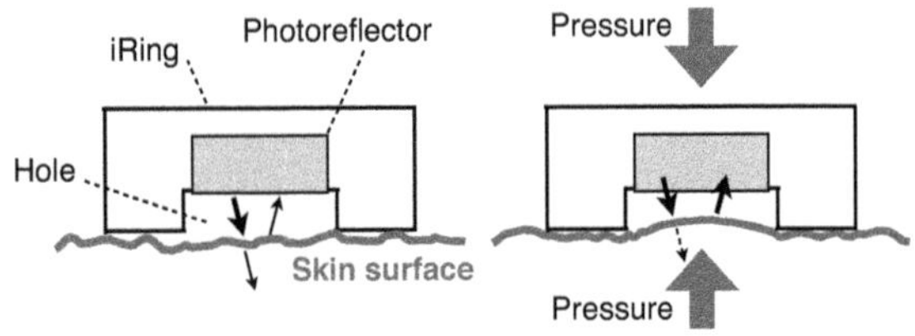

Figure 9. Cross section of iRing. Reflectance of skin changes when force is applied because of smaller distance to the sensor and less skin absorption.

Multiple sensors

As mentioned above, the combinations of various principles provide a ring device with several functions. We describe the functions with respect to sensor position on iRing, as in figure 8. The finger surfaces, named top, side, bottom, and side, correspond to sensor positions named A, B, C, and D, respectively. Concerning the number of sensors, four is the smallest number of formations that guarantees stable sensing of movement, rotation, and external pressure. First, all sensor values are low when the user is not wearing the device. However, once the user wears the device on the finger, the sensor values increase and installation is detected.

IMPLEMENTATION

We selected a small standalone distance sensor, but it can detect IR reflectance. IR light is selected for less interference than visible light for the purpose of distance measurement. This sensor, called photoreflector, combines an IR LED with a phototransistor. The sensor type is GENIXTEK Corp.'s TPR-105. As the sensor gain is controlled to a sufficient level to measure finger skin changes, 470 and 30k Ohm resistor are used for the LED and transistor, respectively. As the maximum number of grasping motions is 5/s, we set a sufficient sensing rate of 20 Hz. iRing recognizes finger clenching, which can also be detected by a pressure sensor. However, compared to conventional pressure sensors, photoreflectors are low-cost, compact, fast, robust, and they do not require an amplifier because they are not attached to the skin.

An Arduino Pro mini microcontroller (based on AT-mega328) was used for reading data from the IR sensor. It has a 10-bit A/D converter that allows photoreflector outputs from 0 to 1023. The power supply was selected as 3.3 V so that graphs and results in this paper shown below have a maximum voltage of sensor gain, which was set to 3.3 V. The hardware used is shown in figure 10.

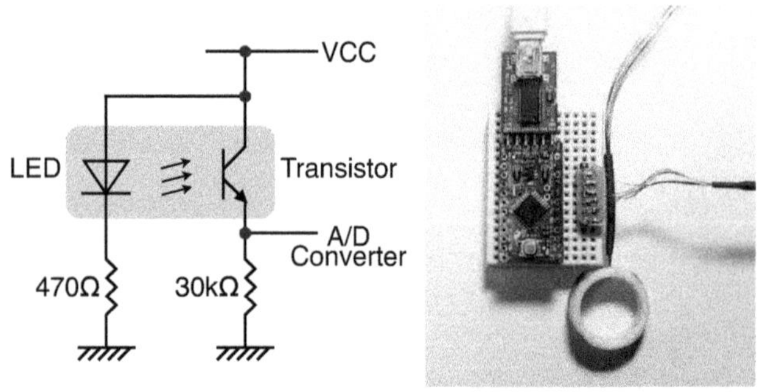

Figure 10. Circuit configuration implemented on iRing shown in the photo with an A/D converter.

RECOGNITION ALGORITHM

All gestures can be distinguished because they give unique sensor values. For example, as bending increases the total sensor value, bending and other functions (including rotation) can be distinguished.

We used four *variables*, S_A to S_D, as values of each sensor A, B, C, and D identified in figure 8. S_{AVE}, the average of S_A to S_D, is useful to roughly evaluate which state finger such as worn and inner pressure occurred.

$$S_{AVE} = (S_A + S_B + S_C + S_D) / 4$$

By calibrating, the *baseline* $B_{X\ (X=A,\ B,\ C,\ D)}$ is set as the sensor value for the straight finger state, and G is set as the distance from baseline when the finger is bent. If the finger is bent, inner pressure occurs, changing all the sensor values. All S_X become higher than B_X so that finger bending can be detected by considering S_{AVE}.

Bending/Inner Pressure

Finger bending can be described as the below equation. R is a ratio that sets the level of recognition (R < 1.0).

$$S_{AVE} > B_{AVE} + R \cdot G_{AVE}$$

However, backward finger bending derives a different relationship shown below. X refers to the sensor on the back of the finger (position of 180° in figure 8), while Y refers to the other sensors. The Y value does not change, but X changes because of bulged skin on the back of the finger.

$$S_X > B_X + R \cdot G_X \cap S_Y < B_Y + R \cdot G_Y$$

Rotation and Degree

According to experiments #2 and #3, the finger has non-uniform reflectance, but it is approximately normally distributed. Supplementing the lack of a maximum at 180° in figure 5, finger reflectance can also be thought as a sine curve distribution. This characteristic brings a uniform value of S_{AVE} in all the angles. Even if S_{AVE} changes, its value is maintained under *threshold T* (*T* can be defined as *G* with a constant ratio). A_A is an *angle* position of sensor A defined in the experiment section.

$$\text{When } S_{AVE} < B_{AVE} + T$$

$$A_A \approx 0°: \quad S_A < S_B \approx S_D < S_C$$

$$0° < A_A < 90°: \quad S_A < S_B, S_D < S_C$$

External Pressure

Because of the rigid body of iRing, external pressure relatively keeps the same sensor state to normal. It means that the opposite side of the pressed side is distanced from the finger, so that S_{SUM} does not change beyond *threshold T*.

$$S_X > B_X + T \cap S_Y < B_Y - T \ (Y \text{ is opposite to } X)$$

In this operation, the rotation parameter can be affected because the relationship among sensors will be changed. To separate two commands, the recognition of external pressure has priority over rotation.

Calibration

The skin reflectance is stable for finger bending and rotation. However, calibration is required for setting the threshold to recognize commands. iRing requires individual calibration. It first records both states of the bending gesture: straight and bent finger. The system then configures the steps to identify to what extent the finger is bent. Other gestures are also calibrated in this way.

1. Putting on finger with sensor position on the right angle.
2. Demanding system to determine the *baseline* of the straight state.
3. Bending finger completely, but not clenching.
4. Demanding system to determine the *gap* of the bent state.
5. Bending finger straight.
6. Rotating the ring and demanding the system to store reflectance data on each point by 90°. The purpose is to standardize for uneven photoreflector sensor characteristics by recording reflectance at four points. The user should perform this task only thrice; the first point is already sensed.

Limitation

As shown in experiments #2 and #3, iRing has a limitation in sensing the entire finger skin equally because of the variety in finger sizes and shapes. However, these problems can be solved by choosing a size fit for each person and using many sensors instead of the current product implementation.

Although the recognition of finger state is described with an equation, the ideal state is achieved when the iRing's sensor is set on the right angle position. It is difficult to sense other states during the intent to do other gestures. For example, iRing cannot detect rotation when the finger is bent because the sensor value relationship can be complicated.

As the photoreflector can detect minute distances from an object, sensing data from different sensors are not even because of the physical gap of the installation. In this paper, the recognition equation premises an even condition of sensor data to simplify calculation. The sample application normalizes the small lag among sensors.

FUNCTIONS

Bending Extent as Input

iRing detects bent finger and the level of bending by calculating *baseline* value and *gap* that can be detected when the hand is clenched. The bending measurement is not linear to the bending angle, but it is linear to pressure.

Inner Pressure Measurement

When the hand is clenched, pressure is exerted on the palm without a visible change on the outside. When the ring is worn, this inner pressure can be sensed during finger bending. Calibrating in advance allows the ring to distinguish the states of the hand—with and without inner pressure—even when the hand is clenched.

Degree and Direction of Rotation

This measurement provides the absolute degree of rotation when the ring is worn. Therefore, the ring can be used as an interface, e.g., as a volume controller or jog dial. The equation described in this paper guarantees constant resolution of 45° (eighth of 360°).

Touch Sensor (Pointing and Flipping Actions and Omnidirectional Movement)

The external operation of a device usually requires a switch. The ring detects the direction of the outer pressure by using the finger skin as the medium that reflects the IR ray. This method allows pointing from the top, bottom, and diagonal directions. Furthermore, values of multiple sensors allow calculation of the time span, direction, and force, which would be useful in understanding user operations such as flipping and tracing. The user can provide a 180° input by holding the ring, which means that it can be omnidirectional, like a joystick.

APPLICATIONS

Music Controller

We used iRing as a music controller to (a) rewind and fast-forward, (b) change the channel, and (c) increase or decrease the volume. The stroke (two directions, right and left), pressure (two sides, top and bottom), and rotation functions are connected to operations (a), (b), and (c), respectively. Therefore, if the ring is used as a jog dial and push button, there is no need for an extra controller for the music player.

Cursor Controller and Wearable Mouse

The user can manipulate a cursor by using iRing in two ways. The first way is to use two rings, on the thumb and index finger, and consider them as horizontal and vertical inputs, respectively. The second way is to use the ring as an omnidirectional input device, e.g., a joystick, by holding and moving it in 2D directions. With this device, users only have to use the ring, which has a socially acceptable shape, unlike other human interface devices.

Enhancement of Tablet Computer

We designed an application that uses finger bending on a tablet computer to control functions such as dragging and turning an object on the display. In this example, a straight finger drags and a bent finger rotates a 3D object. We show the possibility of enhancing existing interfaces in wearable computers.

Rehabilitation Support

iRing can be used as a rehabilitation instrument to visualize improvement in movement at a clinic. According to reports of medical staff, it is difficult to quantify improvement in rehabilitation, and clinicians usually have to perform a qualitative evaluation of some disorders. For example, a quantitative test for a patient with apoplexy is to draw a line along a printed spiral line; the severity of the disease is determined by calculating the difference between the two lines. However, devices available presently for measuring surface electromyograms of patients are expensive, with difficulties in movement of the hand and fingers. iRing not only provides the patient motivation to practice but also helps medical staff monitor improvement over time.

FUTURE WORK

In the future, iRing is expected to be suitable as a wearable controller that can be manufactured on a commercial scale. Conventional user interfaces such as a mouse and keyboard are too large to be carried around and too complicated to be used while walking. If users can operate a device through only finger movements, they can control next-generation devices such as glass computers without additional processing (for example, hand image recognition).

CONCLUSION

We proposed a highly functional, wearable input device that uses infrared reflectance as a basis for sensing pressure. We presented examples of application of this interface device as a controller interface and in human sensing systems.

ACKNOWLEDGEMENTS

This work was supported by the JST PRESTO program.

REFERENCES

1. Wing, A. M., Haggard, P., and Flanagan, J. R. Hand and Brain: The Neurophysiology and Psychology of Hand Movements,, *Academic Press, Inc* (1996).
2. Rekimoto, J. GestureWrist and GesturePad: unobtrusive wearable interaction devices. In *Proc. ISWC '01*, pp. 21–27.
3. Fukui, R., Watanabe, M., Gyota, T., Shimosaka, M. and Sato, T. Hand shape classification with a wrist contour sensor: development of a prototype device. In *Proc. UbiComp '11*, pp. 311–314.
4. Tsukada, K., and Yasumura, M. Ubi-Finger: a Simple Gesture Input Device for Mobile and Ubiquitous Environment, *Journal of Asian Information, Science and Life (AISL)*, Vol.2, No.2, pp. 111–120, 2004.
5. Ashbrook, D., Baudisch, P. and White, S. Nenya: subtle and eyes-free mobile input with a magnetically-tracked finger ring. In *Proc. CHI '11*, pp. 2043–2046.
6. Rhee, S., Yang, B.H. and Asada, H.H. Artifact-resistant power-efficient design of finger-ring plethysmographic sensors. *IEEE Transactions on Biomedical Engineering*, Vol.48, Num.7, pp. 795–805, 2001.
7. Sugiura, Y., Kakehi, G., Withana, A., Lee, C., Sakamoto, D., Sugimoto, M., Inami, M., and Igarashi, T. Detecting shape deformation of soft objects using directional photoreflectivity measurement. In *Proc UIST '11*, pp. 509–516.
8. Mascaro, S.A. and Asada, H.H. Photoplethysmograph fingernail sensors for measuring finger forces without haptic obstruction. *IEEE Transactions on Robotics and Automation*, vol.17, no.5, pp.698-708, 2001.

Bimanual Gesture Keyboard

Xiaojun Bi **Ciprian Chelba** **Tom Ouyang** **Kurt Partridge** **Shumin Zhai**
Google Inc.
Mountain View, CA, USA
{bxj, ciprianchelba, ouyang, kep, zhai}@google.com

ABSTRACT
Gesture keyboards represent an increasingly popular way to input text on mobile devices today. However, current gesture keyboards are exclusively unimanual. To take advantage of the capability of modern multi-touch screens, we created a novel bimanual gesture text entry system, extending the gesture keyboard paradigm from one finger to multiple fingers. To address the complexity of recognizing bimanual gesture, we designed and implemented two related interaction methods, *finger-release* and *space-required*, both based on a new multi-stroke gesture recognition algorithm. A formal experiment showed that bimanual gesture behaviors were easy to learn. They improved comfort and reduced the physical demand relative to unimanual gestures on tablets. The results indicated that these new gesture keyboards were valuable complements to unimanual gesture and regular typing keyboards.

Keywords: Text Entry, Touch Screen

ACM Classification Keywords
H.5.2 [Information Interfaces and Presentation]: Input Devices and Strategies

INTRODUCTION
Among numerous novel methods of text input, gesture keyboards, also referred as shape writing [26, 21], have become a rare exception in gaining large-scale adoption on mobile devices. First published in the user interface literature in the early 2000's [27, 13], gesture keyboards today are commercially available through many products such as ShapeWriter, SlideIT, Swype, T9 Trace, and TouchPal.

A gesture keyboard offers users a variety of advantages. It supports a gradual and seamless transition from visually guided tracing to recall-based gesturing, and also relaxes the requirement of precisely specifying words verbatim by allowing users to express the intention with approximate shape and location finger strokes [13]. Also, it is immune to one major problem plaguing regular touchscreen typing: the lack of tactile-feedback [7, 21].

One frequently raised question is that given the capability of modern multi-touch screens, it seems amiss that gesture keyboards are exclusively unimanual. Traditional typewriting is a two-handed activity. Furthermore, many mobile device users often hold the device with both hands and type with two thumbs (Figure 1). On many tablets the virtual keyboard can be split to two parts to support this mode of operation. Additionally, a split keyboard consumes only a small amount of screen space, which has been shown to boost user experience on portable touch screens. [15]. For example, the sizes of the split keyboards in Figures 1a and 1b are only 25% (landscape) and 47% (portrait) of the sizes of default virtual tablet keyboards. In recognition of these advantages, split keyboards are now supported on iPad, Windows 8 and Android tablets. However, despite the popularity of split keyboards, current gesture keyboards are incompatible with two-thumb use. We aim to overcome this limitation by enabling bimanual operation of gesture keyboards.

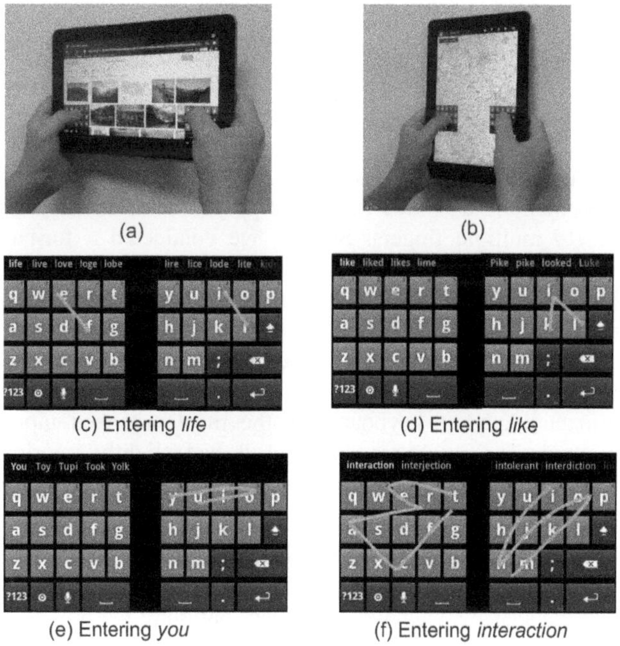

Figure 1. (a) and (b): two-hand holding postures for tablets with split keyboards. (c), (d), (e), and (f): entering words on split keyboards with bimanual gestures. Note that the actual gap between the two sides of a split keyboard is greater than illustrated. Blue strokes represent finger strokes.

Other than supporting two-handed holding and typing, and freeing screen real estate, another benefit of enabling bimanual operation lies in movement efficiency. Instead of frequently moving the same finger from one side of the

UIST '12, October 7–10, 2012, Cambridge, Massachusetts, USA.

keyboard to another, each thumb only moves in its vicinity on one side of the keyboard, hence eliminating the long movements common on unimanual gesture keyboards. For example to enter the word *life*, a unimanual gesture approximates the trace *l-i-f-e* on the keyboard. On a standard Qwerty keyboard the trace from *i* to *f* moving from the right side to the left side of the keyboard is the longest segment of the *l-i-f-e* gesture. With a bimanual gesture keyboard, the word *life* can be gestured with *l-i* movement by the right hand and *f-e* by the left hand, eliminating the *i-f* segment (Figure 1). In another example, the bimanual gesture for the word *like* can be drawn as *l-i-k* by the right hand and a tap (a zero length gesture) on *e* by the left hand, saving the long distance travel from *k* to *e* on Qwerty (Figure 1).

It is important and in fact necessary to design bimanual gesture keyboards to be fully compatible with existing modes of keyboard operation. First, bimanual gestures algorithm should be compatible with unimanual gestures. Any additional flexibility or benefits that bimanual gestures may bring should be at little or no cost of unimanual gestures. Second, tapping is still the preferred mode of touch screen keyboard operation for many users today (if not the majority). Gesture keyboards should not be viewed as competition or as a replacement for tapping. They should be compatible with the tapping mode of keyboard as well.

The contribution of this paper is two-fold. First, we designed and implemented a bimanual gesture text entry system, based on the *multi-stroke gesture recognition* algorithm as well as two interaction methods (i.e., *finger-release* and *space-required*). This system enabled a novel form of bimanual gesture input that was not previously possible, and extended the gesture keyboard from one finger to multiple fingers. Second, we conducted a formal experiment to evaluate the strengths and weaknesses of bimanual gesture input. The results showed that the bimanual behavior was easy to learn. It raised the comfort level and reduced the physical demand over the unimanual counterpart. 42% (15 out of 36) participants chose one of the bimanual gesture keyboards as the most preferred input method. The weakness was that it had slightly inferior speed efficiency over unimanual gesture keyboard, due to the attention and action switches between the two fingers.

In the rest of this paper we first briefly review related work. We then focus on the main bimanual gesture algorithms and the systems we have developed, outlining the pros and cons of each design. We then report and analyze a formal lab experiment evaluating bimanual gesture keyboards on tablets.

RELATED WORK

To our knowledge no bimanual gesture keyboard research has been reported in the literature to date.

In the body of literature on unimanual gesture keyboards, Zhai and Kristensson published the first prototype, experiment and a set of basic principles of gesture keyboards [27]. The first complete and large vocabulary gesture keyboard was published in [13]. Kristensson and Zhai [12] extended the gesture keyboard concepts to gesture keyboard commands whose strokes are defined by the command name but prefixed on a command key. Many of the key concepts of gesture keyboard were summarized in "Introduction to Shape Writing" [26]. The idea of treating typing as a discrete form of "shape writing" was reported in the work of Elastic Stylus Keyboard (ESK) [14_] . Zhai et al analyzed user feedback of ShapeWriter on the iPhone [28]. Rick [21] developed a predictive modele of gesture keyboard and used such a model to estimate keyboard layout's impact on gesture keyboard performance.

A large body of research on two-handed interaction interfaces, beginning with Buxton and Myers [7], can be found in the HCI literature. A focus of this body of work is on the task assignment between two hands [e.g. 4]. The best known model of bimanual action is Guiard's kinematic chain theory [9] explaining the asymmetric relationship between the dominant and the non-dominant hand's role bimanual operation. In this theory the non-dominant hand sets the coarse level frame of reference (e.g. holding a pad) and the dominant hand makes fine control within that frame of reference (e.g. writing with a pen on the pad). In human-computer interaction as well as other real world tasks bimanual operation can also be symmetrical (typing, steering a bicycle). The literature suggests that a number of tasks such as 2D or 3D navigation [3] can be performed effectively with a symmetric assignment of roles to the hand. Factors affecting the performance of symmetric bimanual interaction were also studied [2]. In the field of text entry, symmetric bimanual typing is common on both physical and virtual keyboards. In this work, we extend the bimanual interaction to gesture keyboards.

There is also a long history of research on gesture and sketch based interfaces in the HCI community. These gesture symbols can be drawn using either a single stroke [22, 16] or multiple strokes [1, 19], and have been applied to problems ranging from interfaces for blind users [11] to search on mobile devices [17, 20]. In contrast to our work, these approaches focus on unimanual input where strokes are often drawn sequentially. Furthermore, they represent an inherently different type of interaction where gestures are direct visual recreations of the symbols in the domain, rather than as paths that are defined by virtual keys on a soft keyboard. Finally, strokes are recognized at the word-level on gesture keyboards but mostly at the character-level in other applications.

BIMANUAL GESTURE KEYBOARDS

A bimanual gesture keyboard works similarly to a unimanual keyboard: a word is entered by tracing through all the letters, from the first to last in order. Unlike the unimanual gesture keyboard, on which a word is entered by one continuous stroke, a user can draw multiple strokes for a given word on a bimanual keyboard using both thumbs (Figure 1). In this paper, we define a *stroke* as a continuous trajectory drawn by a finger on the touch screen, with one *touch down*, multiple *touch move,* and one *touch up* events. A *gesture* refers to a collection of *strokes* for a given word. A *unimanual gesture* contains only one *stroke,* while a *bimanual gesture* can contain multiple *strokes* (Figure 1).

As the number of strokes in a *bimanual gesture* is uncertain and previous unimanual gesture algorithms only process single-stroke *gestures*, there are two new challenges to recognizing bimanual gestures: 1) how to *cluster* the *strokes* that belong to the same word into a bimanual gesture and 2) how to *recognize* the target word that the bimanual gesture represents.

Clustering Strokes

On bimanual gesture keyboards, a word can be represented by one or multiple *strokes*, depending on the locations of letters in a word. For example, the word *you* is usually drawn by one *stroke*, because letters *y*, *u* and *o* are on the same side of the keyboard and close to each other, while *"life"* is usually represented by two *strokes*, *l-i* and *f-e*, because *l, i,* and *f, e* are located at different sides and drawn by two thumbs separately. *Interaction* is usually represented by three strokes: *i-n (right), t-e-r-a-c-t (left),* and *i-o-n (right)* (Figure 1).

To recognize words from bimanual gestures, the first step is cluster *strokes* into *gestures*. To be compatible with unimanual gesture and two-thumb typing, and transfer users' experience of using these two methods, we propose two approaches to solve this problem: *Finger-Release* and *Space-Required.*

Finger-Release. Similar to unimanual gestures, which signal the end of a word by the lifting up the finger, this method uses *finger-release* to cluster gestures: lifting both fingers off the screen indicates the end of a word. In other words, the user has to keep at least one finger on the screen while composing the word.

This method is fully compatible with unimanual gesture keyboard. It also allows users to skip inputting the space key, which is a big advantage of gesture keyboards in general.

The disadvantage is that it may require extra mental and physical efforts for users to keep at least one finger on the screen before finishing the word. It may be difficult to get used to such a behavior. If the user accidentally releases both fingers when switching one finger to the other, it would falsely signal the end of a word.

Space-Required. Another approach is to use a space key press to signal the end of a word, the standard method for regular tap-based keyboards.

This method offers users more flexibility than *Finger-Release*, by removing the requirement of keeping at least one finger down. It is also fully compatible with regular typing. Our algorithm even supports mixing regular typing and gesturing for a given word, since both gesturing and typing use the space key press to signal the end of a word. This method can also be viewed as enhanced typing: a user can choose to tap, gesture, or mix tapping and gesturing for a single word.

The disadvantage is that it is somewhat incompatible with unimanual gesture by requiring a space key after finishing gestures. If both unimanual and bimanual gestures are implemented on the same keyboard, it requires pressing a space key for unimanual gestures too.

In short, *finger-release* and *space-required* have their own pros and cons as stroke clustering methods. It is unknown which one fits bimanual gesture keyboards better. We implemented both of them and conducted a formal lab study to understand the strengths and weaknesses of each.

Multi-Stroke Gesture Recognition

A *bimanual gesture* usually consists of *multiple strokes.* To our knowledge, no literature shows how to recognize the word from multiple strokes in the gesture keyboard paradigm.

A straightforward approach is to connect all touch points together to form a unimanual gesture according to the time stamps, and feed it into a unimanual gesture recognition engine [13]. This approach works if all the letters of a word happen to be on the same side of the screen. (e.g., the word *you*, all three letters are on the right side). However, it fails for other words due to the following challenges.

Figure 2. (a) Actual finger strokes for entering *work: w-r* and *o-k*. (b) Final gesture by connecting all touch points according to timestamps: *w-o-w-r-o-k*. Blue strokes are actual finger strokes.

First, unimanual gesture recognition algorithms are based on the assumption that the gesture travels through letters of a word following their natural order. For example, the unimanual gesture template for *work* is *w-o-r-k*. The unimanual gesture algorithm gives the matching score between a unimanual gesture and this template. However, bimanual gestures do not always follow this rule. When a finger slides to a target letter, it may move from the last letter in the word *on the same side*, which might not be the letter preceding the target letter in the word.

For example, *one way* to enter *work* on a bimanual gesture keyboard is as follows (Figure 2):

1. Left thumb presses the letter *w* and right thumb presses *o*. Connecting touch points based on the timestamps creates the stroke *w-o*.
2. Left thumb slides to *r* from its previous location *w*. Connecting all the touch points together creates the stroke *w-o-w-r*.

3. Right thumb slides to k from o. The stroke becomes *w-o-w-r-o-k*, which is different from the unimanual gesture template, *w-o-r-k*.

Second, users might gesture the same word differently, depending on whether the finger slides from its previous location, or starts over from a new location. This variance leads to different gestures for the same word. For example, *interaction* can be gestured in the following two approaches:

Approach #1 (Figure 3a):

1. Right finger gestures *i-n;*
2. Left finger gestures *t-e-r-a-c-t;*
3. Lift right finger from the previous letter *n,* land it on the letter *i,* and gesture *i-o-n;*

The final gesture according to the timestamp is *i-n-t-e-r-a-c-t-i-o-n*. This one is the same with the unimanual gesture template.

Approach #2 (Figure 3b):

1. Right finger gestures *i-n;*
2. Left finger gestures *t-e-r-a-c-t;*
3. Slide right finger to *i* from its previous location *n*, and gesture *i-o-n*.

The final gesture becomes *i-n-t-e-r-a-c-t-n-i-o-n,* different from the unimanual gesture template.

Figure 3. Two approaches for entering *interaction.* (a). Approach #1, (b) Approach #2.

Third, users might move two fingers simultaneously for a given word. For example (Figure 1), *life* is usually gestured by *l-i* (right finger), followed by *f-e* (left finger). Once a user gets familiar with the pattern, she might start the second stroke *f-e* before finishing *l-i*. Therefore, some touch points on the stroke *f-e* have earlier timestamps than those on *l-i*. Simply connecting touch points based on timestamps produces a gesture different from the unimanual gesture template *l-i-f-e*.

To address the above challenges, we designed a novel *multi-stroke gesture recognition algorithm.* Given a bimanual gesture g, it generates a ranked list of candidate words.

It works as follows:

Step 1. Reorganizing touch points based on finger id. Touch points on the gesture g with the same finger id are connected together to generate a sub-gesture based on the timestamps. On a split keyboard, touch points on the same side are connected together, since they are generated by the same finger. This step leads two sub-gestures: g_{left} and g_{right}, with the finger id, *left* and *right* respectively (Figure 4).

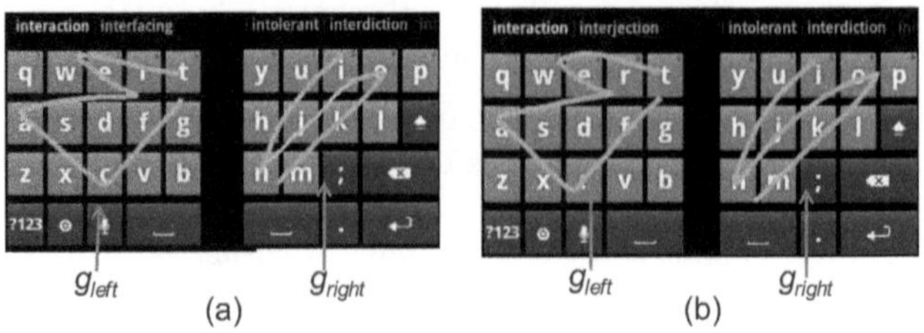

Figure 4. Generating g_{left} and g_{right} by connecting touch points with the same finger id together. (a) and (b) show two approaches for entering the word *interaction.* Blue strokes represent actual finger strokes. The green line in (a) connects the last point of stroke *i-n* with the first point of *i-o-n*, because both of them were drawn by right finger. As shown, (a) and (b) lead to similar sub-gestures.

Step 2. Labeling each letter of a given word *w* with the id of the finger that gestures it, and splitting the word into sub-strings based on finger ids. On a split keyboard, letters on the left and right sides are gestured by left and right fingers respectively. The finger id of a letter is determined based on its location. The word *w* is then split into two sub-strings, $s_{left}(w)$ and $s_{right}(w)$, with the finger id *left* and *right* respectively. Take the word *interaction* as an example. $s_{left}(w)$ = *teract,* and $s_{right}(w)$ = *inion,* because letters *i, n, i, o, n* are gestured by right finger while the others by left finger.

Step 3. Matching sub-gestures g_{left} and g_{right} with sub-strings $s_{left}(w)$and $s_{right}(w)$ respectively. The match scores are recorded as $c_{left}(w)$ and $c_{right}(w)$, reflecting the probabilities of s_{left} and s_{right}, given the g_{left} and g_{right}, respectively. A unimanual gesture recognizer[1] is used here to calculate the matching score between a sub-string and a sub-gesture. E.g., if *w* = *interaction*, $g_{left}(w)$ and $g_{right}(w)$ (Figure 4) are matched with $s_{left}(w)$ = *teract* and $s_{right}(w)$ = *inion*, respectively. The unimanual gesture recognizer first searches for the closest touch point along a sub-gesture for a given letter. The distance between this touch point and the letter is converted to a distance score. The sum of distance scores over all the letters within a word is mapped to the matching score.

Step 4. Obtain the gesture match score *c(w)* for a given word *w* by integrating $c_{left}(w)$ and $c_{right}(w)$:

[1] A detailed description of the unimanual gesture recognition algorithm is beyond the scope of this work, and is independent of the bimanual gesture issues investigated in this paper. We used algorithms different from what has been published in the literature such as Kristensson and Zhai [13], but that approach could also be adapted as building blocks to bimanual gesture algorithm. The algorithms for other unimanual gesture keyboards such as Swype, SlideIt, T9 trace, Touchpal have not been published in the scientific literature, but any of them may be applied here as well.

$$c(w) = \frac{c_{left}(w)c_{right}(w)}{\sum_{i \in W} c_{left}(i)c_{right}(i)}$$

where W is the set of the words contained in the N-best list. N-best list is the set containing the words with top $c_{left}(w)c_{right}(w)$ values. $N = 500$ in our implementation.

Step5. Obtain the final score $c'(w)$ by integrating gesture score $c(w)$ with the language model score $l(w)$:

$$c'(w) = \frac{c(w)l(w)}{\sum_{i \in W} c(i)l(i)}$$

Where $l(w)$ is the probability of the word w based on language model, and W is the set of words contained in the N-best list. The language model in the experiment contained approximately 90,000 unigrams and 300,000 bigrams.

The words in the N-best list are ranked according to the confidence score $c'(w)$. The top candidate is displayed directly in the text input view. Other candidates are displayed on the suggestion bar.

In sum, by reorganizing touch points and splitting letters based on finger id, this algorithm reduces the bimanual gesture recognition problem to two unimanual sub-gesture recognition problems. Since g_{left} and g_{right} are processed separately and independently, it supports both sequential and concurrent finger movements.

Implementation of Bimanual Gesture Keyboards

Based on the aforementioned methods and algorithm, we developed *finger-release* and *space-required* bimanual gesture keyboards on Android Devices. Figure 5 illustrates their architectures.

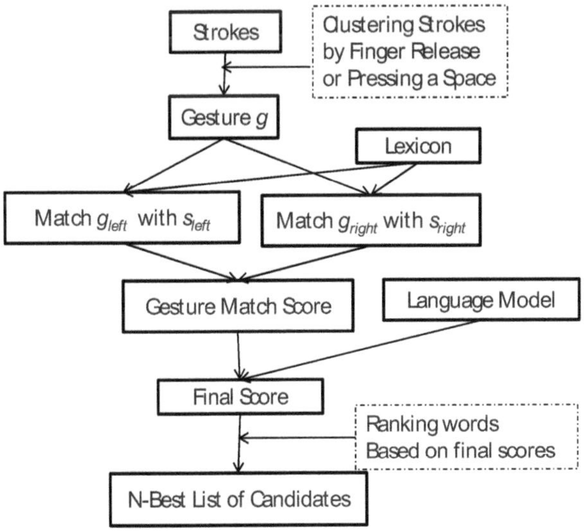

Figure 5. The architecture for bimanual gesture keyboards.

EMPIRICAL STUDY

Our bimanual gesture algorithms enable a new type of interaction behavior that was previously not possible, and we further analyzed and evaluated this design with an empirical study.

The goal of this study was twofold. First it closed the design-iteration loop by testing with participants who had no knowledge of, or bias from, the research and design insight. We wanted to observe users' actual behaviors on bimanual gesture keyboards and evaluate the strengths and weaknesses of two bimanual gesture keyboard methods.

Second, we evaluated bimanual gesture performance along with unimanual gesture performance. Although gestures have already been adopted on a large number of devices, formal user studies of unimanual gesture keyboards are still very limited in the literature.

Note that our basic goal is to expand the flexibility of the gesture keyboard paradigm. If the expanded bimanual mode is completely compatible with existing input modes and is preferred by a meaningful number of users, it does not need to "beat" other modes in performance to be valuable. However it is still important and informative to measure bimanual gestures movement and time difference in comparison to their unimanual counterparts in order to gain empirical insights.

Although the bimanual gesture keyboards work on both smart phones and tablets, this study focused on tablets in order to maintain a manageable scope.

Design

We used a 2 × 3 × 2 mixed-factorial design, with one between subject factor, tablet orientation (Portrait and Landscape), and two within-subject factors: input method and input tasks (phrase vs.word). Input method had three levels: unimanual gesture, finger-release and space-required bimanual gestures.

Figure 6. Left: unimanual gesture keyboards. Right: bimanual gesture keyboards.

Figure 6 illustrates the keyboards used for each method. We chose the sizes based on practical usages. The sizes (in pixels) of unimanual gesture keyboards were 1280 × 360 with each letter key 105 × 90 in landscape mode, and 800 × 304 with each letter key 66 × 76 in portrait. These were also default sizes for Android keyboards on a tablet. The sizes of bimanual gesture keyboards were identical in both landscape or portrait modes: 240 × 240 on each side, with the letter key size 48 × 60. These values were chosen to fit the two hand holding postures. Input task included two levels: *phrase input* and *word repetition* [5,6]. The former simulated regular text entry tasks, while the latter investigated the learnability and expert input speed of each input method. The main measures were *Input Speed* (WPM), *Not Corrected Error Rate*, and *Corrected Error Rate* [22].

Phrase input. In each trial, the participant entered a phrase chosen from MacKenzie and Soukoreff's phrase set [18]. To randomize the starting position of the input finger and also record the beginning time of a trial, participants started each trial by tapping a red start circle (diameter = 110 pixels) on the unimanual keyboard, and tapped the *Enter* key after finishing the phrase. The start circle was centered on one of the 26 English letters. The probability of appearing on a given letter was in accordance with its frequency as an ending letter in English Word, estimated from the American National Corpus.

There were two start circles on a bimanual keyboard, to randomize the positions of two fingers.

Participants were allowed to correct the current word by backspace key.

The input speed was calculated as:

$$WPM = \frac{|T|}{S} \times 60 \times \frac{1}{5}$$

where T was the final transcribed string and S was the elapsed time in seconds from the moment when the finger was lift from staring circle to the finish of the last word in the phrase. Note that the numerator was $|T|$, instead of $|T| - 1$ [23] because the time to input the first character was also included.

The error rates were:

$$Not\ Corrected\ Error\ Rate = \frac{INF}{C + INF + IF}$$

$$Corrected\ Error\ Rate = \frac{IF}{C + INF + IF}$$

where C is the total number of correct words, IF is the number of incorrect but fixed(backspaced) words, and INF is the number of incorrect (but not fixed) words. We used a word-level instead of a character-level error rate [22] because both gesture keyboards were word-level input methods. We randomly chose 32 phrases from MacKenzie and Soukoreff's phrases [18] as the test set and divided them into 4 blocks. The orders of phrases were randomized within a block. The first block was a warm-up session.

Word Repetition. In each trial, the participant entered the same word six times repeatedly. Examining how input speed progressed as a word was repeatedly entered revealed the learnability of a method. Also, assuming that a user became familiar with the gesture pattern of the word after repeating it multiple times, the last one or two repetitions simulated the expert input speed a user can achieve [5, 6].

In each trial, the participant started each repetition by pressing the red starting circle(s). The finish of a word was determined as follows:

1) In unimanual and *finger-release* bimanual gesture conditions, the target word was correctly gestured, or picked from the suggestion bar, or the participant started the next repetition without correcting the current word which was incorrectly gestured.
2) In space-required bimanual, a space key was tapped, or the word was picked from the suggestion bar.

New start circles appear upon the finish of a word.

The input speed was calculated as:

$$WPM = \frac{|W| + 1}{S} \times 60 \times \frac{1}{5}$$

where $|W|+1$ was the length of the target word plus a space character and S was the elapsed time in seconds from the moment when participants lifted fingers from the starting circles to the finish of a word. The error rates were the same with those in *Phrase Input.*

The test set included 32 words randomly chosen from the top 300 frequently used English words. These words were equally divided into 4 blocks and the order within a block was randomized. The first block was a warm-up session.

Subjective measures were collected at the end of the experiments. Participants rated each input method based on *comfort* , *learnability*, *efficiency*, *accuracy*, *absence of frustration*, *mental*, *physical demands*, and *overall preference*, all on 1~10 scales. Some of the measures were adopted from NASA TLX [10].

We also recorded detailed information of each touch event, to analyze participants' gesturing and tapping behaviors.

Participants

We recruited 36 participants (17 females) between ages of 18 and 56. All of them used tablets at least several times a month, 17 used it daily. Eighteen of them participated in the Portrait condition while the others in Landscape. The orders of the three input methods and two tasks were fully counterbalanced across participants. Each participant entered $3 \times 32 = 96$ phrases in *phrase input*, and $3 \times 6 \times 32 = 576$ words in *word repetition* tasks. The study lasted around 1.5 hours for each participant.

Apparatus

The experiment was conducted on a Samsung Galaxy Tab 10.1 with Android OS 2.3. The size of the multi-touch screen was 256.7 × 175.3 mm with resolution of 1280 × 800. The weight was 565g. Participants held the tablet with either one or two hands while sitting in a chair (Figure 7).

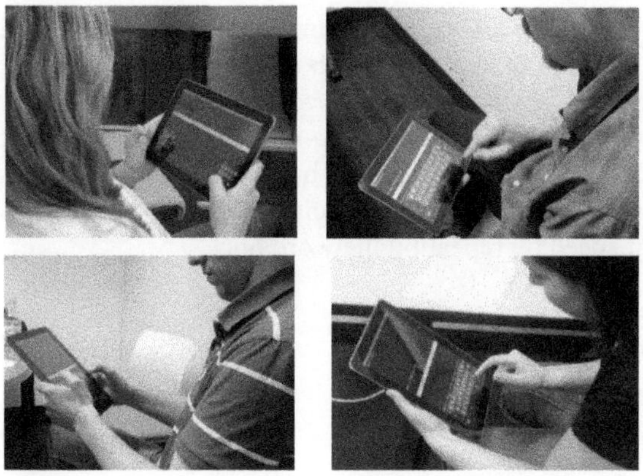

Figure 7. Participants held tablets with two hands (left) or one hand (right).

Results

We first investigated the effect of input method on *input speed* in *phrase input,* and the average input speed of last two repetitions in *word repetition*, which simulated the expert input speed. Similar effects were discovered for both of them. (Figure 8). Input method had a significant main effect on both measures ($F_{(2, 68)} = 87.562$, for phrase input, $F_{(2, 68)} = 153.1$,for last two repetitions; $p < 0.01$). Pairwise comparisons showed significant differences between every two methods ($p < 0.01$). ANOVA did not show a main effect of orientation, or orientation × input method interaction.

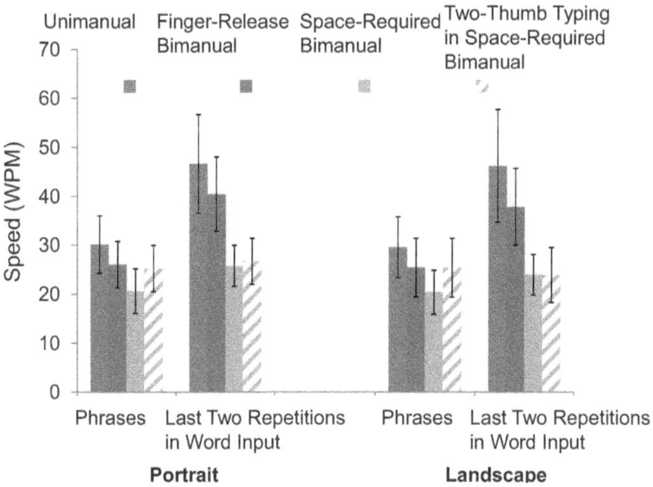

Figure 8. Mean (SD) input speed.

To understand the learnability of each method, we investigate the effect of repetition position (#1~6) on input speed, for each input method separately. The analysis showed similar results across all three methods (Figure 9): participants reached a relatively stable speed from repetition #2. ANOVAs showed that word position had significant main effects on speed ($F_{(5, 170)} = 27.168$ for *unimanual*, $F_{(5, 170)} = 20.443$ for *finger-release bimanual*, $F_{(5, 170)} = 39.671$ for *space-required bimanual*, $p < 0.01$ for all.), pairwise mean comparisons showed significant differences between position #1 with any of other positions ($p < 0.05$), but not between any other two positions. The analysis did not show any significant main effect of orientation on speed.

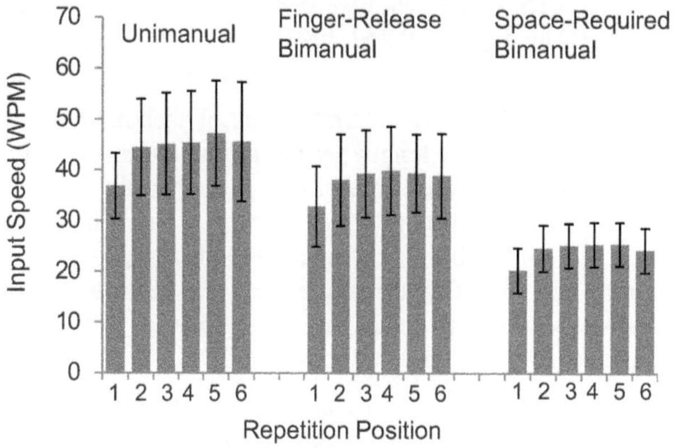

Figure 9. Mean(SD) input speed in Word Repetition Tasks.

We did not explicitly include two-thumb typing as an experimental condition given the limited manageable scope of one controlled study. However, *space-required* bimanual gesture can be viewed as enhanced two-thumb typing: users can tap a word or mix tapping with gesturing. Examining the subset of words that were exclusively entered by tapping provides some insights about two-thumb typing.

On average, 52% (SD = 15%) of words in *phrase input* and 31% (SD = 9%) in *word repetition* were entered by tapping only. Tapping and gesturing were identified by stroke length. A stroke with the length less than half a key-width was identified as a tap. As shown in Figure 8, input speed of *finger-release* bimanual gesture was close to that of two-thumb typing in *phrase input*, but around 50% faster for expert input speed (i.e., last two repetitions in word repetition task). Since these words represent just a subset of the full experimental dataset, we did not perform inferential statistical analysis on them.

Not Corrected Error Rate

ANOVA did not show any significant main effect of orientation ($F_{(1, 34)} = 0.257$, $p = 0.615$) or input method ($F_{(2, 68)} = 0.522$, $p = 0.595$) on *Not Corrected Error Rate*, indicating that participants input texts at the same level of accuracy in both portrait and landscape modes, and across different input methods. The mean (SD) were unimanual at 2.8% (3.2%), *finger-release* bimanual at 3.3% (3.6%), *space-required* bimanual at 3.9% (5.0%). The task type had a significant main effect ($F_{(1, 34)} = 13.53$, $p < 0.05$) with the mean (SD) 4.1%(4.8%), 2.5%(3.0%) for *phrase input* and *word repetition* respectively.

Corrected Error Rate

Unlike Not Corrected Error Rate, Input method has a significant main effect on Corrected Error Rate, i.e., the percentage of words that were backspaced ($F_{(2, 68)} = 10.276$, $p < 0.001$), with the means (SD) of 5.5% (3.1%) for unimanual, 7.6%(4.9%) for *finger-release* bimanual, and 8.1%(5.6%) for *space-required* bimanual. Pairwise mean comparisons show significant differences for *unimanual* vs.

finger-release bimanual, and *unimanual* vs. *space-required bimanual* ($p < 0.05$). ANOVA did not show any significant main effect for either task type ($F_{(1, 34)} = 1.950$, $p = 0.172$), or orientation ($F_{(1, 34)} = 0.252$, $p = 0.619$).

Gesture length

To investigate the movement efficiency of each method, we examined the gesture length per word, i.e., the distance the finger(s) travel on the screen for a given word. ANOVA showed that orientation ($F_{(1, 34)} = 4790$, $p < 0.01$), task type ($F_{(1, 34)} = 36.4$, $p < 0.01$) and input method ($F_{(2, 68)} = 3184$, $p < 0.01$) had significant main effects on gesture length. Pairwise mean comparisons showed significant differences between every two input methods ($p < 0.05$).

As shown in Figure 10, in portrait mode, the gesture length of unimanual gesture was 3.5 and 6.2 times longer than that in *finger release*, and *space-required* bimanual, respectively. In landscape mode, it was 2.1, and 3.4 times, respectively.

Subjective Measures

Participants rated each input method based on the level of *comfort, learnability, efficiency, accuracy, absence of frustration, mental, physical demands*, and *overall preference* in 1-10 scales. Results are illustrated in Figure 11. We performed ANOVAs, as well as post hoc pairwise comparisons with Bonferroni adjustment on each measure (the normality of ratings in each measure passed the Shapiro-Wilk tests). Finger-release and space-required bimanual were rated similarly across all the measures. No significant difference ($p > 0.05$) was observed in any measure.

Unimanual was rated most positive from measure 2 to 6, but most negative in 1 (*comfort*) and 7 (*physical demand*), probably due to the long finger travel distance and the fatigue caused by holding the tablet with one hand. The differences between *unimanual* and other method in both measures 1 and 7 were significant ($p < 0.05$).

The means (SD) of overall preferences rating were *unimanual* at 7.9 (2.3), *finger-release bimanual* at 6.6 (2.7), *space-required bimanual* at 5.7 (2.7). The difference for *unimanual vs. space-required* is significant ($p < 0.05$), but not between every other two methods. Participants were asked to choose one method from the three gesture keyboards and the regular two-thumb typing as the most preferred one for tablets. 19 chose unimanual, 11 chose finger-release bimanual, 4 chose space-required bimanual and 2 chose two-thumb typing.

DISCUSSION

Strengths and Weaknesses of Bimanual Gesture Keyboards

Learnability. Our study results showed that both *finger-release* and *space-required* bimanual gestures were easy to learn. The mean (SD) subjective measure regarding learnability (Figure 11) were 6.3 (2.2) and 7.0 (2.0) for *finger-released* and *space-required* bimanual respectively, indicating the high learnability for both of the two methods. Results also showed that *finger-release* was at the similar level of learnability with *space-required* bimanual method. Also, bimanual gestures can be quickly adopted by users. As shown in Figure 9, participants quickly improved the input speed by repeating the word once.

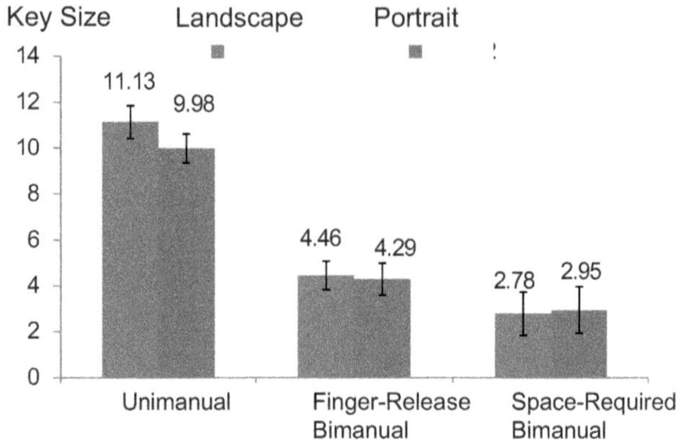

Figure 10. Mean (SD) gesture length per word. Key Size = (Key Width + Key Height) / 2.

Movement Efficiency. Since each thumb only moves in its vicinity on one side of the keyboard, we conjecture that bimanual gesture keyboards have higher movement efficiency over unimanual gesture keyboards. To better understand it, we compared the average length of gesture templates on different keyboards. The gesture template of a word is a set of line segments connecting centers of keys, following the order of letters within the word. For a word with multiple gesture templates on a bimanual gesture keyboard (e.g., Figure 3, two approaches for entering *interaction*). We chose the one with the longest gesture length, to approximate the upper bound.

The average lengths of gesture templates over all words in English Corpus [25], weighted with word frequency, are 11.6 and 5.32 key size long on unimanual and bimanual gesture keyboards respectively, predicting that bimanual gesture keyboard shortens the finger travelling distance by approximately 50% over its unimanual counterpart. The empirical data (Figure 10) echoes this finding: the finger release bimanual gesture keyboard shortens the gesture lengths by 60% (landscape) and 57% (portrait) over the unimanual gesture keyboard.

The shorter travelling distance reduces the physical demands of entering words, and raises the comfort levels (Figure 12). Some participants reported they did not like unimanual gesture on a tablet, especially in landscape mode, because the long distance travelling causes too much friction. Some users even tilted fingers to reduce the friction when drawing unimanual gestures across the screen (Figure 12).

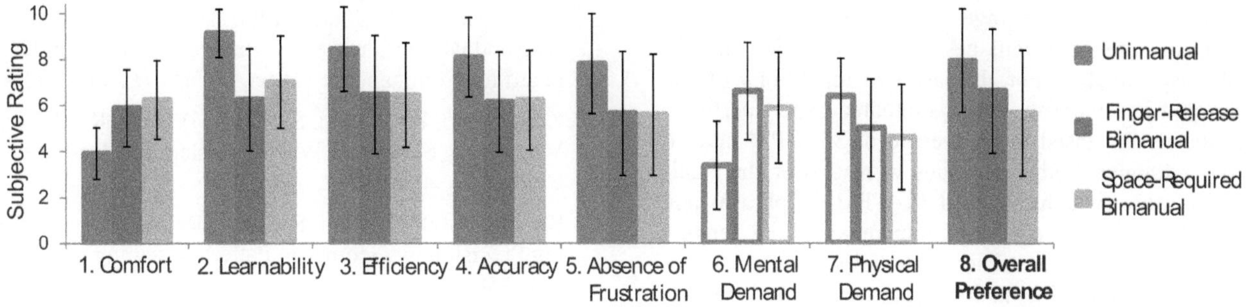

Figure 11. Mean (SD) of subjective ratings, all in (1-10) scales. For measures 1-5, and 8, a score of 10 is the most positive rating. For measures 6 and 7, 10 is the most negative rating (highest demand).

Figure 12. Users tilted fingers to reduce friction on unimanual gesture keyboards.

Time Efficiency. Finger-release is faster than *space-required* bimanual, mainly because it omits the space input. Its phrase input and the expert speed were 26, and 39 WPM respectively. The expert input speed is also around 50% faster than that of two-thumb typing in *space-required* bimanual (Figure 8).

Surprisingly, the movement efficiency of bimanual gesture keyboard does not lead to higher time efficiency over a unimanual gesture keyboard. It was slightly slower than unimanual counterpart, with the margins of 4 and 7 WPM for phrase input and expert speed, respectively. One possible reason is that the attention and action switches between two fingers were costly. They slowed users down and broke the interaction flow. Bimanual gesture might require more effort to coordinate two thumbs. Subjective measures showed that both bimanual gesture methods required more mental effort than bimanual gestures. Participants also corrected the input words more often on bimanual gesture keyboards than on the unimanual gesture keyboard, which reduced the time efficiency.

Screen Space Consumption. As a full keyboard is split to two sides, bimanual gesture keyboards consumed much smaller screen real estate than the unimanual gesture keyboards, which was important to boost the overall user experience on portable touchscreens [15]. In current implementations, the sizes of bimanual keyboards were 240 × 240 on each side (Figure 6), which were just 25% (Landscape), and 47% (Portrait) of unimanual gesture keyboards.

No Keyboard Fits All

Users' preferences varied when they selected the most preferred method. Unimanual gesture keyboard was the fastest, but it did not have the dominance. Only 19 participants, around 50% of all the subjects, select it as the most favorite input method. One disadvantage is that it has high physical demand and lower level of comfort in mobile situations. One female participant explicitly mentioned that the tablet was too heavy to hold with one hand. Also it occupies more screen space then split keyboards, and does not fit the two hand holding, a common posture in mobile situations.

Eleven participants, around 31% of all the subjects, chose finger-release bimanual as the most preferred input method. Four of them entered texts fastest with this method. Other participants mentioned that it well fitted the two-hand holding posture, and omitted the space input. Some participants also reported that they preferred bimanual over unimanual gesture keyboards because they consumed much smaller screen space.

Four participants preferred the space-required bimanual method, even though the inputting speed is slower than others. They reported that it was similar to regular tapping, and they loved the flexibility of mixing gesturing with tapping. They also reported that they did not intensively enter text on tablets, at most a few minutes each time for replying messages. The speed was not a critical factor. Other two Participants selected the two-thumb typing as the most preferred, mainly because of its familiarity.

One important lesson learned from the study was that no one input method fits all the users. Many factors came into play when choosing the input method, and these factors were weighted differently across users. Some users favor speed, while others might consider the ergonomics, familiarity, or the overall balance across different factors.

CONCLUSION

This paper presents a new interaction behavior, bimanual gesture text entry, which expands the gesture keyboard from one finger to multiple fingers.

Recognizing bimanual gesture is challenging and more complicated than recognizing unimanual gesture, because the number of strokes per word can vary, users can draw gestures differently for the same word, and gestures may overlap in time. To address these challenges, we have proposed two interaction methods, *finger-release* and *space-required*, and described the multi-stroke gesture recognition algorithm for recognizing both methods. Furthermore, we have designed and implemented a bimanual gesture text entry system that supports both operation modes. Both are compatible with unimanual gesture and regular typing.

We also conducted an empirical study to evaluate the strengths and weaknesses of bimanual gesture keyboards.

For phrase entry, the average speed of the *finger-release* and *space-required* techniques were 26 WPM and 21 WPM, respectively. For the last two repetitions of the word repetition exercise, which simulated expert performance, speeds increased to an average of 39 WPM and 26 WPM. Although both techniques were slower than unimanual gesture (which averaged 30 WPM for phrases and 46 WPM for word repetition), bimanual stroke lengths were shorter and more efficient. Participants also subjectively reported that bimanual systems were more comfortable and less physically demanding. Fifteen out of thirty-six participants (42%) favored the bimanual gesture keyboards over unimanual. Overall, these results indicate that bimanual gesture keyboards are valuable complements to existing text entry methods.

REFERENCES

1. Anthony, L. and Wobbrock, J.O. (2010). A lightweight multistroke recognizer for user interface prototypes. *Graphics Interface* 245-252.
2. Balakrishnan, R., and Hinckley, K. (2000). Symmetric bimanual interaction. *ACM CHI.* 33-40
3. Balakrishnan, R., and Kurtenbach, G. (1999). Exploring bimanual camera control and object manipulation in 3D graphics interfaces. *ACM CHI.* 56-63.
4. Bier, E. A., Stone, M., Pier, K., Buxton, W. & DeRose. T. (1993). Toolglass and magic lenses: the see-through interface. *SIGGRAPH*, 73-80.
5. Bi, X., Smith, B., and Zhai, S. (2010). Quasi-qwerty soft keyboard optimization. *ACM CHI.* 283-286.
6. Bi, X., Smith, B., and Zhai, S. (2012) Multilingual Touchscreen Keyboard Design and Optimization, *Human Computer Interaction*, to appear. Available online.
7. Buxton, W., and Myers, B. (1986). A study in two-handed input. *ACM CHI*, 321-326.
8. Findlater, L., Wobbrock, O., Wigdor, D. (2011). Typing on flat glass: examining ten-finger expert typing patterns on touch surfaces. *ACM CHI* 2453-2462.
9. Guiard, Y. (1987). Asymmetric division of labor in human skilled bimanual action: The kinematic chain as a model. *Journal of Motor Behavior*, 19(4), pp. 486-517.
10. Hart, S. and Staveland, L. 1988. Development of NASA-TLX (Task Load Index): Results of empirical and theoretical research. In *Human Mental Workload P. A. Hancock and N. Meshkati, Eds.,* North-Holland: Elsevier Science, 139-183.
11. Kane, S.K., Wobbrock, J.O. and Ladner, R.E. (2011) Usable gestures for blind people: Understanding preference and performance. *ACM CHI.* 413~422
12. Kristensson, P.O,. Zhai, S. (2007) Command Strokes with and without Preview: Using Pen Gestures on Keyboard for Command Selection, *ACM CHI.* 1137~1146
13. Kristensson, P-O., Zhai, S., S (2004) SHARK^2: A Large Vocabulary Shorthand Writing System for Pen-based Computers, *ACM UIST,* 43–52.
14. Kristensson, P-O., Zhai, S. (2005) Relaxing Stylus Typing Precision by Geometric Pattern Matching. *ACM IUI* 151–158.
15. Li, F.C.Y, Guy, R.T., Yatani, K., Truong, K.N. (2011). The 1line keyboard: a QWERTY layout in a single line. *ACM UIST*, 461-470.
16. Li, Y. (2010). Protractor: A Fast and Accurate Gesture Recognizer, *ACM CHI,* 2169~2172
17. Li, Y. (2010). Gesture Search: A Tool for Fast Mobile Data Access *ACM UIST*, 87~96
18. MacKenzie, I.S., Soukoreff, R. W. (2003). Phrase sets for evaluating text entry techniques. *Extended Abstracts CHI*, 754-755.
19. Ouyang, T., and Davis, R. (2009). A Visual Approach to Sketched Symbol Recognition, *IJCAI*, 1463~1468
20. Ouyang, T., and Li, Y. (2012), Bootstrapping Personal Gesture Shortcuts with the Wisdom of the Crowd and Handwriting Recognition, *ACM CHI*, to appear.
21. Rick, J. (2010). Performance optimizations of virtual keyboards for stroke-based text entry on a touch-based tabletop. *ACM UIST,* 77-86.
22. Soukoreff, R.W., MacKenzie, I.S. (2003) Metrics for text entry research: an evaluation of MSD and KSPC, and a new unified error metric. *ACM CHI*, 113-120.
23. Wobbrock, J.O. (2007) Measures of text entry performance. In *Text Entry Systems: Mobility, Accessibility, Universality*, I. S. MacKenzie and K. Tanaka-Ishii (eds.) San Francisco: Morgan Kaufmann, 47-74
24. Wobbrock, J.O., Wilson, A.D. and Li, Y. (2007). Gestures without libraries, toolkits or training: A $1 recognizer for user interface prototypes. *ACM UIST* 159-168.
25. www.americannationalcorpus.org/
26. Zhai, S. Kristensson, P.O. Introduction to Shape Writing, *IBM Research Report* RJ10393 (A0611-006), November1, 2006
27. Zhai, S., Kristensson, P-O., (2003) Shorthand Writing on Stylus Keyboard, *ACM CHI.* 97-104.
28. Zhai, S., Kristensson, P.O., Gong, P., Greiner, M., Peng, S., Liu, L. Dunnigan, A., (2009) Shapewriter on the iPhone: from the laboratory to the real world. *ACM CHI Extended Abstracts*. 2667-2670.

Magic Finger: Always-Available Input through Finger Instrumentation

Xing-Dong Yang[1,2], Tovi Grossman[1], Daniel Wigdor[3], George Fitzmaurice[1]

[1]Autodesk Research
210 King St. East, Toronto,
ON, M5A 1J7, Canada
{firstame.lastname}@autodesk.com

[2]University of Alberta,
Edmonton, AB,
Canada, T6G 2E8
xingdong@cs.ualberta.ca

[3]University of Toronto,
Toronto, ON,
Canada, R3T 2N2,
dwigdor@dgp.toronto.edu

ABSTRACT

We present Magic Finger, a small device worn on the fingertip, which supports always-available input. Magic Finger inverts the typical relationship between the finger and an interactive surface: with Magic Finger, we instrument the user's finger itself, rather than the surface it is touching. Magic Finger senses touch through an optical mouse sensor, enabling any surface to act as a touch screen. Magic Finger also senses texture through a micro RGB camera, allowing contextual actions to be carried out based on the particular surface being touched. A technical evaluation shows that Magic Finger can accurately sense 22 textures with an accuracy of 98.9%. We explore the interaction design space enabled by Magic Finger, and implement a number of novel interaction techniques that leverage its unique capabilities.

ACM Classification: H5.2 [Information interfaces and presentation]: User Interfaces. - Graphical user interfaces.

General terms: Design

Keywords: Touch input, always-available input, gesture input, contextual action, texture reorganization

INTRODUCTION

Recent years have seen the introduction of a significant number of new devices capable of touch input. While this modality has succeeded in bringing input to new niches and devices, its utility faces the fundamental limitation that the input area is confined to the range of the touch sensor. A variety of technologies have been proposed to allow touch input to be carried-out on surfaces which are not themselves capable of sensing touch, such as walls [16, 20], tables [20], an arbitrary piece of paper [18] or even on a user's own body [18, 26, 40].

Mounting cameras on the body has enabled these regions to become portable [17, 18, 34, 36]. However, like other vision-based implementations, the range of the sensor is limited to the viewing area of the camera, thus the capabilities of these sensors are in some ways more limited than are non-vision based techniques.

UIST '12, October 7–10, 2012, Cambridge, Massachusetts, USA.

These approaches to instrumentation have all focused on enabling touch capability for surfaces the user will touch with their finger. To overcome their inherent limitations, we propose *finger instrumentation*, where we invert the relationship between finger and sensing surface: with Magic Finger, we instrument the user's finger itself, rather than the surface it is touching. By making this simple change, users of Magic Finger can have virtually unlimited touch interactions with any surface, without the need for torso-worn or body-mounted cameras, or suffer problems of occluded sensors.

Our work has been inspired by earlier projects in always-available input [40]. Like those earlier projects, Magic Finger is capable of sensing the moment of touch and relative finger displacement on a surface. Further, inspired by the versatility of the human finger, Magic Finger can also sense the texture of the object a user touches, allowing for the use of a machine learning classifier to recognize the touched object. Thus, contextual actions can be carried out based on the particular surface being touched. Additionally, Magic Finger can also identify artificial textures and fiduciary markers. This extends its ability to recognize richer information, thus enabling many novel interaction techniques.

Magic Finger is a thimble-like device worn on the user's finger (Figure 1). It combines two optical sensors: a lower-resolution, high speed sensor for tracking movement, and a higher-resolution camera for capturing detail. In addition to this device, the contributions of this work also include an exploration of associated hardware and software design spaces, an evaluation of its texture sensing accuracy levels, and a set of applications and interactions that are enabled by Magic Finger.

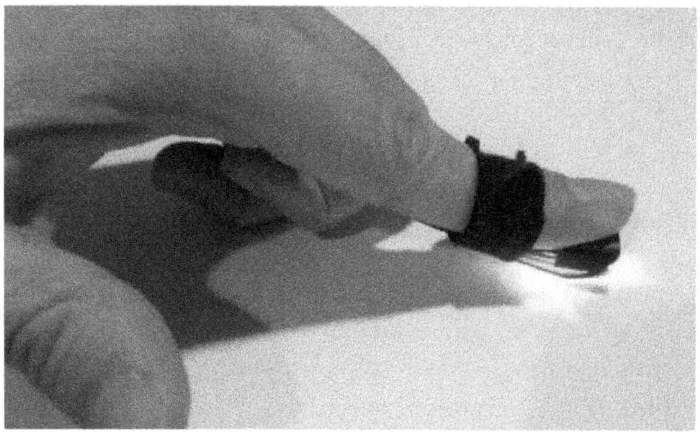

Figure 1: The Magic Finger device.

RELATED WORK

In this section, we review the related literature in the areas of always-available input, research on contextual actions, and augmentation of the user's finger.

Always-Available Input

Advanced sensing technologies have been used to help extend our ability to interact with computers from anywhere, supporting always-available input [40].

One way to accomplish this is to extend the range of devices. SideSight [12] uses an array of proximity sensors to detect a users' finger movement on the side of a cell phone. Therefore, touch input is no longer limited to the small region of the touch screen. Similarly, Portico [7] and Bonfire [30] used cameras installed on a laptop to capture the input occurring around it. PocketTouch allows capacitive sensors to function through fabric [39]. While these devices extend the range of sensors, they also are anchored to a device.

Efforts have also been made to instrument a user's surrounding environment to enable touch. Touché [41] enables touch on everyday objects, including humans and liquids, while Scratch Input [20] recognizes gestures on larger surfaces, but each require a sensor to be connected to the touched object. Wimmer and Baudisch [48] demonstrated that touch gestures can be enabled on an arbitrary object by having the object connect to an electric pulse generator and a Time Domain Reflectometry sensor.

Camera based sensors have also been used to sense input. Wilson 46] demonstrated that a properly positioned depth camera can be used to sense touch on surfaces. In the LightSpace system [47], a small room becomes interactive by combining multiple depth cameras and projectors.

While the instrumentation of environments is promising, it is also limited. Alternatively, the human body can itself be instrumented to sense input. Interactive clothing is one way to do so [28], but requires special clothing.

Many techniques enable body input of taps, postures, and whole body gestures. For example, Saponas et al. [40] used arm mounted electromyography sensors to sense pinch gestures made by different fingers. Cohn et al. [16] proposed a technique to sense whole-body gestures that utilizes existing electromagnetic noise from nearby power lines and electronics. Harrison et al.'s Skinput [26] used arm mounted bio-acoustic sensors to detect finger tap on the different locations of a users' forearm. Tiny sensors could also be embedded on [36], or implanted under [29] the user's skin. These techniques all open up new and interesting interaction opportunities, however they cannot sense detailed finger movements required to emulate touch input.

Several techniques have supported richer input on the human body [24]. The Imaginary Phone [17] uses a 3D camera to detect taps and swipes on a user's palm. OmniTouch [18] uses a depth-sensing camera and a micro projector to turn a user's palm into a touch-sensitive display. SixthSense uses a small projector and camera, worn in a pendant device, to enable touch interactions on and around the body [34]. While such techniques enable always-available input, the input is generally restricted to the body, and can suffer from occlusion. In contrast, we propose *finger instrumentation*, enabling input on almost any surface.

Contextual Interactions

Magic Finger is able to recognize textures and use the information to understand the environment, or object the user is interacting with, and perform associated contextual actions. While texture has been previously explored as an output channel for touch input [8, 22, 31] we are unaware of work where texture is used as an input channel.

Relevant work by Harrison and Hudson used multispectral material sensing to infer the placement of mobile devices, and discussed potential uses, such as tunring off a cell phone when it is placed in a purse [19]. Alternatively a touch sensitive device can respond differently if it knows what caused the touch or who touched it [6, 25, 38, 49]. More broadly, research on contextual interactions in the ubiquitous computing literature is also relevant. We refer the readers to comprehensive surveys [10, 14].

Augment The User's Finger

Early work in augmenting the human finger lies in the virtual reality research, where data gloves are used to track the user's hand position in space [42]. Several projects also exist outside of the VR literature. Marquardt [32] augmented a user's finger with fiduciary markers to inform an interactive tabletop what part of the finger was in contact with the surface. With Abracadabra [21], users wear a magnet on their finger to provide input above a mobile device. FingerFlux [43] also uses a small magnet on the finger, to simulate haptic feedback above an interactive tabletop. While these projects are all related in that they instrument the finger, none had the goal of supporting always-available input.

Logisys's Finger Mouse, a cylinder-shaped optical mouse that can be mounted on a finger, is a relevant commercial product [5]. It is used to control an on-screen cursor with a relative input mapping. Magic Finger extends this basic capability to also support absolute targeting, texture recognition, and fiduciary marker identification. Furthermore, with Magic Finger, we explore a smaller form factor, and a rich interaction design space beyond cursor control.

HARDWARE DESIGN SPACE

In designing a device, our main goal is to enable the finger to sense touch on physical objects, without any environmental instrumentation. In order to emulate traditional touch techniques, the device must be able to sense contact and 2D positional movements. In this section, we present a design space of possible hardware implementations that could enable these goals. For a broader discussion of hardware for small on-body devices, we refer the reader to Ni and Baudisch' s work on *disappearing mobile devices* [36].

Scope of Recognition

We define three scopes of recognition: *none*, *class*, and *instance*. In its simplest form, the device could be able to sense finger movement without the capability of knowing anything about the contact object (*none*). However, when it is the finger itself performing the sensing, it would be helpful to know what the finger is touching, so the input could be directed to an appropriate device. The scope of recognition could be increased to recognize certain classes of objects (e.g. a table or a phone) (*class*), or could be further extended to distinguish between specific instances of objects (e.g. my table vs. your table) (*instance*).

Sensing X-Y Movements

To emulate traditional touch, the hardware must be able to sense X-Y movements. Previous work has shown that an optical flow sensor (found in optical mice) can be used as a small touch sensitive device [9, 36]. As such, 2D finger movements could be detected by affixing an optical flow sensor to the finger. Such sensors can be extremely small and offer reliable 2D motion sensing on a wide variety of surfaces, but a light source is required. Alternatively, a mechanical device, such as a small trackball could be used, but may not be as robust to varying types of surfaces. A mechanical device may also require a larger form factor.

Sensing Material

To increase the recognition *scope*, the device could sense the material that the finger is in contact with. This could be achieved with optics, using texture recognition algorithms [37]. Using an optical flow sensors may be difficult, as their resolutions are typically low (e.g. 18x18). Higher quality cameras may be required to improve the robustness of material recognition or to extend the recognition scope to *instance*. Alternatively, a Multispectral Material Sensor [19] could be used, but would only support a recognition scope of *class*. To sense properties such as roughness, softness, and friction, a texture sensor [35] could be used, but may require the user to touch the surface in specific ways.

Sensing Contact

To sense contact, a hardware switch, which connects a circuit when being pressed by a touching force, may be most accurate. While this would enable explicit sensing of contact, it would require the device to have an additional single-purpose sensor. Contact could instead be inferred from an audio sensor [25], but accuracy may not be as high. Alternatively, contact could be inferred from an optical sensor that is already present to sense movements and material.

Output

In the simplest form, the device could provide no output at all to the user. However, this could be severely limiting, especially in cases where periphery devices that provide feedback are not available. Tactile feedback is possible but may come with high power consumption, and would require an additional component. One or more LEDs could be used to display bit-wise low resolution information [36, 23]. If the device used optical sensing, it may already be equipped with an LED, preventing the need for additional components. Richer forms of output could be provided by a speaker or LCD display, but would require larger form factors and greater power consumption.

Form Factor

The device needs to be small so that it can fit on the users' finger. Ideally, the device would be undetectable when dormant [36]. There are a number of ways which the device could be affixed to the finger. It could be embedded on a ring or thimble like structure worn on the tip of the finger (Figure 2a). This would allow users to remove the device when desired, or twist it to deactivate sensing. Alternatively, if small enough, the device could potentially be embedded under the finger nail (Figure 2b), on the surface of the fingertip skin, or implanted under the skin with exposed components for sensing (Figure 2c) [36]. A larger form factor could be worn above the finger. However this may cause offset problems in the sensing, and could be susceptible to occlusion problems.

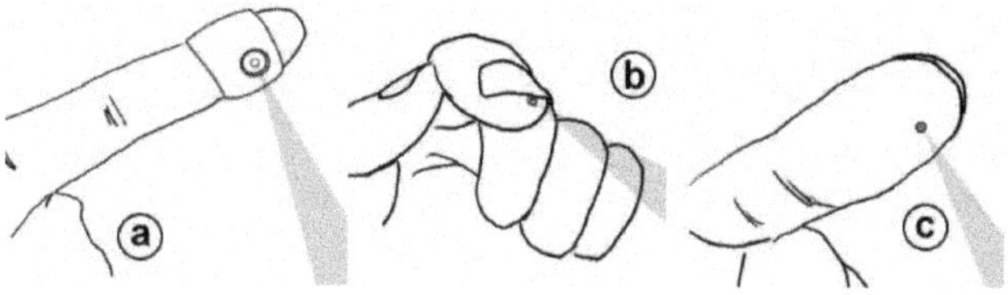

Figure 2: Possible form factors for the hardware.

MAGIC FINGER

After carefully considering the aspects of the hardware design space, we developed Magic Finger, a proof-of-concept prototype that enables always-available input through *finger instrumentation*. In this section we describe our implementation, and the basic capabilities of the device.

Hardware Implementation

To achieve sensing of positional movements *and* sensing of material, our prototype uses two optical sensors. A low resolution high frame rate optical flow sensor is used to sense 2D finger movements, and a higher resolution, lower frame rate camera is used to sense material (Figure 3).

Figure 3. The Magic Finger Device.

Optical Flow Sensor

We used an ADNS 2620 optical flow sensor with a modified HDNS-2100 lens. This sensor is often used in optical mice, and is reliable on a large variety of surfaces. The sensor detects motion by examining the optical flow of the surface it is moving on. The ADNS 2620 sensor is a low-resolution black and white camera (18×18 $63\mu m^2$ pixels). Our initial tests showed that the sensor could be used to recognize textures, but only at the *class* scope of recognition, and only with a very small number of items (4).

Micro RGB Camera

To provide an enhanced scope of recognition, we used an AWAIBA NanEye micro RGB camera [4]. In comparison to the optical flow sensor, NanEye has a higher resolution and smaller pixels, and thus captures more subtle details of textures. The micro camera is 1mm × 1mm × 1.5mm (Figure 4). It captures color images at a resolution of 248 × 248, 3 μm^2 pixels, at 44 fps. For image processing, we converted the signal to greyscale. While it would be desirable to also use the NanEye for sensing optical flow, its low frame rate makes this difficult. We expect future solutions could be achieved with a single miniature sensor.

We embedded the NanEye on the edge of the optical flow sensor. To prevent occlusions from wiring, we crop to only use 70% camera's view to 175 × 175 pixels (Figure 4).

Light Source

In order for the camera and the optical flow sensor to function, an external light source is needed to illuminate the surface underneath it. We used a 5mm white LED, which has similar size and brightness with those used in optical mice. The LED can also be conveniently used for output.

Physical From

Magic Finger is affixed to the fingertip using an adjustable Velcro ring. A small plastic casing holds the components. The case was designed to control the distance between the RGB camera and surface during contact (Figure 1).

Computer Interfacing

The optical flow sensor and the LED were connected to an Arduino UNO board [3], which facilitates communication with the computer, an HP TouchSmart Tm2 running Windows 7. The NanEye is connected directly via USB. Tethering the device to a computer was an enabling technology for our prototype, and not our vision for future implementations. See Future Work for a discussion of power and communication capabilities required for an untethered implementation.

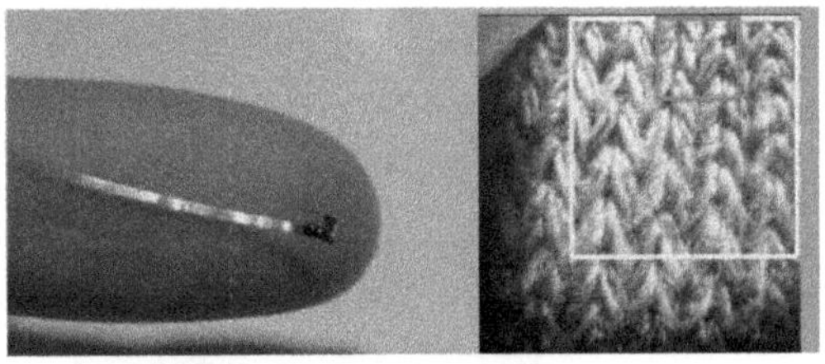

Figure 4: Left: the NanEye camera. Right: the field of view is a 175 x 175 rectangle (yellow region). The red region is used to detect changes in contrast.

Device Capabilities

Relative Positional Movement

Positional movement data is obtained directly from the optical flow sensor using the Arduino. Our program receives (X,Y) coordinates a resolution of 400cpi at 15 fps.

Sensing Contact

Magic Finger uses the micro camera to sense contact with a surface. Rapid changes in contrast (due to reflection of the illuminator) are used to signal changes in contact. To detect contact, we continuously calculate the overall contrast of a 60x60 pixel square of the sensor image, by averaging the square difference between each pixel and its neighbors (in grayscale space). When the Magic Finger is more than 5mm from a surface, light from its built-in LED is not reflected back, and a uniformly darker image is seen. A change within a small window of time form this darker image to a brighter image is measured against threshold values of our contrast metric for changes downward (lift-up) and upward (touch-down) (see Figure 5).

Figure 5. Contrast increases with the finger approaches a surface. Leftmost: the Magic Finger is more than 5mm from a surface. Rightmost: the Magic Finger is in contact with the surface

Identifying Material

When Magic Finger detects a contact event, the current frame of the RGB Camera is used for. texture recognition. Textures are classified using a machine learning algorithm. The first step is to describe the texture using a feature vector. In our implementation, we used Local Binary Patterns (LBP) to retrieve the unique features [37]. The algorithm detects 10 microstructures inside a texture (e.g. edges, lines, spots, flat areas). The histogram of the 10 microstructures uniquely describes a texture. This algorithm is orientation invariant, allowing recognition independent of the angle which the finger touches a surface. The feature vectors are also gray-scale invariant, making it robust in different lighting conditions. To train the classifier, we used Chang and Lin's LIBSVM algorithm using a Support Vector Machine (SVM) [13]. Before we trained the model, we tuned the required SVM parameters that gave high cross-validation scores.

Environmental vs. Artificial Textures

We classify the types of textures Magic Finger can sense as *environmental* and *artificial*. *Environmental* textures are naturally occurring in the user's environment, such as a table or shirt. In contrast, a*rtificial* textures are explicitly created for the purpose of being used by Magic Finger. We found that a simple way to create textures was to print a grid of small ASCII characters (Figure 6).

Fiduciary Markers

The above classification of textures allows Magic Finger to increase its scope to *class* recognition. If we are to further increase the scope to *instance* recognition, further capabilities are required. A common approach to tag specific objects is to use bar codes or fiduciary markers [2, 15]. We used the Data Matrix code, a two-dimensional barcode consisting of a grid of black and white cells. The Data Matrix codes we used were 10×10 cells, representing numerical values between 0 and 9999.

To be properly recognized, the entire Data Matrix must be in the field of view. To ease targeting, we print a cluster of identical Data Matrix codes, each exactly ¼ the size of the RGB camera's field of view to ensure at least one code is fully visible. A library is used to decode the tags [1]. When Magic Finger detects a contact event, an API call is made to decode the frame. This call takes approximately 240ms, and is performed before texture classification occurs.

A future implementation of Magic Finger could utilize grids of fiduciary markers, such as is done by Anoto, in place of the ASCII-based artificial textures we designed. Nevertheless, we found that the ASCII-based technique was an effective way to easily generate artificial-textures.

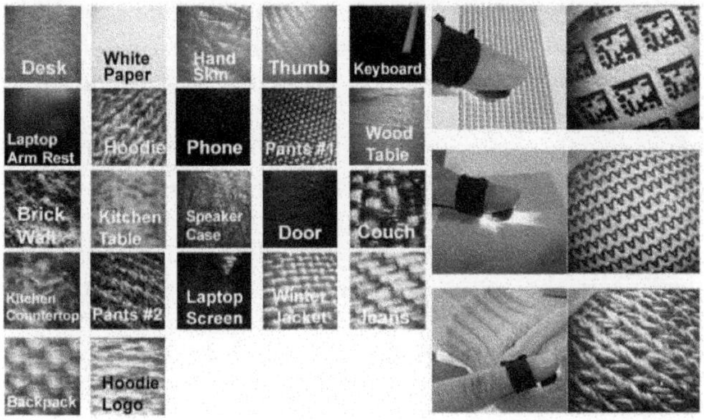

Figure 6: Left: 22 environmental textures used in the study. Right: Data Matrix, artificial texture, and environmental texture, as seen by a human and by the NanEye.

SYSTEM EVALUATION

We conducted a study in order to evaluate the accuracy at which Magic Finger can recognize *environmental* textures, *artificial textures*, and Data Matrix codes. This study was meant to serve as a technical evaluation of Magic Finger's capabilities, not a user study of the device.

For the *environmental* textures, we collected 22 different textures from a large variety of everyday objects, including public items, personal items, and parts of the user's body. The textures we sampled are shown in Figure 6.

To create *artificial textures*, we printed a grid of ASCII characters in black Calibri font, with a font size of 2pt and a line space of 1.6pt. The textures were printed on a Ricoh Aficio MP C5000 laser printer at 1200 DPI. We chose 39 characters found in a standard US English keyboard, including all 26 English capital letters (*A - Z*) and 13 other characters [*~ ! @ # $ % ^ & (- + = . "*]. For the data matrix, we randomly selected 10 out of 10,000 possible codes: 1257, 3568, 9702, 3287, 4068, 5239, 8381, 6570, 0128, and 2633, with each printed clusters of 72 × 15 identical codes.

For each *environmental* texture, *artificial* texture, and Data Matrix, 10 samples were collected twice a day for 3 days (as in [19]). Samples in the same class were obtained from the same object but from different locations. In total, we collected 60 samples for each material. The accuracy of recognition was tested using a 5-fold cross validation procedure. Because training and testing data may include points that were sampled in an adjacent time (e.g. points that tend to be similar), we randomized the order of the points prior to the test [19]. The Data Matrix recognition was evaluated by calculating the accuracy of decoding.

Results

Cross validation achieved an accuracy of 99.1% on the 22 tested *environmental* textures. This is a promising result given that we were only using 175 × 175 pixels (e.g. 70% of the camera's view). To better understand how the classification accuracy is affected by the resolution of the camera, we cropped the sample images from their center into smaller images of $18px^2$, $70px^2$, and $122px^2$. The results of the 5-fold cross validation are shown in Figure 7, left. Samples of $70px^2$ achieved 95% accuracy across the 22 textures. This gives future engineers some flexibility when choosing sensors for finger instrumentation.

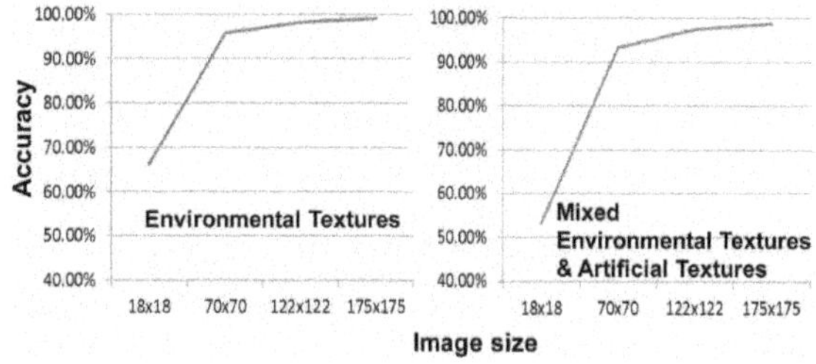

Figure 7: Cross validation accuracy. Left. On *environmental* textures. Right. On and mixed *environmental* and *artificial* textures.

For the ASCII *artificial* textures, cross validation yielded 83.8% accuracy with all the 39 tested characters. Given the large number of textures, this result is also promising. The lower accuracy is due to the larger number of textures, and also because the different textures are less visually distinguishable than the *environmental* textures we selected.

To see how the number of textures impact accuracy levels and find an optimal set of characters to use, we performed another 4 iterations of tests by progressively removing textures that resulted in lower accuracy rates. The accuracy levels through each iteration were 86.4% for 36 textures, 89.9% for 31 textures, 97.9% for 13 textures, and 99.5% for 10 characters [B G I ! # % ^ (+ .].

The above results indicate that Magic Finger can recognize 22 *environmental* textures *or* 10 *artificial* textures with an accuracy of above 99%. We also tested accuracy levels when combining these two sets, for a total of 32 textures. The Cross validation accuracy was 98.9% using the 175x175 pixel image. We also tested the classification accuracy with the smaller cropped images. The results of the 5-fold cross validation are shown in Figure 7, right.

The Data Matrix codes were correctly decoded for 598 of the 600 samples we collected, which yields an accuracy of 99.7%. In both failure cases (one for 3568, one for 9702) the API reported that no Data Matrix was recognized.

Summary

The results of our evaluation are very promising. Accuracy levels indicate that Magic Finger would be able to distinguish a large number of both *environmental* and *artificial* textures, and consistently recognize Data Matrix codes. Compared to Harrison and Hudson's multispectral material sensing, which was able to classify 27 materials with an accuracy of 86.9% [19], we have obtained an accuracy of 98.9% across 32 textures. Overall, this demonstrates the feasibility of using a Magic Finger device for interactive tasks. In the following sections, we explore the interaction techniques and usage scenarios that Magic Finger supports.

INTERACTION DESIGN SPACE

Having developed a robust device, we sought to develop interaction techniques to facilitate its use. Here, we define the interaction design space for Magic Finger using 5 dimensions, described below.

Input Texture

The input textures vary according to the degree of specificity and information bandwidth they allow. We differentiate our interaction design space by 3 types of textures the user may encounter: *environmental* textures are textures of real objects, unmodified for Magic Finger; *artificial* textures refer to textures engineered for the Magic Finger, as we have discussed previously; and *dynamic* textures are those that change over time. Dynamic textures, for example, can be used to communicate between 2 Magic Finger devices.

Input Type

The possible input type depends on the specific capabilities of an implementation of Magic Finger. That is, our implementation is limited to having the Magic Finger act as a 2-state input device. Thus, input actions can either be *tap input* (sensing contact), or *gesture input* (positional movement).

Texture to Result Mapping

The ability to recognize different textures allows contextual actions to be carried out by the Magic Finger. The mappings of texture to result vary by the degree with respect to their artificiality: *Intrinsic* mappings rely on the semantics of the touched object to define the mapping. For example, tapping on the empty space of a phone always triggers a function of the phone, e.g. fast dial a number. Intrinsic mappings may suffer from a lack of flexibility, and conflicts in mappings. In contrast, *extrinsic* mappings associate commands to unrelated physical objects. Such mappings are flexible but may be less discoverable or memorable.

Resulting Action Type

Many types of actions could result from user input. We classify three main types: perform a *command execution*, provide *continuous control*, or serve as a *mode delimiter*.

Feedback

Based on needs, feedback can be *internal* or *external* to Magic Finger. For example, *internal* feedback could provide information using an LED while richer *external* feedback could be provided by an attached or secondary device.

AUTHORING ENVIRONMENT

We created an application to help users manage their registered and recognized textures (*environmental* and *artificial*) and their associated functional mappings. A window displays a list of the defined texture classes (Figure 8 left). Each texture class in the list contains a sample image of the texture and a user defined title for that texture class. Users can double-click the sample images to view all the samples of that object that are used in training the SVM model. A button in the user interface can be used to create a new texture class. Users can also add samples to a new or existing texture class as input to the recognizer.

Each texture class also has an associated dropdown menu, which shows a list of functions which are preset resulting actions that could be mapped to any texture class (Figure 8 middle). For the purposes of demonstration, we have predefined a variety of resulting actions which can be mapped to Magic Finger input. In some cases, the authoring environment allows the user to adjust parameters of an action. For example, if the user selects the "Send SMS" action (which automatically sends an SMS message) from the drop down list, a pop up dialog is displayed where the user can enter a recipient number and message. To automatically launch external applications, the user can select "external application" from the action drop down list. The user can then drag-and-drop an icon of a desired application onto the menu item (Figure 8 right). This allows the user to link Magic Finger actions to existing applications, as well as to define their own scripts in their preferred languages and link them to Magic Finger.

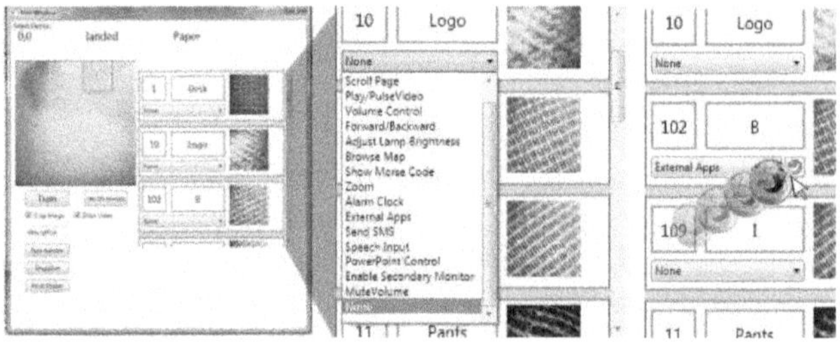

Figure 8: Left: list of texture classes. Middle: the drop down list of functions; Right: external applications

Authoring Artificial Textures

The authoring application also allows users to generate ASCII-based *artificial* textures which can be used, for example, as stickers to be placed on objects. In these textures, the individual ASCII characters are so small that they are indiscernible to the human eye, and can be used as pixels to create two-colour graphical images. While each "pixel" is the same character, the pixels can take-on a foreground or background color. We chose two colors that are distinguishable by the human eye, but are indistinguishable in greyscale during recognition (Figure 9 right).

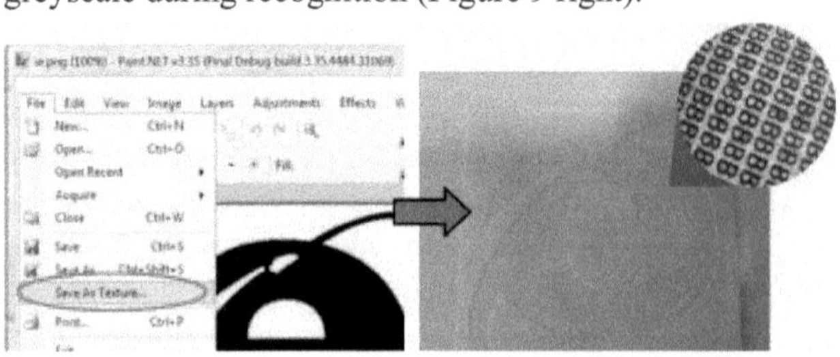

Figure 9: Left: the paint.net application; Right: the resulting texture.

To author these textures, we modified Paint.NET, an image editing application, to include a "*save as texture*" option (Figure 9 left). This option prompts the user to enter a character, and then converts the current image into an HTML document consisting entirely of that character rendered in either the foreground or background color. Such images can be used to give the *artificial textures* user friendly appearances, such as icons representing their functions.

INTERACTION TECHNIQUES

In order to explore the interaction design space we have described, we implemented a number of interaction techniques. Each of the following techniques serves as an exemplar of a point in our design space, as well as a portion of a coherent set of possible uses for Magic Finger. Some of the interactions are novel while others show how Magic Finger can be used to implement previously published techniques that required numerous different hardware configurations. In the example interaction techniques below, we explicitly mention the corresponding design dimension.

Some of the below interactions involve multiple Magic Fingers. To implement these scenarios, we constructed a second Magic Finger without the RGB camera. This device was unable to sense textures, but was sufficient for demonstrating the desired multiple-device interactions.

Tap Input

PocketTouch

Magic Finger can be used to remotely access or control mobile devices. We implemented a resulting action of muting an incoming Skype call (*command execution*), and mapped this to touching a handbag. If the user receives an unwanted call when their Smartphone is in the handbag, the user can simply tap the handbag to mute the notification. This interaction is much like PocketTouch [39], but does not require a phone's capacitive sensor to be placed in a special mode, or require the phone to be placed at a specific location (Figure 10a).

Tap-to-Talk

Because Magic Finger can identify the object that users touch, tapping different surfaces can trigger different *command executions*. In our implementation, the empty surface of a phone is used as a shortcut 'button' to send a frequent SMS message to a predefined recipient, e.g. *"I'm on my way home."* (Figure 10b). This is an example of an *intrinsic mapping*. Users may also take advantage of inherent features of physical artifacts to define input textures. We created an *extrinsic mapping* of tapping on the logo of a t-shirt, to launching the Windows Voice command app. Thus, tapping on this special area of the shirt serves as a *mode delimiter* for entering speech input (Figure 10c).

Skinput

By recognizing skin as a texture, Magic Finger provides a method for using skin as an input surface, without requiring additional sensors. We utilized this to create an "am I late?" gesture – when the user taps their wrist (where a watch might have been – *intrinsic mapping*), Magic Finger checks for an upcoming appointment and either displays it on-screen (*external feedback*), or blinks its built-in LED (*internal feedback*) to indicate "time to head out!" (Figure 10d).

Pinching Finger to Thumb

The finger to thumb pinch action has been shown to be a useful gesture for freehand input [45]. By recognizing the thumb as an *environmental* texture, Magic Finger can easily detect a pinch when the thumb is tapped (Figure 10e). We mapped pinch to a *command execution* of advancing slides in a presentation, as a replacement for holding a wireless presentation mouse.

Data Matrix Buttons

In addition to tapping *environmental* textures, users can also tap *artificial* ones. A grid of printed Data Matrix codes can be used as physical buttons. The decoded numeric data can be used to trigger a command or to retrieve contextual information. In our implementation, we assigned specific numbers to PowerPoint documents. A user can print the

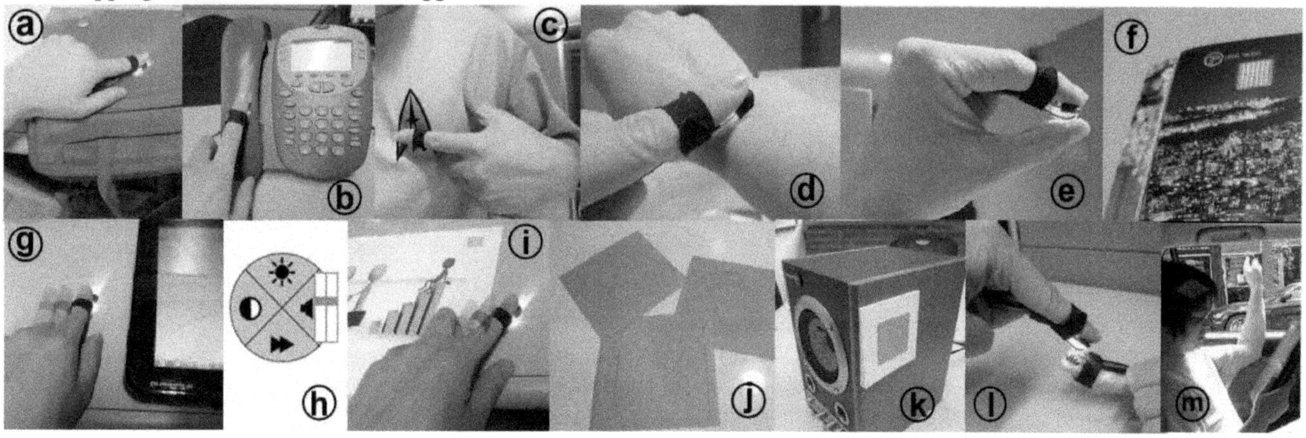

Figure 10. Tap and Gestural-based Interactions. (a) Tap on the bag to mute a Skype call; (b) Tap on the phone to send a frequent SMS message; (c) Using the logo of a t-shirt as a mode delimiter; (d) Tap the wrist to check an upcoming appointment; (e) Pinch gesture (f) Data Matrix Buttons; (g) Occlusion Free Input; (h) FaST slider widget; (i) Multi-surface crossing gesture; (j) Application launch pad; (k) Sticker as disposable remote controls; (l) Passing texture to another Magic Finger; (m) Use Magic Finger as a periscope to check out traffic.

PowerPoint slides with the associated Data Matrix code at the bottom of each page. Tapping the code opens the presentation on the user's computer. We also associated codes on magazine articles with webpages (Figure 10). Tapping the Data Matrix opens a URL associated with the article.

Gesture Input

Occlusion Free Input

Occlusion Free Input allows users to interact with a touch screen device by gesturing on a nearby surface. This eliminates the occlusion of the screen by a users' hand. We implemented a navigation application, where users can pan or zoom a map displayed on a tablet device (*continuous control*). By mapping this action to the back of a tablet, users can carry out back-of-device input [44], without needing a specially instrumented tablet device. Additionally, SideSight [12] can be emulated by mapping the action to the table that the device is resting on (Figure 10g).

FaST Sliders

We implemented a FaST slider widget to control volume and playback of multi-media [33] (Figure 10h). FaST sliders allow manipulation of multiple, discrete or continuous parameters from a single menu. Once activated, the user can select a parameter to manipulate with a directional mark. While the finger remains down, the user can then adjust the value of the selected parameter by dragging. If the user is close to a display device, visual feedback for the menu can be displayed onscreen (*external feedback*). When a display is not available, we blink the Magic Finger's LED to indicate when a parameter has been selected, so the user knows to begin parameter adjustment (*internal feedback*).

Multi-Surface Crossing Gestures

Magic Finger can detect a crossing gesture from one surface to another (Figure 10i). This is accomplished by performing texture recognition any time the finger dwells while still in contact with a surface. We mapped this gesture to activating a slide deck on a projector in a meeting room. The user can tap a Data Matrix on their slide printout to open the PowerPoint, and tap the table to connect the laptop to a secondary monitor (i.e. projector). If a crossing gesture is detected from the Data Matrix to the table, the PowerPoint window is moved from the laptop display to the projector. In this case, the crossing gesture has an *intrinsic mapping*, as it represents a relationship between the two mapped surfaces. These multisurface gestures are similar to stitching [27], but do not require inter-device communication between the surfaces.

Input Stickers

Artificial textures can be used to increase the number of distinguishable surfaces in an area. By printing the artificial textures on adhesive strips, we create Input Stickers. We describe the associated interaction techniques below.

Application Launch Pad

We printed a set of Input Stickers that take-on the appearance of desktop icons (Figure 10j). The user can place these stickers in a convenient location in their work area, and tap the stickers to launch the associated desktop application. This emulates functionality shown in MagicDesk without requiring the entire desk surface to be a touch sensitive surface [11].

Disposable Remote Controls

Input stickers can also be used as remote controls. We printed a stack of stickers and put them beside the physical on-off switch for the speakers in a public room (Figure 10k). When entering a room, a user can pick up a sticker before sitting down. Tapping the sticker plays and pauses music on the room's sound system. When leaving the room, the user can replace the sticker on the stack, or dispose of it.

Additional Features

Identify Awareness

An interesting property of Magic Finger is that it is inherently user-identity aware. We configured the music remote control, described above, to play a user's favorite type of music, based on the identity of the user tapping the sticker. Traditional touch devices are not able to recognize users, without specialized hardware and making potentially error prone inferences [38, 49].

Passing Textures

In some cases, a user may want to virtually pass a texture that has been read by the Magic Finger to a remote receiver or to another user. We use the pinch gesture as a *mode delimiter* for "picking up" a texture. If a pinch is detected immediately after a Data Matrix is tapped, then the Data Matrix code is temporarily stored. When the pinch is released, the LED emits a Morse code pattern, representing the 4 digit number associated with the Data Matrix. We implemented a simple product scanner application that uses a webcam to read the Morse code and display information about the associated item, such as its price. We also implemented a second Magic Finger that can read the Morse code as a *dynamic texture* and carry out the associated functions of the Data Matrix code after it is passed to the user from the source user (Figure 10l).

The Periscope

People often use their fingers to sense areas that they cannot see. For example, we may use our hand to search for a pen dropped between the cushions of a couch. Magic Finger allows users to enhance the capabilities of such probing. By viewing its real-time video feed on a handheld device, the Magic Finger becomes an extension of the user's eyes. For example, a user can look behind them, around a corner or out the window of a car by simply pointing their finger in the associated direction (Figure 10m).

DISCUSSION AND FUTURE WORK

Having used Magic Fingers, we have made several observations which may be of benefit to those seeking to implement one. In this section, we discuss some of the insights we have gleaned from our experiences.

Device Size and From Factor

While our form factor is small enough to fit on a fingertip, it is still larger than what we envision for the future.

The hardware does have room to be made much smaller. Our prototype is limited by the size of the ADNS 2620 chip. The chip was designed to be used in a mouse, and so its form factor is optimized to fit with the other components of the mouse. The core sensor of the chip, however, is only 2 × 3 mm wide. Therefore, reengineering the chip to fit the sensor will significantly reduce the size of Magic Finger.

The NanEye camera has an ideal form factor. However, it is limited by its frame rate. Ideally, Magic Finger would need only one optical sensor to handle all of its functionality. For optical flow to be detected reliably, the sensor would need to have a frame rate of approximately 1500fps. Based on our evaluation, the resolution should be at least 70 × 70px to enable both optical flow and texture recognition. Given existing technologies, we are optimistic that a sensor matching these specifications will soon be available.

The other component that would need to be miniaturized is the LED. Micro LED's are available today; testing would be needed to determine minimum brightness requirements.

Power and Communication

A limitation of our hardware is that it is tethered to a nearby host PC. This simplified our implementations, but for Magic Finger to become a completely standalone device, power and communication needs to be considered. Holz et al. provide a thorough review of potential technologies that can be used for power and communication in a micro form factor [29]. Powering can be accomplished through rechargeable batteries, or harvesting power from the body or the environment [29]. Communication can be provided through a Bluetooth protocol, which consumes little power. Processing responsibilities could be performed by a Bluetooth-tethered mobile phone.

Evaluations

We presented a technical evaluation that demonstrated promising results for sensing accuracy of the Magic Finger. The results should be considered a high bar of what a Magic Finger could achieve, since the samples were collected under controlled conditions. Future evaluations should look at how differences in contact angles may impact captured image quality. Design considerations of the form factor of the device should aim to facilitate capturing good quality samples.

Magic Finger could also benefit from more formal user studies to understand how the device would be used by end users. For example, a user study may help us find a preferred location to mount the device, or identify important topics we have not explored, such as the "Midas touch" and false activations.

Interactions

The interactions which we implemented and demonstrated should be considered exploratory in nature, and only represent a small sample of what is possible with the Magic Finger. In our actual implementation, issues such as conflicts between operating modes and resulting actions would require a more careful examination. Introducing aids to help users learn or remember mappings would also be a fruitful topic for future work.

Magic Finger in its current implementation is limited in absolute positioning. One known technique to enable absolute positioning for artificial textures would be to encode location into the textual pattern (eg: Anoto [2]). For natural textures, absolute positioning may never be possible, although with improved sensing, location could be sensed at higher granularity (e.g. recognize locations of skin rather than simply "skin").

CONCLUSION

In this paper, we introduced the concept of finger instrumentation and our prototype Magic Finger, a novel device that extends users' touch capability to everyday objects. Instead of requiring instrumentation of the user's environment, or external cameras which may be prone to occlusion, Magic Finger is unique in that the finger itself is instrumented to detect touch. Our system evaluation showed that Magic Finger can recognize 32 different textures with an accuracy of 98.9%, allowing for contextual input. We presented a design space of interactions enabled by Magic Finger, and implemented a number of interaction techniques to explore this design space. Future work will focus on investigating topics such as "Midas touch" and false activations, and on understanding how users will use the Magic Finger. We will also explore hardware solutions for miniaturizing the form factor of the Magic Finger.

REFERENCES

1. 2D Technology *http://www.2dtg.com/*
2. ANOTO *http://www.anoto.com/*
3. Arduino *http://arduino.cc*
4. AWAIBA *www.awaiba.com*
5. Finger Mouse *http://www.logisyscomputer.com*
6. Annett, M., Grossman, T., Wigdor, D. and Fitzmaurice, G. (2011). Medusa: A Proximity-Aware Multi-touch Tabletop.*ACM UIST.* 373-382, 2011.
7. Avrahami, D., Wobbrock, J. O. and Izadi, S. (2011). Portico: Tangible interaction on and around a tablet. *ACM UIST.* 347-356, 2011.
8. Bau, O., Poupyrev, I., Israr, A. and Harrison, C. (2010). TeslaTouch: electrovibration for touch surfaces. *ACM UIST.* 283-292, 2010.
9. Baudisch, P., Sinclair, M. and Wilson, A. (2006). Soap: a Pointing Device that Works in Mid-Air. *ACM UIST.* 43-46, 2006
10. Bellavista, P., Corradi, A., Fanelli, M. and Foschini, L. (2013). A Survey of Context Data Distribution for Mobile Ubiquitous Systems. *ACM Computing Surveys.* 1-49, 2013.
11. Bi, X., Grossman, T., Matejka, J. and Fitzmaurice, G. (2011). Magic Desk: Bringing Multi-Touch Surfaces into Desktop Work. *ACM CHI.* 2511-2520, 2011.
12. Butler, A., Izadi, S. and Hodges, S. (2008). SideSight: multi-"touch" interaction around small devices. *ACM UIST.* 201-204.
13. LIBSVM--A Library for Support Vector Machines. *http://www.csie.ntu.edu.tw/~cjlin/libsvm.*
14. Chen, G. and Kotz, D. (2000). A Survey of Context-Aware Mobile Computing Research (TR2000-381).
15. Cheng, K.-Y., Liang, R.-H., Chen, B.-Y., Laing, R.-H. and Kuo, S.-Y. (2010). iCon: utilizing everyday objects as

additional, auxiliary and instant tabletop controllers. *ACM CHI.* 1155-1164, 2010.
16. Cohn, G., Morris, D., Patel, S. N. and Tan, D. S. (2011). Your noise is my command: sensing gestures using the body as an antenna. *ACM CHI.* 791-800, 2011.
17. Gustafson, S., Holz, C. and Baudisch, P. (2011). Imaginary Phone: Learning Imaginary Interfaces by Transferring Spatial Memory from a Familiar Device. *ACM UIST* 283-292, 2011.
18. Harrison, C., Benko, H. and Wilson, A. D. (2011). OmniTouch: Wearable Multitouch Interaction Everywhere. *ACM UIST.* 441-450, 2011.
19. Harrison, C. and Hudson, S. E. (2008). Lightweight material detection for placement-aware mobile computing *ACM UIST.* 279-282, 2008.
20. Harrison, C. and Hudson, S. E. (2008). Scratch input: creating large, inexpensive, unpowered and mobile finger input surfaces. *ACM UIST.* 205-208, 2008.
21. Harrison, C. and Hudson, S. E. (2009). Abracadabra: wireless, high-precision, and unpowered finger input for very small mobile devices. *ACM UIST.* 121-124, 2009.
22. Harrison, C. and Hudson, S. E. (2009). Texture displays: a passive approach to tactile presentation. *ACM CHI.* 2261-2264, 2009.
23. Harrison, C., Lim, B. Y., Shick, A. and Hudson, S. E. (2009). Where to locate wearable displays?: reaction time performance of visual alerts from tip to toe. *ACM CHI.* 941-944, 2009.
24. Harrison, C., Ramamurthy, S. and Hudson, S. E. (2012). On-Body Interaction: Armed and Dangerous. *TEI.* 19 - 22, 2012.
25. Harrison, C., Schwarz, J. and E., H. S. (2011). TapSense: Enhancing Finger Interaction on Touch Surfaces. *ACM UIST.* 627-636, 2011.
26. Harrison, C., Tan, D. S. and Morris, D. (2010). Skinput: appropriating the body as an input surface. In *ACM CHI.* 453-462, 2010.
27. Hinckley, K., Ramos, G., Guimbretiere, F., Baudisch, P. and Smith, M. (2004). Stitching: pen gestures that span multiple displays. *AVI.* 23-31, 2004.
28. Holleis, P., Schmidt, A., Paasovaara, S., Puikkonen, A. and Häkkilä, J. (2008). Evaluating capacitive touch input on clothes. *ACM MobileHCI.* 81-90, 2008.
29. Holz, C., Grossman, T., Fitzmaurice, G. and Agur, A. (2012). Implanted User Interfaces. *ACM CHI.* 503-512, 2012.
30. Kane, S. K., Avrahami, D., Wobbrock, J. O., Harrison, B. L., Rea, A. D., Philipose, M. and Lamarca, A. (2009). Bonfire: a nomadic system for hybrid laptop-tabletop interaction *ACM UIST.*. 129-138, 2009.
31. Lévesque, V., Oram, L., MacLean, K. E., Cockburn, A., Marchuk, N. D., Johnson, D., Colgate, J. E. and Peshkin, M. A. (2011). Enhancing physicality in touch interaction with programmable friction. *ACM CHI.* 2481-2490, 2011.
32. Marquardt, N., Kiemer, J. and Greenberg, S. (2010) What Caused That Touch? Expressive Interaction with a Surface through Fiduciary-Tagged Gloves. *ACM ITS.* 139-142, 2010.
33. McGuffin, M., Burtnyk, N. and Kurtenbach, G. (2002). FaST Sliders: Integrating Marking Menus and the Adjustment of Continuous Values. *GI.* 35-42, 2002.
34. Mistry, P. and Maes, P. (2009). SixthSense: a wearable gestural interface. *CHI EA.* 2009.
35. Mukaibo, Y., Shirado, H., Konyo, M. and Maeno, T. (2005). Development of a Texture Sensor Emulating the Tissue Structure and Perceptual Mechanism of Human Fingers. *ICRA.* 2565-2570, 2005.
36. Ni, T. and Baudisch, P. (2009). Disappearing mobile devices *ACM UIST.*. 101-110, 2009.
37. Ojala, T., Pietikäinen, M. and Mäenpää, T. (2002). Multiresolution Gray-Scale and Rotation Invariant Texture Classification with Local Binary Patterns. *IEEE Transactions on Pattern Analysis and Machine Intelligence (PAMI)*, 24 (7), 971-987, 2002.
38. Richter, S., Holz, C. and Baudisch, P. (2012). Bootstrapper: Recognizing Tabletop Users by their Shoes. *ACM CHI.* 1249-1252, 2012.
39. Saponas, T. S., Harrison, C. and Benko, H. (2011). PocketTouch: Through-Fabric Capacitive Touch Input. *ACM UIST.* 303-308, 2011.
40. Saponas, T. S., Tan, D. S., Morris, D., Balakrishnan, R., Turner, J. and Landay, J. A. (2009). Enabling always-available input with muscle-computer interfaces. *ACM UIST.* 167-176, 2009.
41. Sato, M., Poupyrev, I. and Harrison, C. (2012). Touché: Enhancing Touch Interaction on Humans, Screens, Liquids, and Everyday Objects. *ACM CHI.* 483-492, 2012.
42. Sturman, D. J. and Zeltzer, D. (1994). A Survey of Glove-based Input. *IEEE Computer Graphics and Applications*, 14 (1), 30-39, 1994
43. Weiss, M., Wacharamanotham, C., Voelker, S. and Borchers, J. (2011). FingerFlux: Near-surface Haptic Feedback on Tabletops. *ACM UIST.* 615-620, 2011.
44. Wigdor, D., Forlines, C., Baudisch, P., Barnwell, J. and Shen, C. (2007). Lucidtouch: a see-through mobile device. *ACM UIST.* 269-278, 2007.
45. Wilson, A. (2006). Robust Vision-Based Detection of Pinching for One and Two-Handed Input. *ACM UIST.* 255-258, 2006.
46. Wilson, A. D. (2010). Using a depth camera as a touch sensor. *Tabeltop.* 69-72, 2010.
47. Wilson, A. D. and Benko, H. (2010). Combining Multiple Depth Cameras and Projectors for Interactions On, Above, and Between Surfaces. *ACM UIST.*. 273-282, 2010.
48. Wimmer, R. and Baudisch, P. (2011). Modular and Deformable Touch-Sensitive Surfaces Based on Time Domain Reflectometry. *ACM UIST.* 517-526, 2011.
49. Zhang, H., Yang, X. D., Ens, B., Liang, H. N., Boulanger, P. and Irani, P. (2012). See Me, See You: A Lightweight Method for Discriminating User Touches on Tabletop Displays. *ACM CHI.* 2327-2336, 2012.

YourGloves, HotHands and HotMits: Devices to Hold Hands at a Distance

Daniel Gooch
Department of Computer Science
University of Bath, UK
D.J.Gooch@bath.ac.uk

Leon Watts
Department of Computer Science
University of Bath, UK
L.Watts@bath.ac.uk

ABSTRACT

There is a growing body of work in HCI on the design of communication technologies to help support lovers in long distance relationships. We build upon this work by presenting an exploratory study of hand-holding prototypes. Our work distinguishes itself by basing distance communication metaphors on elements of familiar, simple co-located behaviours. We argue that the combined evocative power of unique co-created physical representations of the absent other can be used by separated lovers to generate powerful and positive experiences, in turn sustaining romantic connections at a distance.

Author Keywords

Hand Holding, Design, Communication Systems, Intimate Communication.

ACM Classification Keywords

H.5.m. Information interfaces and presentation (e.g., HCI): Miscellaneous.
H.4.3. Communications Applications: Miscellaneous

INTRODUCTION

Physical separation can pose many problems for those in romantic relationships. Feelings of dislocation and 'lostness' beset their efforts to construct new routines without diminishing a vital sense of connection with their loved one. People must strive to find a sustainable way to share moment-to-moment experiences. They may be able to preserve an enduring and personally meaningful sense of the absent other using mechanisms they can recruit to somehow be together whilst apart. In these circumstances, communication technologies cease to be tools of convenience but assume a new meaning; they are social lifelines for sustaining personally important relationships.

The exact number of people in long distance relationships (LDRs) is hard to ascertain; what we do know is that they are relatively prevalent. Within our target population, (University students), estimates suggest that between 25% - 50% of students are in an LDR at any one time with around 75% of students being in an LDR at some point [2].

Whilst one might assume that LDRs are somehow inferior to the relationships of co-located couples, the literature suggests otherwise. People in LDRs, on average, report the same or higher levels of relational stability and satisfaction than co-located couples [16]. One reason for this is the way that people in LDRs communicate. LDRs are characterised by a limitation of the amount of face-to-face communication that can take place; additionally there is no evidence that such couples use mediated technologies more than co-located ones. The difference is in what is focussed on during the communicative act; namely that LDRs focus more upon intimacy [16]. Our aim is to understand which design factors are most significant for communication technologies that create such intimacy.

In this paper we consider what a communication system directly aimed at supporting LDRs could be like if based upon a co-located experience. The experience we focus on is hand holding. Our research challenge is to explore what participants think of our prototype devices in terms of the design concepts they embody and then to reflect upon how these concepts could be realised in other interactive systems concerned with intimacy. We examine meaningful qualities of interactivity and communication in romantic personal relationships through several design parameters drawn from the physical act of hand holding. To this end, we report an exploratory qualitative evaluation of three prototype devices. Each device is intended for in-the-moment use by distant couples but is related to enduring values in the relationship. Our immediate aim is to establish the value of hand-holding as the basis of interactive designs. However, we wish to provoke a deeper consideration of paradigmatic approaches to interaction design in the arena of romantic relationships. In particular, we argue that the power of design approaches to communication technologies based on tangible, behavioural metaphors rests on their potential to exploit qualities of 'personalization' and to evoke personal memories.

Designing for Long-Distance Romantic Relationships

We see existing communication systems designed for distance couples falling into three broad categories, based on their design paradigm. These categories are *abstract-*, *object-augmentation-* and *behaviour-based* systems.

Abstract systems are those which in essence have no metaphor behind their use. The Vio system [7] is a good example of this, whereby a simple coloured circle is placed in the taskbar of a person's computer. The colour of the circle changes based on how frequently the person's partner clicked on their own circle. The systems presented by Strong and Gaver in [17] are also abstract, demonstrating how ambiguous movement and scent could be used to create a bond between a couple at a distance.

Object-augmentation systems are those that transfigure existing objects into communication tools. Dodge started this trend back in 1997 (along with an interest in tangible communication systems) when he presented his augmented bed [4]. By integrating heat pads, sound, and moving curtains, the idea was to connect couples that, for whatever reason, were sleeping in separate beds. ComSlipper, [3], is a personal artefact (namely, a pair of slippers) which have been supplemented with technology to develop a rather delightful communication medium. Pressure points on either pair of slippers are connected to an LED and heat pad in the other pair. Various interactions (such as foot tapping) then lead to different outputs. Looking beyond instantaneous experience, Thieme et al. [18] augmented the interior of a lockable antique box with messaging technologies. Their insight was to create a treasured private space, framing messages as intimate to the people who exchange them. In this way, they generated rich emotional experiences by fostering individual reflection on the content of personal messages [18].

Finally, ***behaviour-based systems*** are designed to selectively mimic one or more elements of intimate behaviour over a distance. Interaction with the system is thus intended to resemble an encounter that is already romantically meaningful to those in a relationship. Appearance is deprecated in favour of feel and action. This is an area that thus far has received a little attention. Mueller et al., [11] presented a device that used air pressure to create an enveloping hug sensation when activated. Participants were positive about the concept but were concerned about the practicalities of using such a system. Tsetserukou created the HaptiHug system based on the idea of a full embrace, combining mechanical and thermal emitters into an upper torso harness [19]. Gooch & Watts [5] designed a belt interaction mimicking the idea of an arm around the waist. They showed that using Peltier heat pumps to create an impression of a loved-one's arm increased feelings of Social Presence [5]. The characteristic feature of this third group is the creation of a metaphor around a limited set of physical attributes that are rooted in a familiar intimate act. Our description of these systems as the third grouping should not be confused with the "third paradigm" of HCI [21], where design is emphasized as a process of situated and constructive activity of making meaning rather than as a problem solving activity. Many of the communication systems we have described here fit into this third category of behavioural mimicry.

Before proceeding, it is important to note that there is some overlap between the groups. For example, we could characterize Strong and Gaver's system [17] as augmenting objects; we could also characterize Dodge's bed under behaviour. However, what we have tried to do is classify objects based not on their actual use, but rather, the underlying motivation behind the designs, Strong and Gaver's systems are based around constructing meaning from subtle movements and smells, essentially using abstractness as a resource for design. Likewise, Dodge's bed is not concerned with what occurs in a bed (which would be behaviour-oriented) but is focused heavily upon adaptation of the object itself.

Hand-Holding: Into the Valley

To further elaborate behaviour-based intimate design, we now turn to hand-holding. Within the HCI literature, there is a small amount work based around investigating this specific behaviour. O'Brien and Mueller carried out a technology probe investigating hand-holding [13]. The only similar device of which we are aware is the handshaking system presented in [1]. However, there are some significant differences between their device and our aims. First, a handshake is fundamentally different from holding hands – it is a different action with different emotional overtones. One is a greeting, the other of emotional significance. It is a rare business meeting which would involve the participants holding hands together. Second, the work in [1] uses a force-feedback joystick. Our aim was to build custom communication systems to better understand the factors that would contribute to a good design.

In addition, there are at least two different focus groups that have suggested the building of hand holding devices [8, 20]. Although these designs did not go on to be built, the fact that participants requested such a device makes this area a compelling one to investigate. We build on this work by presenting three prototype devices that are based on the metaphor of hand holding.

Robotics researchers have struggled to find ways of realizing acceptable appearance and behaviour. This is the well-known uncanny valley phenomenon, where high-fidelity androids can provoke feelings of revulsion [10]. Whilst increasing android fidelity initially results in more favourable human reactions, this trend becomes dramatically reversed as the ungainliness of robots ceases to look cute and instead is perceived as 'creepy' or 'weird'. Given that our devices are based around the behaviour of human hands, there is a possibility that they could fall within the valley. Thus one of our considerations for designing three distinct prototypes was to deliberately limit realism, to clearly establish which of a limited set of behavioural and appearance cues we would leverage. In this way we wished to gain insights into how far the metaphor could be developed before the device is rejected as being uncanny.

Our perspective is also semiotic: that the physical signals are only meaningful when embedded in elements of the relationship. We conceptualize the interpretation of signals within a close personal relationship as a matter of establishing it as a personification of the remote loved one. This is akin to Thieme et al.'s specialness of an intimate place [18] but more particularly concerned with the uniqueness of the individual, perhaps best thought of as the 'finger print' of the absent other.

THE HAND-HOLDING PROTOTYPES

The three prototypes we present are titled *YourGlove*, *HotHands* and *HotMits*. They use different physical channels (e.g. movement or heat) to communicate intimate signals and thus present the same behavioural metaphor of hand-holding in three distinctive ways. Movement was selected as the tangible signal most like hand-holding. Heat was used as an alternative metaphor as it has been previously associated with emotional communication [9].

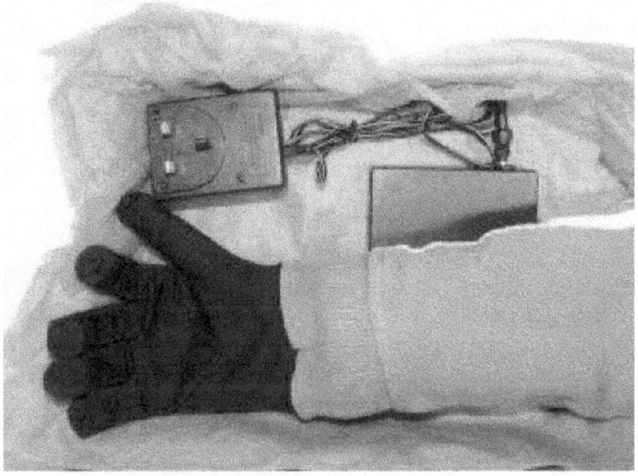

Figure 1. The YourGlove system.

YourGlove is based around the movement of hand-holding (see Figure 1). The device is made up of a robotic hand controlled by strings which, when pulled, cause the hand to contract. YourGlove is mounted onto a tube, approximating the dimensions of a human forearm, and is controlled via a Phidget interface board. The device has the appearance of a limb that can be used to reciprocate hand-holding. Hidden within the back of the glove is a switch that, when pressed, causes an additional paired hand to close. The position of the switch is such that it is activated when someone holds their YourGlove. YourGlove is used by placing the hand within the glove, pressing the aforementioned switch. This sends a signal to the partnered hand making it contract gently around the partner's hand.

YourGlove is designed to be personalized to the absent other by being dressed in a familiar glove, the sleeve of a top and jewellery according to its significance for the particular couple. This means it could gain a familiar and treasured feel (fabric), aroma, and appearance.

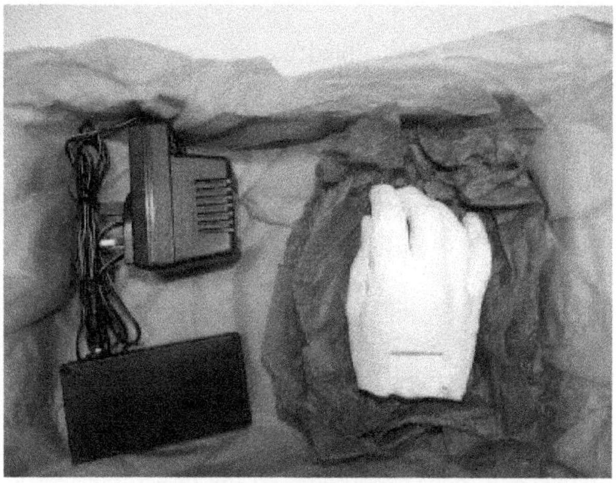

Figure 2. The HotHands system.

HotHands (see Figure 2) uses heat rather than movement as the key physical signal in the medium of the hand. The system consists of two model hands, each with containing a Peltier heat pump. Under each heat pump, a push switch is embedded into the hand. Using a Phidget control board, the heat pump can be controlled in software. When a person places their hand onto their model hand, the other person's model hand warms up. HotHands is personalized to each partner because it is their own unique casting. We envision a co-creation process – making the castings whilst on a visit or before moving away, and including the decoration or embellishment of the device as users see fit.

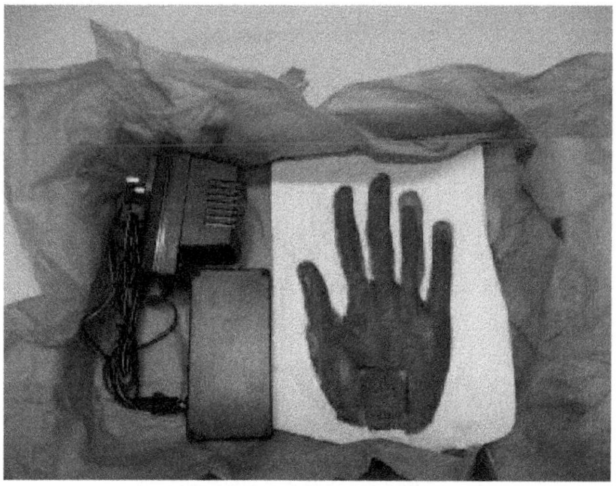

Figure 3. The HotMits system.

HotMits (see Figure 3) again uses heat as the sensory medium, driven by a Phidget-controlled Peltier pump. Instead of casting a hand, HotMits is based around a hand imprint. The device is used by placing one's hand into the imprint. If the partner's hand is within their imprint, both devices warm up. Personalization is again achieved by co-creating the devices but this time as unique imprints of the each person's hand.

METHODOLOGY

The prototypes were intended to explore the design potential around what it could mean to create a communication system based on behavioural qualities of holding hands. We wanted to gather data that would contribute to an understanding of the meaningful qualities of each prototype. To this end, we used a three-phase semi-structured interview process: (1) Introducing the design idea, together with a narrative scenario, (2) a hands-on demonstration of the prototypes device, and (3), a discussion to compare and relate their experience with each device in the context of their own romantic relationship (see Table 1).

The scenarios were used to gather information about the differences in how people viewed the design concept and the actual prototypes. We wanted our participants to engage with the underlying design concept rather than any shortcomings in the way the prototypes had been realized. Along with our design variations on the hand-holding theme, we wanted to better understand the influence of partner uniqueness on the basic design ideas. Scenarios were thus devised in two forms of vignette: device- and person-centred alternatives. Device-centred vignettes were based around giving and receiving a gift in the form of a new remote hand-holding device. Person-centred vignettes described the co-creation of a remote hand-holding device. The YourGlove system was personalised by making it clear that the glove used was that of the person's partner, not just a standard glove. The system could also include other personal items such as bracelets or rings. The HotHands system was personalised by making it clear that the moulds were of the couples' hands rather than a standard meld. It was also made clear that the moulded hands could be painted or decorated. Similarly, the HotMits were personalised by emphasizing that they were imprints of the couples' hands rather than a standardized imprint. HotHands and HotMits also included painting and decoration by the lovers.

12 people in long-term distant relationships took part in the study, 6 male and 6 female. These were 12 individuals, not 6 couples – we interviewed one person from 12 different couples. People were recruited using online noticeboards and posters at a UK university. Participants were paid £10 for taking part. The presentation of the 3 devices was counterbalanced for order. For each order condition, 1 male and 1 female took part. Of these two, one got the person-focused vignettes and the other the device-centred vignettes, counterbalancing for gender. All Device participants were finally introduced to the Person-centred concept in the final phase of the interviews, only after forming impressions based on the relevant device-cantered vignettes.

First Phase – Concept and Scenario
First thoughts on hand holding... do you miss holding hands while you are apart or not?
Do you think you would or wouldn't use a system which represented holding hands?
End of Scenario
What are your first thoughts about the [x] system?
Do you think this is a system you might or might not use? Why/why not?
What do you like about the concepts behind the [x] system? Why?
What do you dislike about the concepts behind the [x] system? Why?
Second Phase - Using the Device
So having used the prototype, has your opinion of the system changed or stayed the same?
Are there any features you thought you would like/dislike which having used you now disliked/liked?
What, if anything, would you change about the device?
If we changed the device by making is more/less personal [by doing Y] would you change your opinion of the device? Or do you think it would stay the same?
What do you think about the way the device is activated? Do you think it would be better if it was activated together? Or do you think separate is better?
Third Phase – Comparison and Discussion
Which of the devices is your favourite? Why? Why don't you like the others as much?
What do you think about the overall idea of trying to support hand holding at a distance? Do or do you not miss holding hands while you're apart? How well do you think the devices I've shown you meet that goal?
Are there other things that you miss more? Do you think those could be supported while you're apart?
These systems are all content free and intended to be used in conjunction with something like IM or Skype, almost like an accessory. Do you use anything like that already? Do you think you would use such a system or not?
Anything else you'd like to add?

Table 1. Three-Phase Exploratory Process.

Vignette Centred on	YourGlove	HotHands	HotMits
Person	2	0	4
Device	0	4	2
Total	2	4	6

Table 2. The favourite device of each participant

Vignette Cantered on	YourGlove	HotHands	HotMits
Person	3	6	5
Device	0	5	4
Total	3 (25%)	11 (91%)	9 (75%)

Table 3. Devices participants 'would use again'

RESULTS AND ANLYSIS

All participant interviews took approximately one hour. The three-phases of the interviews were continuously audio recorded and then transcribed for analysis. Our data are primarily qualitative and are presented as direct quotations from our participants in the form [Px – yz] where x indicates their participant number, y whether they read the Person-centred or Device-cantered scenario and z whether they were male (M) or female (F).

In addition to open-ended questions; we asked each participant to state which device was their favourite (see Table 2) and whether they could imagine using any of the devices, if commercially available (see Table 3). We will discuss these preferences before moving on to consider the specific issues that were raised in response to our prompts.

The first thing to note is that all the prototypes were well received by at least some of our participants but the two casting-based prototypes were much preferred. This indicates that the design concepts behind these devices have a role to play in long-distance relationships. Participants did feel that hand holding was something they missed:

"*Yeah, I think the holding hands is one part of it... if you're away every week for a long period of time... it's that intimacy, the subtle things, just holding hands is something you do miss*" [P10 - DM]

Furthermore, participants felt that these prototypes went some way to helping deal with the distance:

"*if these had been available at the start of my uni life knowing I had 5 years of long distance then I possibly would have considered one*" [P9 - DM]

We now consider these preferences in detail.

Thematic Results

The transcripts were subjected to a three-reading thematic analysis (familiarization, annotation, and consolidation) to form a viewpoint on the interaction factors that were most salient to our participants. Two general themes are used to make sense of our participants experiences: **emotional closeness**, and **practicality**. Our main concern for supporting long-distance romantic relationships is directly addressed though the **emotional significance** of the designs for our participants. **Practical** issues apply across the devices and to communication systems more generally and have an important bearing on situations of use.

Along with describing the themes while using quotes from our interview transcripts to illustrate each, we also indicate how many of our participants raised that particular theme. This in itself provides a guideline as to how significant the theme was. However, we should bear in mind that other participants could agree with the theme but not have thought about it or mentioned it.

Emotional Closeness

Making Connections

The subtle and phatic nature of touch was commended by our participants for helping to "bridge the gap" between them and their partner:

"*its just the little physical thing and something like this wouldn't replace it but help bridge the gap...*" [P11 - PM]

This links to the value that participants saw in the devices. Instead of traditional communication, exchanging news about the day, the devices were liked for "connecting" the couple. Eleven of our 12 participants talked about how the devices would help them to connect to their partner:

"*I'm not sure why but for me there would be more of a connection there because rather than holding something which is fake (YourGlove), you're more putting your hand on a model of something which is creating a reaction on theirs is more like holding your hands together*" [P12 - DF]

People are used to touching their partners; living at a distance prevents this. Couples can still talk to one another but they cannot touch – this is perhaps the most salient thing that changes when a couple start living apart. The tangible interfaces helped to support this change:

"*You just feel the feeling of someone's hand so you feel safe and connected...so you'd associate that more than talking to someone or seeing them on skype*" [P7 - DM]

There was even a view that it didn't even matter what the device did – that it simply has to form a connection:

"*its more about forming that personal connection than the specific action*" [P10 - DM]

One of the things that we wanted to explore in the interviews is what was the best interaction model for the devices. They were configured as synchronous devices in our study – as one put their hand into a device, the partner's device is activated. There was some variation in opinion on whether it might be better to use this synchronicity differently so that *both* hands have to be in their device before they are activated. This was of significance to our participants because it changed the type of connection that was being formed between them and their partner.

Our participants overwhelming preferred to have both people's hands on the device before it was activated because it formed a more personal connection:

"*Making the link... the trouble is, if you put your hand in it and they haven't and it warms up, they cant really get anything from it... so when you're both in it, it probably works better...yeah, I think if you both put it in to form that connection...*" [P8 - DF]

"*Both of you would have to have your hand on because I think that's where the personal connection comes...*" [P10 - DM]

However, it was acknowledged that doing so meant that an element of spontaneity was lost, that arranging the connection did devalue it:

"*I was just thinking that and I don't think that would be as nice as then you'd have to arrange it... cause its not like you'd both spend your evenings sat with your hands in it waiting just waiting for that split second featuring heat and holding his hand... whereas I suppose if you were just sitting there and it warmed up it would be nice... maybe... are you thinking that you just have to sense its warmed up by feeling or you could maybe put a light on it or something...*" [P4 - PF]

The suggestion, then, is that having to use a hand from each partner formed a stronger connection, but if people choose to be spontaneous, some kind of secondary signal would assist this.

We also postulated the option of turning the system into an asynchronous one, a kind of tangible voicemail. We suggested that the system would either consist of recording a short video message with a tangible signal or recording part of a video chat along with the tangible signal. Participants generally disliked this thought as it removed the connection aspect of the experience:

"*I think that's, it is a good idea because as you say then it means you don't have to be there all the time although part of me thinks its slightly impersonal in a way because yes you've recorded the video for them and yes you've triggered the device to respond for them but you're not directly talking to them in a way, I think this sort of device would work better if you were actually in your skype conversation at the time rather than pre-recorded in a way...*" [P9 - DM]

Clearly the asynchronous nature was appealing but the cost of sacrificing the connection with their partner was too high for many participants.

Metaphor

Generally, our participants were able to understand the devices as pointers to hand-holding experiences to form a connection between the couple while they are apart.

"*this is just like feeling closer to someone by almost using holding hands as an inspiration but not trying to imitate the same concept of holding hands but what holding hands represents*" [P3 - PF]

Nine of our participants talked about the different metaphors that the devices were based around. The stronger the metaphor, the more problematic it was for our participants to differentiate the sentiment of the behaviour from the realization of the device. More people would use, and favoured, the devices with the weaker model of hand-holding, the HotMits and HotHands systems. The YourGlove was repeatedly described as being "creepy" and even the HotHands were less accepted than the HotMits:

"*the unfamiliarity people have with just seeing a limb lying around... and I think it's very familiar to see a hand print, and I suppose it's more common and less innovative for people to either dip their hands in paint and put it on the wall or whatever...*" [P5 - PM]

"*just because the imprint it's not something that would be attached to a body whereas these you expect them more to be attached or it's weird to take a part of the body off and have like a dismembered hand or arm or whatever...*" [P3 - PF]

"*I think it's good because [HotHands] was trying to be a hand which it clearly wasn't but this acknowledges that its not a hand, its just an imprint so in a way it's not like trying to trick you into thinking about it... other than that, same as the other one I guess... it doesn't look as nice but it doesn't really matter what it looks like*" [P11 - PM]

The strength of the metaphor helped to determine how "creepy" people found the particular device. Additionally, there was also a practical strand to this thinking. As one participant said:

"*I think I prefer the warmth over the movement because whatever you do, it's never quite going to be the same as an actual movement of your hand... whereas that you can more stimulate something...*" [P8 - DF]

This clearly relates back to the uncanny valley we were discussing earlier. Those devices which tried to copy the behaviour most closely (in this case, the YourGloves) most directly violate expectations of fidelity. Alternative ways of presenting the essence of a behaviour are likely to be successful.

That said, in one particular case, the weak metaphor was seen as a weakness:

"*maybe that seems a bit less personal, its nice again that it's controlled by your partner, but... on the other hand it's sort of, you could just be sat there thinking oh this is warming my hand up rather than thinking im sitting there holding my partners hand...*" [P9 - DM]

It may be enough to convey the envisionment of a behavioural design through a compelling narrative, based on a familiar behavioural experience, as long as it has a simple, direct connection to a tangible facet of that experience. In this instance, our participant points out that heat is inherently less like hand-holding than movement. What keeps it within the realms of believability is the fact that the devices are physically modelled on lovers' hands.

The acceptance or not of a particular metaphor is a difficult thing to design for. Simply going for the lowest common denominator, that which would be acceptable to everyone, runs the risk of forming a weaker connection between the users of the device. Relating that to our own designs, as the process for creating HotHands and HotMits is essentially the same, simply a different cast, any deployment could easily see participants choosing themselves which metaphor they themselves wish to use. As we will discuss, memories played a significant part in people's treatment of the different devices. Allowing users to select which cast they make would have the additional advantage that if people had significant memories based on either of these designs, they could opt for that particular system.

Personalization: private and jointly crafted uniqueness

Personalisation was one of the themes than frequently came up in our interviews, 11 people mentioned it; those who read the person-centred scenarios delighted in it; those who read the device-centred enjoyed the concept more when the personalization idea was raised:

"*maybe because that's a bit more personal... if that were the case, and its made for each of us, it would be really nice to have and maybe id actually consider having it, yeah, I think it would really make a difference...*" [P6 - DF]

There seemed to be three distinct strands that caused personalization to be liked so much. The first is that by being able to personalize the device, it was associated more with their partner. This seemed to be important as it formed an additional connection to their partner as the device was customized to remind them of that individual:

"*it should represent him, so if he painted it boring colours that would be fine, that's what I'd have on my desk. But yeah, it should represent them*" [P2 - PF]

"*[while discussing YourGlove] I like the whole bracelet idea especially cause like I have this bracelet and my partner has the same one and we've had them for like four years so although it's like a pound and worthless to anyone else, there's some sentimental value that means we just don't take them off... so I think that's quite a powerful thing actually...*" [P5 - PM]

The second strand was that of uniqueness. Comparing analogue to digital communication technologies, we can see (arguably) a decrease in uniqueness – no one else has your handwriting but everyone (nearly) uses the same fonts for emails. You use the same phone to talk to your bank manager as you do to your lover. The unique element of these designs seemed to appeal to people:

"*Yeah definitely, because just like a mass produced hand has got nothing personal about it, there's nothing special for you or the person you're with, it's just something everyone else has, it's not unique*" [P11 - PM]

We found that the process of casting HotHands and HotMits was considerably liked. The casting would create something unique and that the effort invested in it would make the device more sentimental:

"*you wouldn't have any qualms about throwing it away... whereas if its someone whose made it, I always feel a bit, like cards and even letters, something someone's written or made or when little kids have painted you something, even though you cant keep it forever, you always feel really bad about throwing it away or getting rid of it... so even if you didn't use it, like you'd still have it on your desk*" [P3 - PF]

The final strand that seemed to contribute to people's feelings of personalization was that of effort. Previous work has indicated that interfaces which require more effort can, sometimes, cause the receiver to value the communication act more [11]. Our participants seem to concur with this assessment but at a different level; the effort that had gone into the creation of the device was definitely appreciated. Whether this appreciation would continue when actually using the device is unknown:

"*its always nice when you have something handmade by someone else, that they put effort into it and you always appreciate that...*" [P3 - PF]

The fact that the personalization seemed so strong could, as one participant pointed out, actually be a downside. They argued that the personalization would remind them of their partner. Because the devices were modelled on a co-located behaviour, they thought that this would simply remind them that they couldn't actually hold hands:

"*Yeah I see, like customise it so it's more like your partner... I suppose that would definitely make it much more personal device so like then you would look at it; then on the other hand that could be quite creepy in a way; like sort of just the arm of your partner in your room... some people might find that a bit strange and actually they might find that a bit emotional in a way, especially if like being in an LDR, if you see things that remind you of your partner, that could be quite hard*" [P9 - DM]

Evocation of Memories

As well as being an act of personalisation, the process of casting the hands created a significant memory that connected the people within the relationship. As our participants said, this memory would subsequently be triggered each time the device was used, making the couple happier and imbuing a sense of attachment to the device:

"*the process of making is important because I imagine they'd be quite fun to make, because the activity is done together, it's a shared memory, so I think each time that you would go to use the system there would be a triggering of the memory of making the cast which I imagine would be a positive memory so that would then influence your mood in a positive way I think*" [P5 - PM]

This illustrates something we did not expect; the power that evoked memories brought to bear on people's attitudes towards the hand-holding devices. Five of our participants talked about memories and connected them to their use of the devices. These memories came in two types – personal memories that were associated with the device and broader cultural memories that made the devices seem less weird. One participant was particularly keen on the HotHands system as it reminded her of an early, but significant, memory within her relationship:

"*it reminds me off a personal memory, just of being in the cinema, it's such a long time ago, I think it was on our second date and my hand was here and he put his hand on mine and I don't know just for me, perhaps not other people, that's why I liked it and when I saw it I thought "wow"*" [P 6 - DF]

One participant recalled an activity they did on holiday, and related it back to the imprint in the HotMits system:

"*we kind of did it when we went on holiday in the sand, It might have been feet, and then like wrote our names in the sand and took a photo of that so that's kind of a similar concept I guess...*" [P3 - PF]

Others related the devices back to more clichéd cultural stereotypes including the imprints in concrete of celebrities' hands in Hollywood and finger painting as children:

"*you know like when you're a kid and you make hand print things and take them back to your parents...*" [P2 - PF]

The cultural memories were useful in so far as they demystified and helped people understand the aim behind the design concepts.

However, what we are really trying to achieve is to tap into those deeper personal memories which were accompanied with a visceral attachment to a particular device. If we can find a way to access this visceral attachment within the communication act then the connection between the couple will be strengthened and hopefully better supported.

Practical Themes

In addition to the themes which had an emotional impact, there were a number of themes which revolved around the practical deployment of these devices, including biomechanical fit, mechanical noise, the possible abuse of the unique lover's channel and the viability of hand-holding devices alongside other media.

Biomechanical Compatibility

The first concern was to do with the simple fact that people have different sized hands. Eight people discussed how best they could actually use the cast hands:

"*well no, actually because this is odd, imagine if my hands were really big and my girlfriends hands are tiny, that still works in real life, but here it's like your putting your hand into a mould of a hand that's not yours so it wouldn't fit. So like that finger there doesn't feel comfortable because it's not resting in there. So even though it sounds odd, it might be better to have a cast of your own hand*" [P1 - PM]

As P1 correctly surmises, couples can have different sized hands and for the participant with larger hands, the device may be uncomfortable. That led to the concept of *not* swapping imprints. That concept had different concerns:

"*I think id find it weird if it was an imprint of my hand because im just holding my own hand*" [P8 - DF]

This suggests that this kind of decision should be left up to individual couples. Whether they choose to be more comfortable or to form a closer connection, it seems to be a personal decision for the couple.

There was also some debate as to the best way to deploy the heat within HotMits and HotHands. Some participants would like the whole device to warm up:

"*I'd say the whole hand, yeah*" [P10 - DM]

While others would have preferred the heat to be across the whole hand:

"*I think it might be weird if the whole thing heated up but actually I think it's good it's the bit in the middle cause if you're holding someones hand, that's the bit that kind of gets warm... but maybe a bigger area like the whole palm...*" [P3 - PF]

Again, these concerns seem to be something dependent upon an individual's own preferences.

Mechanical noise

Only one of the devices caused noise due to the motors in it – the YourGlove system. Four participants complained about the noise that the YourGloves made. As one said:

"*the mechanical noise is a bit odd as it reminds you, you couldn't like close your eyes and pretend it was them because im pretty sure [my partner's] hand doesn't go [buzzzzz] [giggles]...*" [P2 - PF]

And another:

"*I'm not to keen on the noise but obviously the noise has to be there, doesn't it... the noise makes it more robot-like which makes it less human-like...*" [P12 - DF]

Similar findings were reported by Mueller et al. when discussing their compressed air hug-belt [8]. It seems, perhaps unsurprisingly, that any kind of noise that distracts from the moment stands to ruin the communicative act. As tangible devices continue to be experimented with, this is something the design community needs to be aware of.

Channel Abuse

A concern that a two people shared was that somebody other than their partner might use the system, either deliberately or by accident:

"*one thing that stood out was, it is essentially, nothing stopping another person putting their hand in the device... if you're not currently having a conversation with your partner then they could potentially be under the false assumption that you're trying to communicate with them...*" [P5 - PM]

"*if you can see them and see that it's them using it rather than some other person who's hacked into the system and started holding your hand with a stranger...*" [P3 - PF]

The concern seems to be with the possibility that using the system could create issues with their partner by thinking that they were using the system with their partner when in fact they were using it with someone else. Additionally they thought they might use the system without their partner being there. The relationship problems that could stem from either of these situations are clear.

Channel Complementarity

Using the devices with an additional communication system was seen as a plus. Not only did it help overcome the concern of other people using the device, the ability to integrate the prototypes into people's existing communication practices was considered a major positive:

"*the way that you can combine the device with other communication devices is quite a nice idea... so the fact that you could be on skype or a phone, you don't have to be using a technical device; as long as the actual device is in the room with you, you could be using pretty much any method of communication... so I think that's quite a cool thing to have...*" [P5 - PM]

One participant travelled a great deal and as such was concerned about the portability of the devices:

"*the portability too I suppose... it doesn't seem too sort of cumbersome, something that you have to wear; you could potentially just carry it with you... so if you travel a lot, you could take this with you, it's nothing which is too restrictive in that sense... so I think its very convenient; it can be used with multiple communication tools*" [P5 - PM]

In that respect, HotHands and HotMits have a clear advantage over the rather bulky YourGloves.

Practical potential

What these practical concerns tell us is that creating designs based on a familiar intimate behaviour is not straightforward. Although the metaphor is extremely powerful, it is by its nature almost unique to individual relationships. Designing something that provides meaningful interpretation for all potential users is challenging, and thus an approach that leverages small, familiar behaviours could have wide applicability. One possibility for overcoming these concerns would be to modularize the system. This would allow users the opportunity to customize the system to their personal preferences without sacrificing any design innovation.

DISCUSSION

As well as a number of practical considerations, our data indicate that all three devices are valued, to different extents, for their ability to form connections between romantic partners at a distance. Our data suggests that the desirability and ability of our devices to bridge the distance gap is based on the interplay between a number of factors, including personalization, evocation and metaphor.

Some of our themes may seem somewhat unsurprising to designers (e.g. people preferred having both people's hands on the device to make it work) but others are more speculative (e.g. that holding a hand would make them feel more connected). However, we have discussed four key themes that could be of use to others who are designing intimate devices for LDRs.

The first of these concerns the way that co-creation invests special significance in the communication device. The casting process is a form of super-personalisation; not only is each participant customising the device for their own use, they are actually creating the device from scratch, creating a highly personal memory which is of significance to the relationship. As a design concept, it is possible to see how the embedding of memory in the creation or use of communication technologies could benefit LDRs.

We found that the stronger the metaphor of the device, the less participants seemed to enjoy using it. We've previously discussed how our devices relate to the Uncanny Valley phenomenon. Our data seems to indicate that people appreciate the use of underlying behaviours (in this case, handholding) as a starting point for design but that simply replicating the behaviour will not be successful. Given the large number of different behaviours and the different ways of representing such behaviours, this seems to be an area of untapped design potential.

A number of people discussed using our devices along with other communication technologies. People build up strong routines within their relationships, especially regarding the communication technologies they use. These become a necessary backdrop to significant communication activity. As such, designing to augment current technologies could be more successful than creating completely new devices. Although this limits the potential for new technologies, it increases the chance of a device being used. Evolutionary changes can be just as beneficial as revolutionary ones.

Finally, spontaneity was highlighted as a design factor worth considering. Several participants spoke of seeing things during their day which would encourage them to communicate, something which cannot be accomplished through a fixed desktop-based system. Spontaneity is something which can easily be lost within the routine of an LDR and as such, designing it into their communication ecology could be beneficial.

Through this work, our key insights centre on the design of devices based around small, tangible, intimate behaviours intended for long distance couples. We agree with the creators of 'Lovers' Box' that it is inherently hard for designers to direct interaction design for couples because it depends on elements of users' personal history [18]. We argue that co-construction of the designed artefact, whether by casting or decoration, and the traces of loved ones that thereby embed some aspect of the person, are powerful contributors to the user experience. The memories created through the process, and other memories that the simplicity of the behavioural paradigm can evoke, are both mechanisms created by designers that allow couples to direct their own experiences. Our study indicates that it is possible to inspire visceral attachments to particular devices and an appreciation of how these devices can be used to connect them to their distant partner. By no means do we suggest that these are the only design themes that are important; indeed we are working to expand the design space for these devices [6]. Our work here indicates that these key themes (co-creation, metaphor, channel complementarity and spontaneity) have demonstrable relevance for communication devices for LDRs.

FURTHER WORK

Our participants understood the value behind the 'unique physical' designs for tangible presence technologies we have presented here. However, there are two main challenges for the approach we have reported. The devices, especially the cast hands, were not actually made unique for our individual participants. Their responses were to the ideas behind our devices rather than to their individualized realization. It is unclear how much of a difference this made. Given that personalization was such a key theme running through participants' responses, the impact seems likely to have been minimal.

Our exploratory study indicates that devices based on co-located behaviour using tangible interfaces can be successful in supporting long distance romantic relationships. However, there is a substantial difference between understanding concepts and their realization in a design studio and incorporating them into everyday life. Although there are substantial practical barriers to real-world evaluation of relationship-centred technologies, it is clear that more work is required in this area.

REFERENCES

1. Alhalabi M O and Horiguchi S. Tele-Handshake: Cooperative haptic shared virtual environment. *Eurohaptics 2001*, pp. 60-64.
2. Aylor, B. (2003). Maintaining long-distance relationships. In DJ Canary & M. Dainton (Eds.), *Maintaining relationships through communication: Relational, contextual and cultural variations* (pp. 127-140). Mahwah, NJ: Lawrence Erlbaum.
3. Chen, C., Forlizzi, J. & Jennings, P. Comslipper: an expressive design to support awareness and availability. In *Proc CHI 2006*, ACM Press. pp. 369–374.
4. Dodge, C. The bed: a medium for intimate communication. In *Proc. CHI 1997*, ACM Press (1997), 371–372.
5. Gooch, D., and Watts, L., 2010. Communicating Social Presence Through Thermal Hugs. In Proc. Ubicomp 2010 SISSE Workshop.
6. Gooch, D. and Watts, L. A Design Framework for Mediated Personal Relationship Devices. In *Proc. British HCI* (2011).
7. Kaye, J. I just clicked to say I love you: rich evaluations of minimal communication. In *Proc. CHI 2006*, ACM Press (2006), 363–368.
8. Kaye, J. and Goulding, L. Intimate Objects. In *Proc DIS 2004*, ACM Press, pp. 341 – 344.
9. Lee, W. and Lim, Y. Thermo-Message: Exploring the Potential of Heat as a Modality of Peripheral Expression. In *Proc CHI 2010*, ACM Press. pp 4231 – 4236.
10. Mori, M. The Uncanny Valley. 1970. (MacDorman, K.F. and Minato, T., Trans.) Energy, 7(4), pp. 33-35.
11. Mueller, F., Vetere, F., Gibbs, M., Kjeldskov, J, Pedell, S. and Howard, S. Hug over a distance. In Proc CHI 2005, ACM Press (2005), 1673–1676.
12. Neustaedter, C.; Elliot, K. & Greenberg, S. Interpersonal awareness in the domestic realm `in *Proc. OZCHI2006* pp. 15-22. (2006)
13. O'Brien, S. and Mueller, F. Holding hands over a distance: technology probes in an intimate, mobile context. In *Proc. OZCHI 2006*, ACM Press (2006), 293–296.
14. Romero, N.; Markopoulos, P.; van Baren, J.; de Ruyter, B.; Ijsselsteijn, W. & Farshchian, B. Connecting the family with awareness systems. *Personal and Ubiquitous Computing* 11: 299-312. (2007)
15. Short, J., Williams, E. and Christie, D. The Social Psychology of Telecommunications. John Wiley & Sons, London, UK, 1976.
16. Stafford, L. (2010) Geographic Distance and Communication During Courtship, Communication Research 37(2), pp. 275-297.
17. Strong, R., and Gaver, W. W. Feather, scent, and shaker: Supporting simple intimacy. In *Proc. CSCW 1996*, ACM Press (1996).
18. Thieme, A.; Wallace, J.; Thomas, J.; Chen, K.L.; Krämer, N. & Olivier, P. Lovers' box: Designing for reflection within romantic relationships *International Journal of Human-Computer Studies* 69(5): 283–297 (2011)
19. Tsetserukou, D. 'HaptiHug: A Novel Haptic Display for Communication of Hug over a Distance' In *Haptics: Generating and perceiving tangible sensations* LNCS 6191: 340-347 (2010)
20. Vetere, F., Gibbs, M., Kjeldskov, J., Howard, S., Mueller, F., Pedell, S., Mecoles, K. and Bunyan, M. Mediating Intimacy: Designing Technologies to Support Strong-Tie Relationships. In *Proc CHI 2005*, ACM Press. pp 471 – 480.
21. Ylirisku, S., Halttunen, V., Nuojua, J. & Juustila, A. 2009. Framing design in the third paradigm. In *Proceedings CHI '09*. ACM Press, New York, USA, pp. 1131-1140.

Digits: Freehand 3D Interactions Anywhere Using a Wrist-Worn Gloveless Sensor

David Kim[1,2], Otmar Hilliges[1], Shahram Izadi[1], Alex Butler[1], Jiawen Chen[1], Iason Oikonomidis[1,3], Patrick Olivier[2]

[1]Microsoft Research, 7 JJ Thomson Ave, Cambridge, UK
[2]Culture Lab, Newcastle University, Newcastle, UK
[3]FORTH, University of Crete, Heraklion, Greece

{b-davidk, otmarh, shahrami, dab, jiawen}@microsoft.com, oikonom@ics.forth.gr, p.l.olivier@ncl.ac.uk

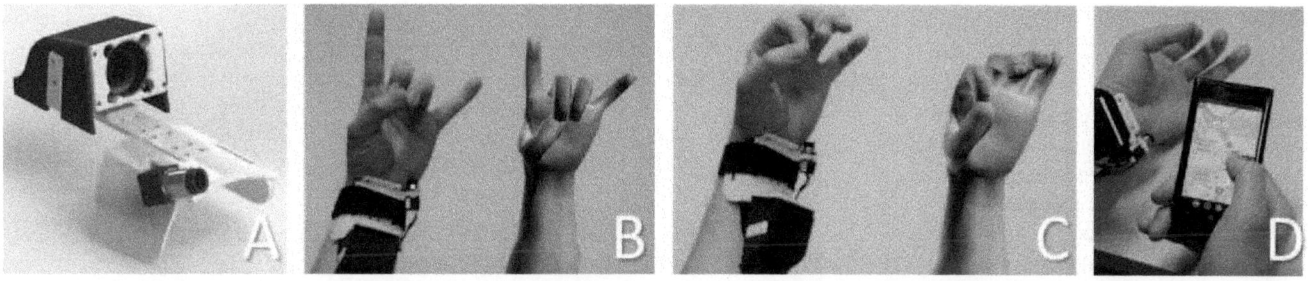

Figure 1: A) Digits is a wrist-worn sensor for freehand 3D interactions on the move. By instrumenting only the wrist, the user's entire hand is left to interact freely without wearing a data glove. B and C) Digits recovers the full 3D pose of a user's hand. D) Spatial interactions using a mobile phone and Digits.

ABSTRACT

Digits is a wrist-worn sensor that recovers the full 3D pose of the user's hand. This enables a variety of freehand interactions on the move. The system targets mobile settings, and is specifically designed to be low-power and easily reproducible using only off-the-shelf hardware. The electronics are self-contained on the user's wrist, but optically image the entirety of the user's hand. This data is processed using a new pipeline that robustly samples key parts of the hand, such as the tips and lower regions of each finger. These sparse samples are fed into new kinematic models that leverage the biomechanical constraints of the hand to recover the 3D pose of the user's hand. The proposed system works without the need for full instrumentation of the hand (for example using data gloves), additional sensors in the environment, or depth cameras which are currently prohibitive for mobile scenarios due to power and form-factor considerations. We demonstrate the utility of Digits for a variety of application scenarios, including 3D spatial interaction with mobile devices, eyes-free interaction on-the-move, and gaming. We conclude with a quantitative and qualitative evaluation of our system, and discussion of strengths, limitations and future work.

ACM Classification Keywords

H.5.2 [Information Interfaces And Presentation]: User Interfaces - Interaction styles;

UIST'12, October 7-10, 2012, Cambridge, Massachusetts, USA.

Author Keywords

Hand tracking, 3D interaction, mobile, wearables.

INTRODUCTION

Our hands are extremely dexterous, making them the primary mechanism to manipulate and interact with the physical world. Understandably a considerable focus of HCI research has been in transferring such 'natural' hand manipulations into the digital domain. However, current user interfaces rarely leverage the full dexterity of our hands. This is largely due to the technical challenges in sensing the full 3D pose of the hand, with its many degrees-of-freedom (DoF).

Consequently, systems constrain the problem along different dimensions, such as limiting hand tracking to 2D input only [9, 24], focusing on fingertips or other specific parts of the hand [19, 35], only supporting interactions through surfaces and other tangible mediators [5, 10, 11], or supporting a small discrete set of hand gestures [14, 32, 33]. Until recently, real-time 3D hand tracking required full instrumentation of the hand (see [7]). Researchers (particularly in the computer vision community) have begun to demonstrate algorithms for real-time 3D hand pose recovery [27, 31] and their applications for HCI [37].

Whilst sensing the full 3D pose of the hand is becoming more tractable, particularly with the advent of consumer depth cameras, there are certain domains where it still remains a fundamental challenge. The mobile domain is one such example, and the focus of this paper. In mobile settings, computational cost, power consumption, form-factor, everyday use, and self-containment are all key requirements. This makes hand tracking solutions impractical that require the sensor to be embedded in the environment, leverage currently bulky and power inefficient depth cameras, or that require the hands of the user to be fully covered.

This paper explores this very challenge and enables dexterous 3D hand interactions on the move. Our system, called Digits, is a compact form-factor wrist-worn device, built using easily reproducible off-the-shelf hardware, which is orders of magnitude lower power than current depth cameras. The sensor is fully contained on the body, requiring no external sensing infrastructure in the environment, and allows diverse bare hand interactions.

This focus on mobile use does not come at the cost of sensing fidelity. We present efficient processing techniques for robustly detecting features of the hand using the wrist-worn device, and new algorithms, which leverage knowledge regarding the biomechanical constraints of the hand to recover a fully articulated 3D model of the hand.

We leverage the recovered 3D hand pose to recognize diverse hand gestures, including discrete and continuous 3D gestures. We demonstrate interactive scenarios, including: eyes-free spatial interactions on the move, in-air 3D interactions around the periphery of the mobile device, combinations of on surface and above the surface input on mobile phones, controlling large displays from a distance using freehand gestures, and immersive 3D gaming experiences.

Our main contributions can be summarized as follows:

- A wrist-worn system that senses the full 3D hand pose without external sensing infrastructure or full instrumentation of the hand (unlike existing data gloves).
- A real-time signal processing pipeline that robustly tracks points on the user's hand.
- Two new kinematic models that allows for full reconstruction of the hand pose from these sparse points.
- A demonstration of compelling interactive scenarios that Digits enables.
- An evaluation of the feasibility of this approach through preliminary qualitative and quantitative studies.

RELATED WORK

Given their dexterity, sensing the full 3D pose of a user's hand is a technically challenging and active area of research. One approach is to instrument the hand directly by wearing a glove with embedded sensors or markers (see [7] for an overview). Originally designed for AR/VR, such sensors have since been leveraged for mobile scenarios. However, gloves can be cumbersome and uncomfortable to wear, can degrade tactile sensation and limit interaction with capacitive touch sensors, which are now standard on mobile phones.

An approach that avoids user instrumentation is to place a camera in the environment pointed directly at the user's hand. Many systems focus purely on fingertip detection for on surface (see [5]) or in-air input (see literature review in [20]). Other systems have recognized a small set of discrete 3D hand poses (e.g. [14]), or leveraged 3D shape and motion analysis for approximating freehand interactions [12].

The vision community has explored higher fidelity 3D hand tracking methods (see [8] for a detailed survey). Real-time 3D pose recovery is becoming feasible, using either non-parametric methods that typically use nearest neighbor lookup into a database of RGB [31] or depth images [37], or attempt to fit a parametrized model of the hand to observed images [27]. These systems offer some of the most sophisticated mechanisms for 3D hand tracking, without the need for direct user instrumentation. However, these approaches clearly lack mobility, requiring sensors embedded in the environment and high computational cost.

Depth Cameras On the Move The rise of consumer depth cameras has led to interest in 3D interaction on the move. Researchers have explored handheld [15, 25], shoulder- [10] or even shoe-worn depth cameras [3], all requiring line of sight of the user's hands. None of these systems however support full 3D hand pose recovery, but instead focus on sensing touch interaction with planar [10] or more complex physical surfaces [15, 25]; or detect simple pinch gestures for interaction [3]. Handheld systems can restrict freeform hand interactions that require both hands. Shoulder and shoe mounted systems alleviate this issue, but can suffer from occlusions of the hands from other parts of the body. In addition, whilst compelling in terms of sensor fidelity, there are practical barriers in making depth cameras mobile, in particular power consumption and form-factor.

Ultra-mobile Wearable Gesture Systems The wearables literature has proposed many lightweight systems for mobile gestural interaction. Instead of supporting high-fidelity sensing, they use IR proximity sensors to detect coarse motion of fingers [13, 17, 18, 26], sense muscle or tendon activity to recognize a small set of discrete hand gestures [30, 32], or leverage acoustics to coarsely localize touch on the body [11]. Given their lightweight form-factor, a variety of on-body placements including forearm [32] and wrist-worn [17, 18, 30] have been demonstrated.

Our work builds upon these systems in that we aim to provide always-available body-worn input but extend the interaction scope from sensing discrete events or coarse motion gestures to much richer continuous 3D input.

Body-Worn 2D Camera Systems One final class of wearable systems uses 2D cameras to add higher fidelity sensing without greatly compromising form-factor. These systems use either monochrome cameras and diffuse IR illumination [9, 33] or RGB cameras [19, 24, 28, 34, 35]. Inferring the full 3D pose of the hand is clearly challenging from such 2D input. Currently systems have only demonstrated simple 2D pinch gestures [9] or detecting fingers using marker [24] or markerless approaches [19, 35] for simple pointing, open and closed hand gestures. [33, 34] classify a wider set of discrete hand postures e.g. for sign language. The form-factor of these systems allows for various body-worn placements (see [22]). These include placement on shoulder or head [19, 34] and around the neck [9, 33], which have the benefit of capturing both hands for bimanual input, but restrict the interaction space to a fixed region directly in front of the user's upper body. Interactions often cannot be subtle and are publicly visible (a potential barrier for adoption in public [3]). Arm fatigue can be an issue for prolonged use.

A viable option to closer couple hand and sensor are cameras directly looking across the hand of the user. [35] use a watch-like camera to count visible fingers for coarse input. [28] presents a prototype of a wrist-worn camera that looks across the hand and images fingertips with markers placed on each finger, inferring hand pose from the 3D fingertip estimate using inverse kinematics (IK). The system is fairly large in terms of form-factor and the requirement of wearing markers on each finger is a clear limitation.

Design Considerations As illustrated by the breadth of the related work, this is a rich and challenging design space. With Digits we aim to bring some of the high fidelity sensing found in data gloves and environment-based vision techniques to mobile settings. This requires the full recovery of 3D articulated hand poses in real-time without the requirement to wear a glove. We strive to build a system that is more practical than using today's depth camera technologies, which as outlined carry serious limitations for mobile use. We identify an interesting area in this design space and focus on a wrist-worn device to recover the full 3D hand pose, but do this with only a 2D camera.

We build upon learnings from the wearables literature that have shown the benefits of wrist-worn devices [17, 18, 13] for supporting eyes-free, always-available interactions [1], as well as overcoming some of the limitations of other sensor placements, including occlusions of the hands by other body parts, imposing interactions that are overly performance-centric (instead of private or subtle [3]), and physically constraining the interaction space due to line of sight requirements of the sensor.

DIGITS – SYSTEM OVERVIEW

Digits is a small camera-based sensor attached to the wrist that optically images a large part of the user's bare hand. The camera is placed so that the upper part of the palm and fingers are imaged as they bend inwards towards the device. Two separate infrared (IR) illumination schemes are used to simplify signal processing. The use of IR allows the illumination to be invisible to the user, and offers a level of robustness to ambient visible light. Both illumination schemes use low cost, readily procurable, and low-power components.

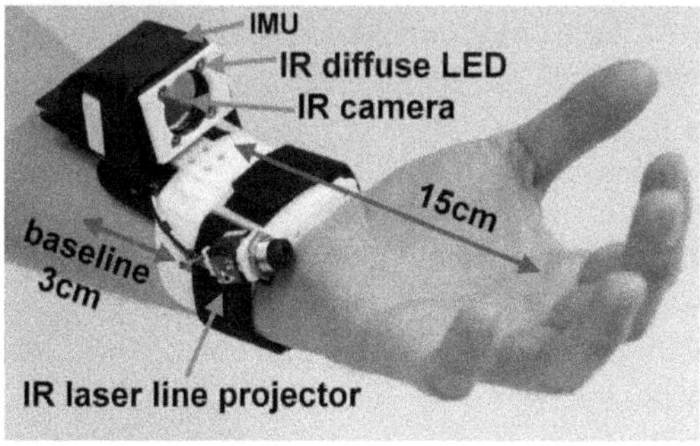

Figure 2: Digits main hardware components attached to a wrist brace.

First, an IR laser line generator projects a thin IR line across the user's hand which intersects with the fingers as they bend inwards [36]. This approach can be used to robustly sample a single 3D point on each of the fingers and thumb. From these five sparse samples, and by exploiting biomechanical constraints, we derive a forward kinematics (FK) algorithm to reconstruct a fully articulated hand skeleton. This initial approximation allows us to support a variety of 3D hand poses as shown in Fig. 9. However, each fingertip is essentially reduced to a single dimension of input, limiting its motion to curling either towards or away from the sensor (see Fig. 7B).

To more faithfully replicate the pose of the hand, more features need to be sampled on the hand. A complimentary method uses a ring of modulated IR LEDs to uniformly illuminate the user's hand. We demonstrate how to robustly extract the 2D positions of fingertips from this IR image, with an associated coarse depth estimate, by modeling the light falloff from the IR LEDs. This fingertip sensing approach can be coupled with the laser line sensing method to derive a new inverse kinematics (IK) based algorithm for computing the full joint-angle configuration of the hand. This method allows for even more realistic reconstructions of the hand as shown in Fig. 12, resulting in higher DoF input.

These methods work together to help constrain the otherwise ill-posed problem of recovering the full 3D hand pose from a 2D image. Because each method may be useful by itself, we keep the description of the two approaches separate. This also aids in understanding the underlying concepts, techniques and algorithms presented in this paper. Finally, an inertial measurement unit (IMU) can be used to approximate wrist and forearm motions in 3D (see Fig. 2).

Digits is primarily a new type of sensor and an enabling technology for interaction, however before describing the system in full, we demonstrate its interactive capabilities.

Interactive Scenarios

We have explored a number of interactive scenarios enabled by our system which we briefly illustrate here. Each scenario looks at a different configuration of output coupled with Digits. The first scenario looks at spatial interaction with a situated display (see Fig. 3A+B). For example, interacting with a TV at home or a large public display. Here the user interacts at a distance using a Digits device. Application scenarios can include gaming or CAD, where the user can perform a variety of continuous or discrete hand gestures to support spatial navigation, pointing or selection in 3D (Fig. 3A+B). From this tracked 3D hand model, discrete gestures can be robustly recognized by looking at the joint angle configuration (Fig. 3C).

Figure 3: Illustration of potential Digits application scenarios. A+B) Continuous interaction with 3D content on a large display. C) Gesture recognition performed on reconstructed hand model.

Mobility was a strong motivation in our work. We envision Digits will expand the physical interaction area of mobile devices beyond the display. In one application scenario (see Fig. 4A+B) the user holds and interacts with a tablet (or phone) using the dominant hand and uses the non-dominant hand to provide 3D input to the application. For example, semantic zooming is initiated with an in-air pinch gesture, and the zoom factor is controlled with the remaining digits.

An interesting possibility here is to support on-screen interactions and simultaneous freehand interactions. For example, dividing between fine-grained interactions on the touch-

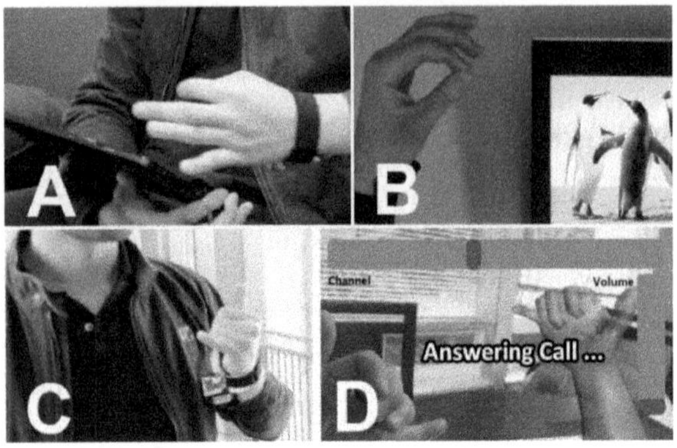

Figure 4: Digits application scenarios. A+B) Extending interaction space around a mobile device into 3D. C+D) Non-visual UIs allow users to manipulate application parameters without looking at or touching a physical device (GUI elements are for illustration only).

screen and coarser navigation tasks using the non-dominant hand and Digits. Our tracker is gloveless and enables the user to interact with the mobile device and operate Digits with the same hand. This allows standard 2D touch gestures to be coupled with above-the-surface interactions in 3D. For example, for quickly changing the Z-order of a selected object by first touching the target and then performing an in-air pinch-based zoom.

Finally, the display could be removed entirely in an eyes-free interaction scenario. The 3D input capabilities of Digits can allow spatial interactions with invisible UIs, such as dials, sliders, or buttons without visual output (see Fig. 4C+D). For example, we can leverage both proprioceptive knowledge and spatial memory to allow the user to set the volume on a mobile phone by directly reaching out and interacting with a virtual dial; turning their hand to the right of the body and performing typing gestures on a virtual number pad to place a call; or moving the hand to the left of the body and touching their thumb and individual fingers to activate other phone functions. One interesting possibility here is to detect the type of action by the initial 3D shape of the hand. For example, if the user requires to change the volume, they simply configure their hand as if they are holding a virtual dial, which can then be rotated to set the desired level.

These scenarios illustrate the utility of the Digits as a general purpose platform for a variety of hand-based interactions. In the next sections, we describe the system implementation in full, focusing on how we sense features of the hand and from these build different articulated models of the hand, with varying levels of fidelity.

SENSING HARDWARE

The Digits hardware is shown in Fig. 2. A PointGrey FireFly MV IR camera (640x480 resolution capturing frames at 90Hz) is attached to a wristband worn on the anterior (inner) side of the wrist. An IR laser line generator (Gated Cameo 1260 from Global Laser) operating at 850nm, with 105° angular spread is positioned at a fixed baseline from the camera. 4 diffuse IR LEDs (OSRAM CHIPLED SFH 4053) again operating at 850nm are attached around the lens of the camera. Finally, an IMU (x-IMU from x-IO Technologies) provides absolute tri-axis orientation data of the forearm at 120Hz.

The hardware is designed to be simple, easily reproducible with off-the-shelf components, and low-power. The setup is powered entirely over USB, both laser and the 4 LEDs powered and driven by strobes from the camera General Purpose Input/Output (GPIO) pins. This results in a total power draw of less than 400mW (16mW for the laser, 60mW for the IR LEDs, and 300mW for remaining camera hardware). This compares favorably to the 3.4 to 5W consumption of the current generation Kinect cameras. A Digits device weighs around 75g, 124g with the wireless IMU, and is lighter than standard watches with a metal wristband (160-180g). The device is attached to the forearm with a 2cm wide Velcro band around the wrist, and the contact area at the inner wrist is covered with soft padding (5x5cm).

SIGNAL PROCESSING

The main processing pipeline is broken down into the following steps:

Background Subtraction We reduce the influence of ambient IR light by capturing three consecutive frames from the IR camera under different illumination conditions (giving an effective frame rate of 30Hz). The first frame turns all active illumination off, capturing only ambient IR. This is subtracted from the other two frames; the first with only the laser on, and the second with just LEDs on. As shown, ambient IR light is greatly reduced in our input images e.g. from room lights or sunlight (Fig. 5).

Image Rectification Rectifies both actively lit images based on a previous intrinsic camera calibration step.

Finger Separation Splits the LED lit IR image into regions that correspond to different unique fingers or thumb.

Laser Line Sensing Triangulates the 3D points where each finger or thumb intersects with the laser line generator.

Forward Kinematics These 3D points are passed to a new forward kinematics algorithm, which reconstructs the full 3D hand pose, based on assumptions regarding the biomechanical constraints of the hand.

Diffuse IR Fingertip Detection Additionally, depending on the hand pose, we can also use the LED illuminated image to robustly extract high-quality surface normals and coarse depth estimation for robust detection of fingertips.

Inverse Kinematics The 3D points sensed from the laser and 2D fingertip locations are passed onto a new IK model for higher DoF recovery of hand poses.

Finger separation One of the important initial pipeline steps associates regions of the image with each of the digits of the hand. A technique utilized in *seam carving* [2] is used to disambiguate the main vertical boundary between pairs of fingers in the IR illuminated image. A one dimensional sobel filter finds vertical edges in the IR image. We detect *valleys* [20] between two fingers as concavities in the traced hand contour. At each valley location, we trace multiple vertical paths along the edges, and use dynamic programming to detect the path with the lowest overall energy by penalizing paths not following the edge (see Fig. 5F). This method divides the image into five areas each mapped to a unique digit.

Laser Line Sensing The laser line generator projects a horizontal line above the palm that intersects with parts of

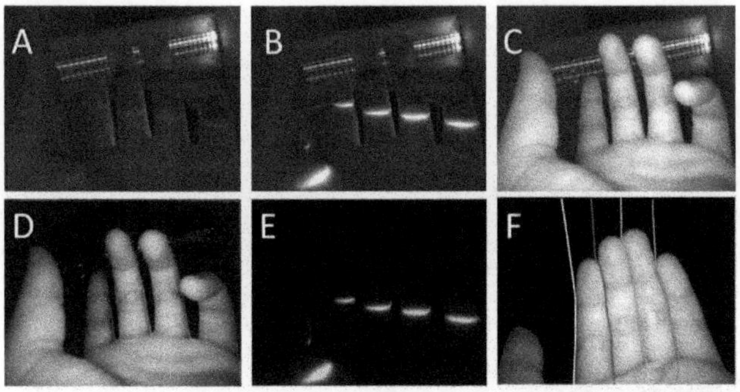

Figure 5: Background subtraction. A) Active illumination off. B) IR laser + background IR. C) IR LEDs + background IR. D) Background subtracted IR LEDs. E) Background subtracted IR laser. F) Finger separation via seam carving.

each finger. These intersections appear as bright regions in the 2D IR camera image, and move towards the palm as the finger is bent, and in the opposite direction when the finger is straightened (see Fig. 7). With a fixed known baseline between laser and the camera, it is possible to triangulate the exact 3D position of each laser line segment (our current implementation uses a 3cm baseline as a reasonable trade-off between depth accuracy and ergonomics, see Fig. 2).

In a one-off process, the camera and laser are calibrated: The camera's intrinsic parameters are retrieved using a checkerboard calibration method [39], and are used for image rectification. Next, the user moves the same target and intersects it with the laser line (see Fig. 6A). The 6DoF extrinsic pose of the target is computed relative to the camera center [39]. The user clicks on an intersection point, and the associated 3D point is recorded. The process is repeated until three non-coplanar points are selected to define the laser plane relative to the camera.

To triangulate the 3D intersections of the finger and laser, the background subtracted and rectified image is first binarized for connected component analysis. Intersections are clearly visible as elongated ellipsoids which are filtered based on size and shape. Merged connected components (when fingers are close to each other) are separated using the previous seam carving output. The centroid of each connected component is reprojected using the camera intrinsics. From the camera center a ray through the centroid is intersected with the derived laser plane (see Fig. 6B). This defines a 3D point for each finger, relative to the camera.

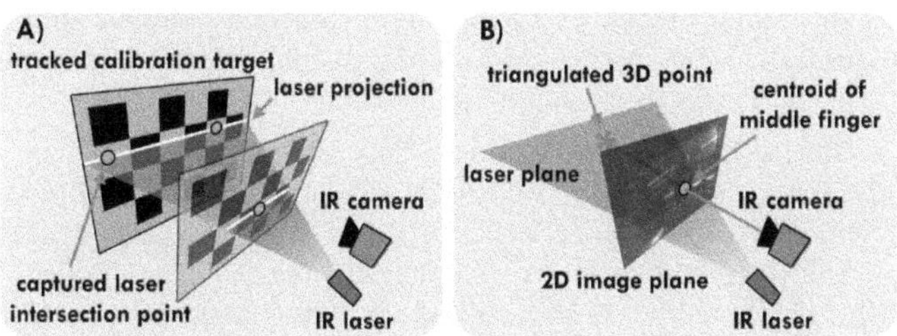

Figure 6: A) Laser plane calibration procedure. B) Reprojected ray intersecting with the laser plane.

A SIMPLE KINEMATIC HAND MODEL

After retrieving the 3D intersections of laser with fingers, we use a new kinematic method to recover the hand pose. Fig. 7 shows the main finger bones and joints in a hand. Each finger is comprised of three bones, namely proximal, middle, and distal phalanges. From fingertip to palm, these bones are interconnected by a 1DoF revolute joint called the distal interphalangeal (DIP) joint, a 1DoF revolute proximal interphalangeal (PIP) joint, and a 2DoF spherical joint called the metacarpophalangeal (MCP) joint [4].

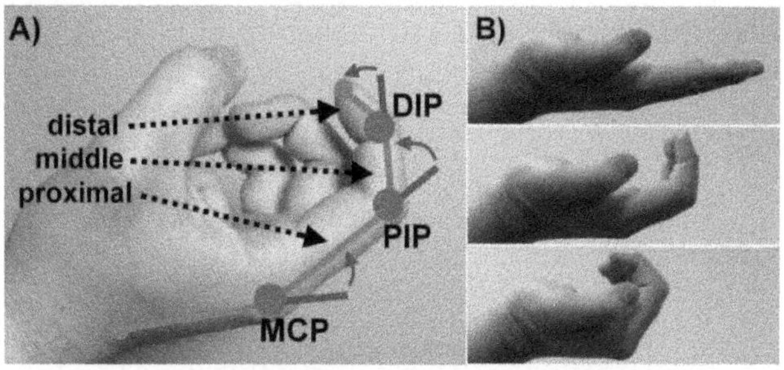

Figure 7: A) Illustration of main finger bones and joints. B) Natural flexing of fingers. Proposed forward kinematics model reconstructs this behavior.

These bones do not move in an entirely independent fashion. Specifically, it has been shown that the DIP joint angle depends on the PIP angle owing to interaction of tendons attached to middle and distal phalanges [4]. Furthermore, as shown experimentally by [16] during natural flex of the finger (i.e. when not explicitly controlling MCP independently of other joints) MCP joint angles depend on the PIP angle when bending the middle and distal phalanges. We leverage the interdependency of these bones and joints to map from sparsely sensed 3D locations on each finger to a 3D articulated model of the hand.

Specifically, during natural flex of each finger (see Fig. 8 Right) a linear relationship exists between all three joints of the finger, such that both MCP and DIP can be derived if the PIP angle is known. Kamper [16] experimentally found the ratio between PIP and DIP is $\frac{1}{0.84}$ and $\frac{1}{0.54}$ for PIP to MCP respectively. Using these ratios, we can approximate a common finger motion, when an outstretched finger curls inwards until it touches the palm, only with a single parameter.

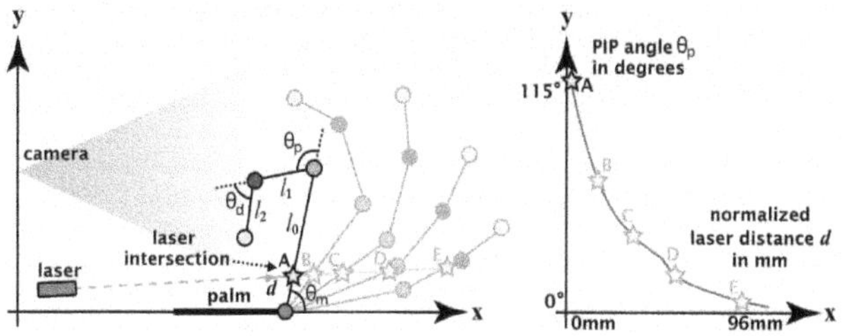

Figure 8: Left: Forward kinematics model for a single finger intersecting with laser line. Right: Graph mapping between laser distance and PIP joint angle.

Calculating joint angles

To determine the articulation of each finger during natural flex, we experimentally derived the mapping between 3D intersection points and the PIP joint angle using a simple forward kinematic model Fig. 8. We simulate each of the bones with predefined lengths (l_0, l_1, l_2 respectively). Average bone lengths can be taken from the literature [4, 16] or measured per user. We compute the PIP angle at simulation time as θ_p $[0°, 120°]$. MCP and DIP are calculated as $\theta_m = a\theta_p$ and $\theta_d = b\theta_p$ respectively where a and b are the joint ratios derived from [16].

During calibration, we also derive the 6DoF pose of the palm with respect to the camera (using a checkerboard placed on the palm), which allows us to determine the offset of the laser and its direction with respect to the palm. We simulate the forward kinematics model by changing the joint angle θ_p. At 0° the finger is outstretched and fully bent at 120°. For each of the angles of θ_p we measure the intersection between the laser ray and each of the bones, and take the minimum distance. The sampled data is plotted in Fig. 8 and used to map from laser distance to θ_p. The graph can be fitted using the following cubic function (where d is the distance to the intersection in mm):

$$\theta_p = -0.0003 * d^3 + 0.059 * d^2 - 4.07 * d + 119.75 \quad (1)$$

As fingers have similar anatomy, it is reasonable to assume that this function is valid for all fingers. We therefore provide a simple one-off online calibration process for each finger, where we plot the principal axis of motion for each finger. New intersections are normalized along this axis. Because we normalize along a 3D line, this approach also works for the thumb which moves more diagonally in the sensor image. While articulated thumb motion is reasonably tracked in practice, results could be further refined by explicitly building a similar model as in Fig. 8 purely for the thumb. Our model can be extended to lateral motions of fingers (i.e. allowing fingers to move left and right), by mapping deviation from the calibrated principal axis to a 3D rotation, which is applied to each finger after articulating finger bend.

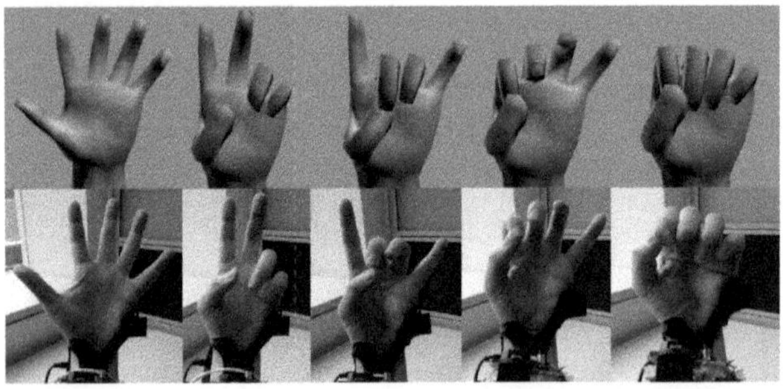

Figure 9: Top: Various hand poses supported by our forward kinematics model. Bottom: User's real hand poses.

Strengths and limitations

This approach provides a simple, but yet natural approximation of hand poses. Fig. 1 and Fig. 9 show a number of real-world hand poses and how these can be replicated using Digits. Whilst the combination of laser line sensing and forward kinematics model is powerful in its own right, there are limitations. In particular, it assumes a strong relationship between all of the joints of each finger. However, there are also common cases where for example the MCP joint moves independently of the PIP. To deal with these wider range of hand poses, we need to sense other parts of the hand and provide an extended kinematics model. Through experimentation we have found that illumination from IR LEDs can be used to robustly detect fingertips, which allows us to define a more complete kinematic model of the hand.

FINGERTIP DETECTION

Despite it being unfeasible to place a full depth camera on the wrist (due to form-factor and power), we demonstrate how to generate high-resolution normal maps and coarse depth estimates, by modeling the light falloff from the LEDs. This provides a robust method for identifying fingertips in the 2D image, even when fingers are directly facing the camera.

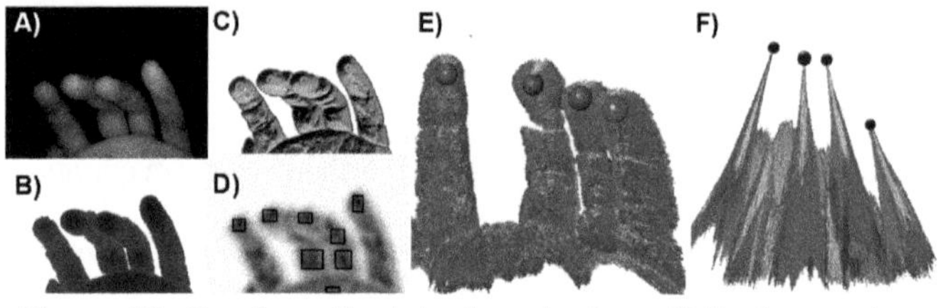

Figure 10: Our fingertip detection pipeline. A) Background subtracted imaged fingers. B) Estimated depth encoded in red color channel. C) Normal map computed from depth map. D) Response map from template matching (darker is closer match), black rectangles mark fingertip candidates. E) Recovered mesh viewed from the physical camera's view. F) Depth distortion visible when viewed from off-center viewpoint. Note the distinct peaks caused by fingertips.

Depth approximation Our approach adapts work on shape-from-shading (SFS) (see overview in [29]). Our scenario makes SFS more tractable, given partially known parameters for (LED) light position, light power and radial intensity falloff, as well as the ability to approximate the skin reflectance model as purely Lambertian (given the typically small angle of incidence between surface and light source [21]).

We first estimate distance measurements for each pixel under the *inverse-square law*. The intensity at distance d is $I = 1/d^2$ solving for d this gives us an initial distance estimate for each pixel u as: $d(u) = \sqrt{I(u)}$. This distance estimate is then attenuated according to the radial falloff in light intensity for pixels further away from the light's central ray. The final distance value is computed as:

$$D(u) = \sqrt{I(u)} * \frac{1}{\cos(\arctan(\frac{(u-pp)}{fl}))}$$

with known principal point pp and focal length fl from camera calibration. This computes a depth map, where each pixel can be reprojected as a 3D point in camera coordinate space. Finally, we compute surface normals for each pixel from adjacent pixels in the depth map (see Fig. 10).

Strengths and Limitations This technique provides only approximated depth values, as pixel intensity depends on many factors beyond distance to the light source and light falloff. In particular, we do not model the shape and material of the imaged 3D surface nor do we take the surface orientation into account. While the resulting depth map looks plausible when viewed from the cameras perspective, distortions and non-linearity of the signal become clearly visible when viewed off-center (Fig. 10F).

However, this approach can be powerful in detecting fingertips and computing a relative depth estimate. Because fingertips are fairly spherical in shape (in particular when pointing towards the camera) they produce a distinct signal as it can be seen clearly in the normal map (Fig. 10C) and the mesh rendering (Fig. 10F). Each fingertip produces a very distinct peak in depth very similar in shape to a Gaussian sphere centered around the finger's most protruding part.

To detect and track these peaks many methods are viable. We have obtained robust results with just simple template matching (based on matching scores as squared distances between a sliding synthetic fingertip template and the live normal map). Fig. 10D-F shows the final result of our technique, reliably detecting fingertip locations. In particular, our technique works for fingertips pointing towards the camera and multiple fingers touching each other, situations in which simple 2D techniques such as peak-and-valley algorithms, or connected component analysis alone would have difficulties.

A NEW KINEMATICS MODEL

Fingertip estimates can be combined with the laser line intersections to recover a more accurate hand model using inverse kinematics (IK). IK typically derives joint angles from the 3D position of the end effector – the fingertip. We do not have an accurate 3D measurement for fingertips, and the 3D point sampled with the laser is not directly associated with the end effector. However, the two sensing modalities can be combined to derive a new IK model enabling separate articulation of the MCP joint and the PIP/DIP joints.

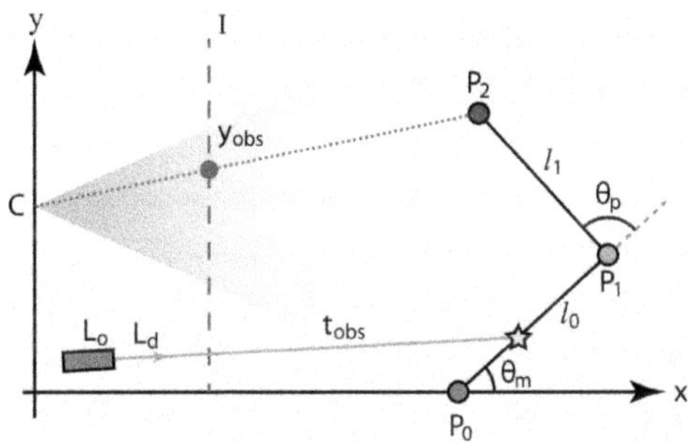

Figure 11: IK model that articulates both the MCP joint and the PIP/DIP joints based on an sensor fusion approach

Fig. 11 illustrates a simplified parametrization of our IK model. Note for illustrative purposes we have reduced the problem to 2D and combined PIP and DIP joints, which cannot be moved independently unless the finger is pressed against a surface. In this parametrization, the palm is again assumed to be resting directly on the X axis. The position of the MCP joint is given by P_0, the position of the PIP joint is P_1 and the end effector is at P_2. Whilst the 3D location of the end effector is not known, we can observe the projection of the point (y_{obs}) on the image plane (I) (as this equates to the centroid of the detected fingertip in the IR image). Given the calibration matrix of the camera, we can project a ray from the camera center (C) through the image plane. We know that P_2 exists somewhere along this ray.

The length of each of the bones (l_0, l_1), of the finger are again assumed to be known, either by measurement or from assuming predefined values. We are solving for the MCP and PIP joint angles given as θ_m and θ_p respectively. We can also parameterize the laser as an offset from the origin (L_o) and direction (L_d). We also have an observed 3D point with distance t_{obs}, sensed from the laser (L_{obs}) which we know intersects one of the bones (the specific bone is unknown).

P_0 is known ahead of time, using the laser line to calculate the minimum 3D extent of each finger (as described previously). This allows us to calculate P_1 by applying a local transform (translation by bone length l_0 and rotation around the joint angle θ_m) to P_0. So that $P_1 = \mathbf{R}(\theta_m) \cdot [l_0, 0]^T + P_0$ and $P_2 = \mathbf{R}(\theta_p) \cdot [l_1, 0]^T + P_1$.

Our aim now is to find the optimal combination of θ_m and θ_p to best describe the observed data (the location of the 2D fingertip sensed using the LEDs and 3D point measured with the laser). For our fingertip location, we define the following energy function:

$$E_{led} = |proj(P_2) - y_{obs}|^2 \tag{2}$$

This function generates estimated positions for P_2 given variations of θ_m and θ_p, and projects these onto the image plane I (using the intrinsic camera calibration parameters). It has a low energy for points that are close to the observed point on the image plane y_{obs}.

Our second energy function first calculates intersections between the laser line and each bone in the finger, based on variations of θ_m and θ_p and takes the minimum:

$$\begin{aligned} t = &\min\{\text{isect}(\overrightarrow{L_0 L_d}, \overline{P_0 P_1}), \\ &\text{isect}(\overrightarrow{L_0 L_d}, \overline{P_1 P_2})\} \end{aligned} \tag{3}$$

It then minimizes the distance between the observed 3D laser point L_{obs} and this estimated intersection:

$$E_{las} = |tL_d + L_o - L_{obs}|^2 \tag{4}$$

Our full energy function is specified as:

$$\arg\min_{\theta_m, \theta_p} E = E_{led}\lambda_{led} + E_{las}\lambda_{las} \tag{5}$$

This allows us to weight the contribution of either the LED or laser based sensing accordingly, using a scalar (λ). In our current implementation, we evaluate this energy function across θ_m $[0°, 100°]$ and θ_p $[0°, 90°]$ in a brute force manner and select the value with the minimum energy.

This new kinematic model give us even higher DoF input sensing. As shown in Fig. 12 a wider range of hand poses can be more accurately predicted from the raw sensor data. This includes a wide range of poses that are difficult to predict using our simpler kinematics model. The combination of the two sensing modalities – both laser line and light falloff – allow us to solve the otherwise ill-posed IK problem.

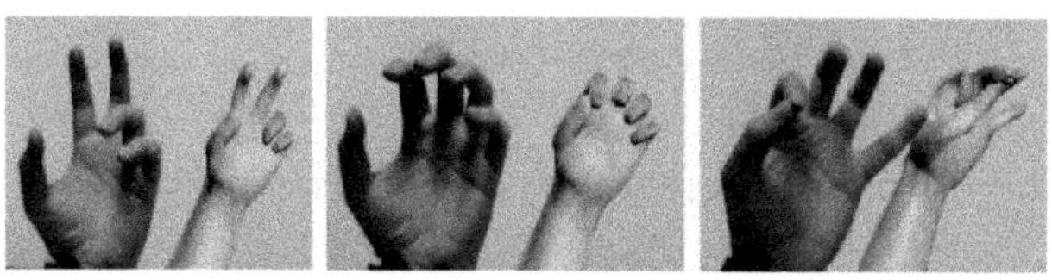

Figure 12: Truer hand pose recovery with inverse kinematics. Note PIP and MCP joint angles recovered correctly.

INITIAL EVALUATION

We performed a preliminary evaluation of Digits, to get a sense of the *accuracy* and *repeatability* of the system at reconstructing different hand poses. Whilst not a detailed user or system evaluation, this study was meant to provide an initial feasibility test for this approach to 3D hand tracking.

Gesture Feasibility Experiment

To provide a first step towards quantifying accuracy and repeatability, we asked participants to mimic hand postures rendered on screen in an interactive 3D application. We used ground truth data gathered using a Vicon motion tracking system as proposed in [23]. Six static hand poses, as shown in Fig. 13, were generated. In the experiment we tested the full IK model described in the previous section.

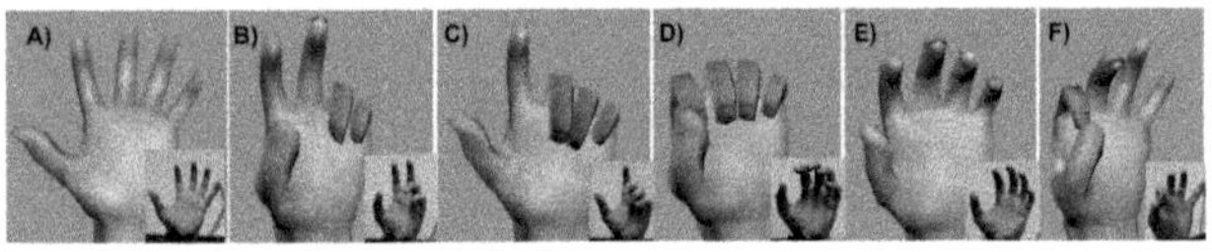

Figure 13: Hand postures in experiment. A) Open palm B) Counting two C) Pointing D) Grasping small object E) Grasping large object F) Pinching.

Participants We recruited 12 participants aged 24 to 39, with a mean age of 32. 10 participants were right handed. None of the participants had any physical disabilities or limited range of motion. Related literature has shown that anthropometric differences in the upper limbs can make comparisons across genders incorrect [6]. Therefore for this first experiment we only tested Digits with male participants.

Procedure and Task The system was mounted on each user's wrist, as in Fig. 13. The system was calibrated for each user's hand (including bone lengths and finger motion range and trajectory). For left handed users, the camera and laser placement was adjusted and a full camera/laser calibration performed. During the study phase participants were presented with the six reference 3D hand configurations on screen (Fig. 13). A second 'live' hand model, driven by the participant's input, was rendered on-top of the reference hand. We ignored wrist and forearm reconstruction in this study (and hence did not use the onboard IMU). Left and right-handed reference postures were selected based on the participant's handedness.

Participants started each trial in a neutral pose (fully closed fist). The experimenter triggered each task. Subsequently a reference pose was rendered on screen and users were asked to align their instrumented hands as closely as possible (labeled as the 'acquisition' phase). Users self-reported once they were satisfied with their pose (by pressing a button with their uninstrumented hand), at which point they were asked to hold the pose for 3 seconds (labeled as the 'static' phase). Each user completed 3 blocks each consisting of 6 trials, which included all the 6 hand postures in random order. Users had 10 minutes training time with the application.

Results and Discussion The mean *acquisition time* was 4074 ms. The first block averaged 4417 ms, second 3981 ms and third 3823 ms. A repeated measures ANOVA reveals that there is a significant main effect for *acquisition time* across blocks ($F_{2,28} = 48, p < 0.01$). Post-hoc analysis (Bonferroni corrected $\frac{\alpha}{n} = \frac{0.05}{3} = 0.0167$) reveals linear improvement between blocks 1 and 2 ($p < 0.01$) but no significant difference between blocks 2 and 3 ($p > 0.35$).

Repeatability As a measure of repeatability we compute intraclass correlation coefficients (ICC), the standard test for repeatability [6, 23, 38] for this kind of time series data. For each of the six poses we computed ICC scores per finger and per joint between the three blocks of repetition (static phase only). We repeatedly selected two blocks randomly. Then for each block a trial was selected randomly and a ICC score was computed between them. This procedure was repeated 40 times to ensure consistency and ICC scores were averaged together. For brevity we only report individual scores for the PIP angles but overall the ICC scores were in the range of 0.6 to 0.97 (moderate to strong correlation). Correlation between repetitions was found to be moderate for little finger ($ICC = 0.66$) and good for thumb ($ICC = 0.74$) to strong for index finger ($ICC = 0.88$), ring finger ($ICC = 0.81$) and middle finger ($ICC = 0.84$). Overall these results suggest that Digits produces moderate to strongly correlated joint-angle measurements when the same pose is repeated multiple times and by multiple participants.

Accuracy To determine accuracy, data was averaged across blocks and participants, keeping joints and gestures separate. Averaging across fingers would not be very meaningful as finger motion is not entirely independent (see discussion on biomechanical constraints earlier). Again for brevity we only report results for PIP bend angles but results for PIP bend and MCP bend and tilt angles are comparable.

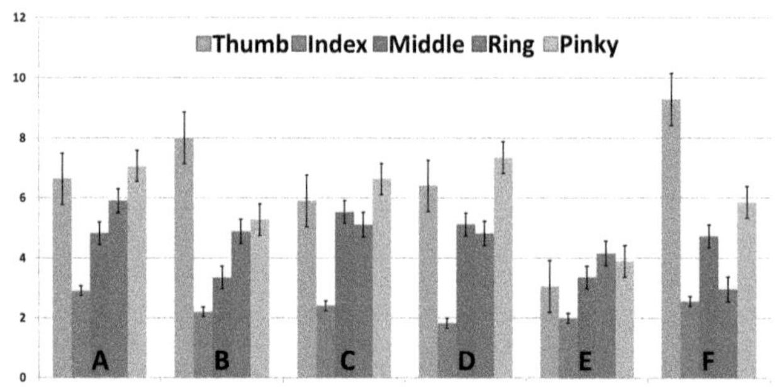

Figure 14: Mean error in PIP joint-angle (in degrees) per finger and for all six gestures. Error bars show std deviation.

Fig. 14 summarizes results for the five fingers and all six gestures. Mean errors throughout the data remain relatively small for all fingers and gestures (all $< 9°$). The best accuracy is usually found with the index finger (min $1.8°$ pose "D", max $2.9°$ pose "A") this could be attributed to the importance of the index finger for many everyday activities (e.g., pointing, pinching, scratching). For most poses the error is largest for the thumb, this maybe explained by the fact that our IK model treats the thumb as a regular finger while in reality the thumb shows a more complex motion (cf. [23]). The mean error for the pinky is also comparatively high (min $3.8°$ pose "E", max $7.3°$ pose "D") this may be explained by the camera placement in our setup – to achieve a compact form factor the camera was moved very close to the palm so that the pinky may not be visible in certain circumstances.

Although preliminary, these overall results are promising.

The achieved accuracy of the tracking and specifically the joint-angle error rates are comparable to those reported in studies on data gloves [6, 38]. Furthermore, the average accuracy (between 2° and 9°) is better than that defined in the literature for manual goniometry (between 7° and 10°) which is considered *"in clinical practice to be the gold standard of joint angle measurement"* [23].

DISCUSSION

Digits is a general purpose wearable 3D hand tracker. It avoids direct instrumentation of the user's hand, but instead is wrist-worn. We have shown how the full 3D pose of the user's hand can be inferred, without requiring high-fidelity and currently impractical hardware such as a depth camera to be worn on the body. The preliminary evaluation of our prototype system demonstrates tracking close to existing data gloves, but without direct instrumentation of the hand.

A tale of two kinematic models In this paper we have introduced two complementary ways to recover 3D pose from a small number of samples on the user's hand. While the different models (based on forward and inverse kinematics respectively) provide different levels of interactive expressiveness they should not be seen as one fully replacing the other. Both have their own strengths and weaknesses and utility in different contexts. Our first model has the advantage of simplicity. It allows reconstruction of rich 3D hand poses from a single measurement on each finger which already enables a number of compelling spatial continuous gestural interactions (Fig. 1 and Fig. 9) and can facilitate gesture recognition in mobile applications. The second model adds higher DOF sensing and more independent movement of each finger joint, and therefore provides more fidelity in recovering the user's hand pose. This model also allows a truer reconstruction of the hand as shown in Fig. 15. This can be useful for example in a physics-enabled application where you wish to model grasping of an arbitrary virtual object or a medical application where accurate joint-angle measurements are needed. We enable this by adding only simple additional hardware, although there is more algorithmic complexity.

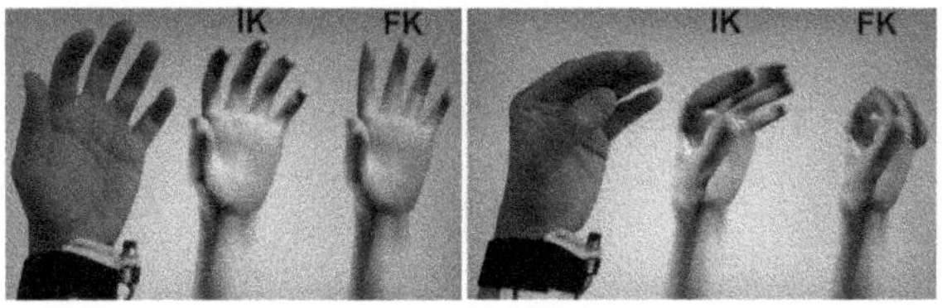

Figure 15: Failure cases for our forward kinematics (FK) model. Notice mismatch in PIP angle (left) and MCP angle (right). Using our inverse kinematics (IK) model we can mitigate such issues, and offer a truer reconstruction.

Limitations With our current implementation being a vision based technique, occlusions resulting from crossed fingers, overly bent thumb and handheld objects are problematic for hand pose reconstruction. However, these are special cases and we anticipate they can be avoided by careful gesture design. Furthermore, more advanced techniques for finger separation and identification could be used to mitigate these issues. In the current Digits prototype we do not model wrist bend and rotations about the forearm explicitly. In particular a fully flat or over-arching hand is problematic, while our image processing techniques can cope better with lateral motion of the hand relative to the camera.

Our proof-of-concept implementation already is wearable and not overly bulky but requires user instrumentation. Furthermore, the device is still tethered to a PC or laptop where computations are being performed. It is however conceivable to further miniaturize the device until it is either a standalone watch-like device or fully integrated into a regular watch. Future depth camera technologies such as time-of flight might enable such compact form factor devices. For the time being we argue that our approach is the best trade-off between practicality and availability concerns but also between computational complexity, power consumption and form-factor.

Always available input It is worthwhile noticing that with Digits input is *not* restricted to a fixed space around the user, but instead moves with the user's hand. For example, gestures can be conducted in front of the body (much like other body-worn systems [10, 24, 33]). However, gestural input may also happen in a more subtle, effortless way. For example, performing hand gestures whilst the hand is lowered by the side of the body or resting on a physical surface, avoiding arm fatigue during long periods of use. Examples of this are shown in the accompanying video figure.

Emergent interactions There are other emergent interactive features of Digits which can be fruitful to explore in future work. For example, Digits may be used to track the spatial positions of fingers from the other (non-instrumented hand) when both hands interact. Using the palm of the reference hand as a track pad, or using the segments of fingers on the reference hand to control sliders in a GUI.

Whilst Digits has been designed to be a general purpose interaction platform, we have demonstrated both in this paper and accompanying video interactive scenarios using this technology. We believe Digits is particularly useful for mobile scenarios, where the sensor can coexist with existing personal devices such as mobile phones and tablets. The combination of touch and 3D input in free space around the device is particularly interesting. Also of interest are eyes-free interfaces which allow for interactions without needing to remove mobile devices from our pockets. One final application area for Digits is in gaming, where technologies such as the Xbox Kinect, or Nintendo Wii do not currently support the level of fidelity of hand sensing. Again such a device could be complimentary to these existing sensing modalities. For example, combining the Kinect full body tracker with high fidelity freehand interactions of Digits.

CONCLUSION

We presented Digits a wrist-worn system for sensing the full 3D pose of the user's hand. The system targets mobile settings, and is specifically designed to be low-power and easily reproducible using only off-the-shelf hardware that is both smaller and more power efficient than current consumer depth cameras. We have shown two complimentary methods for robustly tracking features of the hand, and we demonstrated the evolution of a kinematics model for reconstructing the full articulated hand from these sparse samples. We demonstrated the utility of Digits for a variety of application scenarios, including 3D spatial interaction on mobile phones, eyes-free interaction on the move, and gaming.

REFERENCES

1. Ashbrook, D. L. *Enabling mobile microinteractions*. Phd thesis, Georgia Institute of Technology, 2010.
2. Avidan, S., and A. Shamir. Seam carving for content-aware image resizing. *SIGGRAPH Comput. Graph. 26*, 3 (July 2007), 10.
3. Bailly, G. et al. ShoeSense: A New Perspective on Hand Gestures and Wearable Applications. In *ACM SIGCHI* (2012), 1239–1248.
4. Becker, J. C., and N. V. Thakor. A study of the range of motion of human fingers with application to anthropomorphic designs. *IEEE Trans. Biomed. Eng. 35*, 2 (1988), 110–117.
5. Buxton, B. Multi-touch Systems that I have Known and Loved. Tech. rep., Microsoft Research, 2007.
6. Dipietro, L., A. M. Sabatini, and P. Dario. Evaluation of an instrumented glove for hand-movement acquisition. *Int. J. Rehabil. Res. 40*, 2 (2003), 179–189.
7. Dipietro, L., A. M. Sabatini, and P. Dario. A Survey of Glove-Based Systems and Their Applications. *IEEE Trans. Syst. Man Cybern. Part C Appl. Rev. 38*, 4 (2008), 461–482.
8. Erol, A. et al. Vision-based hand pose estimation: A review. *Comput. Vision Image Understanding 108*, 1-2 (Oct. 2007), 52–73.
9. Gustafson, S., D. Bierwirth, and P. Baudisch. Imaginary interfaces. In *ACM UIST* (2010), 3–12.
10. Harrison, C., H. Benko, and A. D. Wilson. OmniTouch: Wearable Multitouch Interaction Everywhere. In *ACM UIST*, ACM (2011), 441–450.
11. Harrison, C., D. Tan, and D. Morris. Skinput: Appropriating the Body as an Input Surface. *ACM SIGCHI 3*, 8 (2010), 453–462.
12. Hilliges, O. et al. HoloDesk: Direct 3D Interactions with a Situated See-Through Display. In *ACM SIGCHI* (2012), 2421–2430.
13. Howard, B., and S. Howard. Lightglove: Wrist-worn virtual typing and pointing. In *IEEE ISWC* (2001), 172–173.
14. Izadi, S. et al. C-Slate: A Multi-Touch and Object Recognition System for Remote Collaboration using Horizontal Surfaces. In *IEEE TABLETOP* (2007), 3–10.
15. Izadi, S. et al. KinectFusion: Real-time 3D Reconstruction and Interaction Using a Moving Depth Camera. In *ACM UIST* (2011), 559–568.
16. Kamper, D. G., T. George Hornby, and W. Z. Rymer. Extrinsic flexor muscles generate concurrent flexion of all three finger joints. *J. Biomech. 35*, 12 (2002), 1581–1589.
17. Kim, J. et al. The Gesture Watch: A Wireless Contact-free Gesture based Wrist Interface. In *IEEE ISWC* (2007), 1–8.
18. Lee, S. C., B. Li, and T. Starner. AirTouch: Synchronizing In-air Hand Gesture and On-body Tactile Feedback. In *IEEE ISWC* (2011), 3–10.
19. Lee, T., and T. Hollerer. Handy AR: Markerless Inspection of Augmented Reality Objects Using Fingertip Tracking. In *IEEE ISWC* (2007), 1–8.
20. Malik, S. Real-time hand tracking and finger tracking for interaction. Tech. rep., University of Toronto, 2003.
21. Marschner, S. R. et al. Image-Based BRDF Measurement Including Human Skin. In *Eurographics Rendering Workshop*, vol. 5 (1999), 1–15.
22. Mayol-Cuevas, W., B. Tordoff, and D. Murray. On the Choice and Placement of Wearable Vision Sensors. *IEEE Trans. Syst. Man Cybern. Part A Syst. Humans 39*, 2 (Mar. 2009), 414–425.
23. Metcalf, C. et al. Validation and Application of a Computational Model for Wrist and Hand Movements using Surface Markers. *IEEE Trans. Biomed. Eng. 55*, 3 (2008), 1199–1210.
24. Mistry, P., and P. Maes. SixthSense: a wearable gestural interface. In *ACM SIGGRAPH ASIA Sketches*, K. Anjyo, Ed., ACM (2009), 60558.
25. Molyneaux, D. et al. Interactive Environment-Aware Handheld Projectors for Pervasive Computing Spaces. In *Pervasive Computing* (2012), 197–215.
26. Nakatsuma, K., and H. Shinoda. Touch interface on back of the hand. In *ACM SIGGRAPH Emerging Technologies* (2011), 4503.
27. Oikonomidis, I., N. Kyriazis, and A. A. Argyros. Full DOF tracking of a hand interacting with an object by modeling occlusions and physical constraints. In *IEEE ICCV* (Nov. 2011), 2088 – 2095.
28. Pamplona, V. The image-based data glove. In *Symposium on Virtual and Augmented Reality* (2008), 204–211.
29. Prados, E., and O. Faugeras. Shape From Shading. In *Handbook of Mathematical Models in Computer Vision*, N. Paragios, Y. Chen, and O. Faugeras, Eds. Springer, 2006, 375–388.
30. Rekimoto, J. GestureWrist and GesturePad: unobtrusive wearable interaction devices. In *IEEE ISWC*, vol. 5 (2001), 21–27.
31. Romero, J., H. Kjellstrom, and D. Kragic. Hands in action: real-time 3D reconstruction of hands in interaction with objects. In *IEEE ICRA* (2010), 458–463.
32. Saponas, T. S. et al. Enabling always-available input with muscle-computer interfaces. In *ACM UIST*, no. 38 (2009), 167–176.
33. Starner, T. et al. The gesture pendant: a self-illuminating, wearable, infrared computer vision system for home automation control and medical monitoring. In *IEEE ISWC* (2000), 87–94.
34. Starner, T., J. Weaver, and A. Pentland. A wearable computer based American sign language recognizer. In *IEEE ISWC*, vol. 1 of *ISWC '97* (1997), 130–137.
35. Vardy, A. The wristcam as input device. In *IEEE ISWC* (1999), 199 – 202.
36. Villar, N. et al. Mouse 2.0. In *ACM UIST* (New York, New York, USA, Oct. 2009), 33–42.
37. Wang, R. 6D hands: markerless hand-tracking for computer aided design. In *ACM UIST* (2011), 549–558.
38. Wise, S. et al. Evaluation of a fiber optic glove for semi-automated goniometric measurements. *Int. J. Rehabil. Res. 27*, 4 (1990), 411–424.
39. Zhang, Z. A flexible new technique for camera calibration. *IEEE Trans. Pattern Anal. Mach. Intell. 22*, 11 (2000), 1330–1334.

Clui: A Platform for Handles to Rich Objects

Hubert Pham, Justin Mazzola Paluska, Robert C. Miller, and Steve Ward
MIT CSAIL
Cambridge, MA 02139
{hubert, jmp, rcm, ward}@mit.edu

ABSTRACT
On the desktop, users are accustomed to having visible handles to objects that they want to organize, share, or manipulate. Web applications today feature many classes of such objects, like flight itineraries, products for sale, people, recipes, and businesses, but there are no interoperable handles for high-level semantic objects that users can grab. This paper proposes Clui, a platform for exploring a new data type, called a Webit, that provides uniform handles to rich objects. Clui uses plugins to 1) create Webits on existing pages by extracting semantic data from those pages, and 2) augmenting existing sites with drag and drop targets that accept and interpret Webits. Users drag and drop Webits between sites to transfer data, auto-fill search forms, map associated locations, or share Webits with others. Clui enables experimentation with handles to semantic objects and the standards that underlie them.

Author Keywords
Cloud; handles; semantic web

ACM Classification Keywords
H.5.2 Information Interfaces and Presentation: User Interfaces - Graphical user interfaces.

INTRODUCTION
As web applications become more popular, it is important to consider the need for and design of visual handles to rich objects on the cloud. Sophisticated web applications today feature an expanding class of objects that users want to manipulate, like flight itineraries, financial accounts, real estate, restaurants, messages, products for sale, and people. While primitive data types on the web (e.g., text, images, links, and pages) might describe those objects, there are no visual handles to high-level, semantically-rich objects for users to grab. Such handles would enable users to efficiently organize, find, and share structured information. For example, a user looking for flights on AA.com could drag and drop a prospective itinerary to other sites to search for competing flights (e.g., on kayak.com), along with related services, like hotel rooms (e.g., on hotels.com) and car rentals (e.g., on alamo.com). The user could then share that handle to ensure friends are on the same itinerary.

UIST'12, October 7–10, 2012, Cambridge, Massachusetts, USA.

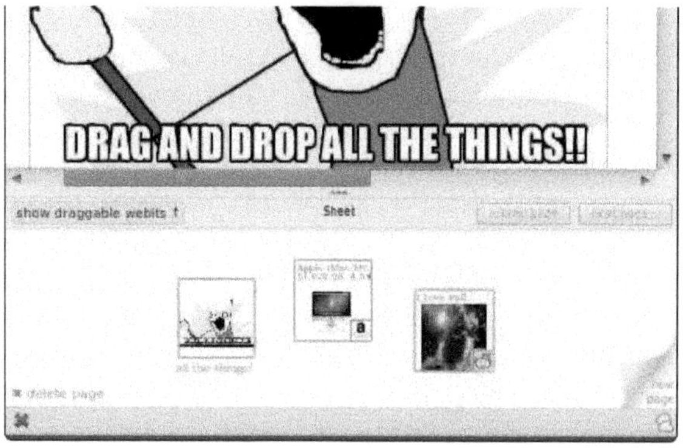

Figure 1. Clui appears as a pane in the browser and is shown here holding several Webits, visual handles to objects on the web.

Without standardized handles to rich data types, each application that requires them must implement its own handles, which invites inconsistency and poses challenges for interoperability across sites. For example, Google Docs features document handles in its document list, which differ from and are not interoperable with Microsoft Office 365's Sharepoint document handles. Similarly, representations of people on Facebook are different from those in GMail. The lack of a generic representation for rich data objects limits what data users may transfer between different web applications; hence, user data tends to remain in silos.

Our hypothesis is that in a web-centric environment, users need a new kind of handle that is generic and designed to represent an evolving set of semantically rich objects. Such handles would 1) enable a simple, direct, and consistent interface for data representation and transfer across the web, and 2) foster new interactions not yet possible with the current web or desktop. For example, handles would allow a user shopping for a tablet device to drag products of interest directly from retailers, like amazon.com or apple.com, to his workspace as he shops, and then drag those products to an online spreadsheet to organize and compare various dimensions (e.g., screen resolution, price, storage size, etc). The user might also drag items to price comparison services. Handles could capture representations of people, allowing a conference program committee chair to drag a paper submission into a group of peers that come from GMail contacts, and then drag that bundle into a conference management system to assign that paper to review to those people. The chair might also drag a group containing all program committee members to a web service that generates a list of names, photos, and affiliations for inclusion in the conference web site.

To explore such interactions, this paper proposes Clui, a platform for experimenting with handles and the workspaces that support them. Clui's primary contributions are:

- an extensible data type, called a *Webit*, that provides uniform handles to rich resources, and
- the Clui platform, a browser extension for experimenting with Webits and Webit-aware workspaces.

In a Clui-enabled system, users interact directly with Webits by dragging and dropping or copying and pasting them to transfer resources between sites. In contrast to typical web URIs, which point to resources, Webits contain an extensible set of associated metadata for the resources they represent. For example, Webits may bundle metadata associated with people (e.g., name, email, address, photo), goods for sale (e.g., price, description, ratings), electronic documents (e.g., authors, title, provenance), and so on.

Clui offers several mechanisms to inject Webit support into existing webpages: 1) by automatically generating them for primitive resources like HTML snippets, links, and images, 2) via a flexible plugin system to augment existing web pages to produce or accept Webits, and 3) through library functions that web developers call to add "native" support for Webits in their web applications.

As a platform, Clui enables experimentation with handles to semantic objects and the data transfer standards that underlie them. In order to test the feasibility and interoperability of Webits, we have built a variety of Clui plugins that augment existing webpages with the ability to generate and consume Webits. We have also built a Webit-aware workspace called Sheets, which appears as a pane below the browser tab, that provides users with a local surface to collect Webits, inspect them, and transfer them between sites (Figure 1).

This paper explores several claims about Webits and verifies those claims by illustration of workflows and examples. The summarized claims are: that Webits can represent a wide range of high-level concepts of interest to users; that they make interaction consistency across sites possible and ease common tasks; and that Webits, with the Clui platform, are easy to create and consume on existing web pages.

The next section is an overview of related work. Following that, we describe Webits in further detail and show various scenarios in which they are useful. We then describe an early, informal user study to obtain a sense of Clui's potential usefulness; that study informs the current design of Clui. Next, we highlight the platform's design and then discuss our experience developing on the platform. We then conclude with future work.

RELATED WORK

Several areas of previous work inspire Clui.

Web Clipping & Scraping

Many web clipping and note taking packages, such as Evernote [3], Microsoft OneNote [9], Zotero [14], list.it [32], and Clipmarks [2], aim to help users organize various snippets of text, images, and references found on the web (or elsewhere). The emphasis of these packages is to provide a digital home for scraps of information [16] as well as tools for their long-term organization and retrieval. Clui differs from these projects by focusing on the use of handles to rich objects, rather than just primitive data types, and by focusing on information transfer instead of organization.

Clui is similar to projects that detect and create structured data in documents and clipboards, like Citrine [29], Apple Data Detectors [27], and Microsoft's Live Clipboard [7]. Clui differs by providing user-visible handles. Data sharing workflows in those projects, like Citrine's ability to paste structured data into forms and spreadsheets, inspire some of Clui's workflows.

Greasemonkey [5] enables users to install JavaScript scripts to alter specific web pages. Clui plugins are similar in that they assumes plugin writers to be expert programmers.

Projects that empower users to clip and scrape structured content from the web typically need to provide interfaces that semi-automate the process of scraping. For example, Dontcheva et al.'s work [18, 17] explores visual techniques that enable users to extract and relate structured content across different sites as a means to summarize and collect information. Fujima et al. [21] explore tools that enable users to construct new interfaces that bridge data between elements clipped from existing pages. Yahoo Pipes [13] provide a similar service that enables users to compose new data flows of content found across the web. Vegemite [25] describes techniques to 1) import web data into spreadsheets via direct manipulation and 2) generate scripts (by observing user action) to run on each row of the data table. d.mix [22] enables developers to obtain code snippets of functionality by clipping representative elements on a webpage. The visual approach of scraping-by-clipping, as proposed in these projects, would improve the development process for Clui plugin authors. The techniques for relating structured content across sites, as discussed in Dontcheva's work, would enable users (or ultimately the system) to merge related Webits found across the web. Techniques reported in Vegemite would be useful for automatically mapping Webit metadata fields to spreadsheet columns.

Piggy Bank [23] scrapes pages open in the user's browser and generates structured data. However, Piggy Bank's aim is to enable users to subsequently browse and query that data within the browser via a Piggy Bank-generated web page. Clui focuses less on allowing users to inspect structured data and more on the interactions for transferring structured data from site to site. Since Piggy Bank is also implemented as a browser extension, it would be fruitful to leverage Piggy Bank as a library within Clui.

Microformat standards [8] enable site authors to embed semantic data within their pages. We imagine that Clui may someday automatically generate Webits on sites with microdata without requiring plugins for those pages.

Desktop Studies

A few common themes emerge from many studies on the traditional desktop, e.g., Malone's in 1983 [26], Barreau and Nardi's in 1995 [15], Ravasio et al. in 2004 [28], and Katifori et al. in 2008 [24]. Barreau and Nardi first observed that users place three types of information on the desktop: ephemeral, working, and archival. The studies agree that the desktop is commonly used for temporary storage, such as a staging area for downloads or uploads, and as a device for reminding users of impending tasks. They also agree that archiving resources (e.g., to tidy the desktop) is difficult because doing so involves classifying each resource, a cognitively difficult task. As such, users tend to put off archiving, leading to desktop clutter. All studies agree that users naturally arrange desktop icons in meaningful, spatial arrangements, such as clustering similarly themed resources together, to aid efficient retrieval. These studies suggested that Clui's initial workspace prototype should borrow from the spatial elements of the desktop.

While studies like these should certainly inform the design of Webit-aware workspaces, we believe that there are some notable differences between traditional desktops and workspaces for Webits. For example, in web-centric workflows (as envisioned by browser-only OSes, like Chromium OS [1]), data scraps not only come from the web but also ultimately return there (e.g., by posts to blogs, tweets, or services that curate and organize content). This suggests that local workspaces for Webits might need to prioritize temporary management rather than long-term retrieval.

Web Authorization Protocols

Cross-site authorization protocols, such as OAuth 2.0 [10], provide mechanisms to enable users to share data between sites. Such protocols rely on site operators to set up pathways between each other before users can transfer data; as such, inter-vendor pathways are likely to be limited in number and driven by business incentives. From the user's perspective, the use of these protocols suffers drawbacks in visibility. For example, when users are prompted to share their data with some external service, they must typically agree to share whole classes of the data (e.g., all their contacts, photos, emails) rather than specific items. Once they agree, there is usually little visibility to alert the user when data is transferred, as it occurs out-of-band, directly between the vendors' systems. In contrast, Clui enables a vendor-neutral approach in which users have fine grained control of the data they wish to share through direct manipulation.

USER INTERFACE

This section overviews Webits, outlines the interaction model that they offer, and describes several scenario workflows.

A Webit is a user-manipulable handle to a collection of rich objects on the web. A Webit bundles properties about the objects that it represents. For example, Webits can provide handles to people, capturing names, contact information, addresses, and so on. Webits can also provide handles to places, like restaurants (bundling addresses, ratings, menus, hours of operation) or apartments for rent (bundling the monthly rent, address, photographs). A Webit may contain other Webits, so a flight itinerary Webit might contain a set of Webits to provide handles to passengers, the flight segments, and the origin and destination cities, while a Webit that represents a trip might embed flight itinerary Webits as well as Webits for hotel and car reservations. The set of objects that Webits may represent is extensible by leveraging existing semantic web technologies to express and interpret object metadata.

User Interaction Model

All Webit workflows in Clui involve three fundamental operations: discovering Webits on a web page, manipulating Webits in a local workspace, and transferring Webits back to the web. Webits appear as icons that, when clicked, reveal a panel containing metadata properties that describe the Webit. Users typically interact with Webits by dragging them from web pages into a temporary workspace and then dragging them to (other) web applications to share the information contained within the Webits. Workspaces are pluggable, and we designed a simple one, called Sheets. Sheets features a chronological notebook (or scrapbook) metaphor, without collections or hierarchy.

Users discover Webits in one of two ways. A web page may explicitly expose Webits to the user, e.g., as a Webit icon to be dragged. Alternatively, the web page may embed Webits inside other draggable elements, such as a picture of a product. To aid discoverability, Clui visually highlights available Webits on command. Clui also displays tooltips during drags to help the user predict the outcome of a drop.

To enhance the consistency of Webit actions across web sites, Clui provides three interface features:

Graceful Degradation Dragging a Webit to a web page results in the Webit being uploaded in its entirety, without loss of information. For example, when dragging Webits to rich-text input boxes, e.g. GMail's message composition window or a Google Docs document, Clui pastes the same iconic representation of the Webit the user dragged and embeds all of the associated metadata, so that it may be dragged by other users (e.g., when they see the Webit in a received email message).

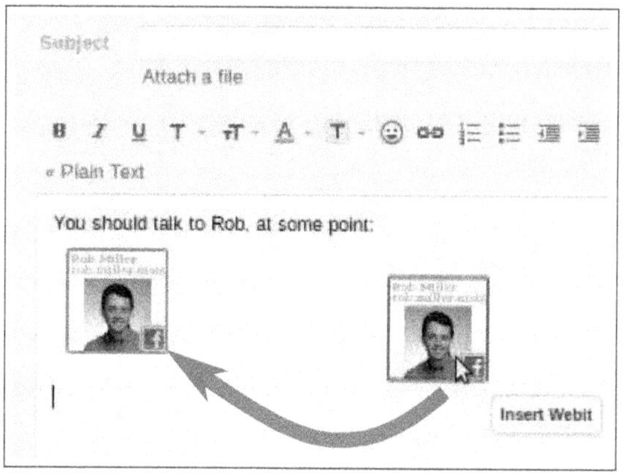

When it is not possible to represent Webits as icons, e.g., when pasting a Webit into a plain-text input box, Clui pastes a short description of the Webit as well as a globally dereferenceable identifier for that Webit.

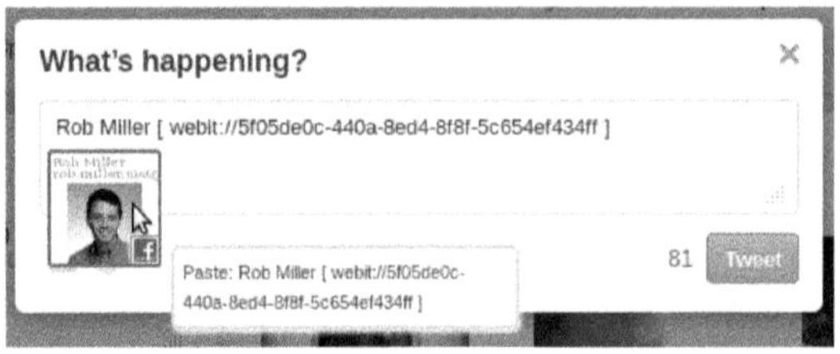

When the data is rendered later (e.g., in this example, as a tweet), Clui restores the iconic version of the Webit (Figure 4) by dereferencing the Webit's identifier.

Customizable Drop Behavior Clui enables web applications or plugins to modify the default drop behavior and provides hooks so that those apps may specify tooltips to describe the altered behavior. For example, when dragging a Webit representing a person onto the "To" field of an email composition form, Clui pastes the person's email address rather than the person's name.

Webit Metadata Transparency A Webit combines many attributes that describe the represented object. Users may override what is pasted by inspecting the Webit's metadata panel and dragging the desired piece of metadata. For example, the user may paste a friend's homepage URI by dragging the "Homepage" field in the metadata panel.

These three features play key roles in user workflows, shown in the example scenarios below.

Scenario 1: Finding An Apartment

Jack is looking for a new apartment and roommates. He searches sites like craigslist.org for potential leads. A plugin generates a Webit on each page that represents an apartment, capturing metadata like the cost of the monthly rent, the location of the apartment, the landlord's contact information, and the description of the property (Figure 2). To keep track of a promising apartment, he drags the apartment's Webit into his Clui workspace. After collecting a few candidate apartments, Jack drags the Webits to Google Maps, which, with the help

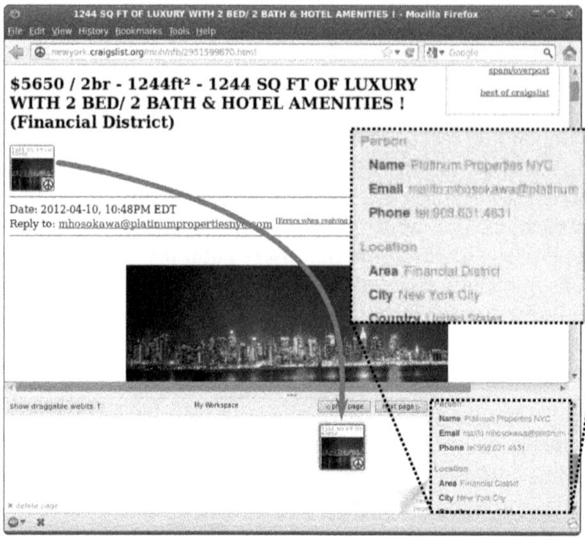

Figure 2. A Craigslist plugin generates an inline Webit to represent the apartment for rent. The Webit contains embedded Webits that represent the contact person and location of the apartment, as shown in the inset.

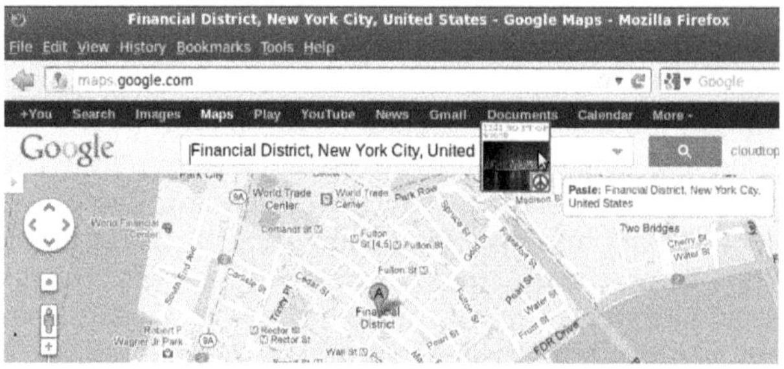

Figure 3. Dragging a Webit to Google Maps maps the location data present within that Webit.

of an installed Google Maps plugin that parses dropped Webits for locations to search, maps the locations of the apartments he likes (Figure 3). When he chooses the apartment in the best location, Jack composes an email to the landlord. Rather than typing the address, Jack drops the apartment's Webit onto the "To" field, which pastes the email address of the landlord. Finally, Jack advertises for roommates by sharing the Webit with his friends over email, Facebook, and Twitter. While the Twitter input box for tweets only accepts plain-text, Clui pastes enough context such that those who view the tweets will see an inline, draggable Webit (Figure 4), assuming they have Clui installed.

Scenario 2: Organizing a Reading Group

Sarah organizes a weekly reading group. She selects papers from the ACM Digital Library (DL) and emails a group member of her choosing to lead the discussion. To obtain contact details, Sarah opens the discussant's Facebook profile page. Pages on Facebook may contain many possible Webits embedded in existing elements; she presses the Clui "Show Webits" button, as shown in Figure 7 to visually highlight the elements that have associated Webits. After finding the appropriate colleague, she drags in the picture of the discussant to Clui.

Figure 4. Even though some services, like Twitter, accept and store only plain-text input, they can still embed Webits with dereferenceable Webit identifiers. Clui can later re-create interactive Webits in the viewer's browser.

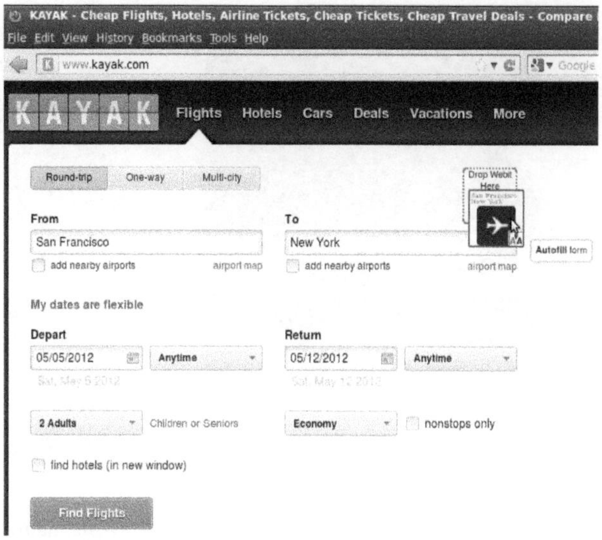

Figure 5. Dragging Webits onto a form auto-fills its inputs. Here, a Kayak.com plugin inspect the metadata in an itinerary Webit and maps it to form elements.

Next, Sarah opens the ACM DL page for the paper up for discussion to gather its bibliographic information, abstract, PDF, and so on. Sarah drags just the image thumbnail for the paper, which represents a Webit containing all the metadata for that paper, including a cache of the PDF file. Figure 6 shows the resulting Webit and some of the metadata captured by the ACM plugin.

Sarah opens GMail to send the paper details to the discussant and other participants. Sarah may drag the Webit that represents the paper directly into the message body to share the paper and all of its metadata. However, to provide context, she pastes a copy of the abstract by dragging the "Abstract" item in the metadata panel into the email.

In both of the scenarios above, Webits improve efficiency in several ways. Bundling relevant bits of information into one handle alleviates the need for users to manually parse, copy, and paste those bits from site to site. Sharing Webits keeps that information intact for the recipient. Plugins that customize the behavior of Webits when dropped in various contexts can scan for and paste the relevant data types, without requiring the user to hunt for that information.

Scenario 3: Booking a Trip

Mary is shopping for flights. She first visits AA.com and enters the origin and destination airports, along with the relevant dates. After perusing several options, she finds an itinerary that is potentially satisfactory, but she still wants to comparison shop in case there are cheaper alternatives. The AA.com plugin generates a Webit that represents her candidate itinerary, so before leaving AA.com, she drags that Webit to her Clui workspace.

Mary opens kayak.com to find alternative flights. Rather than re-enter the airports and dates, she drags the Webit from AA.com into the kayak.com form, which auto-fills the relevant fields with the help of a kayak.com Webit plugin (Figure 5). In contrast to browser auto-fill features that fill already-visited forms with values cached from previous submissions, Webits enable users to auto-fill forms with new values as well as auto-fill never-before-seen forms.

Scenario 4: Shopping

Previous scenarios illustrate the use of plugins to enable existing pages to create and process Webits. This scenario illustrates an example of a web application that natively consumes and generates Webits.

Jim is shopping for camera equipment to start a new photography business with a business partner. As Jim shops various vendors, e.g., amazon.com and newegg.com, he drags Webits of products, produced either natively or with the help of Clui plugins, from these vendors into his Clui workspace. To share his selections with his partner, Jim uses a shared shopping cart service, which is independent of any vendor. The shopping cart natively understands Webits; when he drags Webits to the page, it displays and can sort relevant parameters for each product, as shown in Figure 8, along with product descriptions, as shown in Figure 9.

When done, Jim clicks a button to generate a Webit that represents the cart, housing the individual Webits within. Jim shares that Webit with his partner, who may inspect and purchase the cart.

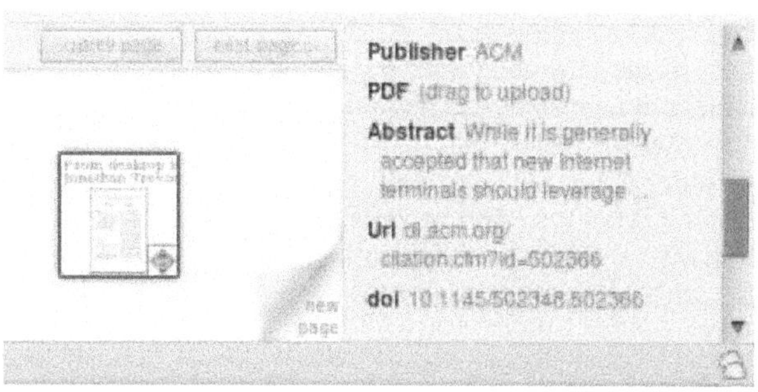

Figure 6. Webits capture metadata that may be dragged and dropped.

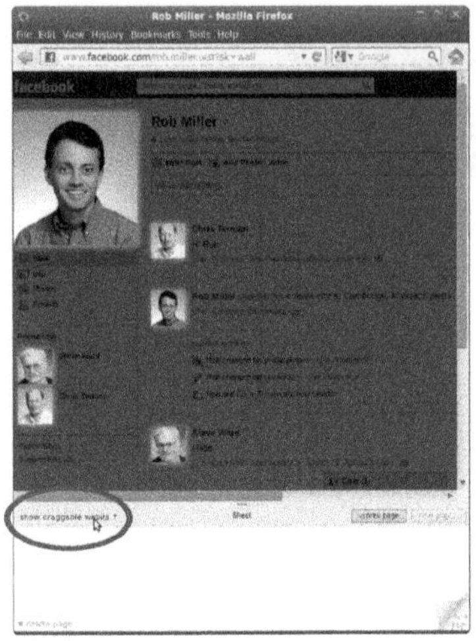

Figure 7. The "Show Webits" button helps users discover Webits that are embedded in existing page elements.

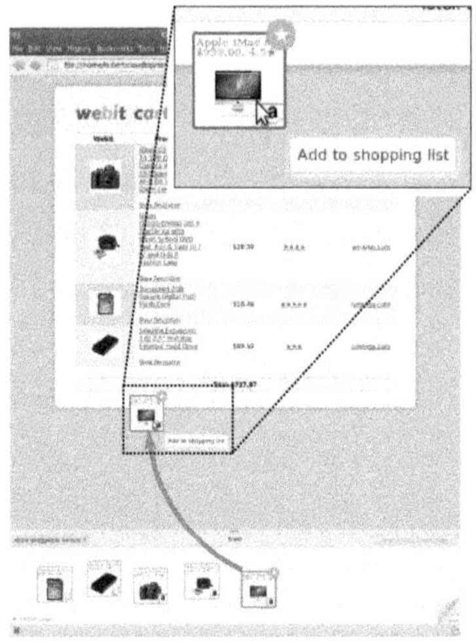

Figure 8. The "Webit Cart" understands Webits natively; thus, it can directly extract Webit data and change tooltips.

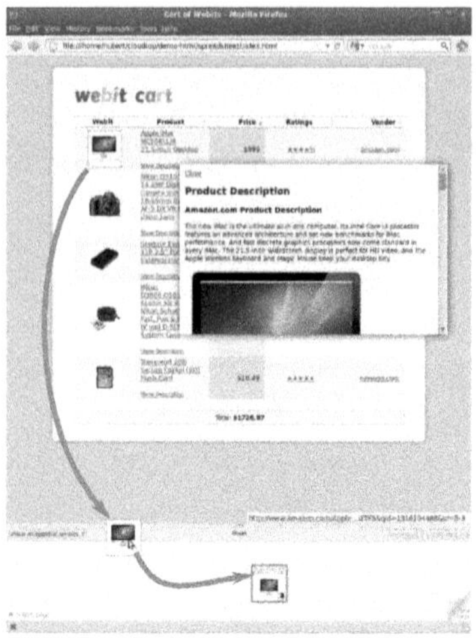

Figure 9. Since the "Webit Cart" understands Webits natively, it can also render information embedded in the Webits.

PRELIMINARY STUDY

We designed Clui using an iterative process. First, we built a simple prototype called Vapor that supports the drag and drop of only text, links, and images. We ran a pilot user study using Vapor to gain feedback on what kinds of interactions users expect when dragging and dropping web resources. We discovered that users of Vapor needed handles to rich data types rather than just primitive ones, informing our design of the Clui platform.

Vapor Prototype and User Study

Vapor displays a drag-and-drop zone like Sheets. Vapor creates primitive Webits that capture the resource (i.e., a text snippet, link, or image) and two pieces of provenance metadata: the URL of the item (for images and links) and the URL of the page containing the item.

We conducted an informal pilot study, consisting of seven volunteers within our university computer science laboratory, to get a general sense of how users may use Vapor in typical workflows. After demonstrating features of Vapor in a brief tutorial, we asked each subject to carry out an early version of the "reading group" scenario using Vapor and observed their usage.

User Feedback

In the reading group task, participants needed to compose an email with paper abstracts and titles, gathered from non-adjacent text snippets on ACM Portal pages, along with the URI of the relevant Portal pages. Some participants immediately dragged abstract and title snippets from the page into Vapor, while others habitually relied on using the operating system clipboard, repeatedly switching back and forth between GMail and the Portal page. Ultimately, subjects who initially used the clipboard realized that they could use Vapor to gather all the information first and proceeded to do so.

Every subject successfully completed the tasks without material intervention or help. In their feedback, participants believed that Vapor would work well for their daily workflows, especially tasks that involved gathering resources first, followed by an aggregation or synthesis process. Participants noted that Vapor alleviated the need to repeatedly context-switch between browser tabs, as a clipboard-based workflow necessitates. Subjects also noted that they especially liked the visible nature of Vapor, and likened it to a powerful cross between a desktop and clipboard.

All subjects noted that spatial element of Vapor was important, and often clustered related Webits into groups, reinforcing earlier findings [15, 28]. Many participants noted that they enjoyed the "freedom" that Vapor affords, especially for collecting and "quickly organizing" (spatially) different information scraps throughout a task. Subjects approved of the fact that Vapor was part of the browser, instead of being in the area behind the browser (like the traditional desktop), with some citing quicker access and constant visibility. However, subjects did resize the visible area of Vapor (to make it larger or smaller). Some suggested that they might keep a separate browser window open, dedicated to displaying Vapor full-screen, while others preferred Vapor to be more "integrated" with and customized to the current, active tab.

Vapor often needs to upload resources to the web, which introduces variable network delays into user operations. We observed that users expect drag and drop operations to be "instant"; without adequate feedback (e.g., the status of the file upload process when users dragged a file into GMail), some users were confused when nothing appeared to happen immediately. This observation hinted that general visibility was an important requirement to address.

Design of Clui

Vapor's primitive Webits do not capture extensible metadata, so unlike the Clui reading group scenario in the previous section, in Vapor users must manually drag individual snippets of text. This observation suggested that users actually need more than just an easier way to collect web snippets; they also need a way to access and transfer objects with all of the associated metadata bundled. The need to collect related information inspires the current design of Clui Webits as handles for rich semantic objects.

ARCHITECTURE

Clui is composed of three components: the core platform, plugins, and the workspace (Figure 10). The core provides common library code, notably for storage and rendering of Webits, and coordinates data flow between plugins and the workspace. Workspaces (e.g., Sheets) implement the user-facing interface and are pluggable. Only one workspace may be active at a time. There are two types of plugins. *Web plugins* add Webits to existing web pages by scraping those pages for metadata. They also augment drop targets on web pages with functionality to accept and parse dropped Webits. *Presentation plugins* translate classes of Webit metadata into user-friendly representations in the metadata panel. Any number of plugins may be in use at any given time. The core is the only fixed component of Clui, but it is relatively small. Workspaces and plugins may evolve independently.

The Clui core reacts to two main types of events: browser page load events and user import events. When a page loads, the browser sends Clui a page load event which causes the core platform to call the onPageLoad(document) function of each relevant Web plugin. The plugin's onPageLoad implementation modifies the page to facilitate drag and drop and information scraping. onPageLoad may optionally return a context object which is used to enable scraping of asynchronously loaded content.

Users import data into the Clui workspace by dragging it in from the web or copying it to the clipboard. Clui also creates Webits to represent downloaded files, which may be later dragged to the web to upload the associated files. When users import resources into Clui, the browser sends an event to the core platform, which forwards the event to the workspace, allowing the workspace to either handle or filter the event. If the workspace accepts the import, it asks the core to create a Webit from the event. In response, the core allocates storage for the new Webit object, assigns the Webit an identifier, and calls the appropriate import function on all relevant Web plugins. For example, for dropped resources, the core calls the onDrop(objectId, event, context) function on each plugin, passing in the Webit's identifier, the drop event, and any context the plugin returned in its onPageLoad function.

The remainder of this section elaborates Clui's use of the HTML5 Drag and Drop API, the internal representation of Webits, the plugins architecture, and system limitations.

HTML5 Drag and Drop

The primary way in which Clui interacts with web pages is through the HTML5 Drag and Drop API [6]. The API specifies a set of events to track and handle drags (using dragstart, dragenter, and dragleave events) and drops (drop events). All drag and drop events carry a DataTransfer structure that contains a list of MIME-typed representations for the item being dragged. For example, the DataTransfer for a text snippet holds a text/html representation containing an HTML string as well as a text/plain one containing the string without markup.

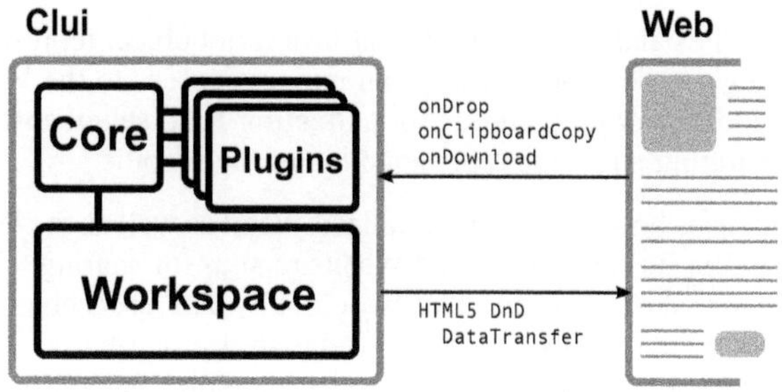

Figure 10. Components of and dataflow between Clui and the web.

Web pages and browser extensions may add their own custom MIME types to the DataTransfer. During the lifetime of a single drag and drop gesture, all associated drag and drop events share the same DataTransfer object, allowing handlers fired on drag events to populate the DataTransfer with data that is consumed by drop handlers. In the context of Clui, when a page loads, a Web plugin's onPageLoad function adds drag event handlers to draggable elements. These handlers augment the DataTransfer object with new Clui-specific MIME types that represent Webit metadata. On a drop into the Clui workspace, those additional MIME types are then interpreted by plugins' onDrop handlers to append the metadata to the Webit.

Webits

Clui represents a Webit as an immutable collection containing a Webit UUID, a representation of the Webit's user-facing icon, the Webit's metadata, and browser-specific metadata (like default DataTransfer MIME types to embed).

Webits leverage existing semantic web technologies, like established vocabularies, ontologies, and the Resource Description Framework (RDF) [12], to express and interpret metadata for the objects they represent. Vocabularies and ontologies are extensible, so Webits, in principle, can describe anything for which a vocabulary exists or can be defined. Webits embed metadata by encoding it as RDF/JSON [11], enabling sites receiving Webits to immediately interpret those statements without additional dereferencing.

A system like Clui only works when sites can interpret Webit metadata—that is, if sites understand a common vocabulary and associated semantics for a given resource. Establishing a standard for each resource type takes time and experimentation. However, Webits can embed multiple descriptions, using different vocabularies, each contributed by different plugins, thus increasing the chance that a website will understand one of the descriptions. In providing a user interface handle that abstracts away representations of semantic data, Webits offer an adoption path that enables vocabulary experimentation while supporting interoperability.

Clui provides JavaScript library support for 1) developers who wish to add native Webit support to their websites, and 2) plugin authors who wish to add functionality to websites that they do not control. There are two concrete representations of Webits: an internal JavaScript object representation, used within plugin and website JavaScript code, and an external JSON-serialized representation, used as the wire-format (embedded in the DataTransfer) for transferring Webits between web sites and Clui. The internal JavaScript object representation gives developers full programmatic access to the Webit, including helper methods for extracting RDF statements and generating an iconic representation of the Webit.

Clui uses both the JSON-serialized Webit as well as the Webit identifier to reliably upload Webits to sites for sharing. In order to make the Webit identifier globally dereferencable, Clui uploads the JSON-serialized Webit to a cloud-based Webit sharing service; the sharing service identifies the Webit with a URI of the form webit://UUID. When users drop Webits onto conventional form elements as a means to share those Webits (e.g., in a new email or blog post composition), Clui first attempts to display an iconic representation of the Webit in the target element when possible, and embed the JSON-serialized representation in a manner invisible to the user. For example, when dropping Webits onto a GMail message body that the user is composing, Clui inserts HTML that renders the iconic representation of the Webit and embeds its associated serialized data inside an HTML attribute. When displaying Webits inline on page elements is impossible (e.g., inside plain-text boxes), Clui pastes a human-readable representation of the Webit, along with a dereferencable link to the stored Webit.

When Clui encounters a Webit on a website, it first attempts to read the associated JSON-serialization, if an embedded one exists. If that succeeds, Clui regenerates the Webit icon and makes it draggable. Otherwise, Clui searches for the associated webit:// identifier and dereferences it for rendering.

Web Plugins

Web Plugins fulfill two roles: they 1) augment pages when those pages are loaded, e.g., to implement specialized behavior for Webits dropped onto targets, and 2) generate RDF metadata for new Webits, typically by page scraping. Web plugins declare regular expressions on URIs to indicate the web pages that they are able to handle.

Plugins generally augment or scrape data on web pages by operating on known DOM elements, e.g., by using XPaths. Typically, plugin authors would use a web debugger to select relevant DOM elements and obtain the associated XPaths.

Plugins must wait for elements to load before augmenting or scraping them. Operating on static web pages, in which all elements are loaded before the DOM load event fires, is straightforward: plugins inspect, augment, or scrape the page in their onPageLoad function. However, many sites load content asynchronously or in response to user action. As an extreme example, when loading certain GMail or Facebook pages, the browser may execute JavaScript that programmatically builds the document asynchronously. In such cases, the browser fires the load event once the bare DOM loads, prompting the onPageLoad functions to execute, even though the user-facing page has not fully loaded.

Clui provides hooks to handle changes to document title or location URI (through the onTitleChange and onLocationChange plugin functions), as web pages that lazily construct whole documents typically change the document title and add fragment identifiers to the current location URI once page construction completes. One caveat is that plugins need to gracefully handle spurious title changes. When this technique fails, e.g. due to pages that do not modify the title or URI, plugins can handle asynchronously loaded resources by responding to DOMSubtreeModified events or by polling.

Plugins that scrape or augment DOM elements are inherently brittle and prone to breaking as sites change. While tools that feature visual techniques for clipping and scraping (e.g., [17, 18]) may help ease the development burden of updating plugins, the most resilient approach is for web authors to directly publish semantic data. Web site authors may use the Clui API to create Webits and specify the semantic data in RDF/JSON. In the future, we imagine that web site authors could instead just embed microdata within their pages, from which Clui could automatically generate Webits.

Presentation Plugins

Presentation plugins interpret RDF statements and generate user-visible handles to the metadata. Each Presentation plugin handles a specific class of metadata, e.g., people, products, provenance, or location, and produces a set of key/value pairs shown to the user, e.g., in the metadata panel of Clui's workspace. Unlike Web plugins, which are site-specific, Presentation plugins work with metadata from any site as long as it matches the plugin's RDF vocabularies. In practice, this allows multiple Presentation plugins to extract metadata from a single Webit, enabling the extraction of (e.g.) location and contact information from a single set of RDF statements.

Limitations

When sharing Webits, Clui preserves the information by embedding it inside the drop site, but when that is not possible, Clui must paste a webit://UUID pointer and upload the Webit to a sharing service. One potential limitation is scalability of the sharing service, although existing services (e.g., pastebin.com) already provide Internet-scale pastebins for text and photos.

Another concern is the security and privacy associated with uploading Webits to such services. Currently, nothing prevents unauthorized access to uploaded Webits, though that could be addressed by storing Webits on personal storage servers with adequate access control. Additionally, Webits may contain sensitive information that is opaque or hidden to users. For example, a Webit representing a purchased flight itinerary might contain Webits for credit card accounts and billing addresses. A user that shares the itinerary Webit with colleagues (or on a blog) may be unaware that he is also sharing sensitive data. Future work must address this limitation, e.g., by improving the visibility of embedded Webits.

Webits on web pages currently do not degrade gracefully for users without Clui installed. Those users either see an icon that they cannot drag or a webit://UUID link they cannot dereference. One improvement is to use a dereferencable URI that conventional browsers can load (e.g., http://clui-project.org/webit/UUID). That URI could load a web page that displays a user-friendly description of the Webit and an invitation to install Clui.

Web Plugin	LoC	Comments
facebook.js	390	Scrape. *Async.* Background fetch of email address.
amazon.js	323	Scrape.
craigslist.js	317	Scrape and Augment (to add Webit icon).
acmdl.js	306	Scrape. *Async.* Background fetch of associated PDFs and EndNote bibliographic data.
provenance.js	288	Scrape.
newegg.js	285	Scrape.
reddit.js	275	Scrape. Save permalink of entries and background fetch of linked pictures.
aa.js	218	Scrape.
tooltip.js	199	Augment (general tooltip implementation).
gmail.js	188	Augment (to specially handle Webits dropped in To/Cc/Bcc fields). *Async.*
kayak.js	183	Augment (to add Webit drop zone to autofill form).
gmaps.js	118	Augment (to extract location data from Webits).
webit_uri.js	62	Augment (to display Webits inline).
twitter.js	49	Augment (to display Webits in Tweets).
gdocs.js	30	Augment (to override tooltips). *Async.*

Table 1. Properties of Web plugins. Entries labeled *Async* indicate sites that load asynchronously. LoC means lines of code.

To inspect a Webit's metadata, users currently must drag the Webit to the workspace first. Future work will enable users to inspect metadata inline on web pages containing Webits.

EXPERIENCES WITH CLUI

We implemented Clui as a cross-platform browser extension for Mozilla Firefox. As a browser extension, Clui can thus 1) appear as a central component available in all browser tabs and windows and 2) intercept user interactions with web page elements. We evaluate Clui's flexibility by reporting on our experience developing plugins to create Webits on various sites. Table 1 lists our Web plugins and Table 2 our Presentation plugins.

Provenance Plugin

One way we evaluated Clui's flexibility is by how much functionality is implementable as plugins rather than as built-in code to the core platform. One feature of Vapor, the initial prototype, is that it automatically captures provenance of resources (e.g., the URI of the resource and the URI of the page containing that resource) dragged into the workspace. A plugin-based implementation of provenance capture, as opposed to being a fixed component in Clui's core, enables the feature to evolve independently. Our plugin captures provenance by inspecting the dropped DOM element and the associated `document` object.

Tooltips Plugin

Another example of implementing "core" functionality in plugins is the tooltips feature that displays previews of pasted data. The tooltip plugin modifies web pages to add user-visible DOM nodes that function as tooltips. When the plugin is called to handle a new loaded web page, it augments various standard drop targets (e.g., HTML input boxes, text-areas, file upload zones) to display the appropriate tooltips when the user hovers over each respective target.

Presentation Plugin	LoC	Typical Metadata
publication.js	65	Title, Authors, Journal, doi
product.js	58	Vendor, Price, Ratings
realestate.js	56	Rent, Size, Number of Bedrooms
provenance.js	54	URL, Context, Snippet Text
person.js	45	Name, Email, Homepage, Phone Number
itinerary.js	44	Origin, Destination, Dates, Travelers
social_bookmark.js	37	Comments, Permalink
location.js	35	Area, City, Country

Table 2. Properties of Presentation plugins, including the typical metadata that they parse. LoC means lines of code.

The tooltips plugin also demonstrates communication between plugins, as other plugins (and web pages) must be able to override the default preview text. For example, when dragging Webits representing people over GMail's input boxes for specifying message recipients, the Clui GMail plugin overrides the tooltip preview text to display the associated email addresses.

Background Loading: Facebook, Reddit, & ACM Plugins

For additional flexibility, plugins may also obtain data from pages other than the page with the Webit. Clui provides routines to make network requests in the background, as well as higher-level routines that load other webpages (in an invisible iframe) and return the associated DOM nodes. This enables plugins to follow links on the loaded page, invoke API calls on web services, or even load other pages for scraping.

For example, when users drop a person's thumbnail from Facebook into Clui, the Facebook plugin must attempt to obtain that person's email address, even if it is not displayed on the current page. The Facebook plugin inspects the URI of any page associated with the person, extracts the person's Facebook numeric ID, and scrapes contact information from the associated profile page fetched in the background. Another example is the Reddit plugin, which targets the social news site; the plugin detects news items that are pictures and automatically fetches the high resolution images. Finally, with the ACM Digital Library (DL), scraping bibliographic data is trivial given a paper's EndNote file, which is not initially visible on the DL page. The ACM DL plugin downloads and parses the EndNote file to create Webits.

Asynchrony: GMail and Facebook Plugins

Several sites load resources asynchronously, e.g., GMail and Facebook. The plugins for those sites use the `onTitleChange` hook to detect when the page contents change dynamically, prompting them to inspect the DOM to, e.g., find form elements and override tooltips. As Table 1 suggests, implementation effort is independent of asynchrony but instead is commensurate with the complexity of scraping.

Data Interoperability and Presentation

When users drag a Webit representing a person from Facebook to a recipient field in GMail, the GMail plugin overrides default behavior and pastes the person's email address. The GMail plugin inspects Webits dropped into various fields and must infer whether those Webits represent people. To promote data interoperability, the Facebook and GMail plugins respectively produce and interpret metadata adhering to the RDF Friend-of-a-Friend [4] specification, which defines a standard vocabulary for describing people.

Presentation plugins (Table 2) demonstrate another example of interoperability. Though Webits may originate from different sources and embed multiple Webits, Presentation plugins can each interpret the parts of Webits that it understands. For instance, the products plugin interprets Webits that come from different vendors, like amazon.com and newegg.com. Similarly, the real estate, person, and location plugins parse metadata relevant to each in apartment Webits.

CONCLUSION AND FUTURE WORK

This paper introduces the Clui platform and Webits as interoperable handles to high-level semantic objects on the web, like real estate, flight itineraries, and products. Clui features plugins for creating and interpreting Webits on existing web pages, as well libraries for web site developers to add native Webit support.

Natural extensions for Clui include Webits that represent live information (e.g., stock prices or weather), visual tools for plugin authors, and site-agnostic plugins that interpret microdata. We also hypothesize that having handles to semantic objects enables new interactions. For example, a user might purchase the contents of a shopping cart Webit filled with product Webits by dragging it to a web application that accepts Webit carts and Webits representing locations for the shipping address. The application could then inspect the Webits and use APIs exported by individual retailers to purchase the associated products. Such interactions need not be limited to web pages, but may occur directly on local, Webit-aware workspaces. For example, in addition to holding Webits, workspaces could also provide handles to actions that operate on specific kinds of Webits. A "purchase" action, when applied to product Webits, could prompt for additional Webits to complete the transaction.

Clui is an apt platform for future work in exploring new workspace models that manage Webits. For example, with Clui, we imagine it possible to adapt conventional interfaces, like the traditional desktop area, file system model, or even command line interface, for use with resources in the cloud. However, we suspect that the cloud demands alternative workspace models, such as ones that promote sharing (e.g., [19, 30, 33]) or capture user context to aid resource finding (e.g., [20, 31]). Furthermore, Webits and their workspaces might also provide new approaches for improving consistency in common tasks, like access control specification, which sites today each handle differently. Webit-aware workspaces could bridge those differences; for example, workspaces could consistently represent access control lists on different sites as a Webit containing people Webits, which users manipulate to affect a resource's access.

The cloud's arrival as a dominant application platform demands new user interfaces that leverage its advantages. Clui enables experimentation with handles to semantic objects and the standards that underlie them. We view Clui as a step towards future web environments that offer greater interface uniformity via consistent and interoperable handles.

ACKNOWLEDGMENTS

This work is sponsored by the T-Party Project, a joint research program between MIT and Quanta Computer Inc., Taiwan.

REFERENCES

1. Chromium OS. http://www.chromium.org/chromium-os.
2. Clipmarks :: Add-ons for firefox. https://addons.mozilla.org/en-US/firefox/addon/clipmarks/.
3. Evernote. http://www.evernote.com/.
4. The friend of a friend project. http://www.foaf-project.org/.
5. Greasemonkey. https://addons.mozilla.org/addon/greasemonkey/.
6. HTML5 drag and drop. http://www.w3.org/TR/html5/dnd.html.
7. Live clipboard - wiring the web. http://liveclipboard.org/.
8. Microdata — HTML standard. http://www.whatwg.org/specs/web-apps/current-work/multipage/microdata.html#microdata.
9. Microsoft OneNote 2010. http://office.microsoft.com/en-us/onenote/.
10. OAuth 2.0. http://oauth.net/2/.
11. RDF JSON. http://docs.api.talis.com/platform-api/output-types/rdf-json.
12. RDF/XML syntax specification (Revised). http://www.w3.org/TR/rdf-syntax-grammar/.
13. Yahoo pipes: Rewire the web. http://pipes.yahoo.com/pipes/.
14. Zotero. http://www.zotero.org/.
15. Barreau, D., and Nardi, B. A. Finding and reminding: file organization from the desktop. *ACM SIGCHI Bulletin* (July 1995).
16. Bernstein, M., Van Kleek, M., Karger, D., and schraefel, m. c. Information scraps: How and why information eludes our personal information management tools. *ACM TOIS* (2008).
17. Dontcheva, M., Drucker, S. M., Salesin, D., and Cohen, M. F. Relations, cards, and search templates: user-guided web data integration and layout. In *ACM UIST* (2007).
18. Dontcheva, M., Drucker, S. M., Wade, G., Salesin, D., and Cohen, M. F. Summarizing personal web browsing sessions. In *ACM UIST* (2006).
19. Fass, A., Forlizzi, J., and Pausch, R. MessyDesk and MessyBoard. In *ACM DIS* (2002).
20. Freeman, E., and Gelernter, D. Lifestreams: a storage model for personal data. *ACM SIGMOD Record* (1996).
21. Fujima, J., Lunzer, A., Hornbæk, K., and Tanaka, Y. Clip, connect, clone: combining application elements to build custom interfaces for information access. In *ACM UIST* (2004).

22. Hartmann, B., Wu, L., Collins, K., and Klemmer, S. R. Programming by a sample: rapidly creating web applications with d.mix. In *ACM UIST* (2007).

23. Huynh, D., Mazzocchi, S., and Karger, D. Piggy bank: Experience the semantic web inside your web browser. *Web Semantics: Science, Services and Agents on the World Wide Web* (Mar. 2007).

24. Katifori, A., Lepouras, G., Dix, A., and Kamaruddin, A. Evaluating the significance of the desktop area in everyday computer use. In *ACHI* (2008).

25. Lin, J., Wong, J., Nichols, J., Cypher, A., and Lau, T. A. End-user programming of mashups with vegemite. In *ACM IUI* (2009).

26. Malone, T. W. How do people organize their desks?: Implications for the design of office information systems. *ACM TOIS* (1983).

27. Nardi, B. A., Miller, J. R., and Wright, D. J. Collaborative, programmable intelligent agents. *Commun. ACM* (Mar. 1998).

28. Ravasio, P., Schär, S. G., and Krueger, H. In pursuit of desktop evolution: User problems and practices with modern desktop systems. *ACM TOCHI* (June 2004).

29. Stylos, J., Myers, B. A., and Faulring, A. Citrine: providing intelligent copy-and-paste. In *ACM UIST* (2004).

30. Sun, Y., and Greenberg, S. Places for lightweight group meetings. In *ACM GROUP* (2010).

31. Van Kleek, M., Bernstein, M., Karger, D. R., and schraefel, m. c. Gui — phooey!: the case for text input. In *ACM UIST* (2007).

32. Van Kleek, M., Bernstein, M., Panovich, K., Vargas, G. G., Karger, D. R., and schraefel, m. c. Note to self: examining personal information keeping in a lightweight note-taking tool. In *ACM CHI* (2009).

33. Voida, S., Edwards, W. K., Newman, M. W., Grinter, R. E., and Ducheneaut, N. Share and share alike: exploring the user interface affordances of file sharing. In *ACM CHI* (2006).

DejaVu: Integrated Support for Developing Interactive Camera-Based Programs

Jun Kato[1,2], Sean McDirmid[1], Xiang Cao[1]

[1]Microsoft Research Asia
Beijing, China
{smcdirm, xiangc}@microsoft.com

[2]The University of Tokyo
Tokyo, Japan
jun.kato@acm.org

ABSTRACT

The increasing popularity of interactive camera-based programs highlights the inadequacies of conventional IDEs in developing these programs given their distinctive attributes and workflows. We present DejaVu, an IDE enhancement that eases the development of these programs by enabling programmers to visually and continuously monitor program data in consistency with the frame-based pipeline of computer-vision programs; and to easily record, review, and reprocess temporal data to iteratively improve the processing of non-reproducible camera input. DejaVu was positively received by three experienced programmers of interactive camera-based programs in our preliminary user trial.

Author Keywords

Computer vision; development environment.

ACM Classification Keywords

H.5.2 [Information interfaces and presentation]: User Interfaces - Graphical user interfaces.

INTRODUCTION

Interactive systems beyond desktop computers and mouse/keyboard input continue to increase in popularity, where users can use their hand, body, or passive physical objects to interact with computing devices. At the heart of many these interactive systems are cameras used to capture input from the real world that is then interpreted in real-time by computer vision algorithms. For example, cameras are used to recognize hand gestures on tabletops [29] and in the air [25], detect human faces [28], track tangible implements [3], as well as monitor crowd activity [15]. Moreover, developing these computer-vision-based interactions has become easier through commercial products such as Microsoft Kinect (which performs body skeleton tracking through a depth camera), as well as software development kits (SDK) of well encapsulated algorithms.

However, despite the increasing accessibility of camera hardware and computer vision algorithms, today's development environments do not cater to the distinctive challenges and workflows of developing interactive camera-based programs. For example, the programmer has to monitor data in the debugger as discrete textual values rather than continuous visual representations that more accurately reflect interactive computer vision data. Such disconnects illustrate the gulf of execution [22] as a gap between the programmer's goal and the available means to execute it. As a result, programmers can still find it difficult to develop such programs even if they possess good computer vision knowledge.

To close this gap, we present DejaVu that enhances conventional integrated development environments (IDE) to better support the development of camera-based interactive programs. This work differs from lower-level computer vision algorithm libraries such as OpenCV [2], or rapid prototyping tools for camera-based applications such as Crayons [7] and EyePatch [16] that are aimed at making certain computer vision techniques accessible to non-programmers through a special user interface. Instead our high-level rationale is similar to Gestalt [23], a general-purpose development environment for machine-learning applications, in that we focus on facilitating a general workflow for current developers of interactive camera-based programs without limiting them to certain algorithms or dramatically changing their programming habits. DejaVu aspires to minimize workflow overhead and draw computer vision programmers closer to the essence of their program. More specifically, DejaVu includes two interlinked main components (Figure 1): a *canvas* to visually and continuously monitor the inputs, intermediate results, and outputs of computer vision processing; and a *timeline* to record, review, and reprocess the above program data in a temporal fashion.

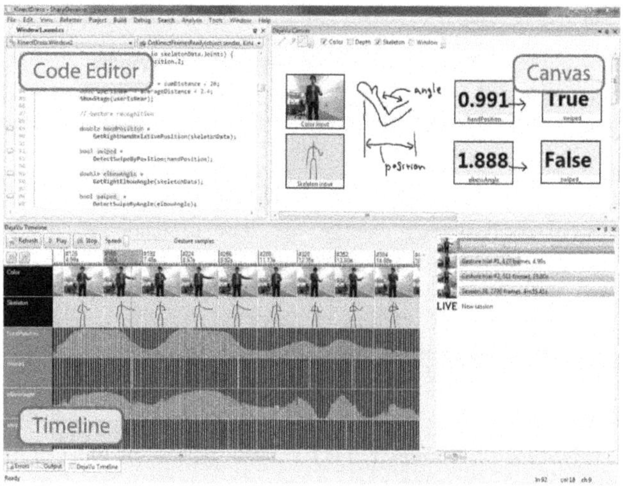

Figure 1: DejaVu Interface.

UIST'12, October 7–10, 2012, Cambridge, Massachusetts, USA.

INTERACTIVE CAMERA-BASED PROGRAMS

To help introduce DejaVu, we first explain how today's IDEs fall short in supporting the development of interactive camera-based programs. This knowledge was obtained both through our own experience (two authors were deeply experienced in developing such programs) and informal interviews with three similarly experienced developers. We first introduce a simple example application named KinectDress to familiarize readers with interactive camera-based program basics, and then elaborate on challenges in their development using today's environments.

A Representative Example

KinectDress (Figure 2a) is a simple virtual dressing room application built with the Microsoft Kinect camera, which provides one color (RGB) image stream and one depth image stream (of which pixel values correspond to distances from the camera). The Microsoft Kinect SDK further uses these inputs to compute a body skeleton of the user in front of the camera, consisting of 3D coordinates of 20 body joints. With KinectDress, users can see themselves dressed in various virtual suits on the computer screen. To start interacting with KinectDress, the user simply walks within a certain distance in front of the camera (Figure 2b). The user's image is dynamically extracted from the surrounding environment and displayed on a virtual background, and overlaid with a suit that follows the user's position as they walk around (Figure 2c). The user can also make a swiping hand gesture to cycle through a list of available suits to wear (Figure 2d).

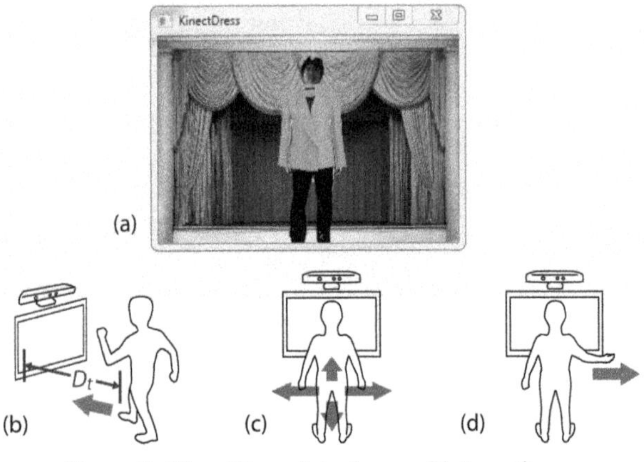

Figure 2: KinectDress interface and interactions.

We carefully designed KinectDress to represent key patterns of general camera-based interactive programs in several aspects:

Interactions. KinectDress includes both the case where the system continuously changes its state in response to the user's current state (e.g., the suit follows the user's body) and the case where the user makes an action to be recognized by the system in order to trigger a command (e.g., a swiping gesture to change their suit). Most camera-based interactions can be categorized into these two main categories.

Program Architecture. KinectDress is typical of most real-time camera-based systems in that the camera is the sole or primary source of input, i.e., the camera "drives" the program. This requires the program to capture and process image frames continuously, hence dictates a frame-based loop architecture. Figure 3 illustrates this classic architecture used in KinectDress. Each iteration of the loop starts with the camera capturing the next frame, followed by the pipeline that processes the frame and updates the system's logical and graphical state accordingly.

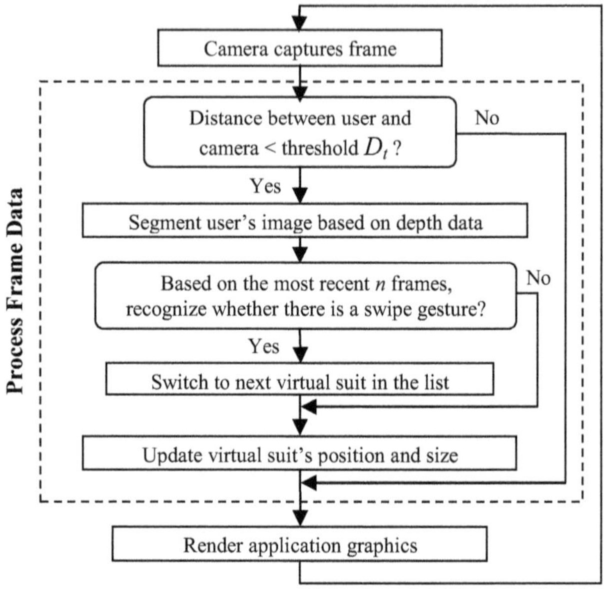

Figure 3: KinectDress program flow.

Processing Paradigms and Components. KinectDress includes both stateless processing that depends only on the current frame (e.g., updating the suit position) and stateful processing that accumulates data over a number of recent frames (e.g., recognizing swipe gestures); both are common in interactive computer vision programs. KinectDress also demonstrates several of the most common processing components in camera-based interaction such as image segmentation, geometric transformation, and heuristic gesture recognition (Figure 3). Finally, KinectDress illustrates how color, depth, and skeleton data are processed in combination as common in Kinect programming.

Attributes and Challenges

Several fundamental attributes of interactive camera-based programs pose challenges for development with today's environments:

First, computer vision processing is inherently *visual*: not only is the raw camera input a stream of image frames (or several streams in the case of stereo or depth cameras), but many of the intermediate processing results are also images (e.g., segmented user image in KinectDress), or have a close geometric correspondence with the input images (e.g., body skeletons) and so are best understood visually. In this respect, today's development environments disregard the visual nature of this data and display their textual value, falling short of the programmer's needs. To ease development, computer vision programmers often write temporary code to visualize some of this data themselves in the application user interface, which is both cumbersome and not scalable.

Second, the inputs of most camera-based interactive applications are *continuous*: the program constantly receives and processes real-time input from the camera, updating intermediate results and final outcomes on a frame-by-frame basis. Such processing continues even when no user actions are occurring, e.g., KinectDress constantly monitors whether there is a user within a certain range. In addition, many user actions, especially gestures, do not happen at a single point in time but rather span multiple contiguous frames. However, today's development environments are usually designed to trace discrete user input events, and programmers cannot directly inspect the temporally continuous dataflow of camera-based programs. For example, debugging using breakpoints can be problematic since they inevitably interrupt the temporal continuity of live input.

Third, camera-based input is mostly *non-reproducible*: input is formed by dynamically observing the real world and often human behavior. Compared to mouse-and-keyboard programs where the programmer can easily reproduce a certain input sequence (even through an automated script) to test them, the dependency on dynamic real world input in camera-based interactions means that it is not only cumbersome but also often impossible to reproduce certain input. For example, a human user can never perform the same action, such as KinectDress's swiping gesture, twice precisely the same way. Other factors such as lighting, environment setup, and even noise in the camera sensor, may also result in different inputs and cause different outcomes. Such non-reproducibility poses a serious obstacle to testing and tuning interactive computer vision programs in today's IDEs.

Finally, developing computer vision programs is often an *iterative* process. The stochastic nature of camera input from the real world along with the somewhat obscure nature of many computer vision algorithms means that predicting the exact outcome of a certain computer vision algorithm is often difficult. Furthermore, given the complexity of real world input, the correctness or quality of a computer vision program's output is often up to the programmer's subjective judgment (e.g., whether a suit's position and size matches the user's body in KinectDress). For these reasons, computer vision programmers more often "tune" an algorithm rather than "debug" it. As a result, developing computer vision programs often involves a great deal of trial-and-error with real world input, such as revising the algorithm, adjusting its parameters (e.g., distance threshold D_t in Figure 3), or comparing multiple variations of the algorithm to find configurations that yield satisfactory behavior. In some cases, this process needs to be repeated when the system is used in a new environment or for a new user group. The need to repeatedly acquire dynamic real world input makes such iterations and comparisons cumbersome and unreliable.

DEJAVU

DejaVu enhances an IDE to reflect the visual and temporally continuous nature of interactive camera-based programs, and to accommodate non-reproducible real world input as well as an iterative development processes. DejaVu is prototyped as an extension to SharpDevelop [26], which is a general-purpose open-source IDE for Microsoft .NET development. DejaVu preserves the full flexibility of the development platforms and patterns developers currently use to write interactive camera-based programs. The only assumption made is that the program follows the previously mentioned canonical frame-based loop architecture where all input and output are synchronized to frames - we do not readily support multi-threaded asynchronous programs, which are nonetheless highly uncommon in real-time camera-based interactions. Without loss of generality, the prototype currently interfaces with a Kinect camera (which may also be used as a regular RGB camera), while extending support for other camera types is straightforward. The DejaVu interface (Figure 1) consists of two tightly interlinked components: the *canvas* and the *timeline*.

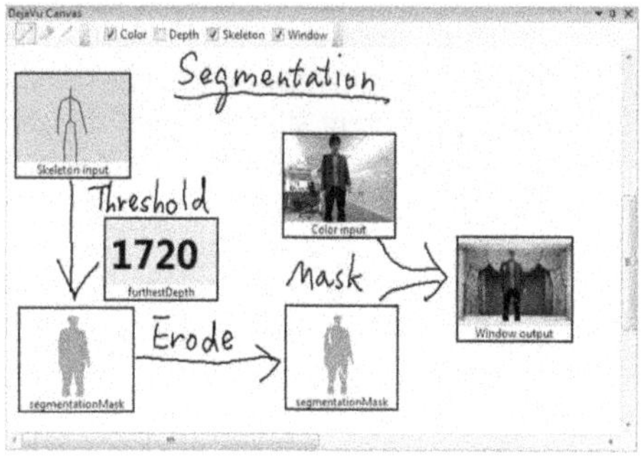

Figure 4: DejaVu Canvas.

DejaVu Canvas

Reflecting the continuous and visual nature of camera input and processing, the canvas (Figure 4) allows the programmer to continuously monitor any number of variables during run-time in an arbitrary layout. For data types that are inherently visual (most notably image and body skeleton), the variable values are automatically shown in their appropriate visual form. To add a variable to monitor, the programmer simply selects it in the code editor and drags it onto the canvas. A display box representing the variable value then appears as labeled by the variable name, which can be freely repositioned through dragging, or deleted when no longer needed. In addition to variables, available types of input from the camera (in the case of Kinect: color, depth, and skeleton) as well as the rendered application window can be inserted into the canvas via a checkbox. The above actions together allow the programmer to monitor any input, intermediate result, or output of the program.

The canvas always reflects variable values at the current frame of interest (FOI). When the program is running with live input from the camera, this is simply the latest frame that has just been captured and processed. Unlike conventional debug watch tables in which the variable values are only updated when the program reaches a break, the canvas is constantly updated at every new frame so the values can be continuously monitored in real time. When the program is not running with live input, the FOI is dependent on the cursor position in the timeline as explained in the next section. In the case that a variable in the canvas has an undefined value in the FOI (e.g., the variable is declared within a conditional branch that is not reached), its display is blank.

The canvas is updated at the granularity of a frame to reflect the frame-based nature of interactive computer vision processing. However, there may be cases where a variable is assigned to values multiple times during the processing of a single frame, which often happens when the programmer applies an image processing filter (e.g., Gaussian blur filter) or transformation (e.g., transforming between color spaces) to an image *in place*, i.e., the result is assigned to the same variable that represents the source image. The canvas maintains a record of not only a variable's name but the source position in the code editor where it was dragged from, and inspects the variable's value just after it is evaluated at that position. In doing so, the programmer can monitor a variable's value at a specific stage in the processing pipeline, or even simultaneously monitor its values at different stages within the same frame by adding the variable to the canvas several times from different positions (Figure 5).

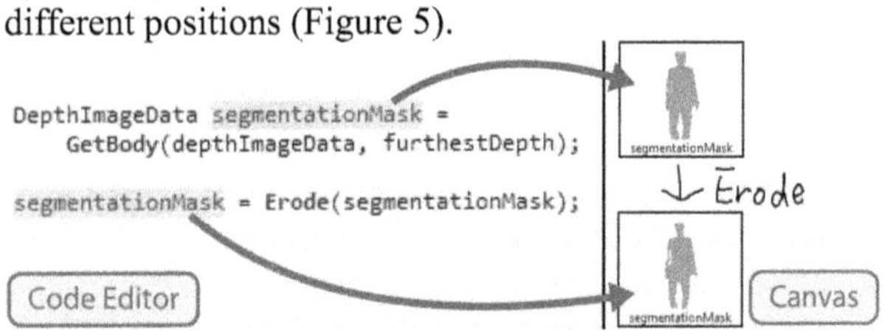

Figure 5: Variable values in the canvas depend on their source positions in the code editor.

Along with displaying variables, the canvas also allows the programmer to freely write or draw on it using a stylus or a mouse to further aid in the thought process of handling visual data. In addition to the obvious use for annotating variables, freehand drawing enables other powerful use cases: by combining static sketches such as algorithm flowcharts with data displays, the programmer can turn the canvas into a "dynamic sketchbook" where sketches come to life with dynamic data. The programmer can then inspect the program dataflow and pipeline on a higher semantic level, providing a more vivid way of conceptualizing and iterating on algorithms. On the other hand, in contrast to visual dataflow authoring tools such as Max/MSP [17], this usage remains lightweight and flexible, and does not dictate literal correspondence between the sketch and program. Alternatively, the programmer may make a coarse sketch of their application UI on the canvas and populate it with data displays to use it as a low-fidelity interactive prototype in lieu of the actual application user interface, which is reminiscent of research on sketch-based prototyping [14].

DejaVu Timeline

The timeline (Figure 6) presents program data recorded or recalculated from historical program sessions. A list of all available program sessions is shown to the right of the timeline as horizontal bars, with their visual length proportional to their temporal duration. Program data in the currently selected session is visualized in the timeline in a style similar to that found in common video editing software such as Windows Movie Maker, where a cursor indicates the current FOI in the timeline. The timeline may consist of multiple data streams (rows), each corresponding to a variable, input, or output that is displayed on the canvas. Streams of visual data are represented as strips of frame thumbnails along the timeline, while a stream of numerical or Boolean data is visualized as a time-graph.

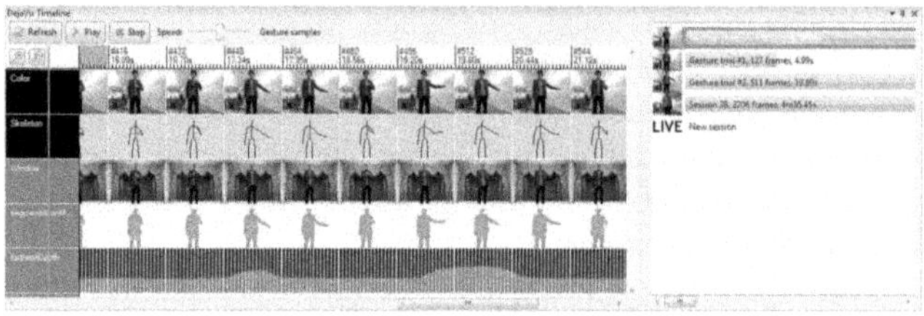

Figure 6: DejaVu Timeline.

The programmer may either review past sessions, or start a live session by running the program with live camera input. DejaVu employs a unified notion of "playing" the session for both cases. To start a live session, the programmer selects the "Live" icon at the bottom of the session list, and clicks the "Play" button. All variables shown on the canvas, along with all available types of live camera input and the rendered application window (regardless of whether they are being monitored on the canvas) are recorded and time-stamped as the program runs. The timeline is populated in the meantime. To stop program execution, the programmer clicks the "Stop" button, and the live session is finished and added to the list of past sessions. Note that the programmer does not need to explicitly trigger program data recording, which happens automatically whenever the program is running live so there is never a risk of missing valuable data or moments.

To review a past session, the programmer selects it from the session list to show it in the timeline. They can then either freely navigate the cursor to an arbitrary frame by clicking on it, or replay the session continuously from the cursor position using the "Play" button. Playing by default happens at the same speed as the original live program, i.e., "real-time", but can also be sped up or slowed down according to the programmer's needs using a slider. When the current session finishes playing, the next session in the list is automatically selected and starts playing. In any case, the canvas always updates and displays the recorded data in the current FOI. When replaying, the recorded application window output is also shown in a separate window, emulating the live program execution experience. An existing session may be duplicated, split into two at any given point, repositioned in the list, or deleted to allow trimming and reorganizing the sessions.

The ability to visually review both past sessions and recent live input in the timeline with all relevant program data addresses the non-reproducibility challenge of interactive camera-based input, and eases the identification and analysis of noteworthy events. The seamless transition between live input and reviewing also allows for the fast recognition and examination of events. When the programmer notices some anomaly while testing with live input, they can immediately switch to reviewing the session to deeply analyze it.

The power of the timeline lies beyond passive review, and in the ability to revise the program and refresh program data by reprocessing recorded input streams, which naturally serves the iterative development process of interactive camera-based programs. After revising their program, the programmer clicks the "Refresh" button so the program is re-executed in the background to recalculate the monitored variable values for all existing sessions in sequence. Sessions and frames are colored green when they are refreshed and ready for reviewing; those yet to be refreshed are colored gray. The refresh functionality allows the programmer to reliably examine the effect of their program revision by comparing to previous outcomes on the exact same input. Finally, the programmer can add variables to the canvas which have not been recorded previously; the sessions will be refreshed to include the new data streams in their timelines.

Example Use Case

We now use the previously described KinectDress application to concretely illustrate how DejaVu can be used by programmers in their workflow.

The programmer's first challenge is to fine tune the distance threshold D_t that determines how close the user should be in front of the camera to trigger the interaction (the program starts displaying the virtual stage to reflect this). Today's programmers usually need to go back and forth several times between adjusting the parameter on the computer, and standing up and walking towards the camera to test the effect until finally satisfied – a very cumbersome and tiring process. With DejaVu (Figure 7), the programmer can add the *userDistance* variable (calculated as the average depth of all body skeleton joints) to the canvas, and monitor its value on the computer screen as they walk from afar towards the camera (only once). When they reach a comfortable distance, they can read the current *userDistance* value on the screen (displayed in a big font for readability from afar), and use this value as a hint for setting the threshold.

Alternatively, the programmer can raise a hand to indicate that they are at a comfortable distance, which is easy to visually identify in the color input stream. Later they can iteratively adjust the threshold in the program code and refresh program data, so that the starting moment of the virtual stage (as seen in the application window stream) aligns with the indication action (as seen in the color input stream) in the timeline.

The programmer next needs to extract the user's image from the color input. This segmentation algorithm involves first finding the farthest point among the skeleton joints whose depth value is then used to threshold the depth input image. The resulting binary mask is applied to the color input to segment the user from the surrounding environment. The programmer can use freehand sketch together with data displays on the canvas to help conceptualize this slightly complex pipeline (Figure 4). Further, to remove some excessive pixels in the binary mask, the programmer may try applying an erosion filter to it. The ability to monitor the same variable's values at different code positions then allows both the original mask and the eroded mask to be monitored and compared simultaneously without confusion.

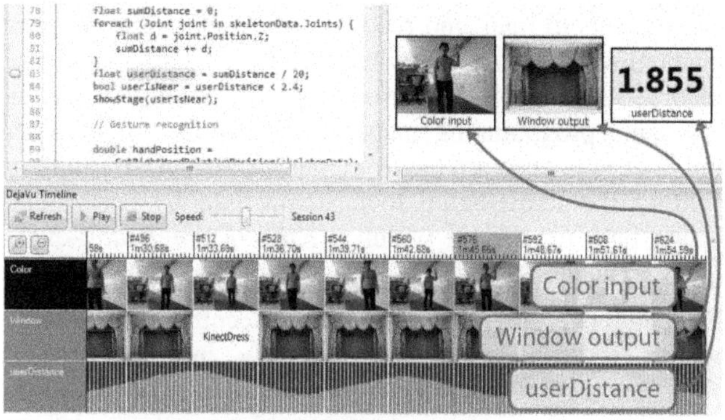

Figure 7: Tuning the distance threshold.

Next, to overlay the suit on the user's image so that it accurately tracks the user's body in position and size, the programmer can fine tune the geometric transformation parameters for the suit picture using both live and recorded input, similarly to how they adjusted the distance threshold in the first step.

Finally, the programmer attempts the gesture recognition algorithm for swiping, which requires observing the user's skeleton over a number of frames to identify the movement. Two simple heuristic algorithms come to the programmer's mind, one based on the change of the hand's horizontal position, the other on the change of the elbow joint angle. Being unsure of which option will work better, the programmer implements both to compare their performance on real world input. Figure 1 illustrates how they use the canvas to monitor the skeleton input, hand position, and elbow angle, as well as the recognition results of both algorithms as Boolean variables. Accounting for variability in real world input, they perform the gesture many times. Once done, they immediately have a visual overview in the timeline of how well each algorithm performs comparatively. They can easily identify cases where either or both fail by skimming the color input and recognition result streams, and then diagnose the cause by examining the corresponding temporal trends in the variables that the algorithms are based on, i.e., hand position or elbow angle. They can also later use the basic session editing functions to clean and trim these sessions to focus on the most relevant gesture samples.

Moreover, to accommodate individual differences between users, the programmer can ask others to trial use the program and collect gesture samples for further analysis and improvement of the algorithms. Such batch (re)processing and visualization of multiple recorded sessions are seamlessly integrated in the DejaVu workflow.

Implementation

DejaVu is implemented in C# based on the existing SharpDevelop IDE. A custom-built thin wrapper API around the Microsoft Kinect SDK acts as the shared medium between the DejaVu components, the programmer's code, and the Kinect camera. The wrapper allows the programmer to access Kinect input and capabilities in an API interface similar to that of the Kinect SDK, while at the same time allows the DejaVu components to track and record Kinect input. The wrapper also allows DejaVu to switch between feeding live and recorded Kinect input streams to the programmer's code via the same programming interface so that the programmer only needs to program for live input. The program naturally follows the frame-based loop architecture by performing frame data processing within a *KinectFrameReady* event handler, which is synchronously generated via the wrapper.

DejaVu's continuous monitoring and recording of variable values is achieved by transparently inserting tracing function calls into the programmer's code during compilation at positions where variables are dragged from onto the canvas, which allows for DejaVu's position-aware variable monitoring capability. Code change in the program are tracked by the code editor and handled during compilation to maintain reference to variables and consistency between canvas/timeline and the code.

Although DejaVu currently supports a finite set of types in terms of data visualization, its architecture is extensible enough so that additional types could be supported in a third-party extension model.

USER FEEDBACK

To gain early feedback about the concept and functionality of DejaVu from target users, as opposed to lower-level usability or technical performance, we invited three professional developers to trial DejaVu. They all had significant experience in developing interactive Kinect-based programs using the mainstream Microsoft Visual Studio IDE. Each participant was first introduced to DejaVu's concept and interface and then asked to use it in the development of a simple interactive program. The program idea was proposed by the participant based on their past experience and generally consisted of a single processing component that can be used in higher-level applications. These included a program to track the object held in the user's hand, a program to shift the user's image to the center of the screen, and a program to detect whether the user's left, right, or both hands are raised.

Given the open-endedness of the programming tasks, and because we were interested in subjective feedback rather than quantifiable productivity at this proof-of-concept stage, we did not enforce the participant to complete the program. Instead the participant worked for an hour regardless of the progress. The participant was asked to raise any feedback they may have during the trial, and was afterwards informally interviewed about their experience and opinions. One participant successfully completed his program in one hour while the other two reached a stage that the substance of the program was ready and needed refinement; both were comfortable leaving the program for later work at that point.

All participants were very positive about DejaVu. They all agreed that it is very useful for developing interactive camera-based programs ("*This IDE is very interesting and useful, awesome.*"), and it matches well with their current workflow in developing such programs. Participants found that the canvas was an indispensable component and cherished the ability to continuously "*see immediate result*" of variable values. They were particularly fond of the direct drag-and-drop interaction to add a variable onto the canvas, and found the capability for the data display to be sensitive to the variable's source position "*very impressive*".

The timeline and its associated recording, reviewing, and reprocessing functionalities immediately resonated with the participants, and were seen as the core competency of DejaVu. One participant described it well: "*(in the past) I just want to check one value, but maybe need to walk around many times... (with DejaVu) no need to run back and forth... it'll save us lots of time to debug this.*" Indeed, similar capabilities had been desired by the participants, even to the point of making their own attempts. One participant used a separate toolbox to record and replay Kinect input data, while another participant wrote his own program to do this. However they both agreed that these separate recording functions were not nearly as powerful and flexible as the visual, integrated, and interactive support in DejaVu. The fact that the timeline is "*pretty much like video making tool like Movie Maker*" was also seen as a reassuring factor.

More importantly, the inseparable link between the canvas and the timeline defines the DejaVu development experience. Both were seen as complementary to each other, e.g., "*the canvas shows the dynamic data*" and "*the timeline provides the alignment of the changing moment*", and the synchronous connection between the two was seen as "*the best advantage*".

Participants made valuable suggestions on how to further improve DejaVu. Beyond lower-level UI and technology polishing, particularly noteworthy are the following:

Simulating and Manipulating Input. It is not always easy to collect input from the programmer's surroundings that satisfies specific realism, precision, diversity, or quantity requirements necessary for program testing. Participants suggested adding the ability to import simulated or prerecorded input such as videos [cf. 4, 21], and to manually or algorithmically manipulate existing real world input such as skeletons.

Visualizing Generic Arrays. Beyond visualizing image data, participants suggested that other array data could benefit as well from compact and intuitive visualization in the form of an image for convenient monitoring and reviewing. The ability to visualize arbitrary arrays as images would be a nice enhancement for the canvas and the timeline.

Composite Visualization. Through freehand sketches and a programmer-defined display layout, the canvas can support the conceptualization of program dataflow beyond individual data displays. Participants suggested going further by compositing multiple data displays into a higher-level visualization that could range from simple graphic combinations such as overlaying the skeleton on the color image, to more semantic compositions such as masking certain regions of an image. However, in the meanwhile we should also be cautious to preserve the central role of the program code in general-purpose data processing.

RELATED WORK

Supporting Applications of Computer Vision

A great deal of previous work endeavor to make employing computer vision for real world applications easier. Several systems aim to make design and prototyping computer vision techniques accessible to non-programmers. For example, Crayons [7] is a design tool that allows users to train image segmentation classifiers using a coloring metaphor, which are then used to prototype interactions. Similarly, Eyepatch [16] supports prototyping camera-based interactions through examples where users train various classifiers and then connect their live outputs to other prototyping tools such as Flash. Concerning more specific application domains, the Papier-Mâché toolkit [13] supports building tangible user interfaces through computer vision, barcodes, and electronic tags; and users of CAMBIENCE [5] can map motions detected by the camera into various sound effects. In contrast to this category of work, DejaVu targets typical programmers and general-purpose interactive camera-based programs by supporting a canonical development workflow rather than individual computer vision components, and preserves the full power and flexibility of standalone computer vision programs.

On the other hand, several software libraries of lower-level computer vision algorithms, such as OpenCV [2] and XVision [9], can readily be leveraged by programmers in their programs. DejaVu fulfills a complementary need, and may be used together with these libraries seamlessly.

Prototyping and Development Tools for Other Domains

In addition to computer vision, rapid prototyping tools also exist for other domains, such as sensor-based interactions that are especially relevant to our work. In specific, d.tools [11] integrates the design, test, and analysis of physical prototypes including sensors, while also providing a visual programming environment for authoring control flow. Exemplar [10] supports the authoring of sensor-based interactions by demonstration. Both d.tools and Exemplar include functionality to capture and visualize temporal sensor data and interface states, which is somewhat similar to the DejaVu timeline. Further, RePlay [21] and FauxPut [4] both support the recording and replaying of sensor input traces for the purpose of testing prototypes. To support mainstream development instead, DejaVu seamlessly integrates these concepts into a general-purpose development environment, extends them to flexibly support arbitrary data variables in the program, and further enables timeline refresh based on iterative program revisions.

Also worth noting is Gestalt [23], a general-purpose development environment that supports the development of machine learning applications. Gestalt shares our design rationale by supporting a general workflow (implementation, analysis, and easy transitions between the two) for machine learning rather than focusing on individual algorithms. Further, the connection between DejaVu and Gestalt could go beyond this philosophical similarity. As apparent in the various computer vision prototyping tools [7, 16] mentioned above, machine learning is an important element of many computer vision algorithms. DejaVu focuses on the distinctive challenges of interactive computer vision; however, future work could consider how aspects of both systems would be combined to support a more comprehensive development process.

General Programming and Debugging Support

DejaVu is also related to general programming and debugging research. DejaVu can record, review, and reprocess input, intermediate results, and program output, which resonates with a long thread of research on temporal debugging where programmers can examine the program state at various points of time in the past. Initially explored in EXDAMS [1], its first graphical example appears in PROVIDE [20] and more recent work includes TOD [24] and URDB [27]. Most relevant to our work is liblog [8], a replay debugging tool for distributed applications that share some of the non-deterministic nature of camera-based applications. These systems focus on tracing and reverse-stepping of individual discrete statements, and do not accommodate or exploit the intrinsic frame-based processing pipeline in interactive camera-based programs as DejaVu does.

Another key capability of DejaVu is to continuously monitor the program data in a visual fashion. The GNU Data Display Debugger (DDD) [30] allows data structures to be visualized as graphs, while Microsoft Visual Studio [19] allows programmers to create custom visualizers of data types (e.g., images) that can be viewed in the debugger. However, these visualizations are built into conventional discrete-step debugging environments and are not updated continuously during program execution.

DejaVu's ability to revise the program and reprocess the input may also remind of research on live programming such as SuperGlue [18] and Subtext [6], where the program is continuously and immediately responsive to any edits in the code. Although DejaVu does not yet provide such a live programming experience, we see this as a promising future direction to further facilitate the iterative development of camera-based programs. Motivated by a similar need, Juxtapose [12] provides an alternative approach that allows the simultaneous testing of multiple program variations, potentially with the same input. Compared to Juxtapose,

DejaVu is more suited to the iterative development and testing process where developers incrementally extend and improve their code over time.

DISCUSSION AND CONCLUSION

DejaVu focuses on supporting real-time interactive programs. Note that non-real-time camera applications, where the user sporadically collect camera input to process in an offline fashion (e.g., QR code reader), are more akin to traditional programming in architecture and workflow, hence do not necessarily require the same special support and are out of the scope of this work.

DejaVu builds on the continuous frame-based update model that reflects the distinctive needs of real-time interactive camera-based programs, and is profoundly different from the conventional discrete step-based debugging model. However, these two models are not necessarily mutually exclusive. Especially when reviewing and reprocessing recorded program data, where there is no concern of interrupting real-time input, we may consider combining these two models to allow stepwise tracing within a frame at statement granularity where needed.

Although DejaVu is a domain-specific tool for camera-based programs, other types of sensor-based interactions or frame-based programs (e.g., games) may share some of their previously mentioned attributes. DejaVu indeed shares some characteristics with existing sensor-based prototyping tools. It is worthwhile to consider how DejaVu's concepts can be generalized to these other domains.

In conclusion, DejaVu provides enhanced integrated support that tightly matches the distinctive nature and workflow of developing interactive camera-based programs. It has been positively received by representative target users, and is a timely exploration facing today's wide adoption of camera-based interactions.

REFERENCES

1. Balzer, R. (1969). EXDAMS: extensible debugging and monitoring system. *Spring joint computer conference*, p. 567-580.
2. Bradski, G. (2000). The OpenCV Library. *Dr. Dobb's Journal November 2000, Computer Security.*
3. Cao, X., Balakrishnan, R. (2003). VisionWand: interaction techniques for large displays using a passive wand tracked in 3D. *UIST*, p. 173-182.
4. Cardenas, T., Bastea-Forte, M., Ricciardi, A., Hartmann, B., Klemmer, S. (2008). Testing physical computing prototypes through time-shifted & simulated input traces. *UIST adjunct proceedings.*
5. Diaz-Marino, R., Greenberg, S. (2006). CAMBIENCE: A Video-Driven Sonic Ecology for Media Spaces. *Video Proceedings of CSCW.*
6. Edwards, J. (2005). Subtext: Uncovering the simplicity of programming. *OOPSLA*, p. 505–518.
7. Fails, J., Olsen, D. (2003). A design tool for camera-based interaction. *CHI*, p. 449-456.
8. Geels, D., Altekar, G., Shenker, S., Stoica, I. (2006). Replay debugging for distributed applications. *USENIX*, p. 289-300.
9. Hager, G. D., Toyama, K. (1998). X Vision: A portable substrate for real-time vision applications. *Computer Vision and Image Understanding*, 69(1), p. 23-37.
10. Hartmann, B., Abdulla, L., Mittal, M., Klemmer, S. R. (2007). Authoring sensor-based interactions by demonstration with direct manipulation and pattern recognition. *CHI*, p. 145-154.
11. Hartmann, B., Klemmer, S. R., Bernstein, M., Abdulla, L., Burr, B., Robinson-Mosher, A., Gee, J. (2006). Reflective physical prototyping through integrated design, test, and analysis. *UIST*, p. 299-308.
12. Hartmann, B., Yu, L., Allison, A., Yang, Y., Klemmer, S. R. (2008). Design as exploration: creating interface alternatives through parallel authoring and runtime tuning. *UIST*, p. 91-100.
13. Klemmer, S. R., Li, J., Lin, J., Landay, J. A. (2004). Papier-Mache: toolkit support for tangible input. *CHI*, p. 399-406.
14. Landay, J. and Myers, B. (1995). Interactive sketching for the early stages of user interface design. *CHI*, p. 43-50.
15. Maynes-Aminzade, D., Pausch, R., Seitz, S. (2002). Techniques for interactive audience participation. *ICMI*, p. 15-20.
16. Maynes-Aminzade, D., Winograd, T., Igarashi, T. (2007). Eyepatch: Prototyping Camera-based Interaction Through Examples. *UIST*, p. 33-42.
17. Max/MSP. Cycling '74. http://cycling74.com/products/maxmsp
18. McDirmid, S. (2007). Living it up with a live programming language. *OOPSLA*, p. 623-638.
19. Microsoft Visual Studio Visualizers. http://msdn.microsoft.com/en-us/library/zayyhzts.aspx
20. Moher, T. G. (1988). PROVIDE: a process visualization and debugging environment. *IEEE Transactions on Software Engineering*, 14(6), p.849-857.
21. Newman, M. W., Ackerman, M. S., Kim, J., Prakash, A., Hong, Z., Mandel, J., Dong, T. (2010). Bringing the field into the lab: supporting capture and replay of contextual data for the design of context-aware applications. *UIST*, p. 105-108.
22. Norman, D. A., Draper, S. W. (1986). User centered system design; new perspectives on human-computer interaction. L. Erlbaum Assoc. Inc.
23. Patel, K., Bancroft, N., Drucker, S. M., Fogarty, J., Ko, A. J., Landay, J. (2010). Gestalt: integrated support for implementation and analysis in machine learning. *UIST*, p. 37-46.
24. Pothier, G., Tanter, E., Piquer, J. (2007). Scalable omniscient debugging. *SIGPLAN*, p. 535-552.
25. Segen, J., Kumar, S. (1998). Gesture VR: Vision-based 3D hand interface for spatial interaction. *Multimedia*. p. 455-464.
26. SharpDevelop. http://www.icsharpcode.net/opensource/sd/
27. Visan, A., Arya, K., Cooperman, G., Denniston, T. (2011). URDB: a universal reversible debugger based on decomposing debugging histories. *PLOS*, p. 1-5.
28. Wang, S., Xiong, X., Xu, Y., Wang, C., Zhang, W., Dai, X., Zhang, D. (2006). Face-tracking as an augmented input in video games: enhancing presence, role-playing and control. *CHI*, p. 1097-1106.
29. Wilson, A. D. (2005). PlayAnywhere: a compact interactive tabletop projection-vision system. *UIST*, p. 83-92.
30. Zeller, A., Lütkehaus, D. (1996). DDD - a free graphical front-end for UNIX debuggers. SIGPLAN Notices, 31(1), p. 22-27.

Homework: Putting Interaction into the Infrastructure

Richard Mortier, Tom Rodden, Peter Tolmie, Tom Lodge, Robert Spencer, Andy Crabtree

University of Nottingham, UK
{firstname.lastname}@nottingham.ac.uk

Alexandros Koliousis, Joseph Sventek

University of Glasgow, UK
{firstname.lastname}@glasgow.ac.uk

ABSTRACT

This paper presents a user driven redesign of the domestic network infrastructure that draws upon a series of ethnographic studies of home networks. We present an infrastructure based around a purpose built access point that has modified the handling of protocols and services to reflect the interactive needs of the home. The developed infrastructure offers a novel measurement framework that allows a broad range of infrastructure information to be easily captured and made available to interactive applications. This is complemented by a diverse set of novel interactive control mechanisms and interfaces for the underlying infrastructure. We also briefly reflect on the technical and user issues arising from deployments.

ACM Classification: H.5.2 [Information interfaces and presentation]: User Interfaces. - Graphical user interfaces.

General terms: Management, Measurement.

Keywords: Home network, infrastructure, interaction.

INTRODUCTION

Domestic networks have become an unremarkable feature of modern life [4], routinely used to generate and consume digital media and to access a burgeoning array of online services. The home network is no longer a novelty for many people, but rather an ordinary background feature of their lives. However, managing domestic networks currently imposes heavy technical overheads and presents critical problems for users. Residents have little or no access to facilities that provide meaningful control over bandwidth use, network access or local network policies.

To address this mismatch between the needs of residents and the nature of the technology we have adopted a user-centred approach to the creation of the next-generation domestic infrastructure. We draw upon empirical studies of home networking to suggest a set of key user-oriented desires for an interactive infrastructure. We then outline how we have re-examined the protocols and architectures of the domestic setting to incorporate these requirements within the infrastructure, opening it up to interactive systems' developers. This allows us to make key features of the domestic infrastructure available to inhabitants in a way that reflects their needs and allows non-technical users to manage and control the network.

Our focus on the underlying network extends consideration of HCI systems beyond interfaces and interaction techniques. Interaction inevitably shapes and is shaped by the nature of the underlying infrastructure. We respond to this *infrastructure challenge in HCI* [5] by undertaking end-to-end systems research that responds to the needs of users. This allows us to push interaction deeper into the infrastructure both *broadly*, in terms of which interactions the infrastructure supports; and *directly*, by adding interactivity to protocols traditionally invisible to users.

End-to-end systems research is a long-term endeavour combining extensive ethnographic study, detailed systems development, and iterative user-centred prototyping. For example, different ways of presenting and controlling the infrastructure represent significant iterative HCI research, requiring repeated deployment and assessment with users.

Our project, *Homework*, has been underway for over three years. We have previously published novel systems elements of our work [15] and the analytical orientation of our ethnographic work towards the unremarkable nature of the domestic network [4]. The core contribution of this paper is the articulation of key requirements arising from our ethnographic work; and the resulting development of a deployable interactive networking infrastructure, informed by empirical understandings of users' needs and capable of supporting a wide range of interesting uses and research interfaces. While we refer to some of our initial interfaces, these are in extensive longitudinal user trials now; their detailed presentation will be the subject of future papers.

SUPPORTING DOMESTIC NETWORK MANAGEMENT

The domestic network has become a significant focus in HCI with researchers offering insights into setting up and maintaining network infrastructure [6,7], in weaving the home network into domestic routines [16], and in users understanding their home networks [11]. As the Internet increasingly underpins more aspects of modern life it becomes a crucial element in how residents access online services and communicate with others. Unfortunately, network remain opaque to users, are often clumsy in use, and lack transparency and local accountability, e.g., [3,16].

Contemporary computer networks are built around essentially the same protocols, architectures and tools

UIST '12, October 7–10, 2012, Cambridge, Massachusetts, USA.

developed for the Internet as a whole in the 1970s. These were designed for a certain context of *use* (assuming relatively trustworthy hosts), made assumptions about *users* (skilled network and systems administrators), and tried to accomplish a particular set of *goals* (e.g., scalability to millions of nodes and resilience against node/link failure).

The role of the digital has changed significantly since the early days of the network, presenting a quite different context of use and set of goals. The home network is really quite different to backbone and enterprise networks. Domestic networks are relatively small in size. They are predominately self-managed by residents not typically expert in networking technology. They connect a highly heterogeneous collection of devices, including desktop PCs, games consoles, and a variety of mobile devices ranging from smartphones to printers to digital cameras. Furthermore, different household members routinely own and individually exercise control over their devices. Finally, home network access and use tends to be locally negotiated between inhabitants where immediate resolution of problems requires direct control over the network [17].

Infrastructure has traditionally been separated from the needs of and control by the user. This separation makes it hard for people to understand and manage their networks in support of their activities. It has also made it hard for interactive systems developers to build applications to meet inhabitants' needs. However, several recent approaches attempt to increase access to domestic networks.

Revealing the Domestic Infrastructure

A range of distinct applications have been developed that expose the underlying infrastructure to users. These include products such as Network Magic[1] that provide simple visualization and configuration wizards to aid users but provide little information on the "traffic" (data flows) in the network and only limited control of the infrastructure itself. More sophisticated support is provided by research systems such as Home Watcher [3] which exploits custom applications (*client agents*) installed on domestic machines to monitor and control network traffic. The system offers users a control panel to throttle (limit) traffic to different machines but its control is limited to those MS Windows-based personal computers where a client is installed.

As the need for users to more effectively manage the network has grown, a range of *middleware* has also emerged. Middleware conceptually sits between the network and the application, offering alternative services and more user awareness and control. Middleware-based approaches tend to offer greater measurement and control by exploiting the role of the router as the main point of contact with an Internet Service Provider (ISP). This has included capturing network layer traffic [2] and storing *flow records*, referring to aggregates of network packets travelling between endpoints, in a database collocated with the web server using custom *DD-WRT*[2] router firmware. Technology probes such as Kermit [2] provide visualizations of this data to users that have been favourably received. Other systems such as Eden [17] also exploit router facilities to offer a graphical UI with drag and drop actions mapped to underlying network facilities.

Existing work has demonstrated the advantages of presenting the underlying infrastructure to residents in domestic settings by exploring a range of visualization techniques and providing new metaphors to allow residents to configure the underlying infrastructure. However, *these researchers have had to work within the limits of the underlying infrastructure* and the specific controls it offers. As Edwards *et al* [5] argue this has restricted the design space for HCI, preventing an exploration of the new possibilities that might emerge if the underlying infrastructure mechanisms were reshaped. We wish to shift this balance of control to allow greater user involvement in the services and protocols of the infrastructure. Rather than treating the infrastructure as a pre-ordained fixed set of facilities, we wish to open it up to allow access to parts of the domestic network infrastructure that are normally either closed to or hidden from both HCI developers and users.

REDESIGNING THE DOMESTIC INFRASTRUCTURE

Our reshaping of the domestic infrastructure is informed by ethnographic studies conducted since 2009 across 24 different households. Distributed geographically around the UK, these have been enormously varied in their make-up: with younger children; with a mixture of younger and older children; with just older children; with young adults still living at home; older couples with children now living elsewhere; younger couples without children; single occupancy households (younger and older); and mixed occupancy shared households. The participants have covered a wide range of different occupations and income brackets, ranging from the unemployed, to factory workers, to a waitress living with her partner (a chef), to highly skilled professional couples.

The empirical approach to the studies has been ethnographic and has included interviews, technology tours, and self-logging of events. Our studies have been complemented by long term "in the wild" studies where we have replaced people's home routers with our infrastructure and undertaken formative assessment of the developed features. The analytic backbone to all our studies has been ethnomethodological: we have sought to elicit how people methodically reason about and account for the operation of their networks as a part of ordinary everyday practice. Details of these studies are the focus of other papers [4]; in this paper we consolidate the key issues these studies raised into a set of basic infrastructure challenges.

Key Domestic Infrastructure Challenges

To drive the reshaping of the underlying infrastructure we have consolidated our own and other ethnographic

[1] http://www.purenetworks.com

[2] http://www.dd-wrt.com/site/index

understandings of domestic settings into four key challenges each presenting distinct challenges to the underlying infrastructure. Residents routinely express the following desires: to understand network bandwidth use and ***manage consumption***; to understand network activity and ***monitor performance***; to respond to demands by ***prioritization*** of network activities and interaction; and to be able to ***police users on the network***. In the following sections we briefly illustrate each of these needs before considering the technical challenges each presents.

Managing Consumption

Residents wished to be aware of bandwidth consumption on both momentary and cumulative bases. Where bandwidth capping exists, this was often articulated at a household level: people want to know when they are approaching or have crossed a threshold above which supplementary charges or other penalties will apply. This can also relate to the bandwidth consumed by specific devices and (implicitly) people, both here-and-now and over longer time periods. Knowledge of such consumption can provide evidence for negotiation of specific rights and responsibilities, and matters of moral accountability:

I would like to see an accumulative/historical record of bandwidth usage. The current month/week/day so I can see patterns of use of time... This is important to me because we keep exceeding the Internet allowance. It has gone up five-fold because we have an international student living with us. I don't think she believes it's her who's eaten up all of the allowance!

A number of HCI researchers have developed technology probes to explore appropriate means of presenting this form of information [2] with existing infrastructures. These have been restricted to the information provided by existing mechanisms in particular infrastructure components, e.g., simple traffic statistics as sFlow/NetFlow records.

The infrastructure challenge is to provide mechanisms that will capture usage information at an appropriate level of abstraction and make it more readily available to the user. The encapsulation inherent within layered protocol stacks limits access to network traffic. HCI developers are thus left to make do with the level of traffic detection provided rather than shaping traffic measurement to meet their needs. Both operational and research approaches to traffic measurement have been driven predominantly by the needs of large backbone networks, where the focus is on capturing information about dominant traffic types to improve network efficiency. These methods do not readily map to the home where the technical context and constraints are quite different, and the need is to link traffic to user activities. It is thus difficult for developers to accurately and efficiently detect key features of importance to users. *The key requirement this challenge imposes is accessibility of data from each protocol layer, in common and extensible representations.*

Monitoring Performance and Activity

Across our various studies people expressed an interest in knowing what others are up to on the network and how the network is performing. Often it is about having a global view of the network as an object so as to reason why your own particular device is behaving the way it is:

I think occasionally we've said, y'know, someone's gone and said "Is someone torrenting?" or "Is someone running a big download?" or something like that. And then they'll go sort of "I've bought a game and it's six gig and it's a download that's gobbling all the bandwidth" ...

A part of this is about having the resources to assess what impact other people's network use might be having upon your own activities. Another part is about troubleshooting, about being able to use different views of the network to disambiguate where problems might lie. Some routers already make part of this functionality available, albeit rarely and in a manner not amenable to construction of UIs:

It [The Router] shows the connectivity ... and if it's wireless or Ethernet. It's just reassuring that- Well J may say I can't link for example and I can see the connection is actually on so it may be something actually on her laptop in settings rather than in the network. It's quite a nice feature.

Understanding and controlling activity can equally be considered in terms of how it is viewed, how we may be informed of it, and how we might shape or prohibit use.

The infrastructure challenge is to provide mechanisms to enable this form of monitoring and to alert users of these issues as they occur. Existing approaches to monitoring assume the recipient of information is an expert network administrator, whether in a corporate or a backbone network. As a result they provide current and historical information at an inappropriate level of detail and without necessary scaffolding for the "uninterested" home user. In the home this leads to the need to develop efficient means to undertake such monitoring in local settings in real time, and to provide the means to detect and alert users of specific traffic issues at a level that makes sense to them. *The key requirement this challenge imposes is for an event notification system that enables applications to dynamically register interest in particular changes in network state.*

Prioritization of Activities

A strongly voiced concern is that the network fails to recognize the ordinary workings of priorities and preferences within a household. Certain people may need to use the network for work, some may need to accomplish particular things at specific times of the day, certain kinds of activity may need to be accommodated on an ad hoc and contingent basis, whilst the actual operation of allocating priority between devices remains opaque. For example, those who work at home often feel that being able to prioritize devices on the network would better recognize the contribution their activities make to the household:

I see myself as using the Internet to bring in income, so I can justify that pretty well ***everything that I do takes priority****.*

On occasion this can even stretch as far as wanting to give priority to specific *individuals*, regardless of which device or application they may be using at the time:

I mean if he is asking for God knows how much to be downloading as I'm trying to download my own stuff, I want mine to take priority over what his requirements are... That would always be the case.

However, sometimes this is more nuanced and the interest is in recognizing certain kinds of higher priority activity and giving preference for however long they may last:

I use a lot of presentations. I do a lot of PowerPoint stuff and I use a lot of photographs in them, so sometimes my computer can be really slow when downloading stuff like that. So... I think that, I'm doing that activity, Give me priority now. Because it's not the sort of thing I do every day. It's the sort of thing I do regularly and when I'm doing it, it's probably over two days where I'm doing that thing on it... And there may be video stuff, that kind of thing.

For other households the interest is in having a network that can recognize the routines of the household and shape the traffic across devices accordingly, giving some priority at one time of day and others priority at another:

M: ... we have had big rows about T stealing the Internet. E said to him "You've stolen the Internet!" coz he's uploading to YouTube and the whole thing just like grinds to a halt for everybody else. We have had a "You put it on overnight T when nobody else needs it".

T: Yeah so normally I just upload overnight. And that's it. ... if the video files are under 50 megabytes I upload it because it only takes 5 or 10 minutes, but normally if it's bigger than that I do it overnight.

The infrastructure challenge is to provide mechanisms to prioritize and control traffic associated with different devices and user activities in real time. Existing approaches to prioritising focus on fine-tuning networks and often deal with large-scale aggregate traffic flows (so-called *traffic engineering*). Reconfiguration of such flows relies on expert judgement by experienced network operators driven by business requirements. Judgement in the home is more closely related to use and, given the subtleties involved, requires human situated judgment. This strongly suggests there is a need to involve the user in such mechanisms, and thus to embed user interaction directly within related control mechanisms. *The key requirement this challenge imposes is for primitives supporting programmable network control, at all protocol layers.*

Policing Users of the Network

A more contentious set of requirements revolves around the control of what people can do on the network. Almost inevitably, interests here frequently relate to parental desires to manage what their children do on the network:

I do use Facebook quite a lot and social networking and I know that a lot of J's friends have asked me to be a friend and I'm very strict on that. At the moment he hasn't even tried to go there but if he does then I would want certain restrictions on that as well.

It can also be about punitive responses to 'bad behaviour':

So if teacher says she's not doing homework and I think she's not doing it because she's spending her life on Facebook, I could block them and say "I'll let you have them back when your homework's done". You see that might be handy, if you could do it at the level of saying- You know, it's easy enough for me to say 'show your homework, right that's done', type something, 'right you can have Facebook now'.

I used to share a house with someone who was- ... largely nocturnal and he used to do a lot of a protocol called direct connect or program and there were some evenings where there was a lot of uploading and swamping the bandwidth and the problem was if you maxed the upload on the Internet connection it just absolutely killed everything else. And, because he was a bit nocturnal, at the times when I'd really want to check email or something in the morning before going off to work- I used to have a hub, which I could sort of disconnect him from, and there were days when I used to do that just so I could get some usage out of the network

An important aspect of the above is the degree to which these things may be reasoned about on the basis of an application or its specific uses. Thus a mother may want to restrict her daughter's access to Facebook but not the whole Internet, as that might be deemed a required homework tool. Existing *platforms* do not typically support such fine grained access control though some tools can, e.g., *StayFocusd*, a Chrome browser extension, *Freedom*[3] and *AntiSocial*.[4] However, they apply to specific client devices/programs, not an *individual's* access.

Another set of requirements here relates to the degree of difficulty people experience giving other people access to their network and the wish to make that more tractable:

...In my parents' house. I think my mum's friend brought a laptop round and then it was sort of, can we get her onto our network so she can copy off her photographs from the holiday that they've all been on across. It caused some problem. I set them up with MAC address only rather than a code. So it was a case of actually having to go and sort that out and log on and add her computer's MAC address to the list. I think for many people this is a big faff...

The infrastructure challenge is to provide mechanisms that make it much easier to police users of the network, managing their access and what exactly they may or may not do when connected. This requires us to consider how we might exercise control locally within the network and to make these controls available to users. Current approaches to policing tend to be removed from the point of use and consequently broad-brush in nature, focusing on wholesale blocking of access to particular sites or services by all, or denying particular devices any form of connectivity and thus access to any site or service. In practice the highly contingent nature of policing in the home is much finer grained and more dynamic in nature. *The key requirement this challenge imposes is for policy and access control primitives that more closely match human practice rather than network state.*

While we have suggested four broad classes of need within the domestic setting we stress the significant diversity of users and uses of the network visible within our, and other, studies. This strongly indicates the need for iterative development of appropriate interfaces and applications with these users. However, before we can begin a process of iterative refinement of these interfaces and applications, we must first develop appropriate underlying interactive mechanisms within the infrastructure. Our aim is to provide open infrastructure that promotes exploration of a range of different styles of interaction with the underlying network.

REALISING A NOVEL INFRASTRUCTURE

The results of our ethnographic work underpin the shaping a new network infrastructure, which we now describe in

[3] http://macfreedom.com/

[4] http://anti-social.cc/

detail. We exploit the arrangement of the home network to adopt a gateway model to changing the infrastructure [12] in response to user needs emerging from our studies. This allows us to reinvent key infrastructure mechanisms locally without changing the Internet as a whole. We have developed a dedicated router from the perspective of the home user, re-examining the means through which network information is collected and the network controlled. As part of this redesign of the infrastructure we have developed:

- A scalable and dynamic measurement infrastructure designed to make available information about the behaviour of the network to interactive user applications.
- A set of mechanisms that exploit user engagement and interaction to allow direct control of the network.

Our aim is to provide an open infrastructure that allows an exploration of a range of different styles of interaction with the underlying network. Our router has been deployed in a range of domestic settings and supports several user interfaces currently undergoing iterative refinement. Our open-source code is online at http://github.com/homework/.

Externally our setup is similar to operator-provided home routers, where one box acts as the wireless access point, uses a wired connection for upstream connectivity to the ISP, and may provide a small number of other wired interfaces. Our router (Figure 1) is deployed over Linux 2.6 on an eeePC. An active database provides an integrated network monitoring facility to applications [15]. We treat the router as an OpenFlow device using the Open vSwitch and NOX implementations – OpenFlow is a network control standard [10] described briefly below. Our router uses OpenFlow datapath rules to control access and connectivity, both upstream and local, of devices.

In the rest of this paper we detail how our router provides the interactive infrastructure needed to capture a rich picture of network behaviour and make this available to users. We then present our distinctive control infrastructure, which enables direct involvement of users in the day-to-day management of the network.

CAPTURING ACTIVITY ON THE HOME NETWORK

"if all the traffic goes through that box ... why can't I see it?"

Home routers embody the invisible nature of current digital infrastructures. They provide a network for wired and wireless devices in the home and act as a gateway to the Internet. Consequently, all traffic in the home typically flows through the domestic router. The router is designed to handle this traffic efficiently and to ensure that it is appropriately *routed*, i.e., correctly passed on toward the correct destination. However, it provides few facilities to capture this information or make it available to applications wishing to surface the nature of the network to users.

The first infrastructure challenge the Homework router addresses is how to capture traffic information efficiently and make this available to applications. To do this our router includes an active measurement database that provides a focal point for information collected about the

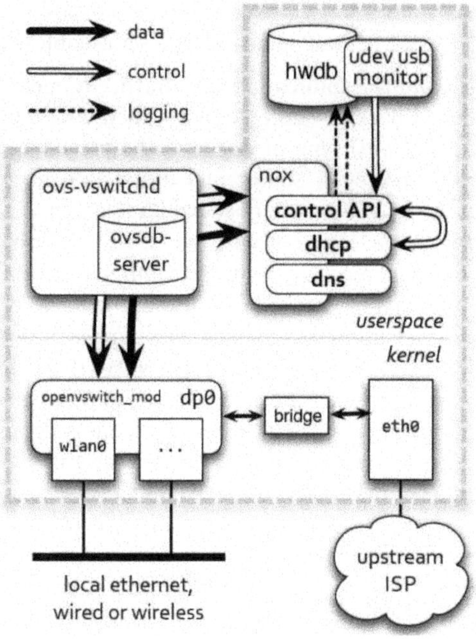

Figure 1. The Homework Router architecture. Open vSwitch and NOX manage the network interfaces. Three NOX modules provide a web services control API, a custom DHCP server, and a DNS proxy.

infrastructure. It offers network visualisation and control applications an extensible facility where dynamic information about the state of the infrastructure is collated.

The measurement database is composed of three distinct components. An *ephemeral timeseries component* holds the most recent (complete) data received from monitoring processes. The continuous, large volume of such data makes it infeasible to persist it all, and demands careful implementation to keep up. A *persistent timeseries component* holds (selected) timeseries data for later use, and a *persistent relational component* stores derived information unrelated to the time of occurrence, e.g., machine details and the daily volume of data.

We use *libpcap* to intercept packets and process to generate appropriate table entries, e.g., flow records. Through careful implementation, no deployment has yet recorded significant loss as a result, in contrast to naïve use of *tcpdump*, reported as initially seeing 10% packet loss [1].

The ephemeral component of the database implements an extended version of the Stanford STREAM Data Manager.[5] Applications access it via a lightweight UDP-based Remote Procedure Call (RPC) system that exchanges request packets (queries) for response packets (data). We have C/C++ and Java bindings that have been tested on Linux, Windows/Cygwin, OS/X, iOS and Android.

Applications periodically query the ephemeral component either for raw events or derived information. This is used

[5] http://infolab.stanford.edu/stream/

directly by user interfaces or stored for subsequent use. There are three default persistent timeseries tables:

- A ***flows table*** captures network traffic by recording the number of packets and bytes associated with a particular (transport level) type of traffic in the preceding second, recording protocol, source and destination information. This allows us to monitor bandwidth usage in the home.
- A ***links table*** captures wireless device information by recording the received signal strength, number of retries, and number of packets associated with a particular device. This allows us to show machines within range of the network, and the wireless topology of the setting.
- A ***leases table*** captures connection to the network by recording when a *DHCP lease* (see below) is granted to a device, or a lease is revoked. This allows us to indicate the status of machines connected to the network.

Figure 2 shows the schema associated with each table.

Table	*Attributes*
Flows	Protocol, src/dst IP addresses, src/dst ports, # packets, # bytes
Links	MAC address, RSSI, # retries, # packets
Leases	Action, MAC address, IP address, host name

Figure 2. The default Homework Database schemas.

The measurement infrastructure is designed to be extensible beyond these core tables allowing additional information about the domestic context to be collected, e.g., arrival and departure of people in the home, or logged interactions with different devices. Applications can exploit and contribute to this time ordered set of heterogeneous data to capture information about users' interactions as they manipulate the infrastructure. The result is a rich log of network activity and user interaction.

Coordination and User Notification

The Homework Database also acts as a central point of coordination for infrastructure services. *Listeners* subscribe to particular tables, and are then invoked when a datum is added to that table. Among these listeners is a user-level notification service that can be configured to notify users of critical network events. It can currently use email, SMS, Twitter and Growl to deliver events to users as desired.

Our notification service plays a critical role in informing users of changes in the infrastructure across a heterogeneous range of devices. For example, if the infrastructure blocks Internet access for a particular device, we can send a message informing the user of this fact.

CONTROLLING THE INFRASTRUCTURE

The router's measurement infrastructure is complemented by a set of user-oriented control mechanisms enabling interactive management of the network. We treat the Homework Router as an OpenFlow device. An OpenFlow *switch* has three parts: a *datapath,* a *secure channel* connecting to a controller, and the *OpenFlow protocol* used by the controller to talk to the switch.

Each OpenFlow *datapath* contains a set of physical ports, plus a table of flow entries with a set of actions associated with each flow entry. Flows are defined in terms of the input datapath and selected values of packet header fields. There are four basic types of action, ranging from simply dropping or forwarding the packet, to forwarding it to the controller for further processing, to forwarding it through the switch's normal processing pipeline. Packets can be selectively modified as they are forwarded.

Open vSwitch[6] is an implementation of OpenFlow running on Linux. It implements a datapath as a kernel module that can be configured to control one or more physical or virtual interfaces. The OpenFlow protocol used to communicate with the datapath is provided as a userspace process, *ovs-vswitchd,* which also maintains a device configuration database. In the current implementation the datapath's flow table supports exact-match rules only; packets that do not have an exact match are forwarded for processing to the *ovs-vswitchd* process that maintains all wildcard rules. Packets that do not match a rule are sent to the controller.

Method	*Function*
/permit: <eaddr>	Permit access by specified client
/deny: <eaddr>	Deny access by specified client
/status: [eaddr]	Retrieve currently permitted clients, or status of specified client
/dhcp-status/	Retrieve current MAC—IP mappings
/whitelist: <eaddr>	Accept associations from client
/blacklist: <eaddr>	Deny association to client
/blacklist-status/	Retrieve currently blacklisted clients
/permit-dns: <eaddr> <domain>	Permit the specified device to access the given domain
/deny-dns: <eaddr> <domain>	Deny access to the given domain by the specified device

Figure 3. Homework Router web API. All methods are prefixed *https://.../ws.v1/.* <*X*> and [*X*] denote required and optional parameters respectively.

In our router, the controller controls just a single datapath that manages all but one of the network interfaces on the eeePC. It implements filtering to control wireless association, and a custom DHCP server. These software processes exercise control by managing rules in the OpenFlow datapath to control both access of devices within the home, and their local and upstream connectivity. The controller presents a simple web RPC interface (Figure 3). The datapath forwards traffic destined upstream for local processing via the built-in bridge, with Linux's *iptables* IP Masquerading rules providing standard NAT functionality.

Having described some of the core technical elements of the router itself, we now discuss how we have extended and used this infrastructure to allow direct involvement of users in the day-to-day management of the network.

[6] http://openvswitch.org/

PUSHING INTERACTION INTO THE INFRASTRUCTURE

Using our infrastructure we have exploited three strategies in response to the challenges involved in managing consumption, prioritization of network activities and interaction, and policing network access. Each illustrates a different means of placing interaction in the infrastructure:

1. **Putting people in the protocol** by embedding user interaction in existing infrastructure protocols. Encapsulation has traditionally meant that these protocols make no reference to users.
2. **Bringing services closer to users** by allowing greater control and configuration. Infrastructures have traditionally designed these services to be remote and neutral with respect to use.
3. **Exploiting the physical arrangement of the home** by manifesting infrastructure in the home. Infrastructures have traditionally sought to be independent of the physical setting and so seldom exploit its affordances.

In the following sections we will briefly illustrate how we exploit each of these strategies in on-going deployments.

Putting People in the Protocol

A key example of this strategy is our manipulation of the *Dynamic Host Configuration Protocol* (DHCP). In order to use IP (i.e., the network layer, and everything above it) a device must have a valid *IP address*. DHCP is an application protocol that allows a device, upon discovering it is connected to a network, to *request* an IP address that is valid for that network. A network's DHCP server allocates addresses to devices and records each device's *MAC address*. This is set in the factory and is often used to identify the device as it never normally changes, even when a device moves between networks. This process is normally invisible to users and there is no mechanism to involve users in responding to the request for a valid IP address. The result is that machines join and leave the network unbeknownst to users who have no opportunity to control access to the network beyond blanket permit/deny policies.

We implemented a DHCP server within our router as a NOX module, enabling interface devices to control which devices will receive an address via the simple web API (Figure 3). As well as recording DHCP leases in the lease table and providing awareness of who is on the network, the server provides control over the leases it grants. When devices are first detected, they are placed in a requesting pool and this is flagged in the leases table. Applications subscribed to the leases table are then made aware of this request and can inform users. Users then respond to the request by interacting in some application specific manner, and the application completes the process by invoking the web API. The router drops all traffic from devices that have not been permitted, allowing machines to be selectively prevented from using the network.

This facility may be exploited in a number of different ways by HCI developers. The interface in Figure 4 is an example of a situated noticeboard interface exercising this functionality that we are currently exploring with users. Requesting machines appear in the central display panel. Any user with access to the display may then choose to drag any device to the right. Doing so invokes the web API on the router to mark the device (specifically its MAC address) as "permitted", granting it an IP address and enabling its traffic to be routed.

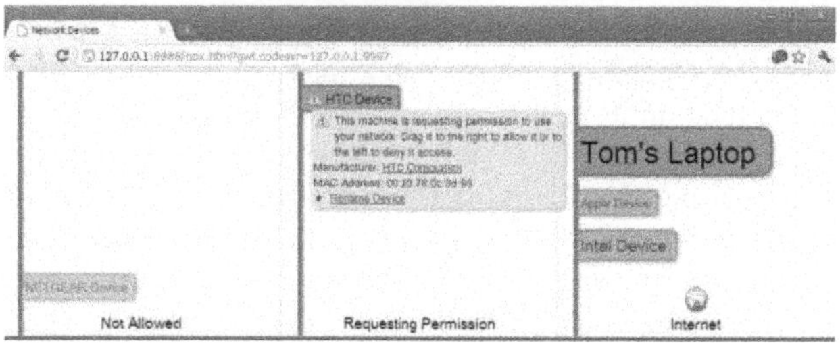

Figure 4. Control panel showing an HTC device requesting connectivity.

This control is enabled by the combination of publishing information about DHCP leases and enabling direct interaction in the protocol by the user to complete address allocation. Obviously, user involvement may take other forms depending on the interaction and management styles at play. For example, we may provide an alert to the mobile device of one of the residents requesting permission for this machine to connect. The means of presenting this facility appropriately and understanding its utility obviously requires significant HCI research. Our contribution is in embedding interaction within the protocol so as to enable different forms of user involvement.

Bringing Services Closer to Users

Our custom realization of another service illustrates our second strategy of localizing standard services to the specific home. The *Domain Name System* (DNS) is a standard Internet service that translates computer names (e.g., as appear in website URLs) into IP addresses. This *must* be done before an application such as a browser can communicate with the named computer because the IP protocol uses only IP addresses, not names. For example, when a user opens *facebook.com* in their web browser the browser first resolves the name 'facebook.com' into an IP address using DNS, and only then can it request page(s) from the Facebook server(s), using that IP address.

In a typical home network DNS requests from every device are sent to the router, which passes them on to a *DNS server* in the ISP's network. This server may query several other servers before returning a response, which may then be *cached* by both the home router (to answer subsequent requests) and the original requesting device.

In contrast, we have incorporated a DNS proxy into the home router itself, which we have extended to allow *specific devices* to be permitted or denied the ability to access *particular names* (such as facebook.com). Shifting the service closer to the point of use allows us to involve users and the context of use, as part of the name resolution in this case. In this way we can provide quite fine-grained control (e.g., per device, per user) over access to external services hosted at those locations.

The DNS proxy is implemented as another NOX module. DNS requests are intercepted by the proxy and dropped if the requesting device is not allowed access to that domain, preventing the initial lookup. In addition, any traffic the router encounters that is not already permitted by an explicit OpenFlow flow entry has a reverse lookup performed on its destination address, using a local cache of recent DNS requests to provide acceptable performance. If the resulting name is from a domain that the source device is not permitted to access, then a rule will be installed to drop related traffic. This prevents access to sites if the user directly enters the IP for a forbidden domain name, or if the device was previously allowed access and has cached the IP address but is no longer permitted access.

Figure 5. Diary showing restrictions for a given user.

Implementing such fine-grained control over the different sites that a given user's devices can access is very difficult, perhaps impossible, to perform successfully *upstream* in the network, e.g., by the ISP. Different users using different devices within the household have different policies for accessing different sites at different times: it is not possible to define a successful one-size-fits-all policy, and the ISP cannot easily identify user devices in any case. In contrast, local intervention in name resolution enables us to build a router that *can* provide the necessary degree of control.

Again this facility may be presented to users in a variety of ways. For example, we exploit an iCal feed to expose this behaviour to the user via a standard calendar application, showing which sites a user is barred from accessing at which times. This enables, e.g., a parent to control access by their children's devices to sites like Facebook, restricting them to (say) particular times (Figure 5).

Designing an appropriate means to present this level of control to users obviously requires iterative user-centred development. It is also likely to surface potentially contentious issues of control, trust, and power. Indeed, we have already started to find these within our own studies of interface deployments. Our contribution of localizing the service within the home enables this fine grained control to be exercised, opened up to user-centred investigation and specialized to the particular household: it will be sensitive to *that household's* specific, complex, changing demands, and able to reflect negotiations that take place between the various actors, homeowner and guest, parent and child.

Exploiting Local Physical Arrangements

The final strategy we explore is to exploit knowledge of the local situation to drive control. Although placed within our homes, devices have few means to access the nature of the setting and exploit this to control the network. Equally, the infrastructure has limited physical manifestation in the home that users can exploit.

As well as monitoring traffic, the database at the core of our router allows us to coordinate network control with user activities and actions in the physical home. This might include recognition of particular devices and individuals with results placed in the ephemeral timeseries database.

We currently use a simple USB memory stick as an exemplar implementation as these are cheap and readily available. Use of the USB key to provide access control is straightforward: inserting the key in the router enables the devices specified on the key to connect to the network. When the key is removed, access by those devices is revoked. A USB hub connected to the router is placed in a publicly available location allowing USB keys to be easily inserted and removed. Physical access to the USB hub is required to gain access to the network.

Our implementation uses the Linux *udev* subsystem to detect insertion and removal of the USB key. When a key containing appropriate metadata is inserted, the router reads the metadata specifying the MAC addresses of the devices to be permitted, and invokes the NOX controller's web service interface accordingly. Upon removal of the USB key, all devices for which it had been permitted access have their OpenFlow rules removed, denying subsequent access.

As with other forms of control the means of presenting this to users will require a significant amount of HCI research. Our redesign of the router provides the mechanism to link between users' activities and actions in the physical space, and the control elements of the router. Placing both detailed network information and interactive activities in the same active timeseries database allows us to explore a wide set of interrelationships between users' activities in the home and the consequent control of the network.

THE INFRASTRUCTURE IN ACTION

This paper has detailed the changes to the underlying infrastructure made in response to the challenges of home networking. Our first deployment of this router began in October 2010. We have since undertaken a rolling programme of deployments to drive interface refinement. The router has subsequently been deployed in 12 homes, each deployment lasting at least 3 months. It has also run continually in two project members' homes since summer 2010. Our deployments have considered both technical and user-related issues and so we conclude with brief reflections on the deployments from both perspectives.

Technical Reflections

The Homework Router has been successfully deployed in a range of homes in the UK as described above with very few issues. Our measurement system has little impact on the performance of the router. The router provides an ideal point of traffic measurement in the home [1]. As in the case of projects such as Bismark [14] we have been able to capture a significant amount of traffic information.

While the Bismark router focuses on ISP measurement, our local measurement facilities allow us to capture a richer picture of traffic within the home. For example, during one month, one of our households the router observed: 16 unique devices obtaining DHCP leases and connecting to the network; 4578 unique devices on the wireless network; ~54GB of data in ~94M packets; and IP flows from 178,321 unique sources to 309,473 unique destinations.

During initial deployments we noted that P2P traffic within the home was not visible to the router. Given the growing importance of traffic from storage and media servers in the home, this was a significant omission in any router-based measurement approach! This invisibility is due to the router switching traffic between wireless devices as if those devices are connected via a single Ethernet segment, rendering it invisible to the router at the IP layer. To compensate for this and ensure that *all* traffic is visible to the router, the DHCP implementation in our router pays careful attention to the way in which IP addresses and subnets are allocated: it ensures each device is allocated a distinct IP subnet forcing all traffic to be IP-routed by the Homework Router, rather than simply Ethernet-switched.

Note that the use of standard WPA2 security mechanisms means that *all non-broadcast traffic incurs no extra overhead.* Under WPA2, each device creates a distinct cryptographically secure channel with the access point: data between two devices must thus travel via the access point anyway so that the necessary decryption and re-encryption can take place. Allocating each device to a distinct subnet simply forces each packet to be made visible to the IP layer on the access point. Extra overhead occurs only for packets broadcast to the local subnet: under normal operation, a shared group key would be used allowing the transmitting client to encrypt traffic so that all other connected clients could receive it directly. Due to the use of distinct subnets such traffic must instead be sent to the access point, which must decrypt it before replicating and retransmitting to each connected receiver.

Usability Reflections

The router has been used to support the development of a range of interfaces that make the infrastructure more visible and promote increased user control. Each interface embodies different interaction styles and raises distinctive issues. These interfaces have been placed in households for extended periods of time and are subject to an on-going process of iterative user refinement. During that time we have seen a broad shift from richly featured applications providing a single management application for the network to a set of lightweight apps with more specific information.

It is worth noting that while iterative refinement of interfaces is relatively straightforward, changes to underlying infrastructure (e.g., our DHCP implementation) require considerably more engineering effort. In this section we wish to reflect on a number of broad lessons can be extracted from our deployments.

The invisible nature of a mundane infrastructure

We are particularly interested in how the infrastructure and its interfaces become a mundane part of everyday live. Consequently, we didn't scaffold our studies with particular user tasks. A notable feature across all deployments is the unremarkable nature of the home network. Users are uninterested in the day-to-day operation of the infrastructure and this was reflected in the orientation to many of the interfaces, which were initially explored as curios reflecting the technical nature of the network. People became less curious about who was routinely consuming resources or even accessing the network, an effect that is mirrored in a variety of smart meter energy displays and other public displays [9]. Our users soon forgot passive network displays unless there was a distinct prompt or purpose. Consequently, we found a growing need to notify users of significant events and exploited the user notification facility of the infrastructure to push network events at users through a range of media.

Increasing network information increases social discord

A striking feature of our deployments was the extent to which everyday family life is now predicated on network-based digital services. Network activity is now intertwined with the moral ordering of the home [4]. Revealing network traffic is not a neutral action in the home and can have significant negative impact on the dynamics of the home. A notable example arose in one household where a member suggested understanding traffic would help dealing with a a long-term overseas student visitor who was causing the household to exceed a bandwidth cap. Our interfaces did indeed reveal that the majority of traffic was from the guest's device. However, resolving the issue was more problematic with a number of tense conversations drawn out over succeeding weeks. The key role the interface served was to draw attention to the phenomenon, which may actually have *increased* tensions, making resolution harder. It remains unclear what might be the most effective ways of revealing information to all stakeholders.

The challenge of privacy

Domestic settings have quite subtle privacy issues often associated with awareness of actions across a family. Monitoring tended to be at client screens by looking over users' shoulders. People were strategic about where they would access services. People also exploited browser histories both to occasionally monitor use and to ensure their past use was no longer available for inspection.

Changing the infrastructure in the manner that we have alters the visibility of the network. Information about the activities of a range of clients is now available through the network, with the router providing a single point of record and audit for network activity. The raises a host of new privacy challenges. Who should control this? How broad should access be? How are activities identified and audited? Consider the current use of browser histories: to view your browser history requires access to your device(s). This allows users significant and subtle control of their privacy. However, if the browser logs of all clients are made available through the router this social mediation is altered. Addressing these challenges is complex and is a focus of our ongoing longitudinal study; even in the early stages our data indicates a need to provide techniques for users to maintain some ambiguity in their online actions.

Managing the network is managing the household

Our deployments also highlight the home network as an everyday social object within the household. Interactions within the network are embedded within a host of other social interactions in the household and must be understood in these terms. This is particularly important in terms of network control where changes to the network are subject to a host of domestic judgments. Throttling traffic from a particular device makes a statement about the relative importance of that family member's activity on that device. Blocking traffic from a device to a particular site makes a clear statement of the acceptability of that particular behaviour. Denying access from a guest's device to your home network inevitably has implications for, and causes inferences to be drawn as to, your relationship to the guest.

While all users in all of our deployments enthusiastically requested control of this form they also shared considerable reluctance in the active *use* of such mechanisms in the network. In fact, they welcomed the potential (threat) provided by the control mechanisms but did not see them as a substitute for the nuanced negotiation involved in discussing network use in the family. Using these network-based control mechanisms was seen as the culmination of a longer process of discussion and negotiation: many felt they would only turn to network control mechanisms as a last resort. Thus, although users did not anticipate routine use of these facilities, they felt their existence was crucial in framing discussions of network use.

CONCLUSION

We have presented a reshaping of the home network informed by studies of network use. This required us to recreate the underlying infrastructure to provide greater access to and control, allowing a broader range of interactive possibilities to manage of the infrastructure. This demanded we move beyond a focus on user interfaces, to place interaction deeper into the infrastructure by amending how the underlying network deals with protocols and services. As users increasingly interact through an ecology of devices connected to a complex network, interactive systems developers must consider how they shape underlying systems and services to meet user needs.

While we have focused on the infrastructure of the digital it is worth observing that a host of other infrastructures (water, energy, transport) are also becoming digitally rich, altering our visibility of them. The interactive issues surrounding an infrastructure are subtle: we wish it to be simultaneously unremarkable and invisible in use while providing enough information to orientate our activities [13]. This sociotechnical balance requires reflection of understanding of users throughout the infrastructure

ACKNOWLEDGEMENTS

We would like to thank Keith Edwards for his comments on a draft of this paper. This work was supported by RCUK/EPSRC awards EP/G065802/1 and EP/F064276/1

REFERENCES

1. Calvert, K. *et al.* (2010) "Instrumenting Home Networks", *ACM CCR*, 41(1), pp. 84–89.
2. Chetty, M *et al.* (2011) "Why is my Internet slow?: Making network speeds visible." *Proc. ACM CHI*, pp.1889 — 1898.
3. Chetty, M. *et al.* (2010) "Who's hogging the bandwidth? The consequences of revealing the invisible home", *Proc. ACM CHI*, pp.659–668.
4. Crabtree, A. *et al.* (2012) "Unremarkable Networking: The Home Network as Part of Everyday Life", *Proc. ACM DIS.*
5. Edwards, W.K. *et al.* (2010) "The Infrastructure Problem in HCI", *Proc. ACM CHI.*
6. Grinter, R. *et al.* (2005) "The work to make the home network work", *Proc. ECSCW*, pp.469–488.
7. Grinter, R. *et al.* (2009) "The Ins and Outs of Home Networking: The Case for Useful and Usable Home Networking" *ACM ToCHI*, 16(2):1–28, June 2009.
8. Grudin. J. (1990) "The computer reaches out: the historical continuity of interface design". *Proc. ACM CHI*, pp.261–268.
9. Huang, E. M. *et al.* (2006) "Displays in the wild: Understanding the dynamics and evolution of a display ecology." Proc. Pervasive, Dublin, Ireland.
10. McKeown, N, *et al.* (2008) "OpenFlow: enabling innovation in campus networks", ACM CCR 38(2).
11. Shehan-Poole, E. *et al.* (2008) "More than meets the eye: transforming the user experience of home network management", *Proc. ACM DIS*, pp.455–464.
12. Shehan, E., Edwards, W. K. (2007). "Home networking and HCI: what hath god wrought?" CHI '07: ACM
13. Star, L., "The ethnography of infrastructure," American Behavioural Scientist, vol. 43, no. 3, pp. 377-391, 1999.
14. Sundaresan, S., de Donato, W., & Feamster, N. (2011). Broadband Internet performance: A view from the gateway. Proc SIGCOMM 2011, Toronto.
15. Sventek, J. *et al.* (2011) "An Information Plane Architecture Supporting Home Network Management", *Proc. IFIP/IEEE IM.*
16. Tolmie, P., *et al.* (2007) "Making the home network at home: digital housekeeping", *Proc. ECSCW*, pp.331–350.
17. Yang, J. *et al.* (2010) "Eden: supporting home network management through interactive visual tools", *Proc. ACM UIST*, pp.109–118.

DataPlay: Interactive Tweaking and Example-driven Correction of Graphical Database Queries

Azza Abouzied
Yale University
azza@cs.yale.edu

Joseph M. Hellerstein
Univ. of California, Berkeley
hellerstein@cs.berkeley.edu

Avi Silberschatz
Yale University
avi@cs.yale.edu

ABSTRACT

Writing complex queries in SQL is a challenge for users. Prior work has developed several techniques to ease query specification but none of these techniques are applicable to a particularly difficult class of queries: *quantified queries*. Our hypothesis is that users prefer to specify quantified queries interactively by *trial-and-error*. We identify two impediments to this form of interactive trial-and-error query specification in SQL: (i) changing quantifiers often requires global syntactical query restructuring, and (ii) the absence of *non-answers* from SQL's results makes verifying query correctness difficult. We remedy these issues with *DataPlay*, a query tool with an underlying graphical query language, a unique data model and a graphical interface. DataPlay provides two interaction features that support trial-and-error query specification. First, DataPlay allows users to *directly manipulate* a graphical query by changing quantifiers and modifying dependencies between constraints. Users receive real-time feedback in the form of updated answers and non-answers. Second, DataPlay can *auto-correct* a user's query, based on user feedback about which tuples to keep or drop from the answers and non-answers. We evaluated the effectiveness of each interaction feature with a user study and we found that direct query manipulation is more effective than auto-correction for simple queries but auto-correction is more effective than direct query manipulation for more complex queries.

Author Keywords

Quantification; Query Specification; Query Correction; Semantic fine-tuning

ACM Classification Keywords

H.5.2 Information interfaces and presentation: User Interfaces - Graphical user interfaces.

General Terms

Design, Human Factors, Languages

INTRODUCTION

Despite decades of work on language and interface design, many database users find it difficult to specify complex queries. Of all query tasks, users find non-trivial quantification to be most difficult [20, 19]. Contemporary query specification paradigms, such as query-by-example, visualization-driven querying and faceted search offer help with specifying simple query blocks, but they offer very little assistance for precisely those queries that are most difficult to specify — quantified queries. For those queries, users are stuck with the powerful but difficult database query language: SQL.

Quantified queries evaluate constraints over *sets of tuples* rather than individual tuples, to determine whether a set as a whole satisfies the query. Inherent in these queries are (i) the grouping of tuples into sets, and (ii) the binding of constraints with either existential or universal quantifiers. Existential quantifiers ensure that some tuple in the set satisfies the constraint, while universal quantifiers ensure that all tuples in the set satisfy the constraint.

People engage in casual quantified-query specification with one another on a regular basis. For example, when buying flowers, we might request a bouquet of 'some red and white roses'. Despite this request being somewhat underspecified, the florist will still try putting together a bouquet. He may add some red and white roses and then add a few lilies. If we wanted *only* roses, we clarify the misunderstanding and say 'only roses'. If we wanted only red or white roses, we might allow the lilies but object to pink roses. Such casual interactions suggest that we are accustomed to specifying quantified queries by trial-and-error, where we adjust our initial query specification by modifying quantifiers — only roses — or modifying dependencies between constraints — only red or white roses but no other rose colors[1].

What makes SQL — the de facto query language for quantified querying — challenging is that it discourages this trial-and-error approach to querying. Effective trial-and-error query specification depends on (i) the facility to incrementally refine an incorrect query through *small tweaks* and (ii) the ability to understand the effect of these tweaks. SQL, however, does not facilitate incremental query refinement because it lacks *syntax locality*: semantically small tweaks, such as changing a quantifier from existential to universal, usually result in large changes in the structure and syntax of a SQL query. Moreover, SQL does not present the complete effects of a query. While SQL presents *answers* or tuples that satisfy a query, it does not present *non-answers* or tuples that do not satisfy the query. Non-answers and answers together

[1]The dependency here is between a constraint on flower type and a constraint on flower color.

UIST'12, October 7–10, 2012, Cambridge, Massachusetts, USA.

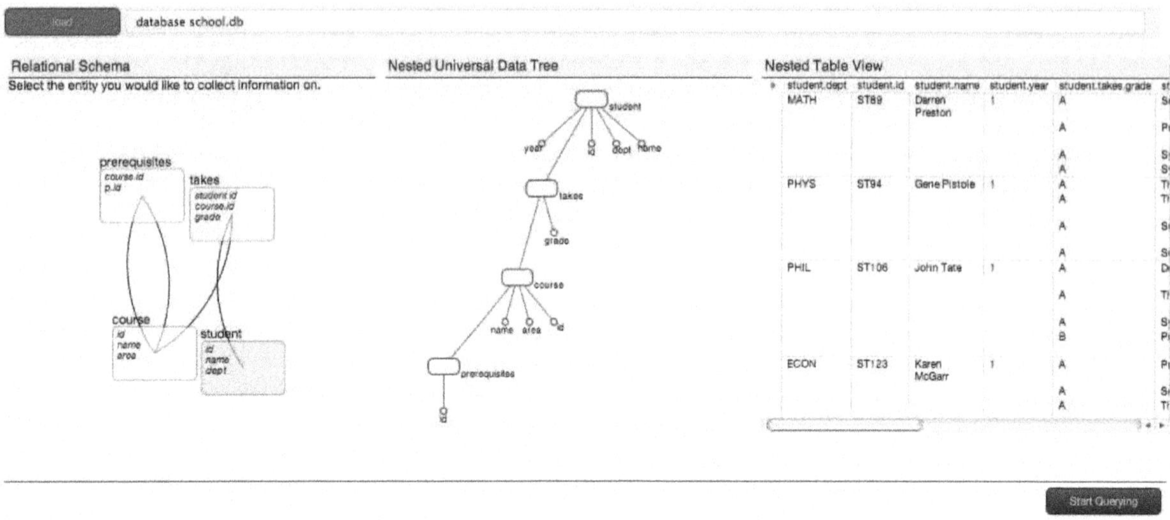

Figure 1. DataPlay's pivot interface: transforming a relational database into a nested data tree

help explain the behavior of quantifiers and help users assess the correctness of a query.

We present the design of *DataPlay*, a query tool that simplifies the specification and debugging of quantified queries by encouraging a trial-and-error approach to querying. DataPlay lets users specify their constraints without worrying about how to assemble them into a complete query. It builds from these constraints a graphical query, which users can *directly manipulate* to semantically refine the query. This is possible because the graphical query language exhibits syntax locality. DataPlay, also, helps users explore the space of query refinements by *visually suggesting possible manipulations*. As users tweak the query, it displays both *answers* and *non-answers* and keeps an *interactive graphical history viewer* of all modifications made to the query.

DataPlay also auto-corrects queries: users mark answers with 'want out' or 'keep in' labels and non-answers with 'want in' or 'keep out' labels and in turn DataPlay generates all modifications to the current query that satisfy the user's revision of answers and non-answers. To help users choose one query from several suggested queries, DataPlay rank-orders the generated queries by the size of their changes to the answers and non-answers, provides visual previews of these changes and also provides side-by-side comparisons of suggested queries.

DataPlay's *mixed-initiative user interface* integrates direct query manipulation with automated query correction. This interface is feasible because of DataPlay's unique data model and graphical query language. In this paper, we describe the data model and query language and how it relates to the relational data model and SQL.

Given the novelty of query auto-correction, we compare its effectiveness against direct query manipulation in a controlled user-study. We asked users to correct an incorrect query by either directly manipulating the graphical query or using the auto-correction feature. Our results show that users prefer direct manipulation to auto-correction for simple queries. As the query complexity increases, users prefer the query auto-correction feature; more users reach the correct query in less time. Thus the study provides evidence that a mixed-initiative query specification interface is superior to only a direct manipulation interface.

QUERYING WITH DATAPLAY

Querying with DataPlay involves four steps: (1) Pivoting, (2) Specifying constraints, (3) Fine-tuning and (4) Auto-correcting. Users typically iterate over steps two and three and occasionally auto-correct a query.

We explain how a user, Jane, performs each of these steps through an example query task. Suppose Jane has a school database and she wants to find students who
a) are in the CS department
b) completed *all* of CS11, CS16 and CS18 and
c) received A's in *all* three courses. She doesn't care about their grades in other courses.

Pivoting

Jane begins by connecting to the school database. DataPlay visualizes the database schema and the relationships between the tables of the database (left panel in Fig. 1). The school database consists of four tables: `student`, `course`, `takes` and `prerequisites`. The `student` and `course` tables represent tangible entities that users may wish to gather information about. Users will most-likely select one of these tables as a *pivot*. The remaining tables represent relationships between these entities. Since Jane is searching for students, she selects the `student` table as the pivot. DataPlay now restructures the database schema into a nested schema, which we call the *data tree* (middle panel Fig. 1). All tables are pivoted by the `student` table: for every student we have a nested-set of all the courses they took along with their grades in each course and for every course taken by a student we have a nested-set

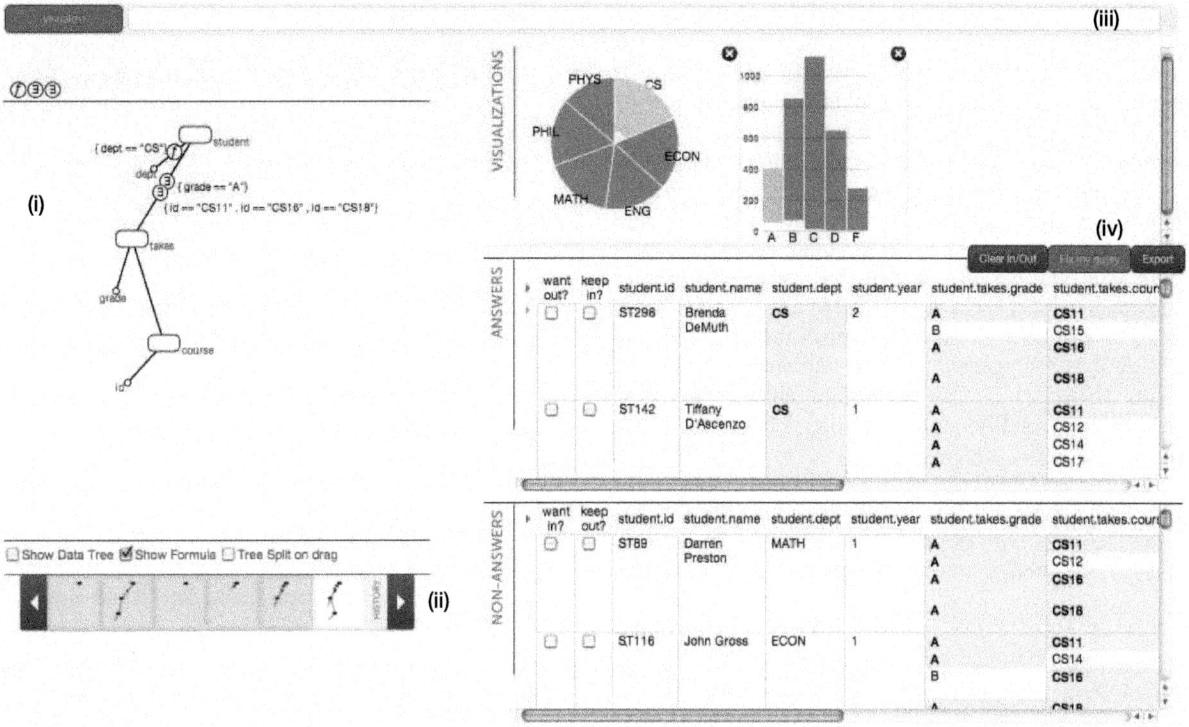

Figure 2. DataPlay's query interface: (i) query tree (ii) interactive graphical history viewer (iii) command bar (iv) data and visualization panel

of all the prerequisites of that course. DataPlay thus transforms the many tables of the database into a single nested-universal table akin to a JSON or XML document. DataPlay shows Jane a tabular presentation of this nested-universal table to help her understand its nested structure (right panel in Fig. 1).

After pivoting, Jane begins querying the data. The query interface (Fig. 2) consists of (i) a query panel that visualizes the current query as a *query tree*, (ii) an interactive graphical history that presents all modifications made to a query, (iii) a command bar to specify constraints or visualizations in, and (iv) a data presentation panel which presents data-visualizations and two tables: an answer table and a non-answer table. At this point, all tuples of the nested-universal table are in the answers table and the non-answer table is empty.

Specifying Constraints

Jane can specify her constraints explicitly by writing simple propositions into a command bar or by brushing data-visualizations and having DataPlay automatically infer the propositions in the style of Tableau [3] or [8]. For the departmental constraint, she decides to visualize the department distribution first. As soon as she types 'dep' into a visualization-bar, DataPlay auto-suggests all attributes with 'dep'. She selects `student.dept`. DataPlay suggests two possible visualizations for the department attribute: a bar chart and a piechart. These suggestions are graphical thumbnails computed on a sample of the data. She picks the piechart; DataPlay adds a piechart to the visualization panel. She brushes the 'CS' pie; DataPlay (i) generates a constraint node with the propositional formula $\texttt{student.dept} =' \texttt{CS}'$, (ii) adds it on the query tree, (iii) executes the query and (iv) updates the answers and non-answers.

Jane then visualizes the `student.takes.grade` attribute in a bar chart. She brushes the A-bar. This causes DataPlay to add another constraint node with the proposition $\texttt{student.takes.grade} =' A'$. Since each student has a *set* of grades, DataPlay binds a default *existential quantifier* to the added constraint. The query tree finds CS students who have an A in their set of grades.

Jane types the following constraint for courses into the command bar:
$\texttt{student.takes.course.id}[= \texttt{CS11}, = \texttt{CS16}, = \texttt{CS18}]$
As a syntactic convenience, DataPlay enables users to specify multiple propositions in the above shorthand. DataPlay treats such propositions as a single constraint. As before, DataPlay generates another constraint node and adds it to the query tree and since each student takes multiple courses, DataPlay binds an existential quantifier to the course constraint.

Every modification made to the query results in the interactive update of answers and non-answers. In addition, a graphical snapshot of the preceding query tree is recorded in history. Jane can revert to a previous query tree by clicking its snapshot in the interactive history viewer; this adds the current tree to history before loading the previous query tree from history.

Jane has now specified all of her constraints and DataPlay has assembled the simplest possible query tree (Fig. 2), which finds students who are in the CS department, **and** took any of CS11, CS16 or CS18, **and** got at least one A in any course.

Fine-tuning

Jane starts fine-tuning the query tree. Any time she hovers over a constraint node on the query tree, DataPlay suggests possible manipulations to the node that will change the semantics of the query. In Figure 3, Jane hovers over the grade constraint and DataPlay suggests (i) toggling the quantifier from existential to universal such that students who *only* got A's are answers (Jane can click the 'Toggle Quantifier' button) or (ii) moving the grade constraint underneath the course constraint such that we only test for the presence of one of the three courses (CS11, CS16 and CS18) in the nested-set of courses taken that have an A grade. Jane drags the grade constraint node to the suggested position underneath the course constraint. She scans the answer and non-answer tables and is happy with the conditional dependence between the grade and course constraint: students who got A's in any of the three courses are answers. The query still needs fine-tuning; Jane wants students who got A's in all three courses. She decides to provide DataPlay with examples of tuples that are answers and tuples that are non-answers and let DataPlay fix her query for her.

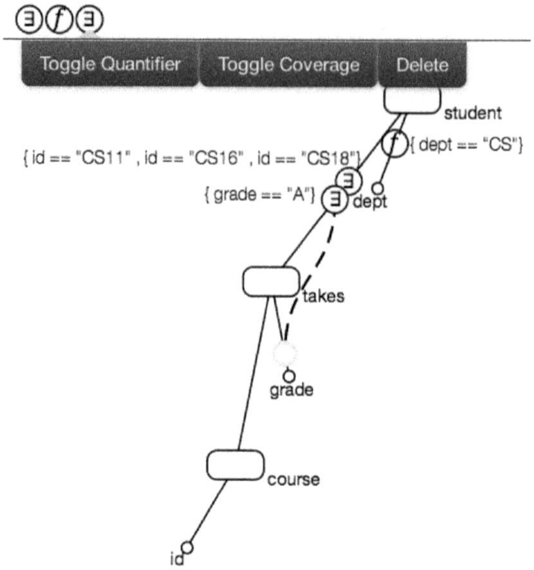

Figure 3. DataPlay visually suggests the different semantic modifications to a query's constraints

Auto-correcting

In Figure 4, Jane marks the 'want out' checkbox for students in the answer table who didn't take all courses. She marks the 'keep in' checkbox for students who took all three courses with A's in them. She only marks a few tuples in the answer table. She decides not to mark any of the tuples in the non-answer table. Jane thus revises the result of the current query to match her intended query. She clicks the 'Fix my query' button. DataPlay constructs all query trees *derivable* from the current query tree and suggests query trees that satisfy the tuple memberships that Jane provided as possible corrections (See Section 'DataPlay's Query Auto-correction' for details).

DataPlay suggests only one correction for Jane's query: *covering* the course constraint. Coverage ensures that all propositions in a constraint are satisfied. Coverage is visually presented as a shading of the constraint node. Jane's accepts this correction and now the query finds all students in the CS department who took all three courses with A's in them.

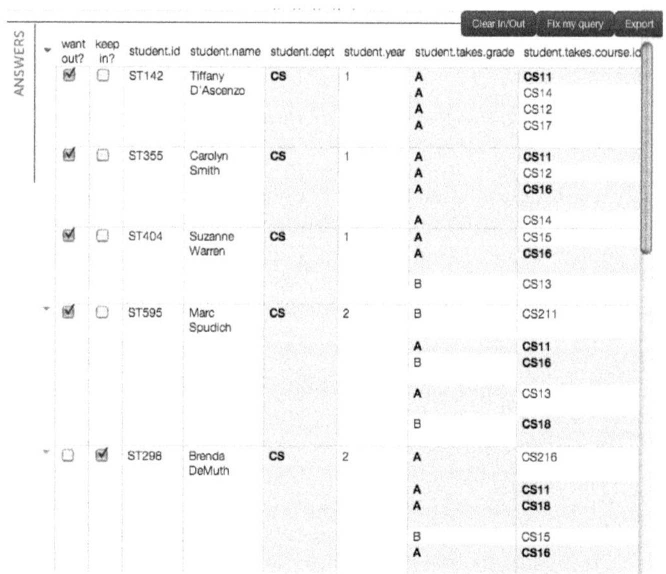

Figure 4. DataPlay's Correction by Example: users mark which tuples they want out or kept in Answers

FROM SQL DEFICIENCIES TO DATAPLAY FEATURES

We designed DataPlay out of a frustration with SQL query tools. We conducted an observational study on thirteen SQL users and analyzed what makes SQL challenging. We identified two key deficiencies, a lack of *syntax locality* and a lack of *non-answers*, which together hinder a trial-and-error approach to querying. We worked from SQL's deficiencies to DataPlay's features: our query language exhibits syntax locality and our data model enables the computation of non-answers for any query.

Figure 6 presents the results of the observational study. It shows the time it takes for trained[2] SQL users to specify a deceivingly complex query task: "find straight-A students

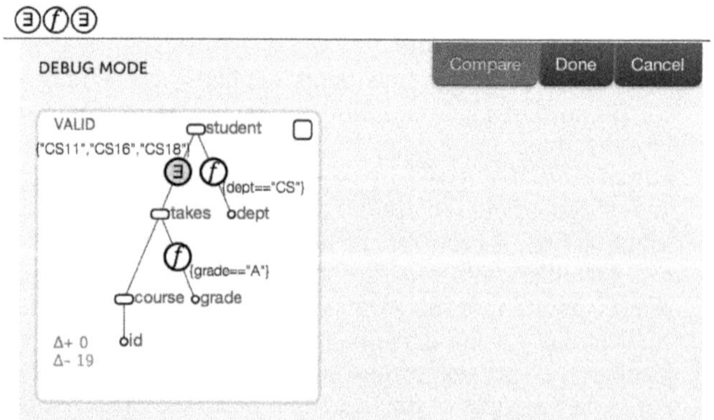

Figure 5. DataPlay searches the space of query trees derivable by manipulating the user's initial query to find query trees that satisfy the user's Answer/Non-Answer markings. Here, DataPlay found one correct query tree.

[2]On a 10-point scale 1 being basic knowledge and 10 being expert, the median self-reported SQL expertise was 5. The study participants were mainly graduate students in Systems research or undergraduate students who recently completed SQL training.

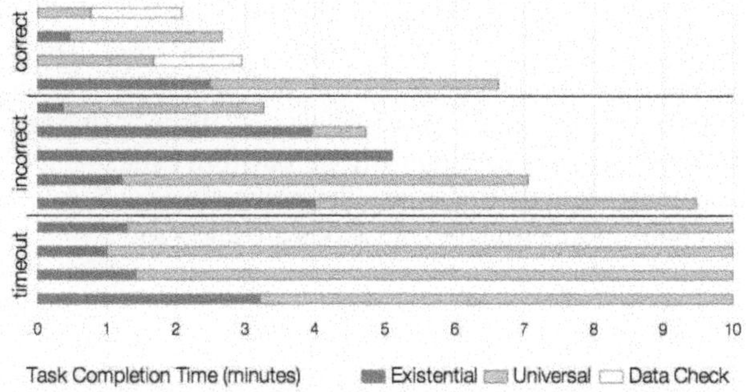

Figure 6. SQL query specification behavior of 13 SQL users.

(students who got A's in all their courses)". Only 4 of the 13 users successfully specified the query within 10 minutes! Most users (11 of 13) began with the simpler existential variant of this query, i.e., they found students with at least one A. This 'existential phase' was followed by a 'universal phase': users attempted to rewrite the existential query to get to the universal query. The prevalence of this two-phase querying behavior hints at the intrinsic trial-and-error nature of quantified querying.

In the following sections, we explain how each SQL deficiency discourages trial-and-error querying.

Syntax Locality

The following two SQL queries find students who got at least one A and students who got all A's respectively.

```
SELECT * FROM student s, takes t,
WHERE  t.grade = 'A' AND t.student_id = s.id;

SELECT * FROM student s, takes t
WHERE t.student_id = s.id AND s.id NOT IN
(SELECT student_id FROM takes WHERE grade != 'A');
```

A key observation about the SQL queries is that their structures are very different. The simple change of the quantifier from existential to universal appears to have global impact on the query syntax. For this reason we say that SQL often exhibits poor syntax locality with respect to changes in quantification. The inability to localize the details of the quantifier make the language confusing to users. Poor syntax locality discourages trial-and-error tuning of query specifications: small changes to query semantics can require large changes to query syntax.

Moreover, SQL users often feel *stuck* after formulating an incorrect query in SQL. Complex SQL queries tend to follow templates or tricks, which users learn with experience: two of the four users who wrote a correct SQL query were directly applying a learned template; they skipped the 'existential phase'. Users who haven't yet learned such templates cannot brute-force their way out of incorrect queries by applying different modifications.

Non-answers

As users write SQL queries, they look at the results to affirm that the written SQL matches their intended query. The presentation of a SQL query's results, however, is insufficient: two of the study's successful users wrote additional queries to check that their query was correct (Data Check phase in Figure 6): they arbitrarily chose a couple of students from the query result and wrote another query to view all the grades of these students to ensure that they indeed had no other non-A grades.

Existential

(a) Answers

Nina Simone	BLUS101	A
Nina Simone	JAZZ101	A
Nina Simone	SOUL101	A
Bill Withers	BLUS101	A
Bill Withers	RYTH101	A

(b) Non-Answers

Bill Withers	**CLAS101**	**C**
Louis Armstrong	REGA101	B
Bob Marley	BLUS101	C
Bob Marley	RYTM101	C
Bob Marley	JAZZ101	C

Universal

(c) Answers

Nina Simone	BLUS101	A
Nina Simone	JAZZ101	A
Nina Simone	SOUL101	A
Frank Sinatra	CLAS101	A
Frank Sinatra	MELD101	A

(d) Non-Answers

Bill Withers	BLUS101	**A**
Bill Withers	RYTH101	**A**
Bill Withers	CLAS101	C
Louis Armstrong	JAZZ101	**A**
Louis Armstrong	REGA101	B

Table 1. Answers and Non-Answers for queries that find students with at least one A and students with all A's

Tables 1a and 1c are example results of executing the existential and the universal SQL queries for finding students who got at least one A and students who got all As respectively.

Without any additional information, it is impossible to determine which query produced which of the sample results in Tables 1a and 1c. SQL interfaces usually provide us with the *answers* or the tuples that satisfy our query, but they do not provide us with the answers' complement: the *non-answers* or tuples that do not satisfy our query. Answers alone, however, may not help us fully understand a query. It is only when we see 'Bill Withers' in both the answers (Table 1a) and the non-answers (Table 1b), that we can deduce that Table 1a is the result of the *at least one A* query. Similarly, it is only when we see A's in the non-answers (Table 1d), that we can deduce that Table 1c is the result of the *straight-A* query.

Without non-answers, a user looking for straight-A students can mistakenly believe that an existentially-quantified query is correct just by examining the answers. Therefore, SQL interfaces that do not present non-answers hinder query interpretation and ultimately correct query specification.

Unfortunately, this problem is not amenable to a quick interface fix: complements are not commonplace in SQL interfaces because the pure relational query and data model make it hard to define and compute complements. Consider the following poorly constructed yet valid query:

```
SELECT * FROM student, takes WHERE
student.id = x AND takes.student_id = x;
```

In this query it is difficult to determine the *universe* from which we complement answers to form non-answers. It is likely that the user's perspective of the universe is `student` $\bowtie$ `takes`, which represents the courses taken by the student. However, the query has no apparent join and one can infer the universe to be `student` × `takes`, which represents all possible combinations of student tuples with takes tuples. If we infer the second universe, we will compute a much larger and an incomprehensible non-answer set.

DataPlay's data model enables the presentation of non-answers and its graphical query language exhibits syntax locality. We describe the data model and query language in the following sections. We describe how the language's syntax locality and the presentation of answers and non-answers enable query auto-correction. We then discuss the inner workings of the query auto-correction feature.

DATAPLAY'S DATA MODEL

DataPlay restricts the relational data model to a *nested universal relation*: while this limits the expressive power of DataPlay compared to SQL to a degree, it enables a far more effective specification interface for a large class of sophisticated queries. We describe the data model, the features it enables and its limitations.

DataPlay uses a user-specified *pivot* to assemble a single nested universal table from the many tables of a database. We refer to the schema of this table as the *data tree*. Any relational schema can be transformed into a data tree: we map the schema of the relational database into a graph where nodes represent relations and edges represent primary-foreign key relationships between relations. We call this graph the *key-graph*. The *data tree* is a rooted spanning-tree of the key-graph with the pivot as the root. Starting with the pivot, we add it as the root of our data tree. We add all its attributes, excluding any foreign keys, as leaves. We then traverse all edges outgoing from the pivot in the key-graph in a depth-first fashion. For each relation that we add as a node to the data tree, we add all its attributes as leaves excluding foreign keys. In the data tree, every attribute is identified by its path from the pivot. We populate the nested universal table by taking the join of a child relation with a parent relation in the data tree.

The nested universal table is an abstract view on top of the relational database; we do need not to physically restructure the database or materialize multiple nested universal tables, one for every pivot.

While the nested universal table is not a new concept [13], it is a largely forgotten one. As the name suggests, it merges universal relations [14] with nested data models, such as JSON or XML. This buys us the following:

1. A natural grouping hierarchy for a large class of quantified-queries: For these queries, users are relieved from two cumbersome SQL steps: *join specification* and *group construction* through sub-queries.

2. A closed-world: Querying in DataPlay is simply the partitioning of the tuples of nested universal table into answers or non-answers. If tuples of the pivot satisfy all our constraints then they are answers, otherwise, they are non-answers. In contrast, non-answers, in the traditional relational-model, are neither well defined nor easy to compute as we discussed in the previous section.

DATAPLAY'S GRAPHICAL QUERY LANGUAGE

A query in our language is called a *query tree*. The class of queries captured by query trees are *Boolean conjunctive quantified* queries over nested relations. Each quantified expression consists of conjunctions or Horn[3] statements over Boolean functions (these are the constraints) and only conjunctions of quantified expressions are allowed.

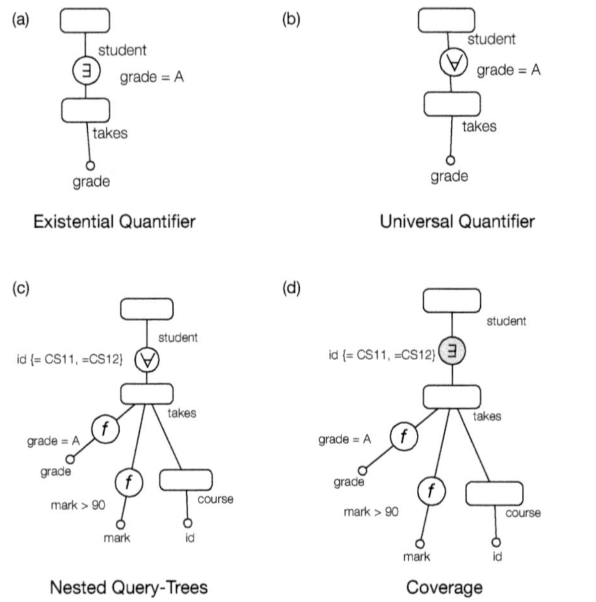

Figure 7. DataPlay's Graphical Query Language

The example query trees in Figure 7 comprehensively describe all aspects of DataPlay's graphical query language. Query trees are *data trees* overlaid with constraints. Every relation node is a query tree that maps its tuples to either answers or non-answers. An empty query tree — one without constraints — maps all its tuples to answers. The trees are conjunctive in nature, they take the conjunction of all constraints on their descendants —attributes or *answer* tuples from a nested query tree.

In Figure 7a, the empty query tree at `takes` maps all its tuples to answers as it has no constraints. For every student, the query tree at the pivot, `student`, determines whether there exists a tuple in the nested set of *answer*-tuples in `takes` where grade is A. Those students are answers. The remaining students are non-answers. In, Figure 7b, the query tree at the pivot, `student`, determines whether all grades of a student in the nested set of answer-tuples in `takes` are A.

Note that when a constraint node operates over a set of tuples, it has one of the following quantifier symbols in it: $\forall$ for the universal quantifier or $\exists$ for the existential quantifier. If the constraint node operates over an individual tuple and not a set of tuples, it requires no quantifier, and instead has the symbol f in it.

In Figure 7c, the query tree at `takes` maps tuples where grade is A and mark is above 90 to answers. The query tree at the

[3] e.g. $a \wedge b \rightarrow c$

`student` pivot, now tests if all of the nested answer tuples in `takes` are either CS11 or CS12 and no other courses. The universally-quantified course constraint here only examines the nested answer tuples of `takes` ignoring the nested non-answer tuples.

The query tree of Figure 7d illustrates a special feature of the language: *coverage*. Coverage allows users to ensure that *all* of a constraint's propositions (assuming it has more than one) are true for a set of tuples[4]. The query tree of Figure 7d ensures that a student has taken both CS11 and CS12 with A's and marks above 90. Coverage is denoted by a shading of the constraint node. Technically, coverage is a redundant feature of the language as one can write separate constraints for every course and the conjunctive nature of DataPlay will ensure coverage. However, users may conceptualize several propositions as a single self-contained constraint. Also, when brushing dense-visualizations, if we generate one constraint for every brushed area or glyph, rather than a list of propositions for a single constraint, we might over-crowd the query tree.

The graphical query language is expressive enough to describe a large class of quantified queries succinctly and with syntax locality: compare the query trees of Figure 7a and 7b with their equivalent SQL queries (see section on SQL 'Syntax Locality'). Notice that to change the semantics of a constraint from existential to universal, only a single symbol change is required. Users can tweak the properties of a constraint independently of other constraints and without re-creating a new query tree. Since each constraint supports a fixed set of manipulations (toggle quantifier, toggle coverage or change position), DataPlay visually suggests these manipulations to users. Users, no longer have to feel *stuck*: they can try out different manipulations until they reach their intended query.

Moreover, the language ensures that for a given collection of constraints, there is a finite and searchable space of possible query trees: this enables auto-correction. Instead of directly manipulating a query tree to achieve a certain partition of tuples into answers or non-answers, users can simply specify this partition by marking tuples as either answers or non-answers and DataPlay will search the space of query trees to find one that achieves the required partition.

Finally, compared to a textual query representation, query trees better reflect the hierarchical structure of the nested universal table and better illustrate the dependencies between constraints; nesting is visually awkward in a linear representation.

DATAPLAY'S QUERY AUTO-CORRECTION

We built the auto-correction feature because as the complexity of a query increases, the more difficult it becomes to debug and fix a query by directly manipulating it as we empirically demonstrate in the following section.

[4]A list of propositions is different from specifying a boolean conjunction or disjunction of these propositions: a list operates at the set level, while the disjunction or conjunction operates at an individual tuple-value.

Users validate a query's correctness by examining its answers and non-answers and searching for misplaced tuples. Enabling users to label offending tuples in answers with 'want out' and actual answers misplaced in non-answers with 'want in' and in turn correcting the query for the user reduces the *gulf of execution* [17] of a query specification tool as users combine validation and debugging in a single process. In DataPlay, we also allow user to label correctly placed answer and non-answer tuples with 'keep in' and 'keep out' respectively. We refer to the user-specified mapping of tuples into answers or non-answers as *tuple memberships*. Users only provide partial mappings of all database tuples to answers or non-answers: unmapped tuples are *free*. Automated query-correction must support such partial mappings as no user will map all tuples of a database to answers or non-answers.

DataPlay generates the space of all possible query trees derivable from the current query tree by (i) toggling quantifiers, (ii) toggling coverage or (iii) changing the positions of constraints. DataPlay suggests all query trees in this space that satisfy the given tuple memberships. If users provide a few or not enough *selective* tuple memberships the space of suggested query trees can be large and it might be difficult for users to understand the semantic differences between the suggested query trees. To reduce this *gulf of evaluation* [17]:

1. We preserve tuple memberships across several iterations of automated query correction. This allows users to pick any one of the suggested query trees and provide more tuple memberships if the selected query tree turns out to be incorrect. Users can explicitly clear tuple memberships by clicking a 'Clear In/Out' button.

2. We provide visual-previews of the effect of a suggested query tree: when users mouse-over over a suggested query tree, DataPlay shades tuples that are non-answers for that query tree.

3. We allow users to *diff* suggested query trees; DataPlay opens up a comparison window containing tuples on which the query trees disagree on whether they are answers or non-answers.

DataPlay rank-orders its query correction suggestions by the number of tuples that change membership from answers to non-answers or vice-versa. We chose this order under the assumption that users might directly manipulate a query to get close to their intended answers/non-answers and then use auto-correction to fix the membership of a few problematic tuples. Thus, we order query trees that drastically change answers and non-answers last. This order, however, does not guarantee that the user's intended query is at the top of all the query tree suggestions.

EVALUATING DATAPLAY'S INTERFACE

As an initial evaluation of our mixed-initiative user interface, we conducted a comparative user study of DataPlay's novel query specification features: direct query manipulation and automated query correction. Our goal was to observe task completion times for each feature to determine which feature users were more effective at debugging queries with.

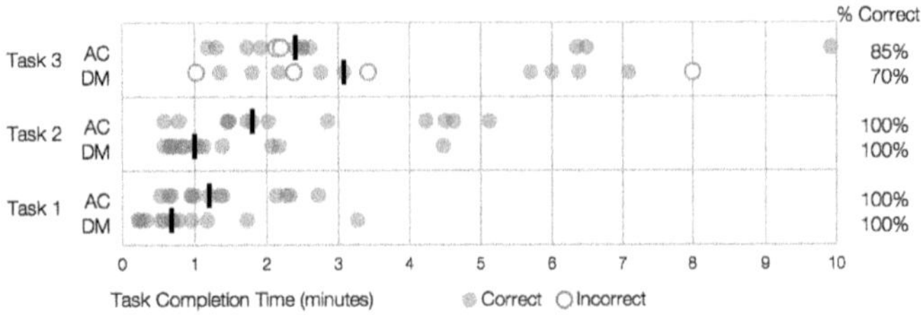

Figure 8. Black bars indicate median task completion times. 'DM' stands for Direct Manipulation and 'AC' for Auto-Correction.

Participants and Methods

We recruited the same 13 participants of the SQL observation study. These subjects are familiar with database querying: undergraduate students from an Introduction to Databases course and graduate students who regularly work with databases. The subjects had never used DataPlay before.

We first presented a 15-minute DataPlay video-tutorial. The tutorial described how to (i) load and pivot a database, (ii) specify constraints, (iii) directly manipulate a query tree and (iv) auto-correct a query tree by providing tuple memberships. We then allowed the participants to play with the tool for 10 minutes. The users directed this play-time and we answered any questions they had about the tool.

We then asked the subjects to fix a set of three incorrect queries of increasing complexity (described below) using only one of the features tested: direct query manipulation or automated query correction. Users then fixed a second set of three incorrect queries of similar complexity to the first three but on a different dataset and using the other, still unused feature. The choice of dataset for each feature was randomized across subjects. The two datasets were (randomly generated) student academic records and US flight arrival and departure records.

Task 1: We gave users a query tree that finds (a) students who got A's in some courses or (b) routes where some flights arrived late. We asked users to fix the query to find (a) students with all A's or (b) routes where all flights arrived late. The complexity of this task is '1-tweak'.

Task 2: We gave users a query tree that finds (a) students who took courses in any of three areas or (b) flights that were delayed by any of three causes. We asked users to fix the query to find (a) students who took courses in all and only the three areas or (b) flights that were delayed by all and only the three causes. The complexity of this task is '2-tweaks'.

Task 3: We gave users a query tree that finds (a) students who took any of three specific courses and got an A in any course or (b) flights that were delayed by any of three causes and some delays lasted more than 10 minutes. We asked users to fix the query to find (a) students who took all three courses with A's in them ignoring grades in other courses or (b) flights that were delayed by all three causes and for each cause the delay lasted more than 10 minutes. The complexity of this task is '3-tweaks'.

Both features are important

We performed a repeated-measures ANOVA of completion times with query complexity and feature used as independent factors. We log-transformed responses to better approximate a normal distribution. We found a significant main effect of query complexity ($F_{2,11} = 36.74, p < 0.001$). In Figure 8, we notice that overall speed and accuracy for both features are adversely affected as query complexity increases. We also found a significant main effect of feature ($F_{1,12} = 7.37, p < 0.02$) and a significant interaction effect of query complexity and feature ($F_{2,11} = 5.39, p = 0.02$); as the query complexity increased (Task 3), performance with the auto-correction tool improved over direct manipulation despite direct manipulation being significantly better than auto-correction for simpler query tasks.

In Figure 8, we observe that the median performance to fix the first two less complex query tasks with direct manipulation is faster than query correction. Users expressed through comments in a post-study questionnaire that when they knew exactly what changes they had to apply to the query tree, they felt query correction slowed them down because they had to spend more time scanning and labeling tuples.

For the third query task, however, we observe the opposite effect: the median performance with query correction is faster than direct manipulation. Even though only three tweaks are required to fix the third query, there were eleven possible query trees. With direct manipulation, users who were still unfamiliar with the query language had many query trees to manually search through, this slowed their overall time. One user expressed: "I really just bruce forced looking for the 2*2*2 options by toggling coverage, quantifier, and position". Those users performed better when they offloaded the mechanical brute-force search to DataPlay. Thus, with auto-correction, task completion time for 75% of the users was under 3 minutes, but with direct-manipulation only 46% of the users completed the task in under 3 minutes.

We also conducted a post-study questionnaire and asked users to rate the utility of DataPlay's features on a Likert scale: users found direct manipulation ($\mu = 4.5$) and query auto-correction ($\mu = 4.6$) to be extremely useful. Users were given the opportunity to elaborate on their ratings. One user explained that with auto-correction: "you no longer really even need to think in sql, just what you want or not [sic] want." Another explained that "auto-correction is useful, but I found marking tuples as 'want in'/'keep out' to be more tedious than [manually] correcting queries". Another user said "It was very useful in the sense that it was simple to manually filter the data elements. I would probably find myself using the manual constraint manipulation first to narrow down results and then using auto-correction if I became confused." As such, we believe that a mixed query specification interface is superior to an interface that only offers direct manipulation.

Users also found answers and non-answers to be very useful for debugging queries ($\mu = 4.6$), however they found the presentation of nested rows to be lacking: DataPlay by default collapses nested rows and shows the top four nested rows; users had to expand some rows to examine relevant data. Users found DataPlay's highlighting of values that satisfy a constraint to be a useful feature when scanning answers and non-answers for correctness.

We note that the first query task in this study is as complex as the query task used in the SQL observational study. A qualitative argument in support of DataPlay can be made here: while only 2 of 11 users successfully transformed an existential SQL query to a universal one, all 13 users successfully transformed an existential query to a universal one in less than 3.5 minutes.

Reducing errors: DATAPLAY v2.0

As query complexity increased, the likelihood of errors also increased: 15% and 30% of users submitted incorrect queries for the third query task when using query auto-correction and direct manipulation respectively (See Fig. 8). We examined screen-recordings of users who failed the third query task and found the following two issues:

1. When users quickly scanned answers or non-answers, they sometimes missed tuples that indicate query-specification errors, especially if those tuples are not within the first few tuples.

2. When correcting queries, users may provide a few or not enough selective tuple-memberships: this results in DataPlay generating a large set of query trees that satisfy the given tuple-memberships. DataPlay's simple ordering of suggested query trees may not bring forward the user's intended query. Users, who submitted incorrect queries, provided a few non-selective tuple-memberships, and then picked the highest ranked query tree from DataPlay's suggestions and hastily concluded that they fixed the query.

The first issue can be resolved if we order answers and non-answers such that they *surface query errors* or at least cluster tuples that have identical data with respect to the constraints and present one tuple from each cluster, hence increasing the diversity of the top-k presented tuples. Alternatively, we can allow users to resample the top-k results, thus extracting more tuples from the database for further query verification.

The second issue is more complex and poses an exciting research challenge. Query trees map an extremely large *data space* to answers and non-answers, user-specified tuple memberships only map a small random sampling of the data space to answers and non-answers. To illustrate, with two constraints over two attributes, for example, grade = A and course.area = Systems, we have 2^2 or 4 possible satisfiability combinations for a two-attribute tuple:

Grade = A	Area = Systems	Example tuples
True	True	[A, Systems]
True	False	[A, Design]
False	True	[B, Systems]
False	False	[C, Theory]

If the attributes are two nesting levels deep then our data space is the number of subsets containing elements from the four possible two-attribute tuples, i.e 2^4 or 16. For example:

Student	Grade, Course Area	Pattern
John	A, Systems B, Design	True, True False, False
David	C, Design B, Systems	False, False False, True

With three constraints on attributes two nesting levels deep, the data space is 256 tuples and with four constraints, it is 65536 tuples. The double-exponential size of the data space means that many semantically-different query trees will satisfy the small sample of tuple memberships that users provide. Convergence to the one correct query may require an unreasonably large sample of tuple memberships: no user will provide tuple memberships for the entire space. Worse, the actual database may not be rich enough in its content and only contain a small sample of the data space. We are currently exploring techniques from learning theory to build an alternate interaction mode of query correction, where DataPlay constructs sample tuples in addition to using existing database tuples to interactively ask users tuple membership questions that guarantee convergence to one correct query tree within a *reasonable* number questions. Depending on the task, users provided as low as one tuple membership and as high as 19 tuple-memberships. The median number of tuple-memberships provided for each task was 4, 6 and 6. This data might help us define the bounds of what is reasonable.

In addition to reducing query specification errors, we would like to create more scalable query and data tree visualizations. In particular, we need to employ techniques such as interactive tree navigation and tree summarization to effectively visualize deeply-nested and bushy data trees (tables with many attributes).

RELATED WORK

DataPlay is influenced by and builds upon years of research on database data models and query languages. Our data model combines the universal relational model [14] with the nested relational model [13]. Our data model closely resembles that of the LORE database and our query language resembles LOREL, a non-graphical query language for nested data models [15].

DataPlay uses techniques from visualization-driven query tools [3, 18, 8]: users can brush visualizations in DataPlay to specify constraints. Similar to tools like Polaris [21] (and its commercial successor Tableau [3]) and Orion [9], DataPlay transforms user-interface actions into formal data-processing specifications. Polaris maps drag-and-drop operations on data variables into database queries and visualizations over single data tables [21]. Orion maps user-interface actions to data transformation statements and visualizations over network data [9].

The visual representation of queries in DataPlay as query trees is influenced in part by the success of code interfaces like Code Bubbles [4] and Stacksplorer [11] in enhancing code readability. These interfaces overlay a graphical 'call-graph' representation over code.

Recent research on *query causality* directed our attention

towards the presentation of non-answers. Query causality provides users with explanations for a particular query result [16]. Users pose questions such as "why is a tuple a non-answer?" and in return the database traces the behavior of the query to identify features of the tuple that make it a non-answer[5, 16]. It is from this research that we borrow the nomenclature of non-answers. We view query correction as the dual of query causality: while causality finds the data that caused a given result set, query correction finds the query that brings about a particular result.

Automated query correction is a novel feature of DataPlay. It applies techniques from *example-driven program synthesis*. While such techniques are currently used for data cleaning and integration [10, 7], we are not aware of any tool that applies such techniques for correcting a database query from example answers and non-answers.

We point out that Query-By-Example (QBE) [22] is not the same as automated query correction. QBE is a graphical *language* for relational data. It allows users to write queries by creating example table layouts and specifying constraints called condition boxes in the columns of these tables. Users find it difficult to specify quantified queries in QBE [19]; like SQL, QBE does not exhibit syntax locality and does not provide non-answers.

Commercial and open-source SQL graphical editors like Postgres' pgAdmin [2] and MS Access [1] enable users to build a graphical SQL query and directly manipulate it. With these editors, users physically draw the query by dropping tables into a drawing board and then connecting the tables with edges to represent joins. Direct manipulation is limited to removing or adding a table, selecting attributes to project and clicking edges to edit joins. Constraints are specified separately and not presented on the drawing board. In MS Access, constraints are specified using QBE. Users then execute the query to view answers only. These graphical editors do not address SQL's lack of syntax locality, thus users still need to learn SQL tricks and templates to specify quantified queries. DataPlay differs from these editors in many ways. DataPlay reverses the steps of query specification: users begin querying by directly specifying their constraints and DataPlay assembles the constraints into a query tree. DataPlay also interactively updates answers and non-answers and maintains a graphical history of all query modifications.

Like DataPlay, two recent research query tools are targeting the apparent gap in usable query tools for complex queries. *QueryViz*, translates SQL into an equivalent graphical language [6] to help users better understand a query, it does not enable direct query manipulation and it does not visually expose possible semantic modifications. SnipSuggest [12] helps users specify queries by auto-suggesting SQL clauses in a manner similar to code-assist tools in IDEs. SnipSuggest learns a variety of SQL templates from database users of a particular domain to provide context-aware suggestions ordered by popularity. SnipSuggest helps users of heavily-queried databases such as scientific data repositories by leveraging the work of the few initial users who write the complex queries. We can extend DataPlay such that, like SnipSuggest, it suggests popular constraints and it orders query trees by popularity during query correction.

CONCLUSION

In this paper, we introduced DataPlay, a query tool that simplifies the specification of quantified queries. We conducted a study to determine what makes quantified querying challenging in SQL. We observed that SQL hinders a trial and error approach to querying because it lacks syntax locality and it lack non-answers.

We designed DataPlay bearing in mind SQL's deficiencies. DataPlay's data model — a nested universal table — enables the computation of non-answers for any query and DataPlay's query language exhibits syntax locality. DataPlay's unique data model and query language help support several interaction features: (i) Users specify simple constraints without worrying about how to assemble these constraints into a whole query (ii) Users semantically tweak a query by directly manipulating a graphical query representation. The syntax locality of the language ensures that such tweaks are equivalent to small manipulations. (iii) Users asses the correctness of a query by examining answers and non-answers. Every query modification interactively updates answers and non-answers.

DataPlay provides automated query correction: users provide tuple memberships (examples of answer and non-answer tuples) and DataPlay suggests the possible manipulations to a given query that will satisfy the user's tuple memberships. We compared the effectiveness of direct manipulation with auto-correction through a user study. The study demonstrates that for simple queries, users perform better with direct manipulation, but as query complexity increases, users perform better with auto-correction.

REFERENCES

1. Microsoft access. `office.microsoft.com/en-us/access/`.
2. pgadmin: Postgresql administration and management tools. `www.pgadmin.org`.
3. Tableau software. `www.tableausoftware.com`.
4. Bragdon, A., et al. Code bubbles: a working set-based interface for code understanding and maintenance. In *CHI* (2010).
5. Chapman, A., and Jagadish, H. V. Why not? In *SIGMOD* (2009).
6. Danaparamita, J., and Gatterbauer, W. Queryviz: helping users understand sql queries and their patterns. In *EDBT/ICDT* (2011).
7. Gulwani, S., Harris, W. R., and Sing, R. Spreadsheet data manipulation using examples. In *CACM* (2012).
8. Heer, J., Agrawala, M., and Willett, W. Generalized selection via interactive query relaxation. CHI (2008).
9. Heer, J., and Perer, A. Orion: A system for modeling, transformation and visualization of multidimensional heterogeneous networks. In *VAST* (2011).

10. Kandel, S., Paepcke, A., Hellerstein, J., and Heer, J. Wrangler: Interactive visual specification of data transformation scripts. In *CHI* (2011).

11. Karrer, T., et al. Stacksplorer: call graph navigation helps increasing code maintenance efficiency. In *UIST '11* (2011).

12. Khoussainova, N., Kwon, Y., Balazinska, M., and Suciu, D. Snipsuggest: context-aware autocompletion for sql. *Proc. VLDB Endow. 4*, 1 (2010).

13. Levene, M. *The nested universal relation database model.* Lecture notes in computer science. Springer-Verlag, 1990.

14. Maier, D., Ullman, J. D., and Vardi, M. Y. On the foundations of the universal relation model. *ACM Trans. Database Syst. 9*, 2 (June 1984).

15. McHugh, J., Abiteboul, S., Goldman, R., Quass, D., and Widom, J. Lore: a database management system for semistructured data. *SIGMOD Rec. 26*, 3 (Sept. 1997).

16. Meliou, A., Gatterbauer, W., Moore, K. F., and Suciu, D. The complexity of causality and responsibility for query answers and non-answers. *Proc. VLDB Endow. 4*, 1 (Oct. 2010).

17. Norman, D. A. *The Design of Everyday Things*, reprint paperback ed. Basic Books, New York, 2002.

18. Olston, C., Stonebraker, M., Aiken, A., Aiken, E., and Hellerstein, J. M. Viqing: Visual interactive querying, 1998.

19. Reisner, P. Human factors studies of database query languages: A survey and assessment. *ACM Comput. Surv. 13*, 1 (1981), 13–31.

20. Reisner, P., Boyce, R. F., and Chamberlin, D. D. Human factors evaluation of two data base query languages: square and sequel. In *AFIPS '75*, ACM (New York, NY, USA, 1975), 447–452.

21. Stolte, C., and Hanrahan, P. Polaris: A system for query, analysis and visualization of multi-dimensional relational databases. In *INFOVIS* (2000).

22. Zloof, M. M. Query by example. In *AFIPS National Computer Conference* (1975), 431–438.

SnipMatch: Using Source Code Context to Enhance Snippet Retrieval and Parameterization

Doug Wightman[1], Zi Ye[1], Joel Brandt[2], Roel Vertegaal[1]

[1]Human Media Lab, Queen's University
Kingston, ON, K7L 3N6, Canada
{wightman, zi, roel}@cs.queensu.ca

[2]Advanced Technology Labs, Adobe
San Francisco, CA 94103
joel.brandt@adobe.com

ABSTRACT

Programmers routinely use source code snippets to increase their productivity. However, locating and adapting code snippets to the current context still takes time: for example, variables must be renamed, and dependencies included. We believe that when programmers decide to invest time in creating a new code snippet from scratch, *they would also be willing to spend additional effort to make that code snippet configurable and easy to integrate.* To explore this insight, we built *SnipMatch*, a plug-in for the Eclipse IDE. SnipMatch introduces a simple markup that allows snippet authors to specify search patterns and integration instructions. SnipMatch leverages this information, in conjunction with current code context, to improve snippet search and parameterization. For example, when a search query includes local variables, SnipMatch suggests compatible snippets, and automatically adapts them by substituting in these variables. In the lab, we observed that participants integrated snippets faster when using SnipMatch than when using standard Eclipse. Findings from a public deployment to 93 programmers suggest that SnipMatch has become integrated into the work practices of real users.

ACM Classification: H.5.2. Information interfaces and presentation: User Interfaces—prototyping.

Keywords: Example-centric development, prototyping, natural language processing

INTRODUCTION

Programmers routinely search online for snippets to integrate into their source code [3, 5, 15, 22, 30]. This find-and-integrate behavior reduces the time to leverage Application Programming Interfaces (APIs), libraries, and algorithm implementations [5, 34]. Even when an API is well understood, snippets provide productivity gains: the time and effort required is often less than writing the code from scratch [3].

Despite the benefits of snippet use, substantial time can still be required to locate and integrate code snippets. Programmers often must locate and combine multiple code

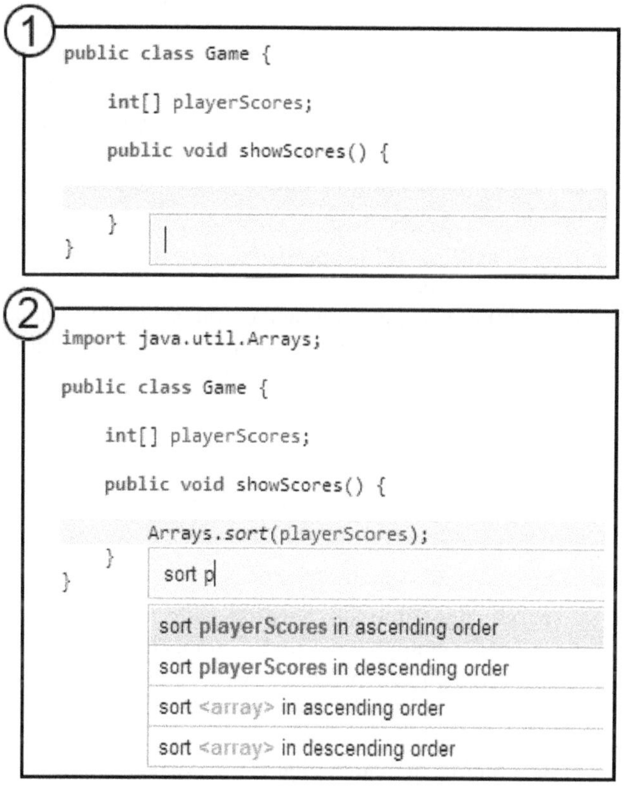

Figure 1. The SnipMatch plug-in for the Eclipse development environment. A keyboard shortcut opens the search window (1) at the programmer's cursor position. Search results (2) are updated as the query is typed. The search query also affects integration: the local variable playerScores is included in the snippet (2). Snippet integration is previewed within the existing code.

snippets, rename or typecast variables, and manually locate and include dependencies [5, 7, 21]. After this complex integration has been performed, a code snippet may be discarded if it contains errors or otherwise does not work as expected [4]. Even a small decrease in the time required to perform this common task — finding and integrating snippets — could cause a qualitative change in behavior [12].

Existing code snippet solutions fall into one of two broad categories: those that leverage a carefully curated set of purpose-built snippets [9, 27], and those that either synthesize new snippets or mine relevant snippets from large repositories [3, 16, 23]. There is a simple trade-off associated with choosing one of these two approaches: curated collections yield higher-quality snippets, but are less complete. Mined or synthesized snippets can cover a much broader set of use cases, but may sometimes yield irrelevant, difficult to understand, or incorrect code.

Our research is driven by two insights:

First, given metadata about integrating a snippet into existing source code, we can build much more powerful tools for snippet retrieval and adaptation. In particular, we can use information provided in the search query, such as local variable names, to semi-automatically tailor snippets and facilitate further adaptation. We can also leverage local code context (e.g. variable types, imported libraries) to rank and filter results in relation to compatibility with the existing code. Unfortunately, gathering rich metadata about a snippet is difficult because users are usually focused on saving time when they are interacting with snippets. When a person is *creating* a snippet, however, she has already decided to invest time now in order to save time later.

Second, when a person creates a code snippet from scratch, she is willing to spend a reasonable amount of effort to make that code snippet configurable and easy to integrate. While creating a snippet, the author might add metadata using a snippet markup language. This is a viable method to obtain search and integration metadata: for example, variables to be renamed and preconditions to verify compatibility with the user's existing code. To explore these insights, we built and evaluated *SnipMatch*, a search interface for finding and integrating curated code snippets.

This work offers three contributions:

1. A search algorithm for curated code snippets that leverages code context — Curated snippets are ranked, filtered, and customized based on the code in the development environment. SnipMatch builds on prior work in Integrated Development Environment (IDE) search [3, 8, 9, 18, 29]. The SnipMatch search algorithm extends the use of code context beyond the current programming language and framework to enhance the ranking of shared, curated code snippets. Our search algorithm uses the following features of the programmer's source code to rank and filter prospective snippet results: variable types and names, the cursor position within the abstract syntax tree, program logic, and code dependencies. We selected these features because they can be used to determine how closely results match the existing code. Results that more closely match the features of the existing code – that is, make use of existing variables and require fewer modifications – are ranked higher.

2. A lightweight markup for specifying integration instructions for code snippets — Other tools suggest error-correction source code modifications [7, 8, 13]: for example, prompting the user to rename variables after a snippet has been inserted. These tools require human intervention because the intended use for a snippet can be ambiguous. Did the programmer intend to use the code snippet "as is", or only part of it? Should the snippet, or the existing code, be modified when there is an error? An integration tool requires more information to answer these questions.

3. Insights about how code snippet search tools are used, derived from the implementation and evaluation of SnipMatch. We implemented SnipMatch, a snippet search plug-in for the Eclipse IDE. To better understand how snippet search tools change the way people program, we conducted a comparative laboratory study with 16 participants and a public deployment with 93 programmers. We observed that SnipMatch was used to reduce context switching and as a memory aid. Participants reported that including snippet arguments in the search box was particularly effective for the two most common usage scenarios: shortcuts and quick reference.

RELATED WORK

Search Interfaces

Search interfaces [14, 26] can be tailored for specific tasks. Prior work includes systems to support data analysis [5, 24], web page revisitation [1, 31], and programming [3, 22]. Programming search interfaces can enhance web search results [15, 22] and, most relevant to our work, locate code snippets [3, 29]. Locating snippets can be time-consuming: in one study, 19% of programming time was spent looking for source code on the Internet [5].

Snippet search interfaces query code repositories to find *keyword* [3, 9, 11] and *structural* [2, 23, 29, 32] matches. Structural search can include building an internal representation of the program, while keyword matching is limited to text analysis. Google code search [11] locates occurrences of keywords in source code files. Uncommon, domain-specific search keywords can improve the relevance of results from this large repository. Blueprint [3] is a development environment plug-in that augments Internet keyword search queries with the language and framework used in the development environment. Snippets are automatically extracted from web pages and can be browsed within the plug-in. While keyword matching can be ineffective for locating many general code structure or program logic patterns, it is easy to use and can match comments, variables, dependencies, and other lexical features.

Structural snippet search interfaces perform static analysis to determine how code functions. For example, structural search interfaces can locate snippets that create an object of a certain type from other objects. Finding a Method Invocation Sequence (MIS) is a common API search task [29, 32, 16, 33]. PARSEWeb [32] ranks code fragments to be incorporated into MISs by frequency of use and length. S^6 [28] allows programmers to include simple test cases and contracts with keyword searches. However, it can be difficult to ensure that snippets do not contain errors [23] and to differentiate between similar structural features: for example, frameworks and class libraries [2]. Further, Jungloid [23] and most other structural search interfaces are less effective when the programmer does not know the names of relevant classes, methods, or types.

SnipMatch is designed to provide more precise results and result rankings than these alternatives, but at a cost: someone must associate additional data with a code snippet for its search ranking and automatic integration to be improved. Snippet creators can also specify alternate search result wording to make snippets easier to find, mitigating the vocabulary problem [10]. SnipMatch allows programmers to enhance the accessibility of snippets that are important to them.

Snippet Integration

Many different types of modifications can be required to integrate a code snippet. EUKLAS [7] highlights source code errors and suggests corrections. EUKLAS can detect and correct missing JavaScript parameters, function and variable definitions, and imports. Eclipse Quick Fix [8] provides similar functionality for Java, and can also correct some unhandled exceptions. These tools allow programmers to quickly resolve many simple errors.

HelpMeOut [13] presents suggestions for correcting compiler and runtime errors. Relevant compiler error suggestions are found by examining the source code line referenced in the error. Relevant runtime exception suggestions are found by examining the stack trace. While HelpMeOut isn't specifically targeted at snippets, this approach could be useful for fixing snippet integration mistakes. Rather than fixing errors, SnipMatch attempts to prevent them from occurring.

The Codelets system [27] allows authors of example code to use a simple markup language to indicate which parts of an example are fixed and which parts the user should edit. Editable regions can be given names that are then referenced in custom user interfaces for configuring the example code. In SnipMatch, we extend this idea of providing users with a lightweight markup language for annotating snippets. In particular, we add syntax for expressing type information, integration instructions, and external dependencies. Additionally, we leverage this semantic information to make our code search more powerful.

Blueprint extracted over 100,000 code examples from blogs, forums, and human-created documentation available on the Internet [3]. In all of these cases, people expressly curated and published these snippets with the intention of sharing. SnipMatch is also dependent on programmers' willingness to curate and share snippets.

Sloppy Interpretation

Sloppy interpreters have lenient syntax requirements [25]. Inky [25] interprets keyword searches as web tasks and allows the user to click a button to perform them. For example, the top search result for the query "johnd@gmail.com leaving the office now" might be "email johnd@gmail.com about "leaving the office now". The keyword interpreter tokenizes the query, detects token types (e.g. email addresses), matches the tokens with pre-defined functions, and returns an ordered list of results. Koala [20] allows users to write scripts to automate web tasks by typing sequences of commands. The interpreter can recognize the commands "type UIST into search field" and "click search button".

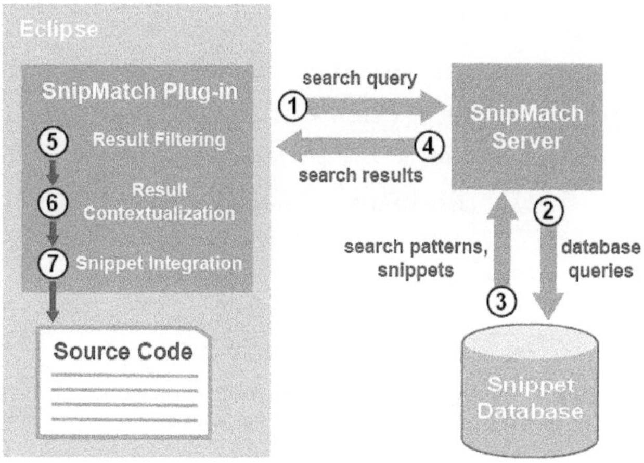

Figure 2. SnipMatch snippet search overview

Koala built on previous work translating keyword commands into executable code [19]. This previous work was also the basis for a project that automatically generated code snippets from search queries [18]. Snippets are created by nesting methods, extracted from open source projects, with names similar to the search keywords. Unfortunately, this alternative to a code repository is often not practical because it can create semantically incorrect code.

SnipMatch does not generate snippets from extracted method calls. Similar to Inky, SnipMatch matches search queries with pre-defined snippets. This prevents semantic errors while preserving the primary benefits of sloppy interpretation: minimal wording and syntax requirements.

ENHANCING SNIPPET SEARCH WITH CODE CONTEXT

Programmers can use SnipMatch to find and integrate Java snippets from within the development environment. Pressing Ctrl-Enter while editing source code opens the SnipMatch search interface. The top search result is previewed inline as the programmer types in the search box. Figure 1 shows the result of typing "sort p" in the search box. The array playerScores is included in the top search result because this snippet has a *search pattern* with a parameter.

The SnipMatch search algorithm matches search queries to search patterns. A search pattern is a text description of the effect of the code snippet, interspersed with placeholders for snippet parameters. For example, this is the text description for the search pattern shown in Figure 1: "sort <array> in ascending order". "<array>" refers to a snippet parameter. To prevent type mismatches, the parameter type can also be specified in the search pattern. Snippets can have multiple search patterns.

When a snippet is submitted to SnipMatch, a lightweight markup language can be used to specify where search pattern parameters will appear in the snippet source code. This markup can also be used to import dependencies as required and define preconditions for snippets to appear in

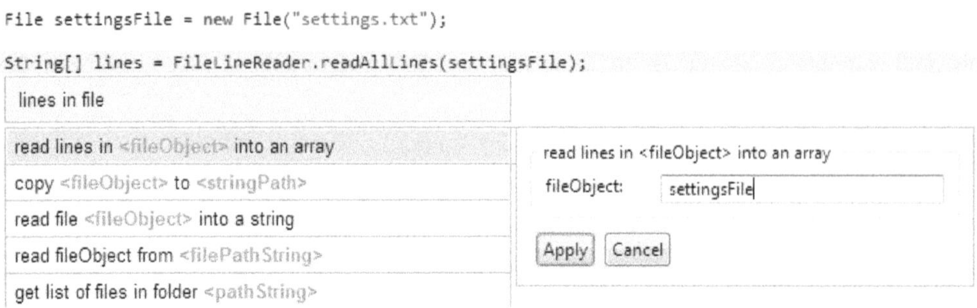

Figure 3. The argument editor (right window) is displayed if the user presses Enter before all arguments have been specified. This structured view prompts the user with text fields for each search pattern parameter. The user's code is modified as the text field is completed.

the search results. After results are returned from the central server, the Eclipse plug-in filters and customizes the snippets based on the markup and the code context in the development environment (Figure 2).

SnipMatch snippets can be private or public. Public snippets are available to all users, while private snippets appear only in the snippet creator's search results. To ensure correctness and maintain a consistent level of snippet quality, system moderators review snippets that are added to the public repository.

Design Rationale

We are interested in reducing the time and effort required to both *locate* and *integrate* code snippets. As described in the introduction, snippet integration can be complicated and time-consuming. Previous approaches for supporting snippet integration include methods that prompt the user with options [7, 8, 13] and methods that generate snippets from keywords based on rules [18, 19]. Although helpful to highlight problems that require attention, user prompts still require code comprehension, decision-making, and manual input prior to testing. Generative methods frequently create semantic errors.

One viable alternative that does not require manual input at the time of integration is for programmers to annotate snippets *when they are created* with additional machine-readable markup language. This information can then be used by the search interface to provide enhanced search ranking and snippet integration. Programmers already create Eclipse Templates for personal use, and share and comment on code snippets online [11, 22]. We believe that programmers will similarly contribute search patterns and integration markups if they will improve snippet usability. As with Wikipedia, relatively few individuals need to contribute for the system to be useful for many.

IMPLEMENTATION

The SnipMatch plug-in was written in Java using the Eclipse Plug-in Development Environment (PDE). The plug-in communicates with the server through HTTP requests. Server-side, the search algorithm is written in C++ and PHP, and snippets are stored in a MySQL database. During the evaluation, our server was located in the United States.

Snippet Search

Search Window. The search window (Figure 1) has two main components: a static text field for the search query input, and a dynamically resizing region below for search results. The ordered list of search results is updated as the contents of the text field are modified. This provides the user with instant feedback, facilitating snippet discovery and step-wise refinement of search queries. To increase readability, search results have basic syntax highlighting; different font colors are used for keywords, arguments, and placeholders for missing arguments.

Argument Editing. If a user attempts to insert a snippet with missing arguments, the argument editor dialog appears to the right of the search window (Figure 3). The dialog presents a structured view of the snippet parameters and includes text fields for entering the arguments. Changes to the arguments are immediately reflected in the source code. The editor can also be manually invoked for any highlighted result by pressing Ctrl-Enter.

Tab Completion. Since search results are updated as the search query is typed, the user can refine the search query based on the results. For example, the search query "read" might return some results that begin with "read lines from file", and other results that begin with "read character from keyboard". The user can narrow the results to only include those pertaining to file operations by changing the search query. Tab completion facilitates this process. When the user presses Tab, the search query text is autocompleted up to the next parameter in the currently highlighted result. For example, if the search query is "read", and the highlighted result is "read lines from file <filePath>", pressing Tab will change the search query to "read lines from file ".

Snippet Icons. A small group of icons is docked in the lower right corner of the currently highlighted result (Figure 5). Most of these icons are buttons that allow the user to send feedback about the result. Feedback options include rating, flagging, and commenting. All user feedback is logged for manual analysis. A yellow warning icon appears when the snippet includes changes to the source code that are omitted from the preview, such as helper classes. Resting the mouse over this icon reveals a summary of all the hidden changes.

Snippet Submission

The SnipMatch Eclipse plug-in includes an interface for adding and editing code snippets. This interface allows users to modify search patterns, and includes features to facilitate the addition of integration markups to the snippet code. SnipMatch uses the Java type hierarchy to recognize standard and user-created parameter types that appear in search patterns.

Search Results

There are three different types of search results: *in-order, unordered, unsigned.* After search results are found, they are ranked, filtered, and shown to the user in a single list.

In-order. An in-order result is a snippet with a search pattern that begins with exactly the same sequence of characters as the search query. For example, the result "read from file <filePath>" is an in-order result for the search query "read from".

Unordered. An unordered result is a snippet whose search patterns do not begin with the search query, but do contain one or more tokens from the search query. For example, the result "read from file <filePath>" is an unordered result for the search query "file".

Unsigned. An unsigned result is a snippet that does not yet have a search pattern, but whose code contains one or more tokens from the search query. These snippets can be retrieved not only from the SnipMatch snippet database, but also from external snippet repositories.

Result Ranking

Results are first ranked by type. In-order results appear first, followed by unordered. Unsigned results appear after all other results. In addition to being ranked by type, each result type uses a different set of ranking criteria.

In-order. In-order results are first ranked by the number of search query tokens matching each search pattern. Next, results are ranked by the number of missing arguments. Results with fewer missing arguments are ranked higher.

Unordered. Unordered results are ranked based on term frequency–inverse document frequency (tf-idf) [17]. Tokens from the search query are matched against search patterns. Search patterns that contain more query tokens or query tokens that appear less frequently in other search patterns are ranked higher. User feedback (e.g. votes and frequency of selection) will be incorporated in the future.

Unsigned. The same ranking criteria as for unordered results are applied, except that the search query is matched against the snippet code instead of the search patterns.

Result Filtering and Contextualization

Since the SnipMatch server has limited information about the user's code, the client modifies the returned search results before they are shown to the user. This is completed in two stages: result filtering and result contextualization.

```
${import(java.io.File)}
${import(java.io.BufferedReader)}
${import(java.io.FileReader)}
${import(java.io.IOException)}
${import(java.util.ArrayList)}

${helper}
class FileLineReader {
   public static String[] readAllLines(File file) {
      ArrayList<String> lines = new ArrayList<String>();
      try {
         BufferedReader br = new BufferedReader(new FileReader(file));
         String line = null;

         while ((line = br.readLine()) != null) {
            lines.add(line);
         }
         br.close();
      }
      catch (IOException e) { return null; }
      return lines.toArray(new String[lines.size()]);
   }
}
${endHelper}

String[] ${freeName(lines)} = FileLineReader.readAllLines(${fileObject});
```

Figure 4. Integration markup

Filtering. Since the SnipMatch server does not have access to the Java type hierarchy, some search results may contain incompatible types. The client performs a type compatibility test on each search result and filters out the results that fail the test. For example, the query "for x" may return a result that tries to create a for loop using a hypothetical local integer x. However, if the client detects a local variable x of another type, this search result will be removed. The client also filters results that are incompatible with the existing code. For example, if integration markup preconditions are not met.

Contextualization. If the user omits an argument, or does not finish typing an argument, the client analyzes the user's source code to find variables within the current scope that can serve as arguments. This list of possible substitutions is used to create variations on the original, incomplete search result. These client-generated results are presented to the user instead of the original. In Figure 1, the client detects a compatible local variable (playerScores) and uses it to complete the server's search results. After variables are matched with parameters, the snippet is customized according to the integration markup.

Snippet Integration

Instructions for integrating a snippet into the user's source code are expressed using a lightweight markup embedded within the snippet code. The SnipMatch markup is similar to the markup used in Eclipse Templates [9], with several additions. Eclipse Templates is a built-in feature in Eclipse that allows users to create and insert code "templates" (snippets). Like SnipMatch, it allows snippets to be integrated into the source code by taking into account local variables and adding missing import statements. Unlike SnipMatch snippets, each Eclipse Template can only be found through its single-word name. Parameters, helper classes, and precondition checking are not supported. Figure 4 shows the snippet code associated with the search pattern "read lines in <fileObject> into an array". This snippet includes two additions to the Eclipse Templates markup: a search result argument (<fileObject>) and a helper class. In figure 4, ${fileObject} indicates where to insert the argument for the <fileObject> parameter. The helper class is delimited by ${helper} and ${endHelper}. Helper classes are inserted in the current source file.

Helper classes are an optional feature that can make code easier to read and reduce redundancy. For example, a programmer might prefer to read text from a file by calling a method of a helper class instead of having the method code appear inline. SnipMatch maintains a record of inserted helper classes so that future snippet insertions will not create duplicate classes.

Another addition to the Eclipse Templates markup is support for integration preconditions. The SnipMatch markup includes the terms ${startPrecondition} and ${endPrecondition}. The code between these two terms is expected to be a Java method named preconditionTest. Before the snippet is shown to the user, the preconditionTest method is executed in a secure sandbox that prevents access to other local processes or communication with other machines. The return value of the method is a Boolean that determines whether or not the user's code meets the necessary conditions for the snippet to be integrated. This method accepts three arguments with information about the source code file currently open in the IDE. The first argument is an instance of the Eclipse JDT ASTParser class. This argument contains a copy of the abstract syntax tree that can be traversed to perform validations. A copy of the source code and the current cursor position in the file are also included as arguments – for example, so that a snippet creator can alternately write a simple grep when string matching is sufficient.

A graphical interface for specifying preconditions without writing code could be created. For now, video tutorials on the SnipMatch website and an interface for selecting markup within the snippet editor provide usage instructions and examples.

Benefits of Client-Server Search Processing

Allowing both the client and the server to process search results has privacy and efficiency benefits. It mitigates privacy concerns, since source code is not sent from the client to the server. Computation is distributed between the client and server, with the client handling the computationally expensive filtering and integration steps that are dependent on the user's code. Server results can be cached because they are not specific to the user's code.

Extensibility

Extending SnipMatch to support other imperative programming languages is straightforward. In addition to Java, we have tested SnipMatch with C++, PHP, and JavaScript. The search algorithm and markup were not changed. The Eclipse plug-in was modified to extract variable names and types from these different ASTs. Type consistency checking was disabled for the dynamically typed languages, but search pattern parameters were still supported. Wrapper classes have been created to simplify the process of extending the plug-in for third-party developers.

EVALUATION

We conducted three studies: a lab study, an analysis of usage logs following the public deployment of SnipMatch, and interviews with programmers who have used SnipMatch. The lab study was conducted to gather initial feedback and assess ease of use. We then made SnipMatch publicly available and analyzed our logs to gain additional insights and confirm external validity. Finally, we interviewed five SnipMatch users to learn more about their needs and search behaviors.

STUDY 1: EVALUATING SNIPMATCH IN THE LAB

Method

Two sets of 8 computer science students were recruited for this study. Each participant was given two programming tasks to complete. Participants in the first set were given a brief (5-minute) SnipMatch tutorial and asked to use SnipMatch instead of searching online for code snippets. Participants in the second set were allowed to search online and were not trained to use SnipMatch.

To avoid priming our participants with search keywords, we explained the tasks by showing images. For the first task, we showed two images. The first image depicted two file folders, one full of files and the other empty. It was described as the "before" image. The second image contained the same two file folders with the all of the files now in the other folder. Participants were asked to "write a program to change the current state of the system to the second image". They were also shown that the folder that contained the files in the first images existed on the computer and was currently full of files. For the second task, we showed one image, depicting a simple Graphical User Interface (GUI) for moving files from one folder to another. This GUI included two text fields, labeled "Source folder" and "Target folder", and a button labeled "Move files".

At the time of the study, SnipMatch included 29 snippets and 55 search patterns. The snippets included all of the functionality required to complete the tasks. The larger number of search patterns indicates that some snippets were discoverable through more than one search pattern. Approximately half of the snippets were created specifically for this study. Drawing from textbooks and our experiences teaching computer science, we attempted to include snippets to support most standard file input and output operations and many basic GUI features. To narrow the scope of our investigation to features specific to SnipMatch, we did not include search results from external code repositories, such as Google Code Search.

We anticipated that participants using SnipMatch would need to perform a minimum of 7 snippet integrations: 2 for the first task and 5 for the second. This calculation was based on the assumption that participants had memorized the method calls required to complete our tasks. It also assumed that participants do not use SnipMatch for basic programming statements (e.g. to create a for loop) and that they prefer to copy and paste their code rather than use SnipMatch repeatedly.

After completing the tasks, each participant using SnipMatch filled out a questionnaire. We logged all SnipMatch searches and the times required by the server and the client to generate the results.

We recorded web search queries and web pages visited for the participants who did not use SnipMatch. After both tasks were completed, we asked these participants about their programming behavior and experiences working with code snippets found online.

Results

Programming with SnipMatch. All of our participants successfully completed both tasks. On average, participants completed the first task in 12 minutes (*s.e. 1.5*) and the second in 28 minutes (*s.e. 3.3*). On average, participants opened the SnipMatch search window 14.2 times (*s.e. 2.2*) and selected a snippet to integrate 74% of the time. Participants performed many exploratory searches to test the capabilities of the system. Most also used SnipMatch to write the loop required in the first task and to create the multiple labels and textboxes for the second task. Verbs were popular search terms (copy, create, move, open, read).

Two participants mentioned that they did not need to remember syntax. One of these participants explained the process of writing code using SnipMatch as "search to figure out how to do something, resulting in the creation of an object, then search again, including this object, to continue using it". Several participants indicated that they were interested in using SnipMatch to create private snippet repositories.

The mean rating for the question "I would use this tool on a regular basis if it was available in my preferred development environment" is particularly encouraging (μ=4.75 on 5 point Likert Scale). Participants also consistently gave SnipMatch high marks as an efficient alternative to online search (μ=4.75) and for ease of use (μ=4.5).

Programming without SnipMatch. All participants successfully completed the first (file i/o) task. Two participants were unable to complete the second (GUI) task within an hour. Including only data from tasks that were completed, on average participants performed 14 online searches (10 min., 18 max.), 7 for each task. On average, participants viewed 9 (5 min., 12 max.) non-search engine web pages for the first task and 15 (8 min., 21 max.) for the second task. Participants completed the first task in 25 minutes (*s.e. 2.5*) and the second task in 37 minutes (*s.e. 3.6*). All searches were performed on Google, with the exception of four performed on Stack Overflow.

Discussion

Programming with SnipMatch. Study participants understood how to use the tool and were able to use it effectively. We were surprised that all participants successfully completed both tasks. One participant had never programmed in Java and GUI programming can be difficult. Most participants chose to use SnipMatch even when it wasn't necessary. For example, they used it to create the loops and as an alternative to copying code from elsewhere in the file.

One participant began the first task by creating String variables for the directory paths. With the variables in scope, he then typed his first search query and the top search result previewed the exact code required to complete the first step for this task: creating an array of File objects for the files in the directory identified in one of his Strings. Several participants regularly took advantage of this context-sensitivity, adopting a search-based code writing behavior in which objects created from prior searches were included as keywords in future searches.

Some results were not as accurate. Participants requested that synonyms be added to the system. In particular, it was suggested that words referring to the same abstract concept in different programming languages might be interchangeable (e.g. form and frame) for search purposes. Also, preconceived ideas regarding command lines initially biased some participants towards selecting snippets that included string arguments instead of object arguments. This was overcome once SnipMatch displayed results that included local object variable names.

Participant feedback indicates that they were comfortable including arguments within search queries. The inline snippet preview provides code context for the arguments. We observed several participants reading the preview as they entered arguments.

The combination of natural language search results and inline previews was sufficient for participants to understand most snippets before integration. Although snippet integration can be undone with a single undo operation, this option was rarely used.

The average server response time was 64ms (*s.e. 2.0*). The Eclipse plug-in then spent 172ms (*s.e. 15.9*), on average, customizing the server results. While the code is not optimized, we believe that these numbers reflect the substantial offloading of computationally expensive operations to the client. Operations specific to the programmer's existing source code are performed client-side. This preserves privacy. With this approach, it is also possible to cache all server responses. SnipMatch can be provided to a large number of users at relatively low cost, similar to hosting static HTML pages.

Programming without SnipMatch. Only one participant who did not have access to SnipMatch completed the tasks in less time than the slowest participant who used SnipMatch (14 minutes, 19 minutes). These numbers are encouraging, but this comparison has many limitations, including the small number of snippets that were in the SnipMatch database. While we expect that SnipMatch will continue to perform well as the number of snippets increases – since search patterns are short, precise, and can be refined as required – in this study, we are more interested in the differences in search behaviors.

On average, participants performed exactly the same number of search queries (14). However, participants using SnipMatch spent less time finding and integrating snippets. Without SnipMatch, participants were not able to directly select snippets from the search result list. Participants opened and viewed many additional web pages (24 on average) listed in the search results. These web pages contained Java examples, tutorials, and class documentation.

Most participants opened multiple tabs in the web browser and flipped between tabs, comparing examples. When asked about this behavior, participants explained that they were checking for differences in dependencies, attempting to verify that the code would operated as expected, and determine which of the examples would be easiest to integrate. With SnipMatch, participants often did not dwell on the search results. They typically inserted snippets with little hesitation, then experimented inline. We believe that this was partially due to the smaller time commitment required to insert snippets with SnipMatch. Viewing the snippet inline, participants could also benefit from the error and warning highlighting provided by the IDE.

Without SnipMatch, participants frequently revisited search result pages and selected alternate links rather that performing addition searches. After completing the tasks, 4 of our 8 participants indicated that they had difficulty coming up with alternate wording that would "make a difference" to the search results shown. They explained that adding additional words to their search queries often did not improve the search results. SnipMatch users may be less likely to experience this problem, since search queries are matched against search patterns, rather than whole documents, for *in-order* and *unordered* results.

Limitations to the Participant Recruitment Method

While we were careful to recruit participants from the same population (computer science students at our university) and using the same recruitment channel (our faculty mailing list), the first set of participants was recruited before the second set of participants. We initially intended only to obtain first use data, then decided to expand the study. Between sets, participants had similar programming experience (first set: 3-10 years, second set: 2-10 years), age (20-29, 21-26), and gender balance (1 female, 2 female). No statistical tests were performed on the study results.

STUDY 2: DEPLOYMENT TO 93 PROGRAMMERS

Method

We made the SnipMatch plug-in publicly available to gain additional insights and verify external validity. We were specifically interested in better understanding usage in the wild. Will programmers use SnipMatch? How often will programmers use SnipMatch? We were also interested to determine the types of search queries and snippets that are most frequently used.

To obtain users, we created a webpage and embedded links to share it on Facebook, Twitter, and Google+. We then publicly announced SnipMatch on academic and industry mailing lists. With user consent, we logged all search queries and snippet insertions conducted during the first three weeks of public deployment. Before the announcement, we increased the number of SnipMatch snippets (72 snippets, 111 search patterns).

Results

93 programmers performed 516 searches: 345 resulted in snippets being inserted into the existing source code, and 171 were cancelled. Ten programmers used SnipMatch on more than four days. Four programmers used SnipMatch during each of the three weeks. These programmers performed 22-54 search queries. Five programmers created snippets. Two of these programmers are among those who have used SnipMatch on the largest number of days. Programmers created snippets for logging, class creation, object and value comparison, and debugging tasks. To preserve external validity, these results exclude usage by all individuals associated with the research and development of SnipMatch.

Discussion

Programmers are often eager to try new tools, but long-term retention and integration into daily practice is substantially less common. As a comparison point, Blueprint had a 1% user retention rate over a five-month span (where "retention" was measured by *any* use of the tool five or more months after initial installation) [3]. In the unlikely case that SnipMatch can maintain even a moderate portion of its current 4% (4/93) rate of *weekly* use, we will consider the tool to be highly successful.

When we conducted phone interviews (described in the following section) we were surprised to learn that at least two of our regular users are professional programmers, and that they are using SnipMatch in the workplace. Programmers with no direct interest in our work are regularly using SnipMatch while creating commercial software. In particular, this professional interest demonstrates need for a snippet search and insertion tool.

The snippets that print values and perform type conversions were among the most frequently inserted, along with several of the user-created snippets. These popular print and conversion snippets have search patterns with parameters. Some of the frequently used user-created snippets also have parameters and other features that require the snippet markup. This indicates that programmers were able to teach themselves to perform searches and use the markup.

STUDY 3: INTERVIEWS WITH PROFESSIONALS

Method

We sent an email to each of the 49 SnipMatch users who registered for an account, requesting that they participate in a 15-minute phone interview. 5 of our users, all professional programmers, agreed to be interviewed (all male, two living in the United States, one in Germany, and two in India). Two of these individuals are among the four programmers who have used SnipMatch during each of the three weeks of public deployment. We asked our interviewees to describe situations when they had used SnipMatch. We also examined their usage logs and spoke with them about searches they had performed. Then we asked if they had any difficulties using SnipMatch or ideas for improving the tool.

Results and Discussion

Common Usage Scenarios. Our interviewees described two common usage scenarios: shortcuts and quick reference. All interviewees used SnipMatch as a typing shortcut. For example, typing "convert", "log", or "println", along with arguments, in the search box. In addition to saving time by reducing keystrokes, one programmer reported that this helped him to "focus his attention", "staying in flow with the code". Three programmers described specific situations when they had inserted snippets that they could not have written from memory, including design patterns and API calls. One programmer explained that SnipMatch was particularly useful for his Android development, which he found to require many "hard to remember structures". Another mentioned writing snippets so that he would not need to memorize how to call JDBC methods. These programmers did not memorize how to type the search queries to insert these snippets – they trusted that they could find them quickly.

SnipMatch complements libraries. Each call requires some boilerplate code: minimally, importing a library and passing arguments. SnipMatch makes this easier, and shifts the balance towards reuse over code duplication. Further, with SnipMatch, programmers are able to help each other maintain good coding practices by curating the search results: if a snippet duplicates code instead of importing it, users can vote, flag, or comment to provide feedback.

Suggestions for Improvement. The programmers in India both requested that we reduce the server response time. In addition to promising to add a geographically proximate server, we proposed to modify the client to cache most frequently used snippets. This will also allow SnipMatch to function offline.

One programmer requested that search results for recently added snippets appear when the search box is empty. He was concerned that users might otherwise not discover them. For example, if a user had previously searched for image manipulation snippets and hadn't found any, he thought they might not think to search again for some time. We proposed to implement his suggestion and also to update the client to display results from other snippet databases (i.e. *unsigned* results) below SnipMatch results.

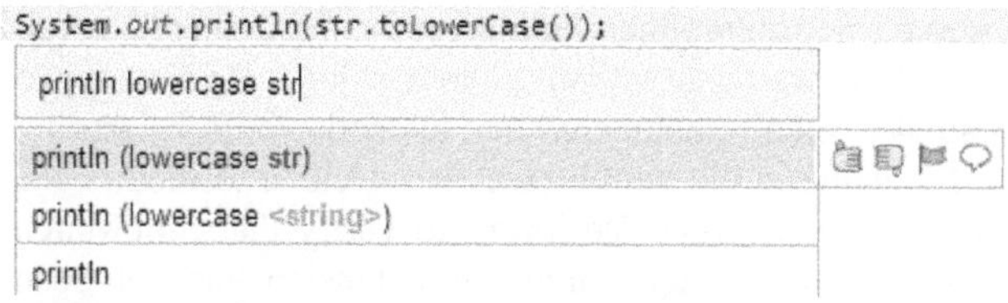

Figure 5. A search result with a nested snippet.

A programmer who uses SnipMatch regularly requested a method for specifying Boolean expressions that could be varied from within the search box. He indicated that he didn't want to have to create snippets for each combination. We then told him about the nesting feature that we are building, not yet released for public use. He thought it would be sufficient for his purposes.

INSERTING MULTIPLE SNIPPETS WITH ONE QUERY

During the lab study, participants spent substantial time manually integrating snippets. For example, most participants in both studies inserted one snippet to retrieve a list of the files in a directory and a second to move files between directories. The participants then modified the snippets to interact. To reduce the time and effort required to integrate snippets, we designed an extension to SnipMatch that allows programmers to insert multiple snippets with a single search query (Figure 5).

For example, if file1 is a Java File object, SnipMatch can recognize that the search query "move file1 to file1 parent directory" can be satisfied by combining snippet results that match the following search patterns: "move <x> to <y>" and "<z> parent directory". In this example, <x>, <y>, and <z> represent search pattern parameters. To reduce ambiguity in the search results, parentheses are inserted: "move file1 to (file1 parent directory)".

To implement this SnipMatch extension, we wrote a context-free parser that interprets search pattern parameters as nonterminal symbols and generates production rules from search patterns. We also added a new, optional, field to store the snippet return type. The left hand side of each production rule is a nonterminal symbol representing the return type of the snippet. This allows programmers to specify, by writing in-order search queries, how multiple snippets are to be combined.

Nested search results – search results that are produced by this extension – are first ranked using the *in-order* result ranking criteria. Next, the results are ranked by nesting depth. Results that have fewer levels of nesting are ranked higher. The ranked list of *nested* results appears below the *in-order* results and above *unordered* results in the search result list.

When performing a nested search, programmers will likely not type the entire query at once. Instead, they might add additional words to a shorter query as results appear. For example, in an informal evaluation of this extension we observed a programmer building up to the search result "read file (lowercase <string>) into a string". He first typed "read file", then remembered that his code could be storing the file name in the wrong case, and decided to modify the search query to "read file lower" to verify that SnipMatch supports this nesting. While this extension has not been formally evaluated, we believe that it is a useful starting point for future investigations.

CONCLUSION

We have documented initial user experiences that demonstrate how search patterns and the snippet markup can improve a snippet search interface. Results from our lab study and public deployment suggest that SnipMatch can be an effective tool for certain tasks. Professional programmers, found to be using SnipMatch in the wild, reported that SnipMatch was useful as a memory aid and reduced context switching.

Unlike prior search tools for curated snippets, results are ranked and filtered based on both a snippet markup and existing code in the IDE. SnipMatch users can include local variables in search queries to pass them as arguments, customizing curated snippets from the search box.

Installation instructions and a quick start tutorial are available at http://snipmatch.org. We have released SnipMatch as open source. The source can be downloaded from the Eclipse Foundation's code repository. Future work includes two main activities: a longitudinal field study and extending the markup to support refactoring.

REFERENCES

1. Adar, E., Dontcheva, M., Fogarty, J., and Weld, D. S. Zoetrope: Interacting with the Ephemeral Web. In *Proc. UIST*. pp. 239-48, 2008.
2. Bajracharya, S., T. Ngo, et al. Sourcerer: A Search Engine for Open Source Code Supporting Structure-Based Search. In *Companion to OOPSLA: ACM SIGPLAN*. pp. 681-82, 2006.
3. Brandt, J., Dontcheva, M., Weskamp, M., Klemmer, S.R. Example-Centric Programming: Integrating Web Search into the Development Environment. In *Proc. CHI*. pp. 513-522, 2010.
4. Brandt, J., Guo, P. J., Lewenstein, J., Dontcheva, M., Klemmer, S. R. 2009. Opportunistic Programming: Writing Code to Prototype, Ideate, and Discover. *IEEE Software*, 26 (5), 18-24.
5. Brandt, J., Guo, P.J., Lewenstein, J., Dontcheva, M., Klemmer, S.R. Two Studies of Opportunistic Programming: Interleaving Web Foraging, Learning, and Writing Code. In *Proc. CHI*. pp. 1589-1598, 2009.
6. Dontcheva, M., Drucker, S. M., Salesin, D., and Cohen, M. F. Relations, Cards, and Search Templates: User-Guided Web Data Integration and Layout. In *Proc. UIST*. pp. 61–70, 2007.
7. Dörner, C., Myers, B. A. EUKLAS, Plug-in for Eclipse IDE. http://www.cs.cmu.edu/~euklas
8. Eclipse Quick Fix. http://wiki.eclipse.org/FAQ_What_is_a_Quick_Fix%3F
9. Eclipse Templates. http://www.ibm.com/developerworks/opensource/tutorials/os-eclipse-code-templates/index.html
10. Furnas, G. W., Landauer, T. K., Gomez, L. M., and Dumais, S. T. The Vocabulary Problem in Human-System Communication. In *Communcations of the ACM* 30, 11 (Nov 1987), 964-971.
11. Google Code Search. http://www.google.com/codesearch
12. Gray, W. D. and D. A. Boehm-Davis. Milliseconds Matter: An Introduction to Microstrategies and to Their Use in Describing and Predicting Interactive Behavior. *Journal of Experimental Psychology: Applied* 6(4). pp. 322-35, 2000.
13. Hartmann, B., MacDougall, D., Brandt, J., and Klemmer, S. What Would Other Programmers Do? Suggesting Solutions to Error Messages. In *Proc. CHI*. pp. 1019-1028, 2010.
14. Hearst, M. *Search User Interfaces*, Cambridge University Press, Cambridge, UK, 2009.
15. Hoffmann, R., Fogarty, J., and Weld, D. S. Assieme: Finding and Leveraging Implicit References in a Web Search Interface for Programmers. In *Proc. UIST*. pp. 13-22, 2007.
16. Holmes, R., Murphy, G. C. Using Structural Context to Recommend Source Code Examples. In *Proc. ICSE*. pp. 117-125, 2005.
17. Jones, K. S. A Statistical Interpretation of Term Specificity and Its Application in Retrieval. Journal of Documentation 28: 11, 1972.
18. Little, G. and Miller, R.C. Keyword Programming in Java. In *Proc. ASE*. pp. 84-93, 2007.
19. Little, G. and Miller, R.C. Translating Keyword Commands into Executable Code. In *Proc. UIST*. pp. 135-144, 2006.
20. Little, G., Lau, T.A., Cypher, A., Lin, J., Haber, E.M., Kandogan, E. Koala: Capture, Share, Automate, Personalize Business Processes on the Web. In *Proc. CHI*. pp. 943-946, 2007.
21. M. Kim, L. Bergman, T. Lau, and D. Notkin. An Ethnographic Study of Copy and Paste Programming Practices in OOPL. In *Proc. ESEM*. pp. 83–92 , 2004.
22. Mamykina, L., Manoim, B., Mittal, M., Hripcsak, G., Hartmann, B. 2011. Design Lessons from the Fastest Q&A Site in the West. In *Proc. CHI*. pp. 2857-2866, 2011.
23. Mandelin, D., Xu, L., Bodík, R., and Kimelman, D. Jungloid Mining: Helping to Navigate the API Jungle. In *Proc. PLDI*. pp. 48-61, 2005.
24. Medynskiy, Y., Dontcheva M., and Drucker, S. M. Exploring Websites through Contextual Facets. In *Proc. CHI*. pp. 2013-22, 2009.
25. Miller, R. C., Chou, V. H., Bernstein, M., Little, G., Van Kleek, M., Karger, D., and Schraefel, M. Inky: A Sloppy Command Line for the Web with Rich Visual Feedback. In *Proc. UIST*. pp. 131-140, 2008.
26. Morville, P., and Callender, J. Search Patterns: Design for Discovery. O'Reilly Media, Inc., 2010.
27. Oney, S., Brandt, J. Codelets: Linking Interactive Documentation and Example Code in the Editor. In *Proc. CHI*. 2012.
28. Reiss, S. P. Semantics-Based Code Search. *ICSE* 2009.
29. Sahavechaphan, N. and Claypool, K. XSnippet: Mining for Sample Code. In *Proc. of OOPSLA*. pp. 413-30, 2006.
30. Stylos, J. and Myers, B. A. Mica: A Web-Search Tool for Finding API Components and Examples. In *Proc. VL/HCC*. pp. 195-202, 2006.
31. Teevan, J., Cutrell, E., et al. Visual Snippets: Summarizing Web Pages for Search and Revisitation. In *Proc. CHI*. pp. 2023-32, 2009.
32. Thummalapenta, S. and Xie, T. PARSEweb: A Programmer Assistant for Reusing Open Source Code on the Web. In *Proc. ASE*. pp. 204-13, 2007.
33. Xie, T., Pei, J. MAPO:Mining API Usages from Open Source Repositories. In *Proc. MSR*. pp. 54-57, 2006.
34. Yeh, R. B., Paepcke, A., and Klemmer, S.R. Iterative Design and Evaluation of an Event Architecture for Pen-and-Paper Interfaces. In *Proc. UIST*. pp. 111-120, 2008.

ConstraintJS: Programming Interactive Behaviors for the Web by Integrating Constraints and States

Stephen Oney, Brad Myers
Carnegie Mellon University
Pittsburgh, PA 15213 USA
{soney, bam}@cs.cmu.edu

Joel Brandt
Advanced Technology Labs, Adobe
San Francisco, CA 94103 USA
joel.brandt@adobe.com

```
1 friends = cjs.async(fb_request("/me/friends"));
2 pics    = friends.map(function(friend) {
3               return cjs.async(fb_request( "/" + friend.id
4                                              + "/picture"));
5           });
6
7 //...
8
9 {{#diagram friends.state}}
10    {{#state pending }} Loading friends...
11    {{#state rejected}} Error
12    {{#state resolved}}
13       {{#each friends friend i}}
14          {{#diagram pics[i].state}}
15             {{#state pending }} <img src = "loading.gif" />
16             {{#state resolved}} <img src = "{{pics[i]}}" />
17             {{#state rejected}} <img src = "error.gif"   />
18          {{/diagram}}
19          {{friend.name}}
20       {{/each}}
21 {{/diagram}}
```

Figure 1: The code on the right produces the interface on the left. Here, asynchronous calls are made to the Facebook API using the `fb_request` function to fetch a list of friends (line 1) and a profile picture for each friend (lines 2—5). These values are placed into the `friends` and `pics` constraint variables respectively. Lines 9—21 declare a template that depends on thes":e variables. As the list of friends is loading, `friends.state` will be `pending`, so the message "Loading friends..." is displayed (line 10). After the list of friends has loaded (lines 12—20) the picture for each friend is displayed alongside their name. While the application is waiting for the Facebook API to return a picture URL for a friend, a loading image (`loading.gif`) is displayed (line 15). The code also correctly notifies the user of any errors (lines 11, 17).

ABSTRACT

Interactive behaviors in GUIs are often described in terms of states, transitions, and constraints, where the constraints only hold in certain states. These constraints maintain relationships among objects, control the graphical layout, and link the user interface to an underlying data model. However, no existing Web implementation technology provides direct support for all of these, so the code for maintaining constraints and tracking state may end up spread across multiple languages and libraries. In this paper we describe ConstraintJS, a system that integrates constraints and finite-state machines (FSMs) with Web languages. A key role for the FSMs is to enable and disable constraints based on the interface's current mode, making it possible to write constraints that *sometimes* hold. We illustrate that constraints combined with FSMs can be a clearer way of defining many interactive behaviors with a series of examples.

Author Keywords Constraints; Finite-state Machines; Bindings; Web Development; User Interface Technology

ACM Classification Keywords

H.5.2 [Information Interfaces and Presentation]: User Interfaces – Interaction styles.

UIST '12, October 7–10, 2012, Cambridge, Massachusetts, USA.

INTRODUCTION

The World Wide Web is perhaps today's most widely used GUI platform. On the Web, HTML, CSS, and JavaScript define a page's content, style, and interactivity respectively. These three languages interact with each other through a shared representation of the page called the Document Object Model (DOM). JavaScript code defines interactive behaviors with callbacks that modify the DOM using side effects — a paradigm used by most GUI frameworks. However, this paradigm of using callbacks and side effects often results in developers writing interdependent, opaque, and error-prone "spaghetti-code," a problem that was identified over 20 years ago [13].

Constraints

Researchers have shown that *constraints* — relationships that are declared once and automatically maintained — can help developers avoid writing spaghetti code [10,13]. However, constraints have only caught on in GUI programming in two special-purpose ways: 1) data bindings for frameworks that use the Model-View-Controller (MVC) or related design patterns to keep the GUI view in sync with its model (e.g., [20,21,22]) and 2) special-purpose graphical constraints that control the layout of graphical elements (e.g., [4]). Android's Java SDK, for instance, contains both a constraint-based approach for specifying UI layout and a completely separate set of Java classes for several pre-defined types of data bindings.

Similarly, for Web programming, CSS offers a limited constraint language for specifying graphical layout, and separately, there are several JavaScript-based data-binding libraries [20,21,22]. While both of these types of constraints are useful to programmers, they are often limited in expressiveness, and further are almost entirely distinct and unaware of each other, despite their conceptual similarities. For instance, while current JavaScript data binding libraries allow developers to create constraints to set the content of DOM nodes, they do not allow them to create constraints that control CSS or DOM attributes.

States in GUIs

One of the main differentiators of interactive behaviors from general programming is that GUIs are often *stateful* [9] – the application state determines its appearance and behavior. Indeed, when thinking about graphical layouts and data bindings, interaction designers often think in terms of states, along with constraints [12]. As an example, consider the requirement: "when the toolbar is docked, it is displayed above the workspace; when it is dragging, it follows the mouse." Here, each constraint ("the toolbar is above the workspace" or "the toolbar follows the mouse") applies in different application states ("when the toolbar is docked" or "when the toolbar is being dragged"). Transitions describe when and how the application changes state – e.g., when the user presses the toolbar header in docked mode, it enters dragging mode.

ConstraintJS

In this paper, we describe the design and implementation of ConstraintJS[1] (CJS), a system that provides constraints that can be used both to control content and control display, and integrates these constraints with the three Web languages – HTML, CSS, and JavaScript. CJS is designed to take advantage of the declarative syntaxes of HTML and CSS: It allows the majority of an interactive behavior to be expressed concisely in HTML and CSS (see Figure 1), rather than requiring the programmer to write large amounts of JavaScript.

In addition, we go beyond the existing constraint literature by integrating the notion of state into our constraint system, allowing developers to write constraints that *sometimes* hold. We show that the development of interactive behaviors in GUIs can be simplified by integrating finite-state machines (FSMs) with constraints in ConstraintJS. Not only can we create more expressive constraints; we can also create many interactive behaviors using only FSMs and constraints, without extra JavaScript. The example in Figure 1, for instance, requires almost no imperative code. Furthermore, we find that state-oriented constraints integrate well with existing event architectures, including JavaScript's.

Contributions

- We provide a new constraint model by integrating FSMs with constraints, allowing programmers to easily enable and disable constraints depending on the application state. This model further enables 1) support for the asynchronous behaviors which are inherent in Web programming, and 2) the full control provided by one-way constraints that programmers desire [11], but with much of the expressiveness provided by multi-way dataflow constraint solvers [16].
- We show in our ConstraintJS system that constraints and FSMs can be effectively integrated with three Web languages – JavaScript, CSS, and HTML.
- We illustrate the effectiveness of the design and implementation of ConstraintJS with example applications.

[1] We invite our readers to read the full documentation and download ConstraintJS at www.constraintjs.com.

CONSTRAINTJS OVERVIEW

ConstraintJS uses *one-way constraints* [18]. A constraint is a relationship that is declared once and maintained by the system automatically. For instance, if `a` is constrained to `b+1` (expressed as `a <- b+1`), then changes to `b` affect `a`. One-way constraints compute the value of a variable based on others, but not vice-versa, and are therefore like spreadsheet formulas (`a <- b+1` solves for `a`). This is in contrast with multi-way constraints, where relationships can be calculated in any direction [16] (`a <-> b+1` solves for `a` *or* `b`).

CJS combines one-way constraints with FSMs in order to make constraints more expressive. An FSM describes a behavior in terms of the states or modes that the behavior can be in, and the triggers (or events) that cause transitions among the states. Surveys have shown that FSMs are commonly used by designers and programmers when they are specifying how an interface should look and behave [12].

Multiple independent FSMs are often required to describe the look and feel of a single interactive element. Consider the everyday example of radio buttons that may be selected with the mouse or keyboard. Each radio button is controlled by a combination of many states: if the radio button has keyboard focus, it should have an outline around it, and there are various events that change which button has keyboard focus. Separately, if the radio button is currently checked, it should have a dot in the center. Finally, the radio button changes its look while it is being interacted with using the mouse, based on whether it is idle, being hovered over, if the mouse is pressed down, or if it is pressed down and moved outside while pressed. Combining all of these independent states into a single diagram would require $2\times2\times4 = 16$ states, many of which will be semantically un-intuitive (e.g., mouse pressed and outside with keyboard focus and checked). CJS allows the programmer to instead create multiple independent FSMs to control GUI behavior and appearance by enabling or disabling constraints while allowing for a much more understandable and maintainable set of states.

MOTIVATING EXAMPLE

To help concretely illustrate our contribution, consider the example shown in Figure 1, which uses the Facebook API to pull in a list of Facebook friends and display their names alongside their pictures. The Facebook API makes this a three-step process: First, the code must retrieve a list of friend IDs. This is done using one Facebook API call, which returns a list of friend IDs and names. After the list of friends

has been retrieved, the second step is to take this list of friend names and retrieve a URL pointing to a picture for each friend. This means that the code must make another Facebook API call for *each* friend the user has. Finally, once these data are retrieved, they must all be correctly displayed.

To further complicate matters, every Facebook API call is *asynchronous*. This means that when a call is made to the Facebook API, Facebook does not provide a return value immediately. Instead, a callback function is executed at a later point when the data are ready. This introduces three types of complications. First, the system must *wait* for the initial API call (which fetches the list of friends) to finish before attempting to make API calls for each friend the user has. Second, when fetching the friends' pictures, the code cannot rely on the API to send return values back in the same order in which they are requested. For example, if the code asks for pictures for Alice and then Bob, the Facebook API might return Bob's picture before Alice's. The developer must take measures to ensure that the right friend is mapped to the right picture. Finally, the code must gracefully handle the failure of any of these asynchronous calls.

The fact that the API calls are asynchronous means that in a naïve implementation, the user will have to wait for all three steps to be completed in series: first, for the list of friends to load, then for the URL for each friend's photo, and finally for the image located at that URL to load. To provide a good user experience, however, the system should indicate progress by displaying whatever information is available: The application should start with a "loading" screen, then add in the name and a picture-loading graphic when it has a friend's name but not a picture, and finally replace the loading icon with the photo when it has a photo URL.

Implementing this in JavaScript *without* ConstraintJS requires writing a large amount of error-prone code: It would require multiple nested callbacks and scope checking to ensure that the pictures are loaded and displayed in the right places, that the friends' pictures do not attempt to load before they are ready, and that images and text indicating loading delays and errors are properly displayed for every profile. It would also require significant code to ensure that the view stays in sync with the model – that the place-holder symbols show up and then disappear when a picture is available, that the list of friends and pictures is in the right order, and that each picture is linked properly to each friend. Standard JavaScript requires around 20 lines of code to replicate the functionality of lines 1–5 in Figure 1, including four nested callbacks and is generally unclean, spaghetti-like interdependent code that would be difficult to adapt to UI specification changes. The root of this problem isn't JavaScript's syntax (addressed by CoffeeScript and others) or its lack of built-in functions (addressed by libraries like jQuery). It's the fundamental callback/side-effect mechanism that JavaScript requires. ConstraintJS represents a better alternative.

With ConstraintJS, things are much easier. The code is shown in Figure 1. At a high level, this code sets up a constraint variable (`friends`) whose value is the list of friends (line 1). This variable will have no value until the list of friends has been fetched. It then declares a constraint variable (`pics`) with a picture URL for each of these friends. `pics` will not have a value until `friends` returns a value. When `friends` returns a list of friends, `pics` takes that list and returns a list of picture URLs for each friend (lines 2–5). Before any of these constraint variables have values, we create an HTML/Handlebars template [23] whose value depends on `friends` and `pics` (lines 9–21). This template looks at every friend and their state. If `friends` has not loaded, it displays the text "Loading friends…" (line 10) When `friends` has loaded, it displays the name of each friend (lines 12–20). For each friend, if the picture URL has not been loaded yet, then the code displays a loading image (line 15). If it has been loaded, then it displays the friend's photo (line 16).

Overall implementing this example with constraints produces relatively clear and straightforward code. Another benefit of using constraints is that if our list of friends were a changing entity (i.e. the code intermittently updates the list of friends) the code in Figure 1 would automatically update (and not completely replace) the list of friends to reflect any changes over time. We will go over the components this example in more detail in the "API" section below.

RELATED WORK

Because ConstraintJS integrates multiple models, its design is informed by work in several domains, including constraints, finite-state machines, and event architectures.

Constraints in Imperative Languages

Several systems have enabled constraint programming in imperative languages. Kaleidoscope [5] mixes imperative and constraint programming by treating variables as streams that are programmatically advanced and allowing programmers to specify time intervals when constraints hold. ConstraintJS uses a model more suited for interactive applications. Rather than allowing constraints to be switched on and off by treating them as streams, CJS switches constraints on and off based on application state.

Several data-binding libraries are also available for JavaScript. Knockout [22], Ember [20], and Backbone [21] are JavaScript libraries that enable declarative bindings between JavaScript objects and DOM objects. They contain templating features that allow DOM nodes created by these templates to be automatically updated when a property's value changes. However, none of them includes states or FSMs in their templating or binding syntaxes. In addition, they do not allow programmers to attach bindings to control attributes or CSS values of arbitrary DOM nodes. Data binding libraries are also available for the related ActionScript language [24]. Tangle [25] also allows for limited types of bindings to be used to affect DOM properties. However, the types of constraints that can be set are limited and once constraints are installed, they are permanent.

Finally, CCSS extends CSS by enabling hierarchical arithmetic constraints to be set on CSS properties [2]. While these types of constraints increase the flexibility of CSS, they do not provide any way to add constraints from JavaScript variables to specify behavior. Standard CSS also has limited support for some device-dependent constraints. For example, media queries allow CSS rules to depend on the user's display size.

States in Imperative Languages

The use of FSMs in user interface toolkits has a very long history (e.g., see [14]). More recently, Chasm [19] has used a tiered representation to describe 3D user interfaces while allowing developers to specify finite state machines as part of the paradigm. However, Chasm does not include any mechanism for specifying constraints or permanent relationships among objects.

IntuiKit [25] allows interface designers to specify how an image should appear in different states but does not enable interaction, constraints, or any other primitives necessary for interaction. Similarly HsmTk [3] allows state diagrams to be used to define interactivity in the context of an imperative language (C++) but has no notion of constraints or relationships between the underlying data and the view. SwingStates [1] also integrates state diagrams into the Java Swing toolkit. It features parallel state diagrams (the ability to have multiple diagrams affect one object) and fits well with the standard Java syntax. SwingStates does not have any notion of constraints or dependencies among objects.

Adobe Flex [24] includes mechanisms for customizing views based on states using its MXML language and also includes the ability to bind data to attributes. However, the notion of states in Flex is specific to components, which makes it difficult for a widget's behavior to depend on other states such as the application or parent widget's state. Also, in Flex, data bindings are restricted to MXML attributes and require extra syntax for dealing with collections of objects.

Dealing with Events

ConstraintJS utilizes events to trigger the transitions between states of an FSM. Event-action mechanisms have a long history in GUI programming [14]. Recently, FlapJax [10], a language implemented as a JavaScript library, introduced an architecture that allows events and constraints to share similar models and syntaxes. Proton [8] also introduced a declarative syntax for describing sequences of events for touch-based devices. The focus of both of these systems is on building more intuitive and understandable event architectures. The focus of ConstraintJS is related, but different: to focus on ways that constraints can help build highly state-oriented interactive behaviors. For this reason, CJS integrates FSMs into its constraint model. Although we opted to build on JavaScript's standard event architecture, CJS and both of these event architectures could be complimentary.

Visualization Tools

Several libraries for producing HTML-based visualizations [4,7] include a limited form of constraints for specifying dependencies between underlying data and graphical visualizations of those data. For example, D^3 [4] is a library for creating visualizations in JavaScript, manipulating DOM properties based on data. D^3 allows designers to create visualizations of data by creating data bindings from the data to DOM properties. ConstraintJS borrows some of the ideas from the ways these systems deal with collections of data. The focus of these libraries is on producing visualizations, whereas CJS is focused on using constraint to help write interactive behaviors.

THE API OF CONSTRAINTJS

The following sections describe the ConstraintJS application programming interface (API). All of ConstraintJS's functionality is accessed via a global `cjs()` JavaScript function[2] to avoid potential conflicts with other libraries.

Basics: Creating Constrainable Variables

Any JavaScript object or widget may be turned into a constrainable variable using the `cjs` function with the JavaScript variable as a parameter. For instance, this code snippet creates `x` as a constrainable variable whose value is `1`:

```
var x = cjs(1); // x <- 1
```

The `.get()` function fetches the value of a constrainable variable and `.set(value)` sets its value:

```
x.get();  // = 1
x.set(2); // x <- 2
x.get();  // = 2
```

Dynamically computed variables can be created by passing a function as the parameter:

```
var y = cjs(function() {
    return x.get() + 1;    // y <- x + 1
});

x.get();  // = 2
y.get();  // = 3
x.set(9); // x <- 9
y.get();  // = 10
```

Constrainable variables also have several utility methods to create new dependent variables. For instance, the declaration of `y` above may seem cumbersome but the same thing can be achieved with:

```
y = x.add(1);  // y <- x + 1
```

In this case, `.add()` is a built-in function that creates a new constrainable variable. Custom constraint functions may also be created, as we describe in "Convenience Methods" below.

Constraints may be "conditional" if an object with a "`condition`" property is passed in:

```
var z = cjs({ condition: x.gt(0)  // if x > 0
            , value: x }          // z <- x
            { condition: "else"   // else
            , value: x.mul(-1)}); // z <- x*-1
```

Constraints from UI Widgets

Developers can also create constrainable variables tied to user widgets. For example, suppose a developer wants to create a constrainable variable whose value is always the value of the jQuery UI slider widget shown in Figure 2,

---

[2] In JavaScript, function objects may have properties, so although `cjs` is a callable function, it also has subfields (e.g., `cjs.mouse`).

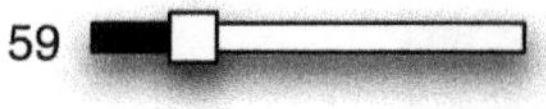

Figure 2: An illustration of a jQuery UI slider widget. Constraint variables can be attached to track the value of this widget.

called `jq_ui`. The constrainable variable `s` will have a getter function that returns the slider's value using the jQuery UI syntax:

```
var s = cjs(function() {
      return jq_ui.slider.option("value");
});
```

The variable `s` now knows *how* to compute its value but it does not know *when* to compute its value. One possible answer is to get its value whenever it is requested. However, for many constrainable variables, recomputing the value is expensive and it is best to avoid recomputing values more than necessary. For this reason, when a constrainable variable's value is requested, its value is cached and not recomputed until the cached value has been *invalidated* using the `.invalidate()` function. Invalidation and evaluation are covered further in the "implementation" section, but the takeaway is that ConstraintJS must be told when the slider should invalidate its cached value, again using the jQuery UI syntax:

```
jq_ui.on("slide change", s.invalidate);
```

Thus, it only takes four lines to create a variable whose value always represents the slider's value. This can now be treated just like any other constrainable variable and have any number of other variables, including DOM elements (as shown below) depend on it.

ConstraintJS includes several built in variables:

- `cjs.mouse.x` – *current mouse x position*
- `cjs.mouse.y` – *current mouse y position*
- `cjs.keyboard.pressed` – *an array of the keys that are currently pressed*
- `cjs.keyboard.modifiers` – `alt`, `ctrl`, *and* `shift` *are* `true` *if pressed,* `false` *otherwise*
- `cjs.touches` – *an array of finger presses on touchscreens*
- `cjs.time` – *milliseconds since midnight 1/1/1970*

Constraining DOM objects to variables

We have shown how to create constrainable variables from regular JavaScript variables. However, to affect any user-visible behaviors, these constraint variables must be linked to the Document Object Model (DOM), the underlying representation for every element on a webpage.

Suppose a developer wants to create the color selection interface shown in Figure 3. As the user selects a color with the sliders, the background color of the `.container`[3] element and the text value in `.hexval` automatically update. Three of the

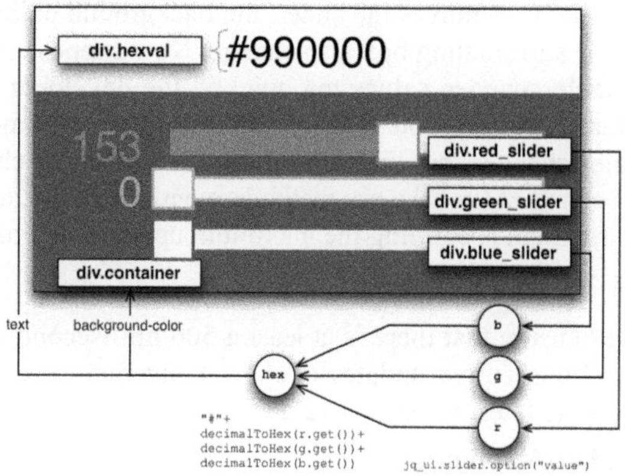

Figure 3: A color selector that uses constraint variables to automatically update the preview color and hex value text. A constraint variable tracks the values for each of the red, green, and blue sliders (`r`, `g`, and `b` respectively.) A fourth constraint variable (`hex`) computes a hex color value. Finally, constraints update the background color and text of the color selector to reflect the slider values.

sliders shown in Figure 2 and implemented in the previous section are used, named `r`, `g`, and `b`. A constrainable variable named `hex` will hold the hexadecimal color value:

```
// decimalToHex converts an integer to hex
var hex = cjs(function() {
          return "#" + decimalToHex(r.get())
                     + decimalToHex(g.get())
                     + decimalToHex(b.get());
        });
```

Now, a constraint is created from `hex` to `.container` (background color) and `.hexval` (text). The code must first search for the appropriate DOM objects, using `cjs.$`. This function takes in a query string as a parameter and outputs a constrainable variable with an array of DOM elements that match that query[4]. As the DOM changes, the value of the array changes automatically[5]. Any of several built-in functions will modify these DOM objects:

- `.class(value)` – *set the class name of a DOM object*
- `.attr(attr_name,value)` – *set any attribute of the DOM obj.*
- `.css(attr_name,value)` – *set a CSS attribute of the DOM obj.*
- `.text(value)` – *set the text value of a DOM obj.*
- `.val(text)` – *set the value of a text input obj.*
- `.children(value)` – *set the child nodes of a DOM obj.* `value` *may be an array.*

In this example,`.css()` sets the background color of `.container` and the `.text()` value of `.hexval`:

```
cjs.$(".container")
    .css("background-color", hex);
cjs.$(".hexval").text(hex);
```

---

[3] A web page's DOM objects have an optional "class" attribute, which can have any number of user-set values. In the standard HTML selector syntax, we can refer to an element with class name "x" as `.x` so here the class is the "container".

[4] In JavaScript, "$" is a legal variable name. The JavaScript library jQuery (jquery.com) popularized the convention of having a function named "$" to search for DOM objects with a query string.

[5] `.snapshot()` can be used to return a non-updating array

Then, as the user moves the slider, the background color and text of the surrounding box also change. Now suppose that if the variable changes values too quickly, the developer does not actually want to update our DOM element *every* time the constraint changes, but limit it to a certain number of changes per second. All of the six methods mentioned take an optional argument specifying the maximum update interval:

```
cjs.$(".hexval").text(hex, 500);
```

This will ensure that there is at least a 500 millisecond delay between consecutive updates to `.hexval` but that `.hexval` always has the latest constraint value.

Finite State Machines

Because many pages have properties and graphics that depend on the current state, ConstraintJS integrates its FSMs with constraints and the page's HTML and CSS. To illustrate, suppose a developer wanted to implement the behavior shown in Figure 4. Here, there are two DOM elements and hovering over one has the effect of highlighting the *other* element. The code to create the FSM shown in the right side of Figure 4 is shown below[6]:

```
var block_a_fsm =
cjs .fsm()
    .add_state("idle")
      .add_transition(cjs.on("mouseover", block_a)
                      , "myhover")
    .add_state("myhover")
      .add_transition(cjs.on("mouseout", block_a)
                      , "idle")
    .starts_at("idle");
```

This snippet uses "chaining," a convention in JavaScript where an object property performs an operation on that object and returns the object back. Here, `cjs.fsm()` creates an FSM and `.add_state("idle")` adds a new state named "idle" to that FSM and returns the FSM back. The `.add_transition()` method then creates a transition from the last state added to any other state. Its first argument specifies *when* the transition should occur. ConstraintJS has several built in event types, including `cjs.on(<event>, <element>)`, which listens for `<event>` to occur on `<element>`. Custom events may also be created. The second argument to `.add_transition()` is the state to which the FSM will transition when the event occurs. Finally, `.starts_at` specifies the initial state of the FSM.

Binding Constraint Values to FSM states

The developer would then create variables and constraints that depend on this FSM. The two blocks shown in Figure 4 would require two FSMs: `block_a_fsm` and `block_b_fsm`. The behavior for `block_a` would be as follows (the code for `block_b` is analogous):

```
block_a.css("background-color",
              block_b_fsm, {
                "idle":    "black",
                "myhover": "yellow"
        });
```

[6] The state name `myhover` is used in this example instead of `hover` to emphasize that this is not the standard CSS built-in hover.

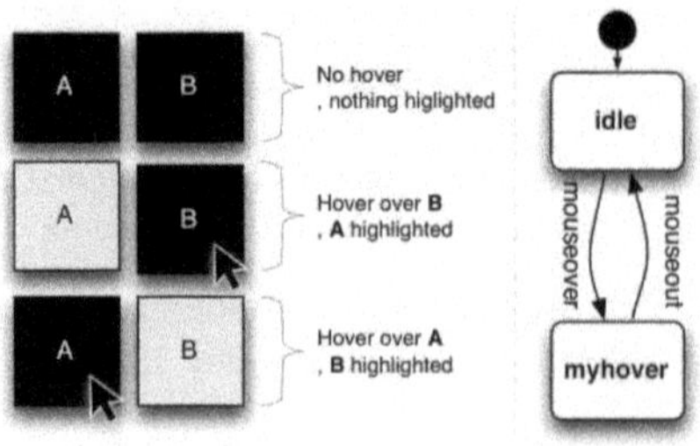

Figure 4: (Left) An illustration of an interactive behavior where hovering over one block highlights the other block. (Right) the FSM used by both blocks to track their state.

The second parameter passed into `block_a.css` is an FSM. The third parameter is an object where the keys ("`idle`" and "`myhover`") represent states in the FSM passed in[7]. The values ("`black`" and "`yellow`" respectively) represent the value for the constraint in the different states. Alternatively, we could create a constraint for the hover color to be whatever color is shown in the `hex` variable in Figure 3:

```
block_a.css("background-color",
              block_b_fsm, {
                "idle" : "black",
                "myhover": hex
        });
```

Every FSM also has a variable called `.state` whose value is the name of its current state. For instance, `block_b_fsm.state.get()` returns either "`idle`" or "`myhover`" depending on the current state of `block_b_fsm`. This allows an alternate implementation approach: the `class` attribute of `block_a` and `block_b` could be constrained to the value of `state`. Then, custom CSS for the classes `idle` and `myhover` could be used to specify how the block is displayed visually:

```
// JavaScript
block_a.class(block_b_fsm.state);
block_b.class(block_a_fsm.state);

// CSS
.idle    { background-color: black;  }
.myhover { background-color: yellow; }
```

Asynchronous Constraints

In JavaScript, developers often have to deal with asynchronous calls: requests that do not provide a return value right away, but instead use a callback to provide the return value at some later time. The Facebook API described earlier in the paper uses asynchronous callbacks. For example, the `fb_request` function takes a query (e.g., "`/me`" to fetch the information of whomever is logged in) and a callback function that will be called whenever the return value is ready. Sometimes, the asynchronous callback will receive an error, (e.g. if we passed in an incorrectly formatted query in the initial call) or might not return at all (e.g., if there was a network problem). To handle these cases in conventional JavaScript code, a developer would need to both create custom error

[7] Multiple states may be selected by joining them with a comma: "`idle, myhover`" or with wildcards: "`*`". Transitions may also be used to instantaneously set constraint values: "`idle -> myhover`".

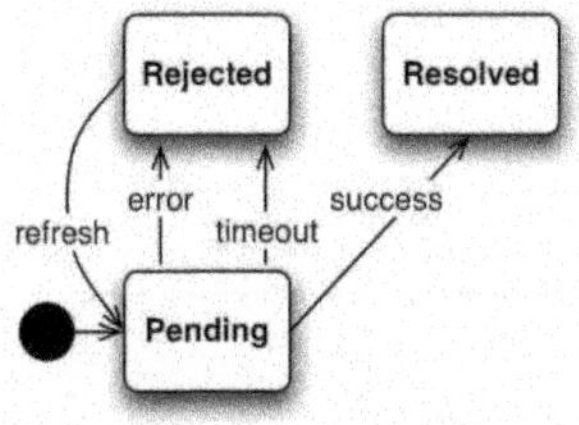

Figure 5: The FSM of asynchronous constraints in ConstraintJS. Asynchronous constraints are constraints that don't have a value until after some delay period, e.g. data returned from network or file system queries. While the constraint is waiting for a value, the FSM is in the "Pending" state. When it successfully receives a value, it enters the "Resolved" state. If there is an error or the request times out, it enters the "Rejected" state.

handling code inside the callback and also manage a timeout after which time a query is considered failed.

Constraints are particularly well-suited to handling asynchronous values because they automatically propagate values when values become available. ConstraintJS handles asynchronous values with a combination of a built-in FSM and a constrainable variable that depends on that FSM. The FSM for asynchronous constraints has three states:

- `"pending"` – waiting for a result
- `"resolved"` – a result was successfully returned
- `"rejected"` – an error occurred

Asynchronous constraints are created with the `cjs.async()` method, which automatically creates the FSM in Figure 5 to track the state of the constraint. `cjs.async()` returns a constraint whose `.state` property is the FSM in Figure 5. This constraint can be treated just the same as normal constraints; we can depend on them, set up dependencies in them, etc. However, the variable will not have a value until the asynchronous callback has returned. If we want to update the variable's value, we can call its `.refresh()` method.

Templates

ConstraintJS also allows HTML templates to be declared in the syntax similar to Handlebars.JS [23] or Ember [20] with values that update with the constraint variables. We extend the syntax of Handlebars by allowing states to be included in the template declaration. These templates accept snippets of HTML code with constraints that automatically update the values of parameters. Templates are created with the `cjs.template` function and variables are specified using double curly braces (`{{x}}`). For instance, this template creates a `<div>` element whose text is constrained to the variables `firstname` and `lastname`:

```
<script id="greeting" type="cjs/template">
    <div>Hello {{firstname}} {{lastname}}</div>
</script>
//...

var fn = cjs("Mary")
    , ln = cjs("Parker");
cjs.template("#greeting"
            , {firstname: fn, lastname: ln});
```

These templates may also include conditionals (omitting the `<script/>` tag in subsequent examples):

```
{{#if logged_in}}
    <div>Hello {{firstname}}
                {{lastname }}</div>
{{#else}}
    <a href="login">Log in</a>
{{/if}}
```

and iterations through collections:

```
{{#each people person}}
   <div>Hello {{person.firstname}}
               {{person.lastname }}</div>
{{/each}}
```

and state diagrams:

```
{{#diagram selected_lang}}
    {{#state english}}
        <div>Hello {{firstname}}
                   {{lastname }}</div>
    {{#state french}}
        <div>Bonjour {{firstname}}
                     {{lastname }}</div>
{{/diagram}}
```

Arrays

ConstraintJS has several functions for dealing with constraints involving arrays. The `.map()` function creates an array whose values depend on the values of a constraint based on another array. For instance:

```
var x = cjs([1,2,3]);
var y = x.map(function(val) {
                return val + 1;
            });
y.get(); // = [2,3,4]
```

When the source array (`x`) changes, `.map()` computes the difference from the previous value in terms of items removed, items added, and items moved. If the value of `x` changes to `[3,4]`, then `y` should get the value `[4, 5]`. `.map()` will detect that `3` was already in the source array and so it only computes the mapped value for `4`. The same difference mechanism is used in the `.children()` method (described above in "Constraining DOM objects to variables") to avoid removing and re-adding DOM child nodes unnecessarily.

Animations

ConstraintJS also includes support for JavaScript animations. Animations are "attached" to any variable using `.anim()`. The resulting variable has the same value as the original variable, but changes are now animated. Animations are currently supported for colors and numbers (which includes objects' positions). For instance, this snippet creates a variable that animates from red to blue over one second:

```
var mycolor = cjs("#FF0000");
var animated_color = mycolor.anim({
                        duration: 1000
                    });
var third_color = cjs(animated_color) ;
mycolor.set("#0000FF");

// mycolor is immediately set to blue
// animated_color and third_color
//    animate from red to blue over one second
```

Convenience Methods

We previously showed that CJS provides a convenience method for add, as in: `x = y.add(z)`. Suppose a developer wanted to be able to express power functions in the same way, as in:

```
var x = cjs(2);    // x <- 2
var y = x.pow(3); // y <- x^3
y.get();           // = 8
x.set(3);          // x <- 3
y.get();           // = 27
```

The developer can define this method as follows:

```
cjs.constraint.mixin("pow",
    function(value, to_the) {
            return Math.pow(value, to_the);
    });
```

Here, the first parameter to `cjs.constraint.mixin` is the name of the method for all constrainable variables and the second is a function whose first argument is the incoming value from the referenced variable (`x` in the snippet above), and the other arguments are whatever are passed into the method.

Working with Third Party Libraries

So far, we have described how to attach constraints to regular DOM objects but JavaScript has a number of libraries that do not use standard DOM objects. We have already extended ConstraintJS to work with the jQuery UI library, as explained above, but we could never provide support for every possible future library ourselves. Therefore, we provide an extension mechanism so that developers can easily get ConstraintJS's constraints, FSMs and other features to work with new libraries. For instance, suppose a developer wants to attach constraints to elements in the RaphaelJS drawing library (found at raphaeljs.com), which uses its own graphics primitives. RaphaelJS objects use the `.attr(prop, val)` method to change display properties, as in:

```
circle.attr("fill", "red");
```

A natural way of expressing a constraint on a RaphaelJS graphics primitive might be:

```
cjs(circle).raphael_attr("fill", constraint_var);
```

ConstraintJS supports this through the function:

```
cjs.binding.bind(context, attr_val, setter, max_updates)
```

which accepts an object (`context`), a value or constrainable value to set that object to (`attr_val`), a function to call to set the object value (`setter`), and an optional maximum update interval (`max_updates`). This provides an easy way to augment the types of constraints that can be made with the `cjs.binding.mixin` function, where the first parameter is the name of the property we are creating and the second is a function that creates a constraint:

```
cjs.binding.mixin("raphael_attr",
 function(obj, attr_name, val, max_updates) {
    var setter = function(obj, val) {
            obj.attr(attr_name, val.get());
    };

    return cjs.binding.bind(context, val
                    , setter, max_updates);
});
```

These ten lines of code are all that is necessary to extend ConstraintJS to work with RaphaelJS graphics primitives. ConstraintJS can be extended to work with any number of third party libraries in a similar fashion.

EXAMPLE APPLICATIONS

We further illustrate ConstraintJS through a series of examples, which we briefly describe below. For the sake of space, we do not include the full example code, but only the relevant snippets. In full, these examples are relatively small, with each example being roughly 200 lines of code.

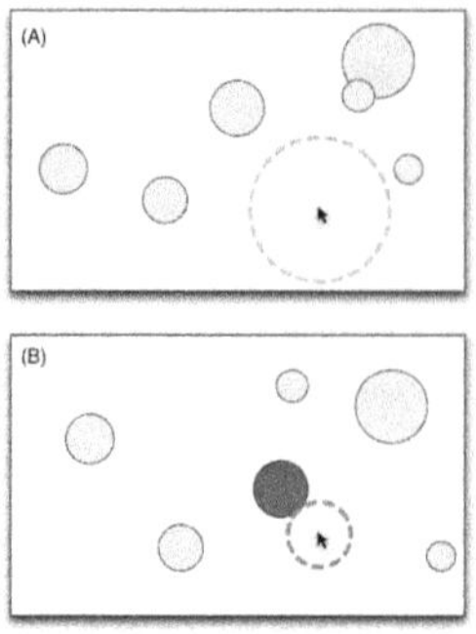

Figure 6: An illustration of Bubble Cursors [6]. Clickable "targets" are light grey-filled circles. When the cursor is too far from any of the targets, a grey dotted halo appears around the cursor (A). When a target is in range (B), the halo becomes red and shrinks enough that it intersects the target, which turns dark grey. The ConstraintJS implementation of this application allows all of this behavior to be expressed declaratively.

Bubble Cursor (Custom Graphics)

Although the most of examples explained in the API section have been standard interaction techniques, constraints and FSMs can also be used to more easily define novel interactions. In this example, we implement a bubble cursor [6] – a cursor that searches for the nearest *target* (represented as grey-filled circles) to the mouse within a maximum radius (the dotted grey circle outline in Figure 6-A). The targets are animated to move continuously, and when there is a single target sufficiently near to the mouse, the dotted outline around the mouse is red and the selected target is a darker grey (shown in Figure 6-B). All of the interaction, including the display colors, position, and movement of the targets and cursor, are defined using constraints. Additionally, this example uses the extensions for the RaphaelJS drawing library, explained in the previous section. In contrast with the equivalent imperative version, the constraint version of the code for the bubble cursor is shorter and uses less interdependent components. For instance, the code to set the radius and color of the cursor is relatively self-contained:

```
// max_bubble_select_distance is a constraint in case
//      we want it to vary based on mouse speed
// select_cursor_radius is a constraint that
//      depends on closest_target
cjs(cursor_halo)
    .raphael_attr("stroke", cjs({ // stroke color
            condition: closest_target.isNull()
          , value: "grey"
        }, {
            condition: "else"
          , value: "red"
        }))
    .raphael_attr("r", cjs({       // radius
            condition: closest_target.isNull()
          , value: max_bubble_select_distance
        }, {
            condition: "else"
          , value: select_cursor_radius
}));
```

In contrast, in a conventional implementation, this functionality would necessarily be spread across callbacks that lis-

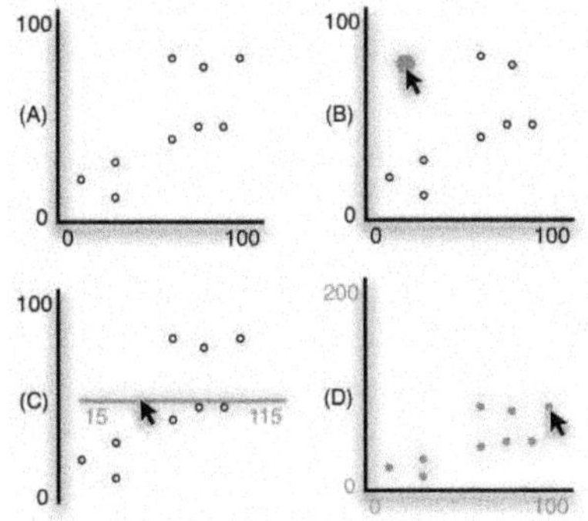

Figure 7: A scatterplot application implemented with ConstraintJS. By default, constraints set the position of every data point to reflect the values of an underlying data model (A). When a point is dragged (B), a constraint in the opposite direction updates the underlying data model based on the position of the point, which in turn, is constrained to the mouse's position. The axes may also be dragged (C) and constraints automatically update the axis labels to reflect its position. Finally, axes' scales may be changed (D) by dragging a point while holding SHIFT. This example illustrates how one-way constraints in ConstraintJS may be combined with FSMs to enable functionality that was previously only possible with multi-way constraints.

tened for changes to the closest target and maximum selection distance.

Scatter Plots (Multi-Way Constraints)

As explained earlier, ConstraintJS uses a one-way constraint solver, as opposed to a multi-way constraint solver. Multi-way constraint solvers have been touted as a way to represent some useful constraints that could not be represented as one-way constraints [15]. In particular, multi-way constraints have been claimed to make it easier to create variables with dependencies that go both ways. Take the scatterplot application in Figure 7. When a data point is being dragged, a constraint sets the model's value for that data point depending on its current display position, which in turn is constrained to follow the mouse. When the user releases the point, a constraint in the opposite direction maintains the x and y display positions based on the underlying model, so if the underlying model's data changes, the point will be updated.

This example was originally used to demonstrate the advantages of multi-way constraints over conventional one-way constraints [15,16]. However, by combining one-way constraints with FSMs, ConstraintJS makes this example easy to implement without the overhead of a multi-way solver. In the default state for every point, a constraint sets the display position based on an underlying data model, where the data model consists of constrainable variables (A). When the user starts to drag a point (B), its state changes, so a different set of constraints are enforced that compute the model's values based on the graphics. When the dragging stops, the state reverts to the default. This is expressed with the following constraint (`div` and `sub` are convenience methods for division and subtraction respectively):

```
cjs(dot_fsm, {
    "init, idle": x.div(scale_x),
    "dragging"  : (cjs.mouse.x).sub(offset.x) });
```

Figure 8: An illustration of a touchscreen-based application written with ConstraintJS. Constraints control the position, scale, and angle of photos, which users can manipulate with one or two fingers. When two fingers touch a photo, a red slider appears that controls the photo's opacity and can be changed using a third finger. Constraints set the position and text of the slider.

A similar pattern is used for the axes and changing the scale. Note that dataflow multi-way solvers required developers to write the constraints in both directions [15,16], just as ConstraintJS does – those solvers just select which set of constraints to use. However, developers often found that they needed to extra features, such as constraint hierarchies [16] to control the direction. In ConstraintJS, FSMs (which are likely to be more understandable and controllable for developers [11,12]) keep track of the dragging state for each point and axis and manages enabling and disabling constraints.

Multi-touch Moveable/Resizable Image (Tablets)

Although all of the examples we have discussed so far are based on mouse and keyboard input, ConstraintJS is not limited to desktop applications. ConstraintJS works with any kind of user input that can be translated into JavaScript events. Figure 8 illustrates a simple multi-touch photo manipulation interface for tablet devices we built with ConstraintJS. In this application, users can move and manipulate photos in a virtual workspace. Touching a photo with one finger drags the photo within the workspace. Manipulating a photo with two fingers changes the rotation, scale, and position of the photo. When a photo is touched with two fingers, a red slider widget that controls the photo's opacity appears and may be manipulated with a third finger. The slider indicates the current value by its position and text.

The layout of every component in this application is controlled by constraints – photo position, scale, rotation, & opacity and the position, visibility & text of the opacity slider. Compared to an implementation of this example that does not use constraints, the ConstraintJS implementation requires fewer lines of code and fewer callbacks.

IMPLEMENTATION

The constraints in ConstraintJS are "pull" constraints, meaning that a constraint's value is never computed until it is asked for. We based our algorithm on the pointer-constraints algorithm outlined by Vander Zanden et. al [17], modifying it to enable more control over when constraints are evaluated (e.g., immediately after FSM state changes). Using this algorithm, dependencies between variables are automatically computed and values are cached until they are invalidated.

Most data-binding libraries have opted for the "push" model, where whenever a constraint's value changes, updates are "pushed" to any constraint that depends upon it. However, in ConstraintJS, constraints may be turned on and off depending on application state, meaning that the "push" implementation for constraints might do unnecessary work if values are pushed to constraint variables that are turned off and do not currently affect the DOM. With the pull model for constraints, we can create any number of constraints, but if they do not affect any DOM objects on screen and are not specifically requested, they will not be updated and therefore will not hinder the performance of the application.

Another potential problem with push-based constraints is that cycles may cause an infinite loop if not handled carefully. With pull-based constraints, we do not have this problem. Cycles are automatically computed using a "once around" algorithm (which evaluates each constraint in the cycle only once per invalidation), which has been shown in previous systems to be understandable and useful for developers [18].

Size & Performance

The current version of ConstraintJS is a 25 KB file when compressed using UglifyJS and Gzip. It can be included in any JavaScript application, including phone/tablet web browsers and server-side JavaScript applications that use the Node platform. In testing the current version of ConstraintJS inside the Safari web browser on a 2.6 GHz Core 2 Duo processor, our system was able to handle without any noticeable delay on the order of 1,000 simultaneously evaluated constraints all affecting DOM objects and simultaneously smoothly animate around 200 DOM properties. This is clearly more than any real interactive behavior is likely to need.

CONCLUSIONS AND FUTURE WORK

We have presented ConstraintJS, a system that integrates constraints and finite-state-machines (FSMs) with Web languages. ConstraintJS can be included in any JavaScript application without browser modifications and it can interoperate with other JavaScript libraries. By integrating constraints and FSMs, ConstraintJS can help simplify the development of interactive behaviors. In fact, many interactive behaviors can be built entirely as a combination of FSMs and constraints, which can both be specified declaratively. For future work, we plan on building an interactive tool to enable non-programmer designers to develop custom behaviors as combinations of FSMs and constraints. However, we feel that in its current form, developers will find that the ConstraintJS language and toolkit is a clearer way to program interactive behaviors for the Web.

ACKNOWLEDGEMENTS

Funding for this research comes from a Microsoft SEIF award, a grant from Adobe, a Ford Foundation Fellowship, and from NSF grant IIS-1116724. Any opinions, findings and conclusions or recommendations are those of the authors and do not necessarily reflect those of any of the sponsors.

REFERENCES

1. Appert, C. and Beaudouin-Lafon, M. SwingStates: Adding state machines to Java and the Swing toolkit. *Software: Practice and Experience 38*, 11 (2008), 1149-1182.
2. Badros, G.J., Marriott, K., Borning, A., & Stuckey, P. Constraint Cascading Style Sheets for the Web. *UIST*,(1999), 73-82.
3. Blanch, R., Beaudouin-lafon, M., and Futurs, I. Programming Rich Interactions using the Hierarchical State Machine Toolkit. *AVI*, (2006), 51-58.
4. Bostock, M., Ogievetsky, V., and Heer, J. D^3: Data-Driven Documents. *Visualization and Computer Graphics 17*, 12 (2011), 2301-9.
5. Freeman-Benson, B. Kaleidoscope: Mixing Objects, Constraints, and Imperative Programming. *OOPSLA*, (1990), 77-88.
6. Grossman, T. and Balakrishnan, R. The Bubble Cursor: Enhancing Target Acquisition by Dynamic Resizing of the Cursor's Activation Area. *CHI*, (2005), 281-290.
7. Heer, J. and Bostock, M. Declarative language design for interactive visualization. *Visualization and Computer Graphics 16*, 6 (2010), 1149-56.
8. Kin, K., Hartmann, B., DeRose, T., and Agrawala, M. Proton: Multitouch Gestures as Regular Expressions. *CHI*, (2012).
9. Letondal, C., Chatty, S., Phillips, W.G., and André, F. Usability requirements for interaction-oriented development tools. *PPIG*, (2010), 12-26.
10. Meyerovich, L., Guha, A., and Baskin, J. Flapjax: A Programming Language for Ajax Applications. *OOPSLA*, (2009), 1-20.
11. Myers, B., Hudson, S.E., and Pausch, R. Past, Present, and Future of User Interface Software Tools. *TOCHI 7*, 1 (2000), 3-28.
12. Myers, B., Park, S.Y., Nakano, Y., Mueller, G., and Ko, A. How Designers Design and Program Interactive Behaviors. *VL/HCC*, (2008), 177-184.
13. Myers, B.A. Separating Application Code from Toolkits: Eliminating the Spaghetti of Callbacks. *UIST*, (1991), 211-220.
14. Olsen, D.R. *User Interface Management Systems: Models and Algorithms*. Morgan Kaufmann, San Mateo, CA, 1992.
15. Sannella, M. and Borning, A. Multi-Garnet: Integrating Multi-Way Constraints with Garnet. *UW Technical Report*, (1992).
16. Sannella, M. SkyBlue: A Multi-Way Local Propagation Constraint Solver for User Interface Construction. *UIST*, (1994), 137-146.
17. Vander Zanden, B.T., Myers, B.A., Giuse, D.A., and Szekely, P. Integrating Pointer Variables into One-Way Constraint Models. *TOCHI l*, 2 (1994), 161-213.
18. Vander Zanden, B.T., Richard, H., Myers, B.A., et al. Lessons Learned About One-Way, Dataflow Constraints in the Garnet and Amulet Graphical Toolkits. *TOPLAS 23*, 6 (2001), 776-796.
19. Wingrave, C.A., Laviola Jr, J.J., and Bowman, D.A. A natural, tiered and executable UIDL for 3D user interfaces based on Concept-Oriented Design. *TOCHI 16*, 4 (2009), 21.
20. Ember. http://emberjs.com/.
21. Backbone. http://documentcloud.github.com/backbone/.
22. KnockoutJS. http://knockoutjs.com/.
23. Handlebars.JS. http://handlebarsjs.com/.
24. Adobe Flex. http://www.adobe.com/products/flex.html.
25. Tangle. http://worrydream.com/Tangle/.

User Interface Toolkit Mechanisms for Securing Interface Elements

Franziska Roesner, James Fogarty, Tadayoshi Kohno
Computer Science & Engineering
DUB Group, Security and Privacy Research Lab
University of Washington
{franzi, jfogarty, yoshi}@cs.washington.edu

ABSTRACT

User interface toolkit research has traditionally assumed that developers have full control of an interface. This assumption is challenged by the mashup nature of many modern interfaces, in which different portions of a single interface are implemented by multiple, potentially mutually distrusting developers (e.g., an Android application embedding a third-party advertisement). We propose considering security as a primary goal for user interface toolkits. We motivate the need for security at this level by examining today's mashup scenarios, in which security and interface flexibility are not simultaneously achieved. We describe a security-aware user interface toolkit architecture that secures interface elements while providing developers with the flexibility and expressivity traditionally desired in a user interface toolkit. By challenging trust assumptions inherent in existing approaches, this architecture effectively addresses important interface-level security concerns.

ACM Classification: H.5.2 [Information interfaces and presentation]: User Interfaces - Graphical user interfaces.

General terms: Security; Human Factors; Design.

Keywords: Security; user interface toolkits.

INTRODUCTION AND MOTIVATION

User interface toolkits help to reduce barriers to the design and development of modern graphical interfaces [24, 25]. In aiming to provide maximal flexibility and expressivity, existing toolkit research generally makes an implicit assumption that developers have full control of an interface (e.g., [6, 7, 8, 17, 24]). However, as applications move towards interfaces composed of elements from different sources, this assumption can pose significant security risks.

Consider the mashup nature of many modern interfaces, wherein multiple elements of an interface are implemented by different developers with varying trust relationships. Such mashups arise both on the Web and within applications. In a common scenario, a mobile application imports a library to display advertisements in a designated portion of its interface. The application must trust that the advertising library will not abuse the application's permissions without user consent (e.g., to access user information or to send a premium-rate SMS). Conversely, the advertising library must trust that the application will not programmatically click its advertisements in order to increase its advertising revenue. In both cases, this trust can be misplaced: Android ad libraries can and have abused the permissions of embedding applications [10, 13] and Android apps can programmatically click on embedded ads. Malicious programmers can also trick users into clicking a sensitive embedded element by manipulating its display, an attack known as clickjacking [14]. For example, a website can trick a user into clicking a Facebook "Like" button by making the element transparent or uncovering it just as the user clicks in a predictable location.

Such risks traditionally go unaddressed or are mitigated in ways that come at the expense of interface flexibility and usability. For example, a conventional solution for preventing an ad library from illicitly accessing a user's location is to insert a system-controlled confirmation dialog when an application requests location information. Although this approach increases security, it can significantly impact the usability of legitimate applications. Consider also guidelines for security-critical interfaces, such as the Microsoft Windows User Account Control (UAC) guidelines specifying that a shield icon be displayed on buttons that result in actions requiring administrative privileges. In current tools, such guidelines cannot be programmatically enforced but must instead be verified through inspection and review (e.g., an app store process).

Existing mitigations for interface-level security concerns are implemented at the system level, not in the user interface toolkit. We argue that this design is a principal reason that these solutions negatively impact interface usability and flexibility. For example, because traditional user interface toolkits do not support securely embedding a sensitive element into another developer's context, system developers are forced to resort to secure system prompts.

UIST'12, October 7-10, 2012, Cambridge, MA, USA.

We therefore propose that such threats be addressed by rearchitecting the user interface toolkit. A well-designed security-aware user interface toolkit could enforce visual security indicators (such as the UAC shield), link a user's actions in an interface to an application's access to sensitive resources (such as location), and strike at the core of security threats that leverage interface manipulation (such as clickjacking). In addition, we believe that securing sensitive interface elements will enable future innovation in the design of interfaces for security-sensitive interactions.

In this work, we consider security as a primary goal in the user interface toolkit. We explore the security assumptions of existing approaches and develop mechanisms that isolate mutually distrusting interface elements while retaining the flexibility that developers enjoy in existing toolkits. Specifically, this paper contributes:

- Scenarios that motivate a security-aware user interface toolkit for interfaces with mutually distrusting elements.
- A set of security properties needed for these scenarios.
- A security-aware user interface toolkit architecture that achieves these system-level security properties while maintaining necessary flexibility for developers.
- Prototype implementations in the context of mobile application (Android) and Web (browser) toolkits.

SCENARIOS AND SECURITY PROPERTIES

In this section, we introduce a set of scenarios motivating a need for security as a primary goal in user interface toolkits and explore the drawbacks of existing approaches to achieving security in these scenarios. We then consider our threat model and extract a set of desired security properties.

Scenarios

Resource Access. Modern systems (e.g., smartphones, browsers, and desktop operating systems) provide applications with access to a variety of system resources (e.g., a camera, user location, a contact list). Systems protect these resources by granting applications access to them only if permitted by the user, who agrees either to a prompt at the time of first access or to a list of permissions requested at the time of installation (known as a manifest). However, these approaches can pose security risks: after an application is granted access to a resource, most systems allow it to continue accessing the resource whenever and however it wishes, even if that access is invisible to the user and/or inappropriate [29]. For example, an app could take photos or send out location information without a user's consent or knowledge.

Existing work on user-driven access control [29] considers using a person's interactions with an interface for resource access control decisions. For example, a person's click on an embedded location button implies the intent to grant the application location access (see Figure 1). By capturing this intent, the system can ensure that the application accesses location only at the appropriate time, when access is expected by the user. However, this solution assumes that applications cannot trick people into clicking on such

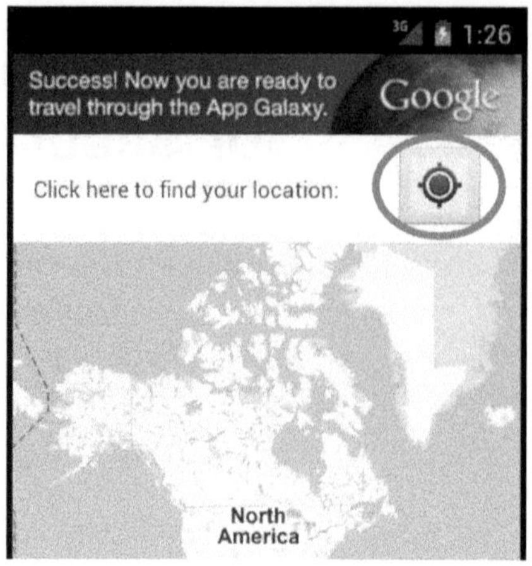

Figure 1: This maps application includes an advertisement generated by an ad library (top) and a system-provided location button (circled).

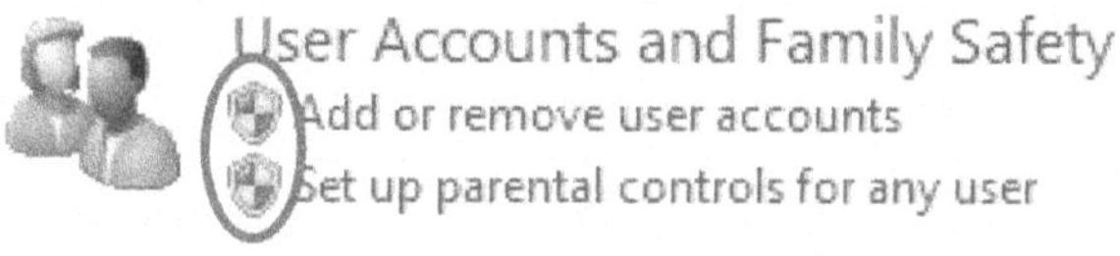

Figure 2: The User Account Control shield in Microsoft Windows (circled) signifies that the resulting action requires administrator privileges.

buttons and cannot manipulate a button's display (e.g., to hide the location icon). Because existing user interface toolkits do not support security for embedded elements, system buttons cannot be embedded in today's interfaces.

Enforcing Interface Requirements. More generally, the system may wish to enforce interface restrictions on elements that can result in restricted operations when users interact with them. For example, Microsoft Windows UAC guidelines [21] state that buttons which will result in actions requiring administrator privileges should be adorned with a UAC shield icon (see Figure 2). As another example, browsers may choose to display visual indicators when users perform insecure actions (e.g., a crossed-out lock icon displayed when using a non-HTTPS connection). If a system wants to require such a visual indicator for all applications making network connections, current tools cannot help in enforcing the requirement. Instead, such a requirement can be enforced only with interface guidelines and application review (e.g., an app store process).

Third-Party Libraries and Transactions. As described in the introduction, applications that embed third-party elements (such as advertising libraries) can present or expose themselves to security risks. Similar concerns arise when applications embed other third-party elements, such as payment elements (e.g., for PayPal), social widgets (e.g., the Facebook "Like" button), or federated login systems (e.g., using a Google account to login to another website).

User interface toolkits currently do not support security in these scenarios. For example, Android applications can easily manipulate interface elements provided by third-party libraries. An application seeking to fraudulently increase its advertising revenue can, for instance, programmatically click on the ads that it embeds. We have implemented a proof-of-concept Android application demonstrating that three separate ad libraries are vulnerable to this type of attack. On the other hand, existing research [10, 13] indicates that some ad libraries inappropriately exploit the permissions of the embedding application (e.g., stealing contact information and tracking location).

Current approaches to securing third-party interface elements embedded in an application restrict the flexibility of interface designers. Consider the popular Facebook "Like" button, which can be embedded by websites as an iframe to allow visitors to "Like" the embedding page and share it on their Facebook profile. Although the Web's same-origin policy [33] prevents the embedding webpage from programmatically clicking on or manipulating the button's iframe, pages can mount clickjacking attacks in which they trick users into clicking on the button (e.g., by uncovering the button just before the user clicks in a predictable location). When Facebook suspects that a particular button is victim to such an attack, it switches that button into a secure mode [11]. In this mode, clicking on the button opens a popup window in which the user must confirm the action. This is clearly a more cumbersome user experience not desired by Facebook's developers.

In these and other scenarios, there may be expected and mutually beneficial interaction between an embedded element and an application (e.g., informing the application when an ad fails to load or when a payment has been completed). It would thus be too restrictive to completely isolate interface elements from different sources.

Threat Model

In this work, we are concerned with protecting interface elements in one part of an application (e.g., the main application itself) from another part of the application (e.g., an included ad library), and vice versa. We consider developers of these different application components to be potentially mutually distrusting. We further consider any application developer to be a potential adversary or accidental adversary of the system. An intentional adversary might attempt to fool a user or attempt to access sensitive resources without legitimate permission; an accidental adversary might fail to adhere to interface guidelines intended to increase system security (e.g., failing to display the UAC shield) or might accidentally expose a user's data to a third party. We make the standard assumption that the system itself is trustworthy and uncompromised (e.g., the operating system or the browser). In selected cases, where noted, we also rely on a trusted app store review process, though we design our toolkit architecture to minimize this reliance. Later sections also discuss additional limitations of our prototypes on two current platforms (i.e., Android and a Web browser).

Desired Security Properties

To refer to code belonging to different parts of an application or the system, we introduce the term *trust group*. We extract from the presented scenarios and threat model the following security properties needed to protect interface elements within mutually distrusting trust groups.

1. *Display Integrity*: Code in one trust group should not be able to alter the content or appearance of an interface element in another trust group, except via APIs explicitly exposed by that element.
2. *Input Integrity*: Code in one trust group should not be able to programmatically interact with interface elements in another trust group (e.g., calling a `performClick()` function), except when explicitly permitted.
3. *Intent Integrity*: Code in one trust group should not be able to mount clickjacking attacks to force or trick users into interacting with an interface element in another trust group. Code should also not be able to prevent intended user interactions with interface elements in another trust group (i.e., a denial-of-service attack).
4. *Data Isolation*: Code in one trust group should not be able to read or extract content displayed by an interface element in another trust group, except following an explicit user interaction within the element that permits this (e.g., pressing "Select" in a file picking menu would allow the application to access the file system and open the selected file). Code in one trust group should not be able to eavesdrop on input intended for a interface element in another trust group.
5. *UI-to-API Links*: It should be possible for application or system APIs to be linked to interface elements. For example, a `takePhoto()` API might be accessible only from a camera button in the system's trust group.

In designing a security-aware user interface toolkit, we aim to support these security properties alongside the traditional goals of minimizing the difficulty of implementing typical interfaces (i.e., minimizing a toolkit's threshold [24]) while still providing maximal expressiveness and flexibility (i.e., maximizing a toolkit's ceiling [24]).

ARCHITECTING A TOOLKIT FOR SECURITY

In this section, we introduce a user interface toolkit architecture that achieves the above properties by (1) isolating interface elements into trust groups and (2) maintaining specific invariants with respect to the interface layout tree. The toolkit does so while retaining developer flexibility to (3) expose model-level APIs, (4) compose elements, and (5) display feedback across trust groups. We describe each of these design points in turn.

Trust Groups and Permissions

Our architecture separates mutually distrusting application components, both interface code and application code, into distinct trust groups. For example, system code belongs to one trust group (referred to as "system-trusted" throughout this paper), an application belongs to another trust group, and third-party elements belong to their own trust groups (e.g., an ad library, a PayPal payment button, or a Google login field). Figure 3 shows how parts of an application

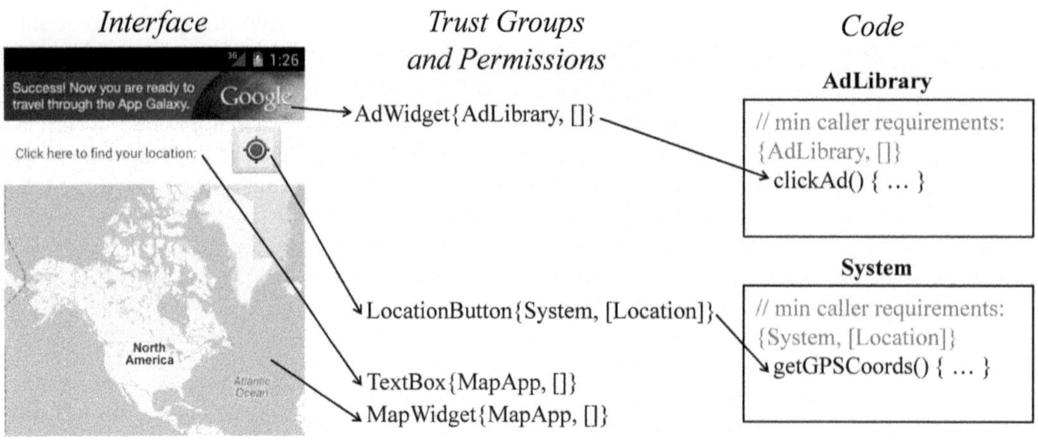

Figure 3: An example of how an element's trust group and permissions map to accessible APIs. An element with trust group A and permissions B and C is designated ElementName{A, [B, C]}. This screenshot is from the Android implementation of our architecture.

might map to trust groups, and we explain the details of this figure throughout this subsection.

Trust Group Assignment. In order to isolate elements from different sources, our toolkit must associate all code and all interface elements with a trust group. We leave it up to applications, libraries, and the system to associate their own non-interface code with trust groups at any granularity, but we must consider the appropriate model for assigning interface elements to trust groups. In particular, our toolkit architecture must support two types of scenarios. In the first, an application embeds a sensitive element exposed by another trust group, such as a system-trusted camera button. In the second, an application simply uses a generic toolkit element (such as a standard button) which should become part of the application's own trust group.

To support these scenarios, we introduce two types of interface elements: *fixed-trust-group elements* and *owner-bound elements*. A fixed-trust-group element has a set trust group that does not depend upon which entity instantiates or embeds it (e.g., a camera button may belong to the "system" group). An owner-bound element, such as a standard button, adopts the trust group of the code that instantiates it.

Restricting Application, System, and Library APIs. Our architecture can use trust groups to create the desired link between interface code and application, system, or library code (UI-to-API Links) by simply denying API access to callers with unauthorized trust groups.

However, trust groups may sometimes not be sufficiently granular for an API's access control policy. For instance, the system may wish to restrict the `takePicture()` API only to the system-provided camera button, not to all system interface elements. This policy embodies the standard security principle of "least privilege", as arbitrary system components do not need access to the camera. Thus, even if other system elements could be manipulated into invoking the `takePicture()` API, those calls would fail.

To allow such fine-grained access control policies, we associate each interface element with a set of permissions in addition to its trust group. Taken together, these allow the system or an application to restrict certain APIs (e.g., `takePicture()`) to code originating from interface elements of an appropriate trust group and with sufficient permissions (e.g., an element with trust group "system" and a permission list containing the "camera" permission).

In this paper, we designate an interface element with trust group A and permissions B and C as Element{A, [B, C]}. Figure 3 shows an example of how elements map to trust groups and permissions, which in turn map to accessible APIs in application, system, or library code. In the common case (such as the AdWidget in Figure 3), an element's permissions list will be empty, giving it access to only those APIs that do not require any additional permissions.

Restricting Interface APIs. Interface elements may need to protect certain methods and expose others. For example, an ad element would not wish to allow `performClick()` to be called by another trust group, but it may wish to expose a method to set advertisement keywords. Similarly, an application should be able to attach a callback to a system camera element to receive a photo after it is taken.

Interface elements are thus responsible for defining an access policy for their methods. By default, only code within the same trust group and the system's trust group can access all of an element's methods. We note that an alternate default would allow all access, relying on developers to selectively restrict sensitive methods. We opt for the stricter default, lowering the threshold to implementing secure interfaces under the assumption that most interfaces do not require crossing security boundaries.

Restrictions on relevant methods provide the following protections, which are subsets of our security properties:

- Code cannot manipulate the display of elements in other trust groups (Display Integrity). For example, the methods `setBackground()` or `setTransparency()` can be inaccessible to code from another trust group.

- Code cannot extract data from elements in other trust groups (Data Isolation). For example, the method `getText()` can be inaccessible.
- Code cannot programmatically click on elements in other trust groups (Input Integrity).
- Code cannot enable or disable elements in other trust groups (Intent Integrity).

Another aspect of Intent Integrity is the ability to prevent clickjacking attacks, in which a malicious parent reveals a sensitive interface element from another trust group just as the user is about to click in a predictable location. An element can use system-provided information about its current visibility to implement a clickjacking-protection policy, such as becoming enabled only after being fully visible for some time (as in Chrome [3] and Firefox [23]).

Interface Layout Tree

Using trust groups and permission lists, our architecture achieves a number of desired security properties. However, applications are still susceptible to security weaknesses stemming from the way in which traditional user interface toolkits organize interface elements into a layout tree (where an element is the parent of any elements it embeds).

- *Insecure layout*: Although trust groups and permissions restrict method calls on elements, code can still manipulate an element's display using layout techniques (i.e., violate Display Integrity). For instance, an application wishing to hide a required interface element (such as a UAC shield) could simply cover that portion of an interface. Similarly, an application wishing to force a user into clicking on a system-trusted location button could simply make this button much larger than surrounding buttons. In traditional user interface toolkits, parent nodes can control the size and layout of their children. As a result, an application that embeds an element of another trust group has complete control over the drawing and layout of the embedded element.
- *Insecure input*: In a traditional layout tree, a malicious application could eavesdrop on or modify events as they trickle down the tree. For example, an application could embed a third-party login element and then steal a user's password by eavesdropping on key events as they propagate down the tree (thus violating Data Isolation). Other attacks could modify the picking code to redirect input to a different interface element (e.g., modifying a legitimate click event to move its location onto a secure button) or prevent an event's propagation entirely. The fundamental challenge is that a single layout tree contains nodes from different trust groups, thus introducing the potential for untrusted nodes to access events before they reach their intended recipient.

Layout Tree Invariants. To mitigate these weaknesses, our toolkit departs from traditional toolkits to enforce the following invariants: (1) the root node of an application's layout tree must be a system node, and (2) only system nodes may have children of a different trust group. Because

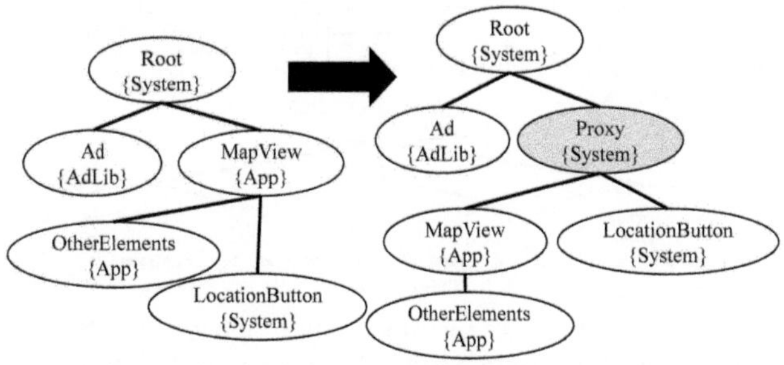

Figure 4: The intended layout tree for the application shown in Figure 1 is transformed to include a proxy node, enforcing the invariant that only system-trusted nodes may have children of a different trust group.

we can trust the system itself to provide elements with the layout attributes they request (subject to any necessary conflict resolution), these invariants mitigate the insecure layout weakness. We can also trust the system to provide accurate information about an element's position and visibility (enabling the clickjacking protection described above). Furthermore, only nodes in the same trust group or the system's trust group will see input events propagating down the tree, thus eliminating the eavesdropping threat.

Conflicts in Visual Space. Although our invariants dictate that only system nodes may have children from another trust group, applications may wish to visually embed elements from different trust groups. Consider the example in Figure 1, where an interface consists of an application map element containing a system-trusted location button. The first invariant is easy to satisfy by placing the entire application in a system-trusted frame. However, the second invariant is more difficult to satisfy while achieving the desired visual effect, as it prevents the map element from being the parent of the location button.

We solve this problem by introducing a system-trusted *proxy node* into the layout tree. Figure 4 shows the resulting transformation of the tree. In particular, the proxy node becomes a parent of both the map element and the location button, overlaying them as intended by the application. This transformation preserves the trust hierarchy for layout and for event propagation. We describe in later sections how this transformation can be implemented automatically and transparently to applications, which can continue to manipulate a view of the layout tree that matches the intended visual layout.

A final issue to resolve is layout requests that are conflicting or otherwise cannot be satisfied. The parent element traditionally controls space available to a child element, but this approach may violate security properties (e.g., an application may tell an element to paint itself so small that important context is hidden from a user). On the other hand, a malicious child that controls its own size could draw outside the acceptable bounds (e.g., a malicious ad library that takes over the entire screen).

In the case of a system-trusted child element (e.g., a location button), we rely on our assumption that the system

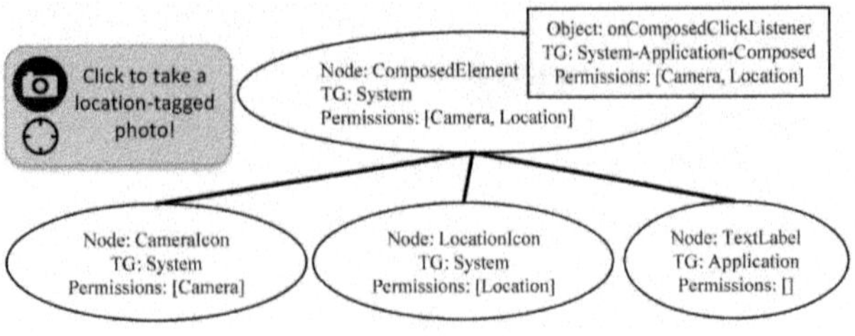

Figure 5: In this example, the application has composed the system-trusted camera and location icons with its own label to create a custom button that has both camera and location permissions.

is trustworthy. Our architecture enforces the minimum requested size for system-trusted elements, even if the size allocated by the parent is smaller than this minimum.

In the general case, we cannot make assumptions about whether the embedding or the embedded node is more trustworthy. We resolve the conflict as follows: if the child element requests a larger size than permitted by the parent element, we draw the child element with the smaller size, visually indicate to the user that the child could not be fully displayed, and allow the user to manually maximize it. This solution can be seen as a sort of generalization of the behavior of typical browser popup-blockers.

Although isolating elements into trust groups and maintaining the described tree invariants supports our desired security properties, naïvely implementing these mechanisms introduces undesired restrictions on interface flexibility. To restore this necessary flexibility, the next sections extend this basic architecture to allow developers to expose model-level APIs, compose elements, and display feedback across trust groups.

Model-Level Event Listeners

In traditional user interface toolkits, interface elements allow applications to attach listeners for various events (e.g., click, key, touch). For sensitive elements, however, these generic listeners may present security risks. For example, an application can use an `onKeyListener` to eavesdrop as a user enters a password into a third-party federated login element. To prevent such attacks, elements in our architecture default to restricting such listener hooks to callers of the same trust group (or the system trust group).

However, recall that elements may wish to expose certain events across trust groups (e.g., to inform an application when an ad has loaded, to provide a captured photo, to update detected GPS coordinates). Unlike generic event listeners, these events have model-level semantics (i.e., they are meaningful at the application level, not at the interface element level). We thus apply *model-level event listeners*, which can be used by a sensitive element to expose higher-level data or events to the trust group that embeds it. For example, a payment library might now allow applications to attach arbitrary listeners to a payment dialog, but could explicitly expose events for successful payment. Existing user interface toolkits use model-level events to provide meaningful notifications related to manipulation of an element (e.g., `ItemListeners` on menu items and `ChangeListeners` on sliders), but security-sensitive interface elements are likely to expose even higher-level events than current examples.

In our architecture, both generic and model-level event listeners execute in the trust group of the defining code, not that of the element to which they are attached. Otherwise, an attacker could inject arbitrary code into another trust group (e.g., by attaching an `onClickListener` to an element in the trust group of the attacker's choice).

Composition Across Trust Groups

We have thus far considered only the *visual* composition of elements belonging to different trust groups. However, interface designers require greater flexibility to *logically* compose elements. For example, consider the Windows UAC scenario in which an arbitrary developer-defined button that includes a UAC shield must be able to access privileged system APIs. To access these APIs, the button must be in the system's trust group. However, its visual layout must be largely defined by the app developer. Conceptually, the developer would like to embed the system-trusted UAC shield element in a custom element and inherit the former's trust group and permissions.

We support composition of elements from multiple trust groups by introducing a system-defined ComposedElement. Any trust group may choose to expose composable sub-elements for inclusion in a ComposedElement (e.g., the system may expose a UAC shield icon with the "administrator" permission or a GPS icon with the "location" permission). Another developer can then mash up these sub-elements with custom elements in a ComposedElement. For instance, Figure 5 shows a composed button for taking a location-tagged photo.

Our toolkit must ensure that allowing compositions does not violate the security properties achieved in previous sections. In particular, a ComposedElement must not allow code to manipulate or observe elements in another trust group or to inappropriately access restricted APIs.

In order to retain the benefits of the layout tree invariants previously described, we assign ComposedElements to the "system" trust group. ComposedElements are thereby allowed to contain sub-elements of other trust groups. Our invariants continue to hold within the ComposedElement. This ensures, for example, that an application cannot use a composition to eavesdrop on a third-party login field.

Recall the goal of a composition is for the resulting element to inherit the permissions of its constituent elements. However, we do not wish to allow applications to inject arbitrary code into a ComposedElement, as this code will run in the system's trust group. To achieve these goals simultaneously, the ComposedElement allows the trust group that embeds it to attach event listeners. Unlike other event listeners (which run in the attacher's trust group), listeners of a ComposedElement run in a temporary trust group derived from the ComposedElement's sub-elements;

its set of permissions is the union of their permissions. For example, the ComposedElement in Figure 5 includes location and camera sub-elements, resulting in an `onComposedClickListener` with trust group and permissions defined as {System-Application-Composed, [Location, Camera]}. The attached listener can thus access the necessary system APIs (but not other system APIs).

Without an additional timeout mechanism, such ComposedElement listeners cannot be prevented from running and taking advantage of these permissions indefinitely. Thus, if a trust group wishes to prevent this risk for certain permissions, it should not expose them via composable sub-elements. For example, if the system wishes to grant camera access only via photos returned directly from a system-trusted camera button, it should not (and does not need to) expose a composable camera icon.

Flexibility of Feedback

Isolating interface elements from different trust groups as described thus far will restrict developer flexibility in displaying feedback that requires access to elements and data across trust groups. We examine drag-and-drop and lenses as canonical examples of such flexible feedback, and we describe how our toolkit architecture preserves developer flexibility for these types of scenarios.

During a drag-and-drop operation, dragging an object over a potential drop target often yields feedback indicating whether it can accept the drop and possibly what effect the drop will have. This feedback may require access to the contents of the drag object (not just its type). For example, a text editor may wish to show what dropped text will look like in the current font before the user completes the drop.

However, the drop target may be in a different trust group than the drag object. Until a user drops the object, it is not clear that the potential drop target is the intended recipient, so it should not receive full access to the drag object. Providing such access would allow a malicious non-target application to steal potentially sensitive information. A challenge for our toolkit architecture is therefore to allow the potential drop target to display feedback that relies upon the content of the drag object.

Similarly, lenses [2] are overlaid on an interface to display flexible feedback about the underlying elements. For example, a lens over a set of map tiles might magnify the underlying map features or highlight certain cities. However, the elements from which a lens requires information in order to paint itself may not all belong to the lens's trust group. System-trusted lenses can have full access, but supporting arbitrary lenses requires allowing the lens element to show feedback based on elements in other trust groups. As with drag and drop, we wish to support feedback in the lens without granting the lens's trust group full access to the underlying interface elements.

Supporting Flexible Feedback. When an element wishes to display this type of cross-trust-group feedback, the system launches a new sandbox that can run and isolate arbitrary code, preventing it from communicating over the network or with other applications (note that our toolkit design is independent of the implementation of this sandbox). Isolated in this way, the system executes feedback generation code provided by the element in question. This code generates feedback by accessing and manipulating a copy of the layout tree and any other restricted data needed to generate appropriate feedback (e.g., the drag object). However, the feedback code cannot break Data Isolation because it cannot communicate outside of the sandbox. It also cannot violate Display Integrity, as it manipulates only a copy of the restricted data

The feedback code produces a temporary version of the relevant portion of the layout tree. The system displays this feedback in a system-trusted overlay element, thus never granting the original element access to the sensitive data. Note that it is possible for malicious feedback code to show inaccurate feedback (e.g., a lens that displays cities not on the underlying map). Thus, while users may interact with the feedback element (e.g., clicking on the map inside the lens), this feedback is not automatically propagated to the underlying elements. If desired, these elements can expose methods allowing for feedback event propagation.

ANDROID IMPLEMENTATION

We prototyped our user interface toolkit architecture with an implementation for Android. Android currently shows only one application interface at a time, with all elements in that interface run in the same process. This can include elements defined by Android's toolkit, by the application itself, by an embedded library, and in a limited way by another application (via `RemoteView`). The embedding application is thus trusted with and trusts any element it embeds, an assumption that we challenge with this work.

We implemented our approach in Android 4.0.3 (Ice Cream Sandwich) by modifying its user interface toolkit (Java packages `android.view` and `android.widget`).

API Restrictions

The base class of all Android interface elements is the `View` class, which is extended by Android's built-in elements and can be arbitrarily extended by developers. We modified all methods in this class to take an additional parameter that specifies the trust group of the caller. This additional parameter is a reference to the calling object (we describe below how we ensure the validity of this parameter and how we extract the correct trust group and permissions list from it). The `View` class and its subclasses can thus use this information to restrict or expose methods based on the appropriate policy. By default, we allow calls only from callers of the same trust group as the `View` itself, as well as from system-trusted objects.

For backwards compatibility with existing Android applications, we did not replace all `View` methods but instead duplicated them and added the additional trust group parameter. An app store review process could ensure new applications use only the new methods (via static analysis or a trusted compiler that replaces deprecated method calls). A non-backwards compatible solution could simply remove the deprecated methods entirely.

Trust Group Declaration and Enforcement

One of the strengths of our toolkit architecture is that it is independent of how the isolation between trust groups is implemented. The main requirement for a trust group implementation is that it prevents a code component from faking its trust group. Our Android implementation uses Java packages to define trust groups. This approach allows applications to split themselves into trust groups of the appropriate granularity, and it naturally separates libraries into separate trust groups (usually included as .jar files). To prevent an application from faking its trust group as that of a library-defined package, the library should seal its package [26]. Package sealing is not currently enforced by Android's Java classloader; this would need to change in order to securely support trust groups based on packages.

Verifying the trust group of a caller requires access to the calling object. Android applications expose and manipulate their interfaces from within Android `Activity` classes, which are in turn extensions of the `Context` class, which contains global information about the application. We modified the `Context` class to include non-overridable `getTrustGroup()` and `getPermissions()` methods; the former returns the trust group of the enclosing object based on the Java package name. Methods that require a trust group must thus be called from within a `Context`; we can again use static analysis at app store review time to verify that callers pass themselves to such methods (i.e., pass `this`). Methods in the `View` class can thereby be assured that the stated trust group of the caller is correct.

Layout Tree Invariants

We further modified Android's user interface toolkit to enforce the layout tree invariants described in the previous section. We achieve this in a manner that is transparent to applications. In particular, we assign to the "system" trust group the Android-defined root element by which each application's interface is attached to its window. When an application attempts to insert a system element as the child of a non-system parent, our modifications rearrange the layout tree to insert the necessary proxy. In practice, we insert a set of three proxies, so that all elements retain a parent of the `ViewGroup` type that they expect (and for which their layout parameters are specified). Figure 6 shows an overview of this transformation.

To make this transformation transparent to the application, our implementation preserves the expected parent and child references for moved nodes. We introduce a dummy child node (see Figure 6) containing a reference to the real child (which has been moved), and we store the original parent reference in the moved child. We return these references for methods requesting parent or child information. Thus, the application can continue to add, remove, and reference elements as if the layout tree reflects the visual tree.

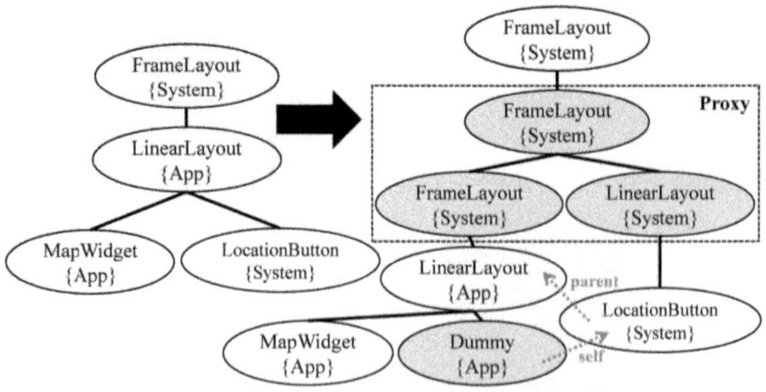

Figure 6: Android layout transformation example. When the LocationButton is added to the tree, two proxy nodes are needed so that both LinearLayout{App} and LocationButton{System} end up with parents of the expected type. The third proxy (a FrameLayout) is used to control the positioning of the other two proxies. The dotted lines indicate pointers tracking intended parent/child relationships.

Flexible Feedback

We modified Android to support flexible feedback for drag-and-drop. We added a new system-trusted element to the toolkit, a `FeedbackView`. When an application wishes to display feedback based on the contents of a passing drag object from another trust group, it creates a new instance of the `FeedbackView` and overlays it upon itself. The `FeedbackView` can thus intercept all drag events intended for the original element.

The application provides the `FeedbackView` a function to generate a bitmap based on drag object data. The `FeedbackView` then provides this function to a sandboxed `FeedbackService` implemented as another Android application with no permissions. The `FeedbackService` generates and returns the appropriate bitmap. The `FeedbackView` displays the resulting feedback bitmap, and the application itself cannot access the contents of the system-trusted `FeedbackView`. The application can thus display drag feedback to a user without gaining access to cross-trust-group drag data.

One limitation of our prototype implementation is that, although the `FeedbackService` runs as an Android application with no permissions, it is not completely isolated. In particular, it may still communicate with other applications via Intents, Android's inter-process communication mechanism. Android currently limits application permissions using manifests. If desired by the Android community, the permission to send or receive Intents could also likely be limited in this way.

Sample Application

We created several sample Android applications to validate our prototype implementation. We summarize one here (shown in Figures 1 and 3), which mashes up an advertisement, a system-trusted location button, and an application's own content. Part of the application interface shows an ad, and another part displays the current location on a map when a user clicks on the location button.

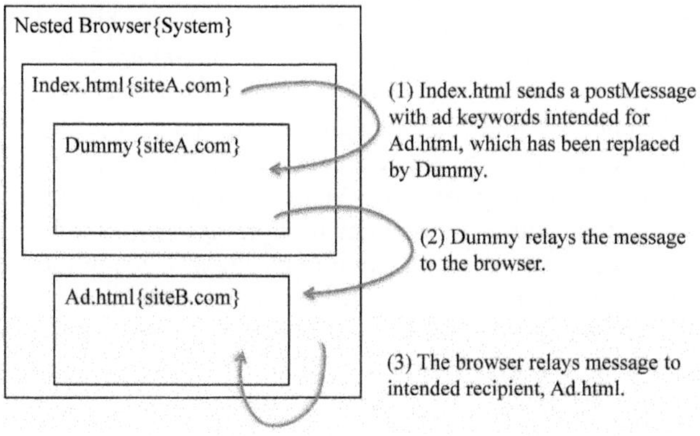

Figure 7: After removing the iframe containing Ad.html from the Index.html page and replacing it with the Dummy, the browser must relay any intended postMessages from Index.html to Ad.html.

The system-trusted location button is a new element that we added to the Android toolkit. It has a fixed "system" trust group and the "location" permission, and it restricts all methods to system-trusted callers, with one exception. It allows any trust group to set a new model-level event listener for location data via `setOnLocationListener()`. Applications can thus embed this button and attach a listener for location data. That data is returned to the application when the user clicks the button. The button also protects itself from clickjacking attacks by responding to input events only while it is completely visible to the user.

The advertisement comes from an ad library embedded by the application. We created a secure ad library by wrapping the existing AdMob library for Android [12]. Our library wraps AdMob's `AdView` in a `SecureAdView`, which sets the `SecureAdView`'s fixed trust group to be the ad library's trust group, thereby restricting all methods to callers in that trust group (or the system group). As a result, our proof-of-concept clickfraud attack for the original AdMob library, in which the embedding application programmatically clicks on the ad, is no longer possible.

WEB IMPLEMENTATION

To further evaluate our approach, we created a prototype implementation for the Firefox Web browser, implemented using iframes and a Firefox add-on.

The Web has long required support for complex embeddings among content from different sources. Web browsers isolate pages and iframes from different origins (based on the same-origin policy [33]). A website containing an iframe has complete control of that iframe's size and the surrounding layout. This control allows the embedding page to, for instance, cover important context and trick the user into clicking on something. Browsers support one-off mechanisms for handling such attacks (e.g., websites can prevent their pages from being framed by another site [30]), but our layout tree invariants ensure that even nested iframes from different origins can securely control their own display properties.

Trust Groups

In our browser implementation, trust groups are defined by standard Web origins (i.e., scheme, domain, and port), which cannot be faked. Interface elements from different trust groups are thus contained within iframes. For example, a webpage in one trust group may embed an advertisement within an iframe from another trust group. As before, an element can have a fixed trust group (defined by its URL) or an owner-bound trust group (defined by the URL of its embedder). These elements use the HTML5 `postMessage` API [15] to expose model-level APIs via cross-origin messages. For example, an advertisement in an iframe from the advertiser's domain might expose a method to set advertising keywords.

Layout Tree Invariants

For simplicity, our current implementation controls the root of all webpages using a browser-within-a-browser (i.e., a trusted webpage that acts as a nested browser, with all navigation done within the nested browser). This simplification allows us to control the root frame of every page (thus satisfying our first layout tree invariant) with minimal changes to the browser itself (see Figure 7).

Our add-on then enforces the second layout tree invariant by modifying pages as they load. In particular, any iframe nested within an iframe of a different origin is removed by the add-on and nested instead within a system-trusted proxy. To preserve the visual effects of the intended nesting, the add-on must move and clip iframes appropriately as their original parent frames are scrolled.

As in the Android implementation, we must retain parent and child pointers expected by the original nodes so that they can continue to communicate with each other via postMessage. We thus replace the moved iframe with a dummy iframe. This dummy, defined by the system but in its embedder's trust group (i.e., owner-bound), relays any postMessages it receives to the moved iframe. This allows the original parent to continue to hold a reference to its visual child, making these modifications transparent to the webpage. Figure 7 shows the sequence of messages sent in the relaying process. Similarly, the browser maintains a mapping of moved iframes to their original parents. If an iframe that has been moved attempts to send a postMessage to its visual parent, the system-trusted actual parent relays this message to the original parent.

DISCUSSION AND RELATED WORK

Considering security as a primary goal in a user interface toolkit presents a unique opportunity to address interface-level security vulnerabilities without sacrificing developer flexibility or expressivity. This approach is a departure from classic security solutions, which operate at a system level or require application review, as well as from conventional user interface toolkits, which have not focused on securing the interaction between multiple mutually-distrusting elements. With the mechanisms that we propose, a security-aware toolkit can ensure that sensitive elements are correctly displayed, that a user's intended interactions are accurately captured, and that private data is not leaked through interface elements. The remainder of this section examines some related work.

User Interfaces

User interface toolkit research generally focuses on reducing the effort needed to develop new interfaces. Because the assumptions embedded in a framework can limit interface designers and hinder the development or adoption of new techniques, research often focuses on achieving maximal expressivity and flexibility for interface developers [6, 7, 8, 17, 24]. For example, prior work has proposed tools to aid in the creation of mashup interfaces on the Web [16, 19, 36]. However, these toolkits are not aimed at addressing security concerns and their implicit trust assumptions can pose challenges to security.

Work by Arthur and Olsen [1] examined protecting user data by separating interface elements based on trust. They provide a methodology that splits an interface across a trusted private device and an untrusted public device (e.g., a connected screen or keyboard) by surfacing a user's trust choices to applications. Although focused on security, the model is more restricted; we consider a broad set of threats and complex trust relationships within an interface.

Other researchers have focused on designing and evaluating interfaces for security-critical interactions, including phishing protection [9], user account control [22], Web SSL certificate warnings [32], and social network privacy policies [20]. Our work focuses on securing interface-level threats, and we believe that advances here can be leveraged to help enable research in how to best design security-related interfaces.

Security

This work naturally draws upon existing security concepts, such as permissions and capabilities used in operating systems [18]. However, the issue of securing interfaces has not been explored in the security community from the user interface toolkit perspective. Instead, prior security work has focused on isolating applications and content from different sources using system-level techniques (e.g., [4, 28, 34]). These approaches do not consider or are not able to address all of the interface-level threats that we consider (e.g., the authors of [34] do not address a parent element's ability to manipulate the layout of its children).

Our work in this paper draws on user-driven access control [29], which uses system-controlled interface elements called access control gadgets (ACGs) to extract a user's intent to grant system-level permissions to an application (e.g., to access the camera). ACGs, which support only limited composition and customization, represent the most restrictive type of interface elements that we consider in this work. By considering security at the level of the user interface toolkit rather than the system, our proposed architecture subsumes ACGs and supports security properties for a broader and more flexible range of interface elements and scenarios.

It is possible to implement trust groups in ways other than those used in our prototypes. For example, Quire [5] fully separates mutually distrusting code components into different Android applications. To approximate the embedding of interface elements from one app within another (not supported by Android), Quire overlays an application with a transparent background (e.g., the main app) over a second application (e.g., the ad), requiring the top layer to delegate user input events to the bottom layer. To prevent clickfraud, Quire authenticates messages legitimately generated by user input events. In this paper, we explore how a user interface toolkit can leverage trust groups of any implementation to support a wide range of security properties and scenarios.

Although a security-aware user interface toolkit can mitigate a large number of concerns, there remain threats that benefit from alternate mitigation techniques. For example, even with a security-aware toolkit, adversaries can still create fake interface elements to mimic legitimate elements. Fake embedded elements taking user input may be used in phishing attacks (e.g., to steal a password). Sensitive elements can apply existing anti-phishing techniques (e.g., Sitekeys). Although not infallible [31], these techniques can make such attacks more difficult. Additionally, our toolkit can assure that a click on a sensitive element was legitimately intended by the user (e.g., an ad click), but it cannot prevent forged requests to backend servers (e.g., direct requests to the advertising server that mimic the requests made when a user clicks an ad). The Web currently protects against this type of attack (via techniques to prevent cross-site request forgery), but Android does not. Other researchers focus on addressing this type of problem with code attestation [27] or by bringing the Web model to mobile operating systems [35].

CONCLUSION

We have presented a user interface toolkit architecture that maintains developer flexibility while achieving a set of security properties: display integrity, input integrity, intent integrity, data isolation, and UI-to-API links. The mechanisms we propose enable scenarios in which interface elements from different trust groups are embedded in a single interface. In today's interfaces, these scenarios are either insecure (e.g., allowing an application to trick a user into clicking on another trust group's button) or inflexible (e.g., forcing security-related interfaces to be displayed as invasive system prompts).

By isolating code and interface elements into trust groups and by enforcing certain layout tree invariants, our toolkit architecture secures sensitive elements and APIs while still providing developers the necessary flexibility for element composition and for communication and feedback across trust groups. Important questions for future work include the ease with which developers can adopt these mechanisms, as well as support for testing and debugging secure interfaces. In both cases, we note that a security-aware toolkit seems to provide advantages over current ad-hoc approaches. Our prototype implementations demonstrate that this toolkit architecture is feasible and that important security properties can be enforced with maximal transparency and flexibility for developers.

ACKNOWLEDGEMENTS

We thank Saleema Amershi, Alan Borning, Morgan Dixon, Alex Moshchuk, Kayur Patel, and the anonymous reviewers for valuable feedback on earlier versions of this work. We thank Werner Dietl and Mike Ernst for their insights about Java static analysis. This work was supported in part by the NSF under Graduate Research Fellowship award DGE-0718124 as well as awards CNS-0846065 and IIS-1053868.

REFERENCES

1. R. B. Arthur and D. R. Olsen. Privacy-aware shared UI toolkit for nomadic environments. In *Software Practice and Experience*, 2011.
2. E. A. Bier, M. C. Stone, K. Pier, W. Buxton, and T. D. DeRose. Toolglass and Magic Lenses: The See-Through Interface. In *ACM Conference on Computer Graphics (SIGGRAPH)*, 1993.
3. Chromium. Security Issues, Issue 52868. https://code.google.com/p/chromium/issues/list?q=label:Security
4. R. Cox, J. Hansen, S. D. Gribble, and H. M. Levy. A Safety-Oriented Platform for Web Applications. In *IEEE Symposium on Security & Privacy*, 2006.
5. M. Dietz, S. Shekhar, Y. Pisetsky, A. Shu, and D. Wallach. Quire: Lightweight Provenance for Smart Phone Operating Systems. In *USENIX Security Symposium*, 2011.
6. M. Dixon and J. Fogarty. Prefab: Implementing Advanced Behaviors Using Pixel-based Reverse Engineering of Interface Structure. In *ACM Conference on Human Factors in Computing Systems (CHI)*, 2010.
7. J. R. Eagan, M. Beaudouin-Lafon, and W. E. Mackay. Cracking the Cocoa Nut: User Interface Programming at Runtime. In *ACM Symposium on User Interface Software and Technology (UIST)*, 2011.
8. W. K. Edwards, S. Hudson, J. Marinacci, R. Rodenstein, T. Rodriguez, and I. Smith. Systematic Output Modification in a 2D User Interface Toolkit. In *ACM Symposium on User Interface Software and Technology (UIST)*, 1997.
9. S. Egelman, L. F. Cranor, and J. Hong. You've Been Warned: An Empirical Study of the Effectiveness of Web Browser Phishing Warnings. In *ACM Conference on Human Factors in Computing Systems (CHI)*, 2008.
10. W. Enck, P. Gilbert, B. Chun, L. P. Cox, J. Jung, P. McDaniel, and A. N. Sheth. TaintDroid: An Information-Flow Tracking System for Realtime Privacy Monitoring on Smartphones. In *USENIX Symposium on Operating Systems Design and Implementation (OSDI)*, 2010.
11. Facebook. Like button requires confirm step. http:// developers.facebook.com/bugs/169544703153617
12. Google. AdMob. http://developers.google.com/mobile-ads-sdk/
13. M. Grace, W. Zhou, X. Jiang, and A. Sadeghi. Unsafe Exposure Analysis of Mobile In-App Advertisements. In *ACM Conference on Security and Privacy in Wireless and Mobile Networks (WiSec)*, 2012.
14. R. Hansen and J. Grossman. Clickjacking. http://www.sectheory.com/clickjacking.htm
15. I. Hickson (ed). HTML5 Web Messaging. W3C Working Draft, 2012. http://www.w3.org/TR/ webmessaging/
16. B. Hartmann, L. Wu, K. Collins, S. R. Klemmer. Programming by a Sample: Rapidly Creating Web Applications with d.mix. In *ACM Symposium on User Interface Software and Technology (UIST)*, 2007.
17. S. Hudson, J. Mankoff, and I. Smith. Extensible Input Handling in the subArctic Toolkit. In *ACM Conference on Human Factors in Computing Systems (CHI)*, 2005.
18. H. M. Levy. Capability-Based Computer Systems. Digital Press, 1984.
19. J. Lin, J. Wong, J. Nichols, A. Cypher, and T. A. Lau. End-User Programming of Mashups with Vegemite. In *ACM Conference on Intelligent User Interfaces (IUI)*, 2009.
20. H. R. Lipford, J. Watson, M. Whitney, K. Froiland, and R. W. Reeder. Visual vs. Compact: A Comparison of Privacy Policy Interfaces. In *ACM Conference on Human Factors in Computing Systems (CHI)*, 2010.
21. Microsoft. User Account Control. http://msdn.microsoft.com/en-us/library/windows/desktop/ aa511445.aspx
22. S. Motiee, K. Hawkey, and K. Beznosov. Do Windows Users Follow the Principle of Least Privilege? Investigating User Account Control Practices. In *ACM Symposium on Usable Privacy and Security (SOUPS)*, 2010.
23. Mozilla Foundation. Known Vulnerabilities, Advisory 2008-08.http://www.mozilla.org/security/known-vulnerabilities/
24. B. Myers, S. Hudson, and R. Pausch. Past, Present, and Future of User Interface Software Tools. In *ACM Transactions on Computer-Human Inteaaction (TOCHI)*, 2000.
25. D. R. Olsen, Jr. Evaluating User Interface Systems Research. In *ACM Symposium on User Interface Software and Technology (UIST)*, 2007.
26. Oracle. Sealing Packages within a JAR File. http://docs.oracle.com/javase/tutorial/deployment/jar/ sealman.html
27. B. Parno, J. M. McCune, and A. Perrig. Bootstrapping Trust in Commodity Computers. In *IEEE Symposium on Security & Privacy*, 2010.
28. C. Reis and S. D. Gribble. Isolating Web Programs in Modern Browser Architectures. In *ACM Eurosys*, 2009.
29. F. Roesner, T. Kohno, A. Moshchuk, B. Parno, H. J. Wang, and C. Cowan. User-Driven Access Control: Rethinking Permission Granting in Modern Operating Systems. In *IEEE Symposium Security & Privacy*, 2012.
30. G. Rydstedt, E. Bursztein, D. Boneh, and C. Jackson. Busting frame busting: a study of clickjacking vulnerabilities at popular sites. In *IEEE Web 2.0 Security and Privacy (W2SP)*, 2010.
31. S. E. Schechter, R. Dhamija, A. Ozment, and I. Fischer. The Emperor's New Security Indicators. In *IEEE Symposium on Security & Privacy*, 2007.
32. J. Sunshine, S. Egelman, H. Almuhimedi, N. Atri, and L. F. Cranor. Crying Wolf: An Empirical Study of SSL Warning Effectiveness. In *USENIX Security Symposium*, 2009.
33. W3C. Same Origin Policy. http://www.w3.org/ Security /wiki/Same_Origin_Policy
34. H. J. Wang, C. Grier, A. Moshchuk, S. King, P. Choudhury, and H. Venter. The Multi-Principal OS Construction of the Gazelle Web Browser. In *USENIX Security Symposium*, 2009.
35. H. J. Wang, A. Moshchuk, and A. Bush. Convergence of Desktop and Web Applications on a Multi-Service OS. In *USENIX Hot Topics in Security*, 2009.
36. J. Wong and J. Hong. Making Mashups with Marmite: Towards End-User Programming for the Web. In *ACM Conference on Human Factors in Computing Systems (CHI)*, 2007.

Cliplets: Juxtaposing Still and Dynamic Imagery

Neel Joshi[1] **Sisil Mehta**[1,2] **Steven Drucker**[1] **Eric Stollnitz**[1]
Hugues Hoppe[1] **Matt Uyttendaele**[1] **Michael Cohen**[1]

[1]Microsoft Research
Redmond, WA 98052, USA

[2]Georgia Institute of Technology
Atlanta, GA 30318, USA

ABSTRACT

We explore creating "cliplets", a form of visual media that juxtaposes still image and video segments, both spatially and temporally, to expressively abstract a moment. Much as in "cinemagraphs", the tension between static and dynamic elements in a cliplet reinforces both aspects, strongly focusing the viewer's attention. Creating this type of imagery is challenging without professional tools and training. We develop a set of idioms, essentially spatiotemporal mappings, that characterize cliplet elements, and use these idioms in an interactive system to quickly compose a cliplet from ordinary handheld video. One difficulty is to avoid artifacts in the cliplet composition without resorting to extensive manual input. We address this with automatic alignment, looping optimization and feathering, simultaneous matting and compositing, and Laplacian blending. A key user-interface challenge is to provide affordances to define the parameters of the mappings from input time to output time while maintaining a focus on the cliplet being created. We demonstrate the creation of a variety of cliplet types. We also report on informal feedback as well as a more structured survey of users.

Author Keywords

Image and video editing; image and video compositing; cinemagraphs; video textures

ACM Classification Keywords

H.5.2 [Information interfaces and presentation]: User Interfaces. - Graphical user interfaces.

INTRODUCTION

A taxonomy of visual imagery may begin with a separation of static images (photographs, paintings, etc.) from dynamic imagery (video, animation, etc.). A static photograph often derives its power by what is implied beyond its spatial and temporal boundaries, i.e., outside the frame and in the moments before and after it was taken. Our imagination fills in what is left out. Video loses some of that power, but being dynamic, has the ability to tell an unfolding temporal narrative. It carries us along through time.

UIST'12, October 7–10, 2012, Cambridge, Massachusetts, USA.

Figure 1: A cliplet that combines loop, mirror loop, and play layers. [Please see `http://research.microsoft.com/cliplets/paper/` for a PDF with embedded videos that better conveys this result.]

In this work, we explore a category of media that in essence is more static image than video, but does contain some temporal elements. The media are derived from a short video, commonly only a few seconds. In particular, our focus is on results that juxtapose static and dynamic elements. Like a still photograph, the resulting piece of media can be "digested" in a short time interval on the order of 10 seconds.

An example of such media, referred to as *Cinemagraphs*, has recently appeared at a number of websites, displayed in the form of animated GIFs [6]. These cinemagraphs derive a visceral power by combining static scenes with a small repeating movement, e.g., a hair wisp blowing in the wind. Carefully staged and captured video coupled with professional tools like Adobe After Effects can result in well crafted cinemagraphs. Recently, at least three mobile-based apps for creating cinemagraphs have also appeared.

At the cost of some confusion, we generalize from cinemagraphs and use a different term, *cliplet*, to denote media in which the dynamic elements do not need to be strictly looping. In addition, the juxtaposition of static and dynamic elements may be spatial (part of the frame is static while other parts are dynamic), temporal (a still followed in time by a dynamic element or vice versa), or both. The tension between these static and dynamic elements works to reinforce both elements within the cliplet.

Our paper makes a number of contributions in this area. First, we describe a set of idioms that characterize elements within cliplets. These idioms greatly simplify the process, relative to existing professional tools, yet provide significant expressiveness beyond the current set of mobile-based apps.

These idioms are essentially mappings from the input video to layers of the result and are used as building blocks in an interactive tool. The tool also provides simple user-driven segmentation and automatic methods to aid in a variety of tasks, including image alignment, loop finding, spatiotemporal layer alignment and compositing, and photometric correction. As a result, our tool allows a wide range of cliplets to be easily produced from informally captured videos.

We also demonstrate a user interface that provides intuitive affordances for defining the parameters of our time-mapping idioms. We exercise the interface on a large number of input videos resulting in a collection of cliplets. In addition, we report on two informal evaluations of the cliplet application, based on extensive one-on-one demonstrations as well as a survey accompanying a publicly released version of the application.

RELATED WORK

Both the research literature and popular media include several examples of visual media that lie between a still and a video. A classic example is the animated GIF, originally created to encode short vector-graphics animations within a still image format. Another common example is simple panning and zooming over large static imagery, sometimes referred to as the Ken Burns Effect [16], which is often used in image slideshows.

More recently, the "Harry Potter" book and film series have popularized the notion that static images can also move. Perhaps the most relevant example, and one of our motivations in pursuing this work, is the "cinemagraph", a carefully crafted juxtaposition of still and moving imagery explored extensively by photographer Jamie Beck and designer Kevin Burg [6].

Until recently, the only widely available tools for creating cliplet-type imagery were general applications like Adobe Photoshop, Premiere, and After Effects. While these tools have the power to create cliplets, they are time-consuming to use in this context, and not easily accessible to an untrained user. Moreover they do not provide all the refinement operations necessary to overcome the inconsistencies and artifacts that commonly arise when constructing a cliplet. Three mobile apps for cinemagraph creation have appeared recently (Cinemagr.am[1], Flixel[2], and Kinotopic[3]). Each of these allows a simple creation of a specific instance of a cinemagraph, a single looping feature within a still. Due to screen real-estate and power constraints, none provide the generality nor the artifact reduction techniques we describe. There are no technical descriptions available for these apps.

Many works in computer graphics and computer vision explore depicting either a static scene or short time sequence with some motion of the scene or observer: e.g., motion without movement [12], video textures [23, 17, 3, 21], animating stills [10], motion magnification [18], parallax photography [28], and spatiotemporal warping of video sequences [20].

Each of these examples adds a temporal element to what is essentially more like a static image than a video; however, none uses the same kind of static/dynamic tension to focus attention as is the emphasis in our work. We do, however, draw inspiration from these works, both in our technical approach and in developing a "language" and taxonomy for cliplets.

Specifically, video textures [23, 17] aim to create seamless video loops, where the entire spatial extent of a video is in motion. Research on panoramic video textures [3, 21] has a similar goal for videos spanning a large spatial extent. While the method of Agarwala et al. [3] may create a mixture of still imagery and video textures, this is a byproduct of an optimization rather than a desired intent, in the sense that the regions of still imagery correspond to mostly static regions in the input video. In our work, the juxtaposition of still and moving imagery is an explicit goal, and our aim is to provide the user several forms of artistic control to extend and guide this process.

Work in video matting [9, 5] and video sprites [22] addresses the problem of extracting video regions, typically in a semantically meaningful way, for later compositing. In our setting, the primary segmentation goal is to find a boundary that forms a seamless composite in the resulting cliplet. In this respect, our work relates particularly to interactive digital photomontage [2], simultaneous matting and compositing [27], and video-to-still composition [14].

Perhaps the most closely related works are those of Tompkin et al. [26] and Bai et al. [4]. Tompkin et al.'s work takes a first step in the semi-automated creation of cinemagraphs. Their tool composites still and animated regions from a source video; it creates motion masks automatically and uses these to drive compositing. However, it offers few creative controls, mainly the ability to enable or disable looping per spatial region. The tool also has little provision to overcome or compensate for the many types of artifacts commonly encountered when creating cliplets. Bai et al.'s work focuses primarily on the challenging aspect of stabilizing subregions in the video. This is done with user-specified image-warping constraints. It does not address the concerns of developing an end-to-end system. Our contribution is to explore intuitive controls and several technical refinements that together enable users to quickly create high-quality results. Our work is also more general in that it develops a small set of idioms beyond simple looping and lets these idioms be sequenced together to develop short narratives.

THE LANGUAGE OF CLIPLETS

We define a cliplet as a 3D spatiotemporal object indexed by time t and 2D location x. A cliplet is formed by composing an ordered set of spatiotemporal output layers $\tilde{L}$, (we use tildes to denote the output), where each layer $\tilde{L}$ is mapped in time (and optionally space) from a corresponding input layer L

[1]http://cinemagr.am/
[2]http://flixel.com
[3]http://kinotopic.com/

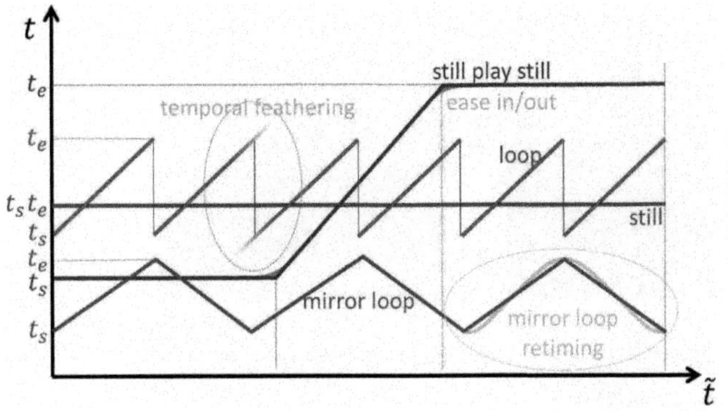

Figure 2: Various cliplet layer types graphed using input video time t as a function of output cliplet time $\tilde{t}$. Subscripts s and e refer to the start and end times respectively. The diagram also illustrates layer refinements which are discussed in the Refinements section.

within the given video. Input and output layers are subsets of the spatiotemporal volume of pixels in the input video and resulting cliplet. One key challenge is to provide the user with intuitive tools to map portions of the input video to the final cliplet.

We explore a number of mapping functions between the input and output layers. We begin by assuming that the *spatial* mapping from each input layer, $L(t,x)$, to output layer, $\tilde{L}(\tilde{t},\tilde{x})$, is the identity. In other words, the effect of each layer is to modify some portion of the cliplet by overwriting each cliplet pixel using an input pixel from the same position, i.e., $x = \tilde{x}$, but offset in time.

Time-mapping idioms. For each layer, the mapping from output to input time is defined by some function $t = \phi(\tilde{t})$:

$$\tilde{L}(\tilde{t},\tilde{x}) = L(\phi(\tilde{t}),\tilde{x}).$$

This temporal mapping function, ϕ, characterizes the behavior of a layer and depends on various layer properties. In principle, an authoring system could provide direct, explicit control over ϕ, which is the approach used by professional tools such as Adobe Premiere, After Effects, and Photoshop.

We initially developed our interactive tool to provide a similar type of direct control over the temporal mapping function, e.g. as a set of key-frames on a time in vs. out plot (as in Figure 2), allowing us to study the affordances of such an interface. After several months of use, we found that this explicit control was unnecessarily complex and made it difficult to perform common operations, like creating simple loops, for all but the most patient and highly experienced users.

Furthermore, we found that the typical mappings functions one needed to create cliplets was actually quite limited. This led us to define a small set of iconic time-mapping idioms, (Still, Play, Loop, Mirror). Figure 2 shows $t = \phi(\tilde{t})$ for each idiom. As we will discuss in the Interactive Authoring System section, our current tool hides this complexity and instead uses simpler, higher-level controls to set the various layer properties.

The simplest idiom is a Still layer, in which the input layer, while spatially covering some or all of the full input, temporally consists of a only single video frame. The still time-mapping repeats this single frame to create an output layer that fills some portion of the cliplet volume. Typically, the first layer in a cliplet is a Still that spans the full spatial extent of the video and is mapped over all frames of the cliplet. This initial layer forms a background layer over which additional layers are composed. These additional, more complex layers include spatial and temporal subregions of the input that are mapped in time via our set of idioms.

In our authoring system, layers are defined using the following attributes: an idiom (Still, Play, Loop, or Mirror), a spatial region $R(t)$, start and end times t_s, t_e within the input video, a playback velocity v relative to the input speed (default=1), start time $\tilde{t}_s$ within the cliplet, and optionally, an end time $\tilde{t}_e$ within the cliplet, otherwise the idiom is assumed to go on indefinitely.

A Still layer freezes a chosen input frame:

$$\phi_{\text{Still}}(\tilde{t}) = t_s, \quad \tilde{t}_s \le \tilde{t} < \tilde{t}_e.$$

For a Play layer, we have

$$\phi_{\text{Play}}(\tilde{t}) = t_s + v\,(\tilde{t} - \tilde{t}_s), \quad \tilde{t}_s \le \tilde{t} < \tilde{t}_s + (t_e - t_s)/v.$$

A Loop layer repeats a snippet of video multiple times:

$$\phi_{\text{Loop}}(\tilde{t}) = t_s + v\,((\tilde{t} - \tilde{t}_s) \bmod T),$$

where the loop period $T = (t_e - t_s)/v$.

Finally, a Mirror layer is a loop where the input is played successively forwards and backwards:

$$\phi_{\text{Mirror}}(\tilde{t}) = t_s + v\,\text{Hat}((\tilde{t} - \tilde{t}_s) \bmod 2T),$$

where $\text{Hat}(u)$ maps time to move forward for one interval T, and then backwards for another interval T:

$$\text{Hat}(u) = \begin{cases} u & \text{if } u \le T, \\ 2T - u & \text{otherwise.} \end{cases}$$

INTERACTIVE AUTHORING SYSTEM

Four snapshots of our tool are shown in Figure 3. The tool is designed to be simple, yet expressive, in order to help users quickly create cliplets. The UI is the result of three primary design decisions: 1) the building blocks of a cliplet are controls corresponding to our set of idioms, 2) the main UI area shows both the input video and resulting cliplet in a single window and is also used to define the layers' spatial boundaries, and 3) the UI uses two separate timelines, one for the input video at the top and one for the output cliplet at the bottom.

The panel on the right has buttons to add new layers (Still, Loop, Mirror, and *compound* Still-Play-Still), including thumbnails of the layer spatial extents. A panel of advanced features (not shown) contains checkboxes to invoke refinements discussed in the Refinements section.

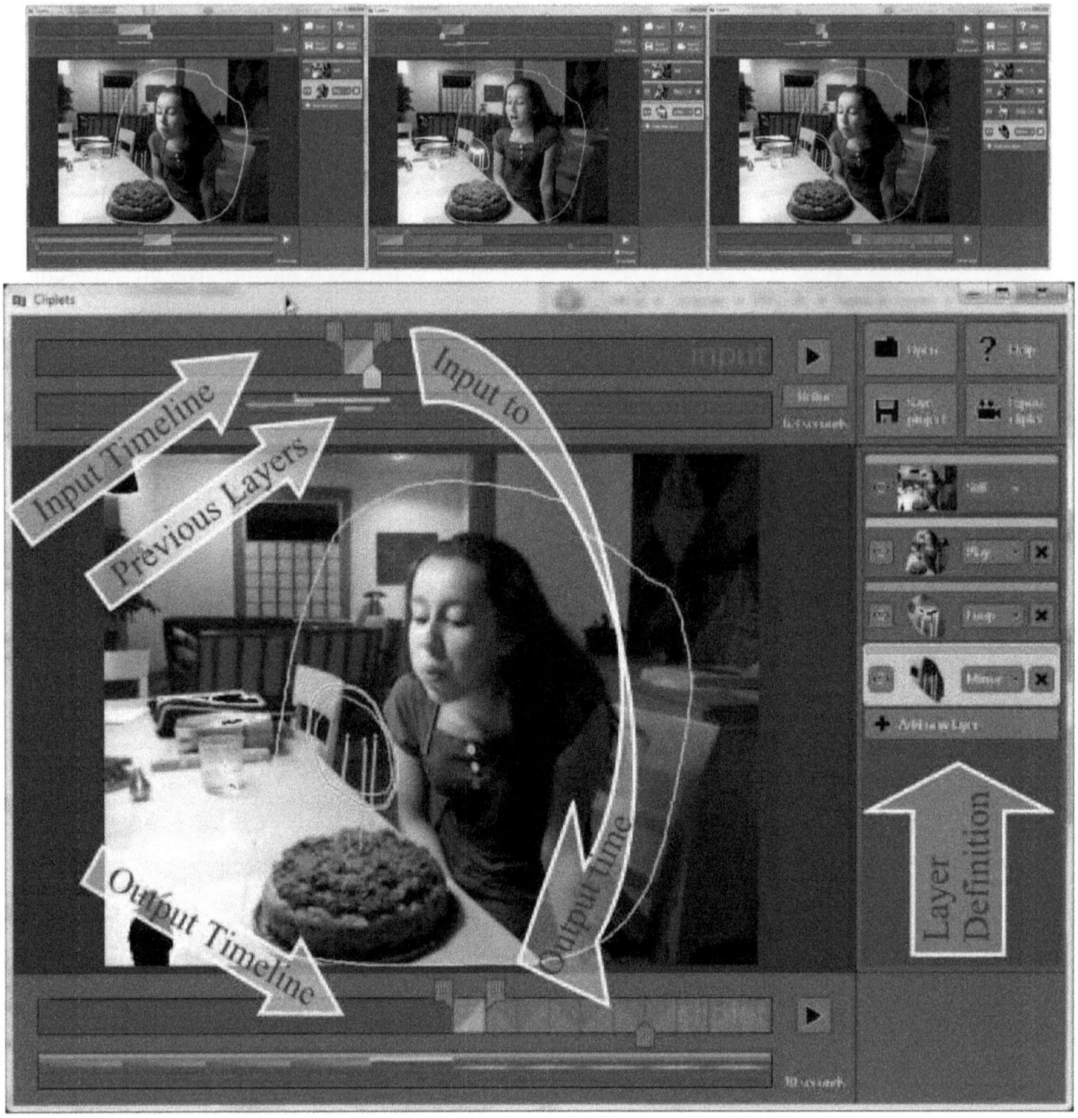

Figure 3: Interactive system for creating cliplets. The main area is used to indicate the spatial boundaries of layers and show the input video and resulting cliplet. The input and output timings for each layer are defined on the top and bottom timelines, respectively. The top three panels depict the process of defining a play layers, followed by a loop, and a mirror layer in sequence. [Please see `http://research.microsoft.com/cliplets/paper/` for a video that shows the system in use.]

Associated with each timeline are representations of the temporal aspects of each layer. The three panels in the top of Figure 3 depict three states of an example cliplet creation session. Four layers are successively defined. The first layer is always a still background. It is indicated on the input timeline as a small blue mark that can be set by the user. This particular layer covers the full frame spatially and also covers the full extent of the output timeline.

The second (yellow) layer (upper-left) shows the definition of a Still-Play-Still *compound* layer (SPS), which is really three individual layers laid consecutively in output time. The spatial extent has been indicated by drawing a selection region with a pencil tool. The input temporal extent is indicated by the yellow bar in the input timeline at the top. The user can drag the input start or end times independently or can drag its center to shift it in time. The layer is next positioned and sized on the output time slider. The wide yellow region indicates when this layer plays in the cliplet. The yellow bars to the left and right on the output indicate the duration of the stills before and after the play. If both are off, it is simply a single play layer. In the figure, the first frame is held as a still before the play layer, and the last frame is held as a still after the play layer.

The third (green) layer is a looping layer, indicated by the sawtooth line on the output timeline. The bright-green region defines the first temporal instance of the loop in the cliplet, while repeated instances are shown in mid-green color. The length of the loop and number of repetitions is set by the user. In this example, four instances are selected, thus this layer disappears from the cliplet at about the same time that the

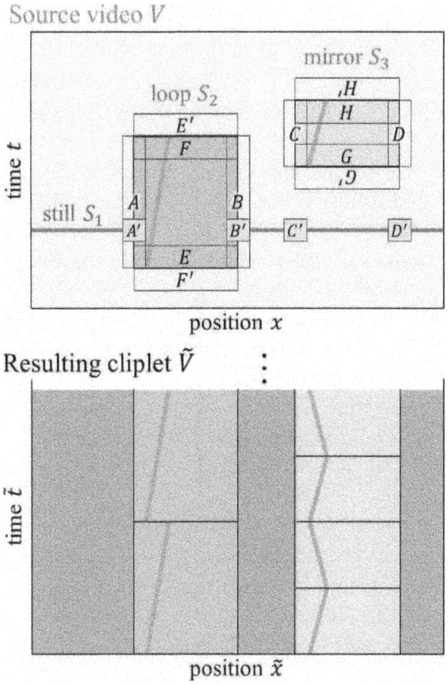

Figure 4: Three layers (Still, Loop, Mirror) access various spatiotemporal regions of the input video. For spatial continuity in the resulting cliplet, pixel colors in regions A, B, C, D should be similar to those in A', B', C', D' respectively. For temporal continuity, pixel colors in regions E, F, G, H should be similar those in E', F', G', H' respectively.

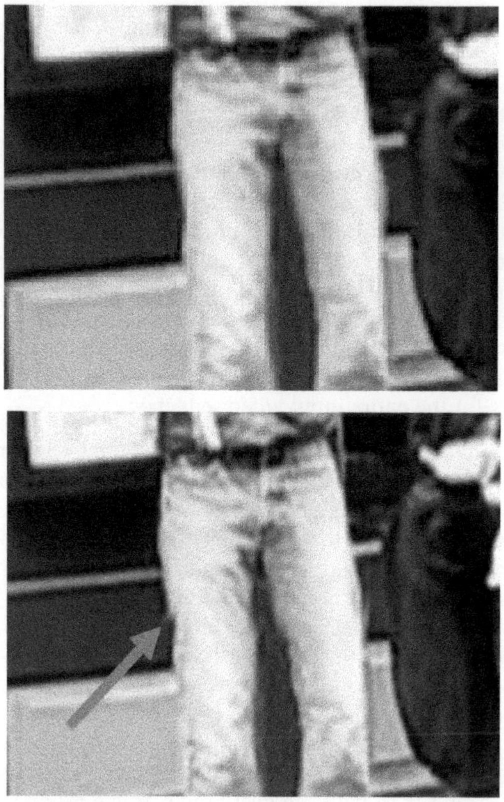

Figure 5: With local alignment (top) and without (bottom). Note that before the alignment the middle part of the person's leg tears on the left edge of his jeans.

previously defined play layer starts. Note the indicators of the previously defined layers are depicted below the timelines. These act as guides to the user in defining subsequent layers. Since the looping layer's spatial extent overlaps that of the SPS, it is composited over it.

Finally, the fourth (blue) layer is a mirror loop. The up-and-down triangle line in the output timeline indicates that each loop instance played forward and backward. In this example, the first mirror loop instance is positioned to begin at the midpoint of the output timeline, so it has no effect during the first half of the cliplet.

To see the system being used to create a cliplet, please visit `http://research.microsoft.com/cliplets/paper/`.

REFINEMENTS

A direct composition of layers can often fail to produce visually perfect cliplets. Handheld camera shake, as well as scene motion at layer boundaries, may reveal seams between layers. Changes in scene illumination or camera exposure can also create photometric seams at the boundaries. Temporal discontinuities created by the looping structure may reveal temporal seams.

We reduce these artifacts by refining the simple mappings (described in the Language of Cliplets section) between input video layers and the output cliplet. Specifically, we improve spatiotemporal continuity using a combination of techniques that (1) warp the layers both geometrically and temporally, (2) optimize the spatiotemporal region segmentation, and (3) blend the pixel colors at layer boundaries. These automatic refinements are presented to the user as a set of simple binary controls to either enable or disable the feature.

Geometric refinement

We begin by modifying the spatial mapping from input to cliplet. Conceptually, we modify the spatial positions of the input pixels. Let us consider the illustration in Figure 4, which shows time-versus-position slices of the input video and output cliplet, in the presence of three layers (Still, Loop, and Mirror). The Still layer, S_1, sources its pixels from a single point in time but spatially across the whole video. Small regions of the still, A' and B', abut a looping layer S_2. The goal of the geometric refinements is to make the corresponding regions in the looping layer, A and B, be as similar to A' and B' as possible, over the *entire time interval* $[t_s, t_e]$. Similarly, for the Mirror layer S_3, we wish C' and D' from the still to match C and D from the spatial boundary of the looping layer. Effectively, each pixel near a looping boundary should have constant color over the loop (i.e., zero optical flow). We vary the source location over time in the input video via global and local alignment operators to accommodate this goal.

Global alignment. Because we allow the flexibility of working with handheld video, it is necessary to account for camera motion. As a preprocess, we use a modified video stabilization pipeline to align the video frames to simulate a still camera[13, 15]. The goal of the global alignment step is to find a sequence of affine transforms, that when applied to the input removes all apparent camera motion (as if the camera had been on a tripod). To accomplish this, for every frame in the video we extract *Harris* features each with a corresponding *Brief* descriptor [8]. Between adjacent frames we do a windowed search to find matching features. The window size is dictated by the maximum frame-to-frame velocity that is expected in handheld videos. A feature is determined to be a match if the Brief descriptor distance of the best match is sufficiently different from that of the second best match (a.k.a. the ratio test[19]). This allows us to produce a set of feature tracks for the entire input video sequence.

To avoid locking onto scene motion, the tracks are analyzed to distinguish foreground motion from background static features. The background feature tracks are assumed to belong to the largest set, such that a single temporal sequence of affine transforms can map all background features back to their positions in frame 0. For this we employ a RANSAC (RANdom SAmple Consensus) [11] technique that runs over all of the frames simultaneously. The RANSAC iterations run by picking a random pair of tracks to determine a putative affine transform $T[n,0]$ between the last frame(n) and first frame(0) of the sequence. If $T[n,0]$ maximizes the set of *inlier tracks*, then that same track pair is used to determine the transform $T[i,0]$ between every other frame (i) and the first frame. For every frame (i) we test the current inlier tracks with $T[i,0]$ and remove any inliers that are not within the RANSAC threshold. The set of feature tracks that maximizes the inlier count in this multi-frame sense are declared to be on the background and used to determine the transformations to stabilize the frames to simulate a still camera.

Local alignment. Subtle scene motion, scene parallax, or small errors in global alignment can still cause spatial seams in a cliplet. For example, in Figure 5, one layer covers a man and his son but cuts though the man's legs. As the man rocks from side to side, a tear occurs at the layer boundary. We reduce this effect as follows. Within an eroded and dilated region near the layer boundary, R, we compute optical flow together with a confidence for the flow values based on local gradient magnitudes. Using a diffusion-based method for sparse data interpolation [24], these flow vectors are interpolated across the layer weighted according to their confidences values. We use the resulting smooth warp field to spatially deform the layer such that it aligns with the background at the boundaries.

Temporal refinement

Much like with the spatial discontinuities above, Loop and Mirror layers may introduce temporal discontinuities at their temporal boundaries, indicated as E, F, G, and H in Figure 4.

Optimized loop transitions. As in Video Textures [23], for Loop layers we desire the frames just before and after the start and end frames to be as similar as possible. Thus, temporal artifacts are minimized if the temporal region E in Figure 4 matches the region E' just beyond the end of the layer and likewise F matches F'. Effectively, the endframes of the loop should be similar in both pixel colors and optical flow. To achieve this we seek start and end time pairs that minimize these differences. The user can let the system search the entire input video for the best candidate loops or can specify an initial layer and have the system search nearby for improved start and end times.

Temporal feathering To further reduce Loop temporal discontinuities, we feather (i.e., morph) across the frames near the layer endframes. Over the small temporal regions (F', E) and (F, E'), we first use optical flow to warp E' to fit E and call the result $\bar{E}$. Similarly, we create an $\bar{F}$ to fit F. Finally, we cross-fade between $\bar{F}$ and F and between E and $\bar{E}$ at the loop transition, as illustrated in the inset diagram and as denoted by the oval marked "temporal feathering" in Figure 2. The effect can be seen in Figure 6.

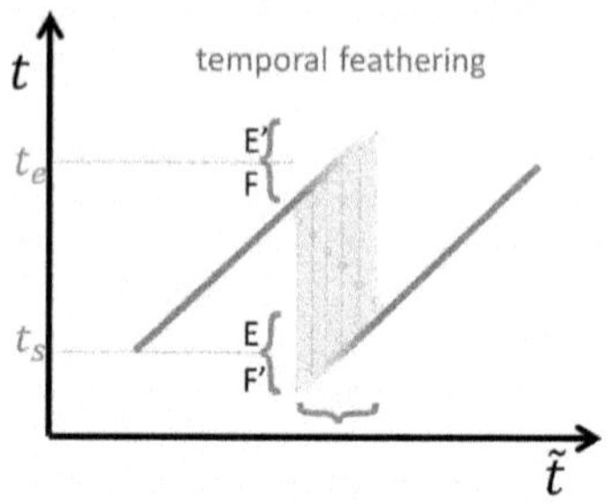

Optimized mirror loop transitions. For Mirror layers, the situation is quite different. We would like the small temporal regions around the start and end, G and H in Figure 4, to match their temporally inverted regions just beyond the temporal boundaries, G' and H'. This can only be true if the endframes have zero optical flow. We thus look for frames with little optical flow within the layer region. As with loop layers, we automatically present candidates near those specified, or the top set of candidates from the full input.

Slow-in/slow-out temporal mapping For Mirror layers any residual optical flow at the layer endframe results in jerky motion. We further reduce this type of artifact by slowing the motion as it approaches the layer endframes. For instance, in the case of Mirror layers, we replace $\text{Hat}(u)$ by $\text{Hat}'(u)$ as shown in the inset.

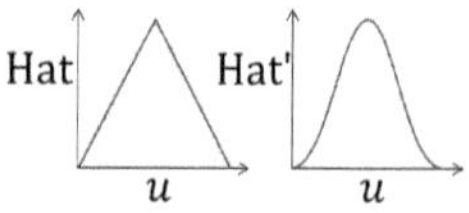

Figure 2 shows this in the oval marked "mirror loop retiming". We perform a similar retiming when transitioning between Still and Play layers as indicated by the "ease-in ease-out" label in Figure 2. Because time is momentarily slowed considerably we generate new in-between frames.

Layer boundary refinement

Recall that to keep the UI simple, the user sketches a single region R for each layer at one selected time frame. Thus the layer's spatiotemporal extent $\tilde{L}_i$ is a generalized cylinder — the extrusion of the user-drawn region R over a fixed time interval $[t_s, t_e]$ obtained by the optimization in the Temporal Refinement section.

At times, the user may not completely encircle an object, or in subsequent frames, objects with significant motion may leave the boundary and/or unwanted objects may enter. In these cases, to improve spatiotemporal continuity, we can refine the extent $\tilde{L}_i$ in two ways. First, we can compute optical flow between frames to advect the user-drawn boundary R to form a time-dependent region $R(t)$.

Second, we perform a binary graph-cut over the spatiotemporal volume to refine the layer boundary. The construction is similar to that in graphcut textures [17]. It also leverages the observation in simultaneous matting and compositing [27] that, since both the layer and the background come from the same source material, a conservative matte that does not cut through the foreground tends to avoid artifacts.

The optimization is governed by a trimap computed from erosion and dilation on the region $R(t)$. Pixels between (and including) the two trimap boundaries are assigned nodes in the graph-cut formulation. A binary cut determines if the pixel is assigned to the new layer $\tilde{L}_i$ or retains its value from the reference image, depending on the spatiotemporal similarity with neighboring pixels. Thus the result of is a modified spatiotemporal extent $\tilde{S}_i$ whose boundaries adapt to both the source video content and the background over which it is composed. An example is in our video at `http://research.microsoft.com/cliplets/paper/`.

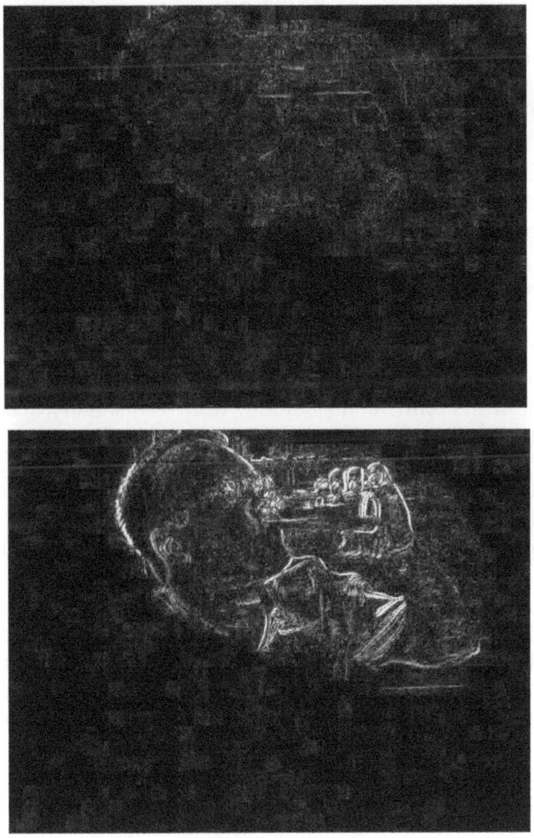

Figure 6: We show the difference between the start and end frame of a loop with temporal feathering (top) and without (bottom). Note that the temporal discontinuity is reduced in the feathered result, resulting in a more seamless loop. [Please see `http://research.microsoft.com/cliplets/paper/` for a PDF with embedded videos that better conveys this result.]

Blending during composition

To reduce any remaining spatial discontinuities, we perform per-frame Laplacian blending [7, 25] when compositing each layer. This reduces any artifacts due to changes in exposure times as well as small misalignments. In the inset comparison, the small gradient at the edge of the layer in the left panel causes a visual jump on each loop iteration which is removed in the right panel and in the resulting cliplet.

EVALUATION

The evaluation of the Cliplets tool has proceeded through two informal means. First, we demonstrated the tool one-on-one to approximately 1000 people during three days at a technical exhibition. This resulted in numerous online articles and blog entries. In addition, we released the tool to the public and recently requested users to voluntarily respond to a short survey about their experiences. We report informally on both personal observations and conversations at the exhibition and the more structured survey responses.

At the exhibition, we created Cliplets on-the-fly in a matter of seconds. The most obvious reaction was one of amazed joy as the juxtaposition of still and motion appeared. Often, we were then asked, "Can you make that part move (e.g., a bird), and freeze the rest?". Most of the time we could satisfy such requests in a few seconds. The most common reason such intents could not be satisfied was due to overlapping motions. There were also some questions that indicated, that the 30 second demo did not make clear the differing roles of the input and output timelines. Such misconceptions could usually be clarified quickly with a second example.

The Cliplets application was placed online along with a few short tutorials showing how to use the tool, much like the demonstrations shown at the exhibition. The application asks users to optionally fill out a short survey after the second usage of the tool. As of this writing, over 60,000 people have downloaded the application. More recently, we added a voluntary survey, and over 400 people have responded. The online survey has helped us understand some of the experiences of those that have tried the Cliplets tool themselves (and were willing to respond to the survey).

The survey respondents were overwhelmingly male (90%), were fairly evenly spread in ages (8% under 20, 26% 20-39, 21% 30-39, 31% 40-59, and 14% 60 and over). Education levels were also well spread (4% completed elementary school, 23% high school, 46% undergraduate, and 27% graduate education). 75% had watched one or more tutorials. Only 11 found the tutorials "not useful". The survey request was triggered after the second time users were about to close the application. At that point, about half had made 2 or more cliplets. About 1/3rd had made only one cliplet and 17% reported making none.

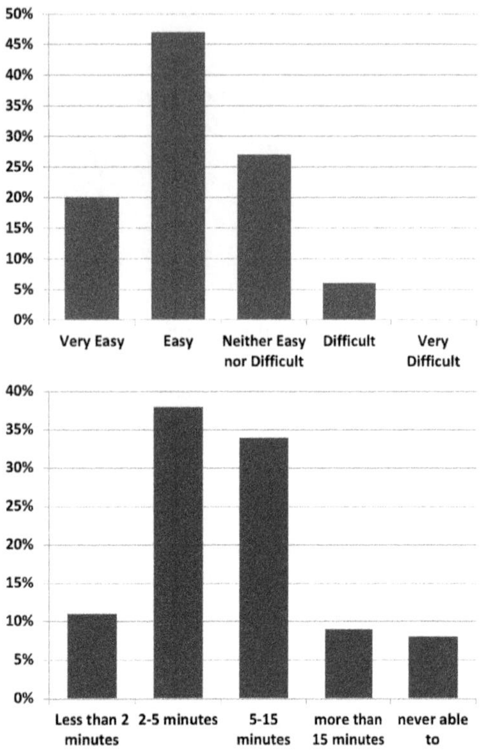

Figure 7: Ease of Use (top) and Completion Time (bottom)

We asked how easy or hard it was to create a cliplet on a 5-point Likert scale. About two thirds found it easy (47%) or very easy (20%), with most of the rest (27%) reporting it was neither easy nor difficult. Only 6% reported it difficult and one respondent reported it being very difficult (see Figure 7(top)). When asked how long it took to create a cliplet they were satisfied with, the most common answer was 2-5 minutes (37%) with 11% reporting success in less than 2 minutes. 34% were able to create a satisfactory cliplet in 5-15 minutes, 9% took more than 15 minutes, and 8% were unable to create a satisfactory cliplet (see Figure 7(bottom)).

We also asked about understanding and usage of some of the features. All but 5% reported a basic or good understanding of the timelines. All but 5% reported understanding the layers concept. Users indicated using 2 layers in a cliplet as the most common, with a quarter creating cliplets with more than 2 layers. Loops were the most used layer type, however each of the other idioms was reported having been used by at least 30% of respondents. Input videos were derived from video cameras (66% indicating this source), mobile devices (27%), as well downloaded videos (26%), with a few indicating other sources. Interestingly, about half of respondents said they had shot videos specifically with making a Cliplet in mind. Half also indicated having shared a resulting cliplet, split almost evenly between using email and posting on a sharing site.

We also asked for freeform comments to indicate particular aspects of the system they liked and disliked, as well as features they would like to see added. There were a large number of very complimentary comments, perhaps our favorite being, "It's very simple to use, I like that very much. So simple I'm not too worried about my dad downloading this to play about and asking me too many questions." There were a number of requests for more advanced features such as being able to specify the changing shape of the mask through time, and to be able to combine layers from more than one video. Professional tools do provide this but at a cost to the simplicity of the interface. This type of tension is an expected one and perhaps impossible to overcome. The most common request was to allow animated GIF output in addition to mp4's and wmv's. We recently added this ability in a new version.

RESULTS AND DISCUSSION

We have created numerous cliplets using our tool. Most of the source material comes from casual, handheld videos shot by the authors. Depending on the complexity of the cliplet, they took from 2 to 10 minutes to construct. A number of examples are shown in Figure 8. We demonstrate cliplets created with combinations of four idioms: Still, Play, Loop, and Mirror. Our results show the interplay of these idioms resulting in a range of imagery from cinemagraphs to short narratives. [Our complete set of video results, including those from external users, can be found at `http://research.microsoft.com/cliplets/paper/`.]

Automation vs. Interaction. The system we describe gives the user creative control over the semantic elements of the cliplets. The refinements automate minor adjustments to clean up the spatiotemporal boundaries of layers. In a few instances, however, the automated refinements change the intended semantics of the cliplet. For example, spatial adjustments may enlarge the layer to include unwanted foreground elements. Adjustments to temporal boundaries may result in a smoother loop transition, but may remove something the user intended to have in the layer. This tension between automatic and interactive operations is not uncommon in many semi-automated systems. In these cases, the user is able to turn off the refinements but may need to manually make precise adjustments to the layer boundary.

Failure cases. There were a few common types of failure cases that do not arise in professionally created cinemagraphs. One failure mode occurs when the video could not be aligned due to excessive camera or foreground motion or when there is no background to lock on to. Another difficult case arises when the object of interest overlaps a moving background. In some cases this could be handled by creating a "clean plate", which is something we are pursuing as future work; however, there are times where there is no possibility of constructing a clean plate since some of the background is revealed only during the loop. The boundary refinement can also fail if the user specified boundary is too far away from the "ideal" boundary, as the trimap will not contain a good region for creating a lower cost boundary. Boundary refinement in its most general form is equivalent to video segmentation and matting, an area of continued, active research, thus there are numerous opportunities for future work here. Given these constraints, we were pleasantly surprised how often a successful cliplet could be derived from spontaneously and casually captured video.

SUMMARY AND FUTURE WORK

We have presented a tool for creating cliplets – a type of imagery that sits between stills and video, including imagery such as video textures and "cinemagraphs". We have identified a few simple time-mapping idioms that, when combined, provide a wealth of freedom for creativity. Our tool allows cliplets to be quickly created from casual, handheld video using simple interactions. Numerous examples are provided.

Further analysis. We made three fundamental design decisions in our work: 1) creating a reduced set of mapping functions that does not allow full control yet is more expressive than the controls in related mobile apps, 2) creating separate in and out timelines instead of a single time-in vs. time-out graph, and 3) using one pane instead of two for displaying the input video and output cliplet. While these choices seem valid given our experiences and initial user feedback, they do depart somewhat from previous work and each choice warrants more formal study, which is an interesting direction for future work.

A new way to see. When one picks up a camera and heads into the world to photograph it, one often *sees* the world differently. One sees shots to frame and instants to grab, rather than buildings, people, and traffic. Ansel Adams describes *seeing the finished photo in your mind's eye* [1]. In a similar way, after using our tool, we began to *see* the world through this new type of lens when thinking about capturing video. Small motions became things to focus on while the rest of the busy world faded away. This, as much as the results, has convinced us that cliplets represent an exciting and provocative new media type, and that intuitive tools for creating such media can be very powerful.

ACKNOWLEDGEMENTS

We would like to thank Bill Freeman for helpful discussions on the earlier stages of this work. We would additionally like to thank the anonymous UIST reviewers.

REFERENCES

1. A. Adams. *Camera*. Number v. 1. Houghton Mifflin Harcourt P, 1980.
2. Aseem Agarwala, Mira Dontcheva, Maneesh Agrawala, Steven Drucker, Alex Colburn, Brian Curless, David Salesin, and Michael Cohen. Interactive digital photomontage. *ACM Trans. Graph.*, 23(3):294–302, 2004.
3. Aseem Agarwala, Ke Colin Zheng, Chris Pal, Maneesh Agrawala, Michael Cohen, Brian Curless, David Salesin, and Richard Szeliski. Panoramic video textures. *ACM Trans. Graph.*, 24(3):821–827, July 2005.
4. Jiamin Bai, Aseem Agarwala, Maneesh Agrawala, and Ravi Ramamoorthi. Selectively de-animating video. *ACM Transactions on Graphics*, 31(4), 2012.
5. Xue Bai, Jue Wang, David Simons, and Guillermo Sapiro. Video snapcut: robust video object cutout using localized classifiers. *ACM Trans. Graph.*, 28(3), 2009.
6. Jamie Beck and Kevin Burg. Cinemagraphs. `http://http://cinemagraphs.com/`.
7. Peter J. Burt and Edward H. Adelson. A multiresolution spline with application to image mosaics. *ACM Trans. Graph.*, 2(4):217–236, October 1983.
8. Michael Calonder, Vincent Lepetit, Christoph Strecha, and Pascal Fua. Brief: binary robust independent elementary features. In *Proceedings of the 11th European Conference on Computer vision: Part IV*, ECCV'10, pages 778–792, 2010.
9. Yung-Yu Chuang, Aseem Agarwala, Brian Curless, David H. Salesin, and Richard Szeliski. Video matting of complex scenes. *ACM Trans. Graph.*, 21(3), 2002.
10. Yung-Yu Chuang, Dan B Goldman, Ke Colin Zheng, Brian Curless, David H. Salesin, and Richard Szeliski. Animating pictures with stochastic motion textures. *ACM Trans. Graph.*, 24(3):853–860, 2005.
11. Martin A. Fischler and Robert C. Bolles. Random sample consensus: a paradigm for model fitting with applications to image analysis and automated cartography. *Commun. ACM*, 24(6):381–395, June 1981.
12. William T. Freeman, Edward H. Adelson, and David J. Heeger. Motion without movement. In *SIGGRAPH Proceedings*, pages 27–30, 1991.
13. Michael L. Gleicher and Feng Liu. Re-cinematography: Improving the camerawork of casual video. *ACM Trans. Multimedia Comput. Commun. Appl.*, 5(1):2:1–2:28, October 2008.
14. Dan B. Goldman, Chris Gonterman, Brian Curless, David Salesin, and Steven M. Seitz. Video object annotation, navigation, and composition. In *Proceedings of ACM Symposium on User Interface Software and Technology*, UIST '08, pages 3–12, 2008.
15. Matthias Grundmann, Vivek Kwatra, and Irfan Essa. Auto-directed video stabilization with robust L1 optimal camera paths. In *IEEE Conference on Computer Vision and Pattern Recognition (CVPR 2011)*, 2011.
16. Randy Kennedy. The still-life mentor to a filmmaking generation. The New York Times, October 6, 2006.
17. Vivek Kwatra, Arno Schödl, Irfan Essa, Greg Turk, and Aaron Bobick. Graphcut textures: image and video synthesis using graph cuts. *ACM Trans. Graph.*, 22(3):277–286, July 2003.
18. Ce Liu, Antonio Torralba, William T. Freeman, Frédo Durand, and Edward H. Adelson. Motion magnification. *ACM Trans. Graph.*, 24(3):519–526, July 2005.
19. David G. Lowe. Object recognition from local scale-invariant features. *IEEE International Conference on Computer Vision*, 2:1150, 1999.
20. Alex Rav-Acha, Yael Pritch, Dani Lischinski, and Shmuel Peleg. Spatio-temporal video warping. In *ACM SIGGRAPH 2005 Sketches*, SIGGRAPH '05, 2005.
21. Alex Rav-Acha, Yael Pritch, Dani Lischinski, and Shmuel Peleg. Dynamosaicing: Mosaicing of dynamic scenes. *IEEE Trans. Pattern Anal. Mach. Intell.*, 29(10):1789–1801, October 2007.
22. Arno Schödl and Irfan A. Essa. Controlled animation of video sprites. In *ACM SIGGRAPH/Eurographics Symposium on Computer animation*, pages 121–127, 2002.
23. Arno Schödl, Richard Szeliski, David H. Salesin, and Irfan Essa. Video textures. In *SIGGRAPH Proceedings*, pages 489–498, 2000.
24. Richard Szeliski. Locally adapted hierarchical basis preconditioning. *ACM Trans. Graph.*, 25(3):1135–1143, 2006.
25. Richard Szeliski, Matt Uyttendaele, and Drew Steedly. Fast Poisson blending using multi-splines. In *IEEE International Conference on Computational Photography*, April 2011.
26. James Tompkin, Fabrizio Pece, Kartic Subr, and Jan Kautz. Towards moment images: Automatic cinemagraphs. In *Proceedings of the 8th European Conference on Visual Media Production (CVMP 2011)*, November 2011.
27. Jue Wang and Michael F. Cohen. Simultaneous matting and compositing. In *IEEE Computer Vision and Pattern Recognition*, pages 1 –8, June 2007.
28. Ke Colin Zheng, Alex Colburn, Aseem Agarwala, Maneesh Agrawala, David Salesin, Brian Curless, and Michael F. Cohen. Parallax photography: creating 3D cinematic effects from stills. In *Proceedings of Graphics Interface*, pages 111–118, 2009.

Figure 8: A variety of cliplets. Our tool has been used to create numerous cliplets. Each cliplet is a juxtaposition of at least two of our four idioms: Still, Play, Loop, and Mirror, and represent imagery from "cinemagraphs" to short narratives. [Please see `http://research.microsoft.com/cliplets/paper/` for a PDF with embedded videos that better conveys this result.]

JellyLens: Content-Aware Adaptive Lenses

Cyprien Pindat[1,2] pindat@lri.fr
Emmanuel Pietriga[2,3,1] emmanuel.pietriga@inria.fr
Olivier Chapuis[1,2] chapuis@lri.fr
Claude Puech[3,2,1] claude.puech@u-psud.fr

[1]Univ Paris-Sud & CNRS (LRI) 91405 Orsay, France
[2]INRIA 91405 Orsay, France
[3]INRIA Chile (CIRIC) 7561211 Santiago, Chile

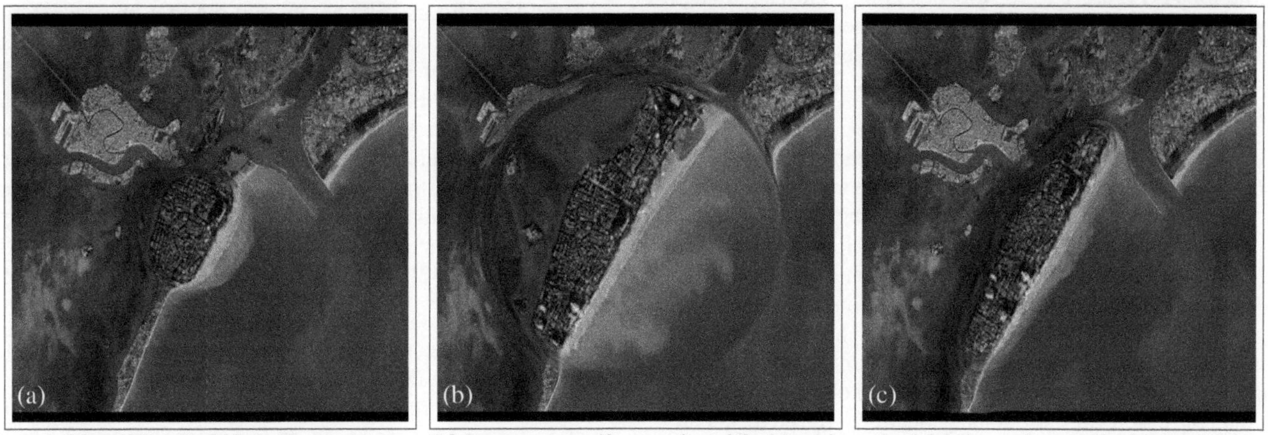

Figure 1. Magnifying the Lido in Venice. (a) a small fisheye can magnify a portion of the island from the Adriatic sea shore to the Laguna Veneta, but fails to show the entire island, requiring extensive navigation to see it in detail; (b) a large fisheye magnifies a bigger portion of the island, but at the cost of severe distortion of almost the entire image, hiding other islands; (c) a JellyLens automatically adapts its shape to the region of interest, magnifying as much relevant information in the focus region as (b) while better preserving the context: surrounding islands are left almost untouched from (a).

ABSTRACT
Focus+context lens-based techniques smoothly integrate two levels of detail using spatial distortion to connect the magnified region and the context. Distortion guarantees visual continuity, but causes problems of interpretation and focus targeting, partly due to the fact that most techniques are based on statically-defined, regular lens shapes, that result in far-from-optimal magnification and distortion. JellyLenses dynamically adapt to the shape of the objects of interest, providing detail-in-context visualizations of higher relevance by optimizing what regions fall into the focus, context and spatially-distorted transition regions. This both improves the visibility of content in the focus region and preserves a larger part of the context region. We describe the approach and its implementation, and report on a controlled experiment that evaluates the usability of JellyLenses compared to regular fisheye lenses, showing clear performance improvements with the new technique for a multi-scale visual search task.

ACM Classification Keywords
H.5.2 [Information interfaces and presentation]: User Interfaces – Graphical user interfaces.

Author Keywords
Multi-scale Interfaces, Focus+Context, Lenses

UIST'12, October 7–10, 2012, Cambridge, Massachusetts, USA.

INTRODUCTION
In many domains, datasets grow in size much more rapidly than computer displays in resolution. This includes maps produced by geographical information systems: rasterizing the OpenStreetMap world map at street level would require an $18 \cdot 10^{15}$ pixel bitmap; satellite or astronomical imagery: Spitzer's recent infrared survey of the inner part of our galaxy is made of thousands of frames stitched together to produce a 4.7 billion pixel image; images several dozens of gigapixels in size assembled from multiple frames taken by conventional SLR cameras; as well as numerous information visualizations such as complex networks represented as node-link diagrams. None of these datasets fit on computer screens, not even high-resolution wall displays. They require multi- scale navigation capabilities that will enable users to transition from high-level overviews to zoomed-in, highly-detailed representations of a region of interest, and conversely.

Multi-scale navigation in large information spaces is typically achieved using one of the following three interface schemes or combination thereof [15]: overview+detail, zooming and focus+context. Techniques based on the latter integrate a detailed representation of a region of interest directly in the surrounding context [17], which essentially corresponds to the original, unmagnified visualization showing more data at a lower scale. One of the main focus+context techniques is the magnification lens and its derivatives, that provides in-place magnification integrated into the context.

Smooth integration of the two levels of detail is generally achieved using spatial distortion to connect the magnified region and the context, as with the so-called fisheye lenses.

While distortion guarantees visual continuity, it also causes problems of interpretation [12, 13], focus targeting [1, 18, 30] and virtual navigation. Indeed, most techniques are based on lens shapes defined statically by distance functions obtained through $L(P)$-metrics [14], that often fail to provide relevant magnifications of the object(s) of interest: either the lens is small, preserving context but requiring extensive navigation to explore the region of interest when the latter does not fit in the focus (Figure 1-a); or the lens is big, showing a larger portion of the region of interest at the expense of the context (Figure 1-b). Moreover, distortion impedes comprehension, even more so when the lens' and objects' shapes differ significantly.

We present interactive focus+context techniques called *JellyLenses*, that dynamically adapt to the geometry of object(s) of interest. JellyLenses optimize what regions fall into the focus, context and spatially-distorted transition regions based on user interaction, providing detail-in-context visualizations of higher relevance than existing distortion-oriented magnification lenses (Figure 1-c). The first technique, *PathLens*, consists of a lens attached to the mouse cursor, that adapts its shape, circular by default, to the graphical objects considered of interest based on the cursor's location. Intuitively, PathLenses behave approximately like water drops on a spider net, or more generally speaking like drops on an irregular surface featuring elements of varying affinity [38]. The second technique, *AreaLens*, consists in the dynamic relayout and resizing of all objects that fall in the lens' scope. The technique tries to preserve the original aspect of those objects as much as possible, magnifying those closest to the cursor while reducing those closer to the lens' periphery, and distorting the regions in-between. As discussed later, the two techniques are complementary, providing solutions to a wide range of tasks and visual configurations. Both work for arbitrary 2D datasets, ranging from networks and maps displayed as vector graphics (Figure 2) to documents and Web pages. They also apply to satellite imagery (Figure 1) and other pixel-oriented datasets, as detailed later in this paper.

After an overview of related work, we describe 1) a method for modeling lenses of arbitrary shape, used in all JellyLenses to enable rendering of magnified regions of interest at interactive frame rates, and 2) two methods for dynamically generating relevant lens shapes based on the geometry of regions of interest, that respectively correspond to the PathLens and AreaLens techniques. We then report on a controlled experiment that evaluated the usability of JellyLenses compared to regular fisheye lenses, showing clear performance improvements with the new technique.

RELATED WORK

Distortion-oriented visualizations often rely on metaphors inspired by the physical world: magnifying glasses [32, 18], stretchable rubber sheets [34] and, more generally, surface deformations [11]. Other techniques work with more fundamental concepts: hyperbolic projection [26], non-linear magnification fields [22] or complex logarithmic views [8].

Early systems made the distortion extend to the boundaries of the representation [26, 27, 32, 33, 34], thus affecting the entire display. More recent techniques use a locally-bounded distortion function, leaving a large part of the context untouched, which reduces the negative impact of distortion [19, 30]. Such lenses, usually termed *constrained lenses*, can be created using 3-dimensional pliable surfaces [11] and the framework for unifying presentation space [14, 13], nonlinear magnification fields [22], conformal mapping [42], or the Sigma Lens framework [1, 30].

Magic Lens filters [6] were among the first interface components based on constrained lenses to actually support elaborate, non-regular shapes. Magic Lenses are graphical filters that can modify the appearance of objects seen through them in various ways. Magnification is only one of the many powerful transformations that they make possible. However, to our knowledge, their shape is defined statically (no dynamic content-aware adaptation), a limitation shared with more recent lenses that support irregular shapes but do not adapt their geometry [11, 42], including the recent undistort lenses [9].

Other techniques have been developed for 3D datasets. A first set of techniques deform 3D representations by projecting a texture on a mesh that models the distortion, as do pliable surfaces for 2D representations [11]. LaMar *et al.*'s magnification lenses [25] are based on homogeneous texture coordinates and special geometries. They can be applied to both 2D and 3D representations but are limited in the type of distortion and lens shapes they can model. Non-linear perspective projections [41] project the RGB image produced by a 3D pipeline on a surface shape inserted in front of the flat projection plane. Related to the latter is Brosz et al.'s single camera flexible projection framework [10], which is capable of modeling non-linear projections through the parametric representation of the viewing volume.

There is also an impressive set of space deformation techniques, ranging from early works on the deformation of solid primitives [3, 36] to view-dependent geometry [31] and deformation based on hardware-accelerated displacement mapping [16, 35] and deflectors [23]. These techniques distort 3D geometry, but often do so in an object-centric manner, and are thus not well suited to the implementation of focus+context navigation lenses, which deform a region of the current display, i.e., a subsection of the current viewing frustum that intersects a set of objects, some of them only partially. Camera textures [37] are among the few to actually apply constrained magnification lenses to 3D meshes, but the technique requires a sufficient level of tessellation of the target mesh to produce distortions of good quality. Wang *et al.*'s technique [39] is designed to minimize distortion, but applies to 3D objects only and, relying on a grid-based energy optimization model, is limited to basic shapes between the magnified and compressed regions.

Böttger *et al.* [7] recently introduced a domain-specific warping technique that distorts a city's geographical map to match the layout of subway stations from the corresponding schematic transit map. Distortion is not used to magnify a region of interest, but rather to establish a correspondence between an ordinary map, that is geographically accurate, and a schematic map optimized for the readability of a specific network. While very different from our approach in terms of visual output, interaction, and usage, map warping and JellyLenses have conceptual similarities: they both make use of the geometry of particular objects of interest in the visualization to adapt the distortion.

Finally, JellyLenses are conceptually related to the numerous content-aware image resizing techniques that have emerged recently, from seminal work on seam carving [2] to Laffont *et al.*'s image zooming technique [24]. However, those are not focus+context interaction techniques, as they do not provide users with explicit control of the magnification (factor, region), and in many cases do not preserve context.

GENERAL APPROACH

JellyLenses magnify a subregion of the visualization and smoothly integrate it in the context by locally compressing the area immediately surrounding the region of interest. But as opposed to previous techniques, JellyLenses dynamically adapt to better match the geometry of the region of interest. Thus, they must be able to take arbitrary shapes (Figure 2).

Adapting a JellyLens to match the geometry of the region of interest is a three-step process. The first step consists of obtaining information about the geometry of objects of interest in the scene, that the lens will adapt to. This step is heavily dependent on the nature of the graphics visualized: the geometry information is readily available in 2D vector graphics scenes, as well as in 3D scenes, but not in pixel-oriented scenes where the objects of interest are arbitrary sets of contiguous pixels on a bitmap. In the latter case, the geometry information has to be obtained through some external means, such as feature extraction algorithms applied dynamically to the image, or metadata generated through manual annotations packaged with the original image. The techniques to achieve this are readily available off-the-shelf, but this particular problem is heavily application-domain dependent and thus not discussed in detail in this paper. At this point we simply emphasize that a JellyLens does not necessarily have to adapt to all graphical objects in a scene; it can ignore those considered as not particularly relevant for some particular task. For instance, the lens in Figure 2 only takes roads on the blue itinerary into account, ignoring all other graphical features in the adaptation process.

The second step consists of computing the lens shape according to its position in the visualization and to the geometry of nearby object(s) of interest (information obtained through the first step). This step, which is the core of the adaptation process and our first contribution, defines how the lens behaves as it gets repositioned by the user in the visualization using the mouse. In Figure 2, the lens adapts its shape to match that of the portion of the object of interest (the itinerary) around the mouse cursor positioned in **P**. We present two methods of adaptation: PathLens, better suited to contours and paths at large, illustrated in Figure 2; and AreaLens, better suited to the magnification of filled shapes, illustrated in Figure 6.

The last step is the rendering of the region seen through the lens. This modeling and rendering method is used by both PathLens and AreaLens to adapt the lens in real-time at interactive frame rates. This second contribution is described in the next section, before the two adaptation methods.

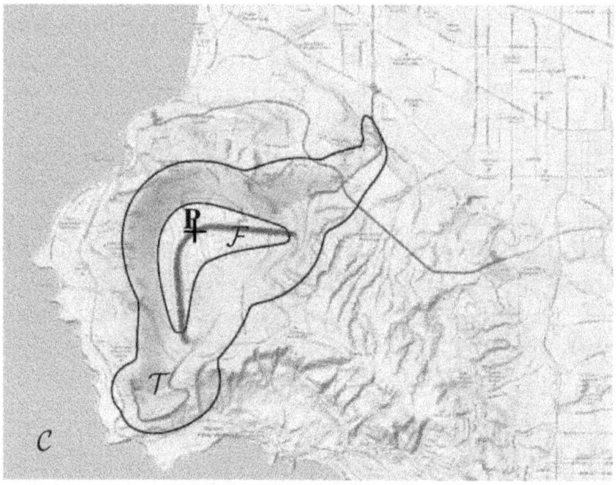

Figure 2. Regions defined by a constrained lens: focus region $\mathcal{F}$ magnifying the region of interest, context region $\mathcal{C}$, and smooth transition $\mathcal{T}$ between $\mathcal{F}$ and $\mathcal{C}$ achieved through distortion.

JELLYLENS MODELING AND RENDERING

Constrained lenses are defined by (Figure 2) a focus region $\mathcal{F}$, often termed *flat-top*; a context region $\mathcal{C}$ left untouched by the lens; a transition region $\mathcal{T}$, sometimes termed *compression region*; a magnification factor μ; a focus point **P** that will be the center of magnification. Focus region $\mathcal{F}$ is the region of interest to be magnified. This region is a flat magnification that is not affected by spatial distortion. It is bounded by a non self-intersecting contour (a simple polygon). Context region $\mathcal{C}$ is the region left untransformed by the lens. It is bounded by two contours: another non self-intersecting contour on the inside and the image's boundary rectangle on the outside. Regions $\mathcal{F}$ and $\mathcal{C}$ are disjoint: $\mathcal{F} \cap \mathcal{C} = \emptyset$. Region $\mathcal{T}$ then corresponds to the region in between the two contours. This is the region where distortion occurs, in the form of compression to allocate more screen real-estate to the magnified region of interest.

In the following, point coordinates are **bold**, scalars are in *italics*, and values defined relative to the source image are primed. The transformation to render points in the focus is straightforward:

$$\mathbf{x} = T_F(\mathbf{x}') = \mathbf{P} + \frac{\mathbf{x}' - \mathbf{P}}{\mu} \tag{1}$$

The transformation is formulated as a reverse mapping. For each pixel coordinates **x** on screen, i.e., in the destination image, we must find the corresponding point in the source image, $\mathbf{x}'$. Pixels in the context region are mapped to themselves: $\mathbf{x}' = \mathbf{x}, \forall \mathbf{x} \in \mathcal{C}$. The inverse of function T_F is applied to pixels falling into the focus region $\mathbf{x}' = T_F^{-1}(\mathbf{x}), \forall \mathbf{x} \in \mathcal{F}$. For pixels that fall in region $\mathcal{T}$, we compute the weighted average of the context and focus regions' contributions:

$$T(\mathbf{x}) = \frac{w_F(\mathbf{x}) \cdot T_F^{-1}(\mathbf{x}) + w_C(\mathbf{x}) \cdot \mathbf{x}}{w_F(\mathbf{x}) + w_C(\mathbf{x})}, \forall \mathbf{x} \in \mathcal{T} \tag{2}$$

where weights are defined as follows:

$$w_F = (\frac{1}{dist_F(\mathbf{x})})^{b_F}, w_C = (\frac{1}{dist_C(\mathbf{x})})^{b_C} \tag{3}$$

with $dist_F$ and $dist_C$ functions returning the distance to the focus and context region contours, respectively. Parameters b_F and b_C determine how the relative influence of the two regions fall off as a function of distance. As pointed out in [14]: *"creating a distortion presentation is all about finding a balance between the magnification required and some compensatory compression"*. Various profiles have been proposed to specify how to distribute the compression in the distortion, including linear, Gaussian and inverse cosine drop-off functions. Setting $b > 1$ will achieve a smooth transition at the boundaries of the corresponding region. Setting $b < 1$ will result in a sharper transition.

The above method makes it possible to generate a wide variety of lens shapes. It can be further generalized to create lenses with multiple foci (flat-tops). Multiple foci can be useful when magnifying disjoint objects of interest that are in close proximity (Figure 5). They make it possible, with a single lens, to have disjoint yet undistorted magnified regions of interest, and are an important feature of AreaLenses.

Let $\mathcal{F}_i$ ($i \in [1, n]$) be n regions of interest. Each region is associated with a transformation T_i with its own $\mathbf{P}_i$ and μ_i. The general mapping function is then a weighted average over the contributions of all involved regions, conceptually similar to the weighted coordinate transformation of multiple pairs of lines in field morphing [5]:

$$T(\mathbf{x}) = \frac{\sum_{i=0}^{n} w_i \cdot T_i^{-1}(\mathbf{x})}{\sum_{i=0}^{n} w_i} \quad (4)$$

$$with \quad w_i = \left(\frac{1}{dist_i(\mathbf{x}) + a_i}\right)^{b_i} \quad (5)$$

where a_i are constants that change the relative flatness of the flat-tops for optimal adaptation. When $a_i = 0$, strength is infinite for pixels on the contour ($dist_i(\mathbf{x}) = 0$) leading to a flat mapping inside the corresponding focus region. When $a_i > 0$, this flatness constraint is relaxed a bit, enabling a better packing of foci through partial distortion. This can be interesting in cases where the information space is densely populated with regions of interest, as illustrated in Figure 6. Indeed, in dense environments, the transition region is small compared to that of the regions of interest and cannot absorb all the distortion. Allowing distortion in the regions of interests distributes it over a wider area and attenuates it. Each parameter b_i has an influence, on the corresponding $\mathcal{F}_i$ region, similar to that of the above parameters b_C and $b_{\mathcal{F}}$ on their respective regions.

We implemented this algorithm in C++ and OpenGL, delegating the spatial transformation to programmable graphics hardware. Mapping function T (Equation (4)) is based on the computation of distance fields to each region involved in the adaptation. Which distance fields get used can vary from one frame to the next. Before each frame update, distance fields are rendered offscreen by the GPU-accelerated technique introduced in [20], and stored into a depth texture, which is then accessed through simple bilinear interpolation. A shading effect can be added at rendering time, to enhance distortion comprehension [12].

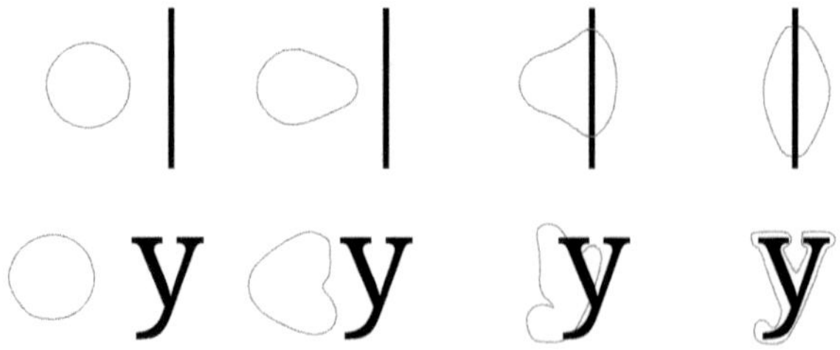

Figure 3. PathLens morphing effect.

ADAPTATION

We present two methods of adaptation, that both rely on the above modeling and rendering method. The first resulting interaction technique, PathLens, consists of a deformable lens, circular by default, that dynamically morphs its shape to roughly adopt that of the closest object of interest. The technique features a single flat-top, and is better suited to magnifying paths. The second technique, AreaLens, considers all regions of interest within a given *area of influence* around the lens' focal point (mouse cursor). Each region gets scaled piecewise to make room for the regions of higher importance, in an attempt to preserve the content of all regions from being significantly distorted.

PathLens

PathLenses assume a default circular shape that gets combined with implicit descriptions of the geometry of some objects in the scene based on distance fields. The actual shape of a PathLens at a given focal point $\mathbf{P}$ in the visualization depends on what objects of potential interest are in the vicinity. As illustrated in Figure 3, when far away from any object, a PathLens adopts the default circular shape, and progressively morphs, conserving the same area, as it approaches an object of interest. Not all objects in the scene are necessarily taken into account, and each application can define what objects the lens will adapt to. For instance, on Google Maps^{TM}, a PathLens could be made to adapt to interstate roads only, ignoring any highway, service road or other geographical landmark such as parks and water bodies.

We define the shape by an implicit function, $f(\mathbf{x})$, as the set of all points $\mathbf{x}$ such that $f(\mathbf{x}) = s$, s being an iso-level. Tesselation of implicit shapes is achieved using the marching square algorithm [28].

The cursor position and the geometry of nearby objects of interest both contribute to the definition of the lens' final shape. These influences are represented in terms of contribution functions: $lens(\mathbf{x})$ represents the contribution of the default lens shape to the final shape, $data(\mathbf{x})$ represents the contribution of proximal objects to the final shape. The shape is thus implicitly represented by:

$$f(\mathbf{x}) = lens(\mathbf{x} - \mathbf{c}) + data(\mathbf{x}) \quad (6)$$

where $\mathbf{c}$ is the cursor's coordinates. The $lens$ contribution is defined as:

$$lens(\mathbf{x}) = \frac{1}{||\mathbf{x}||} - ||\mathbf{x}|| \quad (7)$$

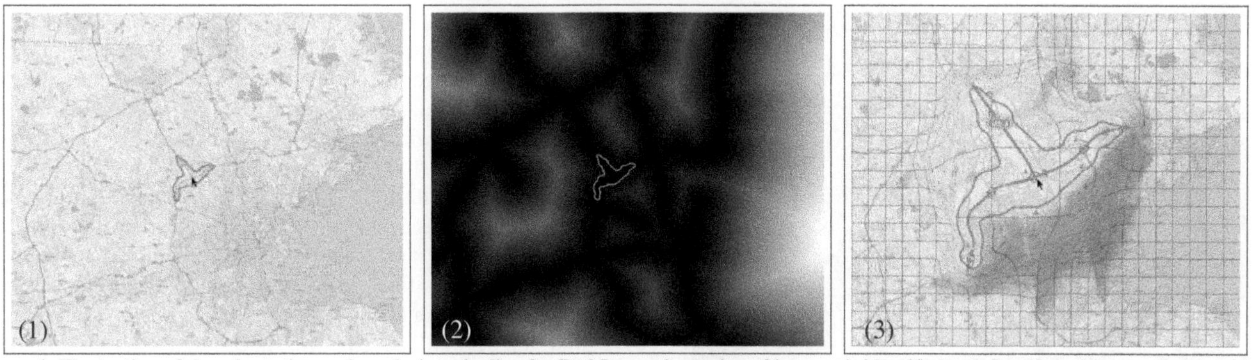

Figure 4. Illustration of the adaptation and rendering pipeline for PathLens: the region of interest is identified as a function of cursor position (1) and distance fields (2); the lens is then adapted to match this shape and rendered with a shading effect (3) – actual rendering displayed to the user, red contour excepted.

We use an adaptation of the function described in [40] to define *data*:

$$data(\mathbf{x}) = G\left(\frac{D(\mathbf{x})}{\beta}\right) \quad (8)$$

where $D(\mathbf{x})$ is the distance between $\mathbf{x}$ and the closest object of interest; G being defined as:

$$G(r) = \begin{cases} 2r^3 - 3r^2 + 1, & if\ r < 1; \\ 0 \text{ otherwise} \end{cases} \quad (9)$$

and β being a parameter bounding the contribution of $data$ to a given radius of influence.

Moving away from the object, as $D(\mathbf{x})$ increases, the contribution of $data(\mathbf{x})$ drops smoothly to zero, the lens reverts to its default circular shape.

We can then define the following set for each cursor position $\mathbf{c}$ and each iso-level s composed of several connected components:

$$E(\mathbf{c}, s) = \{\mathbf{x} \mid lens(\mathbf{x} - \mathbf{c}) + data(\mathbf{x}) > s\} \quad (10)$$

Because a small region around the cursor always yields large values (Equation (7)), it is guaranteed that among the set of all connected components of $E(\mathbf{c}, s)$ there will always be one that encompasses the cursor.

Let $S(\mathbf{c}, s)$ be its boundary. Then $S(\mathbf{c}, s)$ is the shape implicitly defined by the field function of Equation (6) at iso-level s. As s decreases, the shape's area, denoted $area(S(\mathbf{c}, s))$, increases. As mentioned earlier, we want the lens to have a constant area A. This is achieved by means of a numerical minimization method applied to:

$$u(s) = (area(S(\mathbf{c}, s)) - A)^2 \quad (11)$$

We use a gradient descent method, with the gradient defined as follow, P_i ($i \in [1, n]$) being the n vertices of the tessellation of the shape:

$$u'(s) = -2 \times \sum_{i=0}^{n} \frac{||P_i - P_{i+1}||}{||\vec{\nabla} f(P)||} \times (area(S(\mathbf{c}, s)) - A) \quad (12)$$

The above method is used to compute both the focus and context regions' contours. Computation of the context region's contour must also take into account the focus region's magnification by a factor of μ and make the former large enough to fully encompass the latter, so as to avoid intersecting contours that would entail discontinuities in the final result.

As the user repositions the lens in the visualization, $\mathcal{E}(\mathbf{c}, s(\mathbf{c}))$ is likely to eventually merge with another connected component from $E(\mathbf{c}, s(\mathbf{c}))$. This can lead to unwanted discontinuities in the lens' shape between the frame where this happens and the next. This effect can be avoided thanks to parameter β introduced earlier. To understand the influence of this parameter, let us first consider the case when β tends towards infinity. The contribution of function *data* is then flat, leading to $E(\mathbf{c}, s(\mathbf{c}))$ being composed of only one connected component. When β tends towards zero, the iso-level of the field function shrinks (Equation (6)), and tends to fit the object's geometry more accurately, but $E(\mathbf{c}, s(\mathbf{c}))$ is then composed of several connected components. When the cursor is hovering over an object, we want *data*'s contribution to be as in this second case, making the lens shape match the object's geometry more strongly. Conversely, when the cursor gets away from any object, we want to transition to the first case and avoid any discontinuity. This is done by making β depend on thedistance from the cursor position to the object, $D(\mathbf{P})$,ranging from a minimum value as $D(\mathbf{P})$ tends towards 0 and a maximum value as $D(\mathbf{P})$ increases and reaches a maximum radius of influence.

AreaLens

While PathLenses only consider the closest object of interest during the adaptation process, AreaLenses consider all objects of interest within a given area of influence. This makes the second technique better suited to the magnification of filled shapes in dense scenes, while PathLenses are better suited to magnification of paths or filled shapes in sparse scenes (in terms of regions of interest). In the following, regions of interest are referred to as *objects* for the sake of brevity and to emphasize their piecewise processing.

An AreaLens affects each object that falls into its area of influence. Objects that fall outside of it correspond to the context and are left untouched. As illustrated in Figure 5, the object(s) closest to the mouse cursor get magnified, piecewise, so as to preserve their aspect (no distortion). To make room for these objects, the objects that are farther away from the cursor but that still lie within the lens' area of influence get offset and scaled down to prevent overlap between them.

As the user moves the mouse cursor, objects of interest in the area of influence are either smoothly pulled towards the

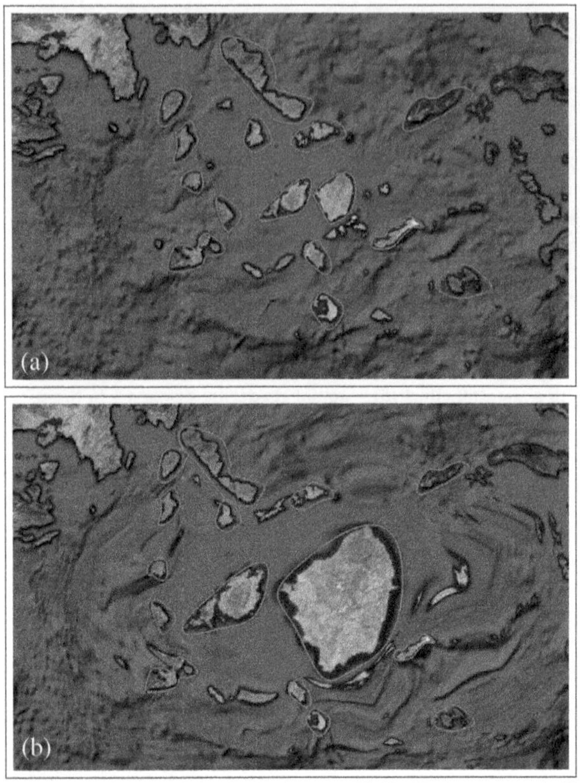

Figure 5. (a) Aegean islands (no lens applied). Red contours indicate regions of interest. (b) an AreaLens preserves the islands' appearance (piecewise magnification), putting most of the distortion in the ocean.

cursor as it approaches them, or pushed away as it gets away from them, eventually reverting to their original location and size when getting out of the area of influence. Achieving this behavior entails the following requirements. Magnified objects should not overlap each other (*R1*); objects should move in a smooth manner (*R2*); the topology of the information space should be preserved as much as possible, i.e., objects preserve their relative positions (*R3*); and finally, objects beyond the area of influence, i.e., that belong to the context region, should neither be moved nor scaled (*R4*).

The area of influence takes the form of a box centered on the lens' focal point, usually corresponding to the cursor. This box delimits the region beyond which the lens no longer affects the visualization, thus leaving the context region untouched (*R4*). We use two concurrent mapping algorithms to achieve the other three requirements: a *dispersion* mapping, and a *magnification* mapping. The purpose of the *dispersion* mapping is to push objects away and shrink them to accommodate the objects that will get magnified. The purpose of the *magnification* mapping is to pull objects towards the cursor and magnify them. The *magnification* mapping takes as input the cursor position and identifies the closest objects, to be magnified. The *dispersion* mapping takes as input this set of magnified objects and spreads out the remaining objects (*R1*). We term *magnified objects* the objects identified by the *magnification* mapping, and *movable objects* the remaining ones, spread out by the *dispersion* mapping.

The *dispersion* mapping consists of two steps. First, it moves every *movable object* according to a displacement vector. Then, it shrinks every one of them according to a scale factor. The displacement vector is computed as a weighted average of displacement contributions from each *magnified object*. Each displacement contribution is responsible for preventing a *magnified objects* from overlaping a *movable object*. Each contribution is computed as $\mathbf{D}_m = \mathbf{x}' - \mathbf{x}$, where $\mathbf{x}$ is the point within the *magnified object* at its initial position (i.e., before magnification) that is closest to the considered *movable object*, and where $\mathbf{x}'$ is the same point on the *magnified object* at its final position (i.e., after magnification). The displacement contribution moves objects away, guaranteeing that objects don't overlap (*R2*) and roughly preserving the relative position of objects (*R3*).

Weights are computed as the inverse distance from a *movable object* to each *magnified object*. An additional contribution is assigned to the area of influence's bounding box to stabilize the position of objects as it approaches them, with a null displacement vector and a weight that is the inverse of the distance to the object. As the first step of the *dispersion* might not be sufficient to guarantee that no overlapping occurs (*R1*), we shrink movable objects by iteratively applying a scaling transformation to them using a constant reduction ratio until they do not overlap anymore.

The *magnification* mapping rescales objects by applying the following transformation to their initial position, where $\mathbf{P}$ is the focal point (cursor) and μ the lens' magnification factor: $T(\mathbf{x}) = \frac{\mathbf{x}-\mathbf{P}}{\mu} + \mathbf{P}$. The closer to the cursor, the more an object gets influenced by the *magnification* mapping. This is achieved through an iterative process. Initially, every object is set to its initial position in the scene, and is considered as a *movable object*. We then process objects one by one, according to their proximity to the cursor (closest one first). Each object is set to its final position: $w \times T(\mathbf{x}) + (1 - w) \times \mathbf{x'}$ with $w = 1 - \frac{dist}{radius}$ where $\mathbf{x}$ is the initial position, $\mathbf{x'}$ the current position, $radius$ a parameter specifying the lens' operating range and $dist$ its distance to the cursor. The object is then added to the *magnified objects* set, and the *dispersion* mapping is applied to all remaining *movable objects*. The iterative process stops when there are no more *movable objects* within range.

The mapping algorithm results in the displacement of each movable object. Each object being associated with a rigid transformation T_i, movable objects in their final position are then used as regions for distortion modeling and rendering.

The above method works well for scenes that contain both low and high numbers of objects, provided that they feature some empty space to absorb the distortion. When objects are densely packed, or even juxtaposed, the method can be adapted to allow for some distortion of movable objects, thanks to parameter a_i associated with each flat-top (introduced earlier). Figure 6 illustrates this case: objects correspond to the different neighborhoods in central Los Angeles. By setting a_i to 0 on the object directly under the mouse cursor (Hollywood), we make sure that this particular neighborhood gets fully magnified, without distortion. The surrounding regions get assigned a_i values greater than 0, allowing the lens to distort those regions if necessary.

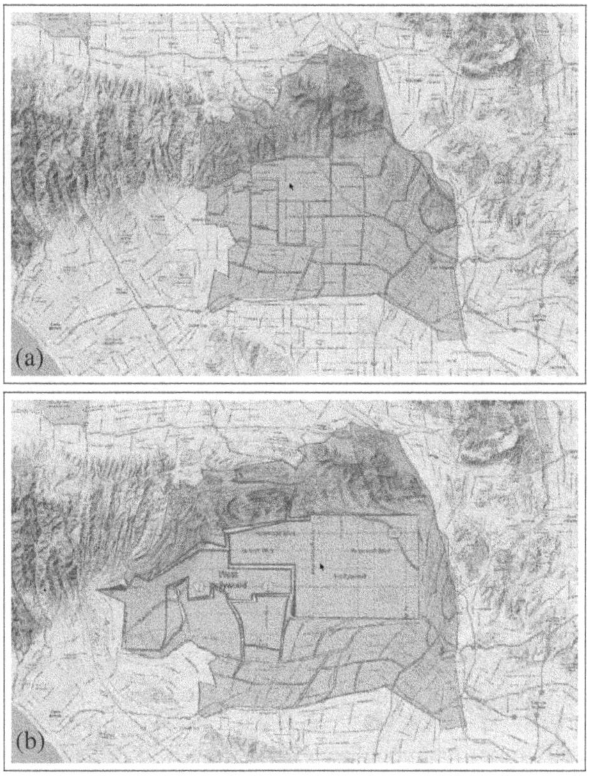

Figure 6. (a) Map of Los Angeles neighborhoods (no lens applied). (b) AreaLens adapting to Hollywood and part of West Hollywood.

EVALUATION

The different multi-scale interface schemes (focus + context, overview + detail, zooming) all have their advantages and drawbacks, depending on the user's task and on the nature of the visualization; their empirical comparison has been the topic of several papers [15, 21, 29]. Our primary goal was to empirically evaluate the potential benefits and pitfalls of adaptive lenses compared to statically-defined lenses. The purpose of this experiment was both to evaluate the actual performance gain under different conditions, if any, and to assess the potential negative impact of the dynamically changing geometry, that might cause confusion and visual discomfort. For this first experiment, we compared regular fisheyes (circular shape, Gaussian drop-off) to AreaLenses, that have a stronger impact in terms of visual changes than PathLenses, as they affect more objects and are thus more likely to suffer from this, especially in dense configurations.

The task was an abstract multi-scale visual search task, operationalized so as to test the following two hypotheses, based on the expectation that by adapting their shape to match that of object(s) of interest, AreaLenses should provide more relevant detail-in-context visualizations than regular fisheyes, requiring less virtual navigation while minimizing the negative effects of distortion that impede comprehension:

H_1 AreaLens performs better than fisheye when the objects of interest have irregular shapes, as the focus of AreaLens adapts to those shapes while that of fisheye does not;

H_2 AreaLens performs worse when the density of objects of interest is high, as this leads to more visual distraction caused by the movement of a larger number of objects.

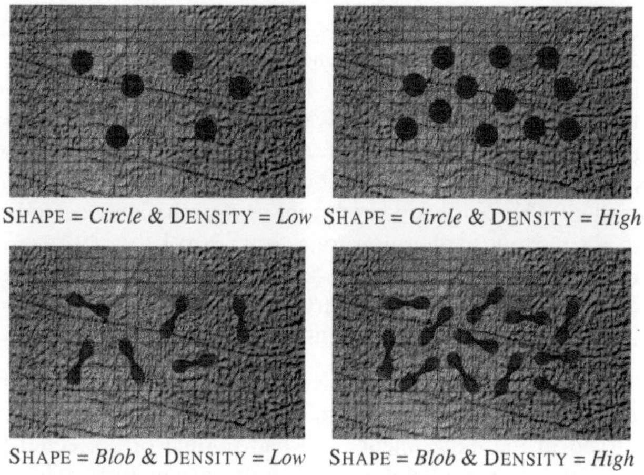

Figure 7. Screenshots for the four SHAPE × DENSITY conditions.

Task and Procedure

In all trials, the information space was made of islands on an ocean (Figure 7). The task consisted in finding a red cross that was positioned on one of the islands, by magnifying each island in turn. The red cross was not visible at context scale and could only be revealed when the corresponding region was magnified through the lens. We used the same texture to represent the ocean in all trials (bathymetric data). Forest textures used to fill the islands all looked similar, so as to ensure that the red cross would be equally difficult to visually differentiate from the background on all islands.

To operationalize *H1*, we considered two types of shapes (factor SHAPE): islands were either circles (*Circle*, Figure 7-top) or elongated blobs (*Blob*, Figure 7-bottom). All islands had the same surface, to make sure that differences could be attributed across conditions to variations in shape, as opposed to area. To ensure fair treatment of both techniques, we made the *Fisheye*'s flat-top the exact same size as the circular islands. Thus, for each condition, the flat-top of both lenses and the islands had the same surface. We did not make the flat-top of the *Fisheye* lens larger to avoid problems caused by the distortion of larger context areas, that impede focus targeting, and thus task performance, and make context information difficult (at best) to understand in real world cases, as illustrated in Figure 1.

To operationalize *H2*, we tested two different object densities (factor DENSITY): a *Low* density with a significant amount of empty space (ocean) between islands (Figure 7-left); and a *High*er density (Figure 7-right) with more islands packed in the same space. AreaLenses would cause more visual disturbance in the *High* condition: more objects had to be moved and resized to accommodate the magnified object of interest, as their was less empty space to "absorb" distortion.

Randomly placing the cross before a trial starts would obviously have been a significant source of noise in the experimental data depending on how lucky participants were in each trial. As this chance factor cannot be balanced across conditions, we artificially forced chance upon participants, following the approach described in previous work on the operationalization of multi-scale search tasks [29]. We introduced a secondary factor, NAVLENGTH, that determines *when*, rather than *where* the cross appears, based on what fraction of the entire scene (considering island surfaces only) the participant had already visited with the lens. Thus, for a value X of factor NAVLENGTH for a given trial, the red cross only appeared after participants had visited $X\%$ of the total surface of all islands, no matter in what order those islands had been visited. The cross appeared right next to the lens, according to the current exploration trajectory. NAVLENGTH was set to one of three values, 30%, 55% or 80%. Participants were completely oblivious of this trick, and were told about it only after the end of the experiment.

Twelve unpaid volunteers (two females), daily computer users, age 24 to 36 year-old (average 30.3, median 30.5), served in the experiment. All had normal or corrected-to-normal vision and did not suffer from any form of color blindness. We conducted the experiment on a 2x2.26GHz Mac Pro workstation running Mac OS X, equipped with an NVIDIA GeForce GT 120 512 MB driving a 30" LCD monitor (2560×1600, 100 dpi), and a standard optical mouse set at 400 dpi resolution and default system acceleration.

To summarize, the experiment was a 2×2×2×3 within-participants design with the following factors:

- 2 techniques (TECH): *Fisheye* and *AreaLens*;
- 2 types of shape (SHAPE): *Circle* and *Blob*;
- 2 types of shape density (DENSITY): *Low* and *High*;
- 3 navigation lengths (NAVLENGTH): 0.3, 0.55 and 0.8.

We grouped trials into two blocks, one per TECH. Half of the participants started with *AreaLens*; the other half with *Fisheye*. Both blocks started with a training session consisting of 3 repetitions of each of the 12 SHAPE × DENSITY × NAVLENGTH conditions presented in a random order. The operator used the first few training trials to explain the task and techniques. After the training trials, each block continued with a series of measured trials, consisting of 6 repetitions of the same 12 conditions presented in a random order. Participants were instructed to perform the task as fast as possible while minimizing the number of errors. To complete a trial, participants had to reveal the red cross through the lens and click the mouse button with the cross still visible. To avoid participants rushing through the experiment, mouse clicks that occurred while the cross was outside of the lens were counted as errors, but did not end the trial; participants still had to find the cross to complete the trial. The average duration of the experiment was 30 minutes per participant.

Quantitative Results

We used R (`http://www.r-project.org`) for our statistical analysis and in particular the `aov` command from the `stat` package. Our main measure was task completion time *MT*. As participants had to successfully complete each trial, errors were integrated in *MT* and were thus not studied on their own. We performed a full factorial nominal ANOVA for the following model:

$$MT \sim \text{TECH}\times\text{SHAPE}\times\text{DENSITY}\times\text{Random(PARTICIPANT)}.$$

We did not include NAVLENGTH in the model as we consider it as a secondary "ecological" factor whose purpose is to prevent noise due to chance, as explained earlier. We removed a few outliers: 1.44% of all trials, with unreasonable (> 1) residual/predicted ratio. Those were equally distributed among *AreaLens* and *Fisheye* conditions.

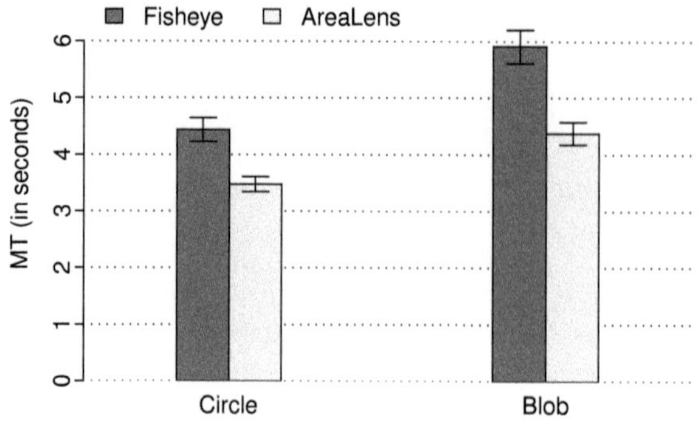

Figure 8. ***MT*** **per TECH by SHAPE. Error bars show the 95% confidence limit.**

The ANOVA reveals a significant effect of TECH on *MT* ($F_{1,11} = 17.3$, $p = 0.0016$). *AreaLens* is significantly faster than *Fisheye* yielding a 24% speed-up. As expected, we find a significant interaction TECH×SHAPE ($F_{1,11} = 13.3$, $p = 0.0039$) that can be observed in Figure 8. A post-hoc t-test with Bonferroni correction shows that *AreaLens* is significantly faster than *Fisheye* for both *Circle* ($p = 0.0002$) and *Blob* ($p < 0.0001$) island shapes, but the magnitude of the difference is larger for *Blob* (25.8%) than for *Circle* (21.6%). Thus, hypothesis *H1* is supported by our data.

The ANOVA also reveals a significant effect of DENSITY ($F_{1,11} = 119.5$, $p < 0.0001$), participants being significantly faster in *Low* density conditions. This was expected as, by design, the *High* density condition requires more navigation for the same value of NAVLENGTH. However, the ANOVA reveals neither a TECH×DENSITY nor a TECH×SHAPE×DENSITY interaction. This implies that we cannot say more than what is said in the previous paragraph on the difference between *AreaLens* and *Fisheye* with respect to the DENSITY factor (*AreaLens* is significantly faster than *Fisheye* for both densities, but the data does not show an effect of DENSITY on this difference). Thus, *H2* is not supported by the results of the experiment. Note, however, that *AreaLens* is significantly faster in *Circle* than *Blob* conditions. This might be due, in part, to the higher amount of visual change in the latter case.

Qualitative Results

At the end of the experiment, participants were asked to rank *AreaLens* and *Fisheye* and were encouraged to provide feedback. Eight participants out of twelve ranked *AreaLens* first. The other four ranked *AreaLens* and *Fisheye* ex-aequo (no participant ranked *Fisheye* first). This is consistent with quantitative results and supports *H1*. Among participants who ranked *AreaLens* and *Fisheye* ex-aequo, two said that they preferred *AreaLens* in the *Blob* condition and *Fisheye* in the *Circle* condition. Two participants found the *AreaLens* deformations sometimes annoying, though this did not impact navigation between shapes significantly. Overall, participants did not find the changing lens shape particularly distract-

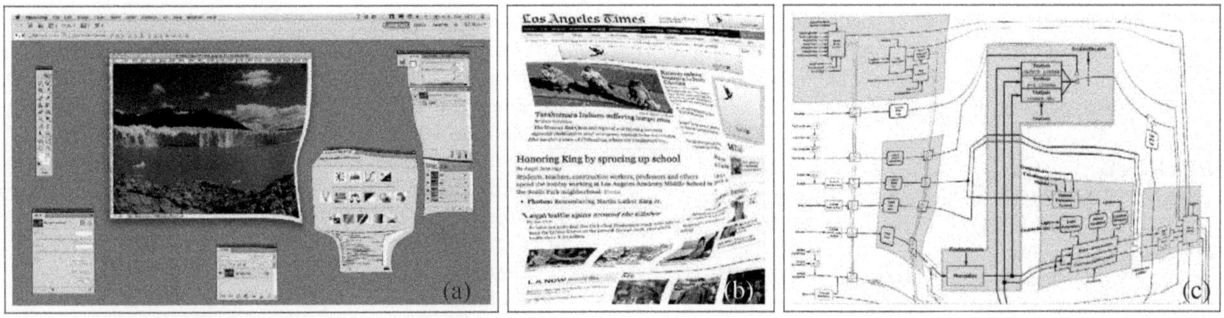

Figure 9. The AreaLens technique applied to: (a) magnifying a group of widgets in a user interface (Adobe Photoshop); (b) the Los Angeles Times Web homepage; and (c) a part of the OpenGL state machine block diagram.

ing; even if more predictable, distortion when moving classical fisheyes also entails constantly changing shapes. Some participants commented on the difference between passively watching the interface and actively operating *AreaLens*, confirming our own observations that while shape changes can be distracting in the former case, they are not in the latter. We tentatively attribute this to operators being more tightly integrated in the feedback/ feedforward loop than people passively watching the screen, and already having their attention focused on the region of interest when relocating the lens, thus better anticipating changes. One remark that came often (formulated differently) is that *Fisheye* requires more concentration because both navigation and visual search (looking for the cross) have to be performed simultaneously. Performing the task with *AreaLens* is cognitively less demanding, as the two tasks can be sequentialized: one can jump to the next shape and then perform the search on the entire island at once. Another frequent remark was that *Fisheye* is more annoying because it deforms (distorts) the islands, something that does not happen with *AreaLens*.

Summary

The results of this experiment are very encouraging: the *AreaLens* significantly outperformed a classical fisheye lens in all conditions, including *Circle*. It was not obvious that dynamic adaptation would provide any advantage in this case, given that a *Fisheye* already provides a good match in terms of shape adaptation, and that it does not suffer from potential problems of visual distraction due to dynamically changing geometry. The results indicate that the latter is actually not a significant usability issue, as it did not negatively impact *AreaLens* performance. In terms of subjective preferences, we received positive feedback from the participants. In accordance with quantitative measurements, participants did not report being distracted by the visual changes in regions of interest when using *AreaLens*. This confirms that this potential problem has a very limited impact, if any, though further investigation is required to generalize this particular finding.

DISCUSSION AND FUTURE WORK

Our implementation of JellyLenses can be applied to arbitrary 2D datasets, provided that objects of interest can be identified in the data. As discussed earlier, identifying objects to take into account during the magnification process is both a matter of deciding what objects are relevant for a given task, a highly domain-dependent problem, and obtaining the geometry of those objects. The latter question is highly dependent on the nature of the graphics. Figures 2 and 4 illustrate the use of JellyLenses on vector graphics, that make geometry information readily available. Figures 1-c and 5 show lenses applied to a satellite picture, i.e., a bitmap that only contains pixels. In such cases, geometry information can be obtained, e.g., using image processing algorithms that can extract relevant features from the original image, or through manual annotations performed by a domain expert.

JellyLenses can also apply to different contexts. For instance, they could be used as accessibility helpers for visually impaired users, to magnify widgets or groups of widgets in desktop user interfaces (Figure 9-a), or to magnify portions of Web pages such as a newspaper homepage (Figure 9-b). The technique makes it possible to display an overview of the full page, and to browse it at a readable level, somewhat like Fishnet [4] does. This can be useful in the context of users who need accessibility features, but also on mobile devices such as tablets and e-readers, that have limited screen real-estate. Note that in both of the above examples, finding objects of interest and obtaining information about their geometry is relatively straightforward: in the case of user interfaces, accessibility/automation APIs enable the automatic discovery of the UI widget hierarchy; in the case of Web pages, the CSS box model and HTML page structure can help identify and segment relevant parts of the web page. Another interesting family of graphics are block diagrams. Figure 9-c shows an example depicting part of the OpenGL state machine. Again, it is possible in such cases to automatically find objects of interest, e.g., sets of boxes, paths connecting components, or coherent sets of connected entities that form components of higher abstraction.

In this paper we break the usual behavior of fisheye lenses by proposing to dynamically change their geometry while preserving visual continuity between the focus and context regions. Our empirical evaluation shows that this approach has strong potential, though this is of course only a first step. More evaluation and more case studies are needed to better understand the advantages and weakness of the approach and of each technique. For instance, it would be interesting to evaluate the PathLens technique in path tracing tasks, and to better understand possible visual distractions caused by the various types of shape (objects of interest) and layout of these shapes. This might lead to novel adaptation techniques that use transformations that go beyond magnification (e.g., rotation). Another avenue for future work is to investigate techniques that would allow users to specify objects of interest on-the-fly, e.g., by sketching, involving them more explicitly in the adaptation process, and to couple adaptive lenses with the recently introduced undistort lenses [9].

REFERENCES

1. Appert, C., Chapuis, O., and Pietriga, E. High-precision magnification lenses. In *Proc. CHI '10*, ACM (2010), 273–282.
2. Avidan, S., and Shamir, A. Seam carving for content-aware image resizing. *ACM TOG 26*, 3 (2007).
3. Barr, A. H. Global and local deformations of solid primitives. In *Proc. SIGGRAPH '84*, ACM (1984), 21–30.
4. Baudisch, P., Lee, B., and Hanna, L. Fishnet, a fisheye web browser with search term popouts: a comparative evaluation with overview and linear view. In *Proc. AVI '04*, ACM (2004), 133–140.
5. Beier, T., and Neely, S. Feature-based image metamorphosis. In *Proc. SIGGRAPH '92*, ACM (1992), 35–42.
6. Bier, E. A., Stone, M. C., Pier, K., Buxton, W., and DeRose, T. D. Toolglass and magic lenses: the see-through interface. In *Proc. SIGGRAPH '93*, ACM (1993), 73–80.
7. Böttger, J., Brandes, U., Deussen, O., and Ziezold, H. Map warping for the annotation of metro maps. *IEEE Comput. Graph. Appl. 28* (2008), 56–65.
8. Böttger, J., Preiser, M., Balzer, M., and Deussen, O. Detail-In-Context visualization for satellite imagery. *Computer Graphics Forum 27*, 2 (2008), 587–596.
9. Brosz, J., Carpendale, S., and Nacenta, M. The undistort lens. *Computer Graphics Forum 30* (2011), 881–890.
10. Brosz, J., Samavati, F. F., Carpendale, S., and Sousa, M. C. Single camera flexible projection. In *Proc. NPAR '07*, ACM (2007), 33–42.
11. Carpendale, M. S. T., Cowperthwaite, D. J., and Fracchia, F. D. 3-dimensional pliable surfaces: for the effective presentation of visual information. In *Proc. UIST '95*, ACM (1995), 217–226.
12. Carpendale, M. S. T., Cowperthwaite, D. J., and Fracchia, F. D. Making distortions comprehensible. In *Proc. VL '97*, IEEE (1997), 36–45.
13. Carpendale, M. S. T., Ligh, J., and Pattison, E. Achieving higher magnification in context. In *Proc. UIST '04*, ACM (2004), 71–80.
14. Carpendale, M. S. T., and Montagnese, C. A framework for unifying presentation space. In *Proc. UIST '01*, ACM (2001), 61–70.
15. Cockburn, A., Karlson, A., and Bederson, B. B. A review of overview+detail, zooming, and focus+context interfaces. *ACM CSUR 41* (2009), 2:1–2:31.
16. Correa, C. D., and Silver, D. Programmable shaders for deformation rendering. In *Proc. GH '07*, EA (2007), 89–96.
17. Furnas, G. W. Generalized fisheye views. In *ACM SIGCHI Bulletin*, vol. 17, ACM (1986), 16–23.
18. Gutwin, C. Improving focus targeting in interactive fisheye views. In *Proc. CHI '02*, ACM (2002), 267–274.
19. Gutwin, C., and Fedak, C. A comparison of fisheye lenses for interactive layout tasks. In *Proc. GI '04* (2004), 213–220.
20. Hoff, III, K. E., Zaferakis, A., Lin, M., and Manocha, D. Fast and simple 2d geometric proximity queries using graphics hardware. In *Proc. I3D '01*, ACM (2001), 145–148.
21. Hornbæk, K., Bederson, B. B., and Plaisant, C. Navigation patterns and usability of zoomable user interfaces with and without an overview. *ACM ToCHI 9*, 4 (2002), 362–389.
22. Keahey, T. A., and Robertson, E. L. Nonlinear magnification fields. In *Proc. INFOVIS '97*, IEEE (1997), 51–58.
23. Kurzion, Y., and Yagel, R. Interactive space deformation with hardware-assisted rendering. *IEEE Computer Graphics and Applications 17*, 5 (1997), 66–77.
24. Laffont, P.-Y., Jun, J. Y., Wolf, C., Tai, Y.-W., Idrissi, K., Drettakis, G., and Yoon, S.-e. Interactive content-aware zooming. In *Proc. GI*, CIPS (2010), 79–87.
25. Lamar, E., Hamann, B., and Joy, K. I. A magnification lens for interactive volume visualization. In *Proc. PG '01*, IEEE (2001), 223.
26. Lamping, J., Rao, R., and Pirolli, P. A focus+context technique based on hyperbolic geometry for visualizing large hierarchies. In *Proc. CHI '95*, ACM & Addison-Wesley (1995), 401–408.
27. Leung, Y. K., and Apperley, M. D. A review and taxonomy of distortion-oriented presentation techniques. *ACM ToCHI 1* (1994), 126–160.
28. Lorensen, W. E., and Cline, H. E. Marching cubes: A high resolution 3d surface construction algorithm. In *Proc. SIGGRAPH '87*, ACM (1987), 163–169.
29. Pietriga, E., Appert, C., and Beaudouin-Lafon, M. Pointing and beyond: an operationalization and preliminary evaluation of multi-scale searching. In *Proc. CHI '07*, ACM (2007), 1215–1224.
30. Pietriga, E., Bau, O., and Appert, C. Representation-independent in-place magnification with sigma lenses. *IEEE TVCG 16*, 03 (2010), 455–467.
31. Rademacher, P. View-dependent geometry. In *Proc. SIGGRAPH '99*, ACM & Addison-Wesley (1999), 439–446.
32. Robertson, G. G., and Mackinlay, J. D. The document lens. In *Proc. UIST '93*, ACM (1993), 101–108.
33. Sarkar, M., and Brown, M. H. Graphical fisheye views. *CACM 37*, 12 (1994), 73–83.
34. Sarkar, M., Snibbe, S. S., Tversky, O. J., and Reiss, S. P. Stretching the rubber sheet: a metaphor for viewing large layouts on small screens. In *Proc. UIST '93*, ACM (1993), 81–91.
35. Schein, S., Karpen, E., and Elber, G. Real-time geometric deformation displacement maps using programmable hardware. *The Visual Computer 21*, 8 (2005), 791–800.
36. Sederberg, T. W., and Parry, S. R. Free-form deformation of solid geometric models. In *Proc. SIGGRAPH '86*, ACM (1986), 151–160.
37. Spindler, M., Bubke, M., Germer, T., and Strothotte, T. Camera textures. In *Proc. GRAPHITE '06*, ACM (2006), 295–302.
38. Wang, H., Mucha, P. J., and Turk, G. Water drops on surfaces. *ACM Trans. Graph. 24* (July 2005), 921–929.
39. Wang, Y.-S., Lee, T.-Y., and Tai, C.-L. Focus+context visualization with distortion minimization. *IEEE TVCG 14*, 6 (2008), 1731–1738.
40. Wyvill, G. Data structure for soft objects. *The visual computer 2*, 4 (1986), 227–234.
41. Yang, Y., Chen, J. X., and Beheshti, M. Nonlinear Perspective Projections and Magic Lenses: 3D View Deformation. *IEEE Comput. Graph. Appl. 25*, 1 (2005), 76–84.
42. Zhao, X., Zeng, W., Gu, D., Kaufman, A., Xu, W., and Mueller, K. Conformal magnifier: A focus+context technique with local shape preservation. *IEEE TVCG* (2012). PrePrint.

PiVOT: Personalized View-Overlays for Tabletops

Abhijit Karnik, Diego Martinez Plasencia, Walterio Mayol-Cuevas, Sriram Subramanian
Department of Computer Science,
University of Bristol, UK
karnik, diegomp1982, wmayol, sriram @cs.bris.ac.uk

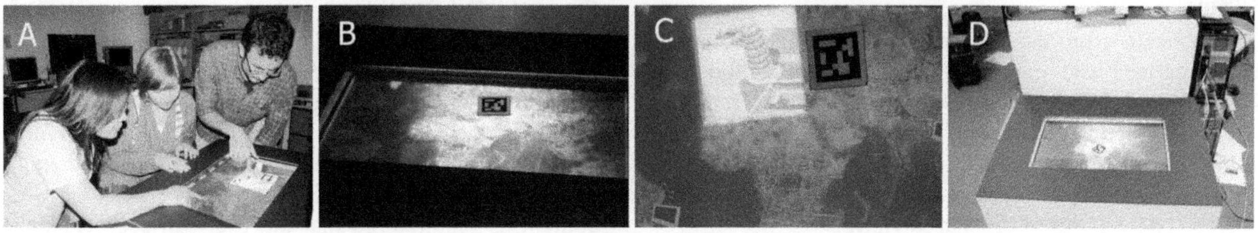

Figure 1: A) One user sees a personalized overlay (*'photoshopped in'* for illustration) which is not visible to the group. The group continues their task unhindered. B) PiVOT in operation; *Shared view* visible to all users. C) *Personal overlay* (visible to one user): A marker placed by user tells PiVOT where to show the overlay. D: PiVOT system.

ABSTRACT
We present PiVOT, a tabletop system aimed at supporting mixed-focus collaborative tasks. Through two view-zones, PiVOT provides personalized views to individual users while presenting an unaffected and unobstructed shared view to all users. The system supports multiple personalized views which can be present at the same spatial location and yet be only visible to the users it belongs to. The system also allows the creation of personal views that can be either 2D or (auto-stereoscopic) 3D images. We first discuss the motivation and the different implementation principles required for realizing such a system, before exploring different designs able to address the seemingly opposing challenges of shared and personalized views. We then implement and evaluate a sample prototype to validate our design ideas and present a set of sample applications to demonstrate the utility of the system.

Author Keywords
Multi-view, Lumisty, multi-user, tabletop.

ACM Classification
H.5.2 **[Information interfaces and presentation]:** User Interfaces. - Graphical user interfaces;

INTRODUCTION
Digital tabletops have been used to support multiple users to perform collaborative tasks such as planning using maps, CAD applications, or educational tutoring. However, such collaborative applications usually involve a mixture of individual and shared activities, and users often need to transition between these two activities [21]. In this context, access to personalized views on-demand becomes a necessity in order to support individual activities. Such a situation arises in planning or design tasks where one or more members break off to complete an action, or when some information is available to or restricted to certain users only. For example, in a war-room discussion, shared views can be presented to all participants to provide general awareness of a situation while personalized situational awareness details are presented to specific users only.

The need for individual, or even private tasks, conflicts with the all-sharing nature of tabletops. Individual tasks usually require dedicated use of a small part of the tabletop, which can affect the shared view of the rest of the users [11]. This is in addition to any privacy requirements. From an implementation viewpoint, the default solution is to use mobile/private devices for personalized views and which is at odds with the needs of a collaborative task.

The ideal situation to address these trade-offs would be the one depicted in Figure 1, a collaborative tabletop able to have exclusive and personal views overlaid on top of the *shared view* and able to operate in a *walkup and use* scenario. These *personal views* include *overlays* that allow each user to carry out individual tasks through views which are exclusive to them and thus not visible to the rest of the group. As a result, no user loses context of the group activity and can also perform individual activities concurrently.

We introduce PiVOT (see Figure 1 D) as a solution to these challenges. PiVOT provides two distinct views - a *shared view* (Figure 1 B) and a *personal view* depending on the zone inside which the user is with respect to the tabletop. The *shared view* is visible to all users while the personal view can be customized to contain *personal overlays* visible only to specific users. These overlays (Figure 1 C) can be used to undertake individual tasks. They co-exist on the same surface of the tabletop and do not interfere with the shared view. This is a key contribution of this paper.

UIST '12, October 7–10, 2012, Cambridge, Massachusetts, USA.

PiVOT uses two display elements in tandem, one to show the *personal views* and the other for the *shared view*. Both elements present information on the same tabletop but their visibility depends on the position (and potentially the identity) of the user. This works because each display acts as a see-through element for the other view. We analyze the principles of operation of these displays and explore different implementation possibilities using suitable see-through elements.

We implement a proof-of-concept prototype that relies on using polarized and unpolarized light sources, modified Liquid Crystal (LC) panels and Lumisty film to present the two non-conflicting views. We finally illustrate the capabilities of the system using several demo applications and evaluate the amount of interference from the *personal view* as perceived by a user of the *shared view*.

The main contributions of this paper are:

- Present a system that displays a *shared view* which is unaffected by collocated *personal overlays*.
- Analyze the operating principles and identify the most promising physical arrangements.
- Implementation of a working prototype to validate our design and evaluate the image quality for *shared* and *personal views*.
- Through a series of example applications demonstrate the capabilities of the implementation.

RELATED WORK

Group activities around interactive tabletops usually involve *mixed-focus collaboration* (individuals work together and break-off for one-person tasks at regular intervals) [3]. This results in *coupling* between individuals as they transition from one activity to another [21].

Some tools have been proposed to support this kind of collaboration. *Filters* [21] or *transparent overlays* [1] affect the whole tabletop, which encumbers simultaneous shared tasks. *Lenses* or *shadow boxes* [21] only apply to a part of the tabletop, alleviating *interference* [11,16] and enforcing *territoriality* [19,22].

Many of the systems using these tools rely on a single-view tabletop. Thus, all the views and personal *territories* are spatially collocated in the same view and interfere with each other for placement. The availability of personal *territories* is limited by the arrangement and size of other *territories* and *workspace coordination* [18] becomes a necessity. Even though increased size and spatial separation can mitigate these conflicts, single-view tabletops will always be subject to *interference.*

As an alternative, some authors propose digital canvas stitched together with multiple display elements, as an alternative to single-view tabletops. As seen with WeSpace [23] and Geospatial [2] multiple devices can be interconnected to facilitate collaboration with spatial separation between shared and personal view spaces. Other implementations like E-conic [12] and LUMAR [13] integrate handheld displays with the tabletop. However as discussed by Ryall et al. [16], the increased size or number of screens doesn't necessarily provide additional advantages.

Another approach is using *overlapping views*, i.e. to display several views, collocated on the tabletop space but with minimal or no interference among them. The position of the user or special devices will determine the view that each user will see. Projection-based systems such as SecondLight [4] and Visibility Control System (VCS) [17] allow *filters* and *lenses* [21] to be implemented as tangible overlays. SecondLight uses a switchable diffuser to produce a *shared view*, while projecting contents in users' personal handheld-diffusers. These diffusers, when lying on the table occlude the *shared view*, and their contents are visible to other users. VCS uses polarizing filters to filter content as required, so that the user can see personalized views. However, this possibility is only made available to one user.

The *overlapping views* based on the user's position can be implemented using the view control made possible by Lumisty film [20]. Lumisight [9], Ulteriorscape [5], TaPS [10], and Bounsight [14] present different alternatives in which people seated around a table can be shown different views based on their position on the same display surface. These systems divide the space around the tabletop in several regions, so that people can see different contents on the tabletop according to the region they occupy. However as the film acts as single-view diffuser over a fixed view area, two users in the same region cannot get different views. Besides, such diffuser film on its own doesn't support stereoscopic views without additional devices (like HMDs).

Some displays have demonstrated the ability to provide multiple users with auto-stereoscopic views (wherein each eye of the user receives a different perspective of the 3D view, without requiring special devices such as HMDs or shutter glasses). IllusionHole [7], Tabletop Autostereoscopic System (TADS) [24] and MUSTARD [6] allow this by the use of blocking masks and viewing holes and deliver multiple views to individuals based on their spatial position relative to the system.

To summarize, delivering overlapping *personal overlays* which do not interfere with the *shared view* can potentially enhance mixed-focus collaboration but challenging to provide with current tabletop display technology. The implementations which currently do support overlapping views do so with restrictions. Some don't restrict the visibility of views to intended for one user only; others fail to support several users. Moreover, existing designs share a common deficiency: all the views support the same kind of content, let it be 2D or stereo 3D. PiVOT provides personalized non-stitching view overlaps to support these functionalities.

PIVOT: DESIGN & PRINCIPLES

PiVOT is a collaborative tabletop display that is designed to support mixed-focus collaboration. PiVOT consists of two view-zones: one that provides the *shared view* and a second zone that provides the *personal view* to all users.

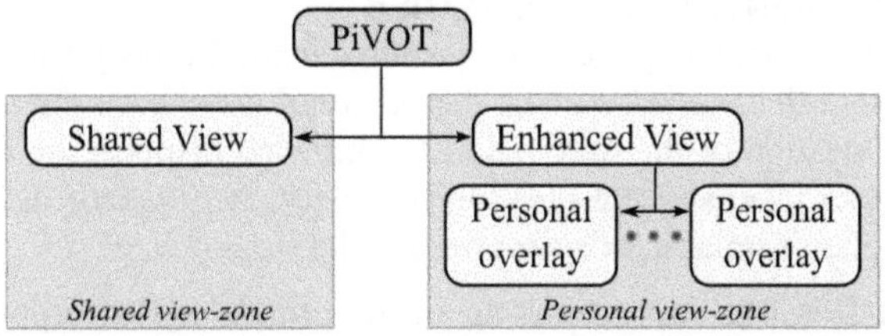

Figure 2: Relationship between different views available in PiVOT.

The relationship between different view-zones and views in PiVOT is illustrated in Figure 2. All users can see the *shared view* at all times but at any moment a user can access his/her *personal view* by changing their position (say for example by leaning forward). This supports the *mixed-focus* collaboration requirement of allowing a user to dynamically transition between individual and group activities by e.g. leaning forward or sitting back. Other users viewing the *shared view* are not affected by the presence of the *personal views* in the same space.

Personal views can either be overlays that are specific to a user or view enhancements that are accessible to any user who enters the personal view-zone. This e*nhanced view* carries additional information that individual users may find useful in a collaborative activity but can interfere with the group activity. Any user can access the *enhanced view* by changing their position to enter the personal view-zone.

The personal view-zone can also contain *Personal overlays* which are individual overlays attached to a specific user. This means, any user entering the personal view-zone will not see the *personal overlay* unless it is meant for him/her. At the same time, multiple users can have their *personal overlays* in the same display location. The system manages the presentation of information on the *personal overlay* such that there is minimal interference between the competing content views.

A final unique feature of PiVOT is that the *personal overlays* support *mixed-content* (both 2D and 3D). While one user is viewing auto-stereoscopic 3D content within one overlay, the other user could be viewing 2D content on another overlay. *Mixed-conten*t also does not affect the requirement that the information meant for one user must be visible only to that user only.

By default, PiVOT operates like a standard tabletop, allowing all users to interact with the *shared view*. In the default mode, all inputs are directed to the *shared view*. But if identity and head-position of the user associated with the input is available then PiVOT also allows users to interact with content in the personal view-zone. The identity and head-position is used to first establish if a user is looking at content in the personal view-zone and if so directs input to that zone. A user positioned in the shared view-zone (and hence not necessarily tracked by PiVOT) can touch the surface where another user's *personal overlay* exists. However PiVOT directs this input to the *shared view* leaving the *personal overlay* unmodified. Only inputs from the owner of the *personal overlay* can affect the *personal overlay*. This approach allows shared and personal views to be considered as two separated workspaces, containing different contexts that the user can interact with depending on the user's head position.

PiVOT Components

PiVOT works by operating two displays simultaneously arranged in tandem, one for displaying the *shared view* and another one displaying the *personal view*, containing the *enhanced view* and *personal overlays* of all the users.

The *shared view* has to be visible to any user located in a specific region. This view is independent of how many users are using the system and if they are also accessing *personal overlays* or not. PiVOT also has to use another region to display *personal overlays* where and when required by the users. The display that contains them must not interfere with the operation of the *shared view* and each overlay must only be visible to its associated user.

As the system consists of two display elements that work in tandem for displaying both the views, each display element needs to be selectively transparent or see-through for the content meant for the other display. This core feature of the two elements to be selectively see-through can be achieved in many ways.

See-through Display Elements

See-through display elements fall into three categories. These are: temporal switching elements; spatial view control elements and polarization dependent elements. Each of these three categories relies on two possible techniques: diffusion or direct display. Diffusion based displays require a projector as their image-source during their operation in diffuser mode or non-see-through mode. Direct displays rely on a light-source but form the image on their own. We briefly discuss each to explore their suitability.

Temporal switching elements: SecondLight [4] is a good example of a temporal switching see-through element. Using a switchable LC diffuser synchronized with fast optical shutters, see-through content can be projected when the diffuser is transparent. When the diffuser is switched to its diffuser mode, content is displayed on it. However, with this implementation, the see-through content needs to be viewed by using a handheld diffuser making it visible to all users and occluding their view of the shared content.

Spatial view control elements: These elements are see through when viewed from certain positions and are transparent from other angles. The two common examples of this type are Holographic Optical Element (HOE) and Lumisty film.

HOE acts as a diffuser surface for projected information. The advantage of HOE is that multiple views can be generated on the same surface, so it could be used to display the *personal overlays*. It also acts as a see-through element. The trade-off with using HOEs is that each user would require one projector per eye for the overlays.

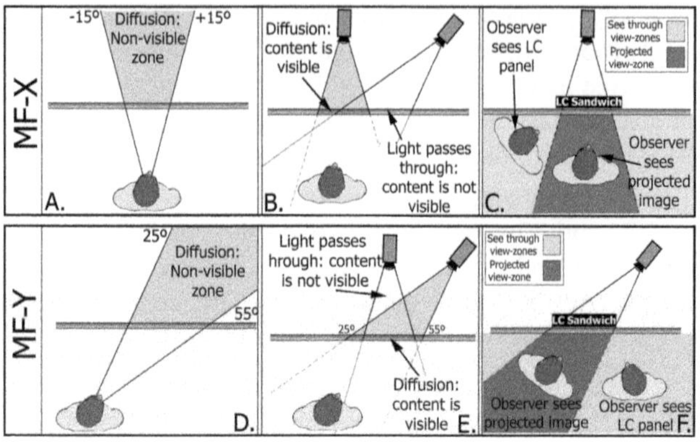

Figure 3: Lumisty film diffuses light at specific angles. Hence objects behind the film are not visible (A, D). The film also acts as a diffuser for projectors (B, F). PiVOT uses both features (C, F): In the *projected view-zone*, observes see the projected image, but not the data on the LC sandwich; the opposite happens in the *see-through zone*.

Lumisty film as used by Lumisight [9] is a view-control film that diffuses light incident at specific angles. A dual projector solution, as shown with Ulteriorscape [5], can hence be used to implement personalized view overlay within the see-through view-zone. A passive tangible overlay made up of the same film can act as the secondary diffuser surface. However as with the switchable diffuser option, once any user is positioned in the view-zone of the second diffuser, only one view is visible. This implies that while Lumisty can serve as the *shared view* display, we need to use a different approach for the *personal view*.

Polarization dependent elements: These elements have selective behavior towards polarized light. With VCS [17], the polarized light is blocked using filters. Another system is the LC sandwich arrangement as shown in MUSTARD [6]. That system is capable of acting as a see-through element for unpolarized light and can deal with multiple personalized views using hole-mask patterns sourced by a polarized light source. Each of the personalized views is only visible at the specific location where the user is situated.

An implementation using static patterns as shown in TADS can also present the view overlays along with the shared view. Both MUSTARD and TADS require precise eye-position information to work and tend to degrade in operation as the number of users increases. However, MUSTARD appears a favorable choice because its see-through capability allows a secondary device to display the *shared view*. MUSTARD could simply display the *personal view*, with no degradation in quality due to the number of users that interact with the *shared view*.

It is clear that as a standalone element none of the see-through elements can provide the solution desired. In the next section we describe a solution using Lumisty film as the *shared view* source and a LC sandwich element as the *personal view* source.

IMPLEMENTATION STRATEGIES

PiVOT brings together a LC sandwich and Lumisty film to present the *shared view* or the *personal view*, according to the location of the user. The LC sandwich displays the *enhanced view* and the *personal overlays*. A projector using Lumisty film as a diffuser presents the *shared view*.

The first two subsections detail the principles that support the correct operation of PiVOT. We first explore the behavior of Lumisty film to produce two non-conflicting co-located views of the table-top. Then we explore the LC sandwich arrangement to support user-specific or personal overlays. In the third subsection we analyze possible strategies to arrange PiVOT's basic components (projector, Lumisty film and LC panels) in order to comply with our requirements.

Selective workspaces with Lumisty film

Lumisty film diffuses light incident on it at a specific angle. This allows it to be used as a selective projection screen that displays its contents based on the position of the user.

Two types of Lumisty films will be analyzed (MF-X and MF-Y), each of them operating on different angles. MF-X film diffuses light incident on it at angles between (-15°, +15°) to the normal. MF-Y film diffuses light incident on it at angles between (+25°, +55°) to the normal. While a third type (MF-Z) exists, we do not discuss its operation in this paper. The film diffuses incoming light in the ranges specified for each film. As a result, an observer will not see any object behind the film in that range (shaded zones in Figure 3 A, D)

This diffusing effect of Lumisty films can also be used for projectors. A projector needs its light to hit a surface and get diffused so that its image becomes visible. As a result, if a projector is positioned so that its light hits the film in the appropriate angle, its contents will become visible to the users. If the projector's light is not incident in the appropriate angle, its light will simply pass through the film and not be visible (see Figure 3 B, E).

However, Lumisty films do not diffuse light in every direction. Observers must be located in a specific area (*projected view-zones* in Figure 3 C, F) to view the image; otherwise, they will not be able to see it (*see-through view-zones* in Figure 3 C, F).

These features have been used in our advantage during the creation of PiVOT to support simultaneous and collocated *shared views* and *personal views*. If a user is in the *projected view-zone,* the user will see the image (i.e. the *shared view*) projected on the Lumisty film. However, if the user is in the *see-through zone* the image from the projector is not visible but he will be able to see the object behind the Lumisty film, that is, the LC sandwich that displays the *personal view* containing the *personal overlays*. Practically, this allows a seated user to switch between these two workspaces by simply leaning forward or sitting back.

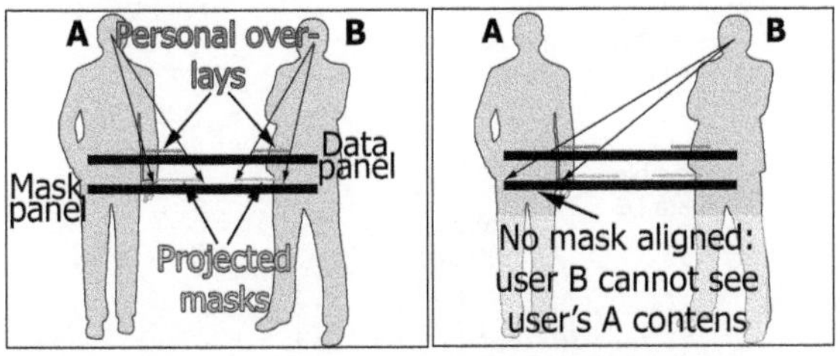

Figure 4: Masks in the data panel align to the personal overlays displayed in the data panel. The position of each user's eyes is used to compute this projection (left). From user B's point of view, there is no mask behind user A's overlay (that region of the mask is black). As a result, user B cannot see user's A contents (right).

LC sandwich for user-specific Personal Overlays

PiVOT uses a pair of LC screens [6] to display *personal overlays*. There are two key features of the LC sandwich setup that allow it to support the unique requirements of *personal overlays* on PiVOT.

The LC sandwich acts as a see-through element for unpolarized light while using polarized light to display content. To achieve this, a setup as shown in Figure 5 is used. The LC sandwich contains an unmodified LC panel that acts as a source of polarized light. This is called the mask panel. The other panel (data panel) is modified by removing its rear polarizer. With this arrangement, the content displayed on the data panel is only visible if illuminated by polarized light from the mask panel. By displaying special light patterns on the mask panels, we can also control which user sees which part of the data panel (see Figure 4 right). By rapidly switching the patterns, it is possible to deliver different content to different users at the same time, without them seeing content meant for other users. It is also possible to deliver different images to each user's eye, providing support for stereo 3D graphics. The operation of mask pattern and underlying methods to do so are explored in detail in MUSTARD [6].

Finally any unpolarized light (e.g. from a projector) passing through the LC sandwich will not make the content on the data panel visible. At the same time, the content carried by the unpolarized light is also not affected. Thus the LC sandwich is included in PiVOT to:

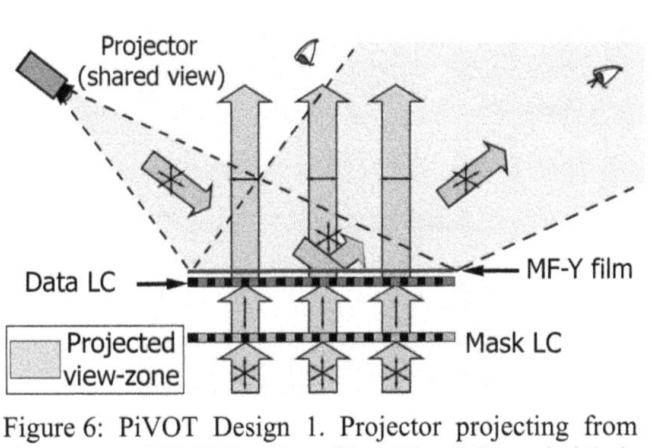

Figure 6: PiVOT Design 1. Projector projecting from above onto MF-Y Lumisty film. The LC sandwich is placed below.

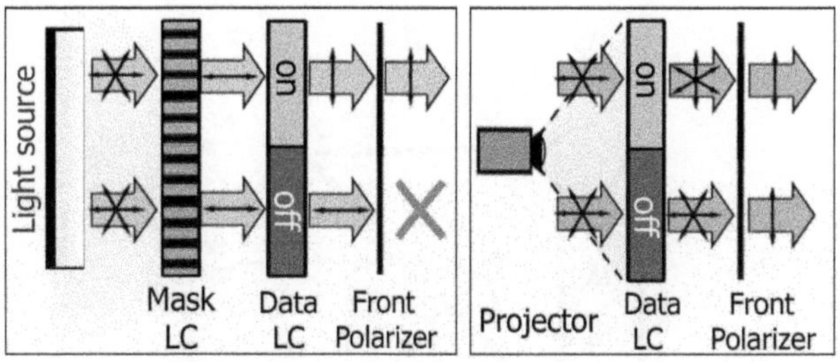

Figure 5: Basic operation of the LC sandwich. The data panel interacts (block/transmit) with polarized light (one axis arrows) coming from the mask panel, according to the information that it wants to display (left). It does not interact with the non-polarized light coming from the projector allowing it to pass through (right).

Present Personal Views: The rear panel (mask panel) acts as a source of light that makes it possible to present *Enhanced views* and *Personal Overlays.* Overlays are visible only from the position of its associated user (see Figure 4 left). As the mask is not aligned for the rest of the users they will not be able to see other users' personal overlays (see Figure 4 right). Even in case of conflict (two overlays in the same space), the mask pattern allows conflict resolution so that each user sees their view only.

Support mixed 2D & 3D content: This is possible by using different masks. A fully white mask can be used to display text, videos or 2D contents in general. Random Hole (RH) masks [6,24] and vertical parallax barriers (VPB) [15] can also be implemented to provide support for stereo 3D contents. The type of mask can be determined based on content and conflict with other users' masks. The RH mask is the default fallback in presence of conflict as it (using conflict functions [6]) can display each user's *personal overlay* with minimal interference from other overlays.

Be transparent to the shared view: The LC sandwich does not disrupt the operation of the projector on the Lumisty film. This is true even if this image is projected through the data panel of the sandwich. As shown in Figure 5 left, the data panel can be used to prevent horizontally polarized light coming from the mask panel to be presented to the user. However, the light coming from the projector is not polarized (see Figure 5 right). As a result, the data panel will remove the part of the light of the projector that is horizontally polarized, but most of the light will still pass through and reach the Lumisty film on the other side.

Possible Arrangements

There are several potential arrangements of the LC-sandwich, the projector and the Lumisty film to support operation of PiVOT. We identify and analyze some of these arrangements here.

1. Top Projection Using Reflection: In this arrangement the projector is placed on top of the table at an angle to hit the MF-Y Lumisty film at its blocking angle. It displays the *shared view* and its image is visible in the *projected view-zone* (see Figure 6). The LC sandwich operates independently, below the Lumisty film and displays the person-

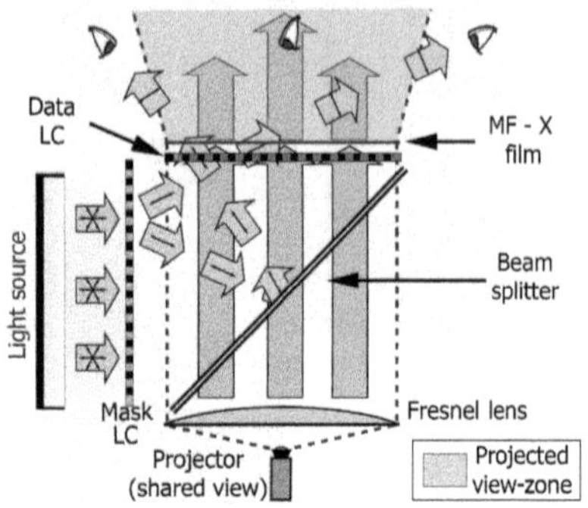

Figure 7: PiVOT Design 2. The projector-Fresnel setup projects the shared view onto the MF-X Lumisty film. Beam-splitter allows overlays to be visible from both sides of the tabletop surface.

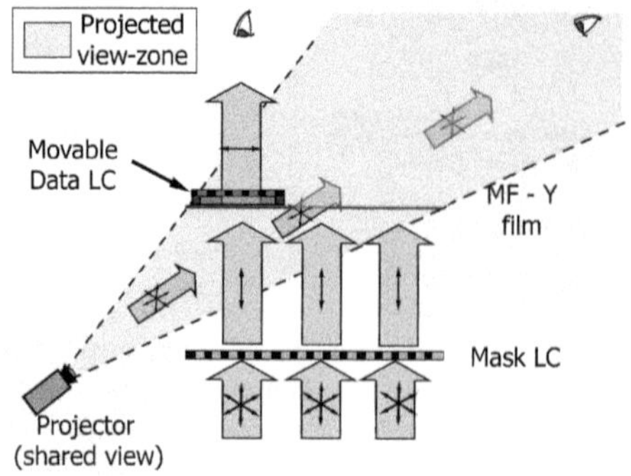

Figure 8: PiVOT Design 3. The overlay as an active element. MF-Y Lumisty film is between the movable LCD data panel and the mask panel of the LC sandwich.

al view. The main benefit of this arrangement is its simplicity, but it fails to provide a good quality for the *shared view.* Lumisty film reflects only ~15% of the light at its blocking angle. Thus a high power projector is required to achieve satisfactory brightness and contrast. Besides, overhead projectors can cause hand-occlusions and cast shadows in a collaborative setting.

2. Beam-splitter with Fresnel lens: This arrangement uses a MF-X Lumisty film and a projector pointing at the tabletop from below displaying the *shared view*. The data panel is located right under the Lumisty film and the mask panel is placed perpendicular to them (see Figure 7). The *projected view-zone* of this setting lies above the tabletop and *see-through view-zones* are available on both sides of the tabletop. A beam-splitter is added to the setup to allow visibility of the personal views from both sides. As shown in Figure 7, on one side, the personal view is in direct line of sight from the user to the mask panel. On the other side the user reflection of the mask panel on the beam-splitter is used.

The projector uses a Fresnel lens to reduce the size of the setting, Having the light hit the Lumisty film in the range of (-15°,+15°) would force a projector covering a table of one meter wide to be placed at 1.86 meters below the tabletop. The Fresnel lens removes this limitations, ensures all beams to pass through the beam splitter at the same angle (to avoid distortion) and hit the Lumisty film at its optimal angle for diffusion. However, the size of the beam-splitter must be equal to the size of the tabletop. This leads to a problem with scalability of this design as a large beam-splitter is not easily available.

3. Active tangible overlay: This arrangement has similarities with LUMAR [13] which uses a small handheld placed on the table to show additional views. The arrangement uses a MX-Y Lumisty film and a short-throw projector to present the *shared view*. The mask panel is located at a fixed distance under the Lumisty film. As a major difference, this setting uses a small LCD panel as an active tangible overlay as seen in Figure 8. This LCD panel is modified to act as the data panel part of the LC sandwich but can be moved and positioned as desired. When placed on the tabletop, data on the panel becomes visible when light from the mask panel passes through it.

However, since the small LCD panel allows the diffuse unpolarized light from the *shared view* to pass through unaffected, the *personal overlay* is only visible to the owner of the overlay. At the same time, other users can continue seeing the *shared view* at the same spot where the overlay rests, even though some distortion can exist. Another benefit of this setting is that the native resolution of the movable LCD panel can be used to display the personal overlay, while other settings only use a relatively small part of the resolution of their data panels.

4. Passive tangible overlay: In contrast to the rest of the arrangements, this uses the LC sandwich to present the *shared view*. These contents are visible from above the

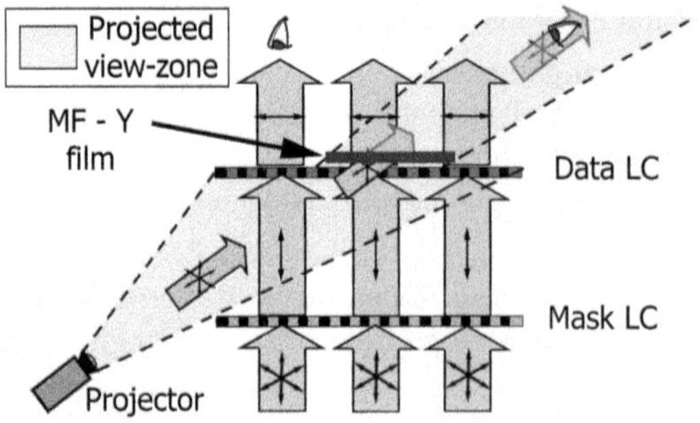

Figure 9: PiVOT Design 4. The overlay as a passive element. MF-Y Lumisty film used to view an overlay while the LC sandwich presents shared view above the tabletop.

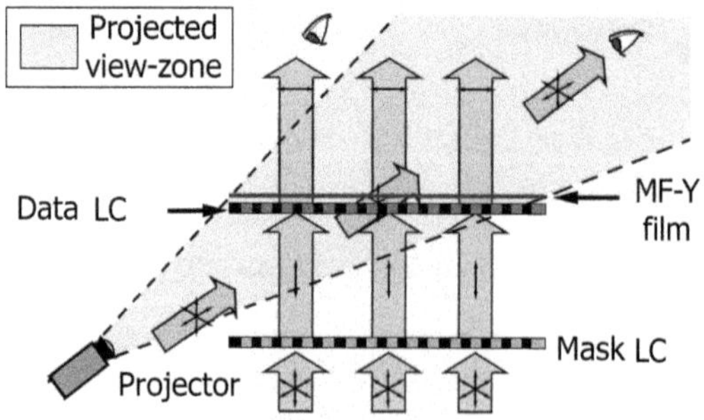

Figure 10: PiVOT Design 5. Projector projecting from below onto MF-Y Lumisty film. The LC sandwich is placed below the film and the overlays are visible from above the tabletop.

tabletop (see *see-through view-zone* in Figure 9). A projector is then used to display *personal overlays* onto small movable patches of MX-Y Lumisty film, which are visible from the size. This setup is advantageous when the tasks involved in the *shared view* require stereoscopic 3D contents, while personal tasks have a preference for 2D contents. In this context, the LC sandwich can be used to render stereo 3D contents for all the users (i.e. using hole masks, as described in [6,24]), while 2D contents can be projected on patches of Lumisty film.

5. Rear Projection Using Diffusion: This arrangement, shown Figure 10, is an alternate form of the passive tangible overlay with some differences. Instead of using Lumisty patch, the whole tabletop is covered with the film. The *shared view* can therefore be presented on the film and the overlays are generated by the LC sandwich. The *shared view* is now limited to 2D content but the overlays can display both 2D and 3D contents. This arrangement leads to a compact design of the tabletop, and its hardware requirements are minimal.

PIVOT PROTOTYPE IMPLEMENTATION

We explored creating a prototype based on the *Active Tangible Overlay* design but we quickly realized that the operation of this prototype didn't work as expected, due to the arrangement of the display elements. Although Lumisty acts as a see-through element it affects the polarization of the light passing through it. So light from the mask panel loses its polarization after passing through the Lumisty film thus destroying the functioning of the LC sandwich. Our working prototype of PiVOT is based on the *Rear projection with Diffusion* design (Design 5) as it offered the greatest flexibility in operation and can be implemented by modifying off-the-shelf components.

The hardware prototype of PiVOT consisted of an LC Sandwich for creating personal view and a projected display for the *shared view* (see Figure 11). For the personal *view* we used two modified LG IPS2321P 23", 1980x1080 LCD monitors to build the LC sandwich. The LC panels

Figure 11: Overview of the project implemented: (a) External appearance; (b) general view of the projector and the LC sandwich; Lumisty film is applied on the data panel (c), the mask panel and the diffuser are located bellow the data panel at a distance of 10 centimeters.

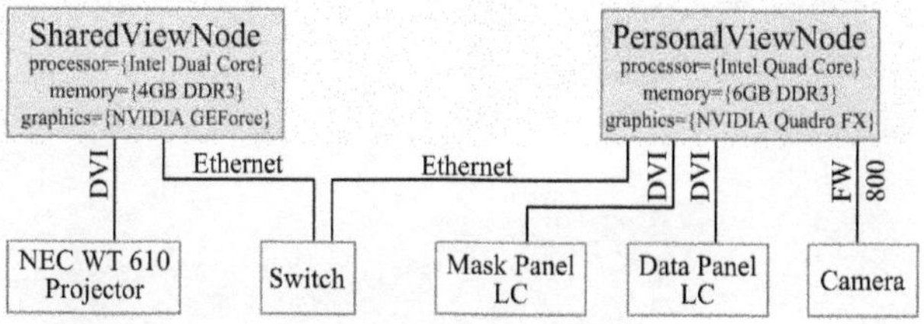

Figure 12: System Architecture for PiVOT.

were dismounted from their frames and the rear polarizer was removed from one LC to use it as the data panel. Both panels were mounted parallel to each other with a separation of 10 cm on a custom frame. The light source and diffuser that comes with the IPS2321P monitor were used as the source of diffused light for our LC sandwich.

The *shared view* was implemented by using a NEC WT610 short-throw projector mounted and adjusted so that it could project its image through the 10 centimeter gap between the two LC panels. Lumisty MX-Y film was stuck to the top LC panel and used as the diffusion surface for the image coming from the projector.

PiVOT requires using a 3D tracking system to determine the position of both the *personal overlays* and the user's eyes. In this prototype, the tracking subsystem was implemented on top of ARToolKitPlus, using a Grasshopper Express GX-FW-10K3M-C Firewire camera working at a resolution of 1024x768 and at 60 fps. The user's heads were tracked using ARToolKitPlus markers worn by the users. The eye positions were estimated using a fixed offset from the markers. The system also tracked tangible fiducial markers and single finger touches to interact with the tabletop. The complete system architecture is described in Figure 12.

A software framework was created to support the creation of applications for the tabletop, supporting three modes of operation: monocular, VPB and RH masks. The first mode works well with 2D contents and non-stereo motion parallax 3D contents. The second and third modes are used to generate stereo 3D contents. Ogre 3D was used as the rendering engine to generate the 3D contents, the masks and to compute the required mask projections. NVidia Cg programs were used to merge the 3D contents and their masks and to run the conflict resolution functions (see [6]). OSC commands on top of UDP were used to synchronize both computers. *PersonalViewNode* acted as a server, running the logic of the application and the subsystems that allowed it to generate the *personal overlays. SharedViewNode* acted as a slave, containing a local copy of the contents to display and reacting to the OSC commands received.

EXAMPLE APPLICATIONS

Two test bed applications have been implemented to illustrate the capabilities of the system.

The first one is a geospatial exploration application using Google maps that is inspired by the Multi-user geospatial system from Forlines et al [2]. Our application provides a

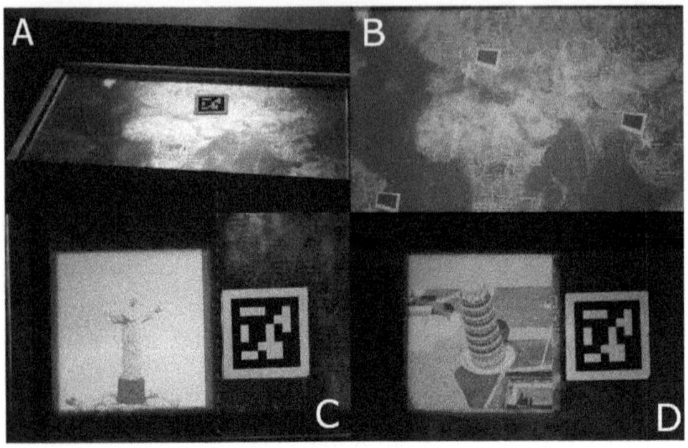

Figure 13: Map application on PiVOT. (A) *Shared view* (B) *Personal overlay* zone with additional information. (C) & (D) Two *personal overlays* showing 3D content.

shared view that allows users to visualize and explore maps (see Figure 13 A). When users lean-forward they get access to an *enhanced view* that is visible inside the personal view-zone and that shows flags on important world landmarks. In this way users know about the availability of important additional information.

The icons in Figure 13 B indicate these locations which include landmarks like the city of Pisa in Italy and Sydney in Australia. This *enhanced view* information is not available in the *shared view,* but available to any user who leans forward to enter the personal view-zone. Once inside the personal view-zone, users can place a tangible marker on map spots to create a *personal overlay* and explore the monuments, by moving the marker or moving themselves (see Figure 13 C, D). These marker-based *personal overlays* are personal to the user placing the tag. Markers are tied to specific users who are also tracked by the system and when the user moves, the *personal overlay* is updated so a perspective corrected 3D rendering of the building is displayed. Furthermore, any other user leaning forward at a different location will *not* see this personal overlay but will instead continue to see the *enhanced view*. We are able to manage the visibility of *personal overlays* by using a Random Hole mask at the location of the marker in mask panels of the LC sandwich.

The second application is from an educational context and meant to teach human anatomy (see Figure 14). The *shared view* allows users to explore a 3D model of a human body (see Figure 14 A). The *enhanced view* which is accessed by leaning forward contains information about the organs that can be examined with a *personal overlay*. Users can access the extra information both by placing fiducial markers on the icon or by touching them with their fingers (see Figure 14 C). In these *personal overlays* users can look at *medical* reports which can contain text, videos or other kinds of information (see Figure 14 D). Organs are displayed using 3D models. The different techniques to display 3D contents (monocular, VPB and RH mask) are available.

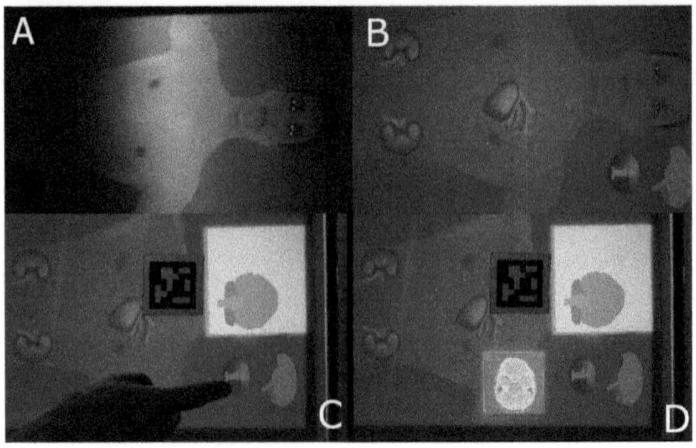

Figure 14: Anatomy application on PiVOT. (A) *Shared view* (B) *Personal view* showing location of additional content. (C) User with access to one *personal overlay* about to trigger one more. (D) User with access to two *mixed-content (2D and 3D) personal overlays.*

EVALUATION

There are two ways in which *personal overlays* may cause interference. First, the *personal overlays* can cause interference with the *shared view*. This interference is what PiVOT proposes to solve.

Second, *personal overlays* can interfere with each other when they are collocated in the same display area. This interference is visually relevant to the LC sandwich only. The LC sandwich approach described in MUSTARD [6] details the use of RH masks and underlying pixel conflict functions to resolve this interference. A detailed evaluation of interference and image quality of views has been performed for MUSTARD [6]. Their results and conclusion are also applicable to PiVOT's LC sandwich, so we do not repeat the study.

We however, carry out a system evaluation to examine the interference caused by the *personal overlays* on the *shared view* for PiVOT.

Metrics

We evaluate using two metrics: Peak Signal to Noise Ratio (PSNR) and the Quality Mean Opinion Score (Q_{MOS}) from Mantuik's HDR-VDP2 [8]. PSNR measures how much noise (from the overlay) is present in the shared view. Q_{MOS} quantifies the interference from the overlays as perceived by human eyes.

Setup

Both metrics use a reference image and a test image for comparison. Two positions that simulated the users sitting around the tabletop were selected to create the images. At each position, the users' eyes were 80 cm from the center of the tabletop. The first position placed the projection center-line, the center of the tabletop and the user's eyes in the same plane.

The second position simulated that of a user sitting next to the first user. We use the PiVOT implementation described earlier to show the images. A Canon 550D camera, placed at the eye positions, was used to capture the images. The zoom was set to maximize the coverage of the tabletop and photographs were taken at f/8; 1/30s; ISO-1600.

Procedure

We evaluate 5 scenarios of operation, three of these depict scenarios with maximum possible interference from the overlays and two are of the system in normal operation. The different content on the LC sandwich are: black background (B in Figure 15), white background (W), black & white pinstripes (Pin), map application showing *shared view* and an *enhanced view* in the LC panels (SV) and finally map application as before but with an additional *personal overlay*.

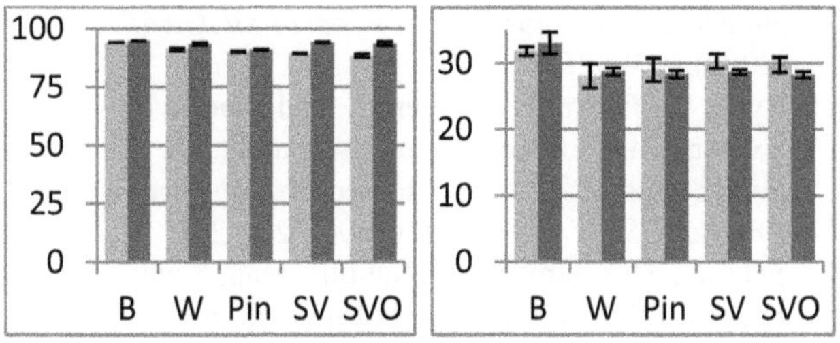

Figure 15: Image quality scores for each position. Q_{MOS} (left) and PSNR (right). Shared View (SV) and Shared View with Overlay (SV+O) depict normal operation mode.

For each position, the reference image was taken with the LC sandwich panels off while the *shared view* from the map application was projected on the Lumisty film. Five test images were captured for each position and each scenario (25 test images per position), with the panels turned on and the *shared view* being shown on the Lumisty film.

Results

Q_{MOS} scores were computed using the reference implementation (version 2.1). The highest possible Q_{MOS} score is 100 and means no difference in the test and reference images. As can be seen from Figure 15 (Left) the Q_{MOS} values in our evaluation are close to 100, implying there is almost no difference between the reference image and the test image. The lowest score obtained was 88.85 for shared view (SV) and SV with overlay (SV+O) were between 88.85 and 94.41. The PSNR scores for all conditions show a similar trend to the Q_{MOS} values. We can infer that the interference from the overlays is low enough for our concept to work.

DISCUSSION

Our evaluation used a range of interfering images in the personal overlays that were designed to explicitly highlight any leakage of *personal overlays* onto the *shared view*. Our results show that there is very little interference and that it is independent of the nature of the content shown in the *personal overlay*. This means that the PiVOT concept works and opens new possibilities in collaborative tabletop that supports mixed-focus collaboration and a wide range of 2D and 3D content in the *personal overlays*.

PiVOT provides the possibility to co-locate two distinct workspaces, shared and personalized, and by tracking the position of each user, the system can know the workspace he/she is viewing. As a result, their interactions (touch inputs, gestures, voice commands) can be interpreted in the appropriate context.

Another relevant capability of PiVOT is its support for *mixed-content*, which offers users the ability to switch between different types of 3D and 2D data and therefore supports a greater number of applications. To date most tabletop systems either support interactive exploration of 2D or 3D content but rarely allow users to dynamically switch between the two of them. However in many applications it is often useful for users to constantly switch between the two types of content. PiVOT provides this flexibility by using the LC sandwich to create the *personal overlays*.

Finally, the distribution of the workspaces that PiVOT uses can change, to adapt to different interaction styles and user preferences. Some usage scenarios will require users to access the *shared view* when they gather above the tabletop (i.e. walk up and use applications) while *personal overlays* are better accessed when sitting back. Others will need a *shared view* to be available to users when they are sitting around the table-top (e.g. meetings). Although our implementation of PiVOT used a specific arrangement of the workspaces it can be easily adapted to support other arrangements. From a range of identified possible designs, we implemented the PiVOT prototype based on the most compact design with the least hardware requirements (Design 5). While this prototype validates our concepts, it is flexible to further adaptations. With minor modifications to the software, it can operate like Design 4 wherein the position of the shared view and the personal views are interchanged. By adding another projector and additional layers of Lumisty film, the table can become accessible from all four sides instead of the current three sides.

Future research can look at the various interaction issues such as how users might move content between the shared and personal views without disrupting group activity or how interactions with PiVOT might affect group awareness and coordination.

CONCLUSION

This paper presents PiVOT, a system that supports mixed-focus collaboration through the use of a Lumisty film, a standard projector and a modified Liquid Crystal in a tandem configuration. The standard projector provides a *shared view* that is visible to all users while the Lumisty film combined with the LCs provide a personal view that support individual work. By moving in and out of the view-zones the user can switch between individual work and group work. PiVOT also supports the use of different types of content such as 2D images, text, auto-stereoscopic 3D and multi-view images in the personal view. Through a system evaluation we show that there is very low interference from the personal overlays on the shared view demonstrating that the PiVOT prototype and concept work.

ACKNOWLEDGMENTS

We thank the members of Bristol Interaction & Graphics group for their support. This work is supported by the

European Research Council (Starting Grant Agreement 278576) under the Seventh Framework Programme and Microsoft Research through the PhD Scholarship Programme.

REFERENCES

1. Cox, D. A., Chugh, J. S., Gutwin, C. and Greenberg, S. The usability of transparent overview layers. In *Proc. of CHI '98,* ACM, (1998), 301-302.
2. Forlines, C., Esenther, A., Shen, C., Wigdor, D. and Ryall, K. Multi-user, multi-display interaction with a single-user, single-display geospatial application. In *Proc. of UIST '06,* (2006), 273-276.
3. Gutwin, C. and Greenberg, S. Design for individuals, design for groups: tradeoffs between power and workspace awareness. In *Proc. of CSCW '98,* ACM, (1998), 207-216.
4. Izadi, S., Hodges, S., Taylor, S., Rosenfeld, D., Villar, N., Butler, A. and Westhues, J. Going beyond the display: a surface technology with an electronically switchable diffuser. In *Proc. of UIST '08,* (2008), 269-278.
5. Kakehi, Y. and Naemura, T. UlteriorScape: Interactive optical superimposition on a view-dependent tabletop display. In *Proc. of 3rd IEEE International Workshop on Horizontal Interactive Human Computer Systems, TABLETOP 2008,* (2008), 189-192.
6. Karnik, A., Mayol-Cuevas, W. and Subramanian, S. MUSTARD: A Multi User See Through AR Display. In *Proc. of CHI '12,* ACM, (2012), 2541-2550.
7. Kitamura, Y., Konishi, T., Yamamoto, S. and Kishino, F. Interactive stereoscopic display for three or more users. In *Proc. of SIGGRAPH '01,* ACM, (2001), 231-240.
8. Mantiuk, R., Kim, K. J., Rempel, A. G. and Heidrich, W. HDR-VDP-2: a calibrated visual metric for visibility and quality predictions in all luminance conditions. In *Proc. of SIGGRAPH '11,* ACM, (2011), 1-14.
9. Matsushita, M., Iida, M., Ohguro, T., Shirai, Y., Kakehi, Y. and Naemura, T. Lumisight table: a face-to-face collaboration support system that optimizes direction of projected information to each stakeholder. In *Proc. of CSCW '04,* (2004), 274-283.
10. Möllers, M. and Borchers, J. TaPS widgets: interacting with tangible private spaces. In *Proc. of ITS '11,* ACM, (2011), 75-78.
11. Morris, M. R., Ryall, K., Shen, C., Forlines, C. and Vernier, F. Beyond "social protocols": multi-user coordination policies for co-located groupware. In *Proc. of CSCW '04,* ACM, (2004), 262-265.
12. Nacenta, M. A., Sakurai, S., Yamaguchi, T., Miki, Y., Itoh, Y., Kitamura, Y., Subramanian, S. and Gutwin, C. E-conic: a perspective-aware interface for multi-display environments. In *Proc. of UIST '07,* ACM, (2007), 279-288.
13. Olwal, A. and Henrys, A. LUMAR: A Hybrid Spatial Display System for 2D and 3D Handheld Augmented Reality. In *Proc. of the 17th International Conference on Artificial Reality and Telexistence,* (2007), 63-70.
14. Oshima, R. and Kakehi, Y. Bounsight table: a view-dependent display with a single front projection. In *Proc. of ITS '10,* ACM, (2010), 281-282.
15. Perlin, K., Paxia, S. and Kollin, J. S. An autostereoscopic display. In *Proc. of SIGGRAPH '00,* (2000), 319-326.
16. Ryall, K., Forlines, C., Shen, C. and Morris, M. R. Exploring the effects of group size and table size on interactions with tabletop shared-display groupware. In *Proc. of CSCW '04,* ACM, (2004), 284-293.
17. Sakurai, S., Kitamura, Y., Subramanian, S. and Kishino, F. A visibility control system for collaborative digital table. *Personal and Ubiquitous Computing 13,*(2009), 619-632.
18. Schmidt, K. and Simonee, C. Coordination mechanisms: Towards a conceptual foundation of CSCW systems design. *Computer Supported Cooperative Work (CSCW) 5,*(1996), 155-200.
19. Scott, S. D., Sheelagh, M., Carpendale, T. and Inkpen, K. M. Territoriality in collaborative tabletop workspaces. In *Proc. of CSCW '04,* ACM, (2004), 294-303.
20. SUMITOMO_CHEMICAL. Lumisty. http://www.sumitomo-chem.co.jp/cgi-bin/product_search/english/products/detail.cgi?pcode=en_a03001.
21. Tang, A., Tory, M., Po, B., Neumann, P. and Carpendale, S. Collaborative coupling over tabletop displays. In *Proc. of CHI '06,* ACM, (2006), 1181-1190.
22. Tse, E., Histon, J., Scott, S. D. and Greenberg, S. Avoiding interference: how people use spatial separation and partitioning in SDG workspaces. In *Proc. of CSCW '04,* ACM, (2004), 252-261.
23. Wigdor, D., Jiang, H., Forlines, C., Borkin, M. and Shen, C. WeSpace: the design development and deployment of a walk-up and share multi-surface visual collaboration system. In *Proc. of CHI '09,* (2009), 1237-1246.
24. Ye, G., State, A. and Fuchs, H. A practical multi-viewer tabletop autostereoscopic display. In *Proc. of ISMAR '10,* (2010), 147-156.

Histomages: Fully Synchronized Views for Image Editing

Fanny Chevalier
Department of Computer Science
University of Toronto, Canada
fanny@dgp.toronto.edu

Pierre Dragicevic
INRIA
F-91405 Orsay, France
dragice@lri.fr

Christophe Hurter
University of Toulouse
ENAC, France
christophe.hurter@enac.fr

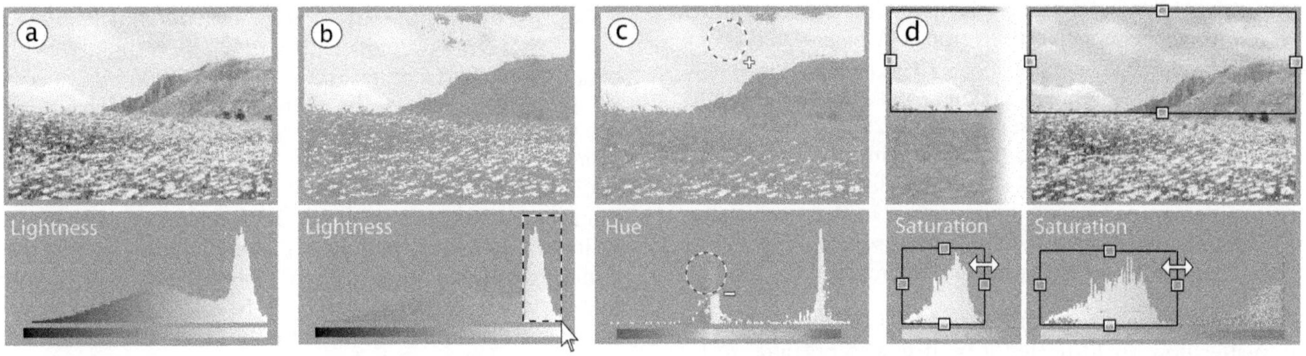

Figure 1: Sky enhancement with Histomages: (a) the image is duplicated and its pixels rearranged into a lightness histogram; (b) bright pixels are selected with the rubber-band selection tool; (c) all pixels are rearranged into a hue histogram and yellow pixels are filtered out with the "subtract" selection brush (bottom). Missing pixels are added with the "add" selection brush on the image (top); (d) the sky is enhanced by resizing the selection on the saturation histogram.

ABSTRACT

We present Histomages, a new interaction model for image editing that considers color histograms as spatial rearrangements of image pixels. Users can select pixels on image histograms as they would select image regions and directly manipulate them to adjust their colors. Histomages are also affected by other image tools such as paintbrushes. We explore some possibilities offered by this interaction model, and discuss the four key principles behind it as well as their implications for the design of feature-rich software in general.

ACM Classification: H5.2 [Information interfaces and presentation]: User Interfaces. - Graphical user interfaces.

Keywords: Image editing, synchronized views, histograms.

INTRODUCTION

Bitmap image editing software like Photoshop or Gimp is extremely powerful in the hands of experts but is hard to master, because of the wealth of functionality and tools that must be learned. Taken individually, most of these tools are relatively easy to learn and to use (e.g., levels, hue shift, color range selection or selection transforms). However, they each follow their own logics and have a different user interface. In order to make image manipulations more flexible and fluent, image editing software needs more unified, coherent interaction models.

UIST'12, October 7-10, 2012, Cambridge, Massachusetts, USA.

We present Histomages, a new interaction model based on synchronized views that supports rich image selection and manipulation operations through simple tools. Although synchronized views have been used in various domains, their support in current image editing software is still rudimentary. In addition to illustrating the benefits of full support for synchronized views in image editing, Histomages more generally demonstrate the benefits that can be gained from focusing on an *interaction model* rather than a *swiss army knife* approach to the design of feature-rich applications.

BACKGROUND

We first briefly review previous work in interaction models, image editing tools and synchronized views.

Interaction Models

An interaction model is "a set of principles, rules and properties that guide the design of an interface" [4]. Interaction models can range from general principles (e.g., direct manipulation) to more specific guidelines and mechanisms. They help achieve logical soundness and consistency in user interfaces, with benefits to both developers and end users of complex software.

Like many authoring and productivity applications, image editors are primarily based on the *swiss army knife* principle (i.e., a large set of specialized, independent and complementary tools), along with transversal mechanisms such as selection, undo and redo, copy and paste, scripts and layers.

Software companies mainly focus on improving existing tools and adding more powerful ones (often through plug-in mechanisms), while the underlying interaction models are considered immutable. Since these models only weakly enforce consistency between tools – each new tool such as an image filter typically comes with specific controls – image editing applications are increasingly difficult to master and more and more intimidating to beginners as new versions appear. In this article we explore an alternative model for two types of image editing tasks: *selection* and *color manipulation*.

Image Selection

Selecting image regions is a key task in image editing and several tools are generally provided. They include *image-space* tools (e.g., lasso or rubber-band selection) and *color-space* tools (e.g., color range selection). Recently, a method based on color naming has been proposed [17]. *Mixed-space* tools combine both approaches. They include the magic wand and other "intelligent" cutout tools whose algorithms are still an active topic of research [22, 28]. Some of these tools dynamically select image regions while the image is being painted [25]. Advanced selection tools can dramatically facilitate common image editing tasks, but the more elaborate they are, the more difficult it is for users to build a clear mental model of how they work and to predict their results.

Since no selection tool alone can address all selection tasks no matter how sophisticated it is, it is also essential to be able to combine different types of selection techniques. This is achieved in image editing software through the support of *boolean operations* on selections, a powerful feature that acts as a bridge between selection methods and allows users to, e.g., select a region using a color picker and tolerance slider, then refine it by lassooing on the image. However, since different types of selections involve different interaction techniques, switching between them can still be tedious.

Color Manipulation

Color manipulation is another key task in image editing, particularly in photo editing. The state-of-the-art interaction model consists in filters whose parameters are set in control panels, with immediate preview on the image. The tools are numerous and include luminosity and contrast correction, color balance, and color replacement. Adobe Photoshop CS5 provides 21 color manipulation tools, 3 of which are automatic and 18 have parameters that are exposed in specialized dialog boxes [1]. Techniques have also been proposed for controlling parameters directly on the image [24, 14].

Popular tools among photographers are image histograms, which give a rapid overview of how color components (e.g., brightness) are distributed in an image and what corrections need to be applied. Most image editors include an interactive histogram that can be stretched by moving control points, which in turn adjusts colors on the image. Although useful, current histogram tools are often difficult to relate to the image and require trial and error, or thorough practice.

A few professional applications provide more advanced interactive histograms, such as Adobe Lightroom 4 where histograms can be locally stretched by direct manipulation, although only the vertical boundaries of a few predefined histogram regions can be moved, which effectively amounts to moving control points [2]. Capture NX 2 provides histograms where value ranges can be selected and the corresponding pixels are shown on the image with a blinking animation [24]. However, this technique cannot be used to select regions of the image for subsequent manipulation.

Synchronized Views

Early uses of the principle of synchronized views can be found in the visual exploration system by Becker and Cleveland [6] and in the MVC design pattern from the Smalltalk programming language [21], later implemented in a number of GUI toolkits. Today, examples of applications with elaborate support for synchronized views include document editing environments that combine a markup editor with a WYSIWYG window [11], and a wealth of visual exploration tools [27, 26]. These tools support *synchronized highlighting*, i.e., hovering over an element in one view highlights the same element in the other, and sometimes *synchronized editing*, i.e., edits in either view are reflected in the other.

Synchronized views have been extensively employed and studied in the field of information visualization under the name of *coordinated views* (see [27] for a survey). The use of multiple data representations is thought to promote effective visual exploration, especially if tools are provided to help analysts relate different views. A popular approach in the domain is synchronized highlighting, termed *brushing and linking* [6, 7]. Other solutions involve drawing links between views [10] or using animated transitions [16]. Synchronized view configuration mechanisms have also been proposed [26], but synchronized editing has comparatively received little attention in this field, with a few exceptions [3].

Image editing applications also involve alternative image representations (mostly histograms) but with very primitive support for synchronized views: interaction with histograms is poor and requires tools that are completely distinct from other tools. Yet histograms are just another way of laying out image pixels and could be therefore treated (at least partly) as images. The similarity between histograms and images has been evoked in art [15] but to the best of our knowledge, it has never inspired any actual tool. In the following we use simple scenarios to illustrate some of the possibilities offered by such an interaction model for image editing.

HISTOMAGES WALKTHROUGH

Histomages employ a classic multi-window image editor interface and a toolbar that contains a small but fully-functional set of traditional image editing tools (Figure 2). The only visible difference is an extra toolbar at the top of each window. One button is for cloning the window (similar to the Clone Window menu command in Photoshop) while other buttons switch between the image view and several types of histogram views (e.g., red, green and blue channels, LAB lightness or hue) and a 2-D lightness/hue scatterplot.

In Histomages, a histogram is a *spatial rearrangement* of the image's pixels (Figure 1a): all pixels are displayed with their initial color but instead of being laid out on a grid, they are grouped into bins depending on the value of the color channel that is visualized. Pixels overlap vertically in case the histogram does not fit the window, and their stacking order reflects their y-ordering in the original image. Thus, pixels remain coherently grouped, which produces a visual effect similar to stacked graphs [8] and makes it easier to identify image regions. In addition, view switches are smoothly animated by having each pixel rapidly move to its new location.

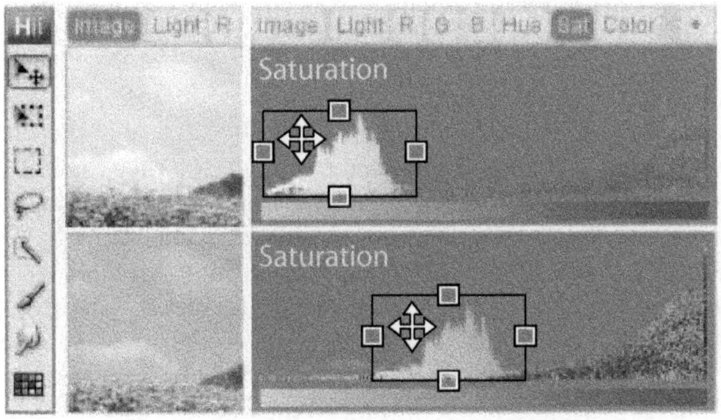

Figure 2: Increasing the saturation of the sky.

Since histograms are merely images with alternative pixel layouts, all operations that can be done on images can also be done on histograms. We illustrate this with a simple scenario: Pamela was asked to illustrate the cover of a new novel called "The Promised Land". She finds a stock photography (Figure 1a top) and feels it would fit perfectly with a few adjustements. She considers making the sky more blue and the hill more verdant. She also finds that the color of the carpet of yellow flowers is too aggressive and needs to be softened.

Adding and Switching Views

After loading the image in Histomages, Pamela duplicates the window so that one view will be kept to display the image while the other view will show histograms. She first selects the lightness histogram. As the image transitions to the histogram, she sees the sky region quickly move to the right while the mountain region piles up at the center (Figure 1a). On the final histogram, she sees that the two regions exhibit a clean separation in terms of lightness, as opposed to the yellow flowers that clearly span the whole luminosity range.

Selecting Regions of Histograms

Pamela first focuses on the sky. She picks the rubber band selection tool and selects the rightmost region of the lightness histogram (Figure 1b). This effectively selects the brightest pixels on both the histogram and the image view. Unselected pixels fade out to better show the selection.

Although unwanted pixels have been included in the selection, Pamela is aware that the sky and the flowers differ enough in hue. She switches to the hue histogram and indeed sees the flower region and the sky region split out into two separate clusters. Using the brush selection tool and holding the key modifier for the "subtract" mode, she quickly removes all yellow pixels as well as other isolated pixels outside the blue range (see Figure 1c, bottom). As some pixels from the sky are still missing, she switches to the "add" mode and brushes over the missing regions directly on the image (see Figure 1c, top). Now the sky is properly selected.

Dragging and Stretching Histogram Regions

Since the sky appears washed out, Pamela switches to the saturation histogram and indeed notices that the selected pixels are all squeezed to the left, in the low saturation range (see Figures 1d and 2). Therefore, she picks the transform tool and drags the selected region to the right, towards higher saturation values on the histogram. This effectively changes the color of all selected pixels so that their saturation match their new x-position on the histogram (see Figure 2). While she drags the selection, Pamela sees the sky change on the image, and she stops once she is satisfied with the color.

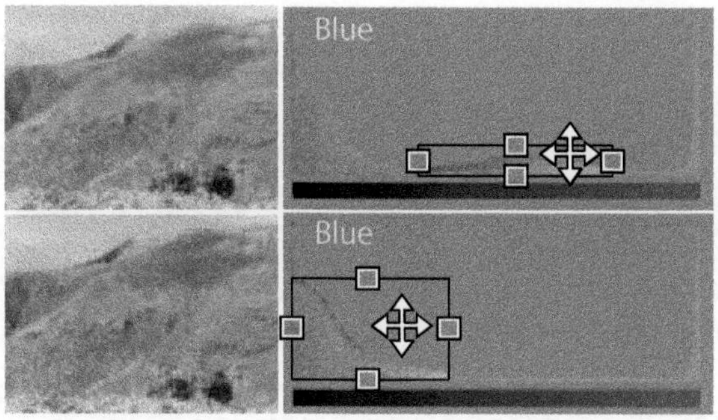

Figure 3: Reducing the blue component of the hill.

Although increasing saturation made the sky more blue overall, Pamela does not find the effect very natural. Since clouds are generally supposed to be white, their saturation should probably be left unchanged. Therefore, Pamela drags the selection back to the left, then grabs the right handle and stretches the selection towards more saturated values (Figure 1d). Her idea is to increase the dynamic range of the selected pixels on the saturation channel, and while she is dragging the handle, she does notice that this type of color transformation works much better visually.

More Selecting and Dragging

The various histograms provide many different ways of selecting and recoloring image regions. As another example, when Pamela switches to the hill, she browses through different histograms and finds that it forms a clear bump in the blue channel (Figure 3 top). She brushes the bump then cleans up the selection on the hue and the lightness channels. She then adjusts the hill to a greener tone by dragging the selection to the left of the blue channel. Again, the image is dynamically updated, which in turn updates the histogram in a way that preserves the y-ordering of pixels and makes them appear to "crawl" over the yellow region (Figure 3 bottom).

Two-Axis Scatterplots

To make yellow colors less aggressive and poppies stand out, Pamela decides to retouch the carpet of yellow flowers. She brings up the hue histogram but realizes that the hue channel does not do a good job at separating yellow and green pixels, which in addition to the stems now also include the hill.

Therefore, Pamela switches to a 2-D scatterplot visualization of the color space, where the vertical axis is mapped to hue and the horizontal one to lightness (Figure 4 left). Although the scatterplot does not show pixel counts like histograms, it is appropriate for selecting complex ranges of colors. In that case, Pamela needs to select dark to light yellows and orange tones while avoiding red, green and dark pixels. She picks the brush selection tool, applies it starting from a bright yellow color, then uses the immediate selection feedback on the image to help her adjust the trajectory of the brush (Figure 4 middle). She occasionally uses the subtract mode to clean the selection or zooms in to gain more precision.

Once the yellow flowers are properly selected, their hue and lightness can be simultaneously adjusted by freely dragging

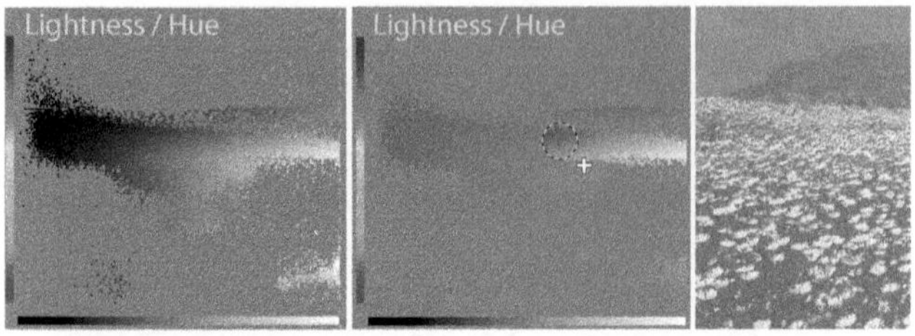

Figure 4: Selection in the Lightness/Hue space.

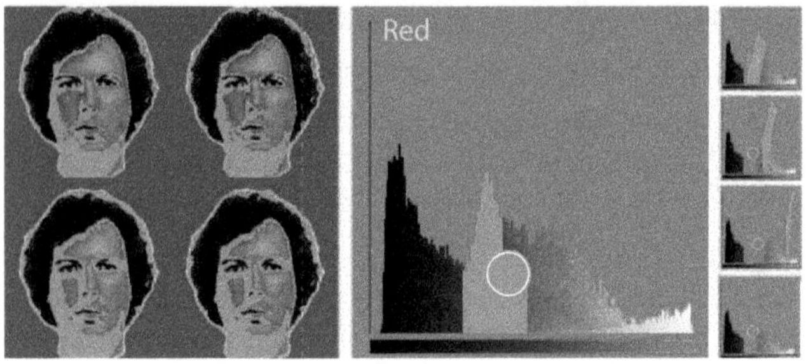

Figure 5: Applying the paintbrush on a view temporarily freezes all histograms (middle). At mouse release, painted pixels jump to their new location (right).

the selection on the scatterplot. However, since Pamela only needs to wash out the colors, she switches back to the saturation channel and drags the selection to the left. By dragging the selection too far she accidentally discovers that a carpet of white flowers produce a soothing and enchanting effect and thus decides to stick to white flowers.

Painting Histograms

Histomages are also compatible with other traditional image editing tools, which opens up a range of other possibilities in terms of color manipulation. Right after she finished her novel cover, Pamela is asked to produce urgently a cover for a special issue of the Garlic Magazine on a personality.

Pamela downloads a photograph of the personality and decides to produce a Warhol-style posterized cover. She makes four copies of the photo then loads the produced image in Histomages. She then picks the paintbrush tool, and on the red channel histogram, she paints a stripe in a uniform orange (Figure 5). She uses the image preview as a guide, while the histogram is temporarily frozen to prevent the brush from accidentally affecting neighboring pixels. At mouse release, all pixels jump to the corresponding bin of the histogram.

Pamela then paints other stripes of the histogram. Since she wants to preserve the lightness component of the hair, she uses the transform tool and shrinks the selection to zero width instead. Finally, she selects one of the faces on the image view and drags it on the lightness/hue scatterplot until she is satisfied with the variant produced. Through the same method, she produces variants for the two remaining faces.

Quick Comparison with Photoshop

The principal strength of Histomages does not lie in its expressive power (the image manipulations shown can be done with any professional photo editing application) but in the elegance and the concision of its interactions. For example, as and far as our expertise goes, carrying out the task illustrated in Figure 1 with Photoshop CS3 would require a user to:

(1) Select the *magic wand* or bring up the *color range selection* dialog (*Selection* menu) ; click on a pixel of the sky and adjust the *tolerance* value (text field or slider) until the sky is properly selected ; possibly change the seed pixel and repeat ; if no combination of seed pixel and tolerance is found to work (which is the case in our example), break down the task into several steps using boolean selections through *key modifiers* ; Close the dialog, pick a tool like *polygon selection* and clean up the selection on the image. (2) Bring up the *Hue/Saturation* dialog (*Image* $\rightarrow$ *Adjustment* menu or Ctrl+U) and push the *saturation* slider to the maximum. This happens to yield a result similar to the one on Figure 1c, but if a result closer to Figure 2 was desired instead, it is not clear how this could be done. Supposing the *Levels* tool supports saturation, the *Hue/Saturation* dialog box would have to be closed (all dialogs are modal), and the *Levels* dialog box would have to be brought up (*Image* $\rightarrow$ *Adjustment* or Ctrl+L) in order to see the histogram and its control handles.

DISCUSSION

We illustrated some of the possibilities of Histomages, a prototype application that is based on a new interaction model for image editing, and rethinks the way selection and color manipulation tasks are carried out. The goal of Histomages is to demonstrate new concepts, more so than to provide a finished product. Therefore, our prototype has limitations and possible extensions that we discuss. We then generalize these concepts and discuss their possible implications for the design of feature-rich applications.

Use by Novices

Retouching images on histograms requires a good understanding of image histograms, i.e., the meaning of different color axes like hue or saturation, and the principle of counting and vertically accumulating pixels of similar value. Although Histomages is initially not meant to be a learning tool, we believe that features like pixel color preservation and animated transitions can help novices understand histograms. We also think that letting users freely explore and manipulate various types of histograms in a consistent manner may have an educational value too. These, however, are only conjectures that need to be further tested in user studies.

Limitations of Selections in Histograms

Selection in histograms is arguably more difficult when there is little contrast between regions. This problem is however common to all color-space selection tools, which are meant to be used when the region of interest differs enough in color. Histomages supports the same tasks but in a more elegant and flexible manner, since it is based on a clear interaction model rather than on black-box color selection algorithms.

Again, no selection tool can solve all selection problems. Intelligent mixed-space selection tools are also limited, as selection is more than automatically detecting contours or color clusters. Ultimately, only the user can tell what is her region of interest so the solution likely lies in familiar, simple and powerful interactions. Boolean operations on selections brought lots of power by allowing selection tools to be combined, while Histomages pushes simplicity and flexibility further by adding logical consistency to these tools.

Currently, Histomages only supports binary selection. A useful extension would be support for fuzzy selections, with support for antialiasing and feathering operations both in the image and in the histogram spaces. Partially selected pixels would travel slower while dragged on a histogram or on a scatterplot, resulting in less prominent edges after color transformation and more natural-looking images. In addition, selected histogram regions are currently manipulated independently from unselected regions, but it could also useful to have a "rubber sheet" feature that preserves boundaries in a similar way to Capture NX 2's direct manipulation tool [24].

Non-linear Color Transfer Functions

Our current prototype allows histogram manipulation with the *selection transform* tool exclusively (move & resize) and therefore only supports linear color transfer functions. Traditional image histograms usually include a third control point and therefore allow for more flexibility in transfer functions, while the Curve tool from Photoshop CS5 supports up to 14 control points. However, in practice 3 to 4 control points are enough to specify transfer functions as complex as S-curves. This is the number of control points supported by interactive geometrical deformation tools such as Photoshop's *warp transform*, so supporting these tools on histograms would allow specifying non-linear color transfer functions.

Generalization to Other Image Editing Tools

We demonstrated two ways of extending traditional image editing tools so that they can be used on histograms: *(a)* having the tool affect histogram pixels the same way as image pixels (selection and paintbrush) and *(b)* interpreting changes in pixel positions within the histogram's coordinate system (the selection transform tool). We experimented with only a few tools, but other common editing tools could be extended to work on histograms following the same two approaches.

A major class of image editing tools are tools that affect pixel colors locally. Beside the paintbrush we implemented, these include the airbrush, eraser, pencil, and brushes that affect pixel lightness or hue. All could be easily modified to work like our paintbrush. We expect these to be useful for retouching non-contiguous close-to-uniform regions. For example, for red eyes removal a user could roughly select the eyes area on the image then paint the hue histogram with a hue brush. This procedure contrasts with current tools, which first require to explicitely select the exact area to be painted.

Another class of tools are pixel displacement tools, of which our selection transform tool is an example. Other geometrical transform tools like the skew, distort, perspective and warp tools could be extended the same way, as well as local displacement tools like the smudge tool. Applied to histograms, these tools could enrich the repertoire of color manipulations. We already mentioned possibilities warp tools could offer in terms of non-linear color transformations.

Other categories of tools would require more experimentation before one can tell whether or not they could be useful on histograms and how to extend their semantics. These include spatial filters (e.g., blur and sharpen) and pixel duplication tools (e.g., copy-paste and the clone stamp). Finally, some tools such as writing text might not make sense at all.

Alternative Pixel Layouts

We illustrated our interaction model on histograms and scatterplots, but other types of pixel layouts can be explored. Visual exploration and complex selections might be facilitated with multidimensional visualizations techniques such as parallel coordinates [18] or scatterplot matrices [13], where data points would be pixels and the dimensions would be color components and pixel coordinates. Some layouts could also be user-defined, in order to let users create meaningful pixel groups and easily reuse them for subsequent manipulations. Especially promising are techniques that combine both approaches such as star plots [20], where users directly manipulate axes to create and explore linear combinations of dimensions, or dynamic filtering lenses [19], where users can switch between different dimension mappings locally.

An Interaction Model for Rich Multi-View Applications

The interaction model behind Histomages reuses and refines the paradigm of synchronized views and is based on the following four general principles:

1. Consistent View Structures. All views are made of similar graphical primitives (pixels in our case) which try to retain their graphical attributes across views. This gives a sense of "conservation of matter" and can make it easier for users to build a mental model of how views are constructed (e.g., what an image histogram means), and how regions of different views relate to each other once they are constructed.

2. Consistent View Interactions. Any tool used to interact with a view can also be used on other views, with identical or similar effects. This is especially relevant for *selection* tools, because if both multi-view selections and boolean operators are supported, powerful "selection sculpting" tasks can be carried out [13]. Furthermore, tool consistency can be beneficial to facilitate learning, since what has been learned for one view can be transferred to other views with little effort (e.g., our paintbrush). Finally, the semantics of some tools can be adapted to the specificities of different views in order to enrich their expressive power (e.g., our transform tool). Overall, applying this principle requires breaking traditional master/slave relationships between views [27] in favor of multidirectional dependencies [26, 12], and removing traditional couplings between tools and views in favor of tool polymorphism [4, 5].

3. Constantly Synchronized Views. The visual consistency between views and the underlying data is maintained at all times, except during modifications that require a view to be temporarily frozen (e.g., using a paintbrush on a histogram). This principle, together with principles 1 and 2, ensures that the system fully supports the traditional synchronized views paradigm: synchronized highlighting (or brushing and linking) is supported through selection tools, while synchronized editing is supported through regular editing tools.

4. Smooth View Transitions. Transitions between views within the same window are smoothly animated, which can further help explain how views are built and clarify how they are mapped [16, 9, 11]. The design and implementation of animated transitions are greatly facilitated by the principle 1. We believe this interaction model can make it easier for both experts and beginners to use multi-view interfaces, and can also make interaction less tedious and more rewarding.

However, this interaction model alone cannot support the large variety of tasks supported by feature-rich commercial applications and is not meant to be used as a replacement. It is rather a complement to existing tools and mechanisms and a way to "polish" their logics. Although integrating this model in existing software might require significant refactoring, it does not necessarily involve many changes from the user's perspective. Histomages is fully integrated with the traditional GUI of image editors: it uses the same multi-window environment and similar visual representations (with some visual enhancements to histograms), and the selection and editing tools it supports are essentially the same.

CONCLUSION

There has been much focus on the problem of "software bloat", often with the assumption that not all features of large applications are useful, or at least not for everyone and not all the time [23]. However, complex activities such as image editing cannot be properly carried out without mastering a wealth of tools that are all complementary and all relevant to many tasks. We believe that the major issue with most feature-rich applications is not an excess of functionalities but a lack of logics and consistency in the way they are exposed at the user interface. Often, most development efforts are spent designing new tools, without much concern for the interaction models that allow these tools to work together.

With Histomages, we show that with a proper interaction model, a small number of tools can provide a large set of functionalities (with sometimes unexpected features), while ensuring some logical coherence. Histomages also suggests that new interaction models do not necessarily have to disorient expert users and can be sometimes integrated into existing GUIs without major changes.

ACKNOWLEDGMENTS

We would like to thank Dustin Freeman and Jean-Daniel Fekete for their comments on this paper.

REFERENCES

1. Adobe. Photoshop CS5. www.photoshop.com, 2011.
2. Adobe. Photoshop Lightroom 4. www.adobe.com/products/photoshop-lightroom, 2012.
3. T. Baudel. From information visualization to direct manipulation: extending a generic visualization framework for the interactive editing of large datasets. In *Proc. ACM User interface software & tech.*, UIST '06, 67–76, 2006.
4. M. Beaudouin-Lafon. Instrumental interaction: an interaction model for designing post-wimp user interfaces. In *Proc. ACM Human factors in computing systems*, CHI '00, 446–453, 2000.
5. M. Beaudouin-Lafon and W. E. Mackay. Reification, polymorphism and reuse: three principles for designing visual interfaces. In *Proc. ACM Advanced visual interfaces*, AVI '00, 102–109, 2000.
6. R. A. Becker and W. S. Cleveland. Brushing scatterplots. *Technometrics*, 29(2):127–142, May 1987.
7. A. Buja, D. Cook, and D. F. Swayne. Interactive high-dimensional data visualization. *Journal of Computational and Graphical Statistics*, 5:78–99, 1996.
8. L. Byron and M. Wattenberg. Stacked graphs & geometry & aesthetics. *IEEE Trans. Vis. & Comp. Graphics*, 14:1245–1252, 2008.
9. F. Chevalier, P. Dragicevic, A. Bezerianos, and J.-D. Fekete. Using text animated transitions to support navigation in document histories. In *Proc. ACM Human factors in computing systems*, CHI '10, 683–692, 2010.
10. C. Collins and S. Carpendale. Vislink: Revealing relationships amongst visualizations. *IEEE Trans. Vis. & Comp. Graphics*, 13(6):1192–1199, 2007.
11. P. Dragicevic, S. Huot, and F. Chevalier. Gliimpse: Animating from markup code to rendered documents and vice versa. In *Proc. ACM User interface software & tech.*, UIST '11, 257–262, 2011.
12. P. Dragicevic, G. Ramos, J. Bibliowitcz, D. Nowrouzezahrai, R. Balakrishnan, and K. Singh. Video browsing by direct manipulation. In *Proc. ACM Human factors in computing systems*, CHI '08, 237–246, 2008.
13. N. Elmqvist, P. Dragicevic, and J.-D. Fekete. Rolling the dice: Multidimensional visual exploration using scatterplot matrix navigation. *IEEE Trans. Vis. & Comp. Graphics (Proc. InfoVis)*, 14(6):1141–1148, 2008.
14. N. Elmqvist, P. Dragicevic, and J.-D. Fekete. Color lens: Adaptive color scale optimization for visual exploration. *IEEE Trans. Vis. & Comp. Graphics*, 17(6):795–807, 2011.
15. D. Friedman. Idea: The histogram as the image. Blog post http://goo.gl/2PfcV, 2007.
16. J. Heer and G. Robertson. Animated transitions in statistical data graphics. *IEEE Trans. Vis. & Comp. Graphics (Proc. InfoVis)*, 13:1240–1247, 2007.
17. J. Heer and M. Stone. Color naming models for color selection, image editing and palette design. In *Proc. ACM Human factors in computing systems*, CHI '12, 237–246, 2012.
18. P. Hoffman, G. Grinstein, and D. Pinkney. Dimensional anchors: a graphic primitive for multidimensional multivariate information visualizations. In *Proc. 1999 workshop on new paradigms in information visualization and manipulation*, NPIVM '99, 9–16, 1999.
19. C. Hurter, A. Telea, and O. Ersoy. Moleview: An attribute and structure-based semantic lens for large element-based plots. *IEEE Trans. Vis. & Comp. Graphics (Proc. InfoVis)*, 17(12):2600–2609, Dec. 2011.
20. E. Kandogan. Star coordinates: A multi-dimensional visualization technique with uniform treatment of dimensions. In *Proc. IEEE Information Visualization Symposium, Late Breaking Hot Topics*, 9–12, 2000.
21. G. E. Krasner and S. T. Pope. A cookbook for using the model-view-controller user interface paradigm in Smalltalk-80. *Object-Oriented Programming*, 26–49, 1988.
22. Y. Li, J. Sun, C.-K. Tang, and H.-Y. Shum. Lazy snapping. *ACM Trans. Graphics*, 23(3):303–308, Aug. 2004.
23. J. McGrenere and G. Moore. Are we all in the same bloat ? In *Proc. Graphics Interface Conference*, 187–196, 2000.
24. Nikon. Capture NX 2 v2.3.0. www.capturenx.com, 2012.
25. D. R. Olsen, Jr. and M. K. Harris. Edge-respecting brushes. In *Proc. ACM User interface software & tech.*, UIST '08, 171–180, 2008.
26. N. H. Riche, B. Lee, and C. Plaisant. Understanding interactive legends: a comparative evaluation with standard widgets. *Comput. Graph. Forum*, 29(3):1193–1202, 2010.
27. J. C. Roberts. State of the art: Coordinated & multiple views in exploratory visualization. In *Proc. IEEE Coordinated and Multiple Views in Exploratory Visualization*, 61–71, 2007.
28. J. Wang, M. Agrawala, and M. F. Cohen. Soft scissors: an interactive tool for realtime high quality matting. In *ACM SIGGRAPH*, 2007.

Sketch-Editing Games: Human-Machine Communication, Game Theory and Applications

Andre Ribeiro
JST, Erato, Igarashi
Design Interface Project,
1-28-1-7F, Koishikawa
ribeiro@media.mit.edu

Takeo Igarashi
JST, Erato, Igarashi
Design Interface Project,
1-28-1-7F, Koishikawa
takeo@acm.org

ABSTRACT
We study uncertainty in graphical-based interaction (with special attention to sketches). We argue that a comprehensive model for the problem must include the interaction participants (and their current beliefs), their possible actions and their past sketches. It's yet unclear how to frame and solve the former problem, considering all the latter elements. We suggest framing the problem as a game and solving it with a game-theoretical solution, which leads to a framework for the design of new two-way, sketch-based user interfaces. In special, we use the framework to design a game that can progressively learn visual models of objects from user sketches, and use the models in real-world interactions. Instead of an abstract visual criterion, players in this game learn models to optimize interaction (the game's duration). This two-way sketching game addresses problems essential in emerging interfaces (such as learning and how to deal with interpretation errors). We review possible applications in robotic sketch-to-command, hand gesture recognition, media authoring and visual search, and evaluate two. Evaluations demonstrate how players improve performance with repeated play, and the influence of interaction aspects on learning.

Author Keywords
Sketch recognition; Machine Learning; Active Learning; Game Theory; Communication; Cooperation.

ACM Classification Keywords
H.5.2. Information interfaces and presentation (e.g., HCI): User Interfaces: Theory and methods.

INTRODUCTION
When a machine learns to understand the symbol "ball!", it is learning an arbitrary convention, one that exists in the minds of a community of English speakers. Acting together, we establish with each other symbols that allow us to solve complex problems in an efficient, truly collaborative manner. Because individuals have no direct access to each others' thoughts, they must communicate to coordinate their distinct mental states and get them to converge (to some extent) in order to work together successfully. This process of "alignment" is necessary even when the parts are rational, cooperative, speak the same language, share much of the same knowledge and culture, but it is essential when they have asymmetric knowledge – such as in current Human-Computer Communication.

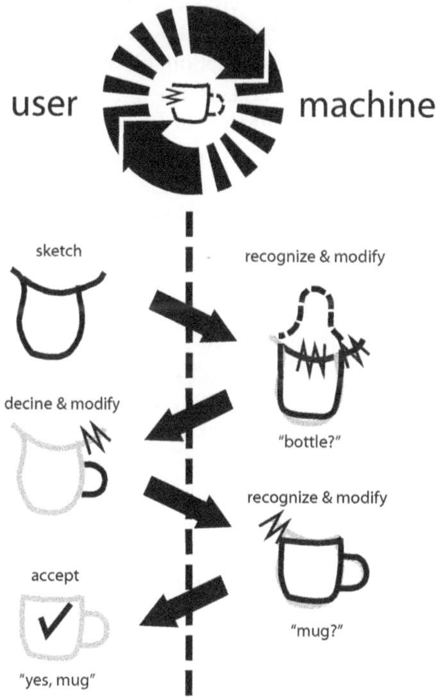

Figure 1. Turn taking in the Sketch-Editing Game.

In this article, we formulate a game theoretical model that captures some important aspects of this difficult problem. We introduce the model with past Human-Computer Communication examples and discuss its application in the learning and recognition of graphical symbols, where a user and a machine take turns modifying a joint sketch, *Fig.1.*

UIST '12, October 7–10, 2012, Cambridge, Massachusetts, USA.

The goal is to establish a two-way symbolic "dialog" between the user and the machine in which the machine not only routinely learns response to cues but also actively creates and manipulates symbols in interaction with humans.

This is an example of Interactive Learning. The problem has particular features not generally found in other learning problems. It consists of individuals that are learning about a process in which others are learning. And a learner in this situation must somehow consider not only the states of a physical process (*medium states*) but also the internal states of others (*knowledge states*). Additionally, learning must happen interactively (may involve turn-taking), transparently (players can observe and test what other's have learned) and be grounded in the common environment.

THE GAME

Suppose, for example, that a user has three types of objects in its kitchen - mugs, glasses and bottles - and that a robot can pass him the objects he sketches. This defines four subgames: need-a-mug, need-a-glass, need-a-bottle and need-nothing. This can be seen as a *coordination* game because user and machine are better off playing the same subgame. The problem is to jointly determine the intended subgame, without the assumption of any prior, common knowledge about these objects (in special, that the robot knows what "mug", "glass" or "bottle" are). A final solution is a symbol, a joint representation between them that unambiguously distinguishes the subgame for both. A solution is reached by a succession of symbolic proposals and modifications. A strategy for each player, at a time, is a specific modification of the current (joint) drawing that makes it less ambiguous (i.e., given the player's current beliefs). Modifications can be contour deletions (scratching), completions (drawing) or substitutions (morphing) – and they, together, are meant as a "is this what you mean?" query. We take this game to be a learning game with many rounds; where each player observes the opponents' moves and adapts its strategy until both are no longer uncertain about the reference. Symbolic communication is then a learning game where players learn better and better each other's references. We suggest that minimizing the expected number of interactions leads to both an attractive new medium for communication, and an effective training procedure.

Seen this way, learning and recognition are not artificially separated. The machine actively prompts the user for specific information whenever it recognizes a specific self-consistency gap (ambiguity) in its model. With better models, less and less interruptions are necessary (and learning transitions into use).

The game is played over a graph by two players, User (*U*) and Machine (*M*). The graph's nodes are shapes and edges are operations a player might perform on the source node (transforming it into the target). A path in the graph is then a progressive modification of some visual structure or structures. Games are often described by a tree (each subgame, a subtree). Imagine then that *M*'s prior knowledge consists of all previous games with *U*. In each round of the current game, *M* proposes a subgraph of this graph (i.e., a subgame) as a way of reducing uncertainty about what subgame is being played.

Figure 2. Game example.

Fig.2 depicts *M*'s graph after several games (sketchings of cans, bottles, and glasses shown in the graph's periphery). At the graph's center (double-circled) is *U*'s most recent sketch. The first set of transformations offered by *M* is seen in depth-1 nodes (first level). They are: adding a "neck" (towards bottle examples), adding a "base" (towards wine glasses) or widening the top (towards cup). The user can accept one of these suggestions and (optionally) use the transformed shape as basis for further editions. The next level shows subsequent transformations if each of these shapes were accepted.

As more is edited, more and more alternatives (or hypotheses) are ruled out as possible. Playing this game, *M* learns new symbols by learning objects' "boundaries" (how they can be deformed and still receive the same name) and coming to share those boundaries through interaction with other individuals. This way, communication serves to make interaction more efficient. A central suggestion in this article is that (visual) symbols are learned to optimize interaction. The first-level shapes in *Fig.2*, for example, make both players imagine an often used shape at a time. While something less likely (like "very tall cup") requires more words, or strokes, for players to jointly construct.

In the next section, we place the work in context. We then turn to the model (first motivating its central concepts and then fully formulating them). After that, we describe an implementation of the model and its possible applications. We finally evaluate two of these applications, with an emphasis on learning performance.

RELATED WORK

The central problem relates to uncertainty and interaction, and thus Machine Learning (ML) and Human-Computer Interaction (HCI). We believe that the natural domain for HCI researchers interested in learning is not unsupervised learning (as sometimes taken as synonymous with Machine Learning), but semi-supervised or active learning [1,2]. Generally, unsupervised algorithms attempt to devise the most accurate classifier according to a provided exemplar set [3,4]. Active learning is of interest when the machine can, instead, query the user (or a database) for the classification of a given exemplar; and the intelligent choice of queries can improve the learning accuracy and/or speed. The user's response is often called a *labeling* of the exemplar. Consider the case of shape matching. A matching is often used as a shape classifier by starting with *U*'s shape (or sketch) and matching it against *M*'s (model) exemplars of different object classes. The resultant (distance) measures lead to a classification decision. In what follows, we consider the problem in the opposite direction: which exemplars should *M* suggest (or query) *U* at a time, to discover the correct class. The labeling (correct shape or not) of each suggestion informs, in this case, subsequent ones and allows *M* to change the shapes it is suggesting progressively, reactively, and quickly.

There has been a surge of research [9,7] tying machine learning techniques and vision problems in the past decade. Some researchers have, in turn, advocated the study, and discussed the power and difficulties of bringing these techniques to everyday computer use and HCI research [5,6]. For example, in [6] authors focused on the efficiency issue. They attempted to make a full re-training *unsupervised* cycle quick enough for interactive training for color and texture classification. For that, they used the popular "bag-of-feature" model [7,8,9] to represent objects (which ends up using over 1000 low-level image features to devise a classification decision). This rendered the interaction as a train-test cycle in a black-box fashion, *Fig.2c*. In this article, we explore an alternative connection between ML and HCI. Besides bringing an active learning perspective and game theoretical concepts to the problem, we address the issue of representation in learning, and we make the representations being learned observable and manipulateable by the user, *Fig.2d*. For the "bag-of-features" approach this seems plain unworkable. *Fig.2a* illustrates the first three features (learned with [8]) to detect cups such as the one in the top. The boxes are Haar-features, where the model expects paired high and low density of edge points. There are not only too many features, each usually at different scales, but few of them have any clear high-level interpretation.

Because ML is often framed in that language, the feature-set approach represents a straight-forward, out-of-the-box application of ML. To better address the unique constraints posed by HCI (semi-supervised, online, efficient, visual and intuitive representations), we believe we have to return to the concept of shape, which (due to the practical success of the feature-set approach) have lost some of its focus in vision. Although maybe not necessary for offline just-detect-the-object technology, it seems that whenever a human user is involved, so should the concept of shape. It's not yet clear, however, how to properly insert shapes into learning. The Shape-Editing game studied here uses the game formulation below and a new shape descriptor [28] to explore such issues in the intersection of shape representation and interactive learning. The descriptor attends to features relevant to HCI. It emphasizes shape regularity and the "gist" (instead of the feature) level of recognition. It represents shapes with a constructive process that recursively edits line-segments, *Fig.3e*. The process constructs rectangles, rectangles with one "bump" (or depression), two "bumps", etc. which are often related to the recognition of affordances [36].

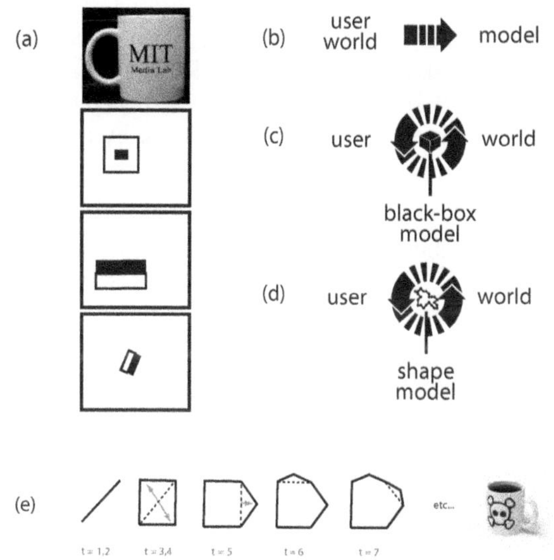

Figure 3. (a) first haar-features for a CART-tree, (b) batch data collection games, (c) iterative data collection and testing scheme, (d) shape learning scheme, (e) shape descriptor.

This top-down descriptor offers an attractive compromise between scalability and accuracy. One implementation [28] can match a shape to over 500 others under a second with accuracy within 5% of the state-of-the-art. We think specialized data-structures could scale the solution further, towards very large datasets (e.g., 1,000,000 shapes), offering a shape-matching alternative (and sketch-editing) to current index-based search solutions [10].

Following the unsupervised paradigm, games have been used as a setting to acquire ground-truth data for images

[11,12] and sketches [13]. After collected, data is then to be used as input for an unsupervised algorithm of choice. The process is one-way and non-interactive (*Fig. 2b*), and the model being constructed drives in no way the data being collected. We have observed that the process is dramatically accelerated when the model's uncertainty is clearly visualized by the user. This way, the interaction is an integral part of the solution (as opposed to the final-product's uninteresting last step). An exception comes from work in automatic translation or transcription [14], which often does have both the model and the user in the loop.

In the online formulation that follows the specific performance measure (otherwise traditionally the error rate [2]) is substituted by the game length (the expected number of interactions in the game). Optimization of large, *perfect*-information games have been studied in networking domains [24,25], while learning in games to a much lesser extent [26]. Models for games of incomplete information remain "laboratorial" (typically non-extensive), dating to Lewis' original signaling game formulation [16]. We studied large coordination games among low-income users, solving common problems, with cooperative (coalitional) game theoretical concepts with very positive results [27]. We are unaware of any other practical use of cooperative concepts, such as the Shapley value [23] used below. The relatively small quantity of game-theoretical concepts in HCI research is surprising, since it studies, by definition, a multi-party (cooperative) phenomenon.

Lee et al. [29] frame human-robot interaction as a "game" but say little about learning, uses no game theory, starts with idealized features, and is mostly descriptive. The solution is similar to work with no "games". Our basic premise (next section) is that people cope with joint problems by adopting hypotheses of what others are thinking and revising these hypotheses with interaction. This adds "cognitive" and "closed-loop" dimensions to general games, and leads to an explicit optimization criterion that doesn't require external models (e.g., markovian matrices) and that is related to principled game theoretical concepts.

In a broader scope, we place importance in mixed-initiative interaction [15], the study of interfaces that support efficient, natural interleaving of contributions by people and computers, aimed at converging on solutions to problems. Our main interest in this direction is to explore a new framework (targeting the visual, instead of the usual conversational medium). The framework developed allows machines to be positioned in a more active stance, ready to obtain information that they need (in as few queries as possible), as opposed to simply receiving information.

The game model proposed takes the user as an adapting creature, and we are interested in user learning (as opposed to assuming that only the machine is changing with interaction). A central motivation in the Shape-Editing game is to study more approachable ways for users to analyze, visualize and modify learned models. We see our work as an extension of efforts in that direction, in special in gesture-based interfaces [17,18]. James and Novins [19] study morphing animations in recognition, aimed at visualization, Lee et al. [20] overlay a cloud of ("completion") strokes recovered from large image datasets as guides for freehand drawing, and Igarashi et al. [21] suggest online candidate interpretations as result of fixed beautification procedures (not editing) for geometric design. The interaction is single-pass and fixed, and does not involve the back-and-forth construction of mutual understanding around complex models. The work here generalizes and enhances these paradigms.

Finally, we explore the issue of representational grounding, how can we represent the user's knowledge, without pre-encoding it in some way? The key seems to be to evolve that knowledge progressively and in collaboration, such that what the user refer to is always grounded in the environment – and so U and M's knowledge can be progressively aligned (i.e., made increasingly similar) through actions in the real world. Work in this direction comes especially from Human-Robot systems. For example, the goal of the Ripley system [30] is to support collaborative human-robot interaction; however, most of the work so far has concentrated on the development of fixed mental models (e.g., perspective taking), involving very little learning and no across-interaction optimization.

HUMAN-COMPUTER COMMUNICATION EXAMPLES

In this section we illustrate how typical Human-Computer communication (HCC) problems can be seen as games. We use the examples listed in *Fig.4b* to motivate and introduce key concepts. We do not study the game here as a general model for HCC, but feel that considering past HCC approaches is essential to better present and contextualize the work.

We see that cooperation, whatever its setting, involves a progressive modification of some structure (the medium). The main components of the model (*Fig.4a*) are two players (and their *knowledge states*) and a medium (and the *medium state*). The crux of the problem for players is that they can play many different games, and must coordinate unequivocally which they want to play at a time, through the medium. We call each a *subgame* to differ from the overall game. A player initially has incomplete information about which subgames the other wants to play. To reduce uncertainty, he changes the medium in some way so as to signal his intentions. The other respond similarly, and turn-taking takes place until they are ready to play a common subgame. Subgames are deterministic games with a fixed payoff structure, where players have shared and settled expectations and behaviors (no uncertainty).

This can be viewed as a series of subgame proposals made by the machine, followed by corrections made by the user, until an unambiguous solution is found for both. We consider strategies for the players, each considering the other's *knowledge state*. The players' *knowledge states* are always subgames subsets (i.e., the set of subgames that a player is considering to play). Careful observation of successive structural modifications generally reveals a basic set of structural medium *operators* or editions (x in *Fig.4a*). The game's risk is the risk of miscoordination (or mis-reference) between players. We sometimes refer to a player's "opponent" to mean "the other player". And we call a user's edition (a correction of the current medium) an *error* in the game.

(a)

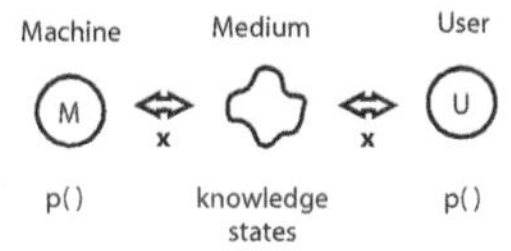

(b)

	Medium	Hypotheses	Operators (U)	Operators (M)
Voting	box, container	candidates	marks	(none, 1 round)
WIMP	widget	action	point-click	state change
Search engine	text	website	string	string edit
Sketch	sketch	examplars	sketch	(none, 1 round)
NL (joint action)	text	action	string	string
Shape Edit	sketch	examplars	sketch edit	sketch edit

(c) (d) (e)

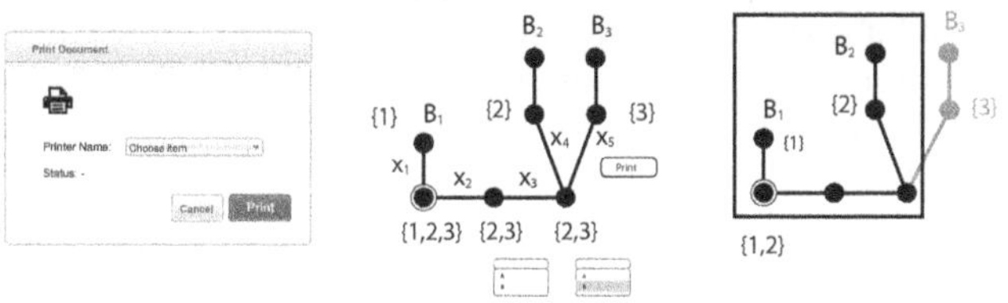

(f)

Figure 4. (a) main elements, (b) example games, (c-e) WIMP example, (f) sketch example hypotheses-sets.

Ballot design is a very simple example of such a game. The medium is typically a paper formulary; the players are the voter and the official interpreting the ballot. The hypotheses-sets for both players are candidate sets (e.g., *{Bush, Kerry}*). The subgames are *vote-for-kerry* or *vote-for-bush*. The medium is typically graphical boxes or containers, and operators are marks. Poor designs lead to confusion and potentially miscoordination between a large numbers of voters and their government. Like in all examples here, the risk is a measure of visual confusion (that tells how well medium states visually distinguish the two hypotheses).

Voting is a simple example because it is a one round/turn game (uncertainty is, supposedly, resolved with a single action). Like voting, WIMP interfaces have also a very simple medium (designed for easy discrimination) and operators, but can have typically more rounds. Media are graphical widgets, and operators are mouse clicks (for *U*) and pre-coded state changes (for *M*). In the simple dialog box in *Fig.4c*, players can play the subgames *close*, *print-on-A* and *print-on-B*. The game's operators are used to construct a graph representation in the next section, *Fig.4d*. To play *print-on-A*, the user may start by clicking on the combo-box (use operation x_2), the machine respond by changing the widget to a popped state, the user click on "*A*" (x_3), the machine change the combo to unppoped (and possibly the "print" button to enabled), which the user clicks (x_4). To play this game *U* must also keep track of the machine's knowledge state (i.e., interaction deteriorate when states are not clear).

These are all graphically mediated interfaces. Search engine interfaces (e.g., google) are contrasting cases with a textual medium (a search string). Operators are often string-edit operations (character insertion, deletion and substitution). The case is interesting because the number of subgames is much larger, and the engine must effectively guess what's on the user's mind. The engine is adaptative (in the long term, across games) but there are typically few turns (within a game), with the engine simply listing its best, current mining matches.

The number of possible medium states is small in this case compared to graphical media. Gestural and sketch recognition interfaces deal with natural input and thus larger medium variation. Subgames are classes over gesture or sketch exemplars. The hypotheses for *M* in this case are the entire set of objects it "knows". The hypotheses-set for the user is the object he wants (or intends to sketch). This can be a set of exemplars of an object (e.g., a "cup") or a more specific set (e.g., a certain cup or any large cup). *Fig.4f* shows example hypotheses-sets for the former case.

Players specify what they are willing to play with their hypotheses-sets. In games here, *M* starts with a full set *H* and rule hypotheses out until it finds *U*'s playable subset in *H*. For the voting and WIMP games, *U* wants to typically play a singleton set (i.e., choose respectively one candidate or action). For others, *U* can specify (with its hypotheses set) a satisficing criteria (i.e., a set of acceptable subgames). The players' hypotheses-sets need not be identical, and learning is necessary if they are not. As result, we can say players "align" their representational sets through learning.

Sketch recognition is typically addressed by pre-training a gesture or sketch classifier, possibly from the two sets of exemplars. This is not convenient, however, when sets (e.g., what the user wants) change with the situation. Approaching the problem this way (offline, or in batch), learning also occurs outside of the interaction.

The previous examples differ in this way from Human-Human interaction where learning can emerge on-line, spontaneously, in response to interaction errors. Natural Language (NL) dialogue is an interesting example of a game that, because of a very large number of subgames, relies on mechanisms of self-adjustment, turn-taking and repair [31]. With larger and more diverse graphical lexicons, errors are always possible and we can expect mechanisms that allow machines to similarly resolve graphical uncertainties online.

That requires both an online learning model and interaction design (i.e., how to present, accept and reject hypotheses online). We present a model next and then an interaction design for the case of sketches (designs for GUIs and other domains are not currently studied).

MODEL

The game is described by a Graph $G = \langle V,X \rangle$. Graph nodes V are medium states, edges X are medium operators. An edge $x \in X$ characterizes a (significant) difference between its two connecting nodes. Training (i.e., learning from previous games) is described by previous graph instances $G_1, G_2, \ldots, G_K$ and constitute the player's hypotheses-set, $H = \{G_1, G_2, \ldots, G_K\}$. The game is more naturally described in extensive form (as opposed to a single payoff matrix). The players' payoff is the game duration. Since players will stop playing only after they have resolved all their individual uncertainties, players must consider each other's knowledge states to minimize the game's duration. And they coordinate on paths with small expected duration for both.

Winning Paths

We first review the game's combinatorial structure, which is similar to [27]. We then introduce new concepts (next section) to formulate an optimal many-rounds game. Let h be the set of operators applied previously by a player (a "path" in G). A player's knowledge state $p(h)$ is a set of possible hypotheses or exemplars (e.g., different objects M thinks U might be thinking of, at a time). The knowledge state can be fundamentally described by a set function, $p : h \to 2^H$, denoting the set of possible hypotheses at a time (note this is merely a convenient functional form for a subset of H). This way, we endow a player with some private information, which is summarized by $p(h)$. Before applying an operator, the player then believes that what is truly being sketched is in the set $p(h)$. After the operation, the player reviews this set by observing the other's response, and so on.

Our overall approach is to first assume that the function $p(h)$ separates hypotheses perfectly (i.e., that no hypothesis is ruled-out erroneously). We then formulate and minimize a risk measure (which indicates the probability of misclassification). Humans often make decisions with nothing close to a complete statistical model. The emphasis here on model selection alleviates the often unpractical data-requirements of ML applications (e.g., [8] or [7] require hundreds of thousands of images, and sometimes days, to generate a classifier).

Let $p^U(h)$ be U's knowledge state after path h. A path is *winning* to M only if U has no more possible plays. That is, the game ends when the opponent has no further possible operations to apply to the medium, which happens when $p^U(h) = \{\oslash\}$, or schematically $h : p^U \to \oslash$. We then say two operations x_i and x_j are dependent for M if $p^U(\{x_i, x_j\}) = \oslash$. The set $\vec{W}_t(H)$ of all winning paths of size t (in a game with hypotheses H) are the set of bases of a matroid [32,27] (which is a generalization of independence in vector spaces). Bases are the matroid maximal independent sets (i.e., sets that become dependent on adding any new element). The set of bases of all sizes up to T (a game parameter) is denoted simply $\vec{W}(H)$.

The winning paths are an equilibrium solution in the game (i.e., neither player has incentive to deviate). Since the bases are the possible (final) plays in a game with hypotheses H, players must coordinate on one such path. They can estimate the opponent's likelihood of playing each path as a discrete probability distribution over the set of bases, $\sum_{B \in \vec{W}(H)} P(B) = 1$.

The structure will allow to calculate efficiently several useful measures. Before devising the game's expected duration (payoff), reconsider *Fig.4d*. Name the subgames 1, 2 and 3 (*close*, *print-A* and *print-B*). M starts with hypotheses $\{1,2,3\}$, if U applies x_2, M reviews the set to $\{2,3\}$. Application of x_4 makes the set $\{2\}$. The path $\{x_2, x_3, x_4\}$ is a basis because the use of any other operation makes M's hypotheses set void. Other bases are $\{x_1\}$ and $\{x_2, x_3, x_5\}$.

Expected Length and Risk

With the bases-set $\vec{W}(H)$, it's simple to calculate the expected duration, or length, L_1 of a game with hypotheses set H:

$$L_1(H) = \sum_{B \in \vec{W}(H)} P(B) \times Length(B) \qquad (1)$$

where $Length(B) = |B|$ in this case[1]. The game's expected duration is given by its bases, which correspond to a set of paths in a graph. The expected duration of the game in *Fig.4d*, for example, is 1.67 (with $H = \{1,2,3\}$ and equiprobable bases).

This is the payoff of a game with fixed initial hypotheses-set, H. The expected duration can be drastically reduced in games where errors are possible (and informative). This is especially true in large games. In this case, players start with a subset of hypotheses, and, in case of errors, review the set (letting interaction feedback control the game).

[1] We assume that operators are associative and contiguous edges belonging to the same set of bases can be, at no cost, combined into a single edge (with length one).

Consider first a game with 2 rounds (and that "\" is typical set contraction). An error is the rejection (by the opponent) of a proposed operation x. The error can be informative, leading the player to reject the set of hypotheses $H \backslash p(x)$. An operation x can then be seen by M as a statistical test performed on U (with a risk $r(x)$). The min-expected length L_2 of a game with 2 rounds is then:

$$L_2(H) = 1 + \min_x [(1 - P_e(x)) L_1(p(x)) + P_e(x) L_1(H \backslash p(x))] \quad (2)$$

where $P_e(x)$ is the probability of x being rejected. The application of operation x splits the game in two, with probabilities $P_e(x)$ and $1 - P_e(x)$ of being played and lengths $L_1(H \backslash p(x))$ and $L_1(p(x))$. For example, in the game of *Fig.4d* consider that $P(B_2) \gg P(B_3)$. In this case, *Eq.2* selects x_5. Players first assume that hypotheses are $\{1,2\}$ (*close* and *print-to-A*), and in case of error $\{3\}$. This corresponds to a design where the combo-box in *Fig.4c* has a default value (and U is forced to further operate the medium to reach the subgame *print-to-B*). Players agree (*Fig.4e*) then to carry the game over the subgraph with edges $\{x_1, \ldots, x_4\}$ first, and move to the subgraph with $\{x_1, \ldots, x_5\}$ as needed.

We can extend this solution by recursion to many rounds, $L_t(H)$, and to encompass the players' risk. In the second, the player, instead of incurring a cost of 1 at each round, incurs a risk $r(x)$. See [28] for a detailed discussion on the implementation of *Eq.2* and its elements in the visual domain (in special, shape operators and bases' risk and probability). This is a computational formulation of the game solution. We relate it now to a cooperative solution concept in game theory. Arrange *Eq.2* in the following way

$$L_2(H) = 1 + \min_x \{L_1(H) - P_e(x)[L_1(H) - L_1(H \backslash p(x))]\}$$
$$L_2(H) = 1 + \min_x \{L_1(H) - S(H,x)\}$$

where $S(H,x) = P_e(x)[L_1(H) - L_1(H \backslash p(x))]$.

Suppose the probability of error of an operation x, $P_e(x)$, is the sum of probabilities of bases that contain x. Then (see [34], proof of theorem 4.2):

$$S(H,x) = \sum_{B \in W(H/x)} \frac{\sum_{B' \in W(H \backslash x)} P(B')}{(T - |B| + 1)\binom{T+1}{|B|}} [L_1(p(x)) - L_1(H \backslash p(x))]$$

In a game with 2 rounds, $S(H,x)$ corresponds to the game's Shapley value [23,35] for operation x over the defined matroid structure. Under this interpretation, the solution removes first the operation with lowest expected Shapley value. Players consequently assume a hypotheses-set with high Shapley value, considering the complementary set with lower value in case of error (requiring, in this case, more editions and thus minimizing the *expected* number of operations). The Shapley value is an ideal measure and generally too expensive to calculate. Due to the matroid structure, the value can be calculated efficiently [33,27].

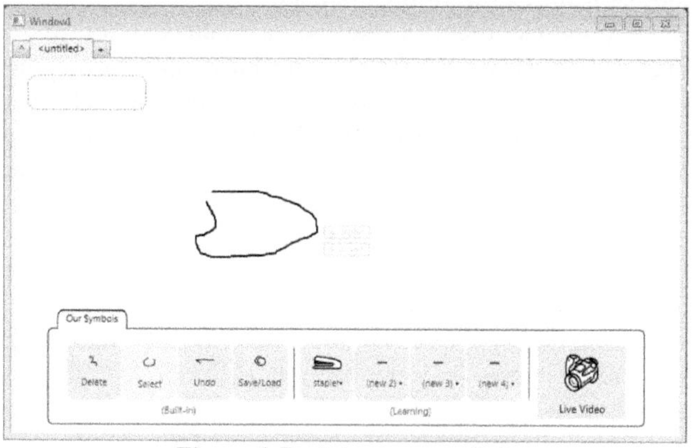

Figure 6. Prototype screenshot.

This view mirrors some intuitive aspects of human communication in general, where we assume at first the most likely aspects of a joint action and negotiate online, as needed, aspects that need alteration. The first-level shapes in *Fig.2* correspond to a reduced-hypotheses (or many-rounds) game. Reference to other (less likely) objects requires extra editions and further rounds.

PROTOTYPE INTERACTIVE SYSTEM

We have built a prototype interactive system to embody the game. *Fig. 6* shows a screenshot. It consists of a sketchboard and a model panel. While the game is played on the sketchboard, the lower bar visualizes the current models and shows recognition in live video.

As U sketches, M presents and updates in realtime its suggestions (shown as a pop-up button list to the side of U's sketch, *Fig.6 light-gray*). Since each is an alternative set of shape operators, they are shown with morph-scratch-draw (substitute, erase, complete) animations on strokes. On hover, the user gets a quick morph (with fade) so he can quickly examine his choices. Each pop-up button corresponds to a set of hypotheses in the (reduced) game selected by *Eq.2* (and in the order of Shapley values). The user can erase or complete contours at any time, observing how changes affect M's hypotheses-set and ordering. By choosing one interpretation, the user rejects all others. Optimization is carried online, stroke-by-stroke (as opposed to a sketch-and-submit model). The user's scratch gesture is pre-trained and cannot be changed.

Either M or U can declare the end of the game at any time. M declares the end when its hypotheses-set is empty and there are no more possible suggestions. U declares the end by choosing an additional ("new") hypothesis, which is always offered. In both cases, M offers U to add the current sketch as a new hypothesis and name it.

USE CASES

We now discuss use cases we have explored for the prototype.

Mobile Robot Sketch-to-Command

M is a mobile robot. *U* sketches a command for *M* to execute. Initially, *U* draws something that carries no meaning to the robot. Through learning, they can establish a common symbolic lexicon. We have prototyped the case where the user can sketch objects, locations, and arrows (*Fig. 7a*). The first two refer to live visual objects in front of both players, and the third to a single action (move source-to-destination). *Fig. 7b* shows data (hypotheses) collected in this scenario for household objects. *Fig. 7c* shows the 4 suggested transformations to the ambiguous user sketch in *Fig. 7a*. An interesting aspect of this scenario is that joint attention, like in human communication, can accelerate dramatically the reference game. Users can "snap" the diagrams to reality, or play the game "grounded" (i.e., *M* only disambiguates among recognized objects – or objects that it "sees"). Although we, for example, may know the shapes for a multitude of objects, there are few that we expect to see in particular joint action situations and places.

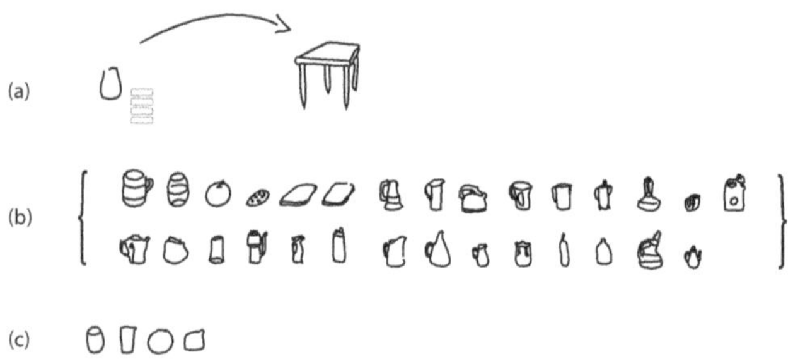

Figure 7. (a) sketch to command, (b) hypotheses, (c) suggestions.

Hand Gesture Recognition

The prototype can be readily used for pen or mouse gesture recognition. We have observed that allowing users to examine the variations or possible deformations in their gestures (similar to Bau's Octopocus technique [22]) makes the process more transparent. This is true for training and for use. The issue of recognition error is important and has been recognized for gestures [18]. The work here offers an alternative way to visualize the error and use it for learning.

Cooperative Sketch Completion

We studied games where users take turns completing sketches "forward". *M* learns such completions and use them in new games (i.e., with the next players). This way, with each new player, the shape editions grow richer and more imaginative and *M* constructs progressively, from playing, a "catalogue" of possible editions. As a first step, we designed a game where *M* starts with a number (*Fig.8*) and *U* is asked to creatively complete it. Children find playing this game after some training a lot of fun.

Figure 8. cooperative sketching.

Media Authoring

We have also used the prototype to assist users draw and animate. To help users draw, we foresee games where *U* draws something (e.g., a circle), and *M* suggests next steps (e.g., add a neck or a leg). *Fig.9a-b* shows editions learned from users drawing animals. To help users animate, we applied the previous framework to shape interpolation. In this case, animations were not only the system's means of communication, but also the final output. Each one of *U*'s deletions was taken to be a new model object. *Fig.9c* depicts an example: *U* drew the first frame, then deleted the arrow (a new model is created); he then drew only the arrow's shaft, which *M* completed with feathers. This was repeated a few times to make 1-stroke keyframes for the arrow wobbling animation. Since animation often compromises the recursive modification of sketch parts, learning parts' models can be useful.

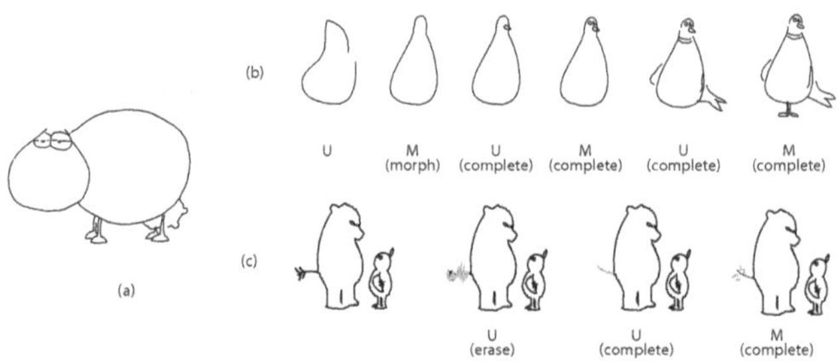

Figure 9. (a,b) assisted drawing, (c) animation.

Interactive Visual Web-Query

We have finally used the prototype to investigate a simplified version of the web search game (*Fig.4b*). Users sketch queries and ambiguity is resolved interactively (with sketch editing). For illustration, consider a simple example. We googled the terms "apple", "tomato" and "lemon" and selected as *M*'s possible hypotheses the top 3 related queries in each case. We used the goggle hit counts as probabilistic priors (see [28]). *Fig.10a* shows one run and *Fig.10b* lists *M*'s hypotheses with subsequent rounds. As in the previous games, the editions are learned from previous users' sketches. In the next section, we evaluate this and the sketch-to-command scenarios in further detail.

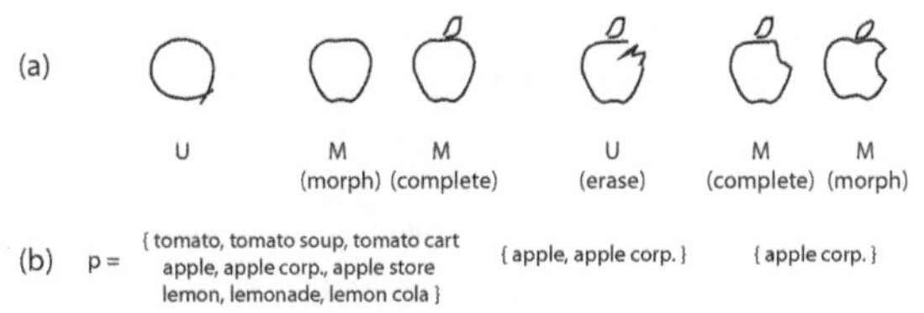

Figure 10. (a) query example, (b) *M*'s knowledge states .

EXPERIMENTS

We study learning and sketch-editing in two user trial studies with 70 participants playing 2 games. Our main goal is to subject the model to actual use – in special, to elucidate how many turns would prove necessary (in avg.) after some initial training and with natural input (which speaks directly to the model's applicability). Other relevant side discussions are also offered: that the designed interaction has an observable effect on these results, a curious benchmark on how humans would play the game, and a very favorable qualitative user evaluation for the web search scenario.

Machine Player (M)

We ran pilot user studies for the sketch-to-command and visual web-query use cases. The goal of these first experiments was to assess *M*'s longitudinal performance across different interactions and games. In the first condition (*U-M*), users played instances of the two games (15 household objects and web query trials each), and we examined the game duration across time (or users). With learning, we expected a progression of reducing game durations. For a baseline, (paired) users played the same games (*U-U*).

Participants were volunteers, aged 17-28, with little or intermediary tablet experience. Before the trials, they were given a 20 minutes training session on its use and the scratch gesture. At the end they were asked to complete a set of 5 exercises completing and erasing a set of shapes. The experiment was performed on two quad-core 2.8 and 2.6 GHz PCs, each connected to a Wacom Cintiq 12WX pen display.

For *U-M*, users were told to imagine they were playing a game where a computer would try to guess an object (or web query) from his/her sketches. They were told to help as much as possible, but that they could end the game at any time. They were asked to press one button for that case and another for a correct guess. Players were told that writing was against the game's rules (including numbers). No further instructions were given, and the experimenter did not answer questions during sessions. Before beginning, participants received a printed list of objects or queries in the games (which they were asked to read beforehand). The list was made available to account for the experimental constraint that *M* only discriminates among objects in the experiment (while *U* in a *U-U* trial, without the list, would consider a much larger number).

U received *M* feedback (hypotheses' labels and editions) with each of his/her strokes, but limited in the trial to a single suggestion. The game ended when either *M* guessed the object correctly, or, *U* or *M* ended the game. In the latter case, the trial was declared *learning-only*.

The *U-U* game reproduced *U-M*'s setup with a Wizard-of-Oz design. The (randomly assigned) initiating user proceeded stroke-by-stroke. The non-initiating user was asked to guess (label) and/or make any number of corrections to the other's sketch (editions). In *U-M, M*'s feedback was presented in less than 2 seconds (after the end of a stroke), while *U* in *U-M* and *U-U* could take any time. Note that this experiment's goal was to study *M*'s performance and not *U*'s perception (of the game). Users could not see each other, only the *GUI* in *Fig.6*, with added "end" and "correct!" buttons, and a "your turn" indicator. Since the response time is very different, we use the number of gestures (and not the more usual time-to-completion) as performance measure. The measure also accounts for *U*'s gesture errors.

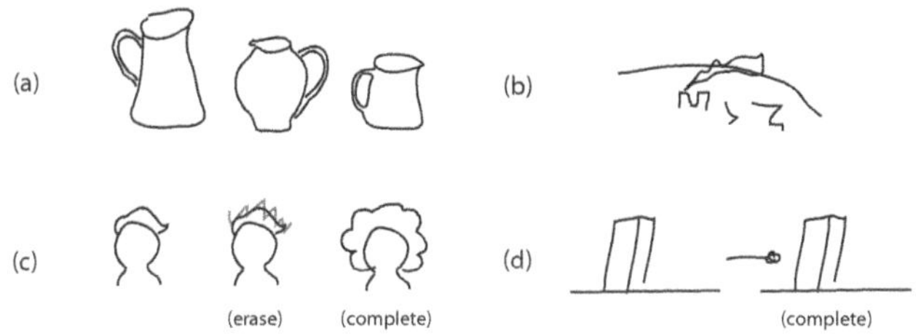

Figure 11. (a) object games examples, (b) learning-only trial, (c,d) web query edition disambiguation examples.

U-U had 20 participants (10 sessions), and *U-M* had 25 (25 sessions). A session consisted of the two games in succession (in random order). In the household objects game, 15 grasp/pushable objects in our lab with obvious names were selected. They were jar, camera, cell-phone, book, glasses, hat, knife, spoon, fork, stapler, plant vase, pen, crayon, tomato and orange. The order of the 15 objects was random. In the web query game, queries were selected (and randomly assigned) from the top 16 google searches in our location. They were "cerebral palsy", "Serena Williams", "World Trade Center", "Ronald Reagan", "college football rankings", "Jacksonville Jaguars", "9/11", "September 11", "flight 93", "mermaid", "Patriots", "Dr. Phil", "White House", "super bowl 2011", "presidencial debate" and "NHL". Two of the searches, "9/11" and "september 11", were merged into one.

Fig.12a shows the percentage of learning-only trials (i.e., without a correct guess) with time for the household object game. *Fig.12c* shows the average number of gestures for the 15 objects over time. In this game, there is a trend towards 1-2 average gestures. The trend is present in *U-U* and emerges in *U-M* after a number of trials. More than one trial (i.e., exemplars) is often necessary to encompass different users' shapes and pose variations (e.g., *Fig.11a*).

Learning is "slower" in the web-query game (*U-M*), *Fig.12b*. It takes 9 users/sessions for *M* to guess correctly all queries for the first time (while only 3 for the household object game). The number of gestures, in both *U-M* and *U-U*, is (on average) also significantly larger for the web-query game, *Fig.12d*. Both observations can be explained by the abstraction level of concepts in this game (which leads to a larger variation on *U*'s depictions). *Fig.11c-d* highlights two trials, where users sketched to disambiguate "Ronald Reagan" and "Serena Williams" and "World trade center" and "11/9". *Fig.11b* shows a trial ended by *U* (learning-only) for "11/9".

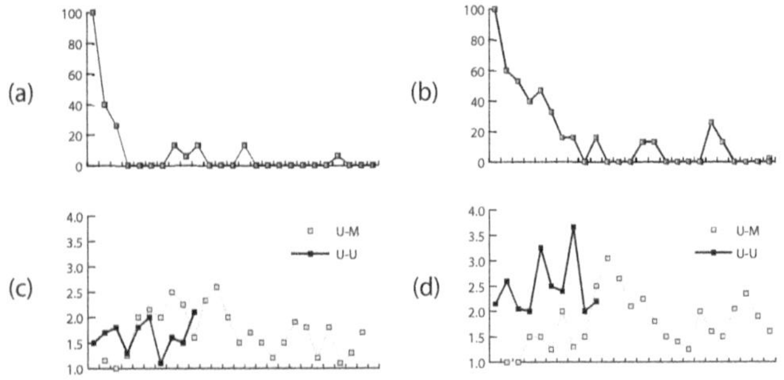

Figure 12. (a,b) average % of learning-only trials resp. in the object and web-query games , (c,d) average number of strokes.

The system is shape-bound and unable to use color and texture cues directly. One could argue that heavily articulated or amorphous objects (e.g., "coat") would take lots of exemplars to learn. Users seem to stick, however, to a surprisingly small set of (prototypical) shapes and poses, making the problem easier. This is arguably intrinsic to how we act together (and expected by the model).

User Player (U)

While the previous study addressed *M*'s learning performance, we addressed "user learning" and representational transparency next. We repeated the *U-M* setup in a two-factor study for 25 users. The control players played with word labels only (as opposed to labels and visual editions). Visual learning happens in the same way (but *M*'s editions are not visualized by *U*). *Fig.13* shows the results. A (paired) t-test for the percentage of correct guesses over trials indicates significant differences ($p = 0.0181$ and $p = 0.0104$) between the distributions in the two conditions, in the two games. The editions induce *U* to directly address *M*'s models (and often demonstrate relevant difference among objects or queries), which is useful to learning.

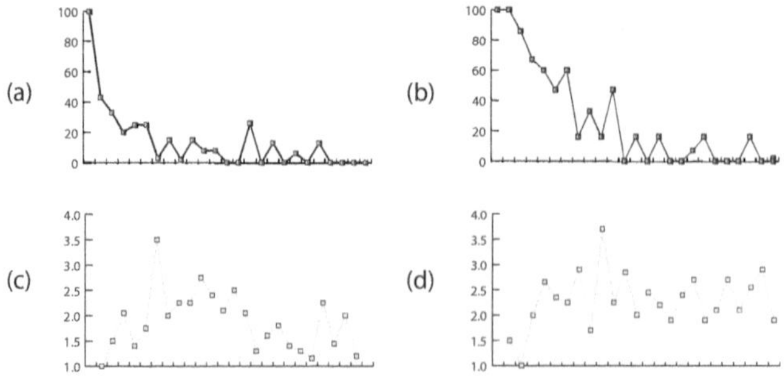

Figure 13. (a,b) average % of learning-only trials resp. in the object and web-query games , (c,d) average number of strokes.

These results point to an interaction between the representation and learning speed in the absolute. They favor the shape over the black-box model (*Fig.3c-d*) in the current tasks. That is, suppression of information about *M*'s current model (summarized by *M*'s editions) has immediate effect on learning performance. As implication, black-box models (where *U* cannot visualize *M*'s model in any practical way) miss an important aspect of the problem. These results suggest, in turn, the relevance of interaction aspects to the problem of learning. In the future, we plan to study learning efficiency across alternative representations.

The shape model has a direct effect not only on the resulting training data, but also on user engagement. A post-study survey asked participants to rank in a 5-point Likert scale if they would use the game to make a web-search (with 0 "not at all" and 5 "definitely"). Participants ranked the shape-model (Mean 4.69, SD 0.83) considerably more favorably than the black-box model (Mean 3.1, SD 0.95).

CONCLUSION

Everyday interaction is misleading in its simplicity. In our initial example game, unlike *U*, *M* does not know what "cup" means (a largely visual concept). Even when it does, does *U* mean that tall cup over there or the one with flowers? Uncertainty is part of any joint action, under any modality. We made the case for a way to address uncertainty in interaction (visually, in special). To articulate uncertainty visually ("tall? with flowers?") is often very powerful (we had users screaming/laughing in surprise, in web and drawing games) and natural (underlies all our GUIs). We demonstrated how such new sketch-based interaction paradigm can improve sketch-based learning. We will study further interaction and representation aspects of *U* and *M* learning performances. We believe that the work can also help understanding other modalities, machine mind-reading (and "writing"), and communication in general.

REFERENCES

1. Tong, S., Koller, D. Active Learning for Parameter estimation in Bayesian Networks. *NIPS* (2000).
2. Chaloner, K., Verdinelli, I. Bayesian Experimental Design: A Review. *Stat. Science* (1995).
3. Alvarado, C., Davis, R. Dynamically Constructed Bayes net for Multi-domain Sketch Recognition. *IJCAI,* (2005).
4. Ulgen F., Flavell C., Akamatsu N., Geometric Shape Recognition with Fuzzy Filtered Input to a Backpropagation Neural Network, *IEICE Transactions on Information and Systems*, 78, 2 (1995).
5. Maynes-Aminzade, D., Winograd, T., Igarashi, T. Eyepatch: Prototyping Camera-based Interaction through Examples, *UIST* (2007).
6. Fails, J., Olsen, D. Interactive Machine Learning. *ICUI (2003).*
7. Opelt, A., Pinz, A., Fussenegger, M., Auer, P. Generic Object Recognition with Boosting, *PAMI* (2006).
8. Viola P., Jones, M. Rapid Object Detection Using Boosted Cascade of Simple Features. *CVPR* (2001).
9. Zhang, J., Marszalek, M. Lazebnik, S., Schmid C. Local Features and Kernels for Classification of Texture and Object Categories: a Comprehensive Study. *IJCV*, 73, 2 (2007).
10. Cao, Y., Wang, C., Zhang, L., Zhang, L. Edgel Index for Large-Scale Sketch-based Image Search. *CVPR* (2011).
11. Russel B., Torralba A., Murphy K., Labelme: A Database and Web-based Tool for Image Annotation, *IJCV*, 77, 1-3 (2008).
12. Von Ahn L., Dabbish L., Labeling Images with a Computer Game, *CHI (2004).*
13. Johnson G., Do E., Games for sketch data collection, *Eurographics (2009).*
14. Vidal, E., Casacuberta, F., Rodrigues, J., Civera, J., Martnez, C. Computer assisted translation using speech recognition. *IEE Transaction on Audio, Speech and Language Processing, 14*, 3 (2006).
15. Horvitz, E. Reflections on Challenges and Promises of Mixed-Initiative Interaction, *AAAI Magazine 28* (2007).
16. Lewis, D., Convention. A Philosophical Study, Harvard University Press, Harvard (1979).
17. Bragdon, A., Zeleznik, R., Williamson, B., LaViola .. GestureBar: Improving the Approachability of Gesture-based Interfaces. *CHI* (2009).
18. Mankoff, J. Providing Integrated Toolkit-Level Support for Ambiguity in Recognition-Based Interfaces. *CHI* (2010).
19. James, A., Novins, K., Fluid Sketches: Continuous Recognition and Morphing of Simple Hand-Drawn Shapes. *UIST* (2000).
20. Lee, Y., Zitnick, L. Cohen, M. ShadowDraw: Real-Time User Guidance for Freehand Drawing. *SIGGRAPH* (2011).
21. Igarashi, T., Matsuoka, S., Kawachiya, S., Tanaka, H. Interactive Beautification: A Technique for Rapid Geometric Design. *UIST* (1997).
22. Bau, O., Mackay, W. OctoPocus: a Dynamic Guide for Learning Gesture-based Command Sets. *UIST* (2008).
23. Owen, G. Game Theory 3rd edition. Academic Press (1993).
24. McKelvey, R., McLennan, A. Computation of Equilibria in Finite Games. *Handbook of Computational Economics, Volume I* (1996).
25. Roughgarden, T. Selfish Routing and the Price of Anarchy. MIT Press (2005).
26. Kerns, M. Graphical Games. Algorithmic Game Theory, Cambridge University Press (2007).
27. Ribeiro, A. A Model of Joint Learning in Poverty: Coordination and Recommendation Systems in Low-Income Communities. *ICMLA* (2011).
28. Ribeiro, A., Igarashi, T. Joint Shape Editing Games: An Implementation. MIT Technical Report (2012).
29. Lee, K., Hwang, J. Human-robot Interaction as a Cooperative Game. O. Castillo (ed.) et al., *Trends in intelligent systems and computer engineering* (IMECS 2007).
30. Roy, D., Hsiao, K., Mavridis, N. Mental Imagery for a Conversational Robot. *IEEE Transactions on Systems, Man, and Cybernetics*, 22 (2004).
31. Clark, H. Using Language. Cambridge Univ. Press (2006).
32. Oxley, J. Matroid Theory Oxford University Press (1992) .
33. Nagamochi, N., Zeng, D., Kabutoya, N., Ibaraki, T. Complexity of the Min. Base Game on Matroids. *Mathematics of Operations Research.* (1997).
34. Bilbao, J., Driessen, T., Jimenez-Losada, A., Lebron, E. The Shapley value for games on matroids: The static model. *Math. Meth. Oper. Res.* (2001).
35. Roth, A., The Shapley Value as a von Neumann–Morgenstern Utility, *Econometrica* 45 (1977).
36. Gibson, J. The Ecological Approach to Visual Perception. Lawrence Erlbaum (1979).

Interpreting Strokes on Paper with a Mobile Assistant

Theophanis Tsandilas
INRIA - Univ Paris-Sud & CNRS (LRI)
F-91405 Orsay, France
Theophanis.Tsandilas@inria.fr

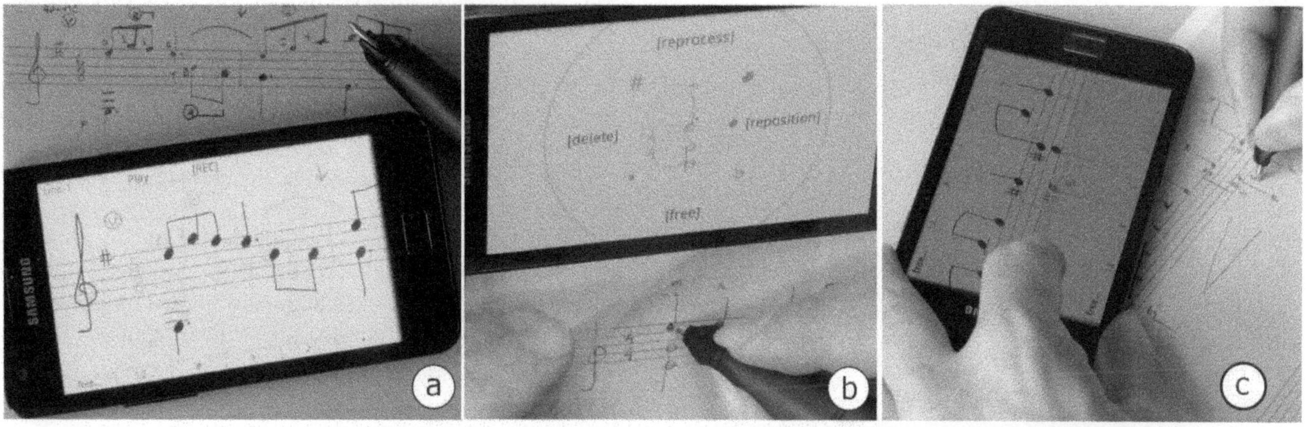

Figure 1. Writing music with an Anoto pen and a smartphone. (a) Handwritten score translated by the device. (b) Correcting the recognition of a note over a small plastic sheet. (c) Guiding the interpretation of strokes with the left hand.

ABSTRACT
Digital pen technology has allowed for the easy transfer of pen data from paper to the computer. However, linking handwritten content with the digital world remains a hard problem as it requires the translation of unstructured and highly personal vocabularies into structured ones that computers can easily understand and process. Automatic recognition can help to this direction, but as it is not always reliable, solutions require the active cooperation between users and recognition algorithms. This work examines the use of portable touch-screen devices in connection with pen and paper to help users direct and refine the interpretation of their strokes on paper. We explore four techniques of bimanual interaction that combine touch and pen-writing, where user attention is divided between the original strokes on paper and their interpretation by the electronic device. We demonstrate the techniques through a mobile interface for writing music that complements the automatic recognition with interactive user-driven interpretation. An experiment evaluates the four techniques and provides insights about their strengths and limitations.

ACM Classification: H.5.2 [Information interfaces and presentation]: User Interfaces. - Graphical user interfaces.

Keywords: Paper interfaces; bimanual interaction; pen + touch; mobile; interactive recognition; music interfaces.

INTRODUCTION

Previous studies suggest that paper is indispensable for several groups of users. Composers of contemporary music are proficient users of computers but still use paper at different stages of the composition process, from sketching initial ideas to working on final scores [11, 24]. Biology researchers use paper to record their field observations [26] or keep a history of their research protocols and results in their lab notebooks [19]. Digital pen technology has eased the connection between paper and computers. Yet, linking handwritten content with the digital world is still a challenging problem. The recognition of handwritten symbols is imperfect, while paper is not interactive by itself and the feedback provided by digital pens is still extremely limited.

Several approaches have succeeded in making paper interactive by using special equipment such as a projector and a tabletop [7] or a graphics tablet and a PDA [19]. More recently, Song et al. [22] explored paper interaction with a pen and a miniature projector. Here, we focus on the use of smartphones as mobile assistants for supporting work on paper and helping users direct the interpretation of their strokes. Smartphones are lightweight, inexpensive and widely available, and afford rich channels of input and output. Yet, how to take advantage of these additional channels when working on paper is a challenging problem that previous work has not examined. The paper explores techniques to help users interactively translate their writing on paper. We examine four forms of bimanual coordination (see Figure 2) that combine pen and finger touch and make use of the smartphone's touchscreen to control how handwritten data are recognized by the computerized system.

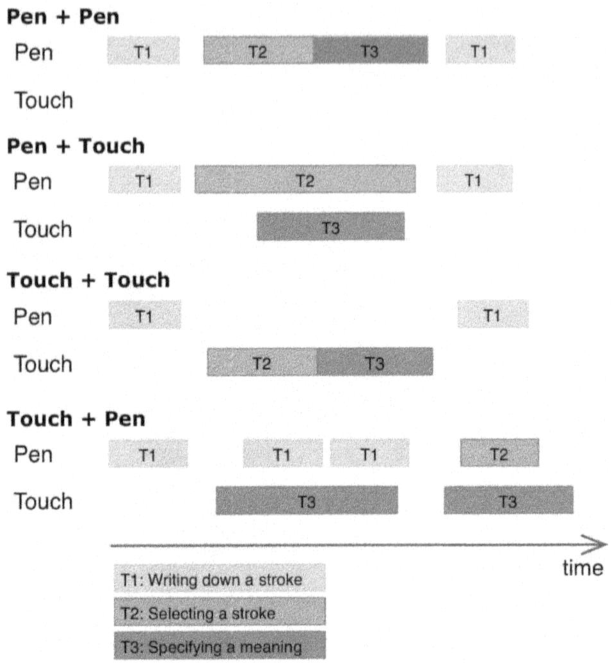

Figure 2. Forms of bimanual coordination. The pen is controlled by the dominant hand. Touch is controlled by the non-dominant hand.

To better understand how these techniques would be used in practice in practice, we apply them to a concrete and challenging task, writing music (see Figure 1), which derives from real user needs [11, 24]. We demonstrate how they can enhance an interactive rule-based recognizer of musical notation by helping users correct recognition errors. We also show how the *Touch + Pen* technique can enable users to override the recognition process by constraining the interpretation of their strokes (see Figure 1(c)). Our approach has been based on Anoto paper technology, Bluetooth pens, and Android devices.

The paper presents an experiment that evaluates the four forms of bimanual coordination when recognition is imperfect. The results show significant performance benefits for the *Touch + Pen* technique, especially when the technique is used to constrain the interpretation of written strokes rather than correct recognition errors. User ratings, however, are not consistent with performance results, as *Pen + Pen* and *Pen + Touch* receive significantly higher scores. Based on our findings, we discuss the strengths and limitations of each technique and proceed with recommendations about their future use.

RELATED WORK

Interpreting Handwritten Data

Paper technology has been studied in range of application domains, from editing documents [17] to composing music [11, 24]. Interpreting the handwriting can be a difficult challenge in such domains, as data can take different representations and forms that vary greatly among different users. Recognition algorithms can help to an extent, but their effectiveness is usually limited. For example, optical musical recognition for handwritten music has been available in commercial software. However, as Rebelo et al. [20] report in a recent survey, there are still no robust methodologies to recognize handwritten musical scores.

Researchers have explored a number of solutions to deal with the problem of recognition, but each solution has limitations. Some restrict the number of recognizable gestures and provide ink delimiters such as pigtails [17] and knotty gestures [25] to differentiate between commands and regular handwriting. Others, such as Mus*ink* [24], provide tools that help users refine the recognition but only after data have been uploaded to the computer. *Paper Substrates* [11] are specialized paper components that only accept certain types of data, which they know how to interpret and process. Finally, commercial products such as Livescribe provide buttons and menus printed on notebooks that activate explicit modes of stroke interpretation.

Pen, Paper and Mobile Feedback

Several solutions have studied the use of portable devices to assist interaction with paper although none of them deals with the problem of stroke recognition. Mackay et al. [19] introduce A-book, a portable device that helps biologists create links between their laboratory notebooks and online resources. A-book acts as a magic lens that displays digital information when positioned over a page. Yeh et al. [26] propose the use of a mobile device together with a digital pen to help biologists record data in the field. Finally, Liao et al. [18] use the camera of a mobile phone to make associations between digital and paper content. More recently, Heinrichs et al. [13] examine how users shift their focus between paper and a smartphone. They observe that users try to minimize the number of transitions between the two media, but transitions are not necessarily disruptive and often go unnoticed. Instead of a mobile phone, Song et al. [22] use a mini-projector to display information and menus on paper. Then, users interact with them by using the pen. Finally, Livescribe pens include a tiny OLED display and a built-in speaker to support live feedback.

Pen + Touch and Bimanual Coordination

Much of the HCI research on bimanual interaction builds upon Guiard's kinematic chain model [12] and its three main principles: (1) the dominant hand moves in the frame of reference defined by the non-dominant hand; (2) the two hands are asymmetric, the dominant one being more precise than the non-dominant one; and (3) the movement of the non-dominant hand precedes the movement of the dominant one. Yet, previous work [2] reports on asymmetric tasks that violate some of these principles. In addition, some results [23] suggest that the dominant hand may lead the non-dominant hand in symmetric tasks [23].

A number of approaches [7, 15, 27] explore forms of bimanual interaction for pen and touch and propose techniques of bimanual interaction that conform to Guiard's model: select an object with the non-dominant hand and bring it under the pen, use the non-dominant hand to define a command mode or context that constrains the interaction with the pen, or make a rough selection with the dominant hand that is then refined by the pen. The pen is always held by the dominant hand, while touch is assigned to any hand. According to Brandl et al. [7], the combination of pen (dominant hand) with touch (non-dominant hand) is faster and more precise than using pens or touch by both hands.

In all the above approaches, the two hands move within the same reference frame and share the same views. Interaction with paper and a smartphone involves two separate spaces of both input and output. Balakrishnan and Hinckley [3] study bimanual interaction with separate reference frames but a common view. They show that users can effectively coordinate their hands as long as visual feedback is provided. In a later study of symmetric bimanual tasks [4], they observe that performance deteriorates when attention is divided between two visual spaces and propose that asymmetric tasks are more appropriate in this case.

BIMANUAL INTERPRETATION OF HANDWRITTING

Our design approach is driven by phrasing [8] principles proposed by Hinckey et al. [15] for pen + touch interaction. Our goal was to avoid the use of persistent modes. We take advantage of the kinesthetic coordination of the two hands to augment the handwriting with computerized commands and user interaction. As a result, we do not require the use of any preprinted paper menus and palettes.

Scenarios

The need for data interpretation when working on paper applies to a range of real-world scenarios:

1. A student adds textual metadata, indexes and audio annotations to handwritten notes.
2. A musician works on a musical score on paper and produces its electronic version.
3. A researcher gets computational assistance while thinking over a set of mathematic equations.
4. A biologist records measurements in a laboratory notebook during an experiment.

In all these scenarios, a full or partial recognition of the handwritten strokes takes place. For example, the system must differentiate between commands, e.g., a command to activate an audio recording, and unrecognized text and identify tags that represent metadata. It must identify numerous symbols in a handwritten musical score, recognize their syntax and separate them from free annotations.

Strategies of Direct User Control

We identify two alternative strategies of user control that aid the interpretation of handwritten data:

S1. The user relies on the system's ability to correctly recognize handwritten strokes and only intervenes to correct mistakes.

S2. The user determines how the system should interpret pen strokes while he or she writes on paper.

The success of each strategy depends on how well the system recognizes the strokes and how easy for users it is to interactively direct or correct recognition. In addition, it depends on how well users could foresee the success or failure of the recognizer to optimize their strategies.

Forms of Bimanual Coordination

We studied the two strategies by focusing on three primitive tasks:

T1. Writing down a stroke or a group of strokes.

T2. Selecting one or multiple strokes.

T3. Specifying a meaning for the selected strokes or a context for their interpretation, e.g., a certain vocabulary that constrains their recognition. The user performs this task with a gesture or a menu selection.

The three primitive tasks can be carried out in various combinations, where pen and touch input can overlap in time. T1 is always performed on paper with the pen. T2 and T3 are performed by using either the pen or the touchscreen on the mobile device. We examined four alternative forms of bimanual coordination, presented in Figure 2. We name them after the sequence of the input channels involved in correcting recognition errors or specifying the interpretation of strokes. We assume that users always use their non-dominant hand to manipulate the mobile device, while their dominant hand holds the pen. All the four techniques allow for a posteriori error corrections (strategy S1). In addition to error correction, *Touch + Pen* can specify or constrain how the system will interpret a group of strokes (strategy S2). Past studies [9, 16] show that this last form of interaction is particularly effective for enforcing commands and switching between modes.

Interestingly, the four techniques do not all strictly obey the principles of Guiard's kinematic chain model [12]. In *Pen + Touch*, the dominant hand determines the reference of interaction and precedes the non-dominant hand, which makes the final selection. In comparison to how menus are activated and selected in the designs proposed by Brandl et al. [7], the technique inverses the use of the two hands. Notice, however, that precise task in our case is the stroke selection (T2). Respecting the second principle of Guiard's model, *Pen + Touch* assigns this task to the dominant hand.

APPLICATION: WORKING WITH MUSICAL NOTATION

We have designed and implemented a user interface for working with musical notation on paper that makes use of a digital pen and a smartphone (see Figure 1). Below, we present how the four techniques of bimanual coordination have been integrated into this interface.

Main User Interface

Figure 1(a) presents an example of a handwritten score and its translation by our system on a smartphone. Several strokes that represent key musical elements such as notes, stems, beams and symbols of intonation (e.g., sharps) have been recognized and replaced by dark glyphs. Other elements, such as rests and annotations, remain unrecognized;

these elements are displayed in a light grey color. Finally, some strokes that represent special functions, such as audio comments on the score, are shown in a yellowish color. The above interpretation has been made by an automatic online recognizer, but a set of bimanual interaction techniques has assisted the recognition process.

At every moment, the smartphone displays only a portion of the active staff. The user uses two fingers to scroll forwards or backwards along the active staff or simply taps the pen on paper to navigate within the score. When the focus of writing exits the active area of the screen, the screen scrolls with a fast animation, and the active stroke is centered at the first half of the screen.

How to represent the recognized symbols on screen turned to be a challenging design problem. The personal writing style of each user bears recognizable landmarks, essential for human recognition and navigation. Such landmarks are destroyed if the system replaces handwritten symbols by fonts that are commonly used in printed and electronic scores. Keeping or simply highlighting the original form of recognized strokes is not a satisfying solution either, because users need feedback about how the system interprets their handwriting. We took an intermediate approach. As shown in Figure 3-6, musical elements such as the head of notes, flats, sharps and keys are replaced by predefined beautified profiles and are positioned with respect to their recognized location in the score structure. Other elements such as stems and beams are slightly beautified but in a way that their relative geometry in the score is preserved.

Automatic Recognition

The user interface uses a custom online recognizer that supports the incremental recognition of the most basic elements of musical notation: notes (whole, half, quarter, eighth, etc.) and chords, ledger lines, dots, beams, flats, sharps, and common keys. Recognition takes place in two steps. Individual strokes are first classified by a tuned Rubine recognizer [21] into basic tokens: parallel and horizontal lines, curved lines or lines with a specific inclination, open and filled circles, special symbols such as G-clefs and flats. The result of this step and the original points of the stroke are then forwarded to a rule engine that keeps information about the changing structure of the score. The rule engine applies a set of syntax rules to derive the type of the new symbol and its connections with the existing score elements, recognized or not. If none of the rules applies, the stroke remains unrecognized. We have implemented a basic set of rules that capture common patterns of writing [1], but the recognizer can be extended with new rules.

The recognizer makes use of three types of rules:

1. *Recognition rules* that handle new strokes.
2. *Reinforcing rules* that reinforce the interpretation of a stroke or a group of neighboring strokes according to explicit user instructions.
3. *Overwriting rules* that handle the interpretation of strokes drawn over existing ones.

Reinforcing the Interpretation of Handwritten Strokes

The user can reinforce the recognition of strokes in a specific manner by using bezel menus around the screen with the left hand while using the right hand to write with the pen (*Touch + Pen*). We opted for a bezel menu as it affords tangible feedback and does not interfere with the content on the screen. Previous work has shown that bezel menus are particularly appropriate for eyes-free interaction [6, 16]. Our design has been inspired by the bezel menu proposed by Hinckley et al. [15] for creating new objects.

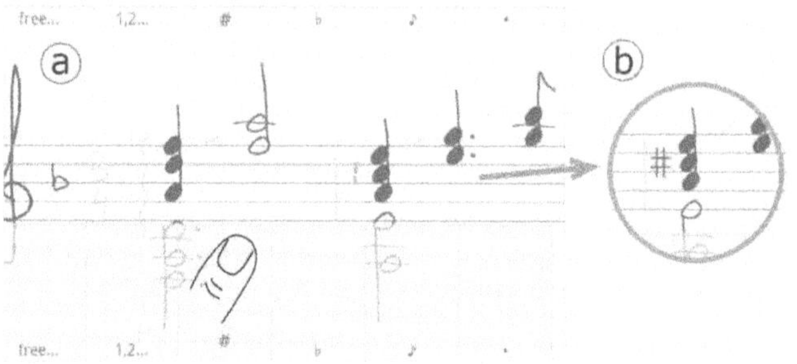

Figure 3. *Touch + Pen*: (a) Activation of the bezel menu at the bottom of the screen to reinforce the recognition of a sharp (#) while writing on paper (finger added only for illustration). (b) The recognized symbol after the entry of the strokes.

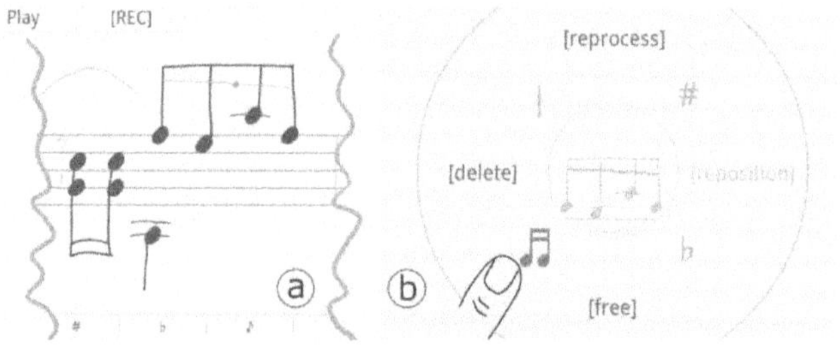

Figure 4. Using *Pen + Touch* to transform an unrecognized horizontal line into a beam: (a) Initial view (truncated). The user holds the pen over the line. (b) After a brief pause of 300 - 350 ms, a radial menu appears. The user selects the correct option with the finger while holding the pen on paper. A thumbnail of the score around the point of menu activation is shown at the center of the menu.

Figure 3 shows the user activating the bezel menu at the bottom of the screen by sliding her finger upwards. A semi-transparent layer follows the movement of the finger. The current selection (#) is shown in red. The menu options are also displayed at the top of the screen, relaxing the problem of hand occlusion as the finger manipulates the bezel menu.

Each option in the menu is associated with a single or multiple reinforcing rules. The rules are applied every time the user writes on paper while the corresponding option is active. For example, the second option ("1,2...") forces the recognition of strokes as numbers, and the 3rd option forces their interpretation as sharps. In contrast, the first option ("free...") deactivates the automatic recognition and handles strokes as free annotations.

Correcting Recognition Errors

The interface allows for correcting recognition errors. We have explored all of the four forms of bimanual coordination. The user can activate *Touch* + *Pen* with the bezel menu and then simply tap on individual or groups of strokes to reinforce their recognition. Figure 4 describes the error-correction mechanism for *Pen* + *Touch*. Holding the pen down over a handwritten stroke activates a radial menu at the center of the screen, enabling the user to assign a meaning from a contextual list of four alternatives or apply a fixed operation: *reprocess* a stroke, *reposition* it, treat it as a *free* annotation, or *delete* it. The menu appears when the pen pauses for 300 - 350 ms. This delay is short enough so that it does not interrupt the flow of interaction and long enough so that it is not accidentally activated when the user writes on paper. Subtle audio feedback informs the user about its activation.

The *Pen* + *Pen* technique provides a similar mechanism. The menu is activated in the same way, but now, the pen instead of the finger makes the final selection, with a marking gesture over the page. Since moving the pen on paper will leave an unwanted trace, the user has to activate the menu over a small transparent overlay that protects the page from inking (Figure 1). The role of the left hand is limited in moving and holding the overlay over the page. For the transparent overlay, we use pieces of plastic transparencies with low friction so that the pen does not leave any ink. The major strength of *Pen* + *Pen* is the fact that it relieves the user from interacting with the mobile device. The role of the device is now limited in providing feedback to the user. Here, we only examine the use of marking pen gestures to correct errors. However, we have also considered the use of quick symbolic gestures, such as the ones introduced by the Music Notepad [10].

To activate the radial menu with the *Touch* + *Touch* technique, the user has to point with the finger on the symbol of interest and perform a short slide movement. Figure 5 illustrates this mechanism. The sliding gesture is fast and relaxes the problem of occlusion: the ring provides a preview of the selection, allowing the user to return to the ring and cancel it before activating the menu.

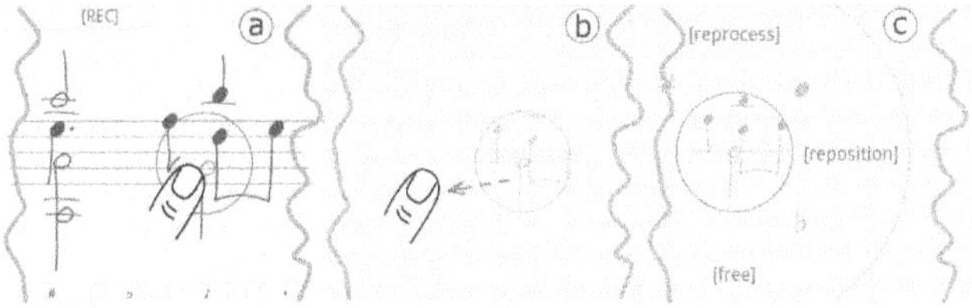

Figure 5. Activation of the radial menu with *Touch* + *Touch*: (a) A ring appears when the finger touches a symbol. (b) The finger slides out of the ring. (c) The finger is raised to activate the radial menu.

In addition to the above four techniques, we have implemented a simple correction mechanism, inspired from how users commonly make corrections on paper: the user rewrites over a symbol to replace it, hoping that the recognizer will make the correct decision. The mechanism is associated with a set of *overwriting rules*. Each rule takes care of the replacement of a different type of symbol, such as the head of a note, a stem, or an unrecognized stroke.

Playing with Sound

The four techniques of bimanual coordination can support functions other than the recognition of musical notation. For example, the user can use the top bezel menu to play a segment of the score or create a link to a recording (Figure 6). To activate the first operation, the user must specify the start position by tapping the pen on the score while holding the *Play* item and release the finger to stop playing it. To create an audio link, the user must draw the linking strokes while holding the *REC* item and keep the finger down while recording. The user can later replay or remove the recording by selecting the strokes that represent the link with the finger (*Touch* + *Touch*) or the pen (*Pen* + *Pen* or *Pen* + *Touch*) and then select the target function (*Replay* or *Remove*) from a contextual menu.

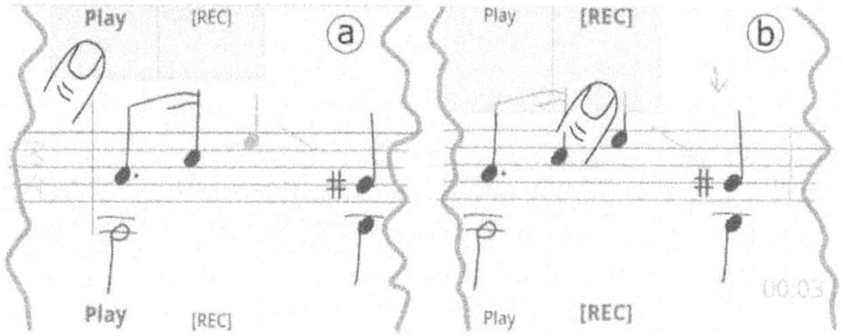

Figure 6. Using *Touch* + *Pen* (a) to play a segment of the score and (b) to create a link (yellow arrow) to an audio recording. The timer of the recording is shown at the bottom right of the screen.

Implementation Details

The implementation has been based on Anoto technology, streaming ADP-301 pens and Android smartphones. As we do not currently own pen drivers for the Android platform, we use a computer to mediate the communication between the pen and the smartphone. For Mac computers, we use the Bluetooth drivers of Letras [14]. In order to accelerate performance, preprocessing of the data with the Rubine algorithm is performed by a Java application on the computer. The rule engine, however, resides on the smartphone. As Android does not yet have support for midi, the computer is also responsible for reproducing the music. We use the JFugue API[1] to turn our internal score model into midi. The computer communicates with the device through OSC messages[2]. Finally, we use the R-Tree structure as implemented by the SpatialIndex library[3] to index strokes and accelerate their access from memory.

EXPERIMENT

We conducted an experiment to evaluate the four techniques of bimanual coordination on abstract tasks that do not require any domain expertise. The design of the techniques was very similar to one presented above. Our goals

[1] *http://www.jfugue.org/*

[2] *http://opensoundcontrol.org/*

[3] *http://trac.gispython.org/spatialindex/*

were to test the performance of the techniques, explore how users would adapt them to their personal writing postures, and gather their personal preferences.

Participants

Sixteen volunteers (five women and eleven men), 25 to 39 years old (Mean = 30.9 years and Std. Dev. = 4.4), participated in the experiment. Two participants were left-handed. They all had experience with touch-based interfaces on mobile devices. Twelve of them were everyday users of smartphones or tablets.

Apparatus

Participants were seated in front of a desk. They interacted with an ADP-301 pen over seven preformatted A4 pages and a 5-inch 800×480 pixel Samsung Galaxy S. The connection between the pen and the Android device was mediated by a 2.66 GHz 15-inch MacBook Pro with 8 GB RAM. Pen data were received by the Android application in real-time with a latency of about 50 ms.

Task

Participants had to complete a series of writing tasks over horizontal lines printed on paper in a portrait orientation. Each writing task consisted of drawing strokes to replicate a group of three pre-printed symbols (see Figure 7). There were eight possible symbols:

| — O • x b ^ +

These symbols were presented in an arbitrary order, but the frequency of the first four symbols was twice the frequency of the rest. Handwritten symbols were drawn over the printed ones. Any stroke drawn away from the indicated symbols was ignored. Participants completed the tasks from left to right and from top to bottom. However, they could draw the three symbols of each task in any order. After finishing with the three symbols of a task, they had to draw a vertical *endline* to indicate the completion of the task. They could scroll along the timeline by dragging the screen with two or three fingers. However, this was generally not necessary as the screen was scrolled automatically whenever a stroke was drawn outside the screen.

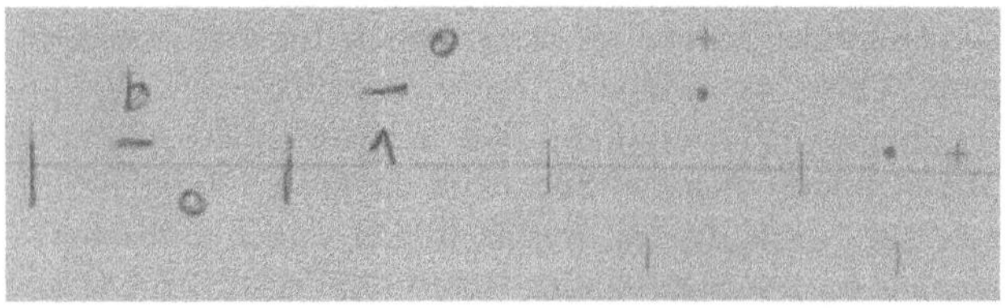

Figure 7. Extract from an experimental page. Symbols were positioned along several horizontal lines (experimental blocks) and organized by groups (tasks) of three symbols. The ending of each group was represented by a vertical *endline*.

Handwritten symbols were not always recognized by the system. The participant had to verify whether strokes were correctly interpreted by following their representation on the screen of the mobile device, shown in Figure 8(a). We expected that the accuracy of the handwriting recognition would affect the performance of the techniques and yield a great variance between participants based on their writing style. Therefore, we decided to simulate and control the recognition instead of using a real recognizer. More specifically, recognition errors were triggered in an arbitrary but controlled manner: 25% of the tasks were error-free, 25% had one error, 25% had two errors, and 25% had three errors. We simplified the task by simulating a single type of errors: wrong negatives. This means that strokes were either correctly recognized or not recognized at all.

A drawback of our approach is the fact that recognition did not depend on how users wrote on paper. We tried, however, to eliminate any side effects of this problem by instructing the participants to write the correct symbols in a way that is proper for human readers. Participants were aware that they did not have any control of how the recognizer behaved. However, they were also informed that their pages would be later verified by a human.

Techniques

The experiment evaluated the four techniques of bimanual coordination discussed earlier: *Pen + Pen*, *Pen + Touch*, *Touch + Touch*, and *Touch + Pen*. Figure 8 illustrates how the interface on the device was adapted to the experimental task. For *Pen + Pen* and *Pen + Touch*, the delay for the detection of a pause and the activation of the radial menu was fixed to 320 ms. Participants used a transparent overlay of about 6×8 cm to interact with *Pen + Pen*. The bezel menu was only displayed for *Touch + Pen* and was positioned at the bottom of the screen. The size of its items was 88×35 pixels.

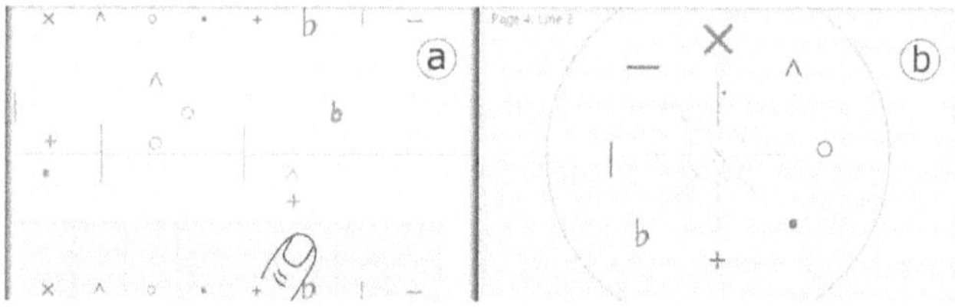

Figure 8. Representative screenshots from the mobile device. (a) The *Touch + Pen* technique over a line with recognized (bluish) and unrecognized (grey) strokes. Strokes are organized into groups of three, where each group represents a task. A vertical *endline* is drawn to complete a task. (b) Example of circular menu of eight items activated to correct a recognition mistake.

The strokes drawn on paper were mapped to the display with a scale of 10.12 pixels/mm. After the user activated the menu with the *Pen + Pen* technique, the scale was doubled, which allowed for menu selections with shorter marking gestures. Symbols on paper could be selected within a range of 0.51 mm around the rectangular boundaries of their strokes. This range corresponds to 5.2 pixels of screen size. Our pre-tests showed that this range was not enough for the *Touch + Touch* technique. Therefore, for this technique, we set the range of touch selection beyond the boundaries of the strokes to 10 pixels.

Conditions

The techniques were tested under two conditions that capture the two extremes of real conditions:

Unpredictable. Participants had no information about whether the system would succeed in recognizing a stroke. Participants had to depend on the visual feedback of the mobile device to anticipate an error.

Predictable. Participants knew beforehand whether recognition would succeed or not. Symbols corresponding to recognition errors were printed in red, which allowed the participant to develop a strategy before starting a task. This condition simulates the situation in which the user writes a special symbol, knowing that the symbol does not belong to the recognizer's vocabulary.

Design and Procedure

We followed a mixed full-factorial design: *Condition* was treated as a between-participants factor whereas *Technique* was treated as a within-participants factor. For each technique, participants completed one page of six lines with eight tasks each. The design can be summarized as follows:

2 Conditions (*Unpredictable, Predictable*)
× 8 Participants per condition
× 4 Techniques
× 6 Lines (blocks)
× 4 Error Levels (0, 1, 2, and 3 errors)
× 2 Repetitions (each with a different set of symbols)
= 3072 tasks in total

In addition to the main tasks, participants completed 2- 3 lines of practice tasks per technique on three separate sheets. The order of presentation of the four techniques was balanced among participants with a Latin square. The position of the items in the menus changed for each page but remained the same for all the tasks on the same page.

We asked participants to complete each task as fast as possible, trying to write clearly for humans and avoid mistakes. Participants could take pauses between tasks. They were encouraged to adjust their posture and re-position the page and the mobile device during the tasks to optimize their comfort and performance. Every time a new page was given to a participant, the experimenter placed the device at the center of the page, which required the participant to move it around. The experimenter also provided a cloth that could be placed under the device to increase the friction with the table and prevent accidental displacements while touching on the screen. The experimenter took notes during the sessions about positioning of the mobile device. After the end of the session, participants completed a questionnaire with 5-level Likert-scale questions about their experience with the four techniques. The whole procedure lasted for approximately 50 - 70 minutes.

Measures and Hypotheses

We measured the time needed to complete a task. It was measured from the point the participant started drawing the first symbol of the task (or from the point that the participant started touching the screen for the *Touch + Pen* technique) to the point the participant finished drawing the vertical end-line. We also counted the number of errors, i.e., untreated recognition mistakes or wrong assignments to symbols, as well as pointing errors occurring during the task, i.e., failure to select a stroke by touch or pen. Finally, we collected participants' responses concerning various qualities of the tested techniques: learning time, performance, precision, physical demand, attention, suitability for real applications and overall preferences.

The experiment was mostly exploratory since we did not have clear hypotheses about the relative performance of the four techniques. Based on past results [7], we expected that the pen would be more accurate than touch in making precise selections. We also expected that the predictability factor would have a clear effect on user performance. The *Unpredictable* condition introduced an additional cost, as participants had to pay continuous attention to the screen of the smartphone, keeping track of how the system interpreted their strokes. We predicted that this effect would be more intense for *Touch + Pen*, as this technique required the user to choose between the two possible strategies: correcting recognition errors (S1) or specifying the interpretation of strokes while writing on paper (S2).

Results on User Performance

We first analyzed task completion times. A total of 154 tasks or 5% of time measurements were disregarded from the analysis due to missing data, errors (2.8% of tasks) and outliers (1.9% of tasks) three standard deviations away from the within-cell mean. The overall results for task completion times are shown in Figure 9.

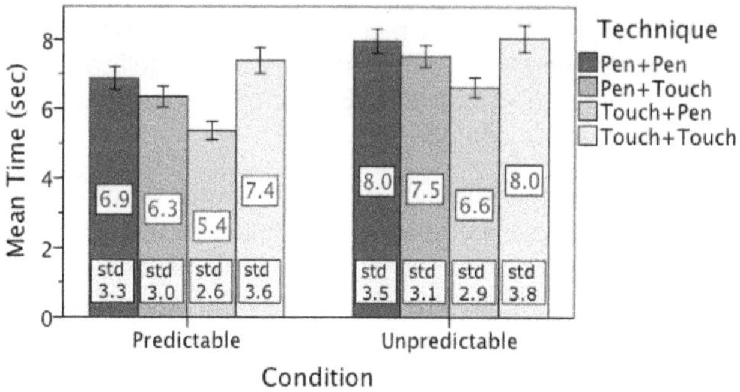

Figure 9. Results for task completion time. Error bars represent 95% Confidence Intervals (CI). Standard deviations are shown at the bottom.

We conducted an ANOVA analysis with *Technique, Line, Error Level* and *Repetition* treated as repeated-measures factors and *Condition* treated as a between-participants factor. The main effect of technique was statistically significant ($F_{3,42}$= 20.6, $p=2.3\cdot10^{-8}$). A pairwise comparison with Bonferroni's adjustment for six pairs of comparisons showed that *Touch + Pen* was statistically faster than any of the other three techniques ($p<.01$). However, we found no significant difference between any other pair. The difference between *Pen + Touch* and *Touch + Touch* was only marginally significant ($p=.086$).

As we expected, the main of effect of *Condition* was statistically significant ($F_{1,14}$=5.04, p =.041). The completion time under the *Predictable* condition (M=6.5 sec, SD=3.3 sec) was about 14% faster than the time under the *Unpredictable* condition (M=7.5 sec, SD=3.4 sec). Interestingly, the mean difference between the two conditions for tasks with no recognition errors (*Error Level* = 0) was 1.3 sec, which translates into a 47.7% increase in time. This difference represents the extra cost due to divided attention between the smartphone and the page as participants tried to keep track of unpredictable errors.

We found no significant interaction effect between *Technique* and *Condition* ($F_{3,42}$=.697, p=.56). Not surprisingly, the main effect of *Error Level* was significant ($F_{3,42}$=704.8, p=$6.0 \cdot 10^{-36}$), with time increasing linearly ($F_{1,14}$=933.4, p= $3.2 \cdot 10^{-14}$) in relation to the number of recognition errors per task. We also found an interaction effect between *Error Level* and *Technique* ($F_{9,126}$=15.7, p=$6.2 \cdot 10^{-17}$). Figure 10 presents the effect of *Error Level* for each technique and summarizes the results for the pairwise comparisons.

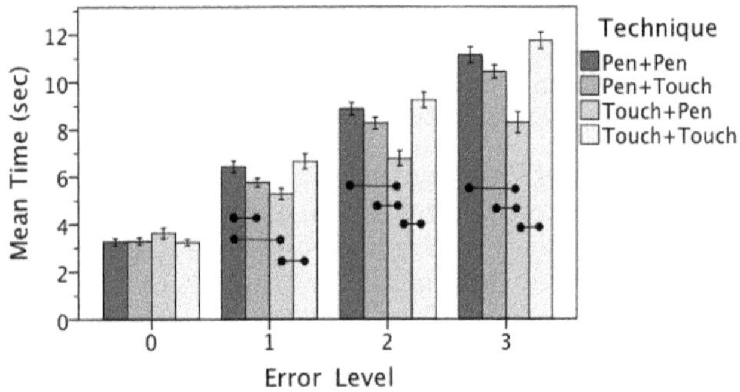

Figure 10. Task completion time per *Error Level* and *Technique*. Error bars represent 95% CI. Connections between bars represent statistically significant differences (p < .05), after Bonferroni's adjustment for 24 pairwise comparisons.

We examined the strategy that participants followed for *Touch + Pen*. Four participants used the bezel menu to only correct mistakes (strategy S1); seven participants used it to assign symbols when drawing strokes (strategy S2); and five participants mixed both strategies. There was no clear relationship between strategy and condition. As shown in Figure 11, S2 seems to be the most effective strategy.

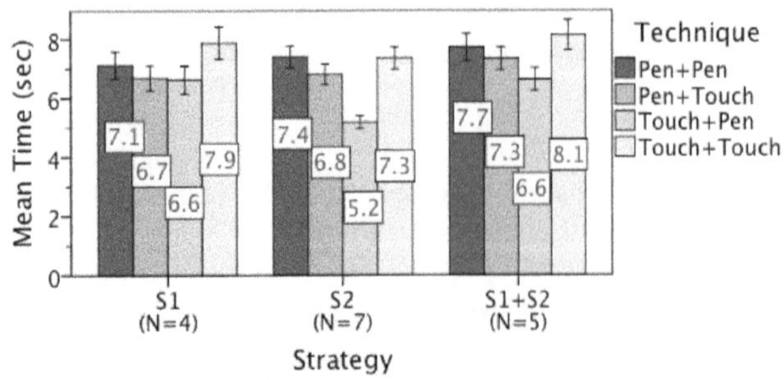

Figure 11. Results by participant group. Groups are based on selected strategies for *Touch + Pen*. Error bars represent 95% CI.

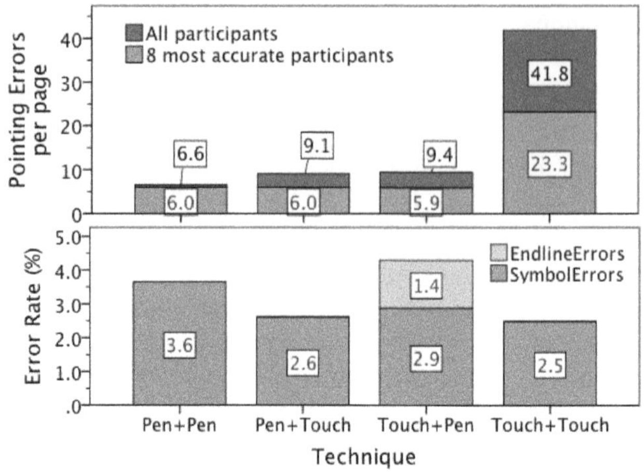

Figure 12. Distribution of errors across techniques

We also analyzed the errors made by participants. Figure 12 (bottom) presents the mean number of untreated recognition errors per task. It also shows the additional errors caused by *Touch + Pen*, when participants kept holding an item of the bezel menu while completing a task. Now, if we examine the error rates with respect to the strategy followed by participants for *Touch + Pen*, we can observe an interesting asymmetry: 0.5% for the four participants that chose the slow strategy (S1), 4.7% for the seven participants that chose the fast strategy (S2), and 1.7% for the five participants that combined both strategies.

The top chart in Figure 12 shows the distribution of pointing errors when participants tried to correct a symbol. Clearly, touch was less precise than the pen. Friedman's non-parametric test showed that the effect of *Technique* on pointing errors was statistically significant ($\chi^2(3)$=30.66, p<.001), while pairwise comparisons showed that *Touch + Touch* produced significantly more pointing errors (adjusted p<.001) than any of the three other techniques.

Positioning the Device in the Physical Space

We observed a variety of strategies concerning the manipulation and positioning of the smartphone. Eight participants were very active in moving the device during the tasks to minimize the distance between the screen and the writing zone and improve the coordination of their hands. Three more participants moved the device but less frequently or only for certain techniques. Finally, five participants were passive, initializing the position of the device before starting writing on a new page and keeping this position for all the tasks. Several of these participants, however, frequently changed the posture of their body and kept moving the page to align the active zone of writing with the device.

Subjective Ratings and User Suggestions

Figure 13 presents participants' subjective ratings. Surprisingly, the ratings are not consistent with performance results. *Pen + Pen* and *Pen + Touch* were rated the highest across all variables. *Touch + Pen* received low ratings even with respect to speed. It seems that participants underestimated the time required to correct recognition errors and the ability of the technique in saving time. Some participants expressed the opinion that *Touch + Pen* required additional concentration and effort because they had to synchronize both hands at the same time and to frequently shift their attention from the page to the device. According to a participant, the technique *"was confusing and [I] always had to keep an eye on the touchpad to make sure I had the correct item selected"*.

We received a number of suggestions about how to improve the design of the techniques. Several participants complained about the occlusion of the finger on the touchscreen and the high precision required to select strokes. Some participants found that the delay (320 ms) required to activate the menu with the *Pen + Pen* technique was too long, as they were tempted to start the marking gesture immediately after putting the pen on the transparent overlay. Two participants suggested that *Pen + Touch* must be enhanced with an additional menu-activation mechanism: the radial menu appears when the user pauses the pen when drawing and disappears if the movement restarts. Another participant asked for richer audio feedback to (1) avoid touch errors when the attention was on the page, and (2) avoid pen errors when the attention was on the screen.

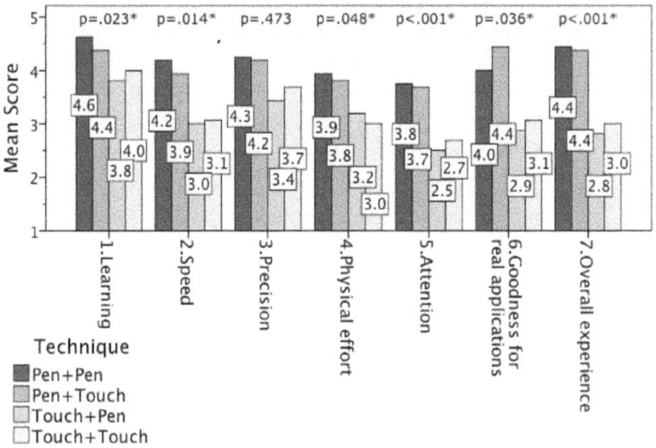

Figure 13. User ratings about various usability variables in a Likert scale (5 = Positive, 1 = Negative). The p values above the bars give the results of Friedman's non-parametric statistical tests for the effect of *Technique* on the score of each variable.

DISCUSSION

Touch + Pen was clearly the fastest technique. This result was independent of the condition, i.e., whether recognition errors were predictable or not. It seems, however, that there was a correlation between the performance of *Touch + Pen* and the strategy that participants followed to complete the tasks. Of course, given the limited number of participants, we cannot make safe conclusions. But our results suggest that participants who consistently used strategy S2 managed to gain a 24 to 30% in speed in comparison to the three other techniques. On the other hand, strategy S2 seems to inflate errors, which may explain why four participants did not use it all and why five other participants mixed it with strategy S1. Reflecting on the use of strategies in real scenarios, a participant commented:

"I would use the technique with both strategies: first, a lot the second one, then I would progressively switch to the first one, provided that the recognizer improves."

Given now the fact that *Touch + Pen* was rated low by most participants, we can conclude that the technique must be used sparingly, in situations in which its use yields significant benefits. It could be especially appropriate for symbols that appear repetitively and in sequence, such as multiple sharps (#) at the beginning of a score, and whose recognition is difficult and imprecise, such as newly added symbols for which the recognizer has not yet training samples. Also, it can be particularly useful for assigning meaning to multi-strokes and groups of symbols, as it is the only technique that can delimit a sequence of pen actions without requiring the use of persistent modes. The fact that *Pen + Touch* was highly preferred to *Touch + Pen* by participants implies that Guiard's principle about the sequential order of the two hands may have exceptions, at least when hands operate in different reference frames, the views are split, and precision is critical for both hands (e.g., making selections in the bezel menu with the non-dominant hand), which means that tasks are not entirely asymmetric.

Pen + Pen and *Pen + Touch* had a similar performance with differences in speed less than 10%. *Pen + Touch* was shown to be significantly faster only for tasks with a single error. In addition, the two techniques received similar ratings by participants. Each technique has different advantages and weaknesses. Fortunately, one technique does not exclude the other, and users can make use of any of the two depending on their work strategies. *Pen + Pen* does not require users to directly interact with the smartphone. They can use it as a peripheral device that supports awareness and only shift their attention to it when they correct an error. A drawback of the current implementation of the technique is the fact that the pen cannot detect the overlay and automatically switch to a command mode. A pause is necessary, which breaks the flow of interaction. As a participant of a pilot study commented, the technique requires the user to mentally switch states that do not directly correspond to the visual and tangible feedback that the interaction instruments [5] provide. Garcia et al. [11] explore the use of active transparent layers detected by the pen, but their mechanism involves a time-consuming calibration phase. We expect, however, that technology of digital pens will soon resolve this limitation.

The *Touch + Touch* technique proved to be the least accurate despite the fact that its stroke selection was given some small advantage compared to the other techniques. We expect that this problem will become more intense in smaller devices. Finger occlusion is not the only issue. The use of the non-dominant hand in conjunction with the varying parallax caused by moving the device around the page aggravates the problem. A participant explained that the technique would be his favorite if the problem of precision were somehow resolved. Consider that *Touch + Touch* is the only technique that makes a clear separation between writing and error correction. When working with musical notation, precision is important as symbols are tiny, are stacked together, and appear in close proximity. The technique, however, could be useful for the selection of larger entities, such as chords and measures, or special elements such as links. Finally, the technique can be valuable in other types of tasks, such as adding tags to text, where interactive elements are sparse, so precision is not an issue.

SUMMARY AND FUTURE DIRECTIONS

We examined how mobile assistants can help users interactively guide the interpretation of their handwriting when working on paper. We identified four techniques of bimanual coordination that serve two strategies of direct user control: (1) correcting recognition errors, and (2) constraining recognition while writing. We explored the design of these techniques with a user interface that helps users work with classical musical notation. An experiment evaluated the four techniques. Its results provide valuable feedback about the performance of the techniques, but also about their strengths and limitations as perceived by users.

Our first future goal is to address current limitations of the techniques: improve the precision of *Touch + Touch*, design state-aware overlays for *Pen + Pen*, support richer audio or vibrotactile feedback to reduce errors. Second, we are planning to evaluate our interface for writing music with expert musicians. This will help us assess its potential but also observe the weaknesses and strengths of the four techniques in more ecological settings.

ACKNOWLEDGMENTS

This work has been partly funded by ANR (ANR-11-JS02-004-01). I thank Jérémie Garcia, Pierre Rossinès, Wendy Mackay, and members of InSitu for fruitful discussions.

REFERENCES

1. Anstice, J., T. Bell, A. Cockburn, and M. Setchell. The Design of a Pen-Based Musical Input System. In Proc. OzCHI '96, 260-267. 1996.
2. Balakrishnan, R., G. Fitzmaurice, G. Kurtenbach, and W. Buxton. Digital Tape Drawing. In Proc. UIST '99, 161-169. ACM, 1999.
3. Balakrishnan, R. and K. Hinckley. The Role of Kinesthetic Reference Frames in Two-Handed Input Performance. In Proc. UIST '99, 171-178. ACM, 1999.
4. Balakrishnan, R. and K. Hinckley. Symmetric Bimanual Interaction. In Proc. CHI '00, 33-40. ACM, 2000.
5. Beaudouin-Lafon, M. Instrumental interaction: an interaction model for designing post-WIMP user interfaces. In Proc. CHI '00, 446-453. ACM, 2000.
6. Bragdon, A., E. Nelson, Y. Li, and K. Hinckley. Experimental analysis of touch-screen gesture designs in mobile environments. In Proc. CHI '11, 403-412. ACM, 2011.
7. Brandl, P., C. Forlines, D. Wigdor, M. Haller, and C. Shen. Combining and Measuring the Benefits of Bimanual Pen and Direct-Touch Interaction on Horizontal Interfaces. In Proc. AVI '08, 154-161. ACM, 2008.
8. Buxton, B. Chunking and phrasing and the design of human-computer dialogues. In Proc. IFIP World Computer Congress, 475-480. 1986.
9. Dillon, R.F., J.D. Edey, and J.W. Tombaugh. Measuring the true cost of command selection: techniques and results. In Proc. CHI '90, 19-26. ACM, 1990.
10. Forsberg, A., M. Dieterich, and R. Zeleznik. The Music Notepad In Proc. UIST '98, 203-210. ACM, 1998.
11. Garcia, J., T. Tsandilas, C. Agon, and W. Mackay. Interactive Paper Substrates to support Musical Creation. In Proc. CHI '12, 1825-1828. ACM, 2012.
12. Guiard, Y., Asymmetric Division of Labor in Human Skilled Bimanual Action: The Kinematic Chain as a Model. Journal of Motor Behavior, 1987. 19(4): p. 486-517.
13. Heinrichs, F., D. Schreiber, J. Huber, and M. Mühlhäuser. Toward a theory of interaction in mobile paper-digital ensembles. In Proc. CHI '12, 1897-1900. ACM, 2012.
14. Heinrichs, F., J. Steimle, D. Schreiber, and M. Mühlhäuser. Letras: an architecture and framework for ubiquitous pen-and-paper interaction. In Proc. EICS '10, 193-198. ACM, 2010.
15. Hinckley, K., K. Yatani, M. Pahud, N. Coddington, J. Rodenhouse, A. Wilson, H. Benko, and B. Buxton. Pen + touch = new tools. In Proc. UIST '10, 27-36. ACM, 2010.
16. Li, Y., K. Hinckley, Z. Guan, and J.A. Landay. Experimental Analysis of Mode Switching Techniques in Pen-based User Interfaces. In Proc. CHI '05, 461-470. ACM, 2005.
17. Liao, C., F. Guimbretière, K. Hinckley, and J. Hollan, Papiercraft: A gesture-based command system for interactive paper. ACM TOCHI, 2008. 14(4): p. 1-27.
18. Liao, C., Q. Liu, B. Liew, and L. Wilcox. PACER: Fine-grained Interactive Paper via Camera-touch Hybrid Gestures on a Cell Phone. In Proc. CHI '10, 2441-2450. ACM, 2010.
19. Mackay, W.E., G. Pothier, C. Letondal, K. Bøegh, and H.E. Sørensen. The missing link: augmenting biology laboratory notebooks. In Proc. UIST '02, 41-50. ACM, 2002.
20. Rebelo, A., I. Fujinaga, F. Paszkiewicz, A.R.S. Marcal, C. Guedes, and J.S. Cardoso, Optical music recognition: state-of-the-art and open issues. International Journal of Mutlimedia Information Retrieval, Springer London, 2012: p. 1-18.
21. Rubine, D. Specifying gestures by example. In Proc. SIGGRAPH '91, 329-337. ACM, 1991.
22. Song, H., F. Guimbretière, T. Grossman, and G.W. Fitzmaurice. MouseLight: bimanual interactions on digital paper using a pen and a spatially-aware mobile projector. In Proc. CHI '10, 2451-2460. ACM, 2010.
23. Swinnen, S.P., K. Jardin, and R. Meulenbroek, Between-limb asynchronies during bimanual coordination: Effects of manual dominance and attentional cueing. Neuropsychologia, Elsevier Science, 1996. 34(12): p. 1203-1213.
24. Tsandilas, T., C. Letondal, and W.E. Mackay. Musink: composing music through augmented drawing. In Proc. CHI '09, 819-828. ACM, 2009.
25. Tsandilas, T. and W. Mackay. Knotty Gestures: Subtle Traces to Support Interactive Use of Paper In Proc. AVI '10, 147-154. ACM, 2010.
26. Yeh, R., C. Liao, S. Klemmer, F. Guimbretière, B. Lee, B. Kakaradov, J. Stamberger, and A. Paepcke. ButterflyNet: A Mobile Capture and Access System for Field Biology Research. In Proc. CHI '06, 571-580. ACM, 2006.
27. Zeleznik, R., A. Bragdon, F. Adeputra, and H.-S. Ko. Hands-On Math: A page-based multi-touch and pen desktop for technical work and problem solving. In Proc. UIST '10, 17-26. ACM, 2010.

High-Performance Pen + Touch Modality Interactions: A Real-Time Strategy Game eSports Context

William Hamilton, Andruid Kerne, Thomas Robbins
Interface Ecology Lab | Department of Computer Science & Engineering
Texas A&M University
{bill, andruid}@ecologylab.net, motasheron@hotmail.com

ABSTRACT

We used the situated context of real-time strategy (RTS) games to address the design and evaluation of new pen + touch interaction techniques. RTS play is a popular genre of Electronic Sports (*eSports*), games played and spectated at an extremely high level. Interaction techniques are critical for eSports players, because they so directly impact performance.

Through this process, new techniques and implications for pen + touch and bi-manual interaction emerged. We enhance non-dominant hand (NDH) interaction with *edge-constrained* affordances, anchored to physical features of interactive surfaces, effectively increasing target width. We develop *bi-manual overloading*, an approach to reduce the total number of occurrences of NDH retargeting. The novel *isosceles lasso select* technique facilitates selection of complex object subsets. *Pen-in-hand interaction*, dominant hand touch interaction performed with the pen stowed in the palm, also emerged as an efficient and expressive interaction paradigm.

ACM Classification: H5.2 [Information interfaces and presentation]: User Interfaces. - Graphical user interfaces.

General terms: Design, Human Factors

Keywords: bi-manual interaction; game design; eSports

INTRODUCTION

eSports is a popular cultural form of playing and spectating digital games. eSports play constitutes one of the world's highest performance HCI contexts. Skilled players practice in order to be able to perform rapid, precise, complex, and sustained interactions to compete. However, despite a shift among casual game players to new interaction modalities such as the Nintendo Wii and Microsoft Kinect, most eSports players continue to favor the keyboard and mouse.

In this research, we develop *Pen-in-Hand Command* (PiHC), pen + multi-touch modality interaction for the real-time strategy (RTS) games genre of eSports. We used the game mechanics and requirements of RTS games to provoke the design of embodied interaction. For detecting pen + touch, we used a Wacom Cintiq augmented with the minimum effort multi-touch interaction of ZeroTouch [18].

UIST'12, October 7-10, 2012, Cambridge, Massachusetts, USA.

In the PiHC design process, we incorporated our experiences observing and playing RTS games, plus principles of direct manipulation, bi-manual interaction, and mode selection. Beyond prior techniques, such as marking menus, we developed new techniques for selection, multi-finger mode selection, and 3D manipulation. To enable real play, these techniques were composed to form a complete interface to an existing open source RTS game.

Through the design process, we developed techniques for increasing the efficacy of interaction with the non-dominant hand. One such is *edge-constrained multi-touch interaction.* We hypothesize that by leveraging physical characteristics of surfaces, such as their edges, we can anchor touch interactions to be performed quickly by the NDH. We also introduce *bi-manual overloading*, an approach to alleviating the difficulties of NDH targeting. Once a target has been acquired with the NDH, the interface should directly enable multiple actions, avoiding extraneous target re-acquisition.

We observed the emergence of the *pen-in-hand* interaction modality, in which the dominant hand alternatively interacts with fingers and stylus. The kinematic chain model postulates that, when performing bi-manual interactions, humans contextualize the dominant hand's action with the other [9]. This research extends the kinematic chain, applying its principles to pen-in-hand direct manipulation's division of labor.

To evaluate PiHC, we recruited RTS players and conducted a user study. These players are highly skilled at playing RTS games with mouse + keyboard. They are attuned to the game interface. They are skeptical of new interaction modalities. We observed participants play against one another. We use data to draw implications for design to support expert, high-performance pen + touch interfaces and new interaction modalities in general.

We begin this paper with interaction techniques and eSports background. We then present PiHC's interaction techniques, evaluation, and results. We synthesize implications for pen + touch interaction, and design for situated expert contexts.

RELATED WORK: INTERACTION TECHNIQUES

The design of PiHC draws from prior research in bi-manual interaction. We further address more specific work involving pen + touch and other new interaction modalities.

Bi-manual Interaction

Yves Guiard developed one of the first models of human bi-manual interaction: the *kinematic chain theory* [9]. The model addresses the relationships between the right and left hand for right handed people. This gets generalized as the dominant hand (DH) and non-dominant hand (NDH). The model has three components: the NDH defines the spatial context for action performed by the DH; the NDH initiates action before the DH; and the NDH performs coarser action than the DH. This model has been applied and investigated in many bi-manual interaction studies [5, 11, 20, 12, 13]. We apply kinematic chain principles in the design of PiHC. We also formulate a new hypothesis: *the kinematic chain extends further into the DH, where the fingers alternatively define the spatial reference, while the stylus is stowed in the palm, then hold and invoke the stylus, for precision action.*

Other research into bi-manual interaction has investigated the performance of the NDH performing Fitt's law tasks. Kabbash et al. confirm Todor and Doane's findings, that for the NDH, performance of Fitt's law tasks is significantly hindered more by target width than the DH [25, 14]. However, they also find that NDH is less affected by target distance than the DH. From these findings, we develop the design principle of physically constrained touch, in which the effective widths of targets for the NDH are increased by using a physical constraint such as the edge of a surface. Prior work has investigated constraining pointing targets to the physical edges of surfaces using mice and on small surfaces[1, 7]. We also develop approaches for minimizing situations in which the NDH must target new interface components.

Wobbrock et al. found that non-expert multi-touch users had trouble differentiating between gestures employing the same motion, like a swipe or tap, but a different number of fingers [27]. Other studies [6], as well as the command set built into Mac OS X, have found that using number of fingers for command differentiation is effective. In bi-manual overloading, we use number of fingers as a quick mode selection technique that minimizes retargeting with the NDH. Our study concurs: with minimal training, number of touching fingers is an effective technique for mode selection.

Pen + Touch Interaction

Pen + Touch interaction is a particular form of bi-manual interaction that seeks to leverage the advantages of both modalities while avoiding the pitfalls. Pen performs well for tasks that require precise path definition, such as inking, while touch is fast and direct, but imprecise. Several designs and studies have investigated the pen + touch modality [5, 3, 12, 13]. Pen + Touch interaction designs are often based on the metaphor of paper-based desk work; the NDH is used to manipulate artifacts, while the DH performs precise interaction using the stylus.

Prior work has investigated the application of pen + touch either in un-situated contexts, such as maze navigation [3], or in those involving electronic drafting tables [3, 12, 13]. The latter directly mimics paper-based desk work. As a RTS game, PiHC is situated in a new high-performance context, which we hypothesize will benefit from the direct manipulation afforded by touch and the high-precision of stylus-based interaction. Without direct correspondence to pen and paper, interaction design must be more abstractly derived. By working in this new context, we aim to develop generalized implications regarding the pen + touch modality.

Performance

Pen, multi-touch, and mouse + keyboard are fundamentally different interaction modalities. It would seem that direct performance comparisons are difficult, as few quantitative studies have achieved this. Odell et al. compared command selection performance across bi-manual marking menus, hotkeys, and toolbars [20]. While they found that hotkeys performed well, no significant differences in completion time were found versus a bi-manual marking menu. PiHC uses fluid in-context techniques, such as marking menus [16], to efficiently perform RTS game mechanics previously executed via hotkeys.

Kabbash et al. conducted an early study investigating the application of Fitt's law to the mouse, stylus, and trackball input modalities, with both the DH and NDH. Results indicated that stylus out-performed mouse on movement time. However, error rates were found to be slightly lower for the mouse [14]. Kurtenbach and Buxton find that for directional interactions, such as marking menus, stylus-based interaction outperforms the mouse [16]. More recent work suggests that for shape tracing tasks, people perform more accurately and quickly with a stylus than a mouse [28]. However, no statistically significant results were found. Brandl et al.'s study investigating performance of a maze task compared pen + touch, touch + touch, and pen + pen [3]. They found that the pen-based modalities outperformed the touch + touch condition. The design of PiHC focuses on leveraging stroke-based interactions, which in light of the prior work, seem to benefit from the stylus modality.

ESPORTS CONTEXT

We use the situated context of eSports as a resource for the design of interaction. *eSports* is the high-level play and spectating of digital games. RTS games are a popular eSports genre. Other eSports genres include first person shooter and arcade style fighting games. The community surrounding eSports is comprised of professional and amateur players, spectators, commentators, and game designers [4]. As with football, professional players are especially skilled. They generate income from tournament winnings, coaching fees, and streaming ads. More players are amateur, practicing skills at home, without pay, for fun and challenge.

eSports games between skilled players are broadcast live from major tournaments. These events are spectated by large co-located and online audiences. The Global StarCraft League (GSL) finals at Blizzcon 2011, Blizzard Entertainment's gaming convention, engaged 25,000 co-located and 300,000 online viewers. They watched two of the world's best StarCraft players compete for a $46,000 prize. We note that only 16,000 attended SIGGRAPH 2011, the ACM's largest annual event, with little live online participation.

Given the complexity of RTS games, it is necessary to play them in order to understand interaction and strategy. Some of the authors have extensive experience playing RTS games, such as Blizzard Entertainment's StarCraft 2 and Riot Games' League of Legends [24, 17]. To better understand high-performance interaction in RTS games, we watched extensive online videos of professional tournament play and explanations of how to perform at a high level [21]. Successful RTS players expertly invoke *game mechanics*, repeated actions that constitute a game's essence [22]. We draw from our experiences playing RTS games, and our observations of experts to form mental models [19] of the game mechanics of RTS eSports. We use this understanding to motivate the design of interaction techniques with new modalities.

eSports play is one of the most extreme interaction contexts that can be readily observed. As with football, players of varying degrees of skill are abundant and may be recruited for studies. We hope that our new interaction modality designs for eSports will create more engaging player and spectator experiences. Pen + Touch is a compelling interaction modality in this context, because it affords fast and precise interaction, the pre-requisites for RTS eSports. Before we present the design of PiHC, we discuss the basic interaction standards for RTS games and investigate eSport player's perceptions of new interaction modalities.

RTS Mechanics and Interfaces

At a low level, RTS game mechanics focus on managing *units*, game entities the player produces and controls. Players may command hundreds of units simultaneously, and make minute adjustments. High-level RTS players rely on reflexes and practice to efficiently perform the suite of mechanics.

RTS game interfaces are usually built around a main view of the game world with limited scope, but high-detail. The main game view is accompanied by a head-up display (HUD) with buttons and a low-detail overview, known as a "mini-map". The common interaction scheme in RTS games is to use the mouse to select units. The mouse is also used to either invoke commands for selected units.

The keyboard serves two primary purposes: activating commands for currently selected units, and accessing saved groups of units. While the mouse can be used to activate HUD buttons, hot-keys are faster, providing a competitive edge.

Using this scheme, players manage the game in macro using the keyboard, with minimal mouse input. This leaves the mouse free for micro-management: performing precise selections and commanding units. Through practice, players become extremely quick at executing game mechanics.

Perceptions of New vs Old Interaction Modalites

Prior play of RTS eSports is dominated by the mouse + keyboard modality. Players are quite skeptical of new interaction modalities; so much so that in 2011, Blizzard Entertainment's April Fool's joke was that they were releasing a version of StarCraft 2 playable with the Microsoft Kinect.

Before running our study, we surveyed 11 RTS e-Sports players to get a sense of how they perceived the potential of new interfaces for RTS eSports. These participants were recruited at a local eSports event. None participated in the later study. Eight of the players were were ranked between StarCraft's Master (Top 2%) and Gold Leagues (Top 20%); the other two did not play ranked games. When asked about Pen + Touch interaction for eSports, they expressd doubt. According to one Master League player: "A mouse and keyboard are very precise and fast. Pen and touch based input in my experience is slow, clunky, imprecise." Other players reported concerns about not having hotkeys, not being able to effectively left or right click, and slow or imprecise input sensors. One player even reported: "Everything in these games is about APM [actions per minute]; no pen or touch based inputs will ever be able to replace it."

Of the ten players surveyed, 80% reported that they thought Pen + Touch interaction in RTS games would hinder their ability to play the game at a high-performance level. However, one of the Masters League players reported that he thought it would *help* his ability to play. At the same time, he reported concern that "easier execution could make the game too easy, which could narrow the skill range." eSport players tend to be very proud of their ability to play at a high-performance level. This is to be expected, as their ability is hard-earned, developed over weeks if not years of practice. Another participant was distressed that pen + touch input would, "drastically change the instinctual feeling of basic game mechanics. I would be relearning EVERYTHING."

Some players thought that interacting with new interaction modalities would provide perceivable benefits. "It would allow you to input more complex actions." "It would encourage less rigid hand movements," and, "could lend itself to creative input schemes". Interestingly, one of the Masters League players reported that he would be excited about, "the difficulties I would have to go through." This indicates that for some high-level players, the challenge of learning a new interaction modality would be rewarding in itself.

SPRING & ZERO-K

Given the RTS eSports context, we present the building blocks of our apparatus. PiHC is built on top of the open source Spring RTS game engine [23], which provides the graphics, unit mechanics, and basic interface features required to create RTS games. We modified Spring to accept TUIO touch inputs [15]. These inputs are then passed through the engine to the game interface. PiHC is more specifically based on Zero-K [29], an open source game built using the Spring engine. We use the units and game mechanics defined in the Zero-K project, along with several existing interface components. We then built the touch and pen based inputs, by modifying Zero-K, adding new interface components, and using the touch and cursor events dispatched by the Spring engine.

PEN + TOUCH APPARATUS

For input, we use a 21" Wacom Cintiq tablet augmented with a ZeroTouch multi-touch sensor (Figure 1), enabling the simultaneous, distinct sensing of pen and touch interactions [18]. The Cintiq's pen sensing resolution is 5080 LPI, with 2048 pressure levels, and tilt sensing $\pm 60°$, at 145 Hz. ZeroTouch's finger sensing resolution is 33 DPI, with a refresh rate of 130 Hz. This sensor can detect up to 28 fingers. The Cintiq was mounted with its display surface tilted ~30° from horizontal, at the edge of a desk.

Table 1: Comparison of RTS game interaction techniques across modalities: prior mouse + keyboard vs. PiHC.

Game Mechanic	Prior Mouse + Keyboard	Pen + Touch in PiHC
Unit Selection	Box selection and single unit clicking.	Extended lasso and single unit tapping.
Command Selection and Invocation	Keyboard hot keys, default command right click, queuing with the shift key, and single-point click invocation.	Number of fingers command selection panel, queuing using scrubbed activation, formation drawing and tap invocation.
Macro	Keyboard factory selection through control groups and keyboard hotkeys for build commands.	In-context menu through direct and proxy selection.
View Manipulation and Selection	Screen edge panning, minimap dragging, control group double-tap, and saved came postion hotkeys.	Direct manipulation multi-touch, bimanual configurable viewpoints, and double tap or two finger press on control group button.
Control Groups	Number hotkeys, shift to add, and cntl to redefine.	Control group buttons. One finger to select/add, two fingers to see in game view and activate default command.

INTERACTION TECHNIQUES

In the following sections, we motivate the design of techniques for pen + multi-touch modality interaction in PiHC. We draw considerations from prior interaction design work, from eSports RTS games, and our own experiences conducting formative user studies and play testing.

The mouse + keyboard modality affords quick performance of discreet actions. RTS games have been designed for these affordances in the extreme. While designing PiHC, we focused on maximizing the performance of pen + touch interaction techniques, while leveraging the fluidity and directness afforded by the modality. This fluidity enabled us to change the nature of several RTS mechanics, giving players more direct control of the game environment.

We designed for expert use. Some interaction techniques may not be considered easily recognizable or intuitive when first encountered; they were designed to be performed quickly after learning. This is the case for most RTS game interaction. Optimal RTS interaction is non-obvious. Most players must practice considerably to become competitive.

We develop new interaction techniques addressing five RTS game mechanics: unit selection, commands, macro, view manipulation, and control groups. For each mechanic, we discuss its importance in the RTS games context, present the traditional mouse and keyboard interaction, and discuss how it is performed by skilled players. We follow with the motivation and design of corresponding pen + touch interaction techniques. Table 1 compares interaction techniques across modalities for the RTS game mechanics.

Unit Selection

Selection is arguably the mechanic that requires the most precision in RTS games. In order to issue commands to units, they must first be selected; subsequent commands are issued to those units. Selection becomes difficult when units are moving or when they are densely packed.

Mouse In the majority of RTS games, selection is performed using box selection. Box selection is performed by specifying the diagonal corners of a rectangle, selecting the units circumscribed by this box. The first corner is placed at the first click location; the second corner is dynamically specified by dragging then releasing the mouse.

The area defined by the box is difficult to accurately define quickly. High level RTS players are known to 'spam' (invoke repeatedly at a very high rate, with little intended effect) boxing while playing in order to practice/hype themselves up. However, even with practice, selection remains difficult to perform, given that game elements are not axis aligned.

Pen In PiHC, we developed the *isosceles lasso select* technique that better suits many selection scenarios encountered during play. Isosceles lasso select is based on prior lasso selection techniques [26]. However, while the path of the lasso is being drawn, its area is extended by projecting a perpendicular vector from the midpoint of the line segment connecting the start and end of the lasso's path (See Figure 2). The magnitude of the perpendicular vector, d, is one half the length of the connecting segment. Two line segments from the extension point create an angle that subtends the current path of the lasso, forming an extension area that is an *isosceles triangle*. The directionality of the extension is defined by the

Figure 1: Cintiq augmented with ZeroTouch sensor.

Figure 2: Isosceles lasso select technique.

user's most recent drawn path curvature. If the lasso end is directed toward the start point, the extension is removed.

Isosceles lasso select enables definition of a selection area with a precise and a non precise edge, reducing the distance of the pen stroke. Consider the scenario of selecting half of a clump of units (Figure 2). Using the leading edge of the lasso, a group may be split (along any direction). The extension selects which half to select by the curvature of the stroke. This contrasts with a normal lasso, which would have to be extended much farther to fully encompass the entirety of the selection. We note that a mouse may be used to perform this interaction. However, a stylus is more direct; it has been shown to more quickly and accurately define paths [28].

Command Selection and Invocation

After unit selection, command selection is among the most commonly invoked mechanics in RTS games. Units are issued one of many commands, including move, attack, repair, guard, reclaim, build, and harvest. Players quickly select and issue commands frequently throughout play, in order to micromanage or *micro* the actions of their units.

Keyboard + Mouse In mouse + keyboard play, commands are either selected specifically by using hot keys, or are automatically invoked as contextual default commands.

With mouse, a default command is issued by right clicking on a game world region. The command issued depends on what units are selected and what is targeted when the default command is invoked. If the cursor is over open ground, the default command is simply *"move"*. If over a unit, it is either *"guard"* or *"attack"*, depending on whether or not the unit is friendly. Non-default commands are issued using keyboard shortcuts, by pressing a key and left clicking the target.

Commands may also be queued, meaning that after finishing the first command issued, the selected unit will execute additional commands. This is useful for minimizing the number of tasks that must be micromanaged by the player. Queuing is enabled by pressing shift while issuing commands.

Pen + Touch We designed an edge-constrained multi-finger command selection panel for quickly issuing common commands (See Figure 3). This panel is positioned in the bottom left corner of the surface; it is approximately 19 x 6.5 cm. Players place a specific number of fingers in this panel to specify what action the stylus will perform upon marking.

Figure 3: Edge-constrained multi-finger command selection panel. The player chooses how the pen performs by selecting a command by number of fingers.

With no fingers in the panel, the pen performs isosceles lasso select. With a single finger in the command selection panel, the pen issues default commands to the selected units. With two fingers in the panel, the pen issues the *"fight"* command. Fight is frequently used in place of regular move to avoid losing units to unexpected enemy units. Finally, if three fingers are used, the stylus invokes a marking menu for selecting structures for construction units to build.

Formative user studies showed that 4 fingers were too difficult to use in the command selection panel. Spacing 4 fingers apart from one another, such that the multi-touch sensor can sense each individual finger, is difficult to reliably perform. This issue is common to many multi-touch sensors. It could be overcome with better blob / area recognition.

Commands are queued when one finger in the command selection panel is to the right of of the queuing activation panel division (Figure 4). This is performed by sliding all of the fingers to the right. We call this interaction technique *scrubbing*, where already placed fingers must simply be slid in an axis aligned direction in order to perform a gesture. This obviates the need to hit a specific target with the NDH.

For less-used commands, we placed an array of buttons above the command selection panel (Figure 3, top). To select a button's command, the player pushes it with the NDH. For buttons that only change state, this is sufficient. For commands that could be invoked multiple times, invocation is afforded by stylus tap or stroke on a target in the game world. These buttons are designed with the technique of Hinckley's springboard: holding the button queues the command [10]. When a finger presses a command button and releases before the stylus marks a target, then the command is issued right away.

When issuing commands with the stylus, instead of only defining a single target point, a stroke may be used, along which selected units will each be given an individual instance of the command (Figure 5). This gives the player more control of unit spacing and formation, a critical tactic. A mouse-based version of this functionality was previously developed by a Spring RTS developer; it is not commonly found in RTS games. The new interaction leverages path definition with the pen to enable more fluid and precise control of units.

Control Groups

Control groups are a fundamental mechanic of RTS games. Instead of invoking the direct selection mechanic, control

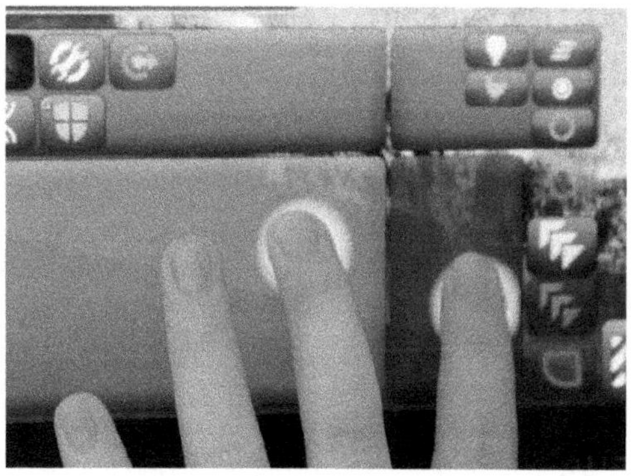

Figure 4: Command queueing is activated when one finger is to the right of queuing activation panel division.

groups let the player save specific unit selections. A group may then be quickly selected, in order to issue commands to it. This saves the player the interaction time required to manipulate the game view to the units and select them directly.

Keyboard Each number key may be assigned to a control group. When a control group's key is pressed, all associated units are selected. If the key is pressed twice, the camera is moved to focus on that group. At this point the user may issue commands to its units. Units are added to control groups using the shift and ctrl modifier keys.

Control groups are used when 'performing macro' (described later). They are also used to control multiple groups of units on the front line. A player may assign all of one type of unit to a control group separate from the rest of his army, to easily invoke those units' special abilities.

Pen + Touch In PiHC, we developed a technique for defining, accessing, and directing control groups. We present a vertical array of buttons, associated with each control group. In order to add units to a control group, the player touches the control group button with one finger, then selects those units using isosceles lasso select. To reset a control group, the player taps its button with the stylus.

When two fingers are used to touch a control group button, the camera automatically moves to focus on it. Interaction performed with the pen, while two fingers are held down, invokes the default command for that group of units. The control group buttons may also be scrubbed, as described for selecting commands. This supports rapidly changing between different views of the game world, and fast control of several control groups at once. Again these control groups are edge-constrained to the left side of the Cintiq tablet, using its physical properties to facilitate NDH targeting.

Macro

In RTS games, 'macro' refers to tasks that a player performs in order not only to control front line units, but also to construct and manage units and buildings in his base. Thus, macro is not macro-management in a strict sense, but really simultaneous micro-management of many elements. Efficient macro is one of the most difficult interactions for new players to master, because it extensively relies on hot-keys and is difficult to observe other players performing.

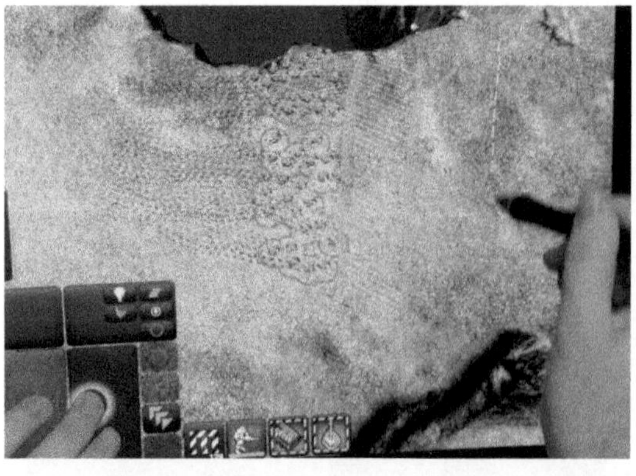

Figure 5: Commands can be placed along a path using the pen. This enables defining unit formations, giving players a higher degree of control over unit placement.

Keyboard One of the most frequently invoked macro tasks is issuing unit construction commands to factories (buildings that produce units). This must be done by first selecting the factory, and then issuing the construction command by either clicking its button, or pressing the hotkey to select the factory's control group. Skilled players almost never use the mouse to perform this task; it is performed via hotkeys because of the speed they afford.

Here is an example macro key sequence in Blizzard's StarCraft. Press '4', to select control group 4, commonly used in StarCraft to select a set of construction buildings, such as a barracks. Once selected, the player builds a 'marine' by pressing the 'A' key. This interaction, once mastered, is quick to execute. It is easy to interweave with other interactions, such as micro of the front line. The keys are pressed without having to change the main view of the screen.

Touch + Pen To support performing macro in PiHC, we developed an in-context touch menu for issuing building commands to factories. To activate the menu, the player touches the building in the game world. The menu appears above and to the right of the touch, avoiding occlusion (Figure 6). The menu interaction is designed so that the NDH brings up the menu, leaving the DH free to interact with the menu using either the stylus or fingers. Thus, menu interaction follows the kinematic chain model: the NDH defines a context for precise DH interaction.

To support the performance of macro while the camera is focused on any location in the game world, the in-context menu may be activated by touching a building's icon in an array at the bottom of the screen (Figure 7). This array includes icons for each of the player's factories. Like graphical hotkeys, this lets the player interweave macro with other mechanics, and saves the player the interaction time required to change the game view to the building's location.

To support issuing various commands to a selected factory, we *overload* the in-context menu with several sub-modes. To interact with all buildings of the same type, a second finger is placed next to the first. Now, the player can issue commands to all factories of this type using the in-context menu. While using the in-context menu, the stylus has several functions. It can be used to press the menu's buttons. As the Cintiq can track the stylus hovering over the screen, the stylus can bring up tool-tips for items in the in-context menu (a very basic

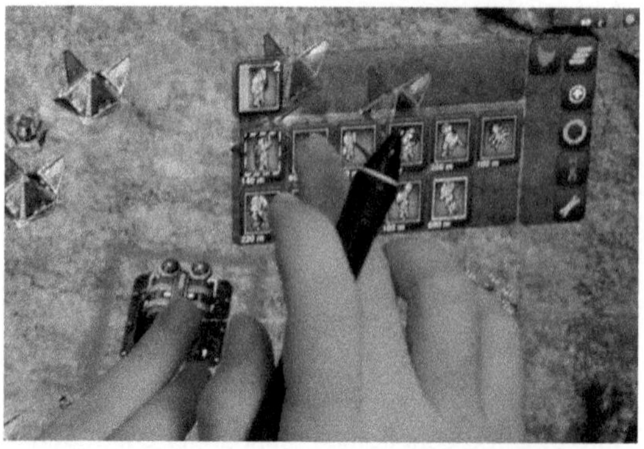

Figure 6: To issue build commands to factories, the NDH is used to activate the in-context build menu.

Figure 7: Macro may be performed at any view location by activating the in-context menu using the factory icons edge-constrained along the bottom of the display.

form of scaffolding). While the in-context menu is activated, the pen can also issue movement commands to the selected factories, enabling setting *rally points* (locations for finished units to move to). By overloading the in-context menu, we aim to reduce the number of targets the NDH must seek.

View Manipulation/Selection

Manipulation of the game world view (camera) is a primary action in RTS games. The position of the camera directly determines what the player can see transpiring in the game world, and at what level of detail. Camera positioning also affects how quickly a player can react to game events.

Mouse + Keyboard The most common camera-positioning technique in RTS games is to move the mouse to an edge of the screen. The game world then gradually pans in the direction of that edge. This interaction has been decried by expert players [21]. They argue that the interaction is slow when you want to move the camera view to a distant location in the game world. It meanwhile prevents the mouse cursor from be used to perform other important interactions. Further, such screen panning can be difficult to perform accurately; it often results in over- or under-shooting a target.

Camera position can also be manipulated in ways more accepted by expert players. The camera is quickly moved to look at a control group by double tapping that control group's assigned key. The player sets predefined camera positions by assigning hotkeys. Another option is to manipulate the camera view by left clicking on the mini-map; this moves the camera to focus on the clicked point. The camera view is also moved by dragging on the mini-map. This last approach is commonly used among skilled players, because its directness affords fast and accurate map manipulation.

Touch In PiHC, the player manipulates the camera directly using touch in the game world. The view is panned using a single finger, zoomed/rotated/panned using two fingers (Figure 8), or pitched by using a three-finger pinch gesture. This interaction may be performed with either hand, and is much more direct than any of the approaches previously implemented in mouse + keyboard RTS games. We note that these gestures may be performed easily using pen-in-hand interaction, with the fingers of the DH, while the stylus is stowed in the palm. This interaction technique emerged early in our design process, through informal use.

Players save and recall camera positions using the viewpoints control. A series of buttons can be touched to target the camera on preset locations. Each button is set by sustained press with the NDH while manipulating the camera view with the DH (Figure 8). When the button is released, it remembers the current camera position. As its icon, the button retains a small representation of its viewpoint (Figure 8, upper left).

Quickly changing the camera viewpoint to observe multiple game world locations is a practice commonly performed in RTS games to maintain awareness. Camera viewpoint buttons can be scrubbed to quickly navigate to preset views. They are edge-constrained in the display's upper left hand corner, so that the NDH can hang off the top edge of the screen, with the thumb touching the control. Again, this edge constraint of the tilted display makes the control easier to target with the NDH, while visually focusing on the main view.

EVALUATION

We conducted an evaluation in which RTS players came to our lab to play PiHC. We recruited 10 participants that reported having previously playing RTS games. All participants were male, university students. Four pairs of participants were friends. All participants were right handed. They were compensated with pizza.

Before the study, we asked participants to fill out a questionnaire that asked about their experience with RTS games and new interaction modalities. After completing the questionnaire, we had them read several pages explaining basics of Zero-K, including how the game economy works, and descriptions of unit types. We conducted a tutorial demo of the pen + touch interface. After this tutorial, we gave participants 15 minutes to try out and learn the interface in a game without enemy units. The proctor answered players' questions during the tutorial.

After the tutorial, players were asked to play against one another for 4 games. We video recorded each game. A high-resolution screen-capture of the game interface and an overhead camera view of the player's hands interacting with the sensor were simultaneously recorded. The independent vari-

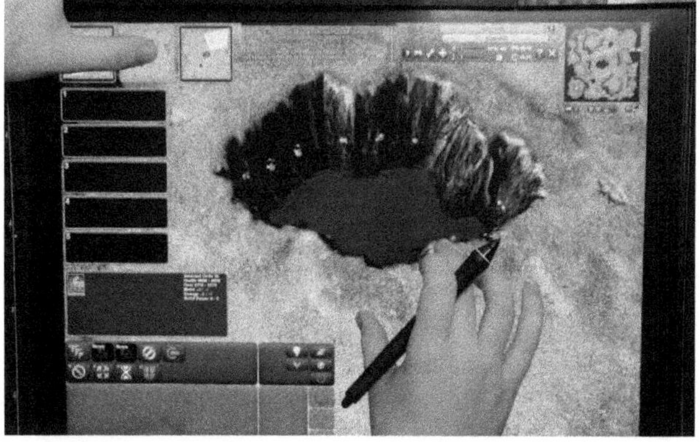

Figure 8: Different game views are saved using the edge-constrained configurable viewpoints control in the display's upper left. A player holds down a viewpoint button with the NDH, manipulating its saved viewpoint with the DH.

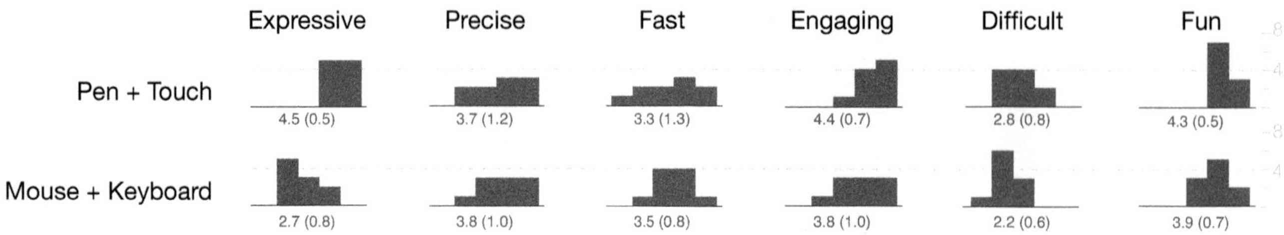

Figure 9: Participant experiences survey distributions. Means and Standard Deviation are given below each distribution.

able was interaction modality: a player used either mouse + keyboard, or pen + touch.

During the first game, each participant played with pen + touch. In the middle two games, players alternated modality conditions. In the final game, both participants played using mouse + keyboard. We decided not to counter-balance the condition order. Because these players already had extensive experience interacting with mouse + keyboard, we thought it best to engage them with the new interaction modality after the tutorial, to create continuity of kinesthetic memory. After playing, participants completed a post-questionnaire.

RESULTS AND DISCUSSION

Despite the findings of our previous survey, the participants were excited about the Pen + Touch interaction modality. We conducted a post-questionnaire survey of participants' experiences of the precision, speed, engagement, difficulty, expressiveness, and fun of the pen + touch, and mouse + keyboard conditions, with a value of 5 for strong agreement and 1 for strong disagreement. The average values reported are shown in Figure 9. A Wilcoxon signed-rank test reported significant differences between the conditions for fun, engagement, and expressiveness ($p < 0.05$). We note that for difficulty, speed, and precision there was more variance in reported ratings: different participants reported strong preference for one condition or the other for these characteristics.

Participants were also asked which condition they preferred in terms of map control, unit control, game awareness, unit selection, and factory control. The results are shown in Figure 10. Unit selection with mouse + keyboard was favored strongly. However, participants' qualitative responses indicated that there was a significant issue with the present implementation of single unit selection. We observed that when players tapped a unit, the tip would travel several pixels between stylus down and up events. This accidentally activated isosceles lasso select, which often failed to select the unit in the small selection area. Many players reported that for group selection, they found that isosceles lasso select was more effective for selecting groups and subgroups of units.

All but one of our participants reported that they felt they could become as good at playing RTS games with pen + touch as they are with mouse + keyboard. Two participants, one of whom was a platinum level StarCraft 2 player, reported that they were already as good with the pen + touch modality by the end of the study. In the following sections, we report on specific qualitative findings concerning the practicability of different interaction components and players' overall engagement with the game.

Engagement

Players reported being more engaged with the game in the Pen + Touch condition. This was found in the Likert scale questions, and also across qualitative data. One participant reported that the experience felt, "more engaging on a visceral level," and that, "somehow the level of control felt more 'real' ". Others reported similar feelings of realness and more physical identification with the game world.

We suspect this is due to the direct nature of the Pen + Touch modality. Several participants reported that the manipulation of the map helped them stay closer to the action. One participant mentioned that he thought he would be more likely to watch someone else playing a RTS game using the Pen + Touch modality, because he would be more engaged watching the physical interactions of another play.

Thus, we see that interaction with new modalities has the potential to transform the experience of engagement in eSports. Part of the spectacle of eSports is being able to observe the skill of high-level players [4]. Because the current mouse + keyboard interactions for RTS eSports are so indirect, the extraordinary skill that high-level players possess can be hard to observe and fully appreciate. The directness of physical interaction in the Pen + Touch modality makes it much easier to connect physical movement and performance. Thus, this aspect of the interaction stands to dramatically augment player and spectator eSports game experiences.

Practicability

Our interaction techniques address efficiency and expression for expert users. Expert use is characterized by extended practice and experience. Our study only lasted for several hours. Meanwhile, our participants reported that they play RTS games with mouse + keyboard for an average of 11.5 hours per week. That constitutes a significant experience level gap. Nonetheless, all but one of our participants felt that with practice, they would become at least as good at playing

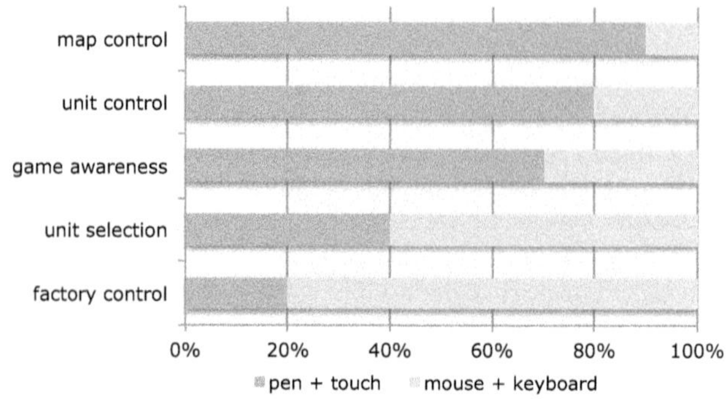

Figure 10: Task performance condition preference.

RTS games using a pen + touch interface.

It is interesting to note that, when asked what they would specifically have to practice to improve their performance, many participants reported that they would practice the in-context build menus for factories. This was the least preferred interaction component (Figure 10). However, no participants reported that they felt they could not practice this component to develop comparable skill.

We observed that few participants used the control group and viewpoints interface components. Typically, these are more advanced skills for RTS players. They are optional and, when practiced, improve overall performance. Several participants noted that they would practice these interactions. Again, none reported that they felt they could not improve their performance by practicing these skills.

IMPLICATIONS FOR DESIGN

Our design process, techniques, and evaluation develop implications for designing pen + touch, and more generally, bi-manual interactions. We first discuss our understanding of pen-in-hand interaction, an emerging paradigm of DH interaction with the Pen + Touch modality. Our experience designing NDH techniques has also led us to a new understanding of how to optimize interaction to minimize the impact of inherent NDH motoric impediments. Finally, we discuss our experiences conducting evaluations with eSports players and present lesson's learned about working with these experts.

Pen-in-Hand Interaction

We first observed DH *pen-in-hand interaction*, touch interaction performed with the pen stowed, early on in informal testing sessions. While we originally intended the NDH to perform map manipulations, as prescribed by Guiard's kinematic chain model, we found ourselves and others manipulating the map using the DH. This is done with the pen stowed between the fingers (see Figure 8). Hinckley et al. observed that this type of interaction is commonly performed when working on desks with pen and paper [13].

We found that Pen-in-Hand interaction increases the capacity of the DH to perform complex interactions. Across the 40 game play sessions of the study, we observed zero instances of a player dropping their stylus. We noticed various stowed positions for the pen. Sometimes, the pen was only moved out of the way for a single finger to pan the map or press a button. At other times, the player would fully stow the pen to perform more complex touch gestures, such as the two or three finger map manipulations.

This data shows us that Pen-in-Hand interaction is particularly useful for direct manipulation. The kinematic chain model is extended further to describe the relationship between the fingers of the DH and an implement held in that hand. Our study indicates that the fingers of the DH effectively define the spatial reference of the held implement, which may be stowed during interaction. It appears that the fingers and stylus have equal priority for interaction order, and may be easily interwoven during interaction.

Edge-Constrained Affordances & Bi-manual Overloading

It has been shown that targeting is more difficult to perform with the NDH [14]. We strove to significantly reduce this problem in two ways. First, we used physical characteristics of the display to *edge-constrain* NDH interactions. Second, we used *bi-manual overloading* to reduce the total number of times that interaction required NDH retargeting.

Designers should place on-screen NDH affordances near a surface's edges and corners. Edge-constraining interactive controls effectively increases target width. The edge of the screen is used as a tactile feedback mechanism for the acquisition of the region. The hand can also grasp or be rested on the edge of the screen to alleviate physical strain from continuous support of the arm. New display technologies, such as curved displays, may offer additional physical properties and tactile feedback to exploit in interaction design.

Another approach to alleviating the difficulty of targeting with the NDH is to simply minimize the number of instances in which new targets must be acquired. We achieve this using the bi-manual overloading design paradigm, which holistically suggests to reduce the number of times that the NDH must retarget. When specifying a mode using the DH, by touching a target, it is best to *overload* the target by providing a number of interactions, likely to be performed together in sequence, that may be performed without retargeting.

An example of bi-manual overloading in PiHC is the in-context build menu. Once a factory has been targeted with the NDH, there are a number of actions that may be performed without moving the NDH. The player may issue build commands to the factory, select all factories of that type by placing a second NDH finger down, and place a rally point using the pen on the game world. All of these options are relevant to the context of the factory and don't require retargeting with the NDH. One of our participants reported that they found this interaction "very smooth and quick".

We note that despite the findings of Wobbrock et al., number of fingers is a very direct way to implement bi-manual overloading. Our experience is that placing a specific number of fingers is a sufficiently coarse action that it may be performed robustly by the NDH, while demanding minimal visual attention. Another approach to bi-manual overloading is the use of *scrubbing*, movement of a finger or fingers of the NDH between multiple axis-aligned interface components without lifting the NDH. Scrubbing avoids retargeting the NDH. The fingers are simply moved in a pre-specified direction. This performs particularly well when feedback can be visualized within the current visual focal point, as when the control group and viewpoint controls are scrubbed. We note that by constraining to an axis-aligned direction, scrubbing requires significantly reduced interactive bandwidth, as prescribed by Balakrishnan and MacKenszie [2]. We utilize scrubbing extensively in the design of the command selection, viewpoint selection, and control group NDH interaction. One participant particularly noted that, "my eyes never had to be averted from the place I was originally looking at".

Situated Evaluation With eSports Players

Situated evaluation with eSports players has many benefits. The foremost is the recruitment of enthusiastic expert participants. All our participants had existing knowledge of how to play RTS games at a relatively high level of performance.

However, we encountered several unforeseen difficulties in our study. The skill levels of the recruited eSports players varied. Even when recruiting participants who were friends and knew they would be playing against each other, almost every pairing of participants resulted in unbalanced skill levels. This makes empirical data from head-to-head matches, such as wins and losses, difficult to interpret, given that the conditions are confounded with the players' prior skill levels. Further, it also makes participation less fun. Few players wanted to stomp or be stomped by their friends.

We found that, given this difference in skill level, another phenomenon emerged during game play. The stronger player would assure their victory early in the game, and would then hold back, not attacking to finish the game. While toying with their opponent, the player would spend time exploring the interface. While this resulted in more observable interaction performance, it also meant that the players were not pushing themselves to perform at the highest level possible.

In future studies, we plan to engage participants in a tournament style study to engage them in more heated play for longer periods of time. We did find that having participants play in pairs sparked interesting discussion and helped players learn more quickly. We may also attempt to have participants play cooperatively against AI opponents.

CONCLUSION

Throughout the design of PiHC, we have encountered many interaction challenges that have pushed us to evolve our understanding of the pen + touch modality. The RTS eSports context has requirements that motived higher performance design. From these requirements comes new designs and implications for new interaction modalities. The isosceles lasso select technique stands as a novel hybrid approach for quick and precise selection. We also developed approaches to enhance NDH interaction using the physical characteristics of surfaces, by edge-constraining affordances, and by overloading NDH interactions. We were excited to see the emergence of the pen-in-hand modality as efficient and expressive DH interaction approach.

Our findings can be generalized in terms of the theory of affordances. Physical properties of objects are perceived, and thus become actionable [8]. We are working with a new form factor for pen + touch. The surface is neither table, nor wall, neither enormous, nor tiny. It is mounted mechanically, and so, unlike a phone or tablet, does not require one hand to hold it. The new physical properties of the surface redefine what can be actionable. The size, proximity to the user, and 30° tilt of this pen + touch surface afford reaching around, and grasping the edges. The constraint of the edge orients the NDH, facilitating the design of new surface-situated interaction techniques involving touch with NDH fingers.

Future research will further investigate edge-constrained NDH interaction, isosceles lasso select, bi-manual overloading, and other affordances and techniques. Their emergence through design for eSports promotes the value of investigating new techniques in this and other situated contexts.

REFERENCES

1. Appert, C., Chapuis, O., Beaudouin-Lafon, M. Evaluation of pointing performance on screen edges. *Proc. AVI* (2008), 119–126.
2. Balakrishnan, R., MacKenzie, I. S. Performance differences in the fingers, wrist, and forearm in computer input control. *Proc. CHI* (1997).
3. Brandl, P., Forlines, C., Wigdor, D., Haller, M., Shen, C. Combining and measuring the benefits of bimanual pen and direct-touch interaction on horizontal interfaces. *Proc. AVI* (2008).
4. Cheung, G., Huang, J. Starcraft from the stands: Understanding the game spectator. *Proc. CHI* (2011).
5. Cutler, L. D., Fröhlich, B., Hanrahan, P. Two-handed direct manipulation on the responsive workbench. *Proc. I3D* (1997).
6. Damaraju, S., Kerne, A. Comparing multi-touch interaction techniques for manipulation of an abstract parameter space. *Proc. ICMI* (2011).
7. Froehlich, J., Wobbrock, J. O., Kane, S. K. Barrier pointing: using physical edges to assist target acquisition on mobile device touch screens. *Proc. SIGACCESS* (2007), 19–26.
8. Gibson, J. J. *The ecological approach to visual perception.* Psychology Press, 1986.
9. Guiard, Y. Asymmetric division of labor in human skilled bimanual action: The kinematic chain as a model. *J. Motor Behavior 19* (1987).
10. Hinckley, K., Guimbretiere, F., Baudisch, P., Sarin, R., Agrawala, M., Cutrell, E. The springboard: Multiple modes in one spring-loaded control. *Proc. CHI* (2006).
11. Hinckley, K., Pausch, R., Proffitt, D., Patten, J., Kassell, N. Cooperative bimanual action. *Proc. CHI* (1997), 27–34.
12. Hinckley, K., Yatani, K., Pahud, M., Coddington, N., Rodenhouse, J., Wilson, A., Benko, H., Buxton, B. Manual deskterity: An exploration of simultaneous pen + touch direct input. *CHI EA* (2010).
13. Hinckley, K., Yatani, K., Pahud, M., Coddington, N., Rodenhouse, J., Wilson, A., Benko, H., Buxton, B. Pen + touch = new tools. *Proc. UIST* (2010).
14. Kabbash, P., MacKenzie, I. S., Buxton, W. Human performance using computer input devices in the preferred and non-preferred hands. *Proc. CHI* (1993), 474–481.
15. Kaltenbrunner, M., Bovermann, T., Bencina, R., Costanza, E. TUIO: A protocol for table-top tangible user interfaces. *Proc. 6th Int'l Gesture Workshop* (2005).
16. Kurtenbach, G., Buxton, W. The limits of expert performance using hierarchic marking menus. *Proc. CHI* (1993), 482–487.
17. *League of Legends.* [PC]. Riot Games, 2009.
18. Moeller, J., Kerne, A. ZeroTouch: An optical multi-touch and free-air interaction architecture. *Proc. CHI* (2012), Full paper in press.
19. Norman, D. A. *The Design of Everyday Things.* Basic Books, September 2002.
20. Odell, D. L., Davis, R. C., Smith, A., Wright, P. K. Toolglasses, marking menus, and hotkeys: a comparison of one and two-handed command selection techniques. *Proc. GI* (2004).
21. Plott, S. Day[9] Daily #242 Secrets of Hotkeys, APM, and Mouse Movement, February 2011.
22. Salen, K., Zimmerman, E. *Rules of Play: Game Design Fundamentals.* MIT Press, Cambridge, MA, USA, 2004.
23. *Spring Engine.* [open source], 2004. http://springrts.com/.
24. *StarCraft II.* [OSX]. Blizzard Entertainment, 2010.
25. Todor, J. I., Doane, T. Handedness and hemispheric asymmetry in the control of movements. *J Mot Behav 10*, 4 (Dec. 1978), 295–300.
26. Wills, G. J. Selection: 524,288 ways to say "this is interesting". *Proc. INFOVIS* (1996).
27. Wobbrock, J. O., Morris, M. R., Wilson, A. D. User-defined gestures for surface computing. *Proc. CHI* (2009).
28. Zabramski, S. Careless touch: a comparative evaluation of mouse, pen, and touch input in shape tracing task. *Proc. OzCHI* (2011), 329–332.
29. *Zero-K.* [open source], 2010. http://zero-k.info/.

GaussSense: Attachable Stylus Sensing Using Magnetic Sensor Grid

Rong-Hao Liang[*‡] **Kai-Yin Cheng**[*] **Chao-Huai Su**[*] **Chien-Ting Weng**[*]
Bing-Yu Chen[†] **De-Nian Yang**[‡]
[*†]National Taiwan University [‡]Academia Sinica
[*]{howieliang,keynes,domossu,ctweng}@cmlab.csie.ntu.edu.tw
[†]robin@ntu.edu.tw [‡]dnyang@iis.sinica.edu.tw

ABSTRACT
This work presents *GaussSense*, which is a back-of-device sensing technique for enabling input on an arbitrary surface using stylus by exploiting magnetism. A 2mm-thick Hall sensor grid is developed to sense magnets that are embedded in the stylus. Our system can sense the magnetic field that is emitted from the stylus when it is within 2cm of any non-ferromagnetic surface. Attaching the sensor behind an arbitrary thin surface enables the stylus input to be recognized by analyzing the distribution of the applied magnetic field. Attaching the sensor grid to the back of a touchscreen device and incorporating magnets into the corresponding stylus enable the system 1) to distinguish touch events that are caused by a finger from those caused by the stylus, 2) to sense the tilt angle of the stylus and the pressure with which it is applied, and 3) to detect where the stylus hovers over the screen. A pilot study reveals that people were satisfied with the novel sketching experiences based on this system.

Author Keywords
Magnetism; Stylus; Sensor; Touchscreen.

ACM Classification Keywords
H.5.2. Information Interfaces and Presentation (e.g. HCI): User Interfaces

General Terms
Design; Measurement; Experimentation.

INTRODUCTION
Stylus input is becoming increasingly prevalent, as people increasingly rely on mobile devices in everyday applications, such as taking notes. To improve the support of these devices for the use of stylus without deploying external optical detectors as shown in Figure 1(a), some manufacturers have started to integrate an additional stylus sensor into devices tightly with the overlain touch panel (Figure 1(b)) or behind the display module (Figure 1(c)). However, since such sensors may be useless through the materials of which the devices are made, they cannot simply be attached behind the devices as retrofit extensions. Some attachable stylus sensors, such as *UnMousePad* [13], can be made transparent overlay onto a back-lit display, but the original touch input capability of the device may thus be disabled.

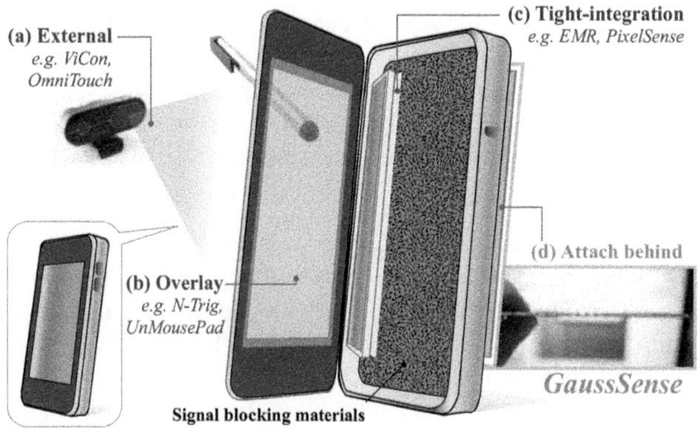

Figure 1. Unlike conventional stylus sensors, the *GaussSense* sensor can be directly attached to the back of the device as a functional extension.

This paper, presents a new back-of-device stylus sensing method, *GaussSense*, which can be directly attached behind a device to enable or enhance stylus input without modifying the front surface (Figure 1(d)). The method is based on the penetrability of magnetism by a magnetic field. A 2mm-thick sensor board is developed for sensing the distribution of a magnetic field from a specially designed magnetic stylus. A user can perform a few calibration steps to enable the stylus to be sensed by the magnetic field sensor board.

The developed technology can be applied in two different manners. For arbitrary non-ferromagnetic surfaces or displays, *GaussSense* can be deployed behind to locate the magnetic stylus on the front of the device. For conventional touchscreens, it can function as an additional sensor that extends the original input capability to stylus detection, including discriminating the stylus events from the finger touch events, determining stylus' tilt angle and stylus tip's pressure, and locating the position above where the stylus hovers.

An initial working prototype made by an 8mm-diameter × 36mm-height magnetic stylus and a 60 × 80mm^2 sensor board with 192 analog Hall sensors in the form of a grid are

UIST'12, October 7–10, 2012, Cambridge, Massachusetts, USA.

implemented and evaluated. The experimental results show that the technology is effective on a non-ferromagnetic device that is under 2cm thick. Finally a sketching application is developed to evaluate the usefulness of the technology, and the results of a pilot study show that people are satisfied with the ability to sketch naturally whatever they want to sketch.

RELATED WORK

Numerous works have been carried out to add stylus detection to displays. The conventional solution is to overlay the screen with a transparent resistive- or capacitive-based panel. With respect to resistive technologies, although the Interpolated Force Sensitive Resistance (IFSR) technology [13] can be used to track a stylus, it cannot easily sense its angle of tilt or position where it hovers. Capacitive technologies [3] allow zero-force manipulation, meaning that the stylus' pressure [18], angle [12] and location of hover [11] can be approximately estimated, but they cannot reliably distinguish between a finger tip event and a stylus tip event.

Another common approach involves external cameras (Figure 1(a)) to capture stylus operations [7] or to assist other stylus input methods to identify subtle operations, such as rolling a stylus [2]. A cuboid stylus, like *Conté* [16], can be used to ease mode switching. However, external detectors are usually not very portable. *OmniTouch* [5] is an exception: it uses a shoulder-worn depth camera that supports multi-touch applications on everyday surfaces with stylus inputs enabled. However, the precision and performance of this system may not suffice for writing or drawing applications, including note-taking and sketching.

With respect to mobility, integrating an additional stylus sensor closely with the overlain touch panel (Figure 1(b)) or behind a display module (Figure 1(c)), as is done with N-Trig DuoSense [9] and electromagnetic resonance[1] (EMR) sensors, respectively, enables advanced stylus detection on a traditional touchscreen. *PixelSense*[2] integrates infrared sensors into every pixel to eliminate external calibrations. These sensing technologies must be tightly integrated with display modules: they cannot be loosely attached behind a device because the physical materials of which the device is made would block signals.

To develop a sensing technology that can be attached to the back of a device as shown in Figure 1(d), the exploitation of directional magnetism is promising because magnetic fields can penetrate most physical materials. *Polhemus*[3] can be used to perform high-resolution tracking by exploiting a strongly penetrating electromagnetic field, but the tracking mechanism requires a heavy external emitter. Ferromagnetic input device deploys an array of coils [8] can be used to sense free-form ferromagnetic objects, but its mobility is constrained by the size of the device. Magnetometers are embedded in most smartphones, but its radial detection range suggests remapping of the input space [1, 6]. The Hall sensor is another widely used magnetic field sensor. It is tiny, inexpensive and consumes low power. *SmartTable* [14] has successfully demonstrated that deploying Hall sensors in a grid can provide 2D detection, but this method is not sufficiently precise for detecting operations with a stylus.

[1]http://www.wacom.com

[2]http://www.microsoft.com/surface/

[3]http://www.polhemus.com/

DESIGN

Hardware

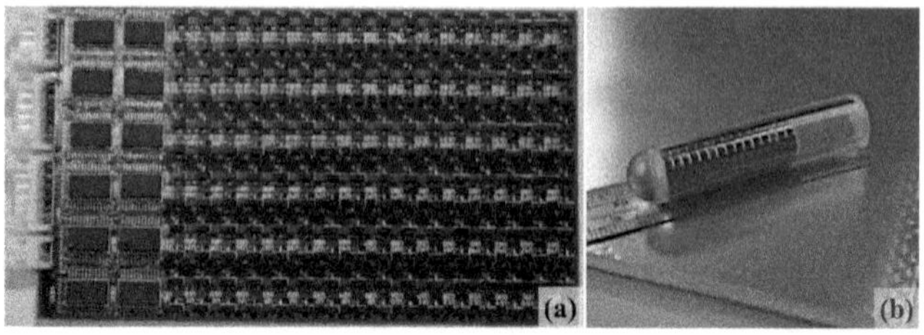

Figure 2. (a) Sensor board with 192 Hall-effect sensors and 12 multiplexers. (b) Magnetic stylus above the example aluminum-coated surface.

The goal of this work is to build an attachable, lightweight sensor system that can detect a magnetic field that penetrates from the opposite side of the device to which it is attached. A 2mm-thick sensor board of dimensions 60(W) $\times$ 80(H) mm^2 is made from 12 $\times$ 16 = 192 Winson WSH138 Hall sensors[4] that are arranged in a grid. Each sensor element is designed to provide N-polar detection linearly in the range of 0 to 200 Gauss on a 512-point scale. All sensor data are multiplexed and transferred to a PC through a Teensy 2.0 microcontroller[5] via USB connection. The captured data are upsampled using the bi-cubic interpolation method (or the bilinear interpolation method for the sensors at the boundaries) to 352 $\times$ 480 (163 dpi), consistently above 60 fps.

A prototype magnetic stylus, in which is embedded an 8mm-diameter $\times$ 30mm-height stack of cylindrical neodymium magnets in a 6mm-radius acrylic pipe, and which has an acrylic hemisphere as its tip, is built.

Signal Processing

Calibration: To eliminate the zero-biasing problem of each sensor element i, a default value v for each element is set by averaging the initial values v_i, while the sensor is turned on, and then calibrating the values of each element at runtime by adding a pre-computed offset between v and v_i.

Sensing: After collecting calibrated raw values v_i' of the sensors, the intensity I_i of each sampling point i is calculated by $I_i = cv_i'^{\gamma}$, where c is a constant and γ is a correction factor. For cylindrical magnets used in the stylus, the γ is set to 0.5 because the sensed intensity of the magnetic field is inverse-cubically related to the vertical distance from sensor to dipole [17]. Thereafter, I_i is utilized to reconstruct the shape of magnetic field exerted from the stylus. The steps of signal processing are listed below:

1. Interpolate the raw data to construct the magnetic field image (Figure 3(a)), and define the global maximum intensity I_{max} as M.

[4]http://www.winson.com.tw/

[5]http://www.pjrc.com/teensy/

2. Clip the image by applying the threshold $T_{clip} = M - k$, where k is a small constant (Figure 3(b)).

3. If the largest connected shape hits the boundary, then shrink the image by increasing T_{clip} until it does not hit the boundary or until $T_{clip} = M$ (Figure 3(c)). This ensures the completeness of the shape to prevent reduced precision when the stylus is close to the boundary of the sensor board.

4. Compute the centroid of the shape as $O = (O_x, O_y)$. Then, the obtained O and M represent the position and the magnitude of the field, respectively.

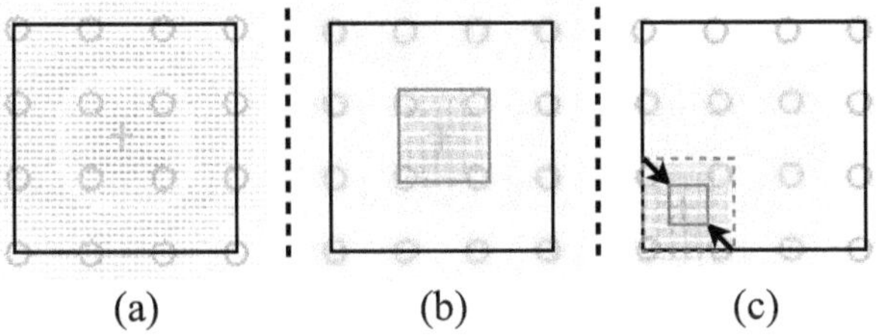

Figure 3. Image of magnetic field (a) without and (b) with clipping. (c) Shrink the image when close to the boundary.

Register a stylus: A user can register the stylus by placing it in contact with the surface without lifting it tip. Sixty consecutive M would be collected after the sensor readings become stable, and the threshold for determining the contacting event of a stylus, $T_{contact}$, can be obtained as $\bar{M} - 2\sigma$, where $\bar{M}$ and σ are the mean value and standard deviation of the collected values, respectively.

Sense through Surfaces

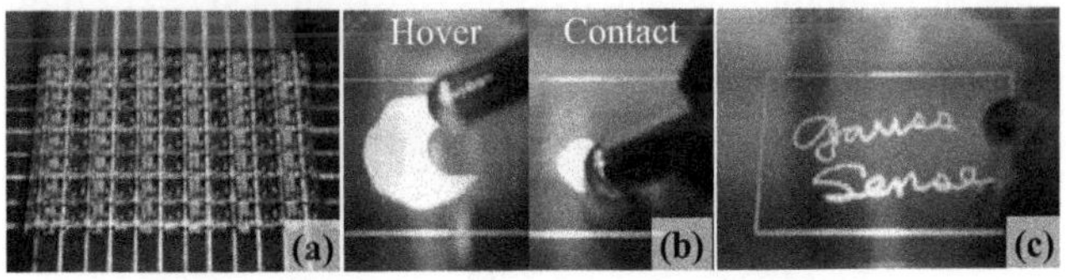

Figure 4. (a) Experimental apparatus. A top-mounted projector is used to provide visual feedback. (b) Image of magnetic field. (c) Results of stylus detection.

An example surface (Figure 2(b)) is made of a 3.5mm-thick wooden board that is coated with a 0.2mm-thick aluminum sheet, which represents the coating of common electronic devices, such as tablet computers. Since this surface is thick, opaque, solid, and made of conductive material, any conventional stylus detection system would fail if it was attached behind it. However, *GaussSense* can accurately detect the stylus through this surface as shown in Figure 4.

Use with Touchscreens

The sensor board also can be attached to the back of touchscreen devices as an extra sensor for stylus input. An unmodified iPod touch[6] was used for prototyping (Figure 5(a)). A sensor board is fixed to an acrylic protection case, which can

[6]http://www.apple.com/ipodtouch/

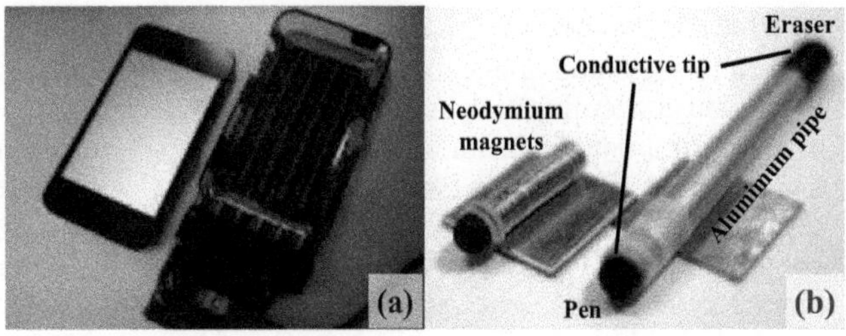

Figure 5. (a) Thin form-factor sensor grid augments magnetic field sensing on the multitouch device. (b) Magnetic stylus with one end as pen point and the other end as eraser.

be easily attached to or detached from the device. The magnetic stylus is also modified for the capacitive touchscreen by encasing in it stacked magnets in a conductive aluminum pipe with a rubber tip, which was taken from an Elecom iPhone stylus[7] (Figure 5(b)).

After the stylus has been registered on the touchscreen, the correspondence between touchscreen inputs and the magnetic sensor inputs is established. Therefore, the actual stylus touch point, $P = (P_x, P_y)$, along with O and M (Figure 6(a)), can be used to perform the following functions.

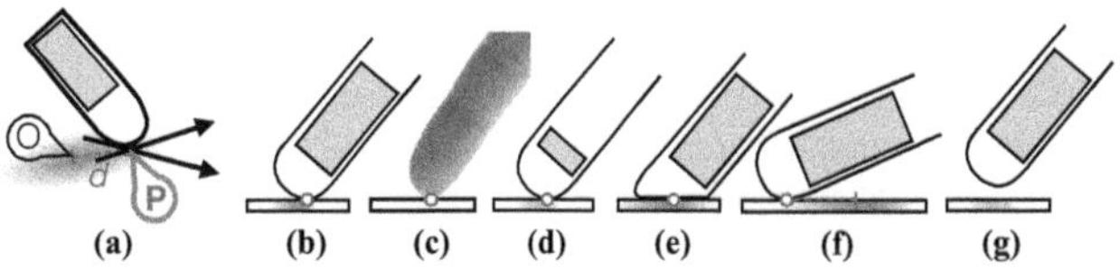

Figure 6. Sensing with touchscreens. Red: Magnetic field intensity. (a) Overview, (b) stylus event, (c) touch event, (d) different stylus, (e) various pressures, (f) different tilt angles, and (g) hover.

Distinguish the magnetic stylus from fingers: A magnetic stylus touch event can be distinguished from finger or conventional stylus touch events. If M exceeds a predened threshold, P will be regarded as a magnetic stylus event (Figure 6(b)) rather than a touch event (Figure 6(c)).

Recognize different styli: Different magnetic styli may yield different values of M when the tip comes into contact with the touchscreen. This fact can be exploited to distinguish among different styli (Figure 6(d)).

Pressure Sensing: When a user applies pressure through the tip, the rubber becomes deformed and the distance between the embedded magnets and the sensor board is shortened. Hence, the sensed value of M increases (Figure 6(e)).

Tilt Sensing: The relative position of O and P may change when the stylus is tilted. Therefore, $\vec{d} = \vec{PO}$ and $d = ||PO||$ can be applied to determine the direction and angle of tilt (Figure 6(f)), respectively.

Hover sensing: When the system senses a magnetic field, but no touching point P within a predefined distance r from the calculated centroid O, then the point O can be treated as the hover point (Figure 6(g)).

[7]http://www.elecom.co.jp/

APPLICATION AND PILOT STUDY

A simple sketching application is implemented to gather information concerning early user experiences. A user can draw a stroke in a natural manner, tilting the stylus (Figure 7(a)) and applying different pressures (Figure 7(b)). If the user wants to erase strokes, he/she can use the other end of the stylus as an eraser (Figure 7(c)), in which is embedded a 6mm-diameter × 1mm-height cylindrical magnet within another conductive rubber tip. The stroke is rendered by a mesh of triangular elements based on the position of the current $\overline{OP}$ and the previous $\overline{O'P'}$ pairs, and the intensity of the color inside the triangles is determined as the corresponding magnitude, M, as shown in Figure 7(d). A higher sensed M corresponds to the rendering of a darker stroke. A finger touch event on the top left-hand corner requests a new canvas. The boundaries of the sensor board can also be utilized for alternative input functions. Causing the stylus to hover at a boundary can call out an off-screen color swatch from which a new color can be selected.

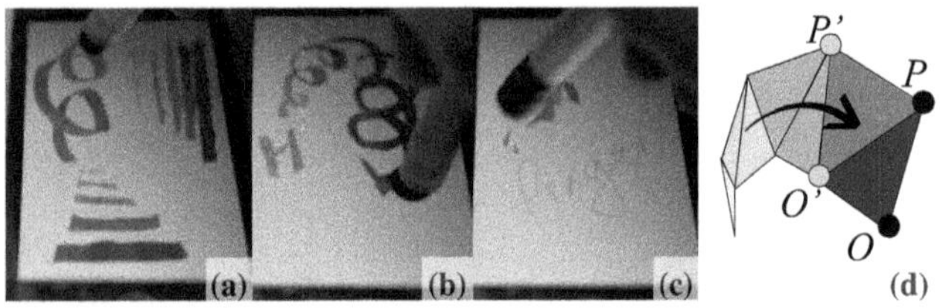

Figure 7. (a) Sensing of tilt angle. (b) Sensing of pressure. (c) Implicit mode switching for erasing. (d) Rendering of a pen stroke.

Pilot Study

Twelve volunteers (five female) were recruited through a designer's workshop as shown in Figure 8. Six of the 12 had more than five years of experience in product design. They were invited to try out all the features of the developed system and share their thoughts.

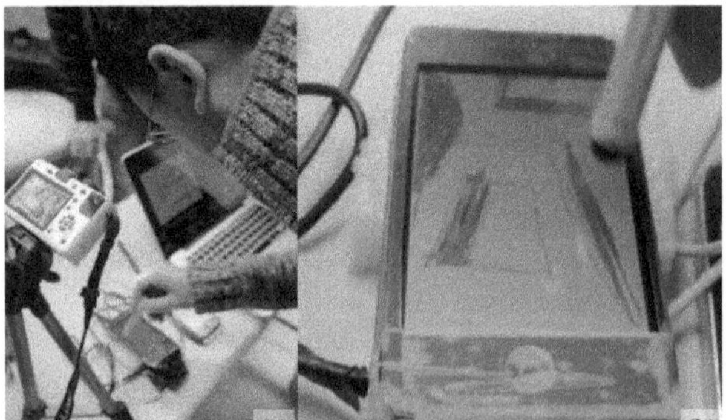

Figure 8. (a) Pilot study is conducted as part of a workshop. (b) A professional designer sketches using *GaussSense*.

All of the participants were surprised that a simple add-on technology could provide all of the aforementioned features. While sketching on the touchscreen, they found that they could use natural movements and they were felt satisfied with the precision. Two of them said that using the stylus reminded them of using a marker pen or a pen brush. Another designer thought that palm rejection should also be provided, because he preferred to place his hand on the screen while sketching. We also observed that several participants spontaneously used their fingers to blur the sketched lines, but this feature was not provided. Some of them suggested that the finger could be utilized to change the color or the simulated type of brush. One designer, who has many years of experience of using a digital pen for sketching, suggested that several well-established UI features, such as hover widgets [4], pressure widgets [10], and tilting menus or operations [15, 19] should be included in the application for advanced editing. Generally, the provided technology aroused the interest of the designers in trying the different combinations of features and discussing possible alternative designs.

EVALUATION

A series of formal measurements are made on the prototype devices to elucidate their various limitations. Measurements were made in two parts. In part I, the capabilities of the magnetic stylus on a *GaussSense*-enabled capacitive touchscreen, including precision, determination of applied pressure and determination of tilt angle, are measured. In part II, the penetrability of the magnetic field from the magnetic stylus through various materials of different thicknesses is measured. The prototype devices that were presented in the preceding section are used in the experiments.

Part I: Use of Magnetic Stylus on Capacitive Touchscreen

Experiment 1 - Precision of the Stylus: An acrylic case was used to hold the stylus perpendicular to the sensor board as Figure 9(a) shown. An arbitrary curve was drawn ten times, and the system registered a total of 13,684 pairs of (P_i, O_i), which is the touchscreen input and the calculated centroid of the magnetic field, respectively (Figure 9(b)). The Euclidian distance from each P_i to O_i is calculated, and the mean of the distances among the paired points is 0.42mm (SD = 0.27mm), which is the calculated precision of positioning.

Figure 9. (a) Apparatus for testing. An acrylic case is used to keep a stylus perpendicular to the sensor board. (b) Drawing an arbitrary curve for sampling; the connected black and red points represent positions P and O, respectively.

Experiment 2 - Tilt Angle of the Stylus: A mechanical arm is used to fix the stylus and a protractor is placed beside to measure the included angle between the stylus tip and the screen as shown in Figure 10(a). The data are sampled every five degrees. At each tested angle, the system samples 100 times and the mean value of the detected angle is calculated. The result is shown in Figure 10(b) Owing to the roundness of the soft tip, the slopes of d in the range from 60 to 90 degrees differ from those in the range from 30 to 60 degrees. Because of physical limitations, the tips cannot be detected at angles from 0 to 30 degrees.

After the measurements were made, we conducted Experiment 1 again to obtain the standard deviations of position SD_p, which was measured to be 0.22mm. Set the range for each level to be 0.88mm, which is $\pm\ 2SD_p$, five angles of tilt were obtained.

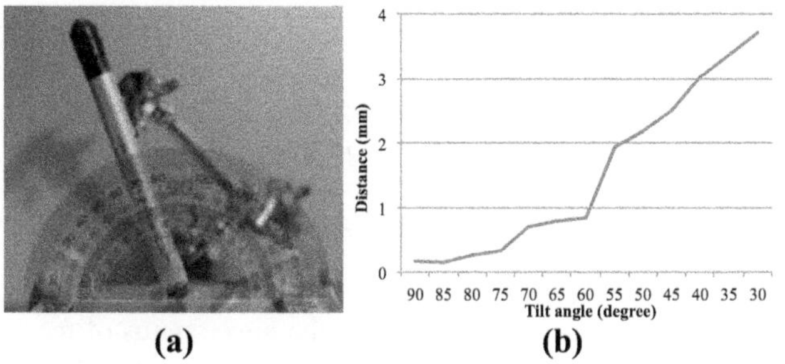

Figure 10. (a) Experimental apparatus. (b) Sensed values. At 90 degrees on horizontal axis, stylus is perpendicular to sensor board.

Experiment 3 - Pressure of the Stylus: An electronic scale with a precision of 0.1gram (g) was used as shown in Figure 11(a). In testing, stainless steel weights were used because stainless steel causes no significant magnetic interference with the magnets in the stylus[8]. An acrylic case was used to hold the soft-tipped stylus perpendicular to the screen. In each trial, a 20g weight was put on the stylus. The total weight never exceeded 400g, and each total weight was used in 100 trials. The mean value was calculated, as shown in Figure 11(b).

After the measurements were made, standard deviations of the magnitude of magnetic field, SD_m, were determined using the same procedures as were used in Experiment 1. The magnitude fluctuated slightly (SD_m=1.15 Gauss) while the stylus was moved around. Set the range for each level to be 4.6 Gauss, which is $\pm\ 2SD_m$, six pressure were obtained.

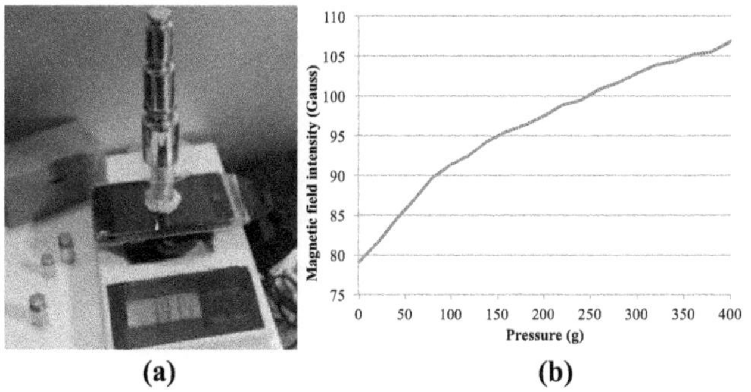

Figure 11. (a) Experimental apparatus. (b) Results of magnetic field intensity using 0 to 400g weights.

[8]Conventional stainless steel is not entirely non-magnetic, but its relative permeability (<1.1; 1 is for non-magnetic) is much smaller than those of most ferromagnetic materials (between 100 and 20000). Given the precision of our developed device, the interference associated with the use of stainless steel is negligible.

Part II: Magnetic Stylus on Arbitrary Surface

Experiment 4 - Surface material: Since a magnetic field can pass through most physical materials, input capability can be enabled on the surface. An initial exploration of this property was conducted by attaching the sensor board behind different materials that were a) opaque, b) conductive or c) ferromagnetic, as shown in Figure 12.

The experimental results reveal that a magnetic field can pass through all of the materials except for the ferromagnetic material. Ferromagnetic materials not only interfere with detection, but also inhibit drawing because of the strong attraction between the magnetic stylus and the ferromagnetic surface.

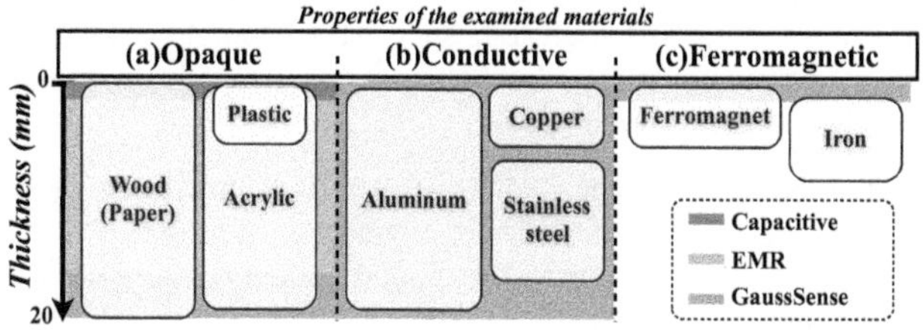

Figure 12. All technologies are effective when opaque materials are thin, but only *GaussSense* works also on conductive and ferromagnetic materials. Except on ferromagnetic materials, *GaussSense* works well with material thicknesses of under 20mm. Generally, *GaussSense* has larger sensing range than capacitive or EMR technology.

Experiment 5 - Thickness of the non-ferromagnetic surface: According to Experiment 4, the sensing ability of on a non-ferromagnetic surface is limited by its thickness. To understand this fact, Experiment 1 was firstly conducted with small magnets to find the minimal magnetic field strength that could be stably detected through the device, iPod Touch, by the sensor board at a distance between the magnet and the sensor board of 8.8mm as shown in Figure 13(a). The input data of the capacitive touchscreen are used as ground truth. After 50 trials, 25 Gauss was found to be the minimal field strength that yielded a mean error of under 1mm.

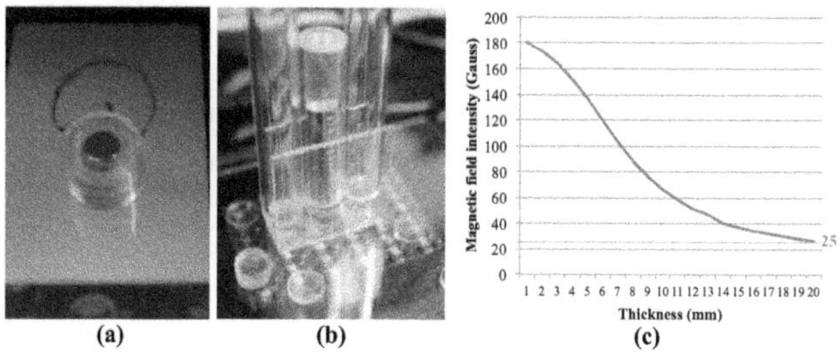

Figure 13. (a) Small magnet is used to find the minimal magnetic field strength, which is determined to be 25 Gauss. (b) Magnetic stylus in a vertical sliding case. Acrylic chips are used to control distance between sensor and stylus. (c) Sensed field strength decreases as distance between stylus and sensor increases.

Thereafter, the magnetic stylus was tested on the sensor board (Figure 13(b)) in the absence of any electronic components within the device, which may otherwise have interfered with the experiment. An acrylic sliding case was used to hold the stylus perpendicular to the sensor board. In each trial, one more 1mm acrylic chip was added between the magnetic pole and the sensor board; 100 measurements of magnitude were made at five fixed sample points, and the mean value was calculated as shown in Figure 13(c). The results show that the developed technology can be used with this device with a thickness of under 20mm. Though iPod Touch is used as the examined material, the results also can be applied to any uniform non-ferromagnetic materials, because the magnetic field penetrates them easier.

DISCUSSION

Limitations

To ensure uniform precision, the sensor board must be kept parallel to the interactive surface on the front of the device. Accordingly, the case that holds the sensor board should not be made of a soft material, such as silicon, to prevent the user from accidentally displacing the calibrated sensor while holding the device.

Since the system exploits magnetism, the *GaussSense* system cannot be combined with some sensors that also use magnetism, such as a magnetometer, and cannot be used with ferromagnetic materials.

A stylus that contains a strong magnet may erase content on magnetic strips on credit cards if they are very close to each other, because magnetic strips are not protected by shielding mechanism. However, the magnet does not affect IC cards, flash storage devices, or well-shielded magnetic storage devices. Crafting a stylus with magnetic shielding materials can mitigate this potential hazard.

Fault Tolerance

In deploying numerous sensors on the board, generally, two problems may be encountered. First, the sensors have different sensitivities, and second, some may be defective. With respect to the first problem, the initially sensed values can be adjusted by the aforementioned calibration process, and with respect to the second, a fault tolerance procedure is developed to recover the values of defective sensors.

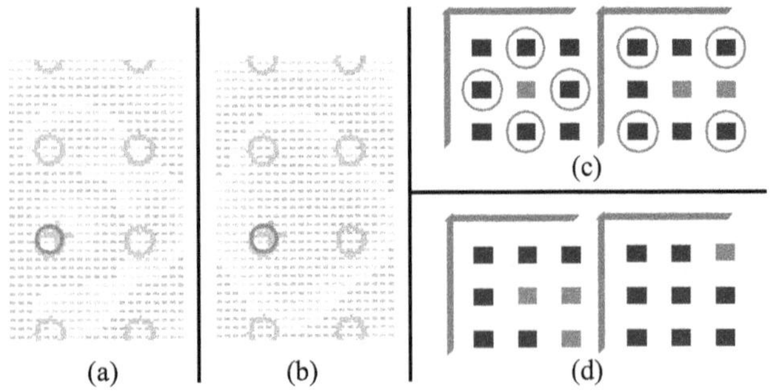

Figure 14. Fault tolerance. (a) Without and (b) with recovery of value that cannot be measured by invalid sensor, which is indicated by red circle. (c) Recoverable cases and (d) unrecoverable cases. Red: Invalid sensor(s). Blue circle: Candidates for recovering.

When the sensors are activated for the first time, a self-validation test records the first n values that are sampled from each sensor i, and the mean $\bar{v}_i$ and standard deviation σ_i are calculated. If the calculated values satisfy the following two conditions, then the sensor will be recognized as operating correctly. First, the $\bar{v}_i$ must lie in a predefined range. Second, the σ_i should not be larger than a predefined threshold. Any sensor that cannot meet these criteria will be regarded as invalid. To recover the measurements would have been made by the invalid sensors, bi-linear interpolation using the values measured by the neighboring sensors can be applied as shown in Figure 14(a). However, if the invalid sensor is at the boundary or no valid neighboring sensor (Figure 14(b)) can be used for interpolation, the values in question cannot be recovered.

Compatibility with Various Surfaces

Integration with a resistive touchscreen: GaussSense is also compatible with resistive touch panels. A well-calibrated 3.8" resistive touchscreen is laid over the screen of an iPod Touch, which is only used for displaying as shown in Figure 15. Because a steady pressure must be applied to the touchscreen, the stylus tip is made of a magnetic cone with 1mm-diameter tip. *GaussSense* not only detects the hover status of the stylus, but also reduces the required initial force that must be applied to the resistive touchscreen. To enable pressure sensing, *GaussSense* can be further integrated with a pressure-sensitive IFSR [13] touch panel.

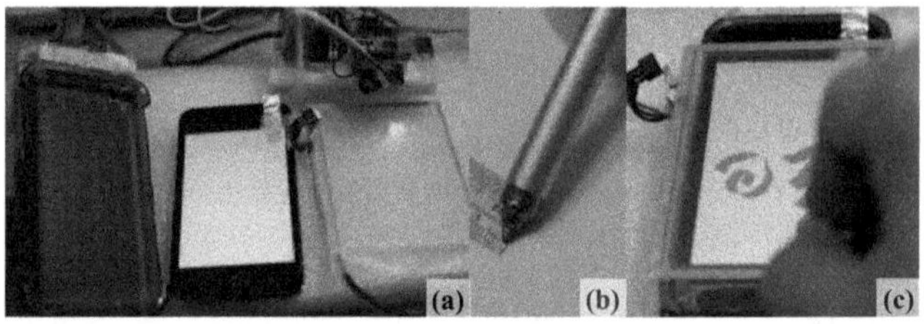

Figure 15. (a) From left to right: modified plastic case, unmodified iPod touch, and well-calibrated resistive touchscreen. (b) Stylus with magnetic cone. (c) Results of stylus detection.

Integration with a LCD Screen: The sensor board can be attached to the back of a laptop monitor as shown in Figure 16. A user can use the registered stylus to write directly on the unmodified LCD monitor. He or she can, for example, sign a personal signature, scribble ideas to be communicated with others, or leave memos.

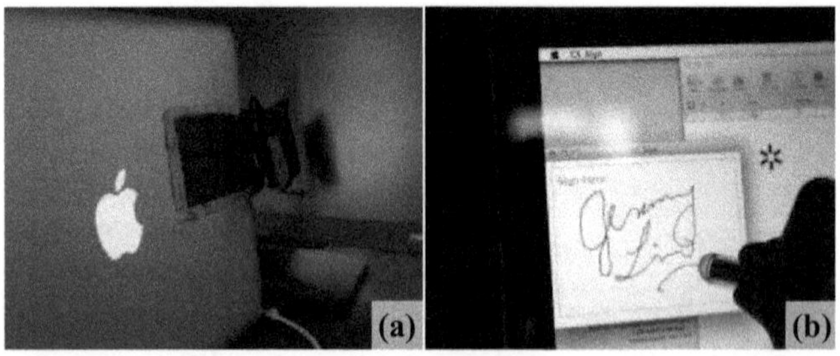

Figure 16. (a) Attaching sensor board to back of laptop monitor, and (b) taking a note.

CONCLUSION AND FUTURE WORK

This paper presents a novel back-of-device sensing method, *GaussSense*, to enable a stylus to be used as an input device on any non-ferromagnetic flat surface that is thinner than 2cm by utilizing directional magnetism. Since most handheld touch devices are thinner than 2cm, the *GaussSense* board can be attached to the back of these devices as an additional sensor to improve their capabilities of stylus input. The board enables touch events that are caused by fingers to be distinguished from those that are caused by the stylus; it also enables the tilt angle of the stylus, the applied pressure, and the position over which the stylus hovers to be detected. Through a series of evaluation, the functions of the developed technology are examined, and the results can be further improved by better manufacturing processes. Since *GaussSense* can discriminate touch points using a finger from those using a stylus, future work should seek to develop richer Pen+Touch interactions. An advanced user study can also be conducted to understand usability issues.

The proposed *GaussSense* technology enables or enhances stylus input without modifying the front surface. The solution is cheap and robust, and the calculations involved are sufficiently simple to be performed in real time.

ACKNOWLEDGEMENTS

We gratefully acknowledge the helpful comments and suggestions of the Associate Chairs and the anonymous reviewers. We also thank Ming Ouhyoung and Mike Y. Chen for their valuable comments. This paper was partially supported by the Excellent Research Projects of the National Taiwan University under NTU10R80919-5, National Science Council of Taiwan under NSC100-2221-E-001-006-MY2, and the MediaTek Fellowship.

REFERENCES

1. Ashbrook, D., Baudisch, P., and White, S. Nenya: subtle and eyes-free mobile input with a magnetically-tracked finger ring. In *Proceedings of ACM CHI 2011* (2011), 2043–2046.
2. Bi, X., Moscovich, T., Ramos, G., Balakrishnan, R., and Hinckley, K. An exploration of pen rolling for pen-based interaction. In *Proceedings of ACM UIST 2008* (2008), 191–200.
3. Dietz, P., and Leigh, D. DiamondTouch: a multi-user touch technology. In *Proceedings of ACM UIST 2001* (2001), 219–226.
4. Grossman, T., Hinckley, K., Baudisch, P., Agrawala, M., and Balakrishnan, R. Hover widgets: using the tracking state to extend the capabilities of pen-operated devices. In *Proceedings of ACM CHI 2006* (2006), 861–870.
5. Harrison, C., Benko, H., and Wilson, A. D. OmniTouch: wearable multitouch interaction everywhere. In *Proceedings of ACM UIST 2011* (2011), 441–450.
6. Harrison, C., and Hudson, S. E. Abracadabra: wireless, high-precision, and unpowered finger input for very small mobile devices. In *Proceedings of ACM UIST 2009* (2009), 121–124.
7. Hinckley, K., Yatani, K., Pahud, M., Coddington, N., Rodenhouse, J., Wilson, A., Benko, H., and Buxton, B. Pen + touch = new tools. In *Proceedings of ACM UIST 2010* (2010), 27–36.
8. Hook, J., Taylor, S., Butler, A., Villar, N., and Izadi, S. A reconfigurable ferromagnetic input device. In *Proceedings of ACM UIST 2009* (2009), 51–54.
9. Perski, H., and Morag, M. Dual function input device and method. U.S. Patent No. 6762752, 2002.
10. Ramos, G., Boulos, M., and Balakrishnan, R. Pressure widgets. In *Proceedings of ACM CHI 2004* (2004), 487–494.
11. Rogers, S., Williamson, J., Stewart, C., and Murray-Smith, R. FingerCloud: uncertainty and autonomy handover incapacitive sensing. In *Proceedings of ACM CHI 2010* (2010), 577–580.
12. Rogers, S., Williamson, J., Stewart, C., and Murray-Smith, R. AnglePose: robust, precise capacitive touch tracking via 3d orientation estimation. In *Proceedings of ACM CHI 2011* (2011), 2575–2584.
13. Rosenberg, I., and Perlin, K. The UnMousePad: an interpolating multi-touch force-sensing input pad. *ACM TOG 28*, 3 (2009), 65:1–65:9.
14. Steurer, P., and Srivastava, M. B. System design of smart table. In *Proceedings of IEEE PerCom 2003* (2003), 473–482.
15. Tian, F., Xu, L., Wang, H., Zhang, X., Liu, Y., Setlur, V., and Dai, G. Tilt menu: using the 3D orientation information of pen devices to extend the selection capability of pen-based user interfaces. In *Proceedings of ACM CHI 2008* (2008), 1371–1380.
16. Vogel, D., and Casiez, G. Conté: multimodal input inspired by an artist's crayon. In *Proceedings of ACM UIST 2011* (2011), 357–366.
17. Vokoun, D., Beleggia, M., Heller, L., and Šittner, P. Magnetostatic interactions and forces between cylindrical permanent magnets. *J. Magnetism and Magnetic Materials 321*, 22 (2009), 3758–3763.
18. Wilson, A. D., Izadi, S., Hilliges, O., Garcia-Mendoza, A., and Kirk, D. Bringing physics to the surface. In *Proceedings of ACM UIST 2008* (2008), 67–76.
19. Xin, Y., Bi, X., and Ren, X. Acquiring and pointing: an empirical study of pen-tilt-based interaction. In *Proceedings of ACM CHI 2011* (2011), 849–858.

FlexAura: A Flexible Near-Surface Range Sensor

Shenwei Liu **Francois Guimbretiere**
Cornell University
301 College Avenue
Ithaca, NY, 14850
{sl2277@cornell.edu, francois@cs.cornell.edu}

ABSTRACT

The availability of flexible capacitive sensors that can be fitted around mice, smartphones, and pens carries great potential in leveraging grasp as a new interaction modality. Unfortunately, most capacitive sensors only track interaction directly on the surface, making it harder to differentiate among grips and constraining user movements. We present a new optical range sensor design based on high power infrared LEDs and photo-transistors, which can be fabricated on a flexible PCB and wrapped around a wide variety of graspable objects including pens, mice, smartphones, and slates. Our sensor offers a native resolution of 10 dpi with a sensing range of up to 30mm (1.2") and sampling speed of 50Hz. Based on our prototype wrapped around the barrel of a pen, we present a summary of the characteristics of the sensor and describe the sensor output in several typical pen grips. Our design is versatile enough to apply not only to pens but to a wide variety of graspable objects including smartphones and slates.

Keywords: Touch sensors; IR range sensing; graspable UI; pen UI;

ACM Classification: H5.2 [Information interfaces and presentation]: User Interfaces. - Graphical user interfaces.

General terms: Human Factors

INTRODUCTION

Multi-touch interfaces have been widely adopted on a variety of devices including smartphones, tablets, and trackpads. Once confined to flat area, the availability of flexible capacitive sensors has led to the development of devices capable of capturing users' grips and gestures on a curved surface. For example, Taylor et al. [11] examined grip recognition on a variety of shapes, including a ball, and Kim et al. [9] explored how the grasp of a smartphone could be used to infer intended use. Microsoft [12] and Apple both developed multi-touch mice, on which users can perform gestures. Finally, Song et al. [10] augmented a pen with a capacitive sensor allowing users to switch drawing tools by simply using different grips.

UIST'12, October 7–10, 2012, Cambridge, Massachusetts, USA.

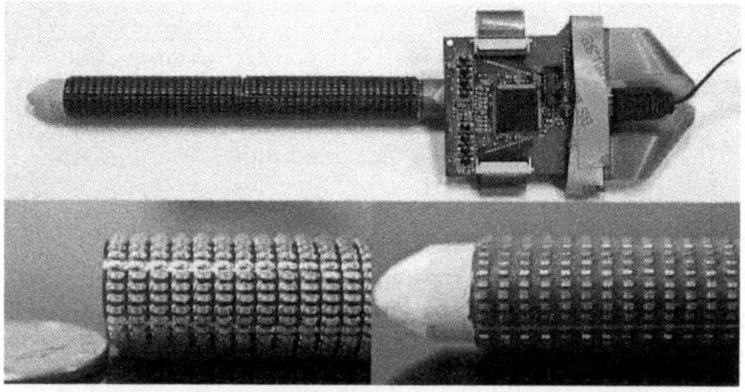

Figure 1. **Top:** The sensor in a pen configuration. We combined two flexible PCBs to create a 16x48 sensing array running at 50Hz. **Bottom left:** A close-up of the sensor with the LEDs and transistors in place. **Bottom right:** The final sensor with black modeling clay applied to limit direct illumination from LEDs to adjacent transistors.

Unfortunately, these capacitive sensors only provide information about contact points, which presents several disadvantages. First, different grips can result in a similar set of contact points posing challenges to recognition. Second, interactions are limited to the surface of the capacitive sensor. This can be problematic since, during a given grip, finger movement is often limited by the constraints imposed by grip itself. Range sensing was shown to significantly increase expressiveness on flat multi-touch surfaces [5, 6]. We believe that graspable interactions will benefit in similar ways.

In this paper, we propose a flexible infrared proximity sensor array capable of capturing range data around graspable objects such as pens (Figure 1). Our system significantly extends the work by Choi et al. [1, 2] by combining a 3.3-fold increase in pixel resolution (10dpi) and a 3-fold increase in range (30mm) with sufficient flexibility to accommodate small radius of curvature. Using the pen as an example, we present the design and characteristics of our sensor as well as its output for typical pen grips. We also illustrate the capability of our system to capture its surroundings.

Our design can be adapted to a wide range of grasp sensing applications including sensing the grasp of a phone or a slate, instrumenting tangible props for tangible interactions, or monitoring the grasp of sport equipment.

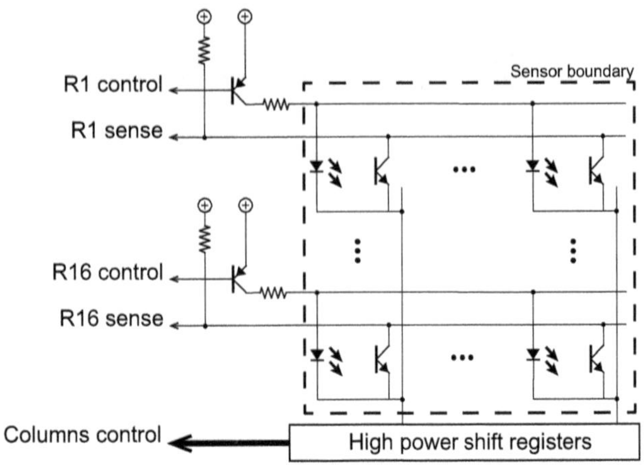

Figure 2: Our system schematic. To simplify wiring, LED and transistors are grounded together.

A FLEXIBLE RANGE SENSOR

In contrast to tabletop interactions, interactions for graspable devices do not benefit much from a typical range camera such as the Kinect. Some of the most important information about grip comes from the shape of the inside of the hand, a part occluded from the camera. One alternative approach is to rely on an array of small range sensors that sense the grasping hand from the inside. Hudson [8] demonstrated the feasibility of this approach by building a reflective range sensor using a matrix of LEDs used as both illuminators and sensors [3]. While this design makes it relatively easy to create dense arrays, LEDs are slow sensors. An alternative is to uses photo-transistors for sensing the reflected light [1, 2, 7] at the cost of a less compact design. Photo-transistors are more sensitive than LEDs resulting in better resolution and range. They also have a fast settling time, which allows for a scanning function that energizes one sensing cell (i.e., a paired LED and photo-transistor) at a time and thus reduces crosstalk among different areas of the reflected surface. Our work improves upon Choi et al.'s hardware [1, 2] in several ways: (1) greater resolution (10dpi instead of 3dpi); (2) greater range (30mm instead of 10mm); (3) sufficient flexibility to be wrapped around many graspable objects.

Our sensor consists of a 16x24 array of sensing cells. Each cell is based on an IR LED (OSRAM SFH 4050) and a photo-transistor (OSRAM SFH 3010) placed side by side such that their long axis corresponds to the main axis of curvature (Figure 1, Bottom left). Our design combines high-side transistors and low-side high-power shift registers to drive each LED with current up to about 300mA, resulting in a greater sensing range (Figure 2). Each photo-transistor current can be read by measuring the voltage of a load resistor (one per row) using one of the 16 analog inputs of our micro-controller. Because only one photo-transistor per column is polarized at any given time, we avoid crosstalk between columns. Note that the same column line polarizes both LEDs and photo-transistors in each cell, resulting in a reduced number of control lines.

Our sensor can be implemented as a 2-layer flexible printed circuit board (minimum bend radius 1.2mm) making it possible to wrap the sensor around a wide variety of surface. In our pen design, two sensors are controlled by a TI LM3S9B90 processor, which transfers sensor data through a USB connection at 50Hz[1].

Calibration

Because of variations in individual components (introduced during manufacturing and manual soldering) each cell is calibrated individually. In a first step, we establish the basic noise level of each cell by placing the pen away from any reflective surface. Noise includes IR light in the environment as well as light traveling directly from the LED to the transistor. To alleviate this latter component, we filled the gaps between LEDs and transistors with black modeling clay (Figure 1 bottom right). The basic noise level is removed from all sensing data before further processing.

Through experimentation, we discovered that the best way to linearize our sensor is to consider two distinct settings (Figure 3). When the target is far away from the sensor, the intensity is proportional to the inverse quartic of the target distance. When the target is less than 0.3" from the sensor, this relation no longer holds because parameters such as the distance between the sensor and the illumination source begin to play a role (Figure 3). At close distances, we observed that the intensity is proportional to the inverse quadratic of the target distance.

To calibrate our sensor in a pen-based setting, we take 3 measurements: 1) a contact measurement where a piece of paper is rolled around the pen; 2) a 0.5" calibration where the pen is placed inside a reflective cylinder whose surface is 0.5" from the sensors; 3) a 1" calibration (same as above but distance from the cylinder surface is 1"). Finally, we apply a median filter on all data to reduce noise.

Sensor Characteristics

We show the sensor linearity after calibration, for a sloped target subtending a 90 degree arc Figure 4 left. This figure also illustrates the maximum range of the sensor at 1.2".

We now consider the level of detail that can be resolved by our sensor. Figure 4b shows the response to a simulated group of 4 fingers (each .75" in diameter and 2" long). Fig-

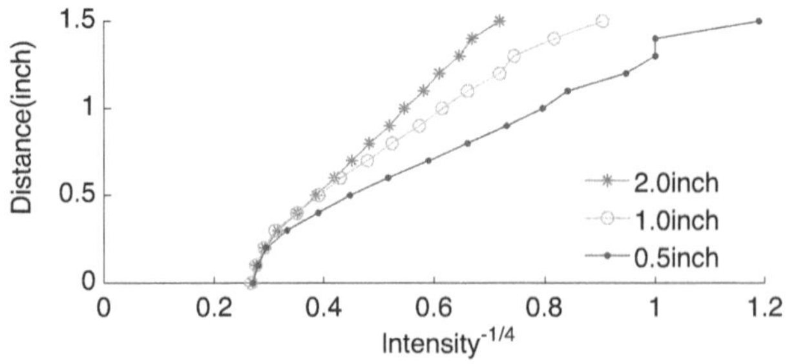

Figure 3: Sensor response to several targets sizes.

[1] The schematic for the sensor and its driving board can be found at this location: http://hdl.handle.net/1813/29087

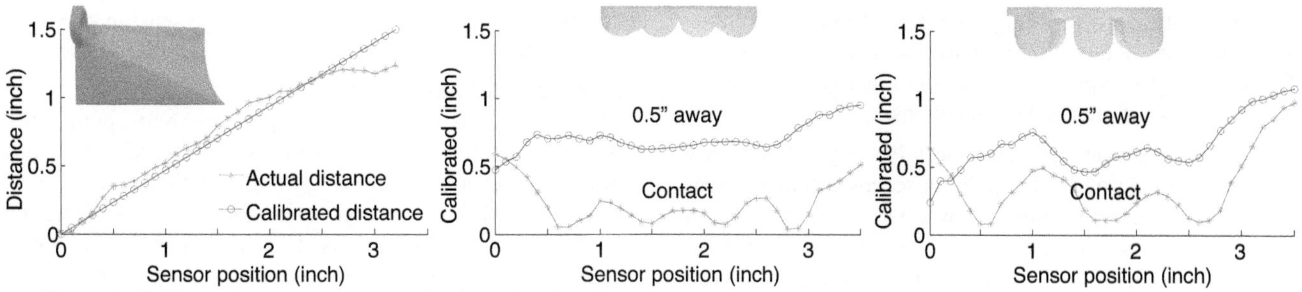

Figure 4: Calibrated sensor characterization showing the sensor response to (from left to right): a ramp, a profile simulating four fingers side by side, and a profile simulating different sized gaps between fingers.

ure 4c shows the detection of 5 and 10mm gaps between fingers. Because our LEDs generate a wide illumination pattern (140 degrees), feature detection diminishes with distance. This issue could be addressed by adding small lenses on top of the LEDs to collimate the light emitted.

When a finger is pressed against the sensor, it reports values greater than the contact value. This is likely caused by IR light being scattered in the skin and could be used to estimate pressure applied to the sensor.

USAGE SCENARIOS FOR A PEN

We now consider how these performance parameters translate into practical usage scenarios. Figure 5a-e shows the 5 different grips described by Song et al. [10]. Our system produces very distinctive range images for each grip. Because the most important features of a given grip are typically close to the barrel, diminished feature detection at higher distances does not seem to be a significant concern. Overall we believe that the richer information provided by our sensor has the potential to significantly improve the performance of machine learning algorithms used for grasp detection [9-11].

An important feature of optical sensing is the capability to detect finger gestures above the surface of the sensor [1]. Figure 5f, for example, illustrates the detection of vertical

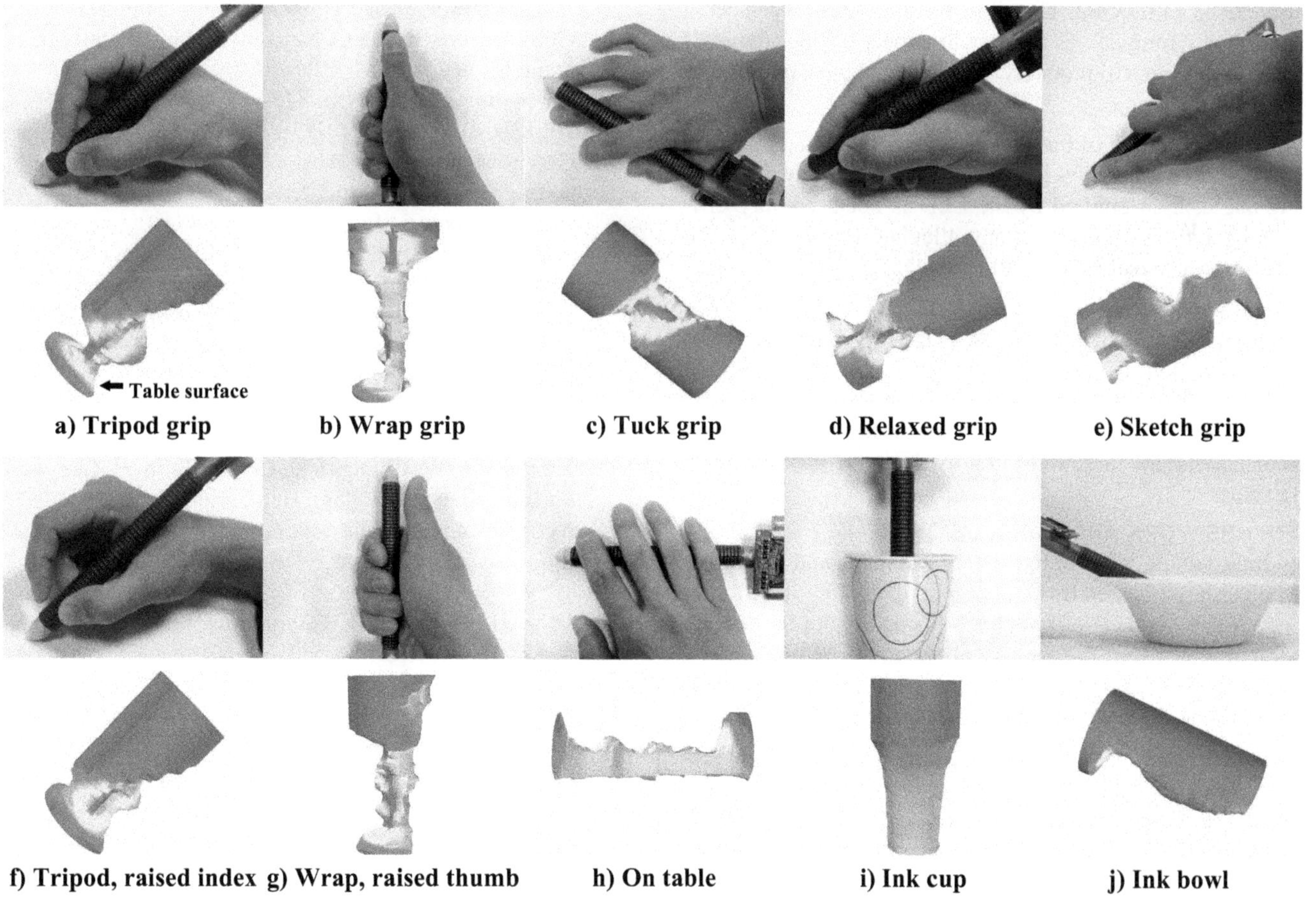

Figure 5: Sensor output for different grips, fingers interactions, and settings. The output is rendered as a 3-dimentional height field above the barrel of the pen using the color coding to the right.

movement of the pointer finger during a tripod grip. Similarly, we can detect thumb movement in a wrap grip (Figure 5g). We expect this will significantly increase the expressiveness of graspable interactions.

Optical range sensing presents the advantage of not only sensing the shape of the hand, but also environmental features. Figure 5a, for example, shows part of the surface on which the grasping hand is resting. This feature facilitates the detection of pen orientation, an important practical concern [10]. Similarly, the system can detect whether the pen is resting on a surface (Figure 5h) or held in an ink cup (Figure 5i) or a bowl (Figure 5j). Information encoded as a depth map would be accessible as well [4].

DISCUSSION

All IR based approaches are affected by ambient light and the properties of the reflective surface. Empirically, our sensor is working very well in an office setting (both day and night, but our system can be blinded by strong direct sunlight. A combination of better filtering, dynamic calibration, and synchronous detection can be implemented to reject background levels of lighting. We have not observed significant changes based on skin complexion, most likely because we sense the inner palm, which tends to show more uniform complexion across individuals. If variations did cause problems, they could be addressed with a simple user based calibration. The situation is different when sensing the environment, as one would expect a wider range of materials. This will probably limit the tracking capability to pre-calibrated objects.

Another limitation of our design is its high power signature (relative to a capacitive sensor). Because of the wide sensing angle, light emitted by the LED is not used very efficiently. Lenses would not only alleviate this problem but also improve resolution at farther distances as noted before.

While we have tested our sensor for pen applications, our design can be adapted to a wide range of grasp sensing applications. For example, it could be used to implement graspable interactions for a phone or a slate, to make the props used in tangible interactions reactive to grasp and near volume interaction, or to provide active grip feedback in sports.

FUTURE WORK AND CONCLUSION

In future work, we plan to increase the range and resolution of our sensor system by exploring the potential of collimating lenses and over-sampling (using multiple sensors around a lit LED). We are also planning to conduct empirical evaluations to quantify the benefits of range sensing for grasp recognition across a variety of contexts.

This paper presents the design of a new optical range sensor flexible enough to be wrapped around a variety of devices. Our system represents an improvement over previous work in terms of spatial and temporal resolution, range, and flexibility. We have illustrated how the sensor encodes typical pen grips and discuss possible improvements to our current design. Ultimately, flexible range sensing may benefit a wide range of graspable interactions.

ACKNOWLEDGEMENTS

This work was supported in part by NSF grant ISS-0916217 and by a gift from Microsoft Research. We thank Steve Marschner, Hyunyoung Song and Nicholas Chen for their insightful discussion, and Corinna Löckenhoff for feedback on previous drafts. Discussions with Andy Wilson and Hrvoje Benko let us to consider developping this sensor. We also thank our reviewers for their feedback.

REFERENCES

1. Choi, S., J. Han, S. Kim, S. Heo, and G. Lee. ThickPad: a hover-tracking touchpad for a laptop. *Proceedings of UIST'11 demonstrations*, pp. 15 - 16.
2. Choi, S., J. Han, G. Lee, N. Lee, and W. Lee. RemoteTouch: touch-screen-like interaction in the tv viewing environment. *Proceedings of CHI'11*, pp. 393 - 402.
3. Dietz, P., W. Yerazunis, and D. Leigh. Very Low-Cost Sensing and Communication Using Bidirectional LEDs. *Proceedings of UbiComp'03*, pp. 175 - 191.
4. Follmer, S., M. Johnson, E. Adelson, and H. Ishii. deForm: an interactive malleable surface for capturing 2.5D arbitrary objects, tools and touch. *Proceedings of Proceedings of the 24th annual ACM symposium on User interface software and technology*, pp. 527-536.
5. Guimbretiere, F. and C. Nguyen. Bimanual marking menu for near surface interactions. *Proceedings of Proceedings CHI'12*, pp. 825 - 828.
6. Hilliges, O., S. Izadi, A.D. Wilson, S. Hodges, A. Garcia-Mendoza, and A. Butz. Interactions in the air: adding further depth to interactive tabletops. *Proceedings of UIST'09*, pp. 139 - 148.
7. Hodges, S., S. Izadi, A. Butler, A. Rrustemi, and B. Buxton. ThinSight: versatile multi-touch sensing for thin form-factor displays. *Proceedings of UIST'07*, pp. 259 - 268.
8. Hudson, S.E. Using light emitting diode arrays as touch-sensitive input and output devices. *Proceedings of UIST'04*, pp. 287 - 290.
9. Kim, K.-E., W. Chang, S.-J. Cho, J. Shim, H. Lee, J. Park, Y. Lee, and S. Kim. Hand grip pattern recognition for mobile user interfaces. *Proceedings of Innovative applications of artificial intelligence*, pp. 1789-1794.
10. Song, H., H. Benko, F. Guimbretiere, S. Izadi, X. Cao, and K. Hinkley. Grips and Gestures on a Multi-Touch Pen. *Proceedings of CHI'11*, pp. 1323-1332.
11. Taylor, B.T. and J. V. Michael Bove. Graspables: grasp-recognition as a user interface. *Proceedings of CHI'09*, pp. 917 - 926.
12. Villar, N., S. Izadi, D. Rosenfeld, H. Benko, J. Helmes, J. Westhues, S. Hodges, E. Ofek, A. Butler, X. Cao, and B. Chen. Mouse 2.0: multi-touch meets the mouse. *Proceedings of UIST'09*, pp. 33-42.

PhantomPen: Virtualization of Pen Head for Digital Drawing Free from Pen Occlusion & Visual Parallax

David Lee, KyoungHee Son, Joon Hyub Lee, Seok-Hyung Bae
I[2]DEA Lab, Department of Industrial Design, KAIST
291 Daehak-ro, Yuseong-gu, Daejeon 305-701, Republic of Korea
david.lee | kyounghee.son | joonhyub.lee | seokhyung.bae @kaist.ac.kr

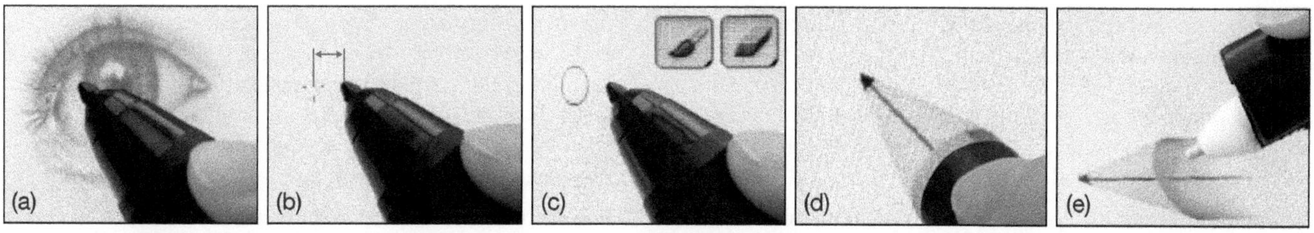

Figure 1: Problems of direct pen input: (a) pen occlusion that covers portions of drawing, (b) visual parallax between a physical pen tip and mouse cursor due to display glass thickness, and (c) hidden pen information such as pen type, color, and thickness, which is not intuitively perceived on the digital canvas. PhantomPen solves these problems by replacing the physical pen head with a virtual pen displayed as if connected to the pen barrel from the user's perspective (d), while an actual pen tip, hidden by the pen barrel, delivers tactile feedback (e).

ABSTRACT

We present PhantomPen, a direct pen input device whose pen head is virtualized onto the tablet display surface and visually connected to a graspable pen barrel in order to achieve digital drawing free from pen occlusion and visual parallax. As the pen barrel approaches the display, the virtual pen head smoothly appears as if the rendered virtual pen head and the physical pen barrel are in unity. The virtual pen head provides visual feedback by changing its virtual form according to pen type, color, and thickness while the physical pen tip, hidden in the user's sight, provides tactile feedback. Three experiments were carefully designed based on an analysis of drawings by design professionals and observations of design drawing classes. With these experiments that simulate natural drawing we proved significant performance advantages of PhantomPen. PhantomPen was at least as usable as the normal stylus in basic line drawing, and was 17 % faster in focus region drawing (26 % faster in extreme focus region drawing). PhantomPen also reduced error rate by 40 % in a typical drawing setup where users have to manage a complex combination of pen and stroke properties.

ACM Classification: H5.2 [Information Interfaces and Presentation]: User Interfaces–input devices and strategies.

General terms: Design, Human Factors

Keywords: pen, occlusion, parallax, visual feedback.

INTRODUCTION

The pen is intuitive, fast, and unconstrained, and has been the tool of choice for artists and designers for a long time. Today, the traditional tool has been digitalized and enables designers to work in ways that were previously impossible. The digitalized device, in conjunction with commercially available software, offers convenient functionalities such as copy, undo, save, diverse colors and textures, and transcends the analog pen in many ways.

Direct pen input technology is evolving to faithfully reproduce the analog pen. However, such a pursuit has made the digital pen a victim of a physical flaw of the analog pen (Figure 1a). Furthermore, the digital technology has generated a new set of problems that were not found in the analog pen (Figure 1b&c).

In this paper we present a new input technique that overcomes the shortcomings of the analog pen and also fixes the new problems of the digital pen. Such improvements will increase drawing performance, and especially so for drawing requiring precise pen control.

By conducting a literature survey and observing drawing classes, we identify the problems of direct pen input in a digital drawing context (Figure 1a~c). To solve these problems we present PhantomPen, a new direct pen input technique that overcomes the limitations of the conventional analog pen and state-of-the the art direct pen input (Figure 1d&e). Then we design and implement a prototype system to evaluate the drawing performance. Three experiments that closely reflect the real drawing context are designed and conducted. The results show that PhantomPen can be applied to the actual drawing situation and improve the drawing performance.

PROBLEMS OF DIRECT PEN INPUT

Pen occlusion and parallax have been reported as major defects of direct pen input [6, 7, 18, 26, 29, 30], but few directly solved the problems. Along with these problems, hidden pen information has also been a problem when drawing. We divided these problems into three categories, defined each of them, and analyzed the conventional approaches to solve them.

Pen Occlusion

When using a direct input device, the hand or the pen can cover certain portions of the display [29]. The hand may cover a larger area than the pen. However, the area occluded by the pen is highly probable to contain important information since it is near the pen tip, where the interaction occurs. The occlusion can be especially problematic in selecting a small UI element or drawing small features.

A common approach to solve occlusion is to shift and magnify information covered by the hand or pen [18, 27, 28]. However, such callout techniques may occlude other visual information in the vicinity. In addition, when the callout is displayed in a vacant, non-occluded area [27], it may place additional load on the user's cognition as the location of the callout changes each time.

Another approach may be to make the styli thinner. However, professional-grade styli require higher precision sensors that are usually larger and thicker [30], so it is difficult to do so without sacrificing the performance.

Visual Parallax

Visual parallax is the difference between the apparent locations of the stylus and the mouse cursor. The parallax error, even a few millimeters of it, can present difficulties to the user in interaction [15]. The main cause of the parallax is the thickness of the protective glass of the display. For example, the thickness for Wacom Cintiq 21UX, which is widely used by design professionals, is about 2 mm. In addition, the coordinate information of the stylus comes from internal coils [30], and there exists a possibility of miscalibration.

One might think that an indirect input device can remove the error caused by the parallax, but it has eye-hand coordination issues. With an indirect input device, movement of the stylus is separated from that of the cursor, making it difficult for users to naturally match the two movements. This is because people tend to aim the target first with their eyes and then move their hand towards the target [11]. On top of that, indirect pen input is slow compared to direct pen input [6], thus it is hard to say that indirect methods are proper solutions for the visual parallax.

Another approach is to minimize the thickness of the glass of the display [15]. An alternative, thinner material can reduce visual parallax [25]. While these efforts can certainly help reduce visual parallax, the tablets that are currently available employ a solid protective glass panel to withhold pen tip pressure, and we expect visual parallax to persist for a while.

Hidden Pen Information

An analog drawing tool has only one set of properties, such as color and thickness, and exhibits its properties through its appearance. On the other hand, a stylus serves various functionalities as a universal apparatus, often without explicitly exhibiting relevant information [5].

Pen information is usually shown in peripheral panels scattered throughout the digital canvas. In this case, users have to frequently displace their line of sight away from the interaction region and search for the panel to obtain the pen information. Such displacements of the line of sight may impair work efficiency [9]. To minimize searching, the current pen status can be shown utilizing a large box and distinctive color coding [22]. However, such an emphasis cannot account for the problem of displacement of the line of sight.

Pen information can be displayed near the pen tip using simple display widgets activated by any one of: pen gesture [8], pen tilting [24], pen rolling [2], and pen projection [21]. These methods can display related information near the pen tip not to displace the line of sight, but information is hidden when the widgets are not activated.

Recent graphics software such as Autodesk SketchBook Pro delivers tool information, such as size, shape, color and transparency through the cursor. However, each tool has its own specialized visualization convention, and there can be confusion over some tool types as they unavoidably share the same cursor convention. While these cursors can be useful, they are limited because they are simplified 2D symbols that must not distract the user from the content, resulting in information visualization not as intuitive or as holistic as the actual analog tools.

The pen device itself can provide pen information with the aid of external modalities such as haptic feedback [17], or light and sound [14]. However, these means provide only ambiguous information about the status of the pen.

DIGITAL DRAWING WITH DIRECT PEN INPUT

Most of the problems identified for direct pen input above are from artificial experimental setups. To better understand the user's natural and unconscious behaviors in practical drawing, we observed drawing classes in an Industrial Design Department at a university.

Drawing Class

The drawing classes consisted of 50 students and lasted for 16 weeks. Students were taught from elementary line drawing to 2D product rendering. The last 2 weeks of the lecture were about digital drawing using tablet displays. The 15th week was an ice breaking period to familiarize the students with the tablets. During the 16th week the students were asked to draw complicated product sketches with the skills they had learned using Wacom Cintiq 21UX tablets, Autodesk SketchBook Pro and Adobe Photoshop. We frequently observed and interviewed the students in and out of the classroom.

Observations

Our first observation revealed that effects of pen occlusion were more problematic in digital drawing. When drawing on paper, students frequently rotated and displaced their sheets using the non-preferred hand. Experts also rotated and displaced their sheets when drawing [4, 19]. However, as a student commented, students "don't move the tablet from the fixed position, because the [Wacom Cintiq 21UX] tablet is too heavy."

Without being able to freely rotate the canvas, students tried to minimize the occluded area by bending their wrist in an arch shape with their pen tip still touching the screen. Such a behavior, also reported by other researchers [26], can increase fatigue during drawing. However, the students simply considered soreness of wrist a "byproduct of hours of drawing."

Because the tablet could not be rotated very easily, students dealt with occlusion by zooming in on an area of interest. However, when working in the magnified state, the overall structure of the drawing became harder to recognize [3]. In addition, when zooming in/out the students pressed hotkeys on the keyboard. Such actions drew the students' attention to the keyboard, distracting them from the actual drawing task.

One interesting observation is that students did not try to avoid occlusion by moving their head. Their occlusion avoidance effort was largely reliant on movements of their wrist and arm. The students almost fixed their head in a position in which they could view the whole screen.

Visual parallax between the cursor and the pen was the other source of complaint in the digital drawing classes. Students who were skilled at using mouse devices to perform graphic tasks pointed out that "the distance between the pen tip and the cursor gave awkward feelings compared to the mouse." Since drawing often requires accurate positional selection [19], some students said that they could draw better by "focusing on the cursor" while drawing small features. However, when not drawing small features, the students "focused on the pen tip." Such an alternation of focus has also been reported by other researchers [6].

In our observation, important pen attributes were not effectively conveyed. For instance, when using pen and eraser tools alternately, students mistakenly erased when they meant to draw because the cursors were the same in shape for both tools. These kinds of mistakes did not occur when the students used analog drawing tools such as color pencils and markers. One annoyed student suggested that "the cursor should contain indicative information about the pen attributes." In addition, other students found it "distracting" that all the information panels were scattered across the screen.

PHANTOMPEN

From the observations above, we discovered that the problems of direct pen input are closely related to the physical form of the *pen head* and the information covered by it. Thus, we judged that we could start to address the three problems of direct pen input – pen occlusion, visual parallax, and hidden pen information – by rethinking the pen head.

Virtualization of Pen Head

We implemented PhantomPen by replacing the head of the stylus with a real-time rendered virtual pen head. With the shape of the pen head rendered to be aligned with the pen barrel in the user's line of sight, and with a hidden pen tip (Figure 2a), it provides visual feedback as well as tactile feedback. PhantomPen addresses the problems of direct pen input:

- By replacing the physical pen head with a virtual pen head, the physical obstacle is removed from the user's perspective (Figure 2b).
- By coinciding the virtual pen tip with the drawing plane, visual parallax is eliminated (Figure 2c).
- By rendering a real-life appearance of the tool, important pen attributes are visualized in the user's focus region, in real time (Figure 2b&c).

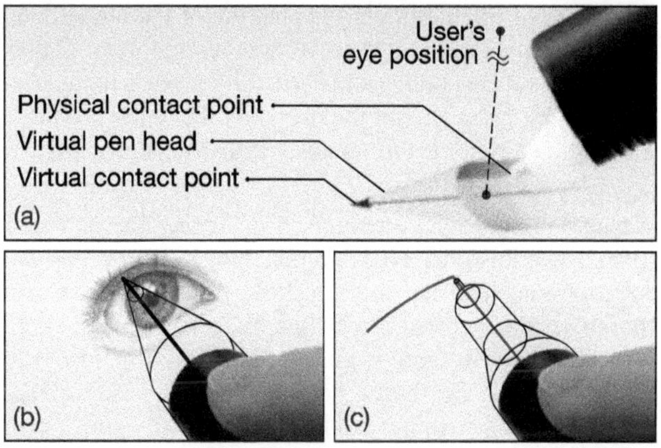

Figure 2: PhantomPen's components (a); virtual pen head does not occlude drawing (b); its virtual tip coincides with the drawing plane, and delivers pen attributes such as pen type, thickness, and color (c).

Geometric Model

The visualization of PhantomPen (Figure 3) changes according to the user's eye position $\boldsymbol{e} = (E_x, E_y, E_z)$, the position of physical contact point $\boldsymbol{p} = (P_x, P_y, 0)$, and the pen tilting direction $\boldsymbol{t} = (\sin\theta\cos\varphi, \sin\theta\sin\varphi, \cos\theta)$ with respect to the frame of reference $\{\boldsymbol{o}, \boldsymbol{i}, \boldsymbol{j}, \boldsymbol{k}\}$ on the tablet display. The tip location $\boldsymbol{q}$ of PhantomPen on the screen is:

$$\boldsymbol{q} = \boldsymbol{p} + \boldsymbol{d}$$

where $\boldsymbol{d} = (-R\cos\varphi/\cos\theta, -R\sin\varphi/\cos\theta, 0)$, and a point $\boldsymbol{r}$ on the axis of PhantomPen is projected onto the tablet display surface as follows:

$$\boldsymbol{r}' = \boldsymbol{r} - \frac{\boldsymbol{r}\cdot\boldsymbol{k}}{\boldsymbol{u}\cdot\boldsymbol{k}}\boldsymbol{u}$$

where $\boldsymbol{r} = \boldsymbol{q} + L\boldsymbol{t}$ and $\boldsymbol{u} = (\boldsymbol{r} - \boldsymbol{e})/\|\boldsymbol{r} - \boldsymbol{e}\|$.

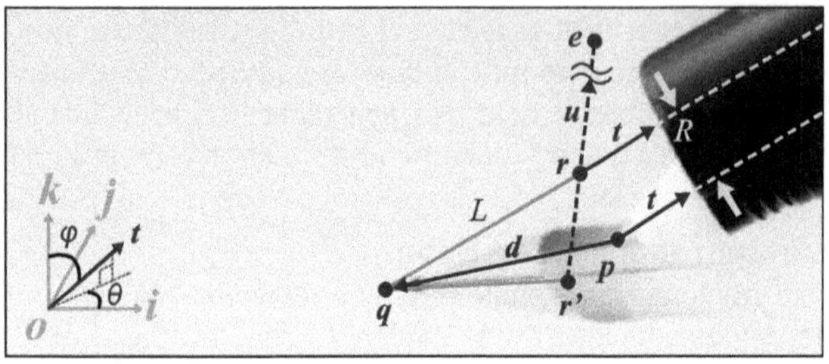

Figure 3: Geometric model of PhantomPen.

PROTOTYPE

We implemented a prototype as a proof of concept to evaluate the drawing performance. We explain the prototype in terms of pen barrel design, sensing of pen status and eye position, and virtual pen head visualization.

Pen Barrel Design

Tactile Feedback

A sense of the pen tip touching physical objects helps precise drawing in general [23]. Since the virtualized pen head cannot provide the required tactile feedback, we employed a surrogate pen tip hidden under the pen barrel that mediates the physical reaction force (Figure 2a). During the design of PhantomPen, the position of the hidden pen tip with respect to the pen barrel was an important factor. When the contact point is pushed further back the occlusion may be reduced, but the user may feel uncomfortable if the contact point is too far away from the virtual tip.

Pen Grip

We also paid special attention in designing the pen grip style. An ellipsoidal cross-section longer in the vertical direction can lead the users to hold the pen with a grip similar to the one used with the Wacom Airbrush Pen. With such a form there is an affordance for users to grab the stylus with the thumb holding the wider side of the pen and the index finger holding the narrower side, a grip that prevents inadvertent rotation.

The final design of PhantomPen is shown in Figure 4.

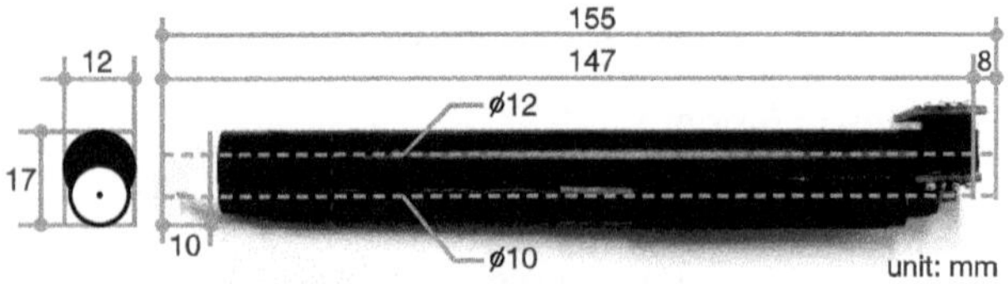

Figure 4: The design of PhantomPen.

Sensing

The geometric model explained above is such that the image of the virtualized pen head of PhantomPen changes according to the direction of the line of sight. To render the virtual pen head, therefore, physical contact point $\boldsymbol{p}$, pen tilting direction $\boldsymbol{t}$, and eye position $\boldsymbol{e}$ are required.

Pen Posture

With the 5 values (P_x, P_y, P_z, θ, φ) provided by Wacom Intuos 4 Art Pen, the physical contact point $\boldsymbol{p}$ is calculated from (P_x, P_y). The tilt values (θ, φ) of the Art Pen, however, contained severe noise to the extent that they could not be used. Such noise was also reported by other researchers [1, 29]. To solve this problem Bi et al. [2] and Lee et al. [13] used Vicon (IR camera) to acquire accurate tilt values. We instead used a 9DOF sensor (E2Box EBIMU-9DOF) to make PhantomPen a stand-alone device. The 9DOF sensor provided 3 geomagnetic, 3 gyro, and 3 acceleration data. We used these data to calculate the tilt angle. The sensor weighed 4.2 g, and set the centroid back by 12 mm (8 %) when attached to the 155 mm, 19 g pen.

In addition, the distance from the pen tip to the screen was measured to render the virtual pen head before and after the pen contacted the screen. Height information (P_z) was not provided by the default Wacom tablet driver, so JTablet driver (http://jtablet.cellosoft.com/) was used. The maximum value measurable was 20 mm from the display.

Eye Position

The virtual pen head of PhantomPen should be rendered with respect to the position of the user's eye and the position and orientation of the pen barrel. In our proof-of-concept prototype, however, we assumed that the line of sight was fixed perpendicular to the tablet surface, based on our observation from the drawing classes and the drawing posture recommended in drawing education [3]. While variable eye position would have been ideal, we excluded eye tracking sensors, which can cause additional delay, to increase the fidelity of the prototype.

Virtual Pen Head Visualization

PhantomPen was developed using Java and JOGL (http://java.net/projects/jogl/). We used a Wacom Cintiq 21UX of which the maximum resolution is 1600×1200. However, there was a lag resulting in a mismatch between the pen barrel and the virtual pen tip for pen movements at high speed. So we set the resolution to 800×600, to boost the rendering speed and perform our formal experiments in a reasonable condition.

Pen Head Model

The virtual pen head is a rendered image of a 3D pen head model (Figure 5). In the model, a semi-transparent cone (pen cap) and a cylinder (pen barrel) are rendered to look connected to the physical pen barrel. The pen tip and lead indicate the color and thickness. The semi-transparency was for indication of pen information and for visibility of the canvas beneath the virtual pen head. As a result, the color of the pen lead seems desaturated, but the pen tip, modeled as a truncated cone, shows the original color.

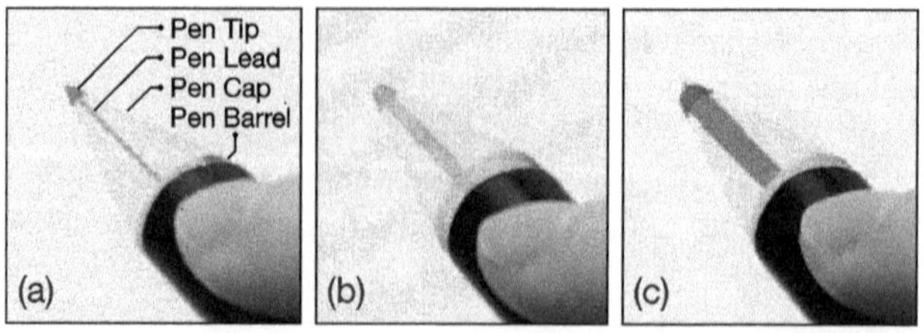

Figure 5: Virtual pen head consists of pen tip, pen lead, pen cap, and pen barrel (a); color and thickness change (a-c).

Transparency Control

PhantomPen is a type of offset cursor that has its cursor position away from the actual contact point, thus disadvantageous in quick pointing because of additional costs for cursor finding, but advantageous in accurate pointing [16]. However, PhantomPen differs from the conventional offset cursors in the following ways. First, with PhantomPen the user can intuitively expect where the cursor will appear based on the direction of the physical pen barrel, reducing the cursor finding cost. Second, the transparency of PhantomPen's pen head changes as a function of the distance from the pen tip to the screen (Figure 6). When the physical tip touches the screen, the pen head is rendered with the predefined maximum opacity, at which point the user can either select (click) or start to draw. This helps to avoid the possible awkwardness of a suddenly appearing or disappearing virtual pen head.

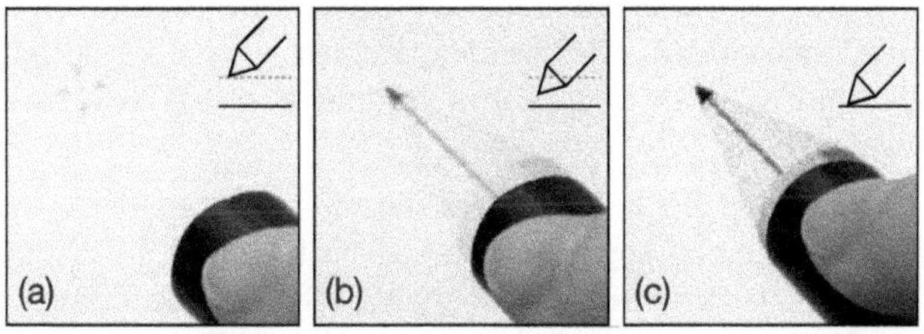

Figure 6: Transparency changes according to proximity of the pen to the display: far away from (> 20 mm) (a), hovering over (b), and in contact with (c) the display.

EVALUATION

We conducted experiments simulating natural drawing to evaluate the PhantomPen concept. The experiments were designed based on design drawing activities [19] and observations from drawing classes. Experiment 1 was to evaluate whether PhantomPen would perform at the same functional level as a normal stylus in basic line drawing. Experiment 2 and 3 were to evaluate whether PhantomPen would increase drawing performance by solving the problems of direct pen input. The participants, procedure, and apparatus were identical in all three experiments.

Participants

12 design major students (2 female, 10 male), with age ranging from 20 to 28, participated in the experiments. Participants were all right-handed and not color-blind. They were all trained in design drawing for at least 4 months.

Procedure

All participants took part in the three experiments sequentially. They were randomly divided into two groups of 6 to counterbalance the order of presentation; one group used the normal stylus first, whereas the other group used PhantomPen first. Before using each pen, participants were given 5 minutes of a warm-up session to familiarize themselves with the pen. They were free to have a break in between the experiments. The combined experiments lasted about 30 to 40 minutes.

Apparatus and Environment

The experiments were conducted using an Intel i5 2.8GHz PC running Windows 7 with OpenGL for graphics. We used a Wacom Cintiq 21UX and oriented the tablet towards the participant at an angle of 10° off the desk. The participants were seated in a height adjustable chair so that they could view the center of the display at an angle of 90°. We asked them to take a straight posture when they bent too much. We attached the flexible USB cable to the participants' forearm with a clip so that they could freely move the arm without being hindered by the cable.

Experiment 1: Basic Line Drawing

In this experiment we intended to test whether the upsides of PhantomPen could make up for its downsides in comparison with the normal stylus in the most frequently performed task in design drawing.

Designers frequently face the situation where they have to draw a line through two specific points. It is typical for designers to initiate the line away from one point so that the stroke can land smoothly on the point at a non-zero velocity. Designers also end the line a short while after passing through the other point to take off smoothly. In addition, designers draw lines away from the body. The first experiment was designed with this continuous drawing technique in mind.

PhantomPen might arouse awkward feelings for designers and therefore lose performance, with its particular shape and distance from the physical contact point to the virtual pen tip. However, it could also gain performance with the three harassing problems of direct pen input alleviated.

Hypotheses

- H1-1. PhantomPen will perform the same as the normal stylus in terms of movement time.
- H1-2. The error rates of the two styli will be the same.

Task

Participants were asked to draw a line between two points displayed on the screen. The starting point was green and the end point orange, so they could recognize the start and end of the line (Figure 7). The angle between the horizontal axis of the screen and the projected line was randomly set between 0° to 45°. The values were set to reproduce natural drawing situations [19]. The color of points changed to gray when the pen passed through them. Whenever the participants missed one or more targets it was considered a failed attempt and no correction, including returning or drawing a second stroke, was allowed.

Figure 7: Basic line drawing task.

Design

A repeated measures within-participant design was used. The independent variables were pen type (normal stylus, PhantomPen), target distance (40, 80, 120 mm), target angle (0, 15, 30, 45° CCW), and target size (2, 3, 4 mm radius). In total, the experiment consisted of:

2 pen types × 3 target distances × 4 target angles × 3 target sizes × 2 blocks = 144 line trials per participant.

Results

Movement time measured in millisecond (ms) was the main dependent variable, and was defined as the time taken to connect the two targets. A paired-samples t-test showed PhantomPen to be faster than the normal stylus (t = 3.333, df = 863, $p < .05$) (Figure 8), with the overall movement time of 470 ms for the normal stylus and 447 ms for PhantomPen. Thus we favorably reject H1-1.

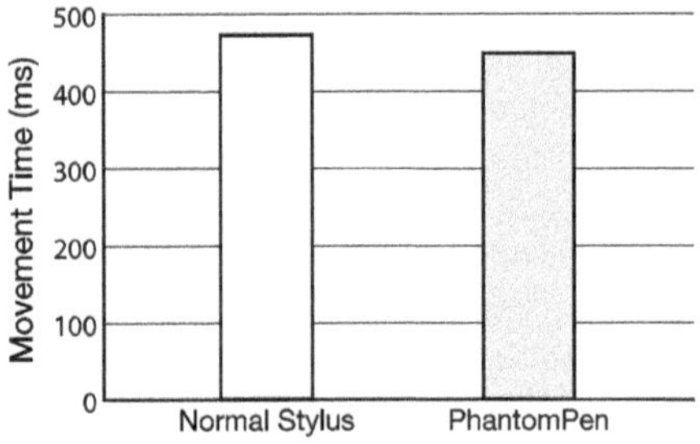

Figure 8: Movement time (basic line drawing).

Repeated measures analysis of variance showed significant main effects for target distance ($F_{2,574} = 625.506$, $p < .05$) (Figure 9), target angle ($F_{3,645} = 4.921$, $p < .05$) (Figure 10), and target size ($F_{2,574} = 16.550$, $p < .05$) on movement time. There was also an interaction effect on movement time for pen type × target distance ($F_{2,574} = 10.246$, $p < .05$). Paired-samples t-test showed no significant main effect on movement time for both pens with the shortest distance, 40 mm (t = 1.239, df = 287, p = .22), but that PhantomPen becomes comparatively faster as target distance increases.

Chi-square analysis showed that there was no difference in terms of error rate between the normal stylus (18.4 %) and PhantomPen (19.3 %) ($\chi^2 = .242$, df = 1, p = .67). Thus, we confirm H1-2.

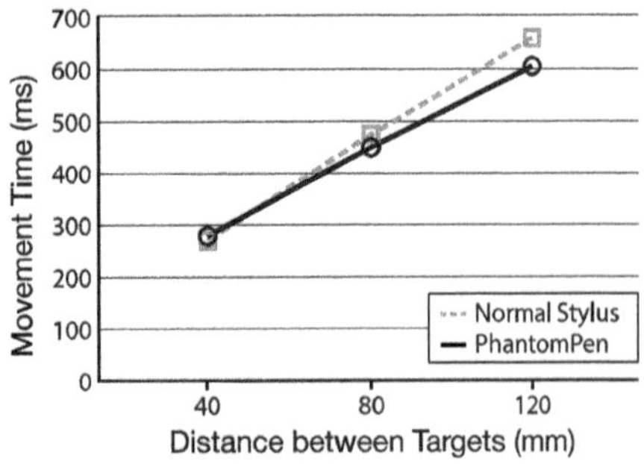

Figure 9: Movement time by target distance (basic line drawing).

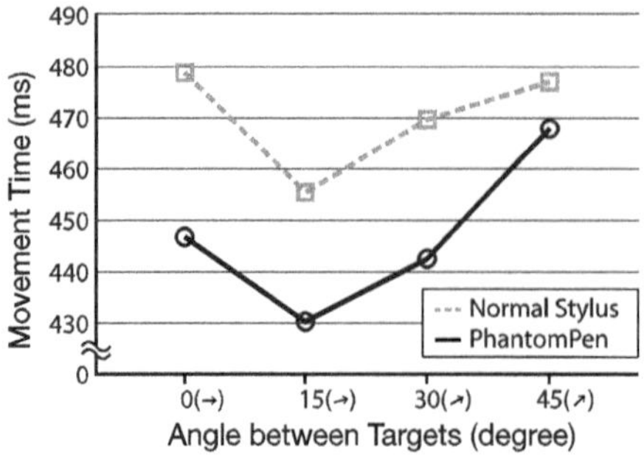

Figure 10: Movement time by target angle (basic line drawing).

Discussion

The distance between the physical contact point and the virtual pen tip could cause usability issues for PhantomPen. In addition, previous experiences with the normal stylus could have had an adverse effect on PhantomPen's performance. Yet PhantomPen was faster, pointing to the possibility of the occlusion and parallax issues being resolved.

PhantomPen might have been faster for larger distances because the end target was clearly visible at all times and enabled users to retain the speed, whereas the drawing speed dropped with the normal stylus because the pen head occluded the target as it approached. The case is analogous to the situation where we underline a phrase in a book. When we cannot see where the phrase ends, we decrease the underlining speed in order not to overshoot, as explained by the impulse variability model [20].

Designers tend to orient the tablet at a certain angle when they draw [4], and there seems to be a comfortable angle to draw lines. If we look at changes in movement time in relations to target angles (Figure 10), both pens show the best performance at the angle of 15°. Such a performance may be due to the anatomical mechanism of the human arm.

Experiment 2: Focus Region Drawing

Pen occlusion can be especially problematic when drawing small and detailed shapes. In the second experiment, we compared PhantomPen and the normal stylus in the focus region drawing context in order to quantitatively validate the effectiveness of PhantomPen in removing pen occlusion.

We referred to the geometric model of hand occlusion proposed by Vogel et al. [29] to determine the size of the pen occlusion region. In the model, the pen tip protruded from the hand by 16 mm on the screen as seen by the user, thus we assumed the pen occlusion area to span about 16 mm on the screen. In addition we designed our target angle range from -90° to +90° where the east is 0°. The range was set wider than that of the first experiment because it is more convenient to draw short lines to various directions [19].

Task

Participants were asked to draw short line segments between points sequentially without taking the pen off the display. Upon crossing the target point, a new target point colored in green was revealed on the right side (Figure 11). This was repeated fifteen times until an orange point appeared as the last target point.

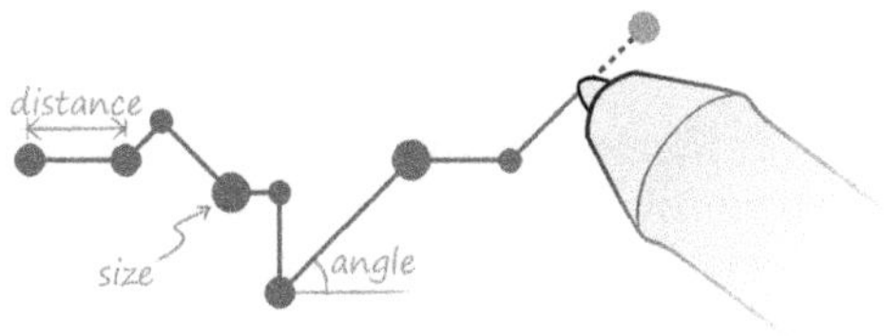

Figure 11: Focus region drawing task.

Hypotheses

- H2-1. PhantomPen will be faster for stroke length of less than 16 mm with the performance benefit diminishing for larger distances.
- H2-2. PhantomPen will be faster than the normal stylus at target angles of 0° and -45° in which occlusion is expected to occur often.

Design

A repeated measures within-participant design was used. The independent variables were pen type (normal stylus, PhantomPen), target distance (8, 16, 24 mm), target angle (-90, -45, 0, 45, 90° CCW), and target size (2, 3, 4 mm radius). All independent variables were presented in random order. In total, the experiment consisted of:

2 pen types × 3 target distances × 5 target angles × 3 target sizes × 2 blocks = 180 line trials per participant.

Results

Movement time was the main dependent variable, and was defined as the time taken in touching two successive targets. Paired-samples t-test showed significant main effect on movement time for pen type ($t = 6.962$, $df = 1080$, $p < .05$) (Figure 12). PhantomPen was 17 % faster (138 ms) on average, with 829 ms for the normal stylus and 691 ms for PhantomPen. A noticeable movement time difference was found in the extreme focus region of 8 mm away, the region in which PhantomPen was expected to excel by eliminating occlusion. PhantomPen was 26 % faster (176 ms) ($t = 7.948$, $df = 360$, $p < .05$) in this region, with 669 ms for the normal stylus and 493 ms for PhantomPen (Figure 13).

Repeated measures analysis of variance showed significant main effects for target distance ($F_{2,574} = 625.506$, $p < .05$) (Figure 13), target angle ($F_{4,860} = 35.246$, $p < .05$), and target size ($F_{2,718} = 40.638$, $p < .05$) on movement time. There was no significant interaction effect for pen type × target distance ($p = .27$). We thus favorably reject H2-1, because PhantomPen was faster for all target distances.

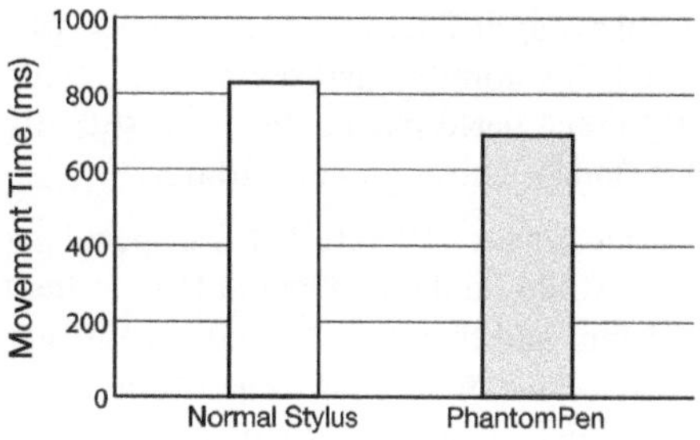

Figure 12: Movement time (focus region drawing).

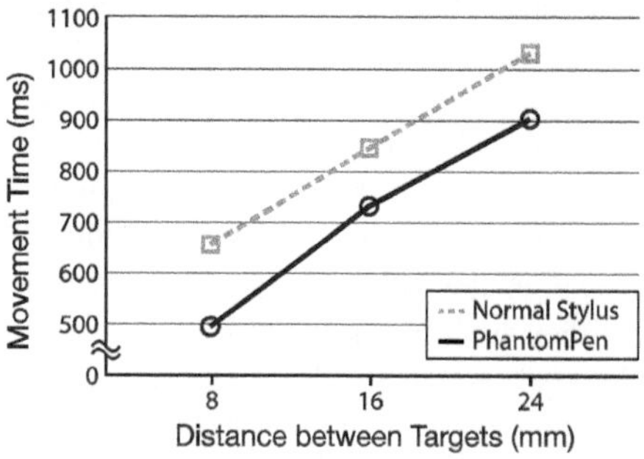

Figure 13: Movement time by target distance (focus region drawing).

There was an interaction effect for pen type × target angle ($F_{4,860} = 51.524$, $p < .05$) (Figure 14). Contrary to our speculation that the performance of 0° and -45° would be impaired due to occlusion, PhantomPen was faster than the normal stylus only at 0° with the normal stylus performing significantly better at -45°. We therefore reject H2-2.

The normal stylus showed the lowest performance at 45° (564 ms difference with PhantomPen), whereas PhantomPen performed the highest at 45°. In the range between 0° and 45° (shaded in Figure 14), which represents a typical range of basic line drawing used in Experiment 1, the average movement time for PhantomPen was 39 % (400 ms) shorter, with the normal stylus at 1013 ms and PhantomPen at 614 ms.

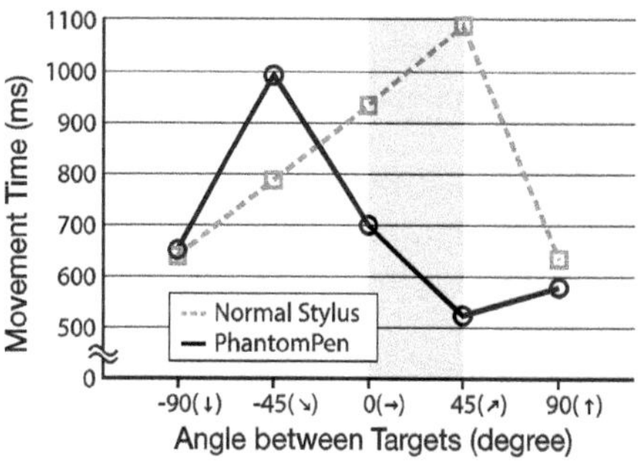

Figure 14: Movement time by target angle (focus region drawing).

Discussion

The overall result of Experiment 2 (Figure 12) shows that pen occlusion is indeed a problem when drawing details in the focus region, and that PhantomPen can increase the drawing performance by solving it. We observed that the participants behaved differently in a number of ways when they used PhantomPen and the normal stylus, and interpreted different performance characteristics for different target distances and angles accordingly.

In terms of target distance (Figure 13), we speculated that hand occlusion would be the dominant effect at the target distance of 24 mm and therefore the movement times for the two styli to be identical. However, PhantomPen was faster at this distance, as well as at 8 mm and 16 mm. We interpreted the result in the following ways. First, when using PhantomPen, out of all the targets, only the target 24 mm away in the -45° was entirely occluded, whereas many targets at different angles and distances were occluded for the normal stylus depending on the hand posture. Because of this, when the participants could not see a target while using PhantomPen, they could immediately guess that it was in the -45° direction, whereas with the normal stylus they had to search for it, increasing movement time. Second, when PhantomPen leant towards the screen (increasing the zenith angle) the non-occluded area underneath the stylus increased, increasing visibility. In evidence, we frequently observed participants leaning PhantomPen, possibly in attempts to avoid occlusion of a wider region.

In addition, the performance characteristics in relation to the target angle (Figure 14) seem to be affected by how the participants hold the styli. When using the normal stylus, the participants swung the stylus back and forth in order to search for the target. In addition, when they found the target, they frequently drew the stroke with their stylus leaning towards it. These behaviors seemed to have a detrimental effect for the target angle of 45°; when they found the target and started to draw, the pen leant toward the target and blocked the view, increasing the movement time (Figure 14). This phenomenon of occlusion in the first quadrant region rather than the fourth quadrant region, has been reported in other studies [27, 29].

On the other hand, we observed that the participants held PhantomPen relatively still at about -45°, possibly because of the stylus form and grip. In addition, there were less searching movements, as PhantomPen had provided a better view of the focus area. Moreover, the participants performed relatively slow translational motion with their elbow and shoulder (Figure 15b) to draw their strokes, rather than relatively fast rotational motion with their wrist and fingers (Figure 15a) as they did with the normal stylus. Translation can be especially slow in the -45° direction, accounting for the peak at -45° for PhantomPen. However, in drawing education [3], using shoulder and elbow rather than wrist and fingers are recommended for better line quality. In this regard, the grip style of PhantomPen and the motion it affords are appropriate.

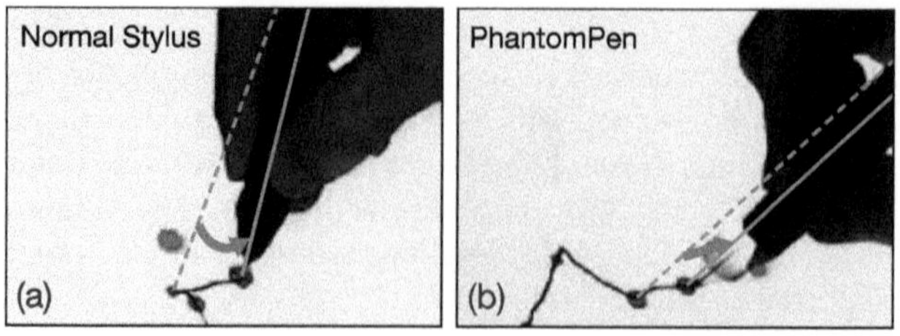

Figure 15: Different pen movement behaviors when drawing a short line to -45° ( ) rotational motion for the normal stylus (a), and translational motion for PhantomPen (b).

Experiment 3: Face Drawing

The third experiment was designed to find out the error reducing characteristic of PhantomPen. Users frequently change pen attributes in drawing, but since the normal stylus does not display much information about pen attributes in the focus region, users are prone to err. Visualization might reduce mistakes when users draw without knowing that they have selected the wrong pen attribute. In this experiment the participants were given a task to draw, without being told that mistakes they make were being counted.

Hypothesis

- H3-1. Mistakes of drawing without knowing that the incorrect pen attribute has been selected will be fewer for PhantomPen.

Task

The task was to draw the right sides of faces so that they would be symmetrical to the provided left sides of faces. Participants were asked to draw 10 faces consisting of 6 lines using the normal stylus and PhantomPen. On the task screen, palette panels with 6 colors (pink, orange, green, blue, purple, black), 3 stroke weights (3, 5, 8 pixels), and two opacity (20, 100 %) options were provided (Figure 16). In addition, 'undo' and 'proceed' buttons were provided, so that the participants could freely correct their mistakes and choose to proceed to the next face.

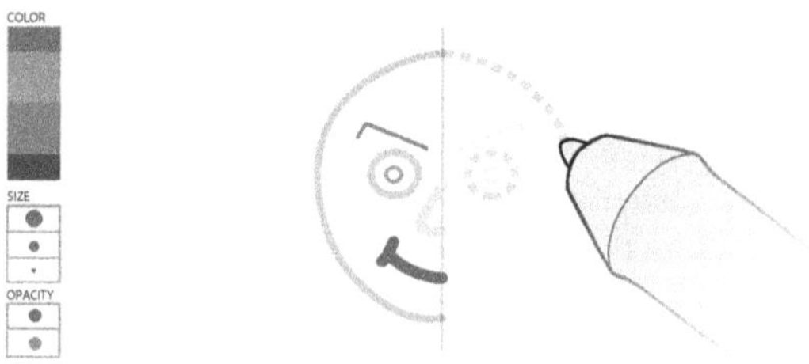

Figure 16: Face drawing task.

Design

The experiment consisted of:

2 pen types × 10 faces × 6 strokes
= 120 stroke attributes per participant.

Results

We considered only the case of drawing a stroke with the incorrect pen attribute as a countable failure. We did not count it as a failure when the participants undid and then drew again with the same pen attribute to adjust the stroke shape.

Chi-square analysis showed a significant difference on error rate between the two pens ($\chi^2 = 9.755$, df = 1, $p < .05$) (Figure 17). Of the total of 720 strokes for each pen there were 87 failures for the normal stylus, and 52 failures for PhantomPen. The participants made 40 % less mistakes with PhantomPen, thus confirming H3-1.

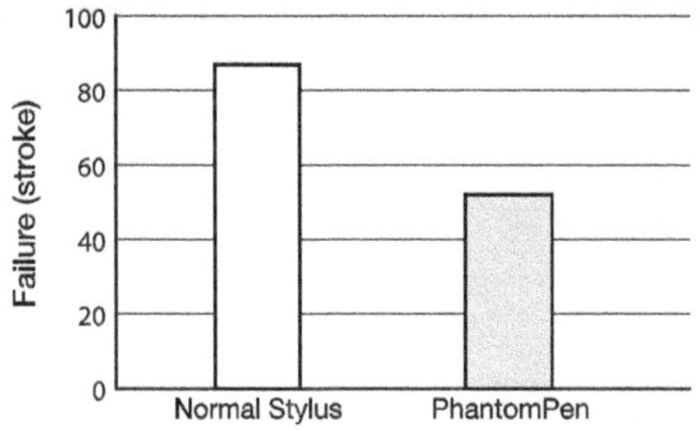

Figure 17: Number of failures (face drawing).

Discussion

We expected PhantomPen to reduce the number of mistakes in selecting the right pen attributes, because it visualizes pen information holistically and intuitively. During the experiment, the participants indeed retracted and reselected the correct pen attribute often by recognizing the incorrect selection through the virtual pen head, before drawing a stroke. PhantomPen thus seemed to lighten the user's workload of checking the selected pen attributes by providing useful visualization at the focus region.

In addition, we had conducted an additional experiment with the same face drawing task as the third experiment to test the information deliverability of two additional virtual pen head designs. We analyzed which elements of the virtual pen head were effective in delivering pen information.

Virtual pen head design 1 (Figure 18a) renders a pen lead, three ellipses, and a cross-hair cursor in 2D. Design 2 (Figure 18b) renders an opaque 3D cap. Design 3 (Figure 18c) renders a pen tip, pen lead, semi-transparent pen cap, and pen barrel in 3D, and is the optimized design used for our formal experiments.

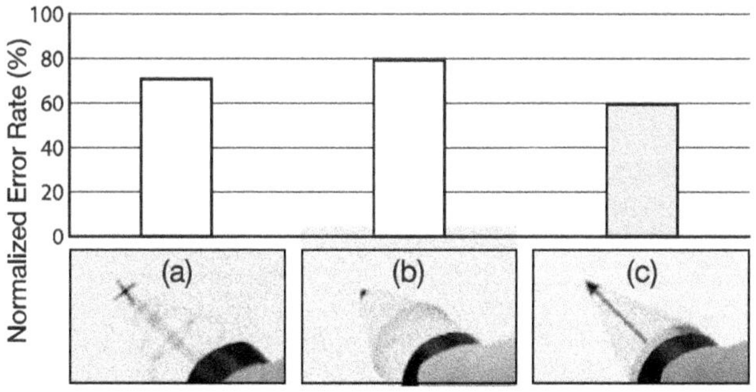

Figure 18: Normalized error rate for three virtual pen head designs: design 1 (a), design 2 (b), and design 3 (c).

We found that design of the virtual pen head matters in reducing errors. With the error rate of the normal stylus normalized as 100 %, the error rate of design 1 was 70 %, design 2 79 %, and design 3 60 %. Design 2 delivered pen information only through the pen tip, and sometimes the participants did not even notice the change of the pen tip. The error rates of design 1 and 3 were relatively low, meaning that delivering pen information such as stroke weight and color through a visible pen lead reduced errors. The error rate of design 3 was lower than that of design 1, indicating that rendering a realistic 3D virtual pen head with appropriate silhouette lines is more effective than a simple pen lead and a cross-hair cursor.

USER FEEDBACK

Before and after the experiments, informal interviews were conducted about the experiments and PhantomPen in general.

First, the participants highly appreciated the possibility of a virtual pen displaying pen attributes, and also commented that they would anticipate for a virtual pen simulating a wider variety of drawing tools. Also, one participant suggested, and we agree, that the virtual pen head can be made to look more realistic by casting a shadow on the canvas [10].

Second, even though our prototype did not consider users' eye motion, when we asked about the mismatch between the pen barrel and the virtual pen head, they did not report any complaint. Thus, we interpreted that our approximation held: the eyes and the head do not move much when drawing with a digital tablet and stylus.

Third, before the experiments some participants doubted the usability of PhantomPen saying that the virtual pen tip not being displayed at the point of physical contact might distract from fluent drawing. However after the experiments, they were satisfied overall, with no participant reporting the tactile difference as a problem.

CONCLUSION AND FUTURE WORK

In this paper, we began by identifying pen occlusion, visual parallax, and hidden pen information as problems of direct pen input. We held the physical form of the pen head liable for these problems, and introduced PhantomPen, a solution involving a drastic change of the form of the stylus.

PhantomPen removes the physical pen head and replaces it with a virtual pen head to secure visibility in the focus region. The virtual pen head is rendered connected to the pen barrel on the display plane to remove visual parallax. In addition, the virtual pen head provides pen information to the user in a more holistic and intuitive way.

We analyzed professionals' drawing behaviors and observed digital drawing classes to design and conduct three experiments that simulate natural drawing contexts (basic line drawing, focus region drawing, and face drawing). The results of the first experiment showed that PhantomPen is as usable as a conventional stylus in non-focus regions. The second and third experiments showed that PhantomPen enhances speed and accuracy by resolving pen occlusion in focus regions, overcoming the limits of the current digital drawing.

In the near future, we intend to explore visualization of the virtual pen head accounting for the user's eye position, design various types of virtual drawing tools (such as a marker or brush), and conduct long-term user studies regarding pen ergonomics.

ACKNOWLEDGMENTS

We thank Woohun Lee, Geehyuk Lee, Hyeon-Jeong Suk, the members of I[2]DEA Lab, and the reviewers for their invaluable comments and assistance. This research was supported by Convergent Design University Program in 2012, funded by the Ministry of Knowledge Economy, Republic of Korea (H1101-12-1001).

REFERENCES

1. Baxter, B., Scheib, V., Lin, M. C. & Manocha, D. DAB: interactive haptic painting with 3D virtual brushes. In *Proc. SIGGRAPH '01*, (2001), 461–468.
2. Bi, X., Moscovich, T., Ramos, G., Balakrishnan, R. & Hinckley, K. An exploration of pen rolling for pen-based interaction. In *Proc. UIST '08*, (2008), 191–200.
3. Curtis, B. *Drawing from Observation: An Introduction to Perceptual Drawing*. MacGraw-Hill (2001).
4. Fitzmaurice, G. W., Balakrishnan, R., Kurtenbach, G. & Buxton, B. An exploration into supporting artwork orientation in the user interface. In *Proc.CHI '99*, (1999), 167–174.
5. Fitzmaurice, G. W., Ishii, H. & Buxton, W. A. S. Bricks: laying the foundations for graspable user interfaces. In *Proc. CHI '95*, (1995), 442–449.
6. Forlines, C. & Balakrishnan, R. Evaluating tactile feedback and direct vs. indirect stylus input in pointing and crossing selection tasks. In *Proc. CHI '08*, (2008), 1563–1572.
7. Goldberg, D. & Goodisman, A. Stylus user interfaces for manipulating text. In *Proc. UIST '91*, (1991), 127–135.
8. Grossman, T., Hinckley, K., Baudisch, P., Agrawala, M. & Balakrishnan, R. Hover widgets: using the tracking state to extend the capabilities of pen-operated devices. In *Proc. CHI '06*, (2006), 861–870.
9. Haider, E., Luczak, H. & Rohmert, W. Ergonomics investigations of work-places in a police command-control centre equipped with TV displays. *Applied Ergonomics 13*, 3 (1982), 163–170.
10. Hilliges, O., Izadi, S., Wilson, A. D., Hodges, S., Garcia-Mendoza, A. & Butz, A. Interactions in the air: adding further depth to interactive tabletops. In *Proc. UIST '09*, (2009), 139–148.
11. Johansson, R. S., Westling, G., Bäckström, A. & Flanagan, J. R. Eye–hand coordination in object manipulation. *The Journal of Neuroscience 21*, 17 (2001), 6917–6932.
12. Langolf, G. D., Chaffin, D. B. & Foulke, J. A. An investigation of Fitts' law using a wide range of movement amplitudes. *Journal of Motor Behavior 8*, 2 (1976), 113–128.
13. Lee, J., Teerapittayanon, S. & Ishii, H. Beyond: collapsible input device for direct 3D manipulation beyond the screen. In *Adj. Proc. UIST '10*, (2010), 393–394.
14. Liao, C., Guimbretière, F. & Loeckenhoff, C. E. Pen-top feedback for paper-based interfaces. In *Proc. UIST '06*, (2006), 201–210.
15. Nescher, T. & Kunz, A. An interactive whiteboard for immersive telecollaboration. *The Visual Computer 27*, 4 (2011), 311–320.
16. Potter, R. L., Weldon, L. J., & Shneiderman, B. Improving the accuracy of touch screens: an experimental evaluation of three strategies. In *Proc. CHI '88*, (1988), 27–32.
17. Poupyrev, I., Okabe, M. & Maruyama, S. Haptic feedback for pen computing: directions and strategies. In *Proc. CHI EA '04*, (2004), 1309–1312.
18. Ramos, G., Cockburn, A., Balakrishnan, R. & Beaudouin-Lafon, M. Pointing lenses: facilitating stylus input through visual-and motor-space magnification. In *Proc. CHI '07*, (2007), 757–766.
19. Robertson, S. *Techniques of Scott Robertson Volume 1: Basic Perspectives Form Drawing*. Design Studio Press (2004).
20. Schmidt, R. A., Zelaznik, H., Hawkins, B., Frank, J. S. & Quinn, J. T. Motor-output variability: a theory for the accuracy of rapid motor acts. *Psychological Review 47*, 5 (1979), 415–451.
21. Song, H., Grossman, T., Fitzmaurice, G., Guimbretiere, F. Khan, A., Attar, R. & Kurtenbach, G. PenLight: combining a mobile projector and a digital pen for dynamic visual overlay. In *Proc. CHI '09*, (2009), 143–152.
22. Sun, M., Cao, X., Song, H., Izadi, S., Benko, H., Guimbretiere, F., Ren, X. & Hinckley, K. Enhancing naturalness of pen-and-tablet drawing through context sensing. In *Proc. ITS '11*, (2011), 83–86.
23. Teather, R. J. & Stuerzlinger, W. Assessing the effects of orientation and device on (contrained) 3D movement techniques, In *Proc. 3DUI '08*, (2008), 43–50.
24. Tian, F., Xu, L., Wang, H., Zhang, X., Liu, Y., Setlur, V. & Dai, G. Tilt menu: using the 3D orientation information of pen devices to extend the selection capability of pen-based user interfaces. In *Proc. CHI '08*, (2008), 1371–1380.
25. Vandoren, P., Claesen, L., Laerhoven, T. V., Taelman, J., Raymaekers, C., Flerackers, E. & Reeth, F. V. FluidPaint: an interactive digital painting system using real wet brushes. In *Proc. ITS '09*, (2009), 83–86.
26. Vogel, D. & Balakrishnan, R. Direct pen interaction with a conventional graphical user interface. *Human–Computer Interaction 25*, 4 (2010), 324–388.
27. Vogel, D. & Balakrishnan, R. Occlusion-aware interfaces. In *Proc. CHI '10*, (2010), 263–272.
28. Vogel, D. & Baudisch, P. Shift: a technique for operating pen-based interfaces using touch. In *Proc. CHI '07*, (2007), 657–666.
29. Vogel, D., Cudmore, M., Casiez, G., Balakrishnan, R. & Keliher, L. Hand occlusion with tablet-sized direct pen input. In *Proc. CHI '09*, (2009), 557–566.
30. Ward, J. R. & Phillips, M. J. Digitizer technology: performance characteristics and the effects on the user interface. *Computer Graphics and Applications 7*, 4 (1987), 31–44.
31. Wood, P. *Scientific Illustraction: A Guide to Biological, Zoological, and Medical Rendering Techniques, Design, Printing, and Display*. John Wiley & Sons (1994).
32. Wu, F.-G. & Luo, S. Performance study on touch-pens size in three screen tasks. *Applied Ergonomics 37*, 2 (2006), 149-158.

Exposing and Understanding Scrolling Transfer Functions

Philip Quinn[1] **Andy Cockburn**[1] **Géry Casiez**[2,3,4] **Nicolas Roussel**[3] **Carl Gutwin**[5]

[1]University of Canterbury
Christchurch, New Zealand
philip.quinn@canterbury.ac.nz
andy@cosc.canterbury.ac.nz

[2]LIFL, [3]INRIA Lille &
[4]University of Lille
Villeneuve d'Ascq, France
gery.casiez@lifl.fr
nicolas.roussel@inria.fr

[5]University of Saskatchewan
Saskatoon, Canada
gutwin@cs.usask.ca

ABSTRACT

Scrolling is controlled through many forms of input devices, such as mouse wheels, trackpad gestures, arrow keys, and joysticks. Performance with these devices can be adjusted by introducing variable transfer functions to alter the range of expressible speed, precision, and sensitivity. However, existing transfer functions are typically "black boxes" bundled into proprietary operating systems and drivers. This presents three problems for researchers: (1) a lack of knowledge about the current state of the field; (2) a difficulty in replicating research that uses scrolling devices; and (3) a potential experimental confound when evaluating scrolling devices and techniques. These three problems are caused by gaps in researchers' knowledge about what device and movement factors are important for scrolling transfer functions, and about how existing devices and drivers use these factors. We fill these knowledge gaps with a framework of transfer function factors for scrolling, and a method for analysing proprietary transfer functions—demonstrating how state of the art commercial devices accommodate some of the human control phenomena observed in prior studies.

Author Keywords

Control-display gain; scrolling; scroll acceleration; transfer functions.

ACM Classification Keywords

H.5.2 [Information interfaces and presentation]: User interfaces – Input devices and strategies.

INTRODUCTION

Scrolling is an essential task in modern computing, and scrolling devices such as mouse wheels and trackpad gestures are ubiquitous. A fundamental element of scroll control that all techniques must address is the *transfer function* that maps the user's actions with the input device (for example, degrees of rotation, millimetres of displacement, or newtons of force) into scrolling movement of the display (typically either pixels, lines, or pages). However, there has been surprisingly little public research on scrolling transfer functions. Notable exceptions include Hinckley et al. [15] and Cockburn et al. [11], but even these studies are ambiguous about the exact functions used or tested—for example, Hinckley et al. stated "We tested the device using the manufacturer's default settings", but precisely determining the corresponding transfer function is now near impossible; Cockburn et al. explicitly acknowledged the need for further research to understand the role that the system transfer function may have played in their experiment.

The poor understanding of scrolling transfer functions creates several problems for researchers. First, existing methods are unknown because they are embedded in 'black box' driver code, making it difficult for researchers to understand the cause of performance differences between devices, or to iteratively improve on the state of the art. Second, replication of scrolling studies is frustrated by ambiguities in experimental settings—researchers lack the tools to examine, report, and replicate transfer functions. Third, researchers may inadvertently introduce confounds into experiments stemming from unknown interactions between particular transfer functions and their experimental treatment.

Casiez and Roussel [8] recently observed similar problems of "bricolage" in research treatment of pointing transfer functions. To address the problem, they developed an electronic device called *EchoMouse* to probe and inspect transfer functions. They also created a software library called *libpointing* that implemented these functions for experimental replication. They used these components to simulate human mouse control at a variety of physical input movement speeds, and to inspect the resultant system response.

Although *EchoMouse* and *libpointing* provide critical hints on how to examine scrolling transfer functions, the mapping from input actions to output effects is more complex for scrolling. While pointing transfer functions attend to two parameters (mouse velocity and user setting), scrolling functions are likely to attend to many more. Multiple parameters are necessary (or advisable) because of the paucity of scrolling input mechanics. For pointing, a modern mouse will register thousands of points per inch, and it can be moved across a two-dimensional area of several inches without clutching (physically disengaging input control in order to reposition a limb to repeat the action); in contrast, a typical scroll wheel can only be moved through five or six detents/notches across ~40° of one-dimensional rotation

UIST'12, October 7–10, 2012, Cambridge, Massachusetts, USA.

between clutching actions; and the muscle groups used to control wheel rotation (finger extensors and contractors) are likely to induce different control capabilities across scroll directions. Scrolling transfer functions, therefore, are likely to attend to input parameters that include the rate of device movement, time between clutched repetitions, scroll direction, and more. But whether they do this, and how they do it, is currently unknown.

These physical and operational characteristics of devices, and the human capabilities when operating them, have clear implications for the design of scrolling transfer functions. To help understand these issues, the following section presents a framework of the factors influencing scroll control. We then reverse engineer the scrolling transfer functions in state of the art commercial scroll drivers, and confirm that some drivers attend to many input parameters, while others are based purely on the velocity of input control.

FACTORS INFLUENCING SCROLL CONTROL

There has been extensive prior work on taxonomies that aid in understanding the design space of input devices, which we draw on to organise the physical characteristics of scrolling devices. Buxton's [4] early taxonomy organised devices by their physical properties—position, motion, or pressure—and by the number of dimensions along those properties that are sensed. Mackinlay et al. [20] and Card et al. [6, 7] expanded this into a *morphological* analysis, placing devices as points in a parametrically described design space that included the eight combinations of linear/rotary, absolute/relative, and position/force across six linear and rotational dimensions. They also composed chains of connections between the physical parameters and the semantics of an application. Buxton [5] and Hinckley and Sinclair [16] expanded this classification to include devices that operate by touch (rather than a mechanical control), and Lipscomb and Pique [19] added several dimensions of physical device characteristics (including the behaviour of the movement axes, bounds of movement, and self-zeroing behaviour).

These taxonomies can be used to classify the physical sensing properties of scrolling devices; for example, that mouse wheels are single-axis rotary controls that sense discretised changes in rotation, or that trackpads sense absolute one or two-dimensional position. They can also classify the features of the physical controls used to input these properties; for example, mouse wheels can rotate in rigid, discrete detents, or the detents can be soft and the wheel can be inertial (supplying sensor data without active user interaction). These design choices promote different methods of interacting with the device in different scrolling scenarios (for instance, rapid clutching on a discrete wheel vs. flicking and inertial one), and consequently influence the range and type of inputs that are likely to be received. However, the input parameters that are derived from these different methods of interaction are not captured by the above taxonomies.

This section presents a framework for the factors influencing scrolling behaviour and prior scrolling research. The framework is organised across considerations of input parameters, a review of the system-oriented view of scrolling, and prior studies of scrolling gain.

Input Parameters

While these taxonomies organise the physical characteristics of scrolling devices, they do not focus on how features of the manipulation can be translated into task-specific semantics.

Despite the apparent simplicity of scrolling as unidimensional translation, there exists a broad variety of devices to support it, each of which may use a multitude of input parameters for inferring the user's scrolling intention. For example, a mouse wheel senses discretised rotary motion, but the user's intention may be inferred from any combination of the following: (1) the degrees of rotation; (2) the speed of rotation; (3) the rate of change in the speed of rotation; (4) the duration of interaction; (5) the direction of interaction; and (6) the period of interaction.

In general, actions performed on a device need to be mapped from a physical manipulation to an interface command. In doing so, several *input parameters* can be considered, increasing expressivity. For example, keyboard arrow buttons are a one-dimensional discrete control, but their use may be interpreted through continuous parameters such as duration of activation or the rate of repetition. These additional input channels can be classified into three types: measures of *instantaneous action*, measures of *action duration*, and *cumulative/relative measures*, described below.

Instantaneous measures. Measures of instantaneous action are the physical properties that are sensed by a device or their derivatives from samples over time. For example, spinning a detented mouse wheel produces discrete events of rotational movement; however, sampling several events produces new input parameters of angular velocity, acceleration, and higher-order derivatives.

These measures may alter the interpretation or mapping of the original property. For example, increasing mouse wheel velocity or acceleration may be used to increase the magnitude of scrolling events generated from the input of each wheel event, or may be used as a signal to switch between scrolling modes (such as between line and page-scrolling).

Action duration. The duration that an input is maintained (or is absent) can also serve as an input to a transfer function. For example, if a key or button is held down for more than a certain duration, it may start issuing repeating events at an increasing rate. Similarly, if scrolling velocity is maintained above a certain level, then gain might increase with the assumption that the user wants to travel a long distance.

Cumulative and relative inputs. Input measures may also have a memory of prior actions to determine resultant effects. For example, Hinckley and Cutrell [17] described a scrolling transfer function that cumulatively adds gain across rapidly repeated wheel rotations in the same direction; the cumulative effect is cancelled if the user pauses too long or reverses direction. Similarly, rate-based scrolling controls scroll velocity using the relative position of the input device with respect to an anchor point set at the action's initiation.

The System's Perspective

Figure 1 depicts the conceptual transformations that form a transfer function's behaviour in converting human action

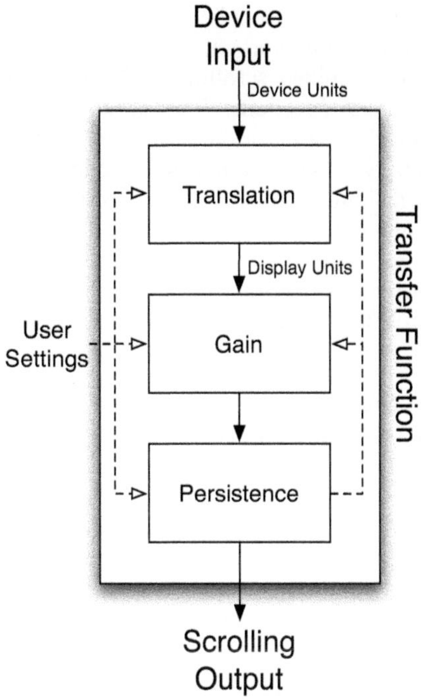

Figure 1: Depiction of the conceptual transformations occurring in a scrolling transfer function.

at the device into resultant display modification in scrolling. Not all of these transformations may be present in any transfer function: some may be absent, some may be combined, and some may be applied multiple times in different components (for example, gain applied by a driver and again by a UI toolkit or application).

Translation converts the device's physically registered events (degrees of rotation, newtons of force, millimetres of displacement, etc.) into units that are comprehensible to the system, such as pixels, lines, or pages. Users may be able to adjust this translation, either through controls on the device, or via a user interface on the system.

A *gain* function may then amplify or attenuate the control signal: for example, to allow slow precise control when the device is manipulated slowly, as well as accelerated scrolling when it is manipulated more aggressively. When gain is supported, users are commonly able to configure its setting.

Finally, a *persistence* component allows for a history of input and calculated parameters (such as input velocity and acceleration) to be preserved, or to allow for effects that are applied across time (such as cumulative effects, inertia, and simulated friction). Data from the persistence component can be used as input into the translation (e.g., allowing a switch from pixel to line scrolling if manipulation is continued for a threshold time), or into the gain (e.g., applying cumulative gain across repeated scroll wheel clutches). Finally, the user may be able to configure parameters of the persistence component (e.g., altering the degree of inertia or friction).

Most scrolling devices conform to the *Human Interface Devices* (HID) class of the USB standard [3]. The HID class provides a common, vendor-independent method for communicating interaction data from common types of devices to a computer system. Devices that implement the appropriate HID usage tables (for example, mice, keyboards, phones, and digitisers [2]) can operate without vendor-specific drivers, allowing a high degree of device/application interoperability.

HID devices report extensive descriptions of their sensing and reporting characteristics to the operating system/driver via HID *descriptors*. Of particular interest to scrolling are the wheel report range (typically 8-bit values interpreted to be between -127 and $+127$, but any size or range may be chosen by a manufacturer), the characteristics of the report (absolute/relative, wrapping/non-wrapping, linear/non-linear, etc.), and the rate at which reports are sent. The resolution and units of these reports can also be specified, but none of the devices we examined did so. System-specific extensions may also exist. For example, starting with Windows Vista, Microsoft allows devices to support horizontal scrolling and high-resolution scrolling by reporting a resolution multiplier and responding to queries from the operating system to configure it [21].

While most of the scrolling devices we examined supplied a 'Wheel' HID usage, notable exceptions to this were trackpads that used configurable gestures to enable a scrolling mode (for example, Apple's laptop trackpads and Magic Trackpad[1]). These devices transmit information about the gestures through proprietary data fields in the HID report, and rely upon manufacturer-specific drivers to interpret them and report scroll events to the operating system.

Despite the vendor-independent nature of the HID specification, drivers from device manufacturers may still play a significant role in defining the device's scrolling behaviour by attending to the input parameters discussed previously (and may be necessary to make exotic hardware that has not been anticipated by the HID usage tables useful at all—for example, trackpad scrolling gestures). Some of these features may include scrolling horizontally, independent transfer functions for each direction to match human capabilities, configurable buttons or gestures to augment or change scrolling behaviour/resolution, or different scrolling modes for each application. For example, the Logitech MX Revolution[2] features a weighted, low-fiction wheel that can have ratchets automatically engaged by the drivers as a user's scrolling behaviour changes.

Prior Studies of Scrolling Gain

In an early scroll wheel description, Gillick et al. [12, 13] described a potential transfer function that treats initial wheel events as line-scrolling, and advanced to page-scrolling once events passed a certain threshold-rate. A similar technique was recently described by Montalcini [22].

Hinckley et al. [15] describe a scroll transfer function that operates on the calculated interval between events received from the scrolling device/driver:

[1]`http://apple.com/magictrackpad/`
[2]`http://logitech.com/428/130`

$$\Delta y = K_1(1 + K_2\Delta t)^\alpha$$

Where K_1, K_2, and α are constants, Δt is the interval between subsequent events, and Δy is the resulting scale factor to apply to reported magnitudes. Hinckley et al. evaluated their function when applied to a driver reporting three lines of scrolling per physical detent, one line per detent, a "standard" three lines per detent without application of the function, and an IBM ScrollPoint (isometric joystick; the configuration parameters of which are not reported) in a repeated tapping task. They found comparable or significantly better performance when using the accelerated functions.

Two further enhancements are detailed in related patents [17, and related continuity data]. One is a feature that detects changes in the scroll direction and temporarily inhibits the application of Δy—aiming to prevent amplification of overshooting errors. The other identifies rapidly repeated clutching of the wheel (in an attempt to travel a long distance) and applies cumulative gain according to the number of successive wheel flicks (N_{flicks}):

$$Z_{\text{scroll}} = \Delta y \cdot G_0 \cdot G_F \cdot N_{\text{flicks}}$$

Where G_0 is the baseline number of lines to scroll per detent, G_F is the additional amount of gain to apply per flick, and Z_{scroll} is the number of lines to scroll.

Kobayashi and Igarashi [18] explored the use of the cursor position as an input parameter to a dynamic transfer function. Their *MoreWheel* technique combines absolute and relative scrolling into the scroll wheel: dragging the mouse with the wheel depressed simulates grabbing the scroll thumb and enables absolute scrolling, while spinning the wheel produces either line or page-scrolling depending on the position of the cursor within the window (for example, line scrolling when the cursor is in the middle of the window, transitioning to page scrolling near the top or bottom edges).

Cockburn et al. [11] describe a method where two transfer functions are transitioned between based on the velocity of the scroll input to enable slow scrolling at a rate akin to Hinckley et al. [15], and rapid scrolling based on a function that utilises information about the length of the document being scrolled. The velocity of incoming scroll events is calculated, smoothed, and used to determine the proportion of each transfer function to apply:

$$g = \left[p \cdot (k_s - k_s\alpha^{-v})\right] + \left[(1-p) \cdot \left(k_f \frac{\text{document length}}{\text{viewport size}}\right)\right]$$

Where k_s, k_f, and α are constants, v is the reported input velocity, p is the proportion of the "slow" function to apply (determined by examining the relationship of v to the user's maximum velocity), and g is the resulting scale factor to apply to reported magnitudes. An evaluation of this function using two wheel-based devices and an isometric joystick against the "additive flicking" technique of Hinckley and Cutrell [17] found it to perform significantly faster for long documents.

The above studies have explicitly examined the impact of scrolling transfer functions, but there are many more studies that have examined scrolling with imprecise and non-replicable transfer functions. This is not a criticism of the studies, but rather an unfortunate state of affairs—there has been a lack of tools supporting rigour around scrolling transfer functions. Some studies evaluate scrolling systems without mentioning the gain levels or transfer function used [e.g., 10, 14, 23]; some explicitly state the absence of acceleration, but do not state the constant translation used [e.g., 9]; and others rely on the default settings without stipulating what behaviour results [e.g., 1, 24].

REVERSE ENGINEERING CURRENT SCROLLING TRANSFER FUNCTIONS

To examine commercial scrolling transfer functions, we used a modified version of the *EchoMouse* [8]: a programmable microcontroller that allowed us to transmit scrolling events to the system in a controlled and systematic manner, emulating an ordinary scrolling device. To inspect the functions inside a particular device driver, the EchoMouse was modified to present itself as a compatible device from the appropriate manufacturer by manipulating its reported HID vendor and product identifiers. Therefore, by triggering the EchoMouse to emit scrolling events in a pre-defined pattern, and inspecting the scrolling events received by a user application, we can examine how the original events have been transformed.

We tested the scrolling drivers found in Apple Mac OS X 10.7.3, Microsoft Windows 7 (SP1), Microsoft IntelliPoint (8.20.468 on Windows), Logitech SetPoint (driver 5.33.14 on Windows), and Logitech Control Center (3.5.1-23 on Mac OS X)—these represent some of the most popular operating systems and device manufacturers. With each driver, we impersonated the characteristics of several representative devices that they supported to gather data (testing low and high-resolution devices, although no differences between devices was found). The Mac OS X and Windows 7 drivers represent generic drivers that are used by the operating system when no vendor-specific drivers are available. We did not test the Mac OS X version of Microsoft's IntelliPoint driver as it conflicted with our EchoMouse control software, nor did we test an X11 environment as pilot testing showed that it (xorg 1.11.4-2; Fedora 16) does not implement scroll acceleration (the interpretation of each count is left to individual UI toolkits or applications).

This section presents an analysis of the publicly available information about these functions, followed by the testing methodology that we used to gather data about their embedded transfer functions.

Analysis of Existing Transfer Functions

Apple Mac OS X. Apple release several of their low-level input processing frameworks under an open source licence, including those for HID devices. Within the `IOHIDFamily` framework[3] (version 368.20, corresponding to Mac OS X 10.7.3 was examined for this study), the `IOHIDFamily/IOHIDPointing.cpp` and `IOHIDSystem/IO-`

[3] `http://opensource.apple.com/source/IOHIDFamily/`

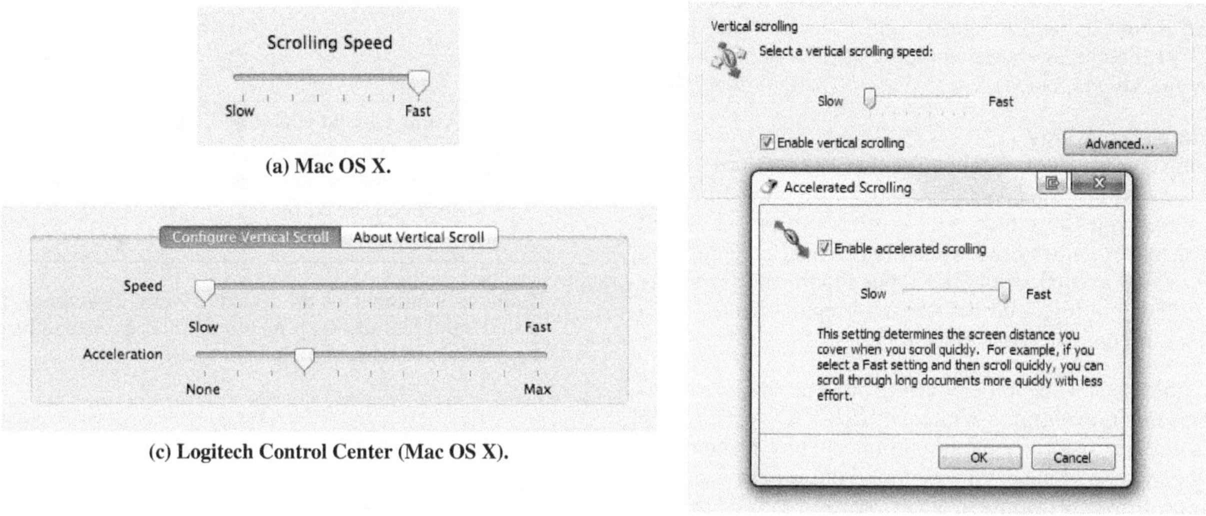

(a) Mac OS X.

(c) Logitech Control Center (Mac OS X).

(b) Microsoft IntelliPoint (Windows).

Figure 2: User interfaces for configuring scroll control.

`HIPointing.cpp` source files contain much of the code pertinent to pointing (and by extension, scrolling) devices.

Drivers can supply an encoded table of acceleration lines (slopes m and intercepts b) to be applied at different input magnitudes; these lines are scaled based on the user's scrolling speed setting (detailed below). When a scroll event is received with magnitude y, it is added to a smoothing window of the last eight events to avoid rapid changes in gain. The average time delta between events in the smoothing window $\overline{\Delta t}$ and average unaccelerated magnitudes $\overline{y}$ is then used to calculate a threshold:

$$l = \left[(K_a \cdot \overline{\Delta t}^2) - (K_b \cdot \overline{\Delta t}) + K_c\right] \cdot r \cdot \overline{y}$$

Where K_a, K_b, and K_c are constants, and r is an input rate multiplier (1 by default).[4] An acceleration line appropriate for an input magnitude larger than l is selected from the table, and applied:

$$y' = y \cdot \frac{b + (l \cdot m)}{|y|}$$

The control exposed to users for this function is a slider in the system preferences to manipulate "Scrolling Speed" with eight intervals from "Slow" to "Fast" (shown in Figure 2(a)), and a corresponding API (`IOHID[Get/Set]ScrollAcceleration()`, where the notches on the slider are mapped to the API values $\{0, 0.12, 0.31, 0.5, 0.69, 0.88, 1, 1.7\}$). An interesting feature of this control is that a negative value (which can only be selected via the API) completely disables scroll acceleration for generic devices, or engages a page-scrolling mode for an Apple trackpad.

Drivers can report scrolling events in units of either lines or pixels, with an automatic conversion by the system between them of 10 pixels per line. We report output in pixels to match the reports given by the system to user applications.

It should be stressed that the behaviour described above is the *default* that is applied should no better drivers match a connected device. Manufacturers are free to use and adjust the described behaviour in part, or as a whole. For example, Apple's closed-source driver for their laptop trackpads supplies a scrolling acceleration table that can be decoded with the source code provided, but that alone does not guarantee that it will be applied in the manner described above.

Microsoft Windows. Windows provides scrolling information to applications via `WM_MOUSEWHEEL` messages with a parameter indicating the distance the wheel has been rotated in units of `WHEEL_DELTA`. These values are intended to be scaled by the user setting `SPI_GETWHEELSCROLLLINES`, indicating how many lines to scroll per unit of `WHEEL_DELTA` (or, a special value indicating that each unit should be interpreted as a page scroll). The interpretation of "lines" or "pages" is left to the application receiving the message. On all current systems, `WHEEL_DELTA` is set to 120, which allows high-resolution devices to indicate scrolling of fractional lines.[5] We report the output from drivers running under Windows in "lines" (i.e. units of `WHEEL_DELTA`).

Microsoft IntelliPoint. Microsoft's IntelliPoint drivers for their branded devices presents two controls for the user to configure the scrolling transfer function (shown in Figure 2(b)). The first controls `SPI_GETWHEELSCROLLLINES` in the range [1, 40]; the second is a seven-interval slider to control accelerated scrolling from "slow" to "fast" (with an option to disable it entirely).

Logitech. Logitech produces two driver packages for their devices: *SetPoint* for Windows, and *Control Center* for Mac OS X. The configuration options and range of supported devices differs between these packages; in particular, *SetPoint* provides options to configure `SPI_GETWHEELSCROLLLINES` for line or page scrolling but with no options for acceleration,

[4] Code also exists for scaling these functions with the screen resolution, but the calculations are currently fixed.

[5] `http://msdn.microsoft.com/library/ms997498`

while *Control Center* allows customisation of the scrolling "speed" (from "slow" to "fast") and "acceleration" (from "none" to "max"), as shown in Figure 2(c) (both of these are continuous sliders, but were tested at the marked intervals).

Testing Methodology

Scrolling events from the EchoMouse have values in the range -127 to $+127$. We observed that reports from devices were typically either -1 (scroll down) or $+1$ (scroll up) with wider values used when the physical manipulation of the device exceeded its HID input report rate (typically 100~125Hz, but high-end devices may report at rates up to 1000Hz); we emulated this behaviour.

A potential issue when impersonating other devices is matching their input resolution. While the USB HID specification allows devices to specify the resolution and physical units of their input, none of the device we tested did so. For instance, a Microsoft Wheel Mouse Optical[6] sends 18 scroll counts per complete revolution of its wheel (20° per detent), while a Logitech MX500[7] sends 24 (15° per detent), but their reports are indistinguishable to a generic driver (similar issues exist for trackpads that transmit events corresponding to millimetres of displacement, or other types of physical control). Because we tested a range of devices with different input resolutions, we report our input velocity in "counts" per unit of time, where one count corresponds to one scroll event of magnitude -1 or $+1$ (issues surrounding device resolution are discussed later).

As we are interested in the various input parameters that transfer functions may attend to (and not only how they operate under levels of velocity), we performed four mechanised tests of each possible configuration of driver and device:

- *Constant velocity:* emulating a constant speed of device operation for five seconds, and measuring the resultant output scrolling velocity as an average over that period.
- *Maintained velocity:* emulating a constant speed of device operation for five seconds, and measuring the resultant output scrolling velocity for each event.
- *Clutching:* we emulated clutching actions, manipulating the speed of device operation, the duration of clutches, and the time between successive clutches.
- *Direction changes:* we emulated direction changes (alternating between scrolling up and scrolling down) while maintaining a constant speed of device operation.

These tests were repeated for each configuration option presented to users (as described above), and across a range of possible user control input rates. Custom software monitored the system's response using the low-level event reporting APIs provided by each operating system (free from potential manipulation by higher-level frameworks or toolkits).

RESULTS AND ANALYSIS

The results of our analyses are summarised in Table 1. We found that neither Microsoft Windows 7, nor Logitech's SetPoint drivers provide any scroll acceleration (the gain is always constant). Due to the large number of configurations tested and the many commonalities discovered between them, the following subsections present a survey of the most salient and interesting behaviour characteristics and parameters attended to (a complete spreadsheet of the acceleration tables collected is also available[8]). Following the main results, we summarise device-specific issues in the analysis.

	Velocity	Direction	Duration	Clutching
Apple Mac OS X	●	◐	○	◐
Microsoft Windows 7	○	○	○	○
Microsoft IntelliPoint	●	●	○	●
Logitech SetPoint	○	○	○	○
Logitech Control Center	●	◐	●	○

Table 1: Summary of the tested drivers' attendance to tested input features—○: no attendance, ●: attendance, ◐: partial attendance (details in text).

Gain with Respect to Velocity

How the different systems alter gain across input velocity is shown in Figures 3(a), (b), and (c) for Mac OS X, Microsoft IntelliPoint, and Logitech Control Center, respectively. The multiple lines in each figure show different levels of user setting for scrolling "speed" (Mac OS X, Figure 2(a)) or scroll "acceleration" (Microsoft IntelliPoint and Logitech Control Center, Figures 2(b) and (c)). The solid and dashed lines in Figure 3(b) differentiate between scrolling direction (up and down); the other drivers respond to both directions equally.

The maximum attainable scale factors range from ~14× with Mac OS X, to ~18× with Logitech, and ~21× with IntelliPoint. The key differences between the three curve shapes is that Logitech's curves for high acceleration show a dramatic drop in gain after peaking at 18× at ~28 counts/s. This is a result of a falling (but still positive) gradient in the output velocity curve; however the rationale for this design choice is unknown. Both Mac OS X and Logitech allow input to be attenuated (with a gain of less than 1) at low input speeds, increasing the expressivity of devices with poor resolution.

Direction as an Input

Figure 3(b) shows that Microsoft IntelliPoint drivers apply differing gain levels across each scrolling direction. This is probably applied to compensate for the differing maximum input velocities attainable in the two directions (Cockburn et al. [11] showed marked differences between maximum scroll wheel rotation speeds upwards and downwards).

Mac OS X and Logitech drivers do not vary gain across direction, but directional changes do momentarily "reset" gain, as shown for Mac OS X in Figure 6(a). This is due to a reset of the smoothing window upon direction change, resulting in reduced gain until the window is re-filled. The same task with Microsoft's IntelliPoint drivers is shown in Figure 6(b), where we observed a very brief drop in gain and the application of different levels of gain for each direction.

[6] `http://microsoft.com/hardware/en-nz/d/wheel-mouse-optical`

[7] `http://logitech.com/428/910`

[8] `http://cortex.p.gen.nz/research/scrolling/`

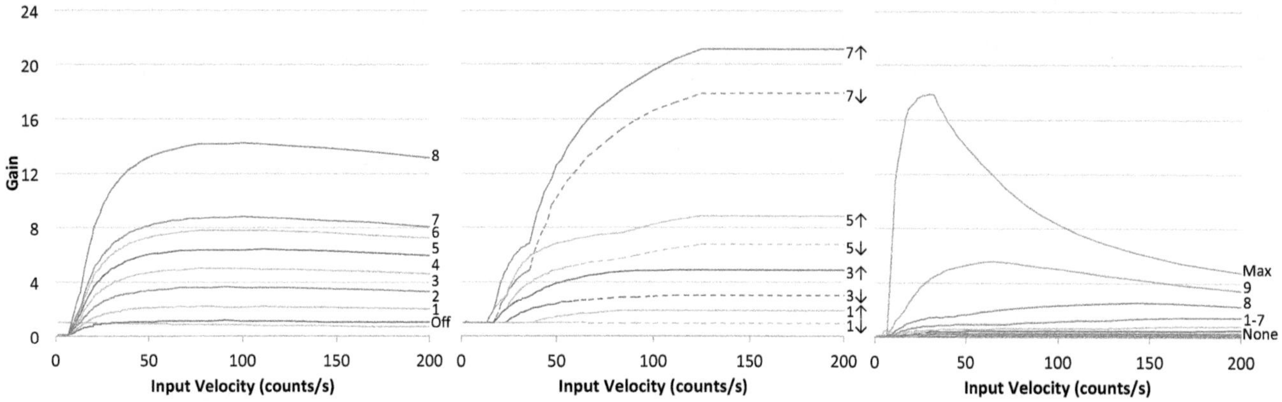

(a) Mac OS X (Generic Device).

(b) Microsoft IntelliPoint: up (solid) and down (dashed).

(c) Logitech Control Center.

Figure 3: Gain scale factors across input velocity (counts per second) with Mac OS X, Microsoft IntelliPoint (under Windows 7), and Logitech drivers under Mac OS X. Gain is measured as the level of amplification in the system's base unit (pixels per count for Mac OS X and Logitech; lines per count for Microsoft IntelliPoint), and is plotted at varying levels of each driver's respective UI sliders for acceleration.

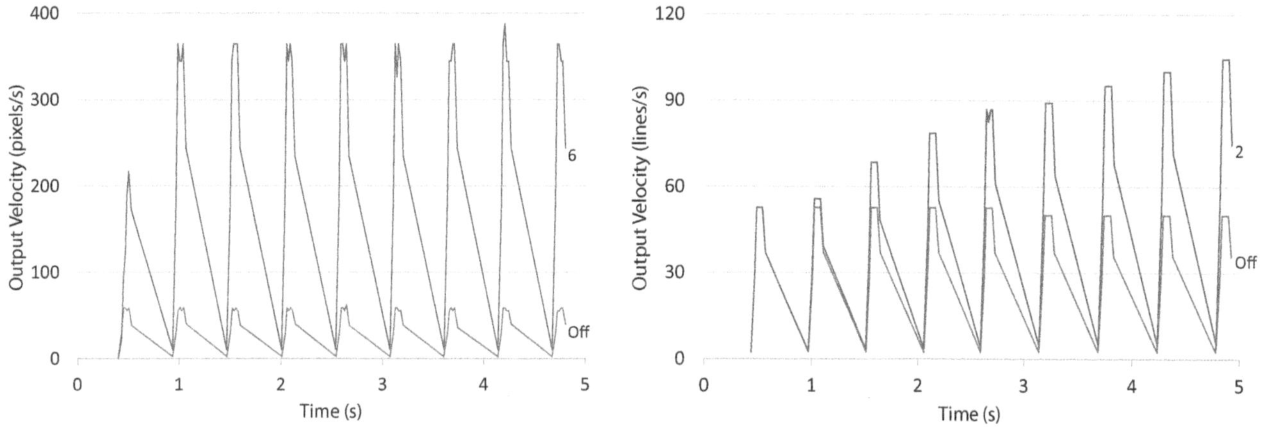

(a) Mac OS X (Generic Device).

(b) Microsoft IntelliPoint.

Figure 4: Output velocity response to repeated clutching.

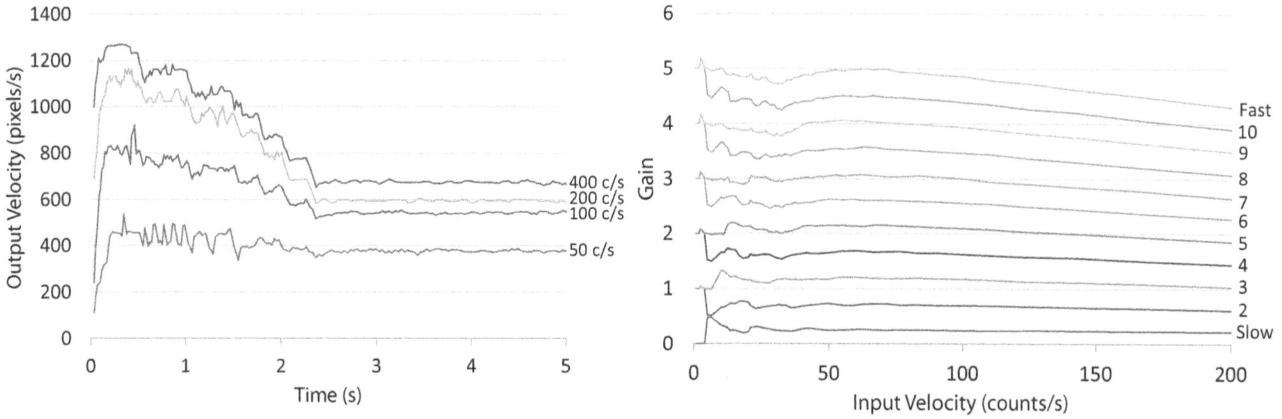

(a) Output velocity over time as a constant input velocity is maintained.

(b) Gain across input velocity at levels of the "speed" slider shown in Figure 2(c).

Figure 5: Logitech's Control Center: Attendance to duration and the control of the "speed" slider.

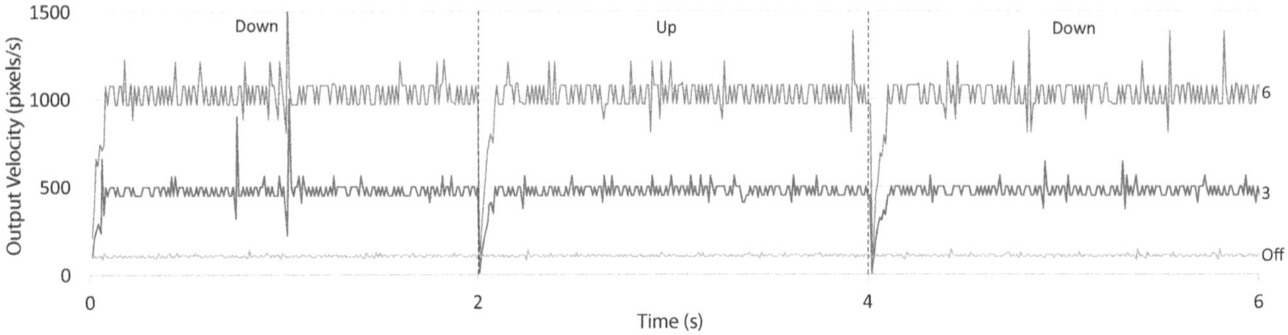

(a) Mac OS X (Generic Device).

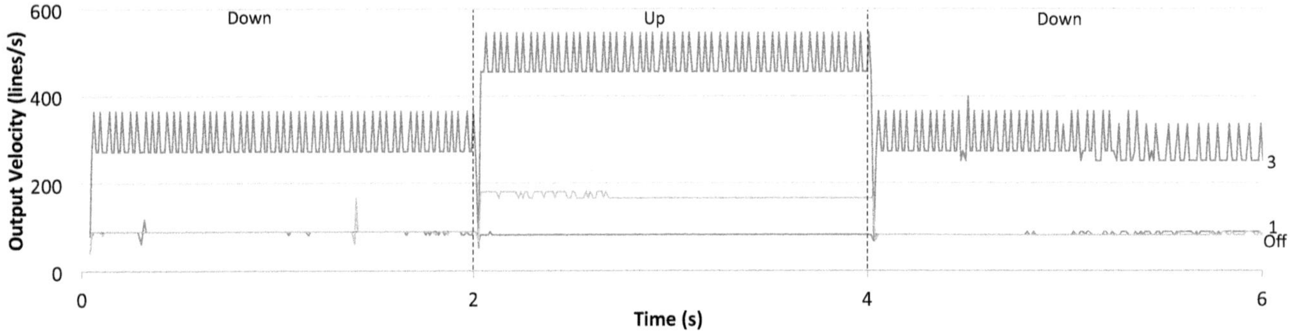

(b) Microsoft IntelliPoint.

Figure 6: Output velocity over time as a constant velocity is maintained but input direction is switched at the dashed lines (2 and 4s). Three curves—two levels of acceleration and one with acceleration disabled—are shown.

Clutching as an Input

Figure 4 shows how Mac OS X and Microsoft IntelliPoint drivers respond to clutching of the scroll wheel (Logitech's response is not shown as it is similar to Mac OS X). The main finding here is that IntelliPoint cumulatively adds gain across successive clutches when acceleration is turned on (similar to the technique described by Hinckley and Cutrell [17]). Mac OS X (Figure 4(a)) and Logitech drivers do not vary their response (the reduced gain for the first impulse is due to an empty smoothing window), however, comments in the Mac OS X driver source code[9] indicate the timeout value for resetting the smoothing window was chosen specifically to avoid doing so between clutches.

Duration as an Input

Figure 5(a) shows that Logitech's driver attends to scroll duration while Mac OS X and Microsoft IntelliPoint do not (not shown). When stimulated with a constant velocity scroll rate, Logitech's output velocity diminishes over approximately 2.5s. This time-based fall-off is particularly marked at high input velocities, and it is therefore likely designed to enhance user performance with Logitech's free-spinning inertial scroll wheels that readily allow high input speeds.

Other Features

It is interesting and potentially important that the speed and acceleration parameters in Logitech's Control Center interact with one another, and that setting acceleration to 'None' does not disable acceleration: Figure 5(b) shows the gain observed at various settings of the speed slider with the acceleration slider set to "None". The noise at low speeds is puzzling, and the lack of constant gain suggests that Logitech Control Center should be used with caution in research experiments.

[9]`IOHIDSystem/IOHIPointing.cpp`, lines 555–559

DISCUSSION

We have presented a framework for understanding the factors influencing the transformation of human action with scrolling devices (particularly scroll wheels) into resultant scrolling output. We have also reverse engineered the scrolling transfer functions from the drivers of popular manufacturers, with results demonstrating substantial variation in both the factors attended to and the manner in which they do so. Key observations include the fact that Microsoft's IntelliPoint drivers apply different levels of gain to each scrolling directions (presumably to accommodate differences in human mechanics), that they also apply cumulative gain across repeated clutching actions, and that Logitech's drivers on Mac OS X apply variable gain even when user settings stipulate that acceleration should be turned off.

The framework and findings have several implications for research that aims to develop new transfer functions or use scrolling devices in experimental conditions, and there are many avenues for further work.

Facilitating Rigour in Scrolling Studies

Scrolling researchers are typically interested in either new input devices [e.g., 24], transfer functions [e.g., 11, 15], or new interactive techniques [e.g., 18]. Scrolling devices are also used in experiments where scrolling is not the focus of an investigation, but as an interaction tool.

In all cases, comparative evaluations are normally conducted to measure performance over the state of the art, and the choices made in the implementation and administration of experimental treatments must be made with the awareness and knowledge of the underlying transfer functions. As experimental software typically operates on-top of existing drivers (rather than replacing them), understanding the interaction between the transfer function of the driver and that of the experimental condition is critical in answering the question of whether the treatment is causing any observed difference, or whether it may be attributed to the interacting transfer functions.

What should researchers do to maximise rigour and facilitate replication? We make three recommendations. First, a constant level of gain (i.e. scroll acceleration is disabled) should be used as a baseline in experiments where gain is not intended to be a factor. Given the complex nature of the gain functions observed in our results, their variation across drivers, and their potential volatility across different versions from the same manufacturer, replicating non-constant gain settings across experiments may be extremely difficult. Note that using constant gain also means that there should be no adaptive *translation*, such as a transition from line to page-based scrolling units reported by Gillick et al. [12, 13] (we are unaware of commercial drivers that do so, however some Logitech mice have a mechanical switch that the driver can activate to transition the wheel from detented to free-spinning when a threshold scroll velocity is exceeded—altering the possible range and behaviour of a user's input).

Second, user settings for disabling acceleration should be treated with suspicion, and researchers should check carefully whether acceleration is actually disabled. Ideally, an inspection similar to that described in this paper should be conducted, but otherwise, researchers should avoid drivers that are known to exhibit non-constant velocity scale factors (e.g., Logitech's drivers under Mac OS X, as reported here). Consequently, when gain is disabled, how this was achieved (user settings, API calls, etc.) should be reported.

The third recommendation is to report details of the transfer function, described next.

Reporting Scrolling Transfer Functions

In reporting a transfer function, there are two components that deserve attention: the *translation* and the *gain*.

The translation concerns the device and display resolutions, the level of action required to generate a scroll event on the device, and the magnitude of those events (in display units). The device resolution considers the number of events reported per unit of physical action: for example, Logitech's MX500 mouse reports 24 events per complete wheel rotation, while Microsoft's Wheel Mouse Optical reports 18 (i.e. a complete revolution of the MX500 is equivalent to 1.33 revolutions of the Wheel Mouse Optical). The level of action required to generate a scroll event considers the lower-bounds of physical action generating scroll events: in a scroll wheel, this would be the minimum wheel rotation and resistance to generate a scroll event, but for trackpad scroll gestures it could concern the minimum velocity of movement, or the minimum total displacement. Finally, the event magnitude considers the number of pixels, lines, or pages that the minimum scroll event moves (which may be fractional with high resolution devices [e.g., 21]).

Where a constant gain is used, the scale factor between the event magnitudes from the translation component should be reported. Where non-constant gain is used, the gain function(s) should be described using formulas, figures, and/or tables with the mapping between the output of the translation component to the final scroll behaviour. In both cases, the mechanics of the device and input/output resolutions should be reported.

Limitations and Further Work

Most of the gain functions analysed in this paper were reverse engineered without source code. It is therefore possible that our descriptions of the functions are incomplete because we failed to probe a salient input parameter: for example, we did not probe for attendance to acceleration or jerk (the derivative of acceleration). Similarly, we analysed the data that is sent from the operating system to user applications, and did not consider possible manipulation of that data by applications or the frameworks/libraries they are built upon. These higher-level systems have access to information about the information space being navigated (for example, the document length [11]) that may be used to augment scrolling behaviour. We have, however, presented a framework for understanding that such parameters could influence behaviour, and a method for inspecting their impact if required.

Our attempt to reverse engineer the behaviour of Microsoft's IntelliPoint driver under Mac OS X failed because the driver prevented us from communicating with the EchoMouse. There are two hardware solutions to this problem: either EchoMouse could be engineered to store a pre-programmed set of signals to be emulated, or it could be designed to support a second USB input (one for sending signals to EchoMouse, and the other for sending messages to the driver).

None of the devices we tested supplied information about their physical units or resolution of input. Our analysis therefore used "counts" rather than physical units (such as degrees). Similarly, to our knowledge, drivers currently do not consider the display resolution when calculating gain (e.g., pixel size, pixel density, and/or scaling factors); but as higher resolution devices and displays become available, there are opportunities for investigating how transfer functions can be better designed to adapt to different input and output resolutions—for example, the interaction between user performance and input resolution (both device resolution, and human capabilities), and similarly for the output resolution (adapting to different display configurations).

There are also other types of scrolling hardware that have not been examined here, most notably trackpads and touch mice (devices that feature a touch-sensitive surface). Some of these devices feature transfer functions that enable features such as simulated momentum and friction when scrolling.

CONCLUSIONS

Scrolling is an elemental interface control, and system transfer functions are fundamental in determining their behaviour. Yet despite their importance, scrolling transfer functions have received little research attention. This paper examined how scrolling transfer functions work and the input parameters they attend to. We described a method to reverse engineer the state of the art in scrolling transfer functions, and we used the method to expose how systems vary with the input parameters they attend to and in their processing of these parameters. As well as providing a firmer foundation for research into improving scrolling transfer functions, the paper's findings also suggest that when evaluating scrolling techniques, researchers should be cautious about potential interactions between the system transfer function and experimental treatment. The method proposed allows system transfer functions to be precisely recorded, aiding experimental replication. In further work, we will examine gesture-based transfer functions on touchscreens and trackpads, and compare user performance with different functions.

ACKNOWLEDGEMENTS

This work was supported by a Royal Society of New Zealand Marsden Grant 10-UOC-020.

REFERENCES

1. Arthur, K. W., Matic, N., and Ausbeck, P. Evaluating touch gestures for scrolling on notebook computers. In *Proc. CHI EA '08*, ACM (New York, NY, USA, 2008), 2943–2948.
2. Bates, B. M., Dezmelyk, R., Ingman, R., Lieb, R., McGowan, S., Ray, K., Schumacher, S., Sherman, N. C., Stern, D., van Flander, M., and Zimmerman, R. HID usage tables, Version 1.12. USB Implementer's Forum (2004).
3. Bergman, M., Peuranch, T., Schmidt, T., McGowan, S., Crowe, J., Dezmelyk, R., Zimmerman, R., van Flandern, M., Nathan, B., Davis, M., and Rayhawk, J. Device class definition for human interface devices (HID), Version 1.11. USB Implementer's Forum (June 2001).
4. Buxton, W. Lexical and pragmatic considerations of input structures. *SIGGRAPH Computer Graphics 17*, 1 (January 1983), 31–37.
5. Buxton, W. Touch, gesture, and marking. In *Human-Computer Interaction: Toward the Year 2000*, R. M. Baecker, J. Grudin, W. Buxton, and S. Greenberg, Eds. Morgan Kaufmann Publishers, San Francisco, 1995, ch. 7, 469–482.
6. Card, S. K., Mackinlay, J. D., and Robertson, G. G. The design space of input devices. In *Proc. CHI '90*, ACM (New York, NY, USA, 1990), 117–124.
7. Card, S. K., Mackinlay, J. D., and Robertson, G. G. A morphological analysis of the design space of input devices. *ACM Transactions on Information Systems 9*, 2 (Apr. 1991), 99–122.
8. Casiez, G., and Roussel, N. No more bricolage! Methods and tools to characterize, replicate and compare pointing transfer functions. In *Proc. UIST '11*, ACM (New York, NY, USA, 2011), 603–614.
9. Chipman, L. E., Bederson, B. B., and Golbeck, J. A. Slidebar: analysis of a linear input device. *Behaviour & Information Technology 23*, 1 (2004), 1–9.
10. Cockburn, A., and Gutwin, C. A predictive model of human performance with scrolling and hierarchial lists. *Human-Computer Interaction 24*, 3 (2009), 273–314.
11. Cockburn, A., Quinn, P., Gutwin, C., and Fitchett, S. Improving scrolling devices with document length dependent gain. In *Proc. CHI '12*, ACM (New York, NY, USA, 2012), 267–276.
12. Gillick, W. G., and Lam, C. C., U.S. Patent No. 5530455. U.S. Patent and Trademark Office (Washington, DC, 1996).
13. Gillick, W. G., and Rosenberg, R. A., U.S. Patent No. 5446481. U.S. Patent and Trademark Office (Washington, DC, August 1995).
14. Gutwin, C., and Cockburn, A. Improving list revisitation with listmaps. In *Proc. AVI '06*, ACM Press (New York, NY, USA, 2006), 396–403.
15. Hinckley, K., Cutrell, E., Bathiche, S., and Muss, T. Quantitative analysis of scrolling techniques. In *Proc. CHI '02*, ACM (New York, NY, USA, 2002), 65–72.
16. Hinckley, K., and Sinclair, M. Touch-sensing input devices. In *Proc. CHI '99*, ACM (New York, NY, USA, 1999), 223–230.
17. Hinckley, K. P., and Cutrell, E. B., U.S. Patent No. 7173637. U.S. Patent and Trademark Office (Washington, DC, 2007).
18. Kobayashi, M., and Igarashi, T. MoreWheel: Multi-mode scroll-wheeling depending on the cursor location. In *UIST 2006 Adjunct Proceedings: Demonstrations* (2006), 57–58.
19. Lipscomb, J. S., and Pique, M. E. Analog input device physical characteristics. *SIGCHI Bulletin 25*, 3 (July 1993), 40–45.
20. Mackinlay, J., Card, S. K., and Robertson, G. G. A semantic analysis of the design space of input devices. *Human-Computer Interaction 5*, 2–3 (1990), 145–190.
21. Microsoft Corporation. Enhanced wheel support in windows. Tech. rep., 2010.
22. Montalcini, A. L., U.S. Patent No. 7661072. U.S. Patent and Trademark Office (Washington, DC, 2010).
23. Wherry, E. Scroll ring performance evaluation. In *CHI EA '03*, ACM (New York, NY, USA, 2003), 758–759.
24. Zhai, S., Smith, B. A., and Selker, T. Improving browsing performance: A study of four input devices for scrolling and pointing tasks. In *Proc. INTERACT '97*, Chapman & Hall, Ltd. (London, UK, 1997), 286–293.

Giving a Hand to the Eyes: Leveraging Input Accuracy for Subpixel Interaction

Nicolas Roussel[1], Géry Casiez[1,2,3], Jonathan Aceituno[1] and Daniel Vogel[4]

[1]Inria Lille & [2]LIFL, [3]University of Lille, France

[4]Cheriton School of Computer Science, University of Waterloo, Canada

nicolas.roussel@inria.fr, gery.casiez@lifl.fr, jonathan.aceituno@inria.fr, dvogel@uwaterloo.ca

ABSTRACT

We argue that the current practice of using integer positions for pointing events artificially constrains human precision capabilities. The high sensitivity of current input devices can be harnessed to enable precise direct manipulation "in between" pixels, called subpixel interaction. We provide detailed analysis of subpixel theory and implementation, including the critical component of revised control-display gain transfer functions. A prototype implementation is described with several illustrative examples. Guidelines for subpixel domain applicability are provided and an overview of required changes to operating systems and graphical user interface frameworks are discussed.

ACM Classification: H.5.2 [Information interfaces and presentation]: User interfaces - Graphical user interfaces.

General terms: Design, Human Factors

Keywords: Display density; indirect pointing; input device sensitivity; device's human resolution; subpixel interaction; direct manipulation

INTRODUCTION

Over the last thirty years, there have been tremendous increases in computer processing power, storage capacity, and network bandwidth. Graphical user interfaces (GUIs) have played a crucial part in making these resources available, enabling the direct manipulation of data, which has also increased substantially in diversity and size. However, while processing, storage, and communication capabilities have experienced a hundred, thousand, or million-fold increase to handle these increased data manipulation requirements, the situation is quite different for computer displays. Most modern displays typically have a pixel density lower than 150 PPI (pixels per inch) and cannot display more than 2.5 megapixels[1]. Display capabilities have increased by only a factor of 21 compared to the original Macintosh.

When data density exceeds display density, direct manipulation becomes a problem. For example, selecting an item from an overview of a large discrete set, or fine adjustment of a continuous variable. Solutions usually involve a scale adjustment in visual space or layering transfer functions to reach the desired control precision. But these approaches take for granted the curious way in which operating systems map input device movements to data.

When you move a pointing device, motion deltas (in device-specific units) are sent to the I/O subsystem and transformed by a transfer function [5] into on-screen pointer motions (in pixels). The system then moves the pointer accordingly and generates *movement events* which are routed via the window subsystem and GUI framework to a widget to manipulate data (Figure 1a). What is curious is that although these are commonly called "mouse events," they are actually "pointer events" because the information they carry describe on-screen *pointer movements*, not *mouse movements*. So, a pointing device is not really how we interact with data: it is a device through which we interact with an on-screen pointer, through which we interact with data. Thirty years ago, mouse sensitivity and display density were comparable, so this kind of input mapping seemed reasonable. The original Macintosh mouse was 90 CPI (counts per inch), quite close to its ≈72 PPI display density. The problem is that this mapping still serves as the basis for all graphical interactions,

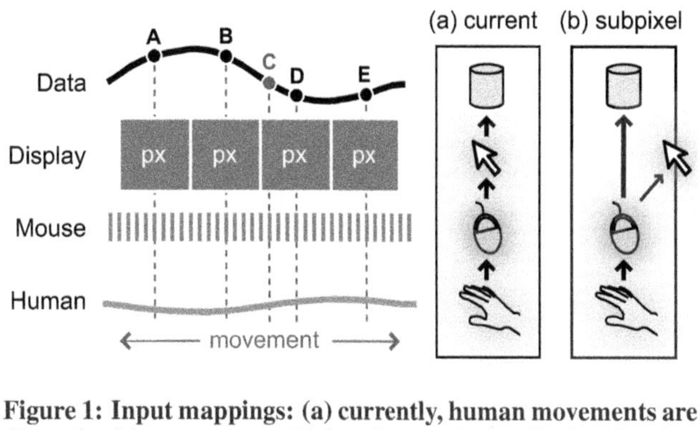

Figure 1: Input mappings: (a) currently, human movements are discretized by mouse sensitivity, then again by display density: data points "in between" pixels like 'C' are unreachable; (b) a subpixel mapping discretizes human movements by mouse sensitivity only, for precise data manipulation.

[1]see `http://libpointing.org/resolution/` for information on the sensitivity and pixel density of commercial mice and displays

UIST'12, October 7–10, 2012, Cambridge, MA, USA.

and since movements are measured in pixels, they are only as accurate as the display density.

Fifteen years ago, in his classic paper "*The Eyes Have It (...)*" [12], Shneiderman pointed out how our remarkable perceptual abilities were often underutilized. From what we just described, it is fair to say that our remarkable motor abilities are currently underutilized. To put it simply, the eyes could surely use a hand. The sensitivity of modern mice is now typically over 800 CPI and can reach more than 10000 CPI, and some touchpads are 1000 CPI — levels of precision more suitable for capturing high human sensitivity [4]. It is time the current input mapping is revised.

We are proposing *subpixel interaction*, a subtle, but critical alteration to current system architectures where device movements are mapped directly to data, enabling interaction "in between pixels" (Figure 1b). Our solution requires a small software-level modification, yet increases the accuracy of standard interaction techniques and remains compatible with complimentary approaches like Focus+Context lenses. After describing motivating situations where pixel-precision is inadequate and reviewing related work, we describe the details of our solution. Specifically, guidelines for useful subpixel resolution and, since our focus is on indirect pointing devices like mice and touchpads, we describe revised transfer function characteristics which leverage subpixel capability. Our work is a rallying cry with implementation details to leverage human input capability for precise direct manipulation.

WHY PIXELS ARE NOT ENOUGH

To illustrate the current problem more concretely, consider navigating a video player where frame selection accuracy is ultimately limited by the pixel width of the display. For example, the Apple OS X QuickTime player has a fixed timeline slider width of 315 pixels (Figure 2a). Moving the slider 1 pixel skips a 5 minute video by 1 second, but a 1.5 hour movie is skipped by 17 seconds (Table 1). This may be fine for coarse positioning, but tasks like skipping *only* commercials becomes tedious or impossible as the video length increases. Even more extreme is accurately selecting specific frames with Apple Keynote's video inspector which uses a 198 pixel, fixed width slider.

There are a myriad of other examples where there are not enough pixels to provide the required precision: picking a particular item in a large list using a slider; image navigation and editing (e.g. accurately cropping a megapixel image, picking a precise location on a map); resizing a calendar event to minute precision (e.g. when booking flight departures or lawyers tracking billing time); high precision vector drawing tasks (e.g. drawing a structural wall to centimeter precision or aligning objects in vertex-dense areas); or manipulating objects in 3D applications (e.g. setting orientation of CAD objects to within 0.1°).

	Duration	Keynote	QT Player
CHI video	05:00	00:01.515	00:00.952
TV Show	52:00	00:15.758	00:09.905
Movie	1:30:00	00:27.273	00:17.143
Gone with the Wind	3:58:00	01:12.121	00:45.333
Bergensbanen	7:14:13	02:11.581	01:22.708

Table 1: Time between pixels in the Keynote inspector and QuickTime Player sliders for different video durations.

A solution to these pixel precision problems could be to simply add more pixels. Returning to the video player example, consider enabling a more reasonable 1 second selection accuracy with a 1.5 hour video by increasing the timeline slider width. Unfortunately, the slider would need to be 5400 pixels wide, the width of three 1080p HDTVs. This is clearly unworkable, so a common way to overcome the limitation is to introduce alternate navigation controls such as arrow keys, but these can be slow and error prone, partly because they no longer follow principles of direct manipulation. Next, we discuss how researchers have approached the pixel precision problem while trying to maintain the benefits of direct manipulation.

RELATED WORK

To make direct manipulation more accurate, previous work introduces explicit *precise pointing modes* such as discrete or continuous zooming and Focus + Context Lenses. In addition to problems inherent with modes, these techniques are impeded by the assumption that whole-pixel input resolution is a hard constraint – they ignore the high resolution capabilities of modern pointing devices and human limb accuracy.

Increasing Pointing Accuracy with Modes

A straightforward way to increase input accuracy is to *zoom* and magnify the desired target area to make pointing easier. For example, the OS X QuickTime Player 10.1 has what is essentially a dwell-while-dragging zoom mode to select video frames more precisely (Figure 2a). Other exam-

(a)

(b)

Figure 2: Manipulating visual space to increase pointing accuracy: (a) dwelling while dragging the OS X QuickTime Player 10.1 timeline slider *zooms* the timeline in to provide 1 second precision in a 10 second window; (b) some YouTube videos have a Focus+Context timeline with a secondary slider providing 1 second precision.

ples include Popup Vernier [3] which supports explicit incremental cursor space magnification during drag operations, and Ramos and Balakrishnan's Zliding technique [10] which continuously maps pen tip pressure to view scale. These examples are part of the more general class of zoomable user interfaces (ZUIs) [8] where the zoom level is adjusted using an explicit control like dwell, pressure, keyboard keys, mouse scroll wheel, or GUI buttons, sliders, or textfields. However, zooming requires an explicit cognitive decision, locating the optimal zoom level to facilitate precise pointing can be time consuming and difficult, and the overall context of the information space is lost while zoomed in.

To maintain context, Focus+Context Lenses embed a magnified portion of the information space in the overview view [9]. Although this addresses some shortcomings of ZUIs, Appert et al. [2] argue that when the input device is used to simultaneously move the lens *and* point at targets in the lens, there is a *quantization problem* limiting the usable range of lens magnification levels. Their solution is also to introduce an explicit mode switch, this time to switch between positioning the lens and pointing at targets inside the lens. Techniques like Alphaslider [1] and YouTube's secondary magnified timeline slider (Figure 2b) are one-dimensional examples of the Focus+Context strategy. Since they are one-dimensional, the switch to the accurate mode is achieved spatially, by acquiring the magnified slider.

Another solution is to switch to a mode with a custom precise pointing transfer function. This can be achieved with a technique called *pointer lock* where "*input methods of applications [are] based on the movement of the mouse, not just the absolute position of a cursor*" [11]. This is often used for first-person navigation in games, but can also be used for modal precise control of parameters like object rotation in 3D applications. Since direct manipulation no longer follows the system pointer, the pointer is usually hidden or "locked" in place to reduce user confusion.

Unfortunately, using pointer lock to enable a modeless subpixel solution is not practical. For the second transfer function to increase accuracy, it must scale down the relatively large integral movement deltas received from the system event (Figure 3). This will increase motor space which lowers comfort and performance due to device clutching. In addition, since precise pointing is necessarily mapped to low speeds which have a lower-bound constrained by integral deltas, then larger 'normal' pointing movements will be harder to control since the speed-to-position mapping is condensed. Finally, since the precise transfer function is layered, it is has to compensate for different hardware, software, and user settings which determine the underlying system transfer function [5]. Like the other techniques above, using pointer lock does not harness the potential precision of modern input devices.

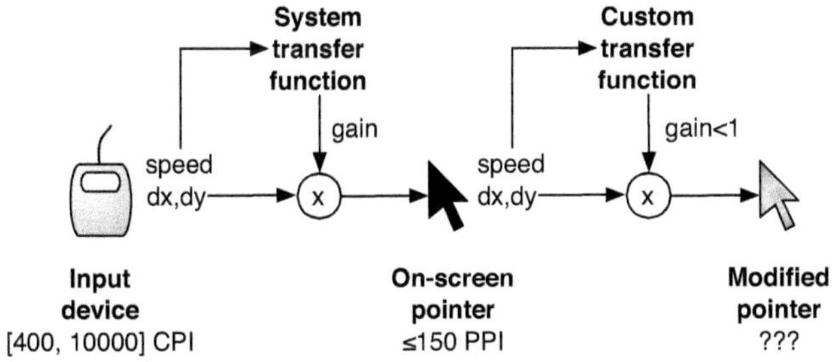

Figure 3: Using pointer lock for subpixel interaction amounts to layering a second precise transfer function in which low speeds are constrained by integral movement deltas.

Lost Capabilities of Input Devices and Human limbs

Traditional GUI toolkits like Java Swing report pointer movement events as integers. Even toolkits like Qt or WPF which are designed for display resolution independence[2] report motion events as integers, regardless whether they are specified as floating point (with WPF, this is due to integral `WM_MOUSEMOVE` messages). On OS X, position events are floating point, but these only hold non-integral values with absolute pointing devices such as tablets. For relative devices, Casiez and Roussel [5] show that pointing transfer functions used by Microsoft Windows, OS X, and X.Org apply a speed-dependent float factor on motion deltas but move the pointer according to the sole integral part of the result. Although the fractional part is preserved internally for later accumulation, it is inaccessible from high-level software.

Raw motion deltas can usually be obtained (e.g. through `WM_INPUT` messages) and are commonly used by games for custom high-sensitivity pointer control. But until recently [5], the lack of appropriate knowledge and tools made it quite difficult for this custom pointer to behave like the system one for "normal" pointing tasks. The idea of using floating coordinates to improve the precision of the system pointer with relative devices was once suggested within the X.Org community[3], but received very little attention.

The sensitivity of modern pointing devices ranges from 400 up to 10000 CPI or more for high-end mice, enabling minimal measurable displacements of 0.0635 mm and 0.00254 mm respectively. Whether people can leverage this level of precision depends on their ability to control fine movements of input devices in motor space. In a multi-scale pointing experiment, Guiard et al. [7] found that users can comfortably acquire 0.06 mm targets in motor space (423 CPI), but this is not an upper bound since it was the smallest width they evaluated. More recently, Bérard et al. [4] defined a *Device's Human Resolution* (DHR) as "*the smallest target size that users can acquire with an ordinary amount of effort using a particular device*". They found that the DHR depends on the input device and the user's sensorimotor capabilities. For computer mice they found DHR values from 700 CPI to 1400 CPI. This means that humans can easily exploit input resolutions up to 7 to 14 times higher than a typical 100 PPI display. The challenge is how to translate these human capabilities into effective control of direct manipulation interfaces.

[2]i.e. where graphical objects are positioned using floating point coordinates in a space independent of the screen

[3]`http://johan.kiviniemi.name/blag/making-x-report-the-mouse-position-with-subpixel-precision/`

LEVERAGING INPUT ACCURACY

Direct manipulation interfaces translate objects of interest into physically manipulatable, graphical representations. Each object is composed of a collection of underlying data, often referred to as a model. Models can represent discrete elements (e.g. integers, video frames) and continuous elements (e.g. floating values). The range of elements may be bounded (e.g. choosing a video frame from a clip) or unbounded (e.g. specifying a CAD object's length). In practice, unbounded models can be considered bounded given reasonable minimum and maximum values for the task, and continuous models may be considered discrete given a reasonable level of precision for the task. By treating all models as discrete, we can define the model's cardinality (N) as the number of elements which users expect to select from.

When display density prevents the object from being represented at the desired granularity (i.e. with the right level of detail), auxiliary representations are needed such as text labels, zoomed views, or even sounds or haptic effects. This solves the output granularity problem, but the problem remains for input. This is what motivates us: we want to overcome the problem of input granularity being limited by display density; we want to support physical actions on objects with a higher precision than the display. As discussed earlier, there is a hidden potential in input devices that is compatible with the degree of control that people can exert. We would like to take advantage of this potential in a way that smoothly integrates with current practices.

In this section we develop a way to provide subpixel input while maintaining current graphical object representations and without introducing any explicit "high precision" mode. We preserve the on-screen pointer since it provides essential visual feedback for direct manipulation. We alter the mapping between movements in motor space and visual space, but we do this without changing the current "feeling" of pointing: we avoid situations where the cursor feels stuck and then suddenly moves quickly, and we do not extend the device operating space. People continue to interact as they do now, but with higher, subpixel precision when needed.

Taking the input device into account

To leverage input accuracy, the system first needs to know the device sensitivity, expressed in device-independent units (such as CPI). This is important so that the system understands what it measures: a higher sensitivity should result in a more precise movement, not a change of magnitude. Unfortunately devices and hardware drivers typically do not provide this information (and probably for that reason, the Windows and X.Org pointing transfer functions completely ignore it [5]).

As already explained, pointing transfer functions apply a dynamic gain factor on device displacements, move the pointer according to the integral part of the result, and store the fractional part internally. We want that information all the way up: the fractional part should be accessible in an easy way to the code actually responsible for the interaction. We propose to generalize what some systems do for absolute devices: expose the fractional part by using floating values for the pointer coordinates. To summarize, we propose first that transfer functions should take into account device sensitivity; and second, that float values resulting from these computations should be forwarded *as is* to higher-level code.

This solution takes the sensitivity of the input device into account so that movements in motor space are no longer magnified by input sensitivity or constrained by display density. In theory, granularity of control can be increased 100 times for a high end 10000 CPI mouse (assuming a display density of 100 PPI). However, standard transfer functions must be adapted to unlock this potential, and this adaptation must be done carefully to maintain normal cursor behavior.

Taking the user into account

Having a device with a high sensitivity does not necessarily mean one can fully take advantage of it: users' capabilities and limitations should also be taken into account. As noted above, Bérard et al. found the *Device's Human Resolution* ($\text{RES}_{\text{human}}$) for mice to be in the range of 700 - 1400 CPI [4]. Devices with a sensitivity ($\text{RES}_{\text{input}}$) below $\text{RES}_{\text{human}}$ are not accurate enough to capture fine movements in motor space. But at the same time, users are not likely to benefit from higher sensitivities. We can thus define the *useful resolution* ($\text{RES}_{\text{useful}}$, in CPI) of a device and *epsilon* (ε, in inches), the smallest measurable displacement one can produce with it:

$$\text{RES}_{\text{useful}} = \min\left(\text{RES}_{\text{input}}, \text{RES}_{\text{human}}\right) \qquad (1)$$

$$\varepsilon = \frac{1}{\text{RES}_{\text{useful}}} \qquad (2)$$

Considering the current unitless gain applied by the pointing transfer function (G), we can calculate the number of practicable subpixels (S) as:

$$S = \frac{1}{\text{RES}_{\text{screen}}} \times \frac{\text{RES}_{\text{useful}}}{G} \qquad (3)$$

where $\text{RES}_{\text{screen}}$ denotes the pixel density of the display (in PPI). S is actually the number of *epsilons* required to move from one pixel to another. Note that S necessarily varies over time since G is dynamic (speed-dependent, based on user movements). Note also that the highest S value $S_{\max}$ corresponds to the lowest gain level $G_{\min}$.

Adapting the transfer function

Modern pointing transfer functions are discrete, speed-dependent, and were generally designed for a 400 CPI mouse sampled at 125 Hz and a 96 PPI display refreshed at 60 Hz [5]. They typically produce gain values between 0.8 and 4.1 for motor speeds under 2.5 $cm.s^{-1}$ and then smoothly transition from these values to high ones at high speeds. Figure 4 shows a sample sigmoid function producing gain values in the same range for a particular hardware configuration. Assuming $\text{RES}_{\text{human}}$ = 1000 CPI and applying Equation 3 to $G_{\min} = 1.0$, this function would provide access to $S_{\max} \approx 11$ subpixels. But what if this was not enough?

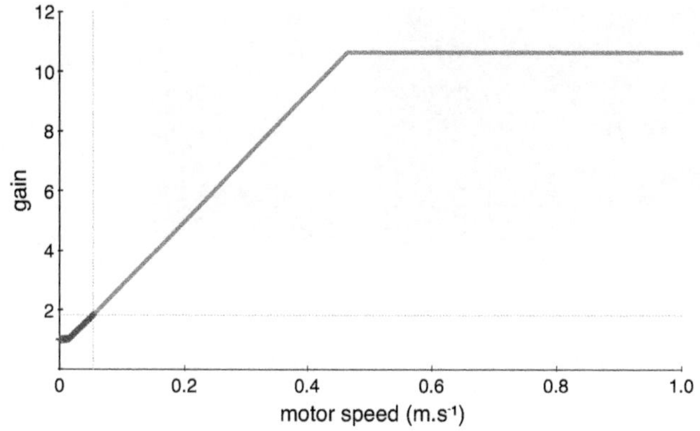

Figure 4: Sample sigmoid transfer function. The plot was made considering a 4000 CPI mouse sampled at 500 Hz and a 90 PPI display refreshed at 60 Hz. Green crosses indicate the 22 gain levels that generate subpixel motion.

We can determine the optimal gain G_{opt} which provides enough subpixels to select among all model elements with cardinality N given P pixels of screen space:

$$G_{opt} = \frac{P}{\text{RES}_{screen}} \times \frac{\text{RES}_{useful}}{N} \quad (4)$$

From this equation, it can be seen that when $P < N$ (i.e. $G_{opt} < \text{RES}_{useful} / \text{RES}_{screen}$) subpixels are beneficial. For example, using the video durations in Table 1 with RES_{useful} = 1000 CPI and RES_{screen} = 90 PPI, a one second accuracy in the QuickTime Player corresponds to a G_{opt} of 1.121 for the TV show, 0.648 for the generic movie, 0.245 for *Gone with the Wind*, and 0.134 for *Bergensbanen*. If we compare these numbers to the gain values in Figure 4, we see that the function should work for the TV show as-is (the corresponding G_{opt} is higher than G_{min}), but not the other videos. Achieving frame accuracy is even more challenging. Assuming a frame rate of 30 fps, G_{opt} values are much lower (0.037, 0.022, 0.008, and 0.004). In order to approach these optimum gain levels, we need a strategy for function adaptation.

To maintain normal pointer behavior, we alter an existing transfer function so that it produces G_{opt} at low speeds. Specifically, we calculate V_{min}, the minimum speed in meters-per-second on which the transfer function operates, and V_{use}, the speed associated with RES_{useful}:

$$V_{min} = \frac{0.0254}{\text{RES}_{input}} \times \text{FREQ}_{input} \quad (5)$$

$$V_{use} = \frac{0.0254}{\text{RES}_{useful}} \times \text{FREQ}_{input} \quad (6)$$

where FREQ_{input} is the frequency of the pointing device. Since there is no guarantee that people can actually move the device at such a slow speed like V_{min}, we maintain the G_{opt} value for all speeds under at least V_{use}. To maintain normal pointer behavior, we smoothly transition between this point (V_{use}, G_{opt}) and the point where the function starts producing motions of 1 pixel or more (V_{pix}, G_{pix}). Note that like G_{min} and unlike V_{min} and V_{use}, the values of V_{pix} and G_{pix} depend on the function definition.

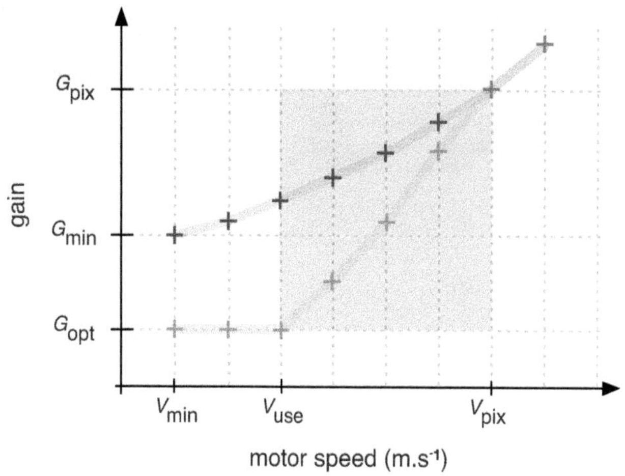

Figure 5: Closeup of the low-speed domain of a transfer function adapted to a particular model. Green and blue crosses show the original gains (subpixel & pixel). Yellow crosses show a possible adaptation.

Figure 5 shows a closeup of the low-speed domain for a hypothetical transfer function that one might want to adapt. The blue crosses show the points of the original function that produce pixel motions, the green ones subpixel motions. The yellow crosses illustrate a possible interpolation between (V_{use}, G_{opt}) and (V_{pix}, G_{pix}). The distance between V_{use} and V_{pix}, the one between G_{opt} and G_{pix}, and FREQ_{input} constrain the interpolation. One needs enough speed steps (n_{steps}, Equation 7) to keep a reasonable distance between interpolated gain levels to reduce the risk of overshooting. At the same time, one does not want to alter the gain values corresponding to pixel motions since this would result in a possibly perceivable modification of the pointer behavior. Note that in a worse-case scenario, there may be no subpixel speed/gain combination (i.e. green cross) in the original function.

$$n_{steps} = \frac{V_{pix} - V_{use}}{V_{min}} \quad (7)$$

In the next section, we provide concrete examples of how this method can be applied to adapt a transfer function to a particular model, taking into account device and human capabilities.

ILLUSTRATIVE EXAMPLES

To create illustrative examples of subpixel interaction (Figure 6), we developed a cross platform software application written in C++ that runs subpixel-enabled applications through the WebKit browser engine. We used libpointing [5] to get raw information from devices, apply transfer functions taking into account hardware characteristics (input and output resolutions and frequencies) as well as DHR, and access remainders to produce floating pointer coordinates to control a custom pointer.

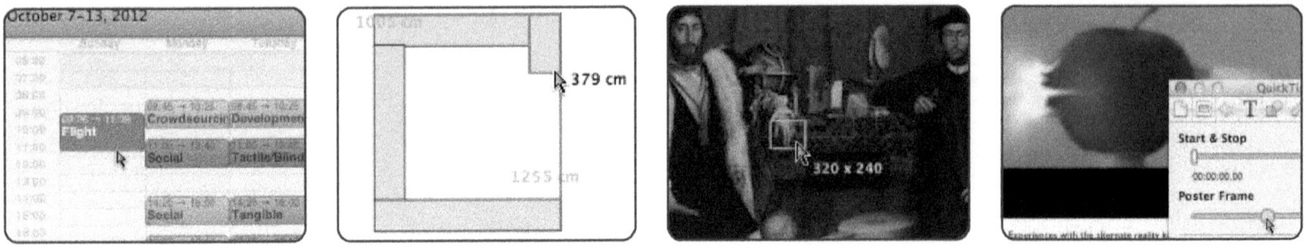

(a) (b) (c) (d)

Figure 6: Illustrative subpixel interaction applications: (a) manipulating calendar events with minute precision; (b) precise CAD object dimensioning; (c) image pixel accurate cropping; (d) selecting one frame of a video.

We used a sigmoid transfer function, similar to Figure 4 which is representative of transfer functions used by modern operating systems. Equation 8 describes this function which we refer to as F_G. It produces unitless gain values between 1.0 and 10.0, where dX represents a relative distance measured in motor space (in meters), dt is the elapsed time since the last input event (in seconds), $v = dX/dt$, and v_1 and v_2 are equal to 0.15 $m.s^{-1}$ and 0.5 $m.s^{-1}$ respectively. Thus, $F(dX,dt) = dX \times F_G(dX,dt)$ is the transfer function used by default to control the pointer.

$$F_G(dX,dt) = \begin{cases} 1 & : v \leq v_1 \\ 1 + 9 \times \frac{v - v_1}{v_2 - v_1} & : v \in]v_1; v_2[\\ 10 & : v \geq v_2 \end{cases} \quad (8)$$

When interacting with an object, we first compute G_{opt} as defined by Equation 4. If G_{opt} is below the minimal gain value defined by Equation 8 ($F_G(dX,dt) = 1$), then the transfer function is blended with G_{opt} to yield the function $H(dX,dt) = dX \times H_G(dX,dt)$, where H_G is described by Equation 9:

$$H_G(dX,dt) = \begin{cases} G_{opt} & : v \leq V_{use} \\ F_G(dX,dt) & : v > V_{pix} \\ (1-q)G_{opt} + q\, F_G(dX,dt) & : \text{elsewhere} \end{cases} \quad (9)$$

$$q = \frac{v - V_{use}}{V_{pix} - V_{use}}$$

We used a 22" Dell 2208WFP display set to its native resolution of 1680×1050 at 60 Hz, providing a pixel density of about 90 PPI. Our input device was a Microsoft Sidewinder X8 mouse with a 500 Hz polling rate. The mouse sensitivity was set to 4000 CPI, corresponding to its maximum configurable value. We fixed $RES_{useful} = 1000$ CPI. Combined with our particular transfer function, this configuration leads to the following values:

$$S_{max} \approx 11 \text{ for } G_{min} = 1.0$$
$$V_{use} = 0.0127 m.s^{-1}$$
$$G_{pix} = 1.0$$
$$V_{pix} = \frac{0.0254}{RES_{screen}} \times \frac{1.0}{G_{pix}} \times FREQ_{input} \approx 0.141 m.s^{-1}$$

$V_{pix}/V_{min} \approx 44$ discrete speed values below V_{pix} are available for subpixel interaction and transfer function blending.

Calendar

It is often convenient to enter and modify calendar events using direct manipulation. Depending on the number of hours in the current view, it may not be possible to set event times like flight or train departures requiring one minute precision: a height of 720 pixels is needed for a 12 hour view and 1080 pixels for 18 hours. These heights may exceed typical calendar window space. For example, an 18 hour view represented in a 400 pixel window requires a modest 2.7 subpixels for one minute precision. With subpixel input, it is even possible to represent a month view while still enabling individual event manipulation to the minute. The calendar application we created represents 17 hours in 272 pixels, yielding 16 pixels per hour (Figure 6a). With our particular setup, this view requires 3.75 subpixels, which our transfer function F_G provides. For subpixel feedback, start and end times are shown on each calendar event.

Computer-aided design

Computer-aided design (CAD) applications require precise specification of object dimensions and placement. Direct manipulation is preferable given the graphical nature of the task, but to achieve the required precision, current applications resort to text entry or zooming. Precise feedback is often shown already as a numerical measurement near the manipulated object, but with subpixel input, the manipulation can be made equally precise. We developed a small subset of an architectural CAD application where it is possible to dimension and position walls with one centimeter precision while maintaining a view of the entire structure. For example, consider a room plan where three walls are already drawn, and a fourth vertical wall of length 2205 cm must be created and aligned exactly. The whole drawing is viewed at a scale which maps 10 cm to 1 pixel (i.e. $1:354$). Here 10 subpixels are required to perform the task with required precision (1 cm), which our transfer function F_G again provides.

Cropping a high resolution image

Many digital cameras capture images exceeding 10 megapixels, yet most computer displays cannot show more than 2.5 megapixels. Cropping such an image to specific dimensions, say 320 by 240 pixels, usually requires zooming. The crop area can be so large that multiple zoom and pan operations are required making the task difficult. For example, consider a 17.8 megapixel image measuring 4215 by 4215 pixels. To show this entire image in a 300 by 300 pixel window, it must be scaled to 7% where one display pixel corresponds to 14 image pixels. To achieve image pixel precision, 14 subpixels are required. Since this is more than S_{max}, we need to switch from F_G to H_G (Equation 9) with $G_{opt} \approx 0.794$ (Equation 4). To facilitate subpixel output, a tooltip shows image-space coordinates for the subpixel pointer and image-space size of cropping rectangle (Figure 6c). When cropping according to visual details, lens-like feedback would be more appropriate.

Selecting a frame in a video

We replicated the Apple Keynote video interface where a 198 pixel wide slider is used to select a single "*Poster Frame*" (Figure 6d). As an example, consider the TV show in Table 1. At 30 frames-per-second, one pixel of the slider corresponds to $52 \times 60 \times 30/198 = 472.72$ frames (i.e. 15.75 s) in the video. To achieve frame-level precision, 473 subpixels are required: we again need to switch from F_G to H_G (Equation 9), this time with $G_{opt} \approx 0.023$ (Equation 4). We informally tested this scenario with several participants. In spite of the low value for G_{opt}, all managed to comfortably reach the intended frame and no one spontaneously noted any change in pointer behavior. Note that selecting one frame in this scenario corresponds to a 16.51 bit pointing task.

The strategies described in the above examples are specific to the transfer function F_G and the particular hardware configuration that we used. Had we used the same monitor with a low-end mouse (400 CPI, 125 Hz) and the default transfer function of Windows, OS X, or Xorg, S_{max} would have been less than 4. In all cases except the simplest Calendar example, it would have been necessary to switch from F_G to H_G.

DISCUSSION

In this section we provide guidelines for applying subpixel in generalized data manipulation situations and enumerate modifications which must be made to current operating systems and GUI toolkits.

Domain of applicability for subpixel interaction

There are three parameters which determine the applicability of a subpixel-enabled floating pointer and custom transfer functions: the number of available pixels (P); the number of practicable subpixels (S, from Equation 3); and the cardinality of the underlying model (N). Using these we can define two critical values for N: $N1 = S \times P$, the value above which custom transfer functions must be used to reach all values of the model; and $N2$, the value above which custom transfer functions can no longer operate due to usability issues. These determine four zones (illustrated in Figure 7):

- $N \leq P$: all values of the model can be addressed with a standard integer pointer, subpixel interaction is unnecessary but compatible;
- $P < N \leq N1$: all values of the model can only be addressed with subpixel interaction, but a standard transfer function is compatible without any change in pointer behavior;
- $N1 < N \leq N2$: to address all model values with subpixel interaction, a custom transfer function like those described earlier is required;
- $N > N2$: all model values cannot be addressed with subpixel interaction.

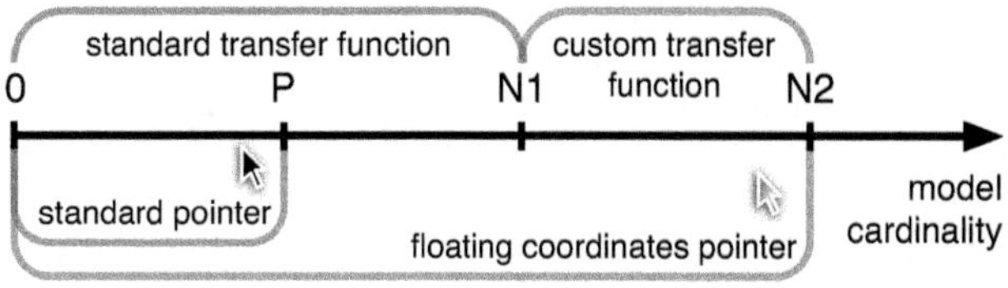

Figure 7: Four zones of applicability for subpixel and custom transfer functions (see text for description).

While N1 is unequivocally specified, N2 is harder to define. As model cardinality increases, G_{opt} decreases but the number of discrete speed steps available to interpolate between (V_{use}, G_{opt}) and (V_{pix}, G_{pix}) remains the same (n_{steps}, Equation 7). For the custom transfer function to remain usable, it must remain gradual. No matter the definition we might choose for this property, there will always be a point where n_{steps} is not enough to preserve it within $[V_{use}, V_{pix}]$. Extending the custom range over V_{pix} might also help, but it will undoubtedly result in a perceivable modification of the pointer behavior after some point. N2 captures this inevitable fact: for a given user and hardware configuration, there will always be an upper limit on the model cardinality that can be smoothly supported while preserving the standard pointer behavior. Note that using devices with higher sensitivity and frequency is the easiest way to push that limit since it reduces V_{min} which increases the number of discrete speed steps available for interpolation.

Impact on operating systems and GUI frameworks

As stated above, our subpixel prototypes were implemented using libpointing [5] to create a custom transfer function taking into account actual input device CPI and screen PPI. We also took into account human precision capabilities (DHR) and the cardinality of the model being manipulated to adjust the transfer function when required[4].

To support subpixel floating point coordinates universally, operating systems and GUI frameworks need to make relatively small, but fundamental changes. First, system transfer functions must take into account input device sensitivity so that higher device sensitivities result in higher precision. Currently, operating systems generally translate higher device sensitivity to faster pointer movements either because they do not take the sensitivity information into account or because it is not provided by the device [5]. Device configuration interfaces definitely need to be re-designed.

[4]Basic source code to create a subpixel libpointing application is available from `http://libpointing.org/`

Operating systems then need to use the remainders stored between two input events to create floating point coordinates. These subpixel coordinates would be dispatched by the windowing system, and ultimately received by the GUI framework. Framework event loops, methods, callback methods, etc. also need to be updated to handle floating point coordinates.

GUI frameworks also need to provide developers with a way to take into account human limb resolution directly or, even better, indirectly. Ideally, a developer would specify model cardinality and the framework would alter the transfer function used when a subpixel widget is manipulated. This also requires that operating system transfer functions can be changed dynamically, which is already achievable to some extent on some systems. Frameworks with dynamic layout capabilities can also adjust the size of widgets, making a subpixel enabled slider smaller without sacrificing precise control of the underlying data. For example, the preferred size of a slider would correspond to $N1$, and the minimal size of a widget would correspond to $N2$.

Since limb resolution varies between individuals [4], the operating system should provide a method to specify the current user's level of limb precision. This could be part of the input device settings with default values set conservatively based on the literature. Ideally, a simple calibration step would tune this value to specific individual, perhaps using a game-like procedure [6] rather than a dry experiment task like Bérard et al. [4]. Since human resolution can improve with practice, the calibration process should be updated intermittently, or automatically adapted over time based on patterns of use – like the strategy of adjusting the offset distance in the Shift pointing technique [13].

CONCLUSION AND FUTURE WORK

Subpixel interaction is a fundamental way to increase direct manipulation accuracy. For too long, positional input has been artificially constrained by design decisions made when input devices were about as accurate as the pixel density of a display. Now that input device sensitivity far surpasses display capabilities, the subpixel methods, transfer functions, and guidelines described above can enable interaction at a level of precision bounded only by human capability. Best of all, subpixel interaction does not change the way people interact, remains compatible with other precision techniques like ZUIs and Focus+Context, and would only require moderate changes to current operating systems and toolkits.

Our focus so far has been to enable subpixel interaction, but there is future work to extend its application context and test the potential benefit in actual settings. For example, formal testing of subpixel-enabled interfaces with realistic direct manipulation scenarios, experimental analysis examining the trade-off between pure subpixel interaction and subpixel interaction augmented by traditional precision techniques like ZUIs and Focus+Context, and investigating subpixel applications to very sensitive absolute touchscreens. There is also opportunity to extend the work of Bérard et al. [4] by measuring DHR with a wider range of devices and a broader range of participants. This will add even more substance to the overarching subpixel philosophy: pixels may be the limit of what we can see, but they should not limit what we can do.

REFERENCES

1. C. Ahlberg and B. Shneiderman. The alphaslider: a compact and rapid selector. *Proceedings of CHI'94*, 365–371. ACM, 1994.
2. C. Appert, O. Chapuis, and E. Pietriga. High-precision magnification lenses. *Proceedings of CHI'10*, 273–282. ACM, 2010.
3. Y. Ayatsuka, J. Rekimoto, and S. Matsuoka. Popup vernier: a tool for sub-pixel-pitch dragging with smooth mode transition. *Proceedings of UIST'98*, 39–48. ACM, 1998.
4. F. Bérard, G. Wang, and J. R. Cooperstock. On the limits of the human motor control precision: the search for a device's human resolution. *Proceedings of INTERACT'11*, 107–122. Springer-Verlag, 2011.
5. G. Casiez and N. Roussel. No more bricolage! Methods and tools to characterize, replicate and compare pointing transfer functions. *Proceedings of UIST'11*, 603–614. ACM, Oct. 2011.
6. D. R. Flatla, C. Gutwin, L. E. Nacke, S. Bateman, and R. L. Mandryk. Calibration games: making calibration tasks enjoyable by adding motivating game elements. *Proceedings of UIST'11*, 403–412. ACM, 2011.
7. Y. Guiard, M. Beaudouin-Lafon, and D. Mottet. Navigation as multiscale pointing: extending fitts' model to very high precision tasks. *Proceedings of CHI'99*, 450–457. ACM, 1999.
8. K. Perlin and D. Fox. Pad: an alternative approach to the computer interface. *Proceedings of SIGGRAPH'93*, 57–64. ACM, 1993.
9. E. Pietriga and C. Appert. Sigma lenses: focus-context transitions combining space, time and translucence. *Proceedings of CHI'08*, 1343–1352. ACM, 2008.
10. G. Ramos and R. Balakrishnan. Zliding: fluid zooming and sliding for high precision parameter manipulation. *Proceedings of UIST'05*, 143–152. ACM, 2005.
11. V. Scheib. Pointer lock. W3C Editor's draft, Web Applications Working Group, Apr. 2012.
12. B. Shneiderman. The eyes have it: a task by data type taxonomy for information visualizations. *Proceedings of VL'96*, 336–343. IEEE Computer Society, 1996.
13. D. Vogel and P. Baudisch. Shift: a technique for operating pen-based interfaces using touch. *Proceedings of CHI'07*, 657–666. ACM, 2007.

UnderScore: Musical Underlays for Audio Stories

Steve Rubin* **Floraine Berthouzoz*** **Gautham J. Mysore†** **Wilmot Li†** **Maneesh Agrawala***
*University of California, Berkeley
{srubin,floraine,maneesh}@cs.berkeley.edu
†Advanced Technology Labs, Adobe
{gmysore,wilmotli}@adobe.com

ABSTRACT
Audio producers often use *musical underlays* to emphasize key moments in spoken content and give listeners time to reflect on what was said. Yet, creating such underlays is time-consuming as producers must carefully (1) mark an emphasis point in the speech (2) select music with the appropriate style, (3) align the music with the emphasis point, and (4) adjust dynamics to produce a harmonious composition. We present UnderScore, a set of semi-automated tools designed to facilitate the creation of such underlays. The producer simply marks an emphasis point in the speech and selects a music track. UnderScore automatically refines, aligns and adjusts the speech and music to generate a high-quality underlay. UnderScore allows producers to focus on the high-level design of the underlay; they can quickly try out a variety of music and test different points of emphasis in the story. Amateur producers, who may lack the time or skills necessary to author underlays, can quickly add music to their stories. An informal evaluation of UnderScore suggests that it can produce high-quality underlays for a variety of examples while significantly reducing the time and effort required of radio producers.

Author Keywords
Radio; music; audio editing; storytelling.

ACM Classification Keywords
H.5.2. [Information Interfaces and Presentation]: User Interfaces - Graphical user interfaces (GUI)

INTRODUCTION
Radio shows, podcasts and audiobooks often use music to emphasize key moments in the spoken content. One common technique is to create a *musical underlay*, which fades in music before the *emphasis point* in the speech, then pauses the speech while the *music solo* plays at full volume, and finally fades out the music as the speech resumes (Figure 1). Professional radio producers use such underlays to enhance the mood of the story and to give listeners time to reflect on the key moment in the speech [3, 4].

Creating an underlay involves four main steps: (1) marking the emphasis point in the speech, (2) selecting music with the appropriate style, mood, tempo, etc., (3) aligning the music solo with the emphasis point, and (4) adjusting the dynamics to achieve a harmonious composition of music and speech (Figure 1). Each of these steps can be time-consuming as producers must carefully refine the timing, alignment and dynamics to generate a high-quality underlay. Moreover, producers often try out several underlay compositions using different music before settling on the best one.

UIST'12, October 7–10, 2012, Cambridge, Massachusetts, USA.

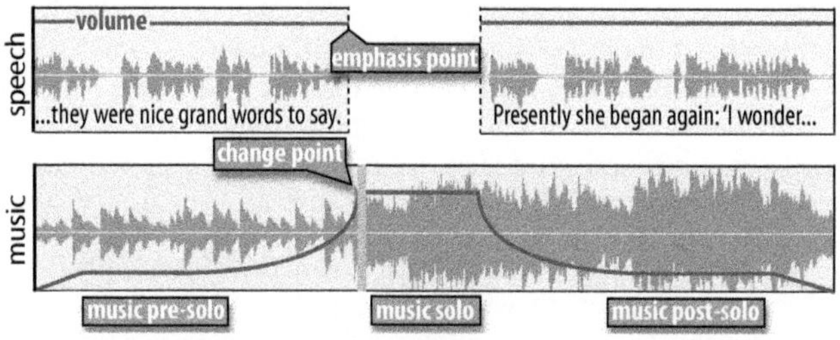

Figure 1. A musical underlay highlights an *emphasis point* in an audio story. The music track contains three segments; (1) a *music pre-solo* that fades in before the emphasis point, (2) a *music solo* that starts at the emphasis point and plays at full volume while the speech is paused, and (3) a music post-solo that fades down as the speech resumes. At the beginning of the solo, the music often changes in some significant way (e.g. a melody enters, the tempo quickens, etc.) Aligning this *change point* in the music with a pause in speech and a rapid increase in the music volume further draws attention to the emphasis point in the story.

We have studied a variety of radio programs [2, 5, 23] and publications on radio production [1, 3, 4, 9, 22] to identify the properties of high-quality underlays. We find that the most effective underlays often introduce a significant change in the music (e.g. in melody, tempo, etc.) at the emphasis point in the speech to further draw attention to that point and underline the emotional tone of the story. This *change point* in the music marks the beginning of the solo. In addition, audio producers carefully adjust the dynamics (volume) of the music to further emphasize the change point while ensuring that it does not interfere with the speech.

In this paper we present UnderScore, a semi-automated system for adding musical underlays to audio stories. To create an underlay the producer simply marks an emphasis point in the speech and selects a music track. UnderScore then applies a sequence of tools that automatically refine the emphasis point, select a suitable change point in the music, align the music with the speech and adjust the dynamics of the composition. The resulting underlay appears in a timeline-based audio editing interface that allows the producer to further tweak any aspect of the underlay as necessary.

UnderScore allows producers to focus on the high-level design of the underlay; they can quickly try out a variety of music and test what it sounds like to emphasize different points in the story. Our automated tools handle the time-consuming, low-level details of aligning the tracks and adjusting their dynamics. Such automation allows amateur producers, who may not have the time or skills to author underlays from scratch, to quickly add music to their stories.

However, our automated results cannot always match the audio quality of underlays created by expert producers. Thus, UnderScore also offers a user-in-the-loop mode in which producers can manually apply each of our underlay tools and immediately decide if the results are acceptable. The producer can always tweak or undo the results of our tools. This mode allows advanced producers to exercise finer-grained control over the design of the underlay.

We demonstrate the effectiveness of UnderScore with an informal evaluation in which three independent experts rated the timing, dynamics and overall quality of our automatically generated underlays. For both timing and dynamics, the vast majority of ratings (89% or more) indicated little or no perceived problems in the underlay, and for overall quality, 86% of the ratings indicated satisfaction with the results (3 or higher on a 5 point Likert scale). We also interviewed both amateur and expert producers who indicated that UnderScore addresses both challenging and time-consuming parts of the editing process. These results suggest that our tools can produce high-quality underlays for a variety of examples while significantly reducing the time and effort required of audio producers.

RELATED WORK

Audio researchers have developed algorithms and interaction techniques to help users edit and compose audio files. Although none of these methods are designed to facilitate the production of audio stories, we consider the set of interfaces and techniques most relevant to our work.

Researchers have developed a variety of low-level techniques to help professional producers edit speech and music recordings [26]. Many of these methods, including automatic dynamics adjustment [11] and noise reduction [12], were introduced several decades ago and have since become standard tools in commercial audio editing software such as ProTools and Adobe Audition. While these tools can help improve the quality of the speech and music tracks in an audio story, they do not directly address the higher level challenge of how to compose these tracks into musical underlays. Thus, we view this existing research as complementary to our work.

Other audio researchers have focused on methods to segment audio into semantically meaningful constructs such as verse/chorus or speech/music [7, 21, 24, 27, 30]. These techniques typically model the global characteristics of each segment and then use the model to detect the transition points between segments. Our system also identifies change points in the song that can then be aligned with the emphasis point in the spoken content. However, we target more localized changes in features such as volume or timbre. Thus, our approach does not require sophisticated models and can instead use a local windowing approach.

The most relevant previous work investigates user interfaces and interaction techniques that simplify various audio editing workflows. Much of this research focuses on the task of creating music and proposes graphical representations [19, 36] and tangible multitouch interfaces [8, 10, 13, 31] that support music composition and live performance. Other researchers have developed tools that leverage metadata and structure (either from automatic audio analysis or manual tagging) to enable users to edit speech and music at a more semantic level (e.g., editing speech via transcripts [15], mixing and matching multiple takes from a recording session [16, 20]) rather than directly working with waveforms or spectrograms. There has also been previous work that supports vocalized user input for selecting specific sounds in audio mixtures [34] and for creating musical accompaniments to vocal melodies [33]. Most of this research adopts the general strategy of identifying the requirements and constraints of specific audio editing tasks in order to design user interfaces that expose only the most relevant parameters or interaction methods to the user. We follow a similar strategy for the task of creating musical underlays.

DESIGN GUIDELINES FOR MUSICAL UNDERLAYS

In developing UnderScore, we follow the approach of Agrawala et al. [6] and first identify a set of design guidelines for creating high-quality musical underlays. We draw on publications describing the best practices of radio production [1, 3, 4, 9, 22] and analyze high-quality radio programs [2, 5, 23] in order to extract guidelines for each step of the underlay creation process.

Marking speech emphasis points. Audio stories usually include a few important segments that present the central ideas, introduce new characters, or set the mood. Producers often emphasize the endpoints of these segments with an underlay. A short break in the speech allows listeners to process the content of the story and can separate long passages into shorter chunks that are easier to understand [3].

Selecting music. Music serves several functions in an underlay. It augments the emotional content of the story and often builds tension leading up to the emphasis point in the story [4]. The music usually exhibits a significant change at the emphasis point to further draw the listener's attention. This change point can correspond to a melody entering, the tempo quickening, new instrumentation beginning, or a strong downbeat [3].

Aligning music and speech. Aligning music to speech requires choosing the entry and exit points of the music, positioning the change point in the music with respect to the emphasis point in the speech and determining the length of the music solo. The entry point of the music pre-solo often corresponds with a rising action or change of tone in the speech. Abel and Glass [3] suggest that the pre-solo should start 12 seconds before the emphasis point in the speech. The change point in the music usually appears slightly after the emphasis point in the speech. This gap ensures that the change in music does not interfere with the speech and can add to the dramatic effect of the change in music. Finally, Abel and Glass suggest that the music solo should last about 6 seconds before the speech resumes. The length of the music post-solo

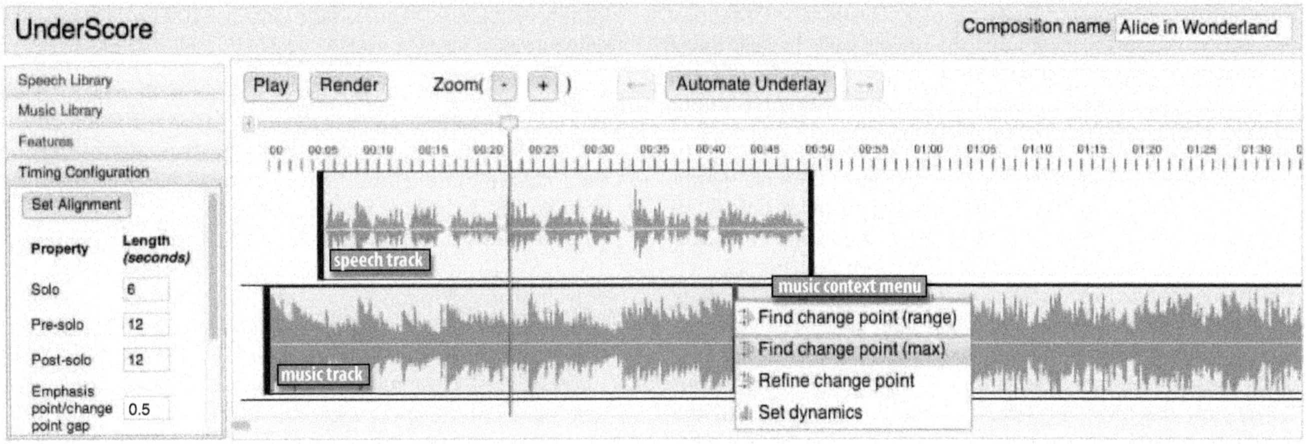

Figure 2. UnderScore is a semi-automated system for adding musical underlays to audio stories. It includes a multitrack timeline-based editor with context menus that provide tools to automate different steps of the underlay creation process. The timing configuration menu allows users to set lengths of the music pre-solo, solo, and post-solo segments to be used in automatic alignment.

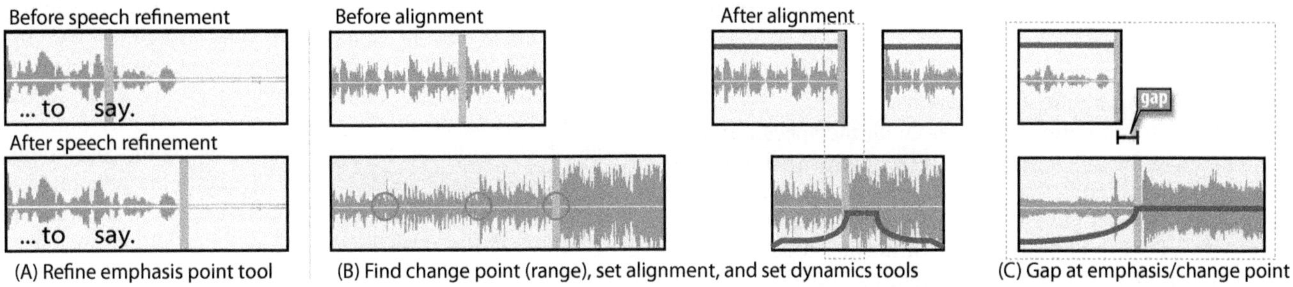

Figure 3. Tools for automating underlay creation. The refine emphasis point tool (A) adjusts a coarsely marked emphasis point in the speech to avoid speech clipping and excessive trailing silence. The find change point (range) tool (B, before) indicates the strongest change points in the music with red circles. The set alignment tool aligns the change point in the music with the emphasis point in the speech and sets the lengths of the audio segments. The set dynamics tool then adjusts the dynamics to ensure that both the music and the speech remain audible. The set alignment tool ensures that there is a small gap between the emphasis point in the speech and the change point in the music, while the set dynamics tool rapidly increases the volume of the music in this gap.

is less consistent. In some cases the end of the music signals another emphasis point in the speech.

Adjusting dynamics. The goal of adjusting the underlay dynamics is to further heighten the impact of the change point in the music while ensuring that the speech is clearly audible. During the pre-solo the music plays softly, gradually increasing in volume. Near the emphasis point the volume quickly increases and reaches its maximum at the change point in the music to create a strong auditory transition. Finally, just before the speech resumes the music quickly fades down for the post-solo.

AUDIO EDITING INTERFACE

Our audio editing interface (Figure 2) offers a set of tools designed to streamline the process of creating musical underlays and transitions. We first describe these tools in the context of a typical editing session for an audio story (Figure 3). We then present the algorithms underlying these tools in the section on Algorithmic Methods.

Step 1: Marking Speech Emphasis Points

The first step in creating an underlay is to select a speech track and mark an emphasis point in the speech. In our example, the producer selects a reading from Alice in Wonderland [14] from the speech library and inserts a mark after the phrase "but thought that they were nice grand words to say" (Figure 3A). Although audio tracks are usually sampled at 44.1 kHz, producers typically work with tracks at the granularity of seconds. At this coarse granularity the mark is often slightly too early and the speech is clipped or slightly too late, which adds a trailing silence to the speech. To mark the speech accurately, the producer can manually zoom in on the waveform to work at finer granularity and then carefully find the end of the sentence.

UnderScore provides a *refine emphasis point tool* that automates this process. The producer accesses this tool through the right-click context menu of the speech track and it automatically shifts the producer's coarse granularity mark to a nearby point that does not clip the speech and minimizes trailing silence (Figure 3A). This tool allows producers to roughly mark the emphasis point without worrying about its sub-second accuracy.

Step 2: Selecting Music

The producer next selects a track from the music library that is stylistically appropriate for the speech and contains a significant change point. Here he picks Damiak's "Tenuous Gears." If the producer knows the music well, he can manually mark the change point and then use UnderScore's *refine change point tool* to automatically shift the mark to the strongest change point within a small range.

If the producer is less familiar with the music, he can apply UnderScore's *find change point (range) tool* which scores the strength of the change at each point in the music and indicates the strongest change points with red circles (Figure 3B). The producer can then listen to each of these potential change points and select the best one, rather than laboriously searching for the best change point throughout the entire song. UnderScore also includes the fully automated *find change point (max) tool* that directly selects the highest scoring change point. This tool further reduces the time required to select the change point. However our fully automated tool may not always find the perfect change point, and in these cases the producer can always use the range tool or manual approach. All of these tools appear in the right-click context menu of the music track.

Step 3: Aligning Music and Speech

The third step is to align the music with the speech and set the lengths of the audio segments. Like many timeline-based interfaces UnderScore allows producers to manually translate audio segments, set the endpoints of a segment and split segments, by clicking and dragging. In manual mode the producer first translates the music so that the change point appears just after the emphasis point in the speech. The small gap between the emphasis point and the change point reduces interference between the music and speech (Figure 3C). UnderScore facilitates this manual alignment process by snapping the change point in place when it is close to the emphasis point. The producer then chooses the lengths of the music pre-solo, solo and post-solo by dragging the endpoints of the music. Finally the producer splits and separates the speech at the emphasis point to create the pause that is filled by the music solo.

UnderScore also provides a *set alignment tool* that automatically performs each of these adjustments. This tool uses default lengths of 6 seconds for the music solo, 12 seconds for both the pre- and post-solo, and 500 ms for the gap between the emphasis and change points. The producer can adjust these default values in the *timing configuration menu*. The resulting underlay segments also appear in the timeline and the producer can further tweak them if necessary.

Step 4: Adjusting Dynamics

To adjust the dynamics the producer can manually set the volume at keyframes within an audio segment and interpolate between them using either a linear or exponential volume transition. In our example (Figure 3B), the producer uses a short linear fade-in at the start of the pre-solo, and then applies an exponential transition so that the music gradually increases in volume at first and then rapidly reaches its maximum at the music change point. Figure 3C shows that the rapid increase in volume falls primarily in the gap between the emphasis point in speech and the change point in music. The producer similarly creates a quick fade-out just before the speech resumes.

UnderScore provides two automated tools that facilitate setting the dynamics. The *set dynamics tool* automatically sets the key frames and volume transitions to create the exponential fades in our example. In some cases large differences in volume levels between the music and speech make it difficult to build a transition in which both tracks remain audible. The *refine dynamics tool* automatically adjusts the overall energy (perceived loudness) of the music and speech to ensure that they fall within a similar range. This tool often improves the clarity of the music when it softly enters during the pre-solo. Both of these tools are available in the right-click context menus of the speech and music tracks.

Automation and Iteration

In each step of the underlay creation process, UnderScore gives producers the option of doing the task manually or leveraging tools that automate the task. This flexibility allows our system to support two main usage modes. In the user-in-the-loop mode, the producer can apply a tool and then manually tweak the results using UnderScore's timeline interface. This mode allows producers to seamlessly jump back-and-forth between using our automated tools and manually exercising finer-grained control. UnderScore also provides a batch mode in which the producer simply marks the emphasis point in the speech and selects one or more music tracks. UnderScore then automatically applies our tools in sequence (refine emphasis point, find change point, set alignment and timing, and set dynamics) to generate an underlay for each selected music track.

Based on informal user feedback (see Results section), we have found that the fully automated batch mode results are often of sufficiently high quality to be used directly (i.e., without any further refinement) by amateur producers. Thus, UnderScore's batch mode gives amateurs a quick and easy way to create underlays without requiring much expertise. Expert producers can also use the batch mode to rapidly iterate through underlays spanning several songs and multiple change points within those songs. These experts can either use our automated results as-is, or treat them as a starting point for further adjustments using our user-in-the-loop mode. In this way, UnderScore provides workflows for both amateurs and experts to create high quality underlays.

ALGORITHMIC METHODS

UnderScore relies on a variety of audio analysis algorithms to facilitate underlay creation. Audio analysis is a well studied area [29] and the algorithms typically operate on features that capture specific properties of music and speech such as volume, harmonic content, and timbre. The features are usually computed on standard 44.1 kHz pulse code modulated (PCM) wave files with their left and right channels summed together. Our tools use the following features:

RMS energy. We measure the perceived loudness of speech and music using root mean squared (RMS) energy, which is defined as $\sqrt{(\sum_n x_i^2)/n}$ where x_i is the value of the ith audio sample in a window of size n.

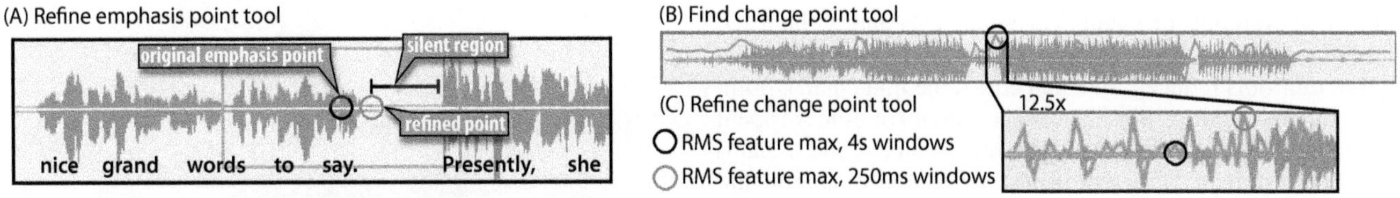

Figure 4. **(A) To refine an emphasis point in speech, our system finds the longest region of silence in a 1 second window centered at the marked emphasis point. It then refines the point to the beginning of that silent region. To generate rough music change point estimations, our system finds the maxima of the RMS energy feature using 4 second subwindows that overlap by 50% and span the entire music track (B). To refine a change point, our system applies the same approach but with 250 ms subwindows that span an 8 second window about the coarse point (C). This two step process first large scale changes in volume and then find the strongest downbeat at the local scale.**

Chroma. We measure the harmonic content of music using chroma vectors [35], which are the projection of the time-frequency spectrum of a song onto the twelve semitones of the chromatic scale ($C, C^\sharp, B^\flat, \ldots$). We use the implementation of Ellis [18].

MFCCs. We measure the timbre of music (which often correlates with instrumentation) by computing its mel frequency cepstral coefficients (MFCCs) as described by Logan et al. [25].

While many of our tools depend on RMS energy, we have found that chroma and MFCCs are useful for finding change points.

Refine Emphasis Point Tool

The refine emphasis point tool is designed to move a coarsely marked emphasis point in the speech to the start of a nearby silent region (Figure 4A). To find this region, we consider a 1 second window centered at the coarsely marked emphasis point. We divide this window into 62.5 ms subwindows with 50% overlap and then compute the RMS energy of each one. We then find the longest span of subwindows whose energies all fall within 10% of the minimum energy of any subwindow.

Refine Change Point Tool

The refine change point tool adjusts a coarsely-marked change point in the music to the strongest change within an 8 second window (Figure 4C). To identify this change, we first compute all three features on 250 ms subwindows with 50% overlap. We then compute the distance between adjacent subwindows using signed difference for RMS energy, and Euclidean distance for both chroma and MFCCs. For each feature, we identify the pair of windows yielding the maximum distance, and set the refined change point to the beginning of the second window in this pair.

Find Change Point Tool

The find change point tool coarsely identifies change points in music. This tool uses exactly the same algorithm as the refine change point tool but with window size set to the length of the entire song and 4 second subwindows (Figure 4B). We then further adjust the coarse change points by applying the refine change point tool.

The find change point (range) tool returns a set of refined change points corresponding to the n strongest coarse changes in the music ($n = 3$ by default). If any of the n refined change points lie within 250 ms of each other, we replace the weaker point with the next strongest change point. The find change point (max) tool returns the refined point with the strongest coarse change in the music. We have found that RMS energy often works well for finding and refining change points because it identifies large changes in volume at the coarse level and strong downbeats at the fine level. We use it as our default feature, but we have found that chroma and MFCCs are useful for music whose variation is primarily in harmonics or timbre rather than in volume.

Set Alignment Tool

The set alignment tool moves the change point in music to just after the emphasis point in speech. It then adjusts the length of the pre-solo, solo, and post-solo. Finally, it splits and translates the speech track to create the pause. The lengths of the resulting segments as well as the gap are specified by the timing configuration.

Set Dynamics Tool

The set dynamics tool adjusts the volume of the music pre-solo, solo, and post-solo. The pre-solo dynamics are a short linear fade-in followed by an exponential increase in volume. The solo plays at full volume, and the post-solo volume adjustment mirrors that of the pre-solo.

Refine Dynamics Tool

The refine dynamics tool further adjusts the volume of the music with respect to the speech to ensure that both tracks are clearly audible. More specifically, we scale the music by $k = \sqrt{RMS(speech)/RMS(music)}$ so that the music and speech are within a similar range of volume. In this case, we compute the RMS energies using only the audio segments within the underlay.

RESULTS

We have created a number of underlays with the user-in-the-loop mode of UnderScore for 3 different audiobook speech clips ("Alice in Wonderland" [14] by Lewis Carroll, "Great Expectations" [17] by Charles Dickens and "Me Talk Pretty One Day" [32] by David Sedaris) representing both male and female voices and a range of emotional tones. We selected the music from tracks commonly heard on the radio documentary program "This American Life" [23]. The resulting underlays are included in our project website[1]. To demonstrate the importance of our automated tools, the website also

[1] http://vis.berkeley.edu/papers/underscore/

includes examples of results generated with and without using our set alignment and dynamics refinement tools. While all of our tools reduced time and effort, the find change point (range) tool significantly reduced the amount of time we spent searching through the music. The set alignment and dynamics tools eliminated much of the tweaking involved in manual creation of underlays.

To evaluate the automated batch mode of UnderScore, we used a speech clip from David Sedaris's "Me Talk Pretty One Day" audiobook [32] and selected 26 songs that are commonly used on the radio documentary program "This American Life." [23]. For each combination we used the find change point (range) tool with the RMS energy feature and automatically generated underlays corresponding to the 3 strongest change points in the music. We asked 3 independent experts who are familiar with "This American Life" to rate the timing, dynamics, and overall quality of each underlay on a 5-point Likert scale (Figure 5).

The underlays generated with the one strongest change point for each song are equivalent to the results of our find change point (max) tool. The ratings for these underlays correspond to the blue bars in Figure 5. With respect to the timing of the change point, the experts gave a rating of 3 (appropriate timing) in 60% of the responses, 89% were rated between 2 (change point arrived slightly too early) and 4 (slightly too late), and 11% were rated either 1 (far too early) or 5 (far too late). For the dynamics of the music, 59% of the ratings were 3 (appropriate volume), 94% were between 2 (slightly too soft) and 4 (slightly too loud), and 6% were rated 1 (far too soft) or 5 (far too loud). To measure overall quality, we asked the experts to evaluate the statement "I am satisfied with the overall quality of the underlay" on a scale from 1 (strongly disagree) to 5 (strongly agree); 50% of the responses were 4 (agree) or higher, 86% were 3 (neutral) or higher, and 14% were 2 (disagree) or lower. On the whole, these ratings suggest that our find change point (max) tool produces high quality underlays with good timing and dynamics.

The ratings for underlays using the second and third strongest musical change points for each song (red and green bars in Figure 5, respectively) are similar to the ratings for underlays using the strongest change point. However, the scores for timing and overall quality do decline somewhat as we move from the first to the third strongest change points. This trend suggests that our algorithm for finding a range of change points produces a useful ordering. For dynamics, there is no clear decline in ratings across the three change points. Note that our set and refine dynamics tools are independent of the strength of the change points. Thus, these tools can produce underlays with the appropriate relative dynamics between music and speech regardless of the strength of the change point.

We have found songs for which the chroma and MFCCs features find effective change points even when the RMS energy feature does not (Figure 6). Although we have found that the RMS energy feature is usually more effective than MFCCs and chroma, this example suggests that producers should consider the other features when RMS energy fails.

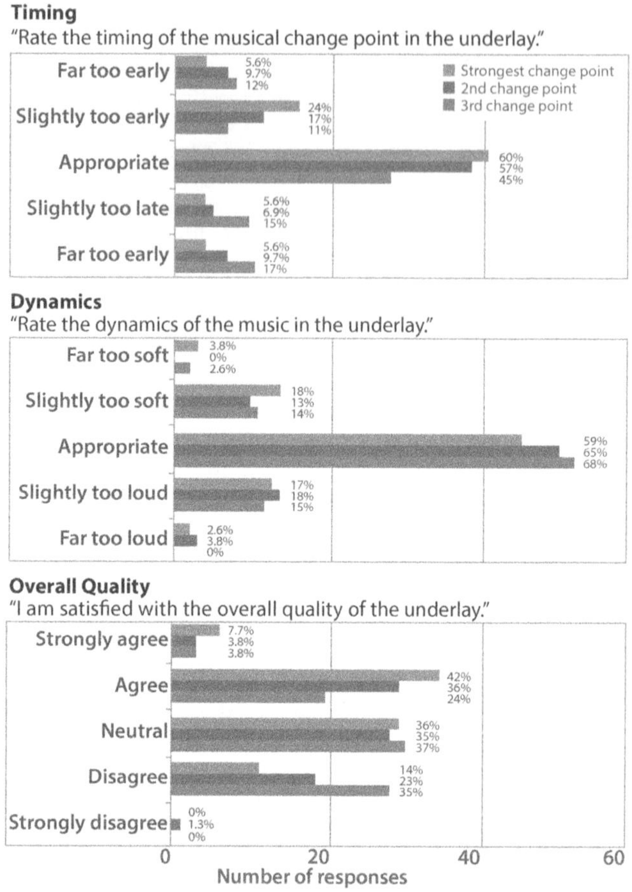

Figure 5. Three experts judged the quality of underlays automatically generated with the 3 strongest change points for each of 26 songs. The percentages are the ratio of a given rating to all ratings for each change point strength. While the strongest change point results in the best ratings, the second and third change points also perform well.

To get a sense for the usefulness of our system, we recruited 6 amateur users, who were either interested in creating audio stories or were casual podcasters, and 1 expert producer. All users were familiar with the technique of adding musical underlays to audio stories. We interviewed the participants about the process of creating musical underlays and showed UnderScore to them. All agreed that underlays enhance audio stories but are too much work to create manually with existing tools. They cited finding musical change points as the most time-consuming step, and most felt refining timing and dynamics would also be difficult. This informal feedback suggests that UnderScore's automated tools address some of the main problems that users face when creating underlays. In addition, all amateurs said they would use our batch mode results without further refinement; the expert said our fully automated results were very good but liked having the option to refine them via our user-in-the-loop mode.

FUTURE WORK

While UnderScore's fully automated tools usually produce good results, at times the change point comes too early or too late, and in rare cases, the music pre-solo can be too soft or too loud even after dynamics refinement. Thus, one direction

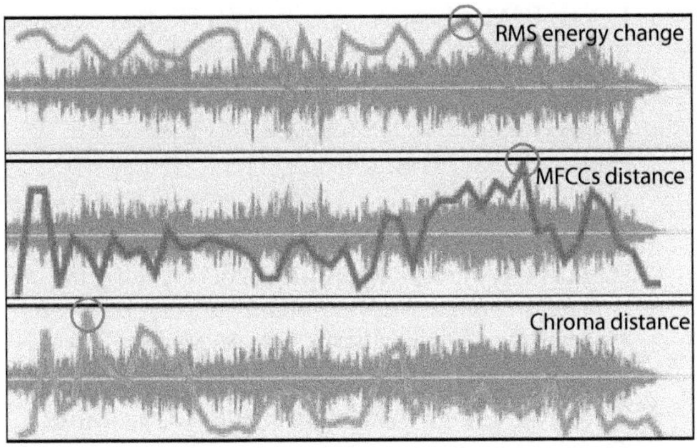

Figure 6. In "Scrapping and Yelling" by Mark Mothersbaugh [28], the maximum of the RMS energy change feature does not correspond to a strongly perceptible change in music. However, the maxima of both MFCCs and chroma distance features give a strong sense of change and lead to an effective underlay (see website).

for future work is to improve the audio analysis algorithms behind our automated system.

We see several other promising directions for further research:

Matching music to stories. Finding the appropriate music for an underlay can be a challenging task that involves searching a large library of songs to find one that best matches the semantic content of the story. Future work could explore and evaluate automated music suggestion techniques that analyze the sentiment of the speech and mood/emotion of the music.

Extended underlays. In some cases, producers may want to emphasize multiple speech points (or an entire story) with a continuous piece of music. Composing such extended underlays automatically would require algorithms that align multiple change points to multiple emphasis points, possibly by extending or contracting musical segments to fit the speech.

Underlays for live performance. In addition to enhancing recorded stories, underlays can emphasize key moments in live performances as well. Future work could investigate algorithms and interfaces that directly support this application.

Music for videos. Enhancing videos with music involves some similar challenges as creating effective underlays for audio stories (e.g., aligning musical changes to the video, balancing the dynamics, etc.). Designing tools that address these challenges for video production is another direction for future research.

Other production techniques. In general, underlays are just one of many production techniques that enhance audio stories. For example, producers sometimes incorporate ambient noise and sound effects to drive narrative development (e.g., in Radiolab [5]) or use music to distinguish multiple on-air performers based on their personalities and musical preferences. We believe that developing and evaluating interactive tools for applying such techniques represents an exciting opportunity for the HCI community.

CONCLUSION

Musical underlays can significantly enhance audio stories. We have identified a set of guidelines for producing high quality underlays. We have also instantiated these guidelines in a set of tools designed to automate the underlay creation process. This automation can help amateur producers who lack the necessary time and skills to add underlays to their stories. It also makes it easier for expert producers to quickly try out a variety of music and test different emphasis points in the speech. Our evaluations suggest that our automated tools create successful underlays on a variety of examples.

ACKNOWLEDGMENTS

This work was supported by NSF grant CCF-0643552.

REFERENCES

1. Stupid fade tricks. `http://transom.org/?p=7543`, September 2003.
2. Third coast audio library. `http://www.thirdcoastfestival.org/library`, April 2012.
3. Abel, J., and Glass, I. *Radio: An Illustrated Guide*. WBEZ Alliance Inc., 1999.
4. Abumrad, J. Music: A force for good (and sometimes evil). `http://www.thirdcoastfestival.org/library/450-music-a-force-for-good-and-sometimes-evil`, 2005.
5. Abumrad, J., and Krulwich, R. Radiolab. `http://www.radiolab.org/`, April 2012.
6. Agrawala, M., Li, W., and Berthouzoz, F. Design principles for visual communication. *Commun. ACM 54*, 4 (Apr. 2011), 6069.
7. Barthet, M., Hargreaves, S., and Sandler, M. Speech/music discrimination in audio podcast using structural segmentation and timbre recognition. In *Proc. of the 7th international conference on Exploring music contents*, Springer-Verlag (2011), 138–162.
8. Berry, R., Makino, M., Hikawa, N., and Suzuki, M. The augmented composer project: The music table. In *Proc. of the 2nd IEEE/ACM International Symposium on Mixed and Augmented Reality*, IEEE Computer Society (2003), 338.
9. Biewen, J. The transom review: John Biewen. `http://transom.org/?p=19659`, September 2011.
10. Bischof, M., Conradi, B., Lachenmaier, P., Linde, K., Meier, M., Pötzl, P., and André, E. Xenakis: combining tangible interaction with probability-based musical composition. In *Proc. of the 2nd international conference on Tangible and embedded interaction*, ACM (2008), 121–124.
11. Blesser, B. Audio dynamic range compression for minimum perceived distortion. *IEEE Transactions on Audio and Electroacoustics 17*, 1 (1969), 22–32.

12. Boll, S. Suppression of acoustic noise in speech using spectral subtraction. *IEEE Transactions on Acoustics, Speech and Signal Processing 28*, 2 (1979), 113–120.

13. Carrascal, J., and Jordà, S. Multitouch interface for audio mixing. *Proc. of New Interfaces for Musical Expression* (2011).

14. Carroll, L. Alice's Adventures in Wonderland, read by Kristen McQuillin. `http://librivox.org/alices-adventures-in-wonderland-by-lewis-carroll/`, Apr. 2012.

15. Casares, J., Long, A. C., Myers, B., Stevens, S., and Corbett, A. Simplifying video editing with silver. In *CHI '02 extended abstracts on Human factors in computing systems*, ACM (2002), 672–673.

16. Dannenberg, R. An intelligent multi-track audio editor. In *Proc. of International Computer Music Conference (ICMC)* (2007), 89–94.

17. Dickens, C. Great Expectations, read by Mark F. Smith. `http://librivox.org/great-expectations-by-charles-dickens/`, Apr. 2012.

18. Ellis, D. Chroma feature analysis and synthesis. `http://labrosa.ee.columbia.edu/matlab/chroma-ansyn/`, April 2012.

19. Farbood, M., Pasztor, E., and Jennings, K. Hyperscore: a graphical sketchpad for novice composers. *Computer Graphics and Applications, IEEE 24*, 1 (2004), 50–54.

20. Fazekas, G., and Sandler, M. Intelligent editing of studio recordings with the help of automatic music structure extraction. In *Proc. of the Audio Engineering Society 122nd Convention, Vienna, Austria* (2007).

21. Foote, J. Automatic audio segmentation using a measure of audio novelty. In *International Conference on Multimedia and Expo (ICME)*, IEEE (2000), 452–455.

22. Glass, I. The transom review: Ira Glass. `http://transom.org/?p=6978`, June 2004.

23. Glass, I. This American Life. `http://www.thisamericanlife.org/`, April 2012.

24. Jensen, K. Multiple scale music segmentation using rhythm, timbre, and harmony. *EURASIP Journal on Advances in Signal Processing 2007* (2007).

25. Logan, B. Mel frequency cepstral coefficients for music modeling. In *Proc. of the International Symposium on Music Information Retrieval* (2000).

26. Louizou, P. C. *Speech Enhancement: Theory and Practice*. CRC Press, 2007.

27. Maddage, N. C., Xu, C., Kankanhalli, M. S., and Shao, X. Content-based music structure analysis with applications to music semantics understanding. In *Proc. of the 12th annual ACM international conference on Multimedia*, MULTIMEDIA '04, ACM (New York, NY, USA, 2004), 112–119.

28. Mothersbaugh, M. Scrapping & yelling, The Royal Tenenbaums soundtrack, December 2001. Audio recording.

29. Müller, M., Ellis, D., Klapuri, A., and Richard, G. Signal processing for music analysis. *Selected Topics in Signal Processing, IEEE Journal of* (2011).

30. Paulus, J., Muller, M., and Klapuri, A. Audio-based music structure analysis. In *Proc. of the International Symposium on Music Information Retrieval* (2010), 625–636.

31. Roma, G., and Xambó, A. A tabletop waveform editor for live performance. *Proc. of New Interfaces for Music Expression* (2008).

32. Sedaris, D. *Me talk pretty one day*. audiobook. Little, Brown and Company, 2000.

33. Simon, I., Morris, D., and Basu, S. MySong: automatic accompaniment generation for vocal melodies. In *Proc. of the twenty-sixth annual SIGCHI conference on Human factors in computing systems*, ACM (2008), 725–734.

34. Smaragdis, P. User guided audio selection from complex sound mixtures. In *Proc. of the 22nd annual ACM symposium on User interface software and technology*, ACM (2009), 89–92.

35. Wakefield, G. Mathematical representation of joint time-chroma distributions. In *International Symposium on Optical Science, Engineering, and Instrumentation, SPIE*, vol. 99 (1999), 18–23.

36. Wright, J., Oppenheim, D., Jameson, D., Pazel, D., and Fuhrer, R. Cyberband: A "hands-on" music composition program. In *Proc. of International Computer Music Conference* (1997), 383–386.

Accessible Skimming: Faster Screen Reading of Web Pages

Faisal Ahmed **Yevgen Borodin** **Andrii Soviak**
Muhammad Asiful Islam **I.V. Ramakrishnan** **Terri Hedgpeth**[†]
Stony Brook University, Computer Science Department, Stony Brook, NY 11790-4400
[†]Disability Resource Center, Arizona State University, Tempe, AZ 85287-3202
{faiahmed, borodin, asoviak, maislam, ram}@cs.stonybrook.edu, [†]terrih@asu.edu

ABSTRACT
In our information-driven web-based society, we are all gradually falling "victims" to *information overload* [5].However, while sighted people are finding ways to sift through information faster, Internet users who are blind are experiencing an even greater information overload. These people access computers and Internet using screen-reader software, which reads the information on a computer screen sequentially using computer-generated speech. While sighted people can learn how to quickly glance over the headlines and news articles online to get the gist of information, people who are blind have to use keyboard shortcuts to listen through the content narrated by a serial audio interface. This interface does not give them an opportunity to know what content to skip and what to listen to. So, they either listen to all of the content or listen to the first part of each sentence or paragraph before they skip to the next one. In this paper, we propose an automated approach to facilitate *non-visual skimming* of web pages. We describe the underlying algorithm, outline a non-visual skimming interface, and report on the results of automated experiments, as well as on our user study with 23 screen-reader users. The results of the experiments suggest that we have been moderately successful in designing a viable algorithm for automatic summarization that could be used for non-visual skimming. In our user studies, we confirmed that people who are blind could read and search through online articles faster and were able to understand and remember most of what they have read with our skimming system. Finally, all 23 participants expressed genuine interest in using non-visual skimming in the future.

Author Keywords
Skimming; Blind; Speed Reading; Screen Reader; Summarization; Accessibility; Assistive Technology.

ACM Classification Keywords
H.5.2 [Information Interfaces and Presentation]: User Interfaces; H.5.4 [Information Interfaces and Presentation]: Hypertext/Hypermedia -*navigation.*

UIST '12, October 7–10, 2012, Cambridge, Massachusetts, USA.

INTRODUCTION
When sighted users look at a random web page, their quick eye movements, called saccades, help them get a quick overview of the page and find what they need. The structure and formatting of the web page further helps them find the information relevant to their goals. In most web pages, this still leaves them a lot of content to read through, imposing a *heavy cognitive load.* But again, saccades help them speed up reading and reduce the cognitive load. The process of quickly glancing over the textual content in order to pick up the gist of the content is called *Skimming.*

Skimming [24, 28] is a speed-reading technique that allows sighted readers to get a general idea of the content and sift through information very quickly, without reading the entire content and, most importantly, without sacrificing basic understanding of the content. Skimming is also very useful while looking for specific information, especially, when keyword searching is not possible. Unfortunately, people who are blind cannot skim through text due to the way screen-reading software works. Screen-readers read all text in a window from start to finish. Though screen-reader users can move through information by character, word, line, paragraph, section, page, etc, these functions are not equivalent to the ability to skim through information [6].

Screen readers [21, 29, 35] are assistive technology software that narrate the content of the screen using text-to-speech and allow users to navigate through the content marked up by HTML tags for headings, paragraphs, links, buttons, etc. Because of the low bandwidth of a serial audio interface and the fact that one has to hear the information before deciding if it is relevant, people who are blind spend considerably more time identifying the information they need [8]. A lot of research [2, 7, 9, 10, 19, 26] has been done to accelerate this process by helping find the main content in web pages. However, little has been done to develop an effective method for skimming, so that blind people could process information faster. For example, having found the beginning of an article in a web page, screen-reader users cannot just scan through the article.

The JAWS screen-reader has a naive implementation of "skimming" [22] that allows users to read the first line or the first sentence of each paragraph. This still does not offer a truly functional tool for skimming, and does not follow the same skimming protocol that sighted folks employ. An earlier experiment with 20 people [1] who are blind showed that skipping sentences with shortcuts and increasing the speech rate are the *only* strategies screen-reader users use to skim through web pages. However, these strategies are no match to visual skimming, in which quick saccades of the eye allow sighted people to pick out snippets of information such as names, dates, phrases, which allow sighted people to get the gist of the content or find the exact information they are looking for much faster.

The earlier study [1] reported the usability of non-visual skimming in listening-and-comprehension and in search scenarios. To simulate skimming, they used several variations of gold-standard (human-generated) summaries. These experiments demonstrated that skimming enabled people who are blind to read faster while maintaining high level of comprehension and retention.

In this paper, we review the related work on summarization and explain why they are not suitable to support non-visual skimming. We propose a new algorithm that can produce summaries for non-visual skimming of *textual* content and report on the experiments over a dataset of human-generated summaries. Finally, we present the results of the user study with 23 blind people to confirm the usability of the approach.

RELATED WORK

Overview of Skimming

People typically read for enjoyment, to search for information, to complete a task, or to explore / review text [24]. Whatever the specific purpose of reading may be, people are often faced with large volumes of information that they need to process. *Cognitive overload* [33]is a fundamental problem that arises while processing a large volume of information in web pages; this is especially true for people with vision impairments who have to listen through most of web content in a sequential manner. Hence, a tool for generating semantic driven summaries that are comparable to the way sighted people skim through information would give screen-reader users, the ability to sift through information reducing the cognitive load.

To reduce the cognitive load, sighted people employ a number of different speed-reading techniques (a.k.a. skimming or scanning). Some people define scanning as looking for specific information in content and skimming as getting the content's gist, others call both of them skimming. Our method covers for both of these fast-reading techniques, and we refer to them collectively as "skimming". While skimming, sighted people quickly scan line by line picking out words and phrases that seem to stand out. This enables sighted people to read several times faster and still get the gist of the content. Skimming can also be very useful when looking for specific information that could not be searched for otherwise. Unfortunately, assistive technology does not provide people who are blind the ability to efficiently skim through information in a manner that is comparable to that of sighted people.

To simulate the skimming process, one could try to use eye tracking devices to figure out what words and phrases are chosen by the human eye. However, different people develop different ad hoc approaches to skimming, and there is no guarantee that the words that "catch the eye" are the ones that carry the most meaning. An alternative approach is to look specifically for the words and phrases that help preserve the meaning of the text. This could be accomplished by using automated summarization.

Automated summarization approaches use computer algorithms [31] to condense textual content while preserving its gist. Broadly, the approaches could be categorized into two main types: summarization by extraction and summarization by abstraction. In short, extraction deals with picking out the most salient sentences or phrases from the original text [3, 14, 15], and abstraction is compressing sentences [4, 13], which involves paraphrasing the content, for example, by automatically filling out a template [20].

Visual skimming is akin to the extractive summarization, because when people scan the text they take it as it is. Interviews with 20 screen-reader users [1] also suggested that the extractive summarization approach that preserves the original content is the most suitable technique for enabling non-visual skimming. We next review the existing extractive summarization approaches and explain why they are not adequate for non-visual skimming of web pages.

Extractive Summarization Approaches

Summarization by Sentence Extraction

The majority of the existing extractive summarization approaches are doing sentence extraction [4, 12, 15, 17]. Such approaches typically analyze the entire text and examine the relationship between sentences to find the ones that have the most meaning or are very different from the rest of the text. JAWS screen reader [21] has a "skimming" feature [22] allowing users to read the 1st sentence or a line of each paragraph of text.

While sentence extraction can help get an overview of text, this approach cannot enable skimming, in which the reader scans through all or most of the sentences picking out the most salient words and phrases. Sentence extraction leaves out most of the original content, which makes it unusable for scanning for information that cannot be found without reading the text, e.g., when keyword search is not possible due to unknown keywords. Sentence extraction assumes coherent text and will not work in web pages, where there is unrelated content, e.g., in front pages of news sites. Therefore, keyword extraction approaches appear to be the only ones suitable for non-visual skimming of web pages.

Summarization by Keyword Extraction

Based on a preliminary study [1] with people who are blind, the authors came up with important criteria for the structure of the summary that can be used for skimming. The study shows that, the subjects were able to understand the gist of the content much better when they were presented word combinations as opposed to separate words. In addition, the subjects did not want information to be skipped or presented out of order. Based on these findings, we can conclude that the desired approach should be able to summarize each sentence in a given document, by extracting meaningful words and word combinations from every sentence, while preserving the original order of the words. To be specific it should summarize each sentence separately, without considering any global features (i.e. word frequency) of the entire document.

We next examine relevant extractive summarization approaches to determine if they fit to our criteria.

In [36], the summary is constructed by extracting word trigrams that frequently occur in the entire document. This approach does not pick words from each sentence and needs long documents.

Marina Litvak presents a keyword extraction approach based on the analysis of a whole document [25]. The approach builds a tree where nodes represent words and edges represent order relationships. Higher weights are given to the words that have higher number of incoming edges, number of outgoing edges, frequency and tf-idf score. Finally, individual keywords that have the highest weights are extracted into the summary.

In [18], the authors build separate graphs for each sentence and weigh each vertex based on the word and structural dependencies within a sentence, as well as word frequency in the entire document. The summary is generated by selection of top ranked words. The compression of the summary depends on the predefined percent value.

An interesting relation-driven summarization algorithm is proposed in [20]. Authors describe three main stages: 1) concept activation, during which they reject the unimportant parts of the document and divide content words into two groups "triggers" and "filters", 2) segmentation, during which they pick the words related to the words defined as "triggers" and decide which of those words should be skipped, and 3) identification of linguistic relations among the words, which helps to extract coherent phrases. Finally, the algorithm removes even more words, and what remains is the summary. While the description of the algorithm is sketchy, we can see that the algorithm runs over a full document and does not guarantee coverage of each sentence.

While these all are viable summarization approaches for many applications, none of these is suitable for generating summaries that satisfy the identified criteria. The major limitation of the reviewed approaches is that they all heavily rely on word frequency, which is a meaningful feature only when summarizing long documents. Unfortunately, the content of web pages is predominantly short. For instance, front pages of news sites typically have a number of short snippets each containing a headline followed by a few sentences from the linked articles; the articles themselves often contain only one long or a few short paragraphs.

In addition, most of the reviewed approaches do not offer any guarantees that keywords will be extracted from every sentence. Some of them do not preserve the original order of the words in the original text or extract separate words instead of word phrases.

In this paper, we propose a Skimming algorithm that satisfies the criteria outlined in the beginning of the section. We next present an overview of our approach.

OVERVIEW OF OUR APPROACH

At a high level, our algorithm works as follows.

Firstly, every sentence is parsed to extract grammatical relations amongst its words. Secondly, a lexical tree based on these relations is constructed, where each node of the tree represents a word in the sentence. Thirdly, for every word in this tree, its grammatical (i.e., POS tags) as well as structural features (related to in-degree/out-degree, etc.) are extracted. These features are given to a trained classifier to determine whether or not to include the word in the skimming summary. Finally a subtree consisting of the selected words is constructed. This subtree represents the skimming summary that users interact with via an interface.

Observe that three key elements of our algorithm are a natural language parser, classifier, and a skimming interface. Below, we describe these three elements necessary for understanding of the Skimming algorithm, as well as its experimental evaluation.

Stanford Parser

A preliminary user study with 20 participants who were blind [1], reported that screen-reader users were able to skim and comprehend text much better if the summary included connected word phrases, as opposed to disconnected word, e.g., "hands down" instead of "hands". To capture the relationships between words in a sentence, we used Stanford Parser [23], which is a probabilistic natural language parser that can analyze the grammatical and syntactical structure of sentences and extract relations.

The relations identified by the parser are very simple and, in the words of the developers, "quite accessible to non-linguists and effective in relation extraction applications". These typed dependencies are represented as relations between pairs of words (i.e., "John likes cake" the object of "John" is "cake"). Apart from the grammatical relations Stanford Parser also identifies the POS (Parts of Speech) of the words.

Stanford parser identifies a total of 48 different binary grammatical relations [27]. A grammatical relationship holds between a governor word and a dependent word. For example, the sentence *"Chewing gum can improve memory, say UK psychologists."* is processed into the following relations:

Relation Name (Governor-Position → Dependent-Position)
Adjectival modifier (gum-2 → chewing-1);
Nominal subject (improve-4 → gum-2);
Auxiliary (improve-4 → can-3)
Nominal subject (say-6 → memory-5)
Clausal complement (improve-4 → say-6)
Noun compound modifier (psychologists-8 → uk-7)
Direct object (say-6 → psychologists-8)

Using the grammatical relations generated by Stanford Parser a directed graph can be constructed, where the nodes are the words and the edges are the relations from the governor to the dependent (Figure 1). In the words of the developers, "the dependency graph is a tree (a singly rooted directed acyclic graph with no re-entrances)." [27]. Throughout the paper, we will treat the dependency graph as a tree and will refer to it as a *sentence tree.*

For training the classifier, we had to create labeled datasets. The details are described below.

Dataset Generation for Training the Classifier

The quality of automated summarization is gradually approaching that of humans [31, 37]. However, in the previous section we explained why the existing automated summarization approaches are not suitable for skimming web pages. Part of the reason is that they have been trained on and fine-tuned for specific type of summaries, which are not suitable for skimming. Since we could not find an existing dataset of human-authored summaries that would be appropriate for skimming, we created our own.

To generate the gold-standard skimming summaries, we recruited 24 sighted participants. All of them were college-educated and were fluent in English. We collected 24 news articles on different topics with 5 paragraphs in each of the articles on average. The total size of the raw text included 674 sentences (17K words).

Each participant was asked to summarize 3 different articles, thus, generating 3 gold-standard summaries for each article. We then used a majority-vote approach to combine each of the 3 summaries into one, i.e., we chose only the words that were selected by at least 2 people, resulting in 43% compression ratio.

Since the purpose of skimming was to pick out the most salient information without rephrasing the original content, we stipulated that the subjects use extractive summarization. Because the point of skimming was to save time to the end users by presenting less information, but still have enough information to understand the content, we requested that the summary length be between 1/3 and 1/2 of the original content. However, we did not want to dictate how exactly to do summarization, so each participant was provided only with the following "loose" guidelines:

- Each sentence is to be summarized separately;
- The summary may only include words and phrases found in the summarized sentence;
- Word order and punctuation has to be preserved;
- Summaries should be as informative as possible.

Interface

Summarization by itself does not satisfy the need for skimming; for screen-reader users, reading a summary is more like reading a separate, albeit shorter, narrative. Therefore, we designed an interface that allowed screen-reader users to switch seamlessly between reading the skimming summary and the original web page preserving the current reading position. This feature emulate the behavior of sighted readers who usually can scan quickly and then, at any point, slow down to read the text regularly. When switching from regular screen-reading to skimming, the reading position is set to the closest preceding word that was in both the original text and the summary.

The skimming interface was integrated into our Non-Visual screen-reading platform, which is a Java application that enables a screen reading interface for the Firefox web browser. It supports all the typical navigation shortcuts available in the mainstream screen-readers such as JAWS [21], e.g., paragraph / sentence / word / character navigation, pause / resume, etc.

A shortcut (i.e. Shift+S) lets the user toggle between skimming mode and full text mode. The skimming interface can be invoked on any web page content regardless of its length as long as the content is organized in sentences (e.g., snippets of news articles along with headlines), but lists of links that can be found in menus, on the other hand, should be read in their entirety.

SKIMMING ALGORITHM

In this section, we describe the underpinnings of the proposed non-visual Skimming algorithm; specifically, we describe feature selection, training classifiers and the skimming algorithm.

Feature Selection

The results obtained from the Stanford parser enabled us to identify a number of features that could be used for training a classifier. The features we chose were the Number of Outgoing Edges, Level in the Tree, Number of descendants, Incoming relation type, and POS tag (Figure 1). Each of the numerical features has been normalized with a scaling factor. The feature, Number of outgoing edges was normalized by the number of nodes in the tree. The feature, Level in the Tree was scaled by the highest level of a node in the tree. Finally, the feature, Number of descendants was normalized by the highest number of descendants a node can have in the tree.

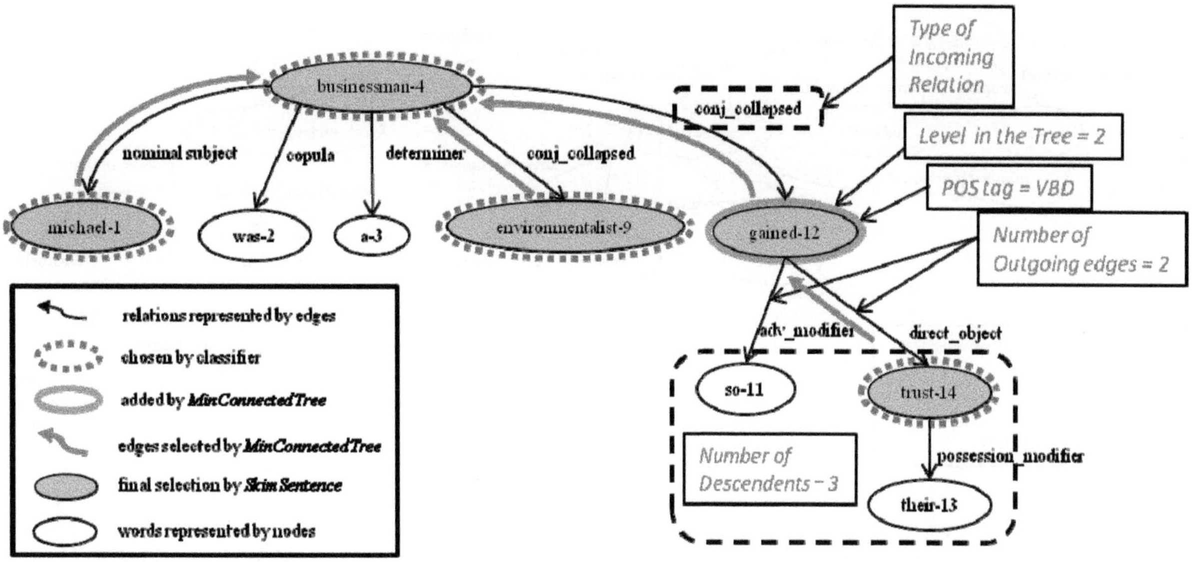

Figure 1. Sentence tree and features for "*Michael was a businessman, as well as an environmentalist, and so gained their trust.*"

Training the Classifier

We used an open source machine learning library, called Weka [16], to train classifiers using various machine learning models. In order to generate training data points we need to generate feature vectors with their label/class. First, we used Stanford Parser [23] to generate feature vectors for each word in each sentence in our dataset. Then, to label/classify a feature vector, we check if the corresponding word appears in the gold summary; if it appears, we label the feature vector as "YES" class otherwise as "NO" class. "YES" class means this word is selected to be used in summary and "NO" class means otherwise. These datasets are used to train different classifiers (i.e., Linear SVM, Multilayer Perceptron, Random Forest) through the Weka machine learning library with 10-fold cross-validation; using 591 sentences (15300 words) for training and 83 sentences (1700 words) for testing.

The classifier-generated summary is formed by selecting words that were classified as "YES" and rearrange them by preserving the order in original sentence. To measure the accuracy of the classifier, we represented both the gold-standard summary and the classifier-generated summary as arrays of words. As many sentences had repeating words, it was necessary to align the words for more accurate measurements. Therefore, we ran the LCS (Longest Common Subsequence) algorithm to align the two arrays and compare the summaries.

We report the results in the first group in Table 1, under the caption "Output of the Classifiers alone". We found Linear SVM performs the best, therefore we decided to use it to classify words (*SkimSentence:Line 12*) in our proposed Skimming algorithm *SkimSentence* (next Section). In section after the next, we discuss this result in details and also show our algorithm *SkimSentence* improves the result.

Skimming Algorithm

The classifier helped us pick up separate words in a sentence, however, the preliminary user studies [1] demonstrated that people tend to understand content better in the presence of phrases. Therefore, we designed the *SkimSentence* Algorithm to extract grammatically related important words of the sentence, while keeping comprehension level almost the same as our Gold-Standard summaries. The algorithm uses a trained classifier and another algorithm *MinConnectedTree* to skim the given sentence. The pseudocode for both algorithms is presented in this section.

Algorithm: *SkimSentence*

R: Set of Typed Dependency Relations $\{(W_{g1}, W_{d1}), (W_{g2}, W_{d2}), \ldots (W_{gn}, W_{dn})\}$ between words in a sentence, where Governor W_{gi} depends on Dependent W_{di} where $1 \leq i \leq n$.

T: Sentence Tree:(Parents:Child) ≡ (Governor : Dependent)

Input: S: sentence to be skimmed
Output: K: skimmed sentence

```
1. SN ← {} //initialize set of summary nodes
2. K ← [] //initialize list of words
3. R ← TypedDependencies(S) //stanford parser
4. T ← ConstructTree(R) //from typed dependencies
5. For each node N in T
6.    Do O ← #ofOutgoingEdges(N)
7.       L ← LevelInTree(N)
8.       C ← #ofDescendants(N)
9.       I ← IncomingRelationType(N)
10.      P ← POSTags(N)
11.      F ← <O,L,C, I, P> //feature vector
12.      Do If InSkimming(F)=True //SVM-classify
13.         Then SN.add(N)
14. MT ← MinConnectedTree(SN)
15. K ← OrderAndListWords(MT)
16. Return K
```

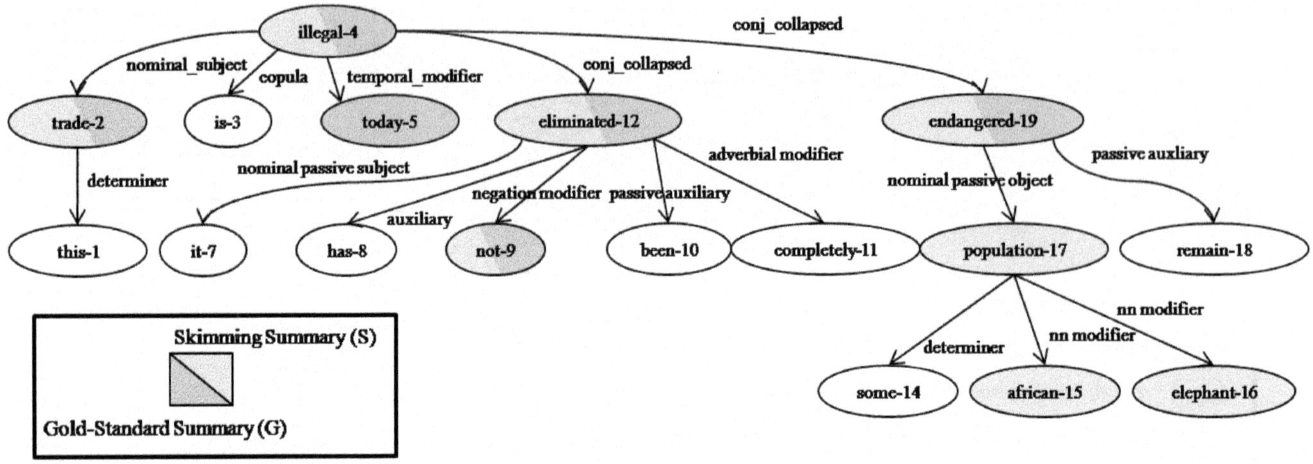

Skimming Summary (S): "*trade illegal, not eliminated, african elephant population endangered.*"
Gold-Standard Summary (G): "*trade illegal today not eliminated endangered*"
(F): *"This trade is illegal today, but it has not been completely eliminated and some African elephant population remain endangered."*

Figure 2. Sentence tree illustration of the typical Skimming algorithm output compared to the human/gold summary

Algorithm: *MinConnectedTree*

TN: Temporary node
Input: **S:** Set of nodes of a sentence tree
Output: MS: Set of minimum connected nodes

```
MS ← {} //initialize set of nodes
For each node N in S
   Do TN ← N
      While TN ≠ NULL and TN.visited = False
         Do TN.visited ← true
            MS.add(TN)
            TN ← TN.Parent
Return MS
```

SkimSentence first uses the Stanford Parser to find all the typed dependencies / grammatical relations in the given sentence (*SkimSentence:Line 3*). Then it uses the list of grammatical relations to construct the sentence tree (*SkimSentence:Line 4*). "*Michael was a businessman, as well as an environmentalist, and so gained their trust.*"; the sentence tree corresponding to this sentence is illustrated by Figure 1 illustrates.

Once the tree is constructed, it creates a set of summary nodes which are chosen by our trained classifier (*SkimSentence:Line 5-13*). In order to choose the summary nodes, it first analyzes each of the nodes in the tree and identifies their features (*SkimSentence:Line 5-10*). #ofOutgoingEdges calculates the number of outgoing edges (normalized by total number of nodes) of a node (*SkimSentence:Line 6*). The method LevelInTree finds the level of a node in the Tree (normalized by the highest level of a node in the tree), where root is at level 1, children of the root is at level 2 and so on (*SkimSentence:Line 7*). #ofDescendents returns the total number of descendents (normalized by the highest number of descendents of a node in the tree) a node has (*SkimSentence:Line 8*).

The type of the relation between a node and its parent is determined by the method IncomingRelationType (*SkimSentence:Lines 9*). POSTags method finds the parts of speech of the word corresponding to a node (*SkimSentence:Line 10*). Going back to our example in Figure 1 let's focus on the node "gained-12". In the figure we can easily identify its features, number of outgoing edges is 2/9, level in the tree is 2/4, number of descendants is 3/8, type of incoming relation is conj_collapsed, POS tag is VBD (Verb, past tense).

With all the node features the algorithm constructs a feature vector F (*SkimSentence:Line 11*). In our example, the feature vector for the node "gained-12" is *<2/5, 2/4,3/9, conj_collapsed, VBD>*. Then the feature vector is fed to the trained SVM model in order to classify it to either "YES" or "NO". The InSkimming method takes a feature vector and returns True/False depending on whether the node is classified to "YES"/"NO" respectively, using the trained linear SVM classifier (*SkimSentence:Line 12*). If InSkimming returns True (which means it can be taken as part of skimmed sentence), the node is added to a set of summary nodes (*SkimSentence:Line 13*). In this example, the nodes "michael-1", "businessman-4", "environmentalist-9", and "trust-14" are chosen as summary nodes. In the figure these nodes are circled with dots (Figure 1).

The set of summary nodes constructed this way, does not guarantee if they have any grammatical relations between them. Moreover, adding more nodes which are grammatically related to these nodes will increase the comprehension level of the skimmed sentence. So to make sure that a minimum relation exists among these summary nodes, a second algorithm *MinConnectedTree* is used, to construct a subtree that connects all the summary nodes with minimum number of edges (*SkimSentence:Line 14*).

The algorithm *MinConnectedTree* constructs a tree with minimum number of edges necessary to cover a given set of tree nodes. The algorithm runs two nested loops. The outer loop iterates over the given set of nodes (*MinConnectedTree:Line 2*). For each node it does a traversal towards root of the tree (*MinConnectedTree:Line 4-7*). In the inner loop, while traversing towards the root, it checks if the node has already been visited or not. If the node has not been visited, it is marked as visited and is added to a set of output nodes (*MinConnectedTree:Line 6*). After the nested loops are executed, a set of nodes are returned, which forms a tree with minimum number of edges (*MinConnectedTree:Line 8*). In Figure 1, from each of the summary nodes (circled with dots), the algorithm traversed towards the root and picked up any non summary nodes on the way. The traversal paths have been marked with bold lines with arrowhead in the figure. The only non-summary node that has been picked up (apart from the summary nodes) by *MinConnectedTree*, is "gained-12". All the nodes that have been selected by *MinConnectedTree* are shaded in the figure.

In the *SkimSentence* algorithm, once the tree with minimum number of edges is constructed (*SkimSentence:Line 14*), a skimmed sentence is made by ordering the nodes according to the position of the corresponding words in the original sentence, using the method OrderAndListWords (*SkimSentence:Line 15*)

Next we present the outcomes of our algorithm on a sample sentence. In Figure 2, we present the corresponding sentence tree and the gold-standard and skimming summaries. For better understanding we color the nodes. The words that appear in the Gold-standard summary are colored with dark red and the words chosen by our *SkimSentence* algorithm are colored with light green. If a word is chosen by our algorithm as well as human/gold skimming, half of the node is colored with dark red and other half is colored with light green.

EXPERIMENTS WITH THE DATASET

Experimental Setup

To evaluate our skimming algorithm, we did experiments on our dataset. In this section we do a comparative study between the "summaries generated by Classifiers alone" and the "summaries generated by *SkimSentence*".

We report the results using the standard metrics of precision, recall, and F-measure, as well as the compression ratio. We define *precision* as the ratio of the number of the words appearing in both arrays to the size of our skimmed summary. We define *recall* as ratio of the number of the words appearing in both arrays to the size of the gold-standard summary. *F-measure* is the harmonic mean of recall and precision. Finally, we define the *compression ratio* as the ratio of the number of words in a skimmed summary to the number of words in the original sentence.

	Random Forest	Multi-Layer Perceptron	Linear SVM
Output of the Classifiers alone			
Precision	58.92%	59.93%	59.27%
Recall	54.01%	66.75%	68.63%
F-measure	0.56	0.63	0.64
Compression	33.62%	41.16%	43.20%
Output of the algorithm *SkimSentence*			
Precision	57.36%	58.34%	63.40%
Recall	63.77%	75.78%	76.57%
F-measure	0.60	0.65	0.69
Compression	40.95%	48.34%	46.81%

Table 1 – Output of three different classifiers

Results and Discussion

Although we tried all of the models available in Weka, in Table 1 we report only on the top three classifiers: Random forest, Multi-layer perceptron, and linear SVM-based model (implemented in the lib-svm [11] software). Of the three classifiers, we chose linear SVM for further experiments as it had the best classification results on our dataset. The comparative performance of different classifiers on our dataset was not in the scope of this paper, especially, because classifier performance often varies depending on the size of the training dataset [30, 34].

The SVM classifier yielded the best combination of the precision: 59.2%, recall: 68.6%, F-measure: 0.64 and, the compression ratio: 43.2%. By running the Skimming algorithm on the classifier results, we improved the precision to 63.4%, recall to 76.5%, and F-measure to 0.69, at the cost of the compression of 46.8%. The 4% improvement of precision and 8% improvement of recall, at the 4% difference in compression justifies the use of the Skimming algorithm on top of the classification results.

While these measures give the overall idea of the algorithm's accuracy, **it should be noted that, for the purposes of skimming, we favored recall over precision**, because the correctly recalled words typically carry the most meaning. At the same time, we balanced recall with precision not to introduce too much "noise"; **it is also notable that the "noise" words that were "erroneously" chosen by the algorithm could carry just as much meaning as the words in the gold-standard summary**, because while shortening a sentence, a human may choose just one of any two equally meaningful words. This observation is supported by the user study that showed no statistically significant difference in the performance of subjects over the gold-standard and skimmed summaries. Finally, in our experiments, we also balanced the compression ratio, so that the skimmed summary was no longer than the gold-standard one.

USER STUDY

Participants

The Disability Resource Center at the Arizona State University helped us recruit 23 participants who are blind to take part in the user study. Gender representation was 7 male and 16 female. The ages of the participants were evenly distributed and varied from early twenties to late sixties. Three of the subjects considered themselves expert computer users, fourteen of them were very comfortable, five were comfortable and one was mildly comfortable with computers. All subjects were well-versed in the use of screen readers, with JAWS as their primary screen reader. Internet usage was more than 20 hours per week for twelve subjects, 11-20 hours per week for eight subjects, 6-10 hours per week for two subject, and 1-5 hours a week for only one subject.

Experimental Set Up

To evaluate our approach, we built the proposed Skimming interface. The articles chosen for the study were typical web news articles. However, they did not contain any links or images to reduce the variation among the articles. We used RealSpeak Samantha voice [32] with the speech rate of 140 words per minute.

To evaluate the interface and the underlying algorithm, the subjects were asked to perform three tasks in each of the listening-and-comprehension and searching scenarios. In each of the three tasks the subjects were either using the Gold-standard summary, Skimming summary, or the original text of the articles.

Listening-and-Comprehension Scenario

In a within-subjects experiment that had a 3 by 3 cell design, we had each subject listen to 3 different articles using 3 types of skimming: Gold-standard summary G, Skimming summary S, and the full text F (Table 2). We varied the order of the tasks for counterbalancing and to avoid bias. Before the experiment, the subjects were given a sample listening-and-comprehension task to practice with. They were not allowed to use navigation shortcuts in this task. Each task took approximately 10 minutes, which included the question answering section as well.

A set of 12 questions was asked to test the overall comprehension and retention of information. The first question was open-ended and the rest were multiple-choice. The questions we formulated to cover the major points of each article without regard for which content actually appeared in the corresponding gold summary. The questions covered several parts of speech that carried information: 1 question was on the article topic (i.e. "What is the article about?" – "African Elephants"), 4 questions on the nouns (e.g., "In search of what do the Mali elephants migrate?" – "Water"), 3 questions on the verbs (e.g., "According to the text, African Elephants cannot be easily" – "Domesticated"), 2 on the numeric values (e.g., "How much does an elephant weigh at birth?" – "200 pounds"), and 2 on the adjectives/adverbs (e.g., "Mali elephants are described as?" – "nomadic"). We approximately followed the distribution of the parts of speech in the original articles and were consistent in this break-down across all articles.

S: Skimming by SkimSentence
Elephants cows live family herds young, adult males bulls tend roam. Having baby elephant commitment. Elephants have longer pregnancy mammal 22 months. Cows give birth to one calf two to four years. Birth, elephants weigh 200 pounds stand 3 feet tall. African elephants, unlike asian relatives, are not domesticated. Range africa rain forests central west africa. Elephants found desert. Herd mali elephants migrates route desert search water.
G: Gold/Human Skimming
Female cows live family herds with young males bulls roam own. Having baby serious commitment. Longer pregnancy 22 months. Birth to calf every two four years. At birth weigh 200 pounds 3 feet tall. African elephants not easily domesticated. Range sub-saharan africa and central west. Northernmost elephants found in malis sahel desert. Herd of mali elephants migrates in circular route search water.
F: Original paragraph:
Female elephants cows live in family herds with their young, but adult males bulls tend to roam on their own. Having a baby elephant is a serious commitment. Elephants have a longer pregnancy than any other mammal almost 22 months. Cows usually give birth to one calf every two to four years. At birth, elephants already weigh some 200 pounds (91 kilograms) and stand about 3 feet (1 meter) tall. African elephants, unlike their Asian relatives, are not easily domesticated. They range throughout sub-Saharan Africa and the rain forests of central and West Africa. The continent's northernmost elephants are found in Malis Sahel desert. The small, nomadic herd of Mali elephants migrates in a circular route through the desert in search of water

Table 2. Skimming and Gold-standard summaries

Searching Scenario

In a within-subjects experiment that had a 3 by 3 cell design, we had each subject skim through 3 different articles using the Gold-standard summary G, Skimming summary S, and the full text F. The conditions were counterbalanced across subjects to avoid bias. Before each task, the subjects were asked a question, the answer to which they had to find in the article. The subjects were instructed not to try keyword searching because some would and some would not depending on their experience with screen readers. However, to make the scenario realistic, the questions were formulated using wording different from those that appears in the actual article, so that one could not easily search for the exact keywords, e.g., if the original sentence was "*Cows usually give birth to one calf every two to four years.*" The question was: "How frequently do female elephants have calves?"

The answer to the question was contained in the 4th and the last paragraph of each article to increase the time required to find the answer. Having the answer in the beginning of the articles would have caused the users to find the answer equally fast with and without skimming, defeating the purpose of the experiment. Varying the location of the answer would have increased the variation of the completion times.

Although the answers in the search scenarios were located in the last paragraph, the subjects would not have been able to notice the pattern because there were only 3 tasks to learn from and the length of passages varied (summary is shorter). The task order was randomized.

In this task, we measured the time it took subjects to answer the question. We also measured the number of keystrokes the subjects pressed to find the answer. The subjects were given a sample task before the experiment and 5 minutes to practice with the skimming interface. They were allowed to use any navigation shortcuts they were used to. Each task took approximately 10 minutes.

Questionnaires

Following each task in either of the scenarios, the participants were asked to rate the perceived difficulty of the task on a 5-point Likert scale (1=Very Easy to 5=Very Hard, Figure 3b, Figure 5b). At the end of the experiments, we read statements about the skimming experience to the subjects and asked them to rate the statements on a 5-point Likert scale (1=Strongly Disagree to 5=Strongly Agree) – Table 3 summarizes the ratings. Finally, we also asked general questions about subjects' computer use, age, comfort level, onset of blindness, etc. We used these questions to test for performance differences among groups of subjects.

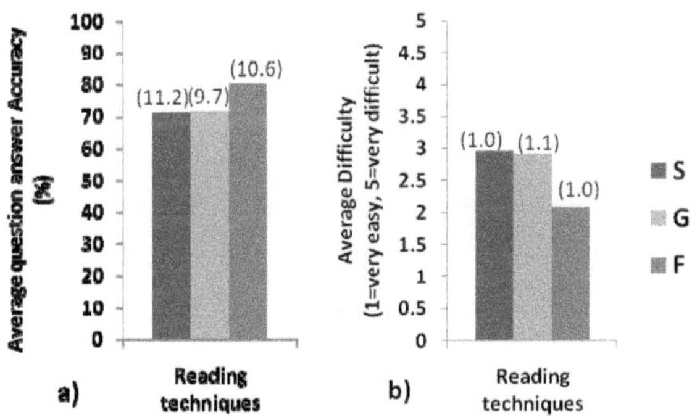

Figure 3. a) Average accuracy and b) Average difficulty (St. Dev.) of question answering with S, G and F

Hypotheses Testing

We formulated a series of specific hypotheses that we accepted or rejected based on the statistical significance testing. In this section, we provide the details on the hypothesis and discuss the results. Finally, we present the results of the analysis of the post-completion questionnaire. *We used a t-test for statistical significance testing with the significance level of alpha = 0.01.* The following are the specific hypotheses tested in the experiments.

H1: After listening to summaries S and G, subjects can answer reading-and-comprehension questions equally well.

Results: Subjects were able to answer the reading-and-comprehension questions correctly with accuracy of 71.01% (St. Dev.=11.19%) for summary S and 71.37% (St.Dev.=9.67%) for summary G (Figure 3a). Using the one-tailed paired t-test, we found that there is no statistically significant difference between the question answering accuracy for summary S and G (t=-0.134, df=22, p=0.894), accepting H1.

We found no statistically significant differences for specific types of questions between summaries S and G (Figure 4).

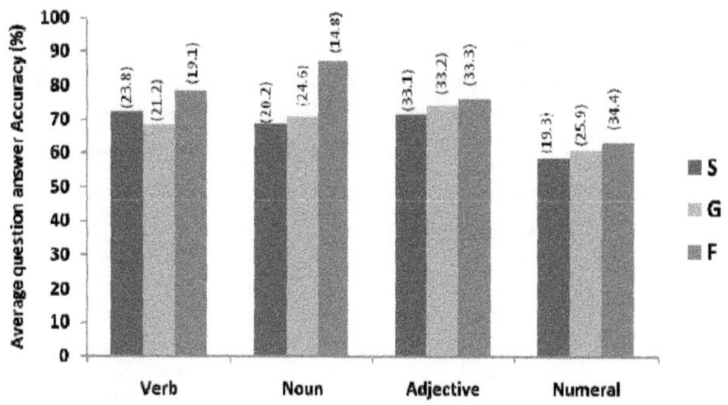

Figure 4. Accuracy of different question types

Discussion: One of the most important findings of these experiments was that the subjects were able to answer accurately about 70% of the questions about the text after listening to either skimming summary S or the gold-standard summary G.

H2: After listening to summary S, G & full text F, subjects can answer reading-and-comprehension equally well.

Results: Subjects were able to answer 71.01% (St. Dev.=11.19%) of the reading-and-comprehension questions correctly for summary S, 71.36% (St. Dev.=9.67%) for summary G and 80.07% (St. Dev.=10.58%) for full text F (Figure 3a). A one-way ANOVA was used to test accuracy differences in answering three types of summaries S, G, and F. The accuracy with which subjects gave answers differed significantly across the three types of summaries, $F(2, 66) = 5.48$, $p = 0.0063$. The post-hoc test for linear trend also shows that there is a trend, that answering accuracies increases as you read summary type S, G and F respectively, (Slope 0.04529, $p = 0.0047$), rejecting H2.

Discussion: This result was as expected, because, after all, full text was easier to understand and contained all the answers to the questions. It is notable that while the length of text shortened by more than 50%, the performance was not compromised significantly (at most 10%). We believe that the subjects could not answer 100% of questions after reading the full text due to information overload.

H3: Subjects perceive question-answering tasks to be of the same difficulty after listening to a summary G/S and full text F.

Results: After the completion of each listening-and-comprehension task, we asked the subject to rate their difficulty on a Likert scale (very easy=1 and very difficult=5). Subjects rated the difficulty level of the task with summary S as 2.95 on average (St. Dev.=1.02), rated summary G as 2.92 on average (St. Dev.=1.16), and rated the full text F as 2.08 on average (St. Dev.=1.06). A one-way ANOVA was used to test the difficulty in answering three types of summaries S, G, and F. The difficulty with which subjects gave answers did not differ significantly across the three types of summaries, $F(2, 66) = 2.501$, $p = 0.0898$, thus we accept H3. (Figure 3b)

Discussion: Reading full text is supposed to be easier than reading a skimmed summary. However, reading the full text may be putting a higher cognitive load on the subject resulting in information overload, and making it harder to remember information and answer questions. The fact that subjects rated both G and S summaries at the same level of difficulty suggests that our Skimming summary is very close to human-generated summaries.

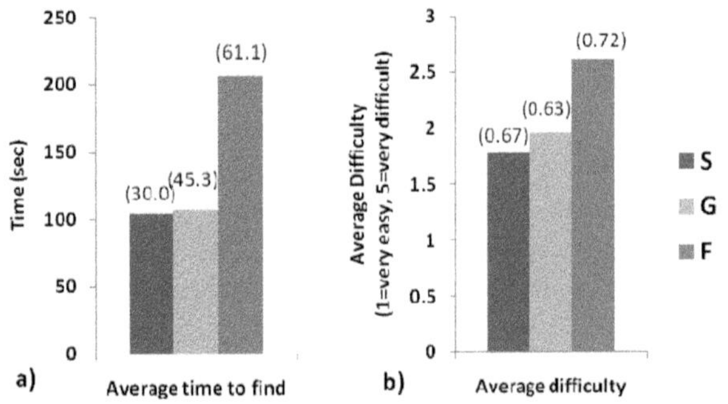

Figure 5. a) Average time and b) Average difficulty in the searching task using skimming vs. regular shortcuts

H4: Subjects could find information faster while skimming with G/S, than when using screen-reader navigation shortcuts.

Results: While using skimming to search for an answer to a question, the subjects took on average 104.13 seconds (St. Dev. 30.00) with S and 107.08 seconds (St. Dev. = 45.33) with G. Using regular screen-reader navigation shortcuts, it took subjects 205.78 seconds (St. Dev. = 61.17) to answer the questions (Figure 5a). A one-way ANOVA was used to test the differences among times subjects took while searching for the answer to a question, with S, G and using regular screen reader shortcuts. The time they took differed significantly across three techniques, $F(2, 66) = 35.02$, $p < 0.0001$. The post-hoc test using Tukey's multiple comparison test shows the difference in time for S and F was significantly different (mean diff = -100.60, q=10.41). Same goes for G and F as well (mean diff = -97.35, q=10.08); thus, we accept H4.

Discussion: Subjects were able to find the answer almost twice as fast using skimming, compared to using regular screen-reader navigation shortcuts. This result demonstrates that skimming can save screen-reader users a substantial amount of time, depending on the size of the text. In our case, since each article had 5 paragraphs, the subjects saved up to 30 seconds per paragraph while searching. The fact that there was no difference between S and G again speaks in favor of our algorithm.

H5: Subjects perceived ad-hoc searching to be more difficult compared to using skimming S or G.

Result: In the search task subjects perceived a difficulty level of 2.60 (St. Dev. = .72) on average while using screen-reading shortcuts without skimming. With skimming S, subjects perceived a difficulty of 1.78 (St. Dev. = 0.67) and with skimming G 1.95 (St. Dev. = 0.63) on average (Figure 5b). Conducting one-way ANOVA test shows significant differences in the perceived difficulty level while finding answers with skimming S, G and using regular screen-reader shortcuts, $F(2, 66) = 9.487$, $p = 0.0002$. The post-hoc test for linear trend also shows: the perceived difficulty increases as you use summary type S, G and screen-reader shortcuts respectively, (Slope 0.4130, $p = 0.0001$). Another post-hoc test, Tukey's multiple comparison test shows that using screen-reader shortcuts is significantly more difficult (mean diff = -0.83, q = 5.84) than skimming S. Similarly using screen-reader shortcuts were more difficult than using skimming G (mean diff = -0.65, q = 4.61); so we accept H5.

Discussion: As the search task using screen-reader shortcuts was involved with listening to full sentences instead of summaries, subjects had to put effort and time to listen in full and find the answer to the question. So using screen-reader shortcuts turns out to be difficult.

H6: The number of keystrokes pressed was the same between searching with skimming and searching with navigation shortcuts.

Result: The average number of keystrokes pressed was 36.60 (St. Dev = 16.21) for Skimming summary S, 35.65 (St. Dev. = 15.85) for Gold Summary G, and 37.08 (St. Dev. = 26.61) for Full text F. A one way ANOVA test showed no statistically significant differences between the number of keystrokes while searching with S, G and using navigation shortcuts $F(2, 66) = 0.0301$, $p = 0.9703$. Thus, we accept H6.

Discussion: These findings demonstrate that skimming does not require more effort in terms of pressing shortcuts, compared to the regular navigation. At the same time, skimming increases the navigation speed twofold (H4).

H7: Subjects were not able to distinguish between human- and computer-generated summaries.

Results: After each listening-and-comprehension, subjects were asked to identify whether the text was written by a human. On average in 66.66% of cases (St. Dev.=48.3%) cases they mistook Skimming Summary S for the Gold-standard summary G. And, on average, in 76.2% of cases (St. Dev. 43.6%) cases they were not able to distinguish between Skimming Summary S and Gold Summary G. The one-tailed paired t-test shows that there is no significant difference between the choices subject made while detecting S and G as human written or not ($t=1.369$, $df=20$, $p=0.186$). This means most of the time they were not able to distinguish between Gold-standard summary and Skimming summary; confirming H7.

Discussion: This is another result that supports the claim that the proposed Skimming algorithm could generate summaries that were almost as good as those written by humans.

We observe no difference in performance on these tasks between groups of subjects:

H8: who lost their eyesight before the age of 10, 15, or 20 and those who lost sight later.

H9: belonging to different age categories.

H10: with different comfort level and different amount of time spent with computers.

Post-Completion Questionnaire Analysis

The post completion questions and answers about the skimming experience are presented in Table 3. The analysis showed that the standard deviation for all questions was within one point, demonstrating high consistency.

General Statements	Avg. (St. Dev.)
I wish I could look through articles faster, than I can with a screen reader	4.30 (0.82)
I often experience difficulties looking for desired information within an article	3.60 (1.11)
Skimming made reading through articles faster	4.22 (0.85)
I understood articles equally well when skimming and when reading the full article	2.82 (1.07)
I want to use skimming in the future	4.26 (1.00)
I would like to see skimming implemented in a commercial screen reader	4.60 (1.15)

Table 3 – Average 5-Point Likert scale values (St. Dev.) (Scale 1=Strongly Disagree to 5=Strongly Agree)

From the statements made by subjects, we can conclude that skimming has a lot of potential to improve the reading experience for screen-reader users. Although the subjects thought that their comprehension was somewhat impeded in the skimming mode, almost all subjects agreed that skimming made the reading faster and they wanted to use skimming in the future.

One of the subjects made a comment that non-visual skimming is "...very useful to glimpse over articles. May be very useful for test takers and also for sighted people (while driving and reading news/articles)". It indicates a possible application of skimming that would allow not only blind but also sighted users to take advantage of audio skimming. Skimming can be useful to sighted users who want to relax their eye and listen to web content faster.

TESTIMONIALS

In this section, we present a short selection of the positive comments made by subjects about skimming:

"It's less labor intensive, I set to skim mode and sit and listen as opposed to reading full sentences. I am more inclined to use skimming now."

"...easier because it was faster. I usually go line by line. I miss important things, when I go line by line. And sometimes I have to go back and start from beginning to double check. But skimming picks the important thing for me"

"it makes efficient and quick access to the document. I can get through a longer doc speedily. I would like to buy this tool. I think this can also be helpful to skim through ads"

Although the majority of comments were highly positive, 3 participants were not as happy with the skimming interface:

"I like detailed information much more."

"People who are not born blind, they can perceive skimming fast. But people who are born blind, it's new to them, needs training."

"I prefer normal reading. I don't like fragmented words."

While it is true that non-visual skimming needs some practice (just like visual skimming), it is notable that the subjects who made those comments did not perform any worse than the rest of the participants; they completed the searching task faster with skimming compared to ad-hoc searching, and they answered most of the questions in the listening and comprehension tasks.

ACKNOWLEDGEMENT

Research reported in this paper was supported by NSF Awards IIS-0808678 and CNS-0751083.

CONCLUSIONS AND FUTURE WORK

The approach proposed in this paper can summarize one sentence at a time without the dependence on the entire document. It can extract meaningful word combinations from most sentences and preserve the original order of the extracted text. All these properties make the proposed summarization approach more suitable for supporting a non-visual skimming interface. Our experiments give reasons to believe that non-visual skimming can enable screen-reader users to browse textual content faster.

This work opens the possibilities to further accelerate non-visual skimming by varying the compression ratio of summarization. This direction of research will require more experiments to evaluate how much information can be retained as we further compress the original text. Armed with the ability to change the amount of information as necessary, people who are blind may be able to battle the information overload more effectively and enjoy the speed-reading commonly used by sighted readers.

There is also room for improving the accuracy of summarization. For instance, we could evaluate more machine learning models. However, as we demonstrated in our user studies, machine-generated summaries do not necessarily have to match those generated by humans to be of equal utility.

Finally, because webpage articles often have formatting, the skimming algorithm can also be extended to take into account the formatting used to emphasize text.

REFERENCES

[1] Ahmed, F., Y. Borodin, Y. Puzis, and I.V. Ramakrishnan, *Why Read if You Can Skim: Towards Enabling Faster Screen Reading*, in *W4A*. 2012.

[2] Ahmed, F., M.A. Islam, Y. Borodin, and I.V. Ramakrishnan, *Assistive web browsing with touch interfaces*, in *Proceedings ACM SIGACCESS*. 2010, ACM: Florida, USA. p. 235-236.

[3] Amitay, E. and C. Paris., *Automatically summarising web sites: is there a way around it?*, in *CIKM*. 2000, ACM. p. 173.

[4] Berger, A.L. and V.O. Mittal., *Ocelot: a system for summarizing web pages*, in *SIGIR*. 2000, ACM Press. p. 144.

[5] Berghel, H., *Cyberspace 2000: Dealing with Information Overload.* COMMUNICATIONS OF THE ACM, 1997. 40-2.

[6] Bigham, J.P., A.C. Cavender, J.T. Brudvik, J.O. Wobbrock, and R.E. Ladner, *WebinSitu: A Comparative Analysis of Blind and Sighted Browsing Behavior*, in *Assets*. 2007, ACM New York, NY, USA ©2007: Tempe, Arizona, USA.

[7] Borodin, Y., F. Ahmed, M.A. Islam, Y. Puzis, V. Melnyk, S. Feng, I.V. Ramakrishnan, and G. Dausch, *Hearsay: a new generation context-driven multi-modal assistive web browser*, in *WWW*. 2010, ACM: Raleigh, North Carolina, USA.

[8] Borodin, Y., J.P. Bigham, G. Dausch, and I.V. Ramakrishnan, *More than meets the eye: a survey of screen-reader browsing strategies*, in *Proceedings of W4A*. 2010, ACM: Raleigh, North Carolina. p. 1-10.

[9] Borodin, Y., J.P. Bigham, R. Raman, and I.V. Ramakrishnan, *What's new?: making web page updates accessible*, in *Proceedings of ACM SIGACCESS*. 2008, ACM, Canada.

[10] Borodin, Y., J. Mahmud, I.V. Ramakrishnan, and A. Stent, *The HearSay non-visual web browser*, in *Proceedings of W4A*. 2007, ACM: Banff, Canada.

[11] Chang, C.-C. and C.-J. Lin, *LIBSVM : a library for support vector machines*, in *ACM Transactions on Intelligent Systems and Technology*. 2011. p. 27:1-27:27.

[12] Chuang, W.T. and J. Yang, *Extracting sentence segments for text summarization: a machine learning approach*, in *Proceedings of ACM SIGIR*. 2000, ACM: Greece. p. 152-159.

[13] DeJong, G., *Skimming stories in real time: An experiment in integrated understanding*, in *Research Report 158*. 1979, Department of Computer Science, Yale Univesity.

[14] Fischer, G. and C. Stevens., *Information access in complex, poorly structured information spaces*, in *CHI*. 1991, ACM Press. p. 63–70.

[15] Goldstein, J., M. Kantrowitz, V.O. Mittal, and J.G. Carbonell, *Summarizing Text Documents: Sentence Selection and Evaluation Metrics*, in *In Research and Development in Information Retrieval*. 1999. p. 121-128.

[16] Hall, M., E. Frank, G. Holmes, B. Pfahringer, P. Reutemann, and I.H. Witten, *The WEKA Data Mining Software: An Update*, in *SIGKDD Explorations*. 2009.

[17] Harper, S. and N. Patel, *Gist summaries for visually impaired surfers*, in *Proceedings of ACM SIGACCESS*. 2005, ACM: Baltimore, MD, USA.

[18] Hori, C., S. Furui, R. Malkin, H. Yu, and A. Waibel, *A statistical approach to automatic speech summarization.* EURASIP J. Appl. Signal Process., 2003. p. 128-139.

[19] Islam, A.M., Y. Borodin, and I.V. Ramakrishnan, *Mixture Model based Label Association Techniques for Web Accessibility*, in *UIST*. 2010: New York, NY, USA.

[20] Jacobs, P.S., *To parse or not to parse: relation-driven text skimming*, in *Proceedings of ACL- Volume 2*. 1990, Association for Computational Linguistics: Finland. p. 194.

[21] JAWS, *Screen reader from Freedom Scientific*. 2011. http://www.freedomscientific.com/products/fs/jaws-product-page.asp.

[22] JAWS_Skimming. *Skim Reading*. 2011; Available from: http://www.freedomscientific.com/Training/Surfs-up/Skim_Reading.htm.

[23] Klein, D. and C.D. Manning., *Accurate Unlexicalized Parsing*, in *Proceedings of ACL*. 2003. p. 423-430.

[24] Lamb, A. and L. Johnson. *Skimming and Scanning*. 1999; Available from: http://42explore.com/skim.htm.

[25] Litvak, M. and M. Last, *Graph-based keyword extraction for single-document summarization*, in *Proceedings of the Workshop on Multi-source Multilingual Information Extraction and Summarization*. 2008, Association for Computational Linguistics: United Kingdom. p. 17.

[26] Mahmud, J.U., Y. Borodin, and I.V. Ramakrishnan, *CSurf: a context-driven non-visual web-browser*, in *Proceedings of WWW*. 2007, ACM: Banff, Alberta, Canada.

[27] Marneffe, M.-C.d., B. MacCartney, and C.D. Manning, *Generating Typed Dependency Parses from Phrase Structure Parses.*, in *LREC* 2006.

[28] MindTools. *Speed Reading*. Available from: http://www.mindtools.com/speedrd.html.

[29] NVDA. *NonVisual Desktop Access*. 2009 [cited 2009]; Available from: http://www.nvda-project.org/.

[30] Popovici, V., W. Chen, B.G. Gallas, C. Hatzis, W. Shi, F.W. Samuelson, Y. Nikolsky, M. Tsyganova, A. Ishkin, T. Nikolskaya, K.R. Hess, V. Valero, D. Booser, M. Delorenzi, G.N. Hortobagyi, L. Shi, W.F. Symmans, and L. Pusztai, *Effect of training-sample size and classification difficulty on the accuracy of genomic predictors.* Breast Cancer Research, 2010.

[31] Radev, D.R., E. Hovy, and K. McKeown, *Introduction to the special issue on summarization.* CL, 2002. 28(4): p. 399-408.

[32] RealSpeak. *RealSpeak Solo Direct Voices for Freedom Scientific Products*. 2011; Available from: http://www.freedomscientific.com/downloads/RealSpeak-Solo-Direct-Voices/RealSpeak-Solo-Direct-Downloads.asp.

[33] Sweller, J., *Cognitive load during problem solving: Effects on learning*, in *Cognitive Science*. 1988.

[34] Wharton, S.W., *An analysis of the effects of sample size on classification performance of a histogram based cluster analysis procedure,* in *Pattern Recognition*. 1984. p. 239-244.

[35] Window-Eyes, *Screen Reader GW Micro*. 2010. http://www.gwmicro.com/Window-Eyes.

[36] Zajicek, M., C. Powell, and C. Reeves, *A Web navigation tool for the blind*, in *Proceedings of the third international ACM conference on Assistive technologies*. 1998, ACM: Marina del Rey, California, United States. p. 204-206.

[37] Zechner, K., *Fast Generation of Abstracts from General Domain Text Corpora by Extracting Relevant Sentences*, in *COLING '96 Proceedings of the 16th conference on Computational linguistics - Volume 2*. 1996.

PICOntrol: Using a Handheld Projector for Direct Control of Physical Devices through Visible Light

Dominik Schmidt[1,2], David Molyneaux[3,2], Xiang Cao[1]

[1]Microsoft Research Asia
Beijing, China
xiangc@microsoft.com

[2]Lancaster University
Bailrigg, Lancaster, UK
schmidtd@comp.lancs.ac.uk

[3]Microsoft Corporation
Redmond, WA, USA
davmo@microsoft.com

ABSTRACT

Today's environments are populated with a growing number of electric devices which come in diverse form factors and provide a plethora of functions. However, rich interaction with these devices can become challenging if they need be controlled from a distance, or are too small to accommodate user interfaces on their own. In this work, we explore *PICOntrol*, a new approach using an off-the-shelf handheld pico projector for direct control of physical devices through visible light. The projected image serves a dual purpose by simultaneously presenting a visible interface to the user, and transmitting embedded control information to inexpensive sensor units integrated with the devices. To use PICOntrol, the user points the handheld projector at a target device, overlays a projected user interface on its sensor unit, and performs various GUI-style or gestural interactions. PICOntrol enables direct, visible, and rich interactions with various physical devices without requiring central infrastructure. We present our prototype implementation as well as explorations of its interaction space through various application examples.

Author Keywords: Handheld projector; physical devices; visible light communication

ACM Classification Keywords: H.5.2 [Information interfaces and presentation]: User Interfaces. – Input devices and strategies

General terms: Design; Human Factors

INTRODUCTION

In everyday environments, we are increasingly surrounded by a growing number of electric devices. At the same time, many of these devices are shrinking in physical size. Both developments come along with their own challenges when it comes to controlling these devices. On the one hand, a plethora of devices imply that not all of them will be in physical reach when needed. Therefore, many people may prefer control at a distance for convenience. On the other hand, small devices are less able to accommodate control interfaces on their surfaces. In fact, user interface hardware is a major limitation to device miniaturization [19].

UIST '12, October 7–10, 2012, Cambridge, Massachusetts, USA.

A common solution to these challenges is to decouple and externalize the user interface onto a separate control device. This not only allows for control at a distance, but may also provide access to a larger set of functions than is accommodated or desired through an on-device interface. For example, current remote controls for home entertainment systems often provide far more functions than are accessible directly on the device itself. Despite this appeal for a decoupled control interface, it also has several drawbacks. Above all, the interaction is no longer *direct*. Users have to divide and switch their attention between the controlling and the controlled. Further, if the user wishes to use a single control device to operate multiple devices in the environment, an explicit selection needs to be made first to indicate the intended target. This becomes cumbersome if the candidate list is long, and requires mental load to map abstract selection to spatially distributed physical targets. Finally, the user is often limited by the size and (lack of) display capability of the control device in hand, which in turn constrains the interaction richness.

Driven by these challenges, we explore *PICOntrol*, a new interaction approach that employs an off-the-shelf pico projector as the handheld control device for users to directly operate various physical devices in the environment. Figure 1 presents a simple example. To use PICOntrol, the user points the handheld projector directly at the device to be controlled (implicit and intuitive selection), and casts a projected graphical user interface (enlarged display capability) directly over a photo sensor unit integrated with the device (no divided attention) to perform a variety of GUI-style or gestural operations (enriched interactions) in order to control the device.

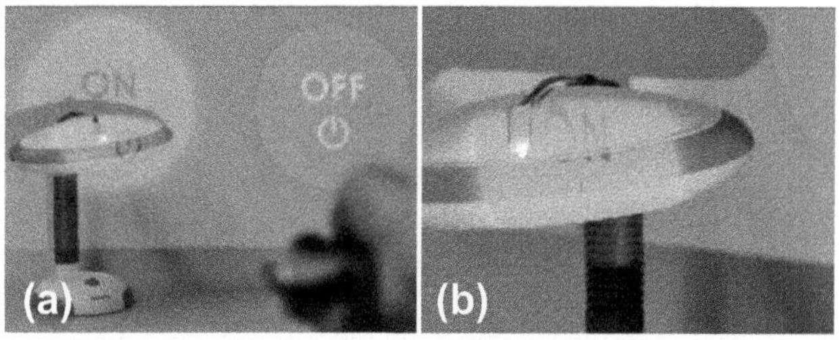

Figure 1. A simple example of PICOntrol interaction. (a) Pointing the handheld projector at a lamp. (b) Casting the projected button "ON" over the sensor unit and pressing an activation pushbutton on the projector turns on the lamp.

PICOntrol is made possible by having the projection simultaneously serve a dual purpose, both for presenting the visual interface to the user, and for transmitting control information to the sensor unit by embedding binary codes in the visible light. In doing so, PICOntrol removes the need for a dedicated channel or central infrastructure for communication. This also results in PICOntrol's technical simplicity. Both the physical size and the hardware complexity of the sensor units are minimal, making them easy to integrate into various physical devices. Based on the prediction that miniaturized projectors will become widely integrated in handheld devices such as mobile phones [17], and since PICOntrol does not require modification or augmentation on the projector, we anticipate future users may use PICOntrol spontaneously without carrying additional devices.

RELATED WORK

Direct Control of Physical Devices

Infrared (IR), radio frequency (RF), or WiFi based remote controls are becoming more widely used to operate various physical devices in the environment. However, given the weak or lack of directionality of the control signal (in the case of IR, the IR light is intentionally diffused, otherwise it is nearly impossible to aim the invisible single light beam to the receiver), it becomes necessary to explicitly select the intended device to control. Currently this is either done by physically choosing from multiple dedicated controllers, or in the case of "universal remote controls", the target device is selected through an abstract hardware or software user interface (e.g. button or touch screen). In addition, the user's attention is divided between the control interface and the device to control. Such an indirect control mechanism may cause both inconvenience and inefficiency.

Motivated by similar goals as us, researchers have explored direct pointing interaction with physical objects using a laser pointer. The laser dot may be detected directly by a photo sensor (e.g. [3, 23]). However, hand tremor makes precise pointing at distant targets difficult [18]. This has caused several systems to increase their sensor size, requiring additional space on the target device [16, 23]. Further, as only a single dot is visible, the richness of direct-pointing interaction using a laser pointer is rather limited. To enrich the interaction space, researchers have explored using a situated camera to track the laser dot position in space, supporting gestural input for devices (e.g. to guide home robots to perform various tasks [12, 13]). Alternatively, as a middle ground between direct-pointing and indirect control, Ringwald [23] uses a laser pointer to select a device, and a handheld device (PDA) as the user interface to perform richer but indirect control. In comparison, PICOntrol not only provides a much richer projected user interface, but also alleviates the hand tremor problem since the user only needs to overlay a relatively large user interface component on the sensor unit rather than aligning a dot to it.

More comprehensive approaches, which aim at supporting both direct and rich interaction, generally rely on a substantial amount of infrastructure. For example, XWand [1] enables natural interaction in smart environments through pointing, gesture, and speech input. The wand's location is tracked by two situated cameras, and each device to be controlled is first represented as a 3D model. WorldCursor [28] avoids cameras, but adds a ceiling-mounted steerable laser pointer to provide a real-world cursor controlled by the wand's motion. Light Widgets [9] uses a set of cameras tracking the users' hands to turn arbitrary surfaces into interactive widgets for controlling physical devices. Further work investigates using photos (e.g. [25]) or augmented live video (e.g. [5]) of the devices as a proxy to "directly" interact with them from a distance. In addition to external tracking of the handheld control device or prior knowledge of the environment or both, all of the above also require a central communication infrastructure to which each device is networked. Neither is needed for PICOntrol, as it directly communicates with the device through visible light in a peer-to-peer fashion, and any motion sensing involved is achieved through the sensor units themselves and relative to the device to be controlled (to be detailed later). In addition, with the user interface projected on the device to be controlled, the directness of the interaction is further increased compared to other solutions.

Handheld Projector Interaction

Using handheld projectors as a novel interaction device has attracted interest of many researchers. However, the majority of work concerns presenting and interacting with digital content, such as for exploring virtual information spaces using a flashlight metaphor [6, 21], supporting GUI-style software applications [2], or augmenting physical objects with digital content [2, 6, 22]. Unlike PICOntrol, all these systems are based on the principle that the projected digital information should remain geometrically static to the physical world, thus relying on constant active stabilization and rectification of the projected image. This requires either an external sensing infrastructure or an onboard camera system to track the projector and compensate for its movement, as well as calibration of the projector and the environment. In contrast, MotionBeam [27] and SideBySide [26] employ an alternative interaction style, not attempting to mitigate projector movement, but instead using it to directly move a digital game character that follows the projection.

In general, many of these works [6, 22] attempt changing the projected information in response to the physical context, but few have explored the opposite direction: controlling the physical world with handheld projection. MotionBeam [27] provides one simple example. Another exception is CoGAME [11] which adopts handheld projectors to manipulate mobile robots from a distance, using a central communication and external tracking infrastructure for both the projection and robots. PICOntrol, in comparison, does not rely on tracking the projector or stabilizing the image, therefore does not require any central infrastructure or calibration.

Encoded Projection

Several researchers have explored transmitting code via visible projection to be received by photo sensors. For example, such code may enable localizing of photo sensors for automatic projection calibration [14], tracking movable surfaces [15, 24], or transmitting payload information such as audio stream [20]. Many of these works rely on Digital Light Processing (DLP) projectors (some with custom hardware modification [15]), given that their fast-flipping mirrors lend themselves to encoding the projected light. Nii et al., in contrast, demonstrate using general luminance variations to embed information using an arbitrary projector [20]. Perhaps the most related to our work is RFIG Lamps [22], which uses dedicated Gray code images that are projected by a handheld projector equipped with RF communication and an onboard camera. This is for the handheld device to recover the 3D locations of active RF tags augmented with photo sensors, and in turn the geometry of surfaces or objects they are embedded in. Like many other handheld projector works, this knowledge was mainly used for subsequently projecting augmenting information to the physical environment, but without the intention to physically influence it. In contrast, PICOntrol addresses a distinctive set of design and technical challenges to support rich interactions to directly control physical devices. By embedding both command and location codes into projected user interfaces, the projection is both to be interpreted by the device being controlled, and at the same time to be viewed and operated by the user.

PROTOTYPE IMPLEMENTATION

PICOntrol consists of two components, the handheld projector as the control device, and the sensor units to be integrated with physical devices to be controlled (Figure 2). The image projected by the handheld projector serves a dual purpose: it presents a visible interface to the user and at the same time embeds codes to be detected by the sensor unit. An off-the-shelf pico projector and inexpensive photo sensors are used to implement PICOntrol. As communication takes place in a peer-to-peer fashion, PICOntrol does not require central infrastructure (e.g. wireless networks); and as selecting the device to control happens implicitly by projecting on it (thus communicating to it), PICOntrol does not need prior knowledge of the layout of physical devices in the environment. Unlike other handheld projector systems, we do not apply image stabilization or rectification, thus do not require tracking or calibrating the projector. In fact, we explicitly use the changing location of the projected user interface for interaction.

Consistent with most of today's remote controls, communication in PICOntrol currently takes place in a unidirectional fashion from the controller to the controlled device. This simplicity allows us to maintain a minimalist system design, not requiring any augmentation on the handheld projector (thus preserving a wider applicability), while still supporting a rich interaction space. Nonetheless, the addition of a similarly simple and peer-to-peer backward communication channel from the sensor unit to the projector (e.g. using similar encoding schemes with the LED on the sensor unit and adding a single photo sensor on the projector) could certainly provide further functionalities, such as automatically selecting a specialized user interface for the device or displaying its internal states to the user using the projector, which we leave for future explorations.

Handheld Projector

We use an unmodified off-the-shelf Microvision SHOWWX pico laser projector to project the user interface. Our encoding and transmission scheme, however, is not reliant on a certain projection technology, and can be generalized to all pico projectors. In our prototype, the projector is connected to a laptop which generates the required image data at 60 Hz. Further, we added a set of simple pushbuttons to the top of the projector (Figure 2a). The buttons are connected via an Arduino nano microcontroller to the same laptop and are used for basic input (i.e. one button to activate control, and two buttons for cycling through different projected user interfaces). In real world usage, however, we envision the projector to be integrated with an existing handheld device (e.g. a mobile phone, as early models already becoming available in the market), and the user can use the input mechanism available on the handheld device in place of the pushbuttons.

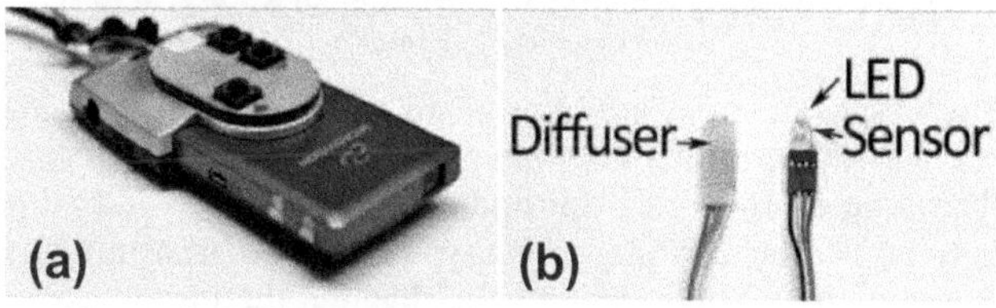

Figure 2. PICOntrol prototype. (a) Pico projector with pushbuttons for basic input. (b) Two sensor units, with and without diffuser attached.

Sensor Unit

A sensor unit (Figure 2b) includes an LED to indicate that a projection signal is being detected, and one or several photo sensors to decode signals (the actual number depends on the target application, as detailed later). Each TAOS TSL13S-LF light-to-voltage photo sensor is connected via a resistor-capacitor (RC) circuit to the same Arduino nano 328 microcontroller, using its analog input pins. The RC circuit acts as low-pass filter to smooth the projected signal and facilitates detection; it comprises an 8 kOhm resistor and a 0.01 μF capacitor. An acrylic diffuser is attached in front of the sensor for it to robustly detect projections from all angles and without requiring accurate pixel alignment. The photo sensor(s) and the LED are the only parts that are visible to the user (costing under $2), while we envision the RC circuit and the microcontroller to be embedded inside the controlled device in the future. Therefore, the required space on the outside of a device is minimal (5 mm^2 for the sensor plus an additional 3 mm^2 for the LED in a single-sensor setup). Moreover, as suggested by Dietz et al. [8], existing LED on the device (such as power indicators) could potentially double as photo sensors by alternating them between emitting and detecting light, further decreasing the space requirement.

Code Transmission

The handheld projector transmits codes to a sensor unit by systematically changing the brightness of pixels in a projected user interface over time. As pixels can be changed independently, multiple arbitrary codes can be transmitted concurrently using different projection regions. However, a sensor unit only receives the codes contained in the projection user interface region directly over it.

Encoding Scheme

We support two types of temporal binary codes: command codes and location codes. A command code encodes an individual command, represented by a discrete region within the projected user interface, such as on or off buttons. In contrast, location codes identify the location of the sensor unit within the projected image, for example to input continuous values when adjusting a virtual slider, or to perform a gesture. Similar to [14, 15, 21], we use Gray codes to encode locations. Each frame consists of bright and dark stripes, subdividing the projection area successively. We first encode horizontal positions, followed by vertical positions, which are projected in a sequence to uniquely identify locations in a grid (Figure 3).

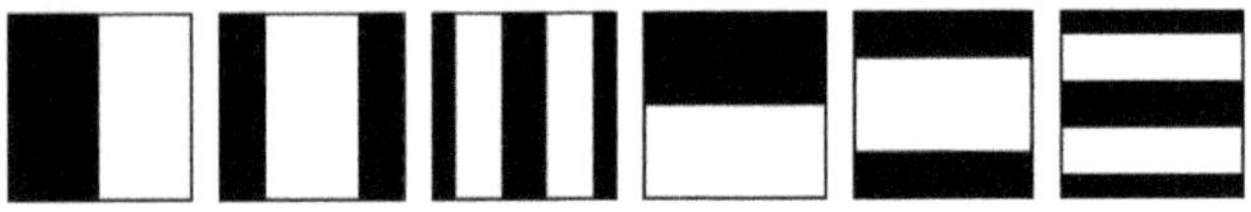

Figure 3. Gray code patterns, encoding an 8 x 8 grid in six consecutive frames.

Both types of codes are transmitted on demand by pressing the activation pushbutton mounted on top of the projector. The same code is transmitted repeatedly while the activation pushbutton is being pressed. To transmit any binary code via the visible light channel, the brightness of pixels is varied accordingly over time. We represent 0-bits by low and 1-bits by high intensities respectively. In doing so, the absolute sensed intensity is not critical, as long as the contrast between low and high is sufficiently large to be detectable. In addition, our mapping ensures that different interface colors yield consistent intensity readings to the hue-insensitive photo sensor. Therefore, we can vary the brightness value of each pixel to represent the binary code while preserving its hue value, and transmit codes at any point in the projected image despite the various user interfaces displayed.

Embedded Synchronization and Calibration Signal

PICOntrol does not require an additional channel for synchronization, but instead embeds this information into the visible light channel used for data transmission. In particular, we project a single frame of black pixels within the code transmission regions, at the beginning and end of each code word to surround and hence delimit it, allowing for variable code lengths. Black image frames are particularly easy to detect with a laser scanning line projectors such as the one we use, as no light is transmitted during them. Minimal backlight during black frames with other projection technologies can also be accounted for by adjusting the detection thresholds accordingly. Such a single black frame (i.e. 16.7 ms) is further highly unlikely to be confused with other conditions (e.g. if the projection was moved away or covered temporarily, this would result in a longer interval of missing signal), and thus serves as reliable indicator to distinguish between normal projection and the start/end of code transmission.

While using PICOntrol, distance and angle between the projector and the sensor unit naturally vary as users are controlling devices from different locations. The sensors thus may receive different light intensities for the same projected brightness, depending on how the projector and the sensor unit are located towards each other. To ensure correct mapping of the sensed light intensity to the intended bit value, we additionally include a short calibration sequence after the synchronization frame, but before transmitting the actual code word. This proved to be more robust than solely relying on brightness contrast. The calibration sequence consists of one 0-bit and one 1-bit to set reference intensity values for the code word that follows. In addition, these two bits also indicate the type of the code being transmitted (i.e. 0-1 for location code, and 1-0 for command code). Figure 4 illustrates the complete transmission sequence for a single code, consisting of header (synchronization and calibration), actual code word, and tail (synchronization). The time that the sensor unit requires to receive and decode a code varies depending on the code type and length, resulting in the system response time ranging between 200 and 400 ms.

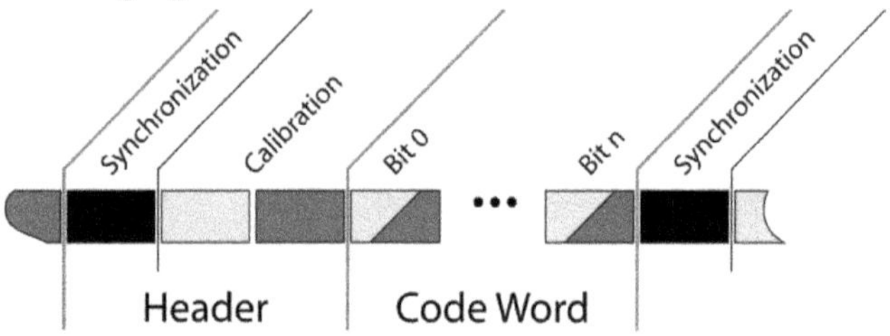

Figure 4. Code transmission sequence.

Rapidly changing the pixel brightness for code transmission inherently results in image flicker. However, this perceivable flickering only happens when the user presses the button, and is further restricted to regions of interest in the user interface. It incidentally serves as a direct visual feedback to the user, indicating an operation is being performed. Further, to ensure that the projected user interfaces are still recognizable by the user during code transmission, they are rendered based on hue contrast rather than brightness contrast. This results in color differences perceivable by human eyes, but the same intensity detected by the photo sensor. During our informal user trials with four participants (one hour each), none complained about the flicker.

Signal Detection

Although the encoding, transmission, and decoding scheme is generic, the way that the sensor unit physically detects the visible light signal may slightly vary between projection technologies, but is generally straightforward. For example, detecting signals from DLP projectors using photo sensors has been demonstrated (e.g. [14]). In our prototype we use a Microvision SHOWWX laser projector, which employs a scan-line-based approach. Three modulated laser sources (red, green, and blue) are combined into a single beam which is then reflected off a scanning mirror to construct each image pixel sequentially in a zigzag fashion. Thus the sensor unit overlaid by the projected image only receives projected light at the time when the laser beam passes over it, and an image frame is detected as a peak in the sensed light intensity. By maintaining the average intensity over a recent time window of 3 μs, we remove the influence of varying ambient lighting on the peak detection. In our prototype implementation, the sensor unit can detect the projector's signal from a distance of up to 4 m.

SENSOR UNIT DESIGNS AND INTERACTIONS

Here, we discuss three distinct sensor unit designs based on the above hardware and code transmission method. These include a single-sensor unit, a dual-sensor unit, and a color-sensor unit (Figure 5). The varying number of sensors enables different sets of interactions in a range of application scenarios. The single- and dual-sensor units, which we focus on in this paper, capture light intensity only. The single-sensor unit detects discrete interface components as well as location and lateral motion within the projection. The dual-sensor unit further enables detection of in-plane rotation and distance between the projector and the unit. Finally, the color-sensor unit enables further interaction possibilities based on color. All sensor units feature an LED that indicates detection of projection, and also facilitates the user to further position the projected interface.

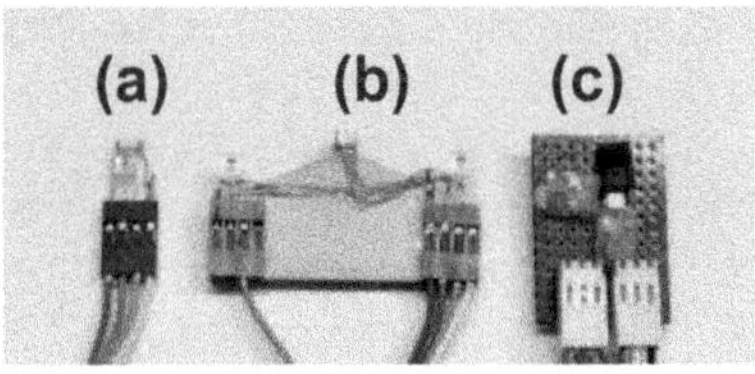

Figure 5. Sensor unit designs (shown without diffuser): (a) Single-sensor unit. (b) Dual-sensor unit. (c) Color-sensor unit.

Interaction Style

PICOntrol interactions share a common style. The projected image comprises one or several active regions which represent interface components, such as buttons or sliders, or an area for gestural input. An interaction is prepared by aiming the projection at the target device and overlaying the interface component in question on the sensor unit. Choosing the device and the function are hence achieved in a single continuous step. To trigger the interaction, the user presses the projector-mounted activation pushbutton. While the button is pressed, all active regions in the image keep transmitting their respective codes simultaneously, but only the code that is directly over the sensor unit will be received. Depending on the application, this may conclude the interaction (*static interaction*, e.g. to execute a command), or may be followed by moving the projector while keeping the activation pushbutton pressed (*motion-based interaction*, e.g. for adjusting a value using a slider or a knob, or for gestural input). In some cases, the active region may cover the entire image to enable larger scale gesture detection by tracking the sensor unit's location across the whole projection area.

Common user interface components (e.g. on-off switches, or sliders and knobs for adjusting a single parameter such as volume) could be made universally applicable to various devices and be interpreted accordingly by the respective device. Therefore, many typical projected interfaces can be reused across various devices with the same layout and codes. Some other functionality may be device-specific, requiring a particular control interface. In this case, device identification headers can be added to the transmitted code to avoid duplicate codes across devices. In our current implementation, the user can cycle through the available set of control interfaces using the two other pushbuttons on the projector. In future applications where the projector is integrated in a smart handheld device, we envision the user may use its touch screen to select or customize a specialized user interface to project. Finally, as we discussed, in future PICOntrol explorations which may feature a backward communication channel, the projector may identify the device it is pointing at and automatically project a specialized user interface, thus eliminating the need for user selection altogether.

Single-Sensor Unit

This unit uses a single sensor to capture projected light intensities (Figure 5a). It decodes the information embedded within the active projection region directly over the sensor to enable the interactions detailed in the following. Both static (using command codes) and motion-based interactions (using location codes) are supported. In both cases, the actions can be thought of as an inverse cursor interaction metaphor: instead of moving a cursor to indicate the location in a static user interface as in conventional GUI, here the sensor unit representing the "cursor" is fixed and the projected user interface as a whole is being moved. This bears some similarity to the Toolglass interface [4] and allows for general two-dimensional input equivalent to conventional GUI.

For the sake of simplicity, we first chose a basic lamp scenario to illustrate both kinds of interaction. In doing so, we attached a single-sensor unit to an off-the-shelf desk lamp. For easy prototyping purposes only, the sensor unit controls the lamp via a digitally switchable power outlet to simulate a direct integration with the lamp. With multiple such lamps, the user can use the same projected interface to individually control each of them simply by pointing at it.

Static Interaction

Figure 1 provides an example of static interaction using a basic interface designed to switch a lamp on or off with two dedicated buttons. Here the user overlays one of the projected buttons on the sensor unit mounted on the lamp's shade, and then presses the activation pushbutton on the projector. While different command codes are transmitted within the two buttons at the same time, the sensor unit only receives the command from the button directly over it. Feedback is provided directly in situ by the lamp's lighting state, without the user's attention being divided between the control interface and the target device.

Motion-Based Interaction

Motion-based control enables a range of different interactions. As shown in Figure 6a and 6b, the sensor unit's location can be used to implement crossing-based interfaces [1]. This further mitigates the difficulty of precise freehand pointing and involuntary movement introduced by pressing the activation pushbutton. Here, the user first overlays the sensor unit with either half of the interface, and then horizontally swipes the projection while holding down the activation pushbutton. Upon crossing the center line, the lamp is switched on or off. This interface uses the entire projection area as an active region by filling it with location codes when the activation pushbutton is being pressed.

Projector motion can be further mapped to set continuous values, such as a lamp's brightness. Figure 6c shows a visual slider, where the region of the slider is filled with location codes when the activation pushbutton is being pressed. Slider positions can be mapped to the brightness values of the lamp. In this case, the user can either drag the slider to adjust values continuously, or directly "click" on one position to set the value. Alternatively, the relative motion of the slider can map to the relative change of brightness to achieve a finer control granularity. In this case, the user can perform a clutching action by releasing the activation pushbutton and drag again.

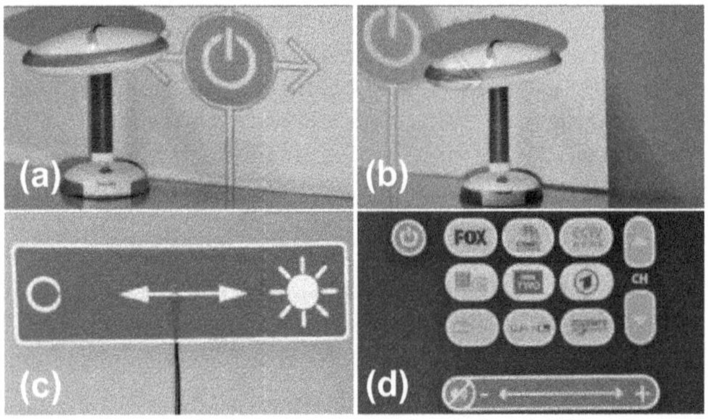

Figure 6. (a, b) A crossing-based switch. (c) Slider for adjusting continuous values. (d) Mixing interface components for controlling a TV.

PICOntrol also supports arbitrary two-dimensional gestures by projecting a location code pattern that spans over the entire image. Again, this pattern is only projected on demand, as long as the user holds down the activation pushbutton. Hence each gesture is demarcated by a pair of button press-release-actions, avoiding random movement to be interpreted as input. To demonstrate this, we simulate a digital photo frame on a standard tablet PC which receives instructions from the sensor unit control circuit via USB (Figure 7). Here, the user can navigate through galleries and photos by aiming the projection at the frame, holding down the activation pushbutton, and flicking to the left or right for going backwards or forwards respectively. A downward flick or an upward flick switches between the photo view and gallery view respectively.

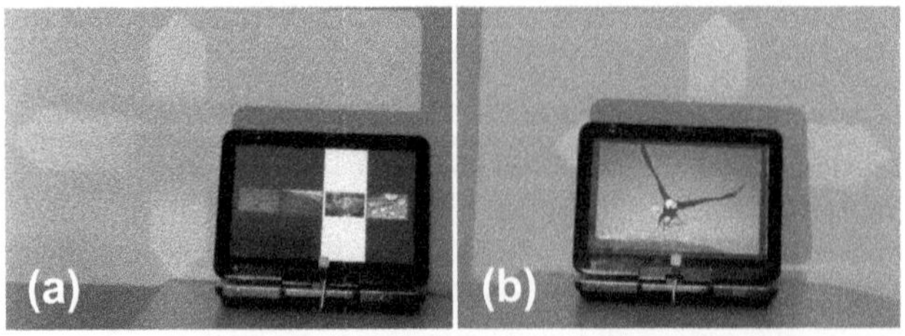

Figure 7. Navigating a digital photo frame with gestures (indicated by arrows) in (a) gallery view (b) photo view.

Obviously, static and motion-based interface components may be mixed to create more complex projected interfaces. Figure 6d illustrates a TV control interface that mixes buttons (static, for selecting channel etc.) and a slider (motion-based, for volume adjustment).

Multi-Device Interaction

As target devices are implicitly selected through pointing, no explicit or abstract device selection step is required. In addition to using the same projected interface to control multiple devices individually, users may also opportunistically combine interactions with multiple devices into one. For example, using the crossing-based switch in Figure 6a, users may hold down the activation pushbutton and swipe the projection over multiple devices to control them all in a single motion. This somewhat resembles the real-world interaction of throwing multiple neighboring light switches at once with a whole hand. In another example, two single-sensor units may be used to control the volume of two neighboring audio speakers respectively, each playing a different audio channel. Instead of using a single slider to control each individually, the user may also use a projection with two parallel vertical sliders to control both sensor units simultaneously. This effectively turns the two independent interface controls into one "macro" control and enables higher-level intuitive operations. Moving the projection up and down changes the overall volume of both channels, while rotating the projection adjusts the balance between the two.

Interaction with Small Devices

PICOntrol interfaces can also provide visible and expressive input for devices too small to accommodate a user interface of their own. To illustrate this, we built a minimalistic music player based on Arduino, which does not have any on-device input mechanisms, but can be entirely operated by PICOntrol using a simple interface echoing the iPod shuffle controls (Figure 8a).

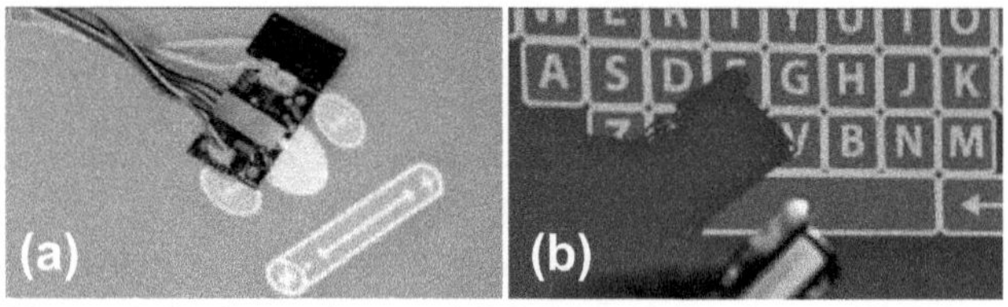

Figure 8. (a) Operating a minimalistic music player. (b) Using the shadow of a device itself as a pointer to enter text.

Similarly, PICOntrol can be used for text input on devices too small to have their own keyboard by projecting a virtual keyboard over it. Following the basic interaction described before, users may input text by moving the projection to overlay the desired character on the sensor unit and then press the activation pushbutton. However, note this motion is relative: the user may instead project the interface statically on a nearby surface and move the device itself to the desired letter, thereby effectively using it as a pointing device for direct interaction with the projection. Alternatively, the user may hold the device between the projector and the surface, hence casting a shadow [cf. 7] on the projected key (Figure 8b). In all cases, when the user presses the activation pushbutton, the respective key input will be transmitted through the sensor unit to the device.

Dual-Sensor Unit

The dual-sensor unit (Figure 5b) extends the previous design by adding a second sensor of the same kind. Both sensors are mounted in the same plane (at a distance of approximately 4 cm in our current prototype, which showed to be a reasonable trade-off between unit size and sensing resolution, to be discussed later) and are connected to the same control circuit. Using location codes as described before, the dual-sensor unit detects two separate locations within the projection simultaneously, one from each of its sensors. Bearing some conceptual similarity to how Minput [10] uses two mouse sensors on the back of a small device to sense its lateral and rotational motion, our dual-sensor unit enables sensing of additional degrees of freedom of the projection (rotation and distance), and extended gestural interaction.

Rotation

The two locations in the projection coordinate space (determined using location code, i.e. Gray codes), in conjunction with the known physical layout of the sensors on the dual-sensor unit, allow for recovering the in-plane (i.e. along the optical axis of the projector) rotation angle between the projector and the sensor unit by the following formula, where (x_1, y_1) stand for the detected location of sensor 1, and (x_2, y_2) for that of sensor 2 respectively:

$$\alpha = atan2(y_2 - y_1, x_2 - x_1)$$

Figure 9 illustrates this. In general, the maximal angular resolution is determined by the detected distance of the two sensors in the Gray code coordinate system, which is in turn dependent on the physical distance between the two sensors (larger distance results in higher angular resolution), the grid density of the projected Gray code (denser grid results in higher angular resolution), and the projection distance between the projector and the sensor unit (smaller distance results in higher angular resolution). In the worst case, if both sensors fall within the same grid cell and report the same location, the rotation angle cannot be determined. While the first two parameters (sensor distance and grid density) are more or less fixed in the system design, and subject to compromise with other design variables (e.g. sensor unit size and code length), the projection distance can be easily changed by the user on the fly, so that the user can choose the best tradeoff point between resolution and convenience that serves them best at the moment.

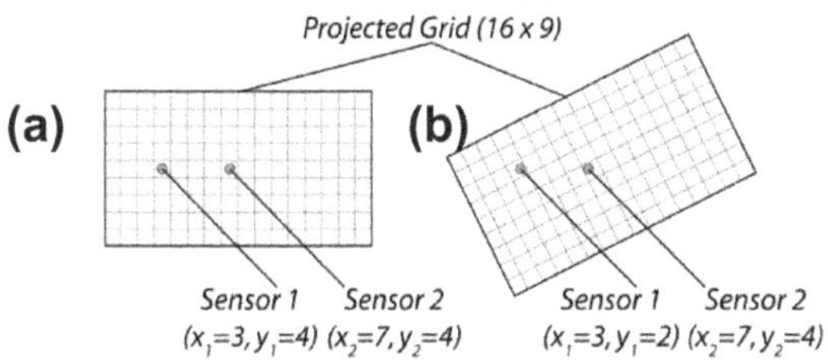

Figure 9. Detecting rotation on a dual-sensor unit. (a) Detected rotation: 0°. (b) Detected rotation: 27°.

Distance

Similarly, the distance between the projector and the sensor unit can be inferred. As shown in Figure 10, moving apart the projector and the sensor unit results in a larger projection, therefore the detected distance between the two sensors with respect to the Gray code coordinates decreases (and vice versa). This allows the dual-sensor unit to detect relative change in projection distance. In addition, if the projector's *ThrowRatio* (i.e. the ratio between the projection distance and the physical width W_{Proj} of the projected image) is known, the absolute physical distance between the projector and the sensor unit, D_{proj}, can also be calculated as:

$$D_{proj} = ThrowRatio \times W_{Proj}$$

where $W_{proj} = \frac{ResolutionX_{code} \times D_{sensors}}{D_{code}}$

$D_{sensors}$ refers to the physical distance between the two sensors, and $ResolutionX_{code}$ refers to the number of Gray code grid cells along the projection's X axis, both of which are fixed. $\boldsymbol{D_{code}} = \sqrt{(\boldsymbol{x_1} - \boldsymbol{x_2})^2 + (\boldsymbol{y_1} - \boldsymbol{y_2})^2}$ refers to the detected sensor distance in Gray code coordinates, from which we can calculate W_{proj} (physical projection width) and in turn D_{proj}. Here we assume the Gray code grid cells are square, however the formula can easily be adapted for non-square cells. The maximal detectable projection distance is reached once both sensors fall within the same Gray code grid cell (i.e. report the same location).

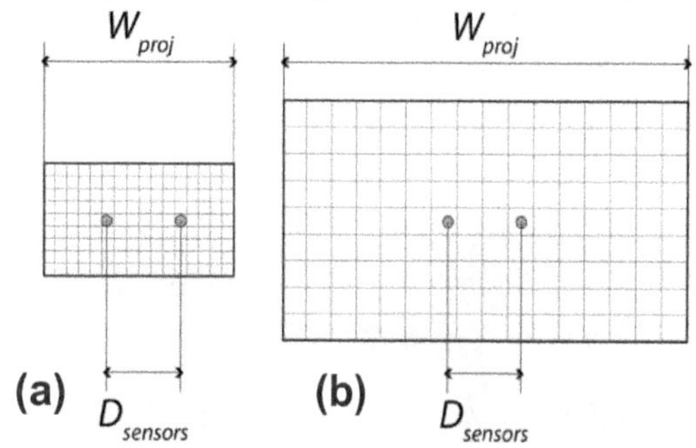

Figure 10. Detecting projection distance on a dual-sensor unit. (a) D_{code}=7. (b) Moving the projector further away, D_{code} decreases to 4.

Note rotation and distance is detected without internal sensors on the projector (e.g. accelerometers/gyros, or camera and RF transponder as used in RFIG lamps [22]) or external tracking infrastructure. Further, as we directly sense the relative position and orientation between the projector and the sensor unit, all projector interactions based on them are also relative to the sensor unit, agnostic of its absolute position and orientation (e.g. it could be mounted on the ceiling facing downwards). This inherently matches the point-and-interact paradigm of PICOntrol and allows the deployment of the sensor units to be entirely flexible. The sensor unit or the device it is connected to may be freely repositioned by the user, or itself may even move during the interaction, as demonstrated in later examples. To achieve the same with absolute sensing such as with internal sensors or external tracker, it would require continuously tracking the positions and orientations of both the projector and the controlled device as well as real-time coordinate transform between the two, a much more complex system to maintain.

The rotation and distance detection algorithm of the dual-sensor unit assumes that the projector's optical axis is approximately perpendicular to the sensor plane. Projecting at an angle may cause less accurate detection results. However, for interaction purposes such inaccuracies are unlikely large enough to be detrimental, as the obliquity is usually reasonably small thanks to the user trying to project a legible user interface. We could potentially create a three-sensor unit capable of sensing full 3D rotation and translation between the projector and the unit, however we suspect interactions based on them may become too complex and subtle to be useful for controlling everyday devices.

Example Applications

We now demonstrate two example applications using a dual-sensor unit. Similar to the linear slider input used with single-sensor units, rotation can also be used to input continuous values. For an intuitive example, to set the hour or minute of an analog clock equipped with a dual-sensor unit, the user points either the minute or the hour control component at the clock with the projected hand at the desired angle. Pressing the activation pushbutton transmits the location codes within both interface components. Thus the rotation between the projector and the clock is detected and used to directly set the respective clock hand to the indicated angle. Continuing rotating the projection while holding down the activation pushbutton allows for further tuning. As shown in Figure 11 we simulated a virtual analog clock displayed on a computer screen.

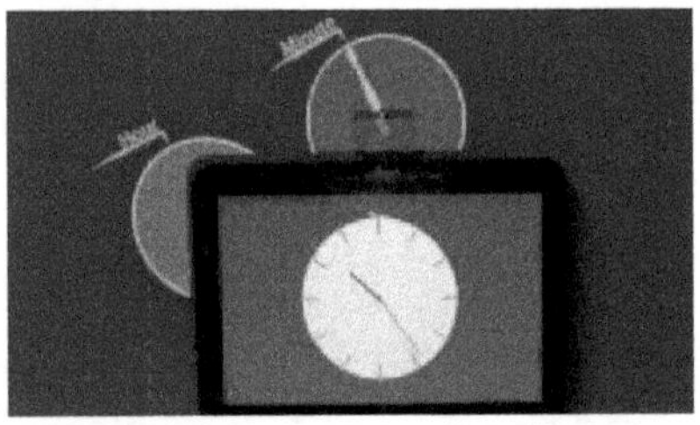

Figure 11. Adjusting a clock by directly setting angles.

In the interactions discussed so far, only the projector is moved or rotated. PICOntrol, however, also lends itself to interaction with moving devices (e.g. home robots such as Roomba™). When controlling such devices, both the projector movement and device movement need to be taken into account. Thanks to our relative detection mechanism, these two types of movements are not differentiated by PICOntrol, and can be seamlessly incorporated into the same interaction, agnostic of whether one or both entities are actually moving. Based on this principle, we demonstrate remotely controlling a toy car with a dual-sensor unit mounted on its roof, using two interaction paradigms: *direct-manipulation* and *follow-the-center*.

With the direct-manipulation paradigm, the user can overlay the projection with the car's dual-sensor unit, press the activation pushbutton, and rotate the projector to rotate the car on the spot. The sensor unit records the initial angle between itself and the projector when the location code is first projected, and subsequently keeps rotating the car if this angle is being changed in order to match the initially recorded angle. By doing so, the car preserves its initial angular alignment with the projection, as if the user is directly rotating the car itself (Figure 12a).

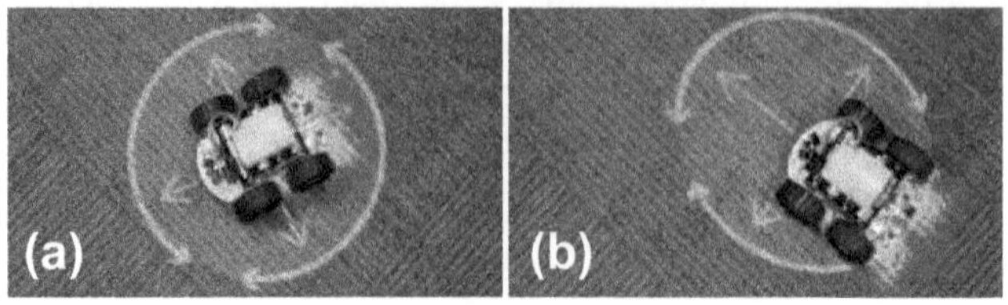

Figure 12. "Direct-manipulation": (a) Rotating on the spot. (b) Swiping to accelerate or decelerate the car.

Swiping the projection along the car's main axis while holding the activation pushbutton will cause it to start moving in the direction of motion (i.e. either forwards or backwards as shown in Figure 12b). The projection itself can be at an arbitrary angle to the car, as long as the direction of the swipe roughly aligns with the car's main axis (as the sensor unit can compensate for lateral motion in different directions by knowing the angle between itself and the projection). Further, if the car is currently already moving when the swiping happens, it will accelerate or decelerate depending on whether the detected swiping direction is the same as or opposite to the current car motion. As the swiping motion is sensed relatively between the projection and the car, this also inherently allows a static projection to serve as a barrier to slow down and eventually stop a moving car, as from the car's perspective a motion opposite the current driving direction is detected.

Note that although the car is interpreting all the control relative to itself, from the users' perspective they are always directly manipulating the car in absolute terms (i.e. world coordinates), as if using their hand to directly manipulate it. Hence the control mechanism remains the same regardless of which direction the user and the car face. This poses a clear advantage over most of today's remote control car interfaces, where the user must operate from the car's perspective and perform counterintuitive mental rotation when facing a different direction.

Figure 13. "Follow-the-center": (a) The car moves to and follows (b) the projection's center.

With the follow-the-center paradigm, the robot car always moves towards the center of the projected image, marked by inwards pointing arrows (Figure 13). In this mode the projector sends location codes continuously. By sensing the rotation and location of the sensor unit with respect to the projection, the car can determine the position of the projection center relative to itself and move accordingly. Users can "catch" the car by aiming the projection at it, and the car will move to and follow the projection's center, with the projection acting as a virtual leash. Hence, the user can guide the car through an arbitrary route.

Color-Sensor Unit

While this paper focuses on sensor units that sense light intensities, here we briefly explore a unit that detects RGB color. We prototyped our color-sensor unit (Figure 5c) using three photo sensors, each equipped with a different narrow band-pass color filter matching the wavelength of the respective color channel (R, G, B) of the projector. The three sensors are mounted with minimal spacing in a triangular arrangement to sense the same projected area. Other off-the-shelf RGB sensors may also be used for this purpose.

The color-sensor unit can support direct codification of locations within the projection based on variations in color in a static image, rather than a temporal code sequence. However, the color-sensor unit may potentially also be combined with temporal codes, for example to increase the transmission bandwidth by using n-ary codes with n colors, or by separating code transmission and user interface to different color channels to minimize interference and perceived flicker. We leave a full exploration of the capability of color-sensor units to future work, and provide one simple application example here: Mood lamps, such as Philips' LivingColors product, allow the user to set the emitted light to an arbitrary color in order to create a certain ambient atmosphere. PICOntrol's visual control interface can make this more intuitive, enabling the user to directly choose a color in a single interaction. The projector projects a color spectrum. To set a specific color, the user presses the activation pushbutton and moves the projection to align the desired color with the lamp's color-sensor unit (Figure 14). While the projection is moved the lamp's color is continuously updated, and to confirm a color selection the user releases the activation pushbutton.

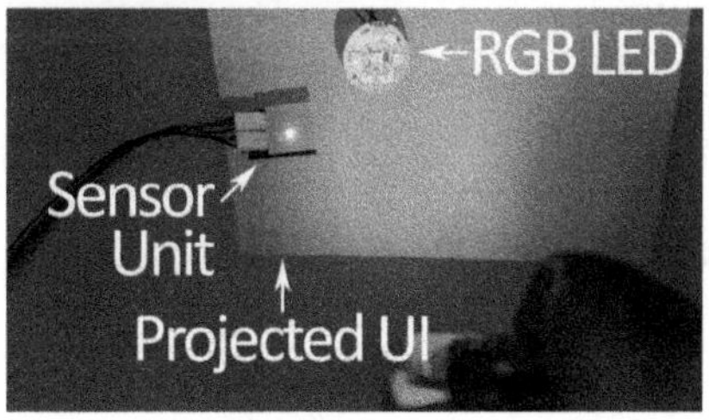

Figure 14. Setting the color of a mood lamp.

DISCUSSION

As mentioned earlier, while we consider a systematic evaluation premature for our proof-of-concept stage, we conducted an informal user trial with four participants (about one hour each) for preliminary feedback. All participants understood the PICOntrol interaction style easily, and were able to use it immediately. They frequently commented on the intuitiveness and "coolness" of the approach, and appreciated its usefulness in supporting everyday tasks. Such feedback supported that our exploration of PICOntrol interactions was successful.

That said, PICOntrol is not without its limitations. Although no participants complained about the visual flicker when control information is transmitted, and it incidentally serves as a feedback mechanism, we do aim to further lower its intrusiveness. We have conducted initial experiments with promising results, which limit code transmission to specific color channels that human eyes are less sensitive to so as to reduce perceivable flicker. This generic solution would work with any off-the-shelf projector. Whereas in scenarios which allow employing specific projection technologies (e.g. higher-frequency projectors, or those based on DLP [15] technology or include an IR projection channel), the visible flicker can be further reduced or removed entirely.

Another limitation is the need for the user to choose a specialized projected interface in some cases. However, with careful interface design, the number of such cases can be considerably reduced. Generic interfaces such as on/off buttons and sliders or knobs for parameter adjustment can be used across a variety of devices, not to mention multiple devices of the same category. In some other cases, the difference between two interfaces is purely visual, for easier understanding by the user, while the underlying codes being transmitted stay the same (e.g. the gestural interface used in Figure 7 and the "follow-the-center" interface used in Figure 13 are both transmitting location codes across the entire image), therefore the interfaces can indeed be used interchangeably. As a result, the burden for the user to select a user interface is lower than that of selecting a device to control with conventional universal controllers. Furthermore, as mentioned previously, the requirement for manually selecting interfaces could ultimately be eliminated by expanding the PICOntrol concept to include a lightweight (likely also via visible light) peer-to-peer backward communication channel in the future.

In everyday environments, the controlled device may not always have a large enough surface or be surrounded by a relatively clean background to accommodate a complete, clear, or undistorted projection. Although this may cause slight inconvenience for users (especially novices) to visualize the full user interface, it does not pose any difficulty to the system, as technically as few as one pixel needs to be projected on each sensor for the code to be detected. Whereas from the user's perspective, once they are sufficiently familiar with the interface layout, only the one interface component being triggered (or part of it thereof) needs to be visible for aiming the projector and controlling the device.

Interfaces become larger when projected at a farther distance. For the most part, this is a beneficial property. Not only their apparent visual size remains relatively constant to the user (since the user is also looking from a farther distance), but also it requires the same amount and precision of angular movement to overlay an interface component on the sensor unit regardless of the distance. Having said that, when several devices are positioned in close proximity and the user is controlling from afar, there is a risk of involuntarily covering and controlling multiple devices at the same time. Introducing mechanisms for the user to optically or digitally zoom the projection on the fly may solve this.

Finally, although we have demonstrated PICOntrol with a variety of concrete and familiar application examples, these are merely starting points for exploring an even richer set of applications. For example, the ability to intuitively control moving devices, as exemplified by the toy car example, may open a new space of human-robot interaction using handheld projectors. We should also note that PICOntrol is not necessarily the best answer for all scenarios, as each control mechanism has their pros and cons, but it should be seen as an alternative interaction approach and technology that addresses some of today's challenges and offers a new interaction space.

CONCLUSION

This work explored the concept of using handheld projectors for direct control of physical devices, using the visible projection to simultaneously present the user interface and transmit the control information. PICOntrol provides direct, visible, and rich interactions with various devices using off-the-shelf handheld pico projectors and inexpensive photo sensors without requiring central infrastructure. We have successfully demonstrated the feasibility of this new approach and presented a first exploration of its rich interaction space. As pico projectors become increasingly integrated with mobile devices, and because our sensor units can be easily integrated with devices at little additional cost, we hope our approach can be readily adopted in the future.

ACKNOWLEDGMENTS

We thank Masahiko Inami, Paul Dietz, Desney Tan, Martina Pagura, and colleagues at Microsoft Research Asia for valuable suggestions and discussions.

REFERENCES

1. Accot, J., and Zhai, S. More than dotting the i's — foundations for crossing-based interfaces. *CHI* (2002), 73–80.
2. Beardsley, P., van Baar, J., Raskar, R., and Forlines, C. Interaction using a handheld projector. *IEEE Comp. Graph. and App.* 25 (2005), 39–43.
3. Beigl, M. Point & Click - interaction in smart environments. *HUC* (1999), 311–313.
4. Bier, E. A., Stone, M. C., Pier, M. C., Buxton, W., and DeRose, T. D. Toolglass and Magic Lenses: the see-through interface. *Computer Graphics and Interactive Techniques* (1993), 73–80.
5. Boring, S., Baur, D., Butz, A., Gustafson, S., and Baudisch, P. Touch projector: Mobile interaction through video. *CHI* (2010), 2287–2296.
6. Cao, X., and Balakrishnan, R. Interacting with dynamically defined information spaces using a handheld projector and a pen. *UIST* (2006), 225–234.
7. Cowan, L. G. and Li, K. A. ShadowPuppets: supporting collocated interaction with mobile projector phones using hand shadows. *CHI* (2011), 2707–2716.
8. Dietz, P. H., Yerazunis, W., and Leigh, D. Very low-cost sensing and communication using bidirectional LEDs. *UbiComp* (2003), 175–191.
9. Fails, J. A., and Olsen, D. Light widgets: Interacting in every-day spaces. *IUI* (2002), 63–69.
10. Harrison, C., and Hudson, S. E. Minput: Enabling interaction on small mobile devices with high-precision, low-cost, multipoint optical tracking. *CHI* (2010), 1661–1664.
11. Hosoi, K., Dao, V. N., Mori, A., and Sugimoto, M. VisiCon: A robot control interface for visualizing manipulation using a handheld projector. *ACE* (2007), 99–106.
12. Ishii, K., Zhao, S., Inami, M., Igarashi, T., and Imai, M. Designing laser gesture interface for robot control. *INTERACT* (2009), 479–492.
13. Kemp, C. C., Anderson, C. D., Nguyen, H., Trevor, A. J., and Zhe, X. A point-and-click interface for the real world: Laser designation of objects for mobile manipulation. *HRI* (2008), 241–248.
14. Lee, J., Dietz, P. H., Maynes-Aminzade, D., Raskar, R., and Hudson, S. E. Automatic projector calibration with embedded light sensors. *UIST* (2004), 123–126.
15. Lee, J., Hudson, S. E., Summer, J. W., and Dietz, P. H. Moveable interactive projected displays using projector based tracking. *UIST* (2005), 63–72.
16. Ma, H., and Paradiso, J. The FindIT flashlight: Responsive tagging based on optically triggered microprocessor wakeup. *UbiComp* (2002), 655–662.
17. Markets and Markets. Global pico projector market. http://www.marketsandmarkets.com/ Market-Reports/ pico-projector-market-196.html, 2010.
18. Myers, B. A., Bhatnagar, R., Nichols, J., Hong, C. H., Kong, D., Miller, R., and Long, A. C. Interacting at a distance: Measuring the performance of laser pointers and other devices. *CHI* (2002), 33–40.
19. Ni, T., and Baudisch, P. Disappearing mobile devices. *UIST* (2009), 101–110.
20. Nii, H., Sugimoto, M., and Inami, M. Smart light-ultra high speed projector for spatial multiplexing optical transmission. *CVPR* (2005), 95–102.
21. Rapp, S., Michelitsch, G., Osen, M., Williams, J., Barbisch, M., Bohan, R., Valsan, Z., and Emele, M. Spotlight navigation: Interaction with a handheld projection device. *Pervasive,* (2004).
22. Raskar, R., Beardsley, P., van Baar, J., Wang, Y., Dietz, P., Lee, J., Leigh, D., and Willwacher, T. RFIG lamps: interacting with a self-describing world via photosensing wireless tags and projectors. *SIGGRAPH* (2004), 406–415.
23. Ringwald, M. Spontaneous interaction with everyday devices using a PDA. *Supporting Spontaneous Interaction in Ubiquitous Computing Workshop* (2002).
24. Summet, J., and Sukthankar, R. Tracking locations of moving hand-held displays using projected light. *Pervasive* (2005), 97–113.
25. Suzuki, G., Aoki, S., Iwamoto, T., Maruyama, D., Koda, T., Kohtake, N., Takashio, K., and Tokuda, H. u-Photo: Interacting with pervasive services using digital still images. *Pervasive* (2005), 190–207.
26. Willis, K. D. D., Poupyrev, I., Hudson, S. E., and Mahler, M. SideBySide: Ad-hoc multi-user interaction with handheld projectors. *UIST* (2011), 431–440.
27. Willis, K. D. D., Poupyrev, I., and Shiratori, T. MotionBeam: A metaphor for character interaction with handheld projectors. *CHI* (2011), 1031–1040.
28. Wilson, A. D., and Pham, H. Pointing in intelligent environments with the WorldCursor. *INTERACT* (2003).
29. Wilson, A. D., and Shafer, S. XWand: UI for intelligent spaces. CHI (2003), 545–55.

DuploTrack: A Real-time System for Authoring and Guiding Duplo Block Assembly

Ankit Gupta, Dieter Fox, Brian Curless
University of Washington
Seattle, WA, USA
{ankit,fox,curless}@cs.washington.edu

Michael Cohen
Microsoft Research
Redmond, WA, USA
mcohen@microsoft.com

ABSTRACT

We demonstrate a realtime system which infers and tracks the assembly process of a snap-together block model using a Kinect® sensor. The inference enables us to build a virtual replica of the model at every step. Tracking enables us to provide context specific visual feedback on a screen by augmenting the rendered virtual model aligned with the physical model. The system allows users to author a new model and uses the inferred assembly process to guide its recreation by others. We propose a novel way of assembly guidance where the next block to be added is rendered in blinking mode with the tracked virtual model on screen. The system is also able to detect any mistakes made and helps correct them by providing appropriate feedback. We focus on assemblies of Duplo® blocks.

We discuss the shortcomings of existing methods of guidance — static figures or recorded videos — and demonstrate how our method avoids those shortcomings. We also report on a user study to compare our system with standard figure-based guidance methods found in user manuals. The results of the user study suggest that our method is able to aid users' structural perception of the model better, leads to fewer assembly errors, and reduces model construction time.

Author Keywords

Active visual feedback; Depth camera; Assembly tasks; Tracking; Augmented reality; Virtual reality.

ACM Classification Keywords

H.5.2. Information Interfaces and Presentation: User Interfaces.; H.5.1. Information Interfaces and Presentation: Multimedia Information Systems.; I.2.10. Artificial Intelligence: Vision and Scene Understanding.; I.3.6. Computer Graphics: Methodology and Techniques.; I.4.8. Image Processing and Computer Vision: Scene Analysis.

INTRODUCTION

Block model assembly toys have retained their popularity over time. These are particularly liked by children who start assembling models at an early age, developing spatial skills useful throughout life. Lego® and their larger cousin Duplo® blocks are well known snap-together blocks for assembling models. These blocks are designed to be easily assembled into interesting models and de-assembled for reuse.

UIST'12, October 7–10, 2012, Cambridge, Massachusetts, USA.

Figure 1: System setup. The user builds the model in the *Play area* and uses the *Add/Remove/Recheck boxes* to interact with the system. The Kinect® looks down from the right and passes the captured video/depth stream to our system to track the model and infer the assembly process in realtime. Visual feedback is shown on the display in front of the user.

Model assembly often follows printed step-by-step instructions as shown in Figure 3. Such step-by-step instructions can be hard to follow and are not very robust to mistakes during the assembly process. Also, rebuilding a model that we created at some earlier point in time would require re-finding the instructions. Or if we want to share our original physical models with friends who want to build a replica, there are no easily generated instructions. We could save/share the completed model in its physical state but then we might run out of blocks while building more models, and even so, the completed model serves as a poor instructional device. The Lego Designer Tool [26] allows users to create virtual models using a keyboard and a mouse and can then generate instructions for them. But making a model virtually can be far less intuitive than actually making the physical model.

Ideally, we can save the construction of the model in some digital format from which it is easy for the same user or others to rebuild it later in future. One could take photographs or video of the model during construction. Casually captured videos of the construction process may be useful in guiding the rebuilding process, but can be confusing or tedious to fol-

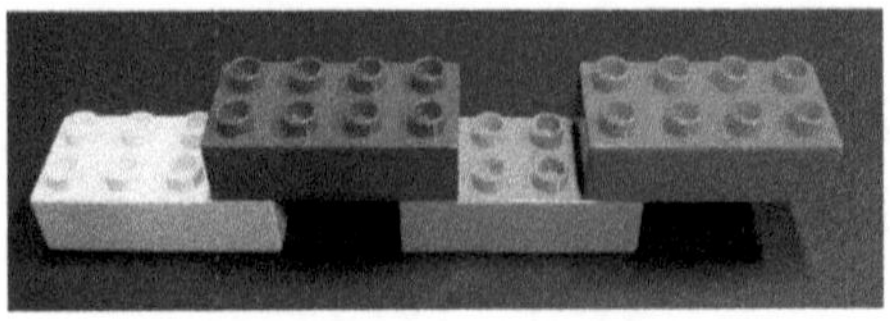

Figure 2: Our system uses 2 × 4 Duplo® blocks.

low especially if there is any back-tracking in the construction process. A user could also create a well-annotated set of instructions in form of photos or figures like standard Lego® blocks instructions; however, this requires great skill and significant effort. We would like to enable users to build models with minimal interference from the recording mechanism and to be able to store and transmit instructions to rebuild that model later with ease.

In this paper, we design and implement a system which watches the user assemble a model using a camera with depth sensing and infers the assembly process in realtime. Figure 1 shows the setup of our system. It dynamically tracks the physical model and displays a virtual replica on the screen in front of the user in the same pose as the in-hand physical model. In *Authoring* mode, it records the step-by-step addition of blocks. Removal of blocks is also handled, effectively deleting the previous addition of that block. In *Guidance* mode, step-by-step instructions are superimposed on the digital replica, again following the dynamically changing pose of the physical model being constructed. The system detects mistakes made and gives appropriate feedback to the user, thus avoiding the user's frustration of undoing and redoing multiple steps for making a correction in the assembly.

The Authoring and Guidance system uses a combination of color-based and depth-based (3D) tracking. We leverage the widely available Kinect® sensor which gives us depth information along with color. Although blocks come in varying shapes and sizes, to keep the inference problem computationally tractable, we work here only with Duplo® blocks that each have a 2 × 4 arrangement of studs, as shown in Figure 2. We later discuss how our solution can be extended to include other different types of blocks. Even with both color and depth sensors and the single block type, inconsistent and noisy depth sensing, specular reflections, and the partial occlusions caused by the user's hands present significant challenges to creating a responsive and robust system. We counter all these challenges in our work both through sensor fusion, and by designing the user interface to lead the user gracefully through the block modeling process. We present a working system which allows for realtime inference and feedback in block model assemblies.

We report on a user study to answer some specific questions related to the guidance system, comparing it to traditional guidance via static images. We measure time taken to complete assembly tasks and count the number of mistakes made by users.

We explore two broad directions in this paper - a novel way of guiding assembly process and a realtime system to track

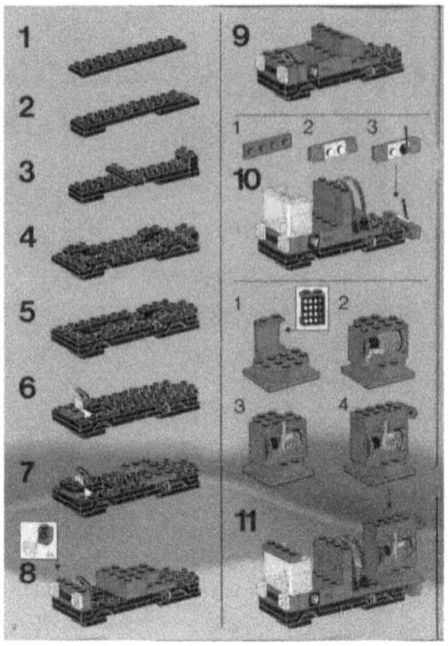

Figure 3: Traditional method of guiding model assembly tasks using images.

and infer the assembly process. In the next two sections, we review the prior work in these directions. We then present the design, implementation and potential applications of our system. After that, we describe the user study, analyze its results and conclude the paper by discussing potential future work.

RELATED WORK: GUIDING THE ASSEMBLY

Agrawala et al. [1] provide an excellent summary of the issues in designing the presentation of many assembly tasks. Heiser et al. [10] and Agrawala et al. [2] have studied design principles for producing visually comprehensible and accessible instructions for assemblies, and develop algorithms for producing such instructions. A key observation is that creating effective static instructions for three dimensional tasks is difficult and should follow established design principles.

We now discuss some common modes of presenting assembly instructions to the users and discuss what depth perception cues they provide.

Figure-based guidance. Figures (as drawings or photographs) are the most common way of providing instructions in assembly tasks. The user is shown a figure or multiple figures depicting the current state of the model and showing where the new block goes as in Figure 3. This type of instruction is used both for toy models such as Lego® as well as in many other assembly tasks such as IKEA® furniture assembly. Each figure provides monocular depth cues such as occlusion, perspective, relative size, and shading. While all these cues can aid structural perception, the spatial perception literature [7] has shown that motion cues also play a central role in understanding shape. Motion parallax [8] and the kinetic depth effect [28] can greatly enhance the structural perception of the model. In addition, any structure that the user understands from static figures needs to be mentally aligned to the physical model in his hand. Once done, the user can add the new block. We call this perceptual alignment from virtual model to physical model *perception transfer*. Perception transfer can induce errors in structural understanding which we hope to minimize in our guidance system.

Video-based guidance. An alternative to figure-based instructions is video-based guidance, presenting the user with recorded videos of the assembly steps. The user can then pause, play or repeat each video clip to understand the instruction and then perform it. Videos can provide the same depth cues as figures, but also provide motion cues that lead to better structural perception. Video instructions can also show the motion of the parts as they are being placed which can be particularly useful if the task requires complex moves. However, the user may find it hard to control the system, needing to pause the video sometimes to understand or replay the clip multiple times. Further, the problem of perception transfer discussed for the figures still remains. Pongnumkul et al. [21] have developed a system for generating Pause-and-Play video tutorials and discuss these common problems.

Kraut et al. [16] have done experiments that show a significant increase in the performance of users on a bicycle assembly task when they work in a collaborative work space getting video instructions from their own viewpoint from an expert compared to doing the tasks using an online figure-based manual. Our system is related to this work in the sense that we provide live feedback from the user's viewpoint by tracking the model being built.

It is known that the spatial perception skills of an individual depend on many factors [9, 25, 22, 6] and while an instructional figure/video may be clear for one user, it might be confusing for another. This observation suggests that an interactive system adapting to the users' handling of the model could improve the assembly process.

Augmented Reality-based guidance. Augmented Reality (AR) techniques try to minimize the problem of perception transfer by creating an immersive environment to merge the virtual instructions and the physical model. Augmented Reality has been applied to assembly tasks and tested in user studies such as Tang et al. [27], Henderson et al. [11] and Boud et al. [5], which evaluate and demonstrate the advantages of using AR techniques over the traditional figure-based techniques. Hou et al. [12] have argued the benefits of using augmented reality and also mention the idea of playing pre-recorded animation clips at each step of the assembly which are better than static figures. In all these systems, highly specialized equipment is needed, the models are typically stationary and the motion cues are due to parallax caused by head motion. In our system, we use an inexpensive, widely available color+depth sensor along with a common computer display to provide motion cues based on the motion of a real model held in the hand.

Guidance in our system. One of our goals is to solve the problems of perception transfer and lack of control while providing the same visual cues as figures or video for structural perception. The system tracks the physical model's motion and continuously shows the replica on the screen in approximately the same orientation as the user's viewpoint with the instruction step superimposed on it. The continuous rendering on the screen can be seen as a video that is being generated on the fly from the user's viewpoint along with the instruction. This instruction mode overcomes the problems of lack of control and perception transfer.

Since the rendering on the screen is governed by the user's handling of the physical model, the user is in complete control of the pose of the model in which the instruction is being shown to him. This minimizes the need for perception transfer. The system also provides all the depth perception cues provided by the static images and the recorded video.

We experimentally compare our system with the figure-based guidance method that is most commonly used. We do not compare with the recorded video-based systems because, in essence, our system is also a video-based guidance system where the video is not pre-recorded but generated on-the-fly based on how the user views the physical model.

RELATED WORK: TRACKING THE ASSEMBLY

There has also been work to track and evaluate the correctness of assembly steps presented to the user. Molineros et al. [20] put encoded markers on each part for tracking it and detecting connections with other parts. They also precompute a connection graph between parts and feature descriptors for all configurations. Ju et al. [15] presented a system called Origami Desk which uses special hardware built into paper to sense folds and hence detect completion of predefined steps. These frameworks can be extended to a *free* mode where the user is allowed to connect any part anywhere or make a fold anywhere. However, this involves precomputation to learn descriptors for the complete space of allowed manipulations over all the parts. Searching over this space in realtime will be even harder. Our work presents a realtime system which can track and evaluate an assembly process of Duplo® blocks.

Recently, there has also been work on tracking manipulations done by user in the *free* mode. Jota et al. [14] present a system which captures and projects virtual replicas of physical objects put together by the user. However, the quality of the virtual replicas suffers due to the inherent noise in Kinect®'s depth sensing. There is no inference to establish connections between the parts. Anderson et al. [3] use special circuitry-augmented blocks to determine the assembly process of a model and then convert it to a more detailed and less blocky virtual model. Our system understands the model assembly without any special hardware and also focuses on guiding the model's re-creation in a sequential manner.

In a contemporaneous work, Miller et al. [18] solve a similar problem of tracking and inferring how a Duplo® block model is built. They assume that the model always stays with its base on the table to reduce the tracking to 3 degrees of freedom (DOF): two for in-plane translation and one for in-plane rotation. Their representation is voxel-centric, rather than part-centric, requiring all voxels occupied by the model to be seen to correctly model the assembly. These restrictions limit their system to simple block models, usually built layer by layer. Their user study to measure model acquisition ac-

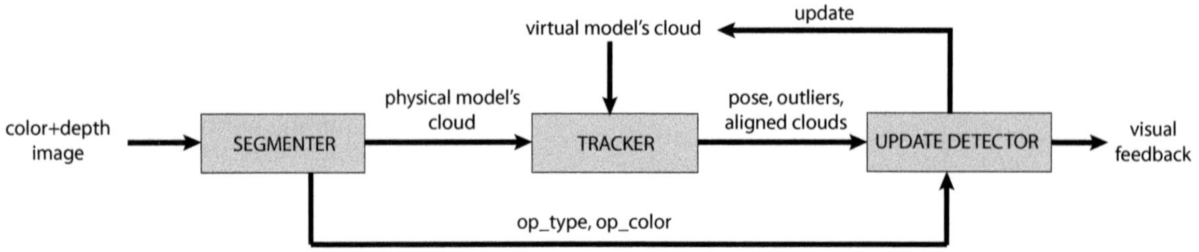

Figure 4: Processing pipeline: The Segmenter receives a color plus depth image from the camera and segments out the background and user's hands. The remaining image is passed as a 3D point cloud to the Tracker which aligns the virtual model's point cloud with that from the camera to output the pose. The Segmenter also detects the user's choice of operation and passes this to the Update Detector as operation type and color of block being added or removed. The Update Detector takes this information and the tracked pose to detect any update. Appropriate visual feedback is rendered to the user and the virtual model is updated.

curacy shows scanning errors due to tracking misalignment, hand pixels, and parts that are less visible. In comparison, our work uses 6-DOF tracking, allowing in-hand manipulation, and belief accumulation from multiple views for inference of whole-part additions/subtractions, and subsequently avoids many errors inherent in their system. Further, we enable two-way feedback between the user and the system compared to only system-to-user feedback in their work. We believe this leads to richer human-computer interaction experience. Additionally, we report on a user study comparing motion-tracked guidance to traditional methods.

SYSTEM OVERVIEW

Our system consists of a Kinect® depth+color camera above and to the right of a table surface in front of which the user sits as shown in Figure 1. The Kinect® looks obliquely down on the table surface. At the back of the table is a monitor facing the user; when the physical model is being tracked, the monitor shows a virtual replica of the model from the point of view of the user. A set of 2×4 Duplo® blocks sits off to the side of the table within reach of the user. The table surface has four demarcated regions - *Play area, Add box, Remove box* and *Recheck box*. We refer to the last three together as *Control boxes*.

The system operates in two modes - Authoring and Guidance. In the Authoring mode, the user builds a model by adding or removing blocks one at a time. The user can freely move around the model in the *Play area* during the whole process. A tracked virtual replica is shown on the screen. To add a new block, he first places the new block in the *Add box* and then adds it to the model. The system checks where the block has been added. Once the system detects the block's most likely position, it shows the update in blinking mode superimposed on the virtual replica in the display. If the detection is correct, the user can move to the next step directly. Otherwise, the user puts his hand in the *Recheck box* and the system checks again for the update. To remove a block, the user removes it from the model and places it in the *Remove box* and the system again starts the cycle of update detection.

In the Guidance mode, there is a pre-loaded model and a sequence of block additions required to build it. As before, a tracked virtual replica of the model in the *Play area* is shown on the screen, but with the block to be added next also shown in blinking mode superimposed on the replica. To add the block, the user first places the new block in the *Add box* and then adds the block to the partial assembly. The system verifies the update. If the update is correct, it loads the next instruction. Otherwise, a notification is displayed providing feedback about the mistake and asks the user to correct it. Please see the supplementary video for a recordings of system usage.

For tracking the model and inferring updates, the system needs an internal representation for the block model. We now describe that representation, followed by the processing pipeline for the Kinect®'s data stream.

Representation for Block Models

We assume that the model resides in a voxelized space where each voxel is of size 16mm $\times$ 16mm $\times$ 19.2mm, the official size of a 1×1 Duplo® block. The model is made of 2×4 Duplo® blocks either red, green, blue or yellow in color. Each block occupies a volume equivalent to 8 voxels.

The following structures are maintained for the model at any point -

- List of blocks where each block has a color and list of voxels it occupies.
- Map of the complete voxelized space where each voxel is either unoccupied or maps to the block occupying it.
- Mesh model used in rendering.
- Point cloud of the model, denoted as P_v, used for 3D alignments.

We also have a mesh model and point cloud representation for one 2×4 block which can be added to or removed from the virtual model in any color. The mesh model is from Google's 3D warehouse, converted into a dense point cloud using *MeshLab*. The point cloud P_v is a union of translated and rotated copies of this block point cloud, with points removed in areas that are covered by other blocks.

Processing Pipeline

Figure 4 shows the work flow of the system. The Kinect® camera provides a continuous stream of images with an RGB color and depth at each pixel. The *Segmenter* module takes each color+depth image from the camera and prunes it to the pixels corresponding to the physical model in the *Play area*. It also checks for user inputs through *Control boxes* and converts that into an *op_type* (add, remove or recheck) and *op_color* (for add or remove). The *Tracker* module aligns the model's point cloud with the virtual model's point cloud. This aligned data plus the user inputs are then passed on to the *Update Detector* module.

SEGMENTING THE CAMERA DATA

We first convert the Kinect® color+depth images into colored 3D *camera point clouds*, P_c, by back-projecting the pixels to the known depths from the Kinect®. We filter out pixels which do not correspond to the physical model such as the background and hands. The system starts with an empty work area and we store the background depth for each pixel. For subsequent images, for every pixel in the incoming depth image, if the observed depth is less than 95% of the background depth, we mark that pixel as foreground. The 95% value is empirically determined to counter the depth inaccuracies from the Kinect® camera. We also filter out the pixels whose corresponding 3D points do not lie within the *Play area* or any of the *Control* boxes.

Pixels above the *Control boxes* set the *op_type* and *op_color* based on majority occupancy. The *Recheck* box is given priority over *Add* and *Remove* boxes since it lies further from the user. If *op_type* is add or remove, we set *op_color* by finding the majority color of the points in the corresponding box.

The remaining 3D pixels above the *Play area* are either part of the user's hands or the model. We use a color-histogram-based classifier built prior to the start of the system to distinguish between the hands and Duplo® blocks, and remove the hand pixels. The remaining pixels above the play area form the point cloud corresponding to the physical model, P_c.

TRACKING THE MODEL

A key component of the system is the ability to track the physical model as the user moves it around with or without adding/removing a block. This allows us to render the virtual model from the user's viewpoint on the screen and enables us to render additional feedback or instructions about the next step of the task. The tracking system runs at real-time frame rates. Currently, we do not guarantee robust tracking if the model is turned upside down. This is because the sensor cannot capture enough geometry on the hollow side of blocks and hence leading to less reliable tracking.

For every camera point cloud, P_c, we compute a transformation that aligns the virtual cloud, P_v, with P_c. We use the ICP (Iterative Closest Point) algorithm proposed by Besl and McKay [4] to align the point clouds by solving for a 6D transformation: 3D rotation and 3D translation. As a side effect of the algorithm, we also get a set of outliers, O, points in P_c which do not find a match in P_v. When a user makes changes to the model, these "outliers" correspond to differences between the previous and updated state of the model; thus, we use the outliers later for update detection.

Given an initial transformation T_0 between the point clouds, the ICP algorithm iteratively solves for the final transformation T_f. The algorithm first applies T_0 to P_v to create a transformed virtual point cloud. For each point in P_c, it finds the closest point in the transformed P_v, accelerated with a K-d tree. Correspondences with distances greater than an outlier threshold are rejected (for the purpose of alignment, though retained for model update). The transformation is then updated by minimizing the total squared distances between the remaining correspondences. This optimization is solved in closed form. The same steps are repeated with the updated transformation until convergence. At each iteration, we reduce the outlier-rejection threshold.

Since the ICP algorithm performs a greedy, local optimization, success depends on good initialization, T_0. Typically, T_0 is set to the T_f from the previous tracked frame. However, when the model first appears before the camera, there is no previous transformation available. Further, the system can lose track of the physical model, e.g., when the motion is too fast. We detect loss of tracking when the distance between the nearest point correspondences becomes too large. Thus, when tracking is lost or a model is newly introduced, we require a method for *pose initialization*.

Pose Initialization

To initialize the pose, we need to estimate a suitable 3D translation and 3D rotation. For 3D translation, we simply use the difference between the 3D centroids of P_v and P_c.

To estimate an initial rotation, we exploit the fact that the model primarily consists of mutually orthogonal or parallel planar faces. We estimate the dominant face normal directions, resulting in a small set of possible rotations to align P_c and P_v. In fact, two normal directions suffice, as the third direction can be inferred.

First, we estimate normals at every point in P_c based on each point's position and the positions of its nearest neighbors. We cluster the normals into bins in direction space, i.e., bins over the unit sphere. A Hough-transform finds a pair of mutually-orthogonal bins in the direction space which has the most normals supporting it. Given this pair of directions, there are 24 possible orientations of the X, Y, and Z axes such that any two line up with this pair. We prune out half of the possible orientations by assuming the hollow side of the blocks does not face up. Hence the 3D rotation search space can be pruned to testing 12 candidate orientations, $j = 1...12$.

Then, for each orientation candidate j, we transform the virtual model points P_v using the corresponding candidate rotation as well as the previously estimated translation. The visible parts of the transformed P_v are selected using a depth buffer rendering from the camera's viewpoint. We then run the ICP algorithm to refine the orientation to arrive at a candidate transformation T_j. Applying T_j to P_v results in a candidate point set P_j to match against samples P_c from the Kinect®. We choose the best transformation candidate T_j

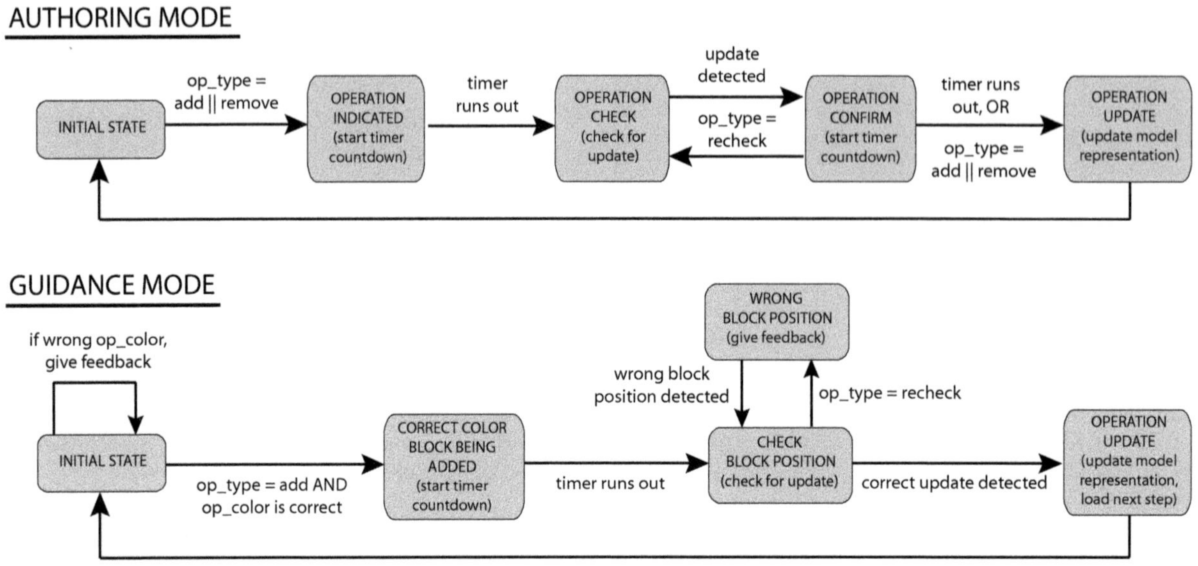

Figure 5: The Update Detector is implemented as a finite state machine with user input and tracked data as input to update the model. In Authoring mode, it detects an update and applies it unless a recheck is requested by the user. In Guidance mode, it detects and performs the update and displays feedback to the user if there is a mistake.

which has the minimum match error between P_c and P_j. For the match error, we render the colored point clouds P_c and transformed P_j from the camera's viewpoint to create two color images. We first quantize the image colors into the possible red, green, blue, and yellow model colors and partition the images into abutting 50×50 windows. For each window, we build a color histogram and cluster the pixels into the bins of corresponding colors. The pixels in P_c's projection may have saturated pixels which cannot be classified as any color. We put them in a separate bin called saturated-color bin. We set the match error between the images as the sum of the match costs between the histograms of corresponding windows.

We use the Earth Mover's Distance (EMD) [23] metric to match any i^{th} histograms in the two images. This metric measures the cost of recreating the latter histogram by moving around the data in former. There is a cost to move data between the bins. We set the cost to move pixels from any color to a different color as 1. We set the cost to move pixels from saturated-color bin to any color bin as 0.

Model Tracking at the Start

The model tracking does not work well for small models below 4-5 blocks. There are two reasons for this:

- **Noise in the camera data.** The data from the Kinect® is particularly noisy near depth discontinuities. For smaller point clouds this noise is a significant fraction of the data and the tracking runs into problems.

- **Structure mismatch.** If the user adds or removes a block, we still track it using a pre-updated virtual model until the update is detected and incorporated into the model. When the model is small, the structural change of even one block confounds the tracking as the outliers from the newly added block overwhelm the points from before the update.

To start a new model we ask the user to place the first block in a fixed position in the *Play area* and add blocks to it at that location. This greatly reduces the possible candidates to search over. We modify the matching algorithms for aligning point clouds to allow for small translations from the known pose. Once the model has 5 blocks, we remove this restriction and allow the user to freely move the model around. The system now dynamically tracks it as described earlier.

DETECTING MODEL UPDATES

When the user indicates an update to the model (add or remove), the system uses the output of the tracker to detect the update. Separate finite state machines implement the Authoring and Guidance modes as shown in Figure 5. These are a formal representation of the system usage already described in detail in the System Outline section.

In Authoring mode, when the user indicates an operation, the system checks for changes in the model as the user moves the model around in front of the sensor. Once the system detects the update, it echoes this in the display. If the user thinks the system is in error and asks for a recheck, the system rechecks; otherwise, it updates the model and moves to the next step.

In Guidance mode, the system checks for the correct color and position of the block and gives appropriate feedback to the user. It goes to the next step automatically if the detected update matches the instruction otherwise it waits for the user to correct the mistake and ask for recheck. Note that only block additions take place in the Guidance mode. Any block removals during the Authoring mode effectively undo the previous addition of that block.

Creating the Candidate Set for Updates

At any stage in the assembly we maintain a set of candidate updates to the model. The candidate updates are one of two types, addition or removal, depending on the indicated operation. In addition mode, we traverse the voxel space and find sets of unoccupied voxels where a new block could be added. To ensure connectivity in the model, these sets must be connected to at least two occupied voxels; i.e., we assume the user is creating a single, rigid model, each piece connected to the model using at least two studs.

In removal mode, the candidates are simply any block that can be removed without leaving the remaining model disconnected, i.e. (1) either the space directly above those blocks or below is completely free and (2) they are not the only connected neighbors to any other blocks connected to them. The second condition does not apply when the remainder model has just one block. We can do this analysis using the voxelized representation to find such candidates.

We also add one more candidate to both modes which corresponds to *no addition/removal*, the state of the model just before the user adds/removes a block.

For each valid candidate, j, we maintain a belief, $b(j)$, which denotes the belief that candidate j should be chosen to update the model. The current belief is based upon the tracked camera data stream consisting of (1) the point cloud seen by the camera, P_c, (2) the transformation T which best aligns the un-updated virtual model's point cloud, P_v, to P_c and (3) the outlier points, O, given T.

Updating the Belief Distribution

After each new block addition or removal, all the $b(j)$ are set to 0. We then update the $b(j)$'s each time new camera data comes in. It is often difficult to determine which block has been added or removed from a single viewpoint due to input noise, occlusion, and structural ambiguities. Thus, we accumulate beliefs from more than one pose of the model as the user turns the model to reveal new views.

From each pose, we score the possible candidates based on how well the camera point cloud P_c, matches with the virtual point cloud corresponding to candidate j, denoted by P_j. For an addition candidate, P_j is obtained by adding the (colored) point cloud of the new block to P_v. For a removal candidate, P_j is obtained by removing the point cloud of the block from P_v. For the no addition/removal candidate, P_j is simply equal to P_v.

To compute the matching score, we first align P_c with each of the P_j's using ICP. The P_j's are structurally close to P_v and we have already aligned P_v with P_c using the transformation T. Hence we use T as the initial transform for these ICP alignments. We then compute the match error for each candidate using the same matching metric as used for comparing poses for tracking . For addition candidates, we also set the error to infinite if the majority of outliers which occupy the voxels of the candidate are not of the indicated color. We do the same for removal candidates if the corresponding block is not of the indicated color.

We sort the match errors in increasing order. The top three ranking candidates get the belief scores of 3, 2 and 1 and the rest get a score of 0. To select a best update candidate, we require beliefs from at least three poses separated by at least 10 degrees of rotation to make a decision (for small models, when the system is working with a fixed pose, we remove this requirement). To accumulate beliefs from three well-separated views, we begin with the initial transformation, call this T_1, and average beliefs into a belief set $b_1(j)$ over subsequent nearby observations until T has changed by at least 10 degrees of rotation from T_1. This establishes a second transformation, T_2, with a new set of beliefs $b_2(j)$ for each candidate. We continue to collect beliefs over subsequent nearby observations, averaging them with the beliefs corresponding to the nearer of T_1 or T_2. We also continuously check for a new transformation, T_3, at least 10 degrees from both T_1 and T_2, and, if found, begin a new average set of beliefs $b_3(j)$. More views and distributions are added if the user continues moving the model to orientations that are at least 10 degrees away from all previous views.

Once belief sets associated with at least three well-separated views have been accumulated, we normalize each set to sum to 1 and then sum all normalized sets to get an overall set, $B(j)$. If the ratio of the highest scoring candidate in this set is at least 1.25 (chosen empirically) times that of the second best candidate, then we declare the highest scoring candidate as the winner. If we cannot declare a winner, then we wait for more camera data from new poses to update the beliefs, continuously checking for a winner as beliefs are updated. If the *no addition/removal* candidate is the winner, which can occur if the user has not yet added/removed a block, we reset the belief sets and re-start checking for an update.

Moving to the Next Step

If the system selects a candidate as the update but the user then asks for a recheck, we remove that candidate from further consideration, reset the belief sets, and the update checking process restarts. In practice, we find that the user needs to request a recheck less than one out of twenty additions or removals.

Once the model update has been identified (and approved by the user in Authoring mode), we update the internal representation of the model. The model's virtual cloud P_v is set to the point cloud corresponding to the winning candidate. For block addition, we append the new block to the list of blocks and map the corresponding voxels in the voxel space to it. For block removal, it is removed from the list and the corresponding voxels are marked as unoccupied.

PERFORMANCE AND APPLICATIONS

The system runs in realtime on a desktop PC with 12-core, 3.33GHz Xeon CPU and uses at most 500MB of RAM. To achieve this performance, the implementation is highly multithreaded with separate threads for tracking, rendering and checking updates. Within the update thread, the candidates are evaluated in parallel.

The system takes about 2-5 seconds to infer each model update. The tracking works in realtime although it lags slightly

(a) (b)

Figure 6: Models authored using our system.

if the model motion is fast. We have used our system to build models up to 85 blocks in size. At that point the tracking speed reduces to about 5 frames per second. Figure 6 shows a few models that users have authored while using our system.

The bottleneck of the system is nearest neighbor correspondence search in ICP alignments for tracking and candidate evaluations. These searches can be done in parallel for 3D points in a cloud, but we were limited by the number of CPU threads that we could use. In the future we believe that our system can benefit from exploiting the parallelization potential in GPUs as shown by recent works like *KinectFusion* [13].

We now describe a few applications of our system.

Generating Tutorials for Model Assembly

The captured assembly of a model is a sequence of add or remove operations. To generate an assembly tutorial, we would like to omit any steps that involve adding and then later removing a block. We delete such add/remove operations from the representation. This may cause the remainder of the sequence to have block additions which do not connect to any blocks added before them. We reorder the steps by postponing the addition of such blocks until they have a connection with the prior model. It is easy to prove that the assembly sequence of any model can be reordered in this way. This representation can then be used to then generate tutorials or explanations in form of images with or without annotations [17, 19].

Ease of Sharing and Recreating Models

The captured assembly sequences from the Authoring mode can also be used as input to our Guidance mode which uses exactly the same hardware setup. This allows for an easier way for people to create and share their models with other users or save these representations for future re-creation.

Access to Virtual Replicas

The output of the Authoring mode is a virtual 3D replica of the model. These virtual models could be used for different purposes, e.g., as content for games and animations.

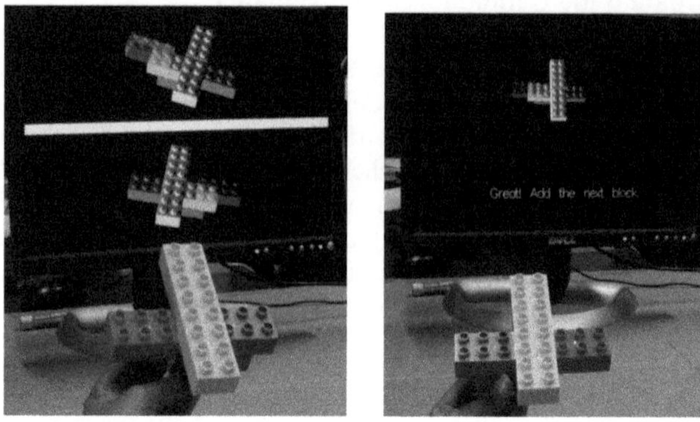

(a) *Baseline* interface (b) *Track* interface

Figure 7: Photographs of the two guidance interfaces that we test in the user study. The *Baseline* interface depicts two static views of the model. In the *Track* interface the orientation of the model tracks that of the model in the user's hand.

USER STUDY

There are many aspects of the Authoring and Guidance system for which we can ask questions that can best be answered by observing user behavior. In this work, we conducted a study that focuses on the Guidance system as it can be compared to other more traditional guidance modes.

In particular, we conducted a user study to focus on the differences between two interfaces for providing instructions for adding blocks to Duplo® models. The first interface (*Baseline*) provides two static views of the model (with the new block) on the screen. The new block blinks, alternating between opaque and semi-transparent. These views were manually chosen to give the best possible view of the new block from two different directions. Figure 7a shows a photograph of this system in progress. This interface is close to the current methods found in user manuals for the assembly tasks. The second interface, (*Track*), is our tracking-based system which shows the virtual model on the screen in the same pose as the physical model in the user's hands. The display updates in real-time as the user moves around the model. The block to be added is again shown in blinking mode as in *Baseline*. Figure 7b shows a screenshot of this interface. Please refer to supplementary videos which show how participants use these interfaces.

For *Baseline*, we decided against using the more traditional way of showing before and after figures of the step. Rather, in the two interfaces being tested, we use the same visualization for the new block to be added to avoid the results being confounded by this difference. Also, we do not use the mistake-detection capability in *Track* since we wish to directly compare the instruction modes.

We conduct two tests, one in which we focus on single-block additions, and the other on multiple sequential-block additions.

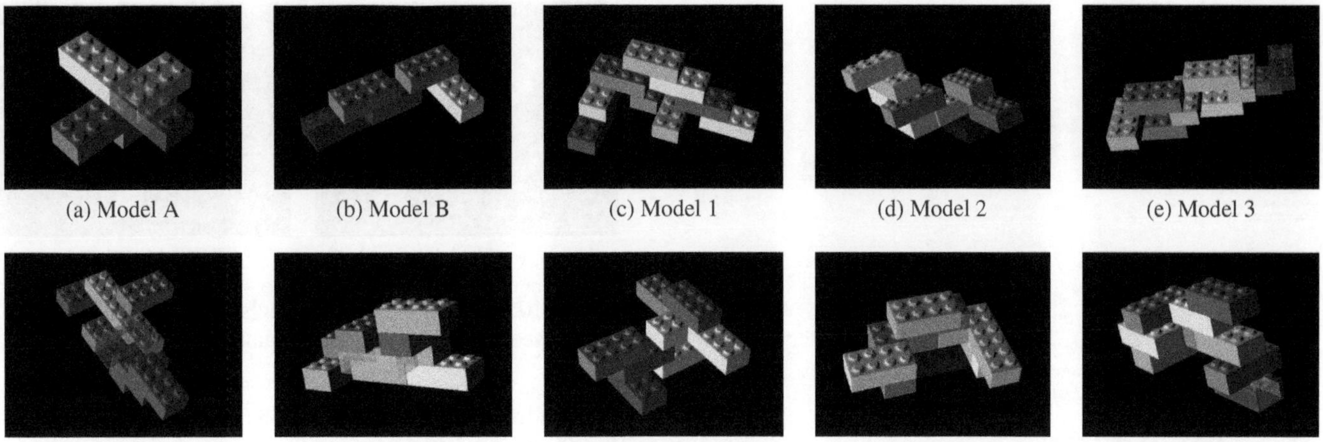

(a) Model A (b) Model B (c) Model 1 (d) Model 2 (e) Model 3

(f) Model 4 (g) Model 5 (h) Model 6 (i) Model 7 (j) Model 8

Figure 8: Initial models used in the user study tasks. Models A and B have 4 blocks each and remaining models have eight blocks each. Participants added one block to each of the 8-block models and 12 blocks in sequence to each of the 4-block models. The transparent block in each of the models is the block that needs to be added next.

Task Design

We assembled ten initial block models, shown in Figure 8. Models A and B initially have four blocks each and Models $1-8$ have eight blocks each. The task in the study was to add one block to each of the 8-block models, and 12 blocks sequentially to the two 4-block models. Each participant had to complete half of the tasks (4 one-block additions and one 12-block addition) with one of the conditions, and then the remaining tasks with the other condition. We shuffled the models randomly between the two conditions for each participant. Also, the order in which the participant used the conditions was randomly decided to counter the effect of any 3D-perception learning that might occur by completing the tasks.

For each block addition, we measured the time taken to add that block. We also noted if the block addition was correct or not. We analyze the effect of the interface conditions on these two dependent variables - the time taken to make the update and correctness.

Procedure

Before starting the assembly tasks, the participants were asked to answer a set of ten questions to test their spatial visual ability. These questions had a mixture of Mental Rotation questions [24] and 3D structure assembly and paper-folding visualization questions, which are commonly part of a spatial IQ test. We might expect that the people with high spatial visual ability perform well in any interface conditions and hence we wanted to test this possible dependence. We also collected information about the gender, education level (undergraduate or graduate) and previous experience with Lego® blocks on a Likert scale of 1 to 5. In our analysis, we wanted to analyze the possible effects of these factors also.

After completing the initial set of questions, the participants started using one of the two interface conditions. Before starting each condition, we gave them a demo of the interface with a training model, separate from those in the tasks, and asked them to practice adding 4 blocks to it sequentially. Under each condition, they first did the single-block additions to four of the 8-block models, and then completed twelve block additions sequentially to one of the 4-block models. After completing every block addition, the participants were provided feedback about the correctness of the block addition. Providing feedback was important for the case of the 4-block models because we did not want the effect of a mistake at an earlier stage to cause a mistake at a later stage. We did not record the time taken for corrective feedback and correction in our time record of the task completion.

After the participants finished all the tasks, they were asked to fill a post-study survey which asked for qualitative feedback about the two conditions. We asked them about their preference for the systems, if any, and also for any other interface ideas that could help guide them better. We report qualitative comments.

Participants

Sixteen participants (eight female, eight male, ages 20 to 30) volunteered. Twelve of them had built models with blocks as a child and all of them had experience in doing some 3D assembly tasks like furniture, electronics etc. Each participant's study lasted for about 45 minutes.

Results

We analyze the results of the experiment in three ways. First, we discuss the one-block additions to eight of the ten models across the users and the conditions to make a quantitative comparison of the two interfaces. Second, we use the measurements from the twelve sequential block additions to the 4-block models to see how the time taken varies when the basic model remains the same. We analyze each of the two models separately for this. Third and last, we report the qualitative feedback from our participants about the two interfaces.

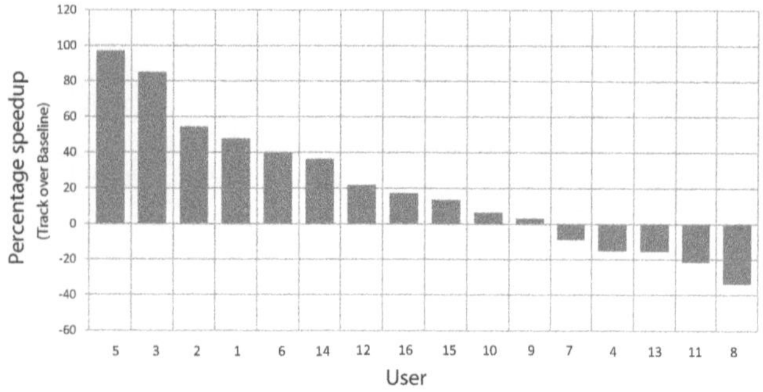

(a) Percentage speedup for users.

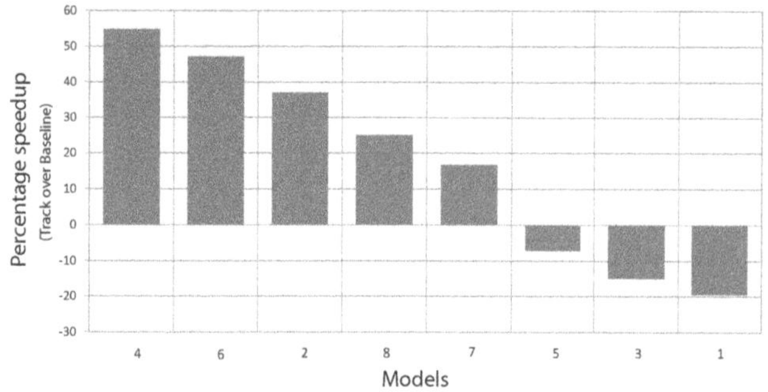

(b) Percentage speedup for models.

Figure 9: Percentage speedup over all the one-block addition tasks (value greater than 0 means that the *Track* interface takes less time).

Comparing the Interfaces for the One Block Additions

We analyze the results using two dependent measures - the time taken to complete the block additions in milliseconds and the correctness.

We perform a mixed-model analysis of variance where *Time* is the dependent factor, and *Participant* and *Model* are random effects. Modeling *Participant* as random effect accounts for any variation in individual performance, and modeling *Model* accounts for any difference in difficulty of block addition across the models. We use the following variables as fixed effects -

- *Gender*
- *Score*: The score of each participant on the set of ten spatial IQ questions.
- *Education*: Level of education - undergraduate or graduate.
- *Experience*: Personal experience with building Lego® models (increasing scale of 1 to 5).
- *Interface*: The interface condition - *Baseline* or *Track*.

The mixed-model analysis reveals that only *Interface* has a statistically significant effect on *Time* ($F(1,104) = 4.4932$, $p < 0.05$). The average time taken for the tasks using *Baseline* is 21.809 seconds (stdev = 10.1s) and for the tasks using *Track* is 18.871 seconds (stdev = 8.1s), an improvement of about 14%. The 95% confidence interval for the difference in the mean times is from 0.189 seconds to 5.687 seconds of improvement for *Track* over *Baseline*.

We define the *speedup* as the percentage increase in the speed of performing the step using *Track* vs *Baseline*. Specifically,

$$speedup = 100 * (\frac{Time(Baseline)}{Time(Track)} - 1)$$

A value above zero indicates that *Track* took less time and vice versa. In Figures 9a and 9b we show the *speedup* for individual users and models respectively. Although the per-user and per-model time averages have been aggregated over a small sample of the models and users respectively, they provide evidence for the statistically significant improvement from the mixed-model variance analysis.

In a second point of comparison between the interfaces, the users made 3 mistakes out of total 64 single-block additions while using *Baseline* while no mistakes were made in the same block additions while using *Track*. We observed that the participants preferred to take longer times to complete a step rather than making a mistake as they were correcting their actions continuously before actually adding the block to avoid making the mistake.

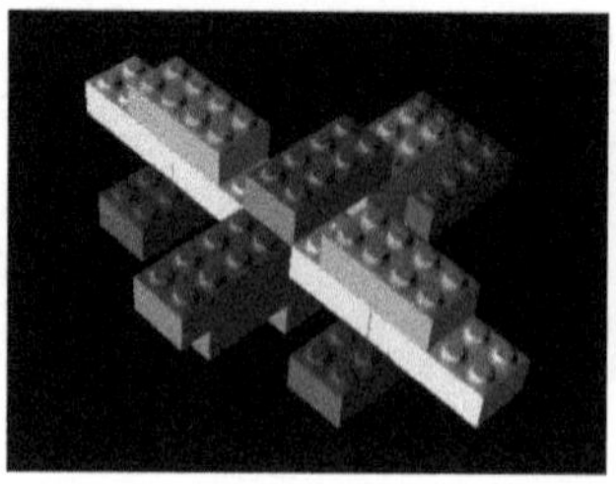

(a) Model A.

(b) Model B.

Figure 10: The two 16-block models, each built by adding 12 blocks sequentially by the participants.

Comparing the Interfaces for Multi-Block Additions

Here, we analyze the times to add blocks one after the other to the same model. We want to see if there is any dependence on the times taken as the model grows, or any dependence on the particular steps or on the interface. For this, we consider two 4-block models to which the participants make 12 sequential block additions using the two interfaces, one interface per model. We do a mixed-model analysis of variance for each of the models separately. Figure 10 shows the two complete models and we refer to them as Model A and Model B. As before, we use *Participant* as a random effect and *Interface* as a fixed effect. We add the size of the model (number of blocks) at every step, denoted by variable *Step*, as another fixed effect. In this analysis, we will call a step harder if it takes a longer time to add that block.

For Model A, the mixed-model analysis reveals that *Time* is significantly affected by both *Interface* ($F(1,11) = 5.3956$, $p < 0.05$) and *Step* ($F(11,154) = 11.6386$, $p < 0.0001$). The mean times for *Track* and *Baseline* interfaces over all the steps are

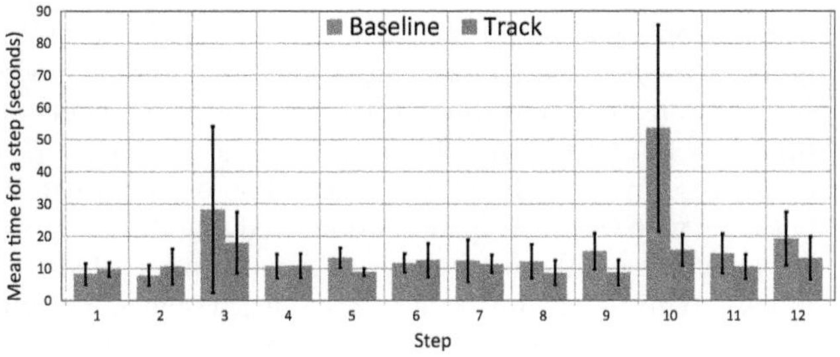

(a) Mean time taken per block addition and standard deviation (seconds). Less is better.

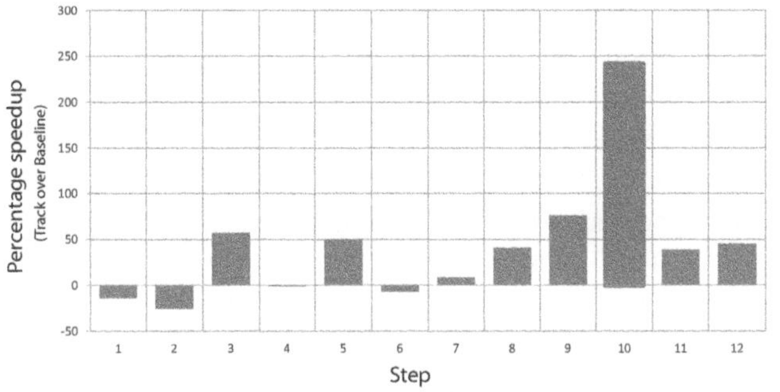

(b) Percentage speedup (value greater than 0 means that the *Track* interface takes less time. The red outline indicates statistically significant result ($p < 0.05$))

Figure 11: Metrics for Model A.

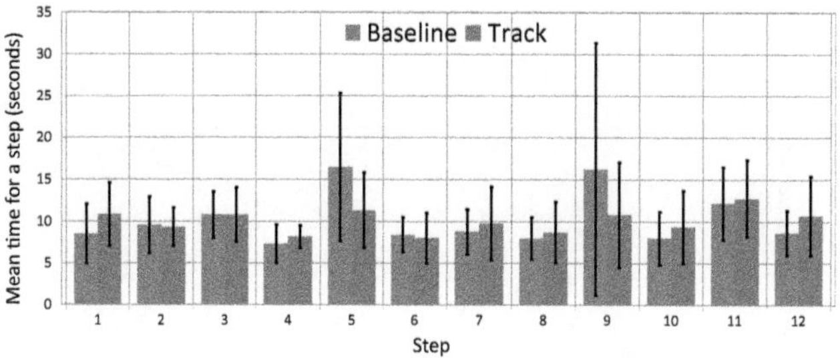

(a) Mean time taken per step and standard deviation (seconds). Less is better.

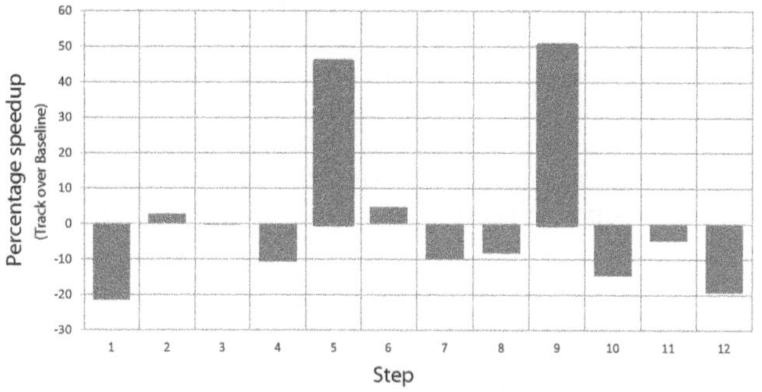

(b) Percentage speedup (value greater than 0 means that the *Track* interface takes less time. The red outline indicates a statistically significant result ($p < 0.05$))

Figure 12: Metrics for Model B.

11.577 seconds (stddev = 5.38s) and 17.303 seconds (stddev = 17.08s) respectively. The 95% confidence interval for the difference in the mean times is from 0.438 seconds to 11.014 seconds of improvement for *Track* over *Baseline*. Figure 11a shows the mean times for the individual steps. We do not observe any correlation between the step (which is also the number of blocks in the model) and the times taken. We do observe that some steps take longer to complete than others, and hence are harder. The *Interface* by *Step* interaction is significant ($F(11,154) = 6.1956$, $p < 0.0001$) with *Track* showing a stronger effect on harder steps. Figure 11b shows the percentage speedup for different steps with the statistically significant data points marked in red. By observing the significant data points, we can infer that using *Track* can help users to understand the structure better particularly when the block update step is harder.

The participants made 7 mistakes in building Model A using *Baseline* compared to none using *Track*.

For Model B, the mixed-model analysis reveals no significant effect of *Interface* on *Time*. The mean times for *Track* and *Baseline* interfaces over all the steps are 10.028 seconds and 10.224 seconds respectively. *Step* does have a significant effect ($F(11,165) = 3.5202$, $p < 0.0002$) which indicates the varying difficulty level across steps. Figure 12a shows the mean times for each step. The *Interface* by *Step* interaction does show significant improvement of *Track* in some cases. Figure 12b shows the percentage speedup for this model with the statistically significant data points in red again supporting the observation that using *Track* can help the harder steps.

The participants made no mistakes while building this model using either of the interfaces.

Perhaps the most interesting observation with the multi-step models is that *Track* provides larger improvements for the steps in the models which are harder than the others. To further quantify this observation, we plot the speedups against the mean time taken to complete a block addition using *Baseline* across both all the ten models. Higher mean time for a step indicates that it was relatively harder. Figure 13 shows this scatter diagram. We fit a line using least squares to the points (shown in red) indicating a positive correlation, ie. the speedup obtained using *Track* over *Baseline* increases with the difficulty of the step.

Qualitative feedback

Eleven of the sixteen users said that they preferred *Track* since it gave them flexibility of moving the model around and understanding its structure better. It was less mentally taxing. Three users preferred *Baseline* since they wanted the guidance to remain static and preferred to move the model around to match the shown view and then add the block. Based on this, we can imagine another interface which does the tracking in the background, and allows the user to ask for the instruction in the current pose of the model if desired.

All the users said that the assembly process using *Track* was more enjoyable experience. They talked about the ability to record stories using models and building virtual models on the fly. As one user said, "This tracking-based system will make playing with Lego® blocks more fun".

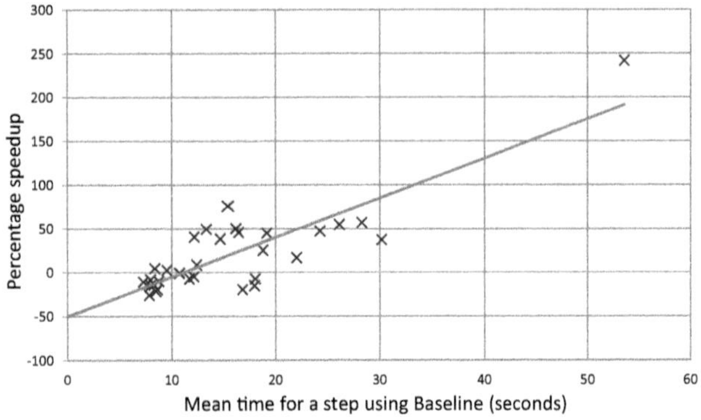

Figure 13: Scatter plot of percentage speedup vs mean time taken to do a block addition using *Baseline* (an indicator of the step's hardness). Fitting a line using least squares (shown in red) indicates a positive correlation between the mean time and speedup obtained by using *Track* over *Baseline*.

Based on our interactions with the users, we feel that the type of guidance varies with users. While the tracking-based system does show improvement in model-building times and fewer mistakes made, some users may still prefer the static views or getting static-views on demand.

Results Summary and Discussion

The results suggest that dynamically updating the pose of a virtual model to correspond with the real model in a user's hands can improve both speed and accuracy. We observed no mistakes made with the *Track* system while a total of 10 mistakes were made with the static *Baseline* instructions. We also observed significant speedups for the tasks with the dynamic systems.

Clearly, we have only scratched the surface of the questions raised. All of the models are quite simple compared to the richness of Lego® models available. We can conjecture that our results may even be stronger as the complexity increases but we have only limited evidence for this from our experiments. The simplicity of our models is also constrained by the technology. The resolution of the Kinect® device precluded using the smaller Lego® block for example. We can hope that this aspect of the system cam improve over time.

CONCLUSION AND FUTURE WORK

We have demonstrated a system which tracks an evolving Duplo® block model in realtime. In Authoring mode, the system learns the assembly through block additions and removals. In Guidance mode, a user is prompted to construct a predefined model by presenting instructions in the same pose as that of the physical model. It also provides feedback about mistakes and appropriate corrections to the model. We discuss the shortcomings of existing static figures or videos of the instruction steps and show how our guidance method avoids these. A user study comparing our system with the traditional figure-based guidance method suggests that our method is able to aid users' structural perception of the model and hence leads them to make fewer mistakes and construct the models in less time.

Some people still prefer the traditional system because they do not want the instruction to move with the physical model. In the future, a system which tracks the physical model continuously but only shows the instruction in the current pose on demand may satisfy all users. Based on our informal discussions with the participants, we noticed that different people tend to use different features of the image for adding the blocks. While some looked at edges, others counted the number of studs in the blocks, and others looked at visibility cues. An interesting future direction would be to analyze what features people tend to use for different types of assembly tasks and adapt the presentation accordingly. Additionally, we can explore new human-computer interactions for guidance like the user being guided to bring the physical model in the same pose as that of instruction. A user study could also be done to correlate people's spatial IQ scores to the guidance method that they prefer.

We hypothesized that depicting the virtual model on the screen in the same pose as the physical model minimized the need of perception transfer. To further reduce that, we are considering replacing the display screen in our current system with a projector attached with the camera. The projector can project the instruction step directly on the physical model or near it on the work surface. Further, the projector can be used to display extra information about the model or its different parts for educational or guidance purposes.

We want to extend this work in future to handle blocks of more sizes and shapes. Rigid blocks made of standard 1×1 Duplo® units are not hard to include as they easily fit into the voxelized representation. We can identify the shape of the block when the user puts in it *Add* or *Remove* box and evaluate the appropriate candidates. In fact, we have already extended our work to initially load a library of parts which the user wants to use in the model. The system uses a learnt area-based descriptor to distinguish parts. However, in the future we would like to handle blocks of curved shapes and articulated parts. It would also be useful to move away from a block-at-a-time update approach and allow for making sub-assemblies and merging them. This might require a different model representation and present more computational challenges.

We would also like to extend our framework for other types of assembly tasks like furniture assembly, and home repairs. This may require waiting for higher resolution sensors than the Kinect® or using multiple sensors and then fusing the data. However we also think some of the complexity can be overcome with better algorithms. Tracking and candidate evaluation algorithms can be vastly sped up by the use of GPUs and we plan to exploit this in future. We hope this initial work inspires others to take on new applications for this type of technology.

ACKNOWLEDGMENTS

We thank the reviewers for their insightful comments. This work was supported by funding from the University of Washington Animation Research Labs, Intel Science and Technology Center for Visual Computing, Microsoft, Adobe, and Pixar.

REFERENCES

1. Agrawala, M., Li, W., and Berthouzoz, F. Design principles for visual communication. *Communications of the ACM* (Apr. 2011), 60–69.

2. Agrawala, M., Phan, D., Heiser, J., Haymaker, J., Klingner, J., Hanrahan, P., and Tversky, B. Designing effective step-by-step assembly instructions. In *Proc. SIGGRAPH '03*, ACM Press (2003), 828–837.

3. Anderson, D., Frankel, J. L., Marks, J., Agarwala, A., Beardsley, P., Hodgins, J., Leigh, D., Ryall, K., Sullivan, E., and Yedidia, J. S. Tangible interaction + graphical interpretation: a new approach to 3d modeling. In *Proc. SIGGRAPH '00*, ACM Press/Addison-Wesley Publishing Co. (2000), 393–402.

4. Besl, P., and McKay, N. A method for registration of 3-d shapes. *IEEE Transactions on Pattern Analysis and Machine Intelligence 14* (1992), 239–256.

5. Boud, A. C., Haniff, D. J., Baber, C., and Steiner, S. J. Virtual reality and augmented reality as a training tool for assembly tasks. In *Proc. IV '99*, IEEE Computer Society (1999), 32–36.

6. Casey, M. B., Winner, E., Brabeck, M. M., Sullivan, K., Gilhooly, K. J., Keane, M. T. G., Logie, R. H., and Erdos, G. Visual-spatial abilities in art, maths and science majors: Effects of sex, family handedness and spatial experience. *Lines of thinking: Reflections on the psychology of thought 2* (1990), 275–294.

7. Domini, F., and Caudek, C. 3-d structure perceived from dynamic information: a new theory. *Trends in Cognitive Sciences 7*, 10 (2003), 444–449.

8. Ferris, S. H. Motion parallax and absolute distance. *Journal of Experimental Psychology 95*, 2 (1972), 258–263.

9. Goldstein, D., Haldane, D., and Mitchell, C. Sex differences in visual-spatial ability: The role of performance factors. *Memory & Cognition 18*, 5 (1990), 546–550.

10. Heiser, J., Phan, D., Agrawala, M., Tversky, B., and Hanrahan, P. Identification and validation of cognitive design principles for automated generation of assembly instructions. In *Proc. AVI '04*, ACM Press (2004), 311–319.

11. Henderson, S. J., and Feiner, S. K. Augmented reality in the psychomotor phase of a procedural task. In *Proc. ISMAR '11*, IEEE Computer Society (2011), 191–200.

12. Hou, L., and Wang, X. Using augmented reality to cognitively facilitate product assembly process. *Augmented Reality* (2010), 99–112.

13. Izadi, S., Kim, D., Hilliges, O., Molyneaux, D., Newcombe, R., Kohli, P., Shotton, J., Hodges, S., Freeman, D., Davison, A., and Fitzgibbon, A. Kinectfusion: real-time 3d reconstruction and interaction using a moving depth camera. In *Proc. UIST '11*, ACM Press (2011), 559–568.

14. Jota, R., and Benko, H. Constructing virtual 3d models with physical building blocks. In *Proc. CHI EA '11*, ACM Press (2011), 2173–2178.

15. Ju, W., Bonanni, L., Fletcher, R., Hurwitz, R., Judd, T., Post, R., Reynolds, M., and Yoon, J. Origami desk: integrating technological innovation and human-centric design. In *Proc. DIS '02*, ACM Press (2002), 399–405.

16. Kraut, R. E., Fussell, S. R., and Siegel, J. Visual information as a conversational resource in collaborative physical tasks. *Hum.-Comput. Interact. 18*, 1 (June 2003), 13–49.

17. Li, W., Agrawala, M., Curless, B., and Salesin, D. Automated generation of interactive 3d exploded view diagrams. In *Proc. SIGGRAPH '08*, ACM Press (2008), 101:1–101:7.

18. Miller, A., White, B., Charbonneau, E., Kanzler, Z., and LaViola Jr., J. J. Interactive 3d model acquisition and tracking of building block structures. *IEEE Transactions on Visualization and Computer Graphics 18*, 4 (Apr. 2012), 651–659.

19. Mitra, N. J., Yang, Y.-L., Yan, D.-M., Li, W., and Agrawala, M. Illustrating how mechanical assemblies work. In *Proc. SIGGRAPH '10*, ACM Press (2010), 58:1–58:12.

20. Molineros, J. M. *Computer vision and augmented reality for guiding assembly*. PhD thesis, Pennsylvania State University, University Park, PA, USA, 2002.

21. Pongnumkul, S., Dontcheva, M., Li, W., Wang, J., Bourdev, L., Avidan, S., and Cohen, M. F. Pause-and-play: automatically linking screencast video tutorials with applications. In *Proc. UIST '11*, ACM Press (2011), 135–144.

22. Preiss, D. D., and Sternberg, R. J. Effects of technology on verbal and visual-spatial abilities. *Cognitive Technology 11*, 1 (2006), 14–22.

23. Rubner, Y., Tomasi, C., and Guibas, L. J. A metric for distributions with applications to image databases. In *Proc. ICCV '98*, IEEE Computer Society (1998), 59–66.

24. Shepard, R. N., and Metzler, J. Mental rotation of three-dimensional objects. *Science 171* (1971), 701–703.

25. Stumpf, H., and Eliot, J. A structural analysis of visual spatial ability in academically talented students. *Learning and Individual Differences 11*, 2 (1999), 137–151.

26. Surhone, L., Timpledon, M., and Marseken, S. *Lego Digital Designer*. VDM Verlag Dr. Mueller AG & Company Kg, 2010.

27. Tang, A., Owen, C., Biocca, F., and Mou, W. Comparative effectiveness of augmented reality in object assembly. In *Proc. CHI '03*, ACM Press (2003), 73–80.

28. Wallach, H., and O'Connell, D. N. The kinetic depth effect. *Journal of Experimental Psychology 45*, 4 (1953).

Capturing Indoor Scenes with Smartphones

Aditya Sankar[1]
[1]University of Washington
Seattle, WA, USA
{aditya, seitz}@cs.washington.edu

Steven M. Seitz[1,2]
[2]Google Inc.
Seattle, WA, USA

(a) Capture data (b) Playback interactive tour (c) Generate indoor floor plan

Figure 1: Our system captures an interactive visual tour and a floor plan of an indoor scene, in real time, on a smartphone.

ABSTRACT
In this paper, we present a novel smartphone application designed to easily capture, visualize and reconstruct homes, offices and other indoor scenes. Our application leverages data from smartphone sensors such as the camera, accelerometer, gyroscope and magnetometer to help model the indoor scene. The output of the system is two-fold; first, an interactive visual tour of the scene is generated in real time that allows the user to explore each room and transition between connected rooms. Second, with some basic interactive photogrammetric modeling the system generates a 2D floor plan and accompanying 3D model of the scene, under a Manhattan-world assumption. The approach does not require any specialized equipment or training and is able to produce accurate floor plans.

Author Keywords
Handheld Devices and Mobile Computing; Visualization; Virtual Reality; Augmented Reality

ACM Classification Keywords
H.5.2 [Information Interfaces and Presentation]: User Interfaces - Graphical user interfaces (GUI); H.5.1 [Information Interfaces and Presentation]: Multimedia Information Systems - Artificial, augmented, and virtual realities

General Terms
Algorithms; Design; Human Factors

UIST'12, October 7–10, 2012, Cambridge, Massachusetts, USA.

INTRODUCTION
In 1979, Lippman et al. [12] used gyrostabilized cameras mounted on top of a car to create an interactive visualization of downtown Aspen. This early hypermedia system, a forerunner of Google's Street View [1], pioneered the use of spatially indexed imagery for generating interactive virtual tours. Their system allowed users to interactively explore an environment and presented the user with a sense of *'being there'*. The desire to enhance and improve the notion of virtual presence has subsequently fueled a sizable body of work around interactive visual tours. However, most of these approaches [24, 21, 1, 9] rely on specialized data acquisition equipment and have complex and time-consuming offline processing pipelines, making them inaccessible to the casual user.

In this work, we present a system to easily create and view interactive visual tours, in real-time, entirely on a smartphone. To create a tour, the user first captures video of an indoor scene by following a few simple guidelines. This video data is then spatially and temporally indexed using sensor readings from the smartphone's gyroscope, accelerometer and magnetometer. Our system then generates an image-based rendering of the scene that allows a viewer to interactively playback a virtual tour in which he/she may explore each room and 'walk' between connected rooms. Once the data capture is complete, we use an interactive photogrammetric modeling scheme to recover room features such as the location of room corners and doors from within the image data. With this information we estimate the position of camera and generate an approximate floor-plan representation of the environment. Our method is designed to capture *Manhattan World* [5] scenes, i.e., scenes wherein all the surfaces are aligned with three dominant directions. The computed floor plans correctly capture the layout of the scene and are used to augment the interactive tour, enabling the user to understand where they are in the scene.

There are several challenges in making such a system work robustly, in real-time, on a mobile device. First, phones lack accurate localization information or odometry (GPS does not work well indoors [26]), making it hard to estimate camera position. Second, the monocular video data lacks depth information about room dimensions or floor plan layout. Extracting this information from video data in real-time is a difficult task. Finally, working within the computational and memory constraints of an embedded device pose additional engineering challenges.

The main contributions of this work are a framework for capturing and spatially indexing visual data by using a combination of measurements from the gyroscope, accelerometer and magnetometer, and a novel interactive technique to estimate room geometry and floor plan layout from monocular video. At a system level, the novelty lies in the implementation of an end-to-end smartphone application capable of capturing and reconstructing indoor scenes. We believe that our application is the first of its kind to deliver an interactive tour experience coupled with a floor plan on-the-fly, entirely on a phone. We foresee the use of our system in areas such as real estate, interior design, indoor localization and mobile robot navigation.

In the remainder of the paper we discuss related work, present an overview of the application from a user's perspective, describe novel components of our system, present floor plan results and evaluate them against ground truth. We conclude with future research directions.

RELATED WORK

The idea of indoor interactive video-based tours has been explored by several authors in graphics, vision and HCI. Brooks [2] in 1986 was one of the first to propose a system to build rapid visual prototypes of buildings for architectural use. More recently Uyttendaele et al. [24] used omnidirectional video to create indoor virtual tours. Similar approaches are used in Google's Streetview [1] and Art Project [9]. Our work is similar, in that the user can can interactively look around an environment, move freely along predefined paths, and branch to different areas at decision points. These prior approaches required sophisticated omnidirectional camera rigs and several hours of offline processing, whereas our method is implemented end-to-end on a commodity smartphone and is able to generate tours in a few of minutes. Our video-based tour approach is similar to that of Quiksee [15] but differs in that they used a hand-held camcorder and an offline processing pipeline. Their method requires manual spatial registration (as camcorders lack gyroscopic sensors) and does not model the geometry of the scene. Quiksee has since been acquired by Google Inc. and no published information is available on their method.

Early mobile robot navigation systems such as those proposed by Ishiguro [10] and Yagi [25] utilized omnidirectional camera systems combined with odometry measurements to reconstruct environments for mobile robot navigation. Taylor [21] also estimated camera position and environment geometry from video data. Their approach required the user to specify several point-and-line correspondences in key-frames of the omnidirectional video, whereas our method requires users to mark each wall corner once in an interactive panorama of the room. The visual SLAM and computer vision communities have developed automatic approaches [6, 7, 19, 4, 20] to reconstruct indoor scenes from images. While computer vision-based 3D reconstruction has demonstrated potential, we avoid explicit reconstruction with computer vision as it tends to be brittle, computationally expensive and does not work well on texture-poor surfaces, e.g. painted walls, which dominate interiors. SLAM-based reconstruction has been shown to work on smartphones by Shin et al. [18] who used sensor data to model indoor environments. Their approach is restricted to modeling only corridors while our method describes rooms, their volumes and also presents an interactive visualization of the space. A Manhattan-world assumption was employed by Kim et al. [11], to acquire indoor floor plans in real-time. Their approach is hardware-intensive, requiring the user to carry a Kinect camera, projector, laptop and a special input device while capturing data around the house.

The recent shift of imaged-based systems to the mobile phone platform is exemplified by the mobile Photosynth application [14] that creates panoramic images in real-time on a smartphone. MagicPlan [17] is a commercial floor plan generation app available for the iPhone. By marking floor corners in the room via an augmented reality interface, their system is able to estimate dimensions of the room and generate a corresponding floor plan. While their algorithms are proprietary and unpublished, they likely estimate and use the height of the observer (in this case the phone camera) and the tilt of the camera to estimate scene depth. By estimating depth in this manner, MagicPlan is able to capture non-Manhattan world scenes. This approach is susceptible to error when floor corners are occluded by furniture, requiring the user to guess at their positions. Our approach uses wall edges (the lines formed where two walls meet), which typically run from floor to ceiling and are often visible in rooms regardless of furniture placement and other occlusions. MagicPlan reconstructs rooms individually and then has a user manually assemble them to form a complete floor plan, whereas in our approach, we solve for correspondences between rooms and assemble the entire floor plan automatically. Finally, the augmented reality approach employed by MagicPlan is quicker and allows users to mark floor corners and doors in a single step. In contrast our two-step approach requires users to first capture imagery of the room and thereafter mark room features over the captured imagery. However, MagicPlan focuses solely on floor plan generation, whereas our goal is to produce a sense of virtual presence, to which end we use the captured imagery to visually reconstruct an immersive tour of the scene. A comparison of floor plans generated by both the approaches is presented in the results section.

APPLICATION OVERVIEW

This section describes the function of our application at a user-level. Our application is implemented on an iPhone 4, running iOS 5.1. However, the technique is designed to work on any device that is equipped with a camera, gyroscope, accelerometer and magnetometer; features that are now standard in the latest smartphones and tablets. We encourage readers to view the accompanying supplementary video [3]

Figure 2: The user may pan left or right in the panorama by dragging

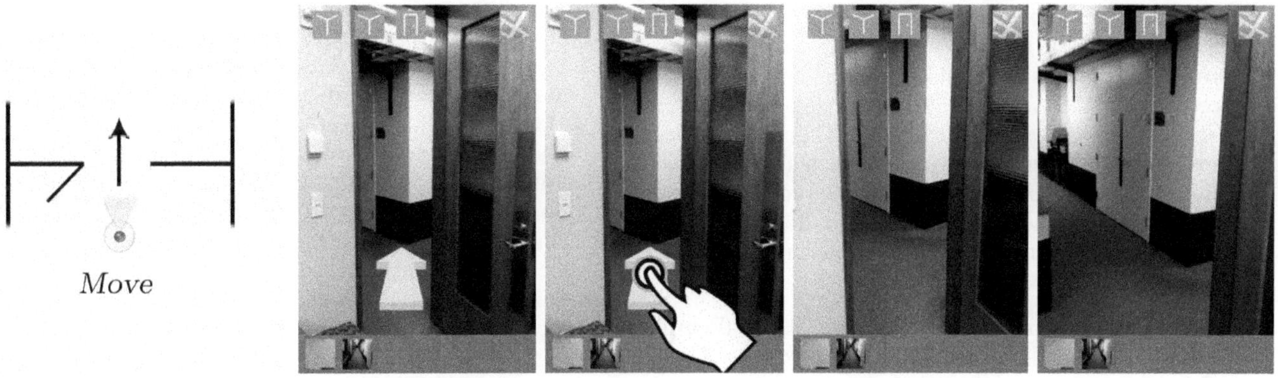

Figure 3: By tapping on the motion arrow, the user may move between rooms

in order to gain a better understanding of the application's interface. The basic steps in the approach are outlined below and in Figures 1, 2 & 3:

1. **Data acquisition**: (Figure 1a) To capture a room, the user stands near the center of the room, holding the phone upright and aiming the phone camera at a wall. He/she then proceeds to rotate 360° to capture a video of the entire room. The application automatically detects when a full rotation has been completed and prompts the user to turn and face the next room. Once in position, the user indicates that he/she is ready to move to the next room by performing a *swipe up* gesture and subsequently proceeds to walk to the next room. Our system records this transition as a video. On reaching the center of the next room, the user performs a *swipe down* gesture and begins to capture the current room. The same process is repeated for every room. If a room is re-visited, the user has an option to indicate this in the interface. Captured rooms appear as thumbnails on the bottom of the screen.

2. **Interactive Tour Playback**: (Figure 1b) Once capture is complete, the user can instantly view a virtual tour of the scene. For each room, the system generates a 360° video panorama, in which the user may pan left of right to explore the scene (Figure 2). The user is afforded two modalities to interact with the panorama. They may drag left or right on the touchscreen or physically move the device in 3D space to '*look around*' the room, in a manner reminiscent of mobile virtual/augmented reality applications [16, 23]. When a door appears in the users current field of view, a motion arrow [8] appears on the screen, indicating that there is a path leading to an adjacent room. Upon tapping the arrow, a transition video is played back giving the user the effect of 'walking' into the next room (Figure 3). At the end of the transition, the system presents the 360° video panorama of the current room, wherein the user may once again explore interactively.

3. **Embedding Close-up Images and Text**: The user has the ability to embed close-up photographs and text in the scene, during playback. To add an embedded object, the user double taps a point of interest on the screen. This instantiates a modal dialog that prompts the user to take a high-resolution photograph of the point of interest and optionally add some descriptive text. Upon completing this task and closing the dialog, the user is returned to the tour and the embedded object now appears as an icon overlaid on top of the panorama. The icon is positioned at the location where the user originally performed the double tap gesture and is pinned to that location as the user pans the panorama left or right. Tapping the icon spawns a modal

popup that shows the hi-res photo along with the annotation text. The embedded objects are saved along with the virtual tour data for future viewing.

4. **Marking Room Features**: In playback mode, the user can mark room features such as wall edges (where two walls meet) and doors via an intuitive touch interface. To mark a wall edge the user first brings the edge into view by panning left or right in the panorama. Once the edge is visible, the user drags a marker to align with the room corner in the image. Similarly, doors are indicated by placing two markers on the extremities of the door. Note that each door is visible from both the rooms that it connects. This door correspondence is also specified by the user, (i.e., which room does a specific door lead to), by tapping the appropriate room thumbnail.
5. **2D Floor Plan**: (Figure 5c) An optimization algorithm uses the corner and door information and other room constraints to generate a 2D floor plan of the space. Alignment errors in the reconstructed floor plan can be manually corrected via a touch interface. To fix an alignment error, the user first taps a wall that requires re-alignment and next taps a wall to which the previously selected wall should be aligned. The walls can be in the same room or different rooms, but they must be parallel. The floor plan is rendered as a top-down map of the environment and indicates the users current position in the tour.
6. **3D Floor Plan**: (Figure 5d) We extrude the 2D floor plan vertically and render a 3D model of the scene. The 3D rendering can be manipulated via the touch interface and users can explore novel views of the environment (e.g., a 45° bird's-eye view).

SYSTEM COMPONENTS

Spatial Video Indexing

Indexing video spatially with camera pose information is a simple yet effective method of creating an interactive viewing experience [12]. During playback, by interactively selecting a desired viewpoint and viewing direction, we can retrieve the closest view from the previously captured video sequence. Interactive video playback has advantages over a traditional composited panorama in that it captures dynamic exposure changes and motion in the environment, which are essential to the richness and realism of the visualization [24]. However, the disadvantage of using a video sequence is the inability to zoom-out. While the idea of spatial video indexing has been explored before [21, 24], we present a few novel developments that help adapt it to a smartphone.

Calculating Camera Pose:

The on-board gyroscope on the iPhone 4 provides fine-grained information about the angular velocity of the device; however integrating this data to calculate relative orientation results in drift and requires calibration. The accelerometer and magnetometer conversely provide more reliable orientation information, but at a lower resolution and refresh rate. We use a simple sensor fusion approach to calculate pose by combining data from the gyroscope, accelerometer and magnetometer as follows. The rotation rate of the device around three axes is obtained by querying the gyroscope at regular intervals. The major axis of rotation is determined by querying the accelerometer to determine the direction of gravitational acceleration and hence the device orientation (portrait v/s landscape). Once the major axis is known, we bootstrap the camera pose with the actual orientation of the device relative to true north, as obtained from the magnetometer. Thereafter current orientation is determined as follows:

$$\theta_t^G = \theta_{t-1}^G + \Delta t \times \omega^{majoraxis} \quad (1)$$

Where θ_t^G represents current device orientation, as calculated by adding the delta change in orientation $\Delta t \times \omega^{majoraxis}$ to the last known orientation θ_{t-1}^G. This value is updated at approximately 100Hz, but suffers from gyroscopic drift of as much as $\pm 10°$ in a full 360° rotation. We then spatially index the current image with the calculated device orientation value.

Countering Gyroscopic Drift:

In order to counter gyroscopic drift, we rely on the magnetometer to inform us when a full 360° rotation has been completed. While the intermediate magnetometer readings are noisy and not useful for updating device orientation, we have found that the resolution is sufficient to indicate when a rotation has been completed. Once we know that the rotation is complete, we can close the "gap" caused due to drift. For this we use the initial and current gyroscopically calculated orientation values and eliminate the drift by uniformly distributing it across the entire rotation.

User Interaction to Mark Room Elements

Once the video and orientation data have been captured, the tour is played back interactively. The playback interface is similar to previous work such as Street View [1] and VideoPlus [21] which allow the user to interactively pan within a 'viewing bubble' and branch to different bubbles at decision points.

During playback, we also present an interface to mark room elements such as corners and doors. In this interface the user is presented with a draggable marker which they can place over the current image to indicate the presence of a corner or door. Marking a corner requires only one marker, whereas marking the extremities of a door requires two. The relative heading of each marker is calculated from the indicated x-coordinate of the marker within an image, by the following equation:

$$\theta_{marker} = \theta_t^G + fov/w_{img} \times (P_{marker} - w_{img}/2) \quad (2)$$

The spatial index, θ_t^G, of the image on-screen corresponds to the heading of the center of the image. The one-dimensional pixel-offset of the marker from the center of the image of width w_{img} is calculated by subtracting the position of the center pixel, $w_{img}/2$, from the position of the marker, P_{marker}. The pixel-offset is then converted into a heading-offset by multiplying by the field of view of the image, fov, and dividing by the total pixel width, w_{img}. Finally, the estimated heading of the marker, θ_{marker}, is determined by adding the heading offset to the current spatial index, θ_t^G.

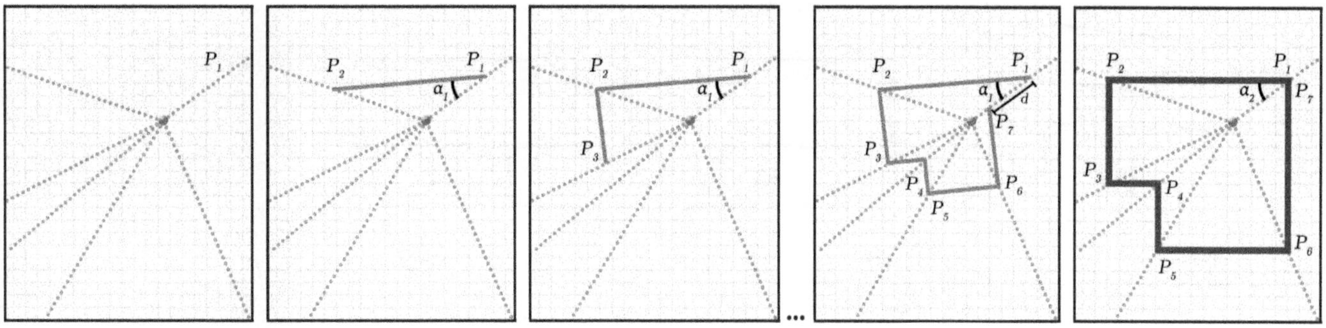

Figure 4: Floor plan reconstruction algorithm: (a) Top-down view of the scene showing the corner rays (dotted green) emanating from the camera. P_1 is unit distance from camera along first ray. (b) Hypothesized wall at angle α_1 intersects second ray at P_2. (c) The next wall is rotated 90 degrees, and intersects at P_3. (d) Incorrect hypothesis results in a distance error d between first and last points. (e) Optimal wall configuration with starting wall angle α_2, minimizes d.

During tour playback, the following equation (2) is used to calculate position, $P_{feature}$, of a feature with a known heading $\theta_{feature}$ within an image.

$$P_{feature} = w_{img}/2 + w_{img}/fov \times (\theta_{feature} - \theta_t^G) \quad (3)$$

This allows us to embed UI elements such as motion arrows and annotations into the scene.

Floor Plan Generation

Computing Room Geometry:

We treat the marked corners and doors as rays emanating from the camera center and reconstruct the room geometry that fits the given set of rays (as shown in Figure 4), based on the following assumptions. First, we assume that the scene satisfies the Manhattan world assumption, i.e., the walls are planar and the room corners are right-angled. Many architectural scenes approximately fit the Manhattan World assumption, and it has previously enabled very high quality reconstruction results across a wide range of scenes [7]. We also assume that the camera is located in a position within the room from which all corners are visible, or if this is not possible, that the user is able to estimate and mark the location of occluded room features. Finally, we assume that the corner ray directions are determined from the spatial indexing data, as described in the previous section.

Search Algorithm:

Our search algorithm over the possible room configurations is described below and in Algorithm 1.

Without loss of generality, assume the camera is located at the scene origin, and the first room corner is at unit distance from the origin (we solve for the room only up to scale). Now suppose we also specify the orientation α (relative to the first corner ray) of the first wall. Under the Manhattan World Assumption, the orientations of all other walls are determined (since they meet at right angles). It also turns out that their lengths can also be inferred from the known corner ray directions (as we will describe shortly). The approach works as follows. Let P_1 be the point at unit distance from the origin along the ray direction of the first corner (Figure 4a). The intersection of the ray from P_1 at angle α with the ray from the origin along the ray direction of the second corner defines the position P_2 of the second corner in the room (Figure 4b). Rotate 90 degrees and repeat this procedure to intersect the ray from P_2 with the ray from the origin along the direction of the third corner to define P_3(Figure 4c), and so on. This procedure will place all of the corners in the plane. The key insight is that for the correct value of α, the final ray from P_N should intersect P_1 (Figure 4e), assuming N corners. An incorrect value of α will generally not satisfy this criterion (Figure 4d). Our approach is therefore to do an exhaustive search over all angles (0 - 360, sampled at 0.5 degree increments), to solve for an α that yields the closest intersection with P_1 (see Algorithm 1). Our algorithm finds an optimal solution in $O(Nd)$ running time where N is the number of corners in the room and d is the number of angles sampled in our search.

Algorithm 1 Calculating optimal wall configuration

```
P_0 = Origin
P_1 = Unit distance from P_0 along the first ray
N = Number of corners
minDistance = MAX_FLOAT
for α = 0 → 360 step 0.5 do
    for i = 2 → N do
        θ_i = direction of i^th corner                ▷ from (2)
        P_i ← intersect(P_{i-1}, α+(i−1)×90, P_0, θ_i)
    end for
    distance = getDistance(P_1, P_N)
    if distance < minDistance then
        minDistance ← distance
        minAngle ← angle
    end if
end for
Return minAngle
```

Note that in Algorithm 1, $intersect(P_A, \theta_A, P_B, \theta_B)$ finds the intersection point of two lines A and B defined in point-

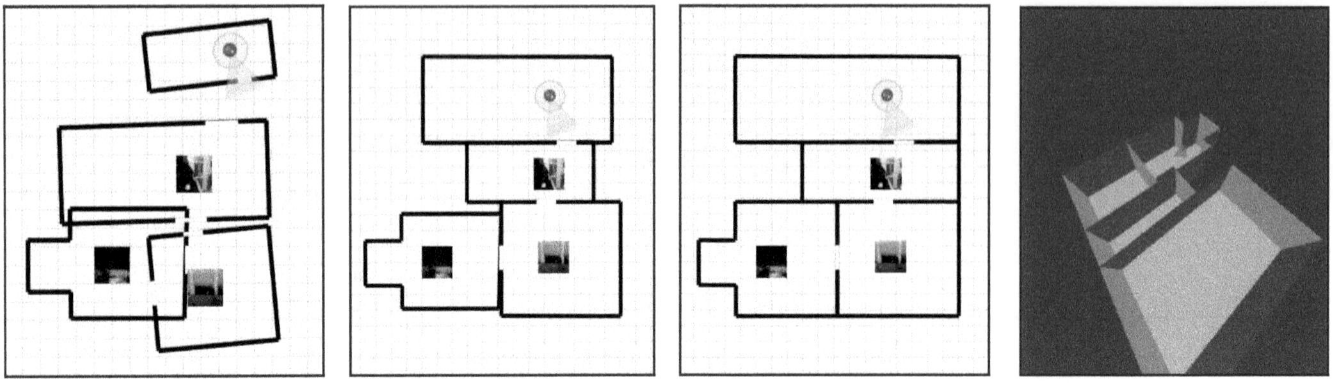

(a) Floor layout as estimated by odometry, with current camera position indicated by the camera frumstum

(b) Solving for the door constraint translates, scales, and rotates rooms to align properly

(c) Layout after manual edits have been made via a touch interface

(d) Reconstructed 3D model of home.

Figure 5: Stages of solving floor layout.

slope form and $getDistance(P_A, P_B)$ calculates the distance between points P_A and P_B in a euclidean space.

Aligning Rooms:
Since our goal is to generate a complete floor plan of an indoor scene, we must calculate relative positions and orientations of rooms to each other. We make an initial best guess with the help of some approximate odometry. If we assume that the user walks at a constant pace between rooms during capture, we can estimate relative positions of rooms, using the user's movement direction and length of the transition video sequence. However this method is prone to error (as is seen in Figure 5a) due to the fact that users may move with a non-uniform velocity and change direction mid-flight.

We can more accurately calculate relative room positioning by using the supplied door rays. Once the walls have been calculated via Algorithm 1, we can find the projected coordinates of the door by intersecting the door rays with the walls. Since each door is visible from exactly two rooms (as indicated in the interface by the user), we can proceed to calculate a 2D rigid body transformation, to align them. The transform is written as:

$$\begin{pmatrix} x'_i \\ y'_i \end{pmatrix} = \begin{pmatrix} c & -s \\ s & c \end{pmatrix} \begin{pmatrix} x_i \\ y_i \end{pmatrix} + \begin{pmatrix} t_x \\ t_y \end{pmatrix} \quad (4)$$

Here c, s, t_x & t_y are unknowns; by substituting the values of corresponding doors in two rooms, we can solve for the transformation that correctly aligns the doors, and hence also aligns both rooms. The matrix equation can be solved by standard least squares fitting methods.

We solve for the transformations between every pair of connected rooms and are able to generate a complete floor plan as shown in Figure 5b. This intermediate solution still contains errors, such as misaligned walls and incorrectly scaled room dimensions. The errors are caused due to several factors; gyroscopic drift not being eliminated completely, human error in marking room features (typically off by a few pixels), error due to discretization of the search angle α and the fact that the physical walls may not be perfectly axis aligned. There may also be error caused due to parallax as the user may slightly move the camera center while capturing the scene.

To alleviate errors, we allow users to manually correct wall alignment using a simple touch interface, as described in the Application Overview section. The end result of this process is depicted in Figure 5c, which more accurately describes the room layout in the house. In this particular example, five corrections were required to produce the final result.

3D Rendering
3D reconstructions of a scene allow for generating novel views and a more immersive spatial visualization. Once we have a suitable 2D floor plan rendering, we extrude it vertically and render a floor plane to obtain a representative 3D model of the environment as shown in Figure 5d. To provide the user with additional spatial context, we render a small camera frustum that represents their current position and orientation in the tour.

RESULTS AND DISCUSSION
We tested our application in four indoor environments. For each environment we generated an interactive visual tour and floor plan. The resulting tour experience has been described previously in the Application Overview section and a demonstration of the interface is available in the supplementary video [3]. In this section we will present the results of floor plan generation.

Recovering Individual Room Geometry
In Figure 6 we present the results of individual room reconstruction by our approach and that of MagicPlan. Since our floor plan reconstruction is not to scale, for the overlay we manually scale and register our result over ground truth. Room 1 took 1 minute and 12 seconds to capture with our approach (44s capture + 28s marking room features) and 53

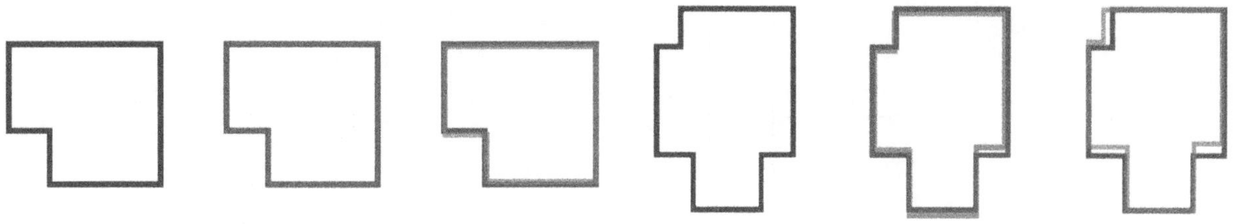

Figure 6: Room geometry recovered by our approach (red) and by MagicPlan (green), when overlaid on ground truth (blue)

seconds to capture with MagicPlan. Room 2 took 1 minute and 34 seconds with our approach (46s capture + 48s marking room features) and 1 minute and 4 seconds with MagicPlan. The running time for both reconstruction algorithms was negligible. Our image capture time remains roughly the same regardless of room configuration, but more complex rooms require longer to mark room features. While the total time taken by MagicPlan is less, our approach also captures imagery of the room for creating an immersive visual tour experience, whereas MagicPlan outputs only a floor plan. The examples in Figure 6 show that our approach is able to capture the shape of the room with similar accuracy to MagicPlan. Note, however that our reconstruction does not provide metric scale, while MagicPlan does.

Generating Floor Plan Layout

In Table 1 and Figure 7 we present results from four indoor environments:

		Features			No. of	Total Time	Error
Env.	*Type*	R	C	D	Frames	Taken	(%)
A	House	5	26	4	1356	7m16s	5.66
B	House	6	42	5	2107	9m42s	13.38
C	House	5	26	5	1571	8m40s	8.76
D	Office	7	28	6	3422	12m35s	13.98
Avg.						9m33s	10.45

Table 1: Experimental results for four environments tested. (Legend: R = Rooms, C = Corners, D = Doorways)

The reconstructed floor plans for each environment are shown in Figure 7, along with manually measured ground truth. Some reconstruction errors can be observed in environments (A) and (D), where an individual room has been misaligned. In environment (C) our system approximates a bay window to be flat, in accordance with the Manhattan-world assumption. We calculate a measure of reconstruction error from the overlay, as the ratio of area incorrectly reconstructed (sum of both overestimated and underestimated areas) to the total ground truth area. The results indicate that our system is able to reconstruct the dimensions and overall floor plan of an indoor scene with an average error of 10.45% for the environments tested. Aside from the previously mentioned failure cases, the floor plan correctly captures the shape, relative position and orientation of most rooms. This meets our goal of capturing an accurate layout that is useful for the purposes of visualization and navigation in the interactive tour.

CONCLUSION AND FUTURE WORK

We presented a novel end-to-end system to capture and reconstruct indoor scenes for the purpose of creating an interactive visual tour. While there is a large body of prior work in this area, our system is the first to allow casual users to quickly and easily create immersive tours on a smartphone. Our method also enables the creation of indoor floor plans and 3D renderings of the scene, without the need to remove furniture or physically measure the environment. In order to achieve our design goals, we have devised a data capture framework, an interactive photogrammetric modeling scheme and an indoor floor plan generation algorithm, designed to run independently on a commodity smartphone in real-time.

While the floor plan generation algorithm is currently unable to model curved walls or non right-angled corners, we believe that the system is sufficient to capture a qualitative sense of most indoor environments.

Several aspects of this system may be improved upon in future work. A hand-held device is susceptible to shake and the resulting imagery is sometimes motion blurred. The gyroscope data from the non-major axes can be used to select frames with minimal shake, thus stabilizing the image data. Another improvement would be to better model complex indoor scenes that contain non-Manhattan world elements. One approach would be to use computer vision techniques to estimate the depth of room features to assist the floor plan generation algorithm. The creation of more detailed 3D renderings of the scene can be enabled by adding textures to the walls and modeling furniture and other items within a room. Finally, to enhance the effect of immersion, it should be possible to capture aspects of physical interaction in the scene, for example operating appliances or turning on/off light switches. These can be captured with our video-based approach but require explicit modeling to incorporate them into the interactive tour.

We believe that real estate is perhaps the most compelling application for our system. Realtors and homeowners can use our smartphone application to generate tours and floor plans of houses without the need for any extra equipment. Mapping is another compelling application area. Commercial map-

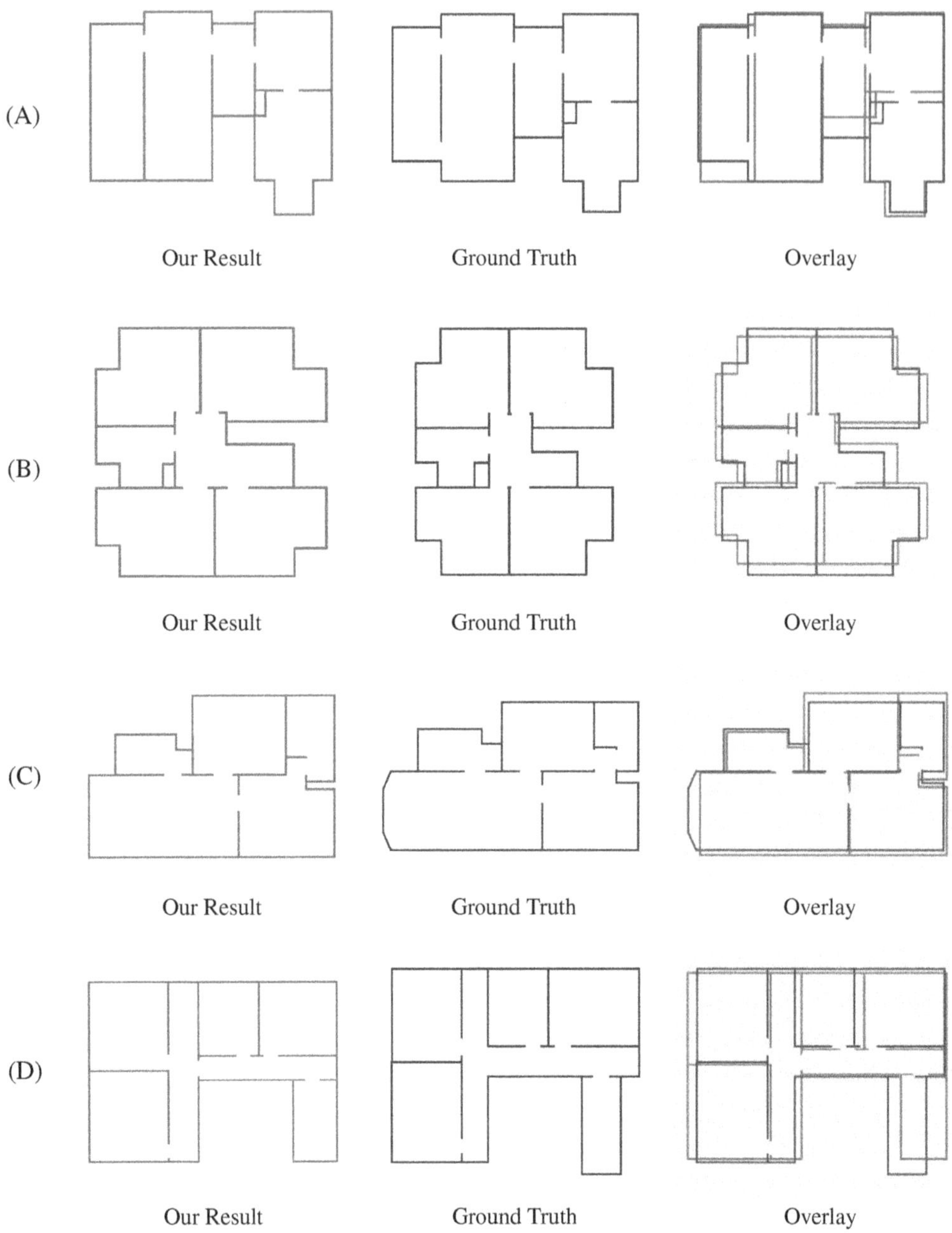

Figure 7: Side-by-side comparisons of floor plans generated by our system to ground truth

ping services such as StreetView [1] and Bing Maps [13] are increasingly incorporating indoor maps into their products. Small-business owners or other operators can use our system to create immersive tours of their establishments (cafés, restaurants, hotels, etc.) and share them with customers through such mapping services. Aspects of our approach may also be useful for other applications, in particular, the floor plans can be used to bootstrap systems for indoor localization (e.g., in a mall) and mobile robot navigation. Finally, the interactive tours give a sense of virtual presence, allowing individual users to share their experience of a space with friends and family.

With almost half (49.7% [22]) of U.S. mobile subscribers now owning smartphones and similar rising trends across the world, we believe that our method will enable casual users to capture, visualize and reconstruct of a wide variety of interesting indoor scenes, from homes and offices to museums and heritage sites.

ACKNOWLEDGMENTS

This work was supported in part by NSF grants IIS-0811878 and IIS-0963657, SPAWAR, the University of Washington Animation Research Labs, and Google.

REFERENCES

1. Anguelov, D., Dulong, C., Filip, D., Frueh, C., Lafon, S., Lyon, R., Ogale, A., Vincent, L. and Weaver, J. Google Street View: Capturing the World at Street Level. In *Computer*, 43(6): pages 32–38, June 2010.
2. Brooks, F. Walkthrough – a dynamic graphics system for simulating virtual buildings. In *Proceedings of I3D'86*, pages 9–21, 1987.
3. Capturing Indoor Scenes with Smarthphones, project page. `http://grail.cs.washington.edu/videotour/`
4. Coorg, S. and Teller, S., Extracting textured vertical facades from controlled close-range imagery. In *Proceedings of CVPR*, pages 625–632, 1999.
5. Coughlan, J.M. and Yuille, A.L. Manhattan World: Compass Direction from a Single Image by Bayesian Inference. In *Proceedings of ICCV*, pages 941–947, 1999.
6. Flint, A., Murray, D. and Reid, I. Manhattan scene understanding using monocular, stereo, and 3D features. In *Proceedings of ICCV*, pages 2228–2235, 2011.
7. Furukawa, Y., Curless, B., Seitz, S. M., and Szeliski, R. Reconstructing Building Interiors from Images. In *Proceedings of ICCV '09*, pages 80-87, 2009.
8. Goldman, D. B., Curless, B., Salesin, D., and Seitz, S. M. Schematic storyboarding for video visualization and editing. In *Proceedings of SIGGRAPH*, pages 862–871, 2006.
9. Google Inc., Google Art Project, 2011. `http://www.googleartproject.com`
10. Ishiguro, H., Ueda, K. and Tsuji, S. Omnidirectional visual information for navigating a mobile robot. In *Proceedings of ICRA*, pages 799–804, 1993.
11. Kim, Y.M., Dolson, J., Sokolsky, M., Koltun, V., Thrun, S., Interactive Acquisition of Residential Floor Plans. In *Proceedings of ICRA*, pages 3055–3062, 2012
12. Lippman, A. Movie-maps: An application of the optical videodisc to computer graphics. In *Proceedings of SIGGRAPH*, pages 32–42, 1980.
13. Microsoft Bing Maps, 2012. `http://www.bing.com/maps/`
14. Microsoft Corporation, Photosynth, 2011. `http://photosynth.net/`
15. Quiksee, 2011. `http://www.quiksee.com/`
16. Reitmayr, G. and Drummond, T. Going out: robust model-based tracking for outdoor augmented reality. In *Proceedings of ISMAR*, pages 109–118, 2006.
17. Sensopia Inc., MagicPlan, 2011. `http://www.sensopia.com`
18. Shin, H., Chon, Y., Cha, H., Unsupervised Construction of an Indoor Floor Plan Using a Smartphone, In *IEEE Transactions on Systems, Man, and Cybernetics*, Volume PP, Issue 99, pages 1–10, 2011
19. Snavely, N., Seitz, S. M., and Szeliski, R., Photo tourism: exploring photo collections in 3D. In *Proceedings of SIGGRAPH*, pages 835–846, 2006.
20. Szeliski, R. and Shum, H. Creating full view panoramic image mosaics and environment maps. In *Proceedings of SIGGRAPH*, pages 251–258, 1997.
21. Taylor, C. J. VideoPlus: A Method for Capturing the Structure and Appearance of Immersive Environments. In *IEEE Transactions on Visualization and Computer Graphics*, 8(2):pages 171–182, 2002.
22. The Neilsen Company: Neilsen Mobile Insights, 2012. `http://bit.ly/HOJ5XU`
23. Tsang, M., Fitzmzurice, G. W., Kurtenbach, G., Khan, A. and Buxton, B. Boom chameleon: simultaneous capture of 3D viewpoint, voice and gesture annotations on a spatially-aware display. In *Proceedings of SIGGRAPH*, pages 698–698, 2003.
24. Uyttendaele, M., Criminisi, A., Kang, S. B., Winder, S., Szeliski, R., and Hartley, R. Image-Based Interactive Exploration of Real-World Environments. In *IEEE Computer Graphics and Applications*, 24:pages 52–63, 2004.
25. Yagi, Y., Kawato, S. and Tsuji, S. Real-time omnidirectional image sensor (COPIS) for vision-guided navigation. In *IEEE Transactions on Robotics and Automation*, 10(1):pages 11–22, 1994.
26. Zandbergen, P. A. Accuracy of iPhone Locations: A Comparison of Assisted GPS, WiFi and Cellular Positioning. In *Transactions in GIS*, 13:pages 5–25, 2009.

Steerable Augmented Reality with the Beamatron

Andrew D. Wilson, Hrvoje Benko
Microsoft Research
One Microsoft Way
Redmond, WA 98052
awilson, benko@microsoft.com

Shahram Izadi, Otmar Hilliges
Microsoft Research Cambridge
7 JJ Thomson Avenue
Cambridge, CB3 0FB
shahrami, otmarh@microsoft.com

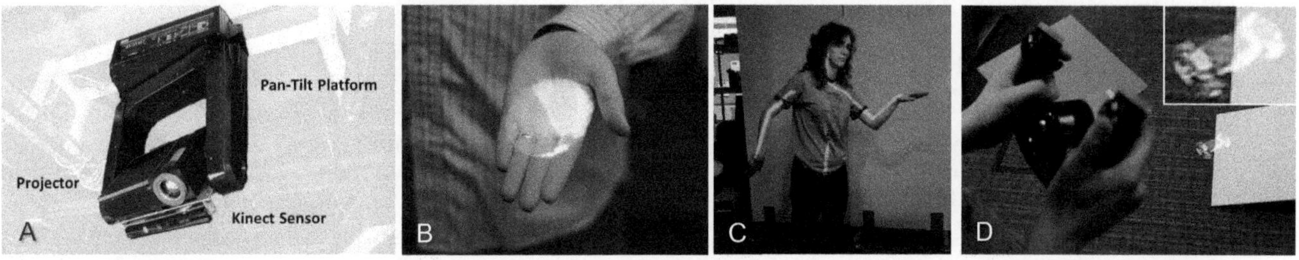

Figure 1. (A) The Beamatron mounts a projector and Kinect sensor to a pan and tilt motorized platform. (B) The Beamatron can project graphics in the user's hand, and follow the user as they move about the room. (C) Skeletal tracking results superimposed on a user. (D) Driving a projected car on real objects in the room with a wireless wheel controller.

ABSTRACT

Steerable displays use a motorized platform to orient a projector to display graphics at any point in the room. Often a camera is included to recognize markers and other objects, as well as user gestures in the display volume. Such systems can be used to superimpose graphics onto the real world, and so are useful in a number of augmented reality and ubiquitous computing scenarios. We contribute the Beamatron, which advances steerable displays by drawing on recent progress in depth camera-based interactions. The Beamatron consists of a computer-controlled pan and tilt platform on which is mounted a projector and Microsoft Kinect sensor. While much previous work with steerable displays deals primarily with projecting corrected graphics onto a discrete set of static planes, we describe computational techniques that enable reasoning in 3D using live depth data. We show two example applications that are enabled by the unique capabilities of the Beamatron: an augmented reality game in which a player can drive a virtual toy car around a room, and a ubiquitous computing demo that uses speech and gesture to move projected graphics throughout the room.

ACM Classification: H5.2 [Information interfaces and presentation]: User Interfaces. - Graphical user interfaces.

General terms: Human Factors

Keywords: Steerable displays, augmented reality, ubiquitous computing, depth cameras

UIST '12, October 7–10, 2012, Cambridge, Massachusetts, USA.

INTRODUCTION

Augmented reality generally refers to viewing the real, physical world with superimposed computer-generated graphics. Today this usually involves rendering graphics onto a live video of the physical world, most commonly on a mobile device such as a smartphone. Graphics are updated continuously to follow the orientation of the device video camera, such that the graphics appear to be inserted into the real world. This approach has the drawback that rather than look at the real world, the user must instead look at a small video feed of it. Near-to-eye displays address this shortcoming, allowing the user to view the real world with superimposed graphics directly, but require wearing exotic gear [4,16].

An alternative approach to achieve direct viewing is to use projectors to render graphics onto the real world directly. *Spatial augmented reality* [4] entails correcting the projected graphics to account for the shape of the projection surface, possibly assuming the user's viewpoint (see [30] for a particularly compelling example). Whereas the effective field of view of a smartphone or near-to-eye display AR system is potentially unlimited as the user moves their head or their device, a projected spatial augmented reality system is limited by the field of view of the projector. This can be overcome somewhat by using multiple projectors and cameras, at the expense of the overall complexity of the system [35]. A handful of research prototypes have explored using a motorized platform to reorient a single projector and camera to view arbitrary locations throughout a room [22, 8, 6, 11]. Such *steerable display* systems trade the shortcomings of the multiple projector and camera approach for the problem of selecting the most appropriate orientation of the projector and camera at each moment.

This paper builds on previous examples of steerable displays by replacing the usual video camera with a depth camera, and by developing algorithms and techniques which allow precise rendering of graphics that appear to be correctly inserted into the real world from the user's point of view. Whereas much of the previous work on steerable displays exploits explicit calibration procedures against a set of discrete static planar surfaces of the real world [22], the real-time update of precise 3D shape information from the depth camera allows interactions with possibly moving objects (including the user's body). This capability allows certain interactions new to steerable displays, such as holding a virtual (projected) object in the hand while walking around the room.

We contribute the Beamatron, a hardware device design, calibration strategy and associated control algorithms to enable the use of a steerable projector and depth camera for spatial augmented reality throughout a room (see Figure 1). We believe the Beamatron is the first steerable display to

- incorporate a depth camera to allow live changes in the 3D environment, such as moving a projection surface, or following a user's hand
- use 3D calculations to allow the application to reason in room coordinates and correctly render 3D objects without regard to the precise orientation of the platform
- use a hardware feedback mechanism to more accurately stabilize projected graphics when the unit is moving
- use projective texturing to appropriately render 3D graphics onto arbitrarily shaped surfaces for a given viewpoint
- incorporate 3D (stereo) projection
- use 3D sound source localization as a means to track user position when the user is not in view, to call the unit to view the user for subsequent gesture-based interaction or adjust rendering viewpoint

In the rest of the paper, we discuss related work, and detail the Beamatron hardware and algorithms. We demonstrate the system in an augmented reality scenario of driving a virtual toy car around the real physical world, and in a ubiquitous computing scenario involving the gesture-driven movement of projected 2D graphics. Finally we discuss a number of possible extensions to the Beamatron.

RELATED WORK

Spatial Augmented Reality

A number of previous works have explored using projectors to superimpose graphics onto the real world [4]. A key technical challenge for these systems is taking into account the shape of the projection surface when rendering graphics, so that the projected graphics either appear "painted" on the object [25], or so that the projection gives the impression of a real 3D object of the correct size and shape [2]. These approaches require the precise calibration of the projector (i.e., focal length and optical center).

Of particular relevance to the present work is the overall rendering pipeline of MirageTable [2], which uses Microsoft Kinect depth image data to distort projected graphics on a per-vertex basis. MirageTable also supports the correct rendering of 3D objects for a given viewpoint; this viewpoint is determined by tracking the user's head. Beamatron adopts a similar approach to rendering graphics.

Immersive Projection

In many application scenarios involving projecting onto the real world, it is desirable to project over wide areas to create an immersive experience [23, 30], and researchers have demonstrated the combination of multiple projectors to create bright, high resolution immersive displays [24].

Underkoffler et al.'s "I/O bulb" [32] is an intriguing vision of a single fixture in the ceiling which projects and senses throughout a room. While it is possible to use wide-angle optics to display and sense over a wide area (for example, see [1]), the limited brightness of projectors and limited sensing of cameras imposes a variety of tradeoffs to make a simple implementation of the I/O Bulb difficult. LightSpace [35] addresses brightness and resolution concerns by mounting multiple cameras and projectors to create a large combined fustrum of display and sensing to approximate an I/O Bulb. As with the present work, LightSpace uses depth cameras to correct projected graphics, and enable a variety of 3D interactions.

Steerable Projector-Camera Systems

Steerable displays use a motorized platform or rotating mirrors to direct projected graphics programmatically. This avoids the complexity of multi-projector, multi-camera systems, but retains the ability to place graphics anywhere in the room. The IBM Everywhere Displays prototype is the first steerable display to demonstrate the correction of projected graphics to account for the orientation of the (planar) projection surface [22]. It consists of a projector and a small mirror with 2 axes of rotation. In contrast with the present work, Everywhere Displays is limited to projecting on a discrete set of planar surfaces which are calibrated beforehand, each modeled by a 2D homography.

The Everywhere Displays project explored many applications of steerable displays, particularly in the retail domain. With the addition of a pan and tilt video camera, a number of gesture-based interactions are demonstrated, including touch-based manipulation of projected graphical widgets [12], as well as person tracking to enable graphics to follow the user.

A small number of later works contribute steerable displays designs which mount the projector and camera directly onto motorized platform with pan and tilt axes of motion [8, 6, 11]. Butz et al. [7] contribute a number of interactions in the tradition of ubiquitous computing, such as the ability to scan a room for special AR Toolkit markers [3] so that they later may be indicated to a viewer by a projected "searchlight" graphic, and to project graphical autonomous agents where they are needed. Molyneaux et al. [19] explore more generic object recognition techniques to find and annotate physical objects.

Ehnes et al. [11] contribute a steerable display design that comes closest to the spirit of the present work. In particular, they address the challenges of stabilizing projected graphics while the projector is in motion. Such functionality can be interesting for a wide variety of applications, such as tracking and projecting onto a moving object (such as a person, or a mobile display). They describe their approach to model the precise pose of the head without use of a hardware feedback circuit, and note the importance of accounting for the latency of the camera when matching image processing results with platform pose.

Handheld and Wearable Projectors

Recent advances in the miniaturization of projectors have encouraged the study of handheld and wearable interactive projectors [36, 33, 9, 13, 20]. These share many traits of the steerable displays described above, including problems related to the distortion of the projected image and device pose [26]. Handheld projectors differ from steerable projectors in at least one important way, however: the onus is primarily on the user to select the appropriate area to project. As we will show with the Beamatron, steerable projectors can split this responsibility between the user and the host computer, as appropriate to the application.

Interacting with Light

A number of early works demonstrate the interactive manipulation of graphics projected onto the environment. For example, Rekimoto at al.'s Augmented Surface [27] allows the user to drag a document off the laptop display and onto the projected desktop, and later bring the object from the desktop to the wall using a laser pointer.

The present work demonstrates the ability for the user to "hold" a projected object in the hand, as if it were a real physical object. This has been demonstrated in previous interactive projection-based interfaces. Micromotocross [34] uses a projector and depth camera to allow a player to drive a virtual projected car over real objects and possibly into the hand, with the projected graphics corrected for the shape of the hand. LightSpace [35] gives the user the capability to move a projected off a tabletop and into the other hand. The projected object stays with the hand until dropped back onto the table top or onto the wall. Furthermore, the motion of the ball is simulated such that it rolls downhill along any real physical surface such as the user's forearm or a piece of paper. MirageTable [2] adds the ability to correctly render 3D virtual objects for a given user viewpoint, as well as stereo rendering for active shutter glasses. Finally, LightGuide [29] demonstrates the use of projected graphics in the hand to guide the user to perform a particular motion in three dimensions.

THE BEAMATRON

Hardware configuration

The Beamatron hardware device consists of a video projector and Microsoft Xbox Kinect sensor rigidly mounted to a City Theatrical Autoyoke [10] moving light platform. The Autoyoke's configuration is similar to that of moving lights found at nightclubs and rock concerts, except that the included spot light is easily removed and replaced with other gear. The Autoyoke tilts 270° and pans 360° with a hard stop (i.e., it cannot rotate past 360°). Product documentation indicates pan and tilt movement speed of 90°/s and positional accuracy of 0.1°.

The Autoyoke uses the DMX lighting protocol and interface. Commands to move to a new pan and tilt configuration are issued programmatically using a USB to DMX adapter. As is common for DMX devices, there is no provision for providing feedback on the actual pan and tilt configuration as the device moves to new target pan and tilt angles. Real-time knowledge of the platform pose is critical to projecting stabilized graphics while the platform is in motion. In lieu of such feedback it may be possible to model and predict the position of the platform, as demonstrated in [11]. Instead, we developed a small circuit board which connects to the pan and tilt optical shaft encoders built into the Autoyoke. This circuit uses the quadrature decoders of an AVR XMega256 microcontroller to relay pan and tilt configuration to the PC by a separate USB interface at 100Hz. As far as we know, the Beamatron is the first steerable display to exploit accurate hardware-based feedback for the purposes of stabilizing graphics.

For projecting graphics, the Beamatron uses the Dell 1610HD 3D-ready projector, rated at 3500 lumens. This projector uses the Texas Instruments' DLP Link technology to optionally render stereo 3D graphics with matching stereo shutter glasses. Whereas other techniques employing active shutter glasses require the careful placement of an infrared beacon to synchronize the shutter glasses with the display, DLP Link instead hides a nonvisible synchronization signal in the projected video. This approach is particularly appropriate for steerable displays because it avoids the problem of placing a synchronization beacon so that it is visible regardless of platform orientation, or the complexity of rigging multiple beacons throughout the room. With DLP Link the glasses will synchronize with the video projection if the user can see the projection.

As with other steerable display prototypes that move the projector and camera directly (e.g., [6, 8, 11]), the Beamatron obtains a wide range of pan and tilt motion at the expense of large and possibly noisy stepper motors. When hung in the ceiling near the center of the room, it can reach most surfaces of the room, but also may operate sitting on a desk or the floor. In contrast, the Everywhere Displays prototypes use a small and quiet rotating mirror in front of a stationary projector and so have a more limited range of motion (pan 230°, tilt 50°). This more limited range of motion may place restrictions on where the unit is best placed for a given application.

Calibration

As in previous steerable displays work, precise calibration of the projector, camera and moving platform is critical to precisely superimpose projected graphics onto real objects. Much of the previous work in steerable displays (e.g., Everywhere Displays) is concerned with projecting graphics on to one or more discrete locations throughout the room while the platform is stationary. In this case calibration involves establishing the 2D transformation which warps the graphics for projection onto a given surface. Usually, this transformation is calculated to ensure that a rectangular source image appears rectangular when projected on a planar surface of arbitrary orientation. For this limited case, a camera is unnecessary.

Ehnes et al. [11] calibrate their projector, platform and camera for a spherical coordinate system. This allows for rendering graphics in precise registration with visual markers (AR tags) found by image processing of the video feed.

The Beamatron goes beyond existing work in steerable displays by performing all calculations in 3D. This is enabled primarily by the use of the depth camera of the Kinect sensor. For example, the platform may be moved such that a given 3D point in the room projects to a given 2D point in the projected graphics. Thus it is possible to place projected graphics precisely on an object in the real world, and, as we will describe later, to account for the shape of the projection surface. We describe the Beamatron calibration procedure in more detail in a later section.

Integrating Depth Images

Depending on the application, it may be necessary to aggressively smooth the depth image data. Later, we present an application which runs a physics simulation benefitting from a smooth surface estimate. Averaging multiple successive frames is challenging if the head is in motion. Minimally, before averaging, the previous smoothed frame must be rotated (in 3D) to match the platform motion. Another challenge is to reuse smoothed depth data for a particular view when the unit leaves and later returns to the same view. It is desirable for the system to build a coherent, smoothed model of the room as it pans and tilts so that smoothed data may be reused over static regions. Certain applications may also make use of such a room model in planning platform motion.

The Beamatron system addresses the problems of smoothing the depth data under motion and incrementally building a model of the room by using KinectFusion [14, 20]. KinectFusion incorporates successive depth images into a voxel representation of the surfaces in the room (see Figure 2). Calculations may be run against this volume directly, or it may be processed by successive ray casting to generate a smoothed depth image which is then processed. In its original formulation, KinectFusion uses 3D image processing techniques to solve for the pose of the camera. At first it may seem that this would obviate the need to calibrate the platform geometry, but in early experiments we experienced tracking loss and drift when relying exclusively on KinectFusion's pose estimate over longer time scales. In the Beamatron, this pose information is instead drawn directly from the known pose of the platform.

The present Beamatron implementation uses Kinect Fusion as a means to obtain smoothed depth images under platform motion, but we expect future iterations to exploit its capability to build a model of the room. This could be useful in determining where to next orient the unit if the desired position is out of view. For example, an application may wish to plan a movement to display a graphic on any available flat surface in the room that is also visible to the user. In our present work, KinectFusion is configured to model a 7.5m cubic volume centered under the unit, covering much of our 6m × 10m space.

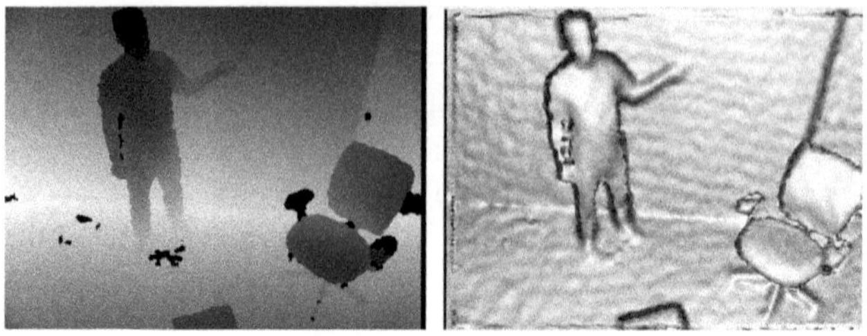

Figure 2. KinectFusion integrates multiple depth camera images (left) as the Beamatron pans and tilts to reveal different parts of the room. Kinect fusion provides stable, smoothed estimates of room geometry suitable for subsequent processing (right).

Rendering

Rendering graphics correctly onto the real world requires using a graphics projection and view matrix that incorporates the pose of the platform, and the projector focal length and principal point found in calibration. For graphics to appear correct when they are projected onto arbitrarily shaped objects, the rendering process must also take into account the shape of the projection surface [25]. Beamatron can use the depth image information to distort the projected graphics so that the projected graphics appear to be "painted" onto the real world object, but it also can correctly render 3D virtual objects for a particular viewpoint while taking into account the varied shape of the projection surface [2] (see Figure 3). This projective texturing-based technique uses multiple rendering passes: the first pass renders the real objects (the room) along with virtual objects from the point of view of the user. The second pass treats the output of the first pass as a texture map for a rendering of the real geometry.

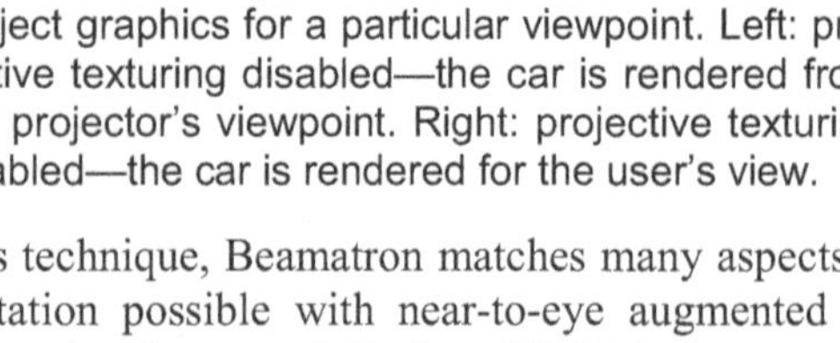

Figure 3. Beamatron rendering pipeline corrects projected graphics to account for projection surface distance and shape. This can be used to correctly project graphics for a particular viewpoint. Left: projective texturing disabled—the car is rendered from the projector's viewpoint. Right: projective texturing enabled—the car is rendered for the user's view.

By this technique, Beamatron matches many aspects of the presentation possible with near-to-eye augmented reality glasses or head mounted displays (HMDs). In some aspects the Beamtron's may be superior. Firstly, the focal distance of the projected graphics may be closer to the correct value, particularly when the virtual object is placed near a real world surface, whereas the focal distance of a rendering on glasses or an HMD is typically fixed. Secondly, graphics rendered on glasses or an HMD must account for the motion of the user's head, particularly if the graphics are meant to be stabilized against the real world. While this can be very difficult given sensor and rendering latencies, projection on the real world would be approximately correct for objects near the real world surface, for any head motion. Such a projection might not show the precisely correct side of a 3D object during motion, but it would not slide across the user's field of view as it might with glasses or an HMD, and therefore would appear more stable.

Beamatron's rendering pipeline supports 3D (stereo) rendering using DLP Link compatible stereo active shutter glasses. Stereo rendering can be used to render virtual objects that appear to have a 3D shape rising from the surface of projection, and even potentially render objects that are located in room coordinate space above any real surface. Consider, for example, a helicopter hovering in space: the projection of the left eye view may fall far from that of the right eye view, depending on the configuration of the room geometry. This can pose a challenge for platform control: instead of controlling the platform to point at the room coordinates of the helicopter, it must instead determine some view that includes the projections of both eyes as they fall on real surfaces. Our current implementation of Beamatron does not support this calculation. The effect of stereo 3D is noticeable, but weaker than that of MirageTable [2], primarily because the distance to the rendered object may be beyond the range in which binocular disparity is a powerful depth cue.

Reasoning in Room Coordinates

The computational strategies described above provide the ability to relate all sensing data to a room coordinate frame, find the real time 3D pose of the moving platform and render viewpoint-corrected 3D graphics regardless of projector pose. Together they provide a fully 3D model of sensing and display.

This model is useful for steerable displays because it allows application developers to perform reasoning in room coordinates, without regard to the pose of the steerable display, provided that any real time changes in the scene are within the field of view of the depth camera.

In fact, for many applications it may be useful to conceptually decouple the reasoning involving the room model (e.g., placing virtual objects in 3D) from the process that controls platform motion, and instead think of the Beamatron as a "camera man" that is controlled by a process that selects the most active or relevant area of the room to monitor. In the case of an augmented reality application where the user controls an object moving around the room, it may be natural to simply have the platform follow the object.

External Sensing with Sound Source Localization

One shortcoming of placing a steerable display in the center of the room is that it is difficult to use the unit's camera to monitor events outside the view of the unit's single camera. KinectFusion could be used to plan the placement of graphics onto known locations throughout the room as long as they do not move while the unit is looking away. However, in applications that would make use of person-tracking or gesture recognition, a model of the room's static surface features may not be useful. In these cases, a means of drawing the unit's attention is needed.

A number of solutions to monitor the wider area come to mind, such as mounting one or more additional Kinect cameras on the unit, using multiple cameras throughout the space, or even moving the unit's single camera to a second moving platform, decoupling the placement of display and sensing. Many of the possible solutions tend towards the more complex immersive setups (such as [34]) and therefore violate the spirit of the steerable display.

Solutions that serve a wide area, but with coarse sensing resolution, seem more appropriate. For example, a single wide angle conventional camera mounted on the unit might be used to detect the presence of the user's gesturing to gain the Beamatron's attention. The unit may then rotate to gain a more detailed view.

Rather than use more cameras and image processing, we exploit the beam-forming array microphone in the Kinect sensor to localize the user as they speak. The Kinect array microphone can be used to find the angle of the dominant sound source in the horizontal plane of the camera to an accuracy of 4° standard deviation at 4m. This is reported over a range of about 100°, approximately double that of Kinect's video camera field of view and well suited for mounting in the corner of a room. We use three Kinect sensors mounted in the corners of the room, one mounted in a vertical orientation, to solve for the 3D position of the dominant sound source. The pose of each sensor in room coordinates is determined by finding the same calibration pattern used to calibrate the Beamatron (described later). The sound source position is found by noting that the angle reported by each sensor constrains the sound to a plane orthogonal to the horizontal plane of the sensor. Thus the 3D position is calculated by computing the intersection of three planes indicated by the reported source angles (see Figure 4). This position is reported along with beam forming confidence values at 10Hz.

A Beamatron application may designate one of the cameras as an audio source for speech recognition. Speech recognition can be an easy way to gate the continuous updates of the sound source localization process: e.g., when a particular user says "Beamatron!" the unit may be commanded to orient itself to bring that user into view, much in the same way that a person reflexively turns their head to look at someone who just called their name from across the room. In the worst case, the platform must pan nearly 360° (about 4s) to put the user in view.

We have found the accuracy of the audio localization to be good enough for the two applications reported in the rest of this paper. To characterize audio localization accuracy, we compared localization results to ground truth at 13 locations throughout the room. Standing at each location, the subject uttered the word "Beamatron". 3D triangulated sound source position was recorded at the precise moment the word "Beamatron" was automatically recognized. This process was repeated four times for each location, with the subject turning to face each of the four walls of the lab. Comparing the audio localization results to ground truth, we notice that accuracy varies depending on the location in the room (RMS error = 0.84m), and that there is a bias that may be caused by imprecise calibration. Translating each sample by the average error can correct for this bias somewhat (RMS error = 0.50m).

Figure 4. Audio sound source localization combines array microphone sound source output angles from three Kinect sensors (red and blue mounted horizontally, white mounted vertically) to find the 3D position of the sound source within the room (yellow). Each array microphone provides a planar constraint on the 3D position of the sound source (illustrated here by long thin rectangles, with minimum and maximum angles indicated by short rectangles). Plan view of the room is shown (6m × 10m).

UBICOMP EXAMPLE: MASTER AND COMMANDER

Our first Beamatron example application is an homage to Bolt's Put-that-there system [5], the grandfather of all natural user interfaces. We also build on LightSpace [34], which demonstrated moving graphics from one surface to another as well as to holding a projected object directly in the hand.

With Master and Commander, the user moves projected graphics around the room with speech and gesture. They can request Beamatron's attention by calling "Beamatron", place projected objects around the room or take them and hold them in their hand. For example, while the Beamatron displays a graphic on the wall, a user in the room may say "take that". This utterance is recognized using the Kinect sensor designated for speech recognition, and the 3D position of the speech audio source is determined as described above. The Beamatron is then oriented to the 3D position of the speaker sound source. With the user now in full view of the onboard Kinect sensor, Master and Commander enables Kinect skeletal tracking (see Figure 5).

Once the user's skeleton is found, a graphical representation of the object previously projected on the wall now appears in the user's hand, thus completing the "take that" command. This projected object may be passed from one hand to the other, and to another tracked user's hand. This is accomplished simply by computing the distance of the hand currently holding the virtual object to all other available hands, and transferring the object to any sufficiently nearby hand, with some hysteresis to prevent instantly handing the object back.

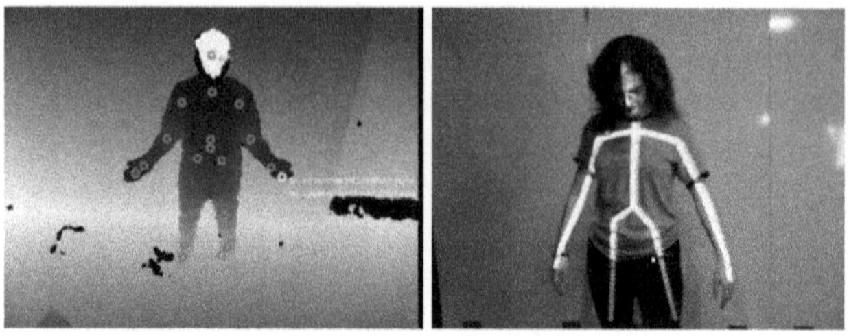

Figure 5. left: Master and Commander skeletal tracking. right: projecting skeleton onto the user.

The user may place the object in the room by pointing with their free hand to a destination position in the room while saying "put that there". Recognition of this phrase triggers the movement of the virtual object from their hand to the 3D point indicated by the ray from the user's head to the user's hand, and its first intersection with a surface in the room (see Figure 6).

Figure 6. Master and Commander allows the user to take projected graphics from the wall into their hand and then place the objects on another part of the room. Here the user is holding a graphic in their left hand while pointing at a destination. Saying "put that there" will cause Beamatron to animate the object to the wall, where it will find a surface to "hang" the graphic.

Computing this destination position can be done in multiple ways. The voxel space representation of KinectFusion holds a representation of all surfaces viewed thus far as the unit has been reoriented to view various points throughout the room. It is thus possible to use this representation to find the intersection of the user's pointing ray with the surface of the room. In the current implementation, we use an approach which does not rely on the model of the entire room. Instead, the Beamatron is continuously moved to look at points along the pointing ray, beginning with the 3D position of the hand. As the Beamatron is moved along the ray, the depth image data in the current view is tested for intersection with the ray after transformation to room coordinates. While this search along the ray is conducted, a graphical representation of the virtual object is rendered along the floor to illustrate the connection between the user's gesture and the movement of the virtual object.

Once the intersection point is found, the virtual object is "hung" on the wall or any other surface by finding the normal at the point of intersection from the depth image. We can also account for gravity by rotating the object to align with the room up vector. This is particularly useful when trying to place graphics or slides on the wall for a presentation.

In Master and Commander, gesture recognition depends on the Beamatron's ability to locate the user well enough that the Kinect skeletal tracking successfully tracks the user. Not all viewpoints work equally well. In particular, locations away from the Beamatron tend to work better, while in the area directly under the Beamatron tracking tends to fail, since the skeleton tracker was trained for frontal views.

In addition, sound source localization can provide noisy position information. When calling its attention, this can cause the Beamatron to move in the right direction, but not center on the user accurately enough to capture their entire body. We address this by randomly moving the Beamatron in a small search pattern around the sound source position until a skeleton is found. In practice, this process can take a few seconds, but due to the limitations of the skeletal tracker is not guaranteed to succeed. When the user's skeleton is found, the Beamatron orientation is trained on the hips of the recovered skeleton, and will then follow the user as they move about room.

AUGMENTED REALITY EXAMPLE: BEAMABUGGY

Our second Beamatron example application takes inspiration from Wilson's Micromotocross tabletop augmented reality depth camera demo [34].

Beamabuggy allows a player to drive a small virtual car throughout the entire room using a wireless steering wheel gaming controller and standard driving controls (see Figure 7 and Figure 1d). Calculations on the KinectFusion surface data enable the car to interact appropriately with real objects placed in the room. Driving the car over a cardboard ramp causes the car to jump appropriately, possibly flipping over. The movement of the car is determined by a gaming physics engine configured to model the dynamics of the car and perform collision detection against the ground mesh derived from the depth image. The Beamatron is programmed to keep the car in the center of the projected image.

Using a smooth surface representation rather than raw depth image data is critical for a reasonable driving experience. Consider that at the scale of a toy car, a bit of noise in the depth data may seem like a giant pothole! KinectFusion provides a smooth depth map for the current view, regardless of the Beamatron motion, as described previously. Transformed to room coordinates, this depth information is used to create the appropriate collisions with the car's wheels and chassis. We use the Newton gaming physics engine [21] for its flexible support of custom collision detection routines.

One of Beamatron's drawbacks in this application is that correct interaction with real world objects is limited to the combined view fustrums of the projector and depth camera. For example, our current prototype does not allow the player to drive under a table. In this case, the depth information at the transition from table to floor leads to a "curtain" in the collision geometry that the car cannot drive through. One approach to addressing this problem is to remove this curtain by rejecting mesh triangles that are at a very oblique angle to the camera, and by providing a dummy ground plane under the table to allow the car to drive under the table. Even with this approach, however, the player will not see the projection of the car under the table.

Beamabuggy uses the multi-pass projective texturing technique described earlier to render the car so that it appears to have the correct 3D shape given a particular user viewpoint, regardless of what surface the car is driving over. In our present implementation, the user viewpoint is deduced by the sound source localization procedure described above. When the user says "Beamatron", the 3D viewpoint is updated with the most recent 3D sound source localization values.

CALIBRATING THE BEAMATRON

To fully calibrate the Beamatron, we first find the focal length and principal point (optical center) of Kinect's infrared (depth) camera and color camera. In the case of the color camera we also find radial lens distortion parameters. These *intrinsic* parameters are computed using the technique described in [37], which uses multiple images of a known 2D printed calibration pattern (i.e., a checkerboard of known dimensions) placed at various orientations.

We must also find the intrinsic parameters of the projector. While it is useful to think of the projector as a camera, with its own focal length and principal point, projector calibration must be handled differently. First, we use the (calibrated) color camera to acquire an image of the calibration pat-

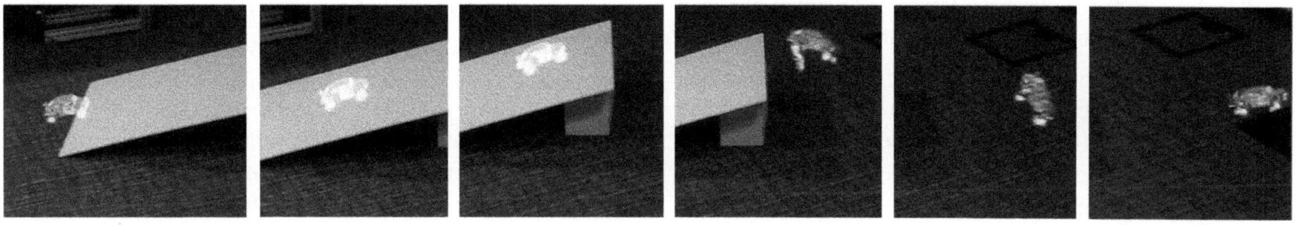

Figure 7. Beamabuggy takes a ramp. A gaming physics engine simulates vehicle dynamics and contact with room geometry modeled by KinectFusion.

tern lying on a large poster board. Because the calibration pattern is known, we can find the plane equation of the calibration pattern (and thus the poster board itself). Then, the printed pattern is taken away, and a similar calibration pattern is projected onto the poster board. This pattern is then imaged by the color camera. In this configuration, the real world dimensions of the projected pattern at the poster board are unknown (the poster board is at an unknown distance and orientation), but because the projected pattern lies in the plane of the poster board, we can compute the 3D position of all points of the calibration pattern using the plane equation. We may then use the usual calibration calculations designed for cameras (see [28] for more detail).

Once the intrinsic parameters of a camera are known, it is straightforward to recover the pose (position and orientation) of the calibration pattern. Thus it is possible to find the *extrinsic* parameters: the relative pose of the Kinect color camera and infrared camera, as well as that of the color camera and projector.

Remaining is the characterization of the moving platform geometry. This includes the conversion of DMX pan and tilt device parameters to radians, the pose of the camera relative to the platform axes of rotation and its pose relative to the room coordinate system. For these calculations we use a procedure described in [15] and [31] which again relies on several images of the same calibration pattern used above, under varying platform pan and tilt angles.

In summary, Beamatron calibration establishes the following quantities, listed here in the approximate order that they should be collected:

- focal length f, principal point (c_x, c_y) and lens distortion parameters of the Kinect color camera
- focal length and principal point of the infrared (depth) camera
- focal length and principal point of the projector
- $\mathbf{T}_{color \to infrared}$, the coordinate transform (rotation and position) relating the pose of the color and depth cameras
- $\mathbf{T}_{color \to proj}$, the coordinate transform relating the pose of the color camera and projector
- scalar values converting DMX pan and tilt commands to pan and tilt angles radians (α, β), and device feedback units (stepper motor counts) to (α, β)
- $\mathbf{T}_{base \to color}$, the coordinate transform relating the pose of the color camera with respect to the pan and tilt axes of rotation
- $\mathbf{T}_{room \to base}$, the coordinate transform placing the pan and tilt axes of rotation in room coordinates

We note that during runtime the color camera is not used, our current calibration formulation is formed around the color camera primarily because of its use in the calibration procedure.

Platform Movement

Two important tasks in working with the Beamatron are controlling its orientation to bring either a real or virtual object within view, and determining the pose of the unit as it moves to the target orientation.

For both we make use of the platform geometry calibration described above to find the pose of the color camera given pan and tilt angle values (α, β). A point in the room coordinate frame can be brought into the coordinate frame of the projector by

$$\mathbf{x}_{proj} = \mathbf{T}_{color \to proj} \mathbf{T}_{base \to color} \mathbf{R}(\alpha, \beta) \mathbf{T}_{room \to base} \mathbf{x}_{room}$$

where $\mathbf{R}(\alpha, \beta)$ is the matrix which rotates about the two axes of the platform. A similar formula may be used to convert a depth camera coordinate point to room coordinates.

To determine the real-time pose of the unit, the encoder feedback values are converted from device units to radians, and the formula for the pose of the color camera is used. The pose of the unit can be used to transform a point in the depth camera to a 3D room coordinate point. In this case it is important to note that if the head is in motion, the latency of the camera will cause the transformed point to be incorrect because the unit will have moved since the image data was acquired. This discrepancy can be eliminated by buffering the encoder feedback values, and selecting older values when dealing with camera-derived information. Our current implementation was manually tuned for a delay of eight encoder frames, which at the 100Hz reporting rate of encoder frames is about 80ms, which corresponds well with the latency of the Kinect depth image. This approach is suggested in [11].

Determining the pan and tilt values to bring an object into view is basic to a steerable display. Given a 3D point in the room, we calculate the pan and tilt angles such that the point projects to a given 2D point in the projected graphics (this 2D point is often chosen to be the center of the projected image). A 3D point in a camera or projector's coordinate is projected to image coordinates by the following standard camera model (neglecting lens distortion):

$$P(\mathbf{x}) = s \begin{bmatrix} u \\ v \\ 1 \end{bmatrix} = \begin{bmatrix} f & 0 & c_x \\ 0 & f & c_y \\ 0 & 0 & 1 \end{bmatrix} \mathbf{x}$$

The relationship between pan and tilt angles and the unit pose is nonlinear due to the rotations involved. Thus it is appropriate to use a nonlinear optimization technique. We minimize an objective function that calculates the distance between the desired projector image position (u, v) and current guess for (α, β):

$$f(\alpha, \beta) = \left\| (u, v) - P_{proj}(\mathbf{x}_{proj}(\alpha, \beta)) \right\|^2$$

The choice of optimization technique is complicated by the fact that for every pan and tilt solution there is a dual solution that pans 180°, and tilts to reflect about the vertical axis. Without constraining the optimization, the platform control algorithm runs the risk of making a drastic and disruptive motion to this second solution, perhaps only to return to the other side in the next moment. Accordingly, we use the Luus-Jaakola nonlinear optimization technique

[17], which is easy to implement to include the constraint that solutions must have a tilt value greater than 0°.

FURTHER WORK

The two very different example applications suggest the broad range of applications enabled by the Beamatron system. The many capabilities of the system, such as the ability to stabilize graphics while the platform is in motion, follow a given point in 3D, render 3D graphics for a given viewpoint and interpret the user's speech and gesture, invite a variety of further investigations into new interactions and applications enabled by the Beamatron. As one example, it is straightforward to contemplate rendering of a 3D object in the user's hand corrected for viewpoint and surface shape as the user wanders about the room, and furthermore use stereo rendering to make the graphic appear to rise off the user's hand.

Here we consider a few areas of further work directed at improving the basic capability of the device.

Automated Calibration

Our current method for calibrating the Beamatron involves several steps and is still very manual in nature. It may be possible to automate much of the calibration procedure. Ultimately, we care most to precisely project graphics on features in the depth image, yet our current calibration procedures are ill-suited to directly minimize any discrepancy between the projected graphics and the target feature in the depth image. Rather, this alignment comes about from multiple independent calibrations, which when composed can accrue noticeable alignment errors. We note that due to the movement of the platform and the need to accurately calibrate its internal geometry, the calibration of the Beamatron is more difficult than the calibration of a static projector and camera pair.

Deeper Integration with KinectFusion

Our present implementation uses KinectFusion primarily as a means to obtain smooth surfaces from noisy depth images even while the platform is moving. There are a number of other ways we could exploit KinectFusion, however.

The original development of KinectFusion includes calculating camera pose by matching features of the image. This pose information is used to correctly integrate new depth image data, and is a potentially useful by-product. Beamatron overrides this pose information with the pose calculated more directly by the known pan and tilt configuration of the platform and the calibration of its internal geometry. Whereas Beamatron's pose estimate will never drift or fail due to tracking failure, it may possess systematic errors due to inaccurate calibration. The complementary nature of these two sources of platform pose suggests that the two could be fused to adjust the calibration of the platform while the unit is used initially, for example.

Additionally, many Beamatron applications could make use of the voxel space model of the room that KinectFusion constructs as the camera is reoriented to view the entire room. This whole-room model could be useful in planning the Beamatron's next movement, such as where best to display a graphic. This model may also be used to integrate data from another camera, possibly a handheld unit or a second Beamatron in the same room. A handheld Kinect sensor, for example, could be used to obtain close-in, high resolution scans of parts of the room, and also complete geometry that is not visible to the camera on the platform, such as under furniture or just around corners. This more complete model could be useful in some applications; e.g., driving the car under the table.

Alternate Hardware Configurations

The Beamatron prototype is large in part because of the use of a regular DLP video projector. The device could be made much smaller with an LED or laser projector. While LED and laser projectors are not nearly as bright as a full size projector, this could be mitigated by the use of longer projection lenses. The smaller projection area of a longer lens is a reasonable tradeoff for a steerable display.

Automated control of focus and zoom might be useful for some applications. In our experience the depth of field of the projector is not a great problem, but it could be for close-in work. Of course, a laser projector requires no focus adjustment.

While the limited viewing and display areas are characteristic of steerable displays, it is tempting to consider more elaborate hardware designs that effectively enlarge the viewing and display areas without resorting to many cameras and many projectors. For example, multiple Beamatron units could be used to cover a large area at relatively little expense. Multiple units could be coordinated in useful ways, such as performing a handoff of projected graphics around a user as they move from one unit's service area to another (see Figure 8).

As suggested earlier, the use of multiple units could address the problem of split attention between the user and some distant focal point of the presentation. In such cases it may be desirable to task a unit with monitoring a user and another unit with monitoring or displaying on another part of the room, and in some cases it may suffice to include units that have only a camera and others that have only a projector.

Figure 8. An arrow directs a man through an airport in Microsoft Office Labs' Productivity Future Vision video [18]. This could be realized by multiple coordinated steerable displays.

CONCLUSION

The Beamatron advances steerable displays by drawing on recent progress in depth camera-based interactions. Through its calibration, control and rendering algorithms, the Beamatron allows applications to reason in the 3D coordinate system of the room, enabling a wide range of augmented reality and ubiquitous computing scenarios with a minimal amount of hardware and computation.

ACKNOWLEDGMENTS

We thank Bruce Cleary for help building the Beamatron hardware prototype.

REFERENCES

1. Benko, H., and Wilson, A.D. Multi-point interactions with immersive omnidirectional visualizations in a dome. In *Proc. of Interactive Tabletops and Surfaces (ITS),* 2010, 19-28.
2. Benko, H., Jota, R., and Wilson, A.D. MirageTable: freehand interaction on a projected augmented reality desktop. In *Proc. of ACM SIGCHI,* 2012, 199-208.
3. Billinghurst, M., Weghorst, S., and Furness, T. Shared space: An augmented reality approach for computer supported collaborative work. *Virtual Reality,* 3(1), 1998. 25-36.
4. Bimber, O., and Raskar, R. Spatial Augmented Reality: Merging Real and Virtual Worlds. A.K. Peters, 2005.
5. Bolt, R.A. "Put-that-there": voice and gesture at the graphics interface. In *ACM Siggraph Computer Graphics.* 14, 3. 1980. 262-270.
6. Borkowski, S., Letessier, J., and Crowley, J.L. Spatial control of interactive surfaces in an augmented environment. In *Lecture Notes in Computer Science*. 2004. 228-244.
7. Butz, A., Schneider, M., and Spassova, M. SearchLight – a lightweight search function for pervasive environments. In *Proc. of Pervasive Computing*, 2004. 351-356.
8. Butz, A., and Kruger, A. Applying the peephole metaphor in a mixed-reality room. In *IEEE Computer Graphics and Applications* 26, 1 (2006). 56-63.
9. Cauchard,, J.R., Fraser, M., Han, T., and Subramanian, S. Steerable projection: exploring alignment in interactive mobile displays. In *Personal Ubiquitous Computing*. 2012. 27-37.
10. City Theatrical, Autoyoke: The First Automated Lighting Solution Designed for Theatrical Use. http://citytheatrical.com/rcyoke.htm, 2012.
11. Ehnes, J., Hirota, K., and Hirose, M. Projected augmentation – augmented reality using rotatable video projectors. In *Proc. of ISMAR*. 2004. 26-35.
12. Kjeldsen, R., Pinhanez, C., Pingali, G., Hartman, J., Levas, T., Podlaseck, M. Interacting with steerable projected displays. In *Proc. 5th Int. Conf. on Automatic Face and Gesture Recognition*. 2002.
13. Harrison, C., Benko, H., Wilson, A.D., OmniTouch: wearable multitouch interaction everywhere. In *Proc. of ACM UIST.* 2011. 441-450.
14. Izadi, S., Kim, D., Hilliges, O., Molyneaux, D., Newcombe, R., Kohli, P., Shotton, J., Hodges, S., Freeman, D., Davison, A., Fitzgibbon, A. KinectFusion: real-time 3d reconstruction and interaction using a moving depth camera, In *Proc. of ACM UIST.* 2011. 559-568.
15. Ngan, P.M., and Valkenburg, R.J. Calibrating a pan-tilt camera head. In *Image and Vision Computing Workshop*. 1995.
16. Levy, S. Google gets transparent with Glass, its augmented reality project, http://wired.com/epicenter/2012/04/epicenter-google-glass-ar/. 2012.
17. Luus, R, and Jaakola, T.H.I. Optimization by direct search and systematic reduction of the size of search region. In *American Institute of Chemical Eng. Journal,* 19(4), 1973. 760-766.
18. Microsoft Office Labs. Productivity Future Vision Video. http://www.microsoft.com/office/labs/index.html, 2009.
19. Molyneaux, D., Gellersen, H., Kortueum, G., and Schiele, B. Cooperative augmentation of smart objects with projector-camera systems. In *Proc. of Ubicomp*. 2007. 501-518.
20. Molyneaux, D., Izadi, S., Kim, D., Hilliges, O., Hodges, S., Cao, X., Butler, A., Gellersen, H. Interactive environment-aware handheld projectors for pervasive computing spaces, In *Proc. of Pervasive Computing*. 2012.
21. Newton Game Dynamics. http://newtondynamics.com.
22. Pinhanez, C. The Everywhere Displays Projector: a device to create ubiquitous graphical interfaces. In *Proc. of Ubiquitous Computing*. 2001. 315-331.
23. Raskar, R., Welch, G., Cutts, M., Lake, A., Stesin, L. and Fuchs, H. The office of the future: a unified approach to image-based modeling and spatially immersive displays. In *Proc. of ACM SIGGRAPH*. 1998. 179-188.
24. Raskar, R., Brown, M.S., Yang, R. Chen, W.-C., Welch, G., Towles, H., Seales, B., and Fuchs. H. 1999. Multi-projector displays using camera-based registration. In *Proc. of Visualization*. 1999. 161-168.
25. Raskar, R., Welch, G., Low, K.-L., and Bandyopadhyay, D. Shader Lamps: Animating Real Objects With Image-Based Illumination. In *Proc. of Eurographics Workshop on Rendering Techniques*. 2001. 89-102.
26. Raskar, R., van Baar, J., Beardsley, P., Willwacher, T., Rao, S., Forlines, C. iLamps: geometrically aware and self-configuring projectors. In *ACM Trans. Graph., 22, 3*. 2003. 809-818.
27. Rekimoto, J. and Saitoh, M. Augmented Surfaces: A Spatially Continuous Work Space for Hybrid Computing Environments. In *Proc. of ACM SIGCHI*. 1999. 378–385.
28. Sodhi, R., and Jones, B. Kinect-Projector Calibration, http://augmentedengineering.com/ProCamCalibration/brjones2rsodhi2Final.pdf. 2010.
29. Sodhi, R., Benko, H., and Wilson, A.D. LightGuide: projected visualizations for hand movement guidance. In *Proc. of ACM SIGCHI.* 2012. 179-188.
30. Sony Entertainment Network. Great films fill rooms, http://greatfilmsfillrooms.com. 2011.
31. Tsai, R.Y, and Lenz, R.K. A new technique for fully autonomous and efficient hand/eye calibration. In *IEEE Trans. on Pattern Analysis and Machine Intelligence,* 5(3), 1989. 345-358.
32. Underkoffler, J., Ullmer, B., and Ishii, H. Emancipated pixels: Real-world graphics in the luminous room. In *Proc. of ACM SIGGRAPH*. 1999. 385–392.
33. Willis, K., Poupyrev, I., Hudson, S.E., Mahler, M. SideBySide: ad-hoc multi-user interaction with handheld projectors. In *Proc. of ACM UIST.* 2011. 431-440.
34. Wilson, A. Depth sensing video cameras for 3D tangible tabletop interaction. In *Proc. of IEEE Tabletop*. 2007. 201-204.
35. Wilson, A., and Benko, H. Combining multiple depth cameras and projectors for interactions on, above and between surfaces. In *Proc. of ACM UIST*. 2010. 273-282.
36. Xiang, C., Forlines, C., and Balakrishnan, R. Multi-user interaction using handheld projectors. In *Proc. of ACM UIST.* 2007. 43-52.
37. Zhang, Z. A flexible new technique for camera calibration. *IEEE Trans. on Pattern Analysis and Machine Intelligence*, 22(11), 2000. 1330-1334.

3D Puppetry: A Kinect-based Interface for 3D Animation

Robert T. Held*, **Ankit Gupta**†, **Brian Curless**†, **and Maneesh Agrawala***
*University of California, Berkeley †University of Washington
{rheld,maneesh}@cs.berkeley.edu {ankit,curless}@cs.washington.edu

ABSTRACT
We present a system for producing 3D animations using physical objects (i.e., puppets) as input. Puppeteers can load 3D models of familiar rigid objects, including toys, into our system and use them as puppets for an animation. During a performance, the puppeteer physically manipulates these puppets in front of a Kinect depth sensor. Our system uses a combination of image-feature matching and 3D shape matching to identify and track the physical puppets. It then renders the corresponding 3D models into a virtual set. Our system operates in real time so that the puppeteer can immediately see the resulting animation and make adjustments on the fly. It also provides 6D virtual camera and lighting controls, which the puppeteer can adjust before, during, or after a performance. Finally our system supports layered animations to help puppeteers produce animations in which several characters move at the same time. We demonstrate the accessibility of our system with a variety of animations created by puppeteers with no prior animation experience.

Author Keywords
Tangible user interface, animation, object tracking

ACM Classification Keywords
I.3.6 [Computer Graphics]: Methodology and Techniques - Interaction Techniques; I.3.7 [Computer Graphics]: Three-dimensional Graphics and Realism - Animation.

INTRODUCTION
Today, the most common way to create 3D animated stories is to use high-end, key-frame-based animation software such as Maya [3], 3ds Max [2] or Blender [7]. While these systems provide fine control over the motion, position, and timing of each element in the scene, users must learn a complex suite of tools and commands to operate their high-threshold, high-ceiling interfaces. Building the expertise to use these tools effectively requires time and patience.

A simpler alternative is to film a performer moving physical puppets with their hands. Real-time, kinesthetic feedback from the puppets allows the puppeteer to concentrate on the performance, rather than how it is being captured. Such direct manipulation significantly reduces the learning curve required to create 3D stories, and even children can readily participate. However, the resulting video usually reveals the puppeteers and their controls. Moreover, video is difficult to modify once it is captured, and the physical nature of a video-recorded puppet show places practical limits on lighting, background complexity, and camera motions.

UIST'12, October 7–10, 2012, Cambridge, Massachusetts, USA.

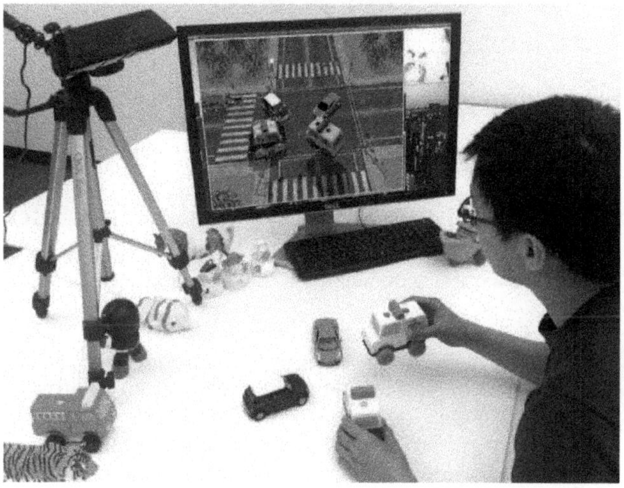

Figure 1. Our system allows puppeteers to use toys and other physical props to directly perform 3D animations.

Motion capture offers another alternative for creating 3D animation that retains the real-time physical performance benefits of video recording a puppet show, but removes the constraints on lighting, background complexity, camera motions and puppeteer visibility. Such systems track the motions of physical props or puppets and map the motions onto virtual objects or characters rendered into virtual sets. However, current motion-capture implementations require complex and often expensive hardware setups (e.g. multiple high-frame-rate cameras, physical markers on the objects, specialized gloves on the hands, etc.) making them inaccessible to casual users [29, 31].

We introduce a 3D puppetry system that allows users to quickly create 3D animations by performing the motions with their own familiar, rigid toys, props, and puppets. As shown in Figure 1, the puppeteer directly manipulates these objects in front of an inexpensive Kinect depth camera [10]. We use the Kinect along with the ReconstructMe 3D scanning software [13] to build virtual 3D models of each puppet as a pre-process. Then, as the puppeteer performs the story,

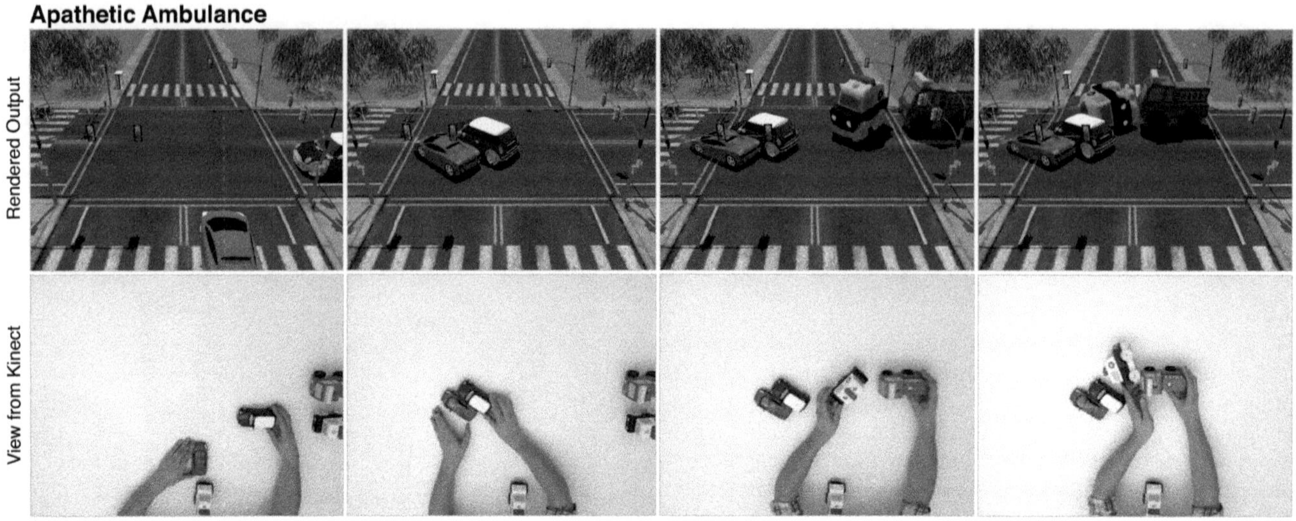

Figure 2. Example frames of our system in action. The bottom row shows the puppeteer manipulating physical puppets. The top row shows the result of our system tracking the puppets in real time and rendering them in a virtual set.

our system captures the motions of the physical puppets and renders the corresponding 3D models into a virtual set (Figure 2). Our system operates in real-time so that the puppeteer can immediately see the resulting animation and make adjustments to the motions on the fly.

We use inexpensive capture hardware and a relatively simple setup to make our system accessible to many users. Our system does not require any markers or specialized gloves for tracking. The performative mode of interaction, which closely resembles a physical puppet show, makes it familiar and approachable to novices. Kinesthetic and proprioceptive feedback gives the puppeteer constant and direct knowledge of the pose of each puppet as it is handled. For instance, the puppeteer can determine a puppet's pose simply by feeling its shape and knowing the spatial positions of her hands relative to the performance space. Moreover, with tangible 3D puppets, the physics of the real world can help to produce natural-looking motions. To animate a car crash, for example, a puppeteer can either manually move two toy cars simultaneously, or more easily, just send one car rolling into the other and rely on momentum to complete the performance.

Our puppet-tracking algorithm does impose a few restrictions on puppeteers. It assumes that puppets are rigid objects—it cannot track articulated joints or easily deformable materials such as cloth. In addition, if puppeteers move the puppets very quickly over long distances our system can lose track of them. However, in practice we have found that a wide variety of toys and props are made of suitably rigid materials and that puppeteers quickly learn the limitations on movement speed.

In addition to its basic tracking functionality, our system includes controls and effects to help users create animated stories. Because our system generates a 3D animated scene, users can adjust the camera, lighting, and background sets of the rendered animation at any time, before, during, or after the performance. In practice we have found that puppeteers sometimes move puppets outside of the tracking volume accidentally, at which point they no longer appear in the virtual set. To warn puppeteers before this happens, we reduce the opacity of the rendered puppets as they approach the edge of the tracking space. Finally, some stories may require a puppeteer to perform with more than two puppets at a time. We provide an interface for creating layered animations to facilitate such multi-puppet animations. Puppeteers can separately capture performances with different puppets, and then combine them into one animation.

We demonstrate the flexibility and accessibility of our approach with a set of animated stories created by first-time puppeteers with no prior animation experience. Our puppeteers combined several features of our system, including 6D camera and lighting controls, physical interactions between puppets, faded entrances and exits, and layered animations to tell engaging short stories. Our results indicate that novice users can quickly generate entertaining 3D animations with our system.

RELATED WORK

Our 3D puppetry system builds on several areas of related work.

Tangible Interfaces With tangible interfaces [16], the user handles physical objects to interact with a computer. These systems use a variety of methods to track objects, including computer vision, electronic tags, and bar codes [21]. For instance, one could use a small paddle to rearrange furniture in a miniaturized virtual room [20], or move two tracked cards together to make virtual characters interact [22].

Our system bears the most resemblance to interfaces that use the identity of everyday objects to guide interactions. Avrahami et al. [4], use a touch-sensitive tablet and stereo cameras to track physical props. Users can roll plastic soccer balls at the tablet to play a sports game, or directly place game tokens on the screen to play tic-tac-toe. Lego OASIS [34] identifies Lego figures using a depth sensor and then projects relevant animations into the physical space. For instance, they can detect a Lego dragon figure and project flames onto it. Finally, Johnson, et al.'s [18] sympathetic interface uses a plush toy with embedded sensors as input. The puppeteer manipulates the limbs of the puppet to control its virtual representation, which can interact with other virtual characters. These systems all use physical input to trigger preset events and interactions, whereas we design our interface to permit free-form creation of new animations.

Kinect-based Interfaces. Researchers have used the Kinect to produce new, low-cost, physical interfaces. The interfaces can track the human body [28] or hands [15] to provide interaction with virtual objects, including medical-imaging data [11]. Though our system also uses the Kinect, we track physical objects, rather than the puppeteer's body. The KinectFusion project [17] allows one to quickly scan a physical environment. We use a similar system, ReconstructMe [13], to convert physical puppets into 3D models. However, the rest of our interface bears less resemblance to these systems, as we focus on object tracking rather than scanning.

Object-based Motion Capture. Motion-capture generally refers to systems that record the movements of physical objects and converts them into animations. Our system most closely parallels object-based motion-capture systems, which track small physical objects and apply their movements to virtual characters [9, 25, 24]. While the prior systems focus on the detailed articulation of one character at a time, we provide a quick way for puppeteers to tell stories by performing with multiple rigid puppets at the same time. The other systems also require multiple cameras [9] or specialized sensing hardware [25, 24], while our system requires only a single Kinect and a tabletop.

Video Puppetry. The 2D video-puppetry system developed by Barnes, et al. [5] lets puppeteers perform animations with paper cut-out characters. It identifies, tracks, and re-renders the characters with the puppeteer removed in real time. Puppeteers operate our system in a similar way, but our use of 3D puppets enables more types of animations. For instance, 3D puppets can be rotated in three dimensions, whereas 2D cutouts are restricted to one axis of rotation and cannot rotate out of the plane. We also allow 6D control of the camera (3D translation and 3D rotation) during performance and playback, while camera changes in the video-puppetry system are limited to translations and zooms. Finally, the mass and shape of 3D objects let the user rely more on physics to tell a story. For instance, one could set a toy car rolling across a scene, which would not be possible with a piece of paper.

SYSTEM OVERVIEW

Our system consists of three main modules: Setup, Capture, and Render. During Setup, puppeteers scan physical puppets into our Puppet Database and build color models of their own skin. The Capture module consists of three components: a Puppet Identifier, a Point-cloud Segmenter, and a Pose Tracker (Figure 3). The Puppet Identifier uses 2D image features to detect the presence of each physical puppet and initialize the Pose Tracker. The Point-cloud Segmenter takes in a colored 3D point cloud from the Kinect and outputs individual point clouds corresponding to each physical puppet. The Pose Tracker then aligns each physical puppet's segmented point cloud with its stored 3D model to determine its pose. In the Render module, our system uses the captured poses to render the corresponding 3D model for each physical puppet in the virtual set. This module provides camera and lighting controls, and the option to swap 3D backgrounds.

SETUP

For tracking and rendering purposes, our system maintains a Puppet Database of defining characteristics for each trackable puppet. The database entry for each puppet consists of a 3D model and several sets of color images and depth maps associated with different example poses. If a puppeteer wishes to use a new puppet with our system, this information must be scanned in and stored in the database once as a pre-processing step. Finally, prior to running our system for the first time, each puppeteer must build a color model of their skin. This model is used by the Point-cloud Segmenter to isolate points that belong to puppets, and not the puppeteer's hands, and is necessary for accurate tracking.

Building the Puppet Database

The Puppet Database includes a 3D model of each physical puppet. To create a 3D model, the puppeteer first uses ReconstructMe [13] to scan the physical puppet with the Kinect sensor. As the puppeteer moves the Kinect around the puppet, casually capturing it from all sides, ReconstructMe converts the stream of incoming Kinect point clouds into an untextured 3D mesh of the puppet in real-time. The raw mesh also includes parts of the environment around the puppet, so we crop out non-puppet points and fill any remaining holes using the MeshMixer modeling software [27].

To add color to the model, the puppeteer loads the untextured mesh into our puppet-tracking system in *Painting mode* and places the physical puppet in front of the Kinect. Painting mode tracks only one puppet at a time, and uses a stripped-down version of the Capture module. It aligns the puppet's 3D model with the incoming Kinect point cloud, and then transfers the colors from the point cloud to the vertices of the 3D model. Figure 4 shows the result of scanning a toy using ReconstructMe and colorizing the model using our approach. Our Painting mode could also be used to colorize models obtained from other sources (e.g., laser scanners). The complete algorithmic details of our tracking approach are given in the Capture Section.

For accurate tracking it is essential that the 3D model match the shape of the physical puppet as closely as possible. However, our system does not require that puppeteers use ReconstructMe, and we also use models from other sources including Google's 3D Warehouse [12] and Autodesk's 123D Catch [1], which uses a multi-view stereo algorithm to produce 3D models from sets of digital photographs. In practice, we found the ReconstructMe pipeline to provide the simplest method for quickly generating suitably accurate 3D models of common objects such as toys, props and puppets.

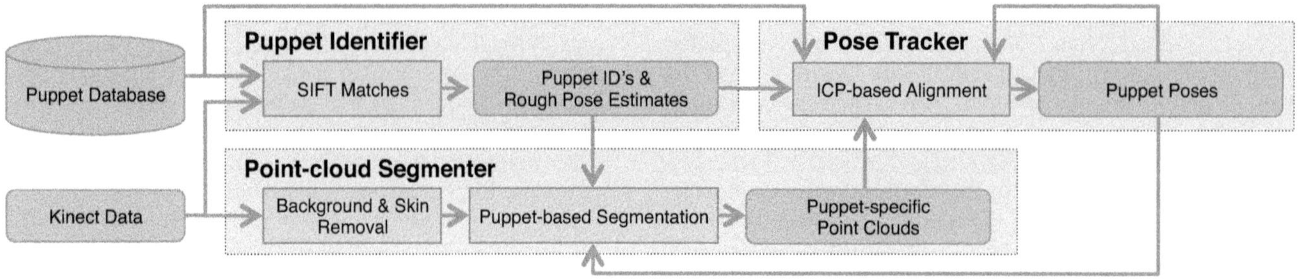

Figure 3. Overview of our system's Capture module. With each frame, the Kinect provides an RGB image and depth map. The puppet identifier compares SIFT features in those data to the features found in a database of image templates to identify puppets and roughly estimate their poses. The RGB and depth information are also combined into point clouds, which are processed to remove the background and the puppeteer's hands, and then matched to stored 3D models using ICP to estimate the puppets' 6D poses.

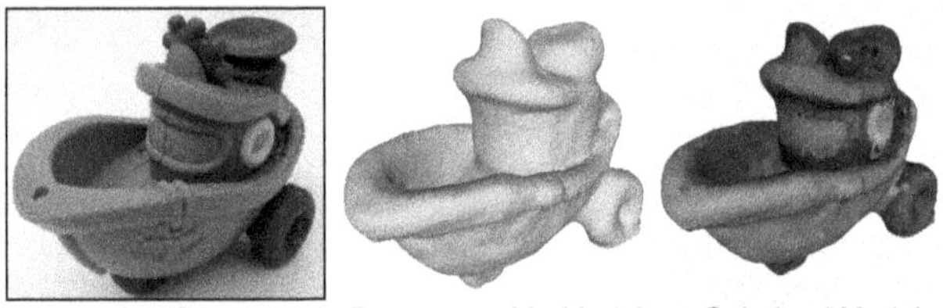

Figure 4. Overview of model-loading using ReconstructMe. Left: A photograph of the toy to be scanned. Middle: An untextured 3D model of the toy produced by ReconstructMe. Right: The same model, with vertex colors assigned using our system.

In addition to the 3D model, our Puppet Database includes roughly 30 color and depth template images for each puppet, along with the pose of the puppet in each image. Our system relies on these templates to detect physical puppets in the Kinect's field of view. Thus, they must sample the range of possible orientations and positions of the puppet throughout the Kinect's field of view. We capture these images with our Capture module in *Template-capture mode*. As with Painting mode, Template-capture mode only tracks one puppet. The puppeteer places the puppet in the Kinect's field of view and the system detects its pose. The puppeteer then presses a key to save the current image, depth map, and puppet pose and repeats this process for several unique poses throughout the Kinect's field of view. We have found that roughly 30 template images spaced in a 2x3 grid with 4-5 orientations in each position is sufficient for accurate puppet tracking. Cropped versions of example image templates can be seen in the bottom two rows of Fig. 5.

Skin Model

Our system uses the 3D point cloud from the Kinect to recover each puppet's 6D pose. However, to ensure accuracy, it needs point clouds that only contain points belonging to the puppets. Therefore, the Capture module must filter out any points that belong to the puppeteer's hands. It uses a histogram-based color model of the puppeteer's skin to perform this filtering. Our system creates this skin model once for each puppeteer as part of Setup.

The color model divides a 3D RGB color space into 96x96x96 bins. The puppeteer uses the Kinect to capture color images of his/her hands, and the system places the skin pixels into the color bins. If the number of pixels assigned to a bin exceeds a preset threshold, the system labels the color range associated with that bin as skin. The result is a tight volume of colors that belong to the puppeteer's skin. This choice of color model is powerful because it can handle arbitrary, non-linear boundaries. However, like any other color-based model, it prevents the use of puppets with colors that are very similar to the puppeteer's skin color.

CAPTURE

Figure 3 gives an overview of the Capture module, which we split into three components: a Puppet Identifier, a Point-cloud Segmenter, and a Pose Tracker. The inputs to the Capture module are the Puppet Database and Kinect data. The Kinect provides color images and depth maps, which are converted to 3D point clouds at 30 frames per second. For a given frame, the Puppet Identifier and Point-cloud Segmenter run first, and then send their data to the Pose Tracker, which determines the pose of each puppet.

Puppet Identifier

The Puppet Identifier serves two main functions: (1) it identifies puppets within the Kinect's field of view, and (2) it roughly estimates their poses as an initialization for the Pose Tracker. The Puppet Identifier runs continuously, but its output is only used in two situations: when a physical puppet first enters the field of view or when the accuracy of the system's pose estimate for that puppet falls below a threshold and tracking must be restarted. See the Pose Tracker module for more details.

Matching Image Features. To identify puppets within the Kinect's field of view, we first find scale-invariant feature transform (SIFT) [23] features within the template images in the Puppet Database. We use SIFT features because they reveal distinctive 2D image elements that are invariant to translation, rotation, and scale. Our implementation uses Sift-GPU [33] to achieve high-performance. We compute the SIFT features for the templates once as a pre-process when we first capture the template images in the Setup module.

During a performance, we compute SIFT features for each color image from the Kinect (or "RGB frame") and compare them to the pre-computed features of each template image. Given the set of feature matches for each template im-

Figure 5. SIFT-based puppet identification. The RGB frame contains two physical puppets that our system has matched to the template images below it. We use color-coded dots to indicate the coordinates of the matched SIFT features. For each puppet, the best-matched template contains the most SIFT matches to the frame.

age, we use Lowe's [23] Hough-transform-based approach to find the subset of that are consistent with a single rigid transformation to the RGB frame. This procedure removes unreliable matches between the RGB frame and each template. Then, for each puppet in the database, we determine the best-matching template image based on the remaining feature matches. We eliminate templates with fewer than 20 feature matches and this usually leaves us with one template match (from the entire database) for each physical puppet in the Kinect's field of view (Figure 5). In some cases this procedure finds more than one best-matching template, each corresponding to a different puppet in the database, for a single physical puppet. In these instances we select the template with the highest ratio of matched features to total features in the template.

Rough Pose Estimation. We compute a rough pose estimate for each physical puppet that we match in the database. Both the template image and RGB frame have corresponding depth maps, which we use to recover the 3D coordinates of each pair of matched features. We then compute the optimal translation between the two sets of matching coordinates. We found that computing the full 6D rigid transform between the points using Horn's method [14] gave unreliable estimates of the rotation component. Instead, we compute just the 3D translation between the points and concatenate this with the transformation stored with the template to give a rough estimate of the physical puppet's pose. When needed, we use this estimate to label points in the Point-cloud Segmenter and to initialize the pose refinement in the Pose Tracker.

Point-cloud Segmenter

The Kinect 3D point cloud generated for each frame is undifferentiated and includes points that belong to each physical puppet as well as the background of the performance space and the puppeteer's hands. The Point-cloud Segmenter first removes the background points and the hands from the cloud and then splits the remaining points into separate clouds for each physical puppet (Figure 6).

Removing Background and Hands. To remove the background points our system captures a *background depth map* of the empty performance space each time the puppeteer first runs our system. Then, during the performance, if the depth of any point in the incoming Kinect point cloud is within 2% of the background, the Segmenter removes it from the point cloud. To eliminate points that belong to the puppeteer's hands, the Segmenter compares the color of each incoming point to the skin color model; if the color of the point matches any bin labeled as skin, the point is removed. Almost all remaining points in the cloud belong to physical puppets.

Segmenting by Physical Puppet. To further segment the point cloud, the Segmenter requires pose information for each physical puppet in the Kinect's field of view. In most cases the Segmenter uses the last known pose from the Pose Tracker. However, whenever a physical puppet is first introduced into the performance space the Pose Tracker cannot provide this pose information. In these cases we use the rough pose estimate produced by the Puppet Identifier. The Segmenter then iterates over each incoming point, computes its distance to the closest point on each visible puppet model, and assigns the point to the closest puppet. To reduce erroneous matches when two physical puppets are close to one another, if the ratio of distances between a point and two puppets is less than 1.2 (i.e., the point is about equally close to both puppets and could belong to either one) we do not assign it to any puppet.

Pose Tracker

The Pose Tracker is responsible for accurately estimating the pose of each puppet in the Kinect's field of view. It computes this estimate by aligning the segmented point cloud for a physical puppet with the corresponding 3D model in the database. The Pose Tracker refines the pose estimate for each puppet by aligning its 3D model from the database to the corresponding cloud produced by the Point-cloud Segmenter. We use the iterative closest point (ICP) algorithm [6] to compute the alignment.

The ICP algorithm aligns two sets of 3D points by 1) determining point-to-point correspondences between the sets, 2) calculating the least-squares optimal rigid transformation between the corresponding points [14], 3) transforming one of the sets to better align the points, and 4) iterating until the fractional reduction in error between iterations drops below a threshold. In our ICP implementation, one set of points is the segmented point cloud for a puppet and the other set is comprised of the vertices of its 3D model (Figure 7). Because

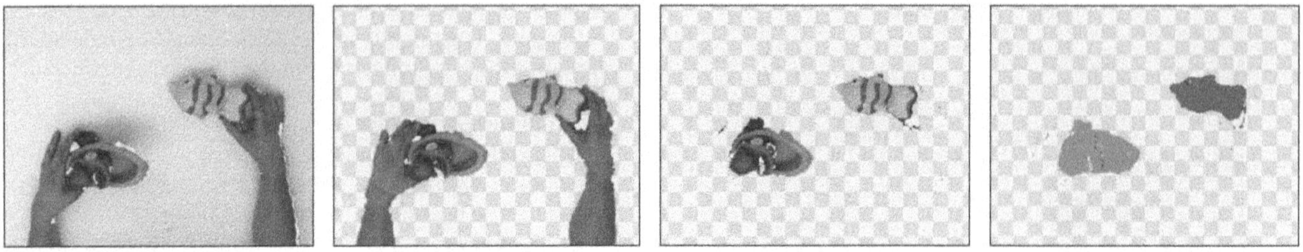

Figure 6. Steps of point-cloud segmentation. Beginning with the raw point cloud from the Kinect, our segmenter removes the background and the puppeteer's skin, and finally produces separate point clouds associated with each puppet.

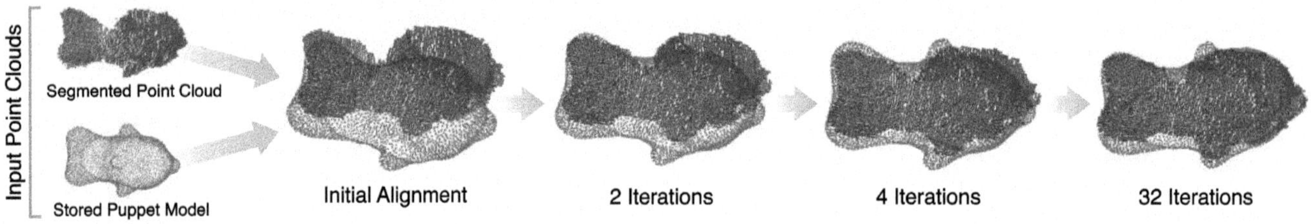

Figure 7. Progression of ICP alignment between a segmented point cloud and a Puppet Database model. Our ICP algorithm begins by transforming the puppet model using its last known pose (if available; otherwise it uses the rough pose estimate from the Puppet Identifier). Then each ICP iteration brings the clouds into closer alignment until the root mean square distance between their points meet an error threshold.

ICP is a greedy, local optimization algorithm, good pose initialization is critical both for finding the global optimum and for fast convergence. To initialize ICP in a given frame, we transform each puppet's 3D model using its pose from the last frame, if it exists. Otherwise we use the rough, SIFT-based pose estimate produced by the Puppet Identifier. Joung et al. [19] use a similar SIFT-based initialization for ICP in the context of 3D environment reconstruction.

Detecting Bad Poses After ICP finishes, we count the number of points in the segmented point cloud that do not have corresponding points in the puppet model. If this number accounts for more than 33% of the points in the segmented point cloud, we assume that we have an incorrect pose estimate. If a puppet fails this test for 20 frames in a row, then we consider the puppet "lost" and wait for a new rough pose estimate from the Puppet Identifier to restart tracking.

Real-time Performance. The point-to-point correspondence search is the main bottleneck of the ICP algorithm. Our implementation uses a kd-tree to accelerate this step of the algorithm. To ensure real-time performance, we also downsample the segmented point cloud as well as the 3D model points. For the segmented point clouds, we keep every n^{th} point, where n is the downsampling rate. For the 3D models, we use Poisson disk-sampling as implemented by Cline, et al. [8] to evenly reduce the number of points. We have empirically found that downsampling to roughly 1000 points for each segmented cloud and 5000 points for the 3D models achieves real-time tracking with minimal loss in accuracy.

Filtering. Sensor noise and imprecise database models can produce noticeable wobble in the tracked poses. To reduce the amount of wobble, we apply separate bilateral filters to the translation and rotation components of the puppet poses. The bilateral filter is an edge-preserving, smoothing filter that is commonly used to reduce noise while preserving strong changes in a signal [30]. It computes a weighted average of the input signal over a small neighborhood of samples to produce each output value. The weights are dependent on both the domain and range of the input signal. In our implementation, we use the last ten pose estimates for a puppet as the sample neighborhood. Since the poses change as a function of time, we treat time as the domain of the signal and either the translation or rotation component as the range. We represent the rotations as quaternions for this computation. We have found that the bilateral filters reduce wobble without introducing noticeable lag or damping intentional puppet motions.

Partially Occluded Puppets. We have found that the Pose Tracker typically requires that the segmented point cloud contain at least 125 points to produce robust pose estimates. However, during a performance, if the puppeteer partially occludes the Kinect's view of a puppet with her hands or another puppet, the size of its point cloud may fall under this threshold. In these cases we simply use the last known pose of the puppet, essentially leaving it in place. In practice we have noticed that this rule is rarely necessary, but that it significantly improves the tracker's robustness to occlusions in the few instances that puppets are mostly occluded.

Entrances and Exits. The segmented point clouds also fall below the 125-point threshold when physical puppets are entering or exiting the performance space. In this case, the thresholding approach we use to handle partially occluded puppets would create artifacts; a puppet exiting the performance space would have its 3D model permanently fixed to the last position in which its point cloud contained at least 125 points. To solve this problem, we add an additional check.

We compute the angle between the Kinect's optical axis and the ray from the Kinect's optical center to the centroid of the puppet's point cloud. If that angle lies within 2.5 degrees of an edge of the system's trackable volume, or the centroid lies within 5cm of the nearest depth detectable by the Kinect, and the puppet's point cloud contains fewer than 125 points, it is labeled as "lost" and not rendered. Our system labels a puppet as "found" only if the Puppet Identifier detects it and its point cloud contains more than 125 points.

Rendering

Our OpenGL-based renderer uses the poses from the Capture module to render each puppet model within a 3D virtual set. It operates in real time and provides visual feedback to the puppeteer during a performance. To allow control over the composition and appearance of a shot, we include 6D virtual-camera and lighting controls. We also provide entrance and exit effects to warn the puppeteer before he/she moves a physical puppet outside the performance space. Finally, we include layered animations to help puppeteers perform animations with more than two simultaneously moving puppets.

Camera Controls. Our 3D animation environment enables 6D virtual-camera control, which aids both the composition and performance of animations. For instance, the puppeteer may capture an animation with the virtual camera at one location, but decide during playback that another vantage point provides a more interesting view of the story. During performance, however, we have found that puppeteers usually place the virtual camera to mimic their point of view of the physical performance space. This setup aids performance by helping the puppeteer avoid difficult mental transformations between the physical space and the rendered scene.

Lighting Controls. Our system allows the puppeteer to adjust the illumination of the virtual set, including the position of a light source, the strength of the ambient and diffuse light levels, and whether or not to render shadows. Puppeteers can switch between day and night scenes by adjusting the strength of the ambient and diffuse components. They can also adjust the light position to cast dramatic shadows on the faces of the virtual puppets.

Entrance-and-exit Effects. The trackable volume of our system is typically smaller than the virtual set. As a result, puppets entering or leaving the trackable volume can spontaneously appear or disappear within the virtual set. Such events can distract from the story. Careful placement of the virtual camera can avoid capturing abrupt transitions, but then the puppeteer's scene-composition options become limited. We address the issue by adjusting a puppet's transparency based on its proximity to the edge of the performance volume. Similar to our process for determining whether we have lost tracking of a puppet, we compute the angle between the centroids of the puppets and the Kinect's optical axis. If that angle lies within five degrees of any side of the performance volume, the puppets are rendered with decreased opacity. We apply the same effect for puppets that move too close to the Kinect sensor for detection. Once a puppet comes within one degree of leaving the side of the volume or within 5cm of leaving the top of the volume, we render it completely transparent. This process renders the puppets invisible before the Pose Tracker labels them as lost. We find this rendering approach to be less distracting to a story than spontaneous entrances and exits. It can also help puppeteers set up animations. The puppeteer can slowly move a puppet to the edge of the tracking region until it is just invisible but still tracked, and then leave it in place. The puppeteer then knows exactly where the puppet will appear if it re-enters the set.

Layered Animations. A key benefit of our system is that it allows the puppeteer to concentrate on the performance, rather than the interface. However, some stories can be difficult to perform. For instance, a story may require three or more puppets to move at the same time. To aid these kinds of performances, we implemented layered animations, which allow the puppeteer to perform a single story using multiple capture sessions. As the puppeteer adds a new layer to a story, we simultaneously play back the previously captured sessions. This mode of performance loses kinesthetic feedback between puppets in different layers, but can be useful for performances with more than two puppets.

RESULTS

We created four animations to demonstrate our tracker, camera and lighting controls, 3D performance space, and layered-animation tools. "Apathetic Ambulance" (Figure 2), "Pool Intruder" (Figure 8), and "Traffic Fight," (Figure 8) were created by the first author, while "Ghost Duck" (Figure 8) was created by a novice user. We also conducted a user study wherein five novices (male and female, 10-30 years old) created animations using our system. All of the animations are on our project website[1]. We first describe the four initial animations and then present the user study.

Animation Details

In "Apathetic Ambulance," two cars crash into each other, and then a fire truck crashes into the police car that has arrived to help. An ambulance arrives, surveys the scene, and decides to go home. The puppeteer made use of physics in this animation to push the physical puppets into each other during the crashes. Our system tracked those motions in real time and reproduced the physical interactions between the puppets in the rendered result. The puppeteer also used the transparent rendering of puppets near the edge of the tracking volume. He placed the virtual fire truck, police car, and ambulance on the roads in the virtual set, and then moved them out until they were rendered invisible, but still tracked by the system. This setup made him confident about where in the virtual set the puppets would appear as they entered the animation. The puppeteer needed five takes to record the animation. He threw out one recording because the system did not accurately track the ambulance model. He discarded the other attempts because he did not like his physical performance (e.g., the motion of the ambulance puppet was too slow).

In "Pool Intruder," a duck goes to take a swim in his pool, but encounters a big fish who refuses to let him in. The duck recruits the help of a wheeled boat, which drags the fish away.

[1] http://vis.berkeley.edu/papers/3dpuppet

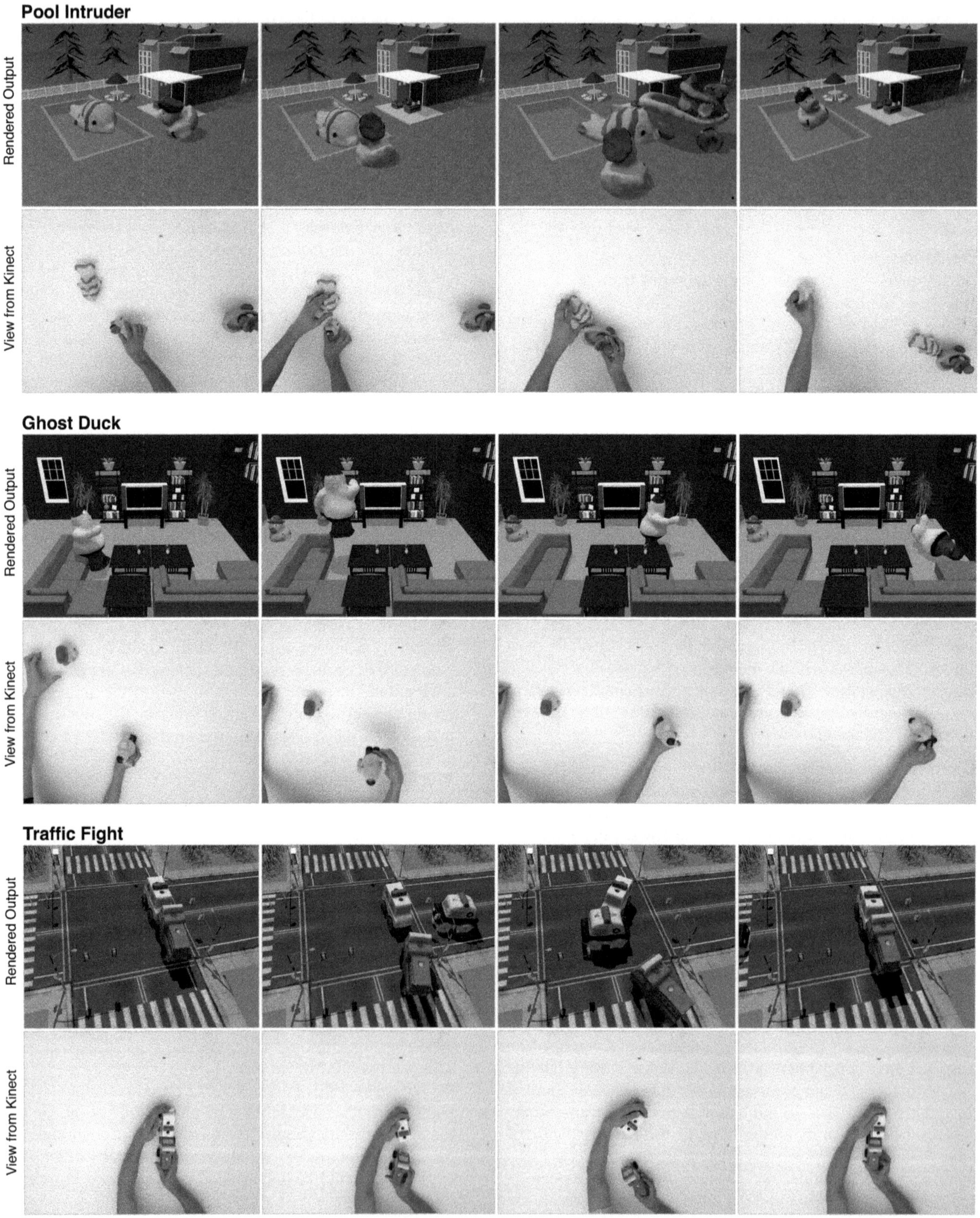

Figure 8. Summaries of three animations created with our system. For each animation, the bottom row shows the view from the Kinect sensor and the top row shows the rendered output of our system. "Traffic Fight" consists of two performances layered together; we include the raw input of only one of them.

Finally, the duck enjoys his pool. The puppeteer needed three takes to produce the final animation, after not being satisfied with the pacing of the first try or the relative positions of the puppets in second try.

In "Ghost Duck," a man enters his living room and goes to his couch. A ghost duck then enters the room and surprises the man, who tries to run away but hits a wall and falls down. The puppeteer creatively applied our system's variable-opacity rendering to give the duck a ghost-like appearance. To show the man's surprise, he made the puppet jump up and down, demonstrating how one can convey emotion even with rigid puppets. The jumps demonstrate how puppeteers can use the full 3D performance space to tell their stories. The puppeteer created this animation after using our system for 40 minutes, including the five minutes we used to explain its controls.

"Traffic Fight" demonstrates our system's layered-animation feature. An ambulance and fire truck fight in the middle of an intersection, move aside as a police car passes through, and then resume fighting. The animation uses three puppets that move simultaneously, and would have been impossible to perform in one take by one puppeteer. In this case, the puppeteer created two layers. In the first layer, he performed the motion of the police car. He then played it back and created a second layer with the fire truck and ambulance. Our system then combined the two layers into one story. This example demonstrates how layered animations rely heavily on the real-time performance of our system. The puppets in each layer interacted with one another, so the puppeteer had to continually monitor the earlier animation and adjust his second performance on the fly to make the interactions believable.

Implementation

We implemented our system with the Robotics Operating System [32], OpenNI Kinect driver [26], and SiftGPU software package [33]. Our system runs on a desktop PC with a 24-core, 3.33GHz Xeon CPU, 12GB RAM, and an NVIDIA GTX 580 video card.

For our physical setup, we place a Kinect sensor 75cm above a tabletop, which we use for a performance space. We orient the Kinect so its optical axis makes a 22.5-degree angle with the tabletop's surface normal. This setup provides a trackable performance volume of roughly 90cm by 60cm by 30cm. We found that this setup maximized the useful performance space while maintaining enough density in the point cloud to allow accurate tracking. While moving the Kinect further away from the table top increases the size of the performance volume it also leads to larger gaps between samples in the point cloud and degrades tracking. Our setup also allows the tabletop to serve as a physical proxy to the virtual ground plane. Thus, a puppeteer can rest a puppet on the tabletop and keep it within the animation while he/she manipulates other puppets. Finally, we chose an oblique view because it usually captures more of the distinguishing, frontal features of the physical puppets than a view pointed straight down.

USER EXPERIENCE

We observed five novice puppeteers (male and female, 10-30 years old) while they produced their first animations with our system. We began by helping each puppeteer create a skin color model. We then took about five minutes to explain the keyboard and mouse controls for changing camera, lighting, and background settings. After this introduction, we asked the puppeteers to play with our system and, when ready, to record a simple story.

The puppeteers began by exploring the capabilities of our system. They put physical puppets in the performance space and watched how quickly our system could detect them. Next, they moved the physical puppets throughout the performance space to test how well our tracker could follow them. They also cycled through the seven virtual sets we provided to explore how characters could interact within them. For instance, multiple puppeteers tried placing puppets under covered bridges and making them hide behind buildings. Three of the puppeteers expressed excitement when they first saw the virtual characters moving in response to their physical actions. In praising its simplicity, one claimed that he could have used it without any introduction.

While playing with our system, puppeteers learned not to occlude too much of each puppet with their hands. Otherwise, the point clouds could become too small for accurate pose detection, and our system would either render a puppet in the wrong pose or stop rendering it altogether. They also learned how quickly they could move each puppet without losing tracking. As we discuss in the Limitations Section, the maximum speed our system can track varies by puppet.

The lack of collision detection confused some puppeteers. They were surprised to see that puppets could pass through walls. We chose to omit collision detection between the virtual puppets and the objects in the virtual sets from our system because handling such collisions would require breaking the one-to-one, physical-to-virtual mapping of our interface. If a virtual wall stopped the motion of a puppet, then the virtual and physical positions of that puppet would no longer correctly match.

On average, our puppeteers took 16 minutes to play with the system before trying to record their first animations. Once they were ready to create an animation, we showed them how to record and export their own performances, and how to produce layered animations. While formulating their stories, they continued to play with our system to plan the motions of the puppets within the virtual sets. We found that first-time users typically needed three or four recording attempts to produce an animation that they liked, with more complex stories taking longer to produce. Puppeteers either discarded animations due to performance errors (e.g., the performance was too slow or a physical puppet's motion did not quite match the puppeteer's intention), or tracking errors. Practice with our system helped reduce the latter issue, as puppeteers learned to avoid motions that were too fast for our tracker.

The final animations produced by our novice puppeteers made full use of the capabilities of our system, including

6D puppet motions, camera and lighting controls, and layered animation. They typically adjusted the camera before performing the motions to set the view so that it resembled their view of the physical performance space but also ensured that all subsequent puppet motions would be visible. They also used camera controls to frame the output movie. One puppeteer chose to change the lighting parameters after she finished her performance. Once we explained our system, each puppeteer took less than one hour to record a story, with some only needing 30 minutes.

LIMITATIONS

Our system is primarily limited by the puppets and puppet motions it can track.

Our system only tracks rigid puppets; the Capture module does not account for articulated or deformable puppets. We also cannot track puppets with sizes much smaller than those in our example animations (the smallest being roughly 7cm x 8cm x 8cm). Smaller puppets do not produce enough unique SIFT features for identification. Puppets that pass the size limitation must also be unique in shape and texture so that they are identified and tracked properly. If two puppets share many of the same SIFT features, our Puppet Identifier can generate false matches. Finally, radially symmetric puppets produce errors during ICP alignment, as multiple orientations provide equally optimal alignment solutions. As a result, the output pose becomes more likely to rapidly jump between the optima and generate temporally inconsistent pose estimates.

Fast puppet motions can also produce tracking errors. We have found that the 3D shape of a puppet has a significant effect on the types of motions it can undergo without error. For instance, the duck puppets seen in our sample animations are the most prone to rotational errors due to their roughly radial symmetry. In general, geometrically simple puppets are more susceptible to tracking errors. For instance, the top of the Lamborghini puppet in the "Apathetic Ambulance" animation is almost completely flat. If that puppet moves quickly in a direction tangential to its roof, the optimal ICP-derived pose can slip and produce a mismatch between the physical and virtual poses. Thus, the puppeteer must take more care with the motions for that puppet.

CONCLUSION AND FUTURE WORK

We have presented a new interface for producing 3D animations by performing with physical puppets in front of a Kinect depth sensor. The system's direct, natural mode of input and simple hardware requirements make it approachable to users of any skill level. We allow puppeteers to tell stories by playing with toys and other physical props, which makes the method of interaction familiar and entertaining. Once puppeteers understand its limitations, the design of our system also allows puppeteers to focus on their physical performance, rather than the interface.

While puppeteers enjoy producing animations with our system, we found that they enjoy free-form play almost as much. In particular, they enjoy seeing how the physical puppets' motions translate into the context of the different virtual sets. This observation suggests other modes of play, for instance where the puppets could explore the virtual world and trigger preset animations, similar to the work in Lego OASIS [34].

Though we have demonstrated its utility for simple 3D animations, our system may be extended in a number of ways:

Integrated Puppet Loading. Our current implementation relies on third-party software like ReconstructMe [13] or 123D Catch [1] to provide 3D models for each puppets, followed by manual capture of the SIFT template images. A more streamlined implementation would combine 3D scanning and template-capture into one process, which could be incorporated directly into our interface.

Articulated Puppets. Our example stories demonstrated how puppeteers could impart emotion onto rigid puppets. However, articulated puppets would provide more expressiveness and widen the range of puppets available to puppeteers. This improvement would require substantial changes to our Puppet Identifier and Pose Tracker in order to handle every possible posture for each puppet.

Deformable Puppets. Our system currently cannot track soft, deformable puppets, including most stuffed animals. In order to track such puppets, we would need to modify our ICP algorithm, which assumes that the shape of a physical puppet does not change throughout a performance. The modification might include deformation models for the ways in which the shape of each puppet can deform.

Multiple Puppeteers. Currently we can easily handle multiple puppeteers using our system at the same time, as long as their skin tones closely match. We might also handle multiple skin tones by combining the skin model for each puppeteer. Beyond multiple puppeteers in one setting, we also envision remote, collaborative puppeteering sessions using our system.

ACKNOWLEDGMENTS

We would like to thank Dieter Fox for providing valuable insight into our tracking algorithm, Evan Herbst and Peter Henry for sharing crucial code, and Nicholas Kong for his help in making the video. We also thank the paper reviewers for their helpful suggestions. This work was supported by NSF grant CCF-0643552 and a gift from the Intel Science and Technology Center for Visual Computing.

REFERENCES

1. Autodesk. 123D Catch. http://www.123dapp.com/catch.
2. Autodesk. 3ds Max. http://usa.autodesk.com/3ds-max/.
3. Autodesk. Maya. http://usa.autodesk.com/maya/.
4. Avrahami, D., Wobbrock, J. O., and Izadi, S. Portico: tangible interaction on and around a tablet. In *Proc. UIST* (2011), 347–356.
5. Barnes, C., Jacobs, D. E., Sanders, J., Goldman, D. B., Rusinkiewicz, S., Finkelstein, A., and Agrawala, M. Video Puppetry: A performative interface for cutout animation. *ACM TOG (Proc. SIGGRAPH) 27*, 5 (2008), 124:1–124:9.
6. Besl, P., and McKay, N. A method for registration of 3-D shapes. *IEEE PAMI 14* (1992), 239–256.

7. Blender Foundation. Blender. http://www.blender.org.

8. Cline, D., Jeschke, S., White, K., Razdan, A., and Wonka, P. Dart throwing on surfaces. *Computer Graphics Forum 28*, 4 (2009), 1217–1226.

9. Dontcheva, M., Yngve, G., and Popović, Z. Layered acting for character animation. *ACM TOG (Proc. SIGGRAPH) 22* (2003), 409–416.

10. Freedman, B., Shpunt, A., Machline, M., and Arieli, Y. Depth mapping using projected patterns. Patent. US8150142 (2012).

11. Gallo, L., Placitelli, A., and Ciampi, M. Controller-free exploration of medical image data: Experiencing the kinect. In *Proc. CBMS* (2011), 1–6.

12. Google. Google 3D Warehouse. http://sketchup.google.com/3dwarehouse/.

13. Heindl, C., and Kopf, C. ReconstructMe. http://reconstructme.net.

14. Horn, B. K. P. Closed-form solution of absolute orientation using unit quaternions. *JOSA A 4*, 4 (1987), 629–642.

15. Iason Oikonomidis, N. K., and Argyros, A. Efficient model-based 3D tracking of hand articulations using kinect. In *Proc. BMVC* (2011), 101.1–101.11.

16. Ishii, H., and Ullmer, B. Tangible bits: Towards seamless interfaces between people, bits and atoms. In *Proc. CHI* (1997), 234–241.

17. Izadi, S., Kim, D., Hilliges, O., Molyneaux, D., Newcombe, R., Kohli, P., Shotton, J., Hodges, S., Freeman, D., Davison, A., and Fitzgibbon, A. Kinectfusion: real-time 3D reconstruction and interaction using a moving depth camera. In *Proc. UIST* (2011), 559–568.

18. Johnson, M. P., Wilson, A., Blumberg, B., Kline, C., and Bobick, A. Sympathetic interfaces: Using a plush toy to direct synthetic characters. In *Proc. CHI* (1999), 152–158.

19. Joung, J. H., An, K. H., Kang, J. W., Chung, M. J., and Yu, W. 3D environment reconstruction using modified color ICP algorithm by fusion of a camera and a 3D laser range finder. In *Proc. IROS* (2009), 3082–3088.

20. Kato, H., Billinghurst, M., Poupyrev, I., Imamoto, K., and Tachibana, K. Virtual object manipulation on a table-top AR environment. In *Proc. ISAR* (2000), 111 –119.

21. Klemmer, S. R., Li, J., Lin, J., and Landay, J. A. Papier-mâché: Toolkit support for tangible input. In *Proc. CHI* (2004), 399–406.

22. Lee, G. A., Kim, G. J., and Billinghurst, M. Immersive authoring: What you experience is what you get (wyxiwyg). *Comm. ACM 48*, 7 (2005), 76–81.

23. Lowe, D. G. Object recognition from local scale-invariant features. In *Proc. ICCV* (1999), 1150–1157.

24. Numaguchi, N., Nakazawa, A., Shiratori, T., and Hodgins, J. K. A puppet interface for retrieval of motion capture data. In *Proc. SCA* (2011), 157–166.

25. Oore, S., Terzopoulos, D., and Hinton, G. E. A desktop input device and interface for interactive 3D character animation. In *Proc. Graphics Interface* (2002), 133–140.

26. OpenNI Organization. OpenNI. http://openni.org.

27. Schmidt, R., and Singh, K. meshmixer: an interface for rapid mesh composition. In *ACM TOG (Proc. SIGGRAPH)* (2010), 6:1.

28. Shotton, J., Fitzgibbon, A., Cook, M., Sharp, T., Finocchio, M., Moore, R., Kipman, A., and Blake, A. Real-time human pose recognition in parts from single depth images. In *Proc. CVPR* (2011), 1297 –1304.

29. Sturman, D. J. Computer puppetry. *IEEE Computer Graphics and Applications 18*, 1 (1998), 38–45.

30. Tomasi, C., and Manduchi, R. Bilateral filtering for gray and color images. In *Proc. ICCV* (1998), 839 –846.

31. Wang, R. Y., and Popović, J. Real-time hand-tracking with a color glove. In *ACM TOG (Proc. SIGGRAPH)* (2009), 63:1–63:8.

32. Willow Garage. Robotics Operating System. http://ros.org.

33. Wu, C. SiftGPU: A GPU implementation of scale invariant feature transform (SIFT). http://cs.unc.edu/ ccwu/siftgpu, 2007.

34. Ziola, R., Grampurohit, S., Landes, N., Fogarty, J., and Harrison, B. Examining interaction with general-purpose object recognition in LEGO OASIS. In *Proc. IEEE VL/HCC* (2011), 65–68.

KinÊtre: Animating the World with the Human Body

Jiawen Chen, Shahram Izadi, Andrew Fitzgibbon
Microsoft Research Cambridge, UK
{jiawen, shahrami, awf}@microsoft.com

Figure 1: KinÊtre allows novice users to easily and quickly create animations of arbitrary real-world objects using just a regular consumer Kinect. From left to right: user scans a real chair using an existing 3D reconstruction system. The Kinect is then placed down so that it can image the user's full body, and a real-time tracked human skeleton is acquired. Our system takes the human skeleton and 3D reconstruction as input. Next, the user physically moves such that the rendered skeleton interpenetrates the mesh. Using a simple voice command, the mesh is rigged (or "possessed") in real-time by the user's skeleton. KinÊtre transfers motions of the user into realistic deformations of the mesh.

ABSTRACT

KinÊtre allows novice users to scan arbitrary physical objects and bring them to life in seconds. The fully interactive system allows diverse static meshes to be animated using the entire human body. Traditionally, the process of mesh animation is laborious and requires domain expertise, with rigging specified manually by an artist when designing the character. KinÊtre makes creating animations a more playful activity, conducted by novice users interactively *at runtime*. This paper describes the KinÊtre system in full, highlighting key technical contributions and demonstrating many examples of users animating meshes of varying shapes and sizes. These include non-humanoid meshes and incomplete surfaces produced by 3D scanning – two challenging scenarios for existing mesh animation systems. Rather than targeting professional CG animators, KinÊtre is intended to bring mesh animation to a new audience of novice users. We demonstrate potential uses of our system for interactive storytelling and new forms of physical gaming.

Author Keywords

3D interfaces; mesh animation; real-time; depth cameras

ACM Classification Keywords

H.5.2 [Information Interfaces And Presentation]: User Interfaces - Interaction styles

INTRODUCTION

Imagine you are asked to produce a 3D animation of a demonic armchair terrorizing an innocent desk lamp. You may think about model rigging, skeleton deformation, and keyframing. Depending on your experience, you might imagine hours to days at the controls of Maya[1] or Blender[2]. But even if you have absolutely no computer graphics experience, it can be so much easier: grab a nearby chair and desk lamp, scan them using a consumer depth camera, and use the same camera to track your body, aligning your virtual limbs to the chair's geometry. At one spoken command, your limbs are attached to the chair model, which follows your movements in an intuitive and natural manner.

KinÊtre[3] is such a system. Rather than targeting professional animators, it brings animation to a new audience of users with little or no CG experience. It allows realistic deformations of arbitrary static meshes, runs in real time on consumer hardware, and uses the human body for input in conjunction with simple voice commands. KinÊtre lets anyone create playful 3D animations.

To realize KinÊtre, we extend the work of Sumner et al. [32] to handle incomplete 3D meshes captured by a real-time 3D reconstruction system [15]. Rather than using mouse or touch, our technique leverages the human skeleton tracked by a Kinect [30] as a more direct and higher degree-of-freedom (DoF) mechanism for mesh animation.

We describe our system pipeline in full, and demonstrate many examples including animation of incomplete physical scans of varying size and shape, retargeting motion to other human and non-human meshes, and animations with multi-

[1] http://usa.autodesk.com/maya/
[2] http://www.blender.org/
[3] A portmanteau of Kinect and Être—"to be."

user input. We describe usage scenarios enabled by this combination of capturing arbitrary real-world objects and bringing them to life using the human body: for example, animating characters for home scripted CG movies or interactive storytelling – imagine enacting the classic Pixar Luxo Jr. scene, by first scanning a household lamp and then controlling it using your body. Other scenarios include creating more realistic avatars for games, where users scan themselves or friends and again control these meshes using their bodies, without any manual rigging or skinning process, as well as leveraging these types of playful mesh animations for physics-enabled gaming. We conclude by discussing qualitative experiences of using the system, its strengths and limitations, and directions for future work.

Our main contributions include:

- A new interactive mesh animation system that allows non-expert users to rapidly create playful animations, using scanned physical objects or existing 3D models.
- A new deformation method, based on [32], capable of performing realistic and detail preserving deformations of incomplete static input scans using the motion of a tracked user's skeleton as real-time input.
- A demonstration of our results operating on input meshes of different topology, size and geometry, and enabling new scenarios for character animation and physics-based gaming previously unavailable to everyday consumers.

RELATED WORK

While considerable advances in real-time virtual character animation have occurred over many decades (see [31] for an overview of pioneering work), this process is still largely based on specialist tools designed for professionals to create high-end animations for movies and games. Our goal is greatly different, we instead target novice users with little or no background in CG tools. Our primary goal is to allow users to rapidly incorporate objects from the real world into their CG applications, and bring these static representations to life in seconds. We leverage the human body for input, instead of mouse and keyboard, to create a more direct performance-based approach to animation, making the process more playful and accessible to a wide range of users.

Manual skinning and skeletal-based deformations remain the de facto method for character animation in a variety of CG applications including gaming. For example, when we see virtual characters coming to life in our games, usually a designer has carefully constructed and *rigged* the mesh, involving embedding a skeleton within the target model and painting individual bone weights onto each vertex. At runtime, motion capture (mocap) data or an inverse kinematics engine drives the character's bones, which then transforms the mesh.

The 3D modeling, rigging, and animation process traditionally requires a great deal of time and expertise and has led to extensive research in automatic animation systems. These include sketch-based interfaces for 2D and 3D animation [33, 9], and the use of multi-touch input for both manipulation of unstructured 2D shapes [13] and 3D articulated human characters [21]. More unusual interfaces include using physical manipulators such as soft toys [18], articulated robots [22], 2D paper cutouts [5], and layering multiple passes of 3D mocap [10]. Mesh manipulation tools can be spatially combined with key-framing to assist artists in scripting animation [14]). Our focus is on real-time 3D shape animation, leveraging the natural and higher DoF input of the entire human body for control.

Another related area explores generating articulated meshes of humans using multi-view video [1] or silhouettes [34], range data [2] and mocap data [3]. These approaches simultaneously acquire and articulate human meshes, but clearly cannot scale to scenarios where animations of non-humanoid characters are desired.

Closer to our goals are systems that leverage recorded or live mocap data to animate meshes [4] or articulated characters [29]. These systems demonstrate compelling examples of character animation on various closed meshes, predominately of humanoid forms. Our method is more flexible in the types of 3D deformations and meshes it supports, including incomplete scans of arbitrary physical objects. Our focus is on a "user in the loop" form of interaction, rather than the more sophisticated technique demonstrated in [4], which works particularly well for closed humanoid meshes but is restricted to watertight shapes. Recent work by Yamane et al. [35] takes a learning-based approach to mapping human motion to non-humanoid characters. Given user-selected correspondences between the poses of the human actor and those of the non-humanoid character, the system builds a statistical mapping; which, combined with physical constraints, transfers the actor's motion to the character. In contrast, KinÊtre is fully automatic and does not require users to pose the character, only themselves. However, the motions that KinÊtre produces are "direct" mappings and not as flexible as those of Yamane et al.

Recently, there has been much work in the area of shape-preserving space deformation algorithms. One approach is to operate on a reduced control *cage* surrounding the mesh, which can have their handles (vertices of the cage) manipulated to cause smooth, detail preserving surface deformations. These cage-based methods typically restrict cage vertex transformations to a series of translations, and use generalized coordinate techniques to uniquely define any possible configuration of the mesh relative to a reference configuration [20, 25, 6, 19]. Another class of techniques support manipulation through unconnected point handles on the mesh. Examples include moving least squares [27], variational methods [6], and inverse kinematics on meshes [28]. These systems all operate on closed meshes, which cannot be guaranteed when scanning real-world geometry. Further, they are optimized to support manipulation of control vertices by mouse or stylus.

The 3D deformation methods described so far all operate on closed meshes. Jacobson et al. [16] demonstrate bounded biharmonic blending weights that produce smooth and intuitive deformations for points, bones and cages of arbitrary topology including incomplete meshes. However, it relies on a volumetric representation and quadratic programming, which incurs a high computational cost each time the user changes the set of constraints. Embedded Deformation by

Sumner et al. [32] supports point-based direct manipulation of meshes, and is agnostic to whether surface data is complete. This method forms the basis of the deformation model used within this paper. We extend embedded deformation in various ways to our novel scenario of use, where data is heavily unstructured and multiple nodes of the graph are manipulated simultaneously by a human skeleton.

SCENARIO OF USE

Before going into the details of our system, we begin with a motivating scenario (shown in Figure 1), to help illustrate the overall user experience and interaction flow.

Imagine that the user wants to introduce and animate an existing static physical object – a chair – into a 3D game. He picks up a Kinect camera and scans in part of the room. KinÊtre automatically generates a 3D mesh of the chair and segments it from the background (Figure 1 left).

At this point we have a static, incomplete and un-rigged mesh in our CG world. To bring this object to life in realistic ways, the user first places the depth sensor back down so that it can image his full body, and a tracked human skeleton is sensed. Our system renders both the human skeleton and scanned object side by side. The user then physically moves such that the desired parts of the rendered skeleton are embedded inside the scanned object (Figure 1 middle). Once in the desired pose, the user issues a voice command to automatically rig (or "possess") the mesh (Figure 1 middle). This attaches joints of his current pose to the mesh.

The user can now move his body and KinÊtre automatically translates his motion into realistic deformations of the previously static mesh (Figure 1 right). Moving his legs causes the legs of the chair to also move. Flexing his knees causes the chair to bend, jumping up makes the chair also jump. Motions of the body propagate in real-time to the mesh and provides a natural way for users to perform playful animations of any object that they wish to bring to life in their CG application or game.

SYSTEM PIPELINE

Although our system works with arbitrary meshes, including complete high-quality 3D models, typically, the input to our system is a real-world object of reasonable physical size and surface reflectance. We acquire the object's 3D geometry by waving a depth camera around it, using a variant of the KinectFusion system [15].

The main pipeline shown in Figure 2 is comprised of two main phases. The first phase can be thought of as *preprocessing* and is broken down as follows:

1. A *3D reconstruction* step estimates the 6-DoF pose of the moving Kinect camera, and fuses depth data continuously into a regular 3D voxel grid data structure.
2. A *segmentation* and *meshing* step automatically extracts and triangulates the desired foreground isosurface stored implicitly in the voxel grid.
3. A *sampling* step traverses vertices of the mesh and constructs a sparse deformation graph [32], with the goal of maintaining key topological features and connectivity of the mesh. This deformation graph is the basis for representing deformations in the higher dimensional mesh.

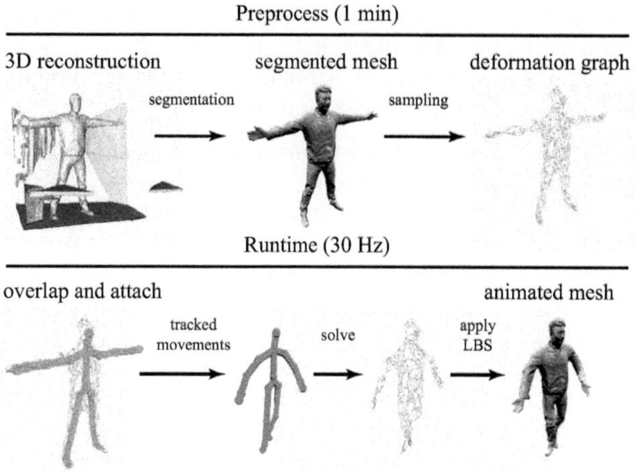

Figure 2: The KinÊtre processing pipeline.

Preprocessing is entirely automatic and can be performed once, before mesh animation occurs per frame. It can be conducted entirely by novice users interactively (the entire preprocessing phase takes about one minute total).

At runtime, KinÊtre computes deformations of the sparsely sampled graph per frame based on real-time human skeleton data captured with the Kinect. We use the publicly available skeletal tracker in the Kinect SDK (a variant of [30]), which gives a prediction of 20 joint positions on the human body. Deformations of the graph are then propagated to the higher resolution mesh. More specifically, the steps are as follows:

1. A "user in the loop" *rigging* step that renders both the input mesh and the tracked human skeleton to the user, and allows the user to pose herself such that her body intersects with the mesh. This metaphorically *attaches* the joints of the tracked skeleton to the surface of the mesh. In practice, the attachment is specified as a set of point constraints on the deformation graph.
2. When the user moves, we solve for the optimal transformations on the deformation graph that is simultaneously smooth, feature-preserving, and satisfies the user's motion constraints. This is formulated as a nonlinear energy minimization (extending [32]), which we solve for each frame in real-time.
3. The final step takes the transformations computed on the sparse deformation graph and applies them to the dense 3D mesh using an algorithm similar to linear blend skinning (LBS) [23, 26].

The following sections describe these steps in more detail.

Acquisition, Segmentation and Meshing

In the KinectFusion system [15], depth data from the camera is integrated into a regular voxel grid structure stored on the GPU. Surface data is encoded *implicitly* into voxels as signed distances, truncated to a predefined region around the surface, with new values integrated using a weighted running average [8]. The global pose of the moving depth camera is predicted using point-plane ICP [7], and drift is mitigated by aligning the current raw depth map with the accumulated model (instead of the previous raw frame).

The system produces a 3D volumetric reconstruction of the scene accumulated from the moving depth camera. To extract a specific object from this full 3D reconstruction two simple segmentation methods are provided. The first described in [15] allows the user to physically remove the desired object from the reconstructed scene. Taking the derivative of the signed distance values over time, we label regions of the voxel grid with high change. A full pass over the voxel grid extracts these labeled connected components and the largest region is chosen as the foreground object. This works well for objects that are physically small enough to be moved. For larger objects, a second method takes the current physical camera pose, raycasts the voxel grid and extracts the dominant plane using RANSAC, segmenting any resting objects (again the largest 3D connected component is assumed to be the desired object).

Next we extract a geometric isosurface from the foreground labeled volumetric dataset using a GPU-based marching cubes algorithm. For each voxel, the signed distance value at its eight corners is computed. The algorithm uses these computed signed distances as a lookup to produce the correct polygon at the specific voxel.

Now that we can acquire, segment, and generate a 3D mesh from a physical object, we next derive a new method that maps tracked user motions to mesh deformations.

Embedded Deformation

We first briefly describe the Embedded Deformation (ED) technique [32] that our system builds upon. Later sections introduce key extensions in the form of a new sampling and point constraint strategy that work on a greater variety of meshes, and a new energy function for the deformation graph. These better accommodate our scenario, which has poorly sampled geometry and a multitude of constraints from a tracked human skeleton.

Like many skinning techniques, ED assumes that shape deformations vary smoothly in space and can be expressed as linear combinations of a sparse set of affine transformations. ED models its lower-dimensional basis as a graph. The nodes of the ED graph are a sparse subset of the samples at locations $\mathbf{g}_j$ on the surface, and its edges are the k-nearest neighbors of each node in $\mathbb{R}^3$, with $k = 4$.

Each node deforms space in a region surrounding its position $\mathbf{g}_j$ with an affine transformation $A_j = (R_j, \mathbf{t}_j)$, where R is a 3×3 matrix and $\mathbf{t}$ a 3×1 vector. This affine transform maps the point $\mathbf{v}$ to:

$$A_j[\mathbf{v}] = R_j(\mathbf{v} - \mathbf{g}_j) + \mathbf{g}_j + \mathbf{t}_j \qquad (1)$$

The deformation defined by multiple nodes is combined linearly as in LBS. Given a point $\mathbf{v} \in \mathbb{R}^3$, the deformation graph maps it to:

$$\phi(\mathbf{v}) = \sum_{j=0}^{k-1} w_j(\mathbf{v}) A_j[\mathbf{v}] \qquad (2)$$

The blending weights $w_j(\mathbf{v})$ are nonzero only for the k nodes closest to $\mathbf{v}$, fall off linearly with distance, and sum to 1. Intuitively, if transformations defined by the nodes vary smoothly, and the nodes are of sufficient density, then the vertices should also deform smoothly.

Energy Formulation To constrain the space of transformations, Sumner et al. make a number of reasonable assumptions and formulate them as an energy minimization problem. The first term minimizes stretching by biasing the solution towards isometry:

$$E_{\text{rot}} = \sum_j ||R_j^T R_j - I||_F^2, \qquad (3)$$

where I is the identity matrix and $||\cdot||_F$ denotes the Frobenius norm. To ensure that the deformation field is smooth, a regularization term encourages each node to map its neighbors near where they would map themselves:

$$E_{\text{reg}} = \sum_j \sum_{k \in N(j)} ||A_j[\mathbf{g}_k] - A_k[\mathbf{g}_k]||_2^2, \qquad (4)$$

where $N(j)$ is the set of neighbors of j in the graph. Finally, the deformation model allows the user to add an arbitrary number of point constraints, mapping each given point $\mathbf{p}_\ell$ to a desired target $\mathbf{q}_\ell$:

$$E_{\text{con}} = \sum_\ell ||\phi(\mathbf{p}_\ell) - \mathbf{q}_\ell||_2^2 \qquad (5)$$

where $\phi(\mathbf{p}_\ell)$ is the result of applying the deformation (Eq. 2) to $\mathbf{p}_\ell$. The total energy is a weighted sum of the three quadratic terms that is minimized using the Gauss-Newton algorithm.

EXTENDING EMBEDDED DEFORMATION

Although standard ED demonstrates impressive results on a variety of shapes, including incomplete polygon soups, we find in our experiments that the technique has difficulty with arbitrary, incomplete meshes that come from 3D acquisition. Dealing with such incomplete scans is key for KinÊtre.

For our scenarios, three major issues arise which require extensions to the work of Sumner et al. [32]. The first is the quality of the deformation graph: standard ED uses Poisson Disk sampling under the Euclidean distance metric to place graph vertices [32]. This sampling strategy tends to miss areas of the surface with high curvature and leads to artifacts where semantically unrelated parts are linked. Figure 3 illustrates how the Euclidean Poisson Disk sampling fails on a scan of a chair and a 3D model of a horse. The output deformation graphs of both meshes have connections occurring across separate legs. This causes undesirable effects as deformations to one leg will influence the other. We address this issue with a new sampling strategy based on a 5D orientation-aware distance metric.

The second issue is graph connectivity: the k-nearest-neighbor deformation graph is not guaranteed to be connected. Figure 4 (labeled a-c) shows one illustrative example, where one of the back legs of a horse model is completely unconnected to the rest of the deformation graph. This leads to unnatural

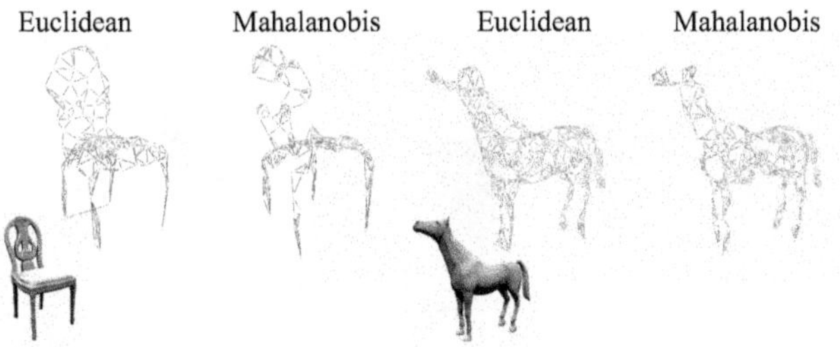

Figure 3: Orientation-aware sampling. With a Euclidean distance, samples are better distributed over the surface, but semantically separate parts tend to be connected. With a 5D Mahalanobis distance, spurious edges are reduced by placing more samples near areas of high curvature.

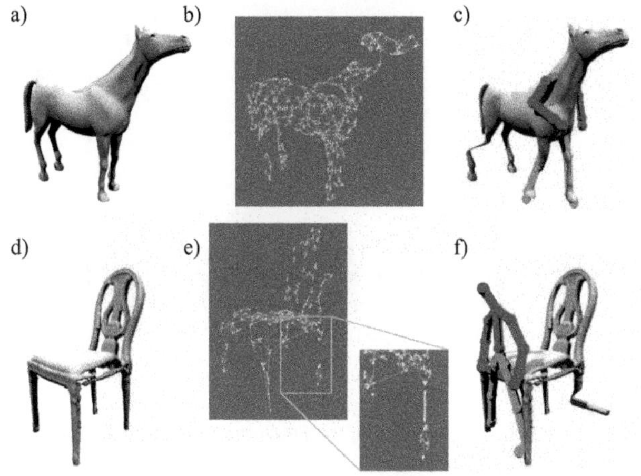

Figure 4: Mesh connectivity and regularization. Top row: a) Input mesh. A disconnected deformation graph b) leads to portions of the mesh not moving with the user and shared regions collapsing unnaturally c). Bottom row: d) Input mesh. e) Disconnected graph connected by spanning tree algorithm (inset). f) Without the rigidity regularizer, the remaining degrees of freedom allows the chair leg to rotate.

deformations in response to user motion. While not considered in [32], in practice these unconnected graphs occur frequently given input scan data or even complex models (such as the horse in Figure 4). We therefore address this explicitly in our sampling strategy.

The final issue arises due to under-constrained parts of the generated deformation graph: even when connected, the graph topology often leads to islands of under-constrained nodes. An example is shown in Figure 4 (labeled d-f), where the chair leg is connected through a single graph edge to the main body of the chair. This results in the chair leg being able to rotate unnaturally, independently of the deformations on the main body. We address this issue by applying an additional rigidity regularizer to these parts of the graph to ensure a well-posed optimization.

Orientation-Aware Sampling We ameliorate the sampling problem near areas of high curvature by adapting the strategy used by Lehtinen et al. [24] for generating Poisson Disk patterns on unstructured geometry. Given surface samples $\mathbf{p}$ and $\mathbf{q}$ with normals $\vec{n}_p$ and $\vec{n}_q$, we can define a 5D orientation-aware distance $D(\mathbf{p}, \mathbf{q})$:

$$\text{dist}_q(\mathbf{p}) = ||\mathbf{p} - \mathbf{q} + 2((\mathbf{p} - \mathbf{q}) \cdot \vec{n}_q)\vec{n}_q|| \quad (6)$$
$$D(\mathbf{p}, \mathbf{q}) = \frac{\min(\text{dist}_q(\mathbf{p}), \text{dist}_p(\mathbf{q}))}{\max(0, \vec{n}_p \cdot \vec{n}_q)}$$

Intuitively, the Mahalanobis distance $\text{dist}_q(\mathbf{p})$ transforms the spherical isosurfaces around $\mathbf{q}$ defined by the Euclidean distance into ellipsoids with the $\vec{n}_q$ axis squashed by a factor of $1/3$. It increases the distance of points that deviate from the plane tangent to $\mathbf{q}$. The symmetric distance $D(\mathbf{p}, \mathbf{q})$ has the nice property that when it is used for Poisson Disk pattern generation, it allows differently oriented samples to be placed arbitrarily close together. We generate such a pattern as the node positions of our deformation graph, with k-nearest neighbor edges defined under the same metric. Since we typically want a fixed framerate, we choose a fixed number of samples N and define the minimum separation radius $R = \sqrt{A/N}$, where A is the total surface area. We use $N = 128$ in our implementation. Alternatively, one can also provide R defined by desired level of detail and vary the number of samples. Actual generation is performed by brute force dart throwing. Finally, the surface normal is stored as part of the graph node for later use in detecting how to attach a user's skeleton to the graph.

Figure 3 shows our Mahalanobis-based sampling strategy compared with the Euclidean-based approach of [32].

Mesh Connectivity and Regularization It is easy to see that a k-nearest neighbor graph is not necessarily connected. The lack of scan data or insufficient sampling can lead to a graph composed of several connected components. Unless there is a user constraint attached to each component, the energy is underconstrained. To illustrate, in the first row of Figure 4, the small disconnected graph component of the horse's rear leg is not influenced by the user constraints and remains stationary. While the rest of the horse moves with the user, the vertices of the leg stays in place and vertices shared by both components collapse unnaturally. We solve this problem by connecting the graph, and guarantee a well-posed optimization problem by introducing an additional regularization term.

We connect the original k-nearest neighbor graph $G = (V, E)$ by first making it undirected: if B is a neighbor of A, then ensure that A is also a neighbor of B. We then compute its connected components and form a new complete, weighted graph $G' = (V', E')$, whose nodes V' are the connected components of G, and every pair of nodes (u', v') has weight equal to the minimum distance between any two nodes $s \in u' \subset V$ and $t \in v' \subset V$. We then compute a minimum spanning tree on G', and add the (undirected) edge (s, t) to E if there is an edge between their connected components in the spanning tree.

A connected deformation graph alone is insufficient to ensure a stable deformation. In particular, the standard ED energy function contains a number of gauge freedoms due to symmetry: a subgraph without user constraints, weakly connected to the rest of the graph through a single *cut vertex* (a vertex whose removal increases the number of connected components), is free to rotate about that point. These cut vertices include the ones where we added additional edges above (see Figure 4, second row). Therefore, at these edges, we enforce a stronger regularization condition:

$$E_{\text{rig}} = \sum_{(j,k)} ||R_k^T R_j - I||_F^2 + ||\mathbf{t}_k - \mathbf{t}_j||_2^2 \qquad (7)$$

The *rigidity regularizer* says that if a piece of the mesh is only loosely connected, the bridge edge (j, k) encourages it to be coupled rigidly with the rest of the mesh. Because this is a stronger condition than the basic regularizer (12 constraints rather than 3), we use a smaller weight. The final energy is then:

$$E = w_{\text{rot}} E_{\text{rot}} + w_{\text{reg}} E_{\text{reg}} + w_{\text{con}} E_{\text{con}} + w_{\text{rig}} E_{\text{rig}} \qquad (8)$$

We use the same weights as [32] for the standard ED terms, and set $w_{\text{rig}} = w_{\text{reg}}/10$.

Constraints

The deformation model supports placement of arbitrary point constraints in space. A basic approach to attach a tracked skeleton to the surface is to simply make each joint a constraint. At attachment time, the position of each joint $\mathbf{p}_\ell$ is stored along with Euclidean distances to the k-nearest nodes in the graph. As the user moves, each joint moves to a new position $\mathbf{q}_\ell$. We update the energy such that the k nearest nodes map $\mathbf{p}_\ell \rightarrow \mathbf{q}_\ell$.

In our experiments, we found that simply attaching joints as point constraints is inadequate for two reasons. First, even with multiple depth cues, the user is not very good at judging whether she is intersecting accurately with the mesh and often places her limbs outside the surface. Secondly, using only two samples on longer limbs such as the femur is insufficient for the deformation graph to faithfully reproduce more complex motions. Therefore, we elected to place additional constraints on bones.

We model each bone of a tracked skeleton as a cylinder with predefined radius (currently 4cm). We place 16 regularly spaced samples along the length and circumference of each bone and also calculate their outward facing normal. We allow a bone sample to be attached to a graph node if it is within 10cm, and the normals are less than 90 degrees apart. Using normals makes our system robust to small misalignments between the user and the surface. For example, if the user is animating another scanned human, her arms may not be perfectly aligned with those of the scan. The surface normal test lets the front of her arm attach to the front of the arm in the scan, and likewise for the back. In practice, this works well with one-sided surfaces that come from KinectFusion.

KINÊTRE IN ACTION

We implemented a prototype system called KinÊtre, which lets users acquire 3D scans and rapidly animate them using their body. Our system also permits existing higher-quality 3D models to be imported and again, animated using human motion. The animations occur in real-time as demonstrated in the accompanying video. We stress that none of the meshes are rigged before being "possessed" within KinÊtre.

Non-Human Animation Figures 1 and 5 illustrates KinÊtre operating on a variety of non-humanoid shapes. In Figure 1,

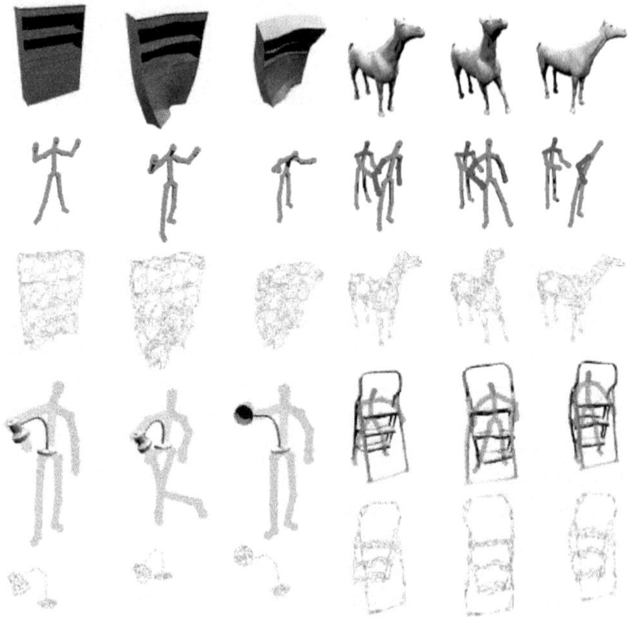

Figure 5: Gallery of non-humanoid animations. Clockwise from top left: making a modeled bookcase walk, two users controlling a horse, a jumping stepladder, and using only the hip and right arm to reenact Pixar's Luxo Jr.

Figure 6: Animating a human scan for realistic avatars. The user can directly embed his skeleton inside the scanned mesh (left and center). Tracked skeletal motions produce realistic mesh deformations (right).

a chair is scanned by the user, automatically rigged and animated when he places his two feet and spine to approximately correspond with the back of the chair. Figure 1 shows how the mesh deformations correspond to the motions of the body. Notice how the deformations propagate across the mesh, so that even when only the back legs of the chair are rigged the front legs move in concert.

Figure 5 (bottom right) shows another example, animating a scan of a step ladder. Our system also works with more detailed closed 3D models, such as the bookcase, which once attached, can start walking, bending or even kicking based on the motion of the user (see Figure 5).

We believe that these types of scenarios where users can animate non-humanoid everyday objects will capture people's imagination, particularly young children. With KinÊtre, children can tell stories where they possess different non-human characters, and record them as home CG movies.

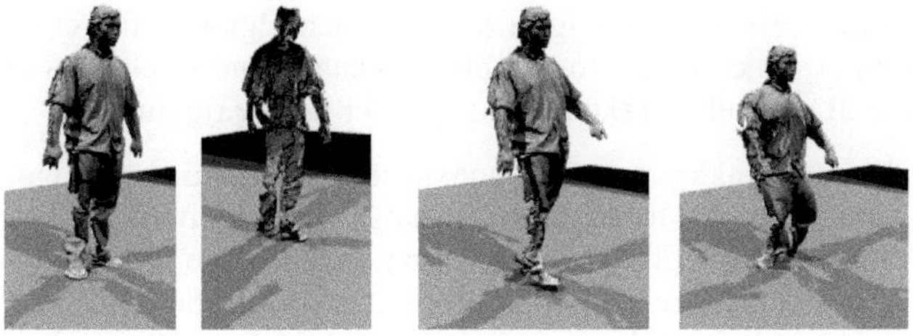

a) partial scan of human b) robust interactive deformations

Figure 7: A partial scan of a human with the back of the mesh completely missing (a). User embeds herself and can still animate the mesh in realistic ways (b).

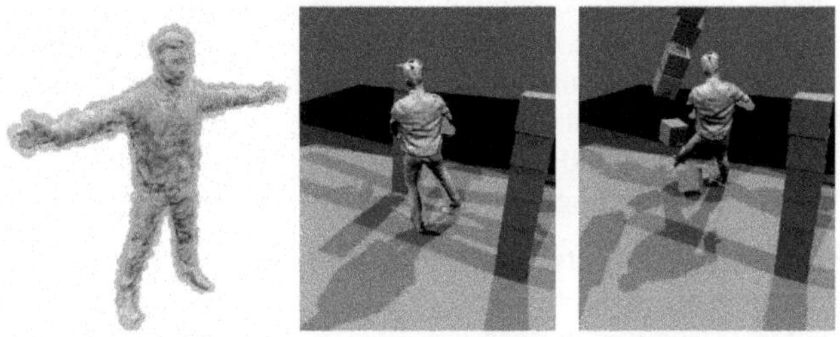

a) sphere proxies b) interactive physical simulation

Figure 8: A user mesh approximated as a series of physics-enabled kinematic spheres (a). This representation allows open ended interactions between the mesh and a virtual physics enabled scene (b).

Possessing and Animating Human Avatars Another key application area for KinÊtre is in creating more realistic avatars for gaming and teleconferencing scenarios. For example, an entire 360° reconstruction of the human body can be acquired, segmented from the ground plane and meshed using KinectFusion in less than a minute. Figure 6 shows an initially static scan of the user's body. Once acquired, he can animate his avatar, and our results show that our method supports fairly large mesh deformations beyond the original pose. *Possessing* one another's avatars can also become a playful activity: KinÊtre treats scans of humans like any other mesh and any user can control the avatar.

For teleconferencing, studies have shown the added benefits of avatar realism for collaboration [11]. KinÊtre is obviously agnostic to whether meshes are textured, and the reconstruction system could be used to create RGB textured meshes for added realism. For gaming, users could control their own avatar for a more immersive experience. Simple 3D modeling techniques such as those demonstrated in [12] could be incorporated if users want to add fun effects or personalize their characters.

Partial Scans One key feature of KinÊtre is to support animation of partial scan data. In Figures 1 and 5 both the chair and step ladder are not closed meshes with incomplete geometry. Figure 7 illustrates KinÊtre's robustness to partial data. The entire back of the mesh is clearly missing and the surface has a number of holes on the lower body. Unlike other animation systems such as [4], we demonstrate how our method can still produce a compelling deformation result even with missing data. These types of partial scans failed with our initial implementation based purely on Embedded Deformation [32]. Our extensions are therefore critical in ensuring that these extreme types of partially scanned meshes (which will be common case in everyday use) can be brought to life.

Figure 9: Users interacting with KinÊtre during informal qualitative sessions. From left: users bind to different parts of a chair to make it walk and jump. A user animates a bookcase. Two users coordinate to control the motion of a virtual horse.

Other Animation Scenarios We demonstrate some more sophisticated usage scenarios. In Figure 5, two users are simultaneously controlling both pairs of legs of the horse, as well as its head and back. This requires only simple additions to the existing pipeline to accept data from a second skeleton; our deformation method is agnostic to this change. We believe these types of multi-user scenarios will be particularly compelling in gaming or storytelling scenarios.

Depending on the scenario, it does not always make semantic sense to use all the joints of the user's body. We assign names to overlapping subsets of joints such as "left arm", "upper body", etc, which the user can toggle using the speech interface. For example, this allows the user to animate a lamp using only his hip and arm to reenact Pixar's Luxo Jr. (see Figure 5).

Physics-based Interactions Finally, once meshes are possessed by the user, they can easily be incorporated into physics-enabled interactions. For example, Figure 8 and the accompanying video show how one person can possess a friend's avatar and rampage through a physics-enabled world, knocking over towers of boxes, or how a possessed chair or stepladder can be used to play dodgeball. While these examples are simple, the combination of capturing the physical world in the digital domain, bringing it to life, and interacting with other virtual objects in physically plausible and implausible ways makes for playful new gaming scenarios.

These scenarios can be simply realized in a physics simulation just by approximating the mesh as a series of kinematic sphere proxies. We perform sphere packing as follows: repeatedly pick a random vertex (until all vertices are processed) on the mesh and place a sphere centered around it, pruning all neighboring vertices inside the sphere. The sphere radius is set to four times the mesh's mean edge length. This step is done alongside the other steps in the preprocessing phase of the pipeline. For each frame, after deformations are computed on the graph, we move the kinematic spheres accordingly. Using sphere proxies enables efficient modeling of collisions with other dynamic objects in the physical simulation, as shown in Figure 8.

Performance

We evaluated the performance of KinÊtre on a workstation with a six-core Intel Xeon W3690 processor running at 3.46 GHz with 6 GB of RAM and an NVIDIA GeForce GTX 580 GPU. With this setup, the "preprocessing" phase (scanning, segmentation, and sampling) takes ~1 minute for a human-sized object. The sampling part runs in ~10 seconds even on multi-million vertex meshes.

Given that the nearest neighbors in the deformation graph and their weights do not change, they can be precomputed and reused during GPU-based skinning. By keeping the deformation graph small, GPU skinning enables our system to scale to highly detailed geometry. Each time the graph transformations A_j change, we upload them to the GPU and all skinning is performed in a vertex shader.

The Gauss-Newton optimization is the performance bottleneck of our system. Our unoptimized CPU implementation, which performs an explicit sparse-sparse matrix multiply to form the normal equations, consistently takes about 0.0254 ms per iteration per graph node with a full set of skeletal constraints, scaling linearly with graph size. Most of our meshes use a deformation graph with 128 nodes. With a budget of 33 ms per frame, we limit our solver to 10 iterations. In practice, the solver converges in 6 iterations, which permits more complex models with larger graphs (256 nodes).

EXPERIENCING KINÊTRE

KinÊtre is only a prototype and we have yet to formally evaluate it. However, we have carried out a number of informal qualitative sessions where over 50 users of diverse background, age and gender have played with the system. While in no way a user study, we share some notable observations, which will hopefully inform our future designs of the system.

A series of non-human scans and 3D models were controlled by users, and animated in convincing ways; i.e., the meshes deformed but yet maintained their overall structure, and overstretching, collapsing, twisting or other mesh artifacts were minimal. As shown in RGB images in Figure 9 and the accompanying video, interacting with KinÊtre is a very physical activity. Users were literally physically animated the majority of the time. This is of course partly a feature of the body-centric input, but also an indicator that users were engaged and immersed in the experience. Although counterintuitive, users were perhaps the most animated when they were controlling non-human objects. We can speculate that the less anthropomorphic the object, the less overloaded or prescribed the methods of control, making users explore many different types of atypical poses.

KinÊtre produced some unexpected animations when users did not attach well to the mesh initially. In our sessions, we found that providing effective visualization and cues to the user is key. In our current implementation the mesh turns partially transparent when it intersects the skeleton, the attachment points are highlighted, and shadows provide further depth cues (see accompanying video). However, attachments were still problematic for users at times. This could be a fruitful area of research to understand how to better represent the lower dimensional representation and constraints to the user, without over complicating the UI. One example, could be that different body parts are locked in turn, with the virtual camera zooming in to show each region in more detail. Another idea is to combine off center and side views of the 3D model and skeleton to the user during rigging.

The other major source of unexpected deformation behavior was mainly due to the limitations of the Kinect body tracker. This was particularly evident when users tried to get into unexpected postures, such as bending to touch the floor with their hands in order to attach to all four legs of the chair simultaneously (with both their legs and arms), lying down or jumping too high. The Kinect SDK's body tracker did not support joint orientations (although this has changed recently) meaning that turning the head or twisting the forearm are not feasible. Given that our system is designed for control of arbitrary objects, a greater range of sensed poses might be a rich area for future work. One interesting area is to try to remove the requirement for a tracked skeleton altogether: because our method works by adding point constraints to the graph, data could be derived directly from the depth map.

Because our objects come from the real world and are acquired using a depth camera, they have physical units (in meters). Again in our sessions, we found direct 1:1 manipulation can be convenient for human-sized objects. However, in many cases the user did not scale correctly to the mesh (or vice versa). Currently, we scale the mesh according to an estimate of the user's physical height (using the Kinect body tracker). However, this remains an open question that begins to head into the mesh modeling arena [12], where of course natural user interfaces (such as hand-based gestures) can also play a part alongside direct animation. These types of exaggerated gestures could be used to add more extreme deformations to the mesh (for example causing stretching or twisting [17]) by selectively reweighting certain parts of the deformation graph (by varying per-node weights).

CONCLUSIONS

We have presented a novel system for using the human body to bring scanned 3D objects to life. The goal of KinÊtre is to let inexperienced home users quickly create animations and incorporate physical objects into games and other CG applications. Our system is not intended to directly create production-quality animation, but rather bring animation to a new audience. We have demonstrated how our method supports a variety of realistic deformations of human and non-human meshes, including 3D scan data, using a simple interface that leverages the user's body and speech. As demonstrated by our results in this paper and the accompanying video, the entire pipeline from geometry acquisition to rigging and animation, runs at interactive rates and requires no manual preprocessing by an artist.

Beyond enabling new interactive scenarios, our system makes technical contributions in the form of a robust deformation model based on the work by [32]. Our model easily handles a wide range of incomplete scans and affords real-time performance in the presence of numerous constraints coming from multiple users, all running on consumer hardware.

We believe that scanning technologies will become more prevalent in the future, particularly given the ubiquity of depth cameras and advances in vision algorithms. This enables a new breed of CG applications where the consumer is now potentially the CG modeler. The logical next step beyond *acquisition* and integration of captured real world data into consumer CG applications is bringing these virtual representations to life. Systems such as KinÊtre, will enable users to enrich games, home movies and other CG applications, by bringing playful animations of arbitrary scans to a wider consumer audience.

Acknowledgments

We thank our colleagues at Microsoft Research for their insightful comments. We are grateful for Robert Wang and Ilya Baran's assistance with numerical optimization. We also thank Emily Whiting for providing the voiceover, and actors Iason Oikonomidis and Angela Yao.

REFERENCES

1. Ahmed, N. et al. Automatic generation of personalized human avatars from multi-view video. In *Proc. VRST*, ACM (2005).
2. Allen, B., B. Curless, and Z. Popović. Articulated body deformation from range scan data. In *Proc. SIGGRAPH* (2002).
3. Anguelov, D. et al. Scape: shape completion and animation of people. *ACM SIGGRAPH* (2005).
4. Baran, I., and J. Popović. Automatic rigging and animation of 3d characters. *ACM SIGGRAPH* (2007).
5. Barnes, C. et al. Video puppetry. *ACM SIGGRAPH Asia* (2008).
6. Ben-Chen, M., O. Weber, and C. Gotsman. Variational harmonic maps for space deformation. In *Proc. SIGGRAPH*, ACM (2009).
7. Chen, Y., and G. Medioni. Object modelling by registration of multiple range images. *Image Vision Computing* (1992).
8. Curless, B., and M. Levoy. A volumetric method for building complex models from range images. In *Proc. SIGGRAPH*, ACM (1996).
9. Davis, J. et al. A sketching interface for articulated figure animation. In *Proc. Symposium on Computer Animation*, ACM SIGGRAPH/Eurographics (2003).
10. Dontcheva, M., G. Yngve, and Z. Popović. Layered acting for character animation. In *Proc. SIGGRAPH*, ACM (2003).
11. Garau, M. et al. The impact of avatar realism and eye gaze control on perceived quality of communication in a shared immersive virtual environment. In *Proc. CHI*, ACM (2003).
12. Igarashi, T., S. Matsuoka, and H. Tanaka. Teddy: A sketching interface for 3d freeform design. In *Proc. SIGGRAPH*, ACM (1999).
13. Igarashi, T., T. Moscovich, and J. F. Hughes. As-rigid-as-possible shape manipulation. *ACM SIGGRAPH* (2005).
14. Igarashi, T., T. Moscovich, and J. F. Hughes. Spatial keyframing for performance-driven animation. In *Proc. Symposium on Computer Animation*, ACM SIGGRAPH/Eurographics (2005).
15. Izadi, S. et al. Kinectfusion: real-time 3d reconstruction and interaction using a moving depth camera. In *Proc. UIST*, ACM (2011).
16. Jacobson, A. et al. Bounded biharmonic weights for real-time deformation. In *Proc. SIGGRAPH*, ACM (2011).
17. Jacobson, A., and O. Sorkine. Stretchable and twistable bones for skeletal shape deformation. In *Proc. SIGGRAPH Asia*, ACM (2011).
18. Johnson, M. P. et al. Sympathetic interfaces. In *Proc. CHI*, ACM (1999).
19. Joshi, P. et al. Harmonic coordinates for character articulation. In *Proc. SIGGRAPH*, ACM (2007).
20. Ju, T., S. Schaefer, and J. Warren. Mean value coordinates for closed triangular meshes. In *Proc. SIGGRAPH*, ACM (2005).
21. Kipp, M., and Q. Nguyen. Multitouch puppetry. In *Proc. ITS*, ACM (2010).
22. Knep, B. et al. Dinosaur input device. In *Proc. CHI*, ACM (1995).
23. Komatsu, K. Human skin model capable of natural shape variation. *The Visual Computer 3*, 5 (1988).
24. Lehtinen, J. et al. A meshless hierarchical representation for light transport. *ACM SIGGRAPH* (2008).
25. Lipman, Y., D. Levin, and D. Cohen-Or. Green coordinates. *ACM SIGGRAPH* (2008).
26. Magnenat-Thalmann, N., R. Laperrire, and D. Thalmann. Joint-dependent local deformations for hand animation and object grasping. In *Proc. Graphics Interface*, Canadian Info. Proc. Society (1988).
27. Schaefer, S., T. McPhail, and J. Warren. Image deformation using moving least squares. *ACM SIGGRAPH* (2006).
28. Shi, X. et al. Mesh puppetry: cascading optimization of mesh deformation with inverse kinematics. *ACM SIGGRAPH* (2007).
29. Shin, H. J. et al. Computer puppetry: An importance-based approach. *ACM Trans. on Graphics 20*, 2 (2001).
30. Shotton, J. et al. Real-time human pose recognition in parts from single depth images. In *Proc. CVPR*, IEEE (2011).
31. Sturman, D. J. Computer puppetry. *IEEE Computer Graphics & Applications 18*, 1 (1998).
32. Sumner, R. W., J. Schmid, and M. Pauly. Embedded deformation for shape manipulation. *ACM SIGGRAPH* (2007).
33. Thorne, M., D. Burke, and M. van de Panne. Motion doodles: an interface for sketching character motion. *ACM SIGGRAPH* (Aug. 2004).
34. Vlasic, D. et al. Articulated mesh animation from multi-view silhouettes. *ACM SIGGRAPH* (2008).
35. Yamane, K., Y. Ariki, and J. Hodgins. Animating non-humanoid characters with human motion data. In *Proc. SCA*, ACM SIGGRAPH/Eurographics (2010).

Dynamic Tactile Guidance for Visual Search Tasks

Ville Lehtinen[1] **Antti Oulasvirta**[2] **Antti Salovaara**[1] **Petteri Nurmi**[1]

[1] Helsinki Institute for Information Technology HIIT,
Aalto University and University of Helsinki
[2] Max Planck Institute for Informatics

ABSTRACT

Visual search in large real-world scenes is both time-consuming and frustrating, because the search becomes serial when items are visually similar. Tactile guidance techniques can facilitate search by allowing visual attention to focus on a subregion of the scene. We present a technique for *dynamic tactile cueing* that couples hand position with a scene position and uses tactile feedback to guide the hand actively toward the target. We demonstrate substantial improvements in task performance over a baseline of visual search only, when the scene's complexity increases. Analyzing task performance, we demonstrate that the effect of visual complexity can be practically eliminated through improved spatial precision of the guidance.

ACM Classification Keywords

H.5.2: User Interfaces – Input devices and strategies.

Author Keywords

Multimodal interaction; tactile guidance; visual search; target selection; user performance models

INTRODUCTION

Finding an object from a complex real-world scene is a common yet time-consuming and frustrating chore. Consider searching for a specific object in a supermarket, parking lot, control room, warehouse, or library, or wayfinding in a place with a lot of signage. These examples illustrate tasks that share the same general characteristics: i) visual search from a complex scene; ii) selection of an object; iii) and physical action, such as picking up or moving towards the target. People struggle with such tasks both in small scale (e.g., a messy desktop) and in large scale (an urban view).

What makes *search and selection* difficult is that the search becomes *serial* when the *visual complexity* of the scene increases, especially when items are similar to each other [20, 29, 30]. In worst cases, search is so slow that it completely dwarfs the time needed for selection of the object once it has been found. A computer can assist the user in the search task if both the location of the object within the scene and the position of the user with respect to the scene are known.

In many domains, such as the ones listed above, the locations of the objects are monitored for logistics purposes. The user position, on the other hand, can be accomplished by sensor-assisted tracking.

The present paper contributes by examining *personal tactile guidance* and demonstrating how it can significantly speed up performance in a complex search-and-select task with a large scene. *Tactition* as a sensory modality is promising for a number of reasons. Tactile cueing does not conflict with visual engagement with the environment, it has minimal cross-modal interference, and it has been shown to enhance performance in a rapid target-acquisition task with a regular desktop display [19]. An additional benefit is that it provides *direct* guidance towards the target of a sort that is intuitive to interpret and to act on. Traditional spatial representations (e.g., maps) on displays are indirect, in that they require the user to perform cognitive matching between the virtual and the real environment. Another alternative is to use direct augmentation – for example, visual highlighting of objects with a pico-projector [20]. Although these techniques allow searching by bottom-up features, which is quicker, they are not private, they add visual clutter, and have problems in bright conditions and over distance. Spatialized audio can be presented as personal guidance through, for example, headphones. However, it inhibits the use of the modality for other purposes and often interferes with the user's primary task. As the results described in the paper demonstrate, tactile guidance can indeed facilitate visual search, especially when the complexity of the task is sufficiently high.

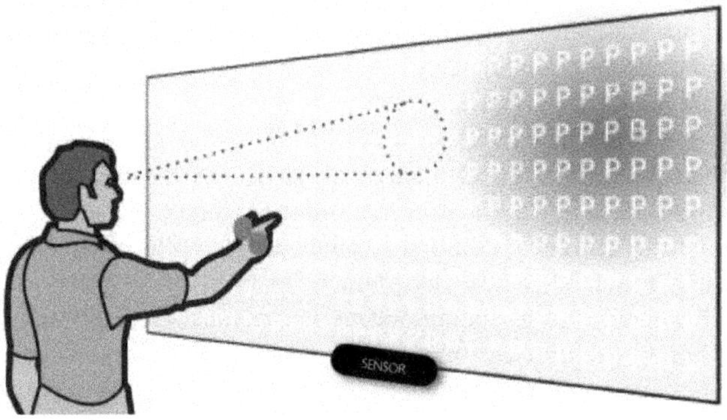

Figure 1: A user searches for an item in a large scene (here, the letter "B" among several "P"s). Vibrotactile stimulus "pulls" the hand toward a subregion (the red-graded area) and visual attention (the blue circle) follows for search of that subregion.

Approach

We build on recent work on *vibrotactile spatial cueing* via the user's hand [8, 14, 18, 19]. Previous work looking at applications of visual search has examined two kinds of cues. *Preview cues* inform about the direction or segment of the display to look at *before* the scene is actually seen [8, 14, 18]. *Dynamic cueing* is based on coupling of hand position with a scene position such that the cue is dynamically updated in view of the distance to and/or direction of the target [19,27]. Analyzing visual search and aimed movements in this task, we argue that dynamic cueing is efficient with large and complex scenes and allows iterative narrowing of the search to a smaller subregion (see Figure 1).

Beyond the realm of visual search, tactile guidance has been used for various applications. For example, a tactile belt has proven itself useful for navigation by indicating two-dimensional directions over a relatively large surface [26]. The chest and the back [25] are other examples of large surfaces where tactile cues can be projected via vibration messages or *patterns* [7, 10]. In the field of motor rehabilitation, cautionary dynamic cues have been proposed for indicating divergence from correct movement trajectories [2].

We expand on current research by applying dynamic tactile guidance to a visual search and acquisition task in a large, complex scene, representative of real-world scenarios. Our implementation is based on a raycasting technique, which projects the position of the user's extended arm with a cursor position in the scene [3, 6, 28]. The position is used in calculation of a feedback pattern that conveys the target's direction and distance. The advantage of such a coupling is that directional cues applied via the raised hand can be interpreted within the spatial frame of reference in which the visual search operates. This is representative of many everyday sensorimotor tasks in which the eye and the hand are in coordinated motion [22] and may, therefore, be natural to learn. We chose "pull" as a guidance metaphor because of direct stimulus–response mapping. Moreover, although the cursor is not *necessary* for the task, seeing the projection of the hand on the scene may reduce the attentional cost of aiming.

There are many options for implementing the tracking of the hand relative to the scene. As we will discuss shortly, the design space of spatial guidance is immense. The contribution of this paper lies in a design of spatial guidance that improves users' performance in visual search tasks and a model of user interaction that informs future efforts. Our solution utilizes a computer vision sensor with depth mapping, mounted in the environment in front of the user [6]. This enables us to accommodate the "non-desktop scenario" wherein the user can move freely in front of a large scene. The scene can contain many more items than a computer display can; in our study, we include a condition with close to a thousand items. Moreover, the user does not need to hold a separate tracking device. The only encumbrance is posed by the actuators, which in our case are woven onto a glove. However, the glove is thin and does not obstruct other manual tasks. Given that the sensors and actuators we utilize are commodity hardware, the proposed system is inexpensive and thus feasible for practitioners.

While this kind of guidance has become feasible, it is unclear whether it can actually facilitate performance. Performance-degrading factors, such as spatial imprecision and latency of hand tracking, as well as ambiguity in interpretation of the actuator signal, could imply that searching the scene with vision only is more efficient than is waiting for the guidance. For critical evaluation of the technique, we present results from an experiment that compares it to search by vision only. We systematically manipulated the visual *complexity* of an item grid projected onto a wall-sized canvas. Our operationalization of search complexity was to manipulate *set size* – that is, the number of visually similar items – which is one of the strongest determinants of search performance [20, 29, 30]. This manipulation enables us to identify the crossover point at which guidance becomes more efficient than opportunistic visual search. To our knowledge, ours is the first study to follow this approach. The data show a strong benefit of tactile guidance as visual complexity increases. We conclude the paper by discussing further development in light of the findings, especially the importance of improving spatial precision and temporal latency of the tracking and actuator components.

ANALYSIS OF TACTILE GUIDANCE IN VISUAL SEARCH

Let us consider the task in Figure 1: a target is in a random location among N equidistant and visually similar items on a plane perpendicular to the forward field of view. The user needs to 1) find the target and 2) select it by pointing. We here model performance with and without guidance. The model parameters will be empirically derived in the section *Model Calibration and Predictions*.

Performance is explained here in terms of two components: *visual search* and *aimed movement*. Aimed movement follows a widely used form of Fitts's law [16]. Visual search is more challenging. The only study we are aware of that has modeled a search-and-select task with tactile feedback obtained poor fit since it was unable to account for visual search [1]. Previous work has used the Hick–Hyman law to model search in menu selection [5]. However, the Hick-Hyman law models *choice reaction*, not visual search, and is not applicable here. Our search model draws from *space-based theories of attention* wherein the focus of attention is assumed to be defined by a spatial region [21].

We now analyze performance in the general case, while the study-specific parameters are presented further on in the paper. Throughout, we assume that pointing and searching start at the center of the scene. Head movements and reaching for the object found are not covered.

The Non-augmented Case

With *no* tactile guidance, task time is a compound of two phases: visual search and target-acquisition:

$$t_{\text{non-augmented}} = t_{\text{search}} + t_{\text{acquisition}} \quad (1)$$

Visual search: We assume that search operates serially. Each fixation of the "spotlight of attention" examines items falling within the foveal area of high spatial acuity (approx. 2°). In visual search, fixation duration is typically 180–275 ms [23]. Unless the target is found, a saccade spanning about three degrees and lasting about 30–40 ms is programmed to a previously unexamined area [23]. This procedure is repeated until the target is found. These properties imply that t_{search} increases linearly as a function of N [20, 29, 30]. Search rate r in visual search experiments with computer displays is, on average, 14.6 ms/item [29], including both inspection and transition time. However, because many factors affect r, such as the similarity of items and their constellation in the search array [23], r must be derived for each individual case. Given that the estimated number of items that must be scanned is $N / 2$, our model becomes

$$t_{search} = r\,N / 2. \tag{2}$$

Target-acquisition: At this point, the target has been located and the cursor, controlled in our case by the computer vision loop, needs to be moved on top of it. $t_{acquisition}$ is here assumed to follow Fitts's law and therefore depends on distance to target (D) and width of target (W) [16] and on the two empirical parameters a and b. We collapse b and the controller-specific *lag* [17] into b_{cursor}, obtaining

$$t_{acquisition} = a + b_{cursor} \log_2(D / W + 1). \tag{3}$$

With these assumptions, the full model for this case is:

$$t_{non\text{-}augmented} = r\,N / 2 + a + b_{cursor} \log_2(D / W + 1). \tag{4}$$

Augmentation with Dynamic Tactile Guidance

Task performance with dynamic tactile guidance consists of a *cascade of hand–eye coordinations*: the hand directs the gaze iteratively toward a region with fewer items (For an *eye*–hand cascade interaction technique, see [31]). Our model, therefore, has three phases:

$$t_{guided} = t_{approach} + t_{search} + t_{acquisition}\,. \tag{5}$$

Approach: Because mentally projecting vibrotactile signals from the hand to the visual field is hard, the guidance signal cannot pinpoint the target; instead, the user infers it as a subregion contained within the scene (e.g., see Figure 1). As the hand approaches this subregion, it may at any time update the inference and change its path. This iteratively corrected aimed movement is given by Fitts's law, but the parameters are different from those in Equation (3): instead of W, width is defined by the width of the subregion S from the angle of approach. With dynamic cueing, S is jointly determined by the accuracy of hand tracking and the subjective ambiguity of the guidance signal. Parameter b hereof is shaped by the additional latency of the tactile feedback loop ($b_{guidance}$). We assume that the hand is *conservative* in the approach phase and does not move further toward the target than half the width of S from the angle of approach. This assumption is plausible, because users would like to prevent occlusion of the subregion by the hand. With this assumption, the model of approach becomes

$$t_{approach} = a + b_{guidance} \log_2((D - S / 2) / S + 1)$$

$$= a + b_{guidance} \log_2(D / S + 0.5). \tag{6}$$

Visual search: As the tactile feedback suggests for the subregion, gaze shifts to this region and starts to search within it. Rate of search r should be the same as in the non-augmented case. Thus performance follows Equation (2) but with N_S targets. The size of the subregion, the density of targets, and the geometry of the setup jointly define N_S.

Target-acquisition: After visual location of the target within the subregion, the cursor needs to be moved on top of it, to select it. This phase, wherein tactile guidance has become irrelevant, is addressed by Equation (3). However, the movement distance is shorter, because the starting position has moved closer to the target.

Given these considerations, we get:

$$\begin{aligned} t_{guided} = {} & a + b_{guidance} \log_2(D / S + 0.5) + \\ & r\,N_S / 2 + \\ & b_{cursor} \log_2(S / 2 / W + 1). \end{aligned} \tag{7}$$

The insight afforded by this model is that $b_{guidance}$ and S, the two parameters determined by tactile guidance, have differential contributions to performance. An increase in the value of the $b_{guidance}$ parameter makes *approach* faster but contributes mainly when N is small. Increasing S reduces the number of items to be searched, which helps when N is large. Because *static* cues hint at a rougher direction or segment of the target (i.e., larger S), we suspect that dynamic guidance has more potential as a technique. Another observation is that aimed movement to the target consists of *two* phases (interrupted by visual search), each with unique control loop characteristics (for a similar two-phase model of target acquisition, see [24]).

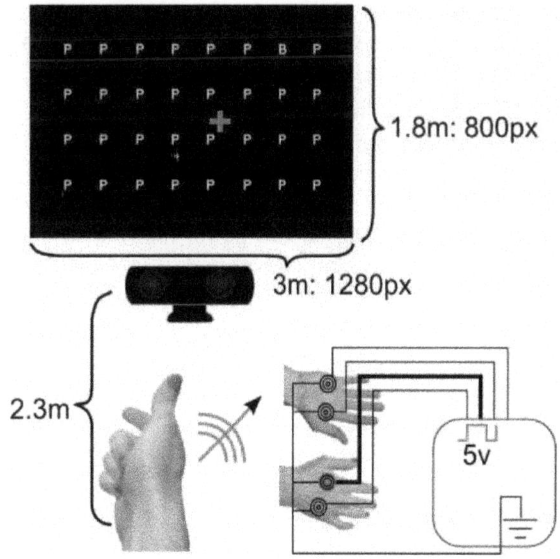

Figure 2: System overview. *Left*: Tracking the pointing arm with a user-facing computer vision sensor and projecting it as a cursor (+) on a wall-sized canvas. *Right*: Positioning of four vibrotactile actuators on the palmar and dorsal aspects of the hand. The radial actuator is active to direct the hand from the cursor position toward the upper right.

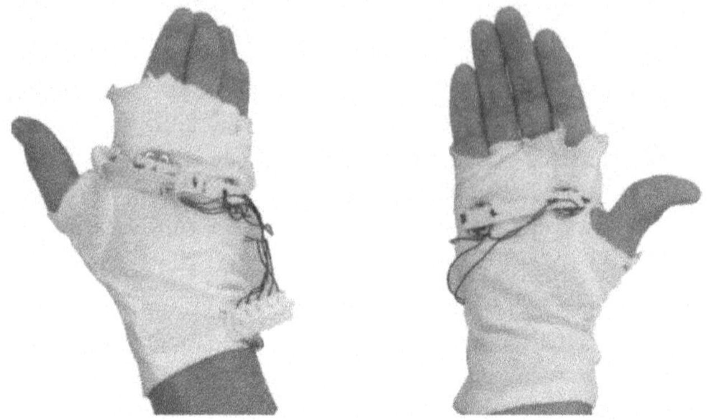

Figure 3: The actuator glove from the dorsal (left) and palmar (right) viewpoints.

DESIGN AND IMPLEMENTATION OF A TECHNIQUE

Figure 2 outlines our setup. The main design challenge was to produce a "pull" sensation that directs the hand and the gaze to the same subregion. *Pull* feedback has been shown to be more effective than *push* in comparable tasks [9]. The tactile display consists of four five-volt LilyPad-mounted vibration boards, an Arduino Uno physical computing platform, and wiring and connectors. The vibration motors are carefully sewn onto a thin-fabric glove, and a rubber band is applied to ensure stability during movement (see Figure 3). For tracking of the arm projection, we employ a user-facing Kinect motion-sensing device mounted on a wall in front of the user. The known constraints of this sensor for pointing with the hand are minimized by considering pointing with *the handshake pose* – that is, thumb upward, palm open, and fingers adducted. We observed that tracking performance is best when wrist, elbow, and shoulder form a straight line. Users should keep the elbow and wrist joints static, controlling pointing with the shoulder only (for a study of this versus other pointing techniques, see [11]).

Dynamic Spatial Cueing

For our vibrotactile spatial cueing, we proceed from dynamic tactile guidance techniques seen in motor rehabilitation [2, 12, 13]. The visual search task, however, is different, in that performance in reaching an end point, rather than correctness of movement trajectories, is emphasized. Quickly overshooting the target in our pointing task does not necessarily hamper performance and may even improve it, thanks to increased information from more data points.

In order to present rapidly recognizable tactile cues, we consider well-known parameters of tactile-cue design: frequency, amplitude, duration, rhythm, and location [4]. *Location* maps naturally to target direction. In the glove, both the dorsal and the palmar side of the hand have two actuators, equidistant from the medial line. With these, we cover the four cardinal directions (up, down, left, right) and the four interstices. To ensure discrimination of cardinal versus diagonal direction, we use distinct *duration* and *rhythm* parameters (for alternative designs, see [4,7,19]). The short diagonal pulses (80 ms on, 40 ms off) are "taps," whereas the cardinal-direction pulses (250 ms on over two adjacent motors, 120 ms off) are longer patterns (see Figure 4). Direction is computed for every frame relative to the cursor shown on the display. *Amplitude* is used as a cue of distance. Amplitude decreases linearly as a function of distance to the target. A varies between A_{min} (a barely noticeable 40% of the maximum vibration amplitude) and A_{max} (the maximum attainable vibration; nominal 0.8 G at 200 Hz).

The calculations of the direction and distance, and the production of the vibration, were implemented as follows:

```
Algorithm: tactile guidance computation
Input: direction (eight 45° blocks), distance from cursor to target
Output: vibration at amplitude A

1.  WHILE NOT onTarget() DO
      /* Update distanceForA_max (amplitude scale) */
2.    IF distance > SceneHeight /2 THEN
3.        distanceForA_max = SceneHeight/2
4.    ELSE IF distance > distanceForA_max THEN
5.        distanceForA_max = distance
6.    ELSE IF direction has changed THEN
7.        distanceForA_max = 0.8 distanceForA_max
      /* Scale the amplitude according to distance to target */
8.    A = (distance / distanceForA_max) (A_max – A_min) + A_min
      /* Vibrate */
9.    IF direction is diagonal THEN
10.       Vibrate at this direction for 80 ms with A
11.       Silence for 40 ms
12.   ELSE /* Main */
13.       Vibrate at 1st diagonal direction for 100 ms with A
14.       Vibrate at both diagonal directions for 50 ms with A
15.       Vibrate at 2nd diagonal direction for 100 ms with A
16.       Silence for 120 ms
17. REPEAT
```

During each iteration, amplitude is updated on the basis of distance and direction (lines 2–8). Amplitude decreases linearly until a change in direction is needed (line 8). However, to react to movement errors, we maintain an amplitude scale, denoted as *distanceForA*$_{max}$, which stores the distance corresponding to the maximum A that should be given for a particular direction. In the case of a wrong direction, this ensures that the maximum A remains the same, thus preventing misinterpretation of the feedback. When the direction indicated needs to be changed – for example, from "up" to "up right" – the amplitude scale is increased to highlight the change in signal (line 7). Finally, once the correct amplitude has been determined, the appropriate tactile feedback pattern is applied (lines 9–16). If the target direction is one of the diagonals, the feedback is simply applied with the corresponding actuator (line 10). Otherwise, the feedback pattern consists of a pseudo-integrated pulse wherein one of the diagonals is triggered, after which the two are triggered simultaneously, before, finally, the second diagonal is triggered (lines 13–16) (see Figure 4). The first and second diagonals were determined by counting clockwise from the "up" cardinal direction. This algorithm iterates until the cursor has been moved within the effective selection radius (60 px, or 1.41°, in our study). When the cursor is within the selection range, we give a strong feedback pulse by driving all motors at maximum. This enables the user to perceive

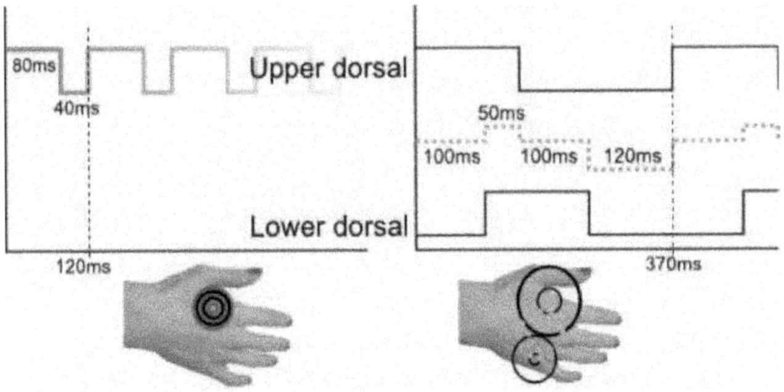

Figure 4: *Left*: The vibration pattern for guidance toward the upper right corner consists of a single active motor producing brief "tapping" pulses. *Right*: Vibration for guidance toward the right consists of a pseudo-integrated signal from both dorsal actuators.

the target even when the hand overshoots it. An example of guidance updating is given in Figure 5.

Hand Tracking and Cursor Updating

The Kinect tracking sensor is placed at a distance of 230 cm from the user. We found this distance to be optimal for precision. A red crosshair was shown on a screen according to the trajectory between the user's elbow and hand joints. These are inferred by the skeletal tracking algorithm of the OpenNI and PrimeSense NITE APIs. For an optimal match between the user's pointing and the cursor displayed, the algorithm must be calibrated for every user by means of the corners of a displayed grid. Some filtering is applied to the signal to reduce jitter further. In addition to tracking arm position, the setup measured *movement speed.* A *selection event* was triggered whenever the speed remained below a designated threshold for longer than 260 ms.

EXPERIMENT

An experiment was conducted wherein tactile guidance was compared to a baseline with no tactile guidance. Participants had to point at a target (the letter "B") on a wall-sized matrix of "P"s (see Figure 2) as quickly as possible. Importantly, *set size* was varied in eight steps. This paradigm is commonly used in studies of visual search. Although it lacks the richness of real scenes, it has been argued to capture the essence of *selective* attention in real-world tasks [30]. Moreover, manipulation of complexity is necessary if one is to derive the technique-specific parameters of temporal latency and spatial precision.

Participants

Twelve users, nine male and three female, were recruited. All participants reported themselves as being in fit physical and mental condition. None of the participants had significant previous experience in using Kinect or tactile displays.

Experiment Design

The study follows a 2 x 8 experimental design with *Feedback* (tactile guidance vs. visual only) and *Set size* (6, 15, 40, 84, 170, 322, 540, 874) as the independent variables. Each participant performed 100 trials with each of the two feedback conditions, such that the feedback condition was changed after every 50 tasks. Half of the participants started these blocks with one and the rest with the other feedback condition. The number of distractors was chosen randomly for each trial. The glove was worn in all conditions.

Physical Setup and Stimuli

The spatial dimensions of the test setup are given in Figure 2 and in the description of the system above. With a distance of 230 cm from the display, the viewing angle was 55°. Users were sitting on a bench with eye level at roughly half a meter above the bottom of the display. The projector was placed behind and above the participant, to minimize occlusion of the scene. The room was quiet and dimly lit.

The stimuli were white capital letters ("B" and "P") presented on a black background on a 1280 x 800 px canvas. The letter grid was center-aligned. The ratio of letters in the x to the y dimension ranged from 1.5 to 1.8 degrees. We scaled the effective canvas size for each set-size condition so as to keep the average distance-to-target within a narrow range (258–381 px from smallest to largest N). The effective area of the canvas ranged from 0.3 degrees, in the $N = 6$ condition, to 0.9, in $N = 874$.

Procedure

Training: To ensure learning of the novel technique, three training steps were taken. First, participants learned inferring signal directions by pointing with eyes closed. When sufficiently correct inference was achieved, the pointing algorithm was calibrated to the participant. Participants then practiced with eyes open. Third, they practiced with at least 10 trials with tactile guidance; they had to point at a given target, starting movement at the center of the display. The experiment was started only after performance in this stage had stabilized. No instructions were given for *visual* search.

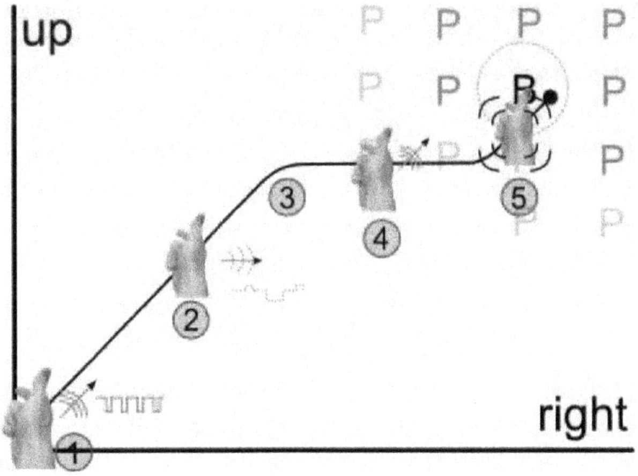

Figure 5: An example scenario: 1) The direction for first approach is provided by the upper dorsal motor with a short pulse, 2) changing to integrated vibration indicating movement right. 3) The user reacts to the feedback and changes movement direction. 4) The direction indicated changes again, soon after which the user reacts. 5) The cursor enters the target's selection range. At this point, signal amplitude has decreased to 10% from that in step 1 before strong feedback from all actuators turns on. Stopping for 260 ms selects the target.

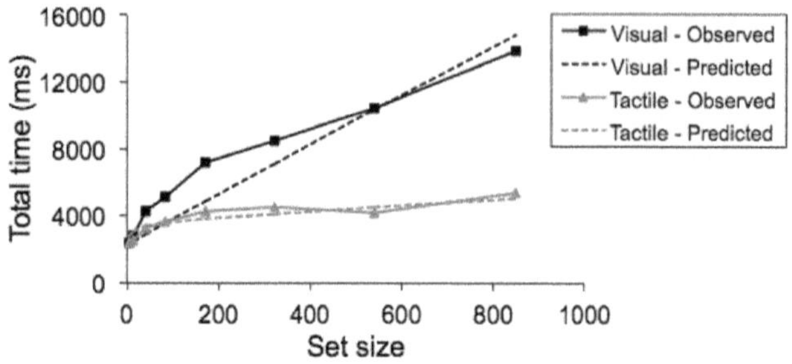

Figure 6: Effects of visual complexity (set size) on total time-in-task. Notice how the slopes differ for the visual-only vs. tactile guidance conditions.

Experimental trials: The experimental task followed the same protocol as the final practice task, with the exception that N items were presented. After a successful selection, the participant had to lower his or her hand for five seconds before starting the new trial at the center of the screen. Participants could rest between trials, and between the 50-trial blocks, they were instructed to relax for a longer time.

RESULTS

Data of three trials were removed from consideration (one trial took over two minutes, and two included an unexpected malfunction in tracking), yielding a dataset of 2,397 trials. All trials ended with a successful selection of the target.

A *repeated-measures analysis of variance* (RM-ANOVA) shows that tactile feedback increased performance, not universally but in conditions where N was large. There were significant effects for *Feedback* [$F(1,8) = 30.73$, $p = 0.001$], *Set size* [$F(7,56) = 27.99$, $p < 0.001$], and their interaction [$F(7,56) = 15.769$, $p < 0.001$]. *Post hoc* paired-samples *t*-tests using the Bonferroni correction showed that performance improvement in the tactile guidance condition was significant for the $N = 40$ condition and for $N \geq 170$. Figure 6 shows the main trends.

Order effects: Any order effects were made visible through division of the trials into four equally sized stages. The RM-ANOVA was repeated with *Stage* as an added independent variable. The analysis showed neither main nor interaction effect for this variable. We conclude that the training procedure sufficed for eliminating learning and order effects.

Direction effects: We examined whether targets in cardinal directions would differ from those in diagonal directions. This was possible because the approach cues differed (see Figure 4). To disentangle the effect of distance, we consider only targets that fit within a circle that touches the top and bottom boundaries of the screen, centered on the screen's middle point. An RM-ANOVA with *Target direction* (cardinal vs. diagonal) as a third independent variable showed an effect of direction but only in the tactile guidance condition [$F(1,8) = 5.77$, $p = .04$]. Targets in diagonal directions were reached about 300 ms *more slowly* than those in cardinal directions. However, this effect is negligible in the context of total task times, and we do not pursue further analysis.

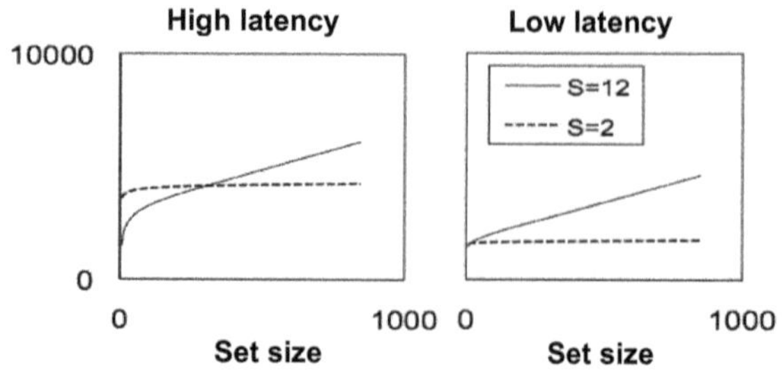

Figure 7: Model's prediction: High spatial precision (here: $S = 2$) will eliminate the set-size effect regardless of the latency of guidance (left vs. right). Y-axis: total time in task (ms).

User assessment: On a Likert scale (range of 1–5, with 5 indicating "best"), the average rating for the claim "The tactile glove helped me significantly in the task" was 4.0.

Self-reporting of strategy: Subjects' retrospective reports confirm the hypothesis that the effect of tactile guidance lies in focusing of visual attention on a subregion. When asked about their search strategies, all subjects mentioned first focusing on the tactile signal and then "*jumping*" to the indicated area with the gaze. Subjects were not convinced that the guidance offers value beyond this phase.

MODEL CALIBRATION AND PREDICTIONS

For learning about the critical factors affecting performance, our interest lies in two factors:

- S, an indicator of *effective spatial precision*
- $b_{guidance}$, an indicator of *effective temporal latency*.

Here, interpreting $b_{guidance}$ as an index of *temporal* latency is justified, because there were no misses in the data and the parameter's value is dictated by differences in movement time. Our approach to deriving the two is this: In the two extreme set-size conditions, $N = 6$ and $N = 874$, motor performance and visual search dominate performance and we use them to approximate the parameters $t_{acquisition}$ and t_{search}, respectively. S and $b_{guidance}$ can be derived when these parameters are known. In all calculations, we use angles (degrees), and D and W are determined by the stimuli and the parameters of the physical setup given in *Experiment*.

In **Step 1**, we derive a and b_{cursor} in Equation (3) from the $N = 6$ condition. In this "easy" condition, task time is dominated by motor performance and we assume that visual search time is close to zero, yielding $a = 995$ and $b_{cursor} = 507$.

In **Step 2**, we derive r in Equation (4) from the $N = 874$ condition in the non-augmented condition, subtracting out the expected value of $t_{acquisition}$ therein by using the parameters a and b_{cursor} found in Step 1. The r obtained is 29.2 ms/item, which is slower but within the regular range of rs [29].

In the final **Step 3**, we use data from the guidance condition to derive the parameters S and $b_{guidance}$ in Equation (6). We make the simplifying assumption that the non-informational parameter a in Equation (6) is equal to that in Equation (4).

Because small changes in a have almost no influence on total time, this assumption does not affect the thrust of the prediction. For simplicity, we consider S to be circular in shape and centered on the target. The parameters $b_{guidance}$ and S are now estimated by fitting to data gained via varying of N. We obtain $S = 8$ and $b_{guidance} = 1120$. Knowing the dimensions of the physical setup and stimuli, we can now calculate N_s. For example, when $N = 874$, 89 items fit within the subregion defined by the obtained S.

We get the following models as the outcome:

$$t_{non\text{-}augmented} = 29.2*N / 2 + 995 + 507 * \log_2(D / 1.41 + 1) \quad (8)$$

$$t_{guided} = 995 + 1120 * \log_2(D / 8 + 0.5) + 29.2 * N_S / 2 + 507 * \log_2(8 / 2 / 1.41 + 1). \quad (9)$$

Model-based predictions are shown in Figure 6 against observations. The models, Equations (8) and (9), yield good fits with observations: R^2 is .95 and .91, respectively. As Figure 6 shows, a slight issue in both models is an additive component in the medium band of N. Because it is similar in the two conditions, we suspect that it is due to *strategic changes* in visual search. Indeed, two strategies were reported by users: Some started scanning the scene by row (or block of rows) or column, or by spiraling from center to the borders, or even by sector. Others consciously adapted either the size of area or their search speed, first taking a quick, general glance at the scene and then decreasing the scope and speed until the target was found. Two subjects reported that they did not consciously utilize any strategy but, instead, just randomly browsed the scene.

SUMMARY AND OUTLOOK

We have presented a novel dynamic cueing technique for supporting visual search in complex two-dimensional scenes. The design space of spatial guidance is vast, and the present paper's contribution lies in identifying a use for 3D dynamic guidance, illustrating how to design it in a way that actually improves user performance, and in modeling the HCI of this task to inform future efforts.

Our technique combines raycasting that projects the user's hand position onto a scene with a vibrotactile glove that uses four actuators to produce a directional pulling sensation. When the arm is raised, it and the projected cursor operate within the same spatial frame of reference as the visual search, facilitating their mutual coordination in the search task. Data from the controlled comparative experiment show a statistically significant benefit in performance in a search-and-select task when set size (N) is increased. In the "hardest" conditions, with $N = 874$, tactile guidance resulted in performance over twice as fast as that in the absence of guidance. This benefit is large enough to warrant consideration of real-world applications.

In the study, the positive effect appeared first for $N = 40$, and reliably only after $N \geq 170$. While few real-world settings have this many items and thus warrant installation of our system, the analysis of task performance suggests that improvements in latency and spatial resolution can virtually remove the set-size effect and render the task as one of aimed movement. The model from Equation (9) suggests directions for improving guidance: The present implementation suffers from lag, which is manifested as the informational factor $b_{guidance}$ of 1120 ms/bit. This lag is likely to be caused by the inclusion of the depth sensor and computer vision in the loop, as well as by the update rate of the tactile display. Moreover, the large S we found suggests that effective spatial resolution was low. In other words, the participants perceived the feedback to refer to a relatively large area. Equation (9) suggests that the two parameters differentially improve performance (see Figure 7): Decreasing latency alone shifts the intercept down but does not eliminate the set-size effect – unless the effective spatial precision improves as well. The effective spatial resolution can be improved through the design of more distinctive feedback patterns and via improved tracking.

The positive result invites research on alternative technical solutions. While our current system setup relies on a projector and a depth sensor, other types of sensor setups could be considered. For example, the tracking of the user's hand could be implemented by means of a combination of accelerometer and gyroscopes, and the cursor projection could be based on pico-projectors, or eliminated altogether once the spatial ambiguity of the techniques has been sufficiently reduced. A solution of this kind would enable our technique not only to be personalized but to function in different environments without the need for infrastructural support.

ACKNOWLEDGEMENTS

This work was supported in part by the Finnish Funding Agency for Technology and Innovation (Tekes), under the project Adaptive Interfaces for Consumer Applications (AICA). Antti Oulasvirta was supported by the Max Planck Center for Visual Computing and Communication (MPC-VCC).

REFERENCES

1. Ahmaniemi, T. T., & Lantz, V. Augmented reality target finding based on tactile cues. In *Proc. ICMI-MLMI '09*, ACM Press (2009).
2. Bark, K., Khanna, P., Irwin, R., Kapur, P., Jax, S. A., Buxbaum, L. J., & Kuchenbecker, K. J. Lessons in using vibrotactile feedback to guide fast arm motions. In *Proc. IEEE World Haptics Conference* (2011), pp. 261–266.
3. Bolt, R. "Put-that-there": Voice and gesture at the graphics interface. *ACM SIGGRAPH Computer Graphics* 14, ACM (1980), pp. 262–270.
4. Brewster, S. A. & Brown, L. M. Tactons: Structured tactile messages for non-visual information display. In *Proc. Australasian User Interface Conference* (2004), pp. 18–22.
5. Cockburn, A., Gutwin, C., & Greenberg, S. A predictive model of menu performance. In *Proc. CHI '07*, ACM Press (2007), pp. 627–636.
6. Gehring, S., Löchtefeld, M., Daiber, F., Böhmer, M., & Krüger, A. Using intelligent natural user interfaces to

support sales conversations. In *Proc. IUI '12*, ACM Press (2012), pp. 97–100.

7. Gunther, E., Davenport, G., & O'Modhrain, S. Cutaneous grooves: Composing for the sense of touch. In *Proc. Conference on New Instruments for Musical Expression* (2002), pp. 1–6.
8. Ho, C., Tan, H. Z., & Spence, C. The differential effect of vibrotactile and auditory cues on visual spatial attention. *Ergonomics* 49 (2006), pp. 724–738.
9. Jansen, C., Oving, A., & van Veen, H.-J. Vibrotactile movement initiation. In *Proc. EuroHaptics* (2004), pp. 110–117.
10. Jansson, G. Tactile guidance of movement. *International Journal of Neuroscience* 19 (1983), pp. 37–46.
11. Jota, R., Nacenta, M. A., Jorge, J. A., Carpendale, S., & Greenberg, S. A comparison of ray pointing techniques for very large displays. In *Proc. GI '10* (2010), pp. 269–276.
12. Kapur, P., Jensen, M., Buxbaum, L. J., Jax, S. A., & Kuchenbecker, K. J. Spatially distributed tactile feedback for kinesthetic motion guidance. In *Proc. IEEE Haptics Symposium* (2010), pp. 519–526.
13. Lieberman, J. & Breazeal, C. TIKL: Development of a wearable vibrotactile feedback suit for improved human motor learning. *IEEE Transactions on Robotics* 23:5 (2007), pp. 919–926.
14. Lindeman, R. W., Yanagida, Y., Sibert, J. L., & Lavine, R. Effective vibrotactile cueing in a visual search task. In *Proc. INTERACT* (2003).
15. Löchtefeld, M., Gehring, S., Schöning, J., & Krüger, A. ShelfTorchlight: Augmenting a shelf using a camera projector unit. In *Adj. Proc. PERVASIVE, Workshop on Personal Projection UBIPROJECTION*, Springer Lecture Notes in Computer Science (2010).
16. MacKenzie, I. & Buxton, W. Extending Fitts' law to two-dimensional tasks. In *Proc. CHI '92*, ACM Press (1992), pp. 219–226.
17. MacKenzie, I. & Ware, C. Lag as a determinant of human performance in interactive systems. In *Proc. INTERACT 1993*, ACM (1993), pp. 488–493.
18. Ngo, M. K. & Spence, C. Auditory, tactile, and multisensory cues facilitate search for dynamic visual stimuli. *Attention, Perception & Psychophysics* 72 (2010), pp. 1654–1665.
19. Oron-Gilad, T., Downs, J. L., Gilson, R. D., & Hancock, P. A. Vibrotactile guidance cues for target acquisition. *IEEE Transactions on Systems, Man, and Cybernetics: Part C, Applications and Reviews* 27:5 (2007), pp. 993–1004.
20. Palmer, J. Attention in visual search: Distinguishing four causes of a set-size effect. *Current Directions in Psychological Science* 4:4 (1995), pp. 118–123.
21. Palmer, S. *Vision Science: Photons to Phenomenology*, vol. 1. Cambridge, MA: MIT Press (1999).
22. Pelz, J., Hayhoe, M., & Loeber, R. The coordination of eye, head, and hand movements in a natural task. *Experimental Brain Research* 139:3 (2001), pp. 266–277.
23. Rayner, K. Understanding eye movements in reading. *Scientific Studies of Reading* 1:4 (1997), pp. 317–339.
24. Rohs, M. & Oulasvirta, A. Target acquisition with camera phones when used as magic lenses. In *Proc. CHI '08*, ACM Press (2008), pp. 1409–1418.
25. Tan, H. Z., Lu, I., & Pentland, A. The chair as a novel haptic user interface. In *Proc. Workshop on Perceptual User Interfaces* (1997), pp. 56–57.
26. Van Erp, J. B. F., Van Veen, H. A. H. C., Jansen, C., & Dobbins, T. Waypoint navigation with a vibrotactile waist belt. *ACM Transactions on Applied Perception* 2:2 (2005), pp. 106–117.
27. Van Erp, J. & Verschoor, M. H. Cross-modal visual and vibrotactile tracking. *Applied Ergonomics* 35:2 (2004), pp. 105–112.
28. Vogel, D., & Balakrishnan, R. Distant freehand pointing and clicking on very large, high resolution displays. In *Proc. UIST '05*, ACM Press (2005), pp. 33–42.
29. Wolfe, J. M. What can 1 million trials tell us about visual search? *Psychological Science* 9:1 (1998), pp. 33–39.
30. Wolfe, J. M., Võ, M. L. H., Evans, K. K., & Greene, M. R. Visual search in scenes involves selective and nonselective pathways. *Trends in Cognitive Sciences* (2011).
31. Zhai, S., Morimoto, C., & Ihde, S. Manual and gaze input cascaded (magic) pointing. In *Proc. CHI '99*, ACM Press (1999), pp. 246–253.

Designing for Low-Latency Direct-Touch Input

Albert Ng[1], Julian Lepinski[2], Daniel Wigdor[2], Steven Sanders[3], Paul Dietz[1]

[1]Microsoft Applied Sciences Group
Redmond, WA, USA

[2]Dept. of Computer Science
University of Toronto
Toronto, Canada

[3]Sanders Capital
New York, NY, USA

{v-albeng | pdietz}@microsoft.com, {lepinski | dwigdor}@dgp.toronto.edu, steven.sanders@sanderscapital.com

ABSTRACT

Software designed for direct-touch interfaces often utilize a metaphor of direct physical manipulation of pseudo "real-world" objects. However, current touch systems typically take 50-200ms to update the display in response to a physical touch action. Utilizing a high performance touch demonstrator, subjects were able to experience touch latencies ranging from current levels down to about 1ms. Our tests show that users greatly prefer lower latencies, and noticeable improvement continued well below 10ms. This level of performance is difficult to achieve in commercial computing systems using current technologies. As an alternative, we propose a hybrid system that provides low-fidelity visual feedback immediately, followed by high-fidelity visuals at standard levels of latency.

ACM Classification: H.5.2 [Information interfaces and presentation]: User Interfaces. - Graphical user interfaces.

General terms: Design, Human Factors

Keywords: touch input, multi-touch, user input, latency

INTRODUCTION

Although long popular in automated teller machines and other kiosk applications, the last decade has seen the mass adoption of direct-touch interfaces. Earlier systems typically utilized soft buttons which the user pressed to interact with the system – hence the popularity of research dedicated to improving the precision of selection using a direct-touch device, beginning with [22]. It wasn't until the emergence of multitouch that swiping, dragging, and pinching became standard interface elements. These operations are typically used in commercial offerings to mimic the manipulation of actual physical objects, leveraging the principles of a "reality-based interface" to render their use more simple for novice users [12].

Unfortunately, the illusion of direct physical manipulation is limited by a number of factors. Among these is the inherent delay between finger movement and the updating of the display. Direct-touch systems are particularly sensitive to this latency, as the unification of input and output makes latency more noticeable than with indirect touch.

UIST '12, October 7–10, 2012, Cambridge, Massachusetts, USA.

Using high-speed cameras, we informally tested a wide variety of iOS, Android, Windows, and Windows Phone devices doing basic OS navigation tasks, and found that this latency typically ranges between 50-200ms in current commercial devices. Past work has found that end users often describe devices with lower latency as feeling more "responsive" [2]. Utilizing a 1ms-latency touch input device, we expanded on this work by conducting a study designed to measure human perception of drag latency in touch. We found that participants could reliably perceive touchscreen latency as low as 5-10ms. Thus, an order of magnitude improvement is required over current commercial offerings before users may begin to perceive response to touch as instantaneous.

Latency in a direct-touch device has many sources, but usually has three main components: 1) the physical sensor that captures touch events; 2) the software that processes touch events and generates output for the display; 3) the display itself. Reducing system latency in a direct-touch system requires addressing latency issues in all three of these components, and is thus a significant challenge. We have constructed a direct-touch device that achieves 1ms of latency by combining a low-latency touch sensor and projector with a dedicated processing system. In order to achieve extremely low latency, our system replaces traditional operating system software and computing hardware with a dedicated, custom-programmed.

Figure 1: An "Accelerated Touch" visualization: the user receives both near-instantaneous visual feedback at low-fidelity (in red), as well as high-fidelity feedback with current-generation latency.

As we will discuss, low latency input and output devices are feasible in the relatively short term. However, overcoming latency due to software execution, while maintaining the convenience of a multi-threaded OS, user interface toolkit, and plethora of other utilities developers rely on, is a significantly greater challenge.

In order to address this, we propose a system we have termed Accelerated Touch, shown in Figure 1. In an Accelerated Touch system, we separate some of the basic visual responses to touch from the broader application logic. The result is a system with a nimble touch processor, capable of providing near-instantaneous visual feedback on user interaction, with a higher-fidelity visual layer rendered at more traditional levels of latency. This is shown in Figure 1, with the Accelerated Touch visualizations shown in red.

The contributions of this paper are fivefold. First, we describe the architectural problems in current systems with respect to latency, and describe possible avenues to reduce them. Next, we introduce our prototype device, which is capable of crude visual feedback at extremely low latency. Third, we present the results of a user study, which demonstrate that the lower latencies made possible by our prototype are perceptible to users, and therefore valuable. Fourth, we present a set of designs for a set of UI controls with bifurcated visual responses between low and high latency, in which users may receive immediate feedback appropriate to context, followed by a more complete response guided by application logic. Finally, we describe options in software architecture to achieve the bifurcated feedback we have presented. First, we present a review of relevant related work.

RELATED WORK

Three areas of related work are illuminating. First, we discuss the impact of latency on user interfaces, with a focus on the oft-quoted "100ms" number. Next, we describe methods by which *perceived* latency (as at least somewhat distinct from actual latency) have been addressed. Finally, we describe various technologies used for touch input.

Impact of Latency on UI

The effects of latency on direct-manipulation based interaction have not been extensively studied. On latency and delay in general, early work by Card, Mackinlay and Robertson [4] is frequently cited, in which the authors claim that that the perception of animation requires a refresh rate no lower than 10Hz. This claim is based on Card, Moran and Newell's [5] work in estimating the cycle time of what they term to be the Perceptual Processor and is itself based on earlier work on visual perception [8, 11]. These figures appear to be frequently used to develop a 100ms rule, by which delays greater than 100ms are considered to be unacceptable [16].

An early paper by Miller [18] estimates that 100ms delay is acceptable when using a light-pen to make slow, deliberate strokes, however this figure is presented without further reference and without explanation of how this value was determined. Miller does not present estimates of acceptable latency for faster light-pen strokes, nor any definition of 'acceptable'.

More recently, Anderson, Doherty, and Ganapathy [2] conducted a study to determine qualitative responses to touchscreen latency during various tasks, such as web browsing, with the aim of determining latencies users find to be "acceptable". The authors found that above a value of 580ms, users found the latency unacceptable, but noted that their experimental tasks were relatively brief (specifically: zooming, panning, and page-turning). We believe that these results are subjective, and are highly influenced by user expectations based on experience with current devices. As technology increases performance, user expectations will rise, along with clear improvement. Thus, we wished to move beyond what users currently find 'acceptable', and instead find the level of latency at which further improvement is no longer perceptible.

A series of works by Pavlovych and colleagues has examined the role of latency on other types of input devices including the mouse [19,20,21]. We build on this work by examining its role in direct-touch input.

Reducing perceived latency

Significant efforts are expended in software and hardware engineering to reduce the latency of a given input device or system. A complete survey of best practices in this field is beyond the scope of this paper, though we will describe some of these in section 3. Also relevant is work in user interface design intended to reduce *perceived* latency – that is, delays perceived by the user, rather than actual delays. Seow [27] argues that the goal of an engineer (be it software or hardware) should be to reduce the perceived latency of a system, which may only be partially a function of the actual latency of that system. Indeed, researchers have found that adding differentiated visual responses to touch input makes a system appear to have improved performance, even when the actual performance is unchanged (e.g.: [31]). While we value this approach, the focus of our efforts has been in understanding the value of reducing *actual* latency.

Touch Input Technologies

Direct touch input can be achieved using a variety of technologies, including resistive [22, 23], direct illumination [30], frustrated total-internal reflection [9], diffuse illumination [24], projective capacitive [3], and capacitive coupling [7]. One property these technologies share is that they contribute to the latency between user action and the system's response. The scale of this contribution varies across technology and implementation. Notable, however, is that in none of the papers cited above is there a measurement of the latency of the device being described.

LATENCY IN TOUCH

We define *touch-to-display latency* as the time delay between a touch action (such as the user moving a finger) and the resulting display change [26]. After testing numerous commercial devices using the method described in the Appendix, we found that, on modern touch systems, this is typically between 50 and 200ms. For example, we used a high-speed camera to examine this delay on an iPad. For this device, there is typically about 75ms of lag between the motion of the finger and the updating of the display. This number varies depending on various factors, including when in the scan and video cycles the user made the movement, the particular application, etc. High latency is particularly problematic on larger displays, such as the iPad, where users are more likely to perform gestures more quickly than with smaller, mobile-phone sized displays.

Direct-touch interfaces are particularly challenging because they make it easy for users to perceive latency. With a mouse or trackpad, a user compares his or her motion to visual perception. Since motor reflexes have 10s to 100s of milliseconds of delay themselves, it is difficult to make the comparison accurately. In contrast, direct manipulation interfaces make latency apparent within a single sensing modality – sight. If a dragged graphical object lags behind a moving finger, the user sees the finger and the misaligned object at the same time, independent of any delay in visual processing. This can even be seen in still photographs, such as in Figure 4. One might think that because the finger is moving, this misalignment will be difficult to notice. However, this is typically not the case. The human eye can easily track a finger moving at moderate speed, and thus the image of the finger and the misaligned graphic can be fairly stable on the retina.

The amount of misalignment between the finger and the tracking graphic can be considerable. For a finger moving at the moderately fast rate of 1 meter/second, a 100ms latency will cause the graphic to lag behind the finger by 100mm, or about 4 inches. At 10ms latency, this reduces to 10mm – about the width of a small finger. This is much better, but still quite noticeable. In designing our test system, we presumed that we would need to get down to about 1/10th of a finger width for the misalignment to be negligible. Thus, our goal was to produce a test system with a touch-to-display latency of 1ms.

There are three major components that contribute to latency in a touch system: 1) the touch sensor itself, 2) processing by the system software, UI toolkits, and ultimately the application, and 3) the display. Reducing the latency of direct touch systems requires understanding, and addressing, the latency introduced by each of these components.

Touch Sensor

Most modern multitouch systems use mutual capacitance sensors that measure the capacitive coupling from each row to each column on a 5-6mm grid. The change in this coupling due to the presence of a finger is very small, typically less than one picofarad. This is a very challenging measurement to make, particularly in the presence of extraneous electric fields such as those produced by an LCD display, backlight, etc. Allowing enough time for each measurement to average away the noise is critical.

Most current touch sensors run at a 60Hz scan rate. This means that each grid point is scanned every ~17ms. Typically, this raw data is then processed into touch points by an embedded touch controller, before being sent out over the communications link. These steps add further delay. Additionally, some touch controllers run at a slower scan rate until they detect a touch event in order to save power. This behavior adds additional delay at first contact, but does not impact tracking performance.

It would be fairly straightforward to decrease the latency of current touch technologies – particularly vision-based techniques, given that high speed cameras are nearly commoditized. However, it would involve running more hardware in parallel, increasing cost and power dramatically. To address this, low latency touch sensors will need to use region of interest, tracking, and related techniques to limit the number of points scanned.

It is worth noting that latency specifications can be extremely misleading. It is common in the industry to refer to frame rate rather than latency. They are not the same thing. If multiple frames are buffered, the latency can be quite high, even with a fast frame rate. Further, it is not uncommon for commercial devices to be advertised with "typical" delays, with no mention of worst case. Our research on this issue has been frustrated by the fact that the industry has not adopted a full disclosure policy that would require specifying the range of latencies and their distribution, hence the need to perform our own measurements.

Processing

Between the sensor and the display there is an arduous path that involves communications, the operating system, UI toolkits, the application layer, and ultimately, the graphics controller. Each of these adds latency.

The latency introduced by the operating system is highly variable. Windows, iOS, OSX, Android, etc. are not real time operating systems. Because of this, there is no guarantee a response will happen within a certain time period. If the processor is heavily loaded, it is possible for latency to increase dramatically. Some operations are handled at a very low level in the software stack, and have high priority. For example, the mouse pointer is typically highly optimized, so that even under heavy load, the perceived latency is relatively low. In contrast, an operation such as resizing a photo with two fingers requires constant rescaling of the image at the application level.

While application developers clearly have an incentive to make their programs seem responsive, there are in fact few constraints on the amount of latency they may introduce. UI threads typically dispatch input events one at a time, requiring that the application finish dealing with one input event before another can be attended to. While the input queue ensures that all input is addressed, this one-event-at-a-time model provides ample opportunity for application developers to introduce significant latency. Unfortunately, developers quickly see diminishing returns on their own efforts to increase application performance given the limits dictated by other latencies in the system.

Display

The display system (including the graphics system as well as the display itself) is another major contributor to latency. Again, an obsession with frame rates obscures the actual latency through the system. For example, a 60Hz monitor may include one or more frames of buffer in order to allow for sophisticated image processing effects. Some display devices, such as projectors, include double-buffering in the electronics, effectively doubling the display latency.

The desire for 3D televisions and reduced motion artifacts is driving the development of faster LCD's. 240Hz displays are now commercially available. Unfortunately, the physics of the liquid crystals themselves appear to make performance beyond 480Hz unlikely. In contrast, Plasma and OLED technologies can run at higher speeds, but face significant commercialization challenges.

In our work, we have developed a high-performance touch demonstration system. Through various engineering efforts, we have been able to reduce the latency in each of the input device, processing of touches, and the display, in order to enable our simple applications to run with a latency of ~1ms. We now describe those efforts.

A HIGH-PERFORMANCE TOUCH TEST SYSTEM

Our ultimate goal is to understand how user perception of a touch system is impacted by touch-to-display latency, and to begin the work of engineering systems which are able to produce appropriately fast responses. To do this, we needed a system capable of generating a wide range of latencies - particularly ones much shorter than those provided by current systems. Unfortunately, no such device is commercially available. Thus, we needed to build our own test system.

The requirements for our test system were very demanding. Presuming a finger moving at 1m/s, we wanted the maximum slippage of dragged-UI elements to be 1mm. This implies a latency of 1ms. To reach this level of performance, our system would require very high speed sensing and display – far faster than typical commercial systems. In addition, any processing would need to be extremely fast. The following sections describe the components of our implementation of such a high-performance touch system. Figure 2 shows a system-level block diagram of the system.

Touch Sensor

We utilized a proprietary multi-touch resistive touch sensor with an active area of 24 cm x 16 cm, with custom electronics that allows very high-speed operation. The delay through this sensor is slightly less than 1ms, with no theoretical upper bound on detected movement speed. Touch data is transmitted serially over an optical link.

Projector

For the display, we chose the DLP Discovery 4100 kit based on Texas Instruments' Digital Light Processing technology [28]. The system utilizes front-projection onto the touch sensor, eliminating parallax error that might disturb a user's perception of finger and image alignment. A DLP projector uses a Digital Micromirror Device (DMD), a matrix of mirrors which turn pixels on or off at very high speed. Typically, the high speed of the mirrors is used to change the percentage time on vs. off to create continuous colored images. If one gives up this capability and only allows simple binary images, these can be produced at an extraordinary rate. Our projector development system displays 32,000 binary frames/second at 1024x768 resolution with latency under 40 μs. To achieve this speed, the video data is streamed to the DMD at 25.6 Gbps.

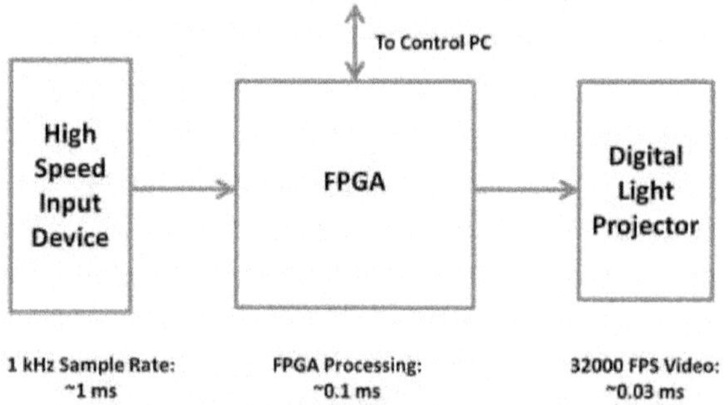

Figure 2: System block diagram of the high-performance touch test system with estimated latency contributions of the individual components.

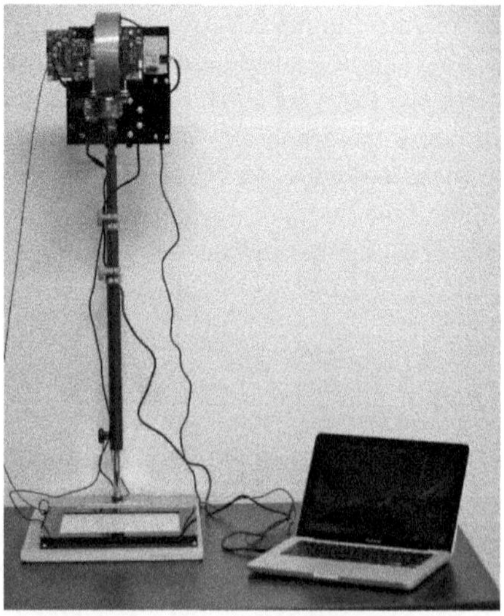

Figure 3: Photograph of device, with the control computer at right. The control computer is used only to set behaviour parameters for the device.

FPGA Processing

To achieve minimal latency, all touch processing is performed on a dedicated FPGA – there is no PC or OS between the touch input and the display output. We used the DLP kit's onboard XC5VLX50 application FPGA for processing the touch data and rendering the video output. To simplify user testing, a USB serial connection to the FPGA allows parameters to be changed dynamically. Latency can be adjusted from 1ms to several hundred ms with 1ms resolution, and different testing modes can be activated. This port also allows touch data to be collected for analysis. Figure 2 shows a block diagram of the FPGA design.

To receive touch data from the sensor, the system communicates through a custom high-speed UART. To minimize the latency, we use a baud rate of 2 Mbps, the highest baud rate we can use without losing signal integrity due to high frequency noise across the communication channel.

The individual bytes of compressed touch data are then processed by a touch detection finite state machine. This FSM simultaneously decodes the data and performs a center-of-mass blob-detection algorithm to identify the coordinates of the touches. The system is pipelined such that each iteration of the FSM operates on the last received byte such that no buffering of the touch data occurs.

The touch coordinates are then sent to a 10-stage variable delay block. Each delay stage is a simple FSM with a counter and takes a control signal that indicates the number of clock cycles to delay the touch coordinate, allowing us to test various levels of latency. The delay block latches the touch sample at the start of the iteration and waits for the appropriate number of cycles before sending the sample and latching the next. The delay block therefore lowers the sample rate by a factor of the delay count. To keep the sample rate at a reasonable level, 10 delay stages are used, so that, for example, to achieve 100ms of latency, the block waits 10ms between samples for a sample rate of 100Hz.

To run basic applications, we chose to incorporate a MicroBlaze soft processor to render the display. Our first prototype originally used a hardcoded control FSM in place of the MicroBlaze for absolute maximum performance, but due to the inflexibility of a hardcoded FSM, we decided to use a soft processor instead. The MicroBlaze is a 32-bit Harvard architecture RISC processor optimized to be synthesized in Xilinx FPGAs [33].

The MicroBlaze soft processor instantiation allows us to select only the cores, peripherals, and memory structures required for our application. For our system, in addition to the base MicroBlaze configuration, we include an interrupt controller, GPIOs for the touch data, a GPIO to set the variable latency, a BRAM memory controller for the image buffer, and a UART unit to communicate with a PC. The MicroBlaze is clocked at 100 MHz.

The MicroBlaze uses an interrupt system to detect valid touch coordinates. A touch ready interrupt event is generated when valid touch data arrives on the GPIOs from the delay block, and the corresponding image is written to the image buffer. Because of the non-uniform nature of an interrupt-based system, the exact latency cannot be computed, but it is insignificant in comparison to the 1ms latency due to the input device.

The image buffer is synthesized in the on-chip BRAM blocks. These blocks provide a dual-port high-speed configurable memory buffer with enough bandwidth to support our high frame-rate display. The image buffer is clocked at 200 MHz with a bus width of 128 bits for a total bandwidth of 25.6 Gbps, as needed by the DLP.

Finally, the DMD controller continuously reads out frames from the image buffer and generates the signals with appropriate timing to control the DMD. This controller can be changed to vary the frame rate in future testing.

Tools

The FPGA design was done using the Xilinx ISE Design Suite 13.2. The MicroBlaze was instantiated and configured using the Xilinx Platform Studio (XPS), and the MicroBlaze was programmed in the C language through the Xilinx Embedded Development Kit (EDK). The image buffer BRAM was instantiated and configured using the Xilinx Core Generator. All VHDL simulations were done using the Xilinx ISim simulator. Synthesis was done using the Xilinx Synthesis Tool (XST).

Having developed a device capable of extremely low latency, we wished to understand precisely what levels of latency would achieve perceptibly improved responses. Thus, we conducted a study to measure the latencies which users are able to perceive while performing drag input.

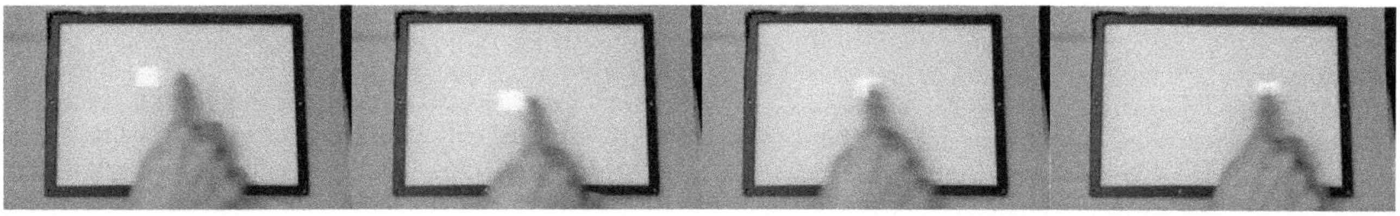

Figure 4: Our high-performance touch device, capable of sensing and responding to input at 1 kHz with only 1 frame of latency. Demonstrating dragging an on-screen object with the same velocity, with latency (from left to right) of 100ms, 50ms, 10ms, and 1ms.

PERCEPTION OF LATENCY IN DRAGGING

While earlier work has demonstrated that users are able to perceive latency down to 100ms, our own use of our prototype device indicated that latency was apparent at far lower levels – as shown in Figure 4. In order to guide our efforts in reducing latency, we wished to understand at precisely what latency value users would no longer notice a difference in performance when performing drags. Thus, we conducted a formal experiment in which we modulated the latency of the system, and measured participants' ability to perceive the differences in performance.

Just Noticeable Difference

We wished to determine the precise level of performance that users are able to perceive when performing common tasks on a touch screen interface. To that end, we conducted an experiment to determine the just-noticeable difference (JND) of various performance levels. The JND is defined as the threshold level at which a participant is able to discriminate between two unequal stimuli – one consistently presented at the same level, termed the reference, and one whose value is changed dynamically throughout the experiment, termed the probe [15]. A commonly accepted value for the JND at some arbitrary reference value is a probe at which a participant can correctly identify the reference 75% of the time [15]. A probe value that cannot be distinguished from the reference with this level of accuracy is considered 'not noticeably different' from the reference.

We conducted a within-subjects experiment to determine the JND level of the probe latency when compared to our maximum performance of 1ms of latency, which served as the reference. While such a determination does not provide an absolute value for the maximum perceptible performance, it does serve as our 'best case' floor condition against which we are able to measure other levels of latency. Our hypothesis was:

H1: Participants will be able to discern latency values that are significantly lower (<20ms) than current-generation hardware provides (~50-200ms).

Apparatus

Our experimental setup, shown in Figure 3, incorporated the previously described system, controlled by a laptop via a USB serial connection. The laptop runs custom software written for the purpose of generating the latency value staircases in real time; each user response is entered and logged on the laptop, and used to generate the following trial's latency level. The experimental task is shown in Figure 4.

Participants

Ten right-handed participants (3 female) were recruited from the local community. Ages ranged between 24 and 40 (mean 27.80, standard deviation 4.73). All participants had prior experience with touchscreen devices, and all participants owned one or more touch devices (such as an iOS- or Android-based phone or tablet). Participants were paid $20 for their participation.

Procedure

Participants were repeatedly presented with pairs of latency conditions: the reference value (1ms) and the probe (between 1 and 65ms of latency). Participants dragged their finger from left to right, then right to left on the touchscreen display. While any dragging task would have been suitable, left/right movements reduce occlusion in high-latency cases. Participants were asked to move in both directions to ensure they did not 'race through' the study Beneath the user's contact point, the system rendered a solid white 2cm × 2cm square. The speed of movement was left to be decided by the participants.

The order of the conditions was randomized for each pair. The study was designed as a two-alternative forced-choice experiment; participants were instructed to choose, within each trial, which case was the reference (1ms) value and were not permitted to make a "don't know" or "unsure" selection [25]. After each pair, participants informed the experimenter which of the two was "faster".

Design

In order for each trial to converge at our desired JND level of 75%, the amount of added latency was controlled according to an adaptive staircase algorithm, which is a more recent and now broadly adopted approach than previous staircase and modified staircase algorithms [15] Each correct identification of the reference value caused a decrease in the amount of latency in the probe, while each incorrect response caused the probe's latency to increase. In order to reach the 75 % confidence level, increases and decreases followed the simple weighted up-down method described by Kaernbach, wherein increases had a three-fold multiplier applied to the base step size, and decreases were the base step size (initially 8ms) [13]. When a participant responded incorrectly after a correct response, or correctly after an incorrect response, this was termed a reversal as it caused the direction of the staircase (increasing or decreasing) to reverse. The step size, initially 8ms, was halved at each reversal, to a minimum step size of 1ms. This continued until a total of 10 reversals occurred, resulting in a convergence at 75% correctness.

Each participant completed eight staircase 'runs'. Four of these started at the minimum probe latency (1ms) and four at the maximum (65ms). The higher starting value of the staircase was chosen because it roughly coincides with commercial offerings, and because pilot testing made it clear that this value would be differentiated from the 1ms reference with near 100% accuracy, avoiding ceiling effects.

Staircases were run two at a time in interleaved pairs to prevent response biases that would otherwise be caused by the participants' ability to track their progress between successive stimuli [15]. Staircase conditions for each of these pairs were selected at random without replacement from 8 possibilities (2 starting levels × 4 repetitions). The entire experiment, including breaks between staircases, was completed by each participant within a single 1-hour session.

Results

Our study was designed to find the just-noticeable difference (JND) level for latency values greater than 1ms. This JND level is commonly agreed to be the level where the participant is able to correctly identify the reference 75% of the time. Participant JND levels ranged from 2.38ms to 11.36ms, with a mean JND across all participants of 6.04ms (standard deviation 4.33ms). JND levels did not vary significantly across the 8 runs of the staircase for each participant. Results for each participant appear in Figure 5.

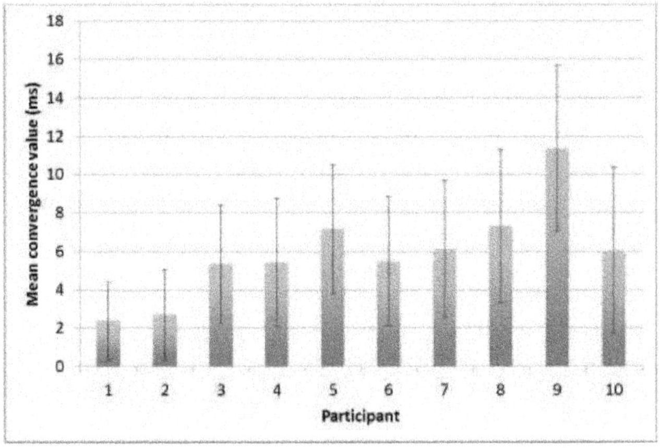

Figure 5: Mean JND by participant. Bars show std-dev.

Discussion

Our results have confirmed our hypothesis. Participants were able to discern differences in latency far below the threshold of current consumer devices [H1] (50-200ms). It should be noted that a baseline of 1ms was a limitation of our experimental hardware, and it is possible that our results are therefore exhibiting the effects of this technical floor; further experimentation is necessary to determine if participants' JND values would be even smaller than those shown here, given a faster reference value.

We should also note that our participants were likely often determining latency by estimating the distance between the onscreen object and their finger as it was moved around the touchscreen; this is an artifact of an input primitives used in modern UIs (specifically, dragging). We have no doubt that testing a different input primitive (tapping, for example) would exhibit different perceptions of latency.

Our results confirm that an order-of magnitude improvement in latency would be noticed and appreciated by users of touch devices. Thus, we set-out to design a software interface which would enable application developers to continue to use toolkit-based application design processes, but enable those toolkits to provide feedback at extremely low latencies, given the presence of a low-latency system.

A TOUCH ACCELERATION TOOLKIT

As we have discussed, input and display devices can conceivably be made in the relatively near term which could enable extremely low-latency interaction. The apparent remaining bottleneck, therefore, is the creation of software that can be executed with sufficiently low latency.

An obvious first step would be to hardware-accelerate application software. While this may be technically feasible, it would require application software be written in a fundamentally new way, foregoing long-standing toolkits and development practices.

We propose a middle-ground, which builds on the model-view-controller model of UI development, upon which many modern UI toolkits are based [14]. The MVC holds that application logic can be separated from the visual representation of the application. In our modified version of MVC, a second, overlaid view is provided for the application. In particular, touch input receives an immediate response from the UI controls, which is based in part on the state of the application at the time the touch is made. Our goal is not to reduce overall system latency, but rather to provide immediate responses that are nonetheless contextually linked to the underlying application.

We aim to extend previous work on application-independent visual responses to touch [31]. While a straightforward port of Ripples might be feasible, a limitation of the visualizations shown in that work is that they are completely separate from even the visual elements of the UI, adding visual complexity [32]. Instead, we aimed to more fully integrate a set of visual responses into the UI elements themselves, so as to reduce visual complexity. Thus, unlike Ripples, where the particular visuals shown provide a *de facto* "mouse pointer" for touch, our goal is to integrate high performance responses into the controls themselves, providing a more unified visualization. We thus designed Accelerated Touch interactions, wherein the traditional direct-touch software runs as it would normally, in a high-latency visual layer, while an additional visual layer contains immediate visual feedback, customized for the UI element at a very low latency.

In our prototype, these two layers are combined by superimposing two projected images – one from the low-latency touch device, and a second from a traditional projector connected to a desktop computer running custom touch software, receiving input from the low-latency subsystem. A commercial implementation would doubtless be architected such that the low-latency layer is generated in hardware, operating directly on touch sensor data, with a high bandwidth link to the display hardware. Our two-display solution is meant only to serve as a demonstrator.

To facilitate future implementations, we now describe our Accelerated Touch user interface designs. We begin by first describing the design constraints which guided our design process, and then present our final designs. We then describe the architecture of our implementation.

User Interface

Design Constraints

In designing a user interface for the low-latency subsystem, we considered a number of constraints:

Information: The low-latency layer has limited information about the current state of the application software; in particular, it is limited to knowledge of the state of the application prior to the beginning of a touch event. This is because any closed loop between the high and low-latency subsystems would necessarily add lag.

Performance: The response of the low-latency layer must be generated very quickly. Even with hardware acceleration, the design of visual responses must be carefully performance-driven.

Fidelity: The low-latency layer is restricted to generating simple visualizations, to the degree that they can be customized at the time of development of the low-latency visual responses. In the case of our prototype, we had the additional constraint that the visuals could be only monochromatic and limited visual primitives. Constraints of this type can be introduced by the acceleration hardware, or by the display hardware.

Non-Interference: Given that some of the application's response will be generated in the low-latency, hardware accelerated layer, and some in the high-latency software layer, a key consideration is how the two will be blended to provide a 'seamless' response to the user's input. Low-latency responses must not interfere with any possible application response, which will necessarily occur later.

Design

We conducted a design process to create a set of UI controls with differentiated low and high latency visual responses to touch. To begin, we sought to find a metaphor which would enable a seamless transition between the two layers of response. These visualizations included such information as object position and state. Our designs were culled based on feasibility under the above constraints.

Our final design was based on a heads-up display (HUD) metaphor, similar to the visualizations used in military aircraft. The HUD was suitable, since traditional HUDs are geometrically simple, and thus was easy to implement such at an authentic fidelity. The HUD, notably, is another example of two visual layers being combined, though in the case of many HUDs, a computerized display is superimposed on video or the real world itself [10]. Accordingly, they are designed to be non-interfering.

Based on the HUD metaphor, we developed a set of touch-event and UI element-specific low-latency layer visualizations for a set of UI elements found in many direct-touch systems. These 3 elements are both common and representative; their interactions (taps, drags, two-finger pinching) cover the majority of the interaction space used in current direct-touch devices. The low-latency responses we developed are described in Table 1, and they are shown in Figure 6 and in our video figure.

ELEMENT	TOUCH DOWN	TOUCH MOVE	TOUCH UP
Button	Outline	(none)	If within bounds, 2nd outline, else none.
Draggable / Resizeable	Bounds outlined	Outline changes / moves	Outline fades when high-latency layer catches up
Scrollable View	List item outlined	List edges highlight to scroll distance.	Edge highlights fade as high-latency layer catches up

Table 1: Accelerated visuals for each element and touch event, which compliment standard high-latency responses to touch input.

These 3 elements represent broad coverage of standard UI toolkits for touch input. Most higher-order UI elements are composed of these simpler elements (eg: radio buttons and checkboxes are both 'buttons', a scrollbar is a "draggable/ resizable" with constrained translation and rotation).

Our Accelerated Touch system depends on the marriage of visuals operating at two notably different latency levels; this latency difference has been incorporated into the design of our low-latency visualizations. Users are informed of the state of both systems, with a coherent synchronization as the visual layers come into alignment.

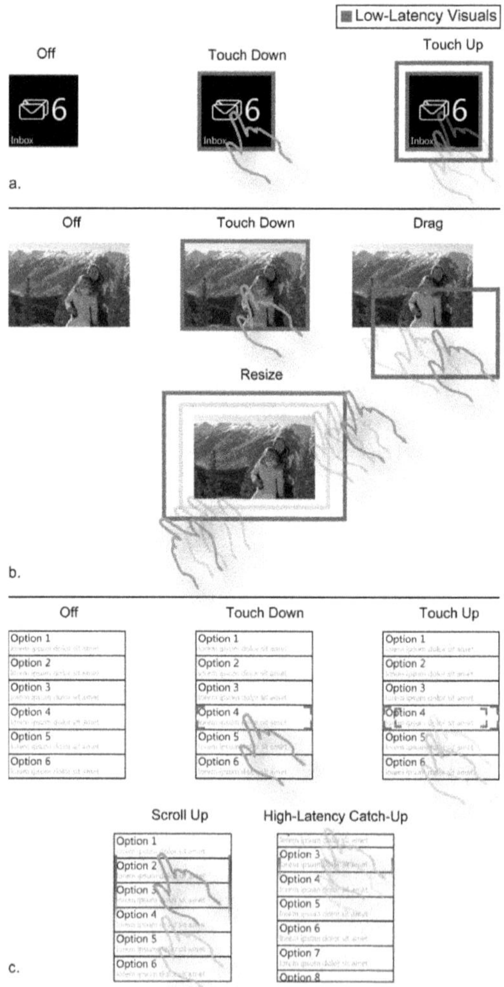

Figure 6: Our element types: a. buttons, b. draggable / resizable elements, c. scrolling viewports.

Architecture

We envision that the application developer utilizing a toolkit such as the one we have described will build their application through the normal process of assembling GUI controls. Upon execution, the UI elements would bifurcate their visualizations, with high- and low-latency visualizations rendered and overlaid on a single display. Information flow through our system is as shown in Figure 7.

As we have described, this bifurcation creates a fundamental communication problem where any parameterization of visualizations provided by the low-latency subsystem required by application logic must be defined before the user begins to give input. Any visualization which requires processing by the application will introduce a dependency of the low-latency system upon the high-latency system, and will therefore introduce lag back into the system.

Therefore it was critical for us to build UI element logic into the low-latency subsystem. Between user touches, the application, which is executing in the high-latency subsystem, has the opportunity to provide parameters for the low-latency subsystem's model of the UI elements. As we have described, our approach was to extend the MVC model of UI software design, by providing a separate controller responsible for low-latency feedback. In our software design, the following can be specified for each control:

- Element type (*button*, *draggable object*, *scrollable list*)
- Bounding rectangle dimensions (*x*, *y*, *width* and *height*)
- Conditional: additional primitive information (for example: *size of list items*, in the case of a scrollable list)

Logic for a given element-type's response to touch input is stored in the low-latency subsystem. In future implementations further parameterization of the low-latency subsystem's responses to user input could be communicated in the same manner, allowing a greater degree of customization.

In our implementation, sensor data is processed on the FPGA to generate events, which are then separately distributed to the low-latency and high-latency subsystems, as shown in (Figure 7). The low- and high-latency subsystems' response to user input is therefore independent but coordinated. In this implementation, the high-latency subsystem acts as the 'master', setting state of the low-latency subsystem between user touches. Future implementations might change this relationship to increase synchronization between the two subsystems, or offload more processing to the low-latency subsystem.

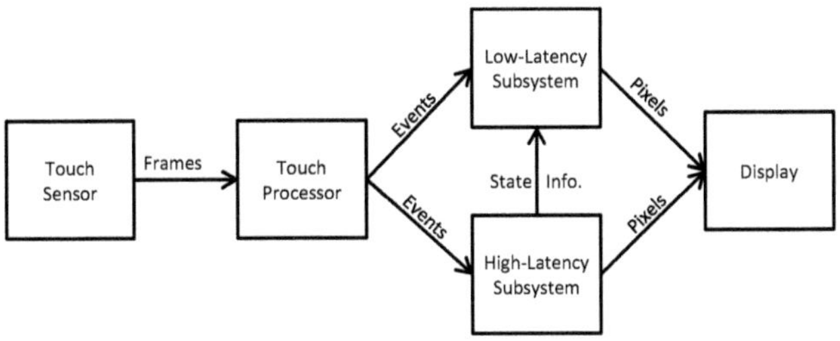

Figure 7: The Accelerated Touch architecture

Synchronization

Communication between the high-latency and low-latency layers is of critical importance. Three issues must be considered in determining how the high- and low-latency subsystems remain synchronized.

Latency differences: Our low-latency visualizations require information about the latency difference between the high- and low-latency visual layers in order to synchronize visualizations. In our system these latency values are static, and thus preprogrammed into the FPGA. In implementations where latency levels vary in either subsystem, it may be advantageous to fix the latency level at an always-achievable constant rather than having a dynamic value that may become unsynchronized.

Hit testing: Hit testing decisions are conditional on additional data regarding the visual hierarchy and properties of visible UI elements. Our implementation resolved this consideration by disallowing overlapping bounding rectangles, requiring a flat, 'hit test friendly' map of the UI. Other implementations may instead provide the necessary information (object state, z-order, listeners) to the low-latency subsystem and have both subsystems conduct hit testing in parallel, or conduct it solely in the low-latency subsystem, providing the results to the high-latency subsystem.

Conditional responses: Many interface visualizations are conditional not only on immediate user input, but on further decision-making logic defined in the application logic. The degree to and method by which application logic might be migrated to the low-latency subsystem is a topic requiring further research. Two illustrative examples of conditional response logic are as follows:

Consider a credit-card purchase submission button, which is programmed to be disabled (to prevent double-billing) when pressed, but only upon validation of the data entered into the form. In such a case, the behavior of the button is dependent not only on an immediate user interaction, but is further conditional on additional information.

Consider also linked visualizations, such as the one shown in Figure 8. In this case, feedback is provided to the user not only by the UI element they are manipulating, but also by a second UI element.

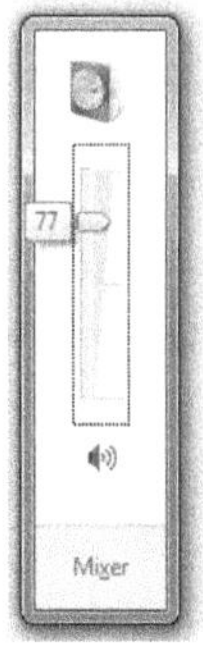

Figure 8: The Windows 7 volume control. When dragging the slider, a tooltip appears showing a numeric representation of the current setting.

These relatively straightforward examples could easily be programmed directly into the low-latency subsystem, even in our relatively primitive FPGA-based demonstrator system. However, how these might be described in general terms that do not require application-specific development within the low-latency subsystem is an open question, and one that is critical to answer to allow developers to continue to use traditional development methods when creating software in an Accelerated Touch-like toolkit.

CONCLUSION & FUTURE WORK

In this paper, we have described sources of latency, and demonstrated how several of these can be eliminated in building a demonstrator system capable of 1ms touch latency. Further, we have described the results of tests which showed that users were able to perceive order-of magnitude improvements in latency over current-generation hardware. Our results suggest that performance beyond 1ms may still yield improvement that is perceptible to users.

We have constructed a prototype Accelerated Touch system, wherein a traditional direct-touch layer is paired with a low-latency layer that displays nearly immediate visual feedback on user interaction, independent of application logic, but visually tied to the underlying UI widget. We have further described the design of this visual language to satisfy the various constraints of a dedicated low-latency touch processor, and we have described a potential architecture for a direct-touch system that pairs Accelerated Touch with more traditional touch interaction.

A common complaint that we heard from people who used our system extensively was that it "broke" them – that they now find the latency of current generation devices completely unacceptable. The implication is that improving latency might be an effective competitive strategy for device vendors. It is our hope that this paper will spark innovation in the design of hardware and software capable of lower latency of response to user input.

We see a wealth of future work in further investigating the limits of human perception of touchscreen computer systems, and better understanding the effect of performance parameters such as latency on the usage of touchscreens. For example, are there performance benefits for input under reduced latency? Further, we have conflated latency and frame rate, future devices may decouple these two parameters, and could optimize one or the other; further investigation is needed into the effects of such a change.

ACKNOWLEDGEMENTS

We thank our experimental participants, the UIST reviewers for their helpful comments, our UIST AC for meticulous feedback, and Ricardo Jota for assistance with the video. We also thank the members of the Dynamic Graphics Project at the University of Toronto, and the Applied Sciences group at Microsoft for valuable discussions.

APPENDIX: MEASURING LATENCY

We use a simple technique for measuring the touch-to-display latency. The device is placed in a mode where a graphic is meant to follow a touch point. (eg: inking, translating an icon). A ruler is placed on top of the device. A finger is then dragged across the screen along the ruler edge at as constant a rate as possible. A high speed camera of known frame rate captures the finger motion as well as the resulting graphical response. By examining individual frames in the video, we can calculate the speed of the finger (distance travelled between successive frames x frame rate). The amount of separation between the finger and the following graphic can be directly observed. The latency is the separation distance / the finger speed. We take two measurements: worst case latency, and best case latency.

We used an inexpensive consumer camera – a Casio EX-FH100 High Speed Exilim – to record 240 fps video at 448x336. This is significantly faster than most display systems, thus the graphic can be seen to jump in discrete increments, while the finger moves between every frame. In addition to this type of variation, latency can also vary with different locations on the screen, OS load, etc.

Figure 9 shows two images taken 12 frames apart from our testing. In the example shown in the figure, the fingers have moved 1.8cm over 12 frames (0.05 seconds, 36 cm/s). The lag distance is 4.2cm, thus the worst-case latency is computed as 116.7 ms.

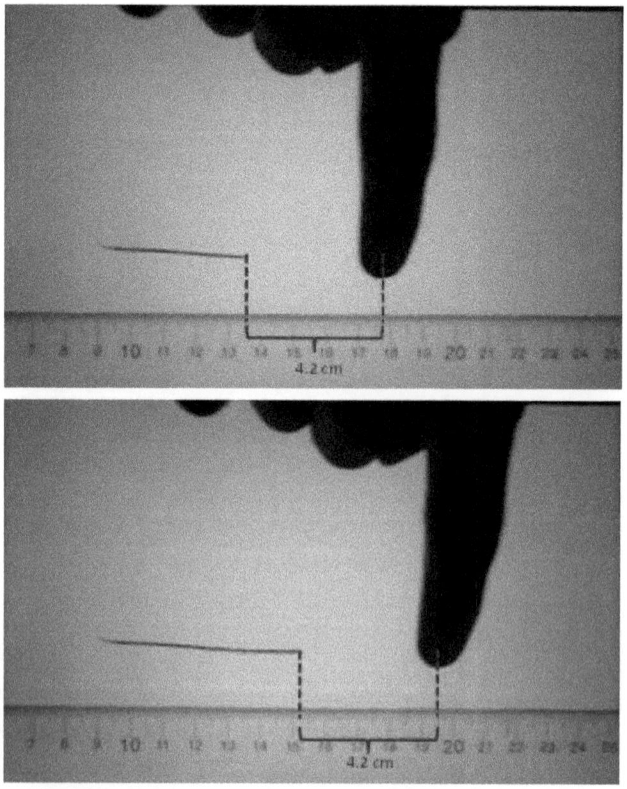

Figure 9. Images of Autodesk Sketchbook Pro running on an iPad 3.

Best-case latency is computed by finding the frame showing the shortest lag distance (among the 10 frames between the samples shown), and assuming the same speed of finger movement. In the case of our example, the best-case lag distance was 2.7cm (shown in Figure 10), thus yielding a best-case lag of 75ms.

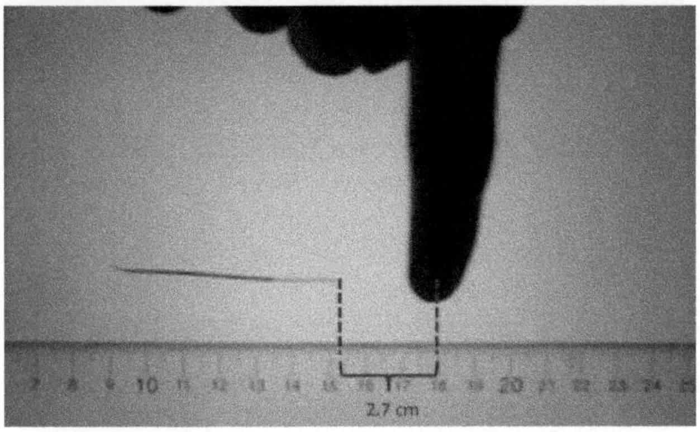

Figure 10. Shortest lag distance among the frames of video between the ones shown in Figure 9.

REFERENCES

1. Accot, J., and Zhai, S. 1997. Beyond Fitts law: models for trajectory based HCI tasks. *Proceedings of ACM CHI'97*, 295-302.
2. Anderson, G., Doherty, R., and Ganapathy, S. 2011. User Perception of Touch Screen Latency. Design, *User Experience, and Usability. Theory, Methods, Tools, and Practice*. 195-202.
3. Boie, R.A. 1984. Capacitive Impedance Readout Tactile Image Sensor. *Proceedings of the 1984 IEEE International Conference on Robotics and Automation*, 370-378.
4. Card, S. K., Mackinlay, J. D., and Robertson, G. G. 1991. The Information Visualizer: An Information Workspace. *Proceedings of (CHI '91)*, 181-188.
5. Card, S.K., Moran, T.P., and Newell, A. 1983. *The Psychology of Human-Computer Interaction*. Erlbaum, Hillsdale, NJ, USA.
6. Cornsweet, TN. 1962. The staircase-method in psychophysics, *American Journal of Psychology*, 75, 485-491.
7. Dietz, P., and Leigh, D. 2001. DiamondTouch: multi-user touch technology. *Proceedings of the UIST' 01*, 219-226.
8. Ganz, L. 1975. Temporal factors in visual perception. In E. C. Carterette and M. P. Friedman, eds. *Handbook of Perception, Vol. V, Seeing*. New York: Academic Press
9. Han, J. 2005. Low-cost multi-touch sensing through frustrated total internal reflection. *Proceedings of UIST '05*, 115-118.
10. Harrison, B.L. and Ishii, H. and Vicente, K.J. and Buxton, W.A.S. 1995. Transparent layered user interfaces: An evaluation of a display design to enhance focused and divided attention. *Proceedings of CHI '95*, 317-324.
11. Harter, M. R. 1967. Excitability and cortical scanning: A review of two hypotheses of central intermittency in perception. *Psychological Bulletin* 68, 47-58.
12. Jacob, R. J. K., Girouard, A., Hirshfield, L. M., Horn, M. S., Shaer, O., Solovey, E. T., and Zigelbaum. J. 2008. Reality-based interaction: a framework for post-WIMP interfaces. *Proceedings of CHI '08*, 201-210.
13. Kaernbach, C. 1991. Simple adaptive testing with the weighted up-down method, *Perception & Psychophysics* 49, 227-229.
14. Krasner, G., Pope, S. 1988. A cookbook for using the model-view controller user interface paradigm in Smalltalk-80. *J. Object Oriented Program.* 1, 3, 26-49.
15. Levitt, H. 1971. Transformed up-down methods in psychoacoustics. *Journal of the Acoustical Society of America*, 49(2): 467–477.
16. MacKenzie, I.S., and Ware, C. (1993). Lag as a determinant of human performance in interactive systems. In *Proceedings of* CHI '93, 488-493.
17. Microsoft Corporation. 2011. Windows Developer Preview: Win 8 Guide. http://windows.microsoft.com/en-US/windows-8/preview, January 2012.
18. Miller, R. B. 1968. Response time in man-computer conversational transactions. *Fall Joint Comp. Conf.* 1968, 267-277.
19. Pavlovych, A. C. Gutwin, (2012) Assessing Target Acquisition and Tracking Performance for Moving Targets in the Presence of Latency and Jitter, *GI 2012*, to appear.
20. Pavlovych, A., W. Stuerzlinger, (2009) The Tradeoff between Spatial Jitter and Latency in Pointing Tasks, *ACM SEICS* 2009, 187-196.
21. Pavlovych, A., W. Stuerzlinger, (2011) Target Following Performance in the Presence of Latency, Jitter, and Signal Dropouts, *GI 2011*, 33-40.
22. Potter, R. Weldon, L. J., and Shneiderman, B. 1988. Improving the accuracy of touch screens: an experimental evaluation of strategies. In *Proceedings of CHI '88*.
23. Rosenberg, I. and Perlin, K. 2009. The UnMousePad: an interpolating multi-touch force-sensing input pad. In *Proceedings of ACM SIGGRAPH 2009 (SIGGRAPH '09)*.
24. Rubine, D., McAvinney, P. 1988. The Videoharp. In *Proceedings of International Computer Music 1988*. Computer Music Association. September, 1988.
25. Savage, W. C. 1970. *The Measurement of Sensation: A Critique of Perceptual Psychophysics*. Berkeley: UC Press.
26. Sears, A., Jacko, J. 2012. *HCI Handbook, 3rd Edition*. Ch. 9.

27. Seow, S. 2008. *Designing and Engineering Time: The Psychology of Time Perception in Software.* Addison-Wesley, NY.

28. Texas Instruments. DLP Discovery 4100 Development Kit. http://www.ti.com/tool/dlpd4x00kit, January 2012.

29. Van Kessel, P. F., et al. 1998. A MEMS-Based Projection Display. In *Proceedings of the IEEE*, 86 (8), pp. 1687-1704.

30. Wellner, P. 1993. Interacting with paper on the Digital Desk. *Communications of the ACM 36* (7), 87-96.

31. Wigdor, D., Williams, S., Cronin, M., Levy, R., White, K., Mazeev, M. and Benko, H. 2009. Ripples: utilizing per-contact visualizations to improve user interaction with touch displays. In *Proceedings of UIST '09.* ACM, New York, NY, USA, 3-12.

32. Wigdor, D., Wixon, D. (2011). *Brave NUI World: Designing Natural User Interfaces for Touch and Gesture* (1st ed.). Morgan Kaufmann Publishers Inc., San Francisco, CA, USA.

33. Xilinx. Microblaze Processor Reference Guide. http://www.xilinx.com/support/documentation/sw_manuals/xilinx13_3/mb_ref_guide.pdf, January 2012.

A User-Specific Machine Learning Approach for Improving Touch Accuracy on Mobile Devices

Daryl Weir, Simon Rogers, Roderick Murray-Smith
School of Computing Science
University of Glasgow
18 Lilybank Gardens
Glasgow, G12 8QQ, UK
darylw@dcs.gla.ac.uk, {Simon.Rogers, Roderick.Murray-Smith}@glasgow.ac.uk

Markus Löchtefeld
German Research Center for Artificial Intelligence (DFKI)
Stuhlsatzenhausweg 3
Campus D3-2
D-66123 Saarbrucken, Germany
markus.loechtefeld@dfki.de

ABSTRACT

We present a flexible Machine Learning approach for learning user-specific touch input models to increase touch accuracy on mobile devices. The model is based on flexible, non-parametric Gaussian Process regression and is learned using recorded touch inputs. We demonstrate that significant touch accuracy improvements can be obtained when either raw sensor data is used as an input or when the device's reported touch location is used as an input, with the latter marginally outperforming the former. We show that learned offset functions are highly nonlinear and user-specific and that user-specific models outperform models trained on data pooled from several users. Crucially, significant performance improvements can be obtained with a small ($\approx$ 200) number of training examples, easily obtained for a particular user through a calibration game or from keyboard entry data.

ACM Classification Keywords

H.5.2. Information Interfaces and Presentation: Input devices and strategies (e.g. mouse, touchscreen)

Author Keywords

Touch; Machine Learning; Regression; Gaussian Processes; Probabilistic Modelling

INTRODUCTION

In this paper, we investigate an alternative, data-driven approach to touch. We treat the problem as a Machine Learning (ML) task where we are interested in learning a function that maps an input (the device's reported touch location or the raw sensor values) to the *intended touch location*. We show later that the functions learned for individual users are highly user-specific and vary greatly across the touch surface, overcoming the limitations of a device specific offset as in [6]. We use a flexible non-parametric regression algorithm based on Gaussian Processes (GPs;[12]) to enable us to model complex nonlinear functions without having to make detailed parametric assumptions about the touch event (as in [14]). We show that using either the raw sensor values or the device's reported touch location as the input we can obtain significant improvements in accuracy using a number of recorded touch events lower than that collected per user in [6].

Given the increasing ubiquity of touch, there is a clear need for techniques which facilitate accurate input. One of the primary causes of touch error is the so called "fat finger problem" [3]: through the act of touching, the user occludes the very targets she is trying to touch and the softness of the finger/thumb produces a much larger, more ambiguous, contact region than intended [8]. This is particularly problematic when users type on a virtual keyboard with their thumbs, both when operating the device one-handed [11] (holding and typing with the same hand) or typing with two thumbs with the device in landscape mode. The result is a user-specific offset between the touch location reported by the device and that intended by the user.

There has been considerable research effort directed at creating models to account for this offset. Studies both in the wild [6, 7] and in the lab [8, 14] have succeeded in compensating for some of the error inherent in touch based interaction. Unfortunately these approaches are either based on custom hardware or on global compensation methods; none of them focused on the needs of specific users. The approach proposed here is both user-specific and uses only data available on commercial smartphones. Further, our model is fully probabilistic in its predictions and is naturally able to incorporate data from sensors other than the touch screen (e.g. accelerometer readings). This approach provides the basis for future research into propagating uncertainty from input to application and potentially opening rich new channels of interaction.

RELATED WORK

Even though HCI research focused on touch screens based on capacitive sensing has been conducted for over 25 years [10], current error rates suggest there is still room for improvement [6]. Precise capacitive touch input is clearly a desirable goal, given the increasing ubiquity of touchscreen devices. Such devices are employed in an extremely broad range of settings

UIST'12, October 7–10, 2012, Cambridge, Massachusetts, USA.

— even input through fabric enclosure (e.g. inside a pocket) has been successfully explored [16].

In lab studies, [8] investigated the relationship between finger orientation and touch error and introduced 'Ridgepad' – a device that could infer finger orientation through fingerprint scanning. Similarly, [14] showed that it is possible to infer finger orientation using an array of capacitive sensors and sophisticated Bayesian statistical techniques. Both [8] and [14] showed that there is considerable diversity between users, and between finger and thumb use. This suggests that significant improvements could be made if user- and context-specific models were built. Unfortunately, the improvements in touch performance described by [8] and [14] come at significant hardware and computational costs respectively and therefore do not offer solutions that are currently practical.

In two recent large-scale studies, [6, 7] used a crowd-sourcing approach to collect vast quantities of touch data from a variety of users and devices. They investigated simple tapping as well as text entry with applications deployed in the Android Marketplace. Their data led them to create a device-specific compensation function which they then showed improved accuracy [6]. For the text-entry scenario a simple shift function helped to decrease the error rate by 9.1% globally [7]. This approach increases the accuracy of touch input, but we argue that there is still room for improvement. In [9] it was shown that the personal perceived touch point is important, in addition to the physical characteristics of the touching finger or thumb. Users tend to use visual features of their fingers for their mental model that determines the corresponding point on the screen that their touch hits. Since these mental models can differ between users, personalized models would have a bigger influence than general models. This is a key motivation for our approach – no matter how good the sensing hardware is at converting sensor inputs into a touch location, there will always be user-specific biases. For example, in Figure 1 we show the smoothed sensor values for a touch event (white is high valued, black low). The grey circle shows the touch location reported by the device, which looks very reasonable given the sensor values. However, the white circle represents the point the user was trying to touch. This offset between the *intended* touch point and the *measured* touch point will be highly user-specific (see e.g. [9, 14]) and it is this error that we aim to reduce in this work.

In both [9] and [6], the techniques proposed give deterministic values for the intended touch location — there is no information about the uncertainty of predictions. There is a growing body of research showing the value of propagating uncertainty from input to the application level [20, 18]. [15] explicitly models the uncertainty in a touch input and uses this to negotiate the handover of control between the user and the system. The authors demonstrate a map browsing application which automatically scrolls towards nearby points of interest when user input is uncertain (i.e. when the finger is lifted from the screen slightly.) The work of Schwarz [17] is also relevant. The authors propose a framework for modelling uncertain interaction which allows a system to consider several possible actions and assign them probabilities based on user input. Definitive action is only taken when the probability for an event reaches a certain threshold. The predictions of our model are Gaussian distributions with full covariance structure, which could be used as input to such a probabilistic interaction framework.

Personalized models have been used commonly for key-target resizing on soft keyboards [2] but the disadvantages of these techniques is that the approach is only applicable for keyboard input since they are based on natural languages technologies. Similarly, in [4] the authors use machine learning to classify which key a given touch was targetting. Again, this requires specific information about the layout of the keyboard and is not generally applicable to all touches. Our approach combines the personalization and learning process with the power of a model which increases touch accuracy for all tasks.

TOUCH AS A MACHINE LEARNING PROBLEM

Our approach to overcome the problems discussed above is to introduce a machine learning technique that allows us to create user specific models based on either raw touch sensor data or the device's reported touch location. We are able to access the raw sensor data for the Nokia N9 MeeGo smartphone, which has an array of capacitive sensors laid out in a grid. We base most of our experimentation on this device as it is the only commercial product for which we have access to raw sensor data. Our task is therefore to find a mapping between either a vector of sensor values or a 2-dimensional reported touch location and the corresponding intended 2-dimensional touch location on the 854x480 pixel display. Figure 1 shows the sensor values for a typical touch towards the top of the device (the intended touch point is represented as a white circle). It is clear that a typical touch produces a significant sensor reading in several sensor positions simultaneously. As already mentioned, the exact pattern of sensor activation for a particular touch will depend on the user and on how they are performing the touch – with a finger or a thumb say – and it is not clear what form this function will take. We therefore turn to a flexible non-parametric regression algorithm: Gaussian Process regression.

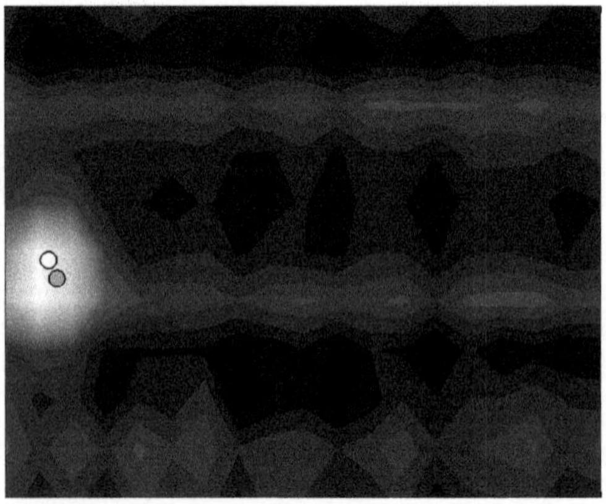

Figure 1. Sensor outputs (black = low; white = high) for a touch aimed at the white circle. The N9's reported touch location is indicated with a grey circle.

Gaussian Process Regression

Gaussian Processes (GPs) [12] are a popular statistical technique for regression and classification. In this work, we are interested in learning a function that can map between inputs $\mathbf{s}$ and intended 2D touch location (x, y): $(x, y) = f(\mathbf{s})$. In our experiments, the input $\mathbf{s}$ will be either the raw sensor values, or the touch location given by the device. GPs allow us to do this without making any parametric assumptions about the form of $f(\mathbf{s})$. Instead, we supply a mean function $\mu(\mathbf{s})$ (which is set to zero in all of our experiments) and a covariance function, $C(\mathbf{s}_n, \mathbf{s}_m)$, which defines how similar the nth and mth outputs should be based on inputs $\mathbf{s}_n$ and $\mathbf{s}_m$. Readers are pointed to [12] for extensive details on GP regression and classification.

Given N training examples, $\mathbf{x}_1, \ldots, \mathbf{x}_n, \ldots, \mathbf{x}_N$ and associated locations, $(x_1, y_1), \ldots, (x_n, y_n), \ldots, (x_N, y_N)$, our GP regression approach proceeds as follows. Firstly, we turn the problem from a two-dimensional regression into a one-dimensional regression by stacking all of the locations into a single vector:

$$\mathbf{z} = [x_1, \ldots, x_n, \ldots, x_N, y_1, \ldots, y_n, \ldots, y_N]^{\mathrm{T}}.$$

Note that this does not preclude us from modelling possible dependencies between x_n and y_n (see below). We now build an $N \times N$ covariance matrix, $\mathbf{C}$, where the n, mth element is calculated by evaluating the covariance function $C(\mathbf{s}_n, \mathbf{s}_m)$. This matrix is then stacked up to produce the full $2N \times 2N$ covariance matrix, $\widehat{\mathbf{C}}$:

$$\widehat{\mathbf{C}} = \begin{bmatrix} \mathbf{C} & \alpha\mathbf{C} \\ \alpha\mathbf{C} & \mathbf{C} \end{bmatrix},$$

where α controls the strength of the dependence between x_n and y_n. Formally, the covariance between x_n and x_m (or y_n and y_m) is given by $C(\mathbf{s}_n, \mathbf{s}_m)$ whilst the covariance between x_n and y_m is given by $\alpha C(\mathbf{s}_n, \mathbf{s}_m)$. If $\alpha = 0$, we are effectively using independent regression models for the x and y locations.

Finally, we assume a small amount of additive Gaussian noise (with variance σ^2). This overcomes possible problems resulting from trying to map very similar input sensor values to different intended touch locations.

Our aim is to be able to predict (x^*, y^*) for a new set of input values $\mathbf{s}^*$. To do this, we create a vector comprising the covariance function evaluated between $\mathbf{s}^*$ and the N input vectors in the training set:

$$\mathbf{c} = [C(\mathbf{s}^*, \mathbf{s}_1), \ldots, C(\mathbf{s}^*, \mathbf{s}_N)],$$

which is then stacked up similarly to the training covariance matrix:

$$\widehat{\mathbf{c}} = \begin{bmatrix} \mathbf{c} & \alpha\mathbf{c} \\ \alpha\mathbf{c} & \mathbf{c} \end{bmatrix}.$$

The GP prediction is a 2-dimensional Gaussian with mean and covariance given by:

$$\begin{aligned} (x^*, y^*) &\sim \mathcal{N}(\boldsymbol{\mu}, \boldsymbol{\Sigma}) \\ \boldsymbol{\mu} &= \widehat{\mathbf{c}}\left[\widehat{\mathbf{C}} + \sigma^2\mathbf{I}\right]^{-1}\mathbf{z} \\ \boldsymbol{\Sigma} &= C(\mathbf{s}^*, \mathbf{s}^*) - \widehat{\mathbf{c}}\left[\widehat{\mathbf{C}} + \sigma^2\mathbf{I}\right]^{-1}\widehat{\mathbf{c}}^T. \end{aligned}$$

Note that the inversion of the $2N \times 2N$ matrix is not prediction specific and can therefore be done just once after training data has been collected. Note that if $\alpha = 0$, this predictive Gaussian will have no covariance between the two dimensions (i.e. the top right and bottom left elements of $\boldsymbol{\Sigma}$ will be equal to zero). Both α and σ^2 are parameters that need to be optimised.

Choice of covariance function

Many different covariance functions have been used for GP regression. In this work, we have used the following, standard, combination of a linear and Gaussian covariance:

$$C(\mathbf{s}_n, \mathbf{s}_m) = b\left(a\mathbf{s}_n^T\mathbf{s}_m + (1-a)\exp\left\{-\gamma||\mathbf{s}_n - \mathbf{s}_m||_2^2\right\}\right),$$

where a controls the relative influence of the linear and Gaussian terms and γ controls the length scale of the Gaussian. Cross validation on a gives an indication of the non-linearity of the mapping from the input space to the intended touch location. We shall see later that using the sensor values as input results in a highly non-linear function, whereas using the device's reported touch location as our input gives an even balance of the linear and non-linear terms. This covariance function provided excellent performance, but an exploration of other covariance functions is an avenue for future work.

EXPERIMENTAL SETUP

We built a simple data collector in Python and PyGame that ran natively on the Nokia N9. The software displayed crosshairs on the screen that the users had to touch. The crosshairs were randomly located in the area that is normally occupied by the landscape keyboard of the N9 to simulate text entry in landscape mode. For each touch on a crosshair, the system recorded the intended location (i.e. the screen location of the crosshair), the values of the capacitive sensors and the location reported by the N9 for the touch event. After the user lifted his finger from the screen another crosshair would be displayed. We obtained data from a total of 8 participants (3 female), aged between 23 and 34, all of whom performed 1000 touches holding the device in landscape mode, using either thumb to touch (see Figure 2). All but one of our participants owned smartphones and therefore were used to operating a touch-screen device.

For all our experiments, we rescaled the touch locations such that they were in the unit square centered on the origin, with no loss of generality. This was done so that the same model parameters can be used across different devices with different native resolutions. We transform the data back to a real world scale when computing virtual button accuracy and RMS error on our predictions.

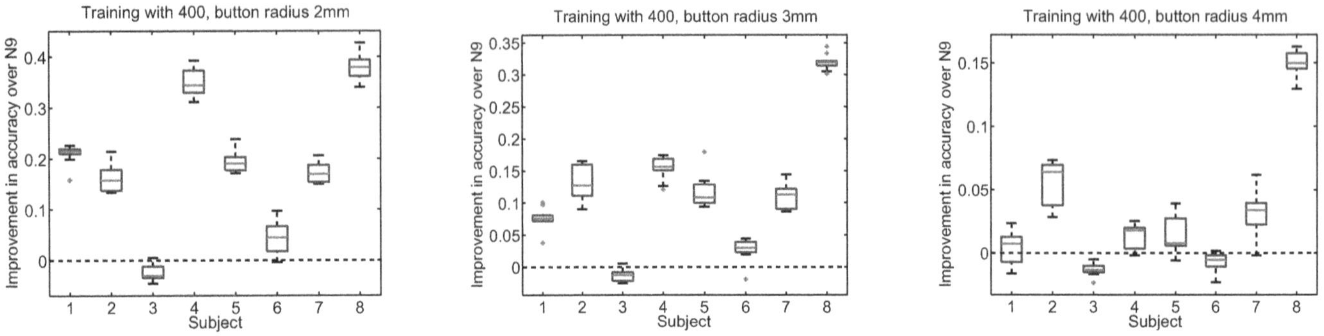

(a) $N = 400$, 2mm button radius. (b) $N = 400$, 3mm button radius. (c) $N = 400$, 4mm button radius.

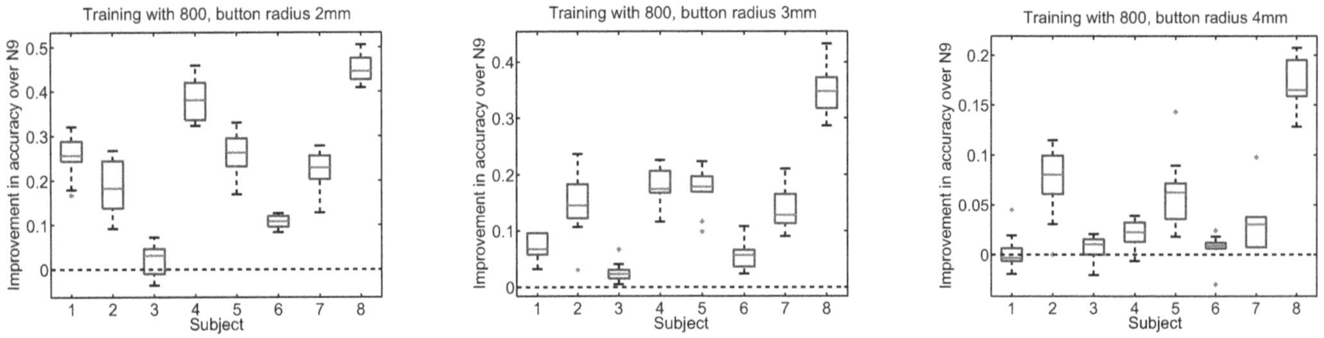

(d) $N = 800$, 2mm button radius. (e) $N = 800$, 3mm button radius. (f) $N = 800$, 4mm button radius.

Figure 3. Improvements in accuracy rate for different virtual button radii and numbers of training examples when the raw sensor values are used as an input. The value on the y-axis is the proportion of touches inside the button for the GP model minus the proportion computed for the N9's native touch location. An increase of say 0.1 corresponds to a 10% decrease in error rate. Boxplots show the distribution of improvement over 10 repetitions.

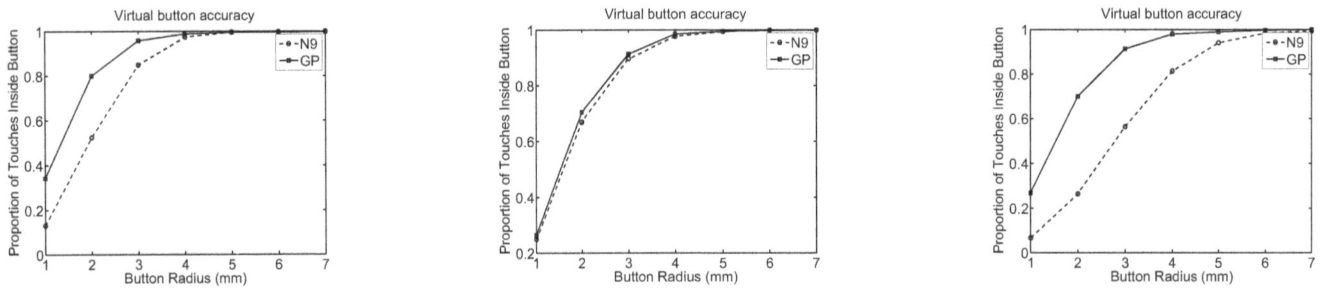

(a) Subject 1 (b) Subject 3 (c) Subject 8

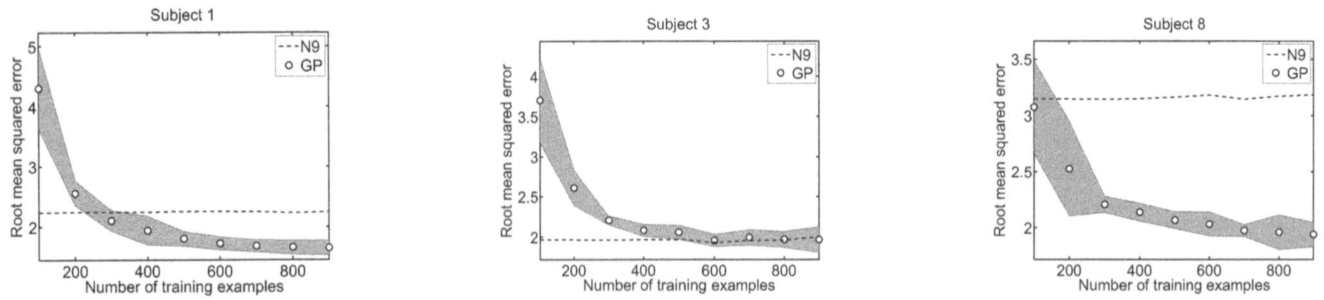

(d) Subject 1 (e) Subject 3 (f) Subject 8

Figure 4. Comparison of performance between the N9 touch events (N9) and our Gaussian Processes predictions using the raw sensor values as input (GP). Top row: Accuracy for different virtual button sizes (800 training points). Bottom row: Learning curves. Subject 1 represents an average user, subject 3 a user that already performs far above average already with the N9 screen and subject 8 represents a user that doesn't own a touch-screen based phone.

Figure 2. Experimental setup: participants held the phone in both hands and used either thumb to touch.

RESULTS

In our first set of experiments, we use the raw values from the capacitive sensor to predict the true touch location. We predict the location directly rather than an offset, since in principle this algorithm could take the place of whatever technique is currently used to predict device location. 5-fold cross-validation was performed for subject 1 over a small range of values for $a, \gamma, b, \alpha, \sigma^2$ and these values were then used across all subjects. It is important to note that these parameters control the GP covariance function, which defines how smooth the resulting predictive functions can be, rather than defining the functions themselves. In practice this means that the results for subject 1 are likely to be slightly optimistic, and those for all other users pessimistic. Ideally, a cross-validation would be performed on a per-user basis but the necessary computation is an unreasonable demand in a mobile setting — any deployment of the system would have to use predetermined covariance parameters such as these. The chosen parameter values were: $\gamma = 0.05, b = 5, a = 0.1, \alpha = 0.9, \sigma^2 = 10^{-3}$. The sensor data is pre-processed prior to use by first setting to zero any values that are less than 150 (we found this was the typical background noise in the absence of touch input) and then normalising each touch so that the sum of the sensor values is equal to 1. The mean of the predictive Gaussian provided by the GP is used as the inferred touch location.

Predicting from raw sensor values

We begin by looking at virtual button accuracy, following [8] and [14]. Assuming a circular button is placed around the centre of the crosshair at which the user was aiming, we can compute the proportion of touches that would fall within this circle. In Figure 3 we show the improvement in proportion for the GP regression over the N9s native location sensing. Positive values mean the model is an improvement over the N9s native algorithm. The data were analysed for three different virtual button sizes (2mm radius, 3mm, 4mm) and two different sizes of training set (400 and 800 touches). In each case, we repeated the experiment 10 times. For each repetition, we randomly sampled $N = 400$ or $N = 800$ touches from the 1000 touches for each user and used the remaining (600 or 200) samples for testing. Note that as we are interested in personalised touch models, separate regression models are trained for each user. The average reductions in error rate across all users are 23.47% (2mm buttons), 14.20% (3mm) and 4.70% (4mm).

For all users except subject 3, we see notable performance increases for buttons of radius 2mm and 3mm. These improvements are all statistically significant (paired t-test, $p < 0.05$), with the exception of subject 3. An increase of 0.2 corresponds to a potential decrease in error rate of 20%. Improvements are lower for 4mm buttons reflecting the acceptable N9 performance at this radius. For 4mm buttons the improvements are statistically significant for subjects other than 1, 3 and 6. To place these results in context, in Figure 4 we show more detailed results from subjects 1,3 and 8 (representing a wide range of performances). The top plots ((a)-(c)) show the button radius results for buttons of radius 1mm to 7mm. The solid curve is the performance of the GP regression and the dashed curve that of the N9s native algorithm. For all subjects, results are indistinguishable at 6mm but large improvements are evident at smaller button sizes for subjects 1 and 8. Subject 3 is the only subject for which we see no improvement. Inspecting Figure 4(b), we can see that both models perform very well for this subject — both the N9s algorithm and the GP perform well, and so very little improvement is possible. It is also interesting to note that subject 8 is the only user in the study who does not own a touch-screen device and is a user for which we see very large improvements.

The bottom row in Figure 4 shows how the root mean squared error between the intended and inferred touch location (in mm) varies as the training set size increases. The solid line gives the GP performance and the shaded area shows plus and minus one standard deviation. This was obtained by randomly taking a subset of touches for training and then testing on the remainder. The N9 performance is averaged over the same set of test points (variance in N9 performance was too small to visualise). We notice that for subjects 1 and 8, there is a large drop up to 400 training examples and then performance appears to plateau. In [6], participants recorded on average ~ 1000 touches each and therefore our proposed approach could be trained using data collected in a similar manner. Subject 3 also plateaus at around 400 training examples, but does not show any improvement. Again however, this can be explained by the excellent N9 performance for this user (a root mean squared error value of less than 2mm).

Prediction from device location

In our second set of experiments, we used the N9's reported touch location as input instead of the raw sensor values. This is motivated by the fact that it is not currently possible to obtain raw sensor data on most touchscreen devices. This approach is similar to the offsets computed in [6] in that it is adding a post-processing step to the device's reported touch location but differs in two respects. Firstly, we are learning a continuous, user-specific offset function which can, in theory, have a different value at any input location and secondly, the GP regression does not restrict us to any particular parametric function family, such as the 5th order polynomials used by Henze et al. We once again optimise the GP covariance parameters by performing a cross-validation (us-

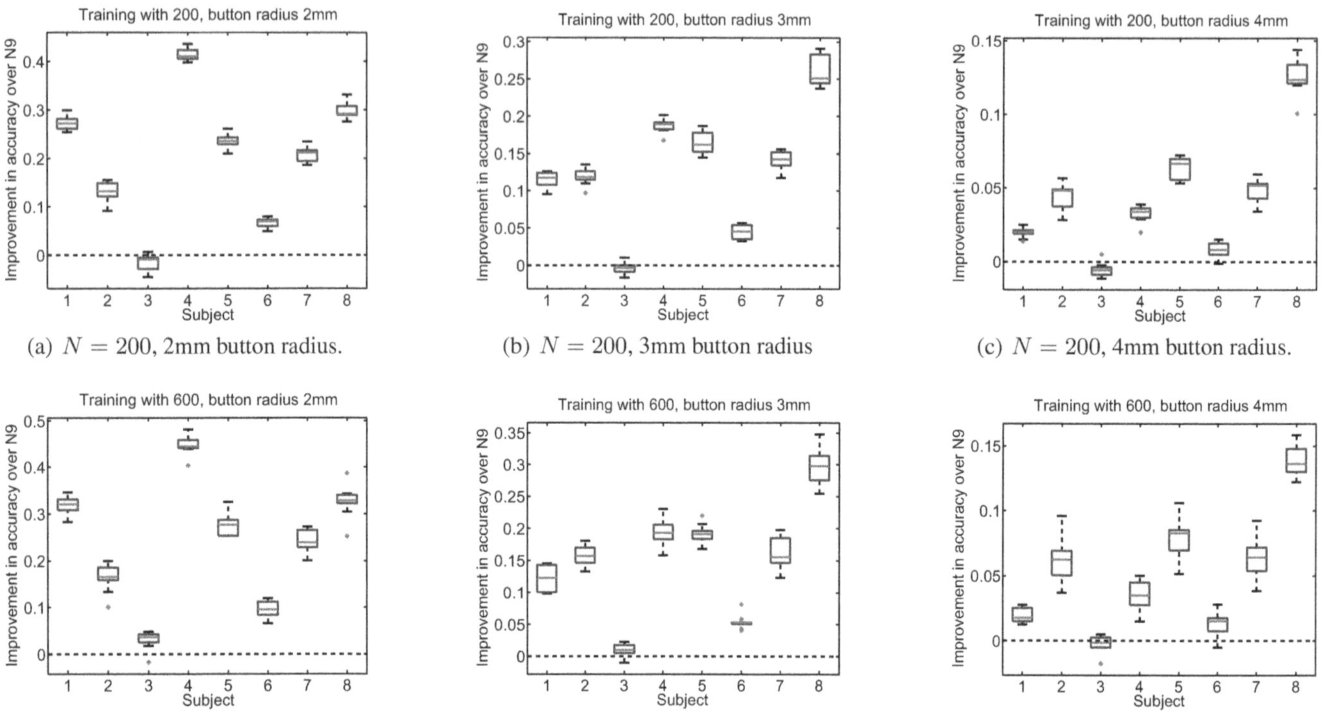

(a) $N = 200$, 2mm button radius. (b) $N = 200$, 3mm button radius (c) $N = 200$, 4mm button radius.

(d) $N = 600$, 2mm button radius. (e) $N = 600$, 3mm button radius. (f) $N = 600$, 4mm button radius.

Figure 5. Improvements in accuracy rate for different virtual button radii and numbers of training examples when the N9's touch location is used as an input. The value on the y-axis is the proportion of touches inside the button for the GP model minus the proportion computed for the N9's reported touch location. An increase of say 0.1 corresponds to a 10% decrease in error rate. Boxplots show the distribution of improvement over 10 repetitions.

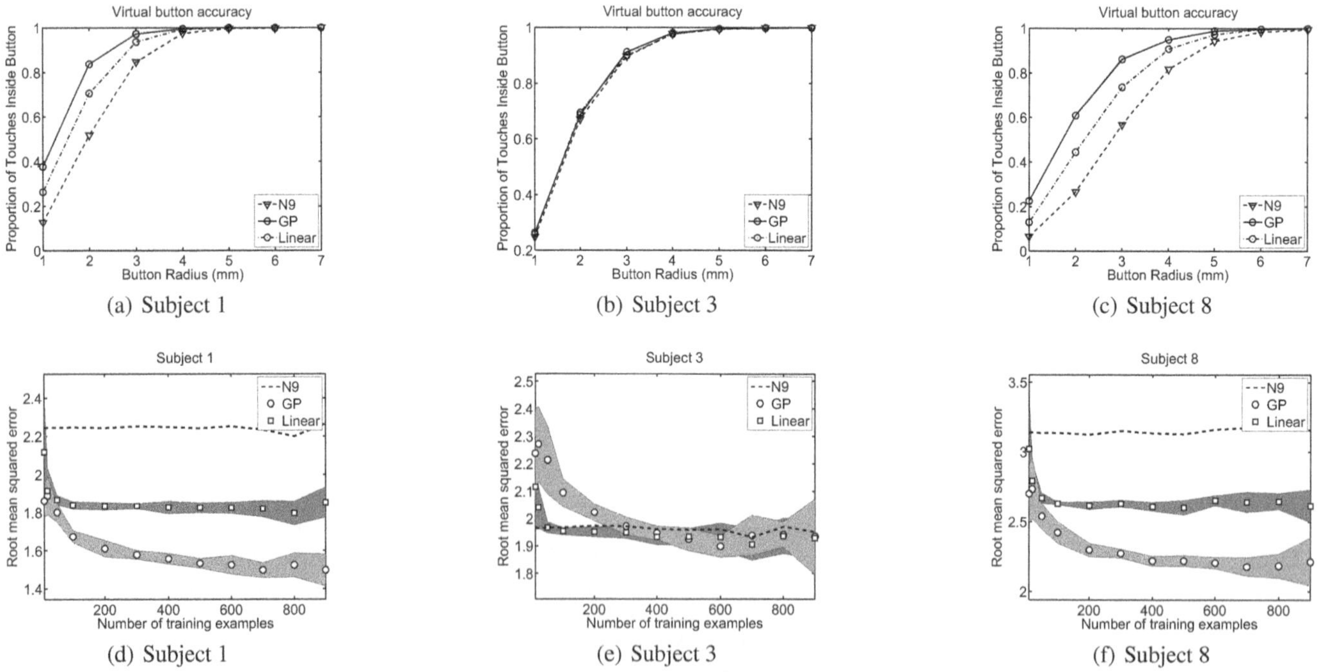

(a) Subject 1 (b) Subject 3 (c) Subject 8

(d) Subject 1 (e) Subject 3 (f) Subject 8

Figure 6. Comparison of performance between the N9 touch events (N9), a simple linear regression model (Linear) (e.g. as in [6] and our Gaussian Process' predictions using the N9's reported touch location as input (GP). Top row: Accuracy for different virtual button sizes (800 training points). Bottom row: Learning curves. Subject 1 represents an average user, subject 3 a user that already performs far above average already with the N9 screen and subject 8 represents a user that never used a touch screen based phone before.

ing user 5; randomly chosen). The optimal parameters were: $\gamma = 100, b = 1, a = 0.5, \alpha = 0.3, \sigma^2 = 10^{-3}$.

Figure 5 shows the improvements in performance offered by this method over the N9's reported touch location. We found that similar improvements can be made with fewer training examples than are required when using sensor data as input and so show the performance for $N = 200$ and $N = 600$ for buttons of radius 2mm, 3mm and 4mm. Once again, we notice significant (paired t-test, $p < 0.05$) performance improvements for all subjects except subject 3. These improvements are for just 200 training examples – collection of which would represent a very low overhead for the user. Assuming that an increase in performance of 0.1 corresponds to a reduction in error rate of 10%, the average reduction in error rate across all users is 23.79% (2mm buttons), 14.79% (3mm) and 5.11% (4mm).

The work in [9] suggests a theoretical lower limit of 2.15mm for the radius of a button which can be acquired with 95% accuracy. Their technique can acquire targets of radius 2.7mm, but doing so requires an overhead camera and an algorithm to extract salient features from the outline of the finger. Clearly these are not reasonable restrictions in a mobile setting. Our method achieves 95% accuracy with targets of radius between 2.8mm and 4mm, depending on the user. For all subjects bar one, this still represents an improvement over commercially available sensing technology of the N9.

In Figure 6 we show more detailed results for subjects 1, 3 and 8. We also give the performance of a simple linear regression model (see e.g. [13] p. 22) trained on the same data. For subject 3 we again see no significant improvement but for subjects 1 and 8 we see that both the linear regression and the GP outperform the N9's native algorithm and that the GP outperforms the linear regression, suggesting that the touch offset is not a linear function of the touch location. Notice also that for subjects 1 and 8, the performance is never worse than that of the N9, whereas in predicting the intended location from the raw sensor values, the performance was worse when there was little training data (see Figure 4(d) and (f)). This can be explained by the GP prior mean function, which is set to zero. When very little data is available, the GP will produce an output close to zero. For the offset prediction, this will give reasonable results as the model output will not vary much from the N9 output. However, when predicting the location rather than the offset, it will give very poor performance unless the touch happens to be close to the origin.

When using the N9 touch location as an input, it is possible to visualise the offset functions that are learned across the 2D input space. These are shown for subjects 1, 3 and 8 in Figure 7. The left hand panels show the predicted offsets across the input space, binned into a 10×5 grid. The size and direction of the offset for each touch which falls in a given box is shown relative to the center of that box. This binning is done only for ease of visualisation — all calculations were done with the continuous offset functions. The centre and right panels show the continuous horizontal and vertical offset functions. White corresponds to a large positive value (to the right or up for horizontal and vertical offsets respectively) and black a

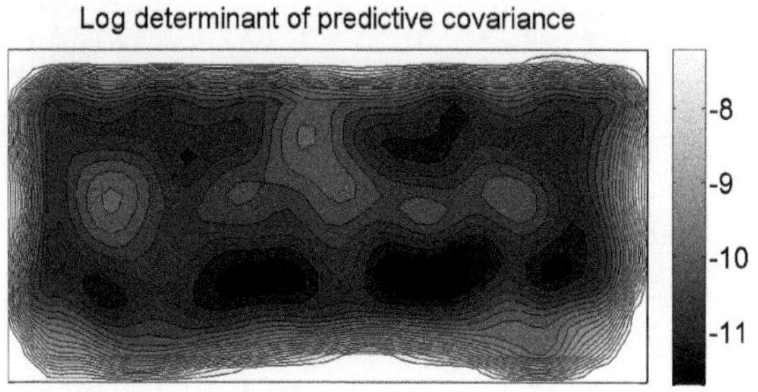

Figure 9. Log determinant of the predictive covariance matrix for subject 1 when the N9's touch location is used as an input.

large negative value (to the left and down). We see very small offsets for subject 3, reflecting the fact that the N9 input is already very accurate. For users 1 and 8, it is immediately clear that the offset functions are highly non-linear. The horizontal offset functions have two reasonably flat areas separated by a steep ridge. Recall that the user is operating the system with two thumbs (see Figure 2) and this ridge represents the point at which the thumb they are using changes. The vertical offsets are more complex, likely reflecting the change in thumb orientation as it reaches up and down.

To show the relative limitations of the linear model, Figure 8 shows the linear offsets learned for subject 8. Comparing these with the bottom row in Figure 7, we can clearly see the subtleties lost by the linear model. In particular, the horizontal offset in the linear model changes smoothly from left to right, completely missing the sharp change required towards the centre of the device where the user changes thumbs.

Predictive covariance

The Gaussian Process prediction consists of a Gaussian density. Thus far we have just used the mean of this Gaussian as a point estimate. The covariance of the Gaussian is also useful as it describes the uncertainty in the prediction and could therefore be used at the application level. In Figure 9 we visualise the log determinant of the predictive covariance matrix (higher corresponds to greater uncertainty) for subject 1 when the N9 touch location is used as an input. The highest uncertainty is at the edges, representing the limit of the recorded data. There are also areas of higher uncertainty down the centre and in the centre left and right areas. The centre area can most likely be explained by the user changing thumbs in this area – they will not always change at exactly the same horizontal position and therefore uncertainty in the required offsets is natural. This information about the uncertainty is a further advantage over the polynomial function of [6], which only gives a point estimate of the offset. We discuss other uses of predictive uncertainty below.

Generalising Results

To ensure that the results described above were not specific to a particular device and orientation combination, we car-

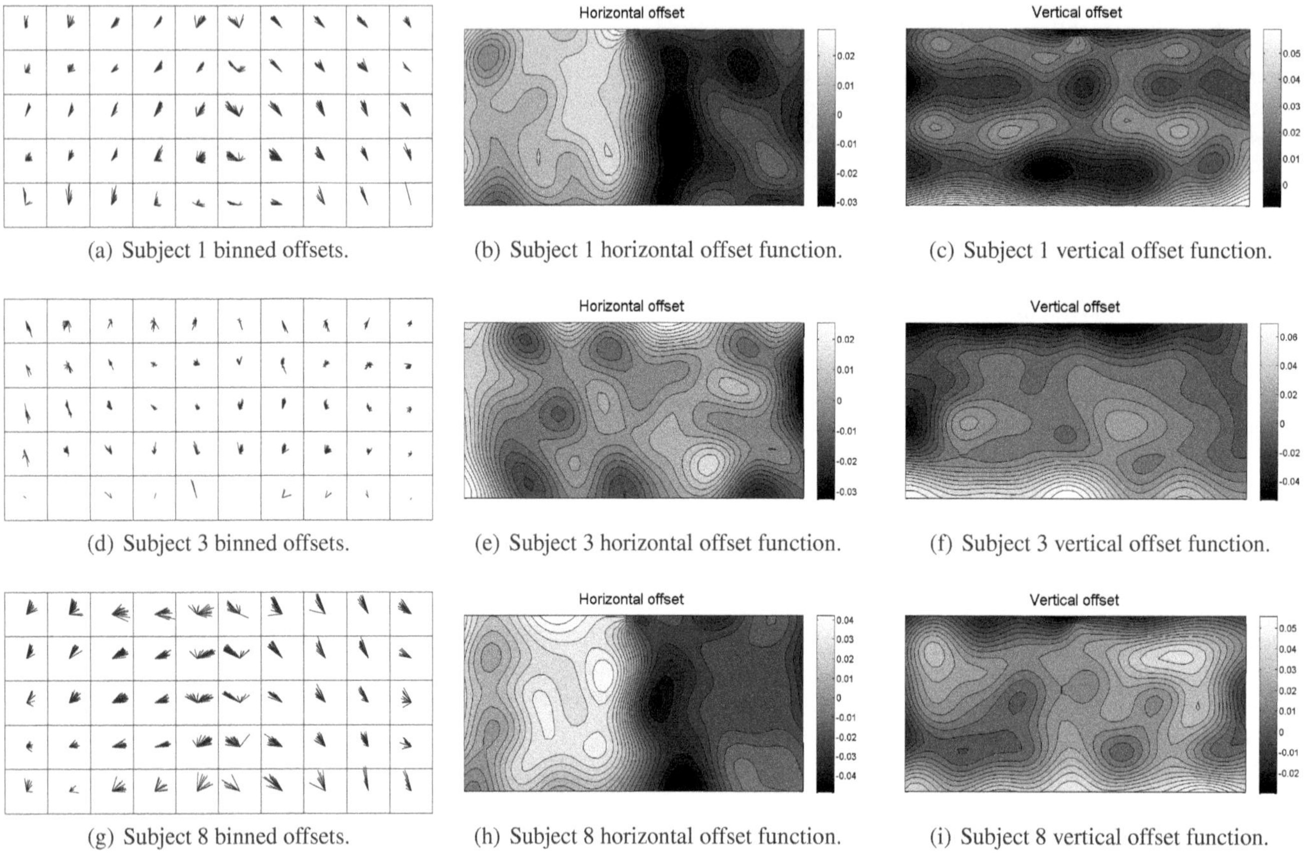

(a) Subject 1 binned offsets. (b) Subject 1 horizontal offset function. (c) Subject 1 vertical offset function.

(d) Subject 3 binned offsets. (e) Subject 3 horizontal offset function. (f) Subject 3 vertical offset function.

(g) Subject 8 binned offsets. (h) Subject 8 horizontal offset function. (i) Subject 8 vertical offset function.

Figure 7. Offsets learned for subjects 1, 3 and 8. All panels represent the lower half of the N9 screen when in landscape mode. The left hand plot shows the offsets inferred by the GP for the actual touch data and the right two the continuous horizontal and vertical offset functions learned by the GP.

ried out a number of additional experiments. First, we had two subjects (1 and 6) each generate 1000 additional touches, with the N9 in a portrait orientation. Users held the device in one hand and touched using the thumb on that hand. The touch targets were generated in the region corresponding to the device's portrait virtual keyboard. While significant conclusions cannot be drawn for a sample of two, the results of this probe are included to contextualise our core results.

Figure 10 shows our results. Again, we computed the virtual button accuracy as our performance metric ((a) and (c)). We used the raw sensor values of the touches as the input to the GP. For both users, we see that the GP is more accurate than the N9's native algorithm. These GPs were based on the optimal parameters found from the cross validation on the landscape data, showing that the covariance parameters generalise well across orientation. The learning curves (10(b) and (d)) show that the GP outperforms the N9 after approximately 300 training points are generated. An interesting future research direction is the development of a model which can predict touch location regardless of device orientation. This is potentially possible since even when touching the same location, the sensor readings are likely to be different across the different orientations.

We also replicated our experiment on a Google Nexus One running Android. Since this device does not expose the raw sensor values in the screen, we were restricted to considering the prediction problem using the device's reported touch location as input. We had two subjects (1 and 3) generate 1000 touches in landscape mode. The protocol was identical to the original experiment. Virtual button accuracies and learning curves for the GP, Android phone and a linear model are shown in Figure 11. Once again we see that the GP outperforms both competing models for all button sizes. Note also that one of the users shown is subject 3, for whom the GP offered no improved performance on the N9. On the Android phone, we see a large improvement for this user when using the GP. As with the N9, the learning curves are below the device performance for even very small quantities of training data. This can again be attributed to the zero mean of our GP.

Importance of user-specificity

In Figure 7 we saw that the offset functions learned varied greatly across users. To quantify what this means in terms of performance, we carried out an additional experiment where we trained on a mixture of data from all subjects and evaluated the test performance of the resulting model on the data for each individual. Figure 12 shows our results. For each subject, two box plots are shown. The first shows the improvement in accuracy for a 2mm button over the N9 when training on 600 of that subject's touches. The second shows the performance improvement when the model is trained on

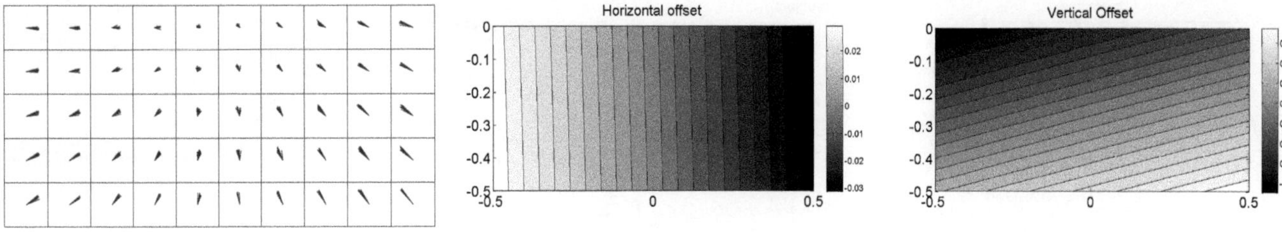

(a) Subject 8 binned offsets. (b) Subject 8 horizontal offset function. (c) Subject 8 vertical offset function.

Figure 8. Offsets learned by linear regression for subject 8.

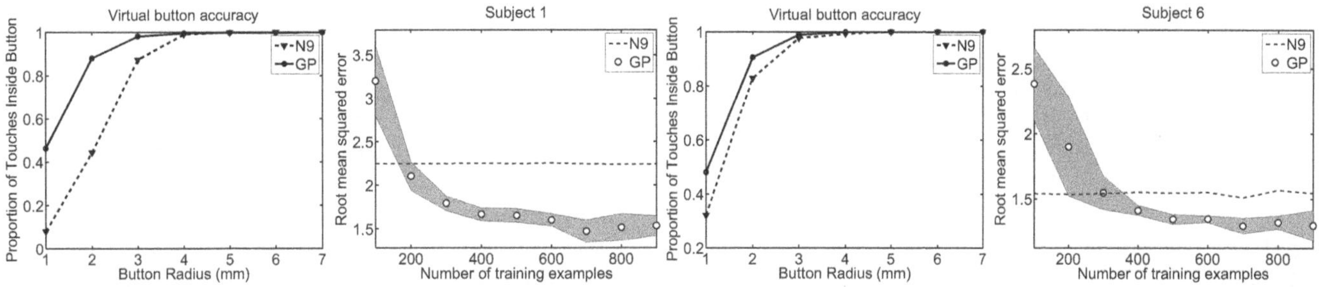

(a) Subject 1 (b) Subject 1 (c) Subject 6 (d) Subject 6

Figure 10. Virtual button accuracy and learning curves for portrait touches

600 touches drawn at random from the data for all subjects. This experiment was done using the device location as the GP input. Improvements were also seen for 3mm and 4mm buttons (results not shown).

In all cases, the performance improvement for the user-specific models is higher than that for the model trained on all subjects. The differences are statistically significant for all subjects (paired t-test, $p < 0.05$). For subject 3, whose touch behaviour is significantly different from the norm (as evidenced by the earlier results), training on the other subjects' data results in a notable *decrease* in performance compared to the N9. Thus it is clear that there is significant variation between users, and that training user-specific models is advantageous.

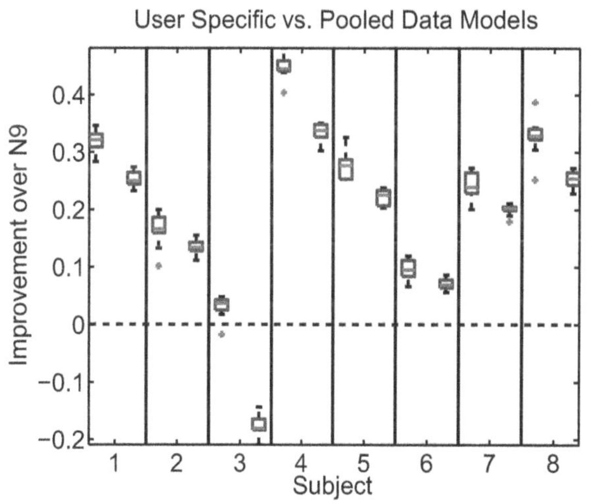

Figure 12. Improvements in accuracy rate for 2mm virtual buttons when using a user-specific model (left hand box plot in each case) and a model trained on all users (right hand box plot).

DISCUSSION AND FUTURE WORK

Data Collection

Key to this approach is the collection of training data. There are several ways in which this could be done with minimal effort from the user, described below. Investigating the practical feasibility of these approaches is an area for future research.

One method for generating the data would be to make use of a calibration game [5]. In [6] a similar approach has been applied and was very successful. With such a tapping game it would be easily possible to generate the required number of touches in a recreational setting. Note that in [6], users provided, on average, many more touches than needed for our approach. An alternative would be to use keyboard entry as a source of training data. Since the approach described in this paper only requires approximately 200 touches (when predicting from the device's reported touch location) to perform significantly better than the native touch location, writing one long email might already provide enough input data to train. Such an approach could be used in conjunction with the automatic keyboard optimisation proposed by [2]. In addition, the success of [7] showed that it is possible to combine typing and a calibration game.

Another possibility would be to introduce a new unlock method that collects the required data. Most mobile phones can be secured by a four digit PIN needed to unlock the device and this can serve as a data collection point. By arranging the numbers randomly on the screen the user

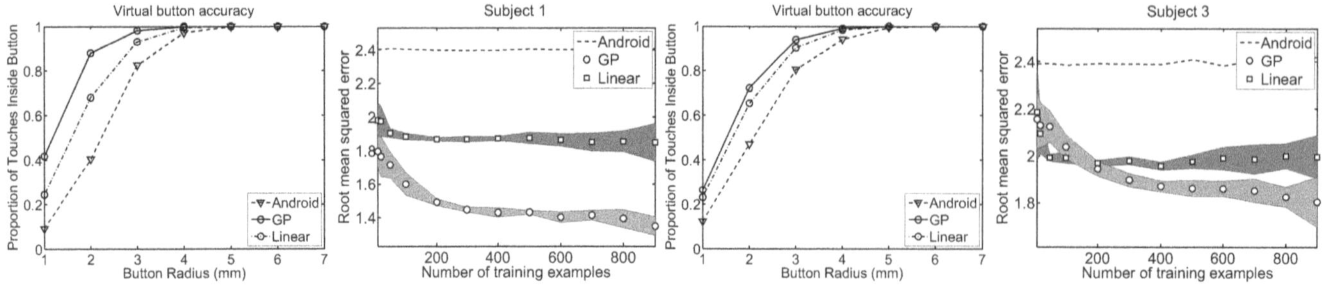

(a) Subject 1, Android (b) Subject 1, Android (c) Subject 3, Android (d) Subject 3, Android

Figure 11. Performance on Android phone

would need to touch on different places each time he wants to unlock his device. This could generate the needed touches in approximately 50 unlock procedures. Furthermore the approach would be safe against so-called smudge attacks [1] - reconstruction of frequently used patterns through oily residues on the screen - since the positions of the unlock digits would vary and no common pattern should emerge. The only drawback of this mechanism would be that users would not be able to generate a muscle memory to quickly unlock the device.

For longitudinal usage an iterative recalibration might be necessary since users might generate certain habits in touching or holding the device. A constant update e.g. using the keyboard approach as discussed above could be a feasible way of adapting the touch accuracy that might actually be capable of coping with temporary impairments such as a sprained thumb.

Predictive variance and uncertainty handover

The GP regression is naturally probabilistic, providing as its prediction a Gaussian density. Whilst we have only used the mean value in our accuracy calculations, the covariance could be useful from both a design perspective and an interaction perspective. Knowing which areas of the input space are the hardest to model (for example, the vertical strip in the centre when the user is using two thumbs in landscape mode, see Figure 9) can help in deciding where to place different sized buttons. Being able to model this in a user-specific manner could lead to devices that could optimise layout for accuracy as more data is acquired. From an interaction point of view, including uncertainty in input opens up the possibility of building schemes where autonomy can be transferred from the user to the device as shown in [15]. For example, uncertainty in touch locations could be used to produce a distribution over which key the user intended to press when operating a keyboard. This distribution could be fed forward into a probabilistic language model allowing for potential improvements in text entry accuracy. In [17] Schwarz et al presented a model which used uncertainty information to select between several small, closely packed buttons. The authors used a Gaussian centered on the detected touch area to represent the uncertain touch, but it is clear that the touch area is not necessarily a good indication of the intended target. The distributions produced by the GP automatically account for the offset and allow the full covariance structure to be learned for all parts of the space — using this information in application frameworks is a promising research direction which could open up new channels for rich touch interaction.

Computational complexity

Key to the success of a method like this is the ability to deploy it in real time on a mobile device. The GP regression approach has two distinct phases: training, involving inverting a square matrix of size $2 \times N$ (where N is the number of training touches) and predicting, which involves creating a covariance matrix and performing a matrix multiplication for each new touch event. The multiplications required for predictions will scale with the number of training examples. In our experiments, we found significant improvements for 400 training points (when the sensor data is used as input) and 200 (when the device's reported touch location is used). With matrices of this size, the operations are easily feasible on all modern mobile devices. In addition, our experiments used randomly placed training locations and it is highly likely that smarter position of these (perhaps using an active learning strategy), coupled with a sparse regression algorithm (e.g. [19]) could reduce the size of training sets further.

Incorporating additional data

GP regression provides a principled and flexible framework for incorporating additional data into the prediction task through combinations of covariance functions (see e.g. [12]). For example, one could include the current output from the accelerometers built into most mobile devices. This could allow the model to automatically adapt to different device orientations or different device usage contexts. For example, the model could adapt to give greater uncertainty in the predictions when the user is walking. In the text-entry scenario described above, the increased uncertainty would automatically give more influence to the probabilistic language model. The ability of the GP to probabilistically incorporate streams of data from multiple sensors is a key strength of our approach, and makes the GP a powerful tool for modelling uncertain interaction.

Multiple users on one device

One drawback of a user-specific model is when multiple users use the same device. One way to overcome this would be to allow the user to switch the adaptive model on or off, depending on who was using the device. Alternatively, it may be possible to automatically infer the particular user from the touch characteristics (particularly if raw sensor data is used) or estimated keyboard error rates (e.g. if the user starts making many mistakes) and switch the predictive model on and off accordingly.

CONCLUSIONS

In this paper we demonstrated the feasibility of a user-specific machine learning approach based on GP regression to increase user specific touch accuracy. Using raw sensor input from a capacitive touch screen we were able to improve touch accuracy on average by 23.47% for a 2mm button, 14.20% for a 3mm and 4.7% for a 4mm button. We also demonstrated that the approach using the touch location reported by the device as input resulted in slightly better performance, with accuracy increasing on average by 23.79% for a 2mm, 14.79% for a 3mm and 5.11% for a 4mm button. This has the potential to both improve the user experience and allow for smaller sized buttons.

We found that our approach worked in both portrait and landscape modes and across two different devices. As shown in [6], user-specific offsets exist in all devices studied and our improvements are therefore unlikely to be restricted to the two devices studied here.

A key finding in this research is that optimal offset functions are highly nonlinear, both horizontally and vertically and vary dramatically over the touch area and over users. For most users, the proposed GP approach considerably outperforms a linear model trained on the same data. User-specific models also outperformed models trained on pooled data, highlighting the diversity in user behaviour.

This work provides the basis for a wide range of further research. We have a flexible GP regression framework with which we can incorporate data from multiple sensors to intelligently deal with the inherent uncertainties of touch interaction. With this rich predictive model, we can easily build improved systems for important tasks such as text entry. Further, we can use the predictive uncertainty to respond appropriately and automatically to a range of usage contexts, or to negotiate the handover of autonomy between user and device.

ACKNOWLEDGEMENTS

Daryl Weir is supported by a PhD studentship from the Scottish Informatics and Computer Science Alliance (SICSA). Nokia provided equipment and funding to support this research.

REFERENCES

1. Aviv, A. J., Gibson, K., Mossop, E., Blaze, M., and Smith, J. M. Smudge attacks on smartphone touch screens. In *WOOT '10*, 1–7.
2. Baldwin, T., and Chai, J. Towards online adaptation and personalization of key-target resizing for mobile devices. In *IUI '12*, 11–20.
3. Baudisch, P., and Chu, G. Back-of-device interaction allows creating very small touch devices. In *CHI '09*, 1923–1932.
4. Findlater, L., and Wobbrock, J. O. Personalized Input: Improving Ten-Finger Touchscreen Typing through Automatic Adaptation. 815–824.
5. Flatla, D. R., Gutwin, C., Nacke, L. E., Bateman, S., and Mandryk, R. L. Calibration games: making calibration tasks enjoyable by adding motivating game elements. In *UIST '11*, 403–412.
6. Henze, N., Rukzio, E., and Boll, S. 100,000,000 taps: Analysis and improvement of touch performance in the large. In *MobileHCI '11*,
7. Henze, N., Rukzio, E., and Boll, S. Observational and experimental investigation of typing behaviour using virtual keyboards on mobile devices. In *CHI'12*,
8. Holz, C., and Baudisch, P. The generalized perceived input point model and how to double touch accuracy by extracting fingerprints. In *CHI '10*, 581–590.
9. Holz, C., and Baudisch, P. Understanding touch. In *CHI '11*, 2501–2510.
10. Lee, S., Buxton, W., and Smith, K. C. A multi-touch three dimensional touch-sensitive tablet. In *CHI '85*, 21–25.
11. Parhi, P., Karlson, A. K., and Bederson, B. B. Target size study for one-handed thumb use on small touchscreen devices. 203–210.
12. Rasmussen, C. E., and Williams, C. K. I. *Gaussian Processes for Machine Learning*. MIT Press, 2006.
13. Rogers, S., and Girolami, M. *A First Course in Machine Learning*. Chapman and Hall / CRC, 2011.
14. Rogers, S., Williamson, J., Stewart, C., and Murray-Smith, R. Anglepose: robust, precise capacitive touch tracking via 3d orientation estimation. In *CHI '11*, 2575–2584.
15. Rogers, S., Williamson, J., Stewart, C., and Murray-Smith, R. Fingercloud: uncertainty and autonomy handover in capacitive sensing. In *CHI '10*, 577–580.
16. Saponas, T. S., Harrison, C., and Benko, H. Pockettouch: through-fabric capacitive touch input. In *UIST '11*, 303–308.
17. Schwarz, J., Hudson, S., Mankoff, J., and Wilson, A. D. A framework for robust and flexible handling of inputs with uncertainty. In *UIST '10*, 47.
18. Schwarz, J., Mankoff, J., and Hudson, S. Monte carlo methods for managing interactive state, action and feedback under uncertainty. In *UIST '11*, 235.
19. Tipping, M. Sparse Bayesian learning and the Relevance Vector Machine. *Journal of Machine Learning Research 1*, 211–244.
20. Williamson, J. *Continuous Uncertain Interaction*. PhD thesis, University of Glasgow, 2006.

Proton++: A Customizable Declarative Multitouch Framework

Kenrick Kin[1,2] **Björn Hartmann**[1] **Tony DeRose**[2] **Maneesh Agrawala**[1]
[1]University of California, Berkeley [2]Pixar Animation Studios

ABSTRACT
Proton++ is a declarative multitouch framework that allows developers to describe multitouch gestures as regular expressions of touch event symbols. It builds on the Proton framework by allowing developers to incorporate custom touch attributes directly into the gesture description. These custom attributes increase the expressivity of the gestures, while preserving the benefits of Proton: automatic gesture matching, static analysis of conflict detection, and graphical gesture creation. We demonstrate Proton++'s flexibility with several examples: a direction attribute for describing trajectory, a pinch attribute for detecting when touches move towards one another, a touch area attribute for simulating pressure, an orientation attribute for selecting menu items, and a screen location attribute for simulating hand ID. We also use screen location to simulate user ID and enable simultaneous recognition of gestures by multiple users. In addition, we show how to incorporate timing into Proton++ gestures by reporting touch events at a regular time interval. Finally, we present a user study that suggests that users are roughly four times faster at interpreting gestures written using Proton++ than those written in procedural event-handling code commonly used today.

Author Keywords
Proton++, custom attributes, touch events symbols, regular expressions, gesture tablature

ACM Classification Keywords
D2.2 Software Engineering: Design Tools and Techniques; H5.2 Information Interfaces & Presentation: User Interfaces

INTRODUCTION
Multitouch gestures can be based on a wide range of touch attributes. At a basic level, each gesture is a sequence of touch events (touch-down, touch-move, touch-up). In addition, developers frequently consider the trajectory of the touches and the timing between the events. New multitouch devices have extended the set of touch attributes to include touch area, touch orientation, finger ID, and user ID. In some cases, applications also derive higher-level attributes such as pressure from lower-level attributes like touch area. Each such attribute increases the expressivity and design space of multitouch gestures.

Incorporating touch attributes into the event-handling code common in today's procedural multitouch frameworks complicates the already difficult task of writing correct gesture recognition code. In these frameworks, developers write event handlers that consider the sequence of touch events and attributes for each gesture. Keeping track of gesture state across many different callbacks leads to *spaghetti code* that is difficult to understand and maintain. Developers must also detect and resolve conflicts between gestures. Conflicts occur whenever a sequence of touch events partially match multiple gestures (e.g., two touches could represent a rotation gesture or a pinch-to-zoom gesture). Current event-handling frameworks force developers to detect such conflicts at runtime through trial-and-error testing.

Recent multitouch frameworks have sought to simplify the creation of multitouch gestures by allowing developers to describe gestures declaratively [14, 30] rather than in procedural event-handling code. Proton [16] is one such framework, which represents multitouch gestures as regular expressions composed of touch event symbols. From these expressions, Proton automatically generates gesture recognizers and provides static analysis of gesture conflicts. This approach reduces the code complexity of event callbacks and facilitates the development and maintenance of gesture sets. However, Proton only considers basic touch event sequences that contain touch ID, touch action (down, move, up), and touch hit-target. It does not support other common attributes such as trajectory, touch area, finger ID, or timing. Finally, Proton is limited to detecting a single gesture at a time.

We present Proton++, an extension to Proton that allows developers to define custom touch attributes and incorporate them into declarative gesture definitions. We demonstrate the benefits of customization with example implementations of five attributes: a *direction* attribute for specifying touch trajectory (Figure 1a,b), a *pinch* attribute for detecting when touches move towards one another, a *touch area* attribute for simulating pressure, a *finger orientation* attribute that provides an additional parameter for selecting menu items, and a *screen location* attribute for simulating hand ID and user ID. We show that such customization allows for more expressive gestures while retaining the automatic generation of recognizers and conflict detection capabilities of Proton.

To facilitate authoring gestures with custom attributes, Proton++ adds attribute notation to the gesture regular expressions and graphical gesture tablature of Proton (Figure 1c-e). Proton++ also allows developers to declaratively specify timing within a gesture by reporting touch events at a regular time interval. In addition, Proton++ allows developers to split the input touch event stream by attribute values. Proton++

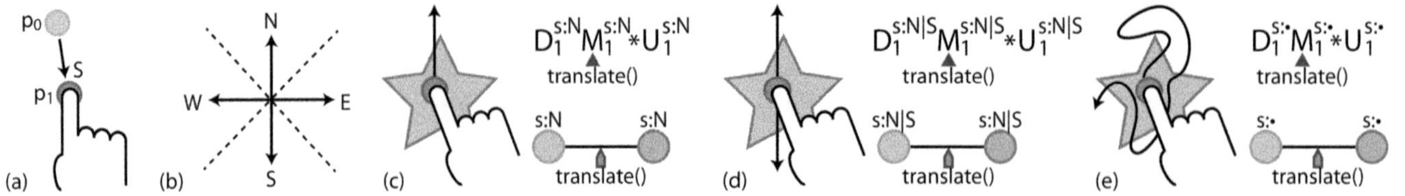

Figure 1. In Proton++ the developer can specify a custom touch direction attribute. (a) The direction is computed by taking the vector formed by the last two positions of the touch and (b) binning it to one of the four cardinal directions. Combining the hit-target and direction attributes, the developer can specify a gesture to translate a star (denoted as 's') with varying degrees of specificity: (c) north only, (d) north and south only, (e) in any direction.

can then process each stream independently in parallel and thereby detect multiple simultaneous gestures. We show how such stream splitting enables multiuser applications in which each user can perform gestures at the same time.

Finally, we contribute a user study that investigates how quickly and accurately developers recognize and reason about gestures described using gesture regular expressions, gesture tablatures, and iOS-style procedural event-handling pseudocode. We find that developers correctly recognize gesture tablatures the fastest of all three gesture descriptions; tablatures are 2.0-2.1 times faster than expressions and 4.2-4.7 times faster than event-handling code. These results suggest that developers are able to more quickly read and understand Proton++ tablatures than expressions and event-handling code.

RELATED WORK

Proton++ builds on a history of frameworks for modeling input. Its custom touch attributes enable recognition of rich, nuanced gestures. We first review work on describing gestures using formal grammars and declarative frameworks. We then survey related work on interaction techniques that leverage touch attributes.

Describing Multitouch Gestures

Proton++ describes multitouch gestures with regular expressions. Regular and context-free languages have been used to model interactions since early work by Newman [24] and Olsen and Dempsey [25]. More recently, CoGesT [10] uses context-free grammars to formally describe conversational hand gestures; GeForMt [13] also uses context-free grammars to model multitouch gestures. Neither system provides recognition capabilities. Gesture Coder [19] recognizes multitouch gestures with state machines, which are equivalent to regular expressions. While Proton++ and Gesture Coder share a recognition approach, their interfaces for authoring gestures differ significantly: developers demonstrate gestures in Gesture Coder; they author gestures symbolically using tablatures and regular expressions in Proton.

In addition to using formal languages, researchers have also developed other declarative frameworks for specifying multitouch gestures. In rule-based frameworks such as GDL [14] and Midas [30], developers author gestures based on spatial and temporal attributes (e.g., number of touches, touch trajectory, etc.). However, to identify conflicts between gestures, developers must rely on runtime testing. In contrast, Proton++'s underlying regular expression formalism enables automatic conflict detection between gestures at compile time.

Proton++ improves upon Proton [16] by increasing the flexibility of the framework. Proton++ allows the developers to customize touch events and expand the space of gestures that can be declaratively represented. In addition, Proton++ lifts the restriction of matching one gesture at a time, by splitting the touch stream into parallel streams with separate gesture matchers. Lastly, Proton++ encodes timing into the touch symbols, so gesture expressions can directly indicate the duration of touch sequences.

Leveraging Touch Attributes

Researchers have used touch attributes provided by multitouch hardware to design a wide range of gestures and applications. We survey representative techniques that use touch positions to create trajectory-dependent gestures, touch shape to increase the design space of gestures, and touch identity to track hands and users in multiuser applications.

Trajectory

Trajectory recognition systems consider touch positions over time. Recognition has been based on comparison to demonstrations [29, 38], and on regular expression matching to a string representation of a gesture [39]. These recognizers can only classify trajectory after the user has completed the gesture. Some systems detect trajectory *online*, as the user performs the gesture. Bevilacqua et al. [4] use a hidden Markov model to perform gesture following and Swigart [32] detects trajectory as a sequence of directions formed by the last two positions of the touch. Proton++ takes a similar approach to Swigart and incorporates direction attributes into touch event symbols. Researchers have used touch trajectories to disambiguate widget selection [23], to implement multitouch marking menus [15, 18], and to detect stroke commands [1].

Touch Shape

All multitouch devices detect position of touches, but many devices also detect touch shape [12, 21, 27, 28, 34]. Researchers have used hand shape in multitouch applications to distinguish between different operations based on analogies to real-world manipulations [5], to control physics simulations [36], to constrain degrees of freedom in shape manipulation [35] and to distinguish commands in multi-user applications [40]. Touch area can be extracted from touch shape, which researchers have used to simulate applied pressure when selecting and manipulating objects [3, 5]. Pressure-sensitive widgets designed for stylus input can also be implemented using touch area [26]. Researchers have extracted touch orientation from touch shape by fitting an ellipse to the shape and calculating the angle of its major axis [6, 33]; they

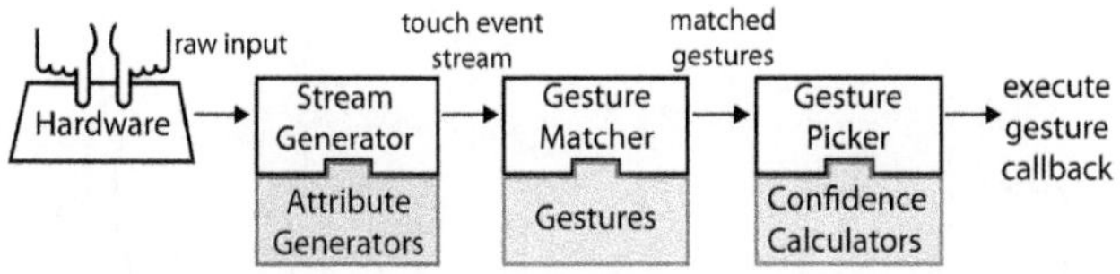

Figure 2. In Proton++, the developer provides the attribute generators (red) that assign attribute values to symbols in the touch event stream. The developer still provides the gestures and confidence calculators (blue) as in Proton.

use orientation as an additional parameter for object manipulation and command selection. With Proton++ developers can integrate touch area and orientation into gesture expressions to detect and execute similar interaction techniques.

Hand and User Identification

Most multitouch devices cannot distinguish the sources of touches, such as from which finger, hand, or person the touch originated. Researchers have augmented multitouch systems with additional vision tracking of hands [7]. With hand identity, developers can assign different gestures and roles to each hand, as promoted by Guiard's Kinematic Chain Model [11]. The DiamondTouch [20] table identifies users through capacitive coupling between the touch surface and a pad on each user's chair. User identity has enabled researchers to develop cooperative gestures for multiple users [22] and player tracking for multiplayer games [8]. Proton++ can integrate hand and user identity into touch events. Since most devices cannot identify hands or users without additional hardware, we describe a heuristic for identifying hands and users based on the screen location of a touch.

PROTON++ ARCHITECTURE AND NOTATION

Proton++ extends the architecture and notation introduced by Proton, while maintaining the gesture matching and conflict detection capabilities of that earlier system. As shown in Figure 2, Proton++ consists of a stream generator that converts touch events into a stream of symbols, a gesture matcher that compares the touch event stream against a set of gesture regular expressions, and a gesture picker that chooses the best gesture when multiple gestures match the user's actions. The developer must provide attribute generators that assign attribute values to the touch events, a set of gesture regular expressions with associated callbacks that describe each gesture the system should recognize, and confidence calculators to help the gesture picker choose the best gesture. The main architectural differences between Proton++ and Proton are in the stream and attribute generation. In this paper we focus on describing these two components of the Proton++ architecture. Detailed explanations of the other components can be found in Kin et al. [16].

A Proton++ touch event consists of a touch action (down, move, up), a touch ID (first, second, third, etc.) and a series of touch attribute values (e.g., direction = NW, hit-target = circle, etc.). Proton++ allows developers to customize touch events with additional touch attributes. Such customization requires writing attribute generators that map hardware touch information (e.g., position, pressure, finger area, etc.) to discrete attribute values. We describe implementations of several different types of attribute generators in the next section.

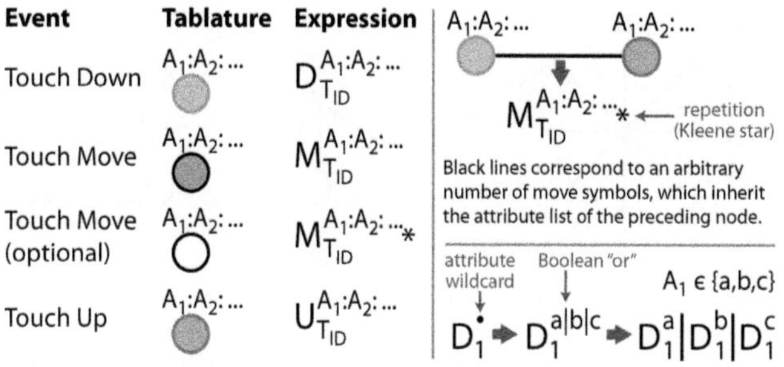

Figure 3. The Proton Syntax. Left: Tablature nodes correspond to different touch symbols. Right top: Tablature lines correspond to move symbols. Right bottom: An attribute wildcard expands into a disjunction of all values of an attribute.

The stream generator converts each touch event into a touch symbol of the form:

$$E_{T_{ID}}^{A_1:A_2:A_3...}$$

where $E \in \{D, M, U\}$ is the touch action, T_{ID} is the touch ID and $A_1 : A_2 : A_3...$, are the attribute values, where A_1 is the value corresponding to the first attribute, A_2 is the value corresponding to the second attribute, and so on. For example, $M_1^{s:W}$ represents *move-with-first-touch-on-star-object-in-west-direction.* We use the 's' attribute value to represent the star-object hit-target and the 'W' attribute value to represent west-direction.

A gesture is a regular expression over these touch event symbols. For example, the expression $D_1^{s:N} M_1^{s:N} {*} U_1^{s:N}$ describes a one-finger northward motion on the star object (Figure 1c). The Kleene star '*' indicates that the move symbol $M_1^{s:N}$ can appear zero or more consecutive times. Often a gesture allows for certain attributes to take on one of several values. The developer can use the '|' character to denote the logical *or* of attribute values. For example, the expression $D_1^{s:N|S} M_1^{s:N|S} {*} U_1^{s:N|S}$ extends the previous gesture to allow both north and south motions (Figure 1d). Proton++ expands the '|' shorthand into the full regular expression $(D_1^{s:N}|D_1^{s:S})(M_1^{s:N}|M_1^{s:S}){*}(U_1^{s:N}|U_1^{s:S})$. Proton++ also allows developers to use the '•' character to denote a wildcard which specifies that an attribute can take any value, effectively ignoring the attribute during matching. For example, if the direction attribute A_2 can take the set of values $\{N, S, E, W\}$, the expression $D_1^{s:\bullet} M_1^{s:\bullet} {*} U_1^{s:\bullet}$ describes any one-finger trajectory on the star object (Figure 1e). In this expression, the symbol $M_1^{s:\bullet}$ expands to $M_1^{s:N}|M_1^{s:S}|M_1^{s:E}|M_1^{s:W}$.

In addition to using regular expressions, developers can describe gestures using the *gesture tablature* graphical notation (Figure 1c-e). In gesture tablature, each touch is represented as a horizontal track. Green nodes represent touch down events and red nodes represent touch up events. The attributes associated with each touch event are listed above the corresponding nodes. Tablature uses the same shorthand as regular expressions for specifying multiple attribute values ('|' characters and '•' wildcards). The black lines connecting nodes represent an arbitrary number of touch move events and inherit the attributes of the preceding node. Ad-

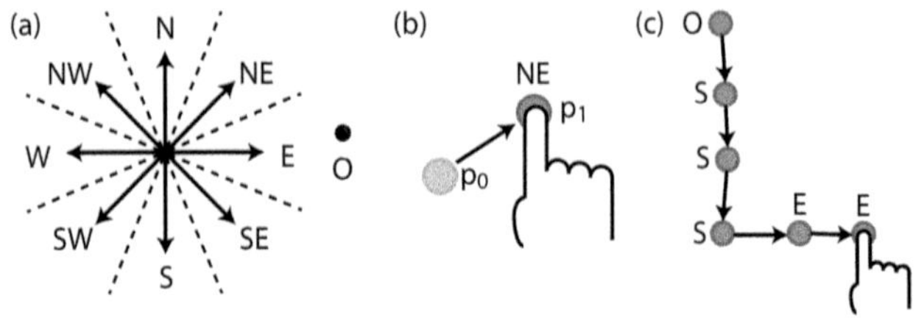

Figure 4. (a) The space of directions is divided into eight ranges representing the four cardinal and four ordinal directions. (b) The vector formed by the last two touch positions is binned to the closest direction. (c) An L-shaped gesture generates south ('S') then east ('E') symbols.

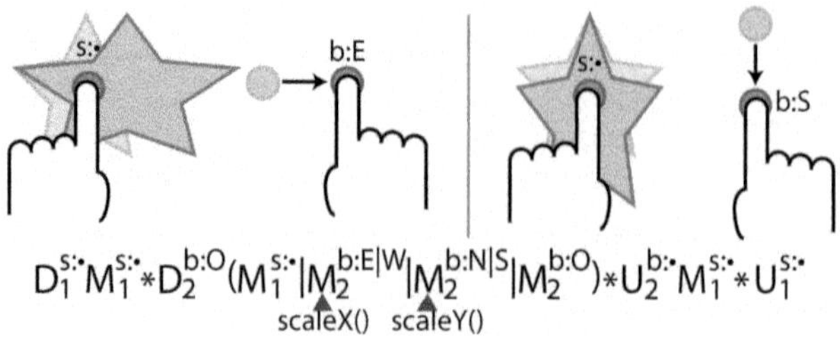

Figure 5. Proton++ continuously tracks the trajectory of the second touch, which allows the developer to provide continuous feedback depending on whether the touch moves east-west (scale in x-axis) or north-south (scale in y-axis).

ditionally, developers can insert gray and white nodes into a touch track. These nodes represent required and optional touch move events, respectively. The developer can use these nodes to change the attribute values associated with a touch. Figure 3 summarizes the mapping between between tablature nodes and expression symbols. Vertically aligned nodes indicate that the corresponding touch events can occur in either order. Tablature uses the same shorthand as regular expressions for specifying multiple attribute values.

A developer can add *triggers* to gesture expressions or tablatures to receive callback notifications. In Figure 1c-e, triggers are shown as blue arrows with the associated callback function name. Triggers are executed when the gesture matcher reaches their positions in an expression or tablature and they allow developers to provide feedback during a gesture.

CUSTOM ATTRIBUTES

To add a new custom attribute in Proton++, the developer must write and register an attribute generator. On each touch event, the attribute generator receives the touch data reported by the hardware sensors, along with the entire sequence of previous touch symbols from the stream generator. It then computes an attribute value based on this information and appends it to the current touch event symbol. Since Proton++ is based on regular expressions composed of discrete touch symbols, the primary constraint on the attributes is that they must take discrete values. Thus, attribute generators are often responsible for quantizing continuous-valued parameters to convert them into attribute values suitable for Proton++.

We have implemented five example attribute generators that produce such discrete attributes and demonstrate the flexibility of our approach: (1) a direction attribute for describing touch trajectory, (2) a pinch attribute for detecting when touches move towards one another, (3) a touch area attribute for simulating pressure, (4) a finger orientation attribute for selecting menu items, and (5) a screen location attribute for simulating hand ID and user ID. The direction and screen location attributes are based on touch position and can work with any multitouch device. Our implementations of the touch area and finger orientation attributes require additional touch information which we obtain from a Fingerworks iGesture Pad [34].

Direction Attribute

The direction attribute allows developers to describe a touch trajectory within a Proton++ gesture expression. Since attribute values must be discrete, we bin the space of all directions into eight ranges representing the four cardinal and four ordinal directions seen in a compass (Figure 4a). To generate this attribute we compute the vector $p_1 - p_0$, between the previous touch position p_0 (as given by the previous touch event with the same touch ID) and the current touch position p_1. Our direction attribute generator then returns the direction bin containing the vector (Figure 4b). If the touch has not moved beyond a distance threshold, the generator outputs an 'O' value. We use a threshold of five pixels.

Trajectory. A sequence of direction attributes describes a gesture trajectory. For example, in an L-shaped gesture (Figure 4c), the touch first moves in the S direction and then in the E direction. The expression to detect this trajectory is thus: $D_1^O M_1^S M_1^S{*} M_1^E M_1^E{*} U_1^E$. In practice we have found that users often slow down at the beginning of the trajectory or when making the turn from S to E, and the gesture expression fails if the user hesitates in this manner. To allow the user to hold a touch position at any point along the trajectory, we modify the expression to include symbols with direction attribute value 'O': $D_1^O M_1^O{*} M_1^S M_1^{O|S}{*} M_1^E M_1^{O|E}{*} U_1^{O|E}$. Note that this gesture expression requires users to execute a perfect right-angle turn. In the section on timing we will describe how we can extend such trajectory-based gestures to allow imprecise turns.

Unlike many recognition systems that detect trajectory at the end of the gesture [29, 38], Proton++ continuously tracks the trajectory as the user performs the gesture. Thus, developers can provide continuous feedback. For example, a shape manipulation application might include a gesture where one touch selects the shape, and a second touch must move E-W to scale the shape along the x-axis or move N-S to scale the shape along the y-axis with continuous feedback (Figure 5). Providing such immediate feedback is an essential feature for direct manipulation interfaces [31].

Pinch Attribute

A pinch in which two or more touches move towards each other is a commonly used gesture in multitouch applications. While the previous direction attribute evaluated the movement of an individual touch, the pinch gesture is based on on the relative movements of multiple touches. Our pinch attribute generator computes the average distance between each touch and the centroid of all the touches. It compares this average distance to the average distance computed for the previous touch event and if it decreases the generator assigns

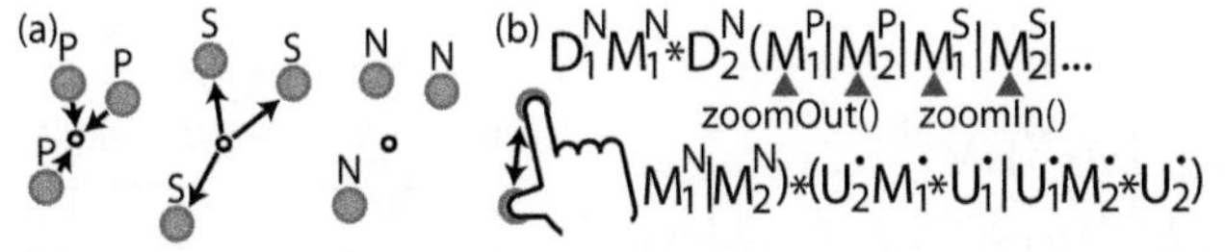

Figure 6. (a) Touches are assigned a 'P' when on average the touches move towards the centroid, an 'S' when the touches move away from the centroid, and an 'N' when they stay stationary. (b) A two-touch gesture that zooms out on a pinch and zooms in on a spread.

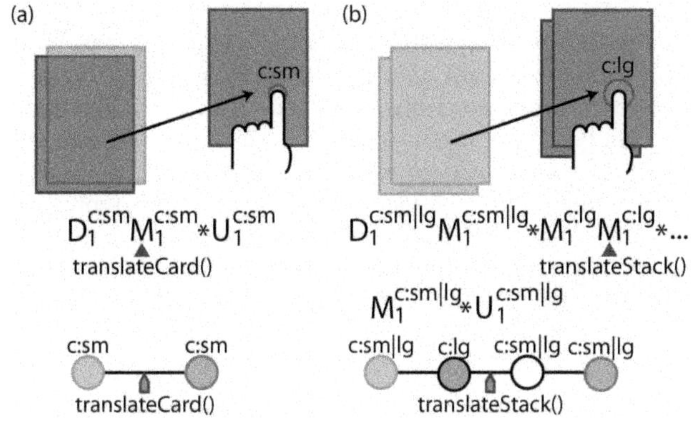

Figure 7. (a) A touch with small ('sm') area translates only the topmost card. (b) A touch with large ('lg') area translates the entire stack.

the touch the attribute value 'P' for pinching. If the average distance increases it assigns the touch the value 'S' for spreading, and if there is no change in average distance it assigns the value 'N' (Figure 6a). We use the pinch attribute to describe a two-touch zoom gesture as shown in Figure 6b. Our approach considers all touches together as a whole and cannot distinguish when only a subset of touches are pinching. For example, if two touches are locally pinching, but moving away from a stationary third touch, this attribute may report the touches as spreading. An alternative approach is to generate an attribute that encodes the pairwise pinch relationships of all possible touches, so the developer can then specify which pairs of touches must be involved in the pinch.

Touch Area Attribute

Many multitouch devices such as the Fingerworks iGesture Pad [34] report the touch area, the contact area between a finger or hand and the device, as a continuous value. Our attribute generator quantizes the size of the touch area to two discrete values, *small* and *large*. Precisely regulating touch area can be difficult. In practice we found that consistently generating more than two distinct levels of touch area was challenging and therefore limited this attribute to two levels.

Simulating Pressure. Although the iGesture Pad cannot detect pressure, we can use touch area to simulate force, using the approach of ShapeTouch [5]: smaller touch area corresponds to lower pressure and larger area corresponds to stronger pressure. As shown in Figure 7a, a touch on a card ('c') with a small ('sm') area $M_1^{c:sm}$ translates the topmost card of a stack, while in Figure 7b, a touch on a card with a large ('lg') area $M_1^{c:lg}$ translates the entire stack of cards. One limitation of touch area is that a user's initial touch area starts small before it grows into a large area. Thus, when using the large touch attribute value, the developer should allow the touch to begin and end on a small area. In general, the developer must carefully consider attributes such as area, where a touch must go through lower attribute values to reach higher attribute values.

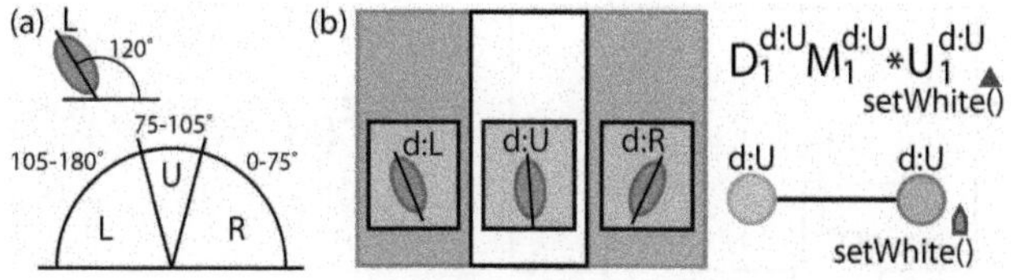

Figure 8. (a) The angle of the major axis of a touch is binned into three finger orientation values. (b) The dial menu ('d') uses orientation to set the background color of an application.

Finger Orientation Attribute

The Fingerworks iGesture Pad provides a continuous orientation value for each touch in the range 0-180°. We bin the orientations to three levels as shown in Figure 8a: up (75-105°), left (>105°), and right (<75°). We define a narrow range for the up bin so users do not have to awkwardly rotate their wrist or fingers from their natural positions to reach the left and right bins. We also minimize the number of orientation levels so that users can easily perform them.

Selecting Menu Items. We use the finger orientation attribute to select from a three-state dial menu (Figure 8b). In this example, the dial sets the background screen color: an up orientation assigns a white background, a left orientation assigns a green background, and a right orientation assigns an orange background. This dial menu is very similar to a marking menu [17], but uses finger orientation instead of stroke direction.

Screen Location Attribute

All multitouch devices provide touch position as a continuous value with each touch event. The screen location attribute generator assigns discrete attribute values to touch positions. Hit testing is one approach for assigning such discrete values; the attribute value is set to the label of the hit-target, the object directly under the touch point. Hit testing is the only attribute generator in Proton [16] and is also available in Proton++. In addition to using scene objects for hit testing, we can define other screen regions to generate attribute values.

Hand Identification. Most multitouch devices cannot detect which hand (left or right) generated a touch event. However, we can simulate hand ID using the screen location attribute as a proxy for hand ID. We divide the screen in half, and assign the attribute value 'L' (for left hand) to touches originating from the left side of the screen. Similarly we assign the value 'R' (for right hand) to touches originating from the right side.

We can combine this simulated hand ID attribute with the direction attribute (Figure 9 Left) to create an ordered two-handed marking menu [15], in which users must start a stroke with the left hand and then start a second stroke with the right hand to select between a large number of menu items. For example, the expression and tablature for the left hand drawing a stroke in the E direction and the right hand drawing a stroke in the W direction are given in Figure 9.

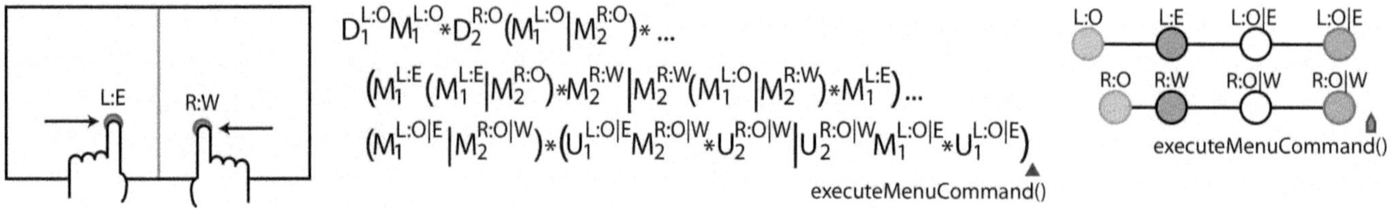

Figure 9. To simulate hand identification, touches beginning on the left side belong to the left hand and touches beginning on the right side belong to the right hand. An ordered two-handed marking menu can be described by adding the direction attribute.

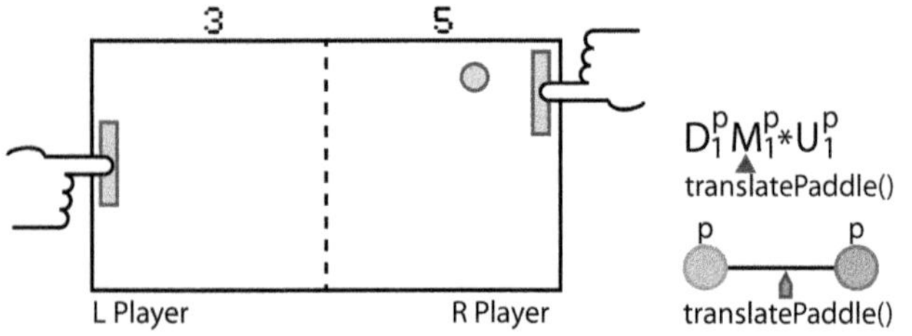

Figure 10. In the Pong game, the touch stream is split so one gesture matcher can process touches from the left player and a second gesture matcher can process touches from the right player. Both gesture matchers use the same gesture for controlling the paddle ('p').

SPLITTING THE TOUCH EVENT STREAM

Proton++ recognizes a gesture when the entire touch event stream matches a gesture regular expression. Each time a match is found, Proton++ executes the callback associated with the gesture expression and flushes the stream. Thus, with a single stream, Proton++ is limited to recognizing at most one gesture at a time.

However, Proton++ also allows developers to split the touch event stream by any custom attribute and run a separate gesture matcher on each stream. Such stream splitting allows Proton++ to recognize multiple simultaneous gestures, as each matcher can detect a different gesture. We use stream splitting in combination with a user ID attribute to enable multiuser applications.

User Identification. Some multitouch devices, such as the DiamondTouch [20], directly provide a different user ID for each person interacting with the device. For multitouch devices that do not provide such identification, we can simulate user ID using the screen location attribute. For example in a two-player Pong game (Figure 10), touches originating on the left side of the screen correspond to one user, and touches originating on the right correspond to a second user. Using a single stream and gesture matcher would restrict the players so that only one of them could move their paddle at any time. Splitting the stream by the location-based user ID removes this restriction. Since each stream has its own gesture matcher, the system can recognize paddle control gestures from both players at the same time. In this example the developer could provide the same set of attributes and gesture expressions to both gesture matchers. However, Proton++ also allows developers to register different sets of attributes and gesture expressions to each gesture matcher.

TIMING

While taps, holds, and flicks are common multitouch gestures, the basic touch event sequence for all three is exactly the same. To distinguish between these three gestures the gesture recognizer must have access to timing information. We introduce timing to Proton++ by adding the constraint that the stream generator reports touch events at a fixed time interval; we use $\frac{1}{30}s$. Thus each touch symbol $M_1^\bullet$ also represents a unit of time t and a sequence of k such symbols represents a time duration of kt. To express gesture timing, the developer can replace $M_1^\bullet{*}$, which matches a touch movement of any duration, with a fixed-length sequence of $M_1^\bullet$ symbols. This sequence matches only when the touch movement lasts for the corresponding length of time.

Writing out a fixed-length sequence of move symbols can be tedious, so we introduce a shorthand for specifying the number of successive touch-move events using the notation

$$(M_{T_{ID}}^{A_1:A_2:A_3\ldots})^{t_1-t_2}$$

which generates the expression that matches t_1 to t_2 successive $M_{T_{ID}}^{A_1:A_2:A_3\ldots}$ events. The t_2 parameter is optional. Proton++ expands the shorthand into t_1 consecutive move symbols if t_2 is not specified. It generates the disjunction of t_1 consecutive move symbols to t_2 move symbols if t_2 is specified. For example, a touch and hold that lasts at least five consecutive move events is expressed as $D_1^\bullet(M_1^\bullet)^5 M_1^\bullet{*}U_1^\bullet$, which expands to $D_1^\bullet M_1^\bullet M_1^\bullet M_1^\bullet M_1^\bullet M_1^\bullet M_1^\bullet{*}U_1^\bullet$. A tap of one to five move events is expressed as $D_1^\bullet(M_1^\bullet)^{1-5}U_1^\bullet$, which expands to $D_1^\bullet(M_1^\bullet|M_1^\bullet M_1^\bullet|\ldots|M_1^\bullet M_1^\bullet M_1^\bullet M_1^\bullet M_1^\bullet)U_1^\bullet$. We also update the tablature with timing notation as shown in Figure 11a. The developer can specify a range t_1 to t_2 within the gray move nodes.

Using timing to detect a hold, we can design a marking menu for novice users that visually displays the menu items if the user holds down a touch for $\frac{1}{3}$ of a second. We use the direction attribute and a sequence of 10 touch-move symbols to specify the $\frac{1}{3}s$ duration of the hold with the expression shown in Figure 11b. We associate a menu drawing callback with the tenth M_1^O.

Our previous L-shaped trajectory example requires the user to make a perfect right-angle turn from the S direction to the E direction. We can use timing to allow the user to momentarily move in any direction during the turn using the expression show in Figure 11c. The timing is specified in the symbol, $(M_1^\bullet)^{1-5}$, which gives the user up to a $\frac{1}{6}s$ window to make a less precise turn.

To capture timing between taps (e.g., double taps), Proton++ utilizes a user-definable timeout as in the original Proton system [16]. If the user releases all touches, the user has the

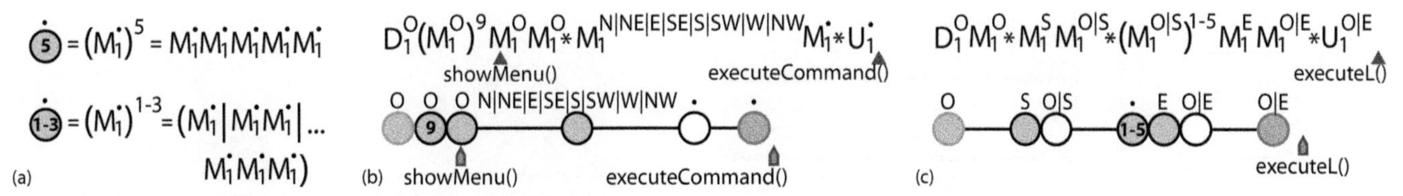

Figure 11. (a) Shorthand for specifying timing in tablature. (b) Novice marking menu using timing notation to specify a touch hold. (c) L-shaped trajectory using timing to permit an imprecise turn from south to east.

duration of the timeout to place the next touch down and continue the gesture. If no such touch occurs within the timeout period Proton++ considers the gesture to have failed. Alternatively, we could extend Proton++ to emit a 'Z' touch event symbol whenever there are no touches on the device. Since each symbol in the stream also represents a unit of time, the developer could use sequences of the 'Z' symbol to specify the duration between taps.

DESIGNING CUSTOM ATTRIBUTES

We have implemented example applications for the direction, pinch, touch area, finger orientation, and screen location attributes. We refer readers to the paper video[1] for demonstrations of these applications. Based on our experience building these applications, we distill several design considerations for creating custom attributes. We then discuss how developers can design new custom attributes to implement two gestures sets that have been recently proposed by other researchers.

Levels and Ranges of Attribute Values. Developers should base the number of levels of an attribute on the specificity needed by the application. More levels provide developers with finer-grain control over gesture specifications. However, more levels also require extra effort to author: developers may have to carefully write complex disjunctions of attribute values in the expressions.

The range of input values binned to each attribute value affects users' ability to perform actions that correspond to each attribute value. For example, if the range of a direction value is small, users may find it difficult to accurately draw a stroke in that particular direction. Noise or variation in user performance may cause matching to fail for attribute values with narrow ranges. Developers should choose ranges such that users can reliably perform actions for each attribute value.

Attribute Value Traversal. Certain attributes such as touch area will require traversal through lower attribute values to reach higher attribute values. Developers should be cognizant of this possibility and design gestures that allow for such traversal. Additional developer tools could aid in integrating these attributes in gestures.

No Asynchronous Attribute Values. Developers must assign an attribute value to each touch event as soon as it is emitted, within the time interval defined by the stream generator's reporting rate. While the history of a touch is available, developers must not wait for future information to determine an attribute value. Delaying assignment of attribute values, and writing expressions that permit such delayed assignments, would diminish the capacity of Proton++ to distinguish gestures from each other and to detect conflicts.

Application Independent Attributes. To create attributes that can be reused across multiple applications, attribute generators should only rely on information contained in the touch stream received from a hardware device and should not access application-specific information. For example, once defined, the direction attribute can be used in any application with gestures that require directional specification.

Implementing Other Gesture Sets in Proton++. Wobbrock et al. [37] present a user-defined gesture set for 27 common multitouch operations. Using Proton++ and our example attributes, the developer can directly implement all but two of the gestures. The remaining two gestures require more specialized attributes. Implementing their lasso gesture requires a distance attribute to differentiate between the longer path of the lasso and the shorter paths of other trajectory-based gestures, such as their check mark. To implement their 'X' gesture the developer could use the Proton++ direction attribute to detect two touch paths with diagonal trajectories (e.g., one SE path then one SW path), but would also have to implement a new intersection attribute that detects when two paths cross.

Freeman et al. [9] present a gesture set containing gestures similar to those of Wobbrock et al. However, half of the Freeman gesture set depends on different hand shapes, such as finger, fist, side of hand, etc. To support these gestures, the developer could implement a new attribute that distinguishes between the possible hand shapes. The gesture set also contains a gesture in which the fingers move counter-clockwise. While the direction attribute generator only uses the last two positions of a touch to detect direction, a counter-clockwise attribute generator requires knowledge of the last three positions of a touch to detect counter-clockwise movements.

USER STUDY

To help us understand whether developers can benefit from the gesture matching and conflict detection provided by Proton++, we conducted a user study evaluating how quickly and accurately developers comprehend gestures described using regular expressions, tablatures, and iOS-style [2] event-handling code. We divided the study into two parts, with the first part focusing on basic gestures that involved only the sequence of touch events and the second part including trajectory-based gestures.

We recruited 12 participants (10 male, 2 female, ages between 20 and 51) who were all experienced programmers. Each participant performed both parts of the experiment and each part contained three blocks. Each block focused on one of the

[1] http://vis.berkeley.edu/papers/protonPlusPlus/

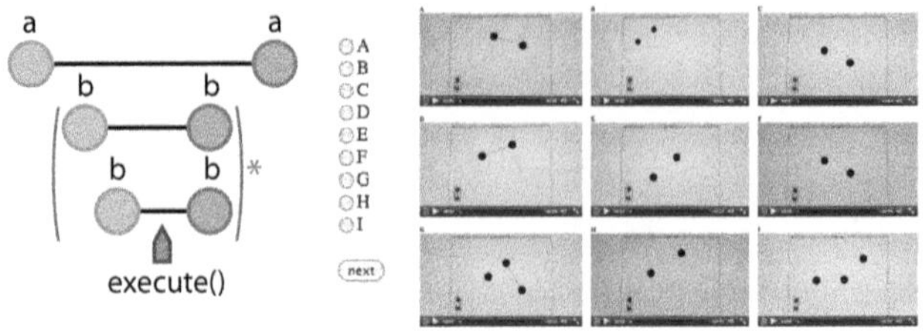

$$D_1^a M_1^a * \left(D_2^b (M_1^a | M_2^b) * D_3^b (M_1^a | M_2^b | M_3^b) *\right.$$

execute()

$$\left.(U_2^b (M_1^a | M_3^b) * U_3^b \,|\, U_3^b (M_1^a | M_2^b) * U_2^b) M_1^a *\right) * U_1^a$$

```
_state = GesturePossible;

touchesDown(Array *touches, Array *allTouches)
  if(allTouches->count() > 3)
    _state = GestureFailed;
  else if(allTouches->count() == 1)
    if(touches[0]->target() != 'a')
      _state = GestureFailed;
  else
    if(touches[0]->target() != 'b')
      _state = GestureFailed;

touchesMove(Array *touches, Array *allTouches)
  for(i = 0; i < touches->count(); i++)
    if(touches[i]->touchId() == 0 && touches[i]->target() != 'a')
      _state = GestureFailed;
      return;
    else if(touches[i]->touchId() != 0 && touches[i]->target() != 'b')
      _state = GestureFailed;
      return;
  if(allTouches->count() == 3)
    execute();

touchesUp(Array *touches, Array *allTouches)
  if(allTouches->count() == 1)
    if(touches[0]->touchId() == 0 && touches[0]->target() == 'a')
      _state = GestureRecognized;
    else
      _state = GestureFailed;
  else
    if(touches[0]->touchId() != 0 && touches[0]->target() == 'b');
    else
      _state = GestureFailed;
```

Figure 12. Top: In Part 1, the participant is shown a gesture tablature and the participant must identify the matching video. Bottom: The corresponding gesture expression and event-handling pseudocode.

three gesture representations: *tablature*, *expression*, and *iOS*. We counterbalanced the orderings of the gesture representations so that each of the six possible orderings was performed by two participants.

Part 1: Basic Touch Event Sequences

The first part of the study tested how each gesture representation affects the participant's understanding of basic touch event sequences in a gesture. Gestures are often dependent on the target of the touches, so we also included a single hit-target attribute: the type of target hit by the touch.

At the start of each block, we gave the participant a tutorial on how to interpret a multitouch gesture using the block's gesture representation. We then asked the participant to perform five gesture identification trials. The gestures were chosen such that each block covered a range of different gestures with one, two, and three touches. For each trial, we presented the participant with a gesture written in the block's gesture representation (Figure 12) and a set of nine videos of a user performing gestures. (Figure 13). We asked the participant to identify which video matched the gesture. To mitigate learning effects, we reordered the nine videos between blocks.

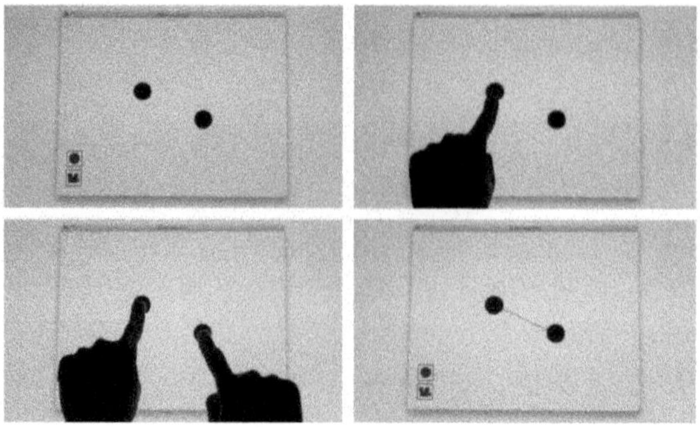

Figure 13. Screenshots of a video depicting a node connection gesture.

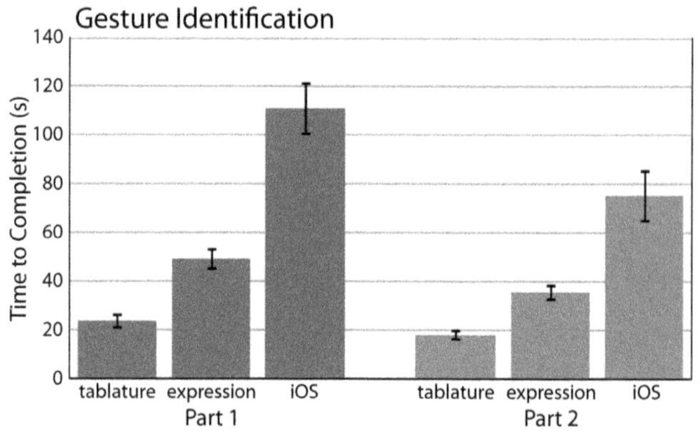

Figure 14. The average time to completion for identifying a gesture in Part 1 and Part 2. Standard error bars are shown.

For each trial, we were interested in only the time spent understanding the gesture. However, participants would often spend significant time rewatching and searching videos for the correct one, after having already understood the gesture. Thus, we measured time to completion of a trial as the total trial time minus the video-playing time. We also checked whether the participant chose the correct video.

Results. The average times to completion (Figure 14 Left) for identifying a gesture were 23.50s for tablature, 49.25s for expression, and 110.99s for iOS event-handling (one way ANOVA $F_{2,22} = 55.37$, $p < .001$; all pairwise comparisons with Bonferroni correction were also significant). Tablature was 2.1 times faster than expression and 4.7 times faster than event-handling. Average accuracies were 100% for tablature, 93.3% for expression, and 95% for iOS event-handling, but differences were not significant ($F_{2,22} = 1.20$, $p = .320$).

Part 2: Trajectory Gestures

In the second part of the study we asked participants to identify gestures that use both hit-target attribute and the direction attribute for specifying trajectory. For each block, we asked participants to perform three trials of gesture identification. In each trial, we presented a gesture and a set of four images, each depicting the gesture trajectory as red directed paths drawn on a target. Participants chose which trajectory would be recognized by the given gesture (Figure 15). As in the first task, for each trial we checked for correctness and measured the time of completion.

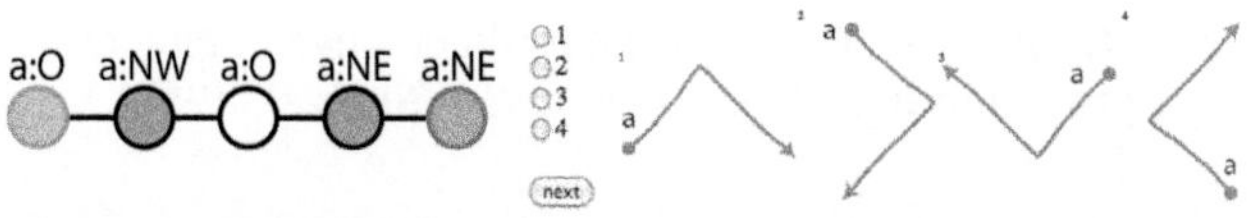

Figure 15. In Part 2, the participant is shown a gesture and must identify the matching trajectory.

Results. The average times to completion (Figure 14 Right) for identifying a gesture were 17.82s for tablature, 35.49s for expression, and 75.29s for iOS event-handling ($F_{2,22} = 21.30$, $p < .001$; all pairwise comparisons were also significant). Tablature was 2.0 times faster than expression and 4.2 times faster than event-handling. All participants had 100% accuracy rate in identifying the gestures for all three representations.

Qualitative Results

In a post-study survey we asked participants to rate the representations for ease of comprehension. On a Likert scale of 1 (easiest) to 5 (hardest), the average scores were 1.33 for tablature, 2.92 for expression, and 4.13 for iOS event-handling. A Kruskal Wallis test revealed a significant effect of condition on Likert ratings ($H = 26.4$, $2df$, $p < .001$). Mann-Whitney tests showed that all pairwise comparisons were also significant. When asked which of the three representations they would most like to design multitouch gestures with, 11 of the 12 participants preferred tablature and the remaining participant preferred expression.

Discussion

Our results show that users are faster at identifying gestures in tablature form than in expression or event-handling form. These results indicate that users can quickly learn and understand gesture tablatures, which suggests users can also more quickly build and maintain multitouch gestures written in tablature. Our results confirm that tablature is an effective graphical representation for the underlying regular expression representation of gestures. Our post-study survey also suggests that users prefer implementing multitouch gestures with tablature over standard touch event-handling.

Participants generally preferred tablature as they found it obvious how "to express temporal order" of the touches. They could mime the touch actions as they read the tablature. They saw similar benefits with regular expressions, but were concerned that the "complexity of the expressions could easily explode." In contrast with tablature and expressions, participants found it difficult to keep track of the gesture state in disparate event-handlers, which required "too much jumping around the code" and "mental book-keeping." However, participants felt by having direct access to touch events, event-handling is "ostensibly more flexible."

CONCLUSION AND FUTURE WORK

We have presented Proton++, a system for declaratively specifying multitouch gestures with custom attributes. We have implemented five such attributes: direction, pinch, touch area, finger orientation, and screen location. We also describe a technique for introducing timing into gesture expressions. A new attribute notation simplifies authoring gestures with custom attributes and timing. We show that splitting input streams by attribute values enables recognition of multiple simultaneous gestures. Finally, our user study suggests that gesture tablatures improve gesture comprehension over gesture expressions, and both representations are easier to understand than procedural event-handling code.

There are several directions for future work. First, as the number of gesture-based input technologies increases, standard event-handling approaches to recognizing gestures cannot scale. Many of these devices also report multiple streams of parallel events. Multitouch devices report multiple fingers; the Kinect [41] reports multiple joint positions; smartphones report acceleration and orientation. It may be possible to support these devices in Proton++ using custom attributes.

Second, expressing variability in the expression can currently lead to complicated expressions that are difficult to author. For example, a developer may want to allow more leeway for performing a certain trajectory, so the user can be less precise when making strokes. More suitable syntactic sugar could help to simplify the authoring of such gestures.

In the longer term, we would like to explore how other formalisms can be used to support developers in authoring gesture-based interactions.

ACKNOWLEDGMENTS

We would like to thank Lora Oehlberg and Wesley Willett for their help in making the video. This research is partially supported by NSF Expeditions in Computing project ExCAPE: Expeditions in Computer Augmented Program Engineering and NSF grant CCF-0643552.

REFERENCES

1. Appert, C., and Zhai, S. Using strokes as command shortcuts: cognitive benefits and toolkit support. *Proc. CHI 2009* (2009), 2289–2298.
2. Apple. iOS. `http://developer.apple.com/technologies/ios`.
3. Benko, H., Wilson, A. D., and Baudisch, P. Precise selection techniques for multi-touch screens. *Proc. CHI 2006* (2006), 1263–1272.
4. Bevilacqua, F., Zamborlin, B., Sypniewski, A., Schnell, N., Guédy, F., and Rasamimanana, N. Continuous realtime gesture following and recognition. In *Gesture in Embodied Communication and Human-Computer Interaction*, vol. 5934 of *Lecture Notes in Computer Science*. 2010, 73–84.
5. Cao, X., Wilson, A. D., Balakrishnan, R., Hinckley, K., and Hudson, S. ShapeTouch: Leveraging contact shape on interactive surfaces. *Proc. TABLETOP 2008* (2008), 129–136.
6. Dang, C. T., and André, E. Usage and recognition of finger orientation for multi-touch tabletop interaction. *Proc. INTERACT 2011* (2011), 409–426.
7. Echtler, F., Huber, M., and Klinker, G. Hand tracking for enhanced gesture recognition on interactive multi-touch

surfaces, 2007. Technical Report, Technische Universität München - Institut für Informatik.

8. Esenther, A., and Wittenburg, K. Multi-user multi-touch games on DiamondTouch with the DTFlash toolkit. In *Intelligent Technologies for Interactive Entertainment*, vol. 3814. 2005, 315–319.

9. Freeman, D., Benko, H., Morris, M. R., and Wigdor, D. ShadowGuides: visualizations for in-situ learning of multi-touch and whole-hand gestures. *Proc. ITS 2009* (2009), 165–172.

10. Gibbon, D., Gut, U., Hell, B., Looks, K., Thies, A., and Trippel, T. A computational model of arm gestures in conversation. *Proc. Eurospeech 2003* (2003), 813–816.

11. Guiard, Y. Asymmetric division of labor in human skilled bimanual action: The kinematic chain as a model. *Journal of Motor Behavior 19*, 4 (1987), 486–517.

12. Han, J. Low-cost multi-touch sensing through frustrated total internal reflection. *Proc. UIST 2005* (2005), 115–118.

13. Kammer, D., Wojdziak, J., Keck, M., and Taranko, S. Towards a formalization of multi-touch gestures. *Proc. ITS 2010* (2010), 49–58.

14. Khandkar, S. H., and Maurer, F. A domain specific language to define gestures for multi-touch applications. *10th Workshop on Domain-Specific Modeling* (2010).

15. Kin, K., Hartmann, B., and Agrawala, M. Two-handed marking menus for multitouch devices. *TOCHI 18* (August 2011), 16:1–16:23.

16. Kin, K., Hartmann, B., DeRose, T., and Agrawala, M. Proton: Multitouch gestures as regular expressions. *Proc. CHI 2012* (2012).

17. Kurtenbach, G. P. *The design and evaluation of marking menus*. PhD thesis, University of Toronto, Toronto, Ont., Canada, 1993.

18. Lepinski, G. J., Grossman, T., and Fitzmaurice, G. The design and evaluation of multitouch marking menus. *Proc. CHI 2010* (2010), 2233–2242.

19. Lu, H., and Li, Y. Gesture Coder: A tool for programming multi-touch gestures by demonstration. *Proc. CHI 2012* (2012).

20. MERL. DiamondTouch. `http://merl.com/projects/DiamondTouch`.

21. Microsoft. Surface. `http://www.microsoft.com/surface`.

22. Morris, M. R., Huang, A., Paepcke, A., and Winograd, T. Cooperative gestures: multi-user gestural interactions for co-located groupware. *Proc. CHI 2006* (2006), 1201–1210.

23. Moscovich, T. Contact area interaction with sliding widgets. *Proc. UIST 2009* (2009), 13–22.

24. Newman, W. M. A system for interactive graphical programming. *Proc. AFIPS 1968 (Spring)* (1968), 47–54.

25. Olsen, Jr., D. R., and Dempsey, E. P. Syngraph: A graphical user interface generator. *Proc. SIGGRAPH 1983* (1983), 43–50.

26. Ramos, G., Boulos, M., and Balakrishnan, R. Pressure widgets. *Proc. CHI 2004* (2004), 487–494.

27. Rekimoto, J. SmartSkin: An infrastructure for freehand manipulation on interactive surfaces. *Proc. CHI 2002* (2002), 113–120.

28. Rosenberg, I., and Perlin, K. The UnMousePad: an interpolating multi-touch force-sensing input pad. *Proc. SIGGRAPH* (2009), 65:1–65:9.

29. Rubine, D. Specifying gestures by example. *Proc. SIGGRAPH 1991* (1991), 329–337.

30. Scholliers, C., Hoste, L., Signer, B., and De Meuter, W. Midas: a declarative multi-touch interaction framework. *Proc. TEI 2011* (2011), 49–56.

31. Shneiderman, B. Direct manipulation: A step beyond programming languages. In *Computer*, vol. 16(8). August 1983, 57–69.

32. Swigart, S. Easily write custom gesture recognizers for your tablet PC applications, November 2005. Microsoft Technical Report.

33. Wang, F., Cao, X., Ren, X., and Irani, P. Detecting and leveraging finger orientation for interaction with direct-touch surfaces. *Proc. UIST 2009* (2009), 23–32.

34. Westerman, W. *Hand tracking, finger identification, and chordic manipulation on a multi-touch surface*. PhD thesis, University of Delaware, 1999.

35. Wigdor, D., Benko, H., Pella, J., Lombardo, J., and Williams, S. Rock & rails: extending multi-touch interactions with shape gestures to enable precise spatial manipulations. *Proc. CHI 2011* (2011), 1581–1590.

36. Wilson, A. D., Izadi, S., Hilliges, O., Garcia-Mendoza, A., and Kirk, D. Bringing physics to the surface. *Proc. UIST 2008* (2008), 67–76.

37. Wobbrock, J., Morris, M., and Wilson, A. User-defined gestures for surface computing. *Proc. CHI 2009* (2009), 1083–1092.

38. Wobbrock, J. O., Wilson, A. D., and Li, Y. Gestures without libraries, toolkits or training: a $1 recognizer for user interface prototypes. *Proc. UIST 2007* (2007), 159–168.

39. Worth, C. D. xstroke. `http://pandora.east.isi.edu/xstroke/usenix_2003`.

40. Wu, M., and Balakrishnan, R. Multi-finger and whole hand gestural interaction techniques for multi-user tabletop displays. *Proc. UIST 2003* (2003), 193–202.

41. Xbox. Kinect. `http://www.xbox.com/kinect`.

Extended Multitouch: Recovering Touch Posture and Differentiating Users using a Depth Camera

Sundar Murugappan[1], **Vinayak**[1], **Niklas Elmqvist**[2], **Karthik Ramani**[1,2]
[1]School of Mechanical Engineering and [2]School of Electrical and Computer Engineering
Purdue University, West Lafayette, IN 47907, USA
{smurugap,fvinayak,elm,ramani}@purdue.edu

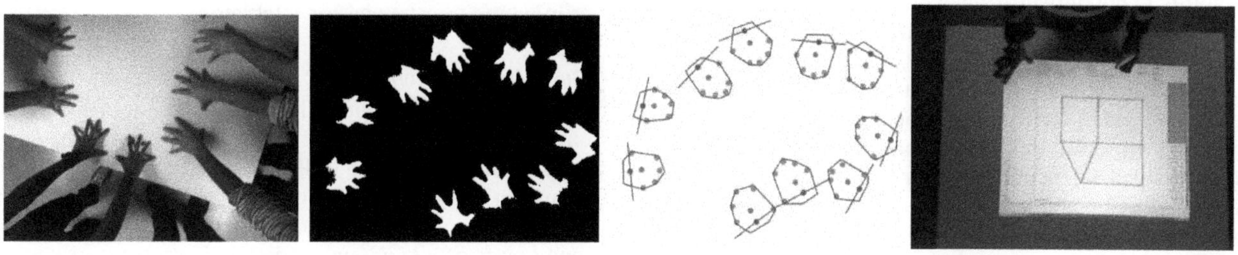

Figure 1. Extracting finger and hand posture from a Kinect depth camera (left) and integrating with a pen+touch sketch interface (right).

ABSTRACT
Multitouch surfaces are becoming prevalent, but most existing technologies are only capable of detecting the user's actual points of contact on the surface and not the identity, posture, and handedness of the user. In this paper, we define the concept of *extended multitouch interaction* as a richer input modality that includes all of this information. We further present a practical solution to achieve this on tabletop displays based on mounting a single commodity depth camera above a horizontal surface. This will enable us to not only detect when the surface is being touched, but also recover the user's exact finger and hand posture, as well as distinguish between different users and their handedness. We validate our approach using two user studies, and deploy the technique in a scratchpad tool and in a pen + touch sketch tool.

ACM Classification Keywords
H.5.2 Information Interfaces and Presentation: User Interfaces—*Interaction styles*; I.3.6 Computer Graphics: Methodology and Techniques—*Interaction techniques*

General Terms
Design, Algorithms, Human Factors

Author Keywords
Multitouch, tabletop, depth camera, pen + touch, evaluation.

UIST'12, October 7–10, 2012, Cambridge, Massachusetts, USA.

INTRODUCTION
Multitouch surfaces are quickly becoming ubiquitous: from wristwatch-sized music players and pocket-sized smartphones to tablets, digital tabletops, and wall-sized displays, virtually every surface in our everyday surroundings may soon come to life with digital imagery and natural touch input. However, achieving this vision of ubiquitous [27] surface computing requires overcoming several technological hurdles, key among them being how to augment any physical surface with touch sensing. Conventional multitouch technology relies on either capacitive sensors embedded in the surface itself, or rear-mounted cameras capable of detecting the touch points of the user's hand on the surface [10]. Both approaches depend on heavily instrumenting the surface, which is not feasible for widespread deployment.

In this context, Wilson's idea [30] of utilizing a front-mounted depth camera to sense touch input on any physical surface is particularly promising for the following reasons:

- **Minimal instrumentation:** Because they are front-mounted, depth cameras integrate well with both projected imagery as well as conventional screens;
- **Surface characteristics:** Any surface, digital or inanimate, flat or non-flat, horizontal or vertical, can be instrumented to support touch interaction;
- **On and above:** Interaction both on as well as above the surface can be detected and utilized for input;
- **Low cost:** Depth cameras have recently become commodity products with the rise of the Microsoft Kinect, originally developed for full-body interaction with the Xbox game console, but usable with any computer.

In this paper, we define a richer touch interaction modality that we call *extended multitouch* (EMT) which includes not only sensing multiple points of touch on and above a surface using a depth camera, but also (1) recovering finger, wrist and hand posture of the user, as well as (2) differentiating users and (3) their handedness. We have implemented a Windows utility that interfaces with a Kinect camera, extracts the above data from the depth image in real-time, and publishes the information as a global hook to other applications, or using the TUIO [16] protocol. To validate our approach, we have also conducted two empirical user studies: one for measuring the tracking accuracy of the touch sensing functionality, and the other for measuring the finger and hand posture accuracy of our utility.

The ability to not only turn any physical surface into a touch-sensitive one, but also to recover full finger and hand posture of any interaction performed on the surface, opens up an entirely new design space of interaction modalities. We have implemented two separate touch applications for the purpose of exploring this design space. The first is a prototype scratchpad where multiple users can draw simple vector graphics using their fingers, each finger on each user being separately identified and drawing a unique color and stroke. The second application is called uSKETCH, and is an advanced sketching application for creating beautified mechanical engineering sketches that can be used for further finite element analysis. uSketch integrates pen-based input that we use for content creation with our touch sensing functionality that we use for navigation and mode changes.

RELATED WORK

Our work is concerned with touch interaction, natural user interfaces, and the integration of several input modalities.

Multitouch Technologies

Several different technologies exist for sensing multiple touches on a surface, including capacitance, RFID, and vision-based approaches. Vision-based approaches are particularly interested for our purposes since they are suitable for surfaces with large form factor, such as tabletops and walls [10, 19, 29]. These systems rely on the presence of a dedicated surface for interaction.

Recently, depth-sensing cameras are beginning to be used in various interactive applications where any surface can be made interactive. Wilson [30] explored the use of depth sensing cameras to sense touch on any surface. OmniTouch [11] is a wearable depth-sensing and projection system that enables interactive multitouch applications on everyday surfaces. Lightspace [31] is a small room installation that explores interactions between on, above and between surfaces combining multiple depth cameras and projectors.

Sensing Touch Properties

Going beyond sensing touch and deriving *properties* of the touches requires more advanced approaches. We classify existing approaches for this into vision-based techniques, instrumented glove-based tracking, and specialized hardware.

Vision-based Techniques

Malik et al. [19] used two cameras mounted above the surface to distinguish which finger of which hand touched a surface, but their system requires a black background for reliable recognition. Wang et al. [25] detect the directed finger orientation vector from contact information in real time by considering the dynamics of the finger landing process. Dang et al. [4] mapped fingers to their associated hand by making use of constraints applied to the touch position with finger orientation. Freeman et al. [7] captured the user's hand image on a Microsoft Surface to distinguish hand postures through vision techniques. Holz et al. [14] proposed a generalized perceived input point model in which fingerprints were extracted and recognized to provide accurate touch information and user identification. Finally, Zhang et al. [35] used the orientation of the touching finger for discriminating user touches on a tabletop.

Glove-based Techniques

Gloves are widely popular in virtual and augmented reality environments [22]. Wang et al. [26] used a single camera to track a hand wearing an ordinary cloth glove imprinted with a custom pattern. Marquardt et al. [20] used a fiduciary-tagged gloves on interactive surfaces to gather input about many parts of a hand and to discriminate between one person's or multiple peoples' hands. Although simple and robust, these approaches require instrumented gear which is not always desirable compared to using bare hands.

Specialized Hardware

Specialized hardware is capable of deriving additional touch properties beyond the mere touch points. Benko et al. [1] sensed muscle activity through forearm electromyography to provide additional information about hand and finger movements away from the surface. Lopes et al. [17] integrated touch with sound to expand the expressiveness of touch interfaces by supporting recognition of different body parts, such as fingers and knuckles. TapSense [12] is a similar acoustic sensing system that allows conventional surfaces to identify the type of object being used for input such as fingertip, pad and nail. The above systems require additional instrumentation of either the user or the surface and take a significant amount of time for setup. Background noise is also a deterrent to use acoustic sensing techniques.

Pen and Touch-based Interaction

A few research efforts have explored the combination of pen and touch [2, 8, 34, 33]. Hinckley et al. [13] described techniques for direct pen + touch input for a prototype, centered on note-taking and scrapbooking of materials. Lopes et al. [18] assessed the suitability of combining pen and multi touch interactions for 3D sketching. Through experimental evidence, they demonstrated that using bimanual interactions simplifies work flows and lowers task times, when compared to the pen-only interface.

OVERVIEW: EXTENDED MULTITOUCH INTERACTION

Traditional multitouch interaction [5] is generally defined as the capability to detect multiple points of touch input on a surface. Here, we enrich this concept into what we call *extended multitouch interaction* (EMT), defined as follows:

- Detecting multiple touch points on and above a surface;

- Recovering finger, wrist and hand postures as well as the handedness (i.e., whether using the left or right hand); and
- Distinguishing between users interacting with the surface.

While previous work has explored various combinations of the above, we are aware of no single work that has addressed all three constraints as a unified framework. To this effect, we propose a two-dimensional hand model that uniquely maps touch points to fingers, hands, and users using depth data. In the following text, we describe our approach to supporting extended multitouch using low-cost depth cameras.

TOUCH SENSING USING A DEPTH CAMERA

Inspired by Wilson [30], our approach to sensing touch using a depth camera simply builds on analyzing the depth image to detect when objects (i.e., fingers) come in close proximity with the physical surface. Our implementation uses a depth camera mounted above a horizontal surface to transform user gestures on and above the tabletop to multitouch events that can be used by a client application. Fully emulating existing multitouch technology using this setup gives rise to several concrete requirements for our system:

- Determine when the surface is being touched and generate the corresponding touch points;
- Track touch points over time when the user is dragging fingers across the surface;
- Map touch points from the physical surface to coordinate space of the display area; and
- Export multitouch events to clients, either using a global Windows hook, or using the TUIO protocol [16].

Below we discuss the physical setup and each of the above components in more detail.

Physical Setup

Our low-cost setup (Figure 2) consists of (1) a horizontal surface, on and above which interactions take place, (2) a projector, which projects on to a surface providing visualization and feedback, (3) a depth sensing camera (like Microsoft Kinect) for capturing touch input, and (4) a computer for processing the input data from the depth camera and projecting visual output using the projector. Again, the surface to be made interactive need not be empty nor flat.

While our focus in this paper is on horizontal (tabletop) setups, there is nothing to prevent the same technique from being used for vertical (wall-mounted) surfaces. The algorithms described below are independent of the configuration and the touch results are not affected as long as a clear line of sight is maintained between the hands and the Kinect.

Basic Touch Sensing

We detect touches by analyzing the image produced by the depth camera. The pixel intensities in the depth image corresponds to the distance from the camera. This allows us to define a "touch input region" as a virtual volume located within a lower and upper distance above the surface. This volume is approximately a cuboid (assuming the surface is flat) offset from the surface with the height equal to the difference of the bounds. All pixels with distance values between these bounds correspond to the contact region(s) of the finger(s) with the surface.

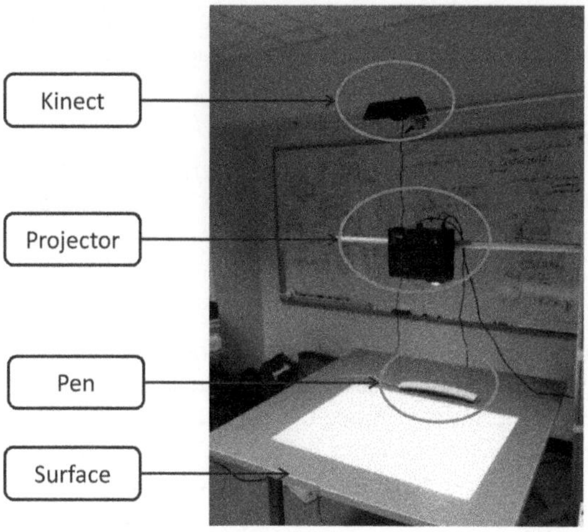

Figure 2. The physical setup showing (from top to bottom) depth camera, projector, pen tracker, and physical surface.

Figure 3. Identifying touch points from the depth data.

Estimating the underlying surface is important for the purpose of obtaining reliable and robust touches using our method. We model the surface as a depth image that can simply be subtracted from the current image to yield the difference. This difference map is then used to detect whether any physical objects in the scene fall within the touch input region. We create a binary image such that the pixels corresponding to these elements are set to white and all the other pixels to black. Figure 3(a) shows the raw depth image with two hands touching the surface and Figure 3(b) is the binary image showing groups of white pixels corresponding to contacts of fingers with the surface.

We use connected component analysis to identify the cluster of pixels from the touch images, yielding touch "blobs." To differentiate between actual touches and noise, we discard the blobs that are below or above a certain area threshold. From experimentation, when the Kinect is at a height of 1.2m from the surface, for a blob to be a candidate for a touch point, the area of the blob must be greater than 20 square millimeter and less than 220 square millimeter, accommodating a wide variety of finger sizes. We use the center of gravity of the white blobs as the location of touch points. Figure 3(c) shows the result of determining the touch points from the raw depth data and the binary touch image.

Note that this approach also lends itself to defining additional volumes at other distances from the surface, allowing us to detect interaction above the surface as well.

Tracking Touch Points

Tracking touch points over time is critical for developing interactive applications that make use of dragging gestures. Without this information, each new depth frame would treat touch points as being new, and the application would not be able to support smooth dragging operations.

In our implementation, we associate touch points in consecutive depth frames by finding the nearest neighbor between points in the frames. Since the Kinect can record at a maximum rate of thirty frames per second, not all depth frames are necessarily used in tracking touches. Our system intelligently discards outlier depth frames by considering the touch points in a sliding window that includes several frames before the current frame, thereby increasing robustness.

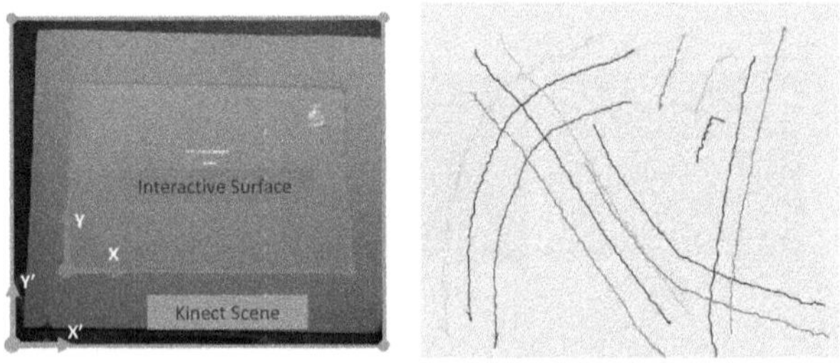

(a) Calibration. (b) Scratchpad.

Figure 4. Touch sensing mechanism.

Mapping Touches to Display Space

Traditional multitouch surfaces have a one-to-one mapping between the physical location that is being touched on the surface and the digital location on the underlying display. This provides users with the feeling of directly touching and manipulating the digital content underneath their fingers.

To facilitate a similar interactive experience in our depth camera-based approach, we need to map the depth camera scene to the projected display area (Figure 4(a)). We employ a technique very similar to how regular touch screen sensors are calibrated with LCD displays using a nine-point calibration grid. This gives us the coefficients needed to transform from camera coordinates to display coordinates while taking scaling, rotation, and translation errors into account.

Generating Multitouch Events

The final step in our implementation is to actually generate multitouch events that a client application can handle in order to support (extended) multitouch interaction. We provide two ways to do this: either through a Windows global hook, or using the TUIO protocol [16]. This enables our implementation to be entirely standalone, and external client applications simply need to interface to the system to receive touch events. Figure 4(b) shows a scratchpad application that demonstrates multitouch tracking using these events.

BEYOND STANDARD MULTITOUCH INTERACTION

Our work so far has concerned itself with detecting the two-dimensional (x and y) locations of touch points on as well as above (i.e., with a z component) the physical surface. However, fully supporting our extended multitouch (EMT) model requires being able to recover finger posture, hand posture, and handedness for all touch points, as well as differentiating users. More powerful and rich interaction techniques can be built if such additional information can be leveraged.

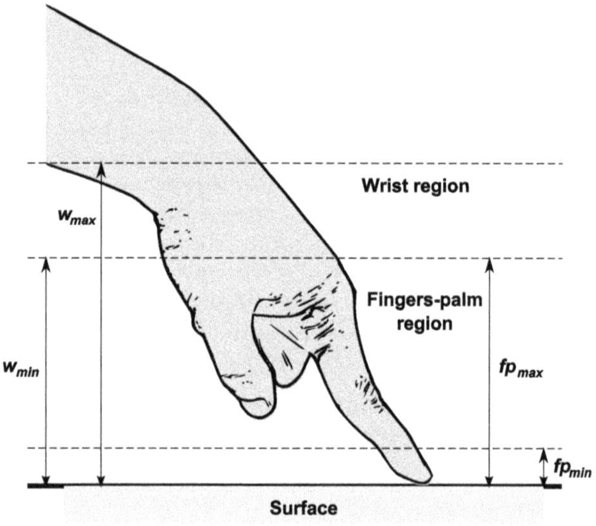

Figure 5. Additional touch regions for extended multitouch.

Extracting Palm and Wrist Data

Similar to the touch input region defined earlier for detecting fingers coming into contact with the physical surface, we can extract the position of the user's palm and wrists from the same depth data. We simply include two additional virtual volumes: the "fingers-palm region" and the "wrist region" (Figure 5). Based on the depth camera image, we construct binary images for each of these regions (Figure 6). These images are then used to recover the touch posture.

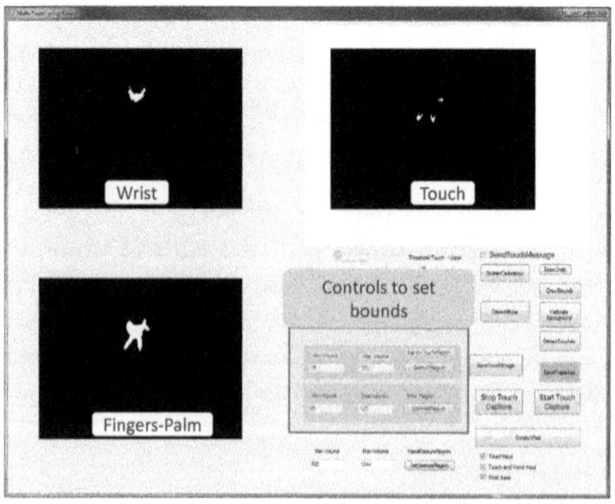

Figure 6. Binary depth images for the three virtual volumes used in our prototype implementation.

A connected component analysis is then performed on the binary image corresponding to 'fingers-palm region' to extract the blobs. For each blob, we compute its a) center of gravity, b) principal directions using principal component analysis and c) convex hull. The center of the palm is approximately the center of gravity of the blob, which is sufficient to map fingers and hands to touch points.

The binary image corresponding to the wrist region is processed in the same manner as above. For each extracted blob, we compute its a) center of gravity and b) principal directions. Wrist orientation can be determined from the principal directions. Tabletop surfaces can take advantage of this information to eliminate the inherent problems that arise due to orientation dependency. Furthermore, this position and orientation information provides an estimate of the hand occlusion region, which can be used to build occlusion-aware interfaces that minimize the impact of occlusion [15, 23, 24]

A Two-Dimensional Hand Model

After processing the three binary images, we combine the results and create a two-dimensional model of the hand. Each hand now has a wrist, fingers-palm, the touch points, and their associations. It can also be noted that the distance value of touches, wrist-center, and palm-center can be obtained from the depth data, which, when added to the two-dimensional model, gives us a three-dimensional model.

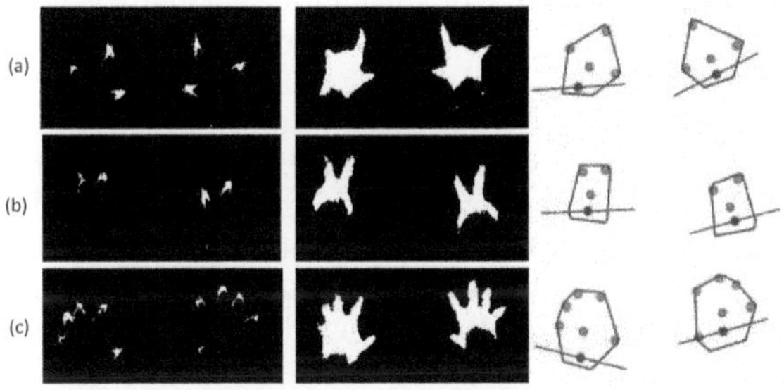

Figure 7. From left to right, each image shows the binary image computed in the touch region, fingers-palm region, and the hand model with touch points, wrist and palm.

Figure 7 shows results from two-hand touches. The red dots on the far right correspond to the touch points, the green dot is the palm center, and the violet dot is the wrist. The blue closed polygon is the convex hull of the fingers-palm blob and the green line represents the first principal component of the wrist showing hand orientation. The principal components of the fingers-palm are not shown to avoid clutter. Figure 1 shows 50 touch points from 10 hands and 5 users.

Modeling Touch Posture

To deduce the mapping between the touch points to the fingers and hand, we take advantage of the geometric properties that can be computed from the abstract hand model derived above. In Figure 8, the purple dot is the center position of the wrist and the purple line represents its first principal component. Similarly, the green dot and green line represent the center position and the first principal component of the fingers-palm region. The yellow arrow (V3) represents the direction of the fingers from the wrist passing through the palm. For every instance of the 2D model, we compute (a) the angles subtended by each touch point with respect to V3, and (b) the distance of each touch point from the wrist.

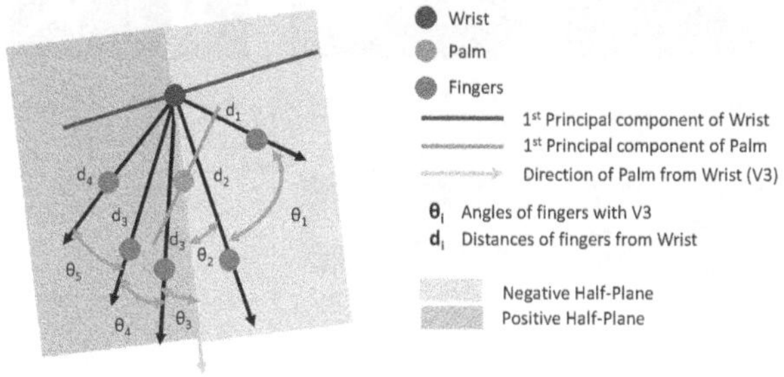

Figure 8. The angles and distances of the hand geometry.

Wobbrock et al. [32] outlined 27 different gestural commands performed on a tabletop surface. From studying these hand poses, we collected the following observations:

- The majority of gestures are performed with one, two, three, or five finger touch points;
- One-finger interactions are always performed using the fore-finger (100%);
- For two-finger interactions, the fingers used are thumb-fore finger and fore-middle fingers;
- For three-finger interactions, the finger combinations used are thumb-fore-middle and fore-middle-ring; and
- For four-finger interactions, the finger combinations are thumb-fore-middle-ring and fore-middle-ring-and-little.

Based on these observations, we propose 16 different touch postures (Figure 9) to be recognized by our system. Detecting handedness, i.e., if it is a right or left hand, can be determined from the location of the thumb, i.e., its signed angle with respect to the orientation vector. If the signed angle is negative, then the input pattern is a right hand, and vice versa. The classification for recognizing touch posture is based on the number of touch points, which is as follows:

- One - Index finger and ambiguous hand.
- Two - We deduce that a thumb is present if the distance between the two fingers (index and thumb or index and middle) is greater than smallest distance of the fingers from the wrist.

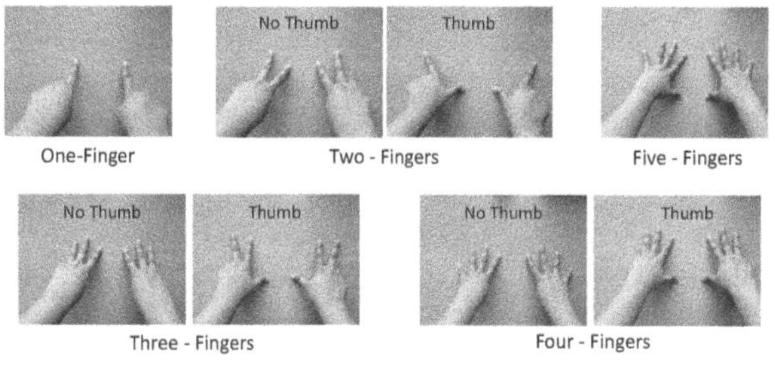

Figure 9. Hand poses during multitouch recognized in our system.

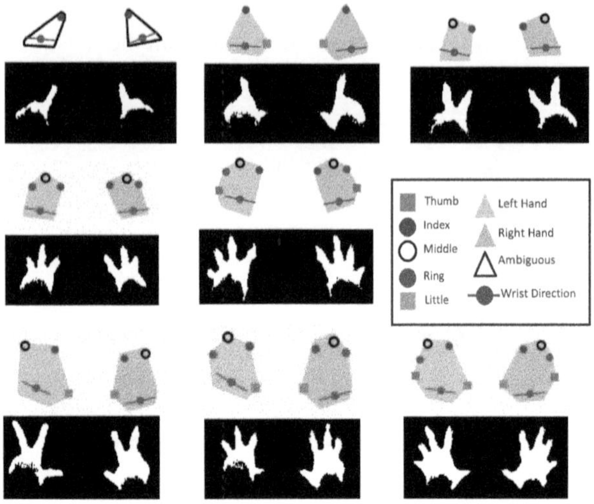

Figure 10. Results (actual snapshots) after mapping touch points to fingers and hands for the poses in Figure 9.

- Three - We deduce that a thumb is present if the angle subtended between extreme fingers (thumb and middle or index and ring) is at least two times greater than the smallest angle made by the extreme fingers with the finger between them (i.e., index and middle or middle and ring finger).
- Four - We deduce that a thumb is present if the angle subtended between the extreme fingers (thumb and ring or index and little) is at least three times greater than the smallest angle made by the extreme fingers with the finger next to them (i.e., ring and little or middle and ring finger.
- Five - the angle and distance between thumb and index fingers is greater than the values between little and ring fingers. Other fingers can now be labeled logically.

Figure 10 shows a sample of the results generated by our system for these 16 different postures. Poses that do not belong to the above classification (for example, Figure 7a) are ambiguous and hence our system cannot identify the fingers reliably. Furthermore, the presence of the thumb and fore finger is crucial in our method for the correct mapping between fingers and touch points, and the thumb is crucial for deducing handedness. Hence, the mapping accuracy decreases for poses which do not have the thumb. In such cases, the distance and angular measures alone do not give conclusive evidence of the correct touch posture and handedness.

Differentiating Users

Finally, being able to match actual touch inputs to individual users is crucial for more advanced collaborative applications where multiple participants are interacting with the tabletop. Our solution builds on the fact that user arms are also partially visible to the depth camera mounted above the tabletop. We use this information to heuristically model user positions that are off-screen of the depth image. However, this approach depends on users maintaining their relative positions around the tabletop surface, as well as not approaching to closely to each other. Also note that our approach does not allow for *identifying users*, only differentiating them.

A future improvement to this solution would integrate a second vision-based tracking system that could follow the participants themselves instead of merely their touch points.

USER STUDIES

To validate our approach, we conducted two empirical user studies: one for measuring the tracking accuracy of the touch sensing functionality, and the other for measuring the finger and hand posture accuracy of our utility.

Study 1: Touch Sensing Accuracy

The accuracy of touch contacts depends on (a) the parameters computed in calibrating the interactive area (projected imagery) to the Kinect scene, (b) the algorithm to detect touch contacts based on depth thresholds, (c) the orientation and size of the finger(s) making the contact, and (d) the user's perception of where they are touching the surface. The above factors all contribute towards the accuracy of the detected touches and as some of them are not controlled, these factors model the real-world performance of our system.

Participants: We recruited 14 volunteers (11 males and 3 females) between the ages of 21 and 32 years for the experiment. Among them, 12 were right-handed and 2 were left-handed.

Task: The task consisted of touching 15 randomly generated locations that were shown on the touch surface. Each location was drawn as a circle with a cross-hair of size 20×20 mm. Each participant was asked to touch every point and hold for two seconds using their index finger. For every location, the system acquired the calibrated touch points repeatedly, between a finger-down and a finger-up event. The system showed one location at a time, and on every finger-up event, a new point was displayed until the end of the experiment.

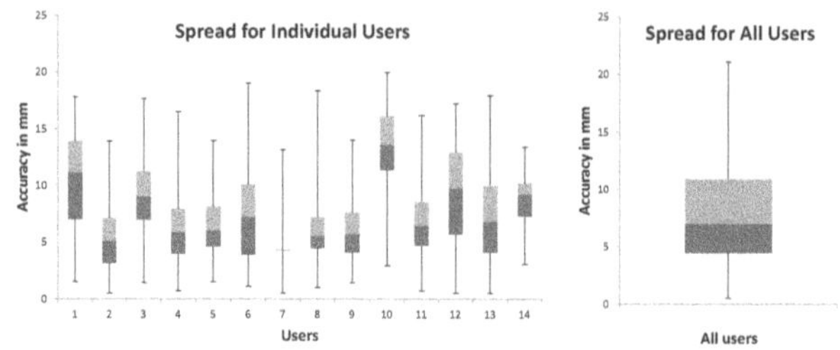

Figure 11. Touch sensing accuracy with average spread for individual users and all users collectively.

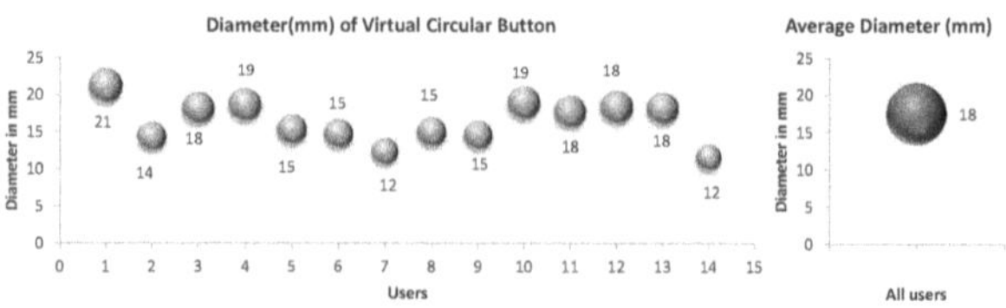

Figure 12. Accuracy of hitting a circular virtual button.

Results: In all, 3715 data points were collected from 14 participants. We analyzed the targeting performance using two

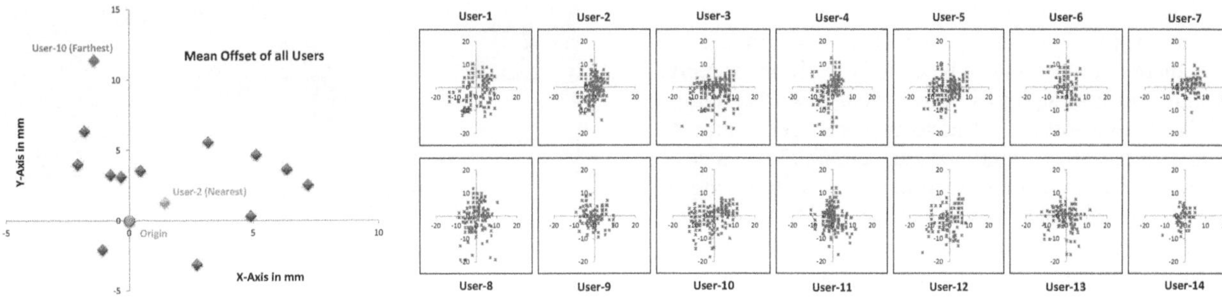

(a) Mean offsets from target (all users).

(b) Distribution of user clicks with compensating mean offsets (mm).

Figure 13. Distribution diagrams.

independent measures: mean offset and spread [11, 14]. Figure 11 shows the average spread for the data collected. The average spread in the best case is 4mm and for the worst case is 13mm. The average spread, taking into account all data points collectively from all users, is 8mm, which is slightly better or in accordance with previous findings in the literature [6, 11]. The mean offset for each user is shown in Figure 13(a) with User-10 having the farthest (largest) offset and User-2 being the nearest (small offset) to the target.

Figure 13(b) shows the distribution of user-clicks for all 14 users with compensating offsets. Here, the origin represents the target locations and the red markers represent the acquired touch points. There were no significant difference in results between the handedness of the users. We also calculated the accuracy of hitting a circular virtual button by accommodating 95% of the touches for each user with compensating offsets. Figure 12 shows the minimum button diameter for every user, with lowest (diameter = 12mm) for User-7 and highest (diameter = 21mm) for User-1. The average diameter for all users is 18mm, which is better than a similar experiment (28mm) conducted in [6]. In comparison, the size of a finger pad is between 10 - 14mm; the fingertip is 8 - 10 mm [3]; the recommended button size for Microsoft Surface is 12mm and for conventional touch input is 15mm [14]. We posit that the accuracy of the touches will decrease with increase in height of the Kinect from the surface. Future studies are needed to study this aspect.

Study 2: Touch Posture and Handedness Accuracy

We conducted a second user study to evaluate the accuracy of recovering touch posture and handedness from depth data.

Participants: We recruited 9 volunteers (7 males and 2 females), between the ages of 22 and 34 for this experiment.

Task: Each participant was asked to perform 8 touch-poses (Figure 9) on the surface with both their left and right hands one after the other. Each pose was to be held for approximately 10 seconds. The participants were not restricted to any position or orientation around the table. No visual feedback was provided to the participant during the study.

Results: A total of 4971 data points were collected during the experiment. The system recognized a hand posture for 4918 of those (approx. 99%). The possible reason for less than 100% recognition is that the users moved their hands either too fast, or that their hands were not in line of sight to the Kinect depth camera, causing data to be lost.

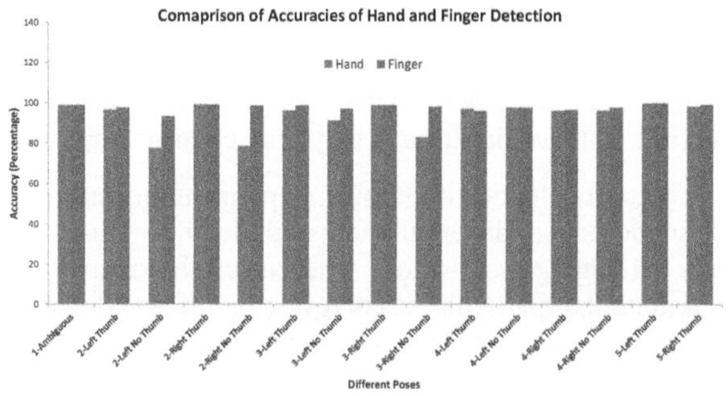

Figure 14. Touch posture and handedness accuracy.

Figure 14 shows the identification accuracies of touch-posture and handedness for the 16 (8 poses × 2 hands each) different touch poses. The overall handedness identification accuracy is 93.2%. We discarded one-finger index pose, as our current implementation cannot distinguish the hands for this particular pose. While the two-finger and three-finger "no thumb" poses had an accuracy of 77% and 86% respectively, their corresponding "thumb" poses had an accuracy of 98% and 97% respectively. Thus, the presence of the thumb is critical in identifying the handedness for two-finger and three-finger poses using our algorithm. Our hand model can be improved by reasoning with the contour of the posture and also convexity defects to better identify the posture. However, this will involve more computation and it is important to consider its trade-offs in real-time applications.

The overall finger identification accuracy was 97.7%. At the end of the user study, each participant was asked to rate their least favorable touch-poses. Among all, seven participants voted the four-finger poses ("thumb", "no-thumb", left and right hands) and 5 participants voted the "three-finger-no-thumb" pose as their least favorites.

DESIGN IMPLICATIONS

Surfaces supporting extended multitouch (EMT) enable a richer and more diverse interaction design space than those merely supporting standard multitouch. Here we briefly review some of these designs in more detail.

Interaction above and beyond the surface. Existing research has already explored interaction on and above a surface, but we think there is more work to be done here. Touch screens traditionally do not support hovering, but this is certainly one of the straightforward ideas to explore. For example, hovering over a surface could bring up a tool palette, a context menu, or simply a tooltip, similar to how hovering is handled in current mouse-based interfaces. More complex modalities are certainly possible, including detecting volumetric and 3D gestures, as suggested by Wigdor et al. [28].

Identifying users. The ability to match touches to users opens the door for personalized touch interaction. For example, instead of relying on social protocols [21], an EMT application can keep track of object ownership and explicitly prevent users lacking permission from interacting with the object. In a command and control setting, this could be utilized to assign different roles to different participants, such as a fire chief having permission to give orders to fire trucks, whereas a police chief instead may only control squad cars.

However, our extended multitouch implementation currently only supports user differentiation, and identifying users is a more challenging proposition. A heuristic solution may simply assume that particular users reside in different locations around the tabletop surface, allowing them to be identified by their physical position around the table alone.

Recognizing posture. Our implementation has proved the validity of recovering finger and hand posture using a very simple and low-cost hardware setup. This in turn brings several of the posture-based ideas devised by other researchers into the realm of possibility: examples include context-sensitive touch menus, complex gestures on and above the surface, and providing explicit gestural feedback during training. We look forward to seeing what the future will bring in terms of exciting new applications of this new touch modality.

EXAMPLE: PENS WITH EXTENDED MULTITOUCH

Although natural, touch input is not suited for tasks such as writing and sketching. These inking tasks are instead particularly suited for pen-based input, which generally has high precision, whereas our multitouch accuracy is approximately 8mm. Multitouch input in general on all forms and modalities suffer from low precision and our system is no exception. Using a pen for input, on the other hand, is a familiar tool that exploits the users' experience of being been trained to use a pen right from their early days.

However, a digital pen realistically allows for only one input point for interaction, constraining the input bandwidth. Augmenting pen-based input with extended multitouch capabilities increases the users' input bandwidth, which can be leveraged by designers to create rich and actually natural interactions for a variety of applications. We outline a division of labor between pen and touch input based on the theme "the pen writes and touch manipulates" [13]. Building on the extended multitouch technique proposed in this paper, we present USKETCH, an advanced sketching application for creating beautified mechanical engineering sketches that can be used for further finite element analysis.

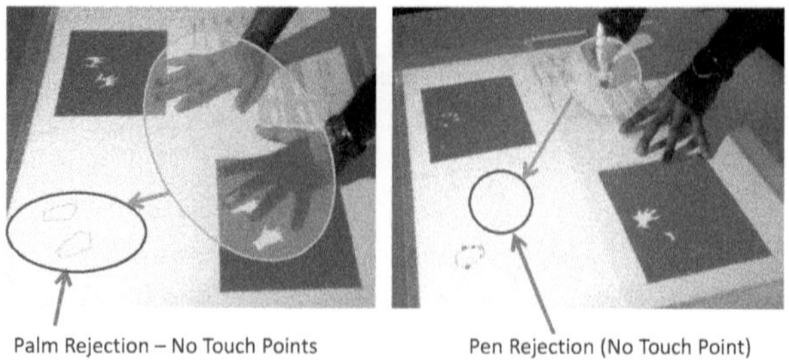

Figure 15. Palm (left) and pen (right) rejection during touch capture.

Combining Pen and Touch Input

For enabling bimanual pen and touch interactions, we added the Mimio™ pen to the setup described in Figure 2. Mimio pen technology tracks the 2D position of a digital stylus using ultrasound and infrared, and wirelessly transmits the location to the computer when the stylus is pressed against any flat surface. The pen can be calibrated to any surface size and works both horizontally and vertically. The pen input can then be processed and visually displayed back on the surface using the projector. This process allows the users to write and sketch on any surface, thus making it interactive.

Any object that touches the surface is identified as a touch point by the Kinect sensor. Hence, the system must be able to negate detecting the contact point of the pen as a touch input (Figure 15). To achieve this, we take advantage of how Kinect senses touch. When the pen is in contact with the surface, it communicates its coordinates to the computer. We take advantage of this coordinate information to negate any touch points detected by the system within a small radius of the pen contact. Similarly, when the whole hand rests against the surface, the system detects a big white blob from the palm's footprint on the surface (Figure 15). The system discards the input since it does not correspond to a touch point. Hence, both pen and palm are conveniently discarded by the design of how the system processes the Kinect data.

uSketch

The right part of Figure 1 shows a snapshot of the uSketch application on the interactive surface, and Figure 16 shows the uSketch interface with (a) a freehand sketch of a 2D-bracket, (b) the beautified sketch with interpreted symbols, and (c) the deformation results in ANSYS™.

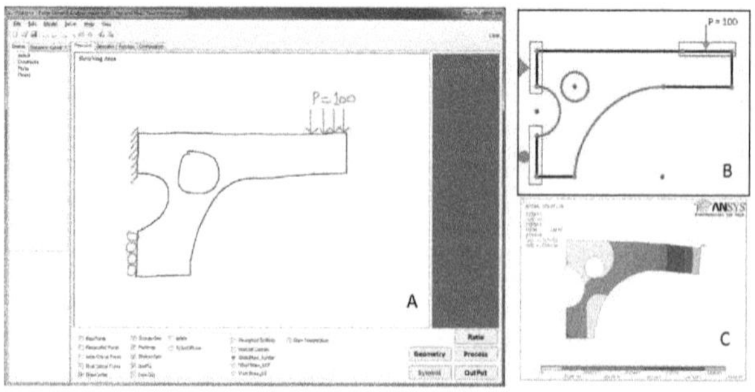

Figure 16. The uSketch interface showing (a) a freehand sketch of a 2D-bracket, (b) the beautified sketch with interpreted symbols, and (c) the deformation results in ANSYS™.

Guiard [9], proposed general principles for asymmetric bimanual actions comprising of three rules: (a) the dominant hand (DH) moves within the frame of reference defined by the non-dominant hand (NDH); (b) the sequence of motion generally sees the NDH setting the reference frame prior to actions with the DH being made within that context; and (c) that the DH works at a higher level of precision than the NDH in both spatial and temporal terms. Hence, the pen is preferably held in the DH and both NDH and DH be used for touch-input with the pen tucked in the DH.

Using bimanual interactions with pen and touch eliminates the need for constant switching between modes and also the need for user interface elements for changing visualizations and other interactions. We posit that using such interactions simplifies work flows and lowers task times, when compared to the pen-only or touch-only interface.

uSketch and EMT

The uSketch tool was designed specifically for taking advantage of extended multitouch. Below we outline some of the supported actions and their motivation:

- **Sketching, symbols, and text:** Pen input only; pens are optimal for content creation [13].
- **Navigation:** One finger from each hand, or one finger and pen; hand is quick and precise enough for navigation.
- **Deletion:** Three fingers on NDH and squiggle with pen or finger on DH; complex gesture to avoid accidental trigger.
- **Context menu:** Three fingers tap or down on NDH, selection using DH pen or finger; complex gesture as above.

Deploying uSketch

We designed uSketch as a design-analysis tool that introduces new ways for mechanical engineering students to interact, explore, and learn design and analysis in the classroom and in the laboratory. The tool provides a complete workflow from early sketching, through beautified imagery, and finally to finite element analysis, and is designed to teach a wide variety of mechanical engineering concepts in courses such as statics, strength of materials, and kinematics. We are currently deploying the tool in a toy design course (Purdue ME 444) where we use it to teach students the connections between early design (creativity) and computer-aided design (final product).

By supporting for hypotheses, calculations, and discussions, uSketch builds a strong intuition for engineering design decisions among students beyond the static content in textbooks.

CONCLUSIONS AND FUTURE WORK

We have presented a multitouch sensing approach based on low-cost depth cameras where any physical surface, flat or non-flat, horizontal or vertical, projected or screen, can be instrumented with touch sensing. Our contribution goes beyond existing depth camera touch sensing approaches into what we call *extended multitouch*, which we define as the ability to not only sense multiple touches, but also detecting interaction above the touch surface, recovering the user's finger and hand posture, and distinguishing between the users interacting with the surface. We validate the work using two user studies gauging the accuracy of touch and posture recognition, as well as using two sketch applications where we begin to explore the design space of this novel idea.

We have only scratched the surface of this extended multitouch interaction approach, and, as discussed in the design implications above, we can see many opportunities for future work in this area. In particular, we envision continuing our investigations into combining multiple interaction modalities for early engineering design and sketching.

ACKNOWLEDGMENTS

This work is partly supported by the National Science Foundation Partnership for Innovation Grant No. 0917959, the Donald W. Feddersen Chaired Professorship, and the Purdue School of Mechanical Engineering. Any opinions, findings, and conclusions or recommendations expressed in this material are those of the authors and do not necessarily reflect the views of the sponsors.

REFERENCES

1. H. Benko and A. Wilson. DepthTouch: Using depth-sensing camera to enable freehand interactions on and above the interactive surface. In *Proceedings of the IEEE Workshop on Tabletops and Interactive Surfaces*, volume 8, 2009.
2. P. Brandl, C. Forlines, D. Wigdor, M. Haller, and C. Shen. Combining and measuring the benefits of bimanual pen and direct-touch interaction on horizontal interfaces. In *Proceedings of the ACM Conference on Advanced Visual Interfaces*, 154–161, 2008.
3. K. Dandekar, B. I. Raju, and M. A. Srinivasan. 3-D finite-element models of human and monkey fingertips to investigate the mechanics of tactile sense. *Journal of Biomechanical Engineering*, 125(5):682–691, 2003.
4. C. T. Dang, M. Straub, and E. André. Hand distinction for multi-touch tabletop interaction. In *Proceedings of the ACM Conference on Interactive Tabletops and Surfaces*, 101–108, 2009.
5. P. Dietz and D. Leigh. DiamondTouch: a multi-user touch technology. In *Proceedings of the ACM Symposium on User interface Software and Technology*, 219–226, 2001.
6. A. Dippon and G. Klinker. KinectTouch: accuracy test for a very low-cost 2.5D multitouch tracking system. In *Proceedings of the ACM International Conference on Interactive Tabletops and Surfaces*, 49–52, 2011.
7. D. Freeman, H. Benko, M. R. Morris, and D. Wigdor. ShadowGuides: visualizations for in-situ learning of multi-touch and whole-hand gestures. In *Proceedings of the ACM Conference on Interactive Tabletops and Surfaces*, 165–172, 2009.
8. M. Frisch, J. Heydekorn, and R. Dachselt. Investigating multi-touch and pen gestures for diagram editing on interactive surfaces. In *Proceedings of ACM Conference on Interactive Tabletops and Surfaces*, 149–156, 2009.
9. Y. Guiard. Asymmetric division of labor in human skilled bimanual action: The kinematic chain as a model. *J Mot Behav*, 19(4):486–517, 1987.

10. J. Y. Han. Low-cost multi-touch sensing through frustrated total internal reflection. In *Proceedings of the ACM Symposium on User Interface Software and Technology*, 115–118, 2005.

11. C. Harrison, H. Benko, and A. D. Wilson. OmniTouch: wearable multitouch interaction everywhere. In *Proceedings of the ACM Symposium on User Interface Software and Technology*, 441–450, 2011.

12. C. Harrison, J. Schwarz, and S. E. Hudson. TapSense: enhancing finger interaction on touch surfaces. In *Proceedings of the ACM Symposium on User Interface Software and Technology*, 627–636, 2011.

13. K. Hinckley, K. Yatani, M. Pahud, N. Coddington, J. Rodenhouse, A. Wilson, H. Benko, and B. Buxton. Manual deskterity: an exploration of simultaneous pen + touch direct input. In *Extended Abstracts of the ACM Conference on Human Factors in Ccomputing Systems*, 2793–2802, 2010.

14. C. Holz and P. Baudisch. The generalized perceived input point model and how to double touch accuracy by extracting fingerprints. In *Proceedings of ACM Conference on Human Factors in Computing Systems*, 581–590, 2010.

15. W. Javed, K. Kim, S. Ghani, and N. Elmqvist. Evaluating physical/virtual occlusion management techniques for horizontal displays. In *Human-Computer Interaction - Proceedings of INTERACT*, volume 6948 of *Lecture Notes in Computer Science*, 391–408. Springer, 2011.

16. M. Kaltenbrunner. reacTIVision and TUIO: A tangible tabletop toolkit. In *Proceedings of the ACM Conference on Interactive Tabletops and Surfaces*, 9–16, 2009.

17. P. Lopes, R. Jota, and J. A. Jorge. Augmenting touch interaction through acoustic sensing. In *Proceedings of the ACM International Conference on Interactive Tabletops and Surfaces*, 53–56, 2011.

18. P. Lopes, D. Mendes, B. Araújo, and J. A. Jorge. Combining bimanual manipulation and pen-based input for 3D modelling. In *Proceedings of the Eurographics Symposium on Sketch-Based Interfaces and Modeling*, 15–22, 2011.

19. S. Malik and J. Laszlo. Visual touchpad: a two-handed gestural input device. In *Proceedings of the ACM International Conference on Multimodal Interfaces*, 289–296, 2004.

20. N. Marquardt, J. Kiemer, D. Ledo, S. Boring, and S. Greenberg. Designing user-, hand-, and handpart-aware tabletop interactions with the TouchID toolkit. In *Proceedings of the ACM International Conference on Interactive Tabletops and Surfaces*, 21–30, 2011.

21. M. R. Morris, K. Ryall, C. Shen, C. Forlines, and F. Vernier. Beyond 'social protocols': multi-user coordination policies for co-located groupware. In *Proceedings of the ACM Conference on Computer Supported Cooperative Work*, 262–265, 2004.

22. D. J. Sturman and D. Zeltzer. A survey of glove-based input. *IEEE Computer Graphics and Applications*, 14(1):30–39, Jan. 1994.

23. D. Vogel and R. Balakrishnan. Occlusion-aware interfaces. In *Proceedings of the ACM Conference on Human Factors in Computing Systems*, 263–272, 2010.

24. D. Vogel and G. Casiez. Hand occlusion on a multi-touch tabletop. In *Proceedings of ACM Conference on Human Factors in Computing Systems*, 2307–2316, 2012.

25. F. Wang, X. Cao, X. Ren, and P. Iran. Detecting and leveraging finger orientation for interaction with direct-touch surfaces. In *Proceedings of ACM Symposium on User Interface Software and Technology*, 23–32, 2009.

26. R. Y. Wang and J. Popović. Real-time hand-tracking with a color glove. *ACM Transactions on Graphics*, 28(3), 2009.

27. M. Weiser. The computer for the twenty-first century. *Scientific American*, 3(265):94–104, Sept. 1991.

28. D. Wigdor, H. Benko, J. Pella, J. Lombardo, and S. Williams. Rock & rails: extending multi-touch interactions with shape gestures to enable precise spatial manipulations. In *Proceedings of ACM Conference on Human Factors in Computing Systems*, 1581–1590, 2011.

29. A. D. Wilson. TouchLight: an imaging touch screen and display for gesture-based interaction. In *Proceedings of the ACM International Conference on Multimodal interfaces*, 69–76, 2004.

30. A. D. Wilson. Using a depth camera as a touch sensor. In *Proceedings of the ACM Conference on Interactive Tabletops and Surfaces*, 69–72, 2010.

31. A. D. Wilson and H. Benko. Combining multiple depth cameras and projectors for interactions on, above and between surfaces. In *Proceedings of the ACM Symposium on User Interface Software and Technology*, 273–282, 2010.

32. J. O. Wobbrock, M. R. Morris, and A. D. Wilson. User-defined gestures for surface computing. In *Proceedings of the ACM Conference on Human Factors in Computing Systems*, 1083–1092, 2009.

33. K.-P. Yee. Two-handed interaction on a tablet display. In *Extended Abstracts of the ACM Conference on Human Factors in Computing Systems*, 1493–1496, 2004.

34. R. Zeleznik, A. Bragdon, F. Adeputra, and H.-S. Ko. Hands-on math: a page-based multi-touch and pen desktop for technical work and problem solving. In *Proceedings of the ACM Symposium on User Interface Software and Technology*, 17–26, 2010.

35. H. Zhang, X.-D. Yang, B. Ens, H.-N. Liang, P. Boulanger, and P. Irani. See me, see you: a lightweight method for discriminating user touches on tabletop displays. In *Proceedings of the ACM Conference on Human Factors in Computing Systems*, 2327–2336, 2012.

FlowBlocks: A Multi-Touch UI for Crowd Interaction

Florian Block[1], Daniel Wigdor[2], Brenda Caldwell Phillips[1], Michael S. Horn[3], Chia Shen[1]
[1]Harvard University, [2]University of Toronto, [3]Northwestern University
[1]{fblock | cshen | phillips}@seas.harvard.edu, [2]dwigdor@dgp.toronto.edu,
[3]michael-horn@northwestern.edu

ABSTRACT

Multi-touch technology lends itself to collaborative crowd interaction (CI). However, common tap-operated widgets are impractical for CI, since they are susceptible to accidental touches and interference from other users. We present a novel multi-touch interface called *FlowBlocks* in which every UI action is invoked through a small sequence of user actions: dragging parametric *UI-Blocks*, and dropping them over operational *UI-Docks*. The FlowBlocks approach is advantageous for CI because it a) makes accidental touches inconsequential; and b) introduces design parameters for mutual awareness, concurrent input, and conflict management. FlowBlocks was successfully used on the floor of a busy natural history museum. We present the complete design space and describe a year-long iterative design and evaluation process which employed the Rapid Iterative Test and Evaluation (RITE) method in a museum setting.

Author Keywords

Crowd Interaction, Multi-Touch UI, Drag & Drop.

ACM Classification Keywords

H.5.m Information interfaces and presentation: User Interfaces. – Graphical User Interfaces.

General Terms

Design, Human Factors.

INTRODUCTION

Interactive tabletops and multi-touch surfaces are a growing area of human-computer interaction research, and recent studies have focused on the use of such devices in real world contexts including museums, galleries, and urban spaces. Indeed, informal learning environments such as museums have emerged as one area in which multi-touch interfaces can be meaningfully applied [15, 16, 17, 30]. The high-bandwidth input capabilities coupled with an inviting form factor seem ideal to facilitate the degree of social learning that is desirable in a museum context Such examinations have discovered that this context creates unique circumstances, that we call *crowd interaction* (CI) [15, 16, 17, 19, 23, 29, 30]. When designing user interfaces for crowds, one has to deal with the known "*chaos*" that arises when groups of strangers from various age groups and backgrounds spontaneously come together to "*collaborate*" (cf. Fig. 1): accidental touches are frequent [17, 36]; parallel interaction is the norm [17, 23, 29, 36]; levels of interference are high [16, 27, 29]; conflicts between participants commonly arise [16, 23, 29]; and mutual awareness amongst users regarding each other's actions and intentions cannot be considered a given [23, 29]. Additionally, UI standards for crowd interaction do not yet exist [40] and users approach gestural interfaces in a variety of different – and often conflicting – ways [16, 17, 42]. At the same time, average dwell times are low (around four minutes for a successful exhibit), making it hard to accommodate the significant training associated with teaching gestures to novice users [5, 6, 8, 11]. Overall, bringing *order* to the "chaos", while providing a UI that *everyone* can almost *instantly use*, is a significant challenge that every interface designer targeting crowd interaction must overcome.

Standard multi-touch UIs (such as the Microsoft Surface SDK [1]) provide a set of conventional widgets adapted for touch, that can be easy to learn (as they facilitate the transfer of desktop idioms, e.g. "click" → "tap") [42], and also scalable by providing functional coverage for most application scenarios. However, widgets that rely on *tapping* graphical elements on the tabletop do not perform well in chaotic crowd interaction circumstances, as they are highly susceptible to interference from accidental and uncoordinated touches [17, 23, 36]. An alternative way of

Figure 1. Chaos in a museum (frame from a video).

UIST '12, October 7–10, 2012, Cambridge, Massachusetts, USA.

circumventing these issues is to design "UI-less" multi-touch applications, such as the "media-sharing"-type of application that primarily relies on the basic manipulation of graphical objects (drag/resize/rotate) [3, 4, 16, 17, 22, 29], or interaction with physical phenomena that inherently lend themselves for multi-point interaction [33, 41]. These types of applications may cope well with the chaos, but the need for scalability limits the degree to which simple physics-based approaches can be effective [42]. This motivated our efforts to go beyond "UI-less" multi-touch applications, and to push towards a fully functional UI that enables a wide spectrum of interaction semantics, while being tailored to the requirements of crowd interaction.

In this paper, we propose *FlowBlocks,* a novel multi-user, multi-touch interface that relies on *drag & drop* as the primary input primitive. Every action is triggered by dragging a *Block* and dropping it over a *Dock* (see Fig. 2). To successfully execute a function, a user has to first pick up the Block, drag it across a certain trajectory – *signaling intent to act* to other users – and drop it over the target Dock to *execute the intended action.*

Promoting Drag & Drop to the primary means of performing all system functions provides inherent advantages in the context of crowd interaction. First, it is less prone to being activated by accidental or uncoordinated touches (or "fiddling" which occurs frequently with children around a multi-touch surface), particularly when the start and end points of the drag & drop are farther apart and when other trajectory-related constraints apply. FlowBlocks provides several design parameters that a designer can use to "fortify" their UI. Secondly, *tapping* and *holding* are freed to act as initiators for feedforward mechanisms that instruct novice users on how to use the application and its UI. Thirdly, as we will demonstrate, drag & drop interaction with UI widgets introduce several design parameters that can help promote mutual awareness and conflict management between users. We have developed FlowBlocks, and established its core qualities, during a year-long process of Rapid Iterative Testing and Evaluation (RITE [24]) in one of our partner museums.

The contribution of this paper is threefold: after discussing related work, we present the FlowBlocks design space, providing details about our core principles, components, and design parameters. We then illustrate how common UI controls can be realized or replaced using FlowBlocks

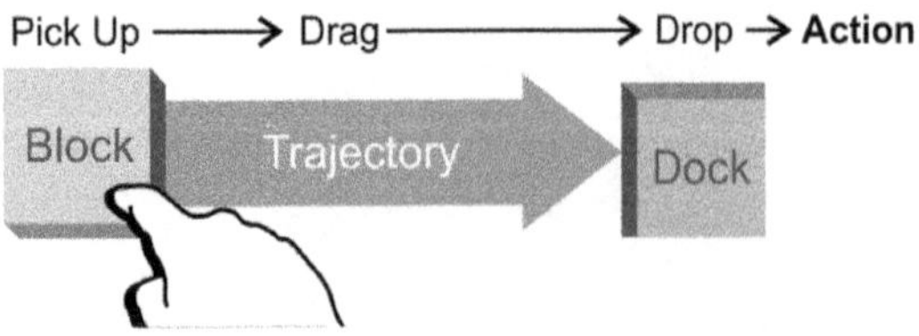

Figure 2. FlowBlocks basic principle: every action is executed by picking up a *Block*, dragging it along a certain trajectory, and dropping it over a *Dock*.

widgets, demonstrating functional coverage for the full range of application scenarios. Finally, we present the evaluation used to yield the current design of FlowBlocks, conducted while they were in use in a deployed application in one of our partner museums, and discuss our findings.

RELATED WORK

Of particular relevance to FlowBlocks is work that addresses multi-user interaction conflict management and mutual awareness, identifies problems with tap-based actions, or provides motivation for drag & drop as input primitive. Additionally, we discuss research that extends existing multi-touch UIs, UIs based on new input primitives, and tangible UIs.

Conflict Management and Mutual Awareness

A series of studies have pointed out that a variety of conflicts that commonly arise in multi-user use of interactive surfaces [7, 22, 25, 26, 29, 32, 36]. This includes conflicts through the sudden occlusion of screen real-estate or unexpected changes to the state of application [7, 29, 32], conflicts caused by accidental touch [36], or power struggles [22, 29]. Several approaches have been presented to address this issue: reducing conflicts through creating mutual awareness [7, 25]; negotiating UI access based on user identity [26, 31]; and enabling physical negotiation techniques [18, 22, 28].

FlowBlocks provides means of addressing conflict through awareness and physical negotiation: similar to the sketching gestures presented by [7]. Drag & drop provides a certain precursor to an action, particularly when performed across shared space. This approach builds on the *Privileged Object* policy [25], which suggests moving actions affecting all users to a shared space. Similar to physical objects, dragable graphical objects afford ways to utilize territoriality and negotiating for access (rather than fighting after the fact), commonly observed as natural behaviors when children interact in groups [18, 22, 28].

Morris et al. propose that social protocols are insufficient for facilitating sharing in some use scenarios, and describe a series of policies that can enforce "good behavior" among users [25]. With FlowBlocks, we follow a fundamentally different philosophy: we believe that social protocols are not inherently insufficient, but rather that UI's based on point-and-click provide insufficient cues to facilitate mutual awareness and thus underserve the needs of social protocols.

Problems with Tap-Based Actions

Existing multi-touch UIs, such as Microsoft's Surface SDK and Apple's iOS, adapt conventional UI widgets (such as buttons, drop down lists or radio buttons) to touch input, utilizing finger-tapping as the equivalent to clicking in the WIMP GUIs. While this allows a transfer of knowledge between traditional UIs and novel multi-touch systems, the lack of a hover state in touch devices eliminates helpful feedforward and feedback mechanisms [11, 40]. Further, studies observing crowd interaction report that erroneous touches lead to the frequent occurrence of false-positive invocation of actions, causing misinterpretation of UI behavior [36], and general confusion [17]. While erroneous touches can be accidental, in many cases they are intentional – caused by users who either don't realize or don't care that their actions will interfere with others. While certain mechanisms can be applied to reduce the negative effect of unintended or unnoticed touches – timeouts to prevent repeated activation [17] and confirmation dialogs [23] – these mechanisms can themselves lead to unresponsiveness, confusion [17], and tension between users [23]. Based on our own experiences in building museum exhibits, we concur with these findings, and consider standard multi-touch UIs unsuitable for crowd interaction.

Drag & Drop

Dragging is one of the most common modalities observed when users spontaneously approach tabletop UIs [16, 42]. Evidence for the success of dragging as an input modality is also provided by a series of "picture-sharing" type of tabletop applications, in which dragging responds well to interference and accidental touches [3, 16, 18, 22, 29]. For example, the "Futura" tabletop game [4] allows users can drag strategic resource tokens from a toolbar (situated at the four sides of the table) and drop them over an environment simulation in board-game like fashion (causing an effect in the outcome of an application). The authors reported that drag & drop worked well despite intense collaboration, and that users quickly learned how to place game tokens. Overall, dragging seems to be an input primitive that can be easily learned and performed by a variety of different users. This motivated us to promote dragging as the primary interaction primitive to prepare the execution of an action.

Extending Existing UIs

There is a series of work that aims at extending aspects of existing conventional UIs to multi-touch operation: the DiamondSpin Toolkit [32] provides a series of novel UI mechanisms to facilitate around-the-table interaction, such as multi-threaded input event streams and concurrent menus; Multi-touch Marking Menus aim to increase the bandwidth of touch input [21]; Attribute Gates utilize dragging trajectories across various graphical gates to adapt the object's attributes to different territories on the tabletop [35]; and Grids & Guides [12] increase the precision of multi-touch manipulations. FlowBlocks is designed for crowd interaction, and thus has less emphasis on some of these aspects, such as precision and throughput.

Graphical UI widgets that are operated through a drag-like gesture have been proposed before, albeit for other devices, motivated by different factors, and afforded with different metaphors [5, 27]. Like FlowBlocks, CrossY [5] replaces WIMP widgets with new UI controlled with a new input primitive: crossing. This is done because crossing is more efficiently and more accurately performed with a pen. Similarly, Moscovich [27] presented a set of widgets selected using sliding motions, aiming to reducing selection ambiguity on high resolution screens in which UI widgets are tightly packed. Gestures similar to "crossing" and "sliding" can be described as sub-primitives of drag & drop and have been incorporated into FlowBlocks.

Teaching Multi-Touch Gestures

One challenge for novel UIs is to be transparent to novice users [4, 5]. Consequently, there has been a series of work aimed at teaching touch and gesture-based input: to learn Marking Menu style gestures [20], OctoPocus [6] provides a dynamic guide that help users execute, learn, and remember gesture sets; ShadowGuides [11] provides in-situ guides that show a visualization of the user's fingers (feedback) alongside possible ways of continuing a gesture (feedforward). OctoPocus and ShadowGuides require the user to first understand the meaning of the visualizations they provide, thus, the process of training itself requires some degree of learning which is not practical in a CI setting where a walk-up-and-use is essential. In contrast, GesturePlay [8] provides an online learning system for teaching gestures through game-like virtual-physical widgets and positive reinforcement. Here, the mechanism for teaching gestures utilizes physical puzzles that the user can solve and in the process learn the execution of a gesture. Just-in-Time Chrome provides UI tailored to evoke various gestures [40]. It is also central to FlowBlocks to provide similar inline mechanisms that can help visitors quickly learn the operation of drag-based widgets. Elements of OctoPocus and GesturePlay have been incorporated in the design of FlowBlocks' inline-feedback and feedforward. ShadowGuide's use of the 'tap' gesture to invoke feedforward mechanisms has also been incorporated.

FLOWBLOCKS DESIGN SPACE

In FlowBlocks, the most elementary functional unit of interaction – invoking a binary command – is triggered by a *compound action* requiring the execution of two binary actions and one continuous action: acquisition of a Block (binary), dragging the Block over a Dock (continuous) and releasing the Block (binary). FlowBlocks intentionally separates the three components previously required for a binary action. In this section we will show how this separation can be beneficially used to address the challenges of crowd interaction. Based on our analysis of related work, we concentrated on designing FlowBlocks to meet these three challenges:

1. *Noise and interference*: minimize the effect of accidental touches and uncoordinated "fiddling".
2. *Mutual awareness and conflict management*: increase awareness between users regarding their intention and actions, and provide tools for negotiating conflicts.
3. *Learning how to interact*: any user must be able to use an interface almost instantly and without training.

The following subsections describe the mechanics relating to each point at the *conceptual* level of FlowBlocks. In the next section we will present *practical* guidelines for applying FlowBlocks in practice.

Dealing with Noise and Uncoordinated Interference

Generally, FlowBlocks widgets are less susceptible to accidental touches, because touches alone do not trigger an action, but only cause feedforward to appear. However, accidental touches could still coincide to form a sequence that mimics a drag operation, potentially triggering an unintended action. For this to happen, an accidental touch would have to start over the position of a Block, move across a certain trajectory, and drop the Block over the corresponding Dock. While we found this to very rarely happen in practical use, FlowBlocks provides three parameters that can further reduce the likelihood, which we will review in turn: increasing the distance between Block and Dock, requiring Dock activation, and constraining the trajectory of the drag component. These methods are not only a means of counteracting accidental touches, but can also be used to reduce the effect of uncoordinated "fiddling", which is especially prevalent among younger children.

Constraining trajectory. Figure 3 provides several examples for trajectory constraints: a) constraining movement to a path, b) using virtual barriers through which Blocks cannot pass, and c) & d) requiring certain speed of drag to allow a Block to reach the Dock. These constraints require more coordination and intent from a user in order to successfully complete an action, which reduces the action's susceptibility to noise and uncoordinated touches.

Dock activation. Docks can be configured to require explicit activation before Blocks can be dropped over their active area, which adds another layer of intent and coordination that is required to execute an action:

- *Tap-to-activate*: tapping a dock "opens" it for a certain time window.
- *Hold-to-activate*: the dock is receptive to a Block for as long as a touch is held in its active area.

While the presented mechanisms of constraining trajectories and dock activation counteract the effect of accidental and uncoordinated touches, they are also useful in the context of mutual awareness and conflict management amongst users. Several other mechanisms of FlowBlocks also help to address this design challenge.

Mutual Awareness and Conflict Management

Mutual awareness is key factor in the fluidity and naturalness of collaboration, and in allowing social protocols to facilitate interaction [13]. By being aware of other's intentions and actions, conflicts can be detected and negotiated [7, 25]. FlowBlocks' core primitive – drag & drop – consciously separates the *intent to interact* – selecting a Block and dragging it towards a Dock – from *executing the intended action* – dropping the Block over the dock (cf. Fig.3). This gives users the chance to become aware of an incoming action, decide if it conflicts with their interests, and intervene. While intervention can always be carried out through social etiquette ("Wait! Don't do that please!"), FlowBlocks also seeks to cater for more physical negotiation strategies that are commonly applied by younger children [16, 22, 28]. Consequently, each of FlowBlocks' basic components – Blocks, trajectories and Docks – affords independent ways of physical intervention. Blocks can be "claimed" and moved into a private space, or shielded from other users. Similarly, Docks can be shielded from an approaching Block, for instance by covering it with the hand, preventing the Block from being dropped. Users can also physically influence the trajectory of a drag-operation, for instance by otherwise "blocking the way", or pushing the respective hand away.

FlowBlocks draws inspiration from tangible computing [10, 14, 39, 37], particularly from the Token and Constraints (TAC) paradigm [34, 38]. Promoting virtual blocks that users can manipulate as the primary UI primitive, makes it possible to apply physical metaphors and constraints to each interface action, opening up a spectrum of design options that are not usually considered by existing, widget-based multi-touch UIs (cf. Fig. 3).

Influencing mutual awareness. FlowBlocks provide three parameters that can be adjusted when designing for awareness. First, positioning of Block and Dock are extremely important, not only because longer distances allow more time to become aware of the drag, but also because it has an impact on what portion of the interactive area has to be crossed. If drags happen in the periphery, they are less likely to cause global awareness than drags that cross shared, central space. Second, the designer can promote awareness using the same trajectory constraints we described for reducing noise and uncoordinated actions (Figure 3). Speed-dependent wrappings ensure easily observed rapid movements (c) or extra time (d). For instance, access to an important global function could be surrounded by "rubber", providing others more time for anticipation and intervention.

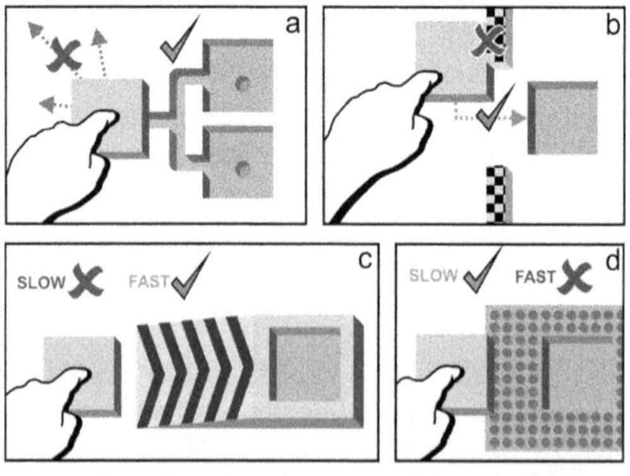

Figure 3. Constraining trajectory of drag operations: a) *rails* limit the movement of a block along a predefined path ("allow" policy); b) *barriers* define regions through which a block cannot pass ("deny" policy); c) *ramps* and d) *rubber pads* require a certain velocity of the drag operation in order to reach the target Dock.

Virtual barriers and paths create recognizable movement patterns and "bottlenecks" through which each action has to pass (a,b). These parameters can be chosen per action: actions that affect all users (e.g. reset the application) can combine any of these factors to achieve the desired global awareness, while more personal functions can omit them.

Learning from others. Existing observations have provided strong evidence that visitors learn from each other [16, 17], by copying each other's actions. This provides further motivation for increasing mutual awareness as it gives particularly novice user approaching the table, as well as younger children or elders, to learn and copy interactions observed from more advanced participants.

Managing simultaneous interactions. A special case of conflict is the simultaneous manipulation of shared resources – dubbed *global coordination* [26]. For instance, in a map application, the current view on the map is a shared resource in that changes will impact on anyone around the table, even if they are engaged in independent sub-tasks (such as looking at different parts of the map). Operations on this shared resource (e.g. jumping to another country) have to be regulated in that only one person can manipulate the resource at a time. In crowd interaction, the common case is that a single person triggers such an action, while others are interrupted in their task, and potentially confused about why this action is happening. FlowBlocks can be used as described previously to create awareness and enable anticipation of global events. Additionally, the Block-Dock metaphor inherently conveys what actions can be executed simultaneously. If a Dock is occupied, it can be "locked", causing any attempt to drop another Block into it to "bounce off", until the associated action is completed (e.g. the view has zoomed to a new country on the map). It is also possible to configure Docks to remain open, so that the existing action can be interrupted by removing the occupying Block, or by dropping a new Block onto the Dock, causing the previous one to "fall out". While this mutual locking is possible with existing multi-touch widget through "graying out" UI elements that are currently inaccessible, FlowBlocks inherently convey and reflect the state of execution, and the availability of functions.

Learning

Due to the lack of UI standards for crowd interaction [40] and a variety of different ways in which users approach gestural interfaces [16, 17, 42], any crowd UI has to clearly convey its meaning to inexperienced users. This aspect is particularly emphasized in a museum context, as dwell times are usually short, and as a consequence, the learning of the interface cannot take up more than a few seconds.

In conventional GUIs, the pointer's hover state can be used to instruct novice users how to interact – such as to show tooltips when the mouse pointer is dwelling over a control. Preview states, however, are sorely missed in a

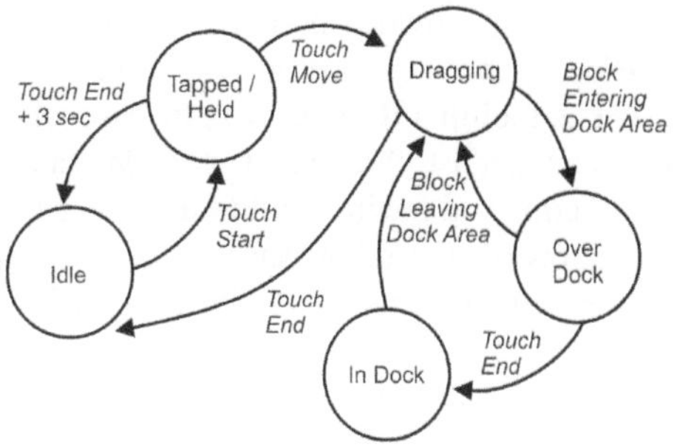

Figure 4. FlowBlocks' *Block* state diagram.

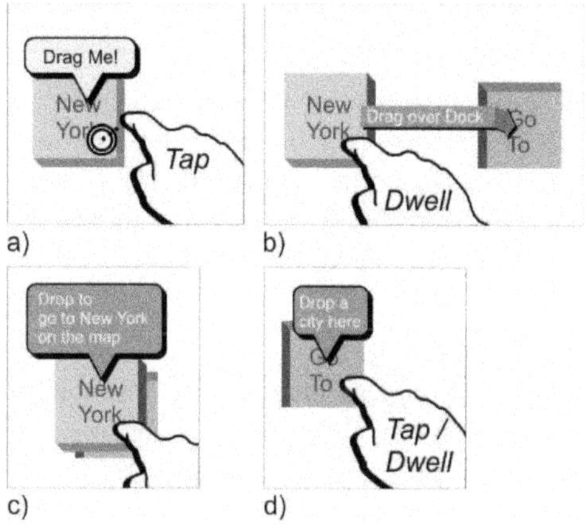

Figure 5. Feedforward help: a) prompting to drag; b) showing directional guides leading towards compatible Docks and c) preview before the execution of an action. Managing screen clutter: d) using relative guides, e) weighing guide strength by distance to Dock.

straightforward port of WIMP UI to touch environments [11, 40]. FlowBlocks introduces a novel state model for its widgets that adds two additional states to existing state models for touch-sensitive input devices [9]. Figure 4 shows the state-transition diagram for a Block. As soon as a Block is touched, it enters a *Tapped / Held* state. This state is also retained for at least 3 seconds in case the user immediately retracts the touch – ensuring that a 'tap' gesture will also activate this state for a short duration. A second state *Over Dock* is entered as soon as a Block is moved over a dock (but not released yet). The remaining states correspond to the traditional three-state model of input [9]: *Idle ~ State 0* (out of range), *Dragging ~ State 1* (tracking) and *In Dock ~ State 2* (state 2 refers to the activation of the input device, in our case, a Block occupying a Dock).

Preview states can be used to teach both mode of operation, and mechanics of the application. Based on our state model, we can provide instructions at three moments where we are able to infer possible user confusion. First, we need to anticipate any graphical element to be tapped, including both Blocks and Docks, as tapping is the most consistently observed way users spontaneously interact with graphical elements [16, 36]. While in the state model *Tapped / Held* does not cause an action in FlowBlocks, we can utilize this state to convey the proper mode of operation to the user.

For Docks, we can provide appropriate feedback (cf. Fig. 5d). For Blocks, we can instruct the user to drag, for instance, via a tooltip (cf. Fig. 5a). In case of a Block, instructions can persist throughout dragging and provide updated instruction and feedforward to help the user with the proper execution of an action, such as guided by arrows (Fig. 5b). Generally, all existing feedforward techniques can be applied, such as OctoPocus [6] or ShadowGuides [11]. The second moment of potential confusion within our state model regards the mechanics of the application. The *Over Dock* state can be used to provide a preview of what *would* happen if the currently dragged Block was dropped over a Dock (cf. Fig. 5c). This is equivalent to a traditional tooltip.

Having designed FlowBlocks' many parameters to overcome specific challenges inherent in crowd interaction, we now demonstrate their functional completeness. To do this, we designed FlowBlocks-based widgets that mimic the logical function of traditional WIMP UI elements.

FLOWBLOCKS WIDGETS

A significant challenge in the construction of UI elements based on a new physical primitive is the need to ensure functional coverage for application development. Previous efforts have accomplished this by redesigning WIMP UI widgets for use with their new primitives [5]. Our intention is not to mimic earlier controls, but rather to use them as a spanning set of logical actions required to create useful applications. Based on common GUI toolkits, we have identified 4 logical types of components that are required to cover most interaction semantics: *Binary Triggers, Selections, Scalar Controls,* and *Menus.* We omit logical compound components as long as they can be constructed using the five types of components we present (e.g. a File Open Dialog is a compound widgets, consisting of a scrollable container and binary controls).

Figure 6 shows each of the five classes of controls that can be supported by FlowBlocks. We provide examples for three different *binary controls*: slider-trigger controls (a), similar to the "Unlock"-slider in iOS; (b) "url" like navigation based on a "Navigation"-Dock and several "URL"-Blocks; (c) an arrangement of two slider-triggers to peek into and open a photo album – combining FlowBlocks widgets in this way might lend itself to playfully teaching multi-point gestures to novice users, similar to [8]. FlowBlocks can support many types of *selectors* through the assembly of Blocks and Docks, as in examples (d) and (e). While Docks usually are limited to one occupant, they can also be considered as containers in which several elements can be placed (e). *Sliders* can be constructed by constraining a handle-Block within a rectangular area using a barrier, and filling the area seamlessly with as many docks as there are steps (f, g, h). Further mechanisms can be put into place to prevent the accidental adjustment of a slider: "gear-box-style" rails require the user to first lift the

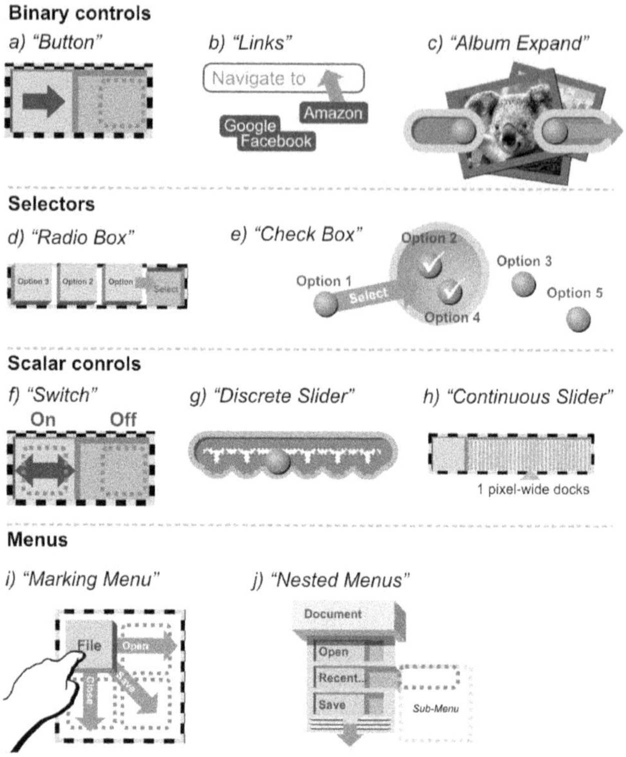

Figure 6. Examples for FlowBlocks versions of common types of UI widget:binary controls, selectors, scalar controls and menus; Legend: = rail, = invisible Dock, = invisible barrier.

handle before it can be horizontally adjusted (g). FlowBlocks also affords various menu styles (i, j). Example (i) shows a menu in the form of a single Block. Once the user touches the Block, arrows point into three distinct directions, and activates invisible docks, as well as an invisible barrier that keeps the Block within the allowed area. If the user now drags the Block in a direction beyond the bounds of the barrier, it will automatically drop over one of the invisible Docks. Thus FlowBlocks are used to implement the scale-independence and free-movement of a Marking Menu [20]. These menus illustrate two more concepts that FlowBlocks can support: dynamically showing and hiding its constituent elements, as well as linking different states from our model to create more complex UI behaviors.

Having demonstrated that FlowBlocks are logically complete across the functions of the WIMP GUI, we now address their design and integration into an application, as well as the iterative design process that led to the development of many of the design parameters we have discussed.

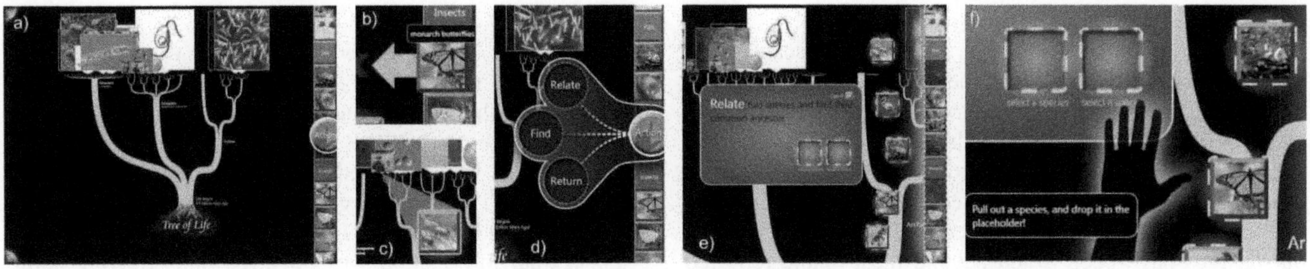

Figure 7. The DeepTree exhibit (a) and FlowBlocks UI (b, c, d, e, f).

APPLICATION AND EVALUATION

FlowBlocks is the outcome of a yearlong iterative design process in which we implemented a Microsoft Surface application, *DeepTree*, as part of a 3-year NSF *Informal Science Education* project. We directly observed over 280 visitors at our DeepTree testing exhibit using talk-aloud protocols. The DeepTree is an interactive and multi-touch visual application that allows visitors to explore the evolutionary relationship and historical time of divergence of all life on earth. This relationship is visualized in the form of a large phylogenetic tree based on data from the Tree of Life Web Project [2] with over 70.000 species, and 20.000 internal nodes. Figure 7a shows DeepTree application and its interface.

The main area shows the Tree of Life, as well as *images* that mark the location of representative species in the tree (in the illustration, the root of the tree is visible, showing the three domains Bacteria, Eukaryotes and Archaea). Users can browse the tree of life with drag-based manipulation, dragging the tree downward to zoom-in towards the leaves, or upward towards the root to zoom-out.

At the right side of the screen, a scrolling image reel of 200 selected species-Blocks are shown. Visitors can scroll through the image reel by standard flicking techniques, or pull any species from the reel and move it above the tree (cf. Fig. 7b). Here, the Blocks gain a "chord" that visually links the block with the location of the species in the tree, to aid navigation and orientation (cf. Fig. 7c). Users can also perform *Find* and *Relate* queries using our Flow Blocks UI. An "Action" marking menu on the right side provides access to *Find*, *Relate* and *Return* (cf. Fig. 7d). Once dragged into a direction and dropped, the action Block morphs into a dialog which occupies the central area of the display (c.f Fig. e). The dialog presents one (*Find*) or two (*Relate*) Docks, respectively. The user executes an action by dragging species-Blocks into the Docks (cf. Fig. 7f). When a species-Block is dropped into a Dock, the tree seamlessly zooms and pans to show an appropriate view (similar to a map flying to a new city). For *relate* queries, this is a view of the most recent common ancestor (the point in the tree were both species separated), as well as visualizations of traits shared by the species which were dropped-in to the Docks. The *Return* dialog contains a trigger-slider (Fig. 6a), which flies the user back to the root of the tree.

The aim of the exhibit was to allow visitors to explore evolutionary concepts and to casually browse the tree for any of the 70,000 species. The comparisons and searches provide a focused activity, and a natural end point, which is recommended in public venues with large crowds [36].

Method

As part of our iterative design process, we used the RITE method (Rapid Iterative Testing and Evaluation [24]) throughout the year, testing the various stages of development and alternative versions of FlowBlocks inside one of the galleries at our partner museum. This method was well suited for our project for reasons of external validity: we wished to carry out our evaluations in the native setting where our exhibit will be installed when it is finished, and with actual visitors that spontaneously interact with our system. Our partner museum has over 170,000 visitors per year from diverse backgrounds. Observations were carried out during weekdays – typically attracting school groups and summer camps – as well as on weekends, when many families visit the museum.

RITE entails expert observations to drive quick design iterations. Both video footage and field notes were collected. Institutional Review Board permission was granted to gather video recordings of visitors without prior written consent, however, a video-taping notice had to be present during observations, and collected footage could only be used for internal analysis. Additionally, an observer was physically present, shadowing the museum visitors and taking notes from a discreet distance. After visitors finished interacting with the DeepTree they were approached by the observer and given the opportunity to provide verbal feedback, which could inform our design iterations. To reduce bias, an independent researcher who was not involved in the development and design of FlowBlocks carried out all observations. The criteria used to evaluate each RITE iteration were based on the three pillars of the presented design space:

1. Create *mutual awareness*, and enable *conflict negotiation*, be it verbal or physical.
2. Reduce (or eliminate) invocations of actions through accidental and uncoordinated touches (*noise & interference*).
3. Visitors should learn to use FlowBlocks during the (typically short) time they interact with the system (*learning to interact*).

New design iterations were begun as soon as it became clear that the design goal was not yet met, or when bugs prevented us from carrying out meaningful observations. Deployments between iterations varied in length and number of users, but were typically 1 week and approximately 20-40 observed users. In total, 10 iterations were conducted over 15 months, with over 280 visitors being observed. With this approach, our designs have been tested beyond most of the reported "*in the wild*" work [16, 23] in that we did not stop at one or two rounds of evaluation. Instead, our designs have been both designed and evaluated in the wild.

Observations & Findings

The *FlowBlocks Design Space* and *Widgets*, and *Application* sections describe the finished product of the RITE process, as well as several design parameters which, while clearly useful in some contexts, did not suit the particular design of the DeepTree exhibit. We now discuss observations gathered throughout the iterative design process, which will be of benefit to researchers and designers seeking to extend and apply FlowBlocks, and to those designing UI for crowd interaction in general.

Everyone can Learn to Drag

We found that nearly all users approach FlowBlocks in one of two ways: some instantly start dragging Blocks around and dropping them into Docks. Particularly children seem to require no instruction as to how FlowBlocks work, which indicates that they could infer the proper use from the visual design of Blocks and Docks shown in Figure 7e. These visuals were the 11th version tested. The second category of user starts by tapping Blocks or Docks. While at this point, feedforward can help the transition from tapping to dragging, we went through several iterations for this transition to happen quickly, and for all age groups. Initially, we used arrow guides that marked the potential routes from the dragged Blocks to the Docks, similar to those described in Octopocus [6]. The arrows persisted through the act of dragging and updated dynamically. While this effectively encouraged hesitant visitors drag, for kids, who readily drag as many species over the tree as possible, this technique lead to significant screen clutter, as many guides cross large parts of the display space.

After several iterations, the final feedforward consisted of four mechanisms. First, if species Blocks within the image reel are tapped, for a brief moment the Block is slightly nudged outwards, and an animated arrow appears (Fig. 7b). This arrow is relatively small, and disappears as soon as the Block is dragged. This was effective in initiating the transition to drag, while not causing screen clutter during dragging, even when multiple elements where pulled out at the same time. Secondly, we used an animated visual effect of an ant-trail (cf. Fig. 7f) that surrounded both Docks and Blocks – to convey their functional dependency. This effect was only visible when an action dialog was in the center of the display (after being selected from the action menu). Thirdly, when tapping a dock, an animated hand shows up, performing a drag operation from the image reel to the Docks (cf. Fig. 7f). The described feedforward was effective for transitioning most visitors to dragging, but particularly seniors still showed hesitance and signs of confusion, even when all three mechanisms where active. Thus, we added a tooltip which was displayed when tapping either the Blocks or the Docks. The tooltip gives instruction in written form, and we found indicators in form of utterances during use that this textual information was effective in instructing adults and seniors, while not hindering kids (who do not read).

After these modifications, FlowBlocks were consistently learned within the first few seconds of interaction. All groups approaching the table, including school groups and seniors, started carrying out actions almost immediately. Considering that UI standards for crowd interaction do not yet exist [40] and that user intuition regarding the "proper" use of such UIs widely differs [16, 17, 42], FlowBlock is effective in teaching a consistent operation of UI widget to a wide range of users. We found less evidence that users noticed the second type of feedforward (shown when a Block is dragged over a Dock). Users seemed willing to try out an action without precise foreknowledge of the result. This may be less true in settings where errors are costlier.

Little Effect of Noise and Fiddling

Our initial prototype of the exhibit was based on tap-activated species-markers. Concurring with existing findings [17, 23, 36], we quickly disqualified this mode of invoking commands for our context, as accidental and random jumps prevented constructive collaboration, particularly in large groups. After introducing FlowBlocks, we did not observe any instances in which accidental touches triggered one of our actions, or in which users seemed to be confused about why a certain action happened. Furthermore, active "fiddling" (children quickly wiping their fingers across the species-Blocks) very rarely caused issues other than multiple feedforward guides cluttering the screen, which led to the described feedforward designs. Overall, we were satisfied with the effectiveness of FlowBlocks regarding both accidental as well as uncoordinated touches, as we generally observed constructive execution of actions despite intense interference.

Drag & Drop is Hard to Ignore and Easy to Prevent

We frequently observed occurrences in which users either verbally or physically reacted to another user's action *prior* to a Block being dropped. We infer from this that users were generally aware of each other's actions, particularly of those actions that we intended to require consent. This was apparent after some initial play and learning about FlowBlocks, children would transition to more constructive interaction with the system, and actively prevent other participants from executing interfering actions. Our observation concurred with existing work in that physical strategies are commonly deployed by younger children, such as blocking one another's hands, pushing each other away, or covering Blocks or Docks to claim "territory" [16, 22].

Many Solutions to Affect Awareness and Collaboration

Throughout our iterations, we tested various parameters of FlowBlocks and their effect on mutual awareness. In an early version (Fig. 8a&b), both the Docks for *Find* and *Relate*, as well as the reset slider were visible at all times, and placed in the top portion of the display. While this created functional overview, we did notice occasions on which visitors seemed surprised and unaware of other visitors triggering a *Find*, *Relate*, or *Return* (then called *Reset*), and at times uncertain about which function (*Find* or *Relate*) was currently executing. This was particularly apparent in a version in which Find and Relate Docks were spatially separated (cf. Fig. b). Several iterations addressed this issue. In one design, we tried to first only show the *Find* Dock (then "Jump To", cf. Fig. 8c), then, after selecting and flying to a species, show a *Relate* Dock (then called "Compare With", cf. Fig. 8d). Consequently, after selecting a species for the *Find*-action, the species is now the starting point for a *Relate*-query. In contrast to the previous versions (Fig. 8a & b), this design made sure that

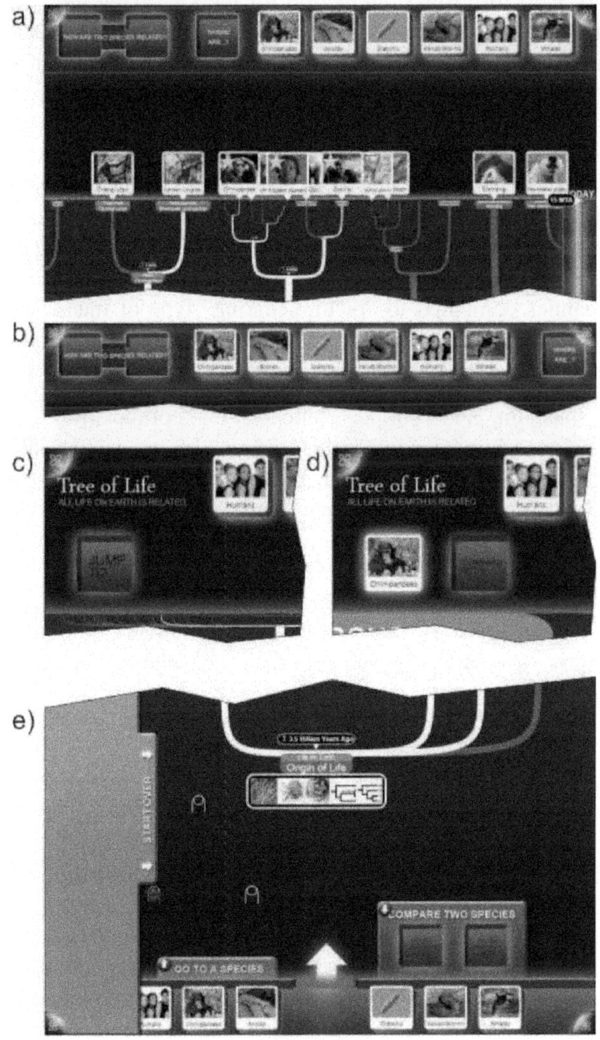

Figure 8. Selection of discarded design iterations of the DeepTree UI.

only the active Docks of *one* function – Find *or* Relate – are visible at a time, and that both actions are presented in the same area on the screen. While this design eliminated the described awareness issues, the mechanism of a Dock changing its function *after* it has been originally occupied with a Block appeared to be a separate source of confusion. Visitors could not anticipate this conditional change when making their initial choice, nor did our design visually communicate this change of functional meaning (the Dock's label is occluded once occupied by a Block). For our exhibit, we dismissed conditionally changing Docks, however, they might be suitable for other scenarios.

An alternative way of addressing the awareness issues observed during earlier iterations (Fig. 8a&b), was to utilize several of the described mechanisms to increase the precursor necessary for each action (Fig. 8e). We place virtual walls so that the species Blocks could only be dragged out of a small bottleneck at the center. The species docks for *Find* and *Relate* are hidden in "drawers", and first have to be pulled out before being accessible (a form of Dock-activation). Additionally, we made the *Reset* (or *Return*) action accessible via a slider, which when pulled out starts to cover the whole screen in a red "curtain". The slider has to be pulled across the whole screen and released in order for the Reset action to trigger.

In a study within one of our iterations in which we compared both interfaces (Fig 8a & e), we found the second version reduced occurrences of confusion, by introducing new constraints that made it harder for a drag to go unnoticed. However, it was also less popular for adults, as the effort of invoking an action was relatively high. In contrast, kids loved this version (cf. "Constraints vs. Play"). In our final design, we utilized the described marking menu and a positioning of the action dialogs in the center of the display (Fig. 7b). This design had three benefits: the marking menu added another precursor to an action; positioning the the action's Docks into shared space (as advocated by [25]) brought the Docks of an incoming action to everyone's attention; and showing only Docks of a single function at a time reduced the confusion observed with earlier designs (Fig. 8a & b). The final UI version balanced suitability for a large age range with good awareness characteristics.

Constraints vs. Play

By providing a set of loose movable tokens, FlowBlocks inherently lend themselves to playful interaction. We have observed various forms of play with the DeepTree UI. FlowBlocks originally implemented inertia, so the species Blocks could be flicked around the table, causing particularly younger kids to "play hockey" (as one of our younger visitors called it). Another popular game among kids was to drag as many species blocks onto the tree as possible. While this form of play seemed enjoyable, it distracted from "deeper" engagement, particularly for younger audiences.

As the DeepTree is focused on learning, we experimented with constraints to "enforce order", such as disabling inertia, introducing the bottleneck (Fig. 8c), and forcing a one-at-a-time order for pulling out species Blocks. While these modifications reduced levels of play, the overuse of such constraints resulted in slow and awkward interaction experiences for adults. Likewise, we observed instances in which the *presence* of constraints encouraged an "obstacle course" style of play (e.g. routing a Block through the mentioned bottleneck). Generally, we feel that certain levels of play are inherent to FlowBlocks, which has to be considered by the UI designer. In our final design, we tried to strike a balance of allowing certain levels of play while minimizing their impact on mature participants (see "Managing Screen Clutter"). This can enable little kids to "participate" alongside more focused and deeper interaction.

Managing Screen Clutter

One issue we have identified is that Blocks scattering around the Display during usage (due to fiddling or directed use) can cause significant screen clutter. We have found two mechanisms that deal with this issue: first, Blocks that are not dropped over a Dock can snap back to their original location; secondly, Blocks can be configured to disappear if they are not actively touched. In our design, the Blocks dragged onto the tree started to slowly fade out when not touched, and eventually move back to the reel. This was successful in reducing clutter.

Sequential vs. Parallel Interaction

As described in the design space, FlowBlocks can be configured to enable parallel interaction or to enforce sequential execution of actions. While one of the obvious strengths of multi-touch technology is its ability to allow multiple users to interact at the same time, we have found that sequential interaction also has merits. For learning, it is preferable for visitors working together rather than working side-by-side. At the macro level, the FlowBlocks UI enforces a parallel execution of actions in order to create a shared context for all participants. However, at the micro-level, phases of negotiation and simultaneous interaction were frequently observed, both verbally, as well as facilitated through moving species Blocks close to the Docks to signal individual preference for which parameter to chose next. We frequently observed turn-based interaction, and at occasion a modality of actor and observer(s). However, both modes of operating the DeepTree were successful in engaging participants in a shared learning activity.

In summary, we found that FlowBlocks, in their current design, and with various parameters, can support a variety of different designs that allow UI designers to actively influence how certain actions are perceived, and enable the creation of successful, crowd-friendly UI.

CONCLUSION

Although the challenges of crowd interaction are widely acknowledged, there are no general UI frameworks or design guidelines that can inform the concrete design of crowd UIs across a variety of application scenarios. Our work starts to fill this gap by providing a general UI, based on the drag-and-drop primitive that is custom-tailored to the challenges of crowd interaction. Our year-long iterative design and evaluation has established the founding qualities of FlowBlocks – enabling crowd interaction in the face of chaos: its robustness regarding accidental touches and interference, its ease of learning and use for a wide spectrum of users, and its capability to provide application designers with a variety of options to influence mutual awareness, and facilitation of conflict management. We have also shown that FlowBlocks provide common interaction primitives that afford the functional scalability of common UI for multi-touch interaction.

While our insights have confirmed that drag-based widgets work well for crowd interaction for the DeepTree museum exhibit, further studies are required to understand how best FlowBlocks can be extended to support wider application scenarios. Theoretically, FlowBlocks can support "desktop-grade" functionality in crowd interaction settings, given their coverage of existing UI primitives. We certainly do not envision to port complex applications, such as photo editing software, to crowd interaction. We do believe, however, that there are many meaningful application scenarios that benefit from more complex interaction semantics compared to "picture-sharing" type of interaction commonly found on surface computer. The DeepTree exhibit serves as an example of more complex interaction flow.

In museum and public contexts, UI composition has significant impact on whether visitors have an enjoyable social experience in which they acquire knowledge, or leave frustrated and confused. Every effort to optimize the UI can thus potentially have significant impact on a wide range of users. DeepTree will soon be deployed in five different museums, with an estimated 4.5 million total visitors in the next year. FlowBlocks will serve to enable visitors to enjoy a meaningful and playful learning experience.

ACKNOWLEDGEMENTS

We thank the Harvard Museum of Natural History, and its Director of Exhibitions, Janis Sacco, for allowing us to conduct this research in their galleries. We also thank Kay Hofmeester and Paul Hoover, formerly of the Microsoft Surface team, for their discussion on drag & drop-based widgets. We thank the National Science Foundation for their support of this project (DRL-1010889). Any opinions, findings and conclusions or recommendations expressed in this material are those of the authors and do not necessarily reflect the views of the National Science Foundation.

REFERENCES

1. Microsoft Surface. http://www.microsoft.com/surface/
2. http://www.tolweb.org
3. http://www.ideum.com/interactive-exhibits/
4. Antle A. Futura: design for collaborative learning and game play on a multi-touch digital tabletop. *TEI'11*, 93-100.
5. Apitz, G. and Guimbretiere, F. CrossY: a crossing-based drawing application. *UIST '04*, 3-12.
6. Bau, O. and Mackay, W. E. OctoPocus: a dynamic guide for learning gesture-based command sets. *UIST '08*, 37-46.
7. Belatar, M. and Coldefy, F. Sketched menus and iconic gestures, techniques designed in the context of shareable interfaces. *ITS '10*, 143–146.
8. Bragdon, A., Uguray, A., Wigdor, D., Anagnostopoulos, S., Zeleznik, R. and Feman, R. Gesture play: motivating online gesture learning with fun, positive reinforcement and physical metaphors. *ITS '10*, 39-48.
9. Buxton, W. A three-state model of graphical input. *INTERACT '90*, 449-456.
10. Cohen, J., Withgott, M. and Piernot, P. Logjam: a tangible multi-person interface for video logging. In Proc. CHI '99, 128-135.
11. Freeman, D., Benko, H., Morris, M. R. and Wigdor, D. ShadowGuides: visualizations for in-situ learning of multi-touch and whole-hand gestures. *ITS '09*, 165-172.
12. Frisch, M., Kleinau, S., Langner, R. and Dachselt, R. Grids & guides: multi-touch layout and alignment tools. *CHI '11*, 1615-1618.
13. Gutwin, C. and Greenberg, S. A descriptive framework of workspace awareness for real-time groupware. *CSCW 2002, 411 – 446.*
14. Hartmann, B., Morris, M. R., Benko, H. and Wilson, A. D. Pictionaire: supporting collaborative design work by integrating physical and digital artifacts. *CSCW '10*, 421-424.
15. Hinrichs, U., Schmidt, H. and Carpendale, S. Emdialog: Bringing information visualization into the museum. *IEEE ToV&CG*, 14(6):1181–1188, 2008.
16. Hinrichs, U. and Carpendale, S. Gestures in the wild: Studying multi-touch gesture sequences on interactive tabletop exhibits. *CHI 2011*, 3023-3032.
17. Hornecker, E. I don't understand it either, but it is cool - visitor interactions with a multi-touch table in a museum. *TABLETOP 2008*, 113–120.
18. Hornecker, E. Interactions around a contextually embedded system. *TEI '10,* 169 – 176.
19. Jacucci, G., A. Morrison, Richard, G., Kleimola, J., Peltonen, P., Parisi, L. and Laitinen, T. Worlds of information: designing for engagement at a public multi-touch display. *CHI '10*, 2267–2276.
20. Kurtenbach, G.and Buxton, W. 1994. User learning and performance with marking menus. *CHI'94*, 258-264.
21. Lepinski, G.J., Grossman, T. and Fitzmaurice, G. The Design and Evaluation of Multitouch Marking Menus. *CHI '10*, 2233–2242.
22. Marshall, P., Fleck, R., Harris, A., Rick, J., Hornecker, E., Rogers, Y., Yuill, N. and Dalton, N.S. Fighting for control: children's embodied interactions when using physical and digital representations. In *CHI '09*, 2149 – 2152.
23. Marshall, P., Morris, R., Rogers, Y., Kreitmayer, S. and Davies, M. Rethinking'multi-user': an in-the-wild study of how groups approach a walk-up-and-use tabletop interface. *CHI '11*, 3033-3042.
24. Medlock, M., Wixon, D., McGee, M. and Welsh, D. The Rapid Iterative Test and Evaluation Method: Better Products in Less Time. *Cost Justifying Usability, An Update for the Internet Age.* Bias, R. and Mayhew, D. (eds). Boston, Morgan Kaufmann, 2005.
25. Morris, M.R., Ryall, K., Shen, C., Forlines, C. and Vernier, F. Beyond social protocols: Multi-user coordination policies for co-located groupware. *CSCW'04* 262 – 265.
26. Morris, M.R., Huang, A. Paepcke, A. and Winograd, T. Cooperative gestures: multi-user gestural interactions for co-located groupware. *CHI'06* 1201 – 1210.
27. Moscovich, T. Contact area interaction with sliding widgets. *UIST '09*, 13-22.
28. Olson, I.C., Leong, Z. A., Wilensky, U. and Horn, M. S. "It's just a toolbar!" Using Tangibles to Help Children Manage Conflict Around a Multi-Touch Tabletop. *TEI'11*, 29-36.
29. Peltonen, P., Kurvinen, E., Salovaara, A., Jacucci, G., Ilmonen, T., Evans, J., Oulasvirta, A., and Saarikko P. It's mine, don't touch!: interactions at a large multi-touch display in a city centre. *CHI'08* 1285–1294.
30. Schmidt, H., Hinrichs, U., Dunning, A., and Carpendale, S. memory [en] codebuilding a collective memory within a tabletop installation. *Proc. CAe*, Eurographics Association, 135–142, 2007.
31. Schmidt, D., Chong, M. K. and Gellersen, H. IdLenses: Dynamic personal areas on shared surfaces. *ITS 2010*, 131-134.
32. Shen, C., Vernier, F. D., Forlines, C., and Ringel, M. DiamondSpin: An Extensible Toolkit for Around-the-Table Interaction. *CHI'04*, 167-174.
33. Scott, S. and Raffle, H. Social immersive media: pursuing best practices for multi-user interactive camera/projector exhibits. *CHI '09*, 1447-1456.
34. Shaer, O., Leland, N., Calvillo-Gamez, E. H. and Jacob, R. J. K. The TAC Paradigm: Specifying Tangible User Interfaces. PUC, vol. 8, no. 5, pp. 359-369, Sept. 2004.
35. Sulaiman, N. S., Oliver, P. Attribute Gates. *UIST 2008*, 57 – 66.
36. Ryall, K., Morris, M.R., Everitt, K., Forlines, C. and Shen, C. Experiences with and observations of direct-touch tabletops. *Tabletop*, 89-96.
37. Ullmer, B., Ishii, H., and Glas, D. mediaBlocks: physical containers, transports, and controls for online media. In Proc. SIGGRAPH '98, 379-386.
38. Ullmer, B., Ishii, H., Jacob, R. J. K. Token+Constraint Systems for Tangible Interaction with Digital Information. *ToCHI 2005*, 81-118.
39. Weiss, M., Wagner, J., Jansen, Y., Jennings, R., Khoshabeh, R., Hollan, J. D., and Borchers, J. SLAP widgets: bridging the gap between virtual and physical controls on tabletops. *CHI '09*, 481-490.
40. Wigdor, D. and Wixon, D. *Brave NUI World | Designing Natural User Interfces for Touch and Gesture*. Morgan Kaufmann, 2010.
41. Wilson, A., Izadi, S., Hilliges, O., Garcia-Mendoza, A., and Kirk, D. Bringing physics to the surface. *UIST '08*, 67-76.
42. Wobbrock, J., Morris, M. R. and Wilson, A. User-defined gestures for surface computing. *CHI '09,* 1083-1092.

PyzoFlex: Printed Piezoelectric Pressure Sensing Foil

Christian Rendl, Patrick Greindl, Michael Haller
Media Interaction Lab,
University of Applied Sciences Upper Austria
Hagenberg, Austria
mi-lab@fh-hagenberg.at

Martin Zirkl, Barbara Stadlober, Paul Hartmann
Institute of Surface Technologies and Photonics,
Joanneum Research
Forschungsgesellschaft m.b.H, Weiz, Austria
materials@joanneum.at

ABSTRACT

Ferroelectric material supports both pyro- and piezoelectric effects that can be used for sensing pressures on large, bended surfaces. We present PyzoFlex, a pressure-sensing input device that is based on a ferroelectric material. It is constructed with a sandwich structure of four layers that can be printed easily on any material. We use this material in combination with a high-resolution Anoto-sensing foil to support both hand and pen input tracking. The foil is bendable, energy-efficient, and it can be produced in a printing process. Even a hovering mode is feasible due to its pyroelectric effect. In this paper, we introduce this novel input technology and discuss its benefits and limitations.

ACM Classification: H.5.2 [Information interfaces and presentation]: User Interfaces. - Graphical user interfaces.

Keywords: piezoelectric, pyroelectric, pressure sensing, input device, bendable

INTRODUCTION

Over the last decade, touch sensing devices have become more and more important. Most researchers tried to improve multi-touch by introducing capacitive [5, 17], resistive [18], or optical [4, 10] sensing devices. Although most of them provide already a multi-touch sensing, it is still often not possible to track input pressure efficiently. Tracking pen and touch separately in combination with pressure tracking provides new possibilities for user interfaces and interaction design [1]. Hinkley et al. [11] point out that entirely new tools or even new interaction modes are possible due to the simultaneous use of pen and touch (e.g. touch input could be used for manipulations or navigation, whereas pen input could be used for accurate annotations). In 2009, Rosenberg and Perlin presented UnMousePad [18], a promising pressure-sensing device that was based on a paper-thin, resistive surface. Their setup had two impressive features: the sensing material was mounted on a paper-thin bendable/flexible material and it was able to accurately sense pressure input.

UIST'12, October 7–10, 2012, Cambridge, Massachusetts, USA.

In this paper, we present *PyzoFlex*, a novel sensing device that is based on a pyro- and piezoelectric sensor matrix, screen-printed on a flexible film (cf. Figure 1). Moreover, the sensor area can detect changes in pressure and temperature respectively.

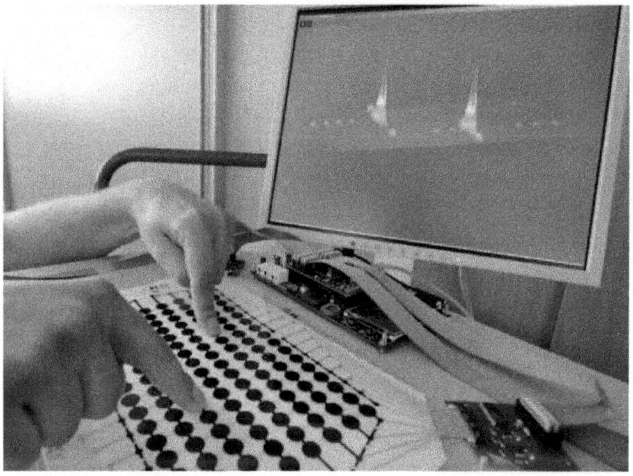

Figure 1: PyzoFlex in action. The current prototype is based on a DIN A4-sized foil that provides real-time pressure sensing feedback with a frame rate of 100 fps.

The piezoelectric effect can be found in any ferroelectric material. Any mechanic stress or force (e.g., touch) applied will result in a change of the electric field. This electric field variation is proportional to the mechanic deformation. Therefore, the piezoelectric effect can be used to measure pressure changes efficiently. All ferroelectric materials also have a pyroelectric effect: a variation in temperature influences the distribution of the electrical charge, which is again measureable. As a result, ferroelectric materials can also be used to measure temperature changes.

The main contributions of this paper are:

- the technical implementation of a pressure sensing device based on piezo- and pyroelectric sensors,
- the presentation of material and sensor electronics,
- the combination with a high accurate pen tracking based on the Anoto[1] technology, and
- the presentation of the key features of PyzoFlex to discuss the pros and cons of the foil.

[1] www.anoto.com

In this paper, we demonstrate the concepts and the development of a novel sensing device based on ferroelectric materials. We will start with a discussion of the related work, followed by our sensing approach and foil design based on ferroelectric materials. Then, we will propose our implementation, including sensing electronics and signal processing. Subsequently, we will discuss interesting material properties and current limitations. Finally, we will conclude our work and give a short preview of the future work.

RELATED WORK

Over the last two decades, researchers tried to develop multi-touch input devices [3]. So far, multi-touch sensing devices are mostly divided into three different categories: optical, resistive, and capacitive tracking devices. The not so common piezoelectric sensing appears to be the fourth.

Optical Sensing

There exists a plenty of different solutions for vision-based multi-touch surfaces developed by researchers [10, 13, 21]. Han proposed a low-cost multi-touch sensing technology based on Frustrated Total Internal Reflection (FTIR) [10]. His back-projected prototype is able to acquire touch information at high spatial and temporal resolutions and is scalable to large surfaces. Matsushita and Rekimoto [13] presented a computer augmented wall, based on Diffused Illumination. With the appearance of the Microsoft Kinect sensor, new multi-touch and interaction solutions based on depth cameras have been developed [21]. However, all optical touch solutions are highly dependent on ambient lighting and the material of the tracking object. In addition, the separation of touch and pen input is not possible.

Resistive Sensing

Resistive array-based sensors usually consist of two layers of conductive material, one with horizontal lanes and one with vertical lanes. Whenever a user touches the surface the horizontal and vertical lanes are alternately connected and enabling the flow of current. This technique is called Force Sensitive Resistance [6, 18]. These solutions are inherently inexpensive and energy efficient, but the tracking resolution is limited to the space between the sensing lanes.

Capacitive Sensing

Capacitive touch sensors [5, 12, 20] consist of a thin conductive layer placed on an insulator, such as glasses. This layer serves as electrode of a capacitor. A touch on the surface results in a distortion of the panel's electrostatic field and is measureable as changes in capacitance. There are several different technologies on to estimate the exact touch position. The DiamondTouch [5] is able to distinguish different users by incorporating them into a unique capacitive circuit. Capacitive sensing can only measure the contact area, so none of these solutions can be pressure sensitive. Another major disadvantage of this technique is that it relies on the dielectric properties of the human body; thus, styluses or objects cannot be tracked.

Piezoelectric Sensing

Existing input devices exploiting the piezoelectric effect are few and very expensive due to the dependence on non-printable piezoelectric materials. Usually they provide only limited user interaction. 3M introduced a system which utilizes the dispersion of touch-generated surface waves across a chemically treated glass plate using piezoelectric sensor elements placed in each corner for detection. Software algorithms then interpret this information and provide the actual location of the touch[2]. The technology claims to be unaffected by dust and scratches, and it works for both fingers and styluses. However, it cannot detect a motionless finger. A similar detection system for surface acoustic waves based on polymer piezoelectric sensors has been introduced by Reis et al. [16]. RIM's Blackberry Storm 2 has embedded a piezoelectric crystalline layer between two glass plates for triggering a haptic feedback. However, the detection of the touch location is not provided by the piezoelectric layer.

Fujita et al. patented a ferroelectric liquid crystal touch panel in 1992 [8]. The touch position gets detected by electrodes measuring the electromotive force which is generated by pushing the ferroelectric crystal layer. Compared to our work, their setup cannot detect different pressure levels. Instead they can only distinguish between touch and no touch.

The company Murata presented a twistable remote controller and a touch-pressure panel which are both based on a piezoelectric film[3]. In contrast to their remote controller, we do detect neither bending nor twisting (which however would be possible with our setup). For their touch panel, they use an additional capacitive approach for position detection and a piezoelectric film for pressure detection. This results in two different hardware components for touch sensing. We avoid this keeping both complexity and costs low. The barely information suggests that only their remote control is transparent, but not their "touch pressure pad".

Pen and Touch

Several research studies consider touch input or pen input in isolation. Only a few systems support both, the simultaneous interaction with pen and touch [1, 11, 22, 23]. Hinkley et al. [11] refined the use of pen and touch by contextual information. Pen input always draws and touch input always manipulates, but if they are used together in the context of an object a new implicit mode is triggered. Yee [23] used single-touch and stylus input on a tablet to support simultaneous drawing and panning within a canvas. Brandl et al. [1] explored the effects of bi-manual pen and touch input on a horizontal tabletop surface, while assigning the pen to the preferred hand and touch to the non-preferred hand. Pen and touch gestures were explored in [2, 7, 22].

[2] www.3Mtouch.com

[3] www.murata.com/new/news_release/2011/0921/

The benefits of combining pen and touch input for digital surfaces have been explored in several research projects [1, 22]. However, many of these systems limit users through their technical restrictions such as constrained scalability. For example, touchscreens overlaid on tablet computers that provide simultaneous pen and touch interaction have been proposed in [23]. Solutions such as the small-scale capacitive multi-touch screen from N-Trig have already been commercialized. They support user-input for both pen and capacitive touch in one single device. For the pen tracking, the developers of the N-Trig device use an electrostatic stylus and an active digitizer that is embedded in the screen.

UnMousePad [18] is a resistive, pressure-sensitive touch-based input device for tracking both touches as well as pens based on Interpolating Force Sensitive Resistance (IFSR), which is completely different to our approach from a technology point of view. The thin and transparent foil can acquire high-quality, anti-aliased pressure images and is able to distinguish touches, objects, or pens. In contrast to UnMousePad our setup is based on ferroelectric material that provides hover capability. Moreover, our transparent foil prototype is ITO-free.

PYZOFLEX APPROACH

Piezoelectric Effect

Piezoelectric materials are like wet sponges, once you squeeze them water/charge pours out. The amplitude and frequency of the signal is directly proportional to the mechanical deformation of the piezoelectric material [14]. The induced deformation of the piezo-element causes a change in the surface charge density of the material resulting in a voltage appearing between the electrodes (cf., Figure 2). The piezoelectric coefficient describes the amount of electrical charge generated per applied force unit.

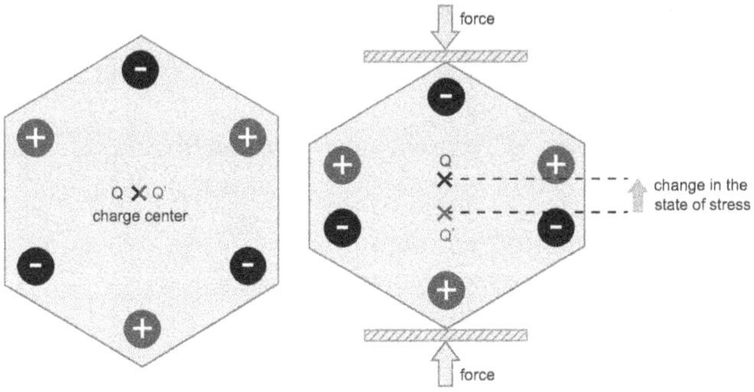

Figure 2: The Piezoelectric Pressure Sensing Effect. *(Left)* Distribution and centers of positive and negative charges. *(Right)* Shifting of the charge centers in the state of stress/force.

Piezoelectricity was discovered over 100 years ago by the Curie brothers studying the dimensional changes of quartz at different electric fields. In the 60's, piezoelectricity was detected in organic materials studying whale bones and tendon thus initiating intense search for piezoelectricity at organic materials. In 1969, Kwai discovered that a stretched and poled film of polyvinylidene fluoride (PVDF) shows large piezoelectric activity (5 pC/N) [9].

A PVDF film, like all piezoelectric materials, is a dynamic material developing an electrical charge proportional to a change in mechanical stress. As a consequence, piezoelectric materials itself are not suitable for static measurements due to their internal resistance. The electric charges generated in the polymer film decay with a time constant determined by the dielectric constant, the internal resistance of the film and the input impedance of the interface electronics to which the film is connected (cf. Figure 3) [14].

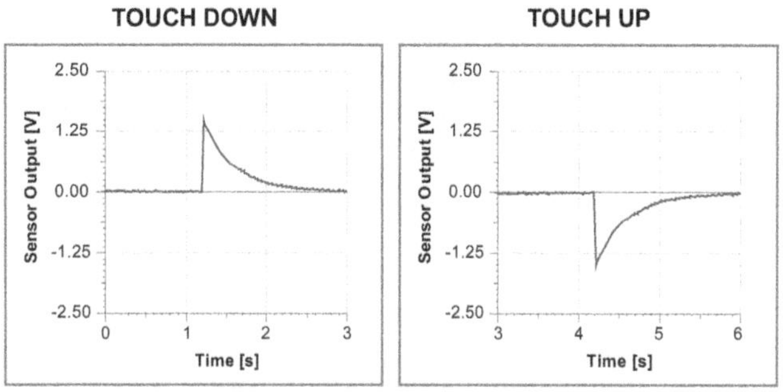

Figure 3: Piezoelectric output voltage once the user is touching the surface *(Left)* and lifting the finger *(Right)*.

Pyroelectric Effect

The pyroelectric effect in orientated and poled PVDF was found in 1971, where a pyroelectric coefficient of about $20\mu C/m^2K$ was identified, comparable to crystalline pyroelectrics [9]. Pyroelectric sensor materials are usually dielectric materials with a temperature-dependent molecular dipole moment. As these materials absorb thermal energy, they expand (or contract). Due to the expansion an indirect piezoelectric signal is caused [14]. A reduction of the average polarization of the film (sum of molecular dipole moments) is caused by random motion of the dipoles upon heating; this generates a charge built up on the film surface. Analog to piezoelectricity and stress, the pyroelectric output current is proportional to the rate of temperature change. The pyroelectric charge coefficient describes the amount of electrical charge generated per degree of temperature change.

Utilizing the afore-mentioned material properties, piezo- and pyroelectric polymer films can be used for sensing of pressure and temperature changes in a large area. By developing a printable formulation of a piezo- and pyroelectric polymer ink, as well as considering a sufficient layout of sensors, the fabrication of cost efficient, large-area sensors by screen printing processes is possible. These sensors are capable of pressure sensing and tracking (touch and/or pen input) as well as detecting the approaching of IR-emitters such as human hands (hovering interaction).

In Figure 4 the piezoelectric and pyroelectric effect are compared, showing a touch with a duration of about five seconds. As seen in the right side of Figure 4, it is highly complex to distinguish the warming and cooling effects from the touch signals. Moreover, in some situations, these effects can get even more blended. Usually, the piezoelectric foil is highly sensitive against any external light sources.

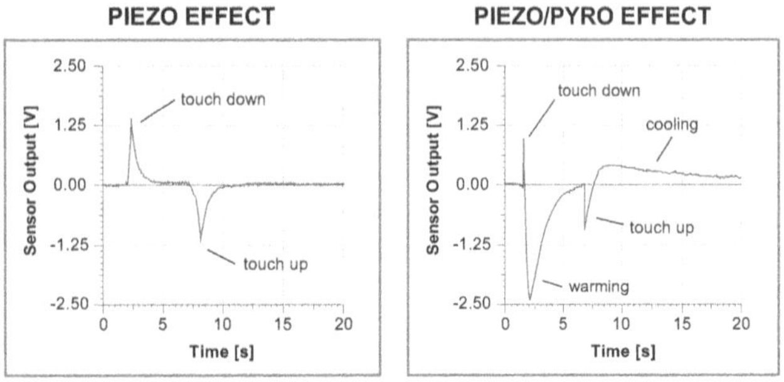

Figure 4: Output signals from the PyzoFlex sensor: Piezoelectric response without pyro effect *(Left)* and combined piezo- and pyroelectric response *(Right).*

These problems can be solved either by adding a temperature absorbing layer – losing the pyroelectric response - or by changing the general foil design. A foil design, which has both piezo- and pyroelectric effects, is discussed later.

Current Foil Design

The current sensing foil is based on a 16 × 8 array of screen printed, flexible, capacitive, circular sensor spots having a diameter of 10 mm (cf., Figure 5). The 128 sensor spots currently cover a 210×130 mm² area.

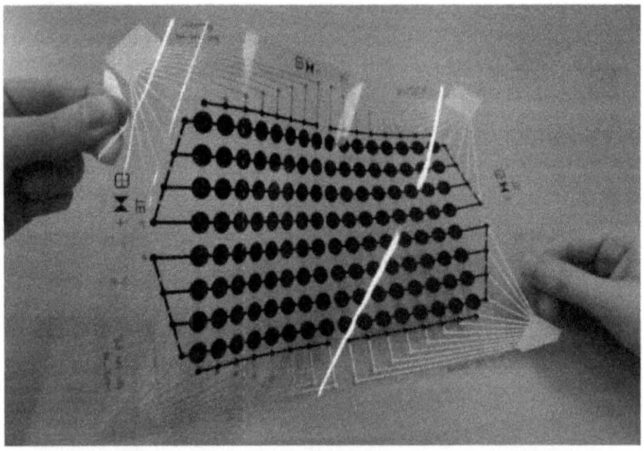

Figure 5: The current version is a 16 x 8 array of printed, piezoelectric sensor spots with a size of 10 mm.

The basis of our touch foil is the transparent plastic substrate, which serves as carrier for the printed materials. In the first step 128 circular spots (electrodes) are printed to the carrier material, which are connected horizontally. Subsequently, the whole plastic substrate gets continuously coated with the ferroelectric material. After that, the second layer with vertically connected electrodes is printed.

The two layers of electrodes are forming a capacitor. Charge changes in the ferroelectric sensor layer cause measureable voltages between the electrodes. Figure 6 shows the sandwich design of our foil prototype.

For our prototype, we used the following materials:

- the first layer is a transparent polyethylene terephthalate substrate (*PET*),
- the electrodes in the second layer consist of a semi-transparent *conductive polymer* material,
- the piezo- and pyroelectric sensor material forms a polyvinylidene fluoride (*PVDF*), which has a transparency of about 85 percent, and
- the top electrodes consist of either non-transparent *carbon* (cf., Figure 5) or again of *conductive polymer* (cf., Figure 16).

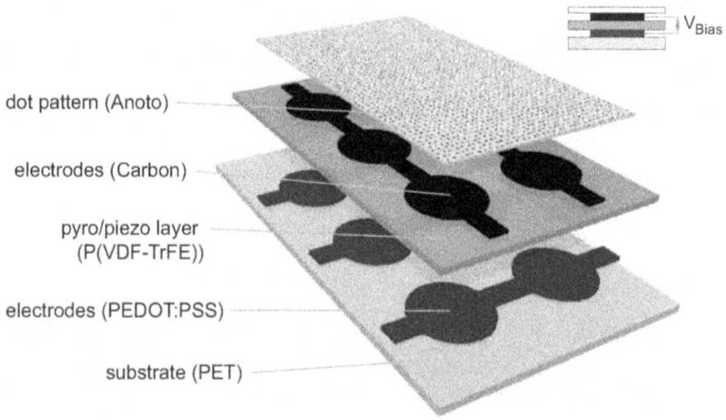

Figure 6: PyzoFlex sensor sandwich technology.

For applications with a strict pen and touch separation, a stable separation of both inputs is highly necessary. A separation based on the blob information of touches [18] is not highly robust, because slight pen and finger contacts result in similar blob sizes and pressure values. Moreover, an accurate pen tracking requires ultra-high input resolutions (e.g., 677 dpi with Anoto[4]), which are hard to achieve with multi-touch sensing technology. We decided to combine the PyzoFlex foil Anoto pen tracking to provide a stable pen and touch tracking. Furthermore, the additional Anoto foil acts as a temperature absorbing layer to reduce the pyroelectric response.

IMPLEMENTATION

PyzoFlex fabrication

The fabrication is done by low-cost printing of a smart active matrix sensor array with four functional inks [24]:

- the fluoropolymer sensor ink[5],
- the conductive polymer ink[6],
- the conductive carbon paste[7], and
- the conductive silver ink[8].

The substrate is formed by a transparent, flexible (175 µm thick) plastic foil[9], thus guaranteeing high flexibility and

[4] http://www.anoto.com/why-anoto.aspx

[5] P(VDF-TrFE) (poly(vinylidene fluoride trifluoroethylene)

[6] PEDOT:PSS(poly(3,4-ethylenedioxythiophene): poly(styrene sulfonic acid)) ink (HC Starck SV3)

[7] DuPont 7201

[8] DuPont 5000

[9] Melinex™ ST725

good adhesion of the functional materials applied during the screen printing process. The sensor ink is based on the pyro- and piezoelectric copolymer P(VDF-TrFE) which has a semicrystalline structure and - in a special formulation - can be printed on the foil thus forming a 5µm thick transparent layer. Silver conductive lines are printed for connecting the sensor electrodes to a Molex 1.00 mm Pitch FFC/FPC connector. After the printing step, each layer needs a short annealing treatment at 100 °C only. This calcination guarantees complete solvent evaporation thus increasing the functional properties (conductivity, piezo- and pyroelectric response) of each layer. Owing to the humble thermal requirements, the overall process can be considered being a low temperature fabrication.

For achieving piezo- and pyroelectric response, the randomly ordered and dipole containing nano-crystallites that are embedded in an amorphous constellation must be aligned vertically to the sensor electrodes. This can be achieved by hysteresis poling of the sensors using a Sawyer-Tower-Circuit [15]. For sufficient dipole alignment, an electric field in the range of 140 MV/m being twice as much as the coercive field strength is needed. This procedure leads to a very high remnant polarization of 70 mC/m^2 at a poling frequency of 10 Hz.

PyzoFlex provides printed, large-area, flexible and durable polymer sensors, showing a piezoelectric coefficient d_{33} of 20-30 pC/N, a pyroelectric coefficient p_{33} of 40 µC/m^{2}K at room temperature, and a Curie temperature of 125 °C.

PyzoFlex sensing electronics

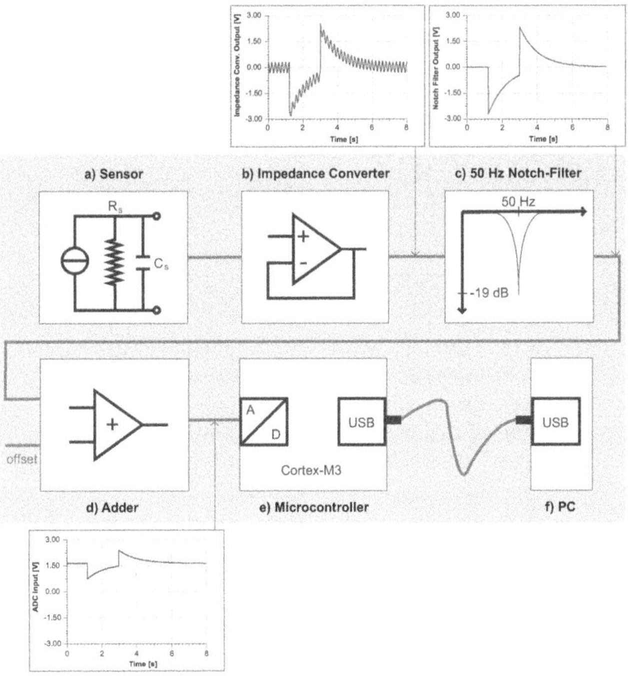

Figure 7: Sensing electronics of the current prototype as block diagram.

The equivalent circuit of a piezoelectric sensor is a current source with an internal resistance R_s (1 GΩ) and an internal capacitance C_s (1 nF), as depicted in Figure 7a. The internal resistance and the internal capacitance of the sensor are dependent on the physical dimensions, the electrical conductivity and the permittivity of the used material.

Touching the foil generates only a small amount of energy, which is difficult to measure. Therefore, an impedance converter is used to amplify the sensor signal (cf., Figure 7b). It forwards the input voltage to the output voltage but amplifies the signal power. In the ideal case the input current should be close to zero Ampere. Hence, an operational amplifier that supports an ultra-low input current (less than 10 fA) would be preferable. The disadvantage of this type of operational amplifiers is the temperature dependency. Therefore, we used a less temperature-dependent operational amplifier with 1 pA input current and added an additional 100 MΩ input resistance. Additionally, the known input resistance provides the back calculation from the signal to the touch force (Newton).

In the next step, the signal noise gets reduced. According to the surrounding mains voltage, the electrical noise is around 50 Hz in the signal spectrum. Therefore, a 50 Hz Notch filter is used to remove this noise (cf., Figure 7c).

In the final step, an offset and attenuation is applied to the signal to satisfy the measurement range (0 to 3.3 V) of the micro-controller's internal analog to digital converter (cf., Figure 7d).

For the current prototype, we chose a highly energy-efficient 32-bit Cortex-M3 microcontroller from ATMEL (cf., Figure 7e). In comparison with other common micro-controllers, the signal processing can be performed on the board more efficiently, because data types are up to 32-bit and high-performance multiplications are supported. Furthermore, it features a 12-bit analog to digital converter (one million samples per second) and an integrated USB core unit.

Scanning the sensor matrix

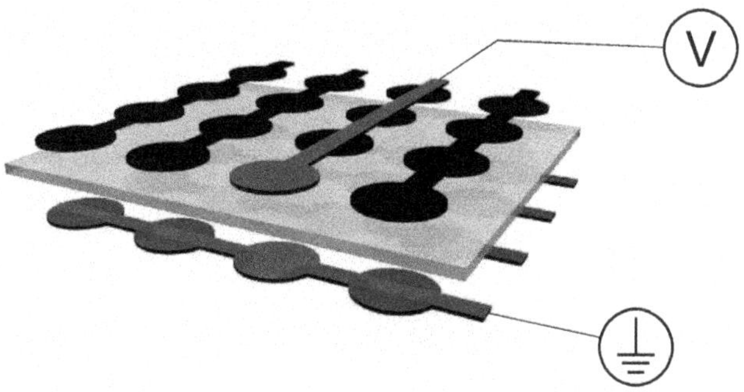

Figure 8: Scanning a single touch point.

The current prototype of PyzoFlex has 128 sensor spots covering a 210×130 mm² area. The electrodes on the bottom are connected horizontally and the electrodes on the top are connected vertically. An ultra-low leakage analog multiplexer is used to connect one horizontal row to ground. Meanwhile, all other rows are on high impedance (cf., Figure 8).

Every column is connected to an impedance converter circuit. Additional analog multiplexers are used to switch one of the impedance converter outputs to one of the analog digital converters' inputs of the micro-controller. Other components between the impedance converter and the A/D converter are described in the sensing electronics section.

All sensor spots are measured and their output voltage is sent to the PC every 10 ms. The scan for all 128 sensors takes 4.352 ms (128×34 μs). To sum up, it takes approximately 1μs for driving the analog multiplexer, 25 μs for waiting for the multiplexer and filtering circuits to settle to the new sensor output, and finally 8 μs for the A/D conversions. After scanning all sensors, it takes additional 2 μs to configure the DMA controller of the USB Core to send the results to the PC. Due to the short processing time enough capacity is left for larger foils or higher touch point density.

Touch Processing

Every pressure-change on a sensor spot generates a charge and eventuates in a measurable voltage. If no further pressure-change occurs, the voltage discharges through internal resistance of the piezoelectric film and the input resistance of the measurement circuit. This discharge follows an exponential function and is well predictable once the parameters of the exponential function are known. Every upcoming sensor value can be predicted with

$$U_{predicted} = U_{current} \cdot e^{\frac{-t}{\tau}}.$$

With a sampling rate of 100 Hz, t would be 10 ms. Every deviation of the predicted value must be caused by a new pressure change on the sensor. This helps us to process the pressure changes from the sensor signal. In an additional step, the pressure progress can be calculated by integrating all pressure changes.

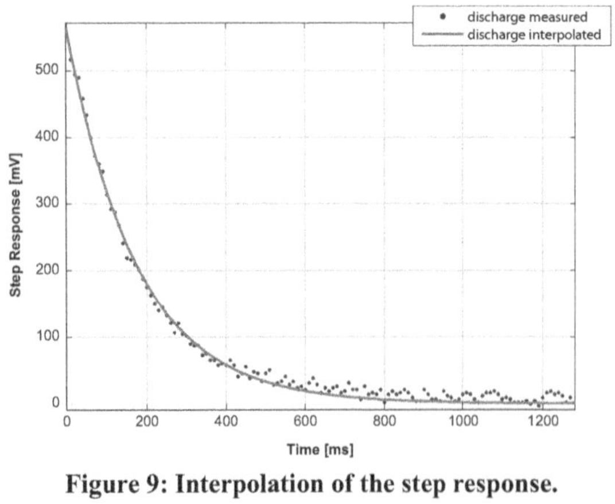

Figure 9: Interpolation of the step response.

The time constant τ of the exponential function depends on the internal resistance and capacitance of the sensor as well as the input impedance of the measurement circuit. We use a pneumatic measurement setup (cf., Figure 11) to apply repeatable forces to a sensor spot. This setup helps to measure the step response of one single sensor spot. We used a fitting tool to interpolate the step response with an exponential function (cf., Figure 9).

The interpolated exponential function has a τ of 177.2 ms. After that, all parameters, which are required to process the pressure progress from the sensor output, are known. Figure 10 shows the back-calculation from the sensor output to calculate the pressure. The applied pressure is illustrated in the first graph. The second graph shows the measured output voltage of the sensor. The deviations between the predicted and the actual values are shown in the third chart. Finally, an integration of the deviations is plotted in the last chart. Notice, that the voltage progress is proportional to the applied pressure.

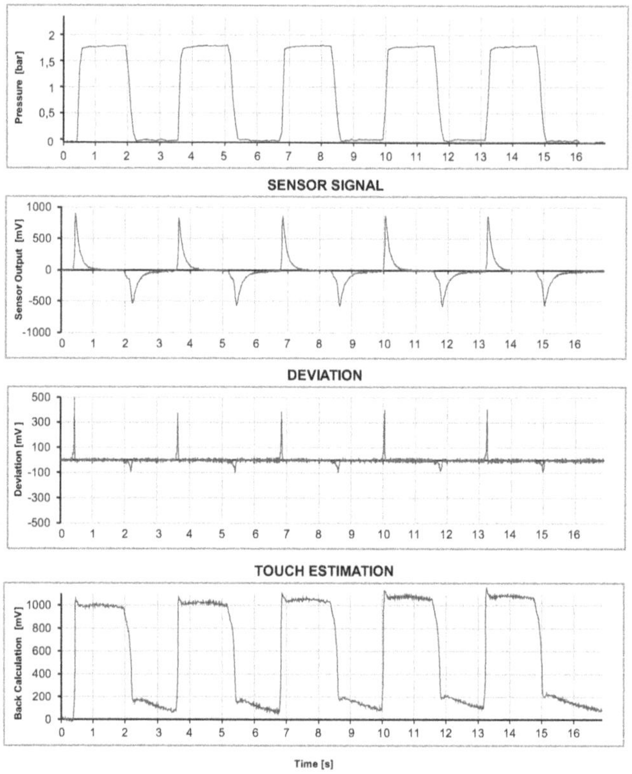

Figure 10: The touch processing. Applied pressure curve *(First)*; resulting in a piezoelectric sensor signal *(Second)*; the deviation between the next estimated and measured signal value *(Third)*; the estimated touch signal, which is achieved by integrating the deviation curve *(Fourth)*.

Pen & touch tracking

To provide a stable solution for a pen and touch tracking, we combine different technologies: the PyzoFlex foil with an additional Anoto dot pattern (cf., Figure 6). The pen and touch separation is realized through software-based solution in the second step. A combined input driver analyses both pen and touch input data synchronously. Whenever a new touch is performed, the input driver waits for about 50 ms for a pen input at the same spot (within a small threshold). This works properly, since each Anoto event has an initial lag of 50 ms as a result of the Bluetooth transmission. During this period, all touch data gets temporarily stored in the input driver. Whenever a pen input is noticed, the input driver forwards only the pen input and ignores the touch input. Otherwise, the temporarily stored touch data gets regularly forwarded to the applications. However, the problem of palm rejection [11] is not yet solved with the suggested separation procedure.

PERFORMANCE OF PYZOFLEX

The piezoelectric response was measured with a special developed air-pressure driven setup shown in Figure 11.

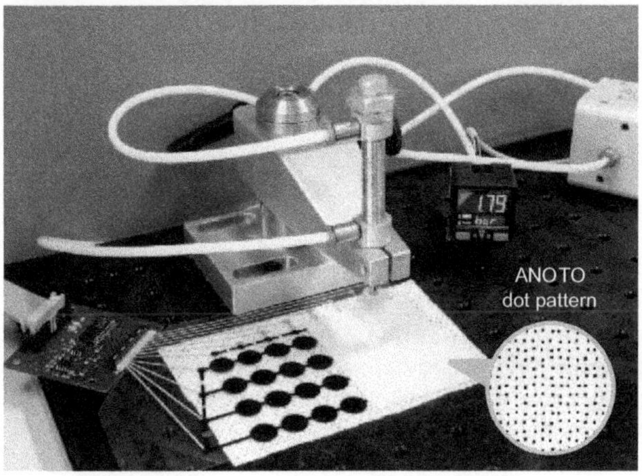

Figure 11: Setup for the piezoelectric measurements. Currently an Anoto covered sensor-spot is excited at 1.8 bar. As a compressable substrate, a thin fabric is used.

A pressurized bar was loaded on the polymer film while the piezoelectrically generated charges were measured with the afore described PyzoFlex sensing electronics. The proportional pressure valve (Festo MS6-LRE-1) regulating the waveform and pressure load applied on the sample is controlled by a function generator (Keithley 6221). The pressure in the air-pipe is monitored with a Festo SPAB-P10R-R18 pressure sensor. The stamp itself consists of a Teflon cylinder with a diameter of 4.5 mm.

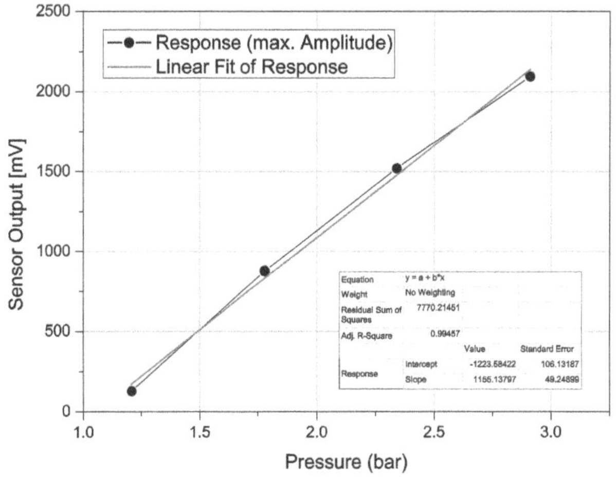

Figure 12: Linearity of the pressure dependent response of the PyzoFlex foil.

Linearity

The generated voltage output from the PyzoFlex foil is perfectly linear (cf., Figure 12). This is important for two reasons: On the one hand it facilitates the tracking of the touch location and on the other hand it enables to utilize the absolute magnitude of the touch force for a selection of different user modi. The exerted pressure is an additional and independent interaction parameter that helps to distinguish intuitively and efficiently between the selection and the movement of an object.

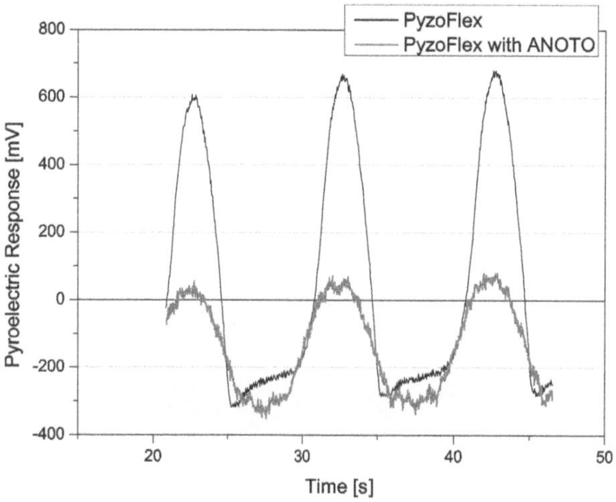

Figure 13: Pyroelectric response to a 70 mW laser diode with a wavelength of 890 nm. The combination with the Anoto pattern significantly reduces the generated (positive) response influencing the touch-signals.

Noise due to external light sources

As shown in Figure 13 the PyzoFlex sensor foil is sensitive to IR-radiation introduced by ambient light.

Thus inducing temperature variations in the pyroelectric layer and therefore generating charges and a detectable voltage signal response.

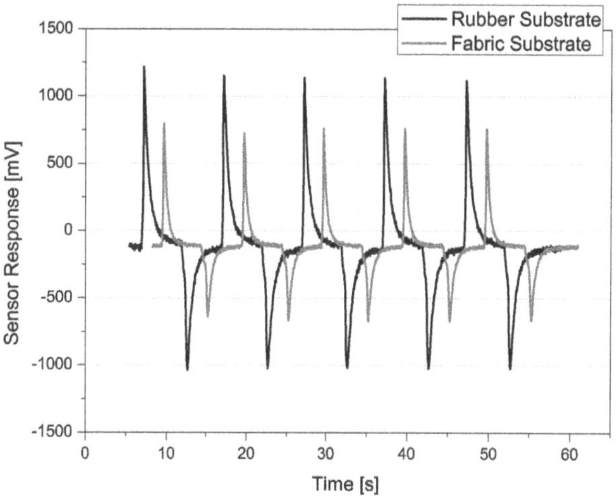

Figure 14: Influence of different substrates to the piezoelectric response. The less elastic fabric-substrate shows only 65 % of the signal generated using the more compressible rubber substrate.

This is an effect that might cause troubles for a multi-touch environment. A combination of the PyzoFlex with the Anoto foil decreases the parasitic pyroelectric effect by several orders of magnitude thus enabling pure touch-based control of the surface (cf., Figure 13). The Anoto foil screens both the IR-radiation from light sources as well as the heat induced by a human body (finger).

Different substrate materials

The type of substrate material is crucial for the magnitude of the harvested piezoelectric signal height. A slightly compressible and/or perforated substrate provides a larger degree of freedom (= stronger bending) in applying a vertical mechanical stress due to the lack of surface confinement (cf., Figure 14).

Geometry

PyzoFlex is a bendable sensor technology, meaning that the sensor can be mounted on different curved surfaces (cf., Figure 15).

Figure 15: The PyzoFlex foil can be also attached to curved surfaces. The metal cylinder has a diameter of 16 cm.

The bending radius depends on the size and the distance of the printed piezoelectric spots. We currently implemented a matrix of circular spots with 10 mm diameter and about 15 mm distance. The spot size is related to the maximum diameter of a human finger-touch. The highest response signal is expected for a fully activated spot surface area (least parasitics). However, too large spot sizes would be detrimental with respect to resolution and higher noise signals trapped from ambient heat sources. Optimization on testing different spot sizes and spot shapes is ongoing.

Transparency

An important topic of touch sensing is transparency, which of course is an important feature for touchscreen applications in mobile devices (e.g. smartphones or tablets). Since the P(VDF-TrFE) sensing layer itself has a transparency over 85 percent, the main limitations come from the black carbon electrodes (cf., Figure 6). One possibility is to replace them by nearly transparent PEDOT:PSS electrodes with the advantage that these are also printable (cf., Figure 16). A further possibility is a high-transparent but less mature metal nanoparticle ink.

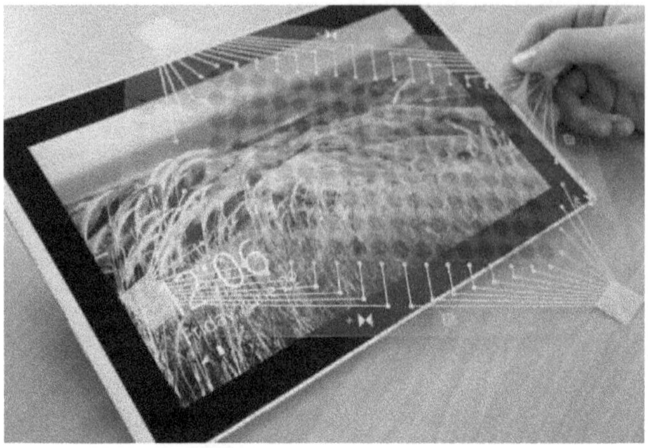

Figure 16: Replacing the black carbon electrodes with PEDOT:PSS electrodes results in a quasi-transparent foil.

Economical tracking & ITO-free

Our approach provides an energy-efficient implementation, since every touch generates a small amount of voltage. Under certain conditions the multi-touch sensing setup could even serve as energy harvesting resource [19]. Another major economic advantage is the ITO-free (*indium tin oxide*) implementation, because common used indium is a very limited resource in our world.

DISCUSSION

We have showed how printed pyro- and piezoelectric materials can be used to produce a pressure and temperature sensitive touch foil. Nevertheless, the following problems have to be solved.

Multi-Touch & Crosstalk problems

Figure 17: Crosstalk problems caused through the matrix-based wiring of the sensor foil.

For a single touch point the back-propagation of the pressure progress works without any problems. Although we are able to capture each sensor point simultaneously with 100 Hz, the recognition of multiple adjacent touches is currently problematic due to *crosstalk problems* between the sensor spots (cf., Figure 17).

The crosstalk is caused by the matrix-based wiring and the used materials. Several solutions are possible. In the next step, we plan to improve our signal-processing algorithm to mathematically remove the crosstalk. We will analyze the crosstalk for characteristic patterns, which can then be subtracted from the original signal. Furthermore, a new sensor design could effectively eliminate crosstalk since a matrix configuration is avoided and each sensor element is separately connected; thus, causing a higher number of connection lines to the electronics. Additional to the previous two solutions, the conductivity of the electrodes (highly conductive printing pastes) could be increased or insensitive discharging elements could be introduced (by applying inactive sensor spots as discharging elements in between the active sensor spots). We are currently working on reducing the crosstalk to mitigate this issue.

Higher Resolution

In the current prototype, 128 circular sensor points with a diameter of 10 mm are arranged in a distance of about 15 mm. The main focus of the current foil design was to prove the concept of using a printed ferroelectric sensor array for pressure sensing. In order to achieve a high-resolution touch foil, we plan to decrease the diameter and distance of the sensor points, since there is enough capacity on the microcontroller left. The current microcontroller can handle easily up to 1024 sensor spots. Furthermore, the use of additional A/D converters will allow us to parallelize the sampling of sensor values, resulting in an even higher resolution.

The current foil uses a different spacing for the horizontal lines (16 mm) of the matrix than the vertical (13 mm). An informal experiment showed that a distance of 13 mm provides accurate linear interpolation, whereas a distance of 16 mm is too large. Thus, by increasing the pixel density of the foil design, we can use a linear interpolation routine to increase the resolution to modern standards. Of course a linear interpolation requires a crosstalk free sensor signal.

Cross-Sensitivity of Piezo- and Pyro-Response

With the current foil design, there is a trade-off between hovering mode and pen input. Currently the additional Anoto pattern (cf., Figure 6) serves as a light reflecting and temperature diffusion layer. By printing the pattern directly on the touch foil, this issue can be solved. To handle piezo- and pyroelectric responses (pressure and hovering) simultaneously, a complete new foil design is required. In the new design, each touch point consists of two side-by-side layers (as half circle electrodes), which are wired separately to the sensing electronics. Whereas one is tuned on piezoelectricity, the other one is tuned on pyroelectricity. This can be accomplished by adding inorganic piezoelectric nanoparticles to the sensing material. Through a smart poling procedure, either pyro- or piezoelectricity can be suppressed, owing to the opposite sign of the piezoelectric coefficient for sensing material and the nanoparticles. This would lead to two separate signals for each touch point and simplifies the signal processing. Currently, we are working on a corresponding foil design.

CONCLUSION & FUTURE WORK

In this paper, we have demonstrated that piezo- and pyroelectric materials are a promising alternative to the existing optical, resistive, and capacitive sensing materials. In comparison to common touch solutions, the proposed approach can sense pressure accurately using piezoelectric materials. Even a hovering mode is feasible due to its pyroelectric effect. Furthermore, the foil is produced by simple low-cost printing. No cleanroom, vacuum or evaporation is required in the manufacturing process. The sensing electronics is able to sample each of the 128 sensor spots with 100 Hz. A software-based input driver calculates the applied pressure from the sensor output. By combining the pressure sensitive touch foil with a high-resolution pen technology (Anoto), a powerful pen and touch solution is achieved. This provides new possibilities for user interfaces and interaction design [1, 11]. We foresee our technology beneficial to the development and use of large surfaces, where pen and touch are used simultaneously (e.g., whiteboards or tabletops). There is also high potential for mobile touch devices due to the quasi-transparency (85%) of the foil.

For future work, we plan to eliminate the discussed problems, including the crosstalk and the cross-sensitivity of the piezo- and pyroelectric response. Furthermore, we want to increase the resolution by changing the sensor arrangement and interpolating between the sensor points. Another goal will be to improve the scalability of the sensor foil – since it can be printed on really large surfaces. In our final version, we would like to fabricate the sensor foil over several square meters in an in-line roll-to-roll process at low cost. Finally, we plan to develop a more transparent sensor foil by experimenting with new materials (e.g., for the use in mobile devices).

ACKNOWLEDGEMENTS

The authors would like to thank our anonymous reviewers for their very useful comments. This work was funded by the Austrian Research Promotion Agency FFG under contract NEUE ENERGIEN 2020, #2690891.

REFERENCES

1. Brandl, P., Forlines, C., Wigdor, D., Haller, M. and Shen, C. 2008. Combining and measuring the benefits of bimanual pen and direct-touch interaction on horizontal interfaces. In *Proc. AVI 2008*, 154-161.
2. Brandl, P., Haller, M., Hurnaus, M., Lugmayr, V., Oberngruber, J., Oster, C., Schafleitner, C. and Billinghurst, M. 2007. An Adaptable Rear-Projection Screen Using Digital Pens And Hand Gestures. In *Proc. ICAT 2007*, 49-54.
3. Buxton, W., Hill, R. and Rowley, P. 1985. Issues and techniques in touch-sensitive tablet input. In *Proc. SIGGRAPH 1985*, 215-224.

4. De los Reyes, I., Roberton, N., Calvery, B., Turner, T. J. E., Chandley, A., Makosi, D., Henderson, P., Nikitin, E., Elabbady, T. and Joe, P. 2007. Function oriented user interface. *U.S. Patent No. 7730426B2.*

5. Dietz, P. and Darren, L. 2001. DiamondTouch: a multi-user touch technology. In *Proc. UIST 2001*, 219-226.

6. Eventoff, F. N. 1979. Electronic pressure sensitive transducer apparatus. *U.S. Patent No. 4313227.*

7. Frisch, M., Heydekorn J. and Dachselt, R., 2009. Investigating multi-touch and pen gestures for diagram editing on interactive surfaces. In *ITS 2009,* 149-156.

8. Fujita, M., et al. 1992. Ferroelectric liquid crystal touch panel. *U.S. Patent No. 5122787.*

9. Fukada, E. 1989. Introduction: Early Studies in Piezoelectricity, Pyroelectricity, and Ferroelectricity in Polymers. *Phase Transitions: A Multinational Journal*, Volume 18, Issue 3-4, 135–141.

10. Han, J. 2005. Low-cost multi-touch sensing through frustrated total internal reflection. In *Proc. UIST 2005*, 115-118.

11. Hinckley, K., Yatani, K., Pahud, M., Coddington, N., Rodenhouse, J., Wilson, A., Benko, H. and Buxton, B. 2010. Pen + touch = new tools. In *Proc. UIST 2010*, 27-36.

12. Jobs, S. P., et al. 2008. Touch screen device, method, and graphical user interface for determining commands by applying heuristics. *U.S. Patent No. 7479949B2.*

13. Matsushita, N. and Rekimoto, J. 1997. HoloWall: designing a finger, hand, body, and object sensitive wall. In *Proc. UIST 1997*, 209-210.

14. Measurement Specialities, Inc. 1999. Piezo Film Sensors. *Tech Report*, Sensor Products Division, Norristown.

15. Naber, R. C. G., Asadi, K., Blom, P. W. M., de Leeuw, D. M. and de Boer, B. 2010. Organic nonvolatile memory devices based on ferroelectricity. *Advanced materials*, Volume 22, Issue 9, 933–945.

16. Reis, S., Correira, M., Martins, M., Barbosa, G., Sousa, M., Minas, G., Lanceros-Mendez, S. and Rocha, J. G. 2010. Touchscreen based on acoustic pulse recognition with piezoelectric polymer sensors. In *ISIE 2010*, 516-520.

17. Rekimoto, J. 2002. SmartSkin: an infrastructure for freehand manipulation on interactive surfaces. In *Proc. CHI 2002*, 113-120.

18. Rosenberg, I. and Perlin, K. 2009. The UnMousePad: an interpolating multi-touch force-sensing input pad. In *Proc. SIGGRAPH 2009*, 65:1-65:9.

19. Sodano, H. A., Inman, D. J. and Park, G. 2005. Comparison of Piezoelectric Energy Harvesting Devices for Recharging Batteries. *Intelligent Material Systems and Structures*, Volume 16, Number 10, 799-807.

20. Westerman, W. 1999. Hand Tracking, Finger Identification and Chordic Manipulation on a Multi-Touch Surface. *PhD thesis*, University of Delaware.

21. Wilson, A. 2010. Using a depth camera as a touch sensor. In *Proc. ITS 2010*, 69-72.

22. Wu, M., Shen, C., Ryall, K., Forlines, C. and Balakrishnan, R. 2006. Gesture registration, relaxation, and reuse for multi-point direct-touch surfaces. In *Proc. TABLETOP 2006.*

23. Yee, K. 2004. Two-handed interaction on a tablet display. In *Proc. CHI EA 2005*, 1493-1496.

24. Zirkl, M., Sawatdee, A., Helbig, U., Krause, M., Scheipl, G., Kraker, E., Ersman, P. A., Nilsson, D., Platt, D., Bodö, P., Domann, G. and Stadlober, B. 2011. An All-Printed Ferroelectric Active Matrix Sensor Network Based on Only Five Functional Materials Forming a Touchless Control Interface. *Advanced Materials*, Volume 23, Issue 18, 2069–2074.

Jamming User Interfaces: Programmable Particle Stiffness and Sensing for Malleable and Shape-Changing Devices

Sean Follmer[1], Daniel Leithinger[1], Alex Olwal[1], Nadia Cheng[2], and Hiroshi Ishii[1]

[1] MIT Media Lab
Cambridge, MA 02139 USA
{sean, daniell, olwal, ishii}@media.mit.edu

[2] MIT Mechanical Engineering
Cambridge, MA 02139 USA
ncheng@mit.edu

ABSTRACT

Malleable and organic user interfaces have the potential to enable radically new forms of interactions and expressiveness through flexible, free-form and computationally controlled shapes and displays. This work, specifically focuses on particle jamming as a simple, effective method for flexible, shape-changing user interfaces where programmatic control of material stiffness enables haptic feedback, deformation, tunable affordances and control gain. We introduce a compact, low-power pneumatic jamming system suitable for mobile devices, and a new hydraulic-based technique with fast, silent actuation and optical shape sensing. We enable jamming structures to sense input and function as interaction devices through two contributed methods for high-resolution shape sensing using: 1) index-matched particles and fluids, and 2) capacitive and electric field sensing. We explore the design space of malleable and organic user interfaces enabled by jamming through four motivational prototypes that highlight jamming's potential in HCI, including applications for tabletops, tablets and for portable shape-changing mobile devices.

ACM Classification: H.5.2 Information Interfaces and Presentation: User interfaces and Evaluation; User Interfaces; Haptic I/O.

General terms: Design; Human Factors

Keywords: Jamming, Variable Stiffness, Organic User Interfaces, Malleable Input, Haptic Feedback.

INTRODUCTION

The form, function and dynamics of user interface devices have traditionally been limited by the rigidity of materials used for sensing and display. Organic User Interfaces (OUIs) [39] embrace the advances of new technology and materials to enable deformable and actuated interfaces of arbitrary shapes. Major enabling technologies for such interfaces have included advances in sensing [31], display technology and mechanical actuation [18, 30], but few projects investigate computationally controlled material properties, such as stiffness. In this paper, we adapt particle jamming [3, 22] as a simple, effective method of stiffness control in human—computer interaction (HCI). The ability to switch between soft and rigid material states enables novel interactions for malleable, clay-like interfaces, haptic feedback and deformable devices.

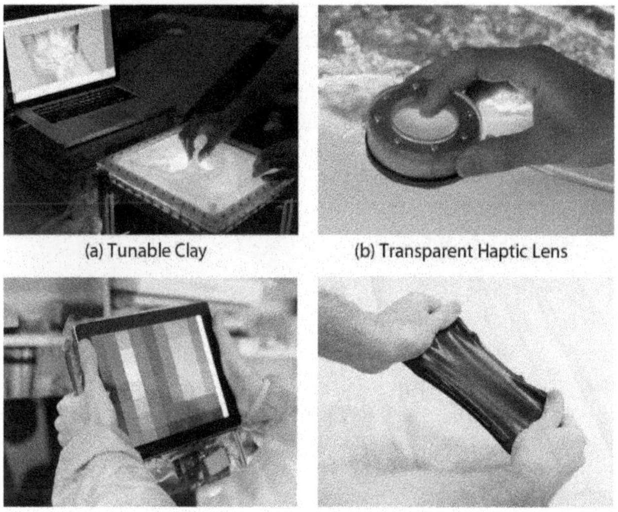

(a) Tunable Clay (b) Transparent Haptic Lens (c) Behind-the-Tablet Jamming (d) ShapePhone

Figure 1: Jamming is a scalable technique for programmatic stiffness control, which can be applied to a variety of malleable and organic user interfaces. Examples include: Tunable stiffness for malleable interfaces on tabletops (a, c), for haptic feedback (b, c), and for mobile shape-changing interfaces (d).

Granular media can exhibit both fluid-like and solid-like states. Liquids typically flow freely due to external forces, while solids require certain applied stresses to deform plastically. Jamming describes a situation when granular media exhibits a yield stress, such that forces can be distributed through chains of grains as if each chain was a rigid object [5]. Thus, groups of particles as a whole can function as a compliant or stiff material, under computational control of this compliance level.

Engineers, architects, and designers have been utilizing these effective phase-change characteristics of granular media to develop devices, tools and systems that can transition between flexible and rigid states. Most applications induce jamming by enclosing grains in a non-porous, flexible membrane inside which a vacuum can be applied. The grains flow when excess interstitial fluid (typically air) is enclosed with the grains, but compact to form an effective solid when vacuum is applied inside the membrane to remove fluid. This enables drastic and reversible shape deformations using a single embedded actuator. Extremely flexible materials such as silicone can be utilized in jamming devices, allowing the system to be stretched, twisted, or bent with the jamming material flowing easily into these new shapes. However, when pressure is decreased these interfaces can become static. This makes jamming an ideal candidate for enabling malleable and shape changing user interfaces.

Jamming has become a popular research topic in the robotics community [3, 35, 36, 6], but its application to user interfaces has received less attention. A successful application of jamming to HCI requires advances in sensing to detect shape deformations and user input, as well as actuation for providing feedback to the user.

Contributions

We introduce techniques that exploit computer-controlled jamming of granular particles as a scalable method to programmatically control the stiffness of malleable devices. This, in combination with our embedded shape sensing, demonstrate the potential for novel interactions and increased expressiveness. Examples of how jamming can be utilized in HCI applications are illustrated in Figure 1 and 2. Our contributions include:

- A review of the state of the art in jamming for use as a variable stiffness material from an HCI perspective.
- A novel hydraulic-based jamming technology, for rapid activation, silent actuation, and embedded optical sensing.
- Two techniques for high-resolution, integrated and embedded sensing for jamming interfaces: optical sensing, using index-matched fluids and particles; and electrical sensing, using capacitive and electric field sensing.
- A small, low-power jamming system for mobile and embedded organic user interfaces.
- Motivating prototypes to highlight how jamming can be applied to HCI

RELATED WORK

Jamming in Mechanical Engineering

Recently, the potential of jamming to control material stiffness has been explored in various engineering fields. A universal gripper, composed of a balloon-like membrane filled with dry grains, will, for example, conform to an external object when the grains are in a loosely packed state. When air is removed to jam the grains into a rigid state, the object is perfectly grasped, as if the gripper was designed to take the form of the target object [3, 1]. The jammable gripper is actuated by a single vacuum pump, while most traditional grippers require one actuator (such as a motor) per joint, or degree of freedom. Jamming has also been explored in soft robotics, where robots transition between compliant and rigid, load-bearing states [35, 36, 6]; for medical devices that need to gently navigate in the body [23]; and for makeshift architectural structures constructed with jammable walls [16].

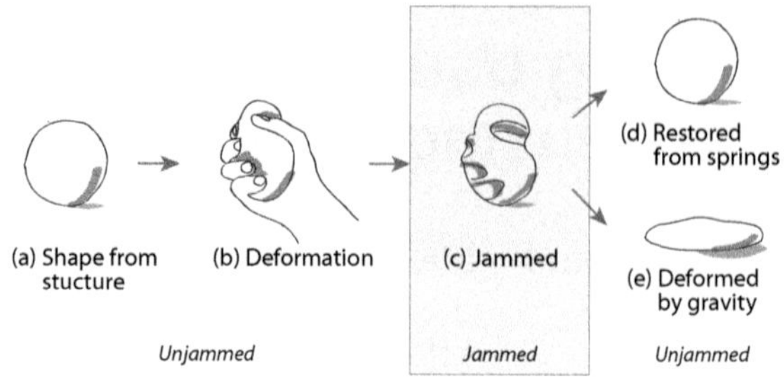

Figure 2: Jamming techniques enables new possibilities for shape state transitions. In this example, an object's shape is informed from structure (a), deformed by a user (b), and jammed to maintain the deformation (c). When unjammed, the object could return to its original shape if there are internal spring forces (d) or deform due to gravity (e).

Malleable and Organic UIs

We position jamming interfaces in the space of malleable and organic UIs. In their unjammed states, jamming user interfaces with flexible skins allow deformation and manipulation, which makes them appropriate as malleable input devices. Particle-based materials, such as beads or sand (e.g., Sandscape [17]), as well as fluids (e.g., [13, 14]), have been previously explored for malleable interfaces. Passive springs can be used to provide haptic feedback for malleable input through the use of mechanical springs [28], gels [40, 8] or foam [34]. All of these interfaces have a static modulus of elasticity, which provides passive feedback to the user. In contrast, jamming interfaces can easily change their material stiffness to emulate interaction with different materials, or to increase the degree of control over the material. Coupled with the sensing techniques described in this paper, jamming enables a wide range of malleable interactions.

Organic UIs have explored bending and stretching as a means for input with flexible devices [32, 21, 12] and jamming can be used to control the degree to which these interfaces can be interacted with and the feeling of interacting with them.

Shape-changing UI

Shape-changing user interfaces can provide users with more affordances for different tasks, allow for greater tactile manipulability, or provide haptic feedback by changing their physical form [7]. Inflatable interfaces have been introduced that allow displays or objects to quickly change shape [20, 10], or to inform the user of program state [11]. Jamming can enable this type of interaction, by increasing the rigidity of a certain shape, while remaining easily actuated in another. In addition, unlike many shape-changing interfaces, jamming interfaces may be user defined and provide a wide design space of possible shapes.

Variable Stiffness for Haptic Feedback

Harnessing jamming for haptic feedback relies on its ability to control stiffness. Previous HCI research has explored variable stiffness materials, such as mechanical actuation for handheld squeezing [9], mouse-like interfaces [24], and rapid localized feedback using Magnetorheological (MR) fluid for touch interfaces [41, 19].

While these techniques can be advantageous for rapid localized haptic feedback, the ability of jamming to vary the stiffness over much larger areas enables a wide variety of other applications and device scales. Jamming can also withstand a much higher loading stress than MR fluid.

Previous uses of jamming techniques in HCI

A wearable force display by Mitsuda et al., is a haptic feedback device for virtual reality applications [27]. It consists of flexible tubes, worn on the body, filled with Styrofoam particles, which can be jammed to constrain user motion. Position sensing is implemented with an embedded magnetic tracker at the end of the jamming tube; it does not measure the exact deformation of the device.

HoverMesh by Mazzone et al. applies a jamming technology with polystyrene beads to a tangible user interface [26]. It consists of a soft mesh that can morph into different shapes through computer controlled pneumatic cells. Jammable chambers in the skin of the interface solidify the shape when its deformation goal is reached. HoverMesh focuses on actuated shape output and does not implement user input through deformation sensing, although the authors discuss the possibility of employing computer vision methods or embedded bend sensors as a future work.

ClaytricSurface by Matoba et al. combines a malleable tabletop jamming surface with a ceiling-mounted depth-sensing camera and projector as a sculpting interface [25]. The malleable surface contains a pneumatic jamming apparatus, which allows for variable stiffness control.

We build upon previous jamming approaches with a systematic analysis of jamming's potential for HCI, with a focus on deformable, organic and mobile user interfaces, and novel complementary sensing techniques.

BACKGROUND: PNEUMATIC JAMMING FUNDAMENTALS

This section provides an overview of how jamming activation techniques enable the control of shape and material stiffness, and thus the degree to which a volume can be physically modified or actuated. This section includes a review and introductory discussion of jamming control to provide readers with the background for implementing their own systems; further details can be found in [35]. We also describe a platform for prototyping jamming user interfaces.

Pneumatic Jamming

Four main elements are required to control a jamming system: the jammable material and housing assembly (usually a non-porous, flexible membrane), a vacuum source or pump, a pressure-controlling valve, and a pressure sensor. We have implemented a closed-loop control system to achieve desired vacuum pressures as a test platform. While pressure relates to the magnitude of jamming, there is not necessarily a linear relationship between pressure and system stiffness [36].

Our system consists of an Atmel AVR microcontroller that interfaces with a 12V DC vacuum pump with a 20 cm^3/s maximum flow rate and a maximum vacuum pressure of 65 kPa, a 12V DC solenoid valve and an analog pressure sensor (see Figure 3). The vacuum pump, solenoid pressure-release valve and pressure sensor are connected in-line to the jammable module with 0.635-cm-diameter tubing. Coffee filters prevent particles from entering the air lines.

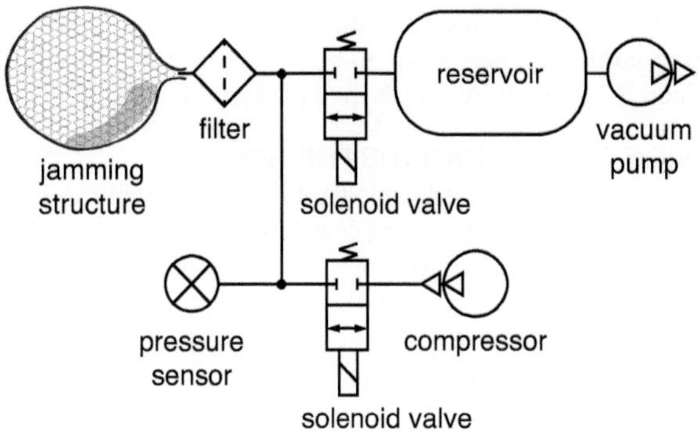

Figure 3: Pneumatic Jamming System. The system measures and controls the difference between atmospheric and internal volume pressure, such that particle jamming in the structure provides varying stiffness.

Differential jamming pressure and activation time

The differential jamming pressure is defined as the difference between atmospheric and internal volume pressure for the jammable module. For example, a balloon that is filled with jamming media and is open to atmospheric pressure, is near the jamming transition, since little fluid volume needs to be removed to induce jamming. The differential jamming pressure can, however, be raised to increase the mechanical stiffness of the system.

We can estimate the time it takes to cause a system to jam based on a pump's rated flow rate. Uniform spheres that are of random, close packing (as opposed to, for example, ordered in a lattice pattern) have a solid volume fraction of approximately 0.64 [38]. Therefore, in a simple system in which a vacuum pump is directly connected to the jammable module, the amount of fluid volume, V_r, which needs to be removed to induce jamming can be approximated as:

$$V_r \approx V_b - V_g(1 + \frac{0.36}{0.64}) = V_b - \frac{m_g}{rho_g}(1.5625)$$

where V_b is current internal volume of the jammable segment (including excess fluid), and V_g, m_g, and rho_g are the solid volume, the mass, and material density of the particles, respectively. Therefore, the time to remove the excess volume, t_r, is:

$$t_r = \frac{V_r}{Q_p}$$

where Q_p is the pump's volumetric flow rate. Any additional vacuum that is applied to the system increases differential jamming pressure and system stiffness.

Accelerated Activation

While jamming speed is typically limited by the vacuum pump's and pressure-control valve's flow rates, it can be increased through the use of in-line reservoirs. For example, a

PVC pipe can be added to build up vacuum pressure to increase jamming speeds. In addition, unjamming speeds can be increased by adding a positive pressure source [1].

DESIGN CONSIDERATIONS FOR HCI

While actuated devices and displays have received extensive attention over the years, less emphasis has been placed on techniques for the control and modification of intrinsic material properties. The application of jamming has great potential to complement shortcomings of traditional shape-changing devices. In addition, due to its unique abilities to affect shape dynamics and kinetics, jamming is valuable as a standalone modality.

Facilitating shape deformation

Malleable interfaces typically need to both enable effortless deformation, while also providing mechanisms to stabilize resulting freeform shapes. Variable stiffness enables continuous transitions between compliant and solid objects. In addition to deformation in the unjammed state, and solidification of the resulting shape in the maximally jammed state, there are interesting nuances related to expression and fidelity in the range of stiffness levels in-between. The type of deformation that is possible, and its effect on the overall shape, depends on material stiffness. It is thus possible to tune the control gain to tweak the precision and scale of user manipulations of the material shape.

Augmenting shape actuation

Most actuation techniques for shape displays employ active elements to displace different types of media. While jamming does not provide actuation per se, it enables straightforward "locking" and "unlocking" of continuous freeform shapes with varying stiffness using a single actuator. The ability to maintain these states without the need to continuously power the jamming actuator is important for mobile, embedded and low-power devices. To change a jamming structure's shape dramatically, another source of actuation is necessary: either a passive source, such as the user's force or gravity, or an active source, such as a pneumatic air muscle. In addition to augmenting existing actuation techniques, novel actuators based on jamming structures could enable completely different shape-changing interfaces [35]. Granular particles can be combined with discrete element matrices as a hybrid approach to achieve smoother, higher-dimensional surfaces with variable stiffness. Passive, deformable shapes, with elastic or spring-loaded properties can also be added to the volume to provide restoring forces, so that when unjammed, the device returns to a certain shape.

The single actuator used to jam the particles may not only be used to accelerate the unjamming in reverse-operation, but could also be employed for inflation the jamming shape (similar to the technique described by Amend et al. [1]). By drastically changing the particle/medium ratio through inflation, we can allow the fluid jamming medium to dominate the shape volume and the user's experience of it.

Haptic feedback through variable stiffness

The capability to control material stiffness can be used as a degree-of-freedom (DOF) for an output device. The device stiffness can be directly mapped to represent object properties in simulation interfaces, such as various materials in a sculpting application. Stiffness can also be mapped to represent parameters, states and action in the user interface, as classical abstract haptic feedback.

Sensing structure and touch

It is often desirable to sense users' freeform deformations of malleable devices, including 3D shapes, as well as interaction on and above surfaces. Sensing proximity and touch allows 2D and 3D non-planar surface manipulations, which can be relevant and useful for a number of interactions [2]. Shape deformation can, besides the direct 1:1 manipulation of geometry representations, also be used in pattern-matching of shapes. This could, for example, allow the embodiment of functionality, such that the device's behavior and interface would adapt to its form factor, or trigger different actions.

Jamming provides great flexibility for adapting the choice of particles and medium to a particular sensing approach, since there are no active electrical or mechanical elements that can cause interference in the volume.

Particle Types, Jamming Quality and Tactile Experience

The effect that different particle properties, such as size and shape, have on jamming performance has been extensively studied [23, 35, 6]. For user interfaces, the tactile experience is an additional important aspect.

For shape-changing interfaces, we are interested in particles that could achieve large changes in stiffness and jam in arbitrary freeform shapes. Ground coffee has previously been demonstrated as an effective material for systems that require large dynamic range in stiffness and strength [3, 6].

Glass beads provide a good balance of control and tactile stiffness response due to their smooth surfaces and low inter-particle friction. This allows for a precise control over levels of stiffness for malleable manipulations, such as sculpting.

Other properties, such as particle weight or membrane thickness and elasticity, can be optimized for a particular system design. The membrane qualities, for example, affect both the user's tactile experience and the jamming performance.

NOVEL JAMMING TECHNIQUES

Mobile Jamming Platform: Pneumatics for Portability

Jamming has great potential in enabling haptic feedback, malleable input, and shape-changing structures for flexible mobile devices, such as future tablets, e-readers or cell phones. Mobile jamming needs to be compact and self-contained, which introduces constraints on size, flow rate, maximum vacuum force, power consumption and sound level (e.g., due to the vacuum pump).

Our Mobile Jamming Platform (MJP) consists of a small vacuum pump, small solenoid valve, control circuit and battery pack, and measures $47 \times 27 \times 8$ mm^3 (see Figure 4). The pump draws 0.12A at 7.4V, and our current 100 mAh LiPo battery allows for one hour of continuous use of the pump, which means several hours in practice, as stiffness changes are rendered intermittently. Our MJP can currently

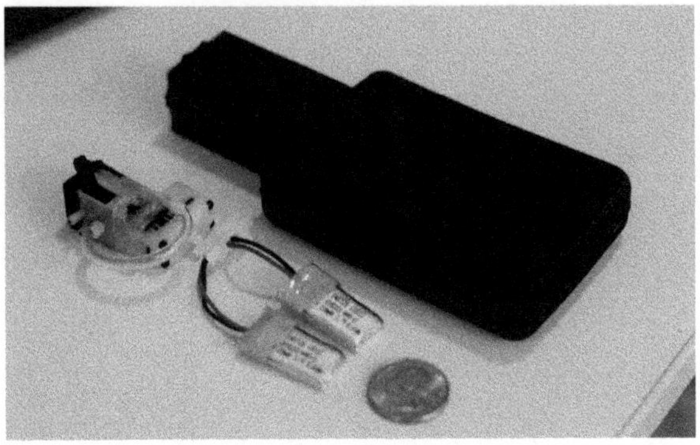

Figure 4: Our Mobile Jamming Platform (MJP) enables pneumatic jamming in a compact, low-power, battery-driven form factor. The MJP consists of a jamming volume, micro air pump, valve and LiPo batteries. (U.S. quarter for scale)

jam/unjam a cell-phone-sized volume of coffee particles in approximately one second.

Hydraulic Jamming: Fast, Silent and Transparent

Hydraulic jamming systems can be created by using liquids as the interstitial fluid between the particles, instead of air (a gas at room temperature). Since liquids are incompressible, hydraulic systems have higher efficiency, can be stiffer, quieter and can withstand more stress and load compared to pneumatic systems [15]. Hydraulic jamming can also enable optical sensing and transparency through the use of index-matched fluids and particles, which we describe in the next section.

We built several hydraulic jamming systems to investigate feasibility and performance compared to pneumatic systems. The system design is similar to a pneumatic system: a DC hydraulic pump, controlled by an H-bridge and microcontroller, moves liquid in and out of the system from a reservoir to change the differential jamming pressure. The pressure is digitally measured with a pressure sensor, and regulated by a control circuit and a hydraulic pump, as shown in Figure 5. Our hydraulic gear pump is $7.62 \times 10.16 \times 5.08$ cm^3, with a 2.3 liter/minute maximum flow rate and a maximum pressure of 151 kPa. Metal mesh filters prevent particles from entering the fluid line and the pump. The pressures required for jamming are significantly lower than pressures used in traditional hydraulic actuation systems because we are not trying to transmit large forces; the goal is to change the interior pressure in reference to the external air pressure of 101.325 kPa.

SENSING FOR JAMMING INTERFACES

In this section, we discuss approaches that are particularly suitable to enable the shape and touch sensing that is necessary to leverage the flexibility and malleability of jamming structures for HCI.

Optical Sensing through Transparent Jamming Volumes

To enable optical sensing of the interface's 3D shape, while avoiding user interference, occlusion and bulky system configurations, it is necessary to integrate cameras below the surface. This, however, requires thin [4] or optically transparent material [8].

Index-matched Hydraulic Jamming A jamming system cannot provide optical transparency simply by using transparent particles, as each particle acts as a light-scattering lens, which makes the overall volume opaque. As light leaves the medium (e.g., air) and enters the particle (e.g., a glass bead), it refracts at an angle governed by Snell's law, due to the different refractive indices. However, by using a fluid that matches the refractive index (n) of the particle, we can suppress refraction and create an optically transparent volume.

Our hydraulic jamming system gives us flexibility to select fluids and particles with matching refractive indices. We chose to use the combination of boroscillicate (Pyrex) glass beads (n=1.474) and vegetable oil (n=1.4674–1.4736, depending on temperature and density). The volume is not completely transparent due to a slight deviation in the refractive indices.

However, our experiments show that the system is sufficiently transparent for optical sensing using projected reference patterns up to an 8 cm thickness of particles. The opacity was measured using a 2 mW red laser and a photometer at different reference thicknesses, and compared to glass beads alone. We determined that 4 cm of glass beads and oil provides 94% transmission, and virtually no transmission for glass beads alone, whereas 8 cm of glass beads and oil provides 47% transmission (see Figure 6). This configuration allows a rear-mounted camera to see through our

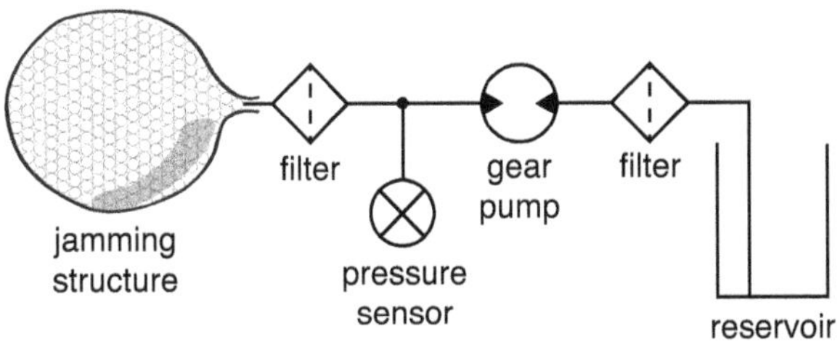

Figure 5: Hydraulic jamming system. Similarly to a pneumatic system, a closed-loop control system measures and manages the differential jamming pressure. Hydraulics can, however, allow higher stiffness, silent operation and faster actuation.

Figure 6: Transparency through index-matched fluid and particles. 3.5 cm of 1 mm Pyrex glass beads immersed in index-matched oil (left), and air (right). The oil reduces refraction as light enters and leaves each glass bead, with a drastic increase in transparency.

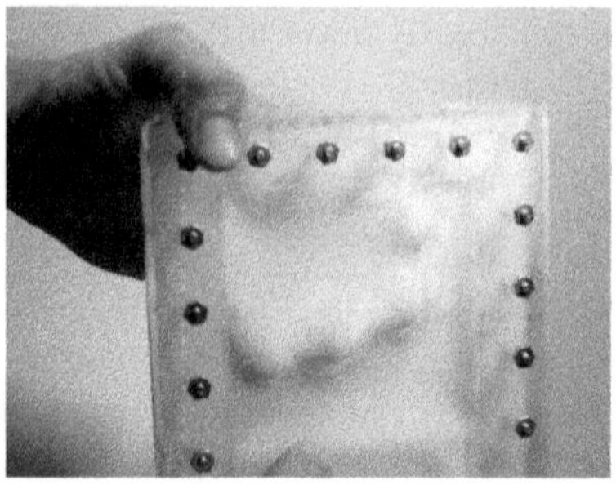

Figure 7: Jamming volume for optical sensing. 3 mm of Pyrex glass beads with index-matched fluid and particles enclosed between a flexible white membrane and a clear plastic sheet. Surface deformations are visible through 8 cm of jamming material.

transparent jammable volume, composed of index-matched fluid and glass beads with a transparent plastic bottom and an upper flexible opaque silicone skin, as shown in Figure 8. This device enables the use of different optical techniques for surface reconstruction, such as shape from shading, photometric stereo, embedded tracking markers in the skin [40], structured lighting, or other custom solutions [8].

Depth from Structured Light through Transparent Volume
For 2.5D sensing through the optical jamming system we choose a custom IR structured light 2.5D scanning system, similar to the deForm system [8], due to its high resolution capture, ability to rear-project visible light content, and its flexibility with regards to changing cameras, projectors, and lenses. Three sequential fringe patterns are rear-projected in IR onto the deformable skin and are captured in 640×480 pixels at 60 frames/s by a side-mounted, synchronized IR camera. The 3 mm-thick silicone skin, with a durometer of 10 shore A, can be stretched and deformed 30 mm above and below its resting height. The deformations of the three patterns are used to reconstruct 2.5D images at 20 frames/s from a 23×18 cm^2 region, at a spatial resolution of 28 pixels/cm, and 0–6 cm depth range, providing a 1–2 mm depth resolution.

Touch Sensing using Structured Light The greyscale surface image from our structured light capture system is also used to track touch points. The system works similarly to an IR diffuse illumination touch system, as the IR projector illuminates the silicone skin. By utilizing a thin, semi-transparent skin made of silicone, the camera captures reflections from fingers as they make contact. Other touch sensing techniques, such as FTIR, could also be explored with our transparent jamming system.

Limitations While this approach provides high-resolution shape and deformation tracking combined with touch sensing, its use is limited to hydraulic jamming systems. Camera and optical sensor placement restricts the system's flexibility, and non-perfect index-matching complicates sensing at greater depths as transparency decreases.

Capacitive Shape Sensing
Capacitive sensing can provide a scalable embedded approach to sensing shape in jamming interfaces, including deformations such as stretching, bending and twisting. In contrast to other techniques, such as resistive pressure sensors or electric impedance tomography, capacitive distance and shape sensing do not rely on a present applied force to the sensor. This makes it advantageous for both absolute and relative input.

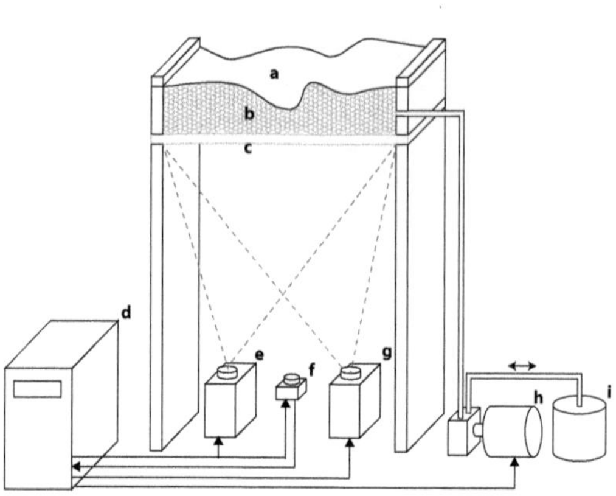

Figure 8: Structured Light Depth Sensing System with Index-Matched Jamming: (a) Silicone Membrane, (b) Pyrex glass beads and oil, (c) acrylic plate, (d) computer, (e) structured light IR projector, (f) IR camera, (g) graphics projector, (h) hydraulic pump, (i) reservoir

Distance Sensing The amount of known dielectric material between two electrodes can be measured through capacitance, and correlated with the distance between them. Pressure sensors have employed this principle [33], which also extends to larger distances and electrodes that can be used for flexible jamming volumes. In our system, an electrode transmits a reference square wave in the 100 kHz range to a receiving electrode, and the signal is sampled by a 12-bit A/D converter in an ARM microcontroller running at 72 MHz. We use synchronous under-sampling to demodulate the signal and recover the original amplitude, which is proportional to the capacitance between the electrodes. 32 samples are averaged to remove white noise.

Dielectric Properties and Sensitivity Stretchable and bendable electrodes are needed for integration in the flexible jamming volume. We use silver-plated 76% nylon, 24% elastic fiber fabric, which has a low surface resistivity, and can be stretched up to twice its length. We insulate the fabric in a non-conductive silicone cast and use Pyrex glass beads as dielectric material. Pyrex glass beads have a dielectric constant of 4.6, whereas air has a dielectric constant of 1.00059. Assuming a random close-packing of glass spheres, 64% of the volume will be glass and 36% will be air [38], resulting in an overall average dielectric constant of 3.3. Hydraulic jamming greatly raises the possibility of increasing this dielectric constant. Using water with glass beads in the jamming volume could approach an average dielectric constant of 30 and increase sensing resolution at larger distances. With simple two-electrode capacitive sensing through glass beads we are able to measure distances of 0–20 cm, with 5 mm or better accuracy (accuracy increases when the two plates are closer to each other).

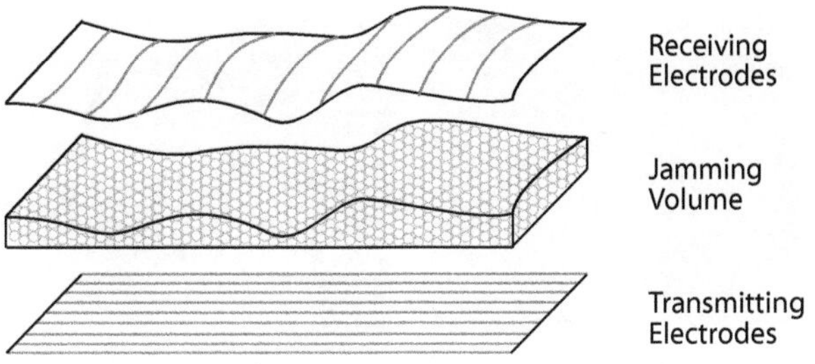

Figure 9: Capacitive shape sensing system. The jamming volume's shape is computed by measuring the capacitance at each transmitter-receiver electrode intersection.

Shape-sensing Prototype Using rows of transmitting electrodes in a rigid back, and columns of receiving electrodes in a flexible skin, we sense the jammable volume's shape through time-division-multiplexing for each of the intersections in the sensing matrix and output a 2.5D depth map. Our prototype of the capacitive shape-sensing input device with jamming haptic feedback uses a 9×9 electrode grid. It measures $25 \times 17.5 \times 3$ cm^3 with an active sensing volume of $18 \times 11.5 \times 3$ cm^3. An overall 25-mm thickness filled with 2 mm glass beads are sealed within a highly flexible upper membrane and a bendable, yet relatively rigid, bottom surface. This device can be placed on a desk, or embedded in the back of a mobile phone or a tablet. Conductive fabric strips (9×1 cm^2 each) are embedded in the flexible skin as receiving electrodes, while strips of copper tape (also 9×1 cm^2 each) on the opposing, bottom surface act as transmitting electrodes, as shown in Figure 9. In addition, a layer of grounded conductive fabric on top of the flexible skin shields the system from the user. An analog multiplexer connects the receiver electrodes to our amplifier circuit and ADC. The current prototype runs at 30 Hz and transmits data over USB serial or wirelessly using Bluetooth. The depth map is filtered and scaled by a factor of ten through bi-cubic interpolation (see Figure 10). The speed and resolution could be increased with dedicated hardware, and code-division-multiplexing could be applied for scalability.

Sensing additional dimensions Separating transmitting and receiving electrodes into rows and columns for deformation sensing is only one approach to capacitive shape sensing electrode layouts; additionally, each electrode can act as both a transmitter and receiver. This can enable stretch, tilt or twist input to be quantified by measuring capacitance between adjacent electrodes with different layouts.

Integrating Capacitive Touch Sensing Our capacitive sensing also supports integrated multi-touch input. By replacing the flexible ground layer with lines of conductive thread that transmit the same reference signal, we enable mutual capacitance touch sensing [31]. When fingers or hands approach the conductive thread transmitting the reference signal, they capacitively couple with the system and decrease the signal. Time-division-multiplexing makes it possible to use the receiving electrodes both for shape-sensing electrodes below, and touch-sensing electrodes above, which reduces the total number of required electrodes for shape and touch sensing. To improve results, we use thin conductive thread (sewn in a zig-zag pattern for flexibility), instead of the thicker conductive stretch-fabric. The thread is more sensitive to capacitive coupling from the user, as its smaller size results in weaker coupling between transmitting and receiving electrode pairs. When not sensing touch, the conductive thread electrodes can be connected to ground to help shield the device. We built a small test system with a 3×3 touch-sensing grid for touch, pressure and hover sensing.

APPLICATIONS AND PROTOTYPES

We built four prototypes that investigate the potential of variable material stiffness for different user interfaces.

Tunable Clay: Precision and Quality through Stiffness

Tunable Clay (shown in Figure 11) is a malleable input device for 3D modeling, where material stiffness can be tuned to comply with different sculpting modes. The interface is inspired by our research group's previous work in 3D modeling in projects such as Illuminating Clay, SandScape [17] and deForm [8]; we are interested in observing how different materials influence the creative process. Tunable Clay is a 30×33 cm^2 malleable tabletop, designed to mimic the malleability of clay, which is a continuous material that users can easily deform. Optical sensing—achieved using structured light through the back of the transparent, hydraulic-

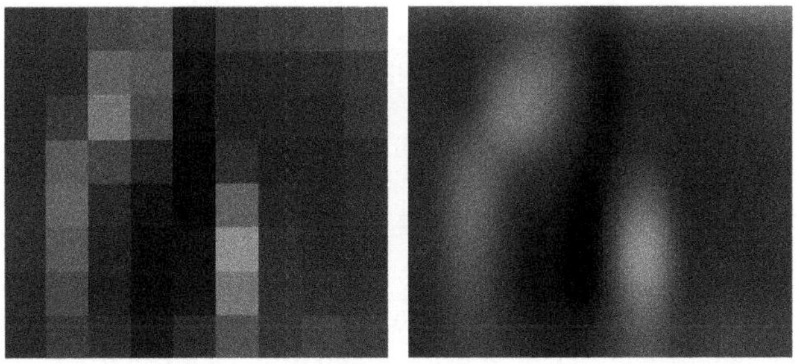

Figure 10: Left) Raw depth map output of 9×9 capacitive shape sensing system. Right) Bicubic interpolated depth map.

Figure 11: Tunable Clay uses material stiffness as an extra dimension for 3D modeling in its malleable interface.

Figure 12: Users can press into the Transparent Haptic Lens to feel the stiffness of the underlying image region on the tabletop display.

activated jamming volume—captures the shape in real-time and applies it to a virtual 3D model. The model is shown both on a separate display and through projected graphics on the malleable surface for direct feedback. The sensing and visible projection is integrated beneath the surface to avoid occlusions from user interactions.

Users can control the stiffness of the malleable surface using a potentiometer. This allows users to modify the resolution of manual input, thereby modifying the interface's control gain. One can increase the stiffness of the interface for detailed work, decrease it to increase malleability or to reset the shape. Tunable Clay highlights the potential benefits of controllable material properties to vary interaction style, precision and feel.

Transparent Haptic Lens: Content Representation

The Transparent Haptic Lens uses varying material stiffness as a haptic information channel. As shown in Figure 12, it consists of a round metal ring with a transparent base and a soft transparent upper skin (Smooth-On Dragon Skin 10) that is tracked on a tabletop display. Users can feel the apparent stiffness of parts of images by moving and pressing into the "lens". An object's haptic information channel is currently represented using 8-bit stiffness values in the alpha channel of the texture. By controlling the degree of jamming inside the lens, the stiffness perceived by the user can vary between a solid object and a liquid.

The jamming device is transparent and controlled hydraulically, as previously described. While haptic output through a tangible tabletop object has been previously explored (e.g., using servo motors [24]), the jamming mechanism inside the Transparent Haptic Lens can present continuous haptic sensations, such as liquids, which would be challenging to render using mechanical actuators. The transparency and shape of the lens also make it possible to provide users with optically magnified view of the objects they are touching.

Behind-the-Tablet Jamming: Haptic Program State

In order to investigate malleable interaction and haptic feedback in the context of mobile devices, we created a jamming

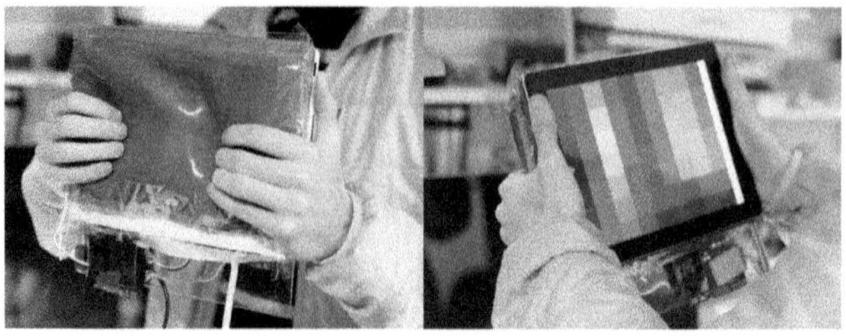

(a) Tablet Back (b) Tablet Front

Figure 13: The Behind-the-Tablet Jamming Interface enables malleable input with varying stiffness as haptic feedback, while avoiding occlusions with on-screen content.

input device mounted on the back surface of a tablet, shown in Figure 13. A custom tablet case has an embedded jamming apparatus and shape deformation sensor for malleable interaction in the back of the tablet. The tablet's rear interface allows users to navigate content on a tablet display by pressing into its malleable surface. This could, for example, be used for browsing information on the tablet using gestures, while receiving jamming-driven haptic feedback. A possible scenario could use kneading on either side of the tablet back to scroll content in that direction, or using both hands to zoom. When a limit is reached, the corresponding part of the tablet could turn stiff, preventing further kneading. This scenario could also allow deformations beyond what is possible in the Tunable Clay interface, since there is no occlusion by the user's hands. As in the previously described interfaces, changes in stiffness can enable different modes of user interaction.

The mobile jamming platform is pneumatically controlled with an on-board vacuum pump and uses capacitive shape sensing. We implemented two variations of the tablet. The first uses Bluetooth to communicate the capacitive shape sensing and jamming control to a tablet, which runs our Android application. The second used an iPad with screen-sharing software to view desktop applications that interface with the hardware over a serial cable.

ShapePhone: Shape-changing Devices

ShapePhone, depicted in Figure 14, is a user-defined mobile device that can be shaped into different forms and then locked into a rigid device for various forms of interaction. With our initial ShapePhone prototype users can transform the affordance of the device—from a phone, tablet (sheet), remote control, watch, game controller, or ball—by stretching, bending and molding ShapePhone when it is unjammed and thus extremely pliable, due to the stretchy silicone skin. The user can control the jamming state using a small switch. When unjammed, ShapePhone returns to its normal state of a phone-sized rectangle, using the silicone skin as a restoring force.

Our prototype uses the Mobile Jamming Platform, described earlier, to control jamming in a small form factor, and enables ShapePhone to be entirely self-contained. The phone-shaped hollow silicone (Smooth-On EcoFlex 0030) body was cast from a 3D-printed three-part mold. This particular silicone

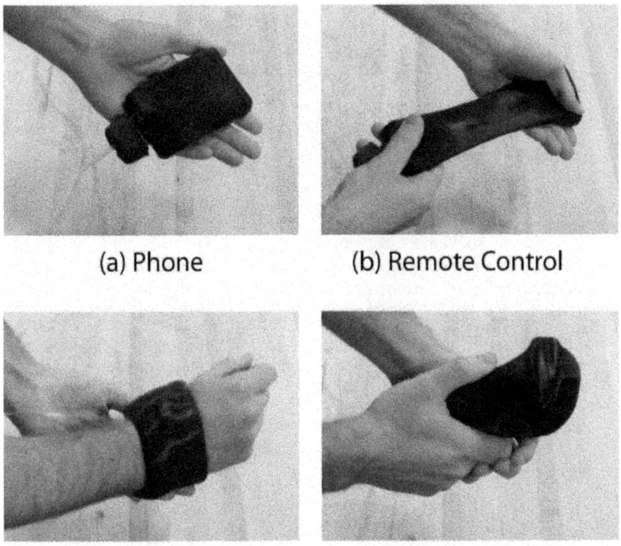

(a) Phone (b) Remote Control (c) Watch (d) Game Controller

Figure 14: The ShapePhone mobile device can be formed into different jammed shapes.

is very flexible and can stretch up to four times its size. The skin is filled with coffee grounds and sealed with a tube for airflow connected to the MJP.

It would be relatively straightforward to add the previously described capacitive shape sensing techniques to ShapePhone to sense a variety of different shapes. These shapes could be used in addition to contextual information gathered through other sensors, or program state, to enable further functionality. Capacitive touch sensing could also be incorporated for user input and recognize how the user is holding the device to enable contextual information [37].

This same jamming phone device could also be used for interaction and haptic feedback while in a pocket. Changes in stiffness could convey battery life, for example, letting the ShapePhone "melt" when it runs out of battery, or allowing user input through the pocket using squeezes or deformations.

DISCUSSION AND DESIGN CONSIDERATIONS

When designing a jamming system with shape and touch sensing, several design decisions are of importance, as demonstrated in our approaches for activation, sensing, and interactive applications and prototypes.

Jamming performance depends on activation technology and particle type, with hydraulic systems and high-friction particles offering wider dynamic stiffness range, while speed of activation can be accelerated using in-line reservoirs. Tactile experience, surface quality and malleability benefit from low-friction particles and thin, elastic membranes.

Hydraulic jamming enables optical shape and touch sensing through transparent volumes, and provides strong, rapid and silent operation. For mobile and embedded devices, pneumatic jamming has the advantages of being lightweight, simple and relatively small, as it can utilize the ambient air as the fluid reservoir. Our MJP demonstrates this with a combination of low-weight particles and compact elements for activation and capacitive sensing.

To address the loudness of most air compressors, such devices can be run at lower voltages if slower actuation speed is acceptable. The effect of gravity in a mobile jamming system can also be addressed using multiple compartments to constrain material placement.

FUTURE WORK

Our prototypes utilize passive actuation either from the user or from restoring forces. There is, however, a large space to explore in actuation. Techniques, such as pneumatic artificial muscles, as well as other inflatable structures, could be used to quickly change state and help jamming enable an even wider array of shape-changing interfaces. Our next steps are also to explore integration of our jamming techniques with actuated displays and devices.

Further work is required to explore other sensing techniques that can be integrated with flexible jamming devices. The conductive fabric we currently use is capable of only half the strain of that of the silicone used, and thus limits system flexibility. We plan to investigate other approaches to embedded electrodes and wiring, such as embedded liquid metal [29] and saltwater, for stretchable capacitive shape sensing.

Once flexible and stretchable displays are widely available, they will enable flexible mobile jamming devices with integrated displays. Until then, such future jamming devices and their related interactions can be prototyped using projection.

While we have focused on tangible, malleable organic user interfaces in this paper, jamming should also be explored in a wider context, as it is applicable to numerous applications such as haptic interfaces for VR, teleoperation, and ergonomic input devices.

CONCLUSIONS

This work demonstrates how jamming of granular particles can be applied to malleable, flexible and shape-changing user interfaces, and the interaction vocabulary made possible through programmable stiffness and control of material properties. By embedding sensing through index-matched optical sensing or capacitive shape sensing, we enable jamming interfaces to become high-resolution input devices. We also show how jamming can be miniaturized for mobile applications. Through four prototypes and two activation technologies, we demonstrate a range of possibilities of jamming user interfaces, and point towards future work. The wide variety of uses of jamming in our work highlights its applicability and potential for HCI in general, and to organic user interfaces, in particular.

ACKNOWLEDGMENTS

This work was supported in part by the National Science Foundation Graduate Research Fellowship under Grant No. 1122374. Alex Olwal was supported by a Swedish Research Council Fellowship and a Blanceflor Foundation Scholarship. We thank Brian Mayton, Rehmi Post, Steven Keating, and Ben Peters for their help with Electric Field Sensing and our jamming prototypes. Thanks also to Dr. Karl Iagnemma and Prof. Anette Hosoi for their continued guidance in jamming-related work.

REFERENCES

1. Amend, J., Brown, E., Rodenberg, N., Jaeger, H., and Lipson, H. A Positive Pressure Universal Gripper Based on the Jamming of Granular Material. *IEEE Transactions on Robotics* (2012), 341–350.
2. Benko, H. Beyond flat surface computing: challenges of depth-aware and curved interfaces. In *ACM MM '09*, ACM Press (2009), 935–944.
3. Brown, E., Rodenberg, N., Amend, J., Mozeika, A., Steltz, E., Zakin, M. R., Lipson, H., and Jaeger, H. M. Universal robotic gripper based on the jamming of granular material. *Proceedings of the National Academy of Sciences 107*, 44 (2010), 18809–18814.
4. Cassinelli, A., and Ishikawa, M. Khronos projector. In *SIGGRAPH 2005 Emerging Technologies*, ACM Press (2005).
5. Cates, M., Wittmer, J., Bouchaud, J.-P., and Claudin, P. Jamming, Force Chains, and Fragile Matter. *Physical Review Letters 81*, 9 (1998), 1841–1844.
6. Cheng, N., Lobovsky, M., Keating, S., Setapen, A., Gero, K. I., Hosoi, A., and Iagnemma, K. Design and Analysis of a Robust, Low-Cost, Highly Articulated Manipulator Enabled by Jamming of Granular Media. *IEEE ICRA* (2012), 4328– 4333.
7. Coelho, M., and Zigelbaum, J. Shape-changing interfaces. *Personal and Ubiquitous Computing 15*, 2 (2010), 161–173.
8. Follmer, S., Johnson, M., Adelson, E., and Ishii, H. deForm: an interactive malleable surface for capturing 2.5D arbitrary objects, tools and touch. In *UIST '11*, ACM Press (2011), 527–536.
9. Gupta, S., Campbell, T., Hightower, J. R., and Patel, S. N. SqueezeBlock: using virtual springs in mobile devices for eyes-free interaction. In *UIST '10*, ACM Press (2010), 101–104.
10. Harrison, C., and Hudson, S. E. Providing dynamically changeable physical buttons on a visual display. In *CHI '09*, ACM Press (2009), 299–308.
11. Hemmert, F., Hamann, S., Löwe, M., Wohlauf, A., and Joost, G. Shape-changing mobiles: tapering in one-dimensional deformational displays in mobile phones. In *TEI '10*, ACM Press (2010), 249–252.
12. Herkenrath, G., Karrer, T., and Borchers, J. Twend: twisting and bending as new interaction gesture in mobile devices. In *CHI EA '08*, ACM Press (2008), 3819–3824.
13. Hilliges, O., Kim, D., and Izadi, S. Creating malleable interactive surfaces using liquid displacement sensing. In *Proc. Tabletop 2008*, IEEE Press (2008), 157–160.
14. Hook, J., Taylor, S., Butler, A., Villar, N., and Izadi, S. A reconfigurable ferromagnetic input device. In *UIST '09*, ACM Press (2009), 51–54.
15. Huber, J. E., Fleck, N. a., and Ashby, M. F. The selection of mechanical actuators based on performance indices. *Proceedings of the Royal Society A: Mathematical, Physical and Engineering Sciences 453*, 1965 (Oct. 1997), 2185–2205.
16. Huijben, F., Herwijnen, F. V. A. N., and Nijsse, R. Vacuumatics 3D-Formwork Systems : Customized free-form solidification. *Nano*, figure 1 (2009), 1–4.
17. Ishii, H., Ratti, C., Piper, B., Wang, Y., Biderman, A., and Ben-Joseph, E. Bringing Clay and Sand into Digital Design Continuous Tangible user Interfaces. *BT Technology Journal 22*, 4 (Oct. 2004), 287–299.
18. Iwata, H., Yano, H., Nakaizumi, F., and Kawamura, R. Project FEELEX: adding haptic surface to graphics. In *SIGGRAPH '01*, ACM Press (Aug. 2001), 469–476.
19. Jansen, Y., Karrer, T., and Borchers, J. MudPad: tactile feedback and haptic texture overlay for touch surfaces. In *ITS '10*, ACM Press (2010), 11–14.
20. Kim, S., Kim, H., Lee, B., Nam, T.-J., and Lee, W. Inflatable mouse: volume-adjustable mouse with air-pressure-sensitive input and haptic feedback. In *CHI '08*, ACM Press (2008), 211–224.
21. Lahey, B., Girouard, A., Burleson, W., and Vertegaal, R. PaperPhone: understanding the use of bend gestures in mobile devices with flexible electronic paper displays. In *CHI '11*, ACM Press (2011), 1303–1312.
22. Liu, A. Jamming is not just cool any more. *Nature 396*, November (1998), 21–22.
23. Loeve, A. J., Ven, O. S., Vogel, J. G., Breedveld, P., and Dankelman, J. Vacuum packed particles as flexible endoscope guides with controllable rigidity. *Granular Matter 12*, 6 (June 2010), 543–554.
24. Marquardt, N., Nacenta, M. A., Young, J. E., Carpendale, S., Greenberg, S., and Sharlin, E. The Haptic Tabletop Puck: tactile feedback for interactive tabletops. In *ITS '09*, ACM Press (2009), 85–92.
25. Matoba, Y., Sato, T., Takahashi, N., and Koike, H. Claytricsurface: an interactive surface with dynamic softness control capability. In *SIGGRAPH '12 Emerging Technologies*, ACM (2012), 6:1–6:1.
26. Mazzone, A., Spagno, C., and Kunz, A. The HoverMesh: a deformable structure based on vacuum cells: new advances in the research of tangible user interfaces. In *ACE '04*, ACM Press (2004), 187–193.
27. Mitsuda, T., Kuge, S., Wakabayashi, M., and Kawamura, S. Wearable haptic display by the use of a Particle Mechanical Constraint. *Proceedings 10th Symposium on Haptic Interfaces for Virtual Environment and Teleoperator Systems. HAPTICS 2002* (2002), 153–158.
28. Overholt, D. The MATRIX: a novel controller for musical expression. In *NIME '01*, AMC (2001), 1–4.
29. Park, Y.-L., Majidi, C., Kramer, R., Bérard, P., and Wood, R. J. Hyperelastic pressure sensing with a liquid-embedded elastomer. *Journal of Micromechanics and Microengineering 20*, 12 (Dec. 2010), 125029.
30. Parkes, A., Poupyrev, I., and Ishii, H. Designing kinetic interactions for organic user interfaces. *Communications of the ACM 51*, 6 (June 2008), 58–65.
31. Rekimoto, J. SmartSkin: an infrastructure for freehand manipulation on interactive surfaces. In *CHI '02*, ACM Press (2002), 113–120.
32. Schwesig, C., Poupyrev, I., and Mori, E. Gummi: a bendable computer. In *CHI '04*, ACM Press (New York, New York, USA, 2004), 263–270.
33. Sergio, M., Manaresi, N., and Tartagni, M. A Textile Based Capacitive Pressure Sensor. *Sensors, 2002.* (2002), 1625–1630.
34. Smith, R. T., Thomas, B. H., and Piekarski, W. Digital foam interaction techniques for 3D modeling. In *Virtual Reality Software and Technology* (2008), 61–68.
35. Steltz, E., Mozeika, A., and Rembisz, J. Jamming as an enabling technology for soft robotics. *Electroactive Polymer Actuators and Devices (EAPAD)* (2010), 764225.
36. Steltz, E., Mozeika, A., Rodenberg, N., Brown, E., and Jaeger, H. JSEL: Jamming Skin Enabled Locomotion. *2009 IEEE/RSJ International Conference on Intelligent Robots and Systems* (Oct. 2009), 5672–5677.
37. Taylor, B. T., and Bove, V. M. Graspables: grasp-recognition as a user interface. In *CHI '09*, ACM Press (2009), 917–926.
38. Torquato, S., Truskett, T., and Debenedetti, P. Is random close packing of spheres well defined? *Physical review letters 84*, 10 (Mar. 2000), 2064–7.
39. Vertegaal, R., and Poupyrev, I. Organic User Interfaces. *Communications of the ACM 51*, 6 (2008), 26–30.
40. Vlack, K., Mizota, T., Kawakami, N., Kamiyama, K., Kajimoto, H., and Tachi, S. Gelforce: a vision-based traction field computer interface. In *Ext. Abstracts CHI '05*, ACM Press (2005), 1154–1155.
41. White, Tom. *Introducing Liquid Haptics in High Bandwidth Human Computer Interfaces*. PhD thesis, MIT, 1998.

A Thin Stretchable Interface for Tangential Force Measurement

Yuta Sugiura[1&2]
[1]Graduate School of Media Design, Keio University, 4-1-1 Hiyoshi, Kohoku, Yokohama, 223-8526 Japan

Masahiko Inami[1&2]
[2]JST ERATO Igarashi Design Interface Project, 1-28-1-7F Koishikawa, Bunkyo, Tokyo, 112-0002 Japan

Takeo Igarashi[2&3]
[3]Department of Computer Science, The University of Tokyo, 7-3-1 Hongo, Bunkyo, Tokyo, 113-0033 Japan

{y-sugiura | inami}@kmd.keio.ac.jp, takeo@acm.org

ABSTRACT

We have developed a simple skin-like user interface that can be easily attached to curved as well as flat surfaces and used to measure tangential force generated by pinching and dragging interactions. The interface consists of several photoreflectors that consist of an IR LED and a phototransistor and elastic fabric such as stocking and rubber membrane. The sensing method used is based on our observation that photoreflectors can be used to measure the ratio of expansion and contraction of a stocking using the changes in transmissivity of IR light passing through the stocking. Since a stocking is thin, stretchable, and nearly transparent, it can be easily attached to various types of objects such as mobile devices, robots, and different parts of the body as well as to various types of conventional pressure sensors without altering the original shape of the object. It can also present natural haptic feedback in accordance with the amount of force exerted. A system using several such sensors can determine the direction of a two-dimensional force. A variety of example applications illustrated the utility of this sensing system.

Author Keywords

Soft User Interface; Tangential Force Input; Transmissivity Measurement; Multiple Sensors;

ACM Classification Keywords

H5.m. Information interfaces and presentation (e.g., HCI): Miscellaneous.

General Terms

Measurement, Design

INTRODUCTION

People have long made use of their skin to communicate intentions and emotions to each other via touching. For instance, people can express affection for children by caressing their head and anger by sharply pinching their cheek. The integration of this property of skin into objects in our daily life or into a smart home environment would enable the implementation of a computer system that could detect user behavior and change the environment accordingly. For example, the user of a robot with sensor-augmented skin could indicate his or her intentions and emotions directly and naturally to a robot through touch interaction. Thus, the objective of this research is to integrate the property of skin into existing objects and thereby enable more natural communication with computer systems.

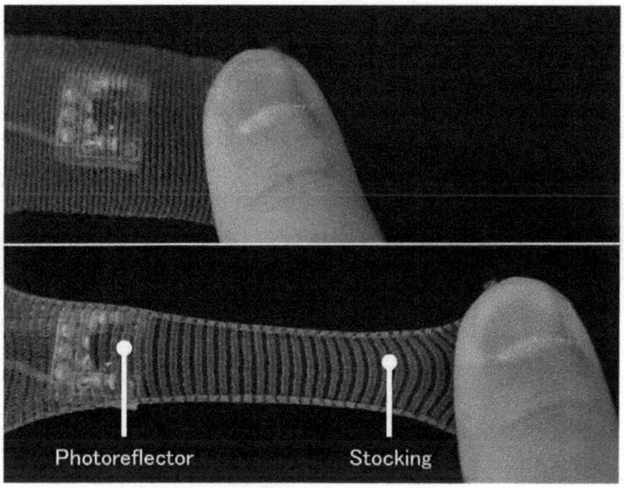

Figure 1: Proposed stretchable sensor measures tangential forces applied to elastic fabric.

There have been several attempts to create artificial skin for use in sense-touch interaction systems, especially in the field of robotics [13, 15]. Many researchers have focused on developing sensors that can detect touch (binary sensing) or measure touch pressure (force in the normal direction) as well as identify the touch points. Interaction via skin involves not only touching and pressing but also pinching, pulling, releasing, twisting, and caressing, thereby creating different tangential forces.

In this paper, we present a simple skin-like user interface that can be easily attached to curved as well as flat surfaces and that can measure tangential forces applied to the surface (Figure 1). The interface consists of several photoreflectors that consist of an IR LED and a phototransistor and elastic fabric such as stocking and rubber membrane. Because a stocking is a stretchable material, it can afford physical interactions such as pinching, pulling, releasing, caressing, and squashing and present natural haptic feedback on the basis of the amount of force applied. We found that photoreflectors can be used to measure the ratio of expansion and contraction of the stocking using the changes in transmissivity of IR light passing through the stocking. This is the key sensing technique used in this research. Since a stocking is thin, flexible, and semi-transparent, it can be attached to various types of objects such as mobile phones, robots, and different parts of the body as well as to various types of conventional pressure sensors, thereby enhancing and providing richer touch interaction. A system using several photoreflectors can determine the direction of a two-dimensional force. We have prototyped a variety of example applications to illustrate the utility of this sensing system.

Our sensor has several advantages over existing technologies. First, the components (stocking and photoreflectors) are commodity products and very inexpensive (less than $1 each). Because the configuration does not require any complex circuitry, users can easily duplicate the system on their own. Second, because a stocking is thin and flexible, it can be attached to various types of objects without changing their original shape and can be used to create powerful and economical ambient sensor environments. Finally, a stocking gives natural haptic feedback in accordance with the amount of force applied. Also, the softness and durability of the sensor can be controlled by using a stocking with a different denier[1] value or by adding another stocking. This can result in more comfortable interfaces.

RELATED WORK

Our work builds upon four distinct areas of prior research that are covered in turn in this section. The first is the augmentation of the sensing area on near-surfaces; the second is tangential force sensing; the third is stretchable sensors and thin deformable displays.

Augmenting Sensing Area on Near-surfaces

There have been several attempts to develop thin skin-like sensors that can be attached to non-planar surfaces and that can detect touch and measure pressure. Lumelsky proposed the concept of "sensitive skin," i.e., the covering of a large area and using a flexible array of sensors with data processing capabilities [11]. The entire surface of a machine or even a part of the human body can be covered. Commercial pressure, position, and bend sensors that are based on the resistance changes of a metal material can be very thin and can be used to augment the sensing area on objects in our daily lives or in the environment. Shimojo et al. developed a thin and flexible sheet-type sensor that can measure two-dimensional pressure and can be used to cover three-dimensional objects. This tactile sensor consists of pressure-conductive rubber with stitched electrical wires [17]. Hoshi et al. constructed a sheet-type sensor that can capture 3D shapes as well as shape deformation in real time by using distributed triaxial accelerometers and triaxial magnetometers [8]. In the field of robotics, several sensors have been proposed for sensing touch interaction on a robot covered with soft skin [13]. Ohmura et al. developed a conformable tactile sensor skin composed of photoreflectors covered with urethane foam [15]. Our method differs from these in that it can measure tangential forces.

Tangential Force Sensing

Strain gauges are commonly used to measure the tangential force on hard objects. Herot and Weinzapfel presented an interface that can measure, via strain gauges, the force vector applied to a screen [7]. Since the voltage change in the gauges is small, an operational amplifier must be used, resulting in complex circuitry. Also, strain gauges are rigid instruments. Since it requires solid attachment to the material, the material's property changes. Our technique allows us to customize the sensor's position and material shape to the target objects or environment because it only requires sensor allocation and cover with stocking.

Heo and Lee modified this interface so that it can measure the tangential forces of gestures applied to the screen of a mobile phone [5]. By combining the normal force with position sensing, this system enables users to use five force gestures. However, because the system components are made of hard materials, they may not produce the expected interactions. Moreover, they are unable to provide haptic feedback.

Several camera-based methods have been proposed for measuring tangential forces applied to soft materials. Kamiyama et al. developed the Gelforce sensor, which enables the measurement of six-degrees of freedom motions by capturing the deformation of color markers embedded in elastic material [10]. Yamane et al. placed many physical bumps on a plate and estimated the tangential forces from images captured with a CCD camera by measuring the mechanical changes in the bumps [22]. While these camera-based methods work well in a limited environment, such as a tabletop, a certain amount of space is required between the material and sensor because a camera is used to track the shape deformation or movement of soft material.

Kadowaki et al. proposed using a phototransistor and multiple IR LEDs to measure a variety of interactions such as push, pinch, and rub [9]. The idea is to measure the gap

[1] Denier is a unit of measure for the linear mass density of fibers. It is defined as the mass in grams per 9,000 meters.

between the top of the silicone material with a phototransistor and its bottom with multiple IR LEDs. However, since phototransistors and IR LEDs have a certain thickness, it is difficult to attach them to object surfaces.

There are several attempts to measure slipping movement on a soft surface by using same optical sensor as that user in an optical mouse [1, 3]. These methods measure the material's relative translational displacement, which leads to cumulative errors. Our sensing method measures the absolute stretch of material, thus it is not prone to such errors. In addition, our method can measure the stretch even if there is no translational move (e.g. measure the stretch of stocking at the center).

Stretchable Sensor and Thin Deformable Display

Slyper et al. proposed using analogue magnetic distance sensors to construct stretchable sensors for measuring the structural changes of silicone [18]. Perner-Wilson and Buechley described a method in which the resistance value of conductive wires knitted into cloth changes with the stretching motion [16].

There have been several attempts to develop thin deformable displays, especially in the media arts field. The "Khronos Projector" is an interactive art installation using a flexible and deformable projector screen [2]. The audience can interact with the screen using physical and dynamic actions, such as pushing. The deformation of the screen is captured using a CCD camera. Heo and Bank developed similar interactive art installations based on Kinect sensing [6]. Miaw presented a high-speed optical motion-capture method that can measure three-dimensional motion, orientation, and incident illumination at tagged points in a scene [12].

PHOTOREFLECTIVITY-BASED RATIO OF EXPANSION AND CONTRACTION MEASUREMENT

Principle

Photoreflectors are generally used to measure the distance between objects. We propose using them to measure the

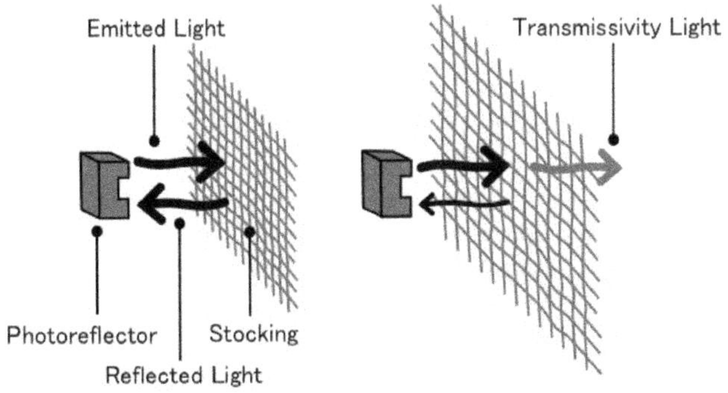

Figure 2: Photoreflector detects ratio of expansion and contraction of stocking on basis of transmissivity changes of IR light passing through the stocking.

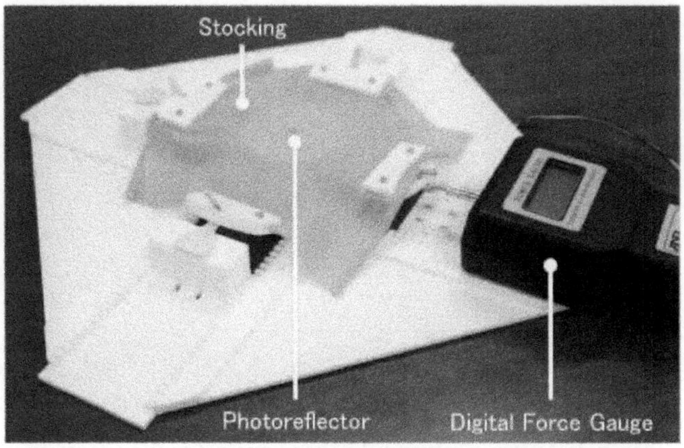

Figure 3: Experimental tool for pulling stocking in a step-by-step manner. Digital force gauge measures pulling force.

ratio of expansion and contraction of stretchable materials. When a material is stretched (i.e., when a stocking is pulled), the amount of emitted IR light passing through the material changes. This phenomenon is illustrated in Figure 2.

Relationship between Photoreflectivity and Ratio of Expansion and Contraction of Stocking

We conducted an experiment to investigate the relationship between photoreflectivity and the ratio of expansion and contraction of a stretchable material. A 20 denier stocking was spread over the center of an experimental tool (Figure 3) and held in place by clamps on three sides. The fourth side of the material was connected to a force gauge (A&D Company, Limited; AD-4932A-50N; resolution: 0.01N). The tool pulled the material in a step-by-step manner. A KODENSHI SG-105 photoreflector was located under the material at the center of the tool.

To check for the effect of hysteresis, we released the material in a step-by-step manner after pulling it until the pulling force was 6N (the maximum force with which 20 denier stocking can be pulled with it being torn apart). The photoreflector measurements were recorded using an Atmel ATmega328 microcontroller. The photoreflector was included in the voltage-divider circuit so that the measured output voltage would be inversely proportional to the light reflected on the sensor.

Experiment Procedure

1. Place 20 denier stocking on experimental tool.
2. Adjust initial force to 0.2N by pulling stocking.
3. Record photoreflector output at 1Hz for 10s.
4. Pull stocking in steps of 2mm.
5. Repeat steps 3 and 4 until force reaches 6N.
6. Release stocking by 2mm.
7. Record photoreflector output at 1Hz for 10s.
8. Repeat steps 6 and 7 until force reaches 0.2N.

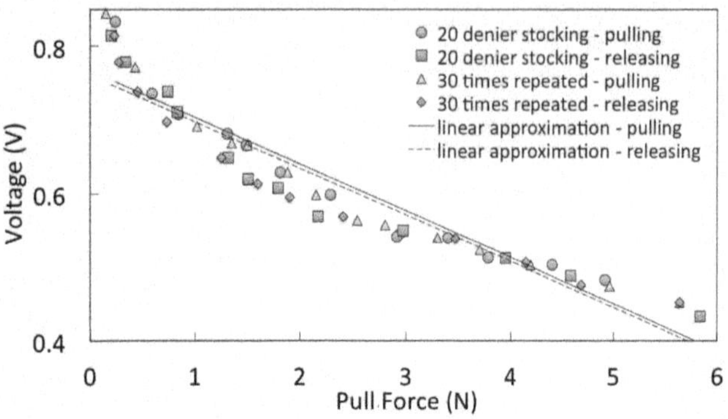

Figure 4: Average measured voltage against pulling force for 20 denier stocking.

Result

Figure 4 plots the sensor value (i.e., the voltage) against the pulling force. The voltage decreased with the force created by pulling, and it increased as the force was reduced by releasing. The effect of hysteresis is evident from 1.3N to 2.8N in the figure. We also plotted the data that was recorded when the stocking was pulled and released at 30 times. We approximated these data by linear.

Other Materials

We also tested other materials in a similar setting. The value of the sensor for a 70 denier stocking decreased linearly from 2N to 11N. The stretch of a thin rubber material used for exercise can also be measured with this sensing method.

IMPLEMENTATION

User Interactions

People interact with skin-like surfaces in various ways. Our sensing method can currently measure three basic interactions (Figure 5). The measurements are made using values obtained from sensors placed on each side of the material. By dragging fingers on the surface, the user can create a tangential force in any direction (Figure 5a). The user can also use pinch-in (Figure 5b) and pinch-out (Figure 5c) gestures. On the basis of changes to the temporal axis, the system can differentiate among a flicking gesture, a double-flick gesture, and so on.

Sensor Module

We constructed a prototype sensor module that can be

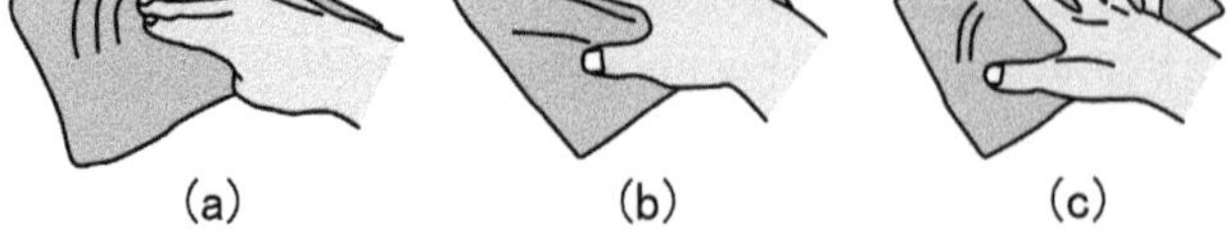

Figure 5: Basic interactions with stretchable surface: (a) dragging, (b) pinch-in, (c) pinch-out.

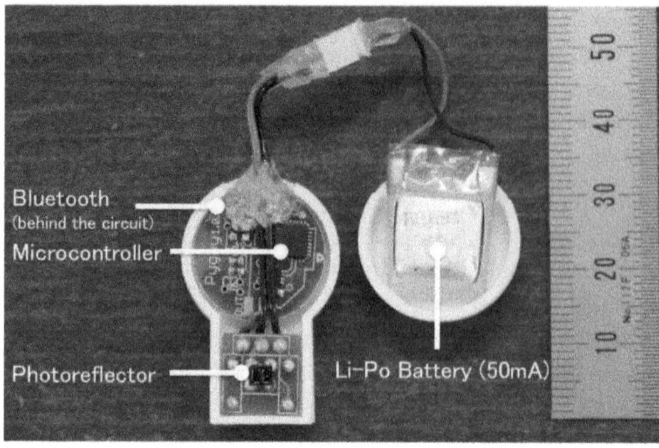

Figure 6: Main components of sensor module.

easily attached to everyday objects and the environment (Figure 6). It consists of photoreflectors, a microcontroller, a Li-Po battery (3.7V, 50mA) and a Bluetooth or ZigBee module (we prototyped both types). Both types of module have a diameter of 35mm, a thickness of 4mm and a weight of 20g. The case is made of laser-cut acrylic. The module requires no physical connection since it is equipped with a wireless communication module and battery. The AT-mega328 microcontroller has a 10-bit A/D converter, so the photoreflector outputs a value of 0 to 1023. It is connected to the Bluetooth or ZigBee module. Since an ID number can be assigned to each wireless module, multiple sensor modules can be used at the same time.

Calculation of Two-dimensional Tangential Force

A dragging interaction is measured by calculating a vector based on the value for each photoreflectors and calibrated sensor location. This calculation is based on the method used to detect the barycenter of multi-mass points. The system detects 1) the direction and 2) the force level of the user's dragging interaction using the following formula.

$$\mathbf{a} = ((\sum_{i=1}^{n} p_i x_i)/M - x_d, (\sum_{i=1}^{n} p_i y_i)/M - y_d) \tag{1}$$

$$M = \sum_{i=1}^{n} p_i \quad , \tag{2}$$

where **a** is the vector for dragging, n is the number of sensor modules, p_i is the photoreflector value for sensor module i, and x_i and y_i represent the x-y coordinates of sensor i. The user specifies the location of the sensors at installation. The default x-y position (when the user is not touching the sensor) is given by x_d and y_d. M is the total value for all the photoreflectors and is used to detect pinch-in and pinch-out gestures. We measured the accuracy of vector direction. The angular range was about ± 4.6 degree compared to real angle. Right now, since the characteristic of the elastic fabrics is not considered in the formula, the system detects these interactions roughly.

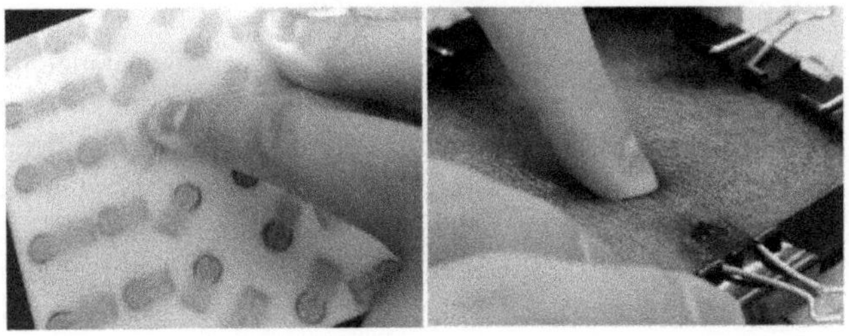

Figure 7: Application to commercial pressure sensor array (left) and FuwaFuwa sensor (right).

Combination with Conventional Pressure Sensors

Since our sensor is thin and deformable, it can be easily combined with conventional touch sensors to enhance the interaction experience. We attached our skin-like surface sensor to two touch pressure sensors: a commercial pressure sensor that can be used to measure not only normal force pressure but also tangential forces (Figure 7, left), and a FuwaFuwa sensor [20], which can detect the shape deformation of cotton on the basis of the cotton's density as measured with a photoreflectors (Figure 7, right). Our sensor did not affect the cotton's softness property, and it expanded the variety of interactions, adding squashing and pulling in addition to interactions based on tangential forces. Also, we can combine our sensor with other soft sensor that is developed by Smith et al. [19].

EXAMPLE APPLICATIONS

Smart Phone – We developed two different types of attachments based on our nearly transparent sensor skin for use with touchscreen mobile phones. The first type is flat and enables the use of both touch and tangential force sensing. The location of a 3D object on the touchscreen is manipulated by normal touch and drag (Figure 8, left). If the user increases the touch pressure when dragging an object, the object rotates (Figure 8, right). Users can thus generate different types of gestures with only one finger. The other type is curved and supports pinching, dragging, and releasing gestures. With these gestures, users can play games with more complicated actions, like shooting at a target with an arrow (Figure 9). The arrow is controlled by dragging them from side to side and up and down and is launched by using a releasing gesture.

Robot – A user would likely feel more comfortable interacting with a robot with soft surfaces than one with hard surfaces [13, 21]. With this in mind, we developed a robotic toy that has soft surfaces and that affords the user physical interactions. The robot is covered with our sensor skin, and two photoreflectors are placed on the front surface of the robot. The robots eyes change direction when the robot is "pulled" using dragging gestures (Figure 10). The robot makes a rocking motion as well when the robot is "caressed" using pinch-in and pinch-out gestures.

Home Appliances – We covered a speaker with our sensor skin (Figure 11). Four photoreflectors were attached at the

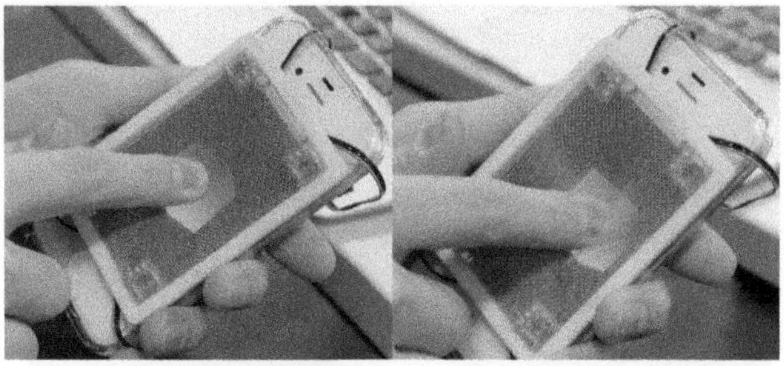

Figure 8: Location of computer graphics object is controlled using normal touch (left); object is rotated using hard touch (right).

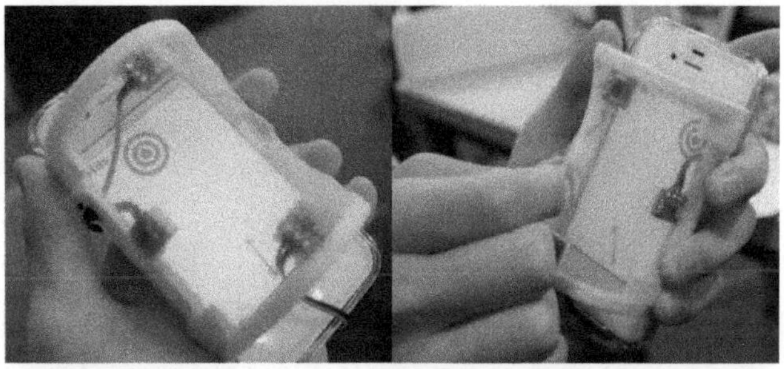

Figure 9: Target shooting game controlled using pinching, dragging, and releasing gestures on the curved type of attachment.

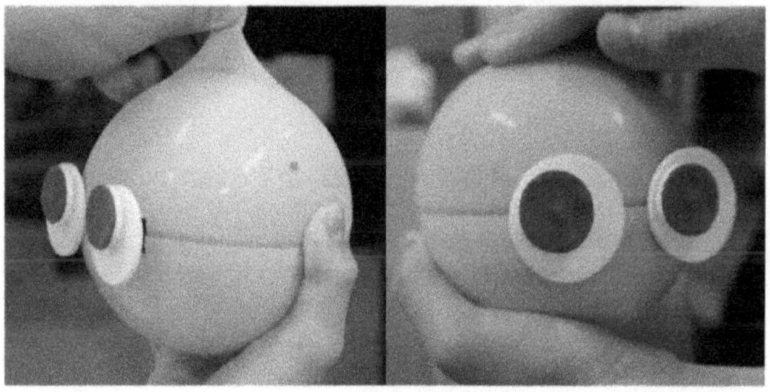

Figure 10: Direction of robot's eyes changes on basis of gestures.

corners of the speaker (one at each corner), enabling it to detect touch interactions. In this prototype, the user can control the volume and track being played by dragging a finger across the skin up and down and from side to side. Tracks can be fast-forwarded by using a rotation gesture.

Chairs – Tangential force interactions occur not only at one's finger tips but also at one's hind end. Postural imbalance affects one's ability to concentrate. There have been several attempts to encourage good postural balance by visualizing the user's own posture [4, 14]. Our sensor skin can be easily attached to an everyday chair and can measure the posture of a person sitting in it, especially slipping (Figure 12). A system combining a conventional pressure sensor with our sensor skin can measure the user's posture in five directions.

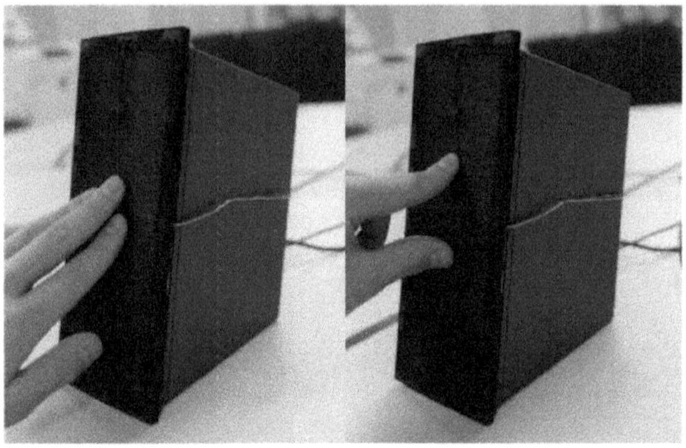

Figure 11: Volume, track-change, and fast-forward functions are controlled using finger dragging gestures.

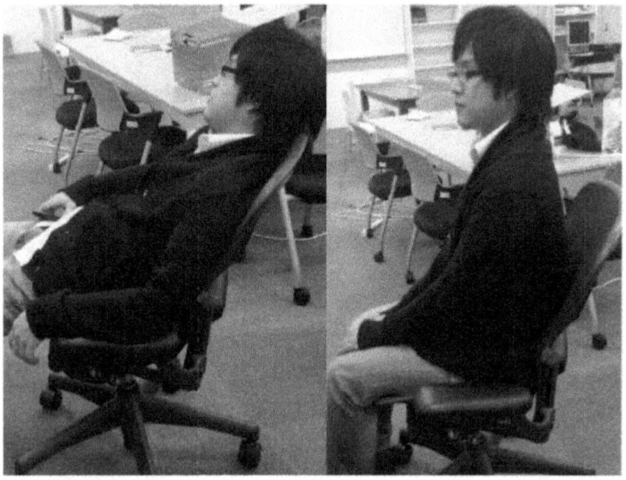

Figure 12: System combining conventional sensor and skin sensor can detect posture of person sitting in a chair, especially slipping movement.

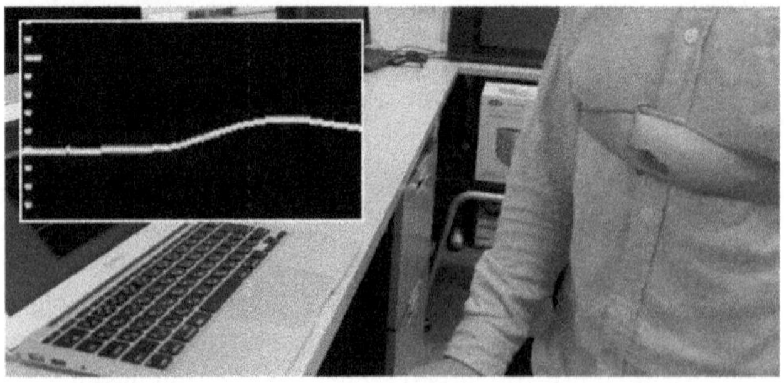

Figure 13: Breathing is captured by our method.

Human Body – Since a stocking is obviously a suitable covering for human skin, we prototyped an application that illustrates the utility of such an application. It is a simple breathing sensor that measures the stretch of a stocking bound around a person's chest (Figure 13). Its continuously detects the respiration rate and depth.

LIMITATION AND FUTURE WORK

Our skin-like sensor is a "proof-of-concept" implementation, so there are some limitations. The photoreflectors are affected by ambient light such as from an electric lamp or sunlight. We plan to implement a filtering system using light modulation that separates IR light emitted by the LEDs in the photoreflectors from ambient light. Photoreflectors also detects the user's hand or other objects if they enter the sensor's detection field. These problems do not occur when using a photo interrupter. However, since a photo interrupter is larger than a photoreflector, we need to establish a method for determining which one to use depending on the application.

Another problem is the durability of the stocking. The 20 denier stocking we mainly used in this research is torn apart when a force greater than 6N is applied. This problem can be overcome by using a stocking with a denier value appropriate for the target application. The color of the stocking affects the sensor value, we plan to generalize the relationship between stocking color and photoreflector sensor value.

As future practical applications, our method is suitable for wearable interface applications. Users can wear the material on the arm to detect interaction. Some of the intended applications are in the medical field: continuous human body monitoring such as muscle movement and body volume changes (edema). Also, it is possible to log dynamic body shape change (e.g. exercising, working, eating).

CONCLUSION

We have demonstrated a simple low-cost skin-like interface that can be easily attached to curved as well as flat surfaces and used to detect and measure tangential force interactions such as pinching and dragging. The sensor consists of photoreflectors and elastic fabric such as stocking and rubber membrane. The photoreflectors are used to measure the ratio of expansion and contraction of the stocking on the basis of changes in the transmissivity of IR light passing through the stocking. Since a stocking is thin, stretchable, and semi-transparent, it can be easily attached to various types of objects such as mobile devices, robots, and different parts of the body as well as to conventional pressure sensors. It presents natural haptic feedback in accordance with the amount of force exerted. Multiple photoreflectors could determine the direction of a two-dimensional force. Prototyping of a variety of example applications illustrated the utility of such a system.

REFERENCES

1. Baudisch, P., Sinclair, M. and Wilson, A. Soap: a pointing device that works in mid-air. In *Proc. UIST '06*, ACM (2006), pp. 43-46.
2. Cassinelli, A. and Ishikawa, M. Khronos projector. In *ACM SIGGRAPH 2005 Emerging technologies*, ACM (2005), Article 10.

3. Dunne, L., A Coarse Desktop Method for Evaluating Transmission of Vibration through Textile Layers. In *Proc. ISWC '09*, pp. 29-32.
4. Haller, M., Richter, C., Brandl, P., Gross, S., Schossleitner, G., Schrempf, A., Nii, H., Sugimoto, M. and Inami, M. Finding the right way for interrupting people improving their sitting posture. In *Proc. INTERACT '11*, in press.
5. Heo, S. and Lee, G. Force gestures: augmenting touch screen gestures with normal and tangential forces. In *Proc. UIST '11*, ACM (2011), pp. 621-626.
6. Heo, Y. and Bank, H. soak, http://megei.jp/recommends/1?locale=en
7. Herot, C. F. and Weinzapfel, G. One-point touch input of vector information for computer displays. In *Proc. SIGGRAPH '78*, ACM (1978), pp. 210-216.
8. Hoshi, T. and Shinoda, H. 3D Shape Measuring Sheet Utilizing Gravitational and Geomagnetic Fields. In *Proc. SICE Annual Conference 2008*, pp. 915-920.
9. Kadowaki, A., Yoshikai, T., Hayashi, M., Inaba, M. Development of Soft Sensor Exterior Embedded with Multi-axis Deformable Tactile Sensor System. In *Proc. Ro-Man '09*, IEEE (2009), pp. 1093-1098.
10. Kamiyama, K., Kajimoto, H., Vlack, K., Kawakami, N., Mizota, T. and Tachi, S. Gelforce. In *ACM SIGGRAPH 2004 Emerging technologies*, ACM (2004), pp. 5-5.
11. Lumelsky, V. J. Sensitive Skin. *IEEE Sensors Journal*, IEEE (2001), vol. 1, no. 1, pp. 41-51.
12. Miaw, D. R. and Raskar, R. Second skin: motion capture with actuated feedback for motor learning. In *Ext. Abst. CHI '09*, ACM (2009), pp. 4537-4542.
13. Miyashita, T., Tajika, T., Ishiguro, H., Kogure, K. and Hagita, N. Haptic communication between humans and robots. In *Proc. ISRR '05*, 2005.
14. Mutlu, B., Krause, A., Forlizzi, J., Guestrin, C. and Hodgins, J. Robust, low-cost, non-intrusive sensing and recognition of seated postures. In *Proc. UIST '07*, ACM (2007), pp. 149-158.
15. Ohmura, Y., Nagakubo, A. and Kuniyoshi, Y. Conformable and scalable tactile sensor skin for curved surfaces. In *Proc. ICRA '06*, IEEE (2006), pp. 1348-1353.
16. Perner-Wilson, H. and Buechley, L. Making textile sensors from scratch. In *Proc. TEI '10*, ACM (2010), pp. 349-352.
17. Shimojo, M., Namiki, A., Ishikawa, M., Makino, R. and Mabuchi, K. A tactile sensor sheet using pressure conductive rubber with electricalwires stitched method. *IEEE Sensors Journal*, vol. 4, pp. 589-596, 2004.
18. Slyper, R., Poupyrev, I. and Hodgins, J. Sensing through structure: designing soft silicone sensors. In *Proc. TEI '11*, ACM (2011), pp. 213-220.
19. Smith, R. T., Thomas, B. H. and Piekarski, W. Digital foam interaction techniques for 3D modeling. In *Proc. VRST '08*, ACM (2008), pp. 61-68.
20. Sugiura, Y., Kakehi, G., Withana, A., Lee, C., Sakamoto, D., Sugimoto, M., Inami, M. and Igarashi, T. Detecting shape deformation of soft objects using directional photoreflectivity measurement. In *Proc. UIST '11*, ACM (2011), pp. 509-516.
21. Wada, K. and Shibata, T. Social effects of robot therapy in a care house - change of social network of the residents for two months. In *Proc. ICRA '07*, IEEE (2007), pp. 1250-1255.
22. Yamane, N., Ohka, M. and Mitsuya, Y. Methods to Enhance Accuracy of an Optical Three-axis Tactile Sensor. *JSME annual meeting 2000(1)*, pp. 229-230. (In Japanese)

Capacitive Fingerprinting: Exploring User Differentiation by Sensing Electrical Properties of the Human Body

Chris Harrison[1, 2]
[1] Disney Research Pittsburgh,
4720 Forbes Avenue,
Pittsburgh, PA 15213 USA
ivan.poupyrev@disneyresearch.com

Munehiko Sato[1, 3]
[2] Carnegie Mellon University,
5000 Forbes Avenue,
Pittsburgh, PA 15213 USA
chris.harrison@cs.cmu.edu

Ivan Poupyrev[1]
[3] Graduate School of Engineering,
The University of Tokyo,
Hongo 7-3-1, Tokyo, 113 Japan
munehiko@acm.org

ABSTRACT
At present, touchscreens can differentiate multiple points of contact, but not who is touching the device. In this work, we consider how the electrical properties of humans and their attire can be used to support user differentiation on touchscreens. We prop0se a novel sensing approach based on Swept Frequency Capacitive Sensing, which measures the impedance of a user to the environment (i.e., ground) across a range of AC frequencies. Different people have different bone densities and muscle mass, wear different footwear, and so on. This, in turn, yields different impedance profiles, which allows for touch events, including multitouch gestures, to be attributed to a particular user. This has many interesting implications for interactive design. We describe and evaluate our sensing approach, demonstrating that the technique has considerable promise. We also discuss limitations, how these might be overcome, and next steps.

Author Keywords
User identification; ID; login; collaborative multi-user interaction; swept frequency capacitive sensing; SFCS; Touché; touchscreens; finger input; gestures.

ACM Classification Keywords
H.5.2 [Information interfaces and presentation]: User Interfaces - Graphical user interfaces; Input devices and strategies.

General Terms
Human Factors, Design.

INTRODUCTION
Touch interaction is pervasive, especially on mobile devices. In a typical touch-sensitive interface, applications receive touch coordinates for each finger, and possibly contact ellipsoids as well. However, there is usually no notion as to who is touching – a valuable contextual cue, which could enable a wide range of exciting collaborative and multiplayer interactions [12,19,25,28,30].

There are two basic classes of touch-centric computing that could be enhanced with user identification and tracking. Foremost are large touchscreens, situated on desktops, mounted on walls, or placed horizontally, such as interactive tabletops [20]. These are sufficiently large to accommodate multiple users interacting simultaneously. Second are handheld mobile devices. Their small size and weight allows for them to be easily passed around among multiple users, enabling asynchronous co-located collaboration [16]. Tablet devices occupy the middle ground: portable enough to be easily shared among multiple users, while also providing sufficient surface area for two or more people to interact simultaneously.

In this paper we consider how the electrical properties of users' bodies can be used for *differentiation* – the ability to tell users apart, but not necessarily uniquely identify them. The outcome of our explorations is a promising, novel sensing approach based on Swept Frequency Capacitive Sensing (SFCS) [26]. This approach, which we call *Capacitive Fingerprinting,* allows touchscreens, or other touch sensitive devices, to not only report finger touch locations, but also identify to which user that finger belongs. Our technique supports single finger touches, multitouch finger gestures (e.g., two-finger pinch), bi-manual manipulations [5], and shape contacts [6], such as a palm press. Importantly, our technique requires no user instrumentation – they simply use their fingers as they would on a conventional touchscreen. Further, our technique could be made mobile and enhance a broad variety of mobile devices and applications. Our experiments show the approach is feasible. In a controlled lab study, touches from pairs of users were differen-

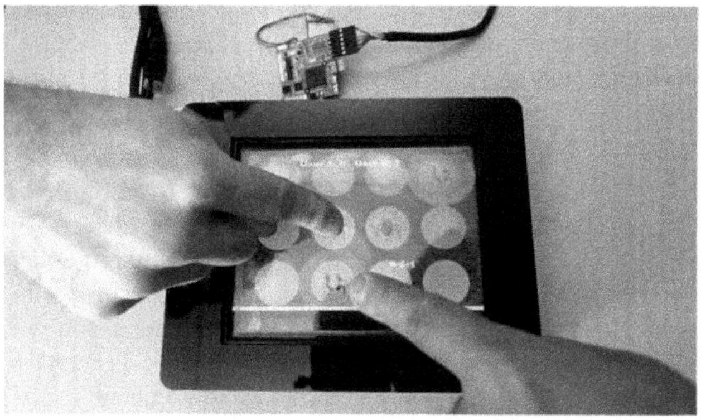

Figure 1. Example two-player "Whac-A-Mole" game. Red highlights indicate user one hits; green for user two. Individual score is kept and shown at top of screen.

UIST '12, October 7–10, 2012, Cambridge, Massachusetts, USA.

tiated with an accuracy of 96 percent. Put simply, four touches in 100 were incorrectly attributed to the other user.

RELATED APPROACHES

User identification has implications in many application domains, including security, personalization, and groupware. The fundamental goal of user identification is to understand *who is controlling the input at any given moment* and adjusts interaction or functionality accordingly. Attempts to support co-located multi-user interaction on shared displays goes back to at least the late 1980's, with systems such as Boardnoter [29] and Commune [3]. The conceptual and social underpinnings of Single Display Groupware have been extensively researched by Stewart, Bederson, Gutwin and others (see e.g., [12,30]). More recently, there have been efforts to develop toolkits to facilitate "identity enabled" applications [19,23,25,28].

There are significant technical challenges in developing and deploying technologies for user identification, particularly on touchscreens. Foremost, and perhaps most challenging, is that the best techniques avoid instrumenting the user. Further, there should be minimal or no instrumentation of the environment, as external infrastructure is costly and prohibits mobility. Furthermore, the technique must be fast and robust, identifying a large number of users both sequentially and simultaneously. Additionally, it should be inexpensive, easily deployable, sufficiently compact, and have low power requirements, thus making integration into mobile devices feasible. Currently, we are not aware of any system that satisfies all of these requirements.

In attempting to answer this challenge, there has been significant effort put forth to develop technical solutions that can support user identification on touchscreens. One approach is to not uniquely identify each user per se, but rather distinguish that there are multiple users operating at the same time. For example, in Medusa [1], the presence of multiple users can be inferred by proximity sensing around the periphery of an augmented table. Touches to the surface can be attributed to a particular user by using arm orientation sensed by an array of proximity sensors on the table bezel. If users exit the sensing zone, knowledge of the user is lost; upon returning, the user is treated as new. Similarly, Dang et al. [8] used finger orientation cues to back-project to a user, achieving a similar outcome. In both systems, occlusion and users in close proximity (i.e., side by side) are problematic.

Another approach to user identification is to capture identifying features, such that each can be uniquely recognized. One option is to instrument the user with an identifying item, for example, fiducial markers [19] or infrared-code-emitting accessories [21,24]. Researchers have also considered biometric features, such as face [35], hand contour [27] and fingerprint analysis [15,31]. MultiToe [2] uses a series of down-facing Kinect cameras to segment users' shoes for identification purposes. DiamondTouch [9] and DT Controls [10] uniquely ground each user (e.g., through a chair or floor mat wired to the sensing electronics). Because the electrical path is unique to each user, touches on a large shared screen can be sensed quickly and reliably. All of these techniques require large, static setups and/or instrumentation of the user, increasing both cost and complexity, and not permitting truly mobile, ad-hoc interaction.

Finally, there are several systems that employ uniquely identifiable pens, such as in Wacom tablets [32], which use electromagnetic resonance sensing to identify several styli, which could be attributable to different users. TapSense [14] used pens with different tip materials, allowing for pen disambiguation through acoustic sensing. Although robust, these approaches do not support the highly popular direct touch interaction.

CONTRIBUTION

The salient distinguishing feature of our user differentiation approach is that it allows direct touch interaction without requiring instrumentation of either the user or environment – sensing electronics are fully contained within the device. This important property sets it apart from all previous techniques. Further, our technology is sufficiently compact, low-powered and inexpensive to enable integration into mobile devices and allow for truly mobile interactions. Additionally, user classification occurs in real time; the initial "first-touch" calibration takes less than a second. Finally, our approach is not sensitive to occlusion, orientation, lighting, or other factors that are problematic for computer vision driven methods.

At present, *Capacitive Fingerprinting* also has several drawbacks. Foremost, it can differentiate only among a small set of concurrent users. Further, users can only touch sequentially, not simultaneously. There are additional limitations regarding the persistence of identification. Finally, although our experimental results are promising, robustness needs to be improved for real world use.

Nonetheless, this work puts forward a novel and attractive approach for user differentiation that has not been proposed previously. This paper assesses and confirms the feasibility of the approach and expands the toolbox of techniques HCI researchers and practitioners can draw upon. Similar to any other user identification approach, *Capacitive Fingerprinting* offers a distinct set of pros and cons. Given that a sensor fusion approach might ultimately prove strongest for user identification, we believe that our approach may fill important gaps in the feature space used for classification. We hope this work will contribute to the ultimate goal of robust and unobtrusive technologies for differentiating and identifying users in a broad variety of applications.

CAPACITIVE FINGERPRINTING

Our approach is based on the fundamental observation that every human body has varying levels of bone density, muscle mass, blood volume and a plethora of other biological and anatomical factors. Furthermore, users also wear different shoes and naturally assume different postures, which alters how a user is grounded. As a consequence, the electrical properties of a particular user can be fairly unique, like a *fingerprint*, from which we derive our system's name. Therefore, if one can accurately measure the electrical properties of a user, it should be possible to identify, or at least differentiate, the person.

Humans have a multitude of electrical properties that can be measured, such as vital signs (e.g., EKG). In this paper, we estimate impedance profiles of users at different frequencies, by using recently proposed SFCS techniques [26]. The advantage of SFCS is that it is trivial to instrument devices, as only a single electrode and wire are needed. Furthermore, it is inexpensive, and it does not require user to wear or hold any additional devices. We are not aware of previous attempts to explore SFCS for user identification.

The fundamental physical principle behind *Capacitive Fingerprinting* is that the path of alternating current (AC) in a human body depends on the signal frequency [11]. This is because the opposition of body tissues, blood, bones, etc., to the flow of electrical current – or body electrical impedance – is also frequency dependent. For example, at 1 kHz bone has a resistivity of approximately 45 Ω•m, but at 1 MHz it's resistivity increases to ~90 Ω•m (Figure 2) [11]. Since the AC signal always flows along the path of least impedance, it is theoretically possible to direct the flow of the current through various paths inside the user's body by sweeping over a range of frequencies.

As the signal flows through the body, the signal amplitude and phase change differently at different frequencies. These changes can be measured in real time and used to build a frequency-to-impedance profile. Different people, by virtue of having unique bodies, should exhibit slightly different profiles. Although we do not specifically model this relationship, our fingerprint-based classification approach relies on it.

Importantly, *Capacitive Fingerprinting* is a non-invasive technique – we do not require a special purpose ground electrode be coupled to users (as in [9,10]). Instead, we use the natural environment as ground (i.e., the floor). This also means shoes influence the impedance profile. As shown in [2], users' shoes are also fairly unique and aid poster classification.

We should note that impedance measurements of the human body have been used since the 1970s in medical diag-

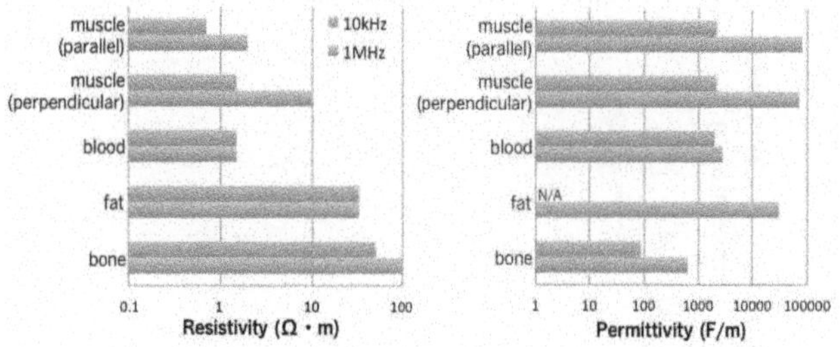

Figure 2. Mean permittivity and resistivity of different tissues (from [11]).

nostics, such as measuring fluid composition and BMI [11,17] and electro-impedance tomography imaging [7]. Despite a long history of such measurements, the correlation between measured body impedance and properties of the human body are still not fully understood [11]. Most often, just one or two frequencies are used for such measurements and we are not aware of any attempts to apply this technique in HCI applications. *Capacitive Fingerprinting* should not be confused with galvanic skin response (GSR), which measures the conductivity of the skin (see e.g., [18,22] for applications in HCI).

PROTOTYPE

We created a proof-of-concept system seen in Figure 1 and schematically described in Figure 3. To capture and classify impedance profiles among a small set of users, we employ Swept Frequency Capacitive Sensing (SFCS), introduced as Touché [26]. Beyond the Touché sensor board, our system consists of a 6.7" LCD panel, a 6.4" IR touch screen, and an Indium Tin Oxide (ITO) coated transparent plastic sheet.

The Touché sensor board generates a 6.6V peak-to-peak sinusoidal wave, ranging in frequency from 1KHz to 3.5MHz, using 200 steps. This signal is injected into an ITO sheet situated on top of the LCD panel. When a user touches the ITO sheet, an electrical connection to the Touché sensor is created (the user is also grounded to the environment). The current of the sine wave is significantly lower than 0.5 mA, safe for humans and on par with commercially available touchscreens [33]. Impedance profiles are sent over USB to a computer approximately 33 times per second. Note that our present sensor board does not measure the true impedance of the body, but rather measures the amplitude component. Specifically, it creates a voltage-

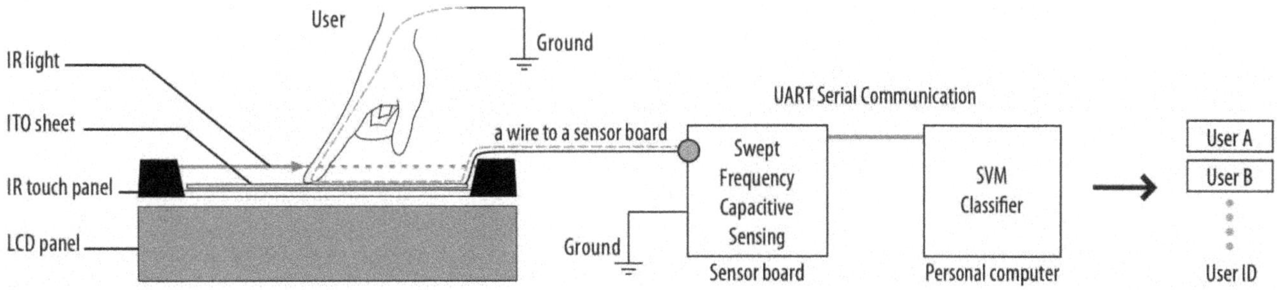

Figure 3. A cutaway view of the touchscreen layers, which are connected to a Touché sensor board. Here, when a user touches the screen; our classifier attributes the touch event to a set of users that have previously logged in.

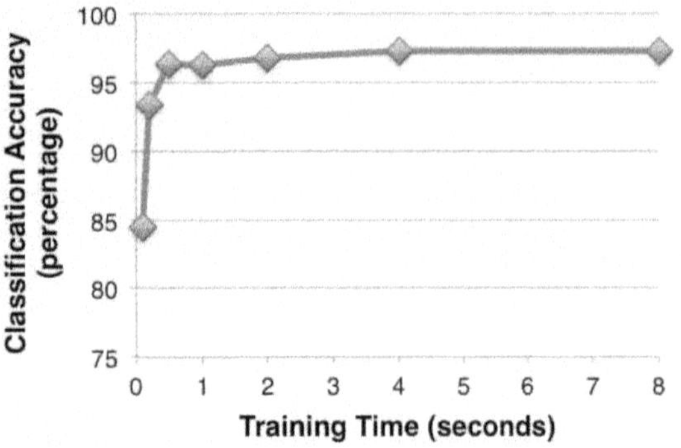

Figure 4. Impact on classification performance by varying classifier training data from 0.1 seconds (1 sample per participant) to 8 seconds (80 samples per participant).

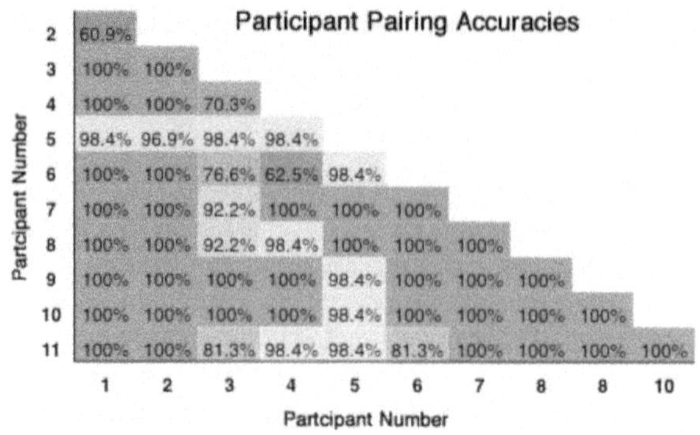

Figure 5. Classification accuracies for all trial participant pairings. Classifer was trained using 0.5 seconds of finger training data (5 samples per participant).

divider circuit with a resistor and samples this with an AD converter. We leave measurement of the phase component to future work.

We first attempted to build our system on top of a capacitive touch input panel. However, we found that the conductive nature of the ITO sheet interfered with touch sensing. Simultaneously, the conductive layers inside capacitive and resistive touchscreens interfered with SFCS. This necessitated the use of an electrically passive sensing technology. We selected an IR-driven touch panel, though several other technologies are applicable (e.g., Surface Wave Acoustic). It is important to note, however, that with tighter hardware integration it may be possible to use e.g., a projective capacitive touchscreen for both touch and impedance sensing.

The final component of our system is a conventional computer running a classification engine. We use a Support Vector Machine (SVM) implementation provided by the Weka Toolkit [13] (SMO, C=2.0, polynomial kernel, e=1.0). We employ the same feature set used successfully in [26]. Our setup provides 200-point impedance profiles 33 times per second. When a user first touches the screen, ten impedance profiles are captured, taking approximately 300ms. Each profile is classified in real time; a majority-voting scheme is used to decide on the final classification. This improves accuracy, as the first 100ms of touch can be unstable due to the user not yet making full contact. This final classification result is paired with the last touch event.

EXPERIMENTAL EVALUATION

The first fundamental question that we aim to answer in this paper is: *can we use measured electrical properties of a user's body for differentiation*? To answer this question, we conducted an evaluation that included 11 participants (two female, mean age 28.1) recruited from our industrial research lab. Our evaluation consisted of two phases. First, we collected data for the purpose of training our classifier. The second phase collected independent data for the purpose of evaluating our classifiers. The experiment took approximately 20 minutes.

Procedure

During the *training data* collection, users were asked to touch a single point in the center of the screen for 8 seconds while rocking their finger back-and-forth and side-to-side (see Video Figure). This helped to capture variability in finger pose and pressure that might be naturally encountered through extended use, but unlikely reflected in a typical, single touch event. During the touch period, 10 samples were collected per second, yielding 80 data points per participant. We were also interested in evaluating how the technique scaled to other gestures beyond simple finger touches. The same procedure was used to collect data for a two-finger pinch (using one hand), a bi-modal two-finger touch, and resting the palm on the screen.

Note that we deliberately chose to collect data from a single touch (i.e., single point) on the touchscreen, as this best simulated a "login button" experience. Although multi-point collection would yield more data, and potentially stronger results, pilot testing suggested that this would be impractical for real world use and applications.

During *testing data* collection, a 4x4 grid of numbered crosshairs was provided as touch targets. Users were asked to touch, with a single finger, each crosshair in order. Two rounds were completed, yielding 32 touch events per participant. In addition, participants performed, in locations of their choosing, ten one-handed pinches, ten bi-modal two-finger touches, and ten palm touches. In total, this process provided 62 touch events, using four different gestures, distributed over the entire surface of the screen.

When investigating a new sensing technique, it is beneficial to control various experimental factors so as to best isolate the innate performance of the technique. Once this has been established, it is then interesting to relax various constraints to explore the broader feasibility. Following this mantra, during the experiment users were asked to stand with both feet on the floor, providing a relatively consistent connection to the floor.

Pairing Users

To assess our system's feasibility, we investigated user differentiation accuracy for pairs of users. Instead of running a small number of pairs live, we used train/test data from our 11 participants to simulate 55 pairings (all combinations of participants). For example, in a trial pairing participant 1 with participant 2, the system was initialized with

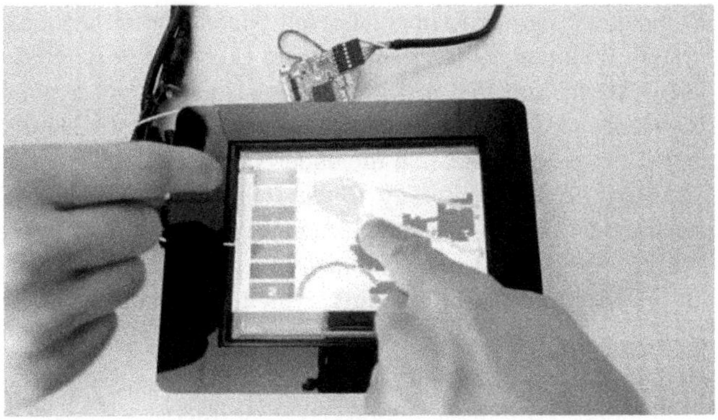

Figure 6. Example painting application. Two users can select colors from a palette on the left of screen. The system records each user's selection, allowing users to paint in a personalized color.

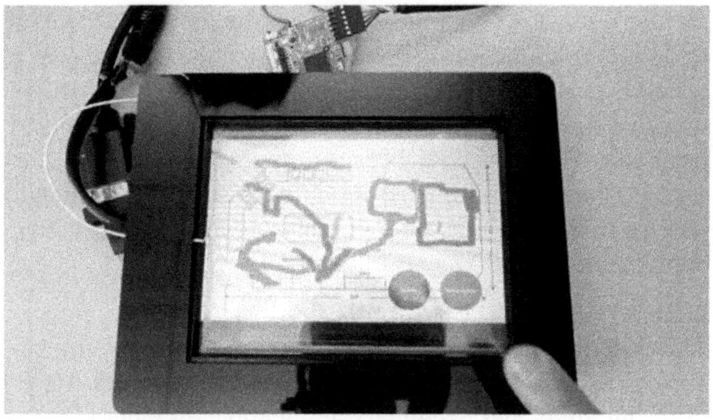

Figure 7. Exampl sketching application. Each user has a different drawing color to attribute edits. An "undo" button is provided, allowing users to undo strokes from their personal edit history.

training data from 1 and 2. The resulting classifier was then fed unlabeled testing data from participants 1 and 2 combined and in a random order. This simulated sequential touch events as if the users were co-located. From the perspective of the classifier, this was no different than real-time operation.

Results

Looking first at single finger touches, performance using all 8 seconds of training data yielded an all-pairs average accuracy of 97.3% (SD=5.9%). Figure 4 illustrates the classification performance with different volumes of training data, varying from 0.1 second (1 training sample per participant) to 8 seconds (80 training samples per participant). Performance significantly plateaus after 0.5 seconds of training data (5 training sample per participant), which achieves 96.4% accuracy (SD=9.0%). Figure 5 shows classification accuracies for all user pairings. Of note, two thirds of pairings had 100% differentiation accuracy.

These findings underscore two key strengths of our approach. Foremost, the fact the system is able to perform at 84.5% accuracy (SD=18.9%) with a single training instance from each user suggests the feature space we selected is highly discriminative between users. Second, 0.5 seconds appears to be a sweet spot, in particular, a nice balance between classification accuracy and training duration. Whereas an 8-second login sequence would significantly interrupt interactive use, 500ms is sufficiently quick to be of minimal distraction. Given that our current approach requires users to login each time they want the system to differentiate them, this interaction has to be extremely lightweight if it is to be practical.

We ran a second, post-hoc simulation that included all gestures: single finger touches, one-handed pinches, bi-modal two-finger touches, and palm touches. The goal was not to distinguish between different gestures, as demonstrated in [26], but rather to distinguish between users performing a variety of gestures. Our classifier was trained on 20 samples per participant (5 samples per gesture), representing 2 seconds of training data. Our testing data consisted of all 62 touch events from our testing data collection. Again using all 55 simulated participant pairings, average accuracy was 97.8% (SD=6.9%). This is very similar in performance to finger-touch-only performance using 2 seconds of training data (both classifiers were trained on 20 samples per participant).

We repeated the latter experiment using a single frequency in order to demonstrate the utility of employing a swept frequency approach. We used attribute selection to identify 753.5kHz as the single best frequency at which to differentiate users. It should be noted that in a real world system this ideal frequency depends on the set of users and environmental conditions, and thus cannot be known *a priori* – thus our estimate is idealized. On average, user differentiation was 87.3% accurate vs. 97.8% when all frequencies were used, or roughly six times the error rate.

EXAMPLE APPLICATIONS

The second research question that we would like to answer in this paper is: *what are the real-world implications of this technique*? To begin to address this question, we designed three simple exemplary applications based on *Capacitive Fingerprinting*. These applications demonstrate different interaction possibilities if user differentiation was available on touchscreens (see also the accompanying Video Figure).

For example, there are many games, especially for tablets, that allow two users to play simultaneously. When individual scoring or control is needed, interfaces most typically have a split view. However, this limits game design possibilities and decreases the available screen real estate for each player. Using *Capacitive Fingerprinting*, it is possible for two players to interact in a common game space. To demonstrate this, we created a "Whac-A-Mole" game [34], seen in Figure 1. Targets appear out of random holes; players must press these with their fingers before they return underground. Each time a player successfully hits a target, he gains a point; individual scores are kept for each player automatically and transparently for each user.

In another example, we created a painting application (Figure 6), where two users can paint with their own selected color. For example, User A can select red and paint in red, while User B can select blue and paint in blue without affecting User A's selection. This could be trivially extended to brush type, thickness, opacity, and similar features. In a general sense, *Capacitive Fingerprinting* ought to allow users to operate on the touch interface with personalized properties [25]. Further, because applications identify the owner of each stroke, it is possible to support individualized undo stacks – a feature we built into a simple sketching application (Figure 7).

LIMITATIONS AND CHALLENGES

The experimental results suggest that measuring the impedance of users is a promising differentiation approach. However, our study and exemplary applications brought to light several limitations and challenges. These include:

Persistence of identification: Calibration seems to be sensitive to changes in the human body over the course of the day. Thus, walking away and returning hours (or certainly days) later is not currently possible. We hypothesize that environmental factors, such as ambient temperature and humidity, as well as biological factors, such as blood pressure and hydration, cause impedance profiles to drift over time. This personal change variability can be larger than between-person variability. This suggests use scenarios where interaction is ad hoc and relatively short, or where the precision of recognition is not critical.

Because of this limitation, we instituted a login procedure for all of our example applications. Specifically, when a user wants to join a multi-user collocated interaction, he must first press and hold a "login button" (see Video Figure). This triggers the system to capture an impedance profile (of the finger pressing the button) and retrain the classifier. As discussed in the evaluation section, this interaction can be completed as quickly as 500ms.

Ground connection: The electrical properties of the user cannot be taken separately from the electrical properties of the environment. However, since the environment is typically the same for co-located users, per-user differences are detectable. The system is sensitive to how a user is connected to ground. For example, if a user logs into the system while seated and then attempts to use it standing, recognition can be poor. By changing the global impedance of a user so dramatically, the user variations are often obscured. The user must re-login so as to register a new impedance profile. Future work is required to study this in more detail, as well as to develop possible techniques to overcome this limitation.

Sequential touch: A further limitation is that our system currently uses a single electrode, covering the entire touch surface. As a consequence, our current prototype can only process a single touch at a time (i.e., two users cannot press the screen simultaneously and be differentiated). It is likely, though not tested, that a mosaic of electrodes, as seen in some forms of projective capacitive touchscreens, could be used to overcome this by sampling the smaller regions that are unlikely to fit two users.

Robustness: Our experimental results suggest a fairly robust system with paired-user accuracies in excess of 96%. However, we caution that a controlled lab study is not a good proxy for real-world use. Our experimental results should be viewed as evidence that the underlying technique is valid and may be a tenable way forward for supporting instrumentation-free, identity-enabled, mobile touchscreen interaction – the first technique to achieve this end. This opens up the possibility of future work, which we discuss next.

FUTURE WORK

Combining *Capacitive Fingerprinting* with other sensing techniques is of great interest. Sensor fusion approaches generally aim to merge multiple imperfect techniques to achieve a superior outcome. Our approach has a unique set of strengths and weaknesses that lend well to this approach. We are also interested in exploring adaptive classifiers, where the system could continuously collect training data from users and integrate changes, including natural drift.

It may also be possible to identify specific situations where the difference between two users is sufficiently dramatic, so that login is no longer necessary and a persistent general classifier can be used. One example application scenario is differentiation between parents and children, or teacher and young student, where games and educational experiences may be designed according to who is providing input. For example, in an educational application a teacher could draw a hint to help a student solve a math problem; the hint then would fade out after a few seconds, prompting the student to complete the problem him or herself.

Finally, we are also interested in exploring applications of *Capacitive Fingerprinting* in highly controlled environments or applications where exact user identification is not necessary - so called *soft biometrics*. In-car entertainment systems are a prime example. We are also curious as to how our approach could be applied to differentiating between humans and non-humans (e.g., bags, drinks) in ride systems and other applications.

CONCLUSION

In this paper we have described how sensing of humans electrical properties can be used for interactive user differentiation. We integrated this approach into a small, touchscreen device and built three simple demo applications to highlight some basic uses of user-aware interaction. The evaluation of our sensing technique demonstrated that the approach holds significant promise. We hope that the current research will encourage HCI researchers and practitioners to investigate this interesting and exciting technology direction.

AKNOWLEDGEMENTS

We are grateful to Zhiquan Yeo, Josh Griffin, Jonas Loh and Scott Hudson for their significant contributions in investigating early prototypes of Touché, on which this work is based. We are also thankful to Disney Research and The Walt Disney Corporation for continued support of this research effort.

REFERENCES

1. Annett, M., Grossman, T., Wigdor, D., and Fitzmaurice, G. Medusa: a proximity-aware multi-touch tabletop. In *Proc. UIST '11*. 337-346.
2. Augsten, T., Kaefer, K., Meusel, R., Fetzer, C., Kanitz, D., Stoff, T., Becker, T., Holz, C., and Baudisch, P. Multitoe: high-precision interaction with back-projected floors based on high-resolution multi-touch input. In *Proc. UIST '10*. 209-218.
3. Bly, S.A., and Minneman, S.L. Commune: A Shared Drawing Surface." In *SIGOIS Bulletin*, Massachusetts, 1990. 184-192.
4. Burges, C.J. A Tutorial on Support Vector Machines for Pattern Recognition. *Data Mining and Know. Disc.*, 2.2, June 1998. 121-167.
5. Buxton, W., and Myers, B. A study in two-handed input. In *Proc. CHI '86*. 321-326.
6. Cao, X., Wilson, A., Balakrishnan, R., Hinckley, K., and Hudson, S.E. ShapeTouch: Leveraging contact shape on interactive surfaces. In *Proc. TABLETOP '08*. 129-136.
7. Cheney, M., Isaacson, D., and Newell, J.C. Electrical impedance tomography. *SIAM Review*, 41(1), 1999. 85-101.
8. Dang, C.T., Straud, M., and Andre, E. Hand distinction for multi-touch tabletop interaction. In *Proc. ITS '09*. 101-108
9. Dietz, P. and Leigh, D. DiamondTouch: a multi-user touch technology. In *Proc. UIST '01*. 219-226.
10. Dietz, P.H., Harsham, B., Forlines, C., Leigh, D., Yerazunis, W., Shipman, S., Schmidt-Nielsen, B., and Ryall, K. DT controls: adding identity to physical interfaces. In *Proc. UIST '05*. 245-252.
11. Foster, K.R. and Lukaski, H.C. Whole-body impedance - what does it measure? *The American Jour. of Clinical Nutrition, 64* (3), 1996. 388S-396S.
12. Gutwin, C., Greenberg, S., Blum, R. and Dyck, J. Supporting Informal Collaboration in Shared Workspace Groupware. HCI Report 2005-01, U. Saskatchewan, Canada. 2005.
13. Hall, M., Frank, E., Holmes, G., Pfahringer, B., Reutemann, P., and Witten, I.H. The WEKA Data Mining Software: An Update. *SIGKDD Explor.*, 11(1), 2009.
14. Harrison, C., Schwarz, J., and Hudson, S.E. TapSense: enhancing finger interaction on touch surfaces. In *Proc. UIST '11*. 627-636.
15. Holz, C. and Baudisch, P. The generalized perceived input point model and how to double touch accuracy by extracting fingerprints. In *Proc. CHI '10*. 581-590.
16. Lucero, A., Holopainen, J., and Jokela, T. Pass-them-around: collaborative use of mobile phones for photo sharing. In *Proc. CHI '11*. 1787-1796.
17. Lukaski, H., Johnson, P., Bolonchuk, W., and Lykken, G. Assessment of fat-free mass using bioelectrical impedance measurements of the human body. *The American Jour. of Clinical Nutrition*. 41, 4 (1985), 810-817.
18. Mandryk, R.L. and Inkpen, K.M. Physiological indicators for the evaluation of co-located collaborative play. In *Proc. CSCW '04*. 102-111.
19. Marquardt, N., Kiemer, J., Ledo, D., Boring, S., and Greenberg, S. Designing user-, hand-, and handpart-aware tabletop interactions with the TouchID toolkit. In *Proc. ITS '11*. 21-30.
20. Matsushita, N. and Rekimoto, J. HoloWall: Designing a Finger; Hand, Body, and Object Sensitive Wall. In *Proc. UIST '97*. 209-210.
21. Meyer, T. and Schmidt, D. IdWristbands: IR-based user identification on multi-touch surfaces. In *Proc. ITS '10*. 277-278.
22. Moore, M.M. and Dua, U. A galvanic skin response interface for people with severe motor disabilities. In *Proc. ASSETS '04*. 48-54.
23. Partridge, G.A. and Irani, P.P. IdenTTop: a flexible platform for exploring identity-enabled surfaces. In *CHI EA '09*. 4411-4416.
24. Roth, V., Schmidt, P., and Guldenring, B. The IR ring: Authenticating users' touches on a multi-touch display. In *Proc. UIST '10*. 259-262.
25. Ryall, K., Esenther, A., Everitt, K., Forlines, C., Morris, M.R., Shen, C., Shipman, S., and Vernier, F. iDwidgets: Parameterizing widgets by user identity. In *Proc. INTERACT '05*. 1124-1128.
26. Sato, M. Poupyrev, I, and Harrison, C. Touché: Enhancing Touch Interaction on Humans, Screens, Liquids, and Everyday Objects. In *Proc. CHI '12*. 483-492.
27. Schmidt, D., Chong, M.K. and Gellersen, H. HandsDown: hand-contour-based user identification for interactive surfaces. In *Proc. NordiCHI '10*. 432-441.
28. Shen, C., Vernier, F.D., Forliens, C., and Ringel M. DiamondSpin: an extensible toolkit for around-the-table interaction. In *Proc. CHI '04*. 167-174.
29. Stefik, M., Bobrow, D. G., Foster, G., Lanning, S., and Tatar, D. WYSIWIS Revised: Early experiences with multiuser interfaces. *IEEE Transactions on Office Information Systems*, 5(2), 1987. 147-167.
30. Stewart, J. Bederson, B., and Druin, A. Single Display Groupware: A Model for Co-present Collaboration. In *Proc. CHI '99*. 286-293.
31. Sugiura, A. and Koseki, Y. A user interface using fingerprint recognition: holding commands and data objects on fingers. In *Proc. UIST '98*. 71-79.
32. Wacom tablet. http://wacom.com/en/Products/Intuos.aspx
33. Webster, J., Editor. *Medical instrumentation: Application and design*. 4th ed. 2008, Wiley. p. 641.
34. Whac-a-mole. http://en.wikipedia.org/wiki/Whac-A-Mole
35. Zhao, W., Chellappa, R., Phillips, P.J., and Rosenfeld, A. Face recognition: A literature survey. *ACM Comput. Surv*. 35(4), Dec. 2003. 399-458.

GripSense: Using Built-In Sensors to Detect Hand Posture and Pressure on Commodity Mobile Phones

Mayank Goel[1], Jacob O. Wobbrock[2], Shwetak N. Patel[1]

[1]Computer Science & Engineering
DUB Group
University of Washington
Seattle, WA 98195 USA
{mayank, shwetak}@cs.washington.edu

[2]The Information School
DUB Group
University of Washington
Seattle, WA 98195 USA
wobbrock@uw.edu

ABSTRACT

We introduce *GripSense*, a system that leverages mobile device touchscreens and their built-in inertial sensors and vibration motor to infer hand postures including one- or two-handed interaction, use of thumb or index finger, or use on a table. GripSense also senses the amount of pressure a user exerts on the touchscreen despite a lack of direct pressure sensors by observing diminished gyroscope readings when the vibration motor is "pulsed." In a controlled study with 10 participants, GripSense accurately differentiated device usage on a table *vs.* in hand with 99.7% accuracy; when in hand, it inferred hand postures with 84.3% accuracy. In addition, GripSense distinguished three levels of pressure with 95.1% accuracy. A usability analysis of GripSense was conducted in three custom applications and showed that pressure input and hand-posture sensing can be useful in a number of scenarios.

ACM Classification: H5.2 [Information interfaces and presentation]: User Interfaces—*graphical user interfaces.*

General terms: Design, Human Factors, Experimentation.

Keywords: Touchscreen; situational impairments; mobile; inertial sensors; gyroscope; hand posture; posture

INTRODUCTION

A typical computer user is no longer confined to a desk in a relatively consistent and comfortable environment. The world's typical computer user is now holding a mobile device smaller than his or her hand, is perhaps outdoors, perhaps in motion, and perhaps carrying more things than just a mobile device. A host of assumptions about a user's environment and capabilities that were tenable in comfortable desktop environments no longer applies to mobile users. This dynamic state of a user's environment can lead to *situational impairments* [28], which pose a significant challenge to effective interaction because our current mobile devices do not have much awareness of our environments or how those environments affect users' abilities [33].

UIST '12, October 7–10, 2012, Cambridge, Massachusetts, USA.

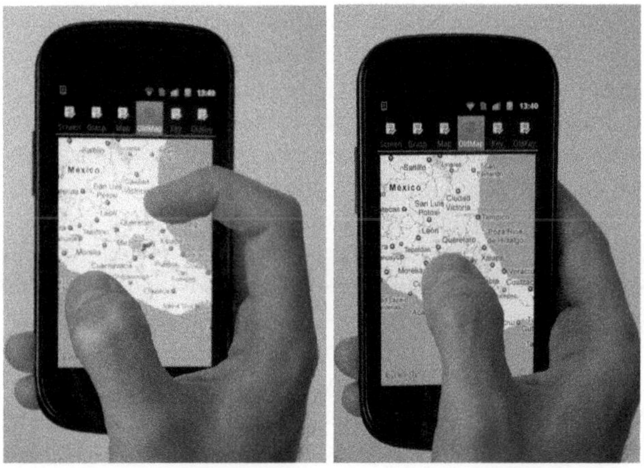

Figure 1. (left) It is difficult for a user to perform interactions like *pinch-to-zoom* with one hand. **(right)** GripSense senses user's hand posture and infers pressure exerted on the screen to facilitate new interactions like zoom-in and zoom-out.

One of the most significant contextual factors affecting mobile device use may be a user's hand posture with which he or she manipulates a mobile device. Research has shown that hand postures including grip, one or two hands, hand pose, the number of fingers used, and so on significantly affect performance and usage of mobile devices [34]. For example, the pointing performance of index fingers is significantly better than thumbs, as is pointing performance when using two hands versus one hand. Similarly, the performance of a user's dominant hand is better than that of his or her non-dominant hand. Research has found distinct touch patterns for different hand postures while typing on on-screen keyboards [1]. And yet our devices, for the most part, have no clue how they are being held or manipulated, and therefore cannot respond appropriately with adapted user interfaces better suited to different hand postures.

Researchers have explored various techniques to accommodate some of these interaction challenges, like the change in device orientation due to hand movement [2,15]. But despite prior explorations, there remains a need to develop new techniques for sensing the hand postures with which people use mobile devices in order to adapt to postural and grip changes during use.

In this paper, we present *GripSense* (Figure 1), a system that uses a combination of the touchscreen and the built-in inertial sensors (gyroscope, accelerometer) and built-in actuators (vibration motors) already present on most commodity mobile phones to infer hand postures and pressure. GripSense detects hand postures over the course of a small number of interaction steps (*e.g.*, tapping, swiping the screen). It infers postures like the use of an index finger, left thumb, right thumb, which hand is holding the device, or whether the phone is lying on a flat surface. GripSense performs this sensing by measuring a device's rotation, tap sizes, and the arc of swiping motions. GripSense additionally leverages the built-in vibration motors in a new way to help infer the amount of pressure being applied to the screen when interacting with the phone, which can be used to enable alternate interaction techniques with mobile devices that have no additional hardware for pressure sensing. As an example, GripSense allows users to zoom-in and zoom-out of maps using pressure input. In addition, GripSense is able to detect when the phone is being squeezed, which could be used to quickly silence a phone while in a pocket. Previous work on hand-posture detection has leveraged accelerometers for detecting whether a device is used in a stationary environment, in a hand, on a table, or in motion [27], and researchers have also used *external sensors* for grip detection [9,22,30]. Leveraging the built-in inertial sensors, vibration motors, and touchscreen for grip and pressure detection has not, until now, been explored.

We evaluated GripSense in a controlled study with 10 participants. Our findings show that GripSense differentiates between device usage in hand or on a flat surface with 99.7% accuracy and various hand postures with 84.3% accuracy and, on an average, makes a decision within 5 "interaction steps"—actions taken by the user that give GripSense information. Based on data collected in our controlled study, we built a three-level pressure detection model for inferring pressure input. GripSense differentiates between three levels of pressure with 95.1% accuracy. Lastly, we also developed three applications that 10 participants used in different settings to qualitatively evaluate the usefulness and usability of GripSense.

The main contributions of this paper are: (1) a new artifact called *GripSense* embodying multiple approaches to sensing mobile device hand-postures using only the built-in sensors present in commodity touchscreen devices; (2) empirical results from an evaluation of GripSense showing that it robustly detects four postures *i.e.*, single-handed operation with left thumb, with right thumb, two-handed operation with either index finger, and operation on a flat surface; and (3) the accurate sensing of three levels of pressure applied to the touchscreen using those hand postures.

RELATED WORK

Our work draws motivation from prior research on exploring solutions for making mobile device interactions easier in different situations and contexts as well as technologies that understand a user's interaction behavior to add new input capabilities to the device.

Situational Impairments and Hand Postures

It has been emphasized by a number of researchers that the devices need to have knowledge of a user's context or situation to provide better support to the user by making interfaces intelligent and invisible (*e.g.,* [18,27]). Recent design approaches have also emphasized this; for example, proactively sensing context is a design principle of *ability-based design* [33], which seeks a better match between interfaces and the abilities of the people who use them. There also has been extensive research in the domain of activity recognition to have a better understanding of the context of a user-in-motion. Choudhury *et al.* [3] developed a small wearable device with number of sensors for activity recognition. Laerhoven and Cakmakci [23] leveraged an accelerometer attached to a phone for recognizing different user motions like walking, climbing stairs, *etc.* Schmidt *et al.* [27] leveraged accelerometers to detect, in addition to user movement, whether a device is held in the hand, is on a table, or is in a suitcase. GripSense contributes to this research area by detecting in which hand and in which hand-posture a device is being used.

Prior to GripSense, others have also proposed techniques for detecting hand postures. Kim *et al.* [22] and Harrison *et al.* [9] used capacitive touch sensors to differentiate between numerous grips. Taylor and Bove [30] additionally leveraged accelerometers to dynamically detect changes in a user's grip for improved interactions. Our system, in contrast, requires no additional instrumentation of a modern smartphone to robustly detect handling grips. The main trade-off for this capability is that the user needs to be interacting with the device for GripSense to make inferences.

Understanding hand posture is important for making devices more intelligent to situational impairments caused by them. Holz *et al.* [16] have evaluated systematic error in target selection due to change in finger posture. Wobbrock *et al.* [34] studied a number of hand postures and evaluated front- and back-of-device finger performance with mobile devices. A number of researchers [14,21,31] suggest that although users prefer single-handed operation while using smartphones, traditional mobile interfaces are designed for two-handed operation. Karlson *et al.* [20] studied such interfaces and evaluated how they impede thumb-based usage. Azenkot and Zhai [1] found that different hand postures induced different touch patterns and affected overall performance while typing on a mobile touchscreen keyboard. AppLens and LaunchTiles [21] attempted to design interfaces mindful of the limited precision and range-of-motion of the thumb. GripSense, using only on-device sensors, robustly detects whether a user is using his left thumb, right thumb, or either index finger to interact with a device.

Inertial Sensors and Force Input

Inertial sensors like accelerometers and gyroscopes have become ubiquitous. Numerous researchers have leveraged these sensors to improve device performance. Joshi *et al.* [19] used them to reduce image blurring due to touch-induced vibrations while using a camera. WalkType [7] used on-device accelerometers to adapt smartphones' keyboards to users' walking movements to reduce text entry errors. Phielipp *et al.* [25] used accelerometers and the sequence of button presses to detect remote control user identity. GripSense derives motivation from such work and uses similar sensors to improve mobile device interaction.

There has been long and consistent interest in augmenting mobile devices with pressure input. Iwasaki *et al.* [17] measured typing pressure on laptop keyboards using on-device accelerometers. Pressure Widgets [26] used a pressure-sensitive stylus for adding pressure-based interactions to PDAs. Clarkson *et al.* [4] instrumented a flip-phone with force sensitive resistors (FSR) to infer continuous pressure applied by the user. Essl *et al.* [5] combined FSR with accelerometers and touch size, inferred from the touchscreen, as a proxy for pressure applied on phone. Force Gestures [12] added detection of tangential forces in a similar setup for richer interactions. Unlike GripSense, most of these efforts required additional device instrumentation.

As with GripSense, there is significant previous work that does not require custom instrumentation. Hinckley *et al.* [14] and Heo and Lee [13] used smartphone accelerometers to leverage touch-induced vibrations as a proxy for pressure. In contrast with our work, these approaches do not get a continuous measure of pressure applied by the user. They provide a coarse proxy of the pressure and only infer the initial velocity with which a user's finger strikes the screen. Although useful in a number of situations, the granularity and frequency of these inferences is limited. Heo and Lee [13] also found that the requirement of increased speed-of-contact results in higher target selection error. We believe this limitation does not impede GripSense.

Grasping and Squeezable Interfaces

Fitzmaurice *et al.* [6] coined the term "graspable user interfaces." Such interfaces allow devices to become more context-sensitive and thereby improve "expressiveness or the communication capacity" of the computer. SqueezeBlock [8] embodies this idea and demonstrates a device that provides feedback by varying its "squishiness." Wimmer *et al.* [32] leveraged computer vision and optical fibers to detect grasping pressure on mobile device surfaces. Harrison *et al.* [9] leveraged FSRs to detect squeezing pressure. These projects required additional device instrumentation to infer grip pressure. GripSense requires no additional hardware for its graspable user interfaces and is a completely software-enabled solution provided one has a commodity smartphone. Another software-only solution, one by Strachan and Murray-Smith [29], used muscle tremor as a proxy for pressure sensing in a squeezable interface. GripSense uses similar phenomenon and combines it with motor-induced vibrations to achieve more fine-grained estimation of pressure.

DESIGN OF *GRIPSENSE*

GripSense uses multiple sources of information to detect a user's hand posture and the amount of pressure exerted in a variety of these postures. Among these sources is the data from device's built-in gyroscope. In case of hand posture detection, the gyroscope is used to measure the direction and amount of rotation of the device in all three axes. For the detection of exerted pressure, the gyroscope is used to measure specific damping characteristics of touch- and motor-induced vibrations. Another source of information is touchscreen interaction data. In this section, we outline the concept and theory behind GripSense.

Inference	Features Used	Sensor Event	Latency
Table *vs.* Hand	Gyroscope (Low frequency in all axes)	Touch Down	1
Thumb *vs.* Index Finger	Gyroscope (Low frequency in *x*- and *y* axis	Touch Down	3
	Swipe Shape	Touch Up	
	Touch Size	Touch Down	
Left Thumb *vs.* Right Thumb	Gyroscope (Low frequency in *y*-axis	Touch Down	5
	Swipe Shape	Touch Up	
	Touch Size	Touch Down	
Pressure in hand	Gyroscope (Low Frequency)	Touch Down	1
	Gyroscope (High Frequency) + Motor		
Pressure on table	Gyroscope (High frequency) + Motor	Touch Down	1
Squeeze	Gyroscope (High frequency) + Motor	Held in Hand	0

Table 1. Summary of all inferences made by GripSense and when and which features were used for each of them.

Inferring Hand Posture

GripSense uses touchscreen interaction and device rotation information to infer whether the phone is (*a*) in a user's left hand and operated with left thumb, (*b*) in a user's right hand and operated with right thumb, (*c*) in either hand and operated with the index finger of the other hand, (*d*) on a flat surface, or (*e*) being only grasped by the user and not operated. Karlson *et al.* [21] discussed how limited precision and extent of the human thumb impedes one-handed mobile touchscreen interaction. We use this information in GripSense to detect hand postures. We use a combination of three features: (1) relative variance in rotation, (2) change in touch size, and (3) direction of arc for finger swipes. These features were extracted on a Samsung Nexus S smartphone running Android OS 2.3.

Rotation of the Device. The first feature is the rotational movement of the device as the user touches the screen. In a one-handed interaction, the phone rotates in response to touches at the top of the screen more than it does to touches at the bottom of the screen (Figure 2). This is to compensate for the limited range of the thumb; fingers move the device as the thumb extends to reach the top of the screen.

In contrast, touches at the bottom of the screen result in less angular motion because that area is usually within the thumb's range. When the user interacts using their index finger, there is no difference in the angular motion from touches at the top or the bottom of the screen. If the device is on a table then there is no change in any of these parameters before the touch event is registered.

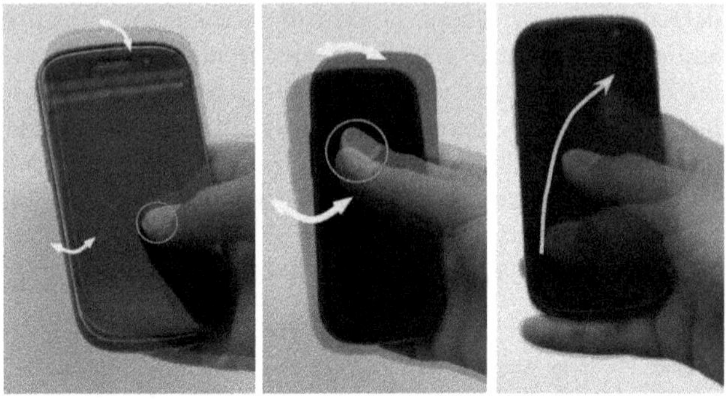

Figure 2. (left) Minimal device rotation in *x*- and *y*-axis, and smaller touch size when the user touches nearby with the thumb. **(center)** Significantly more rotation in *x*- and *y*- axis and larger touch size when the far quadrant of the screen is touched. **(right)** The shape of the swipe arc in the case of right thumb. (All of these phenomena are mirror-imaged for the left thumb.)

To leverage these insights, we store the angular velocities around the *x*-axis sampled at 1 kHz from the gyroscope in a quarter-second buffer. The data in the buffer is passed through a low-pass filter to isolate the low frequency angular velocities. We record the last two angular velocities observed for touches in the top third of the screen and the bottom third of the screen (determined from a pilot with four users). If the difference in variance of angular velocities for touches in the top is five times greater than for touches in the bottom of the screen, we assumed that it was thumb-based interaction.

If the difference in the variances does not exceed the threshold for three consecutive touches, then we bias our final decision towards selecting "index finger."

Similarly, when a user holds the phone in their left hand and interacts with their thumb, touches on the right of the screen cause more angular motion than touches nearer to the palm, again because of the compensation for the limited motion range of the thumb (Figure 2). In the case of the right hand, more motion is seen from touches on the left of the screen. If a thumb-based interaction is inferred, we use a similar approach as before, except now we log the variance in the *y*-axis of the gyroscope for touches on the left third of the screen and the right third of the screen. If the variance in angular velocity of the last two touches on the left side is greater than that on the right side, then we assume the phone is in the right hand (left hand if the variance on the right is greater). Moreover, if the difference in angular velocities is more than ten times greater in consecutive touches, we set a "high confidence flag" which is used to bias our final decision towards using this feature (discussed later).

Touch Size. The second feature is based on the change of size of touch in different regions of the touch screen. We hypothesize that in one-handed interaction when the user interacts with the left and right sides of the screen, the size of the touch changes because of the shape of the thumb and rotation of the device in the user's hand. The touch size on the same side as the thumb will be smaller than the touch size on the far side away from the thumb (Figure 2).

For this feature, we divide the screen into six (2×3) parts and keep track of last two touch sizes. Note that the Android platform provides a method to get the touch size on the screen. This method is supported by most Android smartphones available in the market. We compare touch sizes in the left third and right third of the screen for the same third of the screen height. If the difference in the mean of the touch sizes is more than 25%, we bias the system towards a thumb-based interaction. If the larger tap size is on the left side, then the system believes it is right thumb, and vice versa. Moreover, if the difference in touch sizes is more than 40% for consecutive touches, the heuristic sets a "high confidence flag." If the difference is less than 25%, it biases toward index finger-based interaction.

Shape of the Swipe Arc. This feature is only applicable when the user swipes on the screen. Because of the shape and position of the thumb, users often draw an exaggerated arc instead of a relatively straight line. Karlson *et al.* [21] observed similar arcs and analyzed how an interface can be more effective by limiting interaction within this arc. We use this arc as our "signal" to detect the user's hand posture. While using the phone with the index finger there is no consistent arc. However, with the thumb there is a consistent, exaggerated arc to the right or left depending on which thumb is being used. Figure 2 shows the arc formed by the right thumb while performing a bottom-to-top swipe. A mirror image of this arc will form in the case of the left thumb.

If the difference in coordinates of the start and end position of a vertical swipe are more than 5% of the screen resolution, GripSense biases itself towards one of the two thumb postures. Even so, we observed that sometimes a thumb-based swipe does not result in an arc. Instead, the phone experiences angular motion in the hand. For example, a right-handed swipe from bottom to top results in a counter-clockwise rotation. These two phenomena combine to form a robust heuristic for handling posture detection in the case of swipes. As with the other two heuristics, the final intra-heuristic decision is made when the system biases toward the same posture twice in a row.

Making the Final Decision. If swipes are present, we use majority voting on the output of each heuristic to decide the posture. If all three votes disagree, the posture is marked as "unknown." In the absence of swipe, a final decision is made only if both touch size and rotation heuristics agree or if the "high confidence flag" in one of the heuristics is set. If both heuristics come up with different decisions, then the system chooses the heuristic with a "high confidence flag."

If both confidence flags are set or no confidence flags are set with disagreement, the posture is set to "unknown."

Detecting Pressure Applied to the Touchscreen

GripSense uses the gyroscope and vibration motor to classify the user's touchscreen touches into three pressure categories: *Light, Medium* and *Heavy*. We hypothesize that if we trigger the built-in vibration motor when a user touches the screen (similar to what is already done in a number of smartphones to provide haptic feedback), the user's hand absorbs a portion of these vibrations. Our experiments show that this vibration absorption is proportional to the amount of pressure being applied to the screen (see Figure 3). This damping effect is measured using the on-device gyroscope. We primarily look for the damping of vibrations induced by the vibration motor. We also observed that as the amount of force exerted by the user on the touchscreen increases, there is a subtle oscillating motion between the user's thumb and the four fingers that rest on the back of the device (see the low pass signal in Figure 3). Strachan and Murray-Smith also observed and leveraged this phenomenon [29]. We hypothesize that this oscillation occurs because the user's thumb and fingers try to compensate continually for pressure exerted and this oscillation has much lower frequency compared to that induced by the vibration motor. This subtle motion is not dependent on the vibration motor. In order to make a robust classification of a user's touch intensity, we use both of these features.

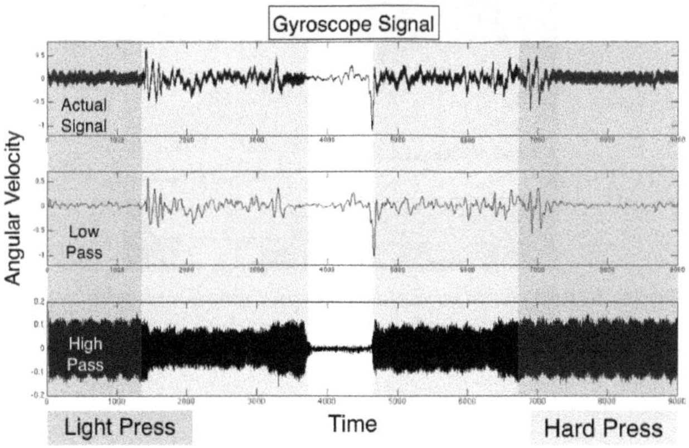

Figure 3. (top) Gyroscope signal when user presses light, then hard, then waits for a second and presses hard and soft again. **(middle)** The lower frequencies generated from touch-induced vibrations *increase* with increase in pressure. **(bottom)** Motor-induced vibrations are diminished as the amount of pressure exerted increases.

The touch-induced vibrations observed in GripSense are different from those used by prior work [13,14]. This prior work used exaggerated vibrations observed when a user "whacks" the phone with higher than usual velocity, moving the phone backward with respect to the finger stroke. This backward motion is proportional to the force with which finger strikes the screen. This technique provides an effective but coarse proxy of the pressure exerted. In contrast, GripSense leverages the subtle shaking of the phone as a user's thumb or finger (depending on the posture) and hand in which the phone is held try to compensate for pressure exerted by each other. An effective combination of these touch-induced vibrations with damped motor-induced vibrations give a much more authentic fine-grained and continuous proxy of pressure exerted on the screen.

We built a custom application on an Android Nexus-S smartphone, wherein any touch triggered the phone's built-in vibration motor. We then gathered angular velocities around the three axes through the built-in gyroscope with a 1 kHz sampling rate (Figure 3, top). Touch-induced vibrations were obtained by passing the signal through a low pass filter (Figure 3, middle). The motor-induced vibrations were obtained by passing the original signal through a high pass filter (Figure 3, bottom).

It is clear from the bottom plot in Figure 3 that in the case of a hard press (blue background), there is an exaggerated damping effect due to vibrations absorbed by the user's hand. We quantify this damping using the 90th percentile of the high-frequency component of the observed signal. For the low frequency signal, we quantify the movement of the phone using the signal variance.

Essl *et al.* [5] have earlier used the size of touch on the screen as a proxy for pressure exerted, and we also use this as a feature in our system. Our analysis shows that this feature alone is a poor measure of pressure (only about 60% accurate in our pilot study), but when combined with vibration analysis it can marginally improve performance by 1.4%, on average. Our pilot study also showed that amount of motor-induced vibrations absorbed by the hand and thumb or finger was also dependent on the location of touch on the screen. Hence, we divided screen into a 4×6 matrix in portrait mode and added "touch zone" as another feature for pressure level classification.

We buffer the gyroscope data at 1 kHz in a 500 ms buffer and analyze it every 250 ms (Figure 4). The data then passes through low pass and high pass filters and appropriate variances and 90th-percentiles are calculated. These features, along with touchscreen features (*zone* and *size*), were used to classify to pressure level using the Weka machine learning toolkit. Weka was used to generate J48 Decision Trees with pruning confidence set to Weka's default (0.25).

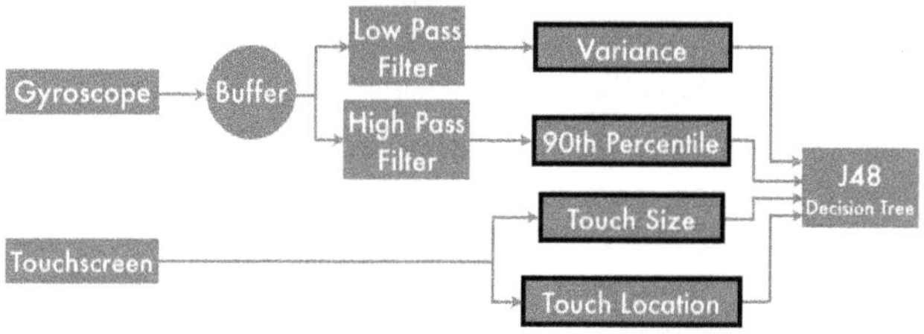

Figure 4. Block diagram of the major components of GripSense's pressure detection module. Low frequency variance, 90th percentile of higher frequencies, touch size and location are the features used for classification.

Squeeze and Grasp GesturesUsing similar techniques as for quantifying pressure exerted on a touchscreen, we implemented a method to detect squeeze or grasp gestures. For example, imagine quickly silencing a phone while it is still in a pocket or in a purse by squeezing it and without the need for fully retrieving the phone. Although grasping provides a significant amount of damping to the motor-induced vibrations, there was no significant variance in low frequency component of the gyroscope data; therefore, only higher frequencies were analyzed and their 90th percentiles were used as features for Weka's J48 decision trees.

EVALUATION

Participants

The performance of GripSense was evaluated in a controlled study. Ten participants (6 males, 4 females) ranging in age from 21 to 32 years (M=26.9, SD=3.6) were recruited. All participants had more than 10 years of experience with computers and self-rated as intermediate to expert computer and smartphone users.

Apparatus

Participants used separate custom Android applications for posture and pressure detection. These applications were deployed on a Samsung Nexus S. The device's angular velocities were recorded at 1 kHz using the built-in gyroscope. The ground truth for pressure detection was obtained using thin-film force sensitive resistors (FSR), affixed to the touchscreen. This was only used to train users to exert different pressures while receiving feedback from the FSR; it was not used to train any of the algorithms.

Pressure Detection Procedure

Pressure Detection. The machine learning system for pressure detection was modeled and evaluated on data collected from participants in a 45-minute study each. Participants were asked to tap the screen using three different and discernible pressure levels with different hand postures detectable by GripSense: (1) thumb-based operation, (2) index-finger operation, (3) on a table, (4) only held by the user but not operated. Twenty taps for each pressure level using each posture were recorded for all participants. Apart from the taps, the participants were also asked to perform seven longer, continuous touches lasting 10 seconds each for each pressure level. These longer touches were recorded because in our pilot study we realized that low frequency touch-induced vibrations lasted for nearly 3 seconds and started attenuating thereafter as the hand became used to the pressure level. Hence we added these gestures in our data collection mode to make for more robust models.

The three different pressure levels were explained to participants and they were asked to practice them. The ground truth from the FSRs was visualized on the screen for feedback during training. Once participants were comfortable entering three distinct levels of pressure, they were introduced to the data collection interface and procedure. Although all participants were comfortable distinguishing for themselves three pressure levels, absolute pressure values were not uniform and varied across participants. The order of postures in which data was collected was randomized to prevent unwanted effects from fatigue.

The procedure for collecting data to evaluate grip pressure was the same as that for collecting touchscreen pressure. Participants were asked to grip the device with three varying intensities. The least pressure was slightly less than what participants would apply while using their phone in general. The middle grip pressure was meant to approximate how participants would normally hold their phones. In the highest-pressure level, participants were asked to grip their phones tightly.

The participants were asked to press a button to trigger the vibration motor. The motor went off 5 seconds after the button was pressed. This gave user ample time to get the phone into the correct grip. Then the device vibrated for 10 seconds. Five such tasks were run for each pressure level and for each participant. Although we collected pressure-based interaction data for our postures separately, using our posture-detection heuristics, applications can seamlessly switch between models for different postures at runtime.

Posture Detection Procedure and Applications

Our heuristics look at different touchscreen interactions like taps and swipes to infer grip; hence, we developed two separate custom Android applications to evaluate performance. One application, *Contact Selection App*, used more swipes than taps; the other, *Text Entry App*, used only taps. The 10 participants recruited for pressure detection data collection also participated in evaluation of these two applications. These applications were evaluated in a separate 30-minute session.

Figure 5. (left) Contact Selection App. Swipe-intensive application that helps to quantify swipe heuristic performance. **(right)** Text Entry App. Tap-intensive app helped in evaluating performance in absence of swipes. The left area of the screen just below the text field prompts the user with current hand posture.

The Contact Selection App presented participants with a list of 100 random names. The investigator asked each participant to select 50 of these names in a random order. Participants were asked to randomly invite some of the names to a fictitious party through a dialog box (Figure 5, *left*). After every 5 name selections, the app prompted the participant to switch postures. The order of postures was randomly generated. The list and dialog box ensured that participants performed a good combination of swipes and taps. The dialog box also ensured participants had a mixture of taps on both the left and right sides of the screen.

The Text Entry App required only tapping. Participants were presented with 15 short English language phrases randomly selected from MacKenzie and Soukoreff's phrase set [24]. At the end of each phrase, the application instructed participants to switch to a new randomly selected posture (Figure 5, *right*). The performance analyses for both of these applications and also for pressure detection models are presented in the next section.

RESULTS

Posture Detection

Accuracy results for posture detection are shown in Figure 6, *left*. This figure shows the confusion matrix for the three hand postures while using the Text Entry App. The *y*-axis has the actual posture and *x*-axis has the prediction made by GripSense. We do not show the performance of detection of the device being on a table or grasped because it was relatively straightforward and the accuracy for that detection was 99.42%.

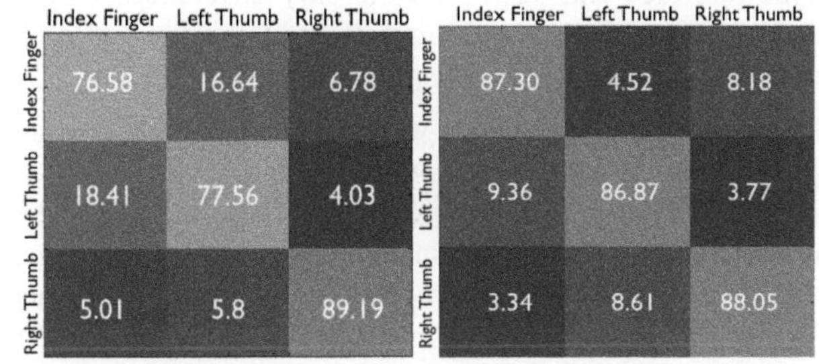

Figure 6. (left) Confusion matrix for classification of hand postures using Text Entry App. The *x*-axis shows the classification and the *y*-axis shows the actual posture. **(right)** Confusion matrix while using the Contact Selection App.

When evaluated using our Text Entry App, GripSense was able to detect correct posture in 81.11% cases. It made a decision after about 5 interaction steps. The number of interactions required to make a decision could be decreased but only at the cost of accuracy. With 5 required interaction steps, GripSense was able to make a decision often when the user completed the first word of a phrase.

The performance of GripSense, expectedly, improved further while using the Contact Selection App, as it permits the use of our third heuristic, the shape of the swipe arc. The accuracy improved to 87.4%. The confusion matrix for the three hand postures is shown in Figure 6, *right*. In this case, GripSense was able to make a decision on hand posture after about 4 interaction steps.

Pressure Detection

Figure 7 shows the accuracy of GripSense in detecting pressure exerted on phone in different postures. The participants were asked to use three levels of pressure and the overall accuracy across all postures was 95.05%.

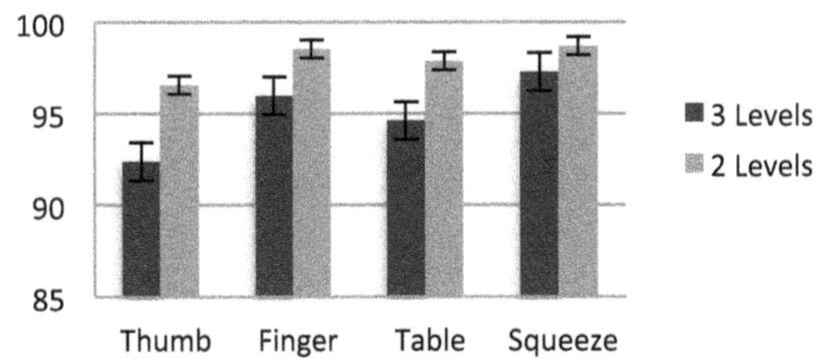

Figure 7. Squeeze gestures performed the best. Reducing the number of pressure levels to two improved accuracy further. Errorbars are standard error.

As discussed earlier, inclusion of Android's built-in touch-size method as a feature provided marginal improvement in performance. We performed an analysis to see how much effect this feature had on the performance of GripSense. The accuracy of GripSense without touch size was found to be 93.46%.

It may be that for many applications, two levels of pressure are adequate so we evaluated performance for two levels of pressure. As expected, the performance of GripSense's pressure detection improved significantly to 97.91%.

We discussed earlier how the touch-induced vibrations attenuate over the duration of the touch. So we collected data for both taps (momentary touch) and long 10 second touches as well. The long touches facilitate functions like zooming-in and out of pictures, maps, *etc.* During our pilot study we realized that different users have different ways of holding the phone and have different types of hands. Hence, we developed personalized pressure classification models for all participants. This meant that participants had to take part in a relatively long data collection study. So we investigated how much data was enough to train the system for acceptable levels of accuracy.

Figure 8 shows the progression of improvement in the average accuracy of GripSense to sense three distinct levels of pressure as we increase the amount of data used for development of models. The investigation has been divided into different accuracies for different tap and continuous gestures in variety of postures. The *x*-axis shows the percentage split in training and test data. Larger values on the *x*-axis signify more training data. It is clear from the figure that in the case of long continuous touches, GripSense does not require a lot of training data. Even for momentary taps, in total, only 20 taps were recorded for each pressure level. In most cases, the classification accuracy reaches above 80% by the 30% split mark, meaning that only six taps for each pressure level are required to train a device per user.

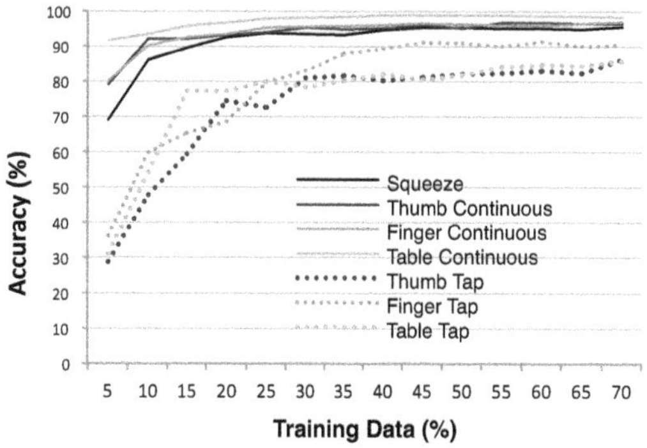

Figure 8. Improvement in average accuracy of pressure level detection for different gestures and touch-types with increasing size of training data. Continuous touches reached maximum performance with significantly less training data.

APPLICATIONS FOR PRESSURE DETECTION

To put GripSense through its paces, we implemented separate Android applications to take advantage of GripSense's posture- and pressure-sensing techniques. Our applications were motivated from the challenges associated with situational impairments [28] and the question of how interfaces may accommodate using only one hand, having one's device in a bag or purse, having limited screen space, *etc.*

The Maps Application

There are circumstances where it is difficult to use multiple fingers on a mobile device. Users often do not have both hands available for interaction. To explore these circumstances, we developed a map application in which user could zoom in by pressing harder on the screen, and could lightly press to zoom out. Hinckley *et al.* [14] have developed a similar application where they used hard and soft onset of taps for similar interactions. As noted previously, our approach differs because we do *continuous* pressure monitoring, not just detection of pressure at touch-onset, and therefore, our users do not have to impact the screen with increased velocity.

In order to assess the usability of our Maps app, we presented participants with a fully zoomed-out view of a world map and asked them to zoom-in to a set location (*e.g.*, Mexico). The participants needed to zoom in until they could see street names, and then they had to zoom-out until they could see the entire country again. To mimic a situational impairment, we required participants to hold a coffee mug in one hand and operate the device in their other hand. We also asked participants to perform same task on an app that did not have pressure-based input capabilities, and they had to use *pinch-to-zoom* to interact with the map using only one hand. After completion of a task on each system, we asked participants to make Likert-scale ratings based on the NASA TLX perceived workload index [10,11]. All 10 participants preferred using GripSense's pressure-sensitive maps, as it was much easier to navigate the map with one hand using pressure input to zoom in and out than to use one hand with pinch-to-zoom. On average, the GripSense-based app did better than traditional maps app on all counts on the Likert scale (Figure 9). A number of participants also liked the fact that the focal point of the zoom did not move while using pressure-based input, which is usually not the case with *pinch-to-zoom* implementations.

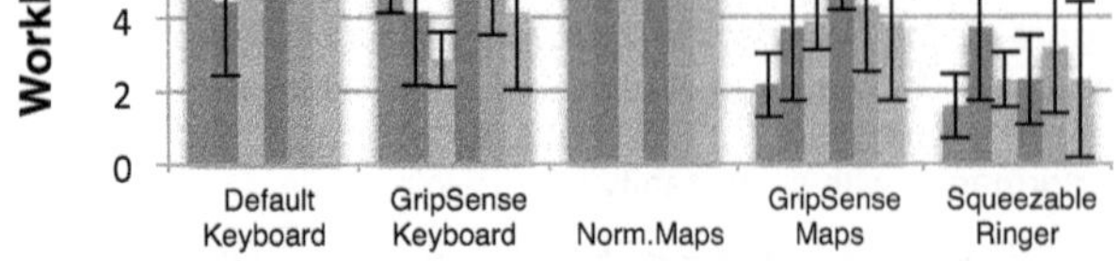

Figure 9. Perceived workload ratings show the GripSense-based applications resulted in relatively low workload. Lower ratings are better. Error bars are standard error.

The Keyboard Application

One obvious utility of having pressure-based input is alternative input. Researchers have used similar input modalities for mimicking right-clicks [14], changing keyboard modes [4], and so on. We use pressure input information to change letter case on a touchscreen keyboard. Users can press harder to enter uppercase letters and press lighter to enter lowercase letters. Participants were presented with 5 phrases randomly selected from the MacKenzie and Soukoreff phrase set [24]. Forty percent of characters in each of these phrases were randomly converted to upper case. We also presented participants with a parallel app having the same interface and task, with the only difference being an absence of pressure-based input. Instead, the app had a separate shift key for uppercasing letters.

The keyboards in both apps were modified to not show any typing errors if participants pressed within three keys of the intended key. We made this choice because the aim of this application was not to measure the user's typing accuracy, but to measure GripSense's pressure-detection accuracy. Participants were asked to use this app while holding the device in one hand and interacting with the index finger of the other hand.

After the completion of tasks on each of the two keyboards, we asked participants to fill out the same Likert scales as for the Maps app. The difference in performance of the two keyboards was not as dramatic as it was in case of the Maps app. Nonparametric Wilcoxon signed-rank tests indicate that our Keyboard application required significantly less perceived workload on the *temporal* and *frustration* Likert scales ($p<.05$). Responses for *effort* showed a trend in favor of our Keyboard application ($p=.07$). Responses for the *mental*, *physical*, and *performance* scales were not significantly different.

The participants were divided on which keyboard they thought allowed them to type faster. For example, P4 said, "[GripSense] felt like it took a lot less time to enter the text because I did not have to keep switching modes." Whereas, P7 said, "While using the pressure one I felt that typing was slower. I had to think more." A Shapiro-Wilk W test of normality indicates the *Time* measure differs significantly from normal ($W=0.95$, $p<.01$). However, a Kolmogorov's D test indicates the *Time* data does not depart significantly from lognormal ($D=0.07$, $p=.15$). Therefore, we log-transformed our *Time* measure before running a repeated measures ANOVA. Although the mean time taken for GripSense was a little less on average than the traditional Shift-based keyboard (14.98 s, $SD=5.29$ *vs.* 16.31 s, $SD=4.55$), the difference was not statistically significant ($F_{1,6}=2.69$, $p=.15$).

Squeeze Application

We developed a fake phone ringer app to check the utility of our squeeze gesture. This application plays a ringtone and goes into silent mode when user squeezes the device. This application was tested by asking participants to keep the phone in their pocket or bag and once the app starts ringing, to reach inside the bag or pocket and squeeze the device. This squeeze action sends the device into silent mode and mimics the behavior of sending the caller to voicemail.

As is evident from the Likert-scale measures, participants frankly loved this application. Many wanted it on their personal phones immediately. P7 said, "There was something satisfying about squeezing the phone and having the vibration stop instantly." P1 said, "When can I get this? This is a really cool feature that I think would be very useful in all kinds of contexts."

DISCUSSION

GripSense successfully infers a user's hand postures and pressure exerted on device in these postures with high accuracy. But, there is slight degradation in the performance of GripSense when deciding between left-handed thumb-based operation and index finger-based operation. We believe this degradation is due to the system confusing one-handed and two-handed operation. This problem is mitigated to a large extent in the swipe-heavy application, Contact Selection App. In the case of the keyboard application, the user's interaction was largely limited to the bottom half of the screen and our current heuristics depend on analyzing differences in device movement when interacting with different parts of the screen. We believe this degradation would not be felt in real world applications that require users to interact with various parts of screen and hence provide much richer data for the algorithms presented in this paper. However, the keyboard app provides ample interaction switching between the left and right sides of the screen, so GripSense's performance is not dramatically affected.

Extended use of the touchscreen, gyroscope, and vibration motor can have significant power implications. But GripSense only leverages these sensors when the device is interacted with. We did not do a direct analysis of energy use, but anecdotally we did not observe any significant reduction in battery life during our user studies. If needed, future iterations of such system could employ a multistage approach by sampling at a low frequency first and then higher rates, as needed.

Because GripSense uses the vibration motor to sense the pressure exerted, the motor is triggered only when the user interacts with the touchscreen or in case of an infrequent event (*e.g.* incoming voice call). We explicitly asked participants about the effects of vibration on their experience with the system. The majority of participants did not feel that their experience deteriorated due to this vibration. Significantly lower levels of frustration in our exit survey after using GripSense-based applications also support this finding.

We implemented our algorithms on a Samsung Nexus S running the Android OS. Although the basic premise would remain the same, our pressure detection algorithms might need to be adjusted somewhat for different phones because of different physical characteristics. The variability of the sampling rate and resolution of different devices may also require algorithmic adjustments on some phones. Current inertial sensors present on commodity mobile devices are not high resolution and the techniques presented in this paper can benefit a great deal from improved resolution. The high performance exhibited by GripSense, particularly in the case of pressure detection, could be even better with improved sensor hardware in the future.

Our use of the built-in motor to produce vibration means that almost half of our features are coming from a relatively high-frequency source. Hence, techniques presented here for pressure detection do not suffer from the usual limitations of inertial sensor-based techniques like the presence of external sources of vibration, *etc.* Although no formal study was conducted to measure the effects due to external vibrations, an informal test was conducted to estimate the efficacy of pressure sensing while sitting as well as walking; results were comparable for both postures. In the case of posture detection, the combination of inertial (gyroscope) and non-inertial (touchscreen) sensors should help mitigate this issue.

As demonstrated by our results, the combination of touch-induced and motor-induced vibrations means that these techniques can be reliably implemented when the device is on a flat surface. Hence these algorithms can be ported to tablets as well, which are used relatively more on a desk when compared to a smart phone. Modern game controller manufacturers can also leverage these techniques with a simple software upgrade to add pressure sensitivity to their devices, as game controllers already have vibration motors and inertial sensors.

In our evaluation of pressure sensing in a variety of postures, we only had three levels of pressure. Three levels were chosen to make it easy for users to discern different pressure levels with acceptable levels of accuracy. We believe our algorithms actually can infer more than three levels of pressure, amply demonstrated by the fact that even though the range of pressure applied by different participants was different, the system maintained high levels of accuracy. That said, a more continuous regression to pressure is possible and algorithms can be built on top of this work that have more than just quantized levels of pressure.

CONCLUSION

The dynamic usage environments of mobile devices can lead to situational impairments that may be overcome with better device awareness and enhanced interaction techniques. In this paper, we presented GripSense, a system that leverages various capabilities of mobile devices like the touchscreen, inertial sensors, and the vibration motor to infer users' hand postures and the amount of pressure exerted on device in these postures. GripSense differentiates between device usage in-hand or on a flat surface with 99.7% accuracy and various hand postures with 84.3% accuracy and, on average, makes a decision within 5 "interaction steps". GripSense differentiates between three levels of pressure on different areas of the device with 95.1% accuracy. A controlled study with 10 participants qualitatively evaluated the desirability of GripSense with the help of three custom applications. Users reported lower perceived workload ratings for GripSense-based applications than for conventional alternatives. GripSense represents an important step in extending the capabilities of our mobile devices to be more aware, responsive, and useful.

ACKNOWLEDGEMENTS

We thank Peter Hornyack for his help in prototyping.

REFERENCES

1. Azenkot, S. and Zhai, S. Touch Behavior with Different Postures on Soft Smartphone Keyboards. *Proc. Mobile HCI 2012*, (2012).
2. Cheng, L.-P., Hsiao, F.-I., Liu, Y.-T., and Chen, M.Y. iRotate: Automatic Screen Rotation based on Face Orientation. *Proc. CHI 2012*, (2012).
3. Choudhury, T., Consolvo, S., Harrison, B., et al. The Mobile Sensing Platform: An Embedded Activity Recognition System. *Pervasive Computing, IEEE 7*, 2 (2008), 32-41.
4. Clarkson, E.C., Patel, S.N., Pierce, J.S., and Abowd, G.D. Exploring Continuous Pressure Input for Mobile Phones. .
5. Essl, G., Rohs, M., and Kratz, S. Use the Force (or something) - Pressure and Pressure- Like Input for Mobile Music Performance. *Organised Sound*, June (2010), 15-18.
6. Fitzmaurice, G.W., Ishii, H., and Buxton, W.A.S. Bricks: Laying the foundations for graspable user interfaces. *Proc. CHI 1995*, ACM Press/Addison-Wesley Publishing Co. (1995), 442-449.
7. Goel, M. and Findlater, L. WalkType: Using Accelerometer Data to Accommodate Situational Impairments in Mobile Touch Screen Text Entry. *Proc. CHI 2012*, (2012).
8. Gupta, S., Campbell, T., Hightower, J.R., and Patel, S.N. SqueezeBlock: using virtual springs in mobile devices for eyes-free interaction. *Proc. UIST 2010*, ACM (2010), 101-104.
9. Harrison, B.L., Fishkin, K.P., Gujar, A., Mochon, C., and Want, R. Squeeze me, hold me, tilt me! An exploration of manipulative user interfaces. *Proc. CHI 1998.*, ACM Press (1998), 17-24.
10. Hart, S.G., California, M.F., and Staveland, L.E. Development of NASA-TLX (Task Load Index): Results of Empirical and Theoretical Research. .
11. Hart, S.G. Nasa-Task Load Index (NASA-TLX); 20 Years Later. *Proc. of the Human Factors and Ergonomics Society Annual Meeting 50*, 9 (2006), 904-908.
12. Heo, S. and Lee, G. Force gestures: augmented touch screen gestures using normal and tangential force. *Proc. CHI EA 2011*, ACM (2011), 1909-1914.
13. Heo, S. and Lee, G. Forcetap: extending the input vocabulary of mobile touch screens by adding tap gestures. *Proc. Mobile HCI 2011*, ACM (2011), 113-122.
14. Hinckley, K. and Song, H. Sensor synaesthesia: touch in motion, and motion in touch. *Proc. CHI 2011*, ACM (2011), 801-810.
15. Hinckley, K., Pierce, J., Sinclair, M., and Horvitz, E. Sensing techniques for mobile interaction. *Proc. UIST 2000*, ACM (2000), 91-100.
16. Holz, C. and Baudisch, P. Understanding touch. *Proc. CHI 2011*, ACM (2011), 2501-2510.
17. Iwasaki, K., Miyaki, T., and Rekimoto, J. Expressive typing: a new way to sense typing pressure and its applications. *Proc. CHI EA 2009*, ACM (2009), 4369-4374.
18. Johnson, P. Usability and mobility; interactions on the move. *First Workshop on Human-Computer Interaction with Mobile Devices.* (1998).
19. Joshi, N., Kang, S.B., Zitnick, C.L., and Szeliski, R. Image deblurring using inertial measurement sensors. *ACM Transactions on Graphics 29*, 4 (2010), 30:1-30:9.
20. Karlson, A.K. and Bederson, B.B. *Understanding Single-Handed Mobile Device Interaction*. 2006.
21. Karlson, A.K., Bederson, B.B., and SanGiovanni, J. AppLens and launchTile: two designs for one-handed thumb use on small devices. *Proceedings of the SIGCHI conference on Human factors in computing systems*, ACM (2005), 201-210.
22. Kim, K.-E., Chang, W., Cho, S.-J., et al. Hand Grip Pattern Recognition for Mobile User Interfaces. *Proc. AAAI'06*, (2006).
23. Van Laerhoven, K. and Cakmakci, O. What shall we teach our pants? *Wearable Computers, The Fourth International Symposium on*, (2000), 77-83.
24. MacKenzie, I.S. and Soukoreff, R.W. Phrase sets for evaluating text entry techniques. *Proc. CHI EA 2003*, ACM (2003), 754-755.
25. Phielipp, M., Lee, R., and Hightower, J. Fast , Accurate , and Practical Identity Inference Using TV Remote Controls. *Artificial Intelligence*, (2010), 1827-1832.
26. Ramos, G., Boulos, M., and Balakrishnan, R. Pressure widgets. *Proc. CHI 2004*, ACM (2004), 487-494.
27. Schmidt, A., Aidoo, K., Takaluoma, A., Tuomela, U., Van Laerhoven, K., and de Velde, W. Advanced Interaction in Context. In H.-W. Gellersen, ed., *Handheld and Ubiquitous Computing*. Springer Berlin / Heidelberg, 1999, 89-101.
28. Sears, A., Lin, M., Jacko, J., and Xiao, Y. When Computers Fade Pervasive Computing and Situationally-Induced Impairments and Disabilities. *HCI International 2*, (2003), 1298-1302.
29. Strachan, S. and Murray-Smith, R. Muscle Tremor as an Input Mechanism. *Proc. UIST 2004*, (2004).
30. Taylor, B.T. and Bove Jr., V.M. Graspables: grasp-recognition as a user interface. *Proc. CHI 2009*, ACM (2009), 917-926.
31. Weberg, L., Brange, T., and Hansson, A.W. A piece of butter on the PDA display. *Proc. CHI EA 2001*, ACM (2001), 435-436.
32. Wimmer, R. FlyEye: grasp-sensitive surfaces using optical fiber. *Proc. of TEI'10.* ACM (2010), 245-248.
33. Wobbrock, J.O., Kane, S.K., Gajos, K.Z., Harada, S., and Froehlich, J. Ability-Based Design: Concept, Principles and Examples. *ACM Transactions on Accessible Computing 3*, 3 (2011), 9:1-9:27.
34. Wobbrock, J.O., Myers, B.A., and Aung, H.H. The performance of hand postures in front- and back-of-device interaction for mobile computing. *International Journal of Human-Computer Studies 66*, 12 (2008), 857-875.

Pressages: Augmenting Phone Calls with Non-Verbal Messages

Eve Hoggan[1], Craig Stewart[1], Laura Haverinen[1], Giulio Jacucci[1] and Vuokko Lantz[2]

[1]Helsinki Institute for Information Technology (HIIT), Department of Computer Science, University of Helsinki, Finland
{firstname.lastname}@hiit.fi

[2]Nokia Research Center
Helsinki, Finland
{firstname.lastname}@nokia.com

ABSTRACT

ForcePhone is a mobile synchronous haptic communication system. During phone calls, users can squeeze the side of the device and the pressure level is mapped to vibrations on the recipient's device. The pressure/vibrotactile messages supported by ForcePhone are called *pressages*. Using a lab-based study and a small field study, this paper addresses the following questions: how can haptic interpersonal communication be integrated into a standard mobile device? What is the most appropriate feedback design for pressages? What types of non-verbal cues can be represented by pressages? Do users make use of pressages during their conversations? The results of this research indicate that such a system has value as a communication channel in real-world settings with users expressing greetings, presence and emotions through pressages.

Author Keywords

Pressure input; haptic feedback; mobile interpersonal communication; squeeze interaction.

ACM Classification Keywords

H.5.2 [Information Interfaces and Presentation]: User Interfaces – Input devices and strategies, Interaction styles Haptic I/O.

INTRODUCTION

Enhancing interpersonal communication is an increasingly important consideration in mobile interaction research as more and more of our everyday communication is conducted remotely via instant messaging, email and phone calls as opposed to face-to-face. Traditional methods of face-to-face communication rely heavily on the sense of touch [1]. In face-to-face interaction, touch is often used to express diverse, private and subtle nonverbal cues [2]. For example, handshakes, holding and squeezing hands, kissing, or pats on the back are all common in everyday communication.

Communication technologies such as mobile devices currently allow people to stay in contact with each other via speech, text and video. Although there have been many developments in this field, these devices make use of touch far less than audio and visual feedback thus perhaps reducing the sense of a physical connection between callers and restricting interaction. Furthermore, mobile users can be in a variety of different situations and contexts during phone calls making certain conversation topics inappropriate at times where tactile communication could still be effective.

Previous research has suggested that using haptic input and output is a good communication channel when used between two people [3]. These techniques, until now, have not been implemented on mobile devices or used during live phone calls. Therefore, this paper focuses on the integration of a haptic interpersonal communication system with a mobile device to establish whether such a system has value as a communication channel in real-world settings.

The prototype developed in this research, ForcePhone, is an augmented, commercially available mobile device with pressure input and vibrotactile output. During phone calls, users can squeeze the side of the device and the pressure level is mapped to vibrations on the receiving phone. The pressure/vibrotactile messages supported by ForcePhone are called *pressages*. This paper discusses the iterative design of ForcePhone from an input, output and field study perspective. Throughout the research, we were interested in answering the following questions: how can haptic interpersonal communication be integrated into a standard mobile device? What is the most appropriate feedback design for pressages? What types of non-verbal cues can be represented by pressages? Lastly, and perhaps most importantly, we wanted to investigate whether users make use of pressages during their normal phone conversations and whether this usage remains constant over time.

RELATED WORK

Multimodal feedback is often used to reduce the visual load on mobile device users. There has been a large body of research into mobile interaction with results of experiments using tactile feedback [4] [5] showing that high recognition rates can be achieved with a small amount of training.

Recent research has investigated pressure as an input technique on mobile touchscreen devices [6]. The results have shown that users can distinguish and apply up to ten pressure levels with high accuracy when navigating through

UIST '12, October 7–10, 2012, Cambridge, Massachusetts, USA.

a standard menu. Another interesting use of pressure can be seen in haptic conviction widgets [7]. The widgets allow users to map conviction to force e.g. emptying the trashcan requires a large amount of pressure. This paper takes the area a step further by examining squeezing as an interpersonal communication technique for mobile devices. We use squeezing in many everyday activities, for example squeezing a loved one's hand.

Interpersonal Communication

There has been a variety of previous research into using alternative modalities in interpersonal communication devices [3] [8 - 11]. Hemmert *et al.* [12] designed a prototype device using tightness actuation with the idea that users can squeeze their device to communicate through hand grasp. The receiving device includes a widening loop positioned around the user's hand that can be extended and contracted. However, this device does not provide any local feedback to the user who squeezes the device and there were no field studies conducted.

Chang *et al.* [3] developed ComTouch, a device that augments remote voice communication. More specifically, the device converts hand pressure into vibration intensity with a single actuator. A study was conducted where pairs of friends took part in a general chatting task and desert survival problem. There were no pre-defined cues and the devices were bi-directional, meaning that users could send and receive signals simultaneously. The results of the study showed that users developed an encoding system like Morse code as well as emphasis, turn-taking and mimicry.

The outcomes of Chang's research are promising but a mobile 'real-world' version of this system was never built, which could allow researchers to investigate this extra channel of communication further. The development of a truly mobile haptic interpersonal communication system is not trivial; there are data transfer, power and feedback issues to consider. In terms of feedback, ComTouch uses a different spatial location to present local feedback to indicate the magnitude of the pressure level. Using spatial location as a design parameter requires the use of multiple vibrotactile actuators. Current mobile devices do not have multiple vibration sources and adding these features leads to an increase in size and energy consumption.

The prototype described in this paper takes a more ecological approach by integrating a haptic interpersonal communication system into a standard smartphone without any external attachments.

Shake2Talk [10] allows users to construct audio-tactile messages through simple gesture interactions, and send these messages to other people. The system was designed to send messages such as "home safely", represented by the sound and sensation of a key turning in a lock and "thinking of you" represented by a heartbeat. Each couple used the Shake2Talk phones for two weeks. Results show the pre-defined messages were used for: coordination of events, awareness and reassurance, playfulness and social touch.

Unlike Shake2Talk, the research described in this paper does not make use of pre-defined cues and synchronises the pressages with a speech conversation. This allowed us to investigate the effects of adding an additional communication channel to a voice call and to establish what types of information can be encoded in the tactile modality when users are allowed to assign their own meanings.

The aim of this research is to extend the boundaries of traditional phone calls by adding an additional channel of communication. Building on the existing research, the prototype development process and studies described here examine the use of pressure input and vibrotactile output over time during standard phone calls.

HARDWARE

The ForcePhone prototype (Figure 1) has been developed by augmenting a Nokia N900[1] with a force-sensing resistor (FSR). The tactile stimuli were presented through the standard rotational motor found within the N900.

Figure 1: The outward appearance of ForcePhone covered with a silicone case and the embedded FSR.

The implementation of the pressure sensor is based on the design proposed by Stewart *et al.* [13] and supported by the datasheet of the FSR manufacturer[2]. As shown in Figure 1, the FSR is attached to the side of the phone using double-sided tape. A 0.5mm wire is then used to connect the FSR to the main sensor board located inside the microSD card slot (visible in Figure 3). The microcontroller communicates with the phone using standard serial communication. This approach is valid for many phone models that include serial ports for debugging purposes.

The op-amp based circuit linearises the sensor output such that changes in the amount of force applied result in a similar change in output voltage across the range of pressure used (Figure 2). The output voltage from the FSR is then sampled by an 8-bit microcontroller (Atmel attiny13) at 30 Hz, and the resulting data is sent to the host system by a hardware-based serial port.

1 http://europe.nokia.com/find-products/devices/nokia-n900

2 http://www.sparkfun.com/datasheets/Sensors/Pressure/fsrguide.pdf

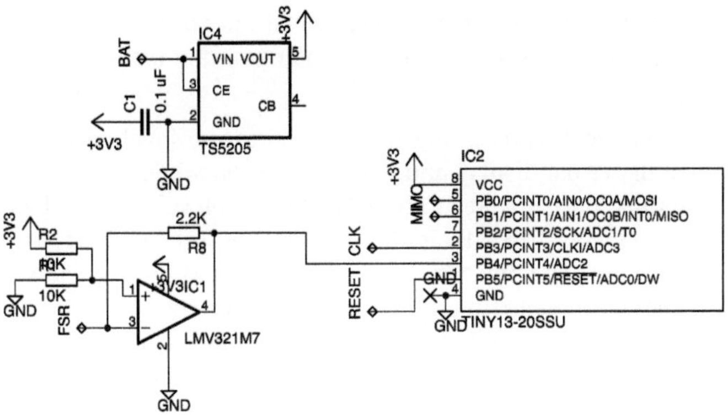

Figure 2: Schematic Diagram

One of our goals was to allow users to explore pressages without any cumbersome additional external hardware. We believe that this approach allows the user experience and subsequent feedback to more accurately reflect the interaction method, rather than the physical implementation. After several iterations, the resulting design can fit within the Micro Secure Digital (microSD) card slot (15mm by 11mm) of the Nokia N900 and has a component cost of less than US $30 (Figure 3).

Figure 3: Completed board compared with microSD card.

PROTOTYPE DESIGN CONSIDERATIONS

The most important aspects of the prototype were centred around the touch communication design variables (as outlined by Chang *et al.* [3]): data direction, data transfer, and data content. Alongside these variables, a variety of additional issues emerged during the design stages of this research such as local and remote feedback, interaction loops and input mechanisms. Our approach to each of these variables and issues is detailed next.

Data Direction and Transfer

ForcePhone allows bi-directional transmission of data. Each user has the ability to send and receive pressages.

One of the main achievements in the development of the ForcePhone hardware and software was the synchronous data transfer feature. As far as the authors are aware, this is the first research in augmented interpersonal communication to allow real time synchronous communication via phone conversations and pressure/vibration messages on a commercially available mobile device. This feature was created using the Extensible Messaging and Presence Protocol (XMPP) so that, when the device receives a call, our program launches a Jabber client to allow information, sent as text, about pressages to be transmitted between phones. Each pressage is represented by a single number (0-3).

Data Content

In contrast to the recommendations by Chang *et al.* [3], the data content in ForcePhone is not continuous. If it was possible for users to continuously send their pressure input levels as vibration messages to the other user, it may be difficult for users to shift their attention between the two competing modalities. It has been found that our auditory sense tends to dominate over the tactile sense in certain tasks [14]. Therefore, the discrete data content is transmitted to the receiver whenever the user explicitly squeezes the phone. The threshold of pressure at which this explicit level occurred was determined to be 0.6N through testing detailed in Stewart *et al.* [15].

Local Feedback for Pressure Input

ForcePhone uses an asymmetric modality mapping where the input modality is translated into the output modality (in our case, pressure to vibrations). A key consideration when designing an interpersonal communication device is the use of local and remote feedback. In terms of our prototype, the remote feedback is the vibration presented on the recipient's phone and local feedback is presented to the sender as a result of their pressure input.

Even though our body provides us with natural feedback about the amount of pressure we apply to something through our muscles and our sense of touch in general, it has been shown that additional feedback can improve our ability to achieve specific target forces [16].

When considering the feedback modality, the combination of pressure input and vibrotactile output seems logical given that both types of stimuli are part of the haptic sense. Rekimoto *et al.* [17] implemented a 3 level pressure-based button ("not pressed", "light pressed", and "hard pressed") and provided vibrotactile feedback for each level. However, there were no user studies conducted to assess the effectiveness of the tactile feedback. Building on this related work, the following section presents an experiment investigating tactile feedback for pressure input.

Pressure Input

The range of pressure, or applied force, our hardware design can measure is approximately 0 – 6 Newton (measured in a similar approach by [13] [6]). The pressure range is separated into 4 discrete levels.

The prototype hardware used in this research allowed users to input pressure using the quick release method. This method has the benefit of allowing much faster selection times than the dwell technique used in [6]. The quick release selection method is performed by applying pressure until the target pressure level is reached and quickly removing the finger to confirm the selection.

Stimuli

Our interaction design requires discrete feedback when the user moves into a new pressure level. Stewart *et al.* [13] explored the use of vibrotactile feedback, providing different feedback for each level. Our design is simpler, with a short burst (50ms) from the N900's built-in vibration motor when moving positively from one pressure level to the next. The duration of the pulse was constrained by two issues: the vibration had to be noticeable, and enable the detection of multiple pulses executed in rapid succession.

The visual feedback design (Figure 4) was based on half of a clock face, with 4 equal segments. The first pressure level was represented by a segment between 12 and 2 o'clock, with the last level, between 4 and 6 o'clock.

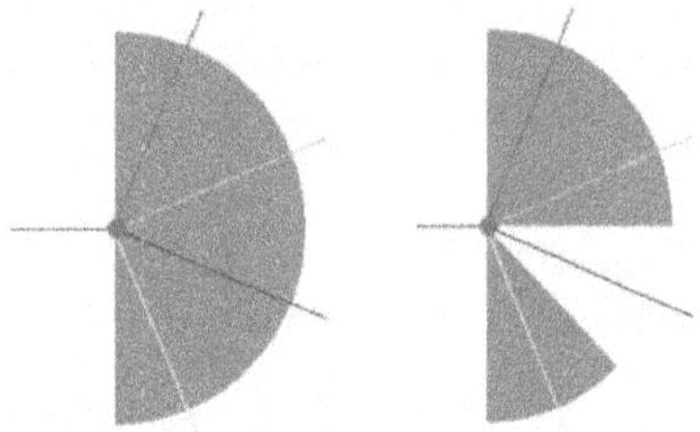

Figure 4: Experimental interface screenshot showing the selection of pressure level 3.

Delayed Interaction Loop

Our basic interaction loop implemented a naive approach without any artificial delay between the presentation of feedback for two consecutive pressure level transitions. This allowed the vibrotactile feedback to 'blur' together and individual pulses may become indistinguishable. Without being able to detect the individual pulses, users may experience difficulty in selecting the correct pressure level. Thus, a second condition, the delayed interaction loop, introduced a 100ms gap between transitions.

Methodology

We designed an experiment to investigate the effects of tactile feedback for pressure input. The experiment compared user performance with visual feedback, visual and vibrotactile feedback, and vibrotactile feedback alone whilst using a basic and delayed interaction loop. The experiment hypotheses were as follows: 1) participants will be able to reach pressure levels with the least errors and greatest speed when using combined visual and vibrotactile feedback; 2) the delayed interaction loop will lead to greater accuracy and speed for all modalities.

We used a within-subjects design with two conditions: basic interaction loop and delayed interaction loop. There were also three sub-conditions for each modality within each of the interaction loops. All conditions were counterbalanced and tested in a static lab environment.

Participants

Twelve participants took part in the experiment. All participants were aged between 18 and 34. There were 6 female and 6 male participants. 1 participant was left-handed. All participants were seated during the experiment and asked to hold the device in their non-dominant hand.

Task

A number, representing the target pressure level, appeared on the visual display and would disappear when participants applied pressure (see Figure 4). Once the level was reached, participants lifted their thumb from the sensor to register the input. The pressure level selected would then be shown, coloured green if the target level was correctly selected, or red if not. For each condition, participants received training with each target being presented 5 times consecutively.

Results - Accuracy

The average error rate (missed targets) for each modality and interaction loop is shown in Figure 5.

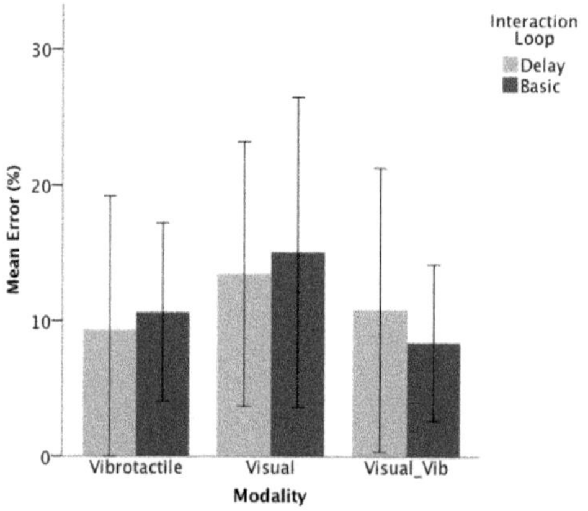

Figure 5: Average error rate for each modality and interaction loop (error bars = SD).

A repeated measures two-factor ANOVA was performed on the mean number of correct pressure levels, comparing the effects of the interaction loop (basic and delay) and feedback modality (Visual, Vibrotactile and Visual/Vibrotactile). A significant main effect for modality was found ($F(2,40) = 4.84$, $p<0.0001$). Tukey tests showed that there were significantly more errors when using visual feedback compared to vibrotactile and combined vibrotactile/visual feedback ($p=0.05$). There was no main effect for the interaction loops and no interaction between the loops and modalities. A further repeated measures two-factor ANOVA for each pressure level, comparing the effects of the interaction loop and modality showed no significant differences in the data.

Results - Speed

Figure 6 shows the average time taken to reach each pressure level for all modalities and interaction loops. A repeated measures two-factor ANOVA on the movement time for each modality and interaction loop showed a significant main effect for modality ($F(2,40)=16.05$, $p<0.0001$). Tukey HSD tests showed that the movement time when using combined visual and vibrotactile feedback was significantly lower than the visual and the vibrotactile version ($p=0.0001$). The vibrotactile version was also significantly faster than the visual version ($p=0.05$). There was no significant main effect for the interaction loops and no interaction between factors.

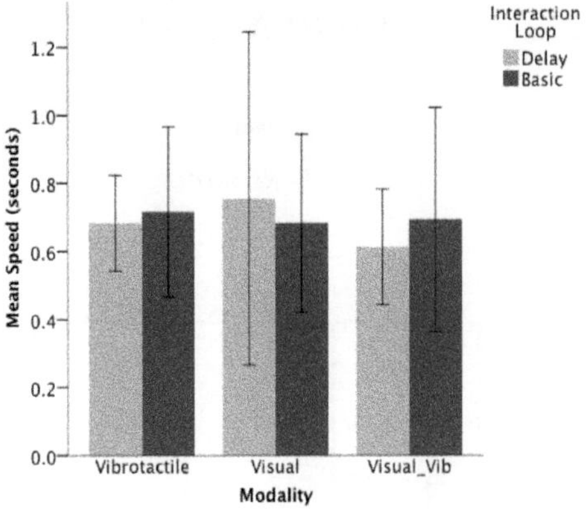

Figure 6: Average movement time for each modality and interaction loop (error bars = SD).

Further analysis of each pressure level showed a significant difference between levels for all modalities and interaction loops ($F(3,30) = 34.87$, $p<0.0001$). Tukey HSD tests showed that pressure level 1 (1.4N) was significantly faster to achieve than the others ($p<0.001$). The analysis also showed that pressure level 2 (2.5N) was significantly faster to achieve than levels 3 (4.7N) and 4 (5.8N) ($p<0.0001$). There were no significant differences between levels 3 and 4. This shows that the lighter pressure levels are quicker to reach. That being said, all of the movement times were reasonably quick (ranging from 0.16 to 1.08 seconds in the basic interaction loop and 0.17 to 1.4 seconds in the delayed interaction loop).

Discussion

Hypothesis 1 can be partially supported because the combined visual and vibrotactile version produced the fastest task times. However, as opposed to our hypothesis, the vibrotactile version of the system produced higher accuracy levels than combined visual and vibrotactile feedback. This may be due to the fact that the vibrotactile feedback allows for completely eyes-free interaction. Furthermore, the coupling of pressure input and vibrotactile feedback may be more direct and simple for users because they are both forms of the same modality. Future studies will investigate this further.

Hypothesis 2 cannot be supported. The delayed interaction loop produced high accuracy scores and low task completion times but there were no significant differences when compared to the basic interaction loop.

Given the results of this study, we chose to incorporate the vibrotactile version of pressure feedback with a delayed interaction loop into ForcePhone.

Remote Feedback for Pressure Input

The local feedback study showed that mapping pressure to vibrotactile stimuli is an effective interaction mechanism. Therefore, the vibrotactile modality was also used for remote feedback. Whenever a user squeezed the phone, a vibration was sent to the recipient's phone.

The choice of feedback for pressages did not follow the traditional guidelines for tactile information transmission. For example, the existing literature on tactons, [18] states that the most effective design parameter is rhythm, followed by spatial location and roughness. However, rhythm is not an appropriate parameter for use during speech conversations, as the durations tend to be a minimum of 500ms. This could distract users from the content of the speech conversation. It was not possible to use spatial location as the N900 only contains one vibrotactile actuator and the use of multiple actuators significantly increases the amount of power used. Lastly, the roughness parameter involves extremely harsh vibrations. Given that pressages are sent during calls when the device is placed beside the user's ear, a very rough vibration is likely to feel particularly unpleasant. Instead, we chose a similar but gentler parameter: texture. Despite the narrow design space, we took inspiration from "The rules of beeping" [19], where useful communication can occur using simple stimuli. The pressure levels were mapped to the vibrotactile textures shown in Figure 7.

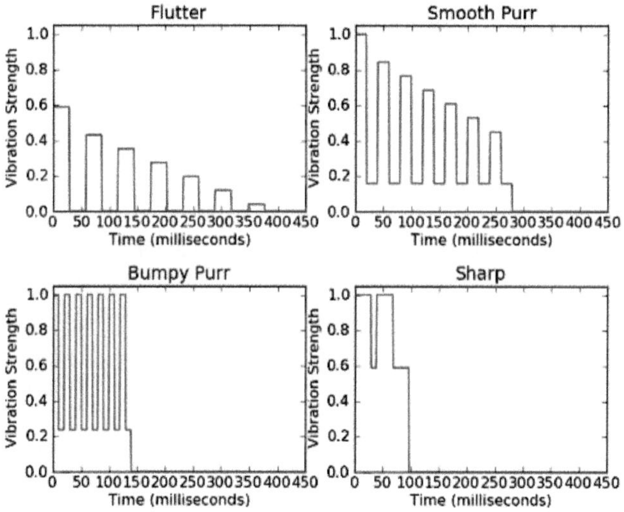

Figure 7: The vibration strengths (max strength = 1) and durations used to create each texture[3].

Based on all of these design considerations and the results of our preliminary experiment, the final version of ForcePhone incorporated bi-directional real-time data transfer, an asymmetric modality mapping (pressure to tactile), discrete data content, vibrotactile discrete local feedback with a delayed interaction loop and textured vibrotactile remote feedback to represent the pressages.

3 The vibration strength is controlled by an 8 bit number, 0 = off and 255 = full power. Pressure level 1 (1.4N) = flutter, level 2 (2.5N) = smooth purring, level 3 (4.7N) = bumpy purring, and level 4 (5.8N) = sharp pulsing.

LONGITUDINAL EVALUATION

A small longitudinal study was conducted to test ForcePhone. Although there are numerous potential use cases for the prototype devices, we decided to conduct our initial study with three couples in long-distance relationships. An introductory session was conducted in the laboratory for one hour before the participants took the devices home and completed the month long study.

The six participants in the study ranged from 24 to 32 years old, three male and three female. Each couple had been in a long-distance relationship for more than six months. The participants stated that they tend to communicate with each other through phone calls, SMS and emails on a daily basis.

Overall the longitudinal study lasted for one month. For the first week, the participants simply used the device for normal phone calls and completed a short questionnaire. This allowed us to log their normal communication behavior without any haptic additions as a baseline. After the first week, participants were asked to use the prototype device instead of their usual phones to call each other. They were informed that they could make as many calls on the prototype device as they liked throughout the study.

We did not define the meaning of the pressages so we conducted this study to answer the following research questions: what types of non-verbal cues can pressure be used to represent and also, does the combination of pressure input and tactile output provide an emotional communication channel? It may be the case that users send the pressages to indicate emotions or to mimic affectionate gestures such as hand squeezes. Then again, the pressages may also be used in a more negative manner to represent nudges or kicks or used simply to surprise the receiver.

ForcePhone logged the duration of all phone calls, the number of pressages sent and received, and the level of pressure used. We did not record any content from the conversations due to privacy concerns raised by the participants. After each phone call, the participants were asked to complete an online questionnaire and at the end of the study, the participants took part in a post-study interview on their experiences with the device.

Results

On average, the participants' phone calls lasted 4 minutes and 43 seconds with an average of 15.56 pressages sent during each call. All phone calls involved the use of pressages. Although the average number of sent pressages reduced from 14.3 to 10.6 by the end of the study, this was not a significant difference ($p > 0.05$). A log of one of the phone calls between participants is shown in Figure 8.

The mean time between received pressages was 5.8 seconds and 7.5 seconds for sent pressages. This indicates that when pressages are used, they are exchanged in rapid succession but as the log in Figure 8 shows, there can be long gaps during the call in which pressages are rarely sent. It would appear as though the participants exchanged pressages frequently at the start and end of calls but focused on the voice content in the middle.

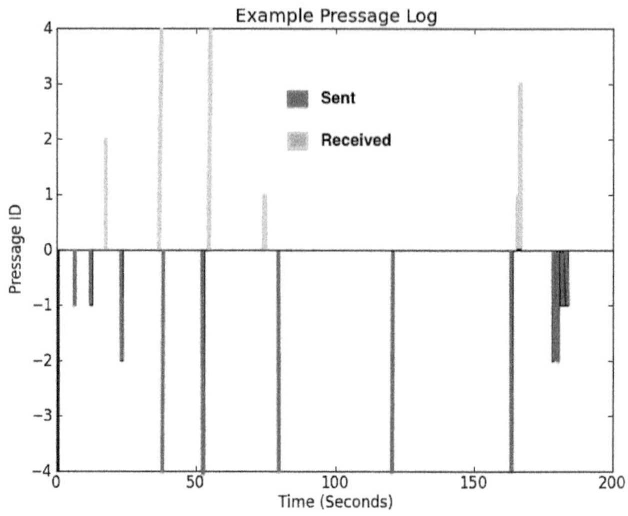

Figure 8: Sent and received pressages during a phone call between participants.

The lower half of the graph shows sent pressages and the upper half shows received pressages. Although the log shows that the participant sent a lot more pressages than he/she received, a small amount of turn-taking can be seen. Furthermore, it appears as though, if a level 4 pressage is sent, then a level 4 pressage is received i.e. the participants attempted to match each other's pressure levels.

Interviews and Questionnaires

After each call, the participants completed an 18-item rapport questionnaire (from [20]). The questionnaire responses show an increase of 5% in ratings for 'involving' and an increase of 3% in 'active' and 'positive' between week 1 with no pressages and weeks 2 – 4 with pressages.

The most interesting results came from the insights of the participants discovered in the post-study interview. The participants explained the ways in which they adapted to the extra channel of communication. All of the participants agreed that it was easy to incorporate pressages into their phone calls and that they "got used to the pressages really quickly". When asked about the specific ways in which they adapted their communication style to accommodate the tactile modality, all of the participants stated that they tended to pause briefly after sending a pressage to "make space for it in the conversation".

When asked about the non-verbal cues that could be represented by pressages, the participants highlighted three different approaches: to emphasise speech, express affection and presence, and to playfully surprise each other.

In the words of one of the participants, pressages help to "express yourself a little bit more". Pressages were found to be useful "especially in noisy situations" and to add emphasis to speech, particularly in terms of greetings: "I would send a pressage whenever I said hi".

In terms of expressing affection, the pressages were used as a mechanism to add an extra emotional element to the conversation. The participants mentioned that they found the pressages reassuring as they gave “a feeling of presence” and “they helped me to show that I was there, I was listening”. In terms of positive emotions, the participants likened the pressage to stroking their partner. In one of the phone conversations, a participant received some good news and she said, “something nice happened to me and suddenly there’s vibration and it was like he was stroking my arm”. The pressages were also used occasionally to express anger. However, the participants found that sending a very strong vibration to their partner to indicate their anger made the receiver angry too.

Lastly, the participants reported that they often used the pressages in a playful manner and to catch attention. In many cases, the participants would send a random pressage just to play with the system and make each other laugh. One of the participants used ForcePhone to communicate privately with his girlfriend in public settings by using the pressages as “a secret message to make her laugh”.

DISCUSSION

As far as the authors are aware, this is the first research prototype developed to transmit pressure and tactile data during calls. Despite the small size of our long-term user evaluation, the interview and data logs yielded a great deal of information. Throughout the development of ForcePhone, we were interested in exploring four areas: the technical issues encountered when integrating haptic interpersonal communication into a mobile device, the most appropriate feedback design for pressages, the types of non-verbal cues that can be represented by pressages, and pressage usage over time.

Integrating Haptic Communication With a Mobile Device

ForcePhone is a haptically augmented mobile device that allows pressure and vibrotactile data to be transmitted during phone calls. ForcePhone makes use of the built-in vibration motor and pressure sensors with a board that is small enough to be placed within the microSD card slot of a mobile device. Pressages are created using XMPP so that, when the device receives a call, a Jabber client is launched to allow information about pressages to be transmitted between phones. The robustness of the prototype was demonstrated by the fact that the participants successfully used ForcePhone as their personal mobile device for one month.

In the future we intend to investigate several technical enhancements for ForcePhone and pressages. Firstly, it may be possible to send pressages through Dual-Tone Multi-Frequency signaling (DTMF). This would make it very easy to synchronise the speech and pressages, and would allow users to send pressages when offline. However, using DTMF means that an audio beep will be sent to the receiver’s phone alongside the pressage. Further studies will examine the effects of this modality combination.

All of the participants in the long-term study expressed an interest in the use of stand-alone pressages. The participants suggested that the pressage functionality should not only be used to augment phone calls but as a completely separate form of communication. The participants said that, in a meeting or in some other situation where it is not appropriate to talk on the phone or spend time typing a message, the pressages could be used to send information discretely. Short messages like ‘I'm coming home’ could be sent without calling or typing. Future versions of ForcePhone will include this functionality.

Pressage Feedback Design

In terms of pressage feedback, our lab-based study showed that discrete vibrotactile feedback for pressure input is as effective as visual feedback. The current version of the prototype uses a rotating vibrotactile actuator that shakes the whole device. This can lead to a reasonably strong sensation on the user’s cheek and hand. This may be part of the reason why angry emotions were amplified when receiving a strong vibration. Additional vibrotactile design parameters or categories of haptic feedback could be included to allow users to choose their own feedback modality depending on the reaction they wish to generate, for example, localized vibrotactile feedback provided by piezo-electric actuators or thermal feedback.

Non-Verbal Cues Encoded in Pressages

Each set of participants used pressages to represent different types of information. Firstly, some of the messages were used as a greeting at the beginning of the conversation, then to get the attention of the person if they had been speaking for too long or if they had been silent for too long and sometimes just to surprise each other in a playful manner. Interestingly, the occasional use of a pressage during a phone call increased the users’ sense of presence. Pressages were also used to emphasise speech or to express both positive and negative emotions. Larger long-term studies will help to establish the most common meanings attached to the pressages.

ForcePhone allows users to input four pressure levels and these are mapped to four vibrotactile textures on the recipient’s phone. During the design stages, it was assumed that users would assign different meanings to the different pressure levels e.g. high pressure/rough vibration for important messages, low pressure/smooth vibration for short or non-urgent messages. However, according to the participants, this was not always the case. The participants did not map specific types of message to each pressure level. Nevertheless, the participants did vary their pressure levels when emphasizing their speech or conveying emotions. Furthermore, the logs show that participants attempted to match their pressure levels when sending the pressages. Similar to the findings by Chang *et al.* [3] , this suggests a form of mimicry in pressage communication. Future longer-term studies will investigate these issues further.

Usage Over Time

Conducting a longitudinal field study allowed us to examine the use of pressages over time to ensure that our findings were not dependent on any novelty effect. The usage logs show that the number of pressages sent and received throughout the study remained consistent. At the beginning of the study, the participants were informed that they could use pressages as much or as little as they wished. All of the participants chose to include pressages in every conversation with their partner.

CONCLUSIONS

To conclude, mobile devices include an increasing number of input and output techniques that are not currently used for communication. Pressure and tactile techniques have been explored in tangible interfaces for remote communication [9] [3] on dedicated devices but these techniques, until now, have not been implemented on mobile devices or used during live phone calls. Therefore, many open research questions have been addressed using ForcePhone and pressages. With the help of lab studies we document concrete design decisions. Finally a month long study helped us gather initial experiences. The results of this research indicate that an additional haptic channel of communication can be integrated into mobile phone calls using a pressure to vibrotactile mapping with local and remote feedback. The longitudinal study showed that such a system has value as a communication channel in real-world settings with users expressing greetings, presence and emotions through pressages.

ACKNOWLEDGMENTS

This work was partially funded by the Nokia Research Center (NRC) Finland and Tekes collaboration project HEI. Many thanks to Anna-Maria Polli for her help with the video.

REFERENCES

[1] Argyle, M., Salter, V., Nicholson, H., Williams, M. and Burgess, P. The Communication of Inferior and Superior Attitudes by Verbal and Non-verbal Signals. *British Journal of Social and Clinical Psychology 9*, 3 (1970), 222-231.

[2] Collier, G. *Emotional Expression*. Lawrence Erlbaum Associates, 1985.

[3] Chang, A., O'Modhrain, S., Jacob, R., Gunther, E. and Ishii, H. ComTouch: Design of a Vibrotactile Communication Device. In *Proc. DIS 2002,* ACM Press (2002), 312 - 320.

[4] Hoggan, E., Brewster, S. A. and Johnston, J. Investigating the effectiveness of tactile feedback for mobile touchscreens. In *Proc.CHI 2008,* ACM Press (2008), 1573-1582.

[5] Ternes, D. and MacLean, K. Designing Large Sets of Haptic Icons with Rhythm. In *Proc. EuroHaptics 2008,* Springer (2008), 199 - 208.

[6] Wilson, G., Stewart, C. and Brewster, S. A. Pressure-based menu selection for mobile devices. In *Proc. MobileHCI 2010,* ACM Press (2010), 181-190.

[7] Chu, G., Moscovich, T. and Balakrishnan, R. Haptic conviction widgets. In *Proc. Graphics Interface 2009*, Canadian Information Processing Society (2009), 207-210.

[8] Rovers, A. F. and van Essen, H. A. Guidelines for Haptic Interpersonal Communication Applications: An Exploration of Foot Interaction Styles. *Virtual Reality 9*, 2 (2005), 177 - 191.

[9] Brave, S. and Dahley, A. inTouch: a medium for haptic interpersonal communication. *Ext. Abstracts CHI 1997,* ACM Press (1997), 363-364.

[10] Brown, L. M., Sellen, A., Krishna, R. and Harper, R. Exploring the potential of audio-tactile messaging for remote interpersonal communication. In *Proc.. CHI 2009*, ACM Press (2009), 1527-1530.

[11] Dobson, K., boyd, d., Ju, W., Donath, J. and Ishii, H. Creating visceral personal and social interactions in mediated spaces. *Ext. Abstracts CHI 2001,* ACM Press (2001), 151-152.

[12] Hemmert, F., Gollner, U., Löwe, M., Wohlauf, A. and Joost, G. Intimate mobiles: grasping, kissing and whispering as a means of telecommunication in mobile phones. In *Proc. MobileHCI 2011,* ACM Press (2011), 21-24.

[13] Stewart, C., Rohs, M., Kratz, S. and Essl, G. Characteristics of pressure-based input for mobile devices. In *Proc. CHI 2010,* ACM Press (2010), 801 - 810.

[14] Jokiniemi, M., Raisamo, R., Lylykangas, J. and Surakka, V. Crossmodal Rhythm Perception. In *Proc.3rd International Workshop on Haptic and Audio Interaction Design 2008,* Springer (2008),111 - 119.

[15] Stewart, C., Hoggan, E., Haverinen, L., Salamin, H. and Jacucci, G. An Exploration of Inadvertent Variations in Mobile Pressure Input. In *Proc. MobileHCI 2012*, ACM Press (2012).

[16] Ramos, G., Boulos, M. and Balakrishnan, R. Pressure widgets. In *Proc. CHI 2004,* ACM Press (2004), 487 - 494.

[17] Rekimoto, J. and Schwesig, C. PreSenseII: bi-directional touch and pressure sensing interactions with tactile feedback. *Ext. Abstracts CHI 2006,* ACM Press (2006), 1253-1258.

[18] Brown, L. M., Brewster, S. A. and Purchase, H. C. Multidimensional tactons for non-visual information presentation in mobile devices. In *Proc. MobileHCI 2006,* ACM Press (2006), 231-238.

[19] Donner, J. The Rules of Beeping: Exchanging Messages Via Intentional "Missed Calls" on Mobile Phones. *Journal of Computer-Mediated Communication 13*, 1 (2007), 1-22.

[20] Bernieri, F. *The Expression of Rapport*. Taylor and Francis, 2009.

Acoustic Barcodes: Passive, Durable and Inexpensive Notched Identification Tags

Chris Harrison **Robert Xiao** **Scott E. Hudson**

Human-Computer Interaction Institute and Heinz College Center for the Future of Work
Carnegie Mellon University, 5000 Forbes Avenue, Pittsburgh PA 15213
{chris.harrison, brx, scott.hudson}@cs.cmu.edu

ABSTRACT
We present acoustic barcodes, structured patterns of physical notches that, when swiped with e.g., a fingernail, produce a complex sound that can be resolved to a binary ID. A single, inexpensive contact microphone attached to a surface or object is used to capture the waveform. We present our method for decoding sounds into IDs, which handles variations in swipe velocity and other factors. Acoustic barcodes could be used for information retrieval or to triggering interactive functions. They are passive, durable and inexpensive to produce. Further, they can be applied to a wide range of materials and objects, including plastic, wood, glass and stone. We conclude with several example applications that highlight the utility of our approach, and a user study that explores its feasibility.

ACM Classification: H.5.2 [Information interfaces and presentation]: User Interfaces - Graphical user interfaces; Input devices and strategies.

General terms: Design, Human Factors

Keywords: Sound, vibration, microphones, identification, ID, tags, markers, classification, location, interaction techniques, ubiquitous and pervasive computing.

INTRODUCTION
Our world is increasingly "tagged" to facilitate information retrieval and to trigger interactive functions. For example, UPC optical barcodes are ubiquitous on consumer goods and QR Codes are being used in smartphone applications. We propose an alternative tagging scheme based on acoustics (i.e., mechanical vibration). Specifically, we use patterned, physical tags composed of a series of parallel grooves (Figure 1). These can be etched, embossed or cut into a variety of surfaces and objects. When a ridged object such as a fingernail is dragged over these notches, they produce bursts of sound that encode a unique ID (Figure 2).

This approach has unique qualities. Foremost, users can trigger acoustic barcodes with their (un-instrumented) fingers. It is also possible to use rings, pens, dry erase markers, mobile phones, keys and many other implements. Moreover, tags are passive, durable, and inexpensive to mass-produce. We used a $6 microphone for sensing, which can monitor roughly 10m^2 of surface area, for example, a large whiteboard or table. Surfaces and objects can be augmented and easily retrofitted with acoustic barcodes. On some surfaces, tags can be made invisible. Overall, they can be smaller and subtler than visual markers (e.g., fiducial markers [10]). Finally, acoustic barcodes can be incorporated in a wide variety of materials.

RELATED WORK
Researchers have explored many approaches for encoding unique identifiers. For example, visual schemes are popular, including 1D barcodes [11], 2D barcodes [19], and fiducial markers [10,17]. Identity can also be time-encoded using infrared light [18]. RFID tags use radio waves (electromagnetic radiation) for identification. Data can also be magnetically encoded, for example, the black strips on credit cards.

Most related to our technique are acoustic or tactile coding schemes. Braille [2] is a human-readable tactile encoding. The Edison Phonograph [4] is an analog system for recording and playing back sound by means of grooves cut in tinfoil. Moving from analog to digital: the Cricket System [15] uses coded ultrasound pulses to locate and identify users in an instrumented room. A listening device is attached to the user's hand and calculates its position in the room by measuring its distance to a set of fixed, coded emitters.

Another approach is acoustic-feature-driven classification. Hambone [3] is a wrist-worn acoustic sensor that detects movement of the arms via bone conduction, and performs gesture recognition by classifying the various sounds produced. Similarly, Skinput [9] uses an acoustic-sensing armband to localize finger taps on the skin (pre-learned locations). TapSense [8] and Sonically Enhanced Touch [12]

Figure 1. An acoustic barcode patterned into an acrylic tag.

UIST '12, October 7–10, 2012, Cambridge, Massachusetts, USA.
Copyright 2012 ACM 978-1-4503-1580-7/12/10...$15.00.

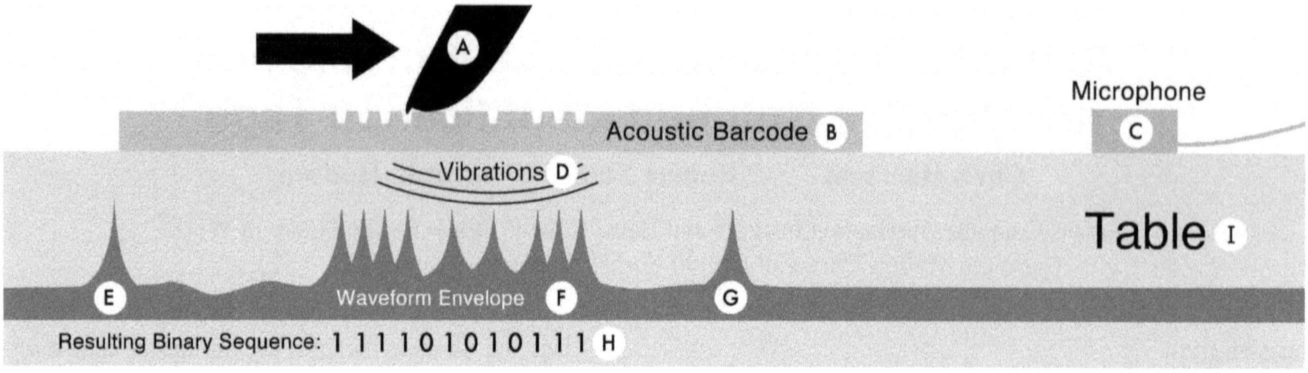

Figure 2. In this example setup, we have an acoustic barcode (B) situated on a table (I), to which a microphone (C) is attached. When a fingernail (A) runs over the barcode, a series of mechanical vibrations result (D), which propagate through the table and are captured by the microphone. The first sound is the initial impact of the finger (E). As the nail passes over the notches in the acoustic barcode, a series of sharp bursts of sound are produced (F). Finally, the finger lifts off or falls off the end of the barcode (G). The resulting waveform is processed, resulting in a decoded binary sequence (H).

use a microphone attached to an interactive surface (e.g., touchscreen) in order to differentiation among taps from different objects and parts of the finger, for example, the knuckle or nail. Stane [13] is a small palm-shaped device with an internal microphone and a multitude of engineered textures on its surface; the device classifies sounds produced by rubbing different areas, which can trigger interactive events. Scratch Input [7] uses a microphone situated on a surface to classify gestures performed on the surface, such as taps, swipes and shapes. Finally, Tapper [14] uses an array of microphones placed on a large sheet of glass to localize taps through time-of-flight correlation.

BARCODE CONSTRUCTION AND ENCODING

An acoustic barcode consists of a series of notches cut into a smooth host material. We use notches that are 0.25 to 0.5mm thick and 0.1 to 0.3mm deep. These are spaced 1.6 or 3.2mm apart. We recommended that notches should be at least 7mm wide to accommodate a fingernail or stylus.

In our encoding scheme, the spacing between notches is variable – the relative lengths of these gaps encode the data payload of the barcode. Specifically, the notches are separated by a small integer multiple of a unit gap distance, either 1.6mm or 3.2mm. Barcodes begin and end with a guard sequence consisting of three grooves separated by unit gaps. This guard sequence serves both to delineate the barcode and to provide a reference for the gap distance.

Following the guard, the payload is encoded. We provide for two different binary encoding schemes: a fixed-notch-count scheme and a fixed-physical-length scheme. Both encodings encode a single bit-sequence of fixed length. The bit sequence may be preprocessed with an error-correction scheme (such as a Hamming code [6] or Reed-Solomon code [16]) to improve the robustness of recognition.

In the fixed-notch-count scheme, 0's are represented as notches followed by a gap of one unit length. Conversely, 1's are notches followed by a gap of two unit lengths. This encoding uses a fixed number of notches, but produces a code that is of variable physical length. Alternatively, the fixed-physical-length scheme encodes each 1 as a notch and each 0 as a blank (i.e., no notch). Every bit is separated by exactly one unit gap. To avoid excessively long runs without notches, we constrain the space of permissible bit sequences to exclude sequences with two consecutive 0 bits. This better assures that a "clock signal" can be recovered, which is used to resolve the binary sequence. Note that this encoding has a fixed physical length, but uses a variable number of notches.

IMPLEMENTATION

We use an inexpensive off-the-shelf piezo contact microphone. An adhesive backing allowed the microphone to be attached to a wide variety of surfaces, such as windows, whiteboards and wooden tables. In general, contact microphones are sensitive only to mechanical vibrations on surfaces to which they are attached, and are robust to ambient noise. The signal is amplified and fed to a conventional laptop computer. Our approach, however, is computationally simple, opening up the possibility of implementation on an inexpensive embedded platform.

Capturing and Filtering Audio

We sample audio at 96kHz to reduce the likelihood of missing the brief transients produced by swiped notches. The audio signal is preprocessed with a high-pass filter at 4KHz to remove human speech and background hum (Figure 3, blue). The system listens for the onset of a swipe by maintaining a moving average of the amplitudes of the last 40ms of audio (4096 samples). Recording initiates if the average exceeds -40dBFS. Once recording begins, the system maintains a moving average of the last 250ms of audio, and stops the recording if this average goes below -40dBFS, or the recording exceeds 1000ms in length.

We then filter the recorded audio to make peak detection more robust. First, we transform the recorded audio by taking the absolute amplitude of each sample. Then, we compute an exponentially-weighted moving average over the recording to remove stray peaks and smooth the waveform slightly. Next, we take the sampled first derivative over the

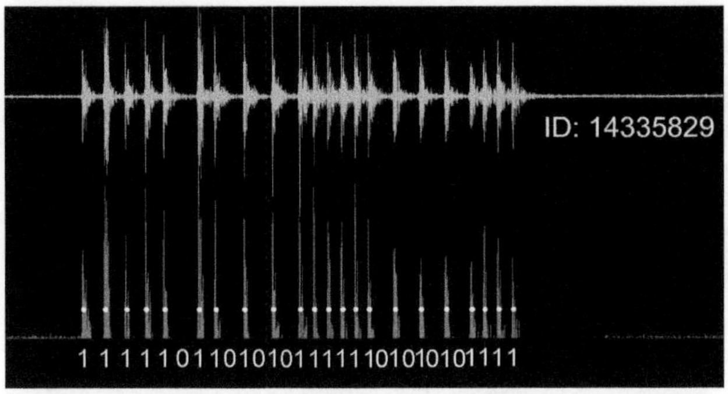

Figure 3. Blue: Example audio signal with 4kHz high pass filter applied. Red: final waveform used for peak detection. White dots indicate segmented peaks - the resolved 24-bit binary sequence is shown below (numerical ID on right).

smoothed recording, which accentuates peaks and subdues constant regions. Finally, we subtract a heavily smoothed copy of the recording from the derivative, which has the effect of removing regions of near-constant amplitude and secondary "echoes" from primary peaks.

Peak Detection

The filtered audio is fed to a peak detection routine (Figure 3, red). Iteratively, the peak detector takes the strongest amplitude value not within 300 samples (3ms) of another identified peak. By enforcing a minimum peak spacing, we avoid extracting echoes as independent peaks. The algorithm stops extracting peaks once the highest peak level is less than 3dB below the Kth largest peak, where K is a lower bound on the number of notches in the barcode. This approach ensures that the algorithm handles variable-notch-count barcodes, while correctly identifying peaks that are stronger or weaker than the average.

Barcode Recovery

A list of time-stamped peaks is fed to a barcode decoder, which recovers the relative gap lengths between peaks. Peaks followed by gaps of 30ms or more are removed. These are assumed to be the product of errant peaks, like those produced when hitting the barcode prior to swiping it (Figure 2, G and E). Next, the peak list is filtered to remove gaps that are much shorter than the median gap length, since they likely represent echoes.

Since the first three notches of the barcode are separated by unit gaps, the decoder assumes that the first gap is the unit length. For each subsequent gap, the system computes the nearest integer multiple of the unit length, and emits that multiplier as the detected relative gap length. When a user swipes an acoustic barcode, it is rarely at a uniform velocity. Thus, reliable decoding must compensate for timing skew (see Figure 3; compare gap length at the start and end of the sequence). To compensate, we calculate the unit length implied by each gap (the gap length divided by the unit multiple). This is then averaged with the previous unit estimates, allowing the value to drift as decoding proceeds.

Materials

Part of our explorations included testing different materials for feasibility (Figure 4). Using a laser cutter, we have been able to etch acoustic barcodes into acrylic, glass, wood, granite, paper, and transparencies (type 1 polyester). The latter two materials are flexible and can be applied to surfaces and objects like stickers. We also successfully laser etched acoustic barcodes into vacuum-formed polystyrene. Acoustic barcodes can also be directly incorporated into 3D printed objects. It is important that a high-density, gloss setting is used. Indeed, an important commonality between these successful materials is a smooth finish. A rough finish will produce excessive noise during swipes, which will obscure sounds produced by notches. There was minimal wear in the materials tested, suggesting acoustic barcodes are durable. Finally it seems likely that metal could be embossed with acoustic barcodes, though we were unable to test this.

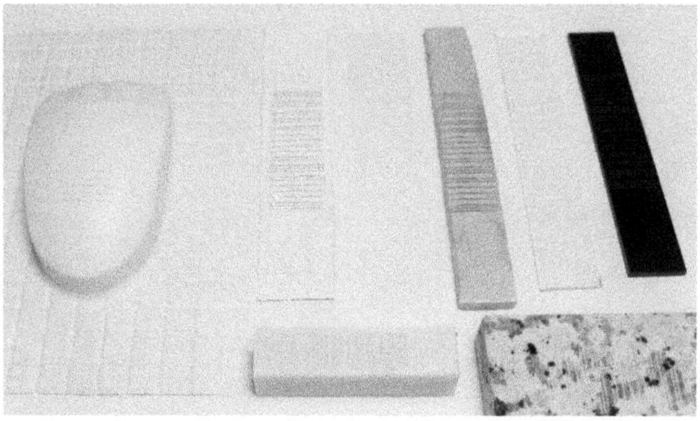

Figure 4. Acoustic barcodes can be incorporated into a variety of materials. Clockwise from top left: Polystyrene (vacuum-formed), paper, transparency, wood, glass, acrylic, granite, and a 3D printed object.

EXAMPLE APPLICATIONS

We devised four example applications, which highlight different aspects, capabilities, and configurations of acoustic barcodes. Please also see the Video Figure.

Acoustic barcodes can be easily patterned into objects (e.g., part of the injection mold for plastic toys). To demonstrate this, we modified a wooden toy ship. Using a pen instrumented with a microphone, users can swipe over different parts of the ship (Figure 5A), which causes the name of the location to be read out loud, for example "port side" or "engine room". This could be easily extended to human models for learning about anatomy, labels on engine parts, and books with audio content.

We also created an acoustic-barcode enhanced storefront (Figure 5B). We fashioned clear acrylic tags and attached them to a large glass window (though ideally the window itself would be patterned). A microphone is attached to the inside of the glass (i.e., all "active" components are safe inside). Passersby can swipe the tags with their nails; the system reads back a description of the item and the price.

Most mobile devices have an internal microphone, which could be used to read acoustic barcodes in the environment - like an acoustic equivalent of QR Codes. As a proof of concept, we attached a microphone to an iPod Touch and created several office widgets. These allow a user to quickly

Figure 5. We created four example applications to highlight different uses of acoustic barcodes.

set the state of a device and the office, for example to "sync phone now" (Figure 5C) and "forward calls to desk."

Finally, we created an example suite of magnetically-backed widgets that can be stuck to whiteboards (Figure 6). The surface of these widgets is patterned with different acoustic barcodes. For example, the four-way arrow has different IDs on each direction and the circle has IDs around its periphery. Teachers, for example, could use these to create class-specific, ad hoc interfaces. Figure 5D shows a left/right arrow used to control a slide deck, and a camera widget used to trigger a photo of the whiteboard to provide students a copy of the non-digital work.

EVALUATION

To evaluate the effectiveness of acoustic barcodes we performed a small user study. Our goal in this study was two-fold. First, we wished to measure the raw accuracy of the recognition system, to determine if the approach was feasible. Second, we wished to empirically determine how much error correction might be required to provide a usable level of accuracy. For reference, 29x29 QR Codes have a raw payload of 841 bits, of which 281 bits are format information, fixed patterns, and other header data, 208 bits are usable data, and 352 bits are used for error correction.

We recruited 7 participants (four female) with a mean age of 26. Participants were paid $10 for their involvement. Before the experiment, participants were given a brief introduction to the acoustic barcodes technique.

Participants were asked to swipe six different types of barcodes with three devices: a fingernail, a dry erase marker, and a mobile phone. The microphone was affixed to the whiteboard in the fingernail and marker conditions and to

Figure 6. Widgets patterned with acoustic barcodes.

the phone in the phone condition. The barcodes varied in bit count (6, 12, and 24 bit codes) and unit gap length (1.6mm and 3.2mm). All barcodes used in the study were encoded using the fixed-physical-length encoding scheme to avoid confounding effects from varying swipe distances.

For each barcode type and device, participants performed a block of 15 trials, swiping 5 different bars 3 times each, for a total of 270 trials over the course of the experiment. Prior to starting each block, participants trained on two random unused bars to familiarize themselves with the swiping technique. The order of blocks was randomized to compensate for order effects. Participants completed all blocks for a single device before moving onto the next device. Participant swipes were processed in real time using the system described above.

RESULTS AND DISCUSSION

We calculated the Hamming distance [6] between each decoded bit sequence and the corresponding expected sequence, including the three guard bits at each end of the sequence. This yields the number of differing bits between the expected and generated sequences.

First, we looked at "raw" zero-error accuracy, that is, sequences that match exactly (Figure 7, left). The phone performed the best of our three input modalities. Across all bit counts and gap lengths, the phone condition correctly resolved 87.4% of the acoustic barcodes without any errors. Fingernail performs second best at 77.9%. Surprisingly, the dry erase marker performed worst overall, achieving an average zero-error recognition accuracy of 66.4%.

Importantly, any real world application would employ error correction for improved robustness. One issue that must be considered when adding error correction is the ratio of data bits to error-correction bits. Adding more corrective bits increases robustness, but decreases the number of available payload bits. Returning to our earlier example of a 29x29 QR Code, over 60% of its available data bits are devoted to error correction, resulting in just a third of its bits being used for data transmission. It should be noted, however, that QR Codes have significantly more data payload owing to their 2D nature (1D data density is comparable).

Correcting a single bit error in a 6-bit code can be done by using a truncated (7,4) Hamming code [6] to produce a barcode with 3 data bits and 3 check bits. Correcting two bit

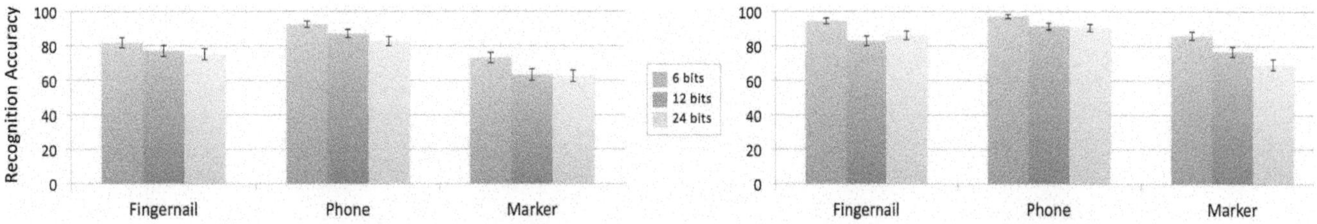

Figure 7. Left: Acoustic barcode recognition rates with perfect recognition (i.e., zero bit errors). Right: Recognition rates when error correction is included in the payload.

errors in a 12-bit code can be done using a truncated (15,7) BCH code [1], giving 4 data bits and 8 check bits. Finally, correcting three bit errors in a 24-bit code can be achieved by using an extended Golay code [5], which yields 12 data bits and 12 check bits, offering 4096 unique acoustic barcodes. Figure 7 (right) illustrates the recognition rates of our acoustic barcodes using these error-correcting schemes. The phone, fingernail and marker conditions achieve average accuracies of 93.1%, 87.4% and 77.3% respectively.

Increasing the size of the barcodes beyond 24 bits will increase the number of expected errors. However, our study suggests that the number of errors will grow linearly with the number of bits (around 10% of bits), which can be corrected with block codes such as Reed-Solomon [16]. For example, using a (63,30) BCH code, a 63-bit sequence, tolerant of up to 6 error bits, provides 30 data bits, offering one billion unique acoustic barcodes. Moreover, we believe that the unit gap length could be further reduced, enabling higher bit densities (there was no significant effect between the two gap lengths we evaluated). With a unit gap length of 1mm (down from 1.6mm), 60 bits can be encoded in roughly 6cm (2.4 inches).

The results in Figure 7 reflect a combination of system and user error. Anecdotally, approximately 5% of swipes were performed incorrectly by participants (e.g., started too close to the guard bits, fell off the side of the tag, ended swipe in middle of tag, used the pad of their finger instead of the nail). When this occurred, the signal was garbled or missing, precluding recognition. Over greater distances, it is harder to maintain a smooth motion, which reduced the accuracy of longer tags. Such user error is inherent in any system. No doubt every person has experienced having to swipe his or her subway or ATM card more than once. Even with recognition error rate of 10%, two swipes will suffice 99% of the time (99.9% for three, and so on).

CONCLUSION

We have described our work on acoustic barcodes, an identifying tag that uses notches to produce sound when dragged across. These could be patterned into a wide variety of materials and incorporated into everyday surfaces and objects. We used our system to prototype four application scenarios. We concluded with an evaluation of our approach, along with a discussion of how the data payload could be coupled with existing error correcting schemes.

ACKNOWLEDGMENTS

Funding for this work was provided in part by grants from NSERC, The Center for the Future of Work, Heinz College, CMU, and also a Microsoft Ph.D. Fellowship.

REFERENCES

1. Bose, R.C., Ray-Chaudhuri, D.K. On A Class of Error Correcting Binary Group Codes. *Information and Control*, 3(1), March 1960. 68–79.
2. Braille, Louis. (1829). Method of Writing Words, Music, and Plain Songs by Means of Dots, for Use by the Blind and Arranged for Them.
3. Deyle, T., Palinko, S., Poole, E.S., and Starner, T. Hambone: A Bio-Acoustic Gesture Interface. In *Proc. ISWC '07*. 3-10.
4. Edison, T. "Improvement in Phonograph or Speaking Machines." USPTO Patent #200521. 1878.
5. Golay, M. J. E. Notes on Digital Coding. In *Proc. IRE*, vol. 37, 1949. 657.
6. Hamming, R.W. Error Detecting and Error Correcting Codes. *Bell System Technical Journal*, vol. 29, Apr. 1950. 147-160.
7. Harrison, C. and Hudson, S.E. Scratch Input: Creating Large, Inexpensive, Unpowered and Mobile finger Input Surfaces. *In Proc. UIST '08*. 205-208
8. Harrison, C., Schwarz, J., and Hudson, S.E. TapSense: enhancing finger interaction on touch surfaces. In *Proc. UIST '11*. 627-636.
9. Harrison, C., Tan, D., and Morris, D. Skinput: appropriating the body as an input surface. In *Proc. CHI '10*. 453-462.
10. Kaltenbrunner M., and Bencina, R. reacTIVision: a computer-vision framework for table-based tangible interaction. In *Proc. TEI '07*. 69-74.
11. Lange, B.M., Jones, M.A., Meyers, J.L. Insight lab: an immersive team environment linking paper, displays, and data. In *Proc. CHI '98*. 550-557.
12. Lopes, P., Jota, R., and Jorge, J.A. Augmenting touch interaction through acoustic sensing. In *Proc. ITS '11*. 53-56.
13. Murray-Smith, R., Williamson, J., Hughes, S., and Quaade, T. Stane: synthesized surfaces for tactile input. In *Proc. CHI '08*. 1299-1302.
14. Paradiso, J.A. and Leo, C.K. Tracking and Characterizing Knocks Atop Large Interactive Displays. *Sensor Review*. 25(2), 2005, 134-143.
15. Priyantha, N.B. Chakraborty, A., and Balakrishnan, H. The Cricket location-support system. *Proc. MobiCom '00*. 32-43.
16. Reed, I.S. and Solomon, G. Polynomial Codes over Certain Finite Fields. *J. SIAM*, 8(2), 1960. 300–304.
17. Rekimoto J., and Ayatsuka, Y. CyberCode: designing augmented reality environments with visual tags. In *Proc. DARE '00*. 1-10.
18. Roth, V., Schmidt, P., and Guldenring, B. The IR ring: authenticating users' touches on a multi-touch display. In *Proc. UIST '10*. 259-262.
19. QR Code. Automatic identification and data capture techniques. Bar code symbology. BS ISO/IEC 18004:2006.

PICL: Portable In-Circuit Learner

Adam Fourney, Michael Terry
Cheriton School of Computer Science
University of Waterloo
{afourney, mterry}@cs.uwaterloo.ca

ABSTRACT

This paper introduces the PICL, the portable in-circuit learner. The PICL explores the possibility of providing standalone, low-cost, programming-by-demonstration machine learning capabilities to circuit prototyping. To train the PICL, users attach a sensor to the PICL, demonstrate example input, then specify the desired output (expressed as a voltage) for the given input. The current version of the PICL provides two learning modes, binary classification and linear regression. To streamline training and also make it possible to train on highly transient signals (such as those produced by a camera flash or a hand clap), the PICL includes a number of *input inferencing* techniques. These techniques make it possible for the PICL to learn with as few as one example. The PICL's behavioural repertoire can be expanded by means of various *output adapters*, which serve to transform the output in useful ways when prototyping. Collectively, the PICL's capabilities allow users of systems such as the Arduino or littleBits electronics kit to quickly add basic sensor-based behaviour, with little or no programming required.

Author Keywords

Toolkits; Machine Learning; Circuits; Tangible User Interfaces

ACM Classification Keywords

H.5.m. Information Interfaces and Presentation (e.g. HCI): input devices and strategies; interaction styles; prototyping

General Terms

Design, Human Factors

INTRODUCTION

The move from desktop to ubiquitous computing has led to the development of a variety of hardware-based toolkits to aid with prototyping and design. These toolkits range from those that depend on computers for both programming and deployment (e.g., Phidgets [10] and d.tools [14]), to those that are completely standalone, such as littleBits [4, 5], a recent hardware platform with individual pieces that snap together. Each of these toolkits lowers the barrier to prototyping hardware-based interfaces by reducing the time and effort required to work with physical sensors, actuators, and electrical circuits in general.

In recent years, interest in machine learning toolkits has also increased. Some of these toolkits are designed to be relatively independent of problem domains (e.g., Weka [11]), while others, such as Exemplar [13] or Crayons [7], are intended to aid in building user interfaces that respond to real-world sensor data. A hallmark of these latter toolkits is that they enable a form of programming-by-demonstration [18] by virtue of allowing the designer to demonstrate desired input.

Inspired by this past research, we envision a more complete integration of these two research trajectories whereby ma-

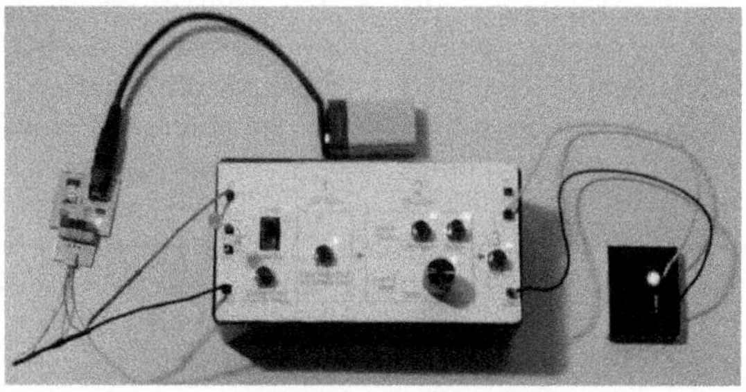

(a) The PICL prototype in a simple circuit involving a battery, a photocell, and an LED output.

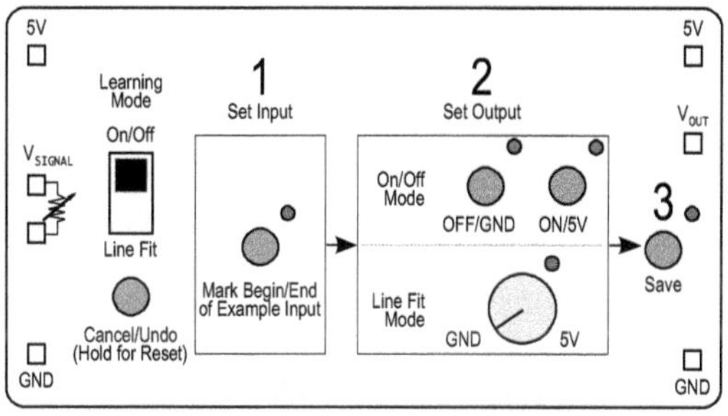

(b) A rendering of the PICL's user interface. The interface consists of five momentary buttons, one rotary dial, one switch, and five small LEDs for feedback. Users attach sensors to the V_{SIGNAL} inputs on the left side. Sensors outputting a voltage connect directly to the top V_{SIGNAL} input port; resistive-based sensors are attached to V_{SIGNAL} and the input directly below it, which attaches internally to a voltage divider.

Figure 1. The PICL prototype.

UIST'12, October 7–10, 2012, Cambridge, Massachusetts, USA.

chine learning capabilities are reified in portable, standalone learning hardware that can integrate with circuits, hardware toolkits, and other computational devices. These learning units should allow designers and developers to attach arbitrary sensors, then teach the learning hardware how to respond when given specific types of input. Ideally, we would like to achieve this goal without requiring a computer for either programming or deployment.

As a step towards this larger vision, we introduce the PICL, the Portable In-Circuit Learner (Figure 1(a)). The PICL is an in-circuit learning unit that accepts arbitrary analog sensors (resistive-based or voltage-based) as input. The sensed input is then mapped by the PICL to an output voltage via a learned function. End-users train the PICL by providing examples of input and the desired output for each input example.

Our current PICL can learn either a linear classifier or a linear regression model. It outputs 0V or 5V for the linear classifier, and a voltage in the range of 0-5V for the linear regression learning mode. These learning algorithms continuously sample input at a rate of 1200Hz on the 16MHz Atmel processor used in our PICL, yielding a 0.83ms response time. These two learning modes, operating at this response rate, enable one to prototype a wide variety of systems without any programming.

To simplify training, the PICL includes a number of *input inferencing* techniques. These input inferencing techniques reduce the number of examples the user must provide when training the PICL, and also infer which parts of an input signal are likely of interest. As an example, consider a scenario whereby the user wishes to turn on a light by clapping their hands. The PICL's linear classifier can be used in this case, but it must be trained on the short-lived, larger amplitudes of the clap's sound wave so it does not accidentally activate at normal, ambient sound levels. To aid with this type of training, the PICL tracks the initial, minimum, and maximum sensor values when it is training. It then chooses the value that leads to the best separation of the training data. This mode of input inferencing is useful when training on transient events, like the flash of a camera, or the previous hand clapping example. It also allows the PICL to be trained without requiring a separate graphical user interface to specify which parts of the signal are of interest.

To further facilitate rapid prototyping, the PICL also includes a number of *output adapters* that transform the output voltage in useful ways. These output adapters are separate components that connect to the PICL. For example, we provide a "toggle" output adapter that acts as a basic flip-flop. The output adapters build on, and extend, previous work exploring programming with tangible eBlocks [19].

The specific contributions of this work are as follows:

- An in-circuit, standalone machine learning hardware component with two learning modes, linear classification and linear regression.
- A programming-by-demonstration style of training that includes a set of input inferencing techniques to minimize training time, and to support training on transient events.
- A series of output adapters that transform the output in meaningful ways, to address a number of common situations and needs when building systems.
- A simplified interface for attaching sensors. Specifically, the PICL includes a built-in voltage divider to allow direct connection of resistive sensors. Active, voltage-based sensors can also be directly attached.

PICLs are aimed at designers, developers, and hobbyists who use platforms such as Arduino or littleBits to develop sensor-based systems. The PICL reduces and simplifies the code necessary to react to sensed input, while eliminating the need to measure sensor values, then write code that reacts to those sensor values. Its use of machine learning algorithms also provides a measure of error tolerance, allowing noisy or imperfect training data. Finally, for users of high-level systems like littleBits, PICLs provide a way to add intelligence to a snap-together system, without requiring programming.

In the rest of this paper, we review related work, then describe the design and implementation of the PICL. We present a set of sample applications, and conclude with a discussion of limitations and possibilities for future work.

RELATED WORK

The PICL draws upon prior research in hardware toolkits; programmable, tangible interfaces; and machine learning toolkits.

Numerous hardware toolkits have been produced to enable rapid prototyping of systems that can sense and interact with the physical world. Phidgets [10] encapsulate sensors and actuators into USB-modules that can be accessed via a rich programming API. In a similar vein, iStuff [3] and the Calder Toolkit [17] attach microcontrollers to physical devices, such as switches and potentiometers, to provide a higher-level interface to these low-level components. d.tools [14] takes an analogous approach, providing a standardized interface for low-level components to attach to a computer. It also includes a software environment to further facilitate programming with the physical sensors. The recent .NET Gadgeteer system [26] provides a similar modular system of sensors, actuators, and a mainboard, and can be programmed using the .NET language. Like these hardware toolkits, the PICL shares the goal of lowering the barrier to designing interactive systems with real-world sensors and actuators, but differs from these previous projects by not requiring a computer for programming or deployment.

A number of embedded systems have been developed that require a computer for programming, but which can otherwise be deployed as self-standing units. Smart-Its [9] are a general purpose development platform for creating context-aware applications using embedded systems. Smart-Its consist of a core board and sensor board, allowing flexibility in the sensors used. The Arduino [1] provides a basic platform for prototyping embedded systems, though it requires basic knowledge of electronics to attach sensors and actuators. Like these systems, the PICL is a self-standing system that can accept arbitrary sensor inputs. However, it is not intended to be a general-purpose system like these other platforms. Instead, its sole function is to learn input-output mappings.

The recent littleBits architecture [4, 5] allows various sensors, controls, and actuators to be chained together, with sensors and controls directly affecting actuators that come after them in the chain. This architecture enables those with no prior electronic experience to snap together basic circuits, but at present, it offers nothing more than AND and OR gates for adding computation to the circuits. The PICL provides a natural way to add intelligence to the littleBits system. We describe this possibility more fully later, and in the accompanying video figure.

The Buttercup system [21] is an embedded system that maps sensor input to effector output via an input-output curve. Users configure the Buttercup on a PC, where they can manually adjust the input-output curve or choose from predefined curves. The PICL performs a similar input-output mapping, but in contrast to Buttercup, PICL users create this mapping by providing example input and the corresponding desired output. The examples are then interpreted in the context of the chosen learning mode (i.e., the linear classifier or linear regression mode).

Research in tangible computing [16] investigates how computation can be embedded in physical objects. In the spirit of tangible user interfaces, a number of research projects have explored how physical objects can be used for programming. For example, AlgoBlocks [24] creates a "tangible programming language" with each block representing a programming construct in a Logo-like language. McNerey's Tangible Programming Bricks [20] provide similar capabilities, allowing individuals to compose basic programs by snapping Lego blocks together, with each Lego block representing a specific operation. While the PICL does not support the traditional form of programming represented by these systems, it does nonetheless allow users to specify desired behavior through demonstration.

More similar to the PICL, eBlocks [19] provide sensor-based blocks that transform their input to logic levels. The output of these blocks can then be connected to logic blocks to perform Boolean logic. Also included in this system are state-based blocks, such as flip-flops (called a "Toggle" block in the system), a "Yes Prolonger" block (which extends the emission of a "yes"/true-valued input), a latch block, and a pulse generator block. The PICL's output adapters are analogous to these state blocks, and serve similar functions when designing circuits. We replicate and extend these blocks with our output adapters, adding line-select and PWM output adapters (described later).

Transitioning to the realm of machine learning toolkits, Hartmann et al.'s Exemplar system [13] provides a bridge between sensor-based toolkits and software that recognizes patterns in sensor data. Exemplar offers a standardized input interface for sensors that allows a designer to illustrate desired sensor input, choose the portion of the sensor signal that is of interest, then train to recognize that type of input. Its use of dynamic time warping enables users to provide a single input to train on. Software can then be notified via an event when that sensor input is later seen. Our PICL shares a similar goal of allowing users to demonstrate desired input with as few examples as possible. However, training the PICL is done entirely with the device itself and does not require a standalone graphical user interface. Furthermore, it possesses a number of input inferencing techniques to lessen training time and effort. Another important difference between these systems is that the PICL does not consider a signal over time, while Exemplar does.

Other toolkits have been developed to lower the barrier to utilizing machine learning techniques, especially by those with little experience developing or using machine learning algorithms. Weka [11] is a general-purpose, low-level machine learning toolkit, while Gestalt [22] provides a number of facilities to assist in developing robust classifiers. While these toolkits help bootstrap the creation of systems with a machine learning component, they are aimed primarily at software developers.

Crayons [7] and CueFlik [8] are both examples of interactive machine learning systems, where end-users interactively label data to train a computer vision classifier. MAGIC [2] similarly allows end-users to create a gesture classifier by providing examples. PICL shares a similar vision to these systems by allowing users to explicitly provide example input and the desired output for that input.

Finally, there have been numerous efforts to embed machine learning capabilities directly in chips such as field-programmable gate arrays (FPGAs) (e.g., [27, 12]). We are inspired by these efforts, but are focused on how to make such functionality accessible to the end-user.

DESIGN DESIDERATA

In designing the PICL, our aim was to construct a learning unit that could enable designers and developers to interface arbitrary sensors with simple electronic circuits using a programming-by-demonstration metaphor. Our specific goals are captured in the following design desiderata:

- **A Standalone Unit**: The PICL should be a standalone unit that does not require a computer for training or deployment.

- **Sensor Agnostic**: The system should be sensor agnostic, and users should not need to know exactly how a given sensor responds to its environment. For example, the PICL should not require users to differentiate between positive temperature coefficient (PTC) thermistors, whose resistance increases with temperature, and negative temperature coefficient (NTC) thermistors, whose resistance decreases under the same conditions.

- **Programming-by-Demonstration**: Users should not need to know anything about machine learning, but rather simply feel like they can demonstrate example input and output, correcting the unit as necessary.

- **Simple and Streamlined Training**: The PICL should require as few training examples as possible, preferably a single training example.

- **Minimalist UI**: The PICL should strike a balance between a minimalist design and a rich, verbose interface that enables easy learning and debugging of the system. The interface should also allow for rapid specification of training data. The desire for a minimalist design is motivated on two grounds. First, a minimalist design can help keep costs down with respect to the required hardware. Second, most of the time, the unit will be responding to input, rather than being trained by the user.

- **Minimal Knowledge of Electronics**: Users should be able to operate a PICL and derive value from it without requiring extensive knowledge of electronics.

Collectively, these goals and constraints are intended to explore a specific area of the design space for hardware-based machine learning, namely, low-cost, standalone learning units that are programmed by demonstration alone.

PICL'S USER INTERFACE

The PICL must support two primary tasks: capturing example input and labeling that input. In support of these tasks, its user interface (Figure 1(b)) consists of five momentary buttons, a rotary dial, a mode switch, and LEDs to signal state. The mode switch allows the user to choose the learning mode (i.e., linear classifier mode or linear regression mode). The choice of learning mode also affects which subset of the interface is active, as described below. This design was a result of an iterative design process that explored dozens of interface possibilities. It represents a balance between a sparse interface with overloaded controls, and an interface requiring more expensive components (such as graphical displays).

Linear Classification

When in linear classification mode (referred to as "On/Off Mode" in the PICL's interface), users train the PICL by providing example inputs and labeling those inputs with a desired output of either "ON/5V" or "OFF/0V". The training process proceeds as follows:

1. The user presses the button labeled "Mark Begin/End of Example Input" to begin recording the training example. The LED next to this button begins flashing to indicate the system is monitoring the input.

2. The user demonstrates the example input by performing some action that is captured by the attached sensor. For example, the user might cover a photocell with their hand, or clap near a microphone attached to the PICL.

3. The user terminates capture of the input by pressing the "Mark Begin/End of Example Input" button for a second time. The LEDs near the "ON/5V" and "OFF/0V" buttons begin to flash to signal to the user that they must specify the desired output for the captured input.

4. The user presses either the "ON/5V" or "OFF/0V" button depending on the desired output. After choosing an output, the PICL begins outputting the corresponding electrical voltage. This allows the user to verify that she has chosen the correct output given her needs. Upon pressing a button, the LED near the chosen value remains on, and the LED near the "Save" button begins flashing to signal the next step of the process.

5. Finally, the user presses the "Save" button. The training example is recorded and the PICL's internal models are retrained. The PICL resumes mapping input voltages to output voltages using the newly trained model.

Linear Regression

The PICL's second mode of operation, linear regression (referred to as "Line Fit Mode" in the PICL's interface), maps input to output through a linear model learned from training data. In this mode of operation, the PICL's output is analog, and varies between 0V and 5V. Training in this mode is identical to the previous mode, except that the end-user specifies the desired outputs using the rotary dial.

Cancel, Undo, and Reset

The PICL has the ability to cancel or undo input via the "Cancel/Undo (Hold for Reset)" button. Pressing this button during any stage of the training processes just described (prior to pressing the "Save" button) discards that training example. If the PICL is not currently being trained, pressing this button undoes the prior training example. This allows users to easily recover from erroneous input. We currently support one level of undo, in part because errors should be readily noticed. As the button's name suggests, holding it down resets the device to its initial state.

Interface Shortcuts and One-Touch Training

To expedite training, the PICL provides a number of training shortcuts. For example, after first pressing the "Mark Begin/End of Example Input" button to start capturing a training example, the user can immediately press either the "ON/5V" or "OFF/0V" buttons, or turn the rotary dial (depending on the learning mode), to simultaneously end capture of the input example and to specify the desired output.

The PICL also supports *one-touch training*, which, when coupled with the input inferencing methods described below, greatly simplifies training of the system. To perform one-touch training, the user can simply press the "ON/5V" or "OFF/0V" button to capture the current input and associate it with the chosen output. That is, the user does not need to explicitly press the "Mark Begin/End of Example Input" or "Save" buttons – they can simply press the desired output button if the sensor is currently reading the desired input. In the linear regression learning mode, users can similarly begin rotating the output knob to set the desired output given the current input. However, the user must explicitly save the training example by pressing the "Save" button, since the PICL cannot infer when the user is done adjusting the output value.

LEARNING MODES AND IMPLEMENTATIONS

We now discuss how the PICL's learning modes are implemented internally. We also describe how the PICL can infer intended training values when capturing input, and how it can learn a linear classifier from a single training example.

Linear Classifier Mode

When operating in linear classifier mode, the PICL examines the input signal voltage and determines if the output voltage should be fully ON (5V) or fully OFF (0V), depending on which side of a learned threshold the input falls. This threshold, V_{THRESH}, is learned from the (x, y) pairs making up the training examples. Here, x can be any input voltage in the range 0-5V, and y is selected to be either 0V or 5V. When there exists a V_{THRESH} that perfectly separates ON examples from OFF examples, the data is said to be linearly separable, and finding a satisfactory V_{THRESH} is trivial. However, in many real-world scenarios, the sensor data is noisy, or otherwise fails to be linearly separable.

In order to better cope with noisy input, and to learn a robust threshold, the PICL employs a one dimensional soft-margin support vector machine (SVM) [6]. While support vector machines are beyond the scope of this paper, it suffices to say that in the one dimensional case, training involves selecting an optimal pair of ON and OFF examples, x_{ON} and x_{OFF}, between which the threshold is placed (i.e., $V_{\text{THRESH}} = (x_{\text{ON}} + x_{\text{OFF}})/2$). These optimal examples are known as the "support", and are chosen so as to maximize their mutual distance from the threshold (i.e., the margins), while minimizing the error contributed by training examples that fall on the wrong side of their respective support. This tradeoff is represented in equations 1 and 2.

$$\text{Cost} = \frac{2}{(x_{\text{ON}} - x_{\text{OFF}})^2} + C \sum_{(x,y)\in\text{Training}} H(x, y) \qquad (1)$$

Where C is a constant which determines how forgiving the support vector machine is of errors, and H is the hinge loss function defined as follows:

$$H(x,y) = \begin{cases} \max(0,\ x - x_{\text{ON}}) & \text{if } x_{\text{ON}} < x_{\text{OFF}} \text{ and } y = 5\text{V} \\ \max(0,\ x_{\text{ON}} - x) & \text{if } x_{\text{ON}} \geq x_{\text{OFF}} \text{ and } y = 5\text{V} \\ \max(0,\ x_{\text{OFF}} - x) & \text{if } x_{\text{ON}} < x_{\text{OFF}} \text{ and } y = 0\text{V} \\ \max(0,\ x - x_{\text{OFF}}) & \text{if } x_{\text{ON}} \geq x_{\text{OFF}} \text{ and } y = 0\text{V} \end{cases} \qquad (2)$$

Linear Regression Mode

When operating in linear regression mode, the PICL employs a simple linear model to map the input signal voltage to an output voltage. Again, the training examples take the form of (x, y) pairs. This time, both the x and the y values can be any voltage in the range 0-5V. From these training examples, standard *simple linear regression* [15] is used to learn a model that maps inputs x to outputs $f(x)$ via the equation $f(x) = \alpha + \beta x$. Here α and β are the usual regression parameters defined as follows:

$$\beta = r_{xy}\frac{s_y}{x_x} \qquad\qquad \alpha = \bar{y} - \beta\bar{x}$$

Where $\bar{x}$ and $\bar{y}$ are the sample means of the x, and, respectively, y components of the training examples. Likewise, s_x and s_y are the sample standard deviations of the x and y components. Finally, r_{xy} is the corresponding correlation coefficient.

When parameters are chosen as described above, the model is said to minimize the sum of squared errors (SSE):

$$\text{SSE} = \sum_{(x,y)\in\text{Training}} (y - f(x))^2 \qquad (3)$$

Input Inferencing

In both the linear classifier and the linear regression modes, users provide training data to the PICL by pressing a button to start and end a recording session. During the time between button presses, the PICL may sample the input many thousands of times. A decision must therefore be made to determine which sample best represents the user's intended training example.

In many cases, the user can demonstrate the desired input the entire time the PICL is capturing the input example. For instance, if the user wishes to capture a sensor value for a photocell that is in a shadow, it may be relatively easy to sustain the shadow during the time the input is being captured. In such situations, while there will undoubtedly be small variations in the input signal, these variations are minor and will not significantly affect training the model.

In other cases, the desired input is transient and difficult for the user to sustain or isolate when providing example input. For example, the user may wish the PICL to trigger its output when the user makes a loud sound (like hands clapping) or when it detects the flash of a camera. In these situations, the desired input value may be close to the minimum or maximum values observed while training. While we could introduce new capture modes to the PICL to allow the user to specify the type of values of interest (e.g., the minimum or maximum sensed values), doing so requires the user to understand how the sensor varies with different input. It would also introduce additional interface requirements. To avoid these requirements, we developed a means to infer the desired training value.

When training, the PICL employs a strategy we call *input inferencing*. Specifically, for each input example, the PICL learns three training examples. Each example has a distinct x value, but an example set shares a common y value (the desired output specified by the user). These three training examples are as follows:

- (x_{INITIAL}, y), where x_{INITIAL} denotes the input at the moment the input capture started

- (x_{MIN}, y), where x_{MIN} denotes the *minimum* input value observed during the input capture

- (x_{MAX}, y), where x_{MAX} denotes the *maximum* input value observed during the input capture

After each input example, the three training examples are added to three corresponding training sets T_{INITIAL}, T_{MIN}, and T_{MAX}. If the PICL is in linear classifier mode, then the three training sets are used to train three distinct support vector machines: $\text{SVM}_{\text{INITIAL}}$, SVM_{MIN} and SVM_{MAX}. The SVM that minimizes the cost represented by equation 1 is then promoted to the final model, while the remaining two SVMs are discarded. This process is similar to feature selection, and selects the input interpretation that yields an SVM with the best margin width-to-error tradeoff (which best separates the classes in the training data).

If the PICL is in linear regression mode, a similar process is undertaken, but with equation 3 in place of equation 1. Intuitively, this has the effect of selecting the training set exhibiting the strongest linear relationship between observed input and desired output. In the special case of only two training examples, the linear model is fit without residuals, and equation 3 evaluates to zero for all three models. These ties are broken by selecting the training set that covers the largest range of input values, relying on the assumption that the user is likely to demonstrate extremes when building regression models.

Baseline input and training with a single example

As a final convenience to users, the PICL records a *baseline* sensor measurement when the device is first powered on, or when it is reset by the user. This baseline measurement is used as a "stand in" for missing training examples when in linear classifier mode. For example, suppose the user resets the device, then provides a training example that is labeled as ON. After receiving this single training example, the PICL will assume the baseline measurement represents the OFF state, and trains the model accordingly. If the user then provides an OFF example, this inferred baseline example is discarded, and the actual user example is used instead. The CueFlik system [8] employs a similar strategy when the end-user has provided only positive examples to the system. In our experience, this simple heuristic often matches the way we think about training the PICL: we first demonstrate exceptional input, then demonstrate more common input. With this mode of input inferencing, it is often possible to train the PICL to classify input with only a single training example and a single button press.

ELECTRICAL AND HARDWARE INTERFACE

The PICL's electrical interface is inspired by the littleBits electrical interface, which provides power rails and an input signal that is transformed to an output signal.

Input electrical interface

At the most basic level, the PICL requires a single input, V_{SIGNAL}. V_{SIGNAL} takes an input voltage in the range 0-5V, which is output by an active sensor (e.g., an ultrasonic rangefinder or amplified microphone). Internally, V_{SIGNAL} is measured by a 10-bit analog to digital converter.

The PICL also includes a second input: *Divider*. When *Divider* is unconnected (floating), V_{SIGNAL} is treated as described above. However, if *Divider* is connected to V_{SIGNAL} through a resistive sensor (e.g., CdS photocell, thermistor, etc.), the PICL employs an internal voltage divider. The voltage divider enables end-users to directly attach resistive sensors without needing to construct their own voltage divider. While a voltage divider is a relatively straightforward circuit, resistive sensors are so common that we felt it worthwhile to include this circuitry in the PICL itself. This built-in divider also lowers the barrier for end-users new to electrical circuits.

Output electrical interface

The PICL provides a single output, V_{OUT}. V_{OUT} provides an output voltage in the range 0-5V, which corresponds to the evaluation performed on V_{SIGNAL} by the internal logic. The V_{OUT} signal is analog, and is generated by an 8-bit digital to analog converter.

Peripheral Compatibility

The PICL's inputs and outputs range from 0V to 5V, making it compatible with a wide range of logic families and microcontrollers (e.g., Arduino [1], PICAXE [23], etc.). Furthermore, with the addition of littleBits' physical magnetic connectors, the PICL can derive power from a littleBits chain, utilize the littleBits sensors as input, and interface with littleBits output modules. Thus, with no other changes beyond the addition of the littleBits physical connectors, the PICL can add basic computational capabilities to that system.

OUTPUT ADAPTERS

In its standard configuration, the V_{OUT} signal generated by the PICL is useful for many applications, such as triggering an external camera flash when detecting a loud noise. Occasionally, more complex output behaviours are desired. To facilitate the construction of more complex responses to input, we designed a set of *output adapters*. As mentioned in Related Work, these output adapters build on and extend the state blocks found in the eBlocks system [19]. They are intended to attach directly to the output line of the PICL.

Adapters for Binary Output

When the PICL is operating in linear classification mode, its output is either 0V or 5V. In many cases, it is useful to condition this output in some fashion. For example, the input may be extremely transient and rapidly vary (e.g., when hands clap), causing the output to change rapidly. To address these, and similar circumstances, we designed the following binary output adapters:

- **Single Pulse**: In its baseline state, the single pulse output adapter emits a steady 0V. This output adapter monitors the PICL's V_{OUT} for instances where the signal transitions from OFF (0V) to ON (5V). Upon observing this rising edge, the adapter raises its output voltage to 5V for a user-configurable period of time (specified by adjusting a dial on the face of the output adapter). This output adapter is useful for extending what would otherwise be very brief high-output signals, and makes interfacing with existing hardware (such as remote controls) more reliable.

- **Toggle**: The toggle output adapter is a basic flip-flop: a rising edge in the PICL's V_{OUT} signal causes the output adapter to flip states (if the adapter is outputting 0V, a rising edge on its input line causes it to output 5V, and vice versa).

- **Latch**: The latch output adapter changes its output state from 0V to 5V upon observing a rising edge in the PICL's V_{OUT} signal. Unlike the toggle and pulse adapters, the latch adapter remains in this high state until manually reset by the user. This reset is achieved by pressing a small button on the face of the adapter.

- **Line Select**: Unlike the aforementioned adapters, the line select adapter has two output lines. The first line simply echoes the PICL's V_{OUT} signal. The second line, $\overline{V_{OUT}}$, transmits the negated signal. This output adapter allows the user to create a system that selects between two circuits.

Adapters for Analog Output

In addition to the binary output adapters, we have developed two output adapters that work with the PICL's linear regression mode.

- **Oscillator**: As the name suggests, the oscillator output adapter outputs a clock signal, whose frequency varies as a function of the PICL's V_{OUT} signal. Specifically, the clock rate is mapped to voltage, with higher voltages yielding higher frequencies. When connected to a speaker, the oscillations are audible, and the result is a tone generator with output tones controlled by the PICL.

- **Pulse-width modulation (PWM)**: The PWM output adapter converts the PICL's V_{OUT} signal to a pulse-width modulated signal. This signal quickly switches on and off, but the percentage of time spent in each state (duty cycle) varies with V_{OUT}. PWM control signals are useful in that they can be used to efficiently control high-current devices. For example, this output adapter allows the PICL to control the speed of a motor, or the brightness of high-power lighting.

Benefits of Output Adapters

In designing the PICL, one of the questions we faced was whether we should include these types of output conditioning on the PICL itself. In the end, we decided to separate this functionality out of the PICL for a number reasons.

First, doing so maintains a minimalist design of the PICL, whose default input and output electrical interfaces are useful in many situations. Second, some forms of output conditioning require setting additional parameters. By offloading output conditioning to separate modules, output adapters can provide interfaces that are specifically designed for manipulating the relevant parameters. This enables very targeted interfaces, while avoiding a cluttered, overloaded interface on the PICL itself. Finally, externalizing the output adapters enables adapters to be chained together to compose more complex behaviours. For example, a Toggle output adapter and Line Select output adapter could be chained together to create a system that switches between two circuits every time the user claps their hands.

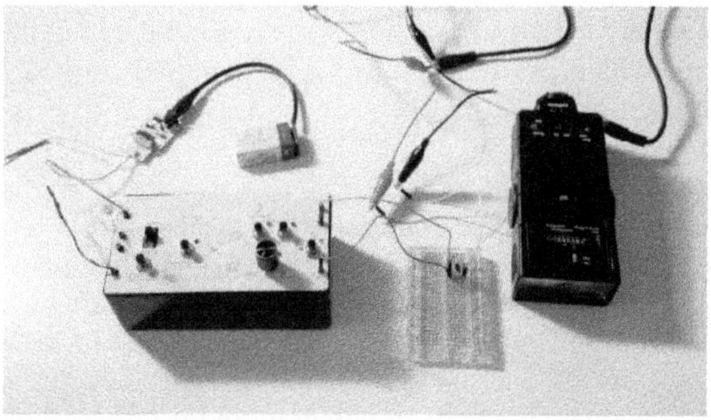

(a) The PICL attached to an external camera flash via a transistor. A photocell also connected to the PICL triggers the flash in response to other bright lights.

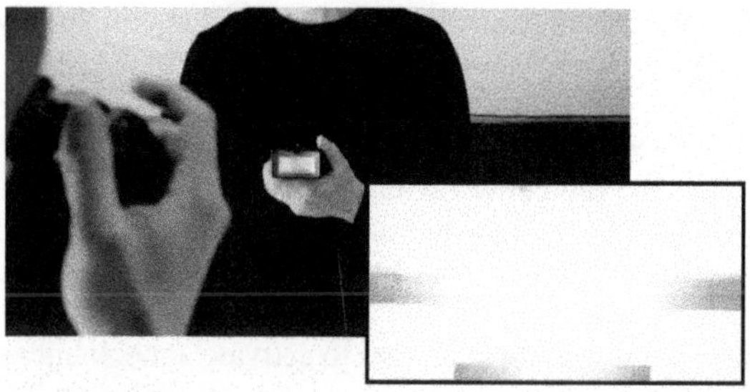

(b) The external flash is triggered by the prior flash of a photographer's camera. Here the external flash is used to defensively overexpose photographs (inset).

Figure 2. Implementation of capture-resistant environments.

SAMPLE APPLICATIONS

Having described the PICL and its output adapters, we now present various sample applications that can be easily developed with our system. All of these examples can be viewed in the accompanying video figure.

Capture-Resistant Environments

Truong et al. [25] describe how spaces can be augmented with a system of directed, pulsing lights to prevent the recording of images by unauthorized camera equipment. With the PICL, we can recreate this effect by detecting camera flashes, and quickly responding by activating a defensive flash to overexpose the recorded image (Figure 2(b)). To construct this system, we attach a passive CdS photocell to the PICL and record instances of camera flashes from various locations in the room. We also record several examples of ambient lighting conditions. The PICL's fast sampling rate and input inferencing features enable the PICL to develop an SVM model that accurately detects the camera flashes. The PICL's output can then be used to interface with a simple switching transistor, which can be used to trigger external camera flashes (Figure 2(a)).

Laser Tripwire Alarm

The PICL can also be configured to create a simple laser tripwire alarm. Using the same photocell as in the previous example, the PICL can be trained to output a low value when the cell is illuminated by a laser beam, and to output a high value when the beam is broken. By attaching a piezoelectric buzzer, the system can be made to output a loud beeping alert whenever the alarm is tripped. If the buzzer is connected through the Latch output adapter, the buzzer will continue to sound even after the laser illumination has been reestablished. To stop the alarm, the Latch adapter needs to be manually reset by pressing a reset button.

Clap Activated Outlet

As a final example, the PICL paired with a remote controlled wall outlet can be used to construct a sound-activated appliance. We accomplish this by training the PICL to output a high signal whenever a clap is detected by a microphone. The PICL's output can then be used to activate a mechanical relay, which closes a connection across the remote's "On" button. In this example, the Single Pulse adapter must be used to prolong the short-lived output signal so that the relay has time to close, and so that the remote detects the input as a proper button press (after debouncing). Now, when the microphone detects a clap, the remote outlet is activated.

In all of these examples, the user can construct a useful circuit with no programming required, and minimal interfacing hardware. For example, a transistor or relay is all that is typically needed to turn an external circuit on or off. In comparison, constructing these applications using a platform like the Arduino would require the user to first take measurements, then write code to trigger an output line when the desired event is observed by the microcontroller.

DISCUSSION

As discussed above, the goal of the PICL is to explore the notion of a low-cost, minimalist, standalone, programming-by-demonstration hardware learning unit. As can be expected, there are limitations associated with the imposition of such severe design constraints. In this section, we discuss the consequences of these design constraints and also outline possibilities for future work.

Limited Interaction

Without an interactive graphical user interface, it potentially can be challenging for the end-user to specify the particular sensor values they wish to train on. For example, they may wish to train on the maximum sensed value, rather than the minimum. In our own uses of the PICL, we have found the input inferencing to work well when inferring the intended training values. However, there may be cases where particularly noisy or widely varying input may lead to the wrong inferences being made. In these cases, the ability to directly select values of interest could be useful (as in the Exemplar system [13]).

Limited Feedback

The lack of a GUI can also make it more difficult to debug the system as a whole. For example, if the system does not seem to be training as expected, the end-user may wish to monitor the current sensor values, the current output values, and the current learned (internal) model. While both the input and output values can be directly measured using tools such as multimeters and oscilloscopes, there is currently no way for the end-user to view the internal model of the PICL. In our own experiences, we have not encountered situations where we were unable to train the PICL, but end-users who are less familiar with sensors and machine learning may run into situations in which they would benefit from a visualization of these values.

Changes in Environmental Context

One particular way in which the PICL may work in unexpected ways for those new to machine learning is when its surrounding context changes. For example, if the PICL is connected to a light sensor and trained indoors, the resulting model will likely fail when taken outdoors. Again, richer feedback could help end-users debug such scenarios and understand why the system does not work as expected.

For this particular problem, we also developed and tested the possibility of allowing the user to shift the learned model. However, we found the resultant interface too clunky. Instead, we opted for a more basic conceptual model of simply retraining the PICL.

Learning temporal patterns

At present, the PICL samples input at a rate of approximately 1200 Hz, and evaluates each sample independently. For example, it trains on inputs such as camera flashes by sensing bright lights, and hand claps by sensing loud noises. While the amplitude of these signals is a strong indication of each event, other key features of these signals are overlooked: their brevity, spectral components, etc. In the future, we look forward to incorporating more temporal features and learning modes into the PICL. Specifically, we are interested in being able to train on features in the frequency domain, as well as the possibility of using dynamic time warping to train on specific patterns. Dynamic time warping is advantageous because it can function with a single training example (e.g., [13]), which is very much in the spirit of the simple training desiderata expressed in the PICL's design.

Input Adapters

As an alternative to enabling temporal models of input, it may be possible to achieve a subset of this functionality through pre-processing of the signal. In this vein, we envision constructing a set of input adapters that are similar in spirit to output adapters, but which filter or transform sensor input. As a simple example, one input adapter may implement a bandpass filter to allow the PICL to detect sounds only within a given frequency range. Similarly, a beat-counter input adapter may allow the PICL to measure tones, or to handle sensors that communicate readings by varying the frequency of an output signal (e.g., some humidity sensors).

Alternatively, it would be useful to develop input adapters that communicate with sensors using common serial interfaces, such as the I^2C serial bus. Such an input adapter would greatly expand interoperability with complex sensors (e.g., accelerometers), but would likely require the input adapters to be preloaded with the communication protocols employed by common I^2C sensors.

Learning with parallel inputs

The PICL's hardware interface accepts a single input signal, V_{SIGNAL}, from which a single feature (discretized voltage) is used to build the PICL's internal models. In the future, we would like to explore the possibility of allowing multiple input signals to train on. For example, one sensor may measure barometric pressures, and another humidity, in order to predict the likelihood of rain. By expanding the feature space, we expand the complexity of the PICL's internal models, and thus increase the need for training data. As such, there are challenges in implementing such models in inexpensive microcontroller hardware. There is also a challenge in maintaining a simplified, low-cost interface to the system.

Cooperating PICLs

As an alternative to accepting multiple parallel inputs, it may be desirable to configure many individual PICLs to work together. In such a scenario, each PICL would monitor a single input or feature. The devices would then communicate with one another to map the ensemble of inputs into a single output signal. Such ensembles are trivial to create by interconnecting current PICLs with standard logic gates or voltage comparators, which is essentially the strategy employed by Exemplar [13]. However, we envision that cooperation could occur earlier in the evaluation process to better model the full input space. For example, one could assemble a group of PICLs to implement a single naive Bayes classifier. In this scenario, each PICL would be independently trained, and would monitor a single feature. The ensemble of PICLs would then communicate with one another to jointly infer the class of an unknown set of sensor readings. Once trained, the individual PICLs could then be swapped in and out, allowing a tangible means of selecting and composing features.

Miniaturization

The current PICL prototype, measuring $16 \times 8 \times 5$ cm, is much larger than it needs to be. This size is mostly a result of our use of an Arduino Mega 2560 microcontroller for prototyping, which itself measures $10 \times 5 \times 1.5$ cm. The enclosure also contains a prototyping breadboard and digital-to-analog converter chip, but much of the PICL's interior is empty space. We have begun the process of miniaturization, and have used surface mount versions of the various electronics to reduce the size of the core assembly (excluding controls) to approximately $7 \times 2 \times 2.5$ cm, for a PICL with only a linear classifier. Miniaturizing the interface will require some simplification of the controls, and remains future work.

CONCLUSION

In this paper, we have presented the PICL, an electronic component that supports basic, in-circuit machine learning. Users wire it into a circuit, then train it by demonstrating example input and desired output. Importantly, the PICL has a minimalist interface, can perform well with minimal training (in many cases, with a single training example triggered with a single button press), is able to infer desired input when recording transient signals, and requires very little knowledge of electronics or machine learning. With the PICL, users can quickly develop interesting applications by simply demonstrating input and specifying the desired output.

This paper also outlined how various simple output adapters can be utilized to expand the behaviour repertoire of the PICL. For example, the Latch or Toggle adapter enables users to develop circuits that maintain state after receiving input, while the Single Pulse output adapter allows users to interface with devices sporting mechanical momentary buttons. Finally, the PICL's electrical interface is compatible with most 5V electronics, including the very popular Arduino microcontroller and the littleBits electronic construction kit. When integrated with such systems, users can quickly interface sensors and transform their input to useful output values, with no programming required.

ACKNOWLEDGEMENTS

We would like to thank Krzysztof Pietroszek for his help in preparing the video figure accompanying this paper. This work was supported in part by an NSERC Discovery Grant and an NSERC Alexander Graham Bell Canada Graduate Scholarship.

REFERENCES

1. Arduino Team. Arduino - homepage. `http://www.arduino.cc/`, Retrieved April 2012.
2. Ashbrook, D., and Starner, T. Magic: a motion gesture design tool. In *Proc CHI '10*, ACM (New York, NY, USA, 2010), 2159–2168.
3. Ballagas, R., Ringel, M., Stone, M., and Borchers, J. istuff: a physical user interface toolkit for ubiquitous computing environments. In *Proc CHI '03*, ACM (New York, NY, USA, 2003), 537–544.
4. Bdeir, A. Electronics as material: littlebits. In *Proc TEI '09*, ACM (New York, NY, USA, 2009), 397–400.
5. Bdeir, A., and Rothman, P. Electronics as material: littlebits. In *Proc TEI '12*, ACM (New York, NY, USA, 2012), 371–374.
6. Cortes, C., and Vapnik, V. Support-vector networks. *Machine Learning 20* (1995), 273–297. 10.1007/BF00994018.
7. Fails, J., and Olsen, D. A design tool for camera-based interaction. In *Proc CHI '03*, ACM (New York, NY, USA, 2003), 449–456.
8. Fogarty, J., Tan, D., Kapoor, A., and Winder, S. Cueflik: interactive concept learning in image search. In *Proc CHI '08*, ACM (New York, NY, USA, 2008), 29–38.

9. Gellersen, H., Kortuem, G., Schmidt, A., and Beigl, M. Physical prototyping with smart-its. *IEEE Pervasive Computing 3*, 3 (July 2004), 74–82.

10. Greenberg, S., and Fitchett, C. Phidgets: easy development of physical interfaces through physical widgets. In *Proc UIST '01*, ACM (New York, NY, USA, 2001), 209–218.

11. Hall, M., Frank, E., Holmes, G., Pfahringer, B., Reutemann, P., and Witten, I. H. The weka data mining software: an update. *SIGKDD Explor. Newsl. 11*, 1 (Nov. 2009), 10–18.

12. Hammerstrom, D. A VLSI architecture for high-performance, low-cost, on-chip learning. *International Joint Conference on Neural Networks 2* (1990), 537–544.

13. Hartmann, B., Abdulla, L., Mittal, M., and Klemmer, S. R. Authoring sensor-based interactions by demonstration with direct manipulation and pattern recognition. In *Proc CHI '07*, ACM (New York, NY, USA, 2007), 145–154.

14. Hartmann, B., Klemmer, S. R., Bernstein, M., Abdulla, L., Burr, B., Robinson-Mosher, A., and Gee, J. Reflective physical prototyping through integrated design, test, and analysis. In *Proc UIST '06*, ACM (New York, NY, USA, 2006), 299–308.

15. Hogg, R., and Tanis, E. *Probability and Statistical Inference*. Prentice Hall, 2001, ch. 7, 402–416.

16. Ishii, H., and Ullmer, B. Tangible bits: towards seamless interfaces between people, bits and atoms. In *Proc CHI '97*, ACM (New York, NY, USA, 1997), 234–241.

17. Lee, J. C., Avrahami, D., Hudson, S. E., Forlizzi, J., Dietz, P. H., and Leigh, D. The calder toolkit: wired and wireless components for rapidly prototyping interactive devices. In *Proc DIS '04*, ACM (New York, NY, USA, 2004), 167–175.

18. Lieberman, H. *Your Wish is My Command: Programming By Example*, 1st edition ed. Morgan Kaufmann, 2001.

19. Lysecky, S., and Vahid, F. Enabling nonexpert construction of basic sensor-based systems. *ACM Trans. Comput.-Hum. Interact. 16*, 1 (Apr. 2009), 1:1–1:28.

20. McNerney, T. S. From turtles to tangible programming bricks: explorations in physical language design. *Personal Ubiquitous Comput. 8*, 5 (Sept. 2004), 326–337.

21. Merlo, M., and Bachman, M. A rapid prototyping tool for interactive device development. In *Proc HCII '11*, Springer-Verlag (Berlin, Heidelberg, 2011), 107–113.

22. Patel, K., Bancroft, N., Drucker, S. M., Fogarty, J., Ko, A. J., and Landay, J. Gestalt: integrated support for implementation and analysis in machine learning. In *Proc UIST '10*, ACM (New York, NY, USA, 2010), 37–46.

23. Revolution Education Ltd. PICAXE. `http://www.picaxe.com/`, Retrieved April 2012.

24. Suzuki, H., and Kato, H. Interaction-level support for collaborative learning: Algoblock – an open programming language. In *Proc CSCL '95*, L. Erlbaum Associates Inc. (Hillsdale, NJ, USA, 1995), 349–355.

25. Truong, K., Patel, S., Summet, J., and Abowd, G. *Preventing Camera Recording by Designing a Capture-Resistant Environment*, vol. 3660 of *Lecture Notes in Computer Science*. Springer Berlin / Heidelberg, 2005, 903–903.

26. Villar, N., Scott, J., Hodges, S., Hammil, K., and Miller, C. .NET gadgeteer: A platform for custom devices. In *Proceedings of Pervasive 2012*, LNCS, Springer-Verlag (2012), 216–233.

27. Zhu, J., and Sutton, P. FPGA implementations of neural networks - a survey of a decade of progress. In *Proc FPL '03*, Springer-Verlag (2003), 1062–1066.

Midas: Fabricating Custom Capacitive Touch Sensors to Prototype Interactive Objects

Valkyrie Savage, Xiaohan Zhang, Björn Hartmann
Computer Science Division & Berkeley Institute of Design
University of California, Berkeley
valkyrie@eecs.berkeley.edu, zhangxiaohan@berkeley.edu, bjoern@eecs.berkeley.edu

ABSTRACT

An increasing number of consumer products include user interfaces that rely on touch input. While digital fabrication techniques such as 3D printing make it easier to prototype the shape of custom devices, adding interactivity to such prototypes remains a challenge for many designers. We introduce Midas, a software and hardware toolkit to support the design, fabrication, and programming of flexible capacitive touch sensors for interactive objects. With Midas, designers first define the desired shape, layout, and type of touch sensitive areas, as well as routing obstacles, in a sensor editor. From this high-level specification, Midas automatically generates layout files with appropriate sensor pads and routed connections. These files are then used to fabricate sensors using digital fabrication processes, e.g., vinyl cutters and conductive ink printers. Using step-by-step assembly instructions generated by Midas, designers connect these sensors to the Midas microcontroller, which detects touch events. Once the prototype is assembled, designers can define interactivity for their sensors: Midas supports both record-and-replay actions for controlling existing local applications and WebSocket-based event output for controlling novel or remote applications. In a first-use study with three participants, users successfully prototyped media players. We also demonstrate how Midas can be used to create a number of touch-sensitive interfaces.

ACM Classification: H.5.2 [User Interfaces (D.2.2, H.1.2, I.3.6)]: Prototyping.

Keywords: Design Tools; Prototyping; Fabrication; Capacitive Touch Sensing.

INTRODUCTION

Ubiquitous, cheap microprocessors have led to a vast increase in consumer products with built-in digital user interfaces. Many of these devices — thermostats, game controllers, and personal medical devices, to name a few — rely on touch sensing to provide input to their user interfaces.

UIST'12, October 7–10, 2012, Cambridge, Massachusetts, USA.

Figure 1: Midas enables users to define discrete and continuous touch sensors with custom shapes and layout. It generates fabrication files and assembly instructions. Designers can also define the interaction events of their prototype.

Digital fabrication processes like 3D printing and CNC machining make it easier to prototype the form of such products, enabling designers to go directly from a digital 3D model to a physical object. In addition, user interface prototyping tools have lowered the threshold to connect sensors to graphical user interfaces. However, one main limitation of current toolkits such as Phidgets [8], d.tools [11], .NET Gadgeteer [29] or Arduino [2] is their reliance on pre-packaged, off-the-shelf sensors such as momentary switches or slide potentiometers. Using pre-packaged sensors has important drawbacks. It *constrains exploration*: pre-defined physical form factors restrict the space of realizable designs. For example, available buttons can be too bulky or too small, or sliders may be too long or too short. Most sensors also lack *physical flexibility*: they are not easily applied to non-planar surfaces or added to existing objects. Finally, a large *gulf of execution* remains between digital design files and physical prototypes: sensors must be manually placed and wired one-by-one. This process is tedious and error-prone; physical prototypes can easily deviate from digital design files if a wire is incorrectly placed or forgotten. While recent research has introduced tools to create touch sensors of different shapes [12, 13, 31], their efforts focus on rapidly constructible, low-fidelity prototypes. In contrast, our work leverages digital design tools and enables designers to use the growing range of fabrication processes to create custom, durable, replicable touch sensors.

We take inspiration from the success of GUI editors. These editors enable designers to specify layout, size, and characteristics of widgets. They also isolate designers from specifying the "plumbing" that connects widgets to event callbacks. *Our research goal is to make the creation of physical touch-sensing interfaces as fluid as the creation of graphical user interfaces in GUI editors.*

As a first step in this direction, we introduce Midas, a software and hardware toolkit to support the design, fabrication, and programming of custom capacitive touch sensors (see Figure 1). With Midas, designers first define the desired shape, layout, and type of touch sensitive areas and obstacles in a *sensor editor* interface. Designers can choose from buttons, 1D sliders, and 2D pad sensors. For discrete (button) inputs, designers can use polygon shapes or import graphics to define custom shapes; other types are adjustable in size and aspect ratio. Once a designer settles on a layout, Midas automatically synthesizes appropriate capacitive touch sensor pads and routes connecting traces, avoiding user-defined obstacles, to a central touch sensing module via a circuit board grid routing algorithm [15]. Midas then generates layout files and step-by-step instructions that designers use to fabricate the sensors using rapid manufacturing techniques. Our prototype cuts sensors from adhesive-backed copper foil and vinyl on a commercial vinyl cutter. We also demonstrate how to use a circuit board milling machine to fabricate Midas sensors. Designers then transfer their flexible, adhesive-backed sensors onto the target object and connect the fabricated sensors to a small microcontroller using the routed connections. The microcontroller detects touch events using charge-transfer sensing [23] and forwards events to a PC. Once assembled, designers can define interactivity on the PC using the sensor editor. Midas supports both record-and-replay actions to control existing local applications, and WebSocket event output for novel and remote applications. WebSockets enable designers to write touch-sensitive applications using standard Web technologies (HTML and JavaScript).

We demonstrate Midas's expressivity with a number of examples and a first-use study. The authors used Midas to create several touch-sensitive interfaces, including recreating prototypes of existing and published systems. In an informal study, three participants using Midas successfully prototyped media player peripherals.

The main contributions of this paper are: 1) a novel method to create custom-shaped, flexible capacitive touch sensors by synthesizing sensor pads and auto-routing connections, as well as instructions for assembly and use, from a high-level graphical specification; 2) a design tool using this method to enable users to to fabricate, program, and share touch-sensitive prototypes; 3) an evaluation demonstrating Midas's expressivity and utility to designers.

The remainder of this paper is organized as follows: we review related work, then describe how designers work with Midas. We present Midas's architecture and limitations, describe author-created Midas interfaces, report on a first-use study, and conclude with a discussion of future work.

RELATED WORK

Midas builds upon prior work in physical computing toolkits and direct touch sensing. We also discuss alternative remote touch sensing approaches for prototyping and Midas's relation to circuit board design and fabrication tools.

Physical Computing Toolkits

A substantial body of work has introduced toolkits that facilitate connecting different types of sensors and actuators to user interfaces. Some research targets software developers, enabling them to extend their reach into the physical world via object-oriented wrappers to physical components [8, 18, 29]. Other research explicitly targets prototyping by interaction designers [3, 10, 11, 13, 16, 17, 20, 21]; such projects employ direct manipulation interfaces or programming by demonstration [7, 10] to enable experimentation by designers who do not write code; our work falls in this group. A third set of projects are aimed at hobbyists and learners: such systems focus on helping users learn how to code and on fostering amateur communities [5, 25].

Many prior toolkits rely on libraries of prepackaged hardware sensors which bring physical constraints with them; it is difficult to create sensors of custom sizes, and it may be difficult to attach them to existing objects. Flexible multi-layer conductive substrates [28] or embedded radio transceivers in each component [16] give designers more freedom of placement, but the components themselves are still fixed in size and shape. In contrast, Midas focuses on only one type of input—capacitive touch sensing—but provides explicit support for defining arbitrary sensor shapes and layouts.

Direct Touch Sensing

Most closely related to our work, BOXES [13] enables designers to create custom touch sensors from office supplies (e.g., thumb tacks); it also enables them to program responses to sensor input using record-and-replay of GUI actions (e.g., mouse clicks). We leverage the same programming approach but target higher-fidelity prototypes: Midas supports continuous as well as discrete (step-wise) sliders, enables construction of more durable prototypes, and permits designers to use digital design tools to create custom sensor layouts. Since layouts are created in software rather than cardboard and thumbtacks, Midas designs can be shared and reproduced. In addition, Midas can also output events to web applications rather than only local applications.

We also draw inspiration from projects that introduce various forms of "sensor tape"—touch-sensitive material that can be unrolled and cut to size to fit custom applications. TactileTape uses resistive graphite to create custom-sized slide potentiometers [12], while Wimmer's time-domain reflectometry approach [31] measures electric pulse reflections in a wire to localize touch points. Both techniques lend themselves to low-fidelity prototyping, but do not contribute design tools to support arbitrary sensor shapes.

"Remote" Touch Sensing

Touch can also be sensed *remotely*, via sensors placed in the environment, instead of the touched surface itself. Depth cameras can be used to detect touch events by segmenting fingers from background areas [30]. OmniTouch [9] uses this

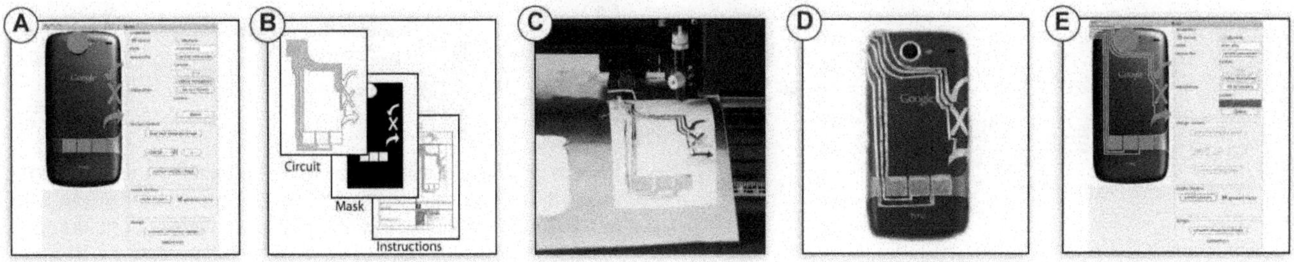

Figure 2: The Midas workflow: (A) A user creates and positions touch elements in the sensor editor. (B) Midas generates fabrication files and instructions. (C) The user fabricates the sensor on a cutting machine. (D) The user adheres sensors to a target object and connects the Midas touch controller. (E) The user authors interactivity in the sensor editor.

technique to make arbitrary surfaces touch-sensitive. Real-time motion capture systems have also been used to detect touch, e.g., Vicon cameras in DisplayObjects [1]. Remote sensing has the advantage that surfaces and objects do not have to be specially prepared. The main disadvantage is that the technique requires an instrumented environment or body-worn hardware. In addition, infrared-based systems often do not work outdoors, may struggle with occlusion, or need significant processing power not available in mobile scenarios. Prototypes that rely on remote sensing may have to be rewritten to change sensing technologies for production.

Design Tools for Fabrication

The placement of sensors and routing of connections in Midas takes inspiration from electronic design automation tools, e.g., Eagle [6] for printed circuit board design. We share the use of auto-routing algorithms with such tools. However, circuit board design tools are usually based on a library of fixed-size components. Midas does not have these restrictions because pads are used for human input sensing, not for placing components. Users can resize and easily import custom shapes in Midas. Finally, our work shares motivation with other applications leveraging digital fabrication equipment. For example, design tools for plush toys [19] and chairs [26] also generate fabrication files from high-level specifications. Our contributions are complementary to and independent from this research.

DESIGNING WITH MIDAS

This section demonstrates the interface affordances and the workflow of Midas (Figure 2) with a concrete running example: A designer would like to explore back-of-device and bezel interactions for a mobile phone. In particular, she would like to scroll through a list of emails with a slider on the back of the device, and open, reply to, and delete messages via sensors on the bezel under the phone user's thumb.

Drawing Sensors

Users start by loading an image of the physical prototype they want to augment into Midas's sensor editor. The sensor editor (Figure 3) allows a user to create the sensor layout, and define interactive behavior for each sensor. The background device image helps designers with correct scaling and positioning. Currently, Midas supports 2D images, including flattened 3D models. Future work will investigate direct support of 3D models. Sensor positioning works analogously to a GUI editor; users choose sensor types and drag them to the desired location on the canvas. Midas supports individual discrete buttons, one-dimensional sliders, and two-dimensional pads. Buttons can take on arbitrary shapes—users can import any graphics file (in PNG format) or draw custom polygons. Sliders and pads are currently restricted to rectangular shapes; however, their size and aspect ratio can be modified to fit the requirements of the prototype at hand. Users may also define *obstacles* using the same drawing tools to restrict routing — Midas will route connections around these obstacles.

In our phone example, the designer creates one slider and three discrete buttons. For the buttons, she loads custom shapes created in a drawing program. She defines a circular obstacle around the phone's camera so the camera will not be obscured during connection routing.

Fabricating and Applying Flexible Sensors

Once users complete a layout, clicking the *create stickers* button generates fabrication files. First, certain components are automatically split into multiple sensing pads. For instance, a slider can generate four interdigitated pads (Figure 6, third template) for continuous finger tracking, while 2D pads result in two separate layers of triangular pads (Figure 7). Second, Midas generates conductive traces that will connect each of the pads to Midas's touch controller. An ad-

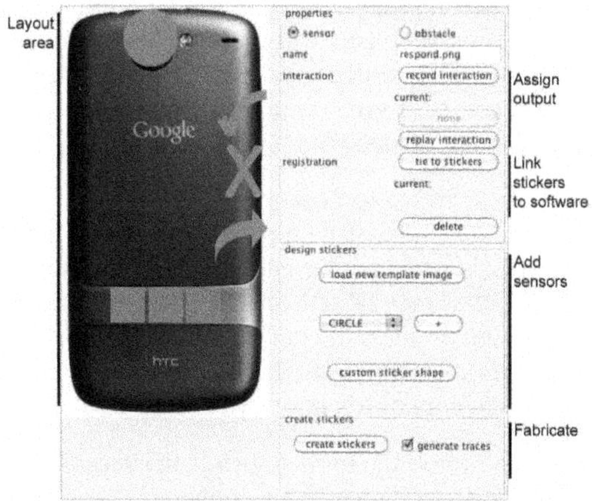

Figure 3: Midas's sensor editor takes its cues from GUI editors: designers first lay out sensing areas through direct manipulation; they later define interactions for each sensor using a property inspector.

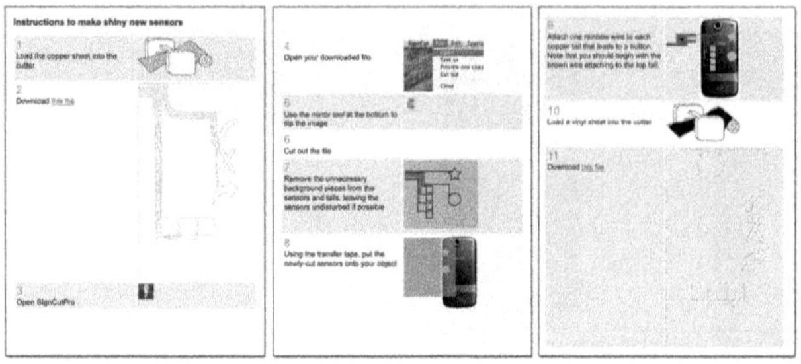

Figure 4: Auto-generated step-by-step instructions in HTML format lead the user through the fabrication and assembly process. Relevant design files are hyperlinked to specific steps; instructions also include general help on processes, e.g., how to use transfer tape to apply a sensor onto an object.

Figure 5: Users start to record GUI interactions in the sensor editor (A); they can for example activate the browser, enter text (B), and click on a search result (C), before concluding the recording (D). This sequence of actions can then be triggered by a touch event.

ditional mask file, to be fabricated in vinyl, includes cutouts of only the sensor shapes: it will cover the traces both for aesthetic reasons and to prevent stray touch events. Midas's connection routing determines the exact position of each touch area. Should the user want to experiment with positioning, Midas can also skip routing and only generate individual touch pads. However, the user must then manually connect wires to each sensor and register the sensor in the interface.

The pad creation and routing step generates a set of graphics files (in SVG format) and an instruction sheet (in HTML) which appears in the user's browser (see Figure 4). This sheet contains step-by-step instructions describing how to fabricate the generated files. For our implementation, instructions include which SVG files to cut in which material and how to transfer the cut designs to the prototype object.

In our phone example, the designer generates one SVG file for the touch areas and one to mask the traces, which prevents stray touch events. Following the generated instruction web page, she feeds copper foil into her vinyl cutter and cuts the corresponding SVG file. She then substitutes a vinyl roll and cuts a mask layer. As both materials have adhesive backing, she sticks the copper and vinyl layers onto the phone she wishes to modify. Once the adhesive layers are applied, she tapes the end of the routed traces to the Midas hardware, which is plugged into her computer via USB. Since the design files for her prototype are digital, she also sends them to colleagues in another office for a second, remote test. With the design files and a vinyl cutter, her colleagues can then recreate a working Midas prototype.

Connecting Hardware to Software

Midas senses touch events with a dedicated touch controller circuit board. Users do not have to program or assemble any electronics — they may treat the entire setup as a prototyping "dongle". Users do have to connect the end of the traces to the controller's rainbow ribbon cable, either by taping the cable leads onto copper traces or by soldering them.

To complete a prototype, users return to the sensor editor. In many toolkits, mapping hardware components to named objects in software can be error-prone—it is easy to swap wires or connect to an incorrect pin. If the user prints a fully routed design, Midas generates instructions for aligning touch areas with specific ribbon cable colors. If the user decided to wire the design herself, this mapping has to be authored. Midas uses *guided demonstration* to assist with this process. For buttons, the user selects an input element in the UI and clicks the *tie to stickers* button; next she touches the corresponding copper sensor. Midas listens for status change events and automatically assigns hardware pins. Midas registers sliders similarly: users are asked to swipe a finger along the slider.

Midas's editor interface displays incoming touch data visually, re-coloring touched sensors in pink on the sensor editor, to aid the user in debugging. If something goes wrong during the connection stage, it is apparent to the user. Midas also reads the data stream for common errors. If it detects that two wires may be too close together and triggering each other, or that there may be a faulty connection from a wire to the board, that information is displayed to the user in a connection status area.

Adding Interactivity

Designers have two options for authoring interactivity: record-and-replay of mouse and keyboard events (a strategy adopted from BOXES [13] and Exemplar [10]), or touch event output to control applications via WebSockets. To record and replay interactions, designers select a sensor in the editor, then click on the *record interaction* button. They can then control any open application (e.g., start or stop a media player application, or drag a volume slider). Midas records the generated keyboard and mouse events and can replay them later in response to touch input (Figure 5).

The types of desktop UI actions that can be executed depend on the button type. Individual buttons can be tied to an *interaction script*, a sequence of keyboard and mouse events recorded by the user. Sliders are linked to exactly one horizontal or vertical line on the screen to be controlled by clicks along its length. 2D pads can control a 2D area on the screen analogous to a slider area. For sliders and pads, the user must capture the location on the screen that she wishes to control with the slider or pad. This is done by clicking at each end of the slider or in opposite corners of the pad, guided by Midas prompts. As the user adjusts the sensitivity (number of discrete buttons) of the slider or pad to be printed, the interaction with the captured on-screen slider or pad becomes more fine-grained, also.

Record-and-replay does not require programming, but it is brittle; changes in application layout or response latency can break a recorded sequence. To let users author more robust interactions, Midas uses WebSockets to send touch events over the Internet. This requires programming, but WebSock-

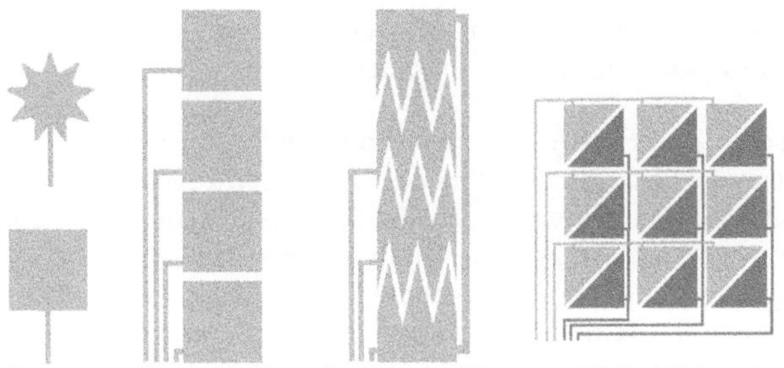

Figure 6: Midas can generate four different types of sensors: discrete buttons, discrete sliders, continuous sliders, and 2D pads. The pad uses row-column scanning and requires multi-layer construction because traces cross.

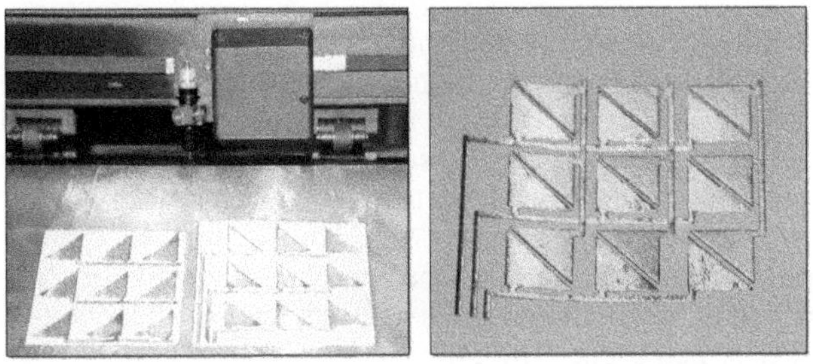

Figure 7: 2D pad sensors are fabricated in two different layers that are then superimposed. Because each copper layer has a vinyl backing, no other inter-layer masking is required.

ets enable designers to work in the languages many are most familiar with: HTML and JavaScript.

In our phone example, the designer chooses WebSockets as she wants to demonstrate how touch events can control a mobile email application. She creates a mockup in HTML and writes JavaScript functions to receive touch events.

ARCHITECTURE AND IMPLEMENTATION

This section describes the architecture and algorithms underlying the Midas system.

Generating Sensor Pads

The Midas sensor editor supports four types of touch sensors: discrete buttons, two types of 1D sliders, and 2D pads. The resolution of pads and segmented sliders can be set through a parameter in the sensor editor. The current editor is written in Java using the Swing GUI Toolkit. Figure 6 shows example templates for each sensor type. The two types of sliders are based on different sensing approaches. The first, *segmented slider*, is made up of individual rectangular touch segments. Users specify how many segments the slider has. *Continuous sliders* offer finer resolution, but require a different detection approach. We use Bigelow's design of interdigitated electrodes [4]. In this design, as a finger slides across the pads, the surface area of the pads underneath the finger changes as pad digits get smaller or larger. Because capacitance is proportional to contact surface area, the measured capacitance of each segment changes during the finger's slide. Though finer in resolution, only one such slider is supported by our current sensing hardware. Increasing the number of supported sliders is possible with additional engineering effort.

2D pads use row-column scanning to reduce connecting traces. For example, a 5×5 array requires 25 individual traces, but only $5 + 5 = 10$ row-column traces. This design requires a dual-layer construction where horizontal traces are isolated from vertical traces. We use copper foil applied to vinyl foil in our cutter, so each layer already has an insulating substrate. Designers thus first apply the bottom conductive layer, then place the top layer directly over it (see Figure 7).

To create a mask layer that covers the topmost copper traces, we generate a design file containing pads from all layers, but no traces. This layer is cut in vinyl. While for other layers designers transfer the pads and traces, for the mask layer they peel and transfer the surrounding "background" shape with sensors and obstacles cut out (see Figure 12, left).

Routing Pads to the Touch Controller

Midas employs an auto-routing algorithm to generate conductive traces connecting electrodes to the Midas touch controller. User-defined obstacles are avoided. We implement Lee's breadth-first maze routing algorithm for single layer paths [15]. For 2D pads, we perform two independent routings: one for the row layer and one for the column layer. Our current algorithm does not generate vias (connections between different conductive layers). When auto-routing fails, we employ an iterative search by adjusting the position where traces connect to sensor pads, routing the sensors in a different order, or moving the position where target traces connect to the touch controller. In our experience, this basic routing algorithm has performed adequately, though there are designs that cannot be successfully routed. For such cases, the algorithm could be replaced with more sophisticated routing techniques that include user input, though such techniques require that the user has a correct mental model of the routing process.

Midas currently offers generic suggestions when routing fails, e.g.: "Sensor *reply* may be too close to sensor *delete*. Try moving sensors away from the edge and each other."

Fabrication

Midas generates vector graphics files in SVG format for the electrode and mask layers. These files can be used to control digital fabrication processes. Our prototype currently cuts conductive, adhesive-backed copper foil on a commercial vinyl cutter—a plotter with a cutting knife instead of a pen. This medium has multiple advantages. First, it is cost-effective and readily available: vinyl cutters are in the same price range as laser printers (ours, a tabletop model with a 35cm bed, cost $200); and copper foil costs a few dollars per foot. Second, copper has excellent conductivity. Third,

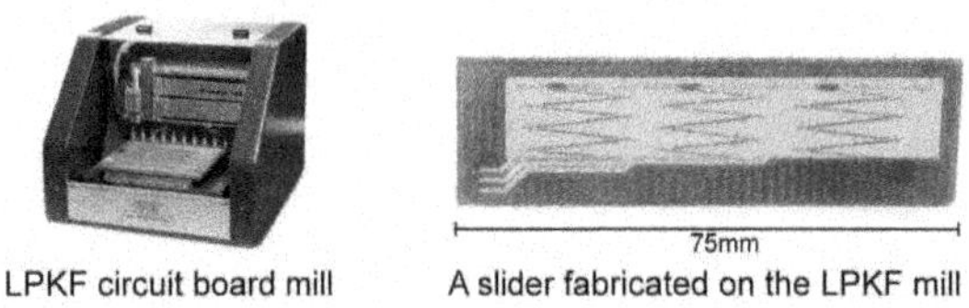

Figure 8: Example of a touch sensor manufactured through an alternative process of circuit board milling.

flexible, adhesive foil is easy to apply to non-planar surfaces. However, there are important drawbacks as well. Most importantly, the cutting process and manual weeding (removing background material) determines a minimum feature size for traces. Thin geometric features can also break during transfer, and the weeding process can be tedious and time-consuming. We found the most success came from adhering the copper sheets to vinyl sheets and cutting both layers at once. This setup has the added benefit of allowing designers to prototype touch interactions on conductive surfaces (e.g., aluminum casing) as vinyl is an excellent insulator.

Alternative fabrication processes may be preferable to copper foil cutting when higher precision or durability is required. Two promising approaches are circuit board milling, which can produce smaller features but is limited to rigid boards; and conductive inkjet printing, which can produce the smallest features, but is not yet available to many end users. As a proof of concept, we produced a touch sensor on an LPKF circuit board milling machine (see Figure 8).

Capacitive Touch Sensing

The Midas touch controller (Figure 9) is based on an Atmel microcontroller board [27] and capacitive sensing chips from Quantum (QT1106) and Freescale (MPR121) Semiconductors. For discrete inputs, both chips rely on charge-transfer sensing using single-wire electrodes: the electrodes are part of a simple RC circuit in which an output pin is set high, and time is measured until an input pin also reads high. This time is proportional to the capacitance of the circuit: when a person touches an electrode, the circuit capacitance and the charge transfer time both increase. The Quantum chip also implements Bigelow's design to extract continuous position readings from interdigitated electrodes [4]. The microcontroller runs software written in embedded C to interface with the sensor chips and communicates touch data to a connected computer over USB. It recalibrates the touch sensing chips periodically to ensure floating sensor values do not lead to erroneous touch readings.

Event Output

Once the user has assigned interface scripts to sensors, Midas listens for events from the touch controller. When a touch event matches the key of a saved interaction, that interaction's associated script is executed.

Record-And-Replay. In record-and-replay, the user selects a sensor and records a sequence of mouse and keyboard actions that should be played back when the sensor is touched. Early prototypes of Midas used Sikuli for this purpose—a scripting language based on computer vision analysis of screenshots [34]. While more robust than hardcoded click locations, Sikuli was designed for automation scripts rather than interactive control, and the latency of invoking and executing scripts was too high. Our current prototype uses the Java Robot API [14] to captures and replay both mouse clicks and keyboard events. We share this approach with the BOXES system [13].

WebSocket Communication with Web Applications. Record-and-replay is restricted to applications running on the same machine as the sensor editor, and it is limited to mouse and keyboard event injection. To surmount this limitation, Midas can also export touch events to remote clients via a built-in server using the WebSockets API. For example, an application running on a smart phone can open a WebSocket connection to Midas and receive a callback for any Midas button, slider or pad event. The callback function receives an event object describing which sensor changed state, and the value of the new state (e.g., on/off, or slider value).

Our WebSockets server is implemented in node.js using the socket.io library. We chose WebSockets because it offers full-duplex communication at low latencies, and, more importantly, is supported by modern web browsers. This means designers can author user interfaces that respond to Midas touch input in HTML and JavaScript. There are two main benefits to these technologies: (1) many designers are already familiar with them from web design; (2) developed interfaces can be deployed on any device with a compatible browser, even if that device does not offer a way to directly connect external hardware. For example, it is difficult to directly connect sensors to Apple's iPhone or iPad.

With our WebSockets architecture (Figure 10), designers open a browser and enter the URL of an HTML file they have placed in the Midas server directory. This file opens a

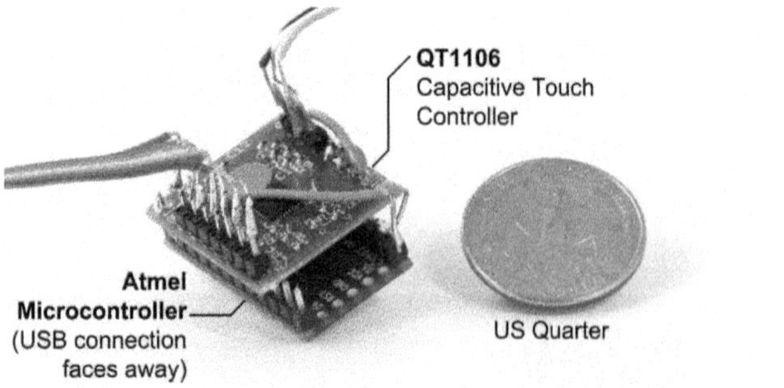

Figure 9: The Midas touch controller board uses a commercial capacitive charge transfer detection chip to sense touch events. Events are relayed to a computer via a mini USB connection on the back. The ribbon cables are used to connect to the end of routed traces. A US quarter is shown as a size reference.

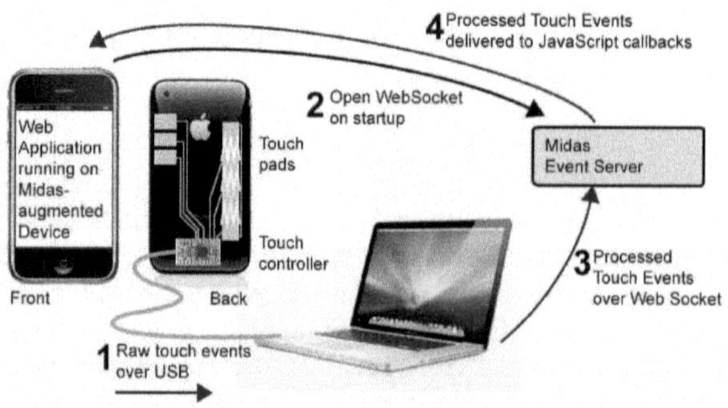

Figure 10: Midas's socket event output enables designers with programming knowledge to create web applications in HTML and JavaScript that react to touch input outside the screen area of a phone or tablet.

socket connection from the phone browser to Midas. When Midas receives events from the touch controller, it forwards them to the client, which can then show visual feedback.

Debugging. Midas offers basic debugging support. The interface displays incoming touch information from the microcontroller, highlighting activated sensors. We have also implemented basic regular expression filtering on the touch stream to help the user identify potential problems. A timestamp and code representing each touch event is stored in a stream. When a sensor is "on" for more than 10 seconds, Midas reports that that sensor may be touching another wire. When a touch sensor "flickers" on and off more than twice within 500ms, Midas suggests that there may be a faulty connection from that sensor to the microcontroller.

LIMITATIONS

Our current prototype has some important limitations. A few are inherent to our chosen approach, while others could be mitigated with additional engineering.

First, the current manufacturing process places certain physical constraints on realizable designs. Both the accuracy of the vinyl cutter on copper and challenges in weeding and transferring cut designs currently restrict traces to approximately 2mm minimum thickness. Our cutter also has difficulties with acute angles such as those in the interdigitated slider. A higher-quality cutter could mitigate these problems.

Second, the touch sensing chips have limited capacity. In addition, continuous sliders use different hardware resources than other inputs and therefore need to be treated differently by the designer. The QT1106 has 7 discrete sensing channels and can support one continuous slider; the MPR121 has 13 discrete channels. The sensor editor keeps track of resources required by the current design and notifies designers if they exceed the capacity of the touch controller. While we currently do not support using multiple touch controllers for a single project, a future circuit board revision could offer such support.

Third, our touch controller must be tethered to a computer. This reduces mobility: prototypes cannot currently be tested outside the lab. Direct connections to mobile devices or integrated wireless radios could address this constraint.

Fourth, Midas does not offer on-device output; a designer must have access to a screen. Use of WebSockets allows this screen to be on any device connected to the Internet, however future work can address on-device output.

Finally, the sensor editor supports only flat, 2D device models. Some 3D shapes can be flattened and these flat files can be imported. Future work could investigate the creation of a plugin for a CAD tool that would aid designers in creating more complex 3D sensor surfaces.

EVALUATION

To understand the user experience of working with Midas, and to assess its expressivity, we implemented some touch-sensitive applications and conducted an informal first-use study of Midas with three participants. We have also released Midas as an open-source toolkit to acquire further usage data.

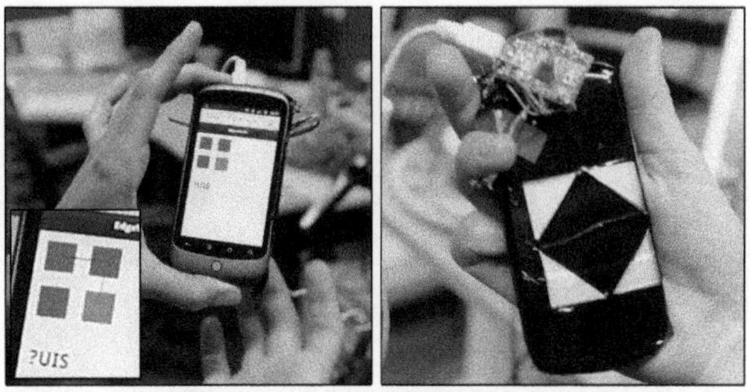

Figure 11: We implemented Wobbrock's Edgewrite on the back of a cell phone using a 2x2 pad and WebSocket events sent to a web page.

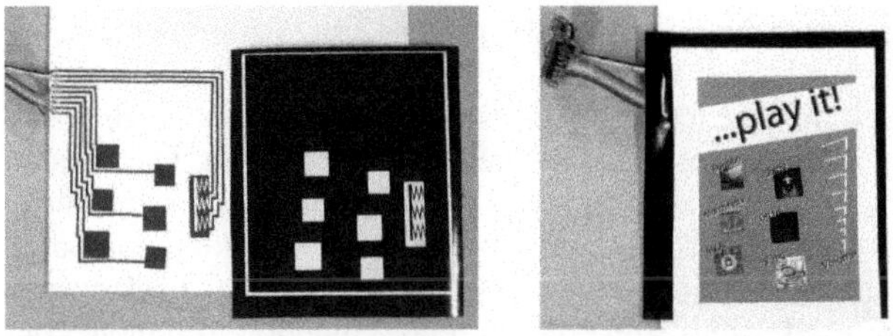

Figure 12: Our music postcard lets users sample tracks by different artists. Left: Circuit and mask layer; Right: assembled postcard.

Example Applications

To demonstrate Midas's expressivity, we built several interactive systems that used all sensor types, and output using both WebSockets and record-and-replay.

Text Entry. Wobrrock's EdgeWrite [33] is a unistroke text entry technique based on activating a series of corner points of a rectangle. Wobbrock demonstrated that this technique can be implemented using four discrete capacitive touch sensors [32]. We cut four discrete buttons and a mask with Midas, attached them to the back of a smartphone, and implemented the EdgeWrite recognition algorithm in JavaScript (Figure 11). Using socket events, we demonstrated how EdgeWrite can be used to enter text on the back of a mobile device, leaving the screen unobstructed. The implementation is functional, though latency for detecting single button presses was higher than expected (>100ms). We plan to investigate ways to increase responsiveness in future work.

Game Controller. To test the responsiveness of Midas's continuous slider, we created a simple game controller for Breakout, in which players horizontally position a paddle to bounce a ball into layers of blocks. In less than fifteen minutes, we attached the slider that we fabricated on the circuit board milling machine to a 7-inch monitor and mapped slider position to paddle position using record-and-replay. The slider is more responsive than individual buttons, and we were able to control the paddle accurately enough for gameplay. The slider's response is non-linear across certain regions, however, and accounting for this is left to future work.

Music Postcard. At a recent media festival, a promotional poster printed with conductive ink enabled passersby to select and play music from a number of artists by touching

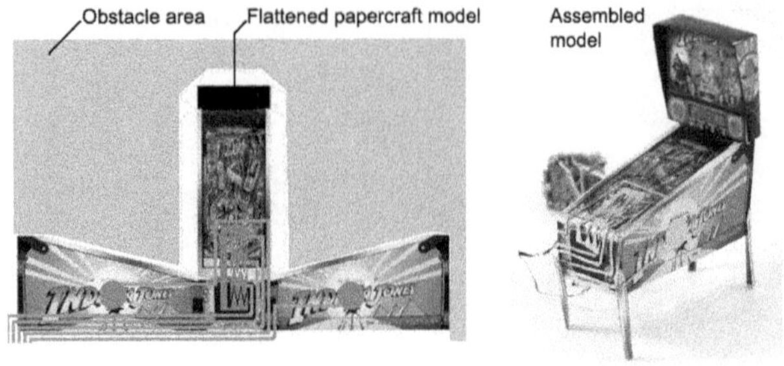

Figure 13: For our papercraft pinball machine, we defined the negative space in the template as an obstacle to restrict sensor routing.

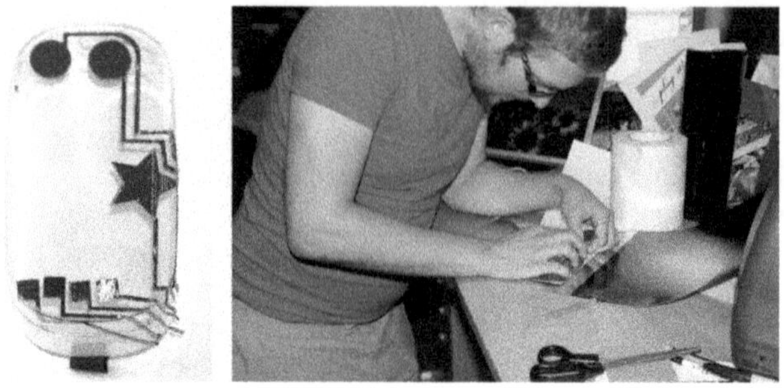
Figure 14: A study participant's sensor layout for a PC media player peripheral.

corresponding areas on the poster [22]. We implemented a postcard-sized version of this poster (Figure 12). We scaled back the size to conserve resources; large designs are possible and only restricted by the cutter's bed width. Our version uses six discrete buttons and one continuous slider to control playback and volume of music clips on a desktop computer. We again cut a vinyl mask layer to prevent stray touch events. We used Midas's record-and-replay function to remote control the iTunes music player.

Papercraft Pinball Machine. Papercraft is the art of cutting and folding paper into 3D models. To demonstrate how Midas can be used for attaching sensors to more complex 3D shapes, we created a papercraft pinball machine which can control a pinball game on a laptop. First we downloaded a template design for a pinball machine [24], cut it out, and assembled it. We then loaded the already-flattened template model into Midas's 2D editor interface and defined the negative space around the model as a routing obstacle (Figure 13). This guaranteed that all trace routing would be on the surface of the model. After attaching the two buttons for the bumpers and a continuous slider for ball release control, we used record and replay to control a desktop pinball game.

Informal Evaluation

To gauge the usability of Midas, we recruited three participants to prototype a media-controlling computer peripheral. Two participants were graduate students at UC Berkeley (in Computer Science and Mechanical Engineering), one was a software engineer at a local technology company. All had some prior experience with prototyping and electronics.

Procedure. Participants received a walkthrough of Midas including a simple record-and-replay task to launch a browser based on a single button input. Participants were then asked to design a physical control interface for a media player (iTunes). No other constraints were given as we wished to encourage exploration. Sessions lasted up to one hour. Participants completed a post-task questionnaire with open-ended questions on interface usability and workflow utility.

Results. All participants successfully designed media players (Figure 14). Participants commented positively on how Midas aided them with the task of physical construction—both by routing connections and through the generated instructions. Record-and-replay was easy to comprehend and effective for the given task. Though the task did not require programming, two participants expressed interest in receiving touch events in their own applications. We take this as corroboration for the utility of our WebSocket server.

Participants identified several areas for improvement. Two participants felt that the instructions, while helpful, did not provide sufficiently detailed information for certain steps (e.g., weeding extra material around the printed sensors). Two desired videos rather than static images. We have since added animations to our instructions to address their request.

Midas's routing algorithm did not find a solution for one version of one participant's design. The participant was unable to identify the underlying problem since he was unfamiliar with auto-routing and the interface did not provide information about the algorithm. In the revised interface we include tips for users on how to adapt designs for successful routing.

Finally, all participants requested richer feedback in the interface about touch events from the hardware controller. The identified challenges are not fundamental to our architecture and have been addressed in recent design iterations.

CONCLUSION AND FUTURE WORK

This paper presented Midas, a software and hardware toolkit to support the design, fabrication, and programming of capacitive touch sensors. Midas leverages the familiar paradigm of the GUI editor to define shape, layout, and interactivity of capacitive touch sensors. To help designers bridge the gap between digital designs and physical realization, Midas auto-routes connections, generates instructions, and offers sensor registration by demonstration. Since generated design files are digital, Midas also enables sharing and replication of prototype designs. Our informal evaluation suggests that working interactive objects can be built with our current implementation and that the interface is accessible for prototyping.

Our future work seeks to address identified limitations and expand into new areas. First, we would like to explore methods to *paint* touch-sensitive areas directly onto 3D CAD models and synthesize pads and routes for more complex objects. Such a function could come as a plugin for modeling software such as SolidWorks. In addition, we are investigating fabrication processes and plan to continue exploring conductive ink printing. We are looking into wireless Midas prototypes to permit testing without a USB tether. Finally, we would like to expand beyond capacitive charge-transfer sensing with a prototyping system that can also assist with other inputs. In general, we are interested in more closely integrating user interface design and digital fabrication tools.

ACKNOWLEDGMENTS

This material is based upon work supported by the NSF GRFP under grant #201246627 and NSF grant #1154235.

REFERENCES

1. Eric Akaoka, Tim Ginn, and Roel Vertegaal. DisplayObjects: prototyping functional physical interfaces on 3D styrofoam, paper or cardboard models. In *Proceedings of TEI '10*, pages 49–56. ACM, 2010.
2. Arduino physical computing platform. http://arduino.cc. Accessed: June, 2012.
3. Daniel Avrahami and Scott E. Hudson. Forming interactivity: a tool for rapid prototyping of physical interactive products. In *Proceedings of DIS '02*, pages 141–146. ACM, 2002.
4. John E. Bigelow. Capacitive touch control and display - us patent 4264903, 1981.
5. Leah Buechley, Mike Eisenberg, Jaime Catchen, and Ali Crockett. The LilyPad Arduino: using computational textiles to investigate engagement, aesthetics, and diversity in computer science education. In *Proceedings of CHI '08*, pages 423–432. ACM, 2008.
6. CadSoft EAGLE PCB Software. http://www.cadsoftusa.com/. Accessed: April 2012.
7. Anind K. Dey, Raffay Hamid, Chris Beckmann, Ian Li, and Daniel Hsu. a CAPpella: programming by demonstration of context-aware applications. In *Proceedings of CHI '04*, pages 33–40. ACM, 2004.
8. Saul Greenberg and Chester Fitchett. Phidgets: easy development of physical interfaces through physical widgets. In *Proceedings of UIST '01*, pages 209–218. ACM, 2001.
9. Chris Harrison, Hrvoje Benko, and Andrew D. Wilson. OmniTouch: wearable multitouch interaction everywhere. In *Proceedings of UIST '11*, pages 441–450. ACM, 2011.
10. Björn Hartmann, Leith Abdulla, Manas Mittal, and Scott R. Klemmer. Authoring sensor-based interactions by demonstration with direct manipulation and pattern recognition. In *Proceedings of CHI '07*, pages 145–154. ACM, 2007.
11. Björn Hartmann, Scott R. Klemmer, Michael Bernstein, Leith Abdulla, Brandon Burr, Avi Robinson-Mosher, and Jennifer Gee. Reflective physical prototyping through integrated design, test, and analysis. In *Proceedings of UIST '06*, pages 299–308. ACM, 2006.
12. David Holman and Roel Vertegaal. TactileTape: low-cost touch sensing on curved surfaces. In *Proceedings of UIST '11 Adjunct*, pages 17–18. ACM, 2011.
13. Scott E. Hudson and Jennifer Mankoff. Rapid construction of functioning physical interfaces from cardboard, thumbtacks, tin foil and masking tape. In *Proceedings of UIST '06*, pages 289–298. ACM, 2006.
14. Java AWT Robots API. http://docs.oracle.com/javase/7/docs/api/java/awt/Robot.html. Accessed: April, 2012.
15. C. Y. Lee. An algorithm for path connections and its applications. *Electronic Computers, IRE Transactions on*, EC-10(3):346 –365, Sept. 1961.
16. Johnny C. Lee, Daniel Avrahami, Scott E. Hudson, Jodi Forlizzi, Paul H. Dietz, and Darren Leigh. The Calder toolkit: wired and wireless components for rapidly prototyping interactive devices. In *Proceedings of DIS '04*, pages 167–175. ACM, 2004.
17. Blair MacIntyre, Maribeth Gandy, Steven Dow, and Jay David Bolter. DART: a toolkit for rapid design exploration of augmented reality experiences. In *Proceedings of UIST '04*, pages 197–206. ACM, 2004.
18. Nicolai Marquardt and Saul Greenberg. Distributed physical interfaces with shared phidgets. In *Proceedings of TEI '07*, pages 13–20. ACM, 2007.
19. Yuki Mori and Takeo Igarashi. Plushie: an interactive design system for plush toys. *ACM Transactions on Graphics*, 26(3), July 2007.
20. Tek-Jin Nam. Sketch-based rapid prototyping platform for hardware-software integrated interactive products. In *Extended Abstracts of CHI '05*, pages 1689–1692. ACM, 2005.
21. Tek-Jin Nam and Woohun Lee. Integrating hardware and software: augmented reality based prototyping method for digital products. In *Extended Abstracts of CHI '03*, pages 956–957. ACM, 2003.
22. BBC News. Playing pop music via paper posters with conductive ink. http://www.bbc.com/news/technology-17339512, 2012. Accessed: April, 2012.
23. Hal Philipp. Charge transfer sensing. *Sensor Review*, 19(2):96–105, 1999.
24. Pinball Paper Toys. http://www.matica.com/paper-craft-toys/61/Classic-Miniature-Pinball-Table-Paper-Toy-Models.html. Accessed: June, 2012.
25. Eric Rosenbaum, Evelyn Eastmond, and David Mellis. Empowering programmability for tangibles. In *Proceedings of TEI '10*, pages 357–360. ACM, 2010.
26. Greg Saul, Manfred Lau, Jun Mitani, and Takeo Igarashi. SketchChair: an all-in-one chair design system for end users. In *Proceedings of TEI '11*, pages 73–80. ACM, 2011.
27. Teensy USB Development Board. http://www.pjrc.com/teensy/. Accessed: April 2012.
28. Nicolas Villar and Hans Gellersen. A malleable control structure for softwired user interfaces. In *Proceedings of TEI '07*, pages 49–56. ACM, 2007.
29. Nicolas Villar, James Scott, Steve Hodges, Kerry Hammill, and Collin Miller. .NET Gadgeteer: A platform for custom devices. In *Proceedings of Pervasive '12*, pages 216–233. ACM, 2012.
30. Andrew D. Wilson. Using a depth camera as a touch sensor. In *Proceedings of ITS '10*, pages 69–72. ACM, 2010.
31. Raphael Wimmer and Patrick Baudisch. Modular and deformable touch-sensitive surfaces based on time domain reflectometry. In *Proceedings of UIST'11*, pages 517–526. ACM, 2011.
32. Jacob O. Wobbrock. Capacitive EdgeWrite implementation. http://depts.washington.edu/ewrite/capacitive.html. Accessed: April, 2012.
33. Jacob O. Wobbrock, Brad A. Myers, and John A. Kembel. EdgeWrite: a stylus-based text entry method designed for high accuracy and stability of motion. In *Proceedings of UIST '03*, pages 61–70. ACM, 2003.
34. Tom Yeh, Tsung-Hsiang Chang, and Robert C. Miller. Sikuli: using GUI screenshots for search and automation. In *Proceedings of UIST '09*, pages 183–192. ACM, 2009.

Printed Optics: 3D Printing of Embedded Optical Elements for Interactive Devices

Karl D.D. Willis[1,2] **Eric Brockmeyer**[1]
Disney Research Pittsburgh[1]
4720 Forbes Avenue
Pittsburgh, PA 15213
{karl, eric.brockmeyer, ivan.poupyrev}
@disneyresearch.com

Scott E. Hudson[1,3] **Ivan Poupyrev**[1]
Computational Design Lab[2], HCI Institute[3]
Carnegie Mellon University
5000 Forbes Avenue
Pittsburgh, PA 15213
scott.hudson@cs.cmu.edu

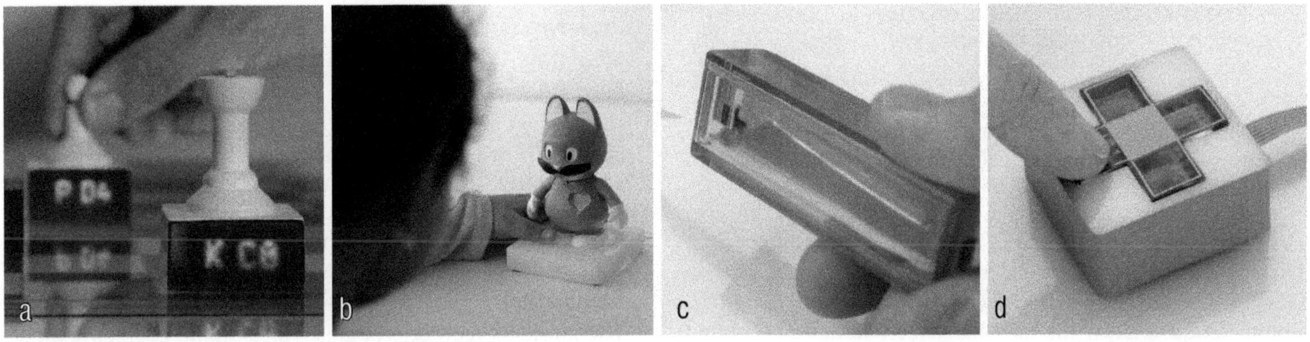

Figure 1: Custom optical elements are fabricated with 3D printing and embedded in interactive devices, opening up new possibilities for interaction including: unique display surfaces made from 3D printed 'light pipes' (a), novel internal illumination techniques (b), custom optical sensors (c), and embedded optoelectronics (d).

ABSTRACT

We present an approach to 3D printing custom optical elements for interactive devices labelled *Printed Optics*. *Printed Optics* enable sensing, display, and illumination elements to be directly embedded in the casing or mechanical structure of an interactive device. Using these elements, unique display surfaces, novel illumination techniques, custom optical sensors, and embedded optoelectronic components can be digitally fabricated for rapid, high fidelity, highly customized interactive devices. *Printed Optics* is part of our long term vision for interactive devices that are 3D printed in their entirety. In this paper we explore the possibilities for this vision afforded by fabrication of custom optical elements using today's 3D printing technology.

ACM Classification: H.5.2 [Information Interfaces and Presentation]: User Interfaces.

Keywords: 3D printing; optics; light; sensing; projection; display; rapid prototyping; additive manufacturing.

INTRODUCTION

3D printing is becoming increasingly capable and affordable. We envision a future world where interactive devices can be printed rather than assembled; a world where a device with active components is created as a single object, rather than a case enclosing circuit boards and individually assembled parts (Figure 2). This capability has tremendous potential for rapid high fidelity prototyping, and eventually for production of customized devices tailored to individual needs and/or specific tasks. With these capabilities we envision it will be possible to design highly functional devices in a digital editor — importing components from a library of interactive elements, positioning and customizing them, then pushing 'print' to have them realized in physical form. In this paper we explore some of the possibilities for this vision afforded by today's 3D printing technology. Specifically, we describe an approach for using 3D printed optical elements, *Printed Optics*, as one category of components within a greater library of reusable interactive elements.

Custom optical elements have traditionally been expensive and impractical to produce due to the manufacturing precision and finishing required. Recent developments in 3D printing technology have enabled the fabrication of high resolution transparent plastics with similar optical properties to plexiglas™. One-off 3D printed optical elements can be designed and fabricated literally within minutes for significantly less cost than conventional manufacturing; greatly increasing accessibility and reducing end-to-end prototyping time. 3D printed optical elements also afford new optical form-factors that were not previously possible, such as fab-

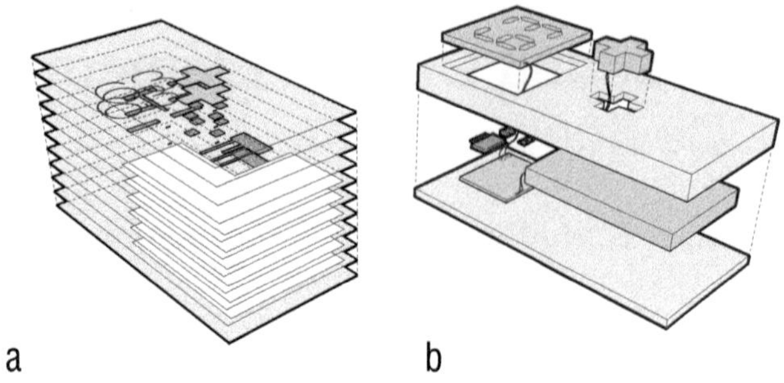

Figure 2: We envision future interactive devices that are 3D printed from individual layers (a) rather than assembled from individual parts (b). These devices will be fabricated from multiple materials to form active functional components within a single 3D print.

ricating structures within other structures, printing multiple materials within a single optical element, and combining mechanical and optical structures in the same design.

Printed Optics opens up new possibilities for interaction. Display surfaces can be created on arbitrary shaped objects using 3D printed 'light pipes' (Figure 1a). Novel illumination techniques allow the internal space within a 3D printed object to be used for illumination and display purposes (Figure 1b). Custom optical sensors can be 3D printed with the structure of interactive devices to sense user input (Figure 1c). Optoelectronic components can be completely enclosed inside optical elements to produce highly customizable and robust interactive devices (Figure 1d).

Our long term vision to digitally fabricate high fidelity, highly customized, 'ready-to-go' devices will be a powerful enabling technology for HCI research. Although much of this novel technology is still in the research stage [7, 26, 33], the simplest forms of 3D printing are rapidly entering the mainstream. A recent cover story in *The Economist* suggests 3D printing is *the* manufacturing technology to "change the world" [32]. A host of consumer-level 3D printing devices are now available and the fundamental photopolymer printing technology behind *Printed Optics* has been demonstrated for less than $200 parts cost [21]. It is reasonable to expect that inexpensive optical 3D printers will be available to researchers in the very near future.

Using today's 3D printing technology we aim to demonstrate that the design of optical systems for interactive devices can be greatly enhanced. We present the following contributions:

1. A general approach for using 3D printed optical elements, *Printed Optics*, embedded in interactive devices to display information and sense user input.
2. Techniques for displaying information using 3D printed optical elements, including the use of 3D printed 'light pipes' and internal air pockets.
3. Techniques for sensing user input with 3D printed optical elements, including touch input with embedded sensors, mechanical displacement of 3D printed light guides, and movement sensed along 3D printed mask patterns.
4. Example applications that demonstrate how *Printed Optics* can be implemented and used in interactive devices.

In the remainder of this paper we introduce the technology that enables us to create *Printed Optics* and outline the fabrication process and its capabilities. We then describe four categories of fabrication techniques for *Printed Optics*: Light Pipes, Internal Illumination, Sensing Mechanical Movement, and Embedded Components. We conclude with discussion of limitations and future research directions. With the continuing emergence of 3D printing technology, we believe now is an ideal time to explore the unique capabilities of 3D printed optical elements for interactive devices.

PRINTED OPTICS

3D printing allows digital geometry to be rapidly fabricated into physical form with micron accuracy. Usable optical elements can be designed and simulated in software, then 3D printed from transparent material with surprising ease and affordability. In this section of the paper we describe the fabrication process for 3D printing optical elements and discuss the unique capabilities that this technology enables.

Fabrication

The fabrication process begins with a digital geometric model that is converted into a series of slices to be physically fabricated layer-by-layer. 3D printing of optical quality materials typically requires a photopolymer-based process. Each layer is fabricated in sequence by selectively exposing a liquid photopolymer material to an ultra-violet (UV) light source, causing the material to cure into a solid state. Traditionally this has been achieved using 'stereolithography', where a precise laser is traced through a vat of liquid photopolymer. Other approaches include controlled exposure to UV light using a projector, or physical deposition of liquid photopolymer in the presence of a UV light source. The fundamental process of layer-by-layer fabrication with photopolymer materials is common throughout each approach.

The range of photopolymer materials for 3D printing is rapidly expanding, with optical-quality transparent plastic, deformable 'rubber', and biocompatible polymers available on the market. In this work we used an Objet Eden260V 3D printer and Objet VeroClear transparent material to fabricate optical elements. VeroClear has similar optical properties to Poly(methyl methacrylate) (PMMA), commonly known as plexiglas^{TM}, with a refractive index of 1.47 (650nm light source). Several other manufacturers also provide similar transparent materials, including DSM Somos' Watershed XC 11122 and 3D Systems' Accura ClearVue.

The Objet Eden260V has a print resolution of 600 dpi (42 microns) that is significantly higher than fused deposition modeling (FDM) 3D printers (e.g. Stratasys Dimension, MakerBot, or RepRap) that are typically around 100 dpi (254 microns). High resolution printing allows the creation of visibly smooth models without internal gaps. Model surfaces can be further enhanced with a manual finishing process to achieve optical clarity. This process consists of removing support material, sanding the surfaces with incrementally finer sandpaper, and then buffing.

Capabilities

3D printing technology enables the fabrication of custom 3D printed optical elements with unique capabilities that are otherwise difficult to achieve.

Multiple Materials Optical elements can be fabricated that combine multiple chemically disparate materials in a single model. 3D printers can often use at least two materials simultaneously: *model material* and *support material*. Model material constitutes the main model itself and support material is used as a sacrificial material to provide structural support under model overhangs and in hollow areas. Typically, support material is removed and disposed of once the printing process is finished, but can also be embedded inside the model to guide, block, and diffuse light. A third 'material' that can be utilized is *air*, hollow pockets of air can be used to guide and reflect light in a similar manner to mirrors and beamsplitters. Advanced 3D printers can combine opaque materials with optical quality transparent materials to mask and block light.

Structures within Structures As the 3D printing process is performed additively layer by layer, geometric structures can be fabricated inside other structures to create optical elements. For example, areas of transparent material can be surrounded by a material with a different refractive index, to transmit light from point to point using total internal reflection (TIR) through the inside of a model. Opaque materials printed within or around a transparent material can be used to block the transmittance of light from one section of the model to another. This can be used to seal internal compartments and avoid optical crosstalk, or to minimize light leakage from the model that may be distracting to the user.

Combined Mechanical-Optical Design 3D printed optical elements can be designed hand-in-hand with the mechanical design of a device. For example, optical elements can be integrated into the body of a device to guide light through the model, act as lenses, or house optical sensors. This combined approach enables a rich new space for prototyping physical interfaces with low-cost optical sensors, such as buttons, sliders, dials, and accelerometers. A single mechanical-optical design can greatly reduce the number of individual parts and the manual labor required for assembly. Optical fiber bundles, that are typically made up of 100s of individual fiber strands, can be 3D printed in a single pass with a solid mechanical structure.

3D printed optical elements currently have some limitations. These include issues of light transmission, surface finishing, clarity, and hollow area fabrication. We describe each of these limitations in the Discussion section. We now introduce four categories of fabrication techniques that demonstrate the wide range of uses for *Printed Optics*.

LIGHT PIPES

'Light pipes' are 3D printed optical elements, similar to optical fiber, that can be used to guide light from point to point. Optical fiber has been used in interactive systems for both display [3, 10, 18] and sensing purposes [3, 12, 20, 23, 34, 39]. Unlike conventional optical fiber, 3D printed light pipes allow arbitrary geometries to be created in software and then fabricated in a single 3D print. Simply by changing software parameters, light pipes can be created with variable widths, rounded caps, and joints with other light pipes. In contrast conventional manufacturing requires considerable effort for individual fiber optic strands to be mechanically assembled, fused/deformed with heat, or chemically bonded.

Internal light pipe geometry can be embedded inside a larger model that has its own independent form-factor, such as a character (Figure 3), mobile device (Figure 4), or tangible chess piece (Figure 5). As each light pipe can be precisely fabricated at a given location, the process of light pipe routing to avoid intersections becomes a well defined software problem. One current limitation of 3D printed light pipes fabricated on the machine we have available is imperfect light transmission with longer pipes or pipes that curve significantly. We outline the characteristics of this light loss in the Discussion section. We have designed around this limitation to produce functional prototypes, but envision our techniques can be expanded using future 3D printers that are optimized for optical performance.

Example Applications

We outline several example applications that demonstrate uses for 3D printed light pipes.

Mobile Projector Displays Mobile projectors have enabled a range of new interactive systems [6, 30, 38]. The small form-factor of mobile projectors makes them well suited to tangible accessories that can map the projector display onto arbitrary surfaces. We have developed a character accessory that uses 3D printed light pipes to guide projected light through the inside of the model and onto outer surfaces. The character is 3D printed with a grid of ⌀0.5 mm light pipes leading from its feet to its eyes (Figure 3a). We paint the outer area of the character except for the ends of the light pipes. When the feet are attached to a mobile projector, the character's eyes become a display surface, responding to user interaction such as sound or physical movement (Figure 3b).

Mobile Touch Sensing Sensing touch has become an important part of interaction with many computing devices [16, 17, 27]. 3D printing is well suited to implement touch [5] and grasp [39] sensing on and around mobile devices. 3D printed light pipes can sense touch by guiding light from arbitrary

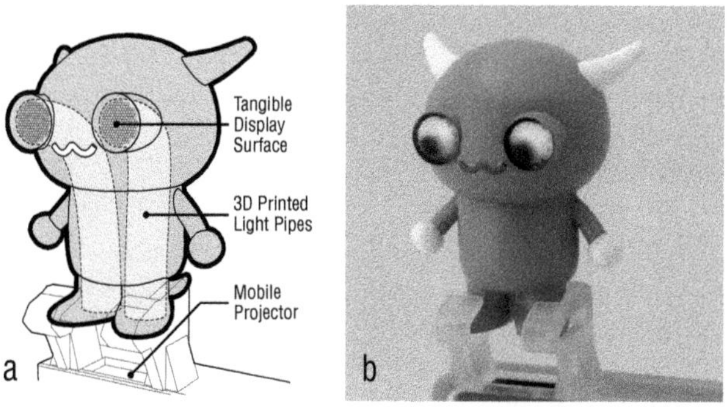

Figure 3: A 3D printed mobile projector accessory using embedded light pipes (a) to map a projected image onto a characters eyes (b).

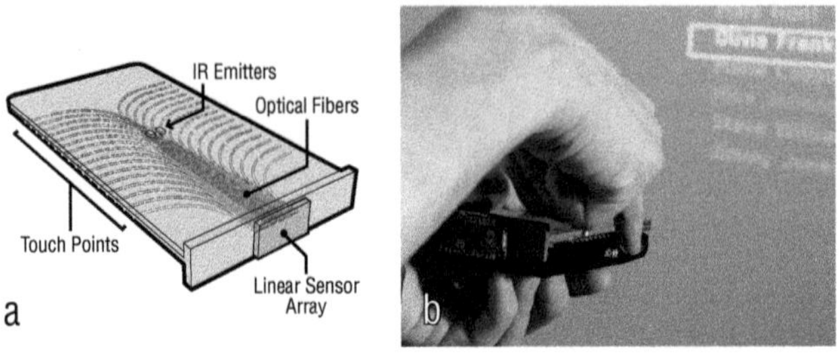

Figure 4: We envision touch sensing using 3D printed light pipes embedded in the walls of future devices. Our proof-of-concept prototype (a) attaches to a mobile projector for gestural control of projected content (b).

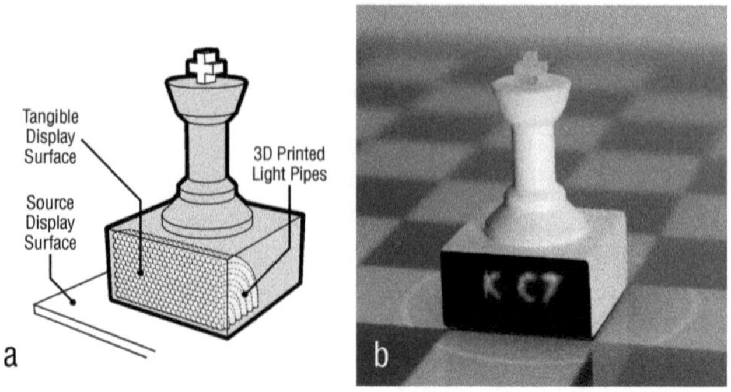

Figure 5: Light pipes are 3D printed inside tangible objects, such as chess pieces (a), to create additional display surfaces for tabletop interaction (b).

locations on the surface of a mobile device to a single sensor array. A key advantage of this technique is the ease with which light pipes can be printed into the walls of a device to create mechanically robust and exceptionally thin (sub mm) embedded sensing with minimal hardware assembly.

We have produced small scale 3D printed prototypes that demonstrate how light can be piped from a 1.5 mm touch point onto a 0.336 mm section of a CCD sensor. When scaled to the size of typical mobile devices however, light loss with 3D printed light pipes currently impacts upon sensing performance. As a proof-of-concept prototype we instead use conventional optical fiber embedded in a 3D printed case to simulate this sensing technique. We arrange 32 'light pipes' so they are exposed on the sides of a mobile projector and piped back to a single 128 pixel photosensor array (Taos TSL202R). The TSL202R is capable of frame-rates up to 40,000 hz for extremely responsive touch interaction on (or near) the device surface. We use two infrared (IR) LEDs embedded in a laser-cut piece of acrylic to provide constant illumination. Figure 4a shows our proof-of-concept prototype demonstrating that the casing of a mobile projector can be embedded with light pipes for robust touch sensing. Single and multi-touch gestures can be used on the side of the device to scroll and zoom in on projected content (Figure 4b).

Tangible Displays Tangible objects have been used to extend the display area of tabletop and touchscreen surfaces with optical fiber bundles [3, 10, 18] and prisms [19]. One of the inherent problems with optical fiber is maintaining alignment with large numbers or long lengths of fiber during mechanical assembly. 3D printed light pipes avoid this issue as individual pipes can be accurately fabricated and enclosed inside a simultaneously printed rigid support structure. Optimal packing patterns can be produced in software to maximize light transmission with large display grids. Although currently the optical quality is inferior to traditional optical elements, light pipes do provide a highly accessible and customizable alternative.

We have developed a set of tangible chess pieces that display content piped from a diffuse illumination tabletop surface. A 62 x 34 grid of ⌀0.5 mm light pipes is embedded in the base of each chess piece and provides a display area perpendicular to the tabletop surface (Figure 5). Contextual information, such as chess piece location and suggested moves, can be displayed on each individual piece using display space that would otherwise be occluded. Fiducial markers cut from transparent IR reflecting film (Tigold Corporation Type 7232) are adhered to the bottom of each chess piece. Projected visible light passes through the transparent marker and into the light pipes, while IR light is reflected back to an IR camera to track and identity each chess piece.

Fabrication Techniques

3D printed light pipes function in a similar manner to optical fiber with light reflecting internally as it travels along the length of the pipe. Internal reflection is caused by a difference in the refractive index of the internal *core* (through which light travels) and the external *cladding* (which surrounds the core) (Figure 6). We fabricate light pipes using model material (Objet VeroClear) for the core and support material (Objet Support Resin) for the cladding. The model material cures into a rigid transparent material and the support material into a soft material designed to be easily broken apart for quick removal. The difference in material density allows for TIR to occur. To create a mechanically sound model, we surround the brittle support material with an outer casing of rigid material. We can fabricate light pipes down to a thicknesses of ⌀0.25mm core with a cladding layer thickness of 0.084mm. To create accurate digital geometry, we programmatically generate light pipe grids using Python inside the Rhinoceros 3D application (www.rhino3d.com). This geometry can then be exported into a mesh-based format suitable for 3D printing.

INTERNAL ILLUMINATION

3D printing is known for its ability to precisely fabricate the *outer* form of physical objects and has been used to create a variety of unique displays [1, 2, 29, 36]. Optically clear material allows for the design and fabrication of *inner* forms

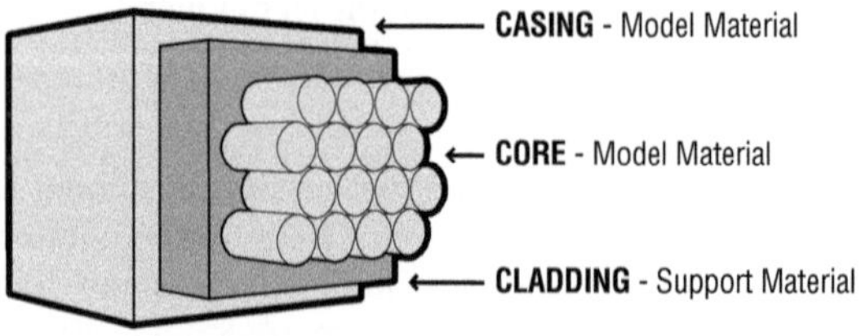

Figure 6: Light pipes consist of a rigid transparent core, a soft cladding, and a rigid outer casing.

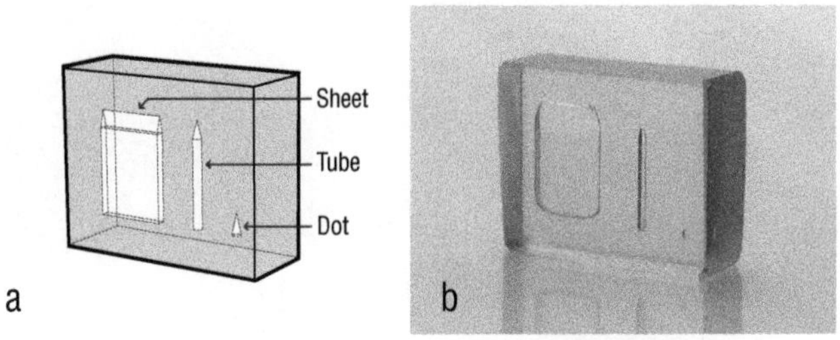

Figure 7: *Sheets*, *tubes*, and *dots* are primitive elements for fabricating reflective pockets of air inside a 3D print. Due to material settling, digital geometry (a) differs slightly from the actual printed form (b).

within a 3D printed model. Internal structures can be viewed from the outside and highlighted with illumination. Internal illumination can be used with interactive devices to display information ranging from simple indicators to complex volumetric displays. In this section of the paper we introduce techniques for internal illumination by creating reflective pockets of air within a solid transparent model.

Example Applications

We outline several example applications that demonstrate uses for internal illumination.

Volumetric Displays 3D printed internal structures are an enabling technology for static-volume volumetric displays, allowing precise alignment of 3D pixels within a volume. Although volumetric displays have been implemented in a number of ways [9, 25], 3D printing allows a new level of control over the shape, size, and resolution of the display. Using the versatility of 3D printing, we implemented a volumetric display based on *Passive Optical Scatterers* [28].

We explored a mobile form factor for a volumetric display by embedding an 4 x 8 x 11 array of ⌀1.2 mm *dot*-shaped air pockets (Figure 7) inside a 40 x 80 x 50 mm volume of transparent 3D printed material (Figure 8). The display is mounted to a laser-based mobile projector (Microvision ShowWX+). 32 x 32 pixel blocks are used to address each of the dots inside the volume. 2D pixel blocks are mapped

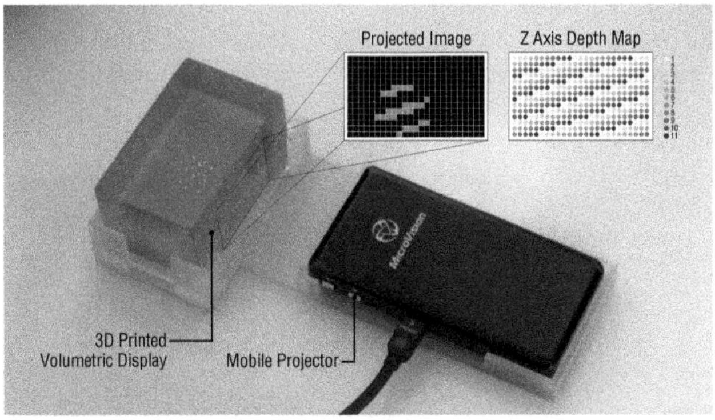

Figure 8: A mobile volumetric display created with embedded *dots* of air inside a 3D printed volume. A sphere is displayed inside the volume by remapping 2D pixels using a Z axis depth map.

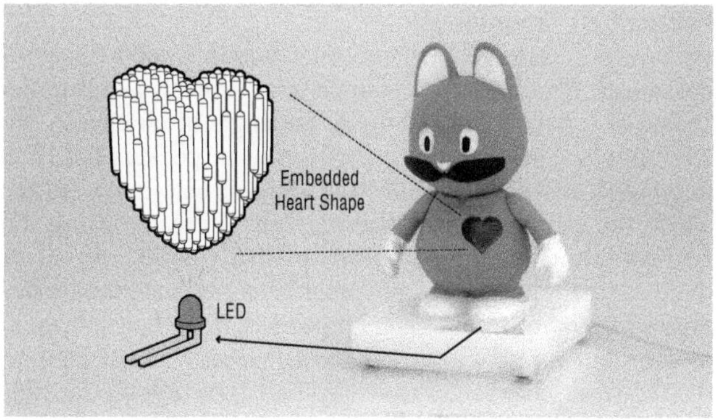

Figure 9: A toy character with an embedded heart shape made from *tubes* of enclosed air and illuminated with an LED.

to 3D dots using a Z axis depth map. An automated camera calibration routine is used to compensate for any slight mechanical misalignments.

Internal Patterns 3D printed *tubes* are hollow cylinder-like structures printed vertically (Figure 7). Tubes are particularly well suited to represent arbitrary shapes inside a 3D printed model. Because it is not yet possible to enclose arbitrary hollow shapes (due to issues of overhang and support material extraction), tubes represent a useful approximation. We created a toy character with a glowing heart embedded inside (Figure 1b). The heart is made from a set of hollow tubes packed together and illuminated from below with an LED (Figure 9). Although a simple example, the internal structures are very difficult to achieve with other manufacturing techniques. We found that tubes can be reliably created down to ⌀0.6 mm and packed together with a minimum distance of 0.6 mm between tubes. This enables relatively good resolution to represent arbitrary internal shapes.

Internal Text 3D printed *sheets* are flat rectangular air pockets that can be used to approximate lines (Figure 7). Text within a 3D printed structure can be fabricated to create robust signage that is resistant to impact and everyday wear. The optical clarity of the material makes it possible to view internal text under normal daylight lighting conditions or with illumination at night. Using 3D printed sheets to fabricate internal text, we created a nixie tube style numeric display (Figure 10a). Individual 3D printed layers with embedded numbers are mounted together and side-illuminated using either an LED or a mobile projector (Figure 10b).

Figure 10: A numeric display (a) created with hollow *sheets* of air that reflect light when illuminated (b).

Fabrication Techniques

By creating enclosed pockets of air within a solid transparent model, light intersects with these air pockets and is transmitted or reflected depending on the angle of incidence. By carefully designing the geometry of the air pockets light can be guided internally within the model or externally out towards the users eye. Air pockets can be created using 3D printers that deposit small beads of material layer-by-layer to build up a model. As individual beads of material are deposited, they must have a supporting surface beneath them or they fall down with gravity. However, a small amount of step-over (overhang) from layer to layer allows for hollow areas to be slowly closed. In practice a step-over angle equivalent to 14°from vertical allows air pockets to be reliably closed with minimum shape distortion. Greater step-over angles cause the material to fall into the air pocket and slowly raise the air pocket location vertically or fill it entirely. Figure 7 shows a series of primitive elements that can be fabricated from air pockets. The digital geometry sent to the printer (left) differs from the actual air pocket shape fabricated (right). This difference is due to beads of material settling without direct support structure during the fabrication process. To programmatically generate patterns from the *dot*, *tube*, and *sheet* primitives, we use the Grasshopper environment (www.grasshopper3d.com) inside Rhinoceros. This allows primitive elements to be mapped to lines, enclosed within solids, or aligned with illumination sources.

SENSING MECHANICAL MOVEMENT

Optical sensing of mechanical movement has been achieved in a number of form-factors [8, 15, 31, 35, 37]. Our approach uses 3D printing to create custom optical sensing embedded in interactive devices. We use low-cost IR emitter/receiver pairs, to sense common user inputs such as rotation, push, linear movement, and acceleration. Our approach offers several benefits. Firstly, custom sensors can be designed and prototyped with minimal effort. 3D printed sensors allow convenient, fast, accurate, and repeatable sensor fabrication. In many cases only a generic IR emitter-receiver pair are required on the electronics side. Secondly, custom sensors can be embedded in the casing or mechanical structure of a device. This enables sensing of user input through the walls of a device, greatly simplifies hardware assembly, and produces robust high fidelity prototypes.

Example Applications

We introduce example applications that demonstrate how 3D printed optical elements can be used to detect common mechanical movements.

Sensing Displacement We have developed a library of mechanical movements that can be mapped to a displacement sensing scheme. In this scheme a flexible light guide mounted below the surface of a device is physically displaced to change the amount of IR light traveling between an emitter-receiver pair (Figure 11, 13a). Displacement sensing provides a versatile way to sense a number of user inputs with 3D printed optical elements.

We sense *push* and *pressure* with a button that applies linear force to displace the light guide (Figure 11a). As the user presses the button the receiver changes from a high to a low state (Figure 13a). Elastic deformation causes the light guide to return to a high state when the user releases the button. The elasticity of the light guide provides clear haptic feedback that can be accentuated with small surface detents on the button shaft.

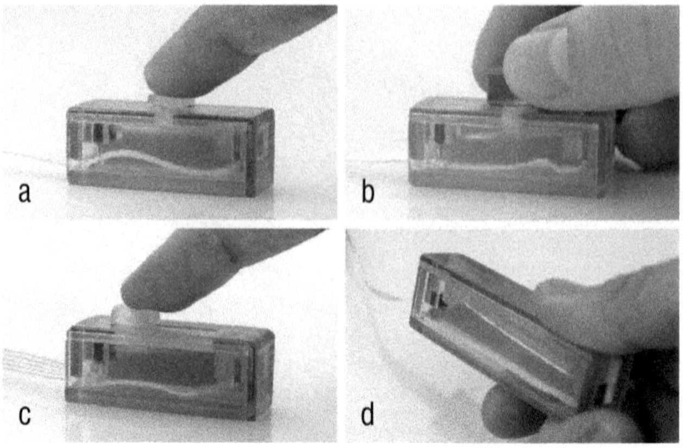

Figure 11: User inputs such as push (a), rotation (b), linear movement (c), and acceleration (d) can be sensed by the displacement of a 3D printed light guide.

We sense *rotation* with a screw dial that gradually lowers to displace the light guide (Figure 11b). When fully inserted the receiver returns a low signal and returns to a high state as the screw dial is extracted. Custom thread pitches can be designed for precise control over how quickly the screw dial transitions between the two extremes.

We sense *linear movement* with a mechanical slider that depresses the light guide when moved from one side to the other (Figure 11c). The light guide is angled downward so that it rests just below the slider at one end and is above the slider at the other end. As the slider is moved by the user, the light guide is displaced to register a low reading.

We sense *acceleration* by printing extra material on the end of a light guide to enhance the effects of outside motion (Figure 11d). The extra weight causes the light guide to be displaced when the the user moves the device along an axis perpendicular to the light guide. The effects of gravity can also be perceived, as the weighted light guide slumps downwards causing displacement.

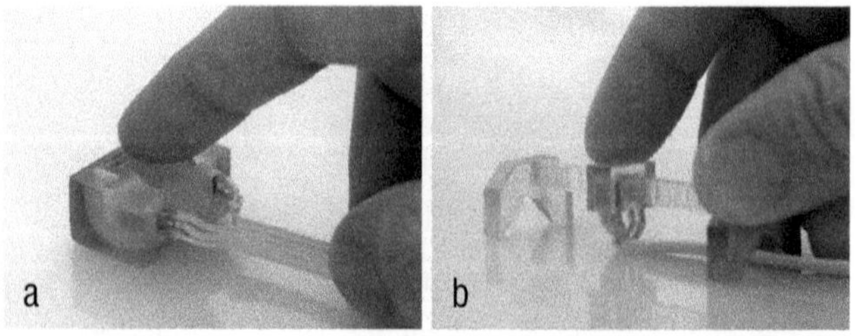

Figure 12: Rotary motion of a scroll wheel (a) and linear motion of a slider (b) can be sensed with IR light passing through 3D printed mask material.

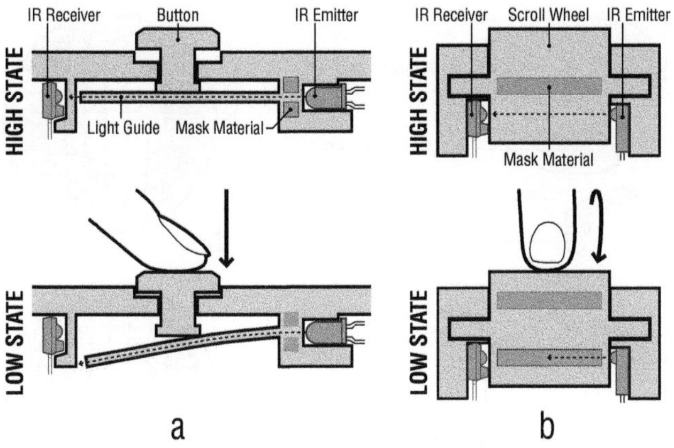

Figure 13: Mechanical force moves a 3D printed light guide below a button (a) and a rotary encoder pattern within a scroll wheel (b) from a high state (top) to a low state (bottom).

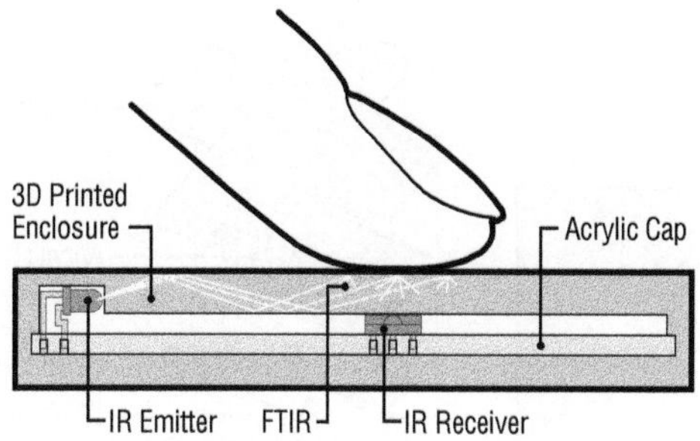

Figure 14: FTIR touch sensing embedded within a 3D printed enclosure.

Sensing With Encoders We fabricate custom linear and rotary encoders with 3D printing by creating a mask pattern from two different materials and sensing the change in light transmission through each material as the encoder moves.

We sense *scroll wheel* motion by embedding sections of mask material in the body of a scroll wheel (Figure 12a). An IR emitter-receiver pair are mounted in the scroll wheel housing on either side. As the scroll wheel is turned, a high-low pattern is returned by the receiver that can be decoded into a relative rotation value based on the mask pattern design. More complex absolute encoding schemes can also be achieved using the same basic principle with multiple emitter-receiver pairs.

We sense *slider* motion by embedding a mask pattern into the shaft holding the slider (Figure 12b). An IR emitter-receiver pair are mounted inside the slider housing on either side of the shaft. As the user moves the slider a high-low pattern is returned to the receiver.

Fabrication Techniques

Sensing Displacement Our displacement sensing scheme uses transparent material to create a flexible light guide between an IR emitter-receiver pair. Light from the emitter travels through a small aperture surrounded by light-blocking mask (support) material and reflects inside the light guide until it meets the receiver. In its normal state light travels into the receiver to register a high reading (Figure 13a, top). The light guide can be displaced with mechanical force, causing the receiver to register a lower reading (Figure 13a, bottom). A range of intermediate values are returned between these two states. In all cases the flexible light guide is positioned just below the surface of the sensor housing and mechanically displaced by outside force. Emitters and receivers are inserted into the housing walls with precisely aligned slots.

Sensing With Encoders To create rotary and linear encoders we use an IR emitter-receiver pair mechanically mounted on either side of a rotary shaft/linear rail. A 3D printed mask pattern is embedded into the rotary shaft/linear rail to produce signal changes. The mask pattern is created with embedded support material so that a distinctive change in light intensity is registered by the receiver. Figure 13b illustrates the high (top) and low (bottom) states of a rotary encoder.

We use standard 3mm or side-look (Honeywell SEP8706) 940nm IR LEDs and light-to-voltage sensors (Taos TSL260R) as the emitters and receivers for both displacement and encoder sensing in this section. Modulation of the emitter-receiver pair would provide further robustness to varying ambient light conditions.

EMBEDDED COMPONENTS

As 3D printing technology grows in sophistication, we envision it will be possible to automatically 'drop-in' components during the fabrication process [4, 22, 33], using part placement robots similar to those employed for PC board manufacture. Drop-in embedded components are physically robust, enable tight mechanical tolerances, and allow easy compartmentalization. Combining optical components with transparent materials allows sensing, display, and illumination to take place through the casing without exposing components directly on the surface of a device. Eventually, we envision it will be possible to 3D print electronic components in their entirety [7, 26]. Although it is not yet possible to automatically insert or print electronic components on commercial 3D printers, it is possible to simulate the results of embedded optical components by manually inserting them during the print process. In this section of the paper we introduce a number of techniques for designing, fabricating, and interacting with optoelectronic components embedded in transparent 3D printed enclosures.

Example Applications

We introduce example applications that demonstrate uses for 3D printed optical elements with embedded optoelectronic components.

Embedded FTIR Sensing Frustrated total internal reflection (FTIR) based sensing is known for its robust and precise touch-sensing performance. Typically individual components are mounted alongside an optical surface that users interact with [13, 17, 27]. In our approach we embed components inside the optical surface to produce a very robust and completely enclosed FTIR implementation. In a basic configuration, an LED emitter is embedded in a hollow area within the 3D print and light is emitted directly into a flat sensing surface (Figure 14). An IR receiver is mounted perpendicular to the sensing surface and detects light reflected

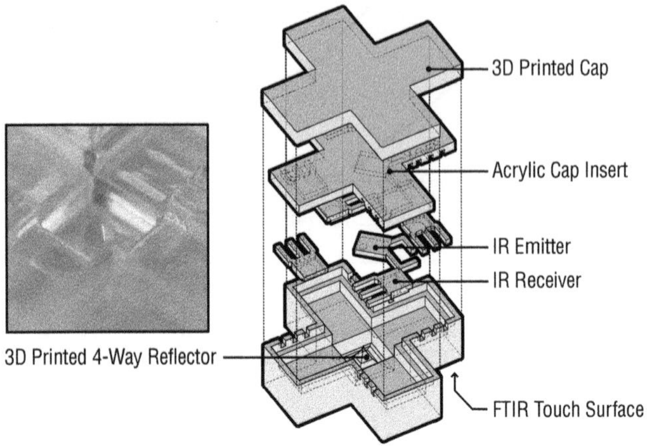

Figure 15: Exploded view of a D-pad made with embedded optoelectronic components. A 3D printed 4-way reflector is used to direct light into a custom shaped FTIR touch surface.

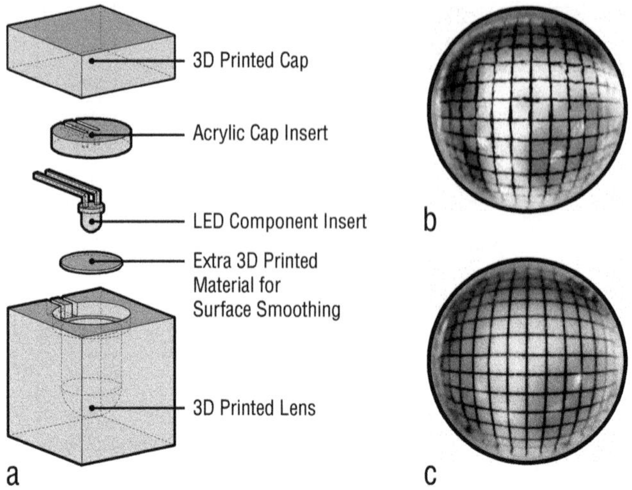

Figure 17: Optoelectronic components are inserted, capped, and enclosed inside a 3D printed model to create a custom lens (a). The quality of the lens surface finish (b) can be improved by depositing additional uniform layers of material (c).

by fingers coming into contact with the outer surface. A more complex variation of the same sensing technique is shown in our four-way D-pad sensor (Figure 1d). A flat side-look LED (Honeywell SEP8706) is embedded facing a four-way reflector that splits light towards four embedded IR receivers (Taos TSL260R) (Figure 15). An analog touch reading is measured at each of the sensors. As with standard FTIR an approximate measurement of pressure is returned based on the amount of skin contact and light reflectivity.

Lenses We embed optoelectronic inside 3D printed plano-convex and plano-concave lenses to better control the directionality of illumination or optical sensing. The base of the 3D print makes up the planar side of the lens and the curved lens surface is fabricated below the component then smoothed with extra layers of material deposition. Figure 16 shows two identical LEDs embedded with 3D printed plano-convave (a) and plano-convex (b) lenses.

Beamsplitters We fabricate rudimentary beamsplitters by creating prisms in front of embedded components. Based on the angle of incidence, some light passes through the prism and the remainder reflects off in another direction. Figure 16c shows an LED with light being split in two directions by the embedded prism.

Fabrication Techniques
We manually insert optical components during the 3D printing process in a similar manner to [22]. The digital geometric model is designed in such a way that a hollow area is left for the component to be inserted. Support material printing must be disabled to ensure that it is not deposited inside the component area. If the component is inserted flush with the top of the model, printing is continued to completely enclose it inside. If an area of air is desired around the component, a laser cut transparent acrylic 'cap' is affixed above the component to seal it in before printing continues (Figure 17).

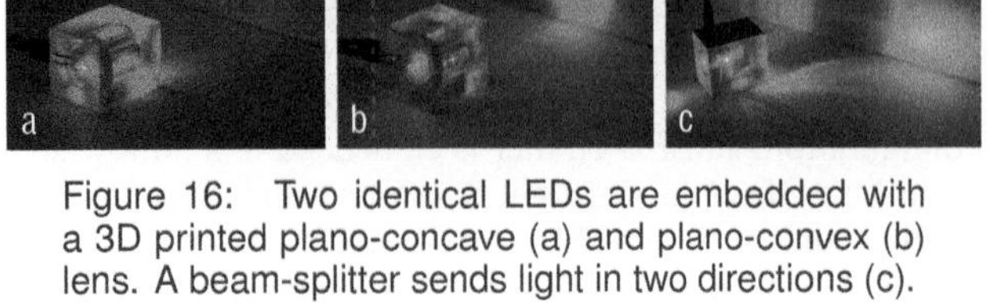

Figure 16: Two identical LEDs are embedded with a 3D printed plano-concave (a) and plano-convex (b) lens. A beam-splitter sends light in two directions (c).

Hollow cavities created for components do not have an optically clear finish (Figure 17b) and it is not practical to sand or buff these small cavities during the print process. However, we discovered a unique technique to improve the surface quality of cavities by depositing additional uniform layers of material. This material is deposited from above and falls into the cavity in a liquid state to smooth its surface. Figure 17c shows the improved surface finish achieved when ten additional layers of material are deposited.

DISCUSSION
3D printed optical elements have unique limitations that should be considered during the design and fabrication process.

Light Pipe Transmission
3D printed light pipes fabricated with our current setup suffer from limited light transmission. To more accurately characterize the conditions under which light loss occurs, we performed light measurement tests with light pipes over varying distances and curvature. To simulate a typical application scenario we used off-the-shelf components: a red 5mm LED emitter and a photodiode-based receiver (Taos TSL12S). For each reading, light was directed into the light pipe with the emitter and a voltage value measured from the receiver at the other end. The emitter and detector were coupled to the test pieces using custom slots, similar to those shown in Figure 11-13, and without surface finishing.

For the distance test we compared the light transmittance of a ⌀2mm 3D printed light pipe, to a commercially produced

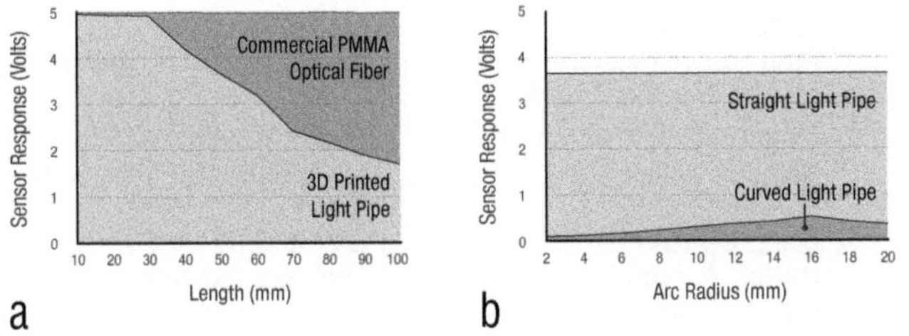

Figure 18: Light transmittance of 3D printed light pipes compared to commercial optical fiber (a) and transmittance of 50mm 3D printed light pipes in 90° arcs with increasing curvature radius (b).

⌀2mm optical fiber made of PMMA. The 3D printed light pipes consisted of a core, cladding, and casing configuration with distances ranging from 10-100mm in 10mm increments. The commercial optical fiber was cut to the same lengths and mounted in a rigid casing. For the curvature test we created a series of light pipes following a 90° arc, each with an incrementally larger radius. The length of the light pipes was extended on each end to be precisely 50mm in total length.

Figure 18a shows that 3D printed light pipes currently suffer from increasing light loss with distance. Adding curvature to a light pipe further increases light loss when compared to a straight light pipe of equal length (Figure 18b). We believe this limited performance is due to two factors. Firstly, the contours where two different materials intersect are currently not perfectly smooth (Figure 19). Microscopic unevenness on internal surfaces result in light being lost or redirected in unpredictable ways. However, we found the consistency between ten identical 50mm straight prints to be high, with a standard deviation of 0.0822V when measuring transmittance as previously described. Secondly, although we know the refractive index of the core material, no information is available for the refractive index of the cladding material. Because we use support material that is not intended as an optical material, its performance as cladding is understandably low. We can assume that the refractive index of each material is close enough to restrict the angle of incidence to a relatively small value and thereby limit internal reflection.

Although the current materials and printing process we use are not optimized for optical performance, promising materials science research has demonstrated that photopolymer waveguides can be fabricated in both planar [14] and non-planar [24] forms with minimal light loss. We are therefore optimistic about the possibilities for fabricating light pipes in the next generation of optically optimized 3D printers. It is worth noting that many commercial display technologies routinely encounter significant light loss, e.g., resistive touch screens reduce display light transmission by up to 20% [11].

Surface Finishing

In current generation 3D printers, unfinished surfaces appear smooth and transparent to the naked eye, but not optically clear. Unfinished surfaces can be used when some amount of light scattering is acceptable, however to maximize light passing to/from the interior of a 3D printed optical element, surface finishing should be performed (i.e. sanding and buffing). Flat surface finishing can be performed using power tools such as a belt sander and buffing wheel. Curved surfaces require hand sanding and are more time intensive. Textured surfaces or surfaces with small micro-facets are difficult to perform finishing on without specialized equipment. Internal surfaces can generally not be reached to perform manual surface finishing, but applying additional layers of uniform material cover can improve the quality of the surface (Figure 17c).

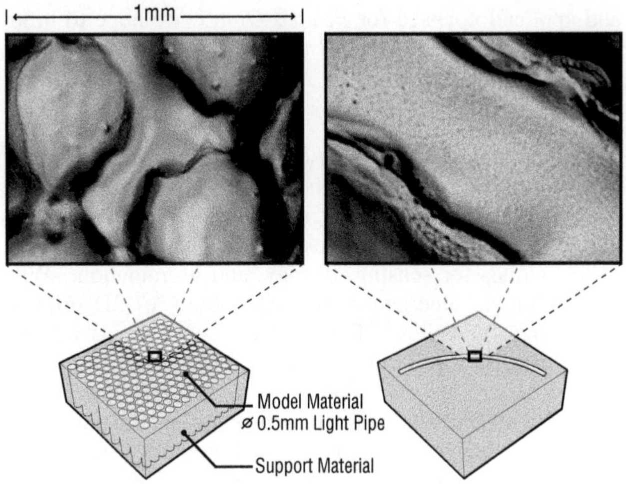

Figure 19: Magnified view of the material intersections in 3D printed light pipes.

Clarity

Based on our experiences with the Objet Eden260V, we have found that the clarity of 3D printed optical elements currently depends on several factors. *Model Thickness*: thicker models tend to lose optical clarity and appear increasingly cloudy. *Print Direction*: the greatest clarity is seen when looking perpendicular to the printed layers, looking parallel to the printed layers appears blurrier. *UV Exposure*: Overexposure to UV light during the curing process can cause a loss in optical clarity, making the model appear yellow in color. *Surface Quality*: greater clarity can be achieved with extra sanding steps during the finishing process.

Hollow Areas

As 3D printed objects are built up layer by layer, hollow areas typically require support material inside the hollow. Printing completely enclosed hollow areas can seal the support material inside with no means for it to be extracted. Completely enclosed hollow areas of air can be fabricated using jet deposition-based machines by disabling support material and using internal geometry with minimal step-over in the vertical axis. This requirement for self-supporting geometry limits the design space when creating hollow areas. In theory, internal geometry can be combined with arbitrary external geometry complete with overhangs and support material. In practice, the 3D printer we made use of did not allow selective use of support material; it must be either enabled or disabled for each print. This restriction, however, can be resolved with an improved software interface to the 3D printer.

Despite these limitations, by demonstrating the capabilities and application space for *Printed Optics*, we hope to influence the design of future 3D printing systems that are fine tuned for optical applications.

CONCLUSION

We have outlined the *Printed Optics* approach for using 3D printed optical elements embedded in interactive devices. *Printed Optics* enable many new possibilities for interactive devices and this initial exploration introduced a range of techniques for sensing, display, and illumination. With the continuing emergence and accessibility of 3D printing technology, we believe 3D printed optical elements will become an important part of future interactive devices that are printed rather than assembled. We foresee future 3D printers with a diverse range of optical printing functionality. The ability to dynamically control optical properties such as the refractive index, reflectivity, transmittance, absorption, and diffusion will enable an even richer design space for sensing, display, and illumination. Although that time is not upon us yet, *Printed Optics* demonstrates what is possible today.

REFERENCES

1. Alexa, M., and Matusik, W. Reliefs as images. *ACM Trans. Graph. 29*, 4 (2010), 60:1–60:7.
2. Alexa, M., and Matusik, W. Images from self-occlusion. In *CAe '11*, ACM (2011), 17–24.
3. Baudisch, P., Becker, T., and Rudeck, F. Lumino: Tangible blocks for tabletop computers based on glass fiber bundles. In *CHI '10*, ACM (2010), 1165–1174.
4. Beck, J., Prinz, F. B., Siewiorek, D., and Weiss, L. Manufacturing mechatronics using thermal spray shape deposition. In *Proc. Solid Freeform Fabrication Symposium* (1992).
5. Butler, A., Izadi, S., and Hodges, S. SideSight: Multi-"touch" interaction around small devices. In *UIST '08*, ACM (2008), 201–204.
6. Cao, X., Forlines, C., and Balakrishnan, R. Multi-user interaction using handheld projectors. In *UIST '07*, ACM (Newport, Rhode Island, 2007), 43–52.
7. Clemens, W., Fix, W., Ficker, J., Knobloch, A., and Ullmann, A. From polymer transistors toward printed electronics. *Journal of Materials Research 19*, 7 (2004), 1963–1973.
8. Dietz, P. H., and Eidelson, B. D. SurfaceWare: Dynamic tagging for microsoft surface. In *TEI '09*, ACM (2009), 249–254.
9. Ebert, D., Bedwell, E., Maher, S., Smoliar, L., and Downing, E. Realizing 3d visualization using crossed-beam volumetric displays. *Commun. ACM 42*, 8 (August 1999), 100–107.
10. Fukuchi, K., Nakabayashi, R., Sato, T., and Takada, Y. Ficon: A tangible display device for tabletop system using optical fiber. In *ITS '11*, ACM (2011).
11. Ge, Z., and Wu, S.-T. *Transflective Liquid Crystal Displays*. John Wiley and Sons, 2010.
12. Go, K., Nonaka, K., Mitsuke, K., and Morisawa, M. Object shape and touch sensing on interactive tables with optical fiber sensors. In *TEI '12*, ACM (2012), 123–126.
13. Han, J. Y. Low-cost multi-touch sensing through frustrated total internal reflection. In *UIST '05*, ACM (2005), 115–118.
14. Hayes, D. J., and Cox, W. R. Micro-jet printing of polymers for electronics manufacturing. In *ADHES '98*, IEEE (1998), 168–173.
15. Hennecke, F., Berwein, F., and Butz, A. Optical pressure sensing for tangible user interfaces. In *ITS '11*, ACM (2011), 45–48.
16. Hodges, S., Izadi, S., Butler, A., Rrustemi, A., and Buxton, B. ThinSight: Versatile multi-touch sensing for thin form-factor displays. In *UIST '07*, ACM (2007), 259–268.
17. Hofer, R., Naeff, D., and Kunz, A. FLATIR: FTIR multi-touch detection on a discrete distributed sensor array. In *TEI '09*, ACM (2009), 317–322.
18. Hoover, P., Cabrera, L. E., and Aumiller, C. Augmented reality, surface style: Extending displays through fiber optics. In *Ext. Abstracts CHI '10*, ACM (2010), 2681–2684.
19. Izadi, S., Hodges, S., Taylor, S., Rosenfeld, D., Villar, N., Butler, A., and Westhues, J. Going beyond the display: A surface technology with an electronically switchable diffuser. In *UIST '08*, ACM (2008), 269–278.
20. Jackson, D., Bartindale, T., and Olivier, P. FiberBoard: Compact multi-touch display using channeled light. In *ITS '09*, ITS '09, ACM (2009), 25–28.
21. Jansen, C. DLP-Based Resin Printer for less than $200. http://www.thingiverse.com/thing:19185.
22. Kataria, A., and Rosen, D. W. Building around inserts: Methods for fabricating complex devices in stereolithography. *Rapid Prototyping Journal 7*, 5 (2001), 253–262.
23. Lee, J. C., Dietz, P. H., Maynes-Aminzade, D., Raskar, R., and Hudson, S. E. Automatic projector calibration with embedded light sensors. In *UIST '04*, ACM (2004), 123–126.
24. Lorang, D. J., Tanaka, D., Spadaccini, C. M., Rose, K. A., Cherepy, N. J., and Lewis, J. A. Photocurable liquid core–fugitive shell printing of optical waveguides. *Advanced Materials 23*, 43 (2011), 5055–5058.
25. MacFarlane, D. L. Volumetric three-dimensional display. *Appl. Opt. 33*, 31 (Nov 1994), 7453–7457.
26. Malone, E., and Lipson, H. Multi-material freeform fabrication of active systems. In *ESDA '08*, ASME (2008), 345–353.
27. Moeller, J., and Kerne, A. Scanning FTIR: Unobtrusive optoelectronic multi-touch sensing through waveguide transmissivity imaging. In *TEI '10*, ACM (2010), 73–76.
28. Nayar, S., and Anand, V. 3D display using passive optical scatterers. *Computer 40*, 7 (July 2007), 54–63.
29. Papas, M., Jarosz, W., Jakob, W., Rusinkiewicz, S., Matusik, W., and Weyrich, T. Goal-based caustics. *Eurographics '11 30*, 2 (2011), 503–511.
30. Rukzio, E., Hollels, P., and Gellersen, H. Personal projectors for pervasive computing. *Pervasive Computing* (2011).
31. Sato, T., Mamiya, H., Koike, H., and Fukuchi, K. PhotoelasticTouch: Transparent rubbery tangible interface using an lcd and photoelasticity. In *UIST '09*, ACM (2009), 43–50.
32. The Economist. Print me a stradivarius: How a new manufacturing technology will change the world, February 10, 2011. http://www.economist.com/node/18114327.
33. Weiss, L., Merz, R., Prinz, F., Neplotnik, G., Padmanabhan, P., Schultz, L., and Ramaswami, K. Shape deposition manufacturing of heterogeneous structures. *Journal of Manufacturing Systems 16*, 4 (1997), 239–248.
34. Weiss, M., Schwarz, F., Jakubowski, S., and Borchers, J. Madgets: Actuating widgets on interactive tabletops. In *UIST '10*, ACM (2010), 293–302.
35. Weiss, M., Wagner, J., Jansen, Y., Jennings, R., Khoshabeh, R., Hollan, J. D., and Borchers, J. SLAP Widgets: Bridging the gap between virtual and physical controls on tabletops. In *CHI '09*, ACM (2009), 481–490.
36. Weyrich, T., Peers, P., Matusik, W., and Rusinkiewicz, S. Fabricating microgeometry for custom surface reflectance. *ACM Trans. Graph. 28*, 3 (2009), 32:1–32:6.
37. Williams, C., Yang, X. D., Partridge, G., Millar-Usiskin, J., Major, A., and Irani, P. TZee: Exploiting the lighting properties of multi-touch tabletops for tangible 3d interactions. In *CHI '11*, ACM (2011), 1363–1372.
38. Willis, K. D., Poupyrev, I., Hudson, S. E., and Mahler, M. SideBySide: Ad-hoc multi-user interaction with handheld projectors. In *UIST '11*, ACM (2011), 431–440.
39. Wimmer, R. FlyEye: Grasp-sensitive surfaces using optical fiber. In *TEI '10*, ACM (2010), 245–248.

Interactive Construction: Interactive Fabrication of Functional Mechanical Devices

Stefanie Mueller, Pedro Lopes, and Patrick Baudisch
Hasso Plattner Institute, Potsdam, Germany
{stefanie.mueller, pedro.lopes, patrick.baudisch}@hpi.uni-potsdam.de

ABSTRACT
Personal fabrication tools, such as laser cutters and 3D printers allow users to create precise objects quickly. However, working through a CAD system removes users from the workpiece. Recent interactive fabrication tools reintroduce this directness, but at the expense of precision.

In this paper, we introduce *constructable*, an interactive drafting table that produces precise physical output in every step. Users interact by drafting directly on the workpiece using a hand-held laser pointer. The system tracks the pointer, beautifies its path, and implements its effect by cutting the workpiece using a fast high-powered laser cutter.

Constructable achieves precision through tool-specific constraints, user-defined sketch lines, and by using the laser cutter itself for all visual feedback, rather than using a screen or projection. We demonstrate how Constructable allows creating simple but functional devices, including a simple gearbox, that cannot be created with traditional interactive fabrication tools.

Author Keywords: interactive fabrication; laser cutting; rapid prototyping; sketching; construction; mechanics.

ACM Classification Keywords: H5.2 [Information interfaces and presentation]: User Interfaces. - Graphical user interfaces.

General Terms: Design; Human Factors.

INTRODUCTION

Rapid prototyping/personal fabrication tools, such as 3D printers and computer controlled milling machines help users create one-off prototypes rapidly.

The process places CAD software at the front-end to personal fabrication tools. The use of CAD provides three main benefits over traditional woodworking tools, such as saws and wood chisels: (1) *Fast interaction*, it is generally faster to describe what to do to a software program than to operate an actual mechanical tool. *(2) Trial-and-error:* Users can *undo* mistakes and even selectively correct flaws.

UIST'12, October 7–10, 2012, Cambridge, Massachusetts, USA

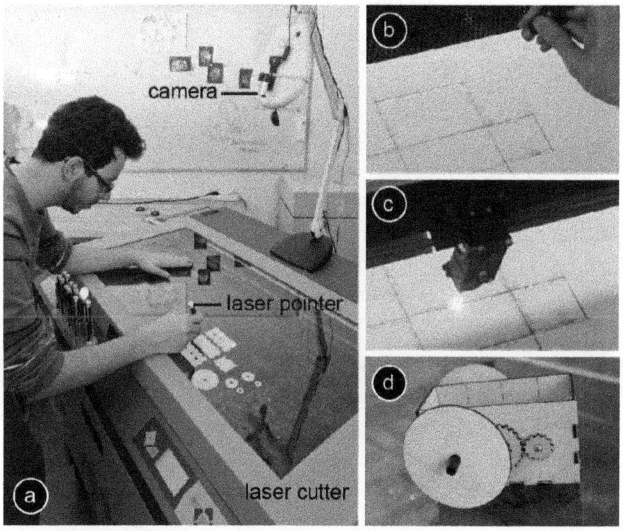

Figure 1: (a) *Constructable* users interact by drafting directly on the workpiece with hand-held lasers. (b) Here the user sketches a finger joint across two objects (c) The system responds by cutting the desired joint using the cutting laser. (d) Constructable allows creating precise & functional mechanical objects, such as this simple motorized vehicle.

(3) *Precision:* constructions aids, such as constraints allow users to precisely manufacture pieces that can perform mechanical functions.

On the flipside, the transition from traditional tools to personal fabrication tools means that all editing is now done on a computer screen, which removes users from the workpiece and prevents users from refining their design interactively along the way [31].

Interactive fabrication

Interactive fabrication systems address this by letting users once again work *directly* with the workpiece [31]. *CopyCAD* [8], for example, allows users to draw on the workpiece.

A key element of interactive fabrication systems is that they provide output to users not at the end of the process, but after every editing step (e.g., *Shaper* [31]). This allows users to (1) validate their designs earlier and (2) build subsequent work steps on the result of earlier steps. The related work suggests that this offers value to artists and designers [31], as their creative process is often inspired by seeing the partially completed workpiece. We argue that similar benefits can be achieved when working on technical projects.

The transition to interactive fabrication, however, comes at a cost. First, since editing is now intertwined with fabrication, editing becomes *slower*, because users have to repeatedly wait for the fabrication engine to finish. Second, as we give up on traditional tools like CAD, users lose the precision required to create functional devices.

In this paper, we attempt to put these qualities back into interactive fabrication, moving it in the direction of what we call *interactive construction.* We present *constructable*, a laser cutter-based interactive construction system that allows users to *construct* functional mechanical devices, while maintaining the immediateness of an interactive fabrication system.

CONSTRUCTABLE

Constructable is a drafting table that produces physical output in every step. As illustrated by Figure 1, all interaction in constructable takes place on the workpiece, mediated through low-power hand-held laser pointers, which we call *proxy lasers* or simply *tools*. In the shown example, the user uses the *finger joint* tool to add finger joints between two pieces by crossing the two involved edges.

Proxy lasers are too weak to affect the work piece. To make the interaction 'real', constructable tracks proxy laser interactions using a camera mounted above (Figure 1b), reconstructs the tool's path, transforms it using a constraint set defined by the current tool, and implements the effect using its high-powered *cutting laser* (Figure 1c). Since all key elements were constructed in the context of constraints, we obtain fully functional mechanical devices, such as the simple motorized vehicle shown in Figure 1d.

The combination of proxy laser and cutting laser is one of the key ideas behind our system, because it allows users to work faster and more interactively than the interactive fabrication systems in the related work. The reason is that the manipulation of materials that are durable enough for making functional mechanical devices requires a *high-powered* tool. These, however, *require* safety measures, such as our glass enclosure. Opening and closing the enclosure for each interaction takes too long, but by letting users point at the workpiece *through* the safety enclosure, constructable allows user's attention to remain *on the workpiece* at all times, despite the enclosure. As intended, users witness how the workpiece changes with their every interaction *first hand* and not mediated by a screen or projector.

Constructable achieves its other main design objective, i.e., *precision,* using a system of constraints implemented by the individual proxy lasers.

Proxy lasers

Figure 2 provides a closer look at the proxy lasers. Each proxy laser features three barrel buttons (Figure 2c). While held depressed, the middle button activates the beam, allowing the system and the user to see where the tool is pointed [21]. The visual feedback allows users to determine a starting point with precision before starting to cut. It thereby implements the *tracking state* of its three-state model [5].

The other two buttons trigger the tool's two modes of operation. The *cut* button allows cutting a tool-specific shape, such as a circle for the *circle* tool. The *sketch line* button creates the same shape, but etches it as a shallow dashed line into the surface of the material. Sketch lines have no direct impact on the mechanics of the workpiece, but instead serve as alignment aids that magnetically attract subsequent cuts (*alignment lines* [3]).

All tools explain themselves exclusively through the cut or sketch line they produce and there is no further visual feedback, i.e., no screen or projector. Since all output is created using the laser cutter itself, constructable's geometry output is extremely precise.

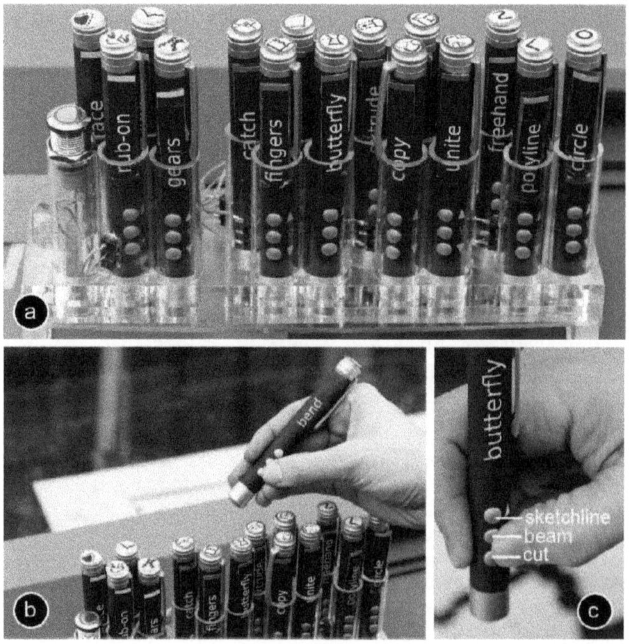

Figure 2: (a, b) Constructable offers 15 different proxy lasers and an undo button. (c) Each proxy-laser offers three barrel buttons.

Creating, Selecting, copying, and pasting using tools

Constructable achieves precision by means of sketch lines and by implementing constraints into every proxy laser. Constraints differ between tools.

Creating: *Polyline*, *Circle*, and *Freehand* are constructable's tools for creating objects from scratch. These tools are only moderately constrained. The *circle* tool, for example, always produces a perfect circle, but diameter and location remain freehand. The *freehand* tool is not subject to any constraints.

Most of constructable's tools connect to or extend an existing object and this spatial relationship adds constraints. Users establish these constraints by *selecting* one or more existing objects. The *finger joint* tool, for example, snaps to existing lines.

Selecting: As illustrated by Figure 3, users select (a) a surface by *clicking* into it, (b) an edge by *crossing* it [2], and (c) a point by drawing a *pigtail* close to it [12]. We designed this selection mechanism so as to extend seamlessly to multiple objects. Users select (d) multiple surfaces by drawing a path across, (e) multiple edges by crossing multiple edges, and (f) multiple points as a sequence of multiple pigtails.

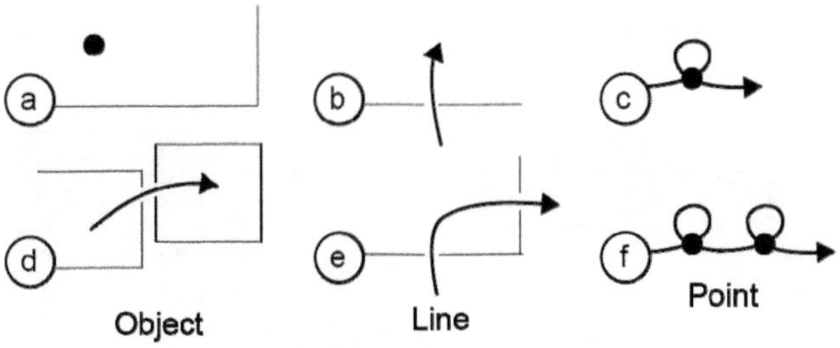

Figure 3: Constructable allows users to select (a) objects by pointing, (b) lines by crossing, and (c) points with pigtails. (d-f) To allow for fast selection, all selection gestures can be extended across multiple objects, lines, and points.

Pasting: A range of tools, such as the *copy* tool, results in the creation of new objects. The size and shape of a new object is determined implicitly, e.g., by the object being copied and does not require or allow for user input. However, to allow users to optimize material usage, we let users show constructable *where* to create it. As illustrated by Figure 4, users point constructable to available material by drawing a directional *cropmark* (see also [19]). The orientation of the cropmark specifies the orientation of the pasted object, allowing users to optimize for material use.

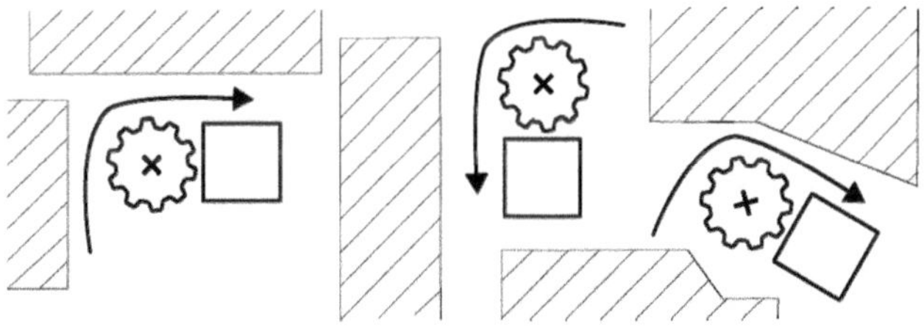

Figure 4: Users paste an object by drawing a cropmark. Constructable places the object into the "inside" of the cropmark. Cropmarks allow users to place objects carefully into available space while preventing them from cutting into adjacent contents.

WALKTHROUGH: CONSTRUCTING A DEVICE

In the following, we illustrate constructable's tools at the example of the simple motorized vehicle that we had briefly touched upon in Figure 1. Figure 5 shows the final outcome and the pieces required to produce it.

We start by creating the housing (Figure 6). (a) We use the *polyline* tool to sketch the rectangular base. (b) Using the *sketch line* button on the *scale* tool we create a sketch line rectangle around the base—this sets the height of the walls. (c) By crossing the north edge of the base with the *Extrude* tool, we create the first wall segment. (d) For efficiency, we create the remaining three walls using a single long stroke that extrudes the base east, south, and west. There is no limit on concatenating, so we could have also extruded all four walls in a single stroke. (e and f) To allow us to assemble the housing later, we add finger joints. We connect the walls by crossing pairs of respective edges using the *finger joint* tool. (g) Finally, we assemble the box by connecting the finger joints.

Figure 5: (a-c) The gearbox in different states of assembly, for use in (d) a simple motorized vehicle.

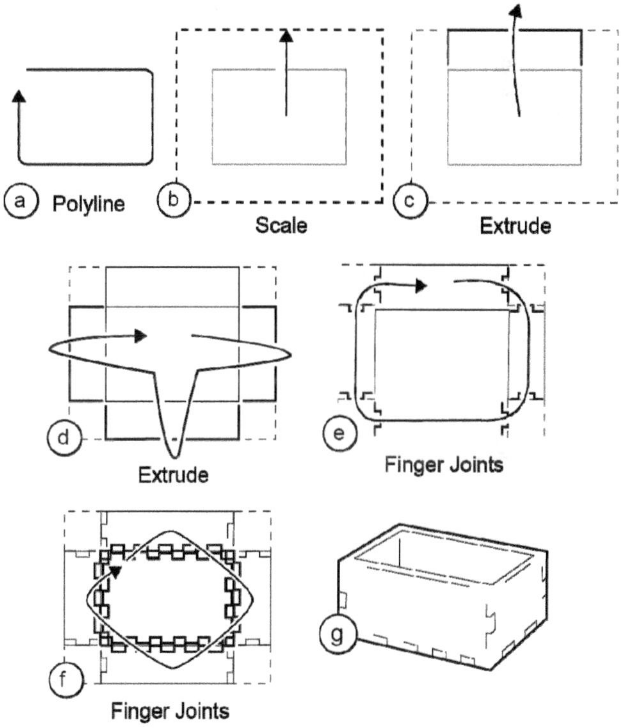

Figure 6: Interactively constructing the housing for the motorized vehicle and gearbox.

Figure 7 shows how we add gearbox and wheels. (a) To make sure that we end up with straight axles we draw three sketch lines using the *polyline* tool. (b) We create the first axle hole using the *hole* tool, the location of which snaps to the intersection of the two sketch lines located close by. (c) We draw all remaining axle holes using a single stroke concatenating multiple pigtails.

(d) We create the first pair of gears by selecting two axle holes, define the transmission ratio by marking the point where we want the two gears to meet, and show constructable where to create the gears using a cropmark. We create the second set of gears accordingly. (f) To create a wheel, we first create an axle hole using the *hole* tool. We then create a wheel around this axle hole using the *scale* tool. (g) We create a second wheel by copying the first one using the *copy* tool.

We are now done creating our parts. We remove them from the machine and assemble them, resulting in the vehicle shown in Figure 5.

The device is mechanically functional, because every mechanical connection was created using tools that embody appropriate constraints.

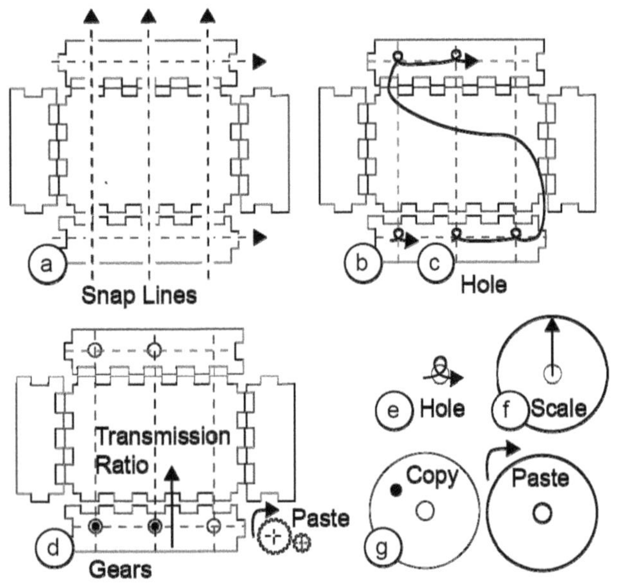

Figure 7: Continuing the previous example, we add axles, a two-stage gearbox, and wheels.

Decorative functionality

While constructable was designed with the goal of supporting interactive *construction*, its underlying concept of tools allows us to integrate form-giving (Figure 8) and decorative functionality as well (Figure 9).

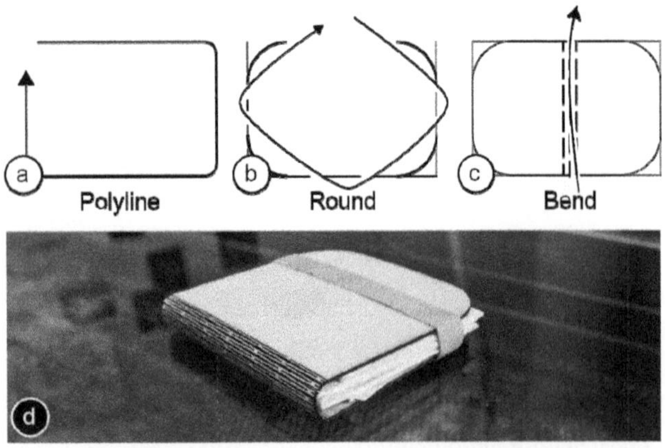

Figure 8: Creating a wooden booklet sleeve by (a) drawing the cover with the *polyline* tool, then (b) smoothing the corners with the *round* tool, and (c) making the wood flexible using the *bend* tool [1].

Figure 9 illustrates how we apply a logo to the housing of our motorized vehicle, á la *CopyCAD* [8]. (a) Continuing our earlier example, we place the housing of our motorized vehicle back into the machine, and position a photo with the desired logo on top of it. (b) We wave the *rub-on* tool across those areas of the photo that we want to transfer. (c) We take the photo back out, and as we close the lid, constructable engraves the logo into the housing.

Figure 9: Adding a decorative logo onto the side of the motorized vehicle using the *rub-on* tool.

Similarly, the *trace* tool cuts the contours of a physical object into the workpiece. Figure 10 shows how to use this to create a holder for two paint jars.

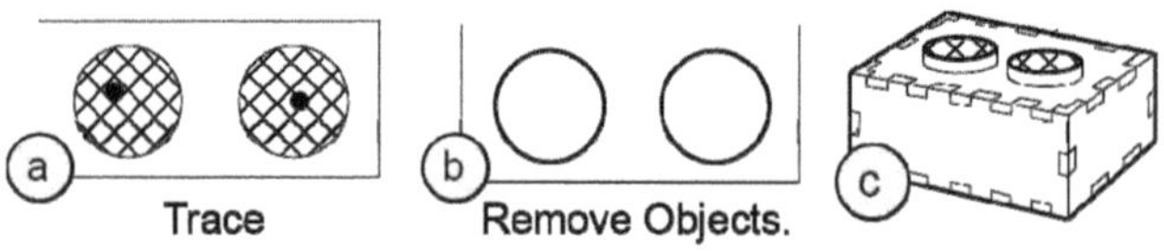

Figure 10: Creating a holder for two paint jars by (a) selecting physical objects inside the cutter using the *trace* tool, (b) After removing the physical objects constructable cuts.

Finally, we can use the *freehand* tool to create unconstrained freehand lines and cuts (Figure 11).

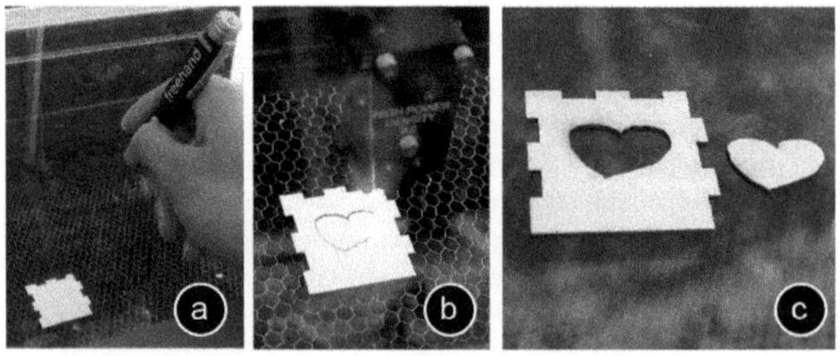

Figure 11: Sketching using the freehand tool.

Trial-and-error support using "undo" tools

Finally, constructable offers basic support for trial-and-error by providing an approximation of *"undo"* tools. Since physical cuts cannot be undone, constructable's *"undo"* tools instead *refabricate* the object — they create a copy that does not have the cut. Users apply the tool by crossing the cuts they want removed; they then *paste* the newly restored object.

While the primary purpose of the tool is to repair and undo, the way it achieves this is by uniting two objects and copying the result. Since this functionality is useful beyond undo, we ended up giving the tool the name *union* tool.

In practice, *any* tool that unites two objects can be used as an *undo* tool. Figure 12 shows the *butterfly joint* tool, which connects two objects using a butterfly connector. This tool produces a butterfly-shaped hole across the cut and lets users paste a matching butterfly-shaped connector. Users repair the cut on assembly by placing the connector into the hole—it sits tight enough to create a lasting connection. While the union tool obviously creates the stronger connection, a butterfly joint consumes less material.

Figure 12: Undoing a cut by re-uniting the pieces using the butterfly tool.

BENEFITS AND LIMITATIONS, SUMMARY OF DESIGN

In the above walkthrough, we demonstrated *interactive construction* using constructable. We showed how constructable allows to interactively construct a functional mechanical device by bringing some of the key qualities of CAD-based personal fabrication into interactive fabrication.

Precise input and output

Constructable achieves the precision required to make functional mechanical devices as follows:

Precise input: Even though all input to constructable is mediated through a hand-held tool, the resulting jerkiness never interfered with precision because all relevant parameters are appropriately constrained. Only parameters with no functional implications, such as the size of the base of the motorized vehicle, were defined free hand.

Constructable uses three types of constraints: (1) *Each tool* implements constraints; the *polyline* tool, for example, draws only rectilinear contents. (2) *Sketch lines* allow users to add constraints explicitly. (3) A special class of tools that create connections, such as finger joints create both halves of the connection at once. As a result, finger joints always fit perfectly even though they involve two parts. The *gear tool* is based on the same concept and one might say that it connects two axles.

Precise output: As mentioned earlier, all tools explain themselves exclusively through the cut or sketch line they produce. Since this allows all output to be created using the laser cutter itself, constructable's geometry output is extremely precise. This offers orders of magnitude higher resolution than projection and is never subject to calibration issues.

No projection

An early version of our system did feature a projector, similar to several systems in the related work, such as *CopyCAD* [8]. Letting go of it not only increased precision, but also made sure we directed users' attention at the workpiece at all times, rather than at a projection collocated with the workpiece.

A side effect of not having a computer display meant that we had to eliminate all hidden state and modes, because there was no way to keep users informed about them. This led us to design the proxy laser model, in which the current set of constraints is represented solely by which physical device the user is currently holding.

As another side effect of using the cutter as the sole visual feedback device, sketch lines became permanent. While users can erase sketch lines by replicating the final object using the *unite* tool, we think that users will typically choose to leave these lines in, the same way that designers leave sketch lines in to illustrate their process or even because they are esthetically pleasing [4].

Trial-and-error using "undo" tools

We implemented trial-and-error using special "undo" functions, such as the *union* and *butterfly joint* tool that allow users to re-create the previous state of an object by re-fabricating it.

Fast interaction via the proxy laser mechanism

As mentioned earlier, constructable achieves fast interaction using the proxy laser mechanism, i.e., drawing with low-power laser tools, the effect of which is implemented by a high-power cutting laser. We found the resulting interaction to invite a powerful conceptual model, namely that the cutting laser *amplifies* the proxy laser, similar to how *power brakes* and *power steering* amplify the driver's muscle strength. We plan to develop this notion further in future versions of constructable, with the ultimate goal of causing at least the *freehand* proxy laser to invite the interpretation that it itself is cutting.

Limitations

Like any tool, constructable is useful for some design problems and less so for others. While constructable extends the range of problems that can be tackled interactively, it is obviously not a CAD system. As with traditional woodworking tools, some types of projects can be tackled tool-in-hand, while more advanced problems require users to sit down with a piece of paper first. The same way that saw and wood chisel cannot replace a detailed design process, constructable cannot replace CAD.

Another limitation is that all construction with constructable is inherently scale 1:1 and constructable offers no way of inspecting a detail in magnification. Similar to working with traditional woodworking tools, this limits users to projects that fit a particular scale.

Finally, constructable was not designed with walk-up use in mind. While some tools, such as the *finger joint* tool have the potential to make complex construction elements accessible to inexperienced users, mechanical construction in general does require know-how. Rather than addressing first time users, we designed the majority of constructable's tools so as to be generic in nature, to apply to each other, and thereby allow for a wide range of constructions.

ERGONOMIC: THE DRAFTING TABLE FORM FACTOR

While constructable is primarily about constructive functionality, we made some observations on ergonomics.

While we initially perceived it mostly as a design hurdle, the laser cutter's glass cover turned out to become one of the key elements creating the affordance of our system. (Figure 13a). By allowing users to rest their body weight on the glass, it allows users to get even closer to the workpiece without worrying about interfering with it. Furthermore, we found ourselves resting proxy lasers on the glass while drawing (Figure 13b), which adds substantial stability, making the interaction even more precise.

Figure 13: (a) The glass cover supports users' weight, allowing them to get close to the workpiece. (b) Resting proxy lasers onto the glass allows for precise interaction.

To invite this interpretation and posture, we positioned the proxy laser tools as shown in Figure 13c. This allows users to reach tools without lifting their arm, but instead pivoting around their elbows similar to the *Lagoon* in *Alias Sketchbook* [6].

We found all of the above to invite the interpretation of constructable as a drafting table, the "drawing" on which is the actual physical object itself. We plan on building on this interpretation in future versions by tilting the glass cover slightly towards the user (e.g., as in *ActiveDesk* [7]).

CONTRIBUTION

The main contribution of this paper is the concept of *interactive construction*, which we support with the functional system prototype constructable. Our demo scenarios illustrate how users can create functional mechanical devices, which exceeds the complexity of examples created in the interactive fabrication literature. We are thus primarily making a systems contribution.

In addition, our system contains a series of novel elements, including (a) the proxy laser mechanism, i.e., drawing with low-power laser tools, the effect of which is implemented by a high-power cutting laser, (b) the use of the laser cutter as a super high precision display, replacing projection, and (c) the notion of undoing a physically destructive action by re-fabricating the broken piece.

RELATED WORK

The work presented in this paper builds on sketching, personal fabrication, and interactive fabrication.

Creating structured drawings from manual input

Several researchers have demonstrated how to create precise input from rough sketchy input (e.g., *ScanScribe* [28]). Many systems simplify the problem by representing additional domain knowledge [16] to resolve ambiguity [11]. Geometric constraints can bring precision for sketching tasks, (e.g., *snap dragging* [3]).

More recently, this style of constrained and precise sketch input has been synergized with interactive surfaces, such as on *Hands-On Math* [32] and *Pen+Touch* [14].

Compared to pen or touch input, lasers are a particularly imprecise input mechanism due to the unsteadiness of the hand, which causes jitter unless resting against a surface [24, 21].

Personal Fabrication

With personal fabrication tools researchers commonly refer to some superset of milling machines, laser cutters, and 3D printing machines. The main goal of personal fabrication is to allow for rapid prototyping, with the intent of reduced costs compared to actual fabrication, thereby allowing for a more iterative design process.

The concept has support not only in research, but also in the open source/DIY community, which is leading the development of more accessible machines, such as *Lasersaur* [17] and *MakerBot* and to the opening of workshops equipped with rapid-prototyping tools (denoted as *fab labs* [10]).

A range of projects aim at lowering the entry barrier to 2D and 3D modeling by restricting the space of possible objects to chairs (*SketchChair* [26]), plush animals (*Plushi* [20]), geometrical 3D shapes (*PaperFactory* [27]), 2D shapes (*Sketch it, Make it* [15]).

Finally, fabrication tools have been used as means to artistic expression, e.g., *Haptic Intelligentsia* [18] users fabricate objects around virtual models using a glue gun attached to a force-feedback haptic device.

Personal Fabrication using Laser Cutters

Laser cutters are one of the preferred personal fabrication devices, since they are powerful and fast.

SpatialSketch [30] and *FurnitureFactory* [23] allow users to sketch objects in 3D. Once the sketching is completed, the system decomposes it into a 2D model that can be batch fabricated with a laser cutter. *SpatialSketch* users draw mid-air gestures, while *FurnitureFactory* users interact via a sketch-based graphical user interface.

LaserCooking [9] uses the laser cutter as a cooking tool. It identifies specific food items by color and handles them appropriately. *MetaCookie* [22] uses a laser to engrave augmented reality markers into cookies with augmented flavors.

Interactive Fabrication

One of the first interactive fabrication tools was *ModelCraft* [29]. It allowed users to draw onto a paper model using an Anoto digital pen, allowing the system to beautify the user's sketches and to keep a history log for versioning and undoing.

While users of ModelCraft still had to manually fabricate the models by printing and folding, combining the approach with personal fabrication tools allowed closing the loop. *Interactive fabrication,* a term introduced by Willis et al. [31] replaces the batch processing common in personal fabrication with alternation between user and system control. Their tool (*Shaper* [31]) allows users to create foam sculptures via a transparent touchscreen.

CopyCAD [8] extends this concept by allowing users to include geometry from real world objects, e.g., by copying the shape of an object (*remixing*) and replicate it using a milling machine.

With *constructable*, we introduce interactive construction, extending interactive fabrication towards precision, thus allowing users to create functional mechanical devices.

IMPLEMENTATION

Figure 14 shows how constructable processes proxy laser input in order to generate cutting laser output.

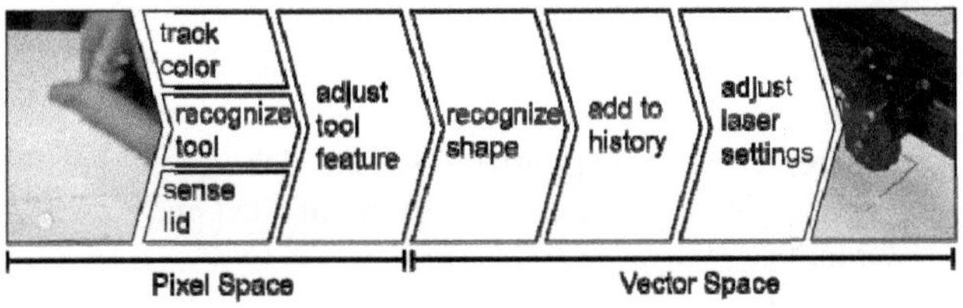

Figure 14: Data processing flow in constructable.

Sensing

Constructable observes the workpiece using a web cam (*MS Lifecam, 844x448px, 30 fps*) and extracts the dot produced by the proxy-lasers using color tracking. Constructable then smoothes tool paths using a Kalman Filter and performs shape recognition on paths using *PaleoSketch* [25] before applying the geometric operations and spatial constraints defined by the tool.

At this point, constructable records the interaction history, which it uses to support *undo* and selective repairs using the *union* tool.

Output to the laser cutter

Constructable now outputs the shape to the laser cutter, currently a *Universal PLS6.150D*. Using the *OpenDraw* API, Constructable draws the shape into an *OpenDraw* document, which it sends to the cutter using the printer interface. As required by *Universal* laser cutter systems, constructable encodes the necessary meta-information into the color of the respective line, i.e., cutting-depth (mm), laser power (percentage), and speed (percentage). A red 0pt line, for example, causes the laser to cut, while green is used to create a shallow, low-power *sketch line*. Constructable sends all communication using the *Open Sound Protocol,* which makes it easy to adapt the system to other hardware components, such as a different laser cutter model.

Remixing: using physical objects as a reference

Constructable captures physical objects using the same camera that tracks the laser dots. A bar of fluorescent light mounted inside the cutter supports this by providing homogeneous, reflection-free illumination of the workpiece. An IR rangefinder sensor informs the system when the lid is open.

Proxy lasers

In order to retrieve the constraint set represented by the current tool, constructable determines which tool is in use using mechanical switches, one of which is installed in each tool holder (similar to pen "recognition" in *SmartBoards*, smarttech.com). This bypass allows us to implement all proxy lasers using a single type of off-the-shelf laser pointer. The buttons on all proxy lasers trigger an IR signal, which Constructable monitors using an IR receiver placed next to the camera.

Similar to the *tracking* button, the *cut* and *sketch line* buttons are spring-loaded in order to eliminate mode errors [13]. Users operate them without letting go of the *tracking* button, which users perform by rocking their finger back and forth between *tracking* button and the center position of *tracking* and *cut* button. For optimized ergonomics during prolonged use [13] constructable offers a dual-footswitch pedal, which is fulfilling the same purpose as the cut and sketch line barrel buttons.

CONCLUSION

In this paper, we proposed *interactive construction* as a way to enable users to interactively create functional mechanical devices. Our prototype called *constructable* serves as a drafting table that produces physical output in every step. By building constraints into tools, providing sketch lines and by using the laser cutter itself for high precision output, constructable offers the necessary precision required to produce simple, yet functional mechanics that cannot be created with traditional interactive fabrication tools.

Equally important, constructable allows for fast fabrication by making a high-power cutting laser accessible to the user via safe low-power proxy lasers.

As future work, we plan to extend *constructable* to allow for collaborative use.

ACKNOWLEDGEMENT

We thank Mike Sinclair for sharing his wisdom on uncommon laser-cut joints, Ken Hinckley, Sean Gustafson, and Christian Holz for feedback.

REFERENCES

1. Booklets—it's just wood! http://www.snijlab.nl/?page_id=358
2. Apitz, G. and Guimbretière, F. CrossY: A Crossing-Based Drawing Application. Proc UIST'04, 3-12.
3. Bier, E. Snap dragging. In *Proc. SIGGRAPH'86*, pp. 233-240.
4. Buxton, B. *Sketching User Experiences: Getting the Design Right and the Right Design*. Morgan Kaufman, 2007.
5. Buxton, W. A Three-State Model of Graphical Input. *Proc. INTERACT '90*, 449-456.
6. Fitzmaurice, G., Khan, A., Pieké, R., Buxton, W & Kurtenbach. G. Tracking Menus. *Proc. UIST'03*, 71-79.
7. Fitzmaurice, G.W., Ishii, H. & Buxton, W. Bricks: Laying the Foundations for Graspable User Interfaces. *Proc. CHI'95*, 442-449.
8. Follmer, S., Carr, D., Lovell, E., Hiroshi, I. CopyCAD: remixing physical objects with copy and paste from the real world. *Adjunct Proceedings UIST '10*, 381-382.
9. Fukuchi, K., Jo, K. Laser Cooking: an Automated Cooking Technique using Laser Cutter. In *TEI'11 Work-in-Progress*.
10. Gershenfeld, N. *Fab: The Coming Revolution on Your Desktop--From Personal Computers to Personal Fabrication*. Basic Books, 2007.
11. Gross, M., and Do, EYL. Ambiguous Intentions: A paper-like interface for creative design. In *Proc. UIST'96*, 183-192.
12. Hinckley, K., Baudisch, P., Ramos, G., and Guimbretiere, F. Design and Analysis of Delimiters for Selection-Action Pen Input Phrases in Scriboli. *Proc. CHI'05*, 451-460.
13. Hinckley, K., Guimbretiere, F., Baudisch, P., Sarin, R., Agrawala, M., & Cutrell, E. The Springboard: Multiple Modes in One Spring-Loaded Control. In *Proc. CHI'06*, 181-190.
14. Hinckley, K., Yatani, K., Pahud, M., Coddington, N., Rodenhouse, J., Wilson, A., Benko, H., Buxton, B. Pen + touch = new tools. *Proc. UIST'10*, 27-36.
15. Johnson, G., Do, E.Y-L. Sketch It, Make It: Sketching precise drawings for laser cutting. In *Extended Abstracts CHI '12*.
16. Landay, J. and Myers, B. Interactive Sketching for the Early Stages of User Interface Design. *In Proc. CHI '95*. 43-50.
17. Lasersaur http://labs.nortd.com/lasersaur
18. Lee, J.H. *Haptic Intelligentsia*. http://studio-homunculus.com/ portfolio/haptic-intelligentsia-human-prototyping-machine.
19. Liao, C., Guimbretière, F., Hinckley, K. PapierCraft: a command system for interactive paper. *Proc. UIST'05*, 241 - 244.
20. Mori, Y., Igarashi, T. Plushie: An Interactive Design System for Plush Toys. *Proc. SIGGRAPH* '07.
21. Myers, B.A., Bhatnagar, R., Nichols, J., Peck, C.h., Kong, D., Miller, R., Long, A.C. Interacting At a Distance: Measuring the Performance of Laser Pointers and Other Devices. *Proc. CHI '02*, 33-40.
22. Narumi, T., Nishizaka, S., Kajinami, T., Tanikawa, T., Hirose, M. Augmented Reality Flavors: Gustatory Display Based on Edible Marker and Cross-Modal Interaction. *Proc. CHI '11*, 93-102.
23. Oh, Y., Johnson, G., Gross, M., Do, E.Y. The Designosaur and the Furniture Factory. *Proc. Design Computing and Cognition'06*, 123 – 140.
24. Olsen Jr, D.R. and Nielsen, T. Laser Pointer Interaction. *Proc. CHI'01*, 17-22.
25. Paulson, B. and Hammond, T. A System for Recognizing and Beautifying Low-level Sketch Shapes Using NDDE and DCR. *Adjunct Proceedings UIST'07*.
26. Saul, G., Lau, M., Mitani, J., and Igarashi, T. SketchChair: An All-in-one Chair Design System for End Users. *Proc. TEI '11*, 73-80.
27. Saul, G., Xu, C., Gross, M.D. Interactive Paper Devices: End-user Design & Fabrication. *Proc. TEI '10*, 205-212.
28. Saund, E., Fleet, D., Larner, D., and Mahoney, J. Perceptually-Supported Image Editing of Text and Graphics, *Proc. UIST '03*, 183-192.
29. Song, H., Guimbretière, F., Hu, C., Lipson, H. ModelCraft: capturing freehand annotations and edits on physical 3D models. *Proc UIST '06*, 13-22.
30. Willis, K.D.D., Lin, J., Mitani, J., Igarashi, T. Spatial sketch: bridging between movement & fabrication. *Proc. TEI '10*, 5-12.
31. Willis, K.D.D., Xu, C., Wu, J.K., Levin, G., Gross, M.D. Interactive fabrication: new interfaces for digital fabrication. *Proc. TEI '11*, 69-72
32. Zeleznik, R., Bragdon, A., Adeputra, F., and Ko, HS. Hands-On Math: A Page-based Multi-touch and Pen Desktop for Technical Work and Problem Solving. *Proc. UIST'10*, 17-26.

Author Index

www.ingramcontent.com/pod-product-compliance
Ingram Content Group UK Ltd.
Pitfield, Milton Keynes, MK11 3LW, UK
UKHW051417290926
15471UKWH00009B/1653

9 781450 315814